19th and 20th Virginia Cavalry

1st Edition

This series is dedicated to the men who served in Virginia Units during the War Between the States. It is the purpose of this series to preserve, as a part of our heritage, the deeds and sacrifices of these men. Your support of this project is greatly appreciated.

Number __651__ of 1,000

Richard L. Armstrong

Copyright 1994 H. E. Howard, Inc.

Manufactured in the United States by
H. E. Howard, Inc., Lynchburg, Virginia

Printed by H. E. Howard, Inc.

ISBN-1-56190-061-3

19th and 20th Virginia Cavalry

1st Edition

Richard L. Armstrong

ACKNOWLEDGEMENTS

While my name appears as author of this volume, the credit cannot be mine alone. To compile the information contained in the history of the 19th and 20th Virginia Cavalry, it was necessary to depend on the generosity of others.

It would be impossible to name everyone who contributed material to the volume. I would, however, like to thank the following persons and institutions for their assistance. Thanks to Sharon I. Lindsay and Jeannette B. Robinson of the Bath County Cooperative Library, for processing innumerable interlibrary loan requests. The Preston Library at the Virginia Military Institute, Lexington, Virginia, is due much credit for allowing me to use their fine resources.

Thanks to Raymond W. Watkins, Robert J. Driver, Jr., Virgil Hart, Jeff Weaver, and Harold Calhoun. Special thanks to Charles Chambers of Houston, Texas for information from the Texas Pension Records, and Shelby G. Moss of Chula Vista, California for sharing information about soldiers from Ritchie County, West Virginia. Thanks are also due Robert K. Krick for sharing information he has compiled concerning soldiers of the Confederacy, and for editing this manuscript.

I would like to take this opportunity to thank Harold E. Howard for undertaking the publication of the Virginia Regimental History Series. This long overdue project has salvaged a great deal of material that may have been lost forever.

To all those who remain un-named, I wish to express my thanks. It is through the generosity of people like you that books like this can be written.

Richard L. Armstrong
Hot Springs, Va.
January 1994

Chapter I

Colonel William Lowther "Mudwall" Jackson received authority from the Secretary of War to raise a regiment of cavalry on February 17, 1863. Colonel Jackson, a second cousin of Major General Thomas J. "Stonewall" Jackson, intended to raise the regiment within the enemy lines (Northwestern Virginia). As the Virginia Legislature planned to disband the Virginia State Line and Virginia State Rangers, Jackson received the recommendation to assume control of these men. When the legislature disbanded the units by March 31, 1863, their men formed the nucleus of the 19th Virginia Cavalry.

In early April 1863, Colonel Jackson delivered a dispatch dated March 31 from the Secretary of War to Major General Samuel Jones. The communication informed Jones that Jackson had successfully raised some "eleven or twelve" companies. The Secretary of War suggested that Jones issue the necessary orders to have field officers elected and form the regiment. The letter continued:

> The authority to Col. Jackson was, on its face, only to raise a Regiment, but it was intended if success crowned his efforts, that he might proceed until Regiments sufficient to constitute a Brigade were organized.

This finally led to the creation of the 20th Virginia Cavalry and the 46th Battalion Virginia Cavalry.

On April 4, General Jones wrote Jackson at Warm Springs, giving him details of the proposed raid by Brigadier General John D. Imboden. The raid into the northwest corner of Virginia would, wrote Jones, begin on April 15. The general urged Jackson to push forward the organization of the regiment and his preparations to move to join Imboden at Huttonsville by April 18. Jackson was to have at least 300 men, and was to take orders from Imboden. General Jones admonished the colonel that all this was "strictly confidential."

The following day, April 5, Jones again communicated with Jackson. Jones informed Jackson that he would send the 37th Battalion Virginia Cavalry (Lieutenant Colonel A. C. Dunn) to join him, if he could arm and use them. The same day, Jones informed the Secretary of War that he was sending troops to aid Imboden in the raid. He wrote that he was sending "all of Col. W. L. Jackson's new regiment that can be armed in time (two or three of his companies are already well armed and have seen service) to join the expedition."

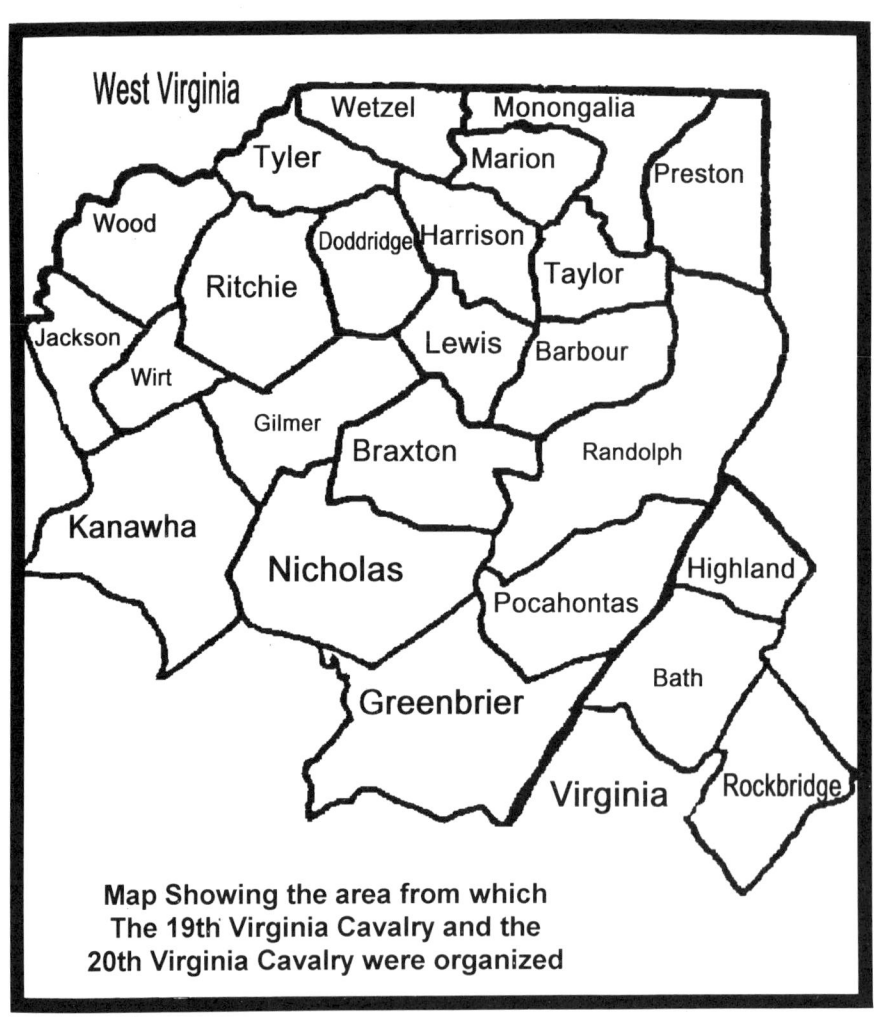

Map Showing the area from which The 19th Virginia Cavalry and the 20th Virginia Cavalry were organized

On April 11, 1863, Jones reported to Imboden that he would supply about 1,500 men for the expedition. Only 400 of them belong to Jackson's regiment. Many of these men were raw recruits. At least one company, and probably others that later belonged to the 20th Virginia Cavalry accompanied Jackson on this expedition. The 19th Virginia Cavalry completed its organization on April 11, 1863, at Warm Springs, Bath County, Virginia, with Jackson as colonel. The War Department officially recognized the 19th Virginia Cavalry on this date. Colonel Jackson, however, wrote later that the War Department had accepted the 19th Virginia Cavalry on March 31, 1863. Jackson established his headquarters at Warm Springs, where he commanded the military post. According to a table of organization dated April 20, the 19th Virginia Cavalry formed part of Brigadier General Albert G. Jenkin's Brigade. Colonel Jackson informed Sam Jones that he had three additional companies of cavalry, and hoped to fill up another regiment soon.

The following companies were assigned to the 19th Virginia Cavalry:

COMPANY A
The Moccasin Rangers

Peregrin Hays and George W. Silcott, of Arnoldsburg, W. Va. organized the Moccasin Rangers as a home guard unit. When Captain Perry Connolly took command of the Calhoun County Home Guards, he began calling them "The Guerrillas." The men disliked the name, and changed it to "The Moccasin Rangers." Nancy Hart, sweetheart of Captain Connolly, may have been a member of this company.

Late in 1861, Connolly moved his base of operations from Calhoun County to Braxton, Nicholas, and Summers counties. This move caused a division in the company. A portion of the men remained in the Little Kanawha Valley, under the command of Captain George Downs.

The United States forces considered the Moccasin Rangers outlaws. Peregrin Hays informed his friend, Governor John Letcher, of this fact. Letcher directed General Henry A. Wise to send a supply of blank commissions to the Rangers, for Downs to use. The Union authorities refused to honor them.

The company commanded by Captain Downs became part of the 3rd Virginia State Line on April 2, 1862. Brigadier General Henry Heth called them "...an organized outlaw band that robbed and plundered...."

The Moccasin Rangers enlisted for service in the 19th Virginia Cavalry on March 1, 1863. A few members of the company transferred to Company F, 20th Virginia Cavalry on July 19, 1863. In 1864, for unspecified reasons, these men returned to the 19th Virginia Cavalry. Other members of this company transferred to Company H, 20th Virginia Cavalry.

Many members of this company were from Calhoun and Wirt counties, West Virginia.

COMPANY B
Braxton County Volunteers

This company enlisted March 7, 1863, with John S. Spriggs as captain. Many of its men formerly had served in Company B, 3rd Virginia State Line. As the name implies, the members of the company were primarily from Braxton County, West Virginia.

COMPANY C

This company enlisted March 15, 1863, with Joseph R. Kessler as captain. Many of the men formerly had served in Company D, 3rd Virginia State Line. Some of them transferred to Company F, 20th Virginia Cavalry, on July 17, 1863. These men transferred back to Company C, 19th Virginia Cavalry, on August 31, 1863. Many of the members of this company were from Jackson and Roane counties, West Virginia.

COMPANY D

This company enlisted March 8, 1863, with John Righter as captain. Many of them formerly had served in Company C, 3rd Virginia State Line. Many of the members of this company were from Marion County, West Virginia.

COMPANY E

This company enlisted March 13, 1863, with James W. Ball as captain. Many of them formerly had served in Company E, 3rd Virginia State Line. Many of the members of this company were from Gilmer County, West Virginia.

COMPANY F
Pocahontas Cavalry

This company enlisted March 9, 1863, with William L. McNeil as captain. Many of them formerly had served in McNeil's Company, 2nd Virginia State Line. Captain McNeil organized this company primarily from Pocahontas County, West Virginia. See note on Company I.

COMPANY G
Dixie Boys

This company enlisted March 12, 1863, with Henry D. Ruffner as captain. Many of its men formerly had served in Company F, 3rd Virginia State Line. Many of the members of this company were from Kanawha County, West Virginia.

COMPANY H

This company enlisted March 19, 1863, with William P. O'Brien as captain. Many of the men formerly had served in Company G, 3rd Virginia State Line. Some absentees from this company later served in Captain Sampson's Company, Major T. S. Davis' Battalion Virginia Cavalry. A large number of the members of this company were from Gilmer County, West Virginia.

COMPANY I

This company enlisted March 19, 1863 with Jacob W. Marshall as Captain. The members of this company were primarily from Randolph and Pocahontas counties, West Virginia. This was one of the largest companies in the regiment, having 104 names on the rolls. Postwar sources show that Captain Marshall organized his company at Huntersville, Virginia (now West Virginia), in November 1861. The same source shows that the company never surrendered, but disbanded in May 1865 at Lexington. Captain Marshall and most of his company then went to Staunton, where they signed paroles.

On February 14, 1864, Captain Marshall wrote the Secretary of War about his company:

> My company was principally formed and organized for the purpose of scouting the roads leading to Beverly, on the right of Gen. Loring's Command then on the Kanawha line, likewise to be used as a police guard in the counties of Bath, Pocahontas & Highland counties. The company was used for this purpose until Col. Jackson came with authority to recruit a command to operate on this the Huntersville line. My company agreed to join his command. When the 19th regt. was ready to be organized we agreed to go into the regt. with the understanding and promise from Col. Jackson that as soon as other companies could be organized to supply our places in the 19th Regt. that Capt. McNeels [McNeils] Co. and my company should be detached or taken out of the Regt.

COMPANY K

This company enlisted March 20, 1863, with Edward Norris as captain. Many of Norris' men formerly had served in Companies H and I, 3rd Virginia State Line. Many of the members of this company were from Gilmer County, West Virginia.

Jackson was to meet Imboden at Huttonsville on April 18, 1863. General Imboden delayed his departure and changed the rendezvous point. It was not until April 20 that Imboden left his camp at Shenandoah Mountain. Jackson joined the 1,825 men who Imboden placed in the field at Hightown, Highland County, on April 21. Many of the men in the 19th Virginia Cavalry did not have horses. The addition of the men from Jones' command brought Imboden's strength to 3,365 men. Fewer than 700 of them owned a horse. From Hightown, Imboden made his way westward toward Beverly, Randolph County.

General Imboden arrived at Camp Bartow on the Greenbrier River on

April 22. There he learned that the "notorious Yankee Scout" John Slayton and a squad of seven Yankees had passed that way about sunrise. Slayton had learned that Imboden was on his way, and intended to warn the Federal garrison at Beverly. Imboden had expected this, and had two days earlier ordered a mounted picket force to go to the Greenbrier River. Their presence caused Slayton to try to reach Beverly through the mountains. At Greenbrier River (Bartow), Imboden sent a detail of 20 men after Slayton, but they did not catch up with him. Slayton, however, did not reach Beverly in time to sound the alarm.

The Confederates arrived at Huttonsville on the evening of April 23. A pouring rain drenched them during most of the 70-mile march. In crossing Cheat Mountain, the Southerners discovered about two feet of snow on the ground. As they made their way through the snow, a severe sleet storm pelted them.

At Huttonsville, Imboden learned that the Federals had recalled their pickets (thirty men) about 11 o'clock that morning. The weary Rebels went into camp for the night. Their rest, however, was not peaceful. About midnight, Imboden's advance picket reported an enemy force moving on the east side of the Tygarts Valley River. Their direction of travel, if continued, would take them to a mountain which overlooked the Confederate Camp at Huttonsville. An hour later, this party returned rapidly toward Beverly. They did not, however, advance far enough up the mountain to see the Confederate Camp.

Rain continued to fall during the night. The dawn of April 24 "was one of the most gloomy and inclement I ever saw" wrote General Imboden.

The advance upon Beverly started at an early hour. General Imboden moved his infantry (including a number of dismounted cavalrymen) along the road on the east side of the river. General Imboden accompanied this column. Some of the dismounted men belonged to the company which later became Company A, 20th Virginia Cavalry. About 40 mounted members of this company accompanied Imboden's cavalry on the other road.

Company F, 19th Virginia Cavalry went before the infantry on the east side of the river. General Imboden assigned them to this post because they were the best mounted. After going several miles toward Beverly, Company F met a Federal foraging train. Private Paul M. McNeil wrote: "We rode right into them before they knew of our presence, and the guard of a dozen or so mounted men surrendered without a shot."

The cavalry and a section of McClanahan's Battery followed the back road, on the west side of the river. Colonel George Imboden commanded this detachment. As soon as they discovered the enemy, they were to rush forward and take possession of the Buckhannon road. This would cut off the Federal retreat in that direction.

The 18th Virginia Cavalry was in the advance. The men of the 20th Virginia Cavalry were toward the rear. The records reveal few details of the role of the 19th Virginia Cavalry during this engagement.

Shortly after 9 a.m., Colonel George R. Latham left Beverly and headed toward Huttonsville. He sent a company of cavalry out on each of the two roads leading to that place. After proceeding about five miles, the Federal cavalry met Imboden's forces on both roads.

Colonel Latham, outnumbered by Imboden's men, fell back slowly. At noon, the Confederates were within two and a half miles of town. The dense fog, which shrouded the valley that morning, finally burned off about 1 pm. From his strong position on the south side of Beverly, Latham for the first time could see Imboden's full strength. Colonel Latham estimated it to be 4,500 men. His own command numbered barely 900 men.

Latham's position was on a plateau 50 or 60 feet above the river bottom. This position commanded the road for more than a mile.

To attack from the front would mean a heavy loss to the Confederates. General Imboden decided to turn Latham's position by making a detour of more than two miles over rough terrain to the north side of Beverly. To mask the flanking party, Imboden ordered Captain McClanahan to open fire with his rifled gun on the enemy artillery.

The Confederate cavalry steadily advanced, and when within a mile of town, Latham ordered his artillery to fire on them. It was now about 2 p.m. Some infantry skirmishing took place at long range.

About 4 p.m., the fighting became general along the entire line. The Confederates drove the Federal skirmishers back in the front. Imboden's cavalry now came under canister fire from Latham's artillery.

The Southern cavalry dashed forward under this dangerous fire and took possession of the Buckhannon road. Latham's only avenue of escape lay in the direction of Philippi, which Imboden was now trying to close.

Lieutenant David Poe, Company A, 20th Virginia Cavalry, commanding the detachment of that company, received orders to bring his men to the front of the column. He reported to Colonel George Imboden, who directed Poe to move around the pike and contact Captain Righter of the 19th Virginia Cavalry. After learning what intelligence he could, Poe was to advance upon and attack the enemy in his front. Poe found Captain Righter, and learned from him that the strength of the enemy in his front was between 70 and 150 men. They concealed themselves behind houses, barns and outbuildings. Colonel Imboden's command would support Poe.

Poe wrote: "There I was, occupying a post of honor, with untried soldiers whom I led through the mountains and the enemies' lines, to go with me, in front of a veteran foe, double in number and sheltered behind buildings." Poe told them "you have followed me through the mountains; now, when I tell you to close up, raise a yell and follow me." Poe recalled "I saw every face brighten." With that, Poe advanced and when fired on by the enemy, gave the command to close up. Lieutentant Poe and his men charged the enemy. The Federals quickly abandoned their position, and fell back about two miles. Poe followed them to near the fortifications near Beverly. There his men halted and the enemy opened fire upon them with their artillery.

Shortly after 4 p.m., Colonel Latham received orders from Brigadier General B. S. Roberts to fall back. The colonel started his train for Philippi at once, destroyed the military stores, and left Beverly about 5 p.m.

Near sunset, Imboden's flanking party arrived on the northern side of Beverly. They were too late to block the road to Philippi. Latham had departed, leaving about a third of the town in flames. Lieutenant David Poe, in his recollections, said the flanking party got lost and allowed Latham to escape.

Southern cavalry pursued the retreating Federals for about six miles, charging upon them twice, without results. The pursuit ended near dark.

General Imboden reported the loss of three men badly wounded, whom he left in private homes at Beverly. They later fell into enemy hands. Colonel Jackson made no report of any loss at Beverly.

Following the capture of Beverly, Colonel Jackson made the comment that he would be coming back to spend the 4th of July there. The comment circulated about town, and eventually reached the ears of the Federal commander. He dismissed it as idle chatter.

After spending the night at Beverly, Imboden marched toward Buckhannon. The road to Philippi was impassable for wagons and artillery because of the deep mud. Their progress was slow. By the evening of April 26, the Confederates crossed the Middle Fork River and went into camp. General Imboden sent his entire cavalry force forward to seize the bridge over the Buckhannon River. Learning of the heavy force at Buckhannon, Imboden decided to retire. He recalled the cavalry sent to the Buckhannon River.

The Confederates marched at 5 a.m. on April 27. After toiling for nine hours through the mud, they managed to cover two miles. Darkness had fallen by the time they went into camp at Roaring Run, exhausted and muddy.

While in camp on the west side of Rich Mountain, Imboden sent his cavalry again in the direction of Buckhannon. Returning after midnight, they reported that the enemy had abandoned Buckhannon. Before leaving the place, the Federals burned the Middle Fork and Buckhannon River Bridges, as well as the military stores in the town.

The Confederates retraced their steps the next day, and camped that evening within four miles of Buckhannon. General Imboden occupied the town on April 29, 1863. General Imboden and Colonel Jackson remained here for two days. During this time the cavalry was busy collecting cattle in the neighborhood.

General Imboden prepared to leave Buckhannon for Philippi on the night of May 1. Early on the morning of May 2, his men crossed the Buckhannon River on rafts. While they did so, a courier arrived with word that Brigadier General W. E. Jones was within six miles of Buckhannon. The courier also brought news that a detachment of the 19th Virginia Cavalry, under Lieutenant Sturms, had been successful in burning all the bridges for 30 miles west of Fairmont.

General Imboden now deceided to change his direction of march toward Weston, to unite with Jones. Once united, the intention was to make an attack on Jane Lew or Clarksburg. He arrived at Weston on the morning of May 3, 1863.

While at Weston, Imboden reported his loss thus far as two men killed and three or four wounded. He sent his scouts out in the direction of Clarksburg. Upon their return, Imboden learned the Federals had fortified Lost Creek Pass, eight miles from Clarksburg. To attack that point now was out of the question.

The general advanced a picket force to Jane Lew. The Federals attacked on May 5 and routed them. All but three escaped.

General Jones' command arrived at Weston on May 4 and remained with Imboden until May 6. Then Jones moved against the Northwest Railroad, while Imboden moved southward toward Summersville. It was their intention to meet again at that place. Imboden sent his sick men, with the captured stores from Beverly and Buckhannon, back to Monterey. At an early hour he marched for Summersville. The roads were horrible, and night found them only five and a half miles from Weston.

On May 7, "with extraordinary labor" Imboden reported, they made two miles. The Confederates spent the next few days marching and on May 12 had reached Bulltown, Braxton County. There the Confederates destroyed the blockhouses and quarters of the Federal garrison. Imboden's command arrived at Summersville about 3 p.m., May 13, 1863. General Jones arrived that evening.

From this point, Imboden took the Cold Knob road. Leaving Summersville, he moved up the Gauley River about 20 miles. There he crossed the river and moved through the mountains to Greenbrier County.

After four days in the wilderness, Imboden's command arrived at Sinking Creek, in Greenbrier County. They rested there the following day, then took up the line of march for Buffalo Gap, near Staunton.

General Imboden, after complaining that the roads preventing him from accomplishing more, gave the following statement of his success:

> I compelled the enemy to destroy large and valuable stores at Beverly, Buckhannon, Weston, Bulltown, Suttonville [Sutton] and Big Birch; captured and brought out over $100,000 worth of horses, mules, wagons and arms; burned their blockhouses and stockades; forced them to burn three important and valuable covered bridges west of Fairmont; enabled the Government agents to buy and bring out to places of safety over 3,100 head of cattle.

In all, Imboden and Jackson had been in the field for 37 days, during which they marched 400 miles. During its time with Imboden, Jackson's command suffered the following losses:

Date	Killed	Captured	Deserted	Total
April 1863	1	1	0	2
May 1863	1	15	4	20
Total	2	16	4	22

Some of the men lost on this expedition belonged to companies that later became part of the 20th Virginia Cavalry.

Imboden's command suffered heavily from desertion during its stay in western Virginia. On the other hand, Jackson's command recruited between three and four hundred men while on the raid. These men served in the 20th Virginia Cavalry and the 46th Battalion Virginia Cavalry.

By May 23, 1863, Jackson had returned to Camp Northwest, on Knapp Creek near Huntersville in Pocahontas County.

While the 19th Virginia Cavalry was with Imboden in the northwest, Major General Sam Jones transferred Jenkins' Brigade to the Army of Northern Virginia. The 19th Virginia, however, remained in Jones' command. They were, wrote Jones, the only troops on the Huntersville Line. He did not think it prudent to pull the 19th Virginia from its position. The commands of Jackson and Imboden were all that stood between the enemy at Beverly and the Shenandoah Valley, guarding the route through Pocahontas and Randolph counties.

On May 25, 1863, the 19th Virginia Cavalry appeared on a table of organization of the cavalry division, Army of Northern Virginia, Jenkins' Brigade. According to a note on the table, the 19th Virginia Cavalry was the largest regiment in the brigade.

CHAPTER II

Colonel William L. Jackson split his command into several detachments to watch the Federals at Beverly and other points. Jackson then sent this intelligence to Brigadier General John Echols at Meadow Bluff and to the department headquarters at Dublin. The department commander, Major General Sam Jones, admonished Jackson to pay close attention to any movement toward Staunton. The general urged Jackson to have the remainder of his men ready for active service as soon as possible. About two months had passed since the organization of the 19th Virginia Cavalry, yet they lacked arms and equipment. Many of the men were without horses.

Not only did the men of Jackson's command have to watch for Union advances; they also were on the alert for suspicious persons moving north and south. Such persons, of course, could be spies for the Lincoln government, or more often Confederate deserters fleeing their commands. General Jones assigned Captain Jacob W. Marshall, Company I, 19th Virginia Cavalry, to duty as Provost Marshal of Pocahontas, Bath, and Randolph counties on June 28, 1863.

On June 20, General Robert E. Lee wrote Major General Jones that he thought now was a good time to threaten western Virginia. If possible, the threat should be an actual attack. Such a move would relieve some pressure from Lee's flanks as he pushed northward to Gettysburg. General Lee wrote, "A more favorable opportunity will probably not occur during the war...." If the expedition accomplished nothing else, it would prevent troops from moving elsewhere. Unknown to Lee and Jones, Colonel Jackson was then piecing together a plan to attack the garrison at Beverly.

Colonel Jackson's command now consisted of the 19th Virginia Cavalry, at least nine unorganized companies of cavalry, and the 37th Battalion Virginia Cavalry. The effective total of his force amounted to 1,210 men.

On June 23, Jackson requested that General Echols send him two pieces of artillery and several ambulances. Echols sent his request to General Jones at Dublin. The department commander quickly responded, directing Echols to honor Jackson's request. The letter from Jackson outlined his plan to attack Beverly. General Jones approved the plan, stating: "Indeed, you have only anticipated my wishes...."

Two days later, June 26, the Federal garrison at Beverly knew of Jackson's intentions. Colonel Thomas M. Harris, commanding the post, estimated that Jackson had 2,000 men. The colonel requested reinforcements in the form of infantry and cavalry "...in order that, after whipping Jackson, I may take the offensive against Staunton...."

The expedition to Beverly started on June 29, 1863, when Colonel Jackson advanced by three different routes. One detachment would advance via Valley Mountain. This column consisted of cavalry, infantry (actually dismounted cavalrymen, used as infantry), and a section of Captain Beirne Chapman's Battery.

The second detachment consisted of Captain Righter's Company (19th Virginia Cavalry), and portions of Captain Arnett's, Campbell's, and Evans' companies. They would follow the Staunton and Parkersburg Turnpike through Cheat Pass. Captain Righter and his command, upon their arrival near Huttonsville, were to capture the Federal picket posts. The scouts supplied Righter with information revealing the location of these posts to a point within five miles of Beverly. None of the pickets must escape.

The third detachment consisted of most of the 37th Battalion Virginia Cavalry (Lt. Col. Ambrose Dunn) and Captain E. M. Corder's company of cavalry. They were to leave their camp at Hightown, Highland County, and proceed west to a point near Slaven's Cabin. There they were to turn to the left and follow a road leading to Philippi. Once they passed Beverly, Dunn was to attack the town from the rear.

Colonel Jackson accompanied the column with the dismounted men and the artillery. Along the way, an assassination attempt against Jackson took place. Sometime earlier Jackson had arrested a Union man and had him sent to a prison in Richmond. A party of Union bushwhackers resolved to kill Jackson. As none of the bushwhackers knew Jackson, they asked for the aid of a young girl who knew him. The aspiring assassins persuaded her to step out into the road as Jackson passed by and hand him a letter. This she did, and as soon as she had reached the safety of her house, the assassins fired a volley at Jackson. Their volley missed, striking no one. Jackson's men immediately returned fire, killing one of the bushwhackers and routing the rest. Jackson promptly arrested the young lady and detained her for a while.

After passing Valley Mountain on the evening of July 1, 1863, Colonel Jackson detached Major John B. Lady with a force of 150 dismounted cavalrymen. Men from the companies of Captains Evans, Arnett, Hayhurst, Duncan and Boggs made up the detachment. These companies became part of the 20th Virginia Cavalry in August.

Colonel Jackson sent Major Lady and his detachment to sieze the Buckhannon Road, to prevent the enemy from retreating in that direction. All forces were to attack when they heard Captain Chapman's guns open fire.

Soon after Major Lady marched, Jackson ordered Sergeant Rader and 20 mounted men to support him. Sergeant Rader went to the Middle Fork Bridge, 18 miles west of the position occupied by Major Lady.

Major Lady and his men followed blind paths over a series of the most rugged and densely timbered mountains for 12 miles. They arrived at the base of Rich Mountain at 3 a.m. on July 2. Major Lady ordered a two-hour halt, which his exhausted men readily welcomed. Many were asleep as soon as Major Lady issued the order.

At 5 a.m., the major roused his men and ordered them to fall in. The march toward Beverly resumed. Many of the men complained of being footsore. Major Lady and his men arrived at their appointed post at 10 a.m., July 2. Beverly lay five miles to the east.

Colonel Jackson, with the main column of his command arrived at Huttonsville about daybreak on July 2. There Jackson found Captain Righter, executing his orders to capture the Federal pickets. Fourteen Federals were now prisoners of war.

It was nearing the time for the Federal relief to arrive. Colonel Jackson sent Captain Marshall with a portion of his company to aid Righter in meeting them. The two captains selected a position which allowed them to surround a point which the relief party must pass. The Federals arrived promptly. They were quickly and efficiently taken prisoner, adding another fourteen prisoners to those already taken that morning.

The road to Beverly was now clear to within a mile and a half of the town. Colonel Jackson wrote in his report that the surprise would have been complete had it not been for a woman. The woman, in some manner, learned of Jackson's approach and immediately went to sound the alarm. Along the way to Beverly, she met 25 Federal troops. One member of this party was Colonel Thomas M. Harris, 10th West Virginia Infantry, the commander of the post at Beverly, out for his morning ride.

When within eight miles of Beverly, Jackson detached about 200 men under the command of Major David Boston Stewart. The men of this detachment were from the companies of Captains Downs and Ball, with part of Young's, Lewis', and Campbell's. Some unorganized recruits and mounted men accompanied him. Jackson ordered Stewart to cross the Valley River, and advance on the back road. At Beverly, Stewart was to strike the Federal left flank and cooperate with Colonel Dunn's column.

Colonel Jackson moved now to the front of Beverly. Near that place, a detachment under Captain Spriggs (Company B, 19th Virginia) went to the burnt bridge. This served as the center of Jackson's line. Major Stewart's command made up the right flank, while Captain Marshall occupied a road leading to the Buckhannon road on the left.

The Federals tried to advance on Jackson by the road occupied by Captain Marshall, but Marshall and Captain Spriggs drove the enemy back.

Colonel Jackson posted his artillery on a hill, opposite the enemy position and about a mile away. The enemy occupied a very strong position on Butcher Hill (now called Mount Iser), in the rear of the town, near the Philippi road. Captain John D. Neal, with his company and portions of two others, supported the artillery. Captain Marshall's detachment was near enough to help them should the enemy make a move against the artillery.

If Colonel Dunn was in place, Jackson's forces would have the enemy surrounded. The Confederate colonel estimated the Union force at Beverly to be 1,000 men. His own command consisted of 1,200 men. A postwar account of the fight states that the Federal force was 800, before General W. W. Averell reinforced them.

At 2 p.m., Jackson ordered his artillery to open fire, which served as the signal for all forces to attack. Something, however, went wrong. Where was Dunn? Colonel Jackson, having a clear view of the field, could see no movement in rear of Beverly.

An artillery duel now started between the two forces. Jackson continued to look for Dunn, who had not yet appeared. The enemy had the advantage of position, number of guns, and quality of ammunition. Colonel Jackson recorded that not more than one in fifteen of his shells exploded.

Colonel Jackson held his men in readiness to attack, waiting for the appearance of Dunn's column. The former judge felt confident he could dislodge the enemy without the aid of Dunn's column. To dislodge them, however, was not the purpose of the attack. He wanted to take them all prisoner.

Soon, it became too dark to continue the artillery engagement. The column under Dunn was still missing. Jackson's efforts to contact him failed. Colonel Jackson sent word to Major Stewart to fall back a short distance, to a safe position for the night.

Major Lady's Detachment

Upon arriving at his appointed post five miles west of Beverly, Major Lady concealed his men in shade and near water. The major ordered Lieutenant John W. Hunt, with 20 men, to proceed carefully to within two miles of Beverly to watch the enemy and to cut off their communications.

When the artillery opened fire, Lieutenant Hunt was to advance and cut off the enemy pickets on the Buckhannon road. A courier went to tell Colonel Dunn that Lady was in position.

When the artillery opened fire at 2 p.m. (Lady says 3 p.m.), Major Lady quickly advanced to within a mile and a quarter of Beverly. He occupied a position which he could hold against any force of the enemy. This position lay just west of Baker's house. Major Lady sent Captain Arnett forward to occupy an eminence to prevent the Federals from using it for an artillery position. Simultaneously, Major Lady sent Captain Evans and a squad to reconnoiter between his position and Beverly. Captain Evans was to examine the fortifications near Baker's house. An hour later Evans reported. A strong position, he said, was available beyond Baker's house, near the old breastworks.

Major Lady advanced his command as far as possible, just out of range of the Federal artillery. His intention was to occupy the position near the old breastworks under cover of darkness. Captain Evans, with 40 men, were placed on the road to blockade and picket it. They were to open an engagement should the enemy try to come that way. Captain Arnett occupied an adjacent height to support Evans' men. Major Lady held the companies of Captains Hayhurst, Duncan, and Boggs in reserve.

About this time the cavalry scouts (Sergeant Rader) reported to Major Lady, reporting they had carried out their instructions. While performing their duty, they had a brush with the notorious spy and bushwhacker, Jacob Simmons. While the Confederates tried to arrest him, Simmons killed one of the Confederate cavalrymen. The Confederates opened fire on Simmons, four balls striking and killing him. Major Lady, taking advantage of now having mounted men, sent a courier to communicate with Colonel Dunn. Lady's detachment remained in this position throughout the night.

Major Stewart's Detachment

Leaving the main column near Huttonsville, Major Stewart followed the back road as fast as the condition of his men would permit. The few mounted men accompanying him acted as scouts in the advance.

When two miles from the home of Henry Harper, Major Stewart deployed Captain Campbell's Company on his right as skirmishers. Advancing cautiously, Stewart discovered a Federal picket force at Harper's house. Detailing 25 men to advance and take possession of the roads beyond Harper's, Stewart prepared to advance upon the Federals. Before he could do so, they saw a rider dash up to Harper's, and the pickets ran headlong toward Beverly.

In his advance on the back road, Stewart met a mounted scout of eight men. Two of the scouts escaped, the others were killed, wounded, or captured. Stewart halted here until 1 p.m.

About 1 p.m., Major Stewart received orders to advance to the support of Captain Marshall's command, if Marshall moved toward Earl Hill. After much difficulty, Stewart collected his scattered men, and moved at 1:40.

Major Stewart arrived at Fontaine Butcher's farm, on a hill south of Files Creek, about 5 p.m. He was now a half mile to the right of Earl Hill, and could see the enemy moving about on Butcher's Hill, northeast of town. Stewart sent his mounted scouts out to see if Captain Marshall had advanced. He intended to occupy Earl Hill after sunset.

About 7:30 p.m., Jackson ordered Stewart to fall back to near Harper's house. Stewart and his detachment arrived at that place at 11:30 and went into camp for the night.

Early on the morning of July 3, 1863, Colonel Jackson determined to attack the enemy. He had wasted much valuable time in waiting for Dunn to arrive. Jackson directed Stewart to advance to the position he had occupied the evening before.

Dismounting most of his cavalry, Jackson advanced on the enemy. The guns of Captain Chapman's Battery opened fire. He then discovered enemy reinforcements, 700 strong, arriving from the direction of Philippi. Major Lady, on the Buckhannon road, and Captain Marshall both reported the arrival of the enemy forces. Colonel Jackson became convinced that Dunn, if he had ever arrived, had fallen back. That being the case, it was not wise to continue the attack. The colonel sent orders to Majors Lady and Stewart to fall back and join the main column east of Huttonsville. Meanwhile, Jackson made a four-hour demonstration in front of Beverly to occupy the Federals attention while Lady and Stewart pulled back. Again, Jackson tried to communicate with Lieutenant Colonel Dunn.

At 2 p.m., Jackson began to fall back slowly, guarding his flanks. The enemy did not follow him that day. About six miles from Beverly, Major J. R. Claiborne arrived with 100 men of the 37th Battalion Virginia Cavalry. The major and his detachment were just returning from detached duty.

Colonel Jackson continued to retire, passing Huttonsville, halting at Crouch's Fortifications for the night. Major Claiborne and his men, in better condition than Jackson's men, watched the rear during the night. They occupied a position between Crouch's and Huttonsville.

Major Lady's Detachment

About 8 a.m. on the morning of July 3, the cavalry which Major Lady had sent the night before to locate Colonel Dunn returned. They had found no sign of Dunn and his men.

An hour later, Major Lady saw the advance of the enemy relief column on the Philippi road. They were advancing rapidly, and had come within a mile of Lady's position. Major Lady sent out his scouts to learn the strength of the column, and informed Colonel Jackson of the situation.

By 9:30 a.m., Major Lady no longer felt secure in his position. He ordered his men to fall back to the position he first had occupied the day before. There Jackson's dispatch arrived, directing him to fall back.

Major Stewart's Detachment

Major Stewart and his men were in motion at 6:45 a.m. Thirty of his men, being unable to march, remained at Harper's house. With his mounted men in advance, Stewart moved to the position he had occupied the evening before. Along the way, he received a message from Jackson. The Confederate commander said he had dismounted Captain Spriggs and his men, and sent them to flank the enemy. Major Stewart should watch for them and not mistake them for the enemy.

The artillery had by 8:45 a.m., nearly ceased firing. Major Stewart could detect no small arms fire. Stewart and his men were now at Daniel's Farm, on a hill east of Files Creek. Captain Young and his company went to scout the road toward Earl Hill. Captain Burns and his company scouted their former position, with Stewart and the dismounted men following.

As Stewart and his men advanced, about 200 of the enemy opened fire upon them. The first fire wounded Major Stewart's horse. The major ordered his men, about 140 strong, to fall in, and opened fire on the enemy. Major Stewart wrote in his report: "This fire at first produced some excitement along the line, and produced a little wavering...."

Major Stewart ordered the dismounted men to charge. They rushed forward with a deafening cheer, firing upon the enemy. Lieutenant William Harris fell while leading his company in this charge.

The men, with few exceptions, pressed forward and routed the enemy, who occupied a position with a fence in his rear and on the left. Another fence lay on the right, leaving a single opening to retreat through. The Confederates poured a deadly fire upon them. Fourteen killed and wounded Federals remained on the field at this point.

The skirmish now became a running fight. About three dozen Federals had been killed or wounded. According to an account in the Richmond *Sentinel*, the Federals had 42 killed and 67 wounded. The same paper reported the Confederate loss as 9 killed and wounded.

The loss in Stewart's command amounted to, according to the available records, three killed and five wounded. The mounted men of Stewart's detachment did not take part in the fight.

Lieutenant Wamsley, Company I, 19th Virginia Cavalry, attached to Stewart's column as a guide, advanced with the first charge. According to Major Stewart, Wamsley yelled: "Come on; don't let the d——d [damned] Yankees whip us on our own soil."

By the time Jackson's order to retire reached Stewart, the skirmish was over. Stewart left his wounded at Daniel's Farm, where they received the necessary care. The citizens in the neighborhood agreed to bury the Southern dead.

On the morning of July 4, 1863, Colonel Jackson at last heard from the missing Dunn, who informed Jackson that he was retiring to Stipe's Hotel. Colonel Jackson immediately ordered Major Claiborne to go to a point near Stipe's, to communicate with Dunn. Jackson ordered Claiborne to fall back to Hightown if the enemy did not appear by 2 p.m. A detachment of the 19th Virginia Cavalry, consisting of Marshall's and Spriggs' companies covered Claiborne's movements from Huttonsville.

When Major Claiborne arrived at Stipe's, he discovered that Dunn had fallen back to Camp Bartow. After 2 p.m., the major fell back as directed by Jackson.

The detachment sent to cover Claiborne commanded by Captain Marshall met the enemy advance near Huttonsville. Captain Spriggs' Company was in front and engaged them. The Federals fell back, trying to draw Spriggs after them. Instead, as ordered, Spriggs and Marshall retired a short distance and waited for the enemy to advance again.

Colonel Jackson at last decided that the enemy would not advance in force or push for an engagement. As the rivers were rising rapidly in his rear, Jackson retired to Marshall's Store and camped for the night. The Federals, commanded by Brigadier General William W. Averell, returned to Beverly.

Colonel Jackson, in his report of the expedition to Beverly, wrote:

> The officers and men of my command, with but few exceptions, performed their duty faithfully and cheerfully throughout the whole expedition, notwithstanding it rained every day but one, and the mud and deep waters through which they were compelled to wade.

One of the "few exceptions" Jackson referred to was Lieutenant Colonel A. C. Dunn of the 37th Battalion Virginia Cavalry. Dunn with part of his command and a company from Jackson's command went to cut off the enemy's retreat on the Philippi road. Colonel Jackson ordered him to attack vigorously the enemy's rear when he heard Jackson's artillery firing. This did not happen. Colonel Dunn, according to his dispatches, was in position two hours before the appointed time. Dunn wrote on July 9 that he "...did everything in my power to carry out your orders, and, in fact, did more than you ordered me to do." Dunn, however, did not elaborate on his deeds. Apparently when he heard the signal, he retired instead of attacking.

One piece of evidence in Dunn's favor has been discovered, which shows he at least reached the position assigned to him. On July 17, 1863, the

Wheeling *Daily Intelligencer* printed an account of the fight at Beverly. The writer, a member of the 10th West Virginia Infantry, states: "The train was left in charge of Capt. Gould's company, B, and was started on the Philippi road. About a mile and a half out the Captain found the road blockaded by Dunn's battalion...."

Reliable persons reported after the war that Dunn's failure was due to the discovery of two barrels of whiskey. The men eagerly consumed the contents and soon did not know if they were Union or Confederate. Another account states that the men lost interest in the expedition because of their intoxication.

Whatever the reason, Dunn did not perform as expected, and was later placed under arrest by Jackson.

Colonel Jackson reported the loss of 13 men: four killed, five wounded, and four missing in action. The loss according to the Compiled Service Records was:

REGIMENT	KIA	CPD	WD	TOTAL
19th Virginia Cavalry	2	2	3	7
20th Virginia Cavalry	1	3	?	4
TOTAL	3	5	3	11

Chapter III

Jackson's command quickly resumed its duties of scouting the movements of the enemy.

During July 1863, rumors of every sort circulated. In the Confederate camp, rumor had it that Averell planned to attack Jackson. In the Federal camp, gossip insisted that Jackson planned to raid Beverly again soon. When the rumor of Averell's attack reached the ears of Colonel Jackson, he gave it no serious thought.

In early August the rumor of Averell attacking became fact. General Averell left Winchester on August 5 on the first of three raids in western Virginia. Five days later, Jackson learned of Averell's movements. General Sam Jones directed Jackson to give whatever aid he could to Imboden in protecting Staunton.

During the summer of 1863, Federals reported the presence of many bands of Confederates in the northwest. Many of these bands, the Federal authorities said accurately, belonged to "Bill" Jackson's command.

Numbers of Jackson's men were absent without leave (AWOL) during that summer. Some of them, perhaps, conducted raids on their own, under the loose guise of the Confederacy.

The problem of deserters from other commands, as well as Jackson's, came to the attention of the Adjutant General's office. On August 6, 1863, Assistant Adjutant General H. L. Clay wrote Major General Samuel Jones:

> ...there are said to be many stragglers from the command of Col. W. L. Jackson, and that even some of the officers of his regiment have been permitted to remain absent several months at a time.

Jones responded:

> I am on my way to Colonel Jackson's command, and if any such abuses exist, I will endeavor to correct them. It is but just to Colonel Jackson, however, to say that his command is new, and is now only in formation and organization, and it is probable that those who are represented as stragglers and absentees have been employed recruiting and collecting men from within the enemy's lines.

A few days after General Jones wrote the above, Jackson completed the organization of his second regiment of cavalry.

Colonel Jackson organized the 20th Virginia Cavalry on August 14, 1863, from the independent companies of his command. He received authority from the War Department to raise a new regiment on August 1, 1863. Captain William W. Arnett became colonel of the new regiment, while Captain Dudley Evans became lieutenant colonel. Major John B. Lady kept his rank in the new regiment. Private John S. Utterback, Company D, 20th Virginia Cavalry, referred to the regiment as "mounted infantry" in his pension application. Utterback, a former infantryman, probably named it so because of the many dismounted men.

The roots of the 20th Virginia Cavalry lay more than a year in the past. The previous spring, Major David Boston Stewart had received authority to raise a battalion or regiment of partisan rangers in the northwest. With the help of Lieutenant David Poe, Stewart collected a small group of men in Highland County. When Colonel Jackson assumed command of the former State Line and Ranger troops, he inherited the handful of men assembled by Stewart.

The companies forming the 20th Virginia Cavalry were:

COMPANY A

Members of this company enlisted at intervals, and included those men collected by Major Stewart during 1862. Captain Dudley Evans completed the organization of the company on April 15, 1863. The company boasted 107 men on its rolls at one point during the war. It accompanied Jackson during the spring and summer campaigns of 1863. Many of the members of this company were from Marion and Monongalia counties, West Virginia.

COMPANY B

This company, organized by Captain William W. Arnett, completed its organization on April 15, 1863. Thirty-one members had formerly belonged to Company D, 19th Virginia Cavalry. Many of the men of this company were from Marion and Monongalia counties, West Virginia.

COMPANY C

This company, organized by Captain Elihu Hutton, completed its organization on April 16, 1863. Most of its members lived in Randolph County, West Virginia.

COMPANY D

The company, only partially organized, entered the service on May 3, 1863. Captain Edward M. Corder completed the organization on June 1, 1863. Many of the members of this company were from Barbour County, West Virginia.

COMPANY E

Captain John W. Young completed this company's organization on May 10, 1863. Many of the men were from Harrison County, West Virginia.

COMPANY F

This company, organized by Captain Asbury Lewis, completed its organization on May 10, 1863. Some members had formerly served in Company A, 3rd Virginia State Line. Others transferred from Companies A and C, 19th Virginia Cavalry, in July 1863. Most of these men returned to their former regiment in 1864. Many of the members of this company were from Harrison County, West Virginia.

COMPANY G
Wood County Grays

This company, partially organized by Lieutenant Paul Neal, entered service before May 12, 1863. The company, under the guidance of Captain John D. Neal, completed its organization in Greenbrier County on May 12, 1863. The members of this company were from Wood and Pleasants counties, West Virginia.

COMPANY H

Captain Joseph Hayhurst completed organization of this company on June 4, 1863. Some of this company's men had served formerly in Company A, 3rd Virginia State Line, and Company A, 19th Virginia Cavalry. Many of the members of this company were from Wirt County, West Virginia.

COMPANY I

This company, raised by Major John B. Lady, completed its organization on May 4, 1863. Henry L. Heiskell served as its captain. The company formed part of Major Lady's detachment in the fight at Beverly, West Virginia, in July 1863. A wartime return shows that Major Lady organized the company in Rockbridge County.

COMPANY K

This company, raised by Major John B. Lady, completed its organization on July 21, 1863. Otho Alexander served as its captain. The company formed part of Major Lady's detachment in the fight at Beverly, in July 1863. A wartime return shows that Major Lady organized the company in Rockbridge County.

General William W. Averell occupied Monterey, the county seat of Highland County, on August 20, 1863, and his men captured a few Southerners. One of the prisoners belonged to the 19th Virginia Cavalry. Three others belonged to the 20th Virginia Cavalry. Averell left Monterey the following day, marching toward Huntersville. Near Gibson's Store, he met 300 Confederates, whom he drove back to within five miles of Huntersville. The Confederates continued to fall back until they reached a ravine about three miles from Huntersville. The Southern force belonged to Jackson's command.

Colonel Jackson, as usual, split his command into several detachments. Jackson had his headquarters at Camp Northwest, east of Huntersville. He

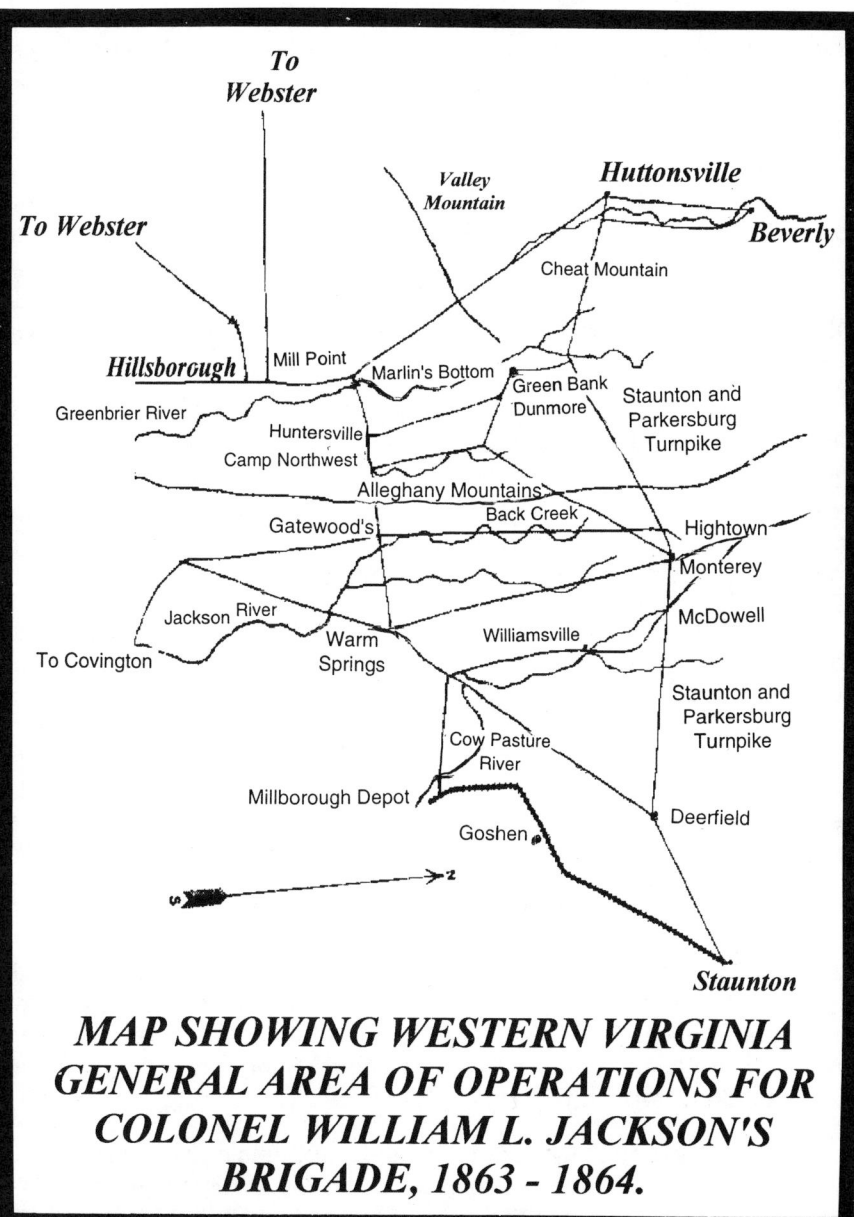

MAP SHOWING WESTERN VIRGINIA GENERAL AREA OF OPERATIONS FOR COLONEL WILLIAM L. JACKSON'S BRIGADE, 1863 - 1864.

had a detachment posted at Hightown (35 miles from headquarters), under Colonel William W. Arnett. Two more detachments camped at Camp Miller (14 miles from headquarters), and Thorny Creek, near Greenbank (10 miles from headquarters).

Colonel Jackson learned of Averell's presence in Highland County at 1 a.m. on August 21. Colonel Arnett of the 20th Virginia Cavalry abandoned his position at Hightown and move to Slaven's Cabin. Jackson ordered Arnett to fall back to Camp Northwest if Averell advanced on him. Couriers rode rapidly to recall the remaining detachments. Jackson sent dispatches to Generals Jones and Imboden in which he expressed the opinion that Averell intended to strike Staunton.

At daylight on August 21, Jackson sent Lieutenant Colonel Dudley Evans with a detachment to Gatewood's (Mountain Grove) in Bath County. That afternoon Jackson received word from Colonel Arnett that Averell was pressing him, and he was falling back down Back Creek. Jackson immediately ordered his dismounted cavalry to Gatewood's, nine miles distant. Only a small mounted force remained at Camp Northwest.

That night the mounted men from Arnett's detachment arrived at Camp Northwest, bringing in his wagon train. They reported Arnett and the dismounted men cut off, and moving down Knapp Creek. Colonel Jackson went to Gatewood's during the early hours of the night. Upon his arrival there, he reinforced Evans' command by two companies. Jackson posted Colonel Evans two miles north of Gatewood's. To support Evans, Jackson ordered Lieutenant Colonel William P. Thompson to take the dismounted men to a position a mile in Evans' rear.

On the morning of August 22, Jackson ordered his cavalry to fall back to Gatewood's. Captain Elihu Hutton (Company C, 20th Virginia Cavalry) remained between Rider's and Camp Northwest to watch Averell's command. Jackson sent Major Kessier with 60 men to McDowell, via the Jackson River and Warm Springs. This detachment was to see if any Federal force was advancing on Staunton. He sent scouts to Warm Springs to watch the route from Back Creek to Warm Springs.

During the evening, Averell's command and Captain Hutton skirmished near Camp Northwest. Averell's men forced Hutton to retire to Rider's. The Randolph County native reported to Jackson that Averell was making a flank movement via Little Back Creek.

Colonel Jackson, feeling vulnerable, moved his dismounted men to the Jackson River, on the road to Warm Springs. The mounted men of his command remained at Gatewood's.

When Averell's men did not appear at Gatewood's on the morning of

August 23, Jackson assumed they had moved toward Lewisburg. He ordered his dismounted men to return to Gatewood's, and moved with his mounted men toward Camp Northwest. As Colonel Arnett had safely returned, he assumed command of the cavalry.

Colonel Arnett met Averell's advance near Camp Northwest, and a skirmish developed. During the skirmish, Arnett discovered a flank movement, and fell back to Rider's. Colonel Jackson joined Arnett at this point, and ordered the men to fall back to Gatewood's for the night. Federal reports show 12 Confederates killed or wounded and six taken prisoner (one lieutenant and five enlisted men). The Compiled Service Records of the 19th Virginia Cavalry show only three men captured on this date in Pocahontas County.

Jackson's position at Gatewood's, according to Lieutenant David Poe (Company A, 20th Virginia Cavalry), was a strong one. He wrote:

> When he [the enemy] came Jackson decided that with the advantage of position he could hold Averill [sic] in check until other forces could reach the scene.

Major General Samuel Jones said of Jackson's position on August 23:

> Colonel Jackson has a strong position on Back Creek, and expressed entire confidence in his ability to hold it, if attacked.

Early on the morning of August 24, Jackson ordered Colonel Arnett to move the cavalry to the Jackson River on the Warm Springs road. Lieutenant G. W. Siple (Company F, 19th Virginia Cavalry) and 30 men remained with Jackson at Gatewood's.

Averell's advance came into sight about 10 a.m., and began skirmishing with Jackson's men. Jackson fell back with Lieutenant Siple acting as rear guard. The skirmishing continued as he retired. Along the way, Jackson posted his dismounted men to make a stand. He ordered Colonel Arnett to send 100 dismounted men to the top of Back Creek Mountain to prevent a flank attack.

Colonel Jackson maintained his position for an hour, then pulled back. Ten minutes later, Averell's men overran the position he had just left. The Federals immediately advanced, forcing Jackson to retire to Warm Springs. Again Jackson posted his men to meet an attack.

An hour passed before Averell's advance came into sight. After some slight skirmishing, Jackson fell back across Warm Springs Mountain. He continued to retire until about 10 p.m., when his dismounted men camped near the Cow Pasture River. The cavalry camped near Bath Alum Springs. Jackson's pickets were between Bath Alum and Warm Springs.

General Averell remained at Warm Springs for the night. He now decided to go to Lewisburg, hoping the occupation of Warm Springs would lead the Confederates to believe he was marching for Staunton. On the morning of August 25, 1863, Averell left his infantry at Warm Springs, and marched toward Lewisburg, via Hot Springs.

That morning Jackson ordered his dismounted men to move to the west bank of the Cow Pasture River. Going to the cavalry camp near Bath Alum, Jackson contacted Colonel Arnett. He ordered Arnett to send his scouts to the top of Warm Springs Mountain to check on Averell's movements. Colonel Arnett, with the main force of cavalry, was ready to move at a moment's notice.

The dismounted men of Jackson's command, through a misunderstanding, fell back to Old Millboro (Millboro Springs). When he learned of the error, Jackson ordered them to go into camp at that place.

During the evening of August 25, Major Kessler returned from McDowell, reporting that he saw no sign of the enemy advancing upon Staunton. The scouts from Warm Springs reported that Averell had moved south, leaving his infantry at Warm Springs. Colonel Jackson ordered Colonel Arnett to occupy Warm Springs the following morning.

On the morning of August 26, Jackson ordered Major Kessler to take a detachment of cavalry to Covington. After reaching that point, if possible, Jackson wished Kessler to go to Lewisburg and scout Averell's movements. By noon that day, Colonel Arnett occupied Warm Springs. Averell's infantry had pulled back to Gatewood's. Jackson ordered Arnett to scout their position.

By the evening of August 27, Averell had returned to Callaghan's, near Covington. He had advanced no farther than Rocky Gap, near White Sulphur Springs. There on August 26 and the morning of August 27, he met a Confederate force which forced him to retire. Averell remained there until nightfall, then moved toward Warm Springs, leaving his campfires burning to mislead the Confederates.

On the morning of August 27, Jackson ordered his dismounted men to move from Old Millboro to Warm Springs. A disheartening rumor awaited Jackson when he arrived at Warm Springs, in advance of the dismounted men. A report was circulating that Averell had forced the Confederates at Lewisburg to retire from that place. Colonel Jackson prepared for the worst. He ordered Lieutenant Siple to take a detachment of men and follow the Hot Springs route until he met the enemy. Captain Lewis and 20 men scouted toward Gatewood's.

Averell's command arrived at Gatewood's about daylight on August 28. They halted here for a short while. About 9 a.m., they resumed their line of march toward Huntersville.

About 3 o'clock on the morning of August 29, Jackson received a dispatch from Major Kessler that Averell was retiring toward Warm Springs. A few minutes later William McClintic, Surveyor of Bath County, contacted Jackson. The citizens, McClintic reported, were blockading the Jackson River Road (also called Boller's or Indian Draft). Colonel Jackson approved their action, and asked McClintic to return and make sure they completed the blockade.

Jackson ordered Colonel Arnett to blockade the road to Hot Springs, as well as one leading from the Jackson River road to the Warm Springs. While Colonel Arnett worked on obstructing the roads, the report arrived that Averell was near Gatewood's, on the Indian Draft route.

Colonel Jackson moved quickly with Colonel Arnett toward Gatewood's. Blockades thrown up by the enemy slowed his progress. Arnett arrived at Gatewood's in time to fire on Averell's pickets and the rear of the column. Jackson wrote that Averell and his men were "in rapid retreat." Arnett and the mounted men followed Averell as far as Little Back Creek. At that point, the Confederates turned to the right to reach the Knapp Creek road.

When Jackson arrived at Little Back Creek and learned what Arnett was doing, he recalled him. Jackson felt sure that Averell would not use the Knapp Creek road, but instead continue to Marlin's Bottom.

Arnett and Jackson followed Averell with the mounted men. Lieutenant Colonel Evans followed him with the dismounted men. About 6 p.m., when between Rider's and Camp Northwest, Jackson received a dispatch from General Jones. The dispatch instructed him to press and destroy Averell. With renewed purpose, Jackson pressed on, catching up with Averell's pickets at Huntersville. Jackson felt confident that Averell would make a stand there.

After dark, with no sign of reinforcements for Jackson, he went into camp for the night near Camp Northwest. Jackson refused to advance any further without sending a flanking party to Big Spring. This party would follow the Clover Lick route to Big Spring, blockade the road and hold Averell until Jackson could move up in his rear.

At 10 p.m., Jackson learned that part of the 8th Virginia Cavalry and the 37th Battalion Virginia Cavalry were at Gatewood's. Jackson requested that they push on to Camp Northwest as quickly as possible.

About 2 a.m., on August 29, Colonel Arnett moved with what cavalry he could muster to Big Spring on the Clover Lick route. At daylight, Lieutenant Colonel Evans and the dismounted men moved toward Huntersville and Marlin's Bottom. While at Huntersville, the detachments from the 8th Virginia and 37th Battalion joined Jackson.

Colonel Jackson immediately asked Colonel James M. Corns of the 8th Virginia Cavalry to send 200 mounted men to aid Colonel Arnett at Big Spring.

Corns consulted with his officers and informed Jackson that his horses could not withstand such a trip. Jackson then asked him to go to Marlin's Bottom, which he consented to do.

Jackson, with his reinforcements, arrived at Marlin's Bottom soon after Averell's command passed over the Greenbrier River Bridge. As Averell's rear was about a mile away, Jackson asked Corns to move up the river and try to cut off some of Averell's stragglers. Colonel Corns informed Jackson that his horses could not "raise a trot." Soon after this, Corns and the 37th Battalion moved to Lewisburg. So much for the reinforcements sent to help Jackson destroy Averell.

By this time, Major Kessler arrived. Jackson ordered him to pursue Averell as rapidly as the condition of his horses and foot soldiers would allow. Kessler moved at once to Edray, where the dismounted men gave out and halted. The major and the mounted men pressed on.

Colonel Arnett arrived at Big Spring in advance of Averell. He quickly blockaded the road, posted his men, and awaited the arrival of Averell's advance. When Averell appeared, Arnett engaged him. The fight lasted only a short time before Arnett fell back. Major Kessler, coming in from the rear, encountered many blockades. Slowed by these and the condition of his horses, he could not reach Big Spring in time to help Arnett. Averell's command safely reached Beverly on August 31, 1863.

During this campaign, Jackson's effective force never exceeded 1,000 men. The colonel wrote of his command: "My command throughout, officers and men, behaved well, enduring patiently great hardships, and conducting themselves as well as any new recruits under the same conditions."

Jackson reported the loss in his command as 20 or less in wounded and captured. A study of the Compiled Service Records does not show any men wounded. They show 22 men taken prisoner by Averell's command.

The Yankees bestowed upon Colonel Jackson the nickname "Mudwall," because they felt he would not stand and fight.

Chapter IV

The men of Jackson's command quickly resumed their duties of scouting and picketing "The Huntersville Line." On September 1, 1863, the issue of stragglers and absentees came up again. Major General Jones' Adjutant wrote Jackson: "...do all in your power to collect together your command, which he [Jones] learns has a large amount of stragglers from your old camp, as far as Millborough."

From his camp at Marlin's Bottom, Jackson informed Jones the next day that he was collecting his stragglers and absentees. Jackson reported that he had left 300 men behind, who could not march.

In the same communication to Jones, Jackson outlined a raid to capture the Federal garrison at Sutton. Major Joseph R. Kessler would move on the Cold Knob route with 200 dismounted men the next day.

A few days before this J. C. Eagle joined Jackson's command. Eagle, a member of the Upshur Militia (133rd West Virginia Militia), had deserted and fled south a short time earlier. He served as a scout and guide for Imboden's command most of the time.

On the morning of September 3, Kessler and Eagle left Jackson's command at Marlin's Bottom. Upon their arrival at Sutton, they discovered that the enemy force there had left. Major Kessler looked about for a new target. Eagle suggested the Upshur Militia, due to assemble in a few days at Rock Cave (Centerville), West Virginia.

Early on the morning of September 12, 1863, Kessler arrived unobserved at Rock Cave. Using the cover proved by the dense woods, he occupied a high hill southeast of the village. This position overlooked the field in which the militia assembled.

On that late summer morning, when the militia formed and the roll was taken, several of the members were absent. Those absent were George and Henry Eagle, father and brother of Confederate Scout J. C. Eagle.

Kessler formed his plan of attack. The situation called for a flanking maneuver. Just before the militia pickets arrived at their assigned posts, part of Kessler's men circled the field. They took a position on a low knoll near the parade ground. Another force moved south and took their position on a high hill, near the cemetery. This position commanded an approach to the rear of the fortifications there.

The detachment on the north side opened fire on the militia. Immediately, Kessler's men advanced and demanded that the militia surrender. The attack brought instant confusion to the militiamen. Four of the citizen soldiers fell wounded in the first fire. Captain Daniel Gould tried to rally his men, but soon gave up and surrendered. The West Virginia Militia did not fire a shot.

The Confederates quickly closed in and disarmed the militiamen. While part of Kessler's men formed the prisoners (87 in all) for the march to Warm Springs, others collected horses and "anything else of value." Major Kessler returned with his prize to the Confederate lines via the Hacker Valley road. From Warm Springs, the prisoners went to Millboro Depot, then by rail to Richmond and Andersonville.

Toward the middle of October, Colonel Jackson launched an attack on the garrison at Bulltown. A few days before moving to Braxton County, Jackson sent a battalion toward Huttonsville. This would draw the attention of the Federal troops in that direction. Taking an estimated 1,000 men (more likely about 800), Jackson left his camp at Marlin's Bottom. Following the Cold Knob road, he arrived near Bulltown late on October 12, 1863.

Jackson's command consisted of elements of the 19th Virginia Cavalry and 20th Virginia Cavalry, and two guns of Captain Warren S. Lurty's Battery. A few independent companies of cavalry accompanied Jackson on the raid. These companies, in a few weeks, would form the 46th Battalion of Virginia Cavalry. Prisoner of war records show that soldiers from several other commands accompanied Jackson to Bulltown.

Jackson and his command arrived at Falls Mills, three miles above Bulltown undetected. The Confederates planned to attack Bulltown from two directions at the once. Jackson divided his command. Major Kessler commanded the right or northwest wing, while Lieutenant Colonel Thompson commanded the left or southwest wing. Colonel Jackson, with the two guns of Captain Warren S. Lurty's Battery, accompanied Thompson. The attack would begin at 4 a.m., October 13, when Lurty's guns opened fire on the unsuspecting Federals.

The garrison at Bulltown consisted of fewer than 200 infantrymen from parts of two companies of the 6th West Virginia Infantry and parts of three companies of the 11th West Virginia Infantry. Captain William H. Mattingly, 6th West Virginia, commanded the post. He had no artillery or cavalry. The fortifications at Bulltown overlooked the village, on property of Moses Cunningham. These fortifications consisted of two lines of breastworks, one inside the other. The addition of blockhouses and rifle pits strengthened the position.

Jackson's men dispersed the Federal pickets early on the morning of October 13. Those not taken prisoner escaped into the mountains. The Federal pickets did not sound the alarm to warn the garrison.

Major Kessler reached his position in advance of Thompson and Jackson. For reasons known only to Kessler, he immediately began the attack without waiting for the signal. As his line drew near the fortifications, an overly zealous officer discharged his pistol and shouted "Charge!" The sharp crack of the pistol shot aroused the Federal garrison. The Yankees quickly awoke and grabbed their weapons to meet the surprise attack.

The defenders eventually forced Major Kessler's line to fall back. As he retired from the field, Jackson and Thompson arrived on a hill opposite the fortifications.

A few minutes after 8 a.m., Colonel Jackson sent in a flag of truce with a message for Captain Mattingly. The note demanded that Mattingly surrender his force. The captain replied "Come and take us."

The battle continued. Early in the fight, Captain Mattingly received a disabling wound, and Captain James L. Simpson (11th West Virginia) assumed command of the post.

Late in the afternoon, Jackson again sent a demand for the garrison to surrender. Captain Simpson replied that he would fight until hell froze over, then escape on the ice. With this, the battle resumed, but with less vigor than before.

About 4:30 p.m., Colonel Jackson began to withdraw his forces. The Confederates fell back to Salt Lick Bridge, about five miles from Bulltown and went into camp. The 12-hour fight was costly, with no clear benefit to the Confederates. Two of the West Virginia soldiers received wounds and eight were taken prisoner. The Confederate loss amounted to 16 killed, wounded, or captured. The 19th Virginia Cavalry lost two killed, three wounded, and three taken prisoner. Two of those taken prisoner suffered wounds. The loss in the 20th Virginia Cavalry was much lighter, with one man wounded and two taken prisoner. One of the prisoners suffered a wound.

A small Federal force caught up with Jackson on the morning of October 14 and attacked him at Salt Lick Bridge. After a brief skirmish, Jackson fell back to his camp at Marlin's Bottom.

Postwar accounts of the fight at Bulltown attribute Jackson's failure to the use of alcohol. The accounts state that Jackson and his men discovered a cache of liquor and consumed it. The same source claims that the Federal garrison actually surrendered, but the intoxicated Confederates did not realize it. A wartime poem by Private Daniel DeWees (19th Virginia) bolsters the truth of these postwar reports. DeWees cited the use of alcohol as the cause of their failure to capture Bulltown. Colonel Jackson, Thompson, and Kessler all were reported as drunk.

These rumors quickly came to Jackson's attention. In a letter to Captain Jacob W. Marshall dated October 22, 1863, Jackson wrote:

> No one can escape slander. I am however surprised at the talk of the Raders. The charges are utterly without foundation both as regards Lt. Col. Thompson and myself. I am sure nothing has emanated from Maj. Kessler to justify what they say.

On November 1, General Averell left Beverly on another raid. His force of mounted infantry, cavalry, and artillery followed the Staunton and Parkersburg Turnpike to Camp Bartow. From that point, the Federals marched by Greenbank to Huntersville on November 3. Averell's advance met some pickets from Captain McNeel's Company near Greenbank. In the skirmish there the Confederates lost one man wounded and five taken prisoner. The Northern troops destroyed the Confederate camp at that place.

At 6 p.m. on November 3, Colonel Jackson learned of Averell's presence near Greenbank via a dispatch from Lieutenant George W. Siple. Jackson at once ordered Siple to find out the strength and intentions of Averell's command. Jackson received no further communications from the lieutenant. Averell's forces got between Siple and Jackson, cutting him off. Lieutenant Siple and his men joined Jackson at Union, Monroe County, after the battle of Droop Mountain.

As usual, Jackson's command occupied several different points. Headquarters were at Mill Point. Colonel Arnett was at Marlin's Bottom, eight miles from headquarters and six miles from Huntersville. Captains Marshall and Hutton were at Edray, a short distance west of Marlin's Bottom. Lieutenant Colonel Thompson, with 120 mounted men and an undisclosed number dismounted, was absent from Camp Miller on a raid to Nicholas County. Colonel Jackson ordered each of these detachments to assemble at Mill Point.

The Federal column arrived at Huntersville about 11 a.m. on November 4. Averell immediately sent the 14th Pennsylvania Cavalry and the 3rd West Virginia Mounted Infantry to Mill Point, to cut off Jackson's retreat to Lewisburg. The rest of the brigade "halted in this forsaken, desolate place." That afternoon, Averell sent the 2nd and 8th West Virginia Mounted Infantry, with a section of artillery, to Marlin's Bottom.

Soon after learning of Averell's approach, Colonel Arnett ordered the loaded wagons to move to Mill Point. He ordered Captain Marshall to retire on a mountain path which entered the road to Mill Point about a mile from Marlin's Bottom. His wagons safely away, Arnett left Marlin's Bottom, leaving Major Lady with a small squad to watch then enemy.

Lieutenant Colonel Thompson received Jackson's order to return to camp at 3 a.m. on November 4, 1863. Soon after his arrival at Camp Miller,

Thompson received orders to report to Jackson's headquarters. Taking the mounted men, Thompson moved rapidly to join Jackson. Captain J. W. Ball and the dismounted men followed.

As soon as Thompson arrived at Mill Point, Jackson ordered him to take his detachment of mounted men out on the Beaver Creek road. Jackson told him to advance until he met the enemy. Once he met them, he was to blockade the road and halt their progress. After Colonel Arnett's column safely passed the intersection of the Beaver Creek road, he could retire.

About 3 p.m. Thompson's detachment met the enemy on the Beaver Creek road. His men at once began blockading the road and skirmishing with the enemy advance. The Confederates fought dismounted and as skirmishers, taking cover behind the blockades. The skirmishing continued for several hours. As night drew near, Thompson learned that Arnett had passed by and began to withdraw. Thompson had one man killed during the fighting; there is no report of any wounded. Thompson and his men fell back to a hill south of Mill Point. Here, he went into camp, within 300 yards of the enemy lines.

Colonel Arnett's column reached Mill Point about sundown, camping on a hill to the southwest. Colonel Jackson later ordered Arnett to take command of the dismounted men of the brigade. Jackson wished Arnett to station them in detachments along Mill Creek, near Mill Point.

Late that evening, about 9 p.m., Averell learned that the force at Marlin's Bottom had retreated. Several hours later, he learned that they had joined Jackson's main force at Mill Point.

Early on the morning of November 5, Averell left Huntersville and followed the Beaver Creek road to Mill Point. The force sent the previous day to Marlin's Bottom advanced on Mill Point from there. Averell's men were confident of capturing "Mudwall" Jackson and his "fleet-footed ragged chivalry."

Skirmishing between Averell's advance forces and Jackson began at daylight. Jackson sent Captain L. R. Exline with 30 men out on a reconnaissance. Exline soon returned and reported to Jackson that the enemy were bringing up some long-range artillery pieces. This was bad news for Jackson. The long-range guns would give Averell the advantage. Jackson decided to retire as soon as the enemy had the guns in place.

Colonel Jackson made the necessary preparations to fall back to the summit of Droop Mountain. He ordered Colonel Arnett to remain in position with the dismounted men until the Federal artillery opened fire. Once they began firing, Arnett was to fall back by the safest route to Droop Mountain. The cavalry, under Lieutenant Colonel Thompson, remained in the rear. After the dismounted men were safely away, the cavalry would follow.

About 11 a.m. the Federal artillery opened fire and Jackson's men began to retire. Shells from the long range guns burst over the heads of Arnett's men, but injured no one. Most of the cavalry followed Arnett. Colonel Thompson, with the companies of Captain Young and Lieutenant Coffman (about 30 men), remained behind. Thompson wrote:

> These men I held on the hill under a terrific shower of shell and grape about forty minutes, until I saw the infantry [dismounted cavalry] in a comparatively safe position, when I slowly retired, the enemy pressing on with his skirmishers and main columns. At one time the enemy prepared to charge in column with his cavalry, but a skillful and determined movement of the detachment under Captain Young deterred him.

Thompson had one man wounded in the fighting.

When Arnett arrived at the summit of Droop Mountain, Jackson stationed him on a high point next to the road. Thompson arrived at the base of Droop Mountain at 3 p.m. A mounted force of the enemy tried to cut him off, but a few well placed shells from Lurty's Battery put them to flight. Jackson placed Thompson's men on picket duty.

During the day, Jackson informed Brigadier General John Echols of his intention to make a stand on the summit of Droop Mountain. He asked Echols for reinforcements. The 14th Virginia Cavalry from Echols' command arrived late in the evening. They relieved Thompson's men on picket duty.

General Averell's men did not press Jackson's rear too vigorously. According to Averell's plan, he was to meet Brigadier General Alfred Duffie at Lewisburg on November 7. He hoped to catch Jackson's command between the two columns and destroy him. The Federals went into camp between Mill Point and Hillsboro, in plain view of Jackson on Droop Mountain. The farm on which the Federals camped for the night belonged to Captain William L. McNeel of Company F, 19th Virginia Cavalry.

Early on the morning of November 6, General Averell sent three companies of infantry out to skirmish with Jackson's men. Their purpose was to learn the exact position of the Confederates. Soon it was clear to Averell that a direct assault would be too difficult because of Jackson's position and the rugged terrain. Instead, the Federals began a flanking movement.

General Averell sent his infantry and a company of cavalry to the right, to turn the Confederate left flank and get in their rear. Colonel Augustus Moor commanded the flanking column of 1,175 men. To draw Confederate attention away from the movement, Averell sent the 14th Pennsylvania Cavalry and Keeper's Battery to the right.

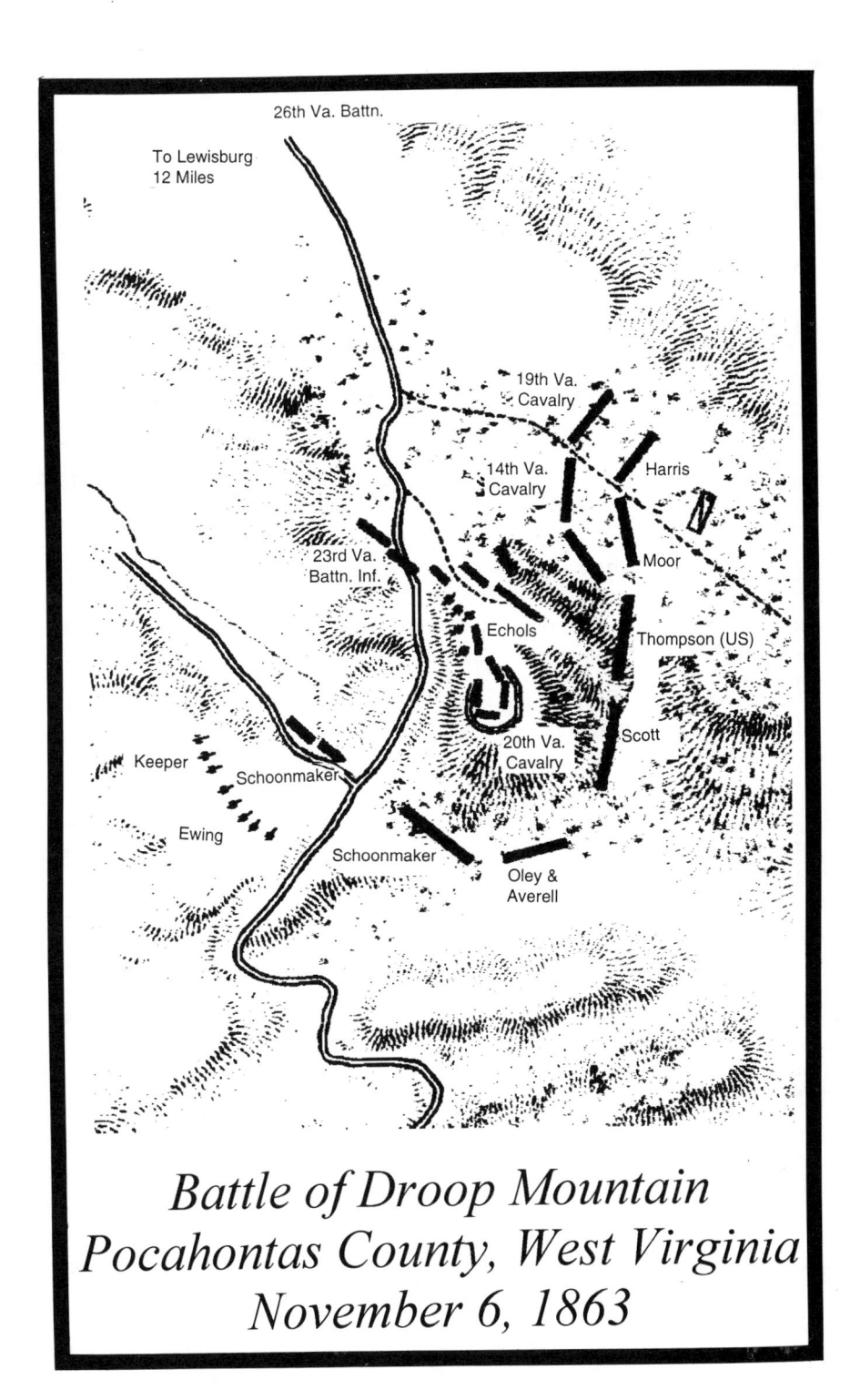

Battle of Droop Mountain
Pocahontas County, West Virginia
November 6, 1863

Colonel Jackson prepared to meet the attack. The right of his line lay near the road across Droop Mountain; he posted his artillery there. Colonel Arnett and his dismounted men occupied the center of the line. During the night, Arnett's men constructed a crude breastwork of logs, rocks, and dirt. Lieutenant Colonel Thompson with the cavalry occupied the left of the line. Only 750 of Jackson's men took part in the fight at Droop Mountain. The rest of his brigade was on the Locust Creek road or cut off in Pocahontas County.

Brigadier General John Echols arrived with his brigade at Droop Mountain about 9 a.m. Upon his arrival, Echols assumed command of the combined force. He examined Jackson's line and found it posted "very advantageously beyond the crest and on the side of the mountain."

The Confederate artillery opened fire soon after Echols came up, then the two armies began skirmishing. Earlier in the morning, Jackson had ordered Thompson to guard the crucial left and rear of his line. A squad of ten men under Lieutenant Boggs moved to that point. Soon Lieutenant Jarrett and 15 men joined them. When Jackson pointed out the importance of the position, Thompson sent Captain Marshall and 100 cavalry to the left. Captain Marshall dismounted his men, sending his horses to the rear. Thompson ordered Marshall to "hold the point at all hazards."

About 11 a.m., Col. Moor and his flanking party arrived on the extreme left of the Confederate line. Echols ordered Jackson to send a force to that point and drive the enemy back. Lieutenant Colonel Thompson with about 175 men of the 19th and 20th Virginia Cavalry rushed to the left. Thompson went too far. Leaving Captain Spriggs to guard that point, Thompson returned to the turnpike with the dismounted men, where he placed them under Major Kessler. Kessler moved at once to reinforce Marshall's line, and push the enemy back. As soon as Kessler and his 50 men reached the line, they charged the enemy, driving them back on their main force. Thompson called for more men.

When the first reports of the Federal advance on Jackson's left arrived, Lieutenant Burns and 18 men of Company A, 20th Virginia Cavalry, advanced to meet them. Burns met the 28th Ohio Infantry and opened fire on them. Taking cover behind trees and rocks, Burns and his squad held the enemy in check for some time. At one point during the fight, the entire Federal line fired upon Burns, but did not dislodge him. Only when the 10th West Virginia Infantry entered the fight did Burns fall back.

When General Echols received Thompson's request, he ordered Major Blessing and six companies of the 23rd Battalion Virginia Infantry to the left. Major Blessing had about 300 men, and deployed on Marshall's right.

About 1:45 p.m., it become clear that Colonel Moor's column had arrived on the left of the Confederate line. Now was the time for the direct assault.

General Averell dismounted the 2nd, 3rd, and 8th West Virginia Mounted Infantry and ordered them to advance. They moved up the face of Droop Mountain at an angle, to join their line with Colonel Moor's.

About 3 p.m. Thompson made another request for reinforcements. Thompson reported that his men drove the enemy back several times, but each time they returned with a stronger force. His troops, he reported, "fought with great gallantry against overpowering odds...." Echols ordered Colonel Patton to take three companies of the 22nd Virginia Infantry to the left and assume command.

By the time Colonel Patton and his men from the 22nd Virginia arrived on the left, Thompson's men were within 300 yards of the turnpike. Even with the additional force, the line continued to retire slowly, bending toward the rear. Colonel Patton informed Echols that he could not hold the line much longer. A few moments later, about 4 p.m., Patton received Echols' order to retire.

Colonel Jackson personally commanded the center of the line. During the afternoon, it repulsed the attackers several times. Only when the left began to give way did the center weaken. Under heavy artillery fire and the assault of four regiments, the center began to waver and fall back, retiring toward the Confederate artillery.

Colonel Arnett wrote of the fight in the center:

> The majority of my command, officers and men, behaved with great courage and coolness, some of them even holding their position until they could and did strike the enemy with their guns. Through fear of being flanked or even cut off by the enemy, then driving our left wing, we fell back to our battery, where we took position and remained until ordered back by yourself [Jackson].

Private Jacob Hall, Company E, 19th Virginia Cavalry, recorded the following about the intensity of the fighting in the center. "The roar of musketry was so regular and volley after volley so we could not distinguish one volley from another. It was so intense that we could scarcely hear the booming of artillery...."

The Confederates retired toward Lewisburg. Parts of Federal regiments followed them. Other troops from Averell's command joined in the pursuit. Colonel Jackson, at the request of General Echols, remained in the rear to hold the enemy in check. Jackson, in turn, ordered Thompson to stay with him until they reached Union. Averell's men followed only a few miles.

Jackson and Echols continued to fall back, passing through Lewisburg about daylight. They halted at Union, in Monroe County. Lieutenant Colonel Thompson recorded the following incident on the retreat:

> The enemy were pressing with great vigor, and the cavalry held in the rear (who had been fighting all day) were momentarily demoralized when Lieutenant Beard of McNeel's company; Lieutenant Justice, of Ruffner's company, and George B. Pollard, of McNeel's company, and one or two others threw themselves in the rear of all the command and gallantly charged the advancing columns of the enemy, and took a prisoner, with his horse and accouterments, from the head of the columns.

Thompson also described the fighting on the left, where his loss was very heavy:

> On the left my men were deployed so as to keep the line extended to prevent flank movements, which were constantly attempted. Our men were sheltered by the timber while the enemy advanced in line of battle, and as our men shot with coolness and precision, the enemy suffered considerably.
>
> In this battle the command under me suffered very heavily in killed and wounded. The fight occurred in the woods, where the undergrowth was very thick. It is therefore impossible for me to approximate our loss, and from the further fact that a large part of my command were strangers to me.

Colonel Jackson, in his report, wrote: "The command and the officers and men of the others, so far as they came under my immediate notice, made a splendid fight against overwhelming odds as long as the position was tenable." Jackson specifically mentioned the bearing of Captain J. W. Ball's company in the fight: "The officers and men of Capt. J. W. Ball, Nineteenth Regiment Virginia Cavalry, never were in disorder during the fight or retreat."

The Union loss at Droop Mountain amounted to 119 killed, wounded and captured. The records show only one Federal soldier captured. The Confederate loss, according to General Echols, amounted to 275 killed, wounded, and missing. Colonel Jackson reported only 150 men killed or wounded.

The Compiled Service Records show the losses in the 19th and 20th Regiments as:

DROOP MOUNTAIN, W. VA.
November 6, 1863

Regiment	Killed	Wounded	Captured
19th Virginia Cavalry	3	7	8
20th Virginia Cavalry	8	6	20*
Total	11	13	28

* Includes at least two wounded, not counted elsewhere.

General Averell's command entered Lewisburg at 2 p.m. on November 7. He found General Duffie's command in possession of the town with four regiments and a section of artillery. Averell and his men left Lewisburg at noon on November 8. They marched to Callaghan's, five miles from Covington, and went into camp for the night. The Federals marched through the snow to Gatewood's the next day. They reported the capture of six or eight prisoners at that place.

Near Covington, Averell met Brigadier General John D. Imboden's Brigade, on its way to join Echols. Imboden reported that about 200 "stragglers" from Jackson's command joined his command. He organized them into two companies, arming those who had lost or thrown away their arms. As soon as Averell appeared, Imboden said, "a large number ran off to the woods and mountains...." Part of Jackson's men remained to fight. Those who ran did so before Averell was closer than two miles to their position. On December 1, 1863, Secretary of War James A. Seddon endorsed Imboden's report: "Colonel Jackson's attention should be called to the conduct of his men who had straggled."

Before leaving Gatewood's on November 10, Averell's men destroyed Jackson's winter camp at that place and burned the nearby saltpeter works. The Federal troops camped for the night at Hightown. The next day the march continued to Franklin, and to Petersburg, where the column arrived on November 13.

Chapter V

By December 1, 1863, Colonel Jackson made his headquarters (Headquarters Hunterville Line) at Warm Springs. Most of his command camped several miles to the west near the Jackson River, at "Camp Cameron." With forage being very scarce, Jackson dismounted most of his men and sent the horses to outlying areas to graze. Small squads of men accompanied the horses as guards, further diminishing the effectiveness of his command. He kept 150 mounted men.

A few days later, Brigadier General Averell began his third, and most successful, raid into Virginia. Averell and his command left New Creek (Keyser), West Virginia on December 8.

This raid called for the cooperation of several different commands. Averell asked the commands of:

1. Brigadier General E. P. Scammon to be at Lewisburg by December 12. Averell wished Scammon to remain there until December 18.

2. Colonel Augustus Moor, 28th Ohio Infantry to be at Marlin's Bottom on December 11. Averell wished Colonel Moor to scout toward Lewisburg the next day.

3. Brigadier General J. C. Sullivan to be at Woodstock on December 11. Averell wished Sullivan to remain there until December 18, then threaten Staunton on December 20 and 21.

4. Colonel Joseph Thoburn to leave Averell's command at Monterey and move toward Staunton.

The Federal force under Averell spent the night of December 11 near Monterey. The next morning Averell moved down Back Creek toward Gatewood's in the pouring rain. Colonel Thoburn, as planned, moved with most of Averell's wagon train toward McDowell.

Detachments of Jackson's command occupied various posts in Bath, Highland and Pocahontas counties. Captain J. W. Marshall, with a detachment of about 150 men (mostly dismounted), occupied an outpost at Huntersville. The captain and his men were busy blockading the roads west of that place. Lieutenant Colonel Thompson, with two companies (McNeel's and Jarvis', totaling about 150 men), scouted to Hillsboro on the morning of December 12. Thompson and his men met a Federal force near Hillsboro and began skirmishing with them. Thompson's command scattered. The next day Thompson informed Jackson that he was marching back to Warm Springs with 35 men.

When Colonel Jackson learned that the Federal forces were moving about, he ordered Marshall's command to fall back to Back Creek, Bath County. Captain Marshall informed Jackson that he thought it would be two days before he could collect his command and fall back, and asked Jackson to send him a few more mounted men.

About 8 a.m. on December 13, Captain Marshall informed Jackson that he was starting his wagon train back toward Warm Springs. He and his men planned to follow. At 5 o'clock that afternoon Marshall and his wagon train met Averell's command at Gatewood's. A brief skirmish followed, in which Averell destroyed four wagons and captured 15 prisoners. Several of the men taken prisoner worked at the nearby Niter Cave. Captain Marshall and his small force escaped into the mountains.

Jackson learned of Thoburn's presence near McDowell at about 2 p.m., and of Averell's advance down Back Creek. Thoburn's force, Jackson believed, planned to march down the Bull Pasture River and get in his rear. Colonel Jackson began making plans to fall back. He sent a courier to the Niter Cave near Gatewood's to warn Superintendent W. W. Heaton to move his equipment to Millboro Depot.

Several hours later the courier returned with sad news. While at the Niter Cave, Averell's advance fired upon him and destroyed the niter works. Captain Marshall's command, according to the courier, had engaged the enemy at Gatewood's. General Averell's command now stood between the commands of Marshall and Jackson.

At sundown, Jackson ordered his dismounted men, artillery, and wagon train to go to Hot Springs. The colonel and a few mounted men remained at Warm Springs for the night. Private Andrew J. Jones of Company B, 20th Virginia Cavalry, noted in his diary: "After traveling six miles of muddy road, we encamp near Hot Springs."

Early on the morning of December 14, Averell and his command marched to the Jackson River, where they skirmished with some of Jackson's men. From that point, Averell forded the swollen river and moved to Callaghan's. After a brief halt there to rest and feed, Averell moved by Sweet Sulphur Springs toward New Castle. Averell and his raiders reached the Virginia and Tennessee Railroad at Salem two days later. After destroying much of the railroad and government property at that place, he began to retrace his steps.

At 1 a.m. on December 14, Lieutenant Colonel Thompson joined Jackson at Warm Springs. He reported the balance of his detachment cut off, captured, or moving to join Jackson at Healing Springs. Later that morning, Captain Jarvis with 20 men joined Jackson.

Three hours later, Jackson went to Healing Springs. His cavalry remained at Warm Springs until sundown. The dismounted men, with the wagon train and artillery, moved at daylight to Healing Springs. They arrived at that place about mid-day, completely soaked. After a brief halt to dry their clothing, Jackson resumed the march. He planned to move to Covington, via Morris Hill, providing he could ford the Jackson River. He could not. Instead, Jackson moved by McGraw's Gap to Jackson River Depot, near Clifton Forge.

On the way, Jackson received a dispatch from General Imboden, asking Jackson to join him at Shenandoah Mountain and help him to repel the enemy. Colonel Jackson regarded the Federal movement as a feint and ignored Imboden's request.

Jackson's command reached the neighborhood of Jackson River Depot late in the evening of December 14, 1863. His men went into camp in the bitter cold. Private Jones, of the 20th Virginia Cavalry recorded in his diary: "The ground was wet and the wind blew high and very cold."

Colonel Jackson and his command arrived at Jackson River Depot about 11 a.m. on the morning of December 15, 1863. The 20th Virginia Cavalry, in advance of the brigade, crossed the Jackson River on the railroad bridge. Once across, the regiment moved past the depot to protect the crossing of the wagons, cattle, and artillery. When all were safely across, the 20th Virginia returned to the bridge and camped.

Several messages awaited Colonel Jackson at the depot. One, dated December 13, from Sam Jones ordered Jackson to move to Callaghan's.

Early that afternoon Lieutenant Colonel Thompson moved to Covington on a scout. Thompson reported he found no sign of the enemy at Covington, and was moving to Callaghan's. At 7:30 p.m., Thompson arrived at Callaghan's, where the mounted men of Jackson's brigade joined him. Colonel Jackson and the remainder of the brigade moved to Covington and camped for the night.

The Federal troops under Averell reached Salem on the morning of December 16. During the day they destroyed large amounts of quartermaster stores and damaged the Virginia and Tennessee Railroad severely. Averell and his men left Salem at 4 p.m. and started to retrace their steps.

On the morning of December 16, Colonel Jackson moved to within a half-mile of Callaghan's. He sent Lieutenant Colonel Thompson with 100 men on a scout toward Sweet Springs to open communication with General Echols. Thompson succeeded and Echols kept him and 30 men of his command. The remainder of Thompson's troops returned to Jackson's Camp.

Colonel Jackson received a message from Major General Sam Jones at 2 a.m. on December 17. Jones directed Jackson to take "some good position" near Clifton Forge and wait for further orders. Jackson and his command moved through the pouring rain and sleet at daylight to a position near Jackson River Depot. From this position, Jackson could watch both the Clifton Forge and Rich Patch roads.

General Jubal A. Early and part of his division now was at Millboro Depot. On December 18, 1863, Early communicated with Jackson, advising him that he was moving part of his command to Bath Alum or Warm Springs. Early ordered Jackson to take possession of the Lick Run Bridge below Clifton Forge, to prevent Averell from passing over it. General Early directed: "Dispose your forces so as to aid in the capture [of Averell]. Do not let him come out by Clifton Forge or Callaghan's."

General Averell's command arrived at New Castle on the evening of December 18. After several hours of rest, the Federals moved toward Sweet Springs, only to find their path blocked by Generals Jones and Echols. General Averell now considered his options. He could use one of two routes: go around Jones into Monroe and Greenbrier counties, or move to Covington. Averell chose to go to Covington as it was the most direct route, and therefore the safest. He immediately ordered his men to take the Rich Patch road.

During the afternoon of December 19, Colonel Jackson learned of Averell's approach on the Rich Patch road from one of his scouts. Jackson immediately ordered Captain John S. Spriggs to take all the mounted men then in camp and move on the Rich Patch road. Jackson wished Spriggs to advance until he met the enemy. Soon afterward, Major Lady came up with an additional force of mounted men, which Jackson ordered to follow Spriggs. Jackson ordered Major Lady to take command of the detachment. The colonel ordered the Alleghany Home Guards, commanded by Captain Thompson McAllister, to prepare the Island Ford bridge for destruction.

By 5 p.m., Jackson received a dispatch from Captain Spriggs at Hook's Hotel, 18 miles from Jackson River Depot. Captain Spriggs reported the Yankee pickets two and a half miles beyond his position. An endorsement on the dispatch told Jackson that Spriggs had engaged the enemy. This information satisfied Jackson that Averell was advancing on the Rich Patch road. He sent Lieutenant Boyd of the engineer corps to ride rapidly to the Island Ford bridge and ensure its destruction.

Jackson sent a dispatch to General Early, telling him: "The enemy are now advancing upon me on the Rich Patch route. I am skirmishing with the advance. I will burn the Island Ford bridge and throw them down this way. Watch Warm Springs at Gatewood's. My force is small. I will do the best I can." General Early ordered General Thomas to reinforce Jackson's small force. The high water and steep grades and poor condition of the railroad beyond Millboro Depot prevented Thomas' Brigade from reaching Jackson.

As darkness settled over the countryside, Jackson moved his dismounted men to the intersection of the Covington and Rich Patch roads. He sent several more couriers to the bridge to ensure its destruction. None of them, however, reached the bridge in time.

Colonel Jackson sent Arnett with the dismounted men up the Rich Patch road to the point where Averell's men had turned off toward the bridge. Jackson directed him to hold that intersection and to prevent any more of Averell's men from passing. If he found that all of Averell's force had passed, he should follow and strike its rear.

As Averell marched toward the Island Ford bridge, he met a detachment of 300 Confederates about eight miles from the river. His advance broke up and drove this force back to the bridge. The Federals reached the Island Ford bridge at 9 p.m. The 8th West Virginia Mounted Infantry, at the head of Averell's column, drove in Jackson's outposts and secured the bridge. Colonel Jackson, in his report, wrote:

> A considerable force of the enemy, by some route that had never been explained to me - although I sought information from every source, and was assured that I was guarding every possible approach - threw themselves between me and the bridge, cut off Lieut. Boyd, fired into or captured my messengers, and as it now appears, rushed upon the bridge, surprising and scattering the home guards before they set fire to the bridge.

The bridge secure, General Averell began crossing his command. To protect against further surprises from Jackson's command, Averell sent a company out on the road toward Clifton Forge. When most of Averell's men had crossed the bridge, Colonel Jackson with a small detachment attacked the rear of the column. Only a few ambulances and wagons, guarded by the 14th Pennsylvania Cavalry, remained on the Clifton Forge side of the river. Jackson's men forced the company guarding the Clifton Forge road back to the bridge. The attack cut off the rear of Averell's command. Colonel Jackson personally tried to set fire to the bridge, but a large force of the enemy drove him back.

While Jackson was at the bridge, Major Lady with about 50 men joined him. Jackson ordered him to take a position on a high cliff, overlooking the bridge. Three times during the night Major Lady kept the enemy from the bridge.

As dawn approached on December 20, Averell decided he must destroy the bridge. He sent orders to the 14th Pennsylvania Cavalry to swim the river, or find a route through the mountains. The Federals set the bridge and wagon train on fire at daylight. As soon as Major Lady saw what was going on, he left the cliff and tried to reach the flank and rear of the Federal regiment. Colonel Arnett and the 20th Virginia arrived in time to take part in the chase.

The 14th Pennsylvania Cavalry followed the railroad tracks to a ford two miles from the bridge and swam the river. Colonel Arnett, only a few minutes behind, arrived as the enemy reached the opposite shore. Colonel Arnett wrote: "We, indeed, pressed them so closely that we drove them from one ford where they tried to cross, capturing 20 prisoners."

Pursuit by Jackson's dismounted men being of no use, Jackson ordered Captain Spriggs to follow with the mounted men of the brigade. Colonel Arnett, with the dismounted men, returned to camp at Jackson River Depot that evening. Private Andrew J. Jones, 20th Virginia Cavalry wrote that the men were "...very much vexed that our insignificant officers had permitted the enemy to escape."

Taking a very obscure road, Averell and his command camped at the base of Droop Mountain on the evening of December 21. When the Federals arrived safely at Beverly, Averell wrote: "My command has marched, climbed, slid, and swum 355 miles since the 8th instant." He reported his loss as seven wounded, seven drowned, one missing in action and 79 taken prisoner.

Colonel Jackson and his command returned to their winter quarters at Warm Springs and Camp Cameron. Jackson reported his loss in the campaign against Averell as one killed, seven wounded, and 30 missing in action. General Averell's command took some of those missing prisoner. A study of the Compiled Service Records shows the following losses in the 19th and 20th Virginia Regiments between December 11 and December 23, 1863.

REGIMENT	KIA	CAPTURED	WOUNDED	TOTAL
19th Virginia Cavalry	0	14	1	15
20th Virginia Cavalry	0	11	1	12
TOTAL	0	25	2	27

Major Edward McMahon charged Jackson and his command with incompetence and criminal activity while in Alleghany County. In a letter to General Jones dated Covington, December 26, the quartermaster charged that Jackson made no preparation to meet the enemy or to prevent his passage to the west. All Jackson did, according to McMahon was build a fence across the road at Alum Rock. The letter declared that Jackson's whereabouts were unknown during a crucial period, and that Colonel Arnett did not obey the orders given him by Colonel Jackson. According to McMahon, the 14th Pennsylvania Cavalry hoisted the white flag three times, and still managed to escape. Instead of gathering up stragglers, the men of Jackson's command "...were running about plundering and gathering up property abandoned by the enemy, and that almost every crime has been perpetrated by the command from burglary down to rape." Major McMahon asked General Jones to investigate the incident. If Jones would not follow through, the major promised to take it to the War Department.

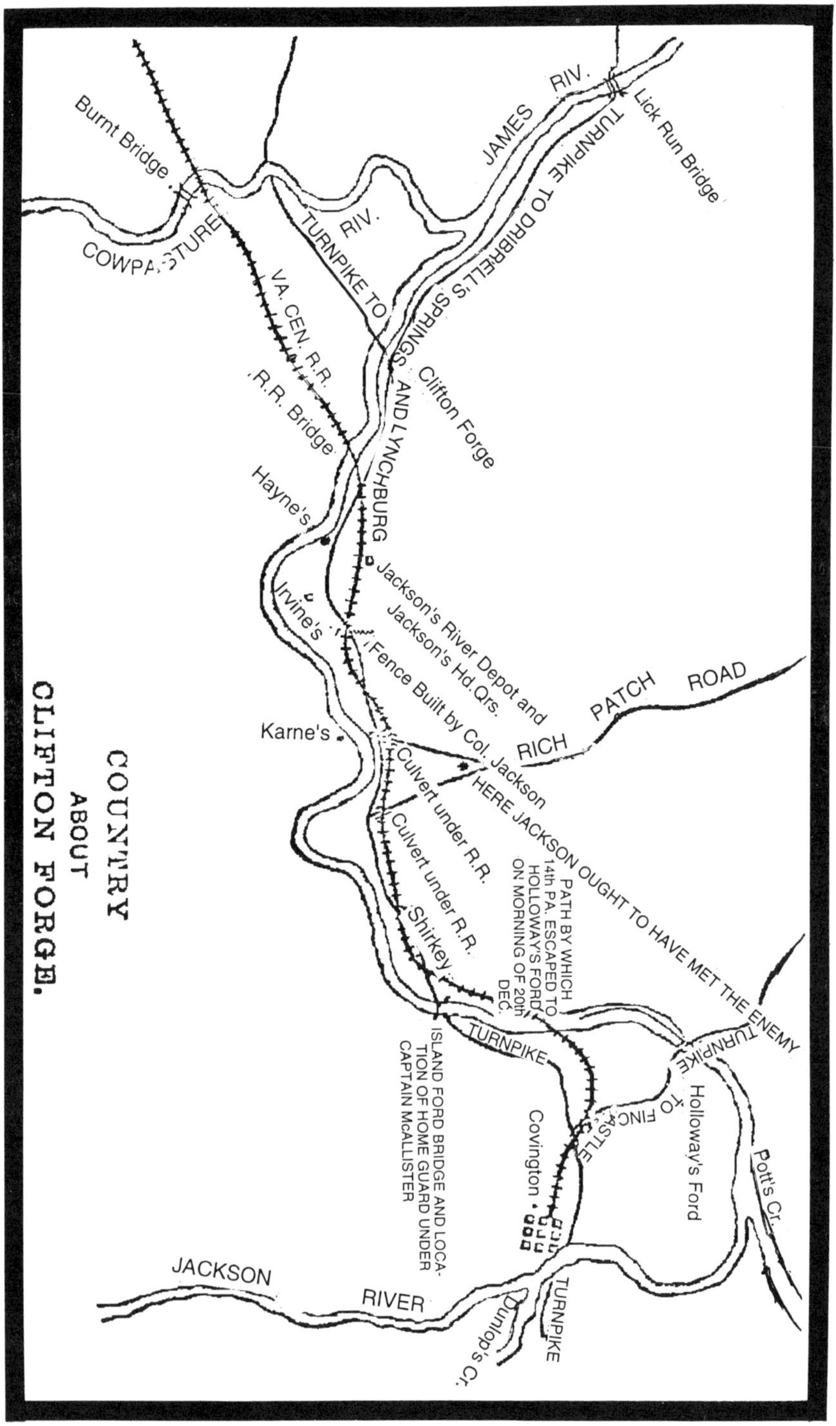
COUNTRY
ABOUT
CLIFTON FORGE.
Burnt Bridge
COWPASTURE
RIV.
JAMES
RIV.
Lick Run Bridge
TURNPIKE TO DRIBRELL'S SPRINGS
TURNPIKE TO
VA. CEN. R.R.
R.R. Bridge
Clifton Forge
AND LYNCHBURG
Hayne's
Jackson's River Depot and
Jackson's Hd.Qrs.
Irvine's
Fence Built by Col. Jackson
RICH
PATCH
ROAD
Karne's
Culvert under R.R.
Culvert under R.R.
HERE JACKSON OUGHT TO HAVE MET THE ENEMY
PATH BY WHICH
14th PA. ESCAPED TO
HOLLOWAY'S FORD
ON MORNING OF 20th
DEC.
Shirkey
TURNPIKE
ISLAND FORD BRIDGE AND LOCA-
TION OF HOME GUARD UNDER
CAPTAIN McALLISTER
TURNPIKE
TO FINCASTLE
Holloway's Ford
Covington
Pott's Cr.
JACKSON
RIVER
TURNPIKE
Dunlop's Cr.

A citizen of Pocahontas County made another complaint against Jackson and his command. Colonel Jackson, the complaint said, did not discipline his men, and was tyrannical and oppressive. The men of his command came and went at their leisure and they were never around when it came time to fight.

Apparently, Jones followed through on the complaints, since Jackson issued a circular to his command on January 18, 1864. The colonel said: "It may not be known that there is now an effort being made by petition, in Alleghany Co. to have this command ordered elsewhere, because of alleged outrages and the utter want of discipline in the command." Jackson continued, asking his officers to consider the reputation of the command and enforce the strictest discipline in their companies.

During late January 1864, several deserters from Jackson's command reported to the Federal authorities at Beverly, West Virginia. In a statement given to the post commander, the deserters reported that Colonel Jackson was under arrest for cowardice during Averell's December raid. The deserters said that Averell "is a terror to them. More so than Stonewall Jackson to us."

The report of Jackson's arrest is apparently only a rumor. No mention of his arrest appears in any Confederate records.

Chapter VI

The brigade commanded by Colonel Jackson spent January and February 1864 recruiting and reorganizing. Second Lieutenant Samuel L. Ruffner, on recruiting duty in Lexington, placed the following notice in the Lexington Gazette:

RECRUITS

For Jackson's Command.

Those persons subject to the last act relating to substitutes, are respectfully informed, that Col. Wm. L. Jackson, is raising a Brigade of Cavalry, to operate in Western Virginia; and especially to protect Pocahontas, Bath, Alleghany, Rockbridge and adjoining counties. Jackson's command is camping in very comfortable quarters near Warm Springs, and is as well provided for as any in the Confederate service. Horses are easily obtained, the prices being much lower at the west than near the Eastern armies. It is confidently believed, that persons in Rockbridge, subject to military duty, cannot do better than to attach themselves to Jackson's command. Anyone desiring further information on this subject, will be cheerfully obliged, at Rev. Wm. H. Ruffner's, Lexington, Va., where I am staying at present.

S. D. RUFFNER,
Recruiting officer for
Jackson's command.

Brigade returns for January and February 1864 show that a total of 133 men joined the brigade by enlistment or transfer. During the same period, the brigade lost 121 men, for a net gain of 12 recruits. Many of the men lost returned to regiments in which they had served before joining Jackson's command.

In mid-February, two companies of the 19th Virginia requested that Jackson release them from duty in the regiment. The captains, William L. McNeel and Jacob W. Marshall, reminded Jackson of the agreement they had made the previous winter.

Soon after Colonel Jackson had received authority to raise a regiment in the northwest, he went to Pocahontas County. There, he met with Captain McNeel and Colonel William W. Fontaine. McNeel's Company belonged to Colonel Fontaine's regiment of the Virginia State Line, which the General

Assembly planned to disband. Colonel Jackson asked McNeel to join his new command. Both McNeel and Fontaine agreed, with one condition.

Colonel Jackson next approached Captain Jacob W. Marshall, who also agreed to join his command, with the same condition as McNeel's Company. Captain Marshall described the condition to Secretary of War James Seddon on February 14:

> When the 19th regt. was ready to be organized we agreed to go into the regt. with the understanding and promise from Colonel Jackson that as soon as other companies could be organized to supply our places in tne 19th Regt. that Capt. McNeel's Co. and my company should be detached or taken out of the Regt.

Captain Marshall informed the Secretary of War of their desire to remain with Jackson's command, as a new battalion. Marshall stated that such an arrangement would provide better service and increase the strength of the brigade.

In early April 1863, when Jackson raised ten companies, McNeel and Marshall both agreed to remain temporarily with Jackson. They asked Jackson to release them as soon as possible.

By the middle of February 1864, nearly a year later, Colonel Jackson presented six new companies to the War Department for battalion status. Captains McNeel and Marshall now asked Jackson to release them and use two of the new companies to fill the gap in the 19th Virginia. Colonel Jackson agreed to the request; however, the Secretary of War must approve the transfer. Colonel Jackson stated that the new companies protested such an arrangement, as did the remaining eight companies of the 19th Virginia.

According to Colonel Jackson, McNeel's and Marshall's companies were large. If allowed to split these two companies, Jackson could add two new companies to his command. If the War Department granted the transfer, Jackson said, he could then raise another battalion. The final decision, of course, belonged to Secretary Seddon. Seddon, in his endorsement a month later, wrote: "I am not willing the 19th Reg. should be broken up and cannot allow the two companies to be detached unless two other companies exist unattached to take their place." Secretary Seddon added "The Department will not interfere and Col. Jackson must arrange the instrument he has allowed to arise."

On February 24, 1864, Jackson wrote Captain McNeel that he had a new company, ready to enter service. Jackson offered to use that company (Captain Apperson's) to replace either Marshall's or McNeel's Company. The alternative, Jackson wrote, was to make it part of the 46th Battalion Virginia Cavalry. As it turned out, Apperson's Company became part of another battalion organized on April 1, 1864 (47th Battalion Virginia Cavalry).

When the 46th Battalion became part of Jackson's Cavalry Brigade, the men elected Major J. R. Kessler to be lieutenant colonel of the new battalion. His election caused a vacancy in the field and staff of the 19th Virginia Cavalry. As February drew to a close, Colonel Jackson wrote Captain McNeel about the vacancy. He informed McNeel that the "contest is between you and Downs." As Captain McNeel was a member of the Virginia legislature, and now absent on that duty, Jackson promoted Captain George Downs to the rank of major.

Colonel Jackson's Brigade consisted of the following units on March 1, 1864:

>19th Virginia Cavalry
>20th Virginia Cavalry
>46th Battalion Virginia Cavalry
>One Unorganized Artillery Company
>Several Unorganized Companies of Cavalry

Jackson and his command remained in camp at and near Warm Springs during March 1864. Early in the month, Major General John C. Breckinridge replaced Major General Samuel Jones as department commander. The new commander inspected Jackson's troops at Warm Springs on March 14.

On April 16, Jackson reported the disposition of his command. Captain McNeel's Company was at Mill Point, scouting to Edray. Captain Marshall's Company was at Camp Northwest, scouting to Green Bank. In addition, Marshall had a small group of scouts concealed near Beverly to watch the enemy. Colonel Arnett, with the 20th Virginia and a company of the 46th Battalion, was at Crab Bottom. Jackson explained the large force at that point: "So large a force is required at Crab Bottom to guard and protect the horses of my command on grass and hay there." The remainder of his command, Jackson said, would move to the Jackson River Depot in a few days.

In the same report, Jackson informed his superiors that he had "...issued strict orders as to discipline, drill, and am making every effort to throughly equip my command."

On April 18, 1864, Captain Marshall and his company met a detachment of the enemy at Marlin's Bottom. Marshall's Company drove the Federal force, consisting of over 200 infantry and cavalry, back to Beverly. Captain Marshall did not suffer any loss in the skirmish.

Ten days later, on April 28, a Federal force from Beverly attacked Marshall's pickets at the bridge in Marlin's Bottom. After a brisk skirmish, the pickets fell back, leaving seven of their comrades behind as prisoners. The Federals took six prisoners back to Beverly. They left the seventh prisoner, seriously wounded, at Marlin's Bottom.

The Federal captain, J. B. Gore, reported that three companies of the 19th Virginia were at Little Levels. Two companies of the same regiment were at Huntersville and Jacktown. The captain reported that 300 men of the 20th Virginia Cavalry were at Crab Bottom.

Jackson's Brigade in late April and early May, numbering about 1,000 strong, scattered from Highland County to Alleghany County. These detachments protected the approaches to the Virginia Central Railroad. Colonel Jackson stationed about half of the 19th Virginia Cavalry in Pocahontas County, watching Beverly.

In the first week of May 1864, two columns of Federals (Crook and Averell) advanced on the Virginia and Tennessee Railroad. By May 5, Jackson's Brigade (part of the 19th Virginia, the 46th and 47th Battalions, and Lurty's Battery), camped at Oakland Church in Alleghany County. Late in the afternoon, Jackson received orders to join General Albert J. Jenkins at Union, Monroe County, West Virginia.

Colonel Jackson started to Union on the morning of May 6, going as far as Callaghan's that day. Portions of his command remained behind to guard the Huntersville Line and several points on the Virginia Central Railroad. Late in the evening, the 20th Virginia Cavalry left their camp in Highland County to join Jackson.

While Jackson was on the way to Union, he received orders to go to the Narrows of the New River, to dispute the retreat of the Federal raiders. Once he arrived at the Narrows, Jackson was to report to Colonel William H. French of the 17th Virginia Cavalry.

Colonel Jackson, in advance of the rest of his command, reported to Colonel French about midnight on May 9, 1864. Jackson expected his brigade, mostly dismounted, to arrive during the evening of May 10, or on May 11. Colonel Jackson left most of the horses of the command, poor and tired, in Monroe County. One mounted company of the brigade arrived at French's camp during the morning of May 10. The balance of the brigade arrived at 2 p.m. Colonel French assumed command of the combined force. The march took a toll on the shoes and boots of the brigade. The roads were in poor condition, full of mud. Shoes and boots fell to pieces. Many of Jackson's men needed new foot gear when they arrived at the Narrows.

Colonel French received orders at 8 a.m. on May 11 to join Colonel John McCausland (now commanding the department) at Christiansburg. The 20th Virginia Cavalry joined Jackson and French during the evening. Colonel Jackson, in his report of the campaign, wrote that the 20th Virginia Cavalry "...made a remarkable march and joined me on the evening of the 11th instant. The officers and men of that command deserve to be complimented."

Jackson and French marched to join McCausland at 9 a.m. on the morning of May 12. Captain McNeel's Company of the 19th Virginia Cavalry was in the advance that morning. Soon his scouts reported that General Crook was approaching on the same road. Jackson and French push onward, hoping to reach the top of Gap Mountain before Crook. When within two miles of the top of the mountain, their scouts reported that Crook has taken possession of the mountain top.

The Confederates met Crook's force between Newport and the junction of the Salt Pond Road and the road to Narrows. The 19th Virginia Cavalry, in advance, began skirmishing with the Federals. As Crook's command outnumbered him, Colonel French decided to fall back on the Salt Pond road to Union. French directed his skirmishers to hold Crook in check long enough for him to move his wagons back to the Salt Pond Mountain road.

After skirmishing for some time, the Federals forced Jackson and French to fall back. Their position was flanked by a large force of Crook's men. The Confederates "...left behind 2 wagons loaded with supplies and 1 dead man, who was killed by our skirmishers."

After Crook's command moved off on the Salt Pond Mountain road toward Union, Jackson and French decided to send a force in pursuit. A hand-picked detachment of between 300 and 350 men from their combined commands followed the Federals. Jackson ordered Lieutenant Colonel Kessler, commanding the detachment, to harass Crook's rear. They caught up with Crook about nightfall and compelled him to abandon some wagons, horses, cattle, and other property.

At daylight of May 13, Jackson and French marched again toward Blacksburg. After crossing Sinking Creek, they learned that Averell and Duffie were advancing from Blacksburg. Jackson and French hastened onward, through Newport to the top of Gap Mountain. The Southern forces reached the gap by 9:30 a.m. and occupied the fortifications constructed there. As they were getting into position, the advance forces of Averell and Duffie came into sight.

The armies skirmished with each other for an hour and a half. Averell's men fell back and retreated on the Catawba road. The loss on both sides was slight. Colonel Jackson reported two men wounded in his command.

The Confederates, having to march on foot, were weary and broken down. After driving Averell and Duffie off, they went into camp for the night on Gap Mountain. Colonel McCausland joined them at 7 p.m. He ordered French to return to the Narrows and take charge of the public property there, while Colonel Jackson was to follow the enemy on the Salt Pond Mountain road the next morning.

Misfortune befell Jackson's command that day on Salt Pond Mountain. When Jackson moved from Jackson River Depot, he left nine wagons and a 12-pounder howitzer, with a small escort, to follow him. After the fight with Crook on May 12, Jackson sent a dispatch to the train, directing it to join him within two hours time. If the train could not reach his position in the allotted time, it was to go to Botetourt County for safety.

When they were about 20 miles away from Jackson's position, the escort became alarmed and abandoned the wagons and artillery. According to Colonel Jackson, several hours later the Federals discovered the abandoned train and destroyed it. General Crook, in his report, says that he came upon a provision train and a 12- pounder brass gun guarded by a small escort. His advance skirmished with the escort and drove the Confederates away. General Crook's men destroyed the wagons and artillery.

Colonel Jackson promised to investigate the matter fully, and punish the guilty parties; however, he never even named the officer in charge of the escort.

Jackson's men set out after the Federals on the morning of May 14 in the pouring rain. They followed the Salt Pond Mountain road, which was knee deep in mud, to John's Creek. There they halted for the night, being unable to cross the swollen stream. The Yankees were three hours away.

Not all of Jackson's command accompanied him to the Narrows. Captain Marshall (19th Virginia Cavalry) and Captain Hutton (20th Virginia Cavalry) remained in Pocahontas County with a force of more than 100 men. While Jackson chased Averell, Marshall and Hutton met 225 Federals troops at the Greenbrier Bridge at Marlin's Bottom. After a brief skirmish, Marshall's men routed the Federals. A contemporary newspaper report contained the following note: "It will thus be seen that the command of Jackson has not been idle, and that it has rendered very efficient service."

On May 28, 1864, Colonel Thomas M. Harris reported that his Federals had scouted parts of Pocahontas and Highland counties. The scouts told Harris, that they found two companies of Jackson's command in these counties. Colonel Harris wrote:

> These are Hutton's and Marshall's Companies. They were always bushwhackers, are strong companies and will do a good deal of mischief and keep the peace of those counties disturbed until they shall have been dislodged. They are broken up in small bands and are very active but afraid to venture out in this direction for any other purpose but to get information of our movements which they do by small parties through their friends in this valley.

The Confederates resumed their march the next morning, crossing John's Creek and making their way to Gap Mills, in Monroe County. They went into camp there for the night, within 300 yards of the Federal pickets. By this time the Yankees were at Union.

The Federal pickets withdrew on the morning of May 16. Captain James S. A. Crawford, Company F, 17th Virginia Cavalry, with 20 mounted men followed the pickets toward Union. Colonel Jackson, in his report, wrote: "My command (not being mounted) will be compelled to stop the pursuit on account of sore feet, want of shoes and rations." The colonel reported "I pressed Averell and Duffie to Greenbrier Bridge, near Lewisburg, drowning and killing between 15 and 20. I have 15 prisoners...."

From that point, Jackson's command marched back to Jackson River Depot, where it arrived on May 20, 1864. After a week's rest and re-fitting, Jackson moved to Callaghan's on May 27. Two days later the men who had horses (125 men) moved to the Falling Springs Valley.

The next day, Jackson moved the main part of his command back to Jackson River Depot. The time of rest was past. General John D. Imboden requested Jackson to move to Millboro to meet a force pressing up the Shenandoah Valley. Later that day, Jackson received permission from General William E. Jones to go to Millboro.

Soon after their return from the raid on the Virginia and Tennessee Railroad, Generals Crook and Averell set out for the Shenandoah Valley. Federal General David Strother Hunter was moving up the Valley to capture Staunton. Averell and Crook were to join him at that place, then move on Lynchburg.

Jackson retired slowly in the direction of Staunton as the Federals advanced. He fell back through old Millboro (Millboro Springs), Panther's Gap, Goshen, and Craigsville. A portion of the 20th Virginia Cavalry skirmished with the enemy advance in Panther's Gap on June 4.

From Buffalo Gap, Jackson sent his scouts on toward Staunton. They soon returned with the sad intelligence that Staunton had fallen. Colonel Jackson and his command moved around Staunton to Middlebrook on June 6, where they joined McCausland's Brigade.

Jackson and McCausland moved in easy stages to a position near Waynesboro where on June 10, Federal troops under General Alfred Duffie caught up with Jackson's rear guard. In the resulting skirmish, Jackson had one man taken prisoner. Two days later, on June 12, Jackson and McCausland cross the Blue Ridge Mountains, en route to Lynchburg. They arrived at Lynchburg at noon on June 16 and went into camp nearby.

On June 13, 1864, General Early had placed the cavalry of his command under the leadership of Major General Robert Ransom. Early hoped Ransom would whip the disobedient cavalrymen into an effective fighting unit. The four brigades assigned to Early (Jackson, McCausland, Imboden, and Johnson) numbered nearly 2,000 mounted men.

Two hours before daylight on June 17, Jackson's command moved back toward Lynchburg. Arriving at the city shortly after daylight, the cavalrymen moved to the west side. There they took up a defensive position and dug rifle pits.

That afternoon, about 4 p.m., the 19th Virginia and 20th Virginia received orders to go out on the Salem Turnpike to support General Imboden's command. Imboden's men were falling back before an overwhelming force of the enemy. Jackson's men met the retreating line after advancing about three miles. Both commands retired back a short distance and erected some breastworks.

The Federals soon appeared. Brisk skirmishing and cannonading started, which continued for nearly an hour. Then the Federals advanced on Imboden's line, driving it back. The position occupied by Jackson's men became untenable because of the chance of a flank attack.

Colonel Jackson gave the order to retreat. Some of his men heard the command, while others did not. As the men began to retire, those who had not heard the order stampeded to the rear. This caused the men who overheard the order to fall back in disorder. The men of Jackson's command ran only a short distance before receiving orders to return to the breastworks. Most of the men obeyed. Once the line was stable again, Jackson gave the order to fall back "in good order." This time the men responded properly. The Federals pursued Jackson and Imboden until they met part of General Jubal A. Early's Division.

Chapter VII

The main battle of Lynchburg took place on June 18, 1864, two miles south of the city. By 2 p.m., Hunter began to retire.

The role played by Jackson's Brigade in the Battle of Lynchburg remains much a mystery. The only wartime account found for this period is the diary of Andrew J. Jones. In his diary for June 18, Jones merely wrote, "The Battle of Lynchburg." A memorandum kept by Captain W. W. Old, aide-de-camp to General Early, states on June 17: "Jackson's Cavalry also ran but were reformed and remained in line all night." Perhaps Jackson's Brigade rested all day on June 18 and did not take part in the fighting around Lynchburg.

The 19th and 20th Regiments suffered slight loss in the two days of fighting around Lynchburg.

LYNCHBURG

Reg't./Date	Killed	Wounded	Captured	Total
19th Va. Cav.				
June 17	—	2	—	2
June 18	—	1	1	2
20th Va. Cav.				
June 17	1	1	—	2
June 18	—	—	1	1
Total	1	4	2	7

The Confederates started in pursuit of Hunter's command on June 19. Jackson's Brigade camped for the night near Liberty (Bedford). They resumed the pursuit the following day, gradually moving toward Lexington and Staunton. Jackson and his command went into camp near Staunton on June 27, and moved down the Shenandoah Valley during the last days of June.

The mounted men of Jackson's Brigade, commanded by Major John B. Lady, were not with the rest of the brigade in early July. They moved through Alleghany County and followed Early's command down the Valley, catching up with it on July 5.

Moving down the Shenandoah Valley, Jackson's cavalry arrived in Winchester about 10 a.m. on July 3, 1864. They moved through the city and took the road toward Martinsburg. At Bunker Hill the cavalry skirmished with the enemy and forced them back.

Diary accounts of the 20th Virginia Cavalry for July 1864 show that Jackson split his command into several detachments. Part of the brigade (the dismounted men) went into camp at Sharpsburg, Maryland, on July 5. The mounted men of the brigade joined McCausland's Brigade and moved through Sharpsburg to Hagerstown. At Hagerstown they engaged the enemy, whipping them and taking nearly 500 prisoners.

The dismounted men of Jackson's Brigade received their horses on July 7 near Maryland Heights. They quickly mounted and moved again toward Sharpsburg. The following day part of Jackson's cavalry moved to Liberty, nine miles from Frederick, Maryland, to gather up horses. Lieutenant J. W. A. Ford, 20th Cavalry, recorded in his diary, "A great many fine and valuable horses were brought into camp...." The remainder of the brigade moved to Middletown, Maryland, going into camp at 11 o'clock that night.

On the morning of July 9, a detachment of Jackson's Brigade moved to Point of Rocks on the Baltimore and Ohio Railroad. After tearing up several miles of track and burning a bridge and some cattle guards, the detachment joined the main force at Frederick. The remainder of Jackson's Brigade accompanied General Early's command into Frederick at daylight. All remained quiet until the afternoon, when the Battle of Monocacy erupted. After a six hour fight, the Confederates drove the Federal forces back in confusion. Lieutenant J. W. A. Ford wrote:

> Our Brigade being all mounted and now under Colonel Jackson, was sent in pursuit of the flying enemy. All that was necessary to make them surrender by day was to let them know the Rebs. were in close proximity and they threw down their guns instantly.

General Early's command left Frederick after the Battle of Monocacy, moving toward Washington, D. C. The Confederates arrived near Washington about noon on July 11, 1864. General Early stationed Jackson's Brigade (with the exception of the 20th Virginia) on the road between Rockville and the 7th Street road. Jackson's men camped near the estate of Montgomery Blair, Lincoln's Postmaster General. The 20th Virginia Cavalry arrived later that day, about 3 p.m., and joined Jackson's Brigade. Lieutenant J. W. A. Ford, wrote of their activity while near the Federal capital:

> We, the cavalry, have been riding around promiscuously, pressing wagon cavalry and artillery horses, tearing up railroad tracks, burning bridges, depots, capturing, occasionally, trains loaded with supplies and living off the fat of the land.

About sundown, on July 12, 1864, Early's command began to retire.

General Early assigned Jackson's Brigade to guard the rear on the retreat. Retiring slowly, Jackson's men arrived at Rockville at daylight on the morning of July 13. Jackson and his men halted here until about noon. Then the rear guard warned Jackson that the enemy were pressing them back. Jackson immediately ordered the 46th Battalion to aid the rear guard. He ordered the 20th Virginia to prepare to meet the enemy.

A portion of Johnson's (formerly W. E. Jones') Brigade joined Jackson at Rockville. Together they waited for the enemy to appear. Not long afterward, the 2nd Massachusetts Cavalry appeared, driving the rear guard and the 46th Battalion before them. Jackson's and Johnson's men opened fire on the advancing enemy, throwing them into confusion. Colonel Jackson now ordered his men to charge the Federal cavalrymen. Lieutenant J. W. A. Ford told his diary: "The whoop and yell was too much for them. They fled in every direction and our boys after them with a vim."

The Confederates captured 58 of Colonel Charles Russell Lowell's men at Rockville. Immediately following the fight, Jackson's command continued its retreat. Being very tired, they went into camp at Darnestown at midnight. The Confederates remained there until the next morning, July 14, when they moved toward Edward's Ferry. Before reaching the crossing of the Potomac River, they met a force of the enemy at Poolesville, Maryland. After a brief skirmish at Poolesville, Early's command moved to White's Ferry (White's Ford), where it crossed back to Virginia soil. From White's Ferry, Jackson's command marched to Waterford, Loudoun County. They arrived at that place at 2 a.m. on July 15 and went into camp.

Jackson's Brigade remained in camp at Waterford all day. During the afternoon, a Federal force advanced upon them from Harpers Ferry and engaged their scouts. The brigade remained in line of battle all night, expecting a fight to begin momentarily.

On July 16, Jackson's Brigade led the advance through Snicker's Gap to the Shenandoah River. There they crossed to Berryville and went into camp. During the next several days, the brigade moved toward Charles Town, Bunker Hill, and Winchester. Jackson's men engaged detachments of Federal troops most every day.

On July 19 Jackson again met his nemesis, Brigadier General William W. Averell. Averell advanced to within four miles of Winchester and engaged Jackson's Brigade. The Federal force drove Jackson's men back. The fighting resumed in the evening of July 20, on the Rutherford Farm, near Winchester.

Jackson's Brigade, with General S. D. Ramseur's Division and General J. C. Vaughn's Brigade, marched toward Martinsburg that afternoon. Ramseur's Division, in advance, met General Averell's command at Rutherford's Farm. The attack by Averell threw the infantry into confusion, forcing them to fall

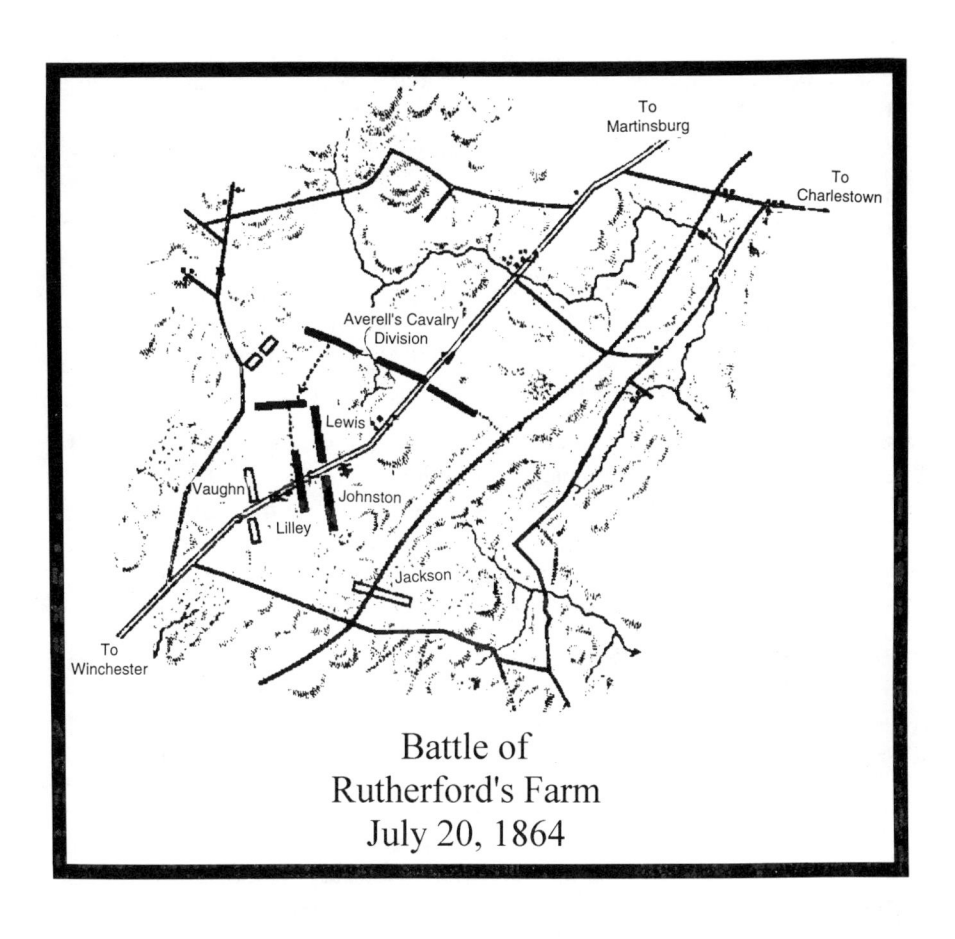

Battle of
Rutherford's Farm
July 20, 1864

back. Colonel Jackson, with his brigade, made a vigorous charge on Averell that allowed Ramseur time to rally his men. The Federals retired. Private Andrew J. Jones, 20th Virginia Cavalry, called the regiment's attack at Rutherford's Farm "a brilliant charge." Private M. P. H. Potts, 20th Virginia Cavalry, recalled:

> Wm. L. Jackson had been by some branded a coward but he was a very brave man, a man that old Kentucky will always be proud of. Ramshur's [Ramseur's] men always respected our brigade. When we would ride by, they would take off their caps and say "That is Jackson's brigade, they saved us at Winchester."

After meeting Averell near Winchester on July 20, Early's command fell back through Winchester, camping near Strasburg for the night. On July 22, Jackson's Cavalry moved to the Middle Road. Once on that road, Jackson moved to a position in the rear of Winchester, going into camp at 9 p.m. Private Andrew J. Jones recorded the following incident: "Two of our men went to [the] pike, fell in with and had [a] conversation with [the] enemy's cavalry."

The next day Jackson's men skirmished near Winchester, then moved that evening back to their old camp near Strasburg. On July 24, the brigade moved to near Kernstown, where Early engaged the enemy. Early stationed Jackson's Brigade on the left flank of his line of battle. The Confederates forced the Federals out of their position, and moved to near Bunker Hill.

From their position near Bunker Hill, Jackson's cavalry moved in the direction of Martinsburg. After some skirmishing, they fell back to their old camp at Bunker Hill. On July 26, Jackson's Brigade moved to Shepherdstown. There it skirmished with the Federal pickets on the opposite shore of the Potomac River.

During the next two days, Jackson's men worked at tearing up the railroad near Shepherdstown. On July 29, Jackson moved toward the river to draw the Federals attention away from McCausland's advance to Chambersburg. After skirmishing all day, Jackson returned to his camp near Shepherdstown.

Before daylight on July 30, Jackson's men left Shepherdstown on the Martinsburg road. Before going too far, Jackson did an about face and moved back toward Shepherdstown in line of battle. A large force of Federal infantry and cavalry (1,500 strong), forced Jackson to fall back to a position two miles from Shepherdstown, on the Martinsburg road. Early the next morning Jackson marched toward Martinsburg. After crossing the railroad and Opequon Creek, Jackson's Brigade went into camp about two miles from Martinsburg.

July was a busy month for Jackson's command, as well as a costly one. The Compiled Service Records and other official sources show the following losses in the 19th and 20th Virginia Regiments for July 1864:

Regiment	Killed	Wounded	Captured	Total
19th Virginia	1	6	21	28
20th Virginia	3	2	12	17
Total	4	8	33	45

August 1864 began much the same way as July. Jackson's Brigade moved to near Charles Town, in Jefferson County, and then back to Shepherdstown. By the evening of August 4, Jackson's cavalry was in camp at Sharpsburg, Maryland. The next morning Jackson's Brigade moved toward Boonsboro. Along the way they met a Federal force and began skirmishing with them. After skirmishing for half an hour, Jackson fell back across Antietam Creek. On the opposite shore the brigade made a stand, repulsing the pursuing Federals. The enemy on the run, Jackson's men again move toward Boonsboro.

Jackson's Brigade on August 6 moved in the direction of Hagerstown. At the junction of the Hagerstown and Williamsport roads, they turned to the left, in the direction of Williamsport. At that place, about 4 p.m., the brigade crossed the Potomac River onto Virginia soil and moved toward Shepherdstown. Resting until the afternoon of August 7, the brigade then moved through Shepherdstown. They went into camp two miles from Shepherdstown, at Keplingers. From that point, Early and Jackson fell back to the east side of Winchester.

Several days later, on August 12, Early moved his command back to Fisher's Hill. While there, Major General Lunsford L. Lomax reported for duty with Early's command. General Early assigned Lomax to the command of the cavalry division lately commanded by Major General Robert Ransom.

On August 17 General Early learned that the Federal forces were falling back and immediately began to pursue them. By nightfall, Early's advance met Federal infantry and cavalry between Kernstown and Winchester. General Early occupied the town of Winchester on August 18, 1864.

The following day, Early moved again in the direction of Martinsburg. General Lomax, with his cavalry, made a reconnaissance to Martinsburg and Shepherdstown. On August 21, Jackson's Brigade and two other brigades advanced toward Leetown. Arriving at Leetown at 10 a.m., Jackson's men moved toward Charles Town. After going about four miles they met a Federal force. Jackson's men, acting as infantry, skirmished with the enemy all afternoon. The next day Jackson continued to skirmish with the Federals and drove them back. The Confederate cavalrymen then occupied Charles Town for a short while before returning to Leetown.

On August 22, 1864, Major General Robert Ransom sent a report to General Samuel Cooper, the Confederate Adjutant General. In his report Ransom mentioned that Jackson's Cavalry Brigade numbered 737 men. The general made the following recommendation:

> Jackson has the Nineteenth and Twentieth Regiments and Forty-sixth and Forty-seventh Battalions Virginia Cavalry; consolidate the two battalions; give Major Lady, Forty-sixth Battalion, the command of the battalion transferred, and place the whole brigade with Lomax's old brigade as part of it.

General Ransom offered an alternative plan. The general recommended combining Jackson's and Imboden's brigades, and appointing a new commander to take charge of the combined organization.

While the main portion of Jackson's Brigade operated in the Shenandoah Valley, apparently some detachment of the brigade annoyed the enemy in West Virginia. On August 24 a detachment of Confederates surprised 70 men of the 8th Ohio Cavalry on picket duty at Huttonsville. The Confederate force consisted of about 100 dismounted cavalrymen, who attacked the Federal pickets at 3 a.m. The Confederates captured the entire detachment of the 8th Ohio Cavalary, then paroled them. When they finished paroling the Ohioans, the attackers retired in great haste toward Crab Bottom, taking with them the captured horses, equipment, and arms. Major General B. F. Kelley, in a letter dated August 26, said: "Jackson's guerrillas are becoming very bold and troublesome in the western part of the State." The identity of the attacking force, other than in Kelley's letter, remains a mystery.

General Lomax moved his cavalry to meet Sheridan at Charles Town on August 24. On this occasion, Lomax placed Major Harry W. Gilmor in command of the 19th and 20th Regiments. The general ordered Gilmor to hold the Leetown road with his command and the two regiments from Jackson's Brigade.

Major Gilmor dismounted the men of the 19th Virginia and stationed them in a patch of woods. Immediately the Federals charged their position. Gilmor wrote of this attack: "The 19th let them come quite near, and then opened upon them a steady fire, which threw them into some confusion...." The Federals fell back after the 1st Maryland Cavalry charged upon them.

Not long afterward, Gilmor learned of a Federal brigade moving to attack his left flank. The Maryland officer wrote: "A whole brigade was then plainly seen winding along. I moved the 19th and 20th to the left, and put them in a splendid position in a belt of woods...." The Federal artillery opened fire on the woods in an attempt to drive the dismounted cavalrymen out.

When the artillery ceased firing, Brigadier General Alfred Duffie advanced his brigade upon the 19th and 20th regiments. Major Gilmor ordered the men of the two regiments to lie down. When the Federal troopers got within 100 yards of the Confederate line, Gilmor ordered them to fire. The men of northwestern Virginia responded "with a deafening yell." Only the 19th Virginia fired on the advancing Yankees. Gilmor held the 20th Virginia in reserve.

After another attempt to break the Confederate line, the Federal troopers fell back and began shelling the woods again. Gilmor wrote:

> My boys laid down under the trees, and not a man was killed; but many were wounded by fragments of shell and limbs of trees cut off and falling on them. They stood it bravely, and expressed their determination to hold out as long as I saw fit to keep them there.

An hour later the Federals charged the woods. The men of the 19th and 20th regiments held their ground, shielded by a crude barricade of rails. Major Gilmor reported four men killed in the 19th and 20th Regiments, and about a dozen wounded, chiefly by saber cuts. The fight ended at sunset, with Gilmor's men sleeping on their arms for the night.

Colonel Jackson's Brigade spent the following week marching and skirmishing, with hardly a day's rest. On August 26, Jackson's Brigade took part in a fight at Shepherdstown. According to Federal reports, "...Jackson's command was crushed...." Colonel Jackson suffered a painful wound that morning at Smithfield, shooting himself in the leg with his pistol. The brigade fell back to Leetown that afternoon.

On the morning of August 28 all of Early's cavalry, except the 20th Virginia, moved toward Smithfield. About 10 a.m. the Federals advanced on the Charles Town road, driving in the scouts of the 20th Virginia. The 20th Virginia fell back slowly from Leetown in the direction of Smithfield, skirmishing all the while. About a mile and a half from Smithfield, the 1st Maryland Cavalry and Major Harry Gilmor's Cavalry Battalion reinforced the 20th Virginia. The combined Confederate force took cover in some nearby woods. The Federals charged the position and drove them back. The Confederates rallied and counter-charged and drove the Federals back. The Federals, not to be out done, returned with reinforcements and again drove the Confederates out of the woods. Again, the Confederates rallied and recovered the position. On the third charge, the Federals brought an overwhelming force against them and chased the Confederates away. Private Andrew J. Jones, 20th Virginia Cavalry wrote in his diary: "During these charges the two parties were mixed together — horses down, sabers, pistols and guns knocked out of men's hands — and the grandest confusion." The Federals did not pursue the Confederate, who retired to a position near Bunker Hill.

The skirmishing about Smithfield continued during the next two days. On August 31, 1864, Early's cavalry received orders to go to Winchester. After moving four miles, they received orders to return to their camp near Bunker Hill.

According to the Compiled Service Records, the 19th and 20th Regiments sustained the following losses during August 1864. This table does not reflect the men mentioned as killed and wounded by Major Harry W. Gilmor on August 26, 1864.

Regiment	Killed	Wounded	Captured	Total
19th Virginia	1	10	1	12
20th Virginia	0	6	4	10
Total	1	16	5	22

Chapter VIII

The next fight for the men of Jackson's Brigade came on September 3, 1864 at Bunker Hill. Early that morning a report arrived that a large Federal force was nearby. The 20th Virginia Cavalry received orders to dismount. Every fourth man remained with the horses. The dismounted men marched a half mile and engaged the enemy until about 2 p.m. At that hour, the men of the 20th Virginia began falling back.

The 20th Virginia Cavalry returned to their horses and quickly mounted. Lieutenant Eugene Hutton, commanding Company C, 20th Virginia, planned to move his men to a nearby hill. A force of Yankee cavalry moved around the extreme left of the Confederate line and attacked the 20th Virginia Cavalry. Lieutenant Hutton fell in the attack, shot through the heart. The men of the 20th Virginia charged the Federal line and recovered Hutton's body. As the Confederates retired, they met part of General Early's infantry advancing to their relief.

Between September 1 and September 19, the cavalry commanded by General Lomax skirmished daily with the enemy. Details of these skirmishes remain a mystery.

By September 14, many of Colonel Jackson's Brigade were absent on horse detail. Federal authorities at Buckhannon, West Virginia, reported on the 14th that Jackson had disbanded his regiment and sent it by squads to the northwest to steal horses. Captain Harrison H. Hagans, 1st West Virginia Cavalry, engaged one such squad of Jackson's men at Centerville that day. Captain Hagans wrote:

> With sixteen men I pursued and overtook thirty horse- thieves thirty miles above this place [Buckhannon]. I killed four, wounded several, and drove them out. Another squad of twelve has made its appearance in another direction to-day.

Hagans concluded his report by saying "The country is infested, and unless I have more force will be overrun." Captain S. H. Campbell, Company K, 19th Virginia Cavalry, was among those wounded in the skirmish.

On September 17, Jackson's Brigade led the way to Bunker Hill, followed by Major General John B. Gordon's Division. Jackson's men went into camp that evening at Bunker Hill. The following day Jackson met Averell's Brigade at Big Spring and drove him back through Martinsburg. That night Jackson's command returned to Bunker Hill, where it went into camp.

Early on the morning of September 19, Jackson's Brigade received orders to return to Winchester as the enemy were advancing on the Berryville road. The Federals threatened General Early's right flank. Lomax sent Jackson's Brigade and later Wickham's to reinforce the right. By order of General Fitzhugh Lee, Lomax took command of the Confederate right.

About noon Jackson's brigade dismounted and met the enemy on foot. The Federals made frequent attacks on the right, attempting to turn it. According to Private Andrew J. Jones, 20th Virginia Cavalry, the fight was "very hot" between 3 and 4 p.m. He described the sound of the musketry as "tremendous" and noted that the smoke rose in columns. The cavalrymen repelled the attacks until about 5 p.m. When Lomax ordered them to withdraw, they did so "unbroken and in good order." The Federals pursued the retreating Confederates and shelled them. Jackson's and Johnson's brigades were the last units to leave the field, and covered the retreat and flank of Early's army.

General Early's army retreated to Fisher's Hill, where it arrived on the morning of September 20, 1864. The Federals followed Early and were in Strasburg by 11 a.m. That afternoon the 20th Virginia Cavalry, while on picket duty, skirmished with the enemy.

The two armies skirmished with each other all morning near Strasburg on September 22. About noon, General Early informed Lomax that the Federals were massing on the left flank. This was Lomax's front, and he reinforced his line. General Lomax dismounted his cavalry, except McCausland's Brigade, and moved in line on the left. The cavalrymen hastily constructed a line of breastworks, joining the infantry on their right. General Lomax sent for the horse holders to leave the horses and join their comrades in the breastworks.

About 4 p.m., Lomax discovered a Federal force moving along the side of the mountain a half mile to the left. He moved to meet them, sending word to the nearest infantry division commander to fill in the gap in the line where his men were. Lomax met two brigades of the enemy and drove them back.

The breastworks formerly occupied by Lomax were open. The Federals took full advantage of the error, moving through the opening to Lomax's rear. The Federal attack forced the Southern cavalrymen to fall back. They rallied at the next line of works. Here Lomax found an infantry brigade (the third one sent for that purpose) to aid him. He formed his dismounted cavalrymen on the left of the infantry and urged the entire line to advance. The cavalrymen obeyed, while the infantrymen broke and ran.

General Lomax now withdrew his men, seeing that the entire army was giving way before the Federal advance. Many reports show that the dismounted cavalry retreated in a general stampede. General Lomax wrote in their defense:

I will mention in connection with this engagement that the cavalry, being on the left and the first attacked, are generally supposed to have been the first to give way, and are accountable for the disaster of that day. I will state that the infantry brigades sent to the support of the cavalry broke while the cavalry were still engaged and did not reach the point of attack. That the only fighting done on the left of the line was by the cavalry, and I believe if they had been supported that the enemy would have been forced back.

General Early retreated during the night and arrived near Mount Jackson on morning of September 23. A force of Federal cavalry commanded by General Averell caught up with Early's rear and attacked it. Colonel Jackson's brigade, in the rear, skirmished with the Federals. In the afternoon a brisk fight took place between Jackson's Brigade and the Federals. The Confederate cavalrymen drove the Federals back. The Confederates went into camp at Rude's Hill for the night.

On the morning of September 24, Lomax's cavalry watched the Middle and Back Roads between Mount Jackson and Harrisonburg. During the day, a superior force of Federals attacked Lomax on the Middle Road and forced him back toward Harrisonburg in disorder. The Confederates reached Harrisonburg after nightfall and moved toward Port Republic several miles before going into camp for the night.

General Early's army marched to Port Republic the next morning, taking a position between Port Republic and Brown's Gap. Jackson's Brigade moved up the Shenandoah River to screen the army. The 20th Virginia Cavalry moved to Mount Sidney, where it performed picket duty.

On the morning of September 26 the Federals advanced on Lomax's cavalry and forced him to fall back. The enemy crossed the river and moved toward Brown's Gap and Staunton, cutting off the 20th Virginia Cavalry. Private Andrew J. Jones, ot the 20th wrote: "We had to take through fields and woods between two roads. 'Twas a narrow escape."

The Confederates fell back to Waynesboro, reaching that point after dark. Marching a short distance farther, they went into camp for the night at the foot of Rockfish Gap.

The next day Early moved back to Port Republic and drove the Federal cavalry from that place. Early's command then went into camp at Port Republic. The 20th Virginia Cavalry of Jackson's Brigade remained near Rockfish Gap and skirmished with the Federals. On the morning of September 28, Early started toward Waynesboro, with part of Lomax's cavalry watching the rear and right flank of the army.

That morning the Federals burned the railroad depot and bridge at Waynesboro. Artillery fire from Rockfish Gap drove them back. About 5 p.m. the Federals advanced again on Rockfish Gap. General Fitzhugh Lee's cavalry, arrived and drove the Federals back to Staunton.

General Early's army spent the remainder of September at Waynesboro, resting. The 20th Virginia Cavalry left Rockfish Gap on the morning of September 29 and rejoined the brigade on the Port Republic road.

The losses in the 19th and 20th Virginia Regiments for the month of September amounted to:

Regiment	Killed	Wounded	Captured	Total
19th Virginia	3	14	13	30
20th Virginia	5	9	15	29
Total	8	23	28	59

Jackson's Brigade spent the early days of October 1864 doing picket duty and skirmishing with the enemy. General Early remained in camp at Mount Sidney until October 6, waiting on the arrival of Brigadier General Thomas L. Rosser and his cavalrymen of the "Laurel Brigade."

General Early learned on October 6 that the enemy had pulled back toward Winchester. He ordered General Lomax to send a portion of his cavalry through the Luray Valley and follow the enemy with the remainder. General Lomax, with Johnson's and Jackson's brigades (about 800 effective men) moved to Keezletown and camped.

The advance continued the following day. Near Mount Jackson, Lomax met the enemy and skirmished for a while. Jackson's and Johnson's Brigades went into camp for the night nearby.

At daylight on the morning of October 8, Lomax moved his two brigades to Edinburg. They discovered two regiments of Federal cavalry on picket at that place, which they drove to Woodstock. At Woodstock, Lomax found a brigade of cavalry drawn up in line of battle, and the village in flames. As the Southern cavalrymen drove the enemy pickets through the town, the support turned and fled. The 19th Virginia Cavalry followed them. General Lomax ordered the 20th Virginia Cavalry and the 46th Battalion Virginia Cavalry to return to Woodstock and extinguish the fires set by the Federals. After dealing with the fires, Lomax's cavalry went into camp in some woods near Woodstock.

Moving at daylight on October 9, Lomax advanced on two brigades of cavalry that had arrived in his front during the night. With his small command, Lomax drove the Northern cavalrymen back on their infantry support. Learning of Rosser's defeat at Tom's Brook, Lomax began to fall back. The Federals followed. When Lomax's men reached the open ground about Woodstock, the

Federals charged and scattered Johnson's Brigade. Jackson's Brigade, on the right of the road, "was unbroken and was detached to meet the force advancing on the left, and retired in good order." The Northerners followed Lomax to Edinburg and to Mount Jackson. General Lomax wrote:

> In the engagement I had but 800 effective men, and was opposed by a division in my front and a brigade on my left (see Sheridan's official report). The officers and men cannot be blamed for giving way when charged in such heavy force, having no arms to resist a charge mounted, not a saber or pistol being in the command. My command being at one time twenty-seven miles from any infantry support, without proper arms or discipline, will explain in a measure why the rout was so complete.

On October 11, Lomax's cavalry division marched toward the Luray Valley, arriving at Luray the following day at 11 a.m. Moving a few miles farther, Lomax went into camp at Milford. He remained until October 18, when orders arrived to move to Front Royal.

Marching at daylight on October 19, Lomax met a Federal force at Front Royal and drove it to within six miles of Winchester. From that point, Lomax moved to the Middletown road, to try to strike Sheridan's flank. When Lomax reached the Middletown road, General Early's troops had not yet reached that point. Lomax moved his division to the left and went into camp for the night. Discovering that Early had fallen back, and that Sheridan's men occupied Fisher's Hill, Lomax moved back to the Luray Valley. He remained here for the remainder of October.

On October 28, 1864, General Lomax recommended Colonel Jackson for promotion to the rank of brigadier general. The recommendation reached General Robert E. Lee's hands, and he endorsed it as follows: "I believe Col. Jackson to be a brave, efficient officer..." General Lomax stated that Jackson's Brigade numbered nearly 1,700 men, of whom about 600 were mounted. The general continued: "The command is completely organized, efficient and composed of a very superior set of men and is daily receiving recruits."

The 19th and 20th Virginia regiments suffered the following losses during October 1864:

Regiment	Killed	Wounded	Captured	Total
19th Virginia	2	9	2	13
20th Virginia	1	4	3	8
Total	3	13	5	21

This table does not reflect the losses to the two regiments in Captain Hall's disastrous raid on Beverly, West Virginia on October 29.

A shortage of horses in Lomax's cavalry division severely reduced the effective strength of his command. Toward the middle of October, General John D. Imboden detailed Captain Hannibal Hill (62nd Virginia Mounted Infantry), to take a detachment in search of horses. Captain Hill led a force of 350 men detailed from 21 regiments to Highland County. Unable to find enough horses there, he conceived a daring raid on the Federal garrison at Beverly.

Near sunset on October 28, 1864, Captain Hill halted his men about a mile west of the camp of the 8th Ohio Cavalry at Beverly. There he and his men spent a long, cold night without heat or shelter. Before daylight on October 29, the sound of a bugle from the Union camp startled the Confederates. Captain Hill quickly formed his men and advanced at about 5 a.m. The Ohio cavalrymen were in ranks for their morning roll call.

As Captain Hill and his men crept forward, the Federal pickets challenged them about 150 yards from the camp. With a shout, the Confederates charged past the pickets into the camp. When the Ohio cavalrymen heard the yell, they scattered in every direction, ducking into their huts to get their weapons.

A confusing hand-to-hand fight followed. The Southern soldiers approached the darkened huts of the Federals in search of the occupants. As they peered into the huts, the Federals had easy shots at them, as their bodies showed clearly against morning sky. Colonel Robert Youart, 8th Ohio Cavalry, wrote: "In the darkness, friend and foe were hardly distinguishable. Both parties were taking and guarding prisoners at the same time."

Captain Hill split his command in half, sending part to the rear of the Federal camp. When day broke, Colonel Youart rallied about 50 of his men and charged upon the Confederate force in his rear. The charge disoriented the Confederates, and a second charge put them to flight. Colonel Youart now turned his attention to the invaders in his front. The Ohio cavalrymen quickly routed the Confederates, who escaped to the safety of the surrounding mountains.

The two-hour fight was over. Colonel Youart and his troopers killed, wounded, or captured one-third of the Confederate force. Those fortunate enough to escape rejoined their commands at Milford.

The following table shows the loss at Beverly among the men detailed from the 19th and 20th Regiments:

Regiment	Killed	Wounded	Captured	Total
19th Virginia	1	3	13	17
20th Virginia	0	5	29	34
Total	1	8	42	51

For the men of Jackson's Brigade, November 1864 brought a time of rest. Still attached to Lomax's cavalry division, the brigade remained in camp near Luray until November 11. On that date Lomax moved his cavalry on General Early's right flank, holding a position between the Valley Pike and the Front Royal Road. General Lomax went into camp near Newtown for the night.

In the afternoon of November 12, Lomax moved his command to the left flank, to reinforce Rosser's cavalry. Colonel Jackson's Brigade, commanded by Brigadier General Henry B. Davidson, accompanied Lomax, but did not take part in any of the fighting. The following day Lomax returned to Milford and went into camp near that place.

A week later, General Lomax moved three brigades of his cavalry to the eastern side of the Blue Ridge. Jackson's Brigade, one of the three, went into camp near Madison Court House to police the area. The brigade, now commanded by Colonel Jackson, remained in camp here until late December 1864.

Chapter IX

On December 20, 1864, Lieutenant David Poe took 20 men of the 20th Virginia Cavalry out on a picket detail. He relieved Lieutenant Hammet of the 46th Battalion Virginia Cavalry near Little Washington, in Rappahannock County. Lieutenant Hammet moved back about five miles and camped for the night near Criglersville.

Before long a large force of Federal troops advanced on the little picket force. The small band of Confederates exchanged shots with the Federal advance, then fell back slowly. At 11 p.m. Lieutenant Poe received orders to return to camp. When he reached Criglersville, he received another order to remain there with Lieutenant Hammet. Poe and his pickets went into camp for the night.

On the following day the Federals advanced, and the Confederates began skirmishing with them. About 3 p.m. Colonel Jackson sent word to Lieutenant Poe to "draw out the enemy." Poe advanced about 150 yards and met the Federal scouts. After firing a few shots, Poe began to fall back. As he retired, Poe received an order from Colonel Jackson to conceal his men near Madison Court House and let the enemy pass by him.

Lieutenant Poe moved as ordered by Jackson. The Federals, General Alfred T. A. Torbert's 1st Cavalry Division, met Jackson's Brigade near Madison Court House.

When the Federals advanced, Jackson's men quickly erected a rude breastwork of rails and poles. From the shelter provided by the breastworks, the two armies exchanged shots until about sundown. As darkness drew near, Jackson's men received orders to be ready to move. Soon afterward, Colonel Jackson and his staff appeared, with the colors flying, and charged down a hill on the Federal left. Unsure of what they faced, the Federal troopers fell back a few paces. At precisely the same moment, the men of Jackson's Brigade mounted their horses and retired. Colonel Jackson and his staff joined the brigade soon afterward.

After Jackson's Brigade fell back, the Federals followed and met Lieutenant Poe. The Confederate lieutenant fell back to the village of Madison Court House, where he made a stand. The Federals continued to advance and forced him out of the town.

As Lieutenant Poe and his men retired and drew close to Jackson's command, Jackson's pickets opened fire on Poe by mistake. Quickly realizing

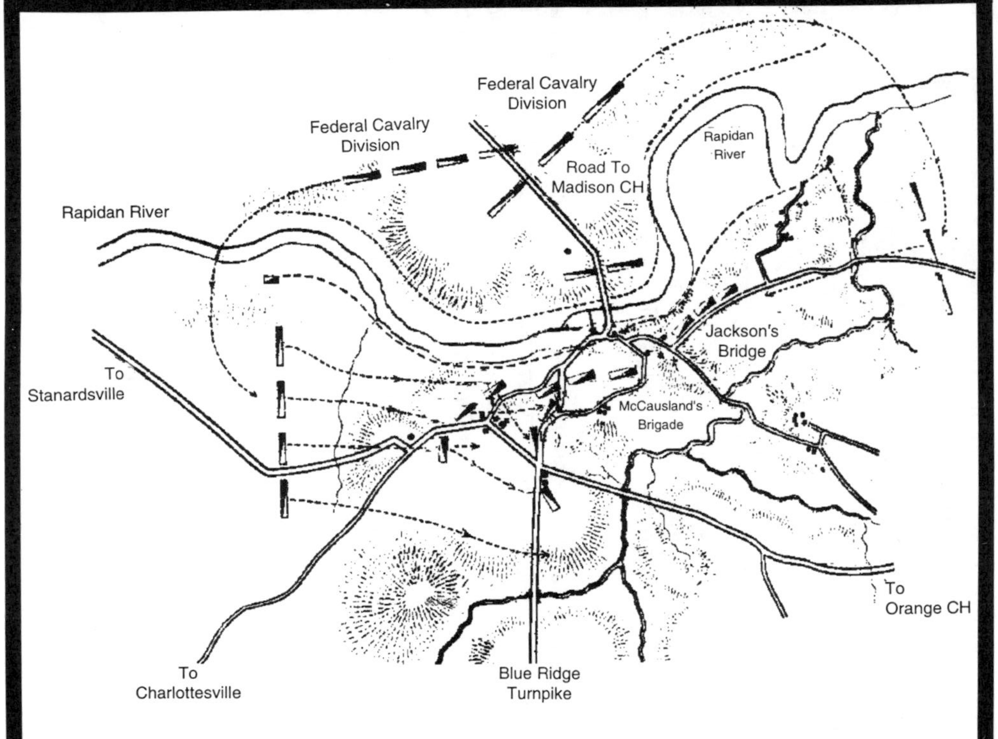

Cavalry Action At Liberty Mills, Va. December 23, 1864

their error, the cavalrymen ceased fire and Poe entered the camp. During the night, Jackson's Brigade moved to Liberty Mills on the Rapidan River.

At Liberty Mills, Jackson joined forces with General John McCausland. The 20th Virginia Cavalry dismounted and took cover in a mill and house, facing a covered bridge. The rest of the Confederates took shelter in rifle pits and behind some breastworks and waited for the Federals to arrive.

As Torbert advanced he drove the Confederate pickets before him. At Liberty Mills, the Confederates fell back across the bridge to their main force. As the Federal cavalrymen drew near the bridge, the Confederates set off an explosion on the bridge. The explosion caused a fire, which quickly consumed the wooden structure.

General Torbert could not cross the river at Liberty Mills because of the bad crossing and the position of the Confederate cavalry and artillery. Instead, Torbert obtained guides from the neighborhood to show his men where to cross the river and strike the Confederate flanks. He sent a detachment of his force to the left and another detachment to the right.

After much delay in crossing the river, the Federal detachment on the right appeared about dark. It immediately charged Jackson and McCausland, driving them toward Orange Court House. Along the way the Confederates met the left-hand detachment of Torbert's command. Caught between two forces, the Confederates turned toward Gordonsville.

The men of Jackson's and McCausland's brigades went into camp before reaching Gordonsville. The night of December 22, recalled Private M. P. H. Potts (20th Virginia Cavalry), was very cold. The temperature hovered near zero. The Confederates huddled around rail fires. Potts recalled that three men shared five blankets that night, and took turns sleeping in the middle.

At daylight on December 23 the fight continued. General Torbert's cavalry drove Jackson and McCausland to within two and a half miles of Gordonsville. The Confederates took a position in the narrow gap at Southwest Mountain, behind rails and earth breastworks.

General Torbert attacked the position with about half of his command, but could not take it. The general then sent a detachment to the left to flank the position. While waiting for this detachment to get into position, about 11 a.m., Torbert saw Confederate infantry coming up. With reinforcements arriving, Torbert withdrew his command to Madison Court House.

In the fighting about Madison Court House, Liberty Mills and Gordonsville, the 19th and 20th Regiments suffered a slight loss. The Compiled Service records show that the 19th Virginia Cavalry lost two men killed and one wounded. The 20th Virginia Cavalry lost one man killed and five wounded.

Not long after the fight at Gordonsville, Jackson's cavalry returned to Bath, Highland, and Pocahontas cunties for the winter. The 19th Virginia Cavalry went into camp near Warm Springs, while the 20th Virginia Cavalry went into camp at Crab Bottom. Detachments from Jackson's Brigade occupied a position at Green Bank in Pocahontas County, West Virginia.

On January 20, 1865, Jackson, now a brigadier general received orders to assume command of the brigade formerly commanded by Brigadier General H. B. Davidson. General Jackson once more led the troops he had organized.

On February 2, Jackson allowed his men to go to their homes, if possible, to procure forage and fresh horses. He directed them to reassemble after 40 days.

By February 11, General Lomax had established his headquarters at Millboro Depot. In a letter dated th 11th, Lomax informed General Early that General Thomas L. Rosser claimed Jackson's Brigade as part of his command. General Lomax, appealing for Early to intervene, stated that Jackson's "...is my best brigade...."

As March began, the troopers of Lomax's cavalry division began to assemble for the spring campaign. General Jackson, at Buffalo Gap, received a dispatch from General T. L. Rosser on March 4, asking for help in recapturing the prisoners taken by Sheridan at Waynesboro on March 2. Jackson responded:

> I have no men with me. One of Regts is at Goshen water bound. I expect about one hundred and fifty men at Buffalo Gap to night, and if they come I will bring them as you desire.

The following day, Jed Hotchkiss visited Jackson at Buffalo Gap. Hotchkiss, a topographical engineer, asked Jackson to send troops to aid Rosser. As the 20th Virginia Cavalry and Imboden's Brigade were now in camp, Jackson agreed to send them to aid Rosser. The 20th Virginia Cavalry went as far as Churchville that day, and reached Harrisonburg the following day.

General Lomax that same day issued orders for his division to assemble as quickly as possible. He wanted them to march to the defense of Lynchburg. Most of his division arrived at Lynchburg in the following week. On March 14, Lomax left Lynchburg and marched toward Charlottesville and Richmond. Four days later Lomax's division went into camp two miles from the "Negro Fort" in Henrico County.

After remaining there for two days, Lomax received orders from General Early to return to Staunton. Back in the Shenandoah Valley, Lomax's men went into camp near Churchville on March 27. Between that date and April 5, 1865, Lomax's troopers skirmished with parties of Federal troops in the Valley.

On April 6, General Lomax and his command left Staunton for Lynchburg. The general with Jackson's and Imboden's brigades of cavalry arrived at Lynchburg about 4 p.m. on April 8.

On April 9, 1865, Lomax prepared to defend Lynchburg. He stationed his two brigades on the Richmond road. In the afternoon McCausland's Brigade arrived from Appomattox Court House, with fragments of other commands. General Lomax learned of the surrender from them. McCausland told Lomax that the Federals were following them with a flag of truce demanding the surrender of Lynchburg.

Lomax sent word to General Jackson and Colonel Smith to resist any Federal advance. He felt that the terms given General Lee at Appomattox did not apply to his command and Lynchburg. Lomax informed Jackson and Smith to retire, if hard pressed, through the city on the Salem Pike, and cautioned them to keep their men under control.

The Army of Northern Virginia, of which Lomax's Division formed a part, surrendered at Appomattox Court House on April 9. Nine men of Jackson's Brigade, Lomax's Division, surrendered that day. Of those nine, only two belonged to the 19th and 20th Virginia Cavalry. One man from each of those regiments surrendered with General Lee's Army.

Three days later, Lomax moved his command to Danville. Two days after that, April 14, Lomax received orders to disband his cavalry for several weeks.

According the Lieutenant David Poe, Jackson marched his brigade into North Carolina and remained there several days. Returning to Buchanan, Botetourt County, on April 15, Jackson disbanded his brigade. He directed the men to rendezvous at Staunton on May 1, 1865.

Before May 1, however, Jackson changed the rendezvous point to Lexington as the Federals occupied Staunton. General Jackson assembled about one half of his brigade at Lexington on May 3. He asked them if they wished him to surrender them, or did they wish to surrender themselves. The men chose to surrender themselves. Some of them, however, never surrendered. General Jackson disbanded his men for the final time on May 4, 1865.

On April 30, Lieutenant Colonel William P. Thompson, commanding Jackson's Cavalry Brigade sent a message to the commanding officer at Staunton. Colonel Thompson asked what terms he could get for the surrender of his men. Colonel Horatio B. Reed, 22nd New York Cavalry, replied he could offer the same terms as General Lee received at Appomattox. When Thompson and his men did not appear to surrender on May 1, Colonel Reed sent his scouts out to learn their position. The scouts soon returned and informed Reed that Thompson's force numbered about 100 men, and had scattered into the mountains.

The last skirmish in which members of the 19th and 20th Virginia Cavalry took part occurred on April 18, 1865. Captain Joseph Badger, 8th Ohio Cavalry, left Philippi with 150 men on April 15 on a scout through Randolph, Pocahontas, Bath, and Highland counties. The Federal scouting party reached Huntersville on April 18 and moved on toward Warm Springs. Lieutenant Swain and 30 men led the advance to Knapp's Creek, seven miles from Huntersville. At that point he turned off the Warm Springs road to search the valley for Confederates. Captain Badger with the main party moved a mile farther and halted to wait for Lieutenant Swain.

As Badger and his men waited for Swain's return, a party of Confederates "suddenly and furiously" attacked Badger's advance. Captain Badger immediately formed his men to meet an attack and galloped to the front. When he arrived at the front, he saw the Confederates running up the side of the mountain. Sending men in pursuit of the fleeing rebels, Captain Badger moved on toward Warm Springs. From the one prisoner taken, Badger learned that the 25 Confederates, with Major Hutton, Captain Marshall, and Captain Harding, were going to their homes.

The pursuit continued for four miles. The Federals caused the Confederates to abandon their horses and run on foot through places a horse could not go.

Major Harding, 20th Virginia Cavalry, provided a slightly different account. According to the major, he had eleven men with him, one of whom the Federals captured. Major Hutton did not accompany them. In the pursuit, Major Harding fired a shot at one of his pursuers and killed his horse. This, Harding claimed, was the last shot fired east of the Mississippi River.

During April and May, many of Jackson's men surrendered to the Federal authorities at various military posts. The Federals treated them as prisoners of war and paroled them for exchange. A lesser number of Jackson's men received their paroles outright, mainly at Charleston, West Virginia, and at Staunton. A few never surrendered.

TABLE OF LOSS AND GAIN
FOR JACKSON'S BRIGADE
FROM NOVEMBER 1863 TO APRIL 1864

Date	Enl.	Transf. To	Transf. Out	Des.	Dropped	Disch-arged	Died	Resigned
Nov. 1863	24	2	-	-	1	1	7	-
Dec. 1863	45	1	-	5	38	-	1	-
Jan. 1864	50	3	-	-	1	42	2	-
Feb. 1864	80	-	-	27	47*	-	-	2
Mar. 1864	18	-	8	6	4	1	-	-
Apr. 1864	33	2	-	-	28	1	1	-
Total	340	8	8	38	119	48	12	2

* The men dropped during February 1864 were turned over to the Enrolling Officer.

STRENGTH OF WILLIAM L. JACKSON'S BRIGADE AS SHOWN BY BRIGADE RETURNS

DATE	PRESENT FOR DUTY OFF	PRESENT FOR DUTY ENL	EFFECTIVE TOTAL	AGGREGATE PRESENT	AGGREGATE PRE. & ABSENT	AGGREGATE LAST RETRUN	NO. OF POW'S OFF	NO. OF POW'S ENL
Nov. 1863	92	777	777	938	1,611	1,598	–	–
Dec. 1863	74	604	604	736	1,607	1,611	3	90
Jan. 1864	72	625	625	772	1,615	1,607	–	–
Feb. 1864	78	660	660	819	1,619	1,615	–	–
Mar. 1864	78	623	623	778	1,617	1,619	–	–
April 1864*	95	823	823	1,026	1,982	1,617	5	201
Aug. 1864*	–	–	737	–	–	–	–	–
Apr. 1864**	80	810	810	1,010	1,994	-----	6	200

1. April 1864 - 47th Va. Battalion Cavalry, 315 men, now first reported. A second return for April (marked **), gives different figures.
December 19, 1864 - Return shows 817 servicable horses and 98 unservicable horses.
2. * August 1864 - The figure here was taken from a letter of Maj. Gen. R. Ransom, Jr. to Gen. S. Cooper, August 22, 1864.

STRENGTH OF JACKSON'S BRIGADE AS SHOWN BY INSPECTION REPORTS

DATE	OFFICERS PRESENT	ENLISTED PRESENT	AGGREG. PRESENT	PRESENT & ABSENT	ABSENT POW'S
10/25/64 Page Co.	55	386	528	2,559	652

STRENGTH OF DAVIDSON'S BRIGADE FORMERLY JACKSON'S, FROM INSPECTION REPORTS

DATE	PRESENT FOR DUTY	AGGREG. PRESENT	PRESENT & ABSENT	EFFECTIVE FOR FIELD	ABSENT POW'S
12/15/64	798	917	3,179	798	691

80

STRENGTH OF JACKSON'S BRIGADE
AS SHOWN ON TRI-MONTHLY FIELD RETURN
OF MAJ. GEN. L. L. LOMAX'S DIVISION
DECEMBER 19, 1864

OFFICERS PRESENT	ENLISTED PRESENT	PRESENT & ABSENT	HORSES	
			SERVICABLE	UN-SERVICABLE
93	781	3,360	817	98

19th Virginia Cavalry
Strength According to Muster Rolls

DATE	COMPANY										
	A	B	C	D	E	F	G	H	I	K
Roll Rec'd 8/1863	NR	NR	NR	NR	NR	NR	NR	NR	NR	NR
6/30/63 - 2/29/64	—	—	—	—	—	—	—	—	132	—
10/31/63 - 10/31/64	—	—	—	—	67	NR	—	—	—	—
11/1/63 - 2/29/64	—	49	—	—	—	—	—	—	—	—
Roll Dated only 1864	—	—	84	—	—	—	—	—	—	—
1/1/64 - 2/29/64	—	—	—	—	—	112	—	—	—	—
2/29/64 - 8/31/64	—	—	—	—	—	—	—	—	115	—
8/31/64 - 10/31/64	—	66	68	—	—	—	42	64	114	—
Previous Roll (1864)*	—	66	—	—	—	—	52	—	115	—

* This roll follows the August 31, 1864 - October 31, 1864 Muster Roll.

82

20th Virginia Cavalry
Strength According to Muster Rolls

DATE	A	B	C	D	E	F	G	H	I	K
Previous Roll*	—	—	109	—	—	—	—	—	—	—
6/30/63 – 8/31/64	—	—	84	—	—	—	—	—	—	—
7/1/63 – 11/1/63	—	—	—	78	—	—	—	—	—	70
7/1/63 – 1/1/64	—	—	—	—	—	33	—	—	—	—
7/1/63 – 8/31/64	—	NR	—	NR	NR	NR	NR	NR	NR	NR
7/25/63	84	—	—	—	—	—	—	31	—	—
About August 1863	84	—	—	—	—	—	—	—	—	—
10/31/63 – 8/31/64	—	64	—	—	—	—	—	—	42	—
11/1/63 – 8/31/64	—	—	—	—	—	—	61	—	—	64
11/1/63 – 2/29/64	—	—	—	—	—	—	—	—	53	—
11/1/63 – 10/31/64	—	—	—	—	—	—	—	—	—	—
12/31/63 – 8/31/64	—	—	—	93	44	—	—	—	—	—
1/1/64 – 8/31/64	—	—	—	—	—	—	—	—	—	53
2/29/64 – 8/31/64	—	—	—	—	—	—	51	—	—	—
3/1/64 – 8/31/64	—	—	—	—	—	—	52	42	—	—
8/31/64 – 10/31/64	—	62	80	—	44	31	—	—	—	—
9/1/64 – 10/31/64	—	—	—	99	—	—	—	—	—	—

* This roll precedes the June 30, 1863 – August 31, 1864 Muster Roll.

STRENGTH OF 19TH VIRGINIA CAVALRY IN DECEMBER 1864

Co.	Officers Present	Officers Absent	Where Raised	Aggreg. Present	Aggreg Absent
Col.		W. L. Jackson			
Lt.Col	W. P. Thompson				
Major		George Downs			
A	Lt. Layne	J. S. Spriggs	Wirt Co.	24	70
B			Braxton Co.	16	57
C	J. W. Gough		Jackson Co.	27	72
D		J. Righter	Marion Co.	18	62
E		J. W. Ball	Gilmer Co.	10	50
F	W. L. McNiel		Pocahontas	12	111
G		W. H. Justice	Kanawha Co.	18	41
H	P. O'Brien		Gilmer Co.	10	30
I		J. W. Marshall	Randolph Co	30	81
K		Jos. Campbell	Gilmer Co.	21	50
TOTAL	4	6	----------	186	623

84

STRENGTH OF 20TH VIRGINIA CAVALRY IN DECEMBER 1864

Co.	Officers Present	Officers Absent	Where Raised	Aggreg. Present	Aggreg Absent
Col.	W. W. Arnett		--------	----	----
Lt.Col	D. Evans		--------	----	----
Major			--------	----	----
A		J. B. Lady	Marion Co.	21	66
B		D. M. Camp	Marion Co.	16	64
C		E. Martin	Randolph	15	75
D		E. Hutton	Barbour Co	14	87
E		W. W. Daniels	Harrison	18	40
F	A. Lewis	J. W. Davis	Harrison	5	27
G		R. D. Neel	Wood Co.	22	54
H		Jos. Hayhurst	Wirt Co.	5	33
I		H.L. Heiskell	Rockbridge	2	70
K	Lt. Murphy		Rockbridge	5	63
TOTAL	4	9	--------	123	579

85

Monument at Mingo Flats, Randolph County, West Virginia. Pictured, left to right: George Washington Painter, Co. I, 19th Va. Cav.; William H. Brady, Co. A, 26th Va. Cav.; John Stewart, 22nd Va. Inf.

Courtesy: Donald R. Rice, Randolph County Historical Society

Thomas Dilley, Co. A, 19th Va. Cav.

Courtesy: J. Dale West Collection, Longview, Tx.

Major George Downs, 19th Va. Cav.

Courtesy: Robert Homer Knotts, Sr., Salisbury, N.C.

Grandison N. Wolfe, Co. E, 19th Va. Cav.

Courtesy: Mrs. Wilbur Hoover, Harrisville, W. Va.

Zachariah Wright, Co. H, 20th Va. Cav.

Courtesy: Mrs. Thelma Hersman

Uriah Hevener (Hefner), Co. F, 19th Va. Cav.

Courtesy: Howard Hevener, Arbovale, W. Va.

Captain Edward M. (W.) Corder, Co. D, 20th Va. Cav.

Courtesy: Lyle K. Corder, Bridgeport, W. Va.

William H. Collins and wife, Caroline Gragg Collins, Co. F, 19th Va. Cav.

Major Joseph French Harding, 20th Va. Cav.

Lieutenant Eugenius Hutton,
Co. C, 20th Va. Cav.

Group of Confederate Veterans, Randolph County, West Virginia.
Back row, left to right: P. C. Collect, W. H. Wilson, J. F. Harding (20th Va. Cav.),
A. J. Collect, Jacob Heater, J. H. DeWitt (20th Va. Cav.);
Front row, left to right: S. N. Bosworth, Eugenius Isner (20th Va. Cav.),
A. C. Weese, Elihu Hutton (20th Va. Cav.).

Courtesy: Randolph County Historical Society and Elizabeth Harding

James Munroe McCann, 19th Va. Cav.

Aaron Bell Young, Co. F, 20th Va. Cav.

Thomas Smith Wade, Chaplain, 19th Va. Cav.

Marcellus F. Wiley, Co. I, 19th Va. Cav.

John Calvin Price, Co. F, 19th Va. Cav.

Courtesy: Mary Price Barlow

John Calvin Price and George McLaughlin, Co. F, 19th Va. Cav.

Brigadier General William L. Jackson, CSA

Headquarters Flag of Brigadier General William L. Jackson

Courtesy: Darrell Collins, Ann Arbor, Mich.

Courtesy: The Museum of the Confederacy, Richmond, Va. Photograph by Katherine Wetzel

THE MUSTER ROLLS

The muster rolls for the 19th Virginia Cavalry contain 1,573 names. These names were compiled from a variety of official and unofficial sources. Foremost on the list of official sources is the Compiled Military Service Records (CSR) from the National Archives in Washington, D. C. Other official sources as well as unofficial ones have been discovered at the Virginia State Library, Virginia Historical Society, and the Eleanor S. Brockenbrough Library at the Museum of the Confederacy, all in Richmond, Va.

The muster rolls for the 20th Virginia Cavalry contain 1,058 names, compiled from the same sources mentioned above.

A number of abbreviations have been used in an effort to reduce the length of the rosters of the 19th and 20th Virginia Cavalry. A list of those used appears at the end of this introduction.

All place names, unless otherwise noted, are in the state of Virginia. Places that were once a part of Virginia and are now in the State of West Virginia, are followed by "W. Va."

All dates are listed as month, day and year. For example: 4/2/40 means April 2, 1840. Dates after 1899 are shown as "19__" to avoid confusion. Whenever a date is not known to be exact, it is accompanied by "c.", which stands for about (circa). Dates on the muster rolls appear as 12/31/63 - 8/31/64 (December 31, 1863 to August 31, 1864.

The format of the entries in the roster is as follows: name of the soldier, along with any variation of spelling and suspected names, followed by the highest rank held in the regiment, and a company letter. Following that is his birth information (when known), prewar occupation, prewar military service, military service record, postwar occupation and residence, death, and burial place (when known).

The oldest soldier in the 19th Virginia Cavalry was Hugh Williams, born in 1801. The youngest was Shedrick Truman, who was born in Ohio in 1853.

The oldest soldier in the 20th Virginia Cavalry was Andrew Radcliff, born in 1809. Several soldiers vie for the position of being the youngest member of the 20th Virginia Cavalry. James C. Coontz, along with several other soldiers, was born in 1849.

ABBREVIATIONS

Ab.	Absent
ACS	Assistant Commissary of Subsistance
Adm.	Admitted
AIGO	Adjutant & Inspector General's Office
AQM	Assistant Quartermaster
Arty.	Artillery
Asst.	Assistant
AWOL	Absent Without Leave
b.	born
Battn.	Battalion
Brig.	Brigadier
Bur.	Buried
c.	Circa (about)
Capt.	Captain
Cav.	Cavalry
CH	Court House
Co.	Company or County
Col.	Colonel
Comp.	Complexion
Corp.	Corporal
Cpd.	Captured
CS	Confederate States
d.	died
Desc.	Description
Disc.	Discharged
Dist.	District
Div.	Division
DOD.	Died of Disease
DOW.	Died of Wounds
Enl.	Enlisted
Ft.	Fort
Gen.	General

Grad.	Graduate
Gov.	Governor
Gov't.	Government
Hosp.	Hospital
HQ	Headquarters
Inf.	Infantry
k.	killed (not in battle)
KIA.	Killed in Action
Lt.	Lieutenant
Lt. Col.	Lieutenant Colonel
Maj.	Major
MIA.	Missing in Action
Mtd.	Mounted
NFR.	No Further Record
No.	Number
POW.	Prisoner of War
Pres.	President
Pt.	Point
Pvt.	Private
QM	Quartermaster
Reg't.	Regiment
Reg'tl.	Regimental
RTD	Returned to Duty
Sgt.	Sergeant
Transf.	Transferred
UCV	United Confederate Veterans
UDC	United Daughters of the Confederacy
Unk.	Unknown
Univ.	University
US	United States
VMI	Virginia Military Institute
Vol.	Volunteer
VSL	Virginia State Line
Wd.	Wounded

19th Virginia Cavalry

ACKER, GEORGE C. - Pvt. Co. K. b.c. 1838. Not on muster rolls. Cpd. Jackson Co., W. Va., 10/20/63. Confined at the Atheneum Prison, 10/29/63. Desc.: age 25, 6' 3 3/4", florid comp., auburn hair, gray eyes and sandy whiskers. Occ. mechanic, residing in Jackson Co., W. Va. Transf. to Camp Chase, 10/30/63. Confined at Camp Chase, 10/30/63. Wished to take the oath and not be exchanged, as he was a conscript and deserter. Transf. to Rock Island, Ill., 1/14/64. Confined at Rock Island, Ill., 1/14/64. Released 10/6/64, joined US Service, to fight on the frontier. NFR.

ADKINS, BERRY - Pvt. Co. H. Prior service, Co. G, 3rd VSL. Enl. Frankfort, Greenbrier Co., W. Va., 3/19/63 (Clay Co., 4/1/63). Not stated if present or absent on muster-in roll dated 3/63. Ab. 9/1/64 - 10/31/64, AWOL; $50 enl. bounty due. NFR.

ADKINS, GEORGE - Pvt. Co. H. Prior service, Co. G, 3rd VSL. Enl. Frankfort, Greenbrier Co., W. Va., 3/19/63 (Clay Co., 4/1/63). Not stated if present or absent on muster-in roll dated 3/63. Ab. 9/1/64 - 10/31/64, AWOL. NFR.

ADKINS, JACKSON - Pvt. Co. H. Prior service, Co. G, 3rd VSL. Enl. Frankfort, Greenbrier Co., W. Va., 3/19/63 (Clay Co., 4/1/63). Not stated if present or absent on muster-in roll dated 3/63. Ab. 9/1/64 - 10/31/64, AWOL. NFR.

ADKINS, PETER - Pvt. Co. H. b.c. 1844. Prior service, Co. G, 3rd VSL. Enl. Frankfort, Greenbrier Co., W. Va., 3/19/63 (Clay Co., 4/1/63). Not stated if present or absent on muster-in roll dated 3/63. Clothing issued 3/1/64; 4/30/64; 6/17/64. Issued a pair of shoes at Lexington, 6/28/64. Ab. 9/1/64 - 10/31/64, AWOL. Deserted. Took oath of allegiance, Charleston, W. Va., 5/23/65, signed by x. Desc.: age 21, 5'7", fair comp., brown hair and gray eyes. Occ. farmer, residing in Nicholas Co., W. Va. NFR.

ADKINS, SILAS - Pvt. Co. H. Prior service, Co. G, 3rd VSL. Enl. Frankfort, Greenbrier Co., W. Va., 3/19/63 (Clay Co., 4/1/63). Not stated if present or absent on muster-in roll dated 3/63. Clothing issued 3/1/64 and 4/30/64, signed by x. Ab. 9/1/64 - 10/31/64, AWOL. NFR.

ALDERMAN, JOHN A. - Pvt. Co. I. b. Pocahontas Co., W. Va., c. 1832. Age 28, laborer, Traveler's Repose, Pocahontas Co., W. Va. 1860 Census. Thought to have served in Co. K. 3rd VSL. Enl. Huntersville, Pocahontas Co., W. Va., 3/18/63. Mustered into service, 3/39/63. Ab. on muster-in roll dated 3/63, sick. Ab. 6/30/63 - 2/29/64, deserted, 6/63. NFR.

ALDERMAN, SOLOMON - Pvt. Co. I. b.c. 1820. Age 50, farmer, Pocahontas Co., W. Va. 1860 Census. Thought to have served in Co. K, 3rd VSL. Enl. Huntersville, Pocahontas Co., W. Va., 3/18/63. Mustered into service, 3/19/63. Present on muster-in roll dated 3/63. Father of Walter F. Alderman. NFR.

ALDERMAN, WALTER FORWARD - 1st Corp. Co. I. b. 4/13/42. Age 18, laborer, Frost, Pocahontas Co., W. Va. 1860 Census. Post war rosters show service in 2nd Co. I, 25th Va. Inf. Thought to have served in Co. K, 3rd VSL. Enl. Pocahontas Co., W. Va., 2/1/63 (Huntersville, W. Va., 3/18/63). Mustered into service, 3/19/63. Present, Pvt., on muster-in roll dated 3/63. Ab., 1st Corp., 6/30/63 - 2/29/64, detailed to wait on sick, not mounted. Present, 2/29/64 - 8/31/64, mounted. Clothing issued 7/64 and 8/64. Present 9/1/64 - 10/31/64, $100 enl. bounty due. Paroled at Charleston, W. Va., 5/10/65 as a Pvt. Desc.: age 23, 6', light comp., light hair, blue eyes and light whiskers. Post war resident of Pocahontas Co., W. Va. Age 38, farmer, Huntersville Dist., Pocahontas Co. 1880 census. Son of Solomon Alderman. d. 1/17/1913.

ALLEN, SAMUEL C. - Pvt. Co. C. Prior service, Co. D, 3rd VSL. Present 1/1/63 - 4/1/63, had one horse. Enl. Alleghany Co., 5/1/64. Ab. 12/31/63 - 8/31/64, in Monroe Co., W. Va., sick since 7/1/64. Ab. 9/1/64 - 10/31/64, in Monroe Co., W. Va., sick since 7/1/64, furlough renewed by physician. Adm. CSA Gen. Hosp., Charlottesville, 9/1/64, Haemoptisis (hemophilia). NFR.

ALLSOP, DAVID O. - Pvt. Co. ?. Not on muster rolls. Deserted and took the oath of allegiance, giving his bond, 12/5/63. NFR.

ALTOP (ALTOPP, ALLTOP), EVAN - 4th Sgt. Co. K. b. Harrison (Gilmer) Co., W. Va., 1839. Age 20, laborer, Gilmer Co., W. Va. 1860 Census. Age 21 (1861). farmer. Prior service, Co. D, 31st Va. Inf. and Co. I, 3rd VSL. Enl. Frankfort, Greenbrier Co., W. Va., 3/20/63. Not stated if present or absent, 4th Sgt., on muster-in roll dated 3/63. Deserted and gave himself up, stating he had taken the oath to the US before joining the rebel army. Arrested at Bulltown, W. Va., 11/13/63. Desc.: age 23, 5'9_", fair comp., light hair and gray eyes. Occ. farmer, residing in Gilmer Co., W. Va. Took the oath again 11/30/63. Confined at the Atheneum Prison, 11/30/63. Transf. to Camp Chase, 12/1/63. Confined at Camp Chase, 12/2/63, charged with violating his oath. Transf. to Ft. Delaware, 2/29/64. Confined at Ft. Delaware 3/4/64 (3/2/64). Took oath of allegiance at Ft. Delaware and was released 6/19/65. Cards in his CSR show service in Co. C. Post war resident of Gilmer Co., W. Va. NFR.

ALTOP (ALTOPP), LEWIS - 2nd Lt. Co. K. b. Harrison Co., W. Va., c. 1827. Age 33, farmer, Gilmer Co., W. Va. 1860 Census. Prior service, Co. I, 3rd VSL. Enl. Frankfort, Greenbrier Co., W. Va., 3/20/63. 1st Sgt., not stated if present or absent on muster-in roll dated 3/63. Promoted to 2nd Lt. Granted 15 days leave, 3/5/64, listed as Lt. Cpd. Loudoun Co. (near Harpers Ferry), 7/15/64. Sent to Washington, DC, before 7/20/64. Confined at the Old Capitol Prison, 7/17/64. Transf. to Ft. Delaware, 7/22/64. Confined at Ft. Delaware, 7/23/64. DOD. Ft. Delaware, 5/8/65 (5/7/65), chronic diarrhoea. Bur. Jersey Shore. CSR shows him as 1st Lt.

AMISS, ANDREW D. - Pvt. Co. F. b. 1828. Age 32, clerk, Academy, Pocahontas Co., W. Va. 1860 Census. Capt., Mill Point Patrol, Pocahontas Co., W. Va., 5/61. Not on muster rolls. Cpd., date and place not known. Confined at Ft. Delaware. Paroled 9/28/64, on account of scurvy. Furloughed at Richmond, 40 days, 10/8/64, unless sooner exchanged. Ordered to report to Richmond at the expiration of his furlough. Clothing issued 10/10/64, listed as a paroled prisoner. Wrote Gen. R. S. Ewell 11/7/64 from Mill Point, Pocahontas Co., W. Va., asking that his furlough be extended. Amiss sends a surgeons certificate, showing that he is "in a bad fix" still suffering from scorbutus (scurvy). Stated that as soon as he learned of his exchange and his health permitted, he would return to his command. "I have a long score to settle with the Yankees." Paroled at Charleston, W. Va., 5/10/65. Desc.: age 37, 5'10", florid comp., sandy hair, blue eyes and sandy whiskers. Age 52, farmer, Edray, Pocahontas Co., W. Va. 1880 Census. NFR.

ANCROM, JOSEPH - Pvt. Co. H. Enl. Roane Co., W. Va., 5/1/64. Ab. 9/1/64 - 10/31/64, AWOL. NFR.

ERSON, DAVID - Pvt. Co. D. Enl. Williamsburg, Greenbrier Co., W. Va., 3/8/63. Not stated if present or absent on muster-in roll dated 3/63. NFR.

ANDERSON, JOHN - 2nd Lt. Co. D. b. Pa., c. 1832. Prior service, Co. A, 3rd VSL. Enl. Williamsburg, Greenbrier Co., W. Va., 3/8/63. Not stated if present or absent on muster-in roll dated 3/63, 2nd Lt. Wd., date and place not given. Ab. 10/25/64, wd. and on 10 day leave, permanently disabled, resigned. Ab. 12/15/64, AWOL since 12/12/64, no steps taken to replace him. Dropped from the rolls, due to prolonged absence from duty, without leave, 2/8/65. Post war rosters show him as Capt., and as being a resident of Marion (Wirt) Co., W. Va. Age 48, no occ., Palentine/Union Dist., Marion Co., W. Va. 1880 Census. NFR.

ANDERSON, MARCUS - Pvt. Co. D. Prior service, Co. C, 3rd VSL. Enl. Williamsburg, Greenbrier Co., W. Va., 3/8/63. Not stated if present or absent on muster-in roll dated 3/63. Clothing issued 1st Qr. 1864; 5/21/64 and 6/17/64. NFR.

ANDREW, WILLIAM - Pvt. Co. K. Prior service, Co. I, 3rd VSL. Enl. Frankfort, Greenbrier Co., W. Va., 3/20/63. Not stated if present or absent on muster-in roll dated 3/63. NFR.

APPERSON, JAMES R. "Jack" - Pvt. Co. ?. b. Hanover Co., 1836. Farmer. Prior service, Co. F, 31st Va. Inf. Transf. to 19th Va. Cav., 11/15/63. Not on muster rolls. Served as Capt., Co. D, 47th Battn. Va. Cav. (later 26th Va. Cav.). Wd. by saber during war. NFR.

ARBAUGH (ARBOUGH), JAMES M. - Pvt. Co. I. b.c. 1845. Age 15, laborer, Edray, Pocahontas Co., W. Va. 1860 Census. Thought to have served in Co. K, 3rd VSL. Enl. Pocahontas Co., W. Va. 2/1/63 (Huntersville, W. Va., 3/18/63). Mustered into service, 3/39/63. Present on muster-in roll dated 3/63. Ab. 6/30/63 - 2/29/64, on furlough, promoted. No record showing to what rank he was promoted, later records show him as Pvt. Present 2/29/64 - 8/31/64. Present 9/1/64 - 10/31/64, $100 enl. bounty due. Paroled at Charleston, W. Va., 5/10/65. Desc.: age 21, 5'5", dark comp., dark hair and dark eyes. May have served in Thurmond's Partisan Rangers. NFR.

ARBOGAST, ADAM MARTIN VAN BUREN - Pvt. Co. I. b. Pocahontas Co., W. Va., c. 1336. Age 24, farmer, Pocahontas Co., W. Va. 1860 Census. Thought to have served in Co. K, 3rd VSL. Enl. Pocahontas Co., W. Va., 3/1/63 (Huntersville, W. Va., 3/18/63). Mustered into service, 3/19/63. Not stated if present or absent on muster-in roll dated 3/63. Present 6/30/63 - 2/29/64, mounted; in arrest. Ab. 2/29/64 - 8/31/64, deserted 6/64. Ab. 9/1/64 - 10/31/64, AWOL since 5/64. NFR.

ARBOGAST NICHODEMUS - 3rd Corp. Co. H. Prior service Co. G, 3rd VSL. Enl. Frankfort, Greenbrier Co., W. Va., 3/19/63. Not stated if present or absent on muster-in roll dated 3/63, 3rd Corp. Ab., Pvt., 9/1/64 - 10/31/64, prisoner of war. Date and place of capture not given. NFR.

ARBOGAST, PAUL McNEIL - Pvt. Co. F. b. Greenbrier Co., W. Va., c. 1846. Age 14, Pocahontas Co., W. Va. 1860 Census. Enl. Warm Springs, 1/20/64 (1/25/64). Present 1/1/64 - 2/29/64, enl. bounty due. Clothing issued 2/6/64, 7/64 and 8/64. Present 9/1/64 - 10/31/64, enl. bounty due. Moved to Hill Co., Tx., 1878. d. Itasca, Hill Co., Tx., 11/8/88. Bur. Itasca, Tx.

ARBOGAST, SAMUEL W. - Pvt. Co. I. b.c. 1847. Enl. Huntersville, Pocahontas Co., W. Va., 2/1/64. Present 2/29/64 - 8/31/64, mounted; enl. bounty due. Ab. 9/1/64 - 10/31/64, left without permission at Fisher's Hill fight, 9/23/64. Clothing issued 7/10/64 and 3rd Qr. 1864. Paroled at Staunton, 5/19/65. Desc : age 18, 5'9", light comp., dark hair and black eyes. NFR.

ARGENBRIGHT, JOSEPH FRANK - Pvt. Co. B. b. Middlebrook, Augusta Co., 3/29/45. Enl. Augusta Co., 3/18/64 (Bath Co., 3/63). Present 9/1/64 - 10/31/64, $100 enl. bounty due. Clothing issued 9/19/64. Deserted and reported at Beverly, W. Va., 10/25/64. Took oath of allegiance and was released, 10/29/64. Desc.: age 18, 5'4", fair comp., light hair and gray eyes. Occ. Tinner, residing in Augusta Co. Post war tinner, and resident of Pulaski Co. d. Pulaski Co., 2/9/1922. Bur. Stonewall Jackson Cem., Lexington.

ARMENTROUT, CHARLES E. - Pvt. Co. F. b. Augusta Co., c. 1840. Age 20, laborer. N. Dist., Augusta Co. 1860 Census. Enl. Warm Springs, 1/2/64 (Hillsboro, W. Va.). Ab. 1/1/64 - 2/29/64, on detail; enl. bounty due. Ab. 9/1/64 - 10/31/64, sick; enl. bounty due. Wartime letter from Col. W. L. Jackson, dated 5/4/64, lists him as being a member of Co. K, 20th Va. Cav., and alleged to be a deserter from another command. Thought to have been a post war resident of Rockbridge Co. Brother of George M. Armentrout. NFR.

ARMENTROUT, GEORGE MARSHALL - Pvt. Co. I. b. Bath (Augusta) Co., 1/26/46. Age 14, student, N. Dist., Augusta Co. 1860 Census. Enl. Huntersville, Pocahontas Co., W. Va., 4/1/64. Present 2/29/64 - 8/31/64, mounted; enl. bounty due. Present 9/1/64 - 10/31/64, $100 enl. bounty due. Post war roster shows he enl. 3/64. Post war farmer and resident of Millboro Springs, Bath Co. Brother of Charles E. Armentrout. d. Bath Co., 6/1/1918. Bur. Windy Cove Presbyterian Church Cem.

ARMSTEAD, JAMES M. - Pvt. Co. G. b.c. 1814. Enl. Pocahontas Co., W. Va., 9/20/63. Clothing issued 3/1/64 and 4/30/64. Present 9/1/64 - 10/31/64, has a serviceable horse. Deserted and surrendered 5/65. Took the amnesty oath, 5/2/65. Desc.: age 51, 5'7", fair comp., fair hair and blue eyes, a farmer. NFR.

ARMSTRONG, ABBOTT L. - Pvt. Co. B. b. Highland Co., 7/5/46. Age 13, McDowell, Highland Co. 1860 Census. Enl. Highland Co., 3/1/64. Clothing issued 7/10/64 and 6/17/64. Present 9/1/54 - 10/31/64, $100 enl. bounty due. Paroled at Staunton, 5/11/65. Desc.: age 18, 5'8", light comp., light hair and blue eyes. Post war rosters show Co. H, 19th Va. Cav. Post war miller, and resident of McDowell. d. 9/7/1922. Bur. McKendree Methodist Church Cem., Highland Co.

ARMSTRONG, JOSEPH H. (W.) - 4th Sgt. Co. B. b.c. 1846. Age 14, student, 1st Dist., Augusta Co. 1860 Census. Enl. Augusta Co., 3/1/64. Clothing issued 6/17/64, Pvt. signed by x. Present, 4th Sgt., 9/1/64 - 10/31/64, $100 enl. bounty due; promoted to 4th Sgt. 7/1/64. NFR.

ARMSTRONG, WILLIAM H. (of S.) - Pvt. Co. B. b. Highland Co., 1/25/46. Age 14, farmhand, Doe Hill, Highland Co. 1860 Census. Prior service, 2nd Co. F, 25th Va. Inf. Enl. Highland Co., 3/1/64. Clothing issued 6/17/64, signed by x. Present 9/1/64 - 10/31/64, $100 enl. bounty due. Post war rosters show service in Co. I, 19th Va. Cav. Post war farmer, and resident of Doe Hill and McDowell. Age 54, farmer, Stonewall Dist., Highland Co. 1900 census. Age 63 in 1907. d. Highland Co., 6/29/1914, heart trouble. Bur. McKendree Methodist Ch. Cem., Highland Co.

ARNETT, THOMAS CALVIN - Pvt. Co. B. b.c. 1833. Prior service, 3rd VSL. Enl. Williamsburg, Greenbrier Co., W. Va., 3/8/63. Not stated it present or absent on muster-in roll dated 3/63. Deserted and surrendered 10/14/63. Desc.: age 30, 5'6", a resident of Monongalia Co., W. Va. Sent North via Wheeling, W. Va., 9/14/63. Served also in Co. B, 20th Va. Cav. Post war resident of Monongalia Co., W. Va. Age 46, carpenter, Clay Dist., Monongalia Co., W. Va. 1880 Census. NFR.

ARNETT, WAITMAN T. - Sgt. Co. A. b. Marion Co., W. Va., c. 1843. Prior service, Co. A, 3rd VSL. Cpd. Braxton Co., W. Va., 5/4/62. Confined at the Atheneum Prison. Desc.: age 18, 5'7", dark comp., brown hair and blue eyes, a farmer. Sent to Camp Chase, 6/30/62. Confined at Camp Chase. Transf. to Vicksburg, Miss., 11/22/62, to be exchanged. Enl. Williamsburg, Greenbrier Co., W. Va., 3/1/63. Not stated if present or absent on muster-in roll dated 3/63. Clothing issued 2/23/64; 5/26/64 and 6/17/64. Promoted to Sgt. Cpd. Marion Co., W. Va., 11/10/64 (11/8/64). Desc.: age 21, 5'8", fair comp., dark hair and blue eyes, listed as Sgt. Sent to Wheeling, W. Va., 11/11/64. Confined at Atheneum Prison, 11/?/64. Transf. to Camp Chase. 11/18/64. Confined at Camp Chase, 11/19/64. Took the oath and was released, 6/11/65. Post war resident of Marion Co., W. Va. NFR.

ARNOLD, FLOYD W. - Pvt. Co. K. b. Harrison Co., W. Va., c. 1847. Age 13, Gilmer Co., W. Va. 1860 Census. Not on muster rolls. Clothing issued 6/17/64, signs roll as Floid Arnold. Paroled at Charleston, W. Va., 5/10/65. Desc.: age 18, 6', light comp., dark hair and blue eyes. NFR.

ARTHUR, JOSEPH D. - Pvt. Co. I. Enl. Huntersville, Pocahontas Co., W. Va., 8/28/63. Ab. 6/30/63 - 2/29/64, went home without leave, 12/12/63, not yet returned; mounted; enl. bounty due. Ab. 2/29/64 - 8/31/64, cpd. near Woodstock, 10/9/64; pay due from enl. Ab. 9/1/64 - 10/31/64, POW. Cpd. Woodstock, 10/9/64. Sent to Harpers Ferry, W. Va., then to Pt. Lookout, 10/13/64. Confined at Pt. Lookout, 10/20/64. Paroled 3/28/65 and sent to Aiken's Landing, to be exchanged. Arrived at Bouleware's Wharf, 3/30/65. NFR.

ARTHUR, RICHARD G. - Pvt. Co. K. Prior service, Co. I, 3rd VSL. Enl. Frankfort, Greenbrier Co., W. Va., 3/20/64. Not stated if present or absent on muster-in roll dated 3/63. NFR.

ARTHURS, R. F. - Pvt. Co. I. Thought to have served in Co. K, 3rd VSL. Not on muster rolls. Cpd. and confined at Camp Chase. DOD. Camp Chase, 12/16/64. Bur. Camp Chase Confederate Cem., grave no. 622.

ASH, DANIEL (DAVID) - Pvt. Co. A. b.c. 1819. Prior service, Co. A, 3rd VSL. Cpd. Tyler Co., W. Va., 8/14/62, listed as guerrilla. Confined at the Atheneum Prison. Desc.: age 43, 5'10", fair comp., brown hair and blue eyes, a farmer, residing in Tyler Co., W. Va. Transf. to Camp Chase, 9/23/62. Transf. to Vicksburg, Miss., 11/22/62, to be exchanged. Judge Advocate L. C. Turner, Washington, DC, ordered his release, 12/8/62. Enl. Williamsburg, Greenbrier Co., W. Va., 3/1/63. Not stated if present or absent on muster-in roll dated 3/63. Deserted. Gave a statement 5/29/63 to the US, stating that he had been imprisoned as a citizen at Johnson's Island. When he was sent to Vicksburg, 11/22/62, he protested, wishing not to be exchanged. Was exchanged on 12/7/62, on a hosp. boat, where he was very sick. States he did not willingly take up arms against the US, "but compelled to do so being without money or subsistence." Came to W. Va. in the late raid (Jones-Imboden Raid) and deserted 5/11/63 near Sutton, Braxton Co., W. Va. Says he now wishes to remain at home. NFR.

ASHCRAFT, JEREMIAH - Pvt. Co. D. Prior service, Co. C, 3rd VSL. Enl. Williamsburg, Greenbrier Co., W. Va., 3/8/63. Not stated if present or absent on muster-in roll dated 3/63. NFR.

ASHCRAFT, PRESTON - Pvt. Co. D. b.c. 1841. Not on muster rolls. Adm. Gen. Hosp. No. 9, 3/4/65. Transf. to Chimborazo Hosp. 3/5/65. Adm. Chimborazo Hosp. No. 5, 3/5/65, rubeola. Deserted 4/1/65. Surrendered at Beverly, W. Va., 4/19/65. Desc.: age 24, 5'5", light comp., brown hair and brown eyes, a resident of Marion Co., W. Va. Took the oath. NFR.

ASHFORD, CLAIBORN - Pvt. Co. ?. b.c. 1839. Post war rosters only, which show him as a resident of Randolph Co., W. Va. Served in Co. C, 20th Va. Cav. Age 41, Green Banks Dist., Pocahontas Co., W. Va. 1880 Census. Listed as a resident of Greenbank, W. Va., 1916. NFR.

ATCHISON (ATKINSON, ADKISON), JOHN E. - Pvt. Co. F. b.c. 1824. Age 36, farmer, Mill Point, Pocahontas Co., W. Va. 1860 Census. Prior service, McNeels Co., 2nd VSL. CSR shows that he deserted and joined the US service. Enl. Hillsboro, Pocahontas Co., W. Va., 3/9/63. Not stated if present or absent on muster-in roll dated 3/63. NFR.

ATCHISON, NATHANIEL S. - Pvt. Co. D. Prior service, Co. C, 3rd VSL. Enl. Williamsburg, Greenbrier Co., W. Va., 3/8/63. Not stated if present or absent on muster-in roll dated 3/63. Clothing issued 2/7/64. Served in Co. A, 46th Battn. Va. Cav. NFR.

AULDRIDGE (ALDERAGE), TILLSON (TILLOTSON) M. - Pvt. Co. I. b.c. 1846. Age 14, Pocahontas Co., W. Va. 1860 Census. Enl. Huntersville, Pocahontas Co., W. Va., 3/1/64. Present 2/29/64 - 8/31/64, mounted; enl. bounty due. Present 9/1/64 - 10/31/64. Age 34, farmer, Huntersville, Pocahontas Co., W. Va. 1880 Census. NFR.

AUSTIN, SAMUEL HENRY (HUNTER) - 2nd Lt. Co. B. b. near Tinkling Springs, Augusta Co., 3/18/40. Resident of West Milford, Harrison Co., W. Va., 1843. Attended VMI 1856-60. Studied medicine under his father, Dr. A. M. Austin. Attended Winchester Medical College (Dr. McGuire), 2 years, 1860-61. Attended lectures at the Medical College of Va. Prior service, Jackson Rifles, 36th Va. Inf. and transf. to Co. B, 22nd Va. Inf. Post war rosters show he enl. in the 20th Va. Cav., spring 1863. Acting Asst. Surgeon, White Sulphur Springs Hosp., W. Va., spring 1863. Enl. Oakland, Alleghany Co., 5/1/64. Present, Pvt., 9/1/64 - 10/31/64, $100 enl. bounty due. Promoted to Lt. Ab. 12/15/64, sick since 12/12/64. Adm. CSA Gen. Hosp., Charlottesville, 12/22/64, debility, listed as Lt. RTD. 1/7/65. Name appears on a list of men surrendered by Gen. R. E. Lee at Appomattox CH, 4/9/65. Served as Asst. Surgeon, 20th Va. Cav. Post war sketch states he was paroled at Staunton, 1865. Moved to Greenbrier Co., W. Va., 1865. Grad. Medical College of Va., 3/1866. Post grad. courses at Philadelphia, Pa. US examining surgeon, Lewisburg, W. Va., 1881, 6 years. Commissioner of Schools, 4 years. Chairman, Democratic Executive Committee. Post war MD, residing at Lewisburg, W. Va., 1894. Surgeon-Major, 2nd W. Va. National Guard. Mason. Member David S. Creigh Camp, UCV, Lewisburg, W. Va. d. Charleston, W. Va., 11/16/1926. Bur. Old Stone Church Cem., Lewisburg, W. Va.

AYERS (AYRES), HIRAM P. - Pvt. Co. ?. b. 8/1/26. Post war rosters only, which show he was from Ritchie Co., W. Va. Post war farmer and resident of Ritchie Co., W. Va. Age 53, farmer, South Grant Dist., Ritchie Co., W. Va. 1880 Census. d. 1919. Bur. Log Church Cem., Cantwell, Ritchie Co., W. Va.

BAILEY, SQUIRE W. W. - Pvt. Co. ?. Post war source only, which states he, Balas C. DeWees and George Casto joined Jackson's command in the fall of 1863. These men took part in the fight at Bulltown, W. Va., 10/13/63. NFR.

BAILY, HIRAM - Pvt. Co. I. Enl. Huntersville, Pocahontas Co., W. Va., 1/19/64. Present, 6/30/63 - 2/29/64, enl. bounty due. Present 2/29/64 - 8/31/64. Clothing issued 3/22/64. Ab. 9/1/64 - 10/31/64, sick. NFR.

BAKELEY (BECKLEY), ISAAC C. - Pvt. Co. D. b. Beverly, W. Va., c. 1841. Prior service, Co. C, 3rd VSL. Not on muster rolls. POW document shows his enl. as Fayette Co., W. Va., 5/61. Cpd. Upshur Co., W. Va., 4/1/65. Desc.: age 24, 5'9", florid comp., dark hair and blue eyes, a carpenter residing at Beverly, W. Va. Confined at the Atheneum Prison, 4/24/65, a resident of Raleigh Co., W. Va. Transf. to Cumberland, Md., where he took the oath of allegiance. NFR.

BAKER, F. M. - Pvt. Co. D. Not on muster rolls. Wd., probably during the fall of 1864. Adm. Chimborazo Hosp. No. 5, 1/29/65, amputation of upper third of right arm. NFR.

BAKER, JOHN W. - Pvt. Co. I. b. Ireland, c. 1823. Age 37, farmer, Randolph Co., W. Va. 1860 Census. Thought to have served in Co. K, 3rd VSL. Enl. Huntersville, Pocahontas Co., W. Va., 3/18/63. Mustered into service, 3/19/63. Present 6/30/63 - 2/29/64, mounted. Present 2/29/64 - 8/31/64. Clothing issued 6/10/64. Present 9/1/64 - 10/31/64, $100 enl. bounty due. Post war resident of Elkins, Randolph Co., W. Va. Age 63, ditcher, Huttonsville, W. Va. 1880 Census. Attended Gettysburg Reunion, 1913. Bur. Mingo Cem., Randolph Co., W. Va.

BALL, EMERY (EMORY, EMEREY) MADISON - Pvt. Co. A. b. Calhoun (Lewis) Co., W. Va., 1841 (1843). Age 17, farmer, Calhoun Co., W. Va. 1860 Census. Prior service, 4th Sgt., Co. A, 3rd VSL. Enl. Williamsburg, Greenbrier Co., W. Va., 3/1/63. Not stated if present or absent on muster-in roll dated 3/63. Served in Co. H, 20th Va. Cav. Post war rosters show him as 4th Sgt. Post war resident of Calhoun Co., W. Va. Age 27, farmer, Center Dist., Calhoun Co., W. Va. 1870 Census. Age 39, farmer, Center Dist., Calhoun Co., W. Va. 1880 Census. d. 1918. Bur. Sand Ridge Cem., W. Va.

BALL, JAMES WILLIAM - Capt. Co. E./Major. b. Gilmer Co., W. Va., c. 1839. Prior service, Pvt., Co. A, 3rd VSL. Enl. Frankfort, Greenbrier Co., W. Va., 3/13/63 (4/1/63). Not stated if present or absent on muster-in roll dated 3/63. Appointed Capt., 3/13/63. Ab. sick, 7/2/63. Present 10/31/63 - 10/31/64. Mentioned for "brave bearing" by Col. W. L. Jackson in his report of the battle of Droop Mtn., W. Va., 11/6/63. Ab. 10/25/64. Ab. 10/25/64, wd., now on leave, temporarily disabled. Promoted to Major. Paroled as Major at Charleston, W. Va., 5/11/65. Desc.: age 26, 5'11", light comp., brown hair, blue eyes and light whiskers. Desc.: "tall, finely proportioned, brown hair and beard." Moved to Roane Co., 1873, engaged in timber business. Age 43, farmer, Reedy Dist., Roane Co., W. Va. 1880 Census. Brother of Samuel Benton Ball. Bur. IOOF Cem., Parkersburg, W. Va.

BALL, SAMUEL BENTON - Pvt. Co. E./F&S Ordnance Sgt. b. Gilmer Co., W. Va., c. 1841. Prior service, Co. E, 3rd VSL. Enl. Frankfort, Greenbrier Co., W. Va., 3/13/63. Not stated if present or absent on muster-in roll dated 3/63. Present F&S MR 9/1/63 - 10/31/63, appointed Ordnance Sgt., 4/1/63; had his own horse. Present, Ordnance Sgt., F&S MR 11/1/63 - 12/31/63, had his own horse. Clothing issued 5/1/64, 6/17/64 and 3rd Qr. 1864. Ab., Ordnance Sgt., F&S MR 9/1/64 - 10/31/64, sick; entitled to $100 Confederate Bond. Paroled as a Pvt. at Charleston, W. Va., 5/11/65. Desc.: age 24, 5'11", dark comp., black hair, blue eyes and dark whiskers. Desc.: "shorter than William and more rugged, brown hair and beard." Moved to Roane Co., W. Va., 1873, engaged in timber business. Age 40, farmer, Reedy Dist., Roane Co., W. Va. 1880 Census. CSR listed as Lemuel B. Ball. Brother of James William Ball. d. 1908.

BALLAH, ASA S. - Pvt. Co. D. b.c. 1841. Resident of Marion Co., W. Va. Prior service, Co. C, 3rd VSL. Enl. Williamsburg, Greenbrier Co., W. Va., 3/8/63. Not stated if present or absent on muster-in roll dated 3/63. Cpd. Highland Co., 12/12/63. Confined at the Atheneum Prison, 1/19/64. Desc.: age 23, 5'11", dark comp., dark hair and dark eyes. Occ. farmer, residing in Marion Co., W. Va. Transf. to Camp Chase, 1/20/64. Age 39, farmer, Paw Paw Dist., Marion Co., W. Va. 1880 Census. NFR.

BALLARD, EDWARD - Pvt. Co. G. Prior service, Co. H, 3rd VSL. Enl. Frankfort, Greenbrier Co., W. Va., 3/12/63. Not stated if present or absent on muster-in roll dated 3/63. Transf. to Co. C, 19th Va. Cav. Pocahontas Co., W. Va., 9/16/63. Ab. 12/31/63 - 8/31/64, AWOL since 6/1/64. Ab. 9/1/64 - 10/31/64, AWOL since 6/1/64. NFR.

BARBER, JAMES - Pvt. Co. A. Served in Co. A, 3rd VSL. Post war rosters only. NFR.

BARKER, DAVID - Pvt. Co. D. b.c. 1828. Prior service, Co. D, 3rd VSL. Enl. Williamsburg, Greenbrier Co., W. Va., 3/8/63. Not stated if present or absent on muster-in roll dated 3/63. Cpd. Randolph Co., W. Va., 4/25/63. Confined at the Atheneum Prison, 4/27/63. Desc.: age 35, 5'8", dark comp., black hair and brown eyes. Occ. farmer, residing in Marion Co., W. Va. Transf. to Camp Chase, 4/28/63. Confined at Camp Chase, 4/28/63. Transf. to Johnson's Island, 6/14/63 and confined the same day. Transf. to Pt. Lookout, 10/30/63. Confined at Pt. Lookout, 11/4/63. Took oath of allegiance and was released 4/11/64. Served in Co. B, 20th Va. Cav. NFR.

BARKER, EDMUND - Pvt. Co. B. b. Hardy Co., W. Va., c. 1813. Prior service, Co. B, 3rd VSL. Enl. Frankfort, Greenbrier Co., W. Va., 3/9/63. Not stated if present or absent on muster-in roll dated 3/63. Cpd. Webster Co. (Bulltown), W. Va., 1/12/65. Sent to Clarksburg, W. Va., 1/12/65. Confined at the Atheneum Prison, 1/14/65. Desc.: age 52, 5'10", fair comp., gray hair and gray (blue) eyes. Occ. Steam Mill (miller), residing in Braxton Co., W. Va. Transf. to Camp Chase, 1/16/65. Confined at Camp Chase, 1/17/65, "bad character." Took the oath of allegiance and was released, 6/13/65. Post war resident of Braxton Co., W. Va. Bur. Cutlip Cem., Braxton co., W. Va.

BARKER (BRAKER), ISAAC - Pvt. Co. B. b. Braxton Co., W. Va., c. 1844. Age 16. Braxton Co., W. Va. 1860 Census. Prior service, Co. B, 3rd VSL. Enl. Frankfort, Greenbrier Co., W. Va., 3/9/63. Not stated if present or absent on muster-in roll dated 3/63. Present 11/1/63 - 2/29/64, has one horse. Clothing issued 1st Qr. 1864, 2/11/64; 6/17/64 and 7/6/64, signed by x. Present 9/1/64 - 10/31/64, $100 enl. bounty due. Cpd. Bulltown, W. Va., 1/8/65 (1/12/65). Sent to Clarksburg, W. Va., 1/12/65. Transf. to Wheeling, W. Va., 1/14/65. Confined at the Atheneum Prison, 1/14/65. Desc.: age 20 (19), 6', dark comp., black hair and blue eyes. Occ. farmer, residing in Braxton Co., W. Va. Transf. to Camp Chase, 1/16/65. Confined at Camp Chase, 1/17/65. Took the oath of allegiance and was released, 6/13/65. Desc.: age 21, 5'10", fair comp., dark hair and gray eyes. Post war resident of Braxton Co., W. Va. Age 35, farmer, Holly Dist., Braxton Co., W. Va. 1880 Census. Bur. McElwain Cem., Braxton Co., W. Va.

BARKER (BABER, BAKER), JAMES K. - 1st Sgt. Co. B. b. Augusta Co., c. 1835. Prior service, Co. A, 3rd VSL. Enl. Frankfort, Greenbrier Co., W. Va., 3/9/63. Not stated if present or absent on muster-in roll dated 3/63. Present, 2nd Sgt., 11/1/63 - 2/29/64, had his own horse. Clothing issued 2/6/64 and 6/17/64. Present, 1st Sgt., 9/1/64 - 10/31/64, promoted to 1st Sgt., 7/1/64; $100 enl. bounty due. Cpd. Upshur Co., W. Va., 2/17/65. Sent to Wheeling, W. Va. Confined at the Atheneum Prison, 2/22/65. Desc.: age 29, 6', sallow comp., brown hair and dark eyes, a farmer residing in Braxton Co., W. Va. Transf. to Camp Chase, 2/24/65. Confined at Camp Chase, 2/25/65. Took the oath of allegiance and was released, 6/13/65. Desc.: age 30, 5'10_". dark comp., dark hair and dark eyes, a resident of Braxton Co., W. Va. NFR

BARKER (BRAKER), JOHNSON - 2nd Corp. Co. B. b. Braxton Co., W. Va., c. 1843. Age 17, Braxton Co., W. Va. 1860 Census. Prior service, Co. B, 3rd VSL. Enl. Frankfort, Greenbrier Co., W. Va., 3/9/63. Not stated if present or absent on muster-in roll dated 3/63, 2nd Corp. Participated in the fight at Bulltown, W. Va., 10/13/63. Present, Pvt., 11/1/63 - 2/29/64, has one horse. Clothing issued 2/11/64, 6/17/64 and 7/10/65, signed by x. Present 9/1/64 - 10/31/64, $100 enl. bounty due. Cpd. Webster Co. (Bulltown), W. Va., 1/13/65. Sent to Clarksburg, W. Va., 1/22/65. Sent to Cumberland, Md., then to Wheeling, W. Va., 1/24/65. Confined at Wheeling, W. Va., 1/24/65. Desc.: age 22, 5'8", sallow comp., light hair and dark eyes. Occ. farmer, residing in Braxton Co., W. Va. Transf. to Camp Chase, 2/7/65. Confined at Camp Chase, 2/8/65. Took the oath of allegiance and was released, 6/13/65. Post war resident of Braxton Co., W. Va. NFR.

BARKSDALE, WILLIAM LEIGH - Surgeon. b. Halifax Co., 11/11/36 (8/29/37). Attended Samuel Davis Institute; UVA Medical School and grad. Jefferson Medical College, 1858. Practiced at Lewisburg, Greenbrier Co., W. Va., 1858. MD, Lewisburg, Greenbrier Co., W. Va. 1860 Census. Prior service, Surg., 3rd VSL, 1st Co. A, 14th Va. Cav., and 22nd Va. Inf. Ass't. Surgeon, Giles CH, 1862. Appointed Surgeon, Swann's Battn. Partisan Rangers. Transf. to Jackson's Cav. Appointed Asst. Surg., 10/14/62, confirmed 4/4/63, to rank from 10/10/63. Appointed Surg. 5/9/63. Present F&S MR 9/1/63 - 10/31/63. Ab. F&S MR 11/1/63 - 12/31/63, on leave. At Warm Springs, 4/12/64. Serving as Brigade Surgeon, 22nd Va. Inf., 1864. Ab. 11/28/64, not at inspection of Wharton's Div., absent attending to the sick, listed as division surgeon. Listed has having served as Brigade Surgeon, W. L. Jackson's Brigade. Listed as having served as a surgeon with the 3rd Va. Inf., Patton's Brigade, until the end of 1864. Served also in the 23rd Battn. Va. Cav. (on leave in Halifax Co., 2/65) and in a staff position. Post war MD, and resident of Lewisburg, W. Va., 1865 - 1874. Moved to Va. for 5 years, then back to W. Va. Resident of Alderson, W. Va., 1/74; Hinton, 1892. Spent 2 years in the lumber business and helped develop the Brownstone Industry. Post war mayor and member of Hinton City Council. d. Hinton, W. Va., 12/17/1913, after a few hours illness.

BARLOW, WILLIAM H. - 4th Corp. Co. G. b.c. 1843 (1845). Prior service, Co. G, 3rd VSL. Enl. Frankfort, Greenbrier Co., W. Va., 3/12/63. Not stated if present or absent on muster-in roll dated 3/63, 4th Corp. Clothing issued, Pvt., 4/30/64. Ab. 9/1/64 - 10/31/64, AWOL; has a serviceable horse. Cpd. Roane Co., W. Va., 10/6/64. Confined at the Atheneum Prison, 10/64. Desc.: age 21, 5'8", fair comp., light hair and blue eyes. Occ. farmer, residing in Kanawha Co., W. Va. Transf. to Camp Chase, 10/28/64. Confined at Camp Chase, 10/29/64, charged with having taken the oath of allegiance, then returning to the rebel army. Took the oath of allegiance and was released, 4/27/65. Age 35, furniture maker, Charleston No. 3 Dist., Kanawha Co., W. Va. 1880 Census. NFR.

BARNES, EDGAR (EDWARD) W. - Pvt. Co. C. b. Harrison Co., W. Va., 10/3/33. Moved to Roane Co., W. Va., 1856 or 1857. Post war source shows service in Co. C, 19th Va. Cav. Transf. to Co. B, 22nd Va. Inf. Post war physician and resident of Countsville, Roane Co., W. Va. Age 46, Harper Dist., Roane Co., W. Va. 1880 Census. NFR.

BARNES, WILLIAM - Pvt. Co. G. b. Alleghany Co., Md., c. 1823. Age 37, farmer, Calhoun Co., W. Va. 1860 Census. Prior service, Co. F, 3rd VSL. Enl. Frankfort, Greenbrier Co., W. Va., 3/15/63. Not stated if present or absent on muster-in roll dated 3/63. NFR.

BARNETT, DAVID - Pvt. Co. E. b.c. 1847. Not on muster rolls. Cpd. Braxton Co., W. Va.. 1/26/64. Confined at the Atheneum Prison, 2/1/64. Desc.: age 17, 5'11", light comp., light hair and black eyes. Occ. farmer, residing in Braxton Co., W. Va. Charged with being a bushwhacker. Transf. to Camp Chase. 2/2/64. Desires to take the oath of allegiance, 6/10/64, stating he was a conscript. Took the oath of allegiance and was released, 5/13/65. Desc.: age ?, 6'1", sandy comp., dark hair and dark eyes, a resident of Braxton Co., W. Va. Signed by x. NFR.

BARNETT (BARNITZ), STEPHEN H. - Pvt. Co. F. b. Pocahontas Co., W. Va., 10/5/36. Age 24, farmer, Thorny Creek, Pocahontas Co., W. Va. 1860 Census. Prior service, McNeel's Co., 2nd VSL. Enl. Hillsboro, Pocahontas Co., W. Va., 3/9/63 (also as 4/17/63). Not stated if present or absent on muster-in roll dated 3/63. Present 1/1/64 - 2/29/64. Clothing issued 2/6/64. Cpd. Pocahontas Co., W. Va., 4/28/64. Confined at the Atheneum Prison, 5/12/64. Desc.: age 29, 5'11", fair comp., dark hair and blue eyes. Occ. farmer, residing in Pocahontas Co., W. Va. Transf. to Camp Chase, 5/13/64. Confined at Camp Chase, 5/14/64. Ab. 9/1/64 - 10/31/64, cpd. 4/28/64; enl. bounty due. Paroled and transf. to City Point, 2/25/65, to be exchanged. Exchanged. Adm. Jackson Hosp., 3/7/65, debilitas. Furloughed 3/9/65, 30 days. Post war resident of Pocahontas Co., W. Va. Age 44, farmer, Green Banks, Pocahontas Co., W. Va. 1880 Census. d. Pocahontas Co., W. Va. 1/12/1915.

BARNETT, WESLEY G. - 1st Sgt. Co. H. b. Braxton Co., W. Va., c. 1835. Age 25, farmhand, Webster Co., W. Va. 1860 Census. Prior service, Co. G, 3rd VSL. Enl. Frankfort, Greenbrier Co., W. Va., 3/19/63 (Clay Co., W. Va., 4/1/63). Not stated if present or absent on muster-in roll dated 3/63. Clothing issued, 1st Sgt., 2/7/64; 3/1/64 and 5/1/64, signs by x. Ab. 9/1/64 - 10/31/64, AWOL; $50 enl. bounty due. Age 46, farm laborer, Glade, Webster Co., W. Va. 1880 Census. NFR.

BARTHLETT (BARNETT), THOMAS - Pvt. Co. H. b.c. 1830. Age 30, farmer, Pocahontas Co., W. Va. 1860 Census. Enl. Pocahontas Co., W. Va., 8/1/63. Ab. 9/1/64 - 10/31/64, AWOL. Age 50, farmer, Green Banks, Pocahontas Co., W. Va. 1880 Census. NFR.

BARTRUG (BARTING), ISAAC - Pvt. Co. A. b.c. 1840. Not on muster rolls. Cpd. Preston Co., W. Va., 7/1/63. Confined at the Atheneum Prison, 7/2/63. Desc.: age 23, 5'10_", light comp., light hair and gray eyes. Occ. farmer, residing in Wetzel Co., W. Va. Transf. to Camp Chase, 8/63. Confined at Camp Chase, 8/11/63. d. Camp Chase, Columbus, O., 8/26/63. Bur. Camp Chase Confederate Cem.

BARTRUG, JOHN - Pvt. Co. A. b.c. 1846. Not on muster rolls. Cpd. Preston Co., W. Va., 7/1/63. Confined at the Atheneum Prison, 7/2/63. Desc.: age 17, 5'10_", fair comp., auburn hair and blue eyes. Occ. farmer, residing in Wetzel Co., W. Va. Transf. to Camp Chase, 8/63. Confined at Camp Chase, 8/11/63. Released by order of the Sec. of War, 1/15/64. Age 34, farmer, Church Dist., Wetzel Co., W. Va. 1880 Census. NFR.

BAUGHFMAN, JAMES A. - 1st Sgt. Co. B. b.c. 1842. Prior service, Co. B, 3rd VSL. Enl. Frankfort, Greenbrier Co., W. Va., 3/7/63. Not stated if present or absent on muster-in roll dated 3/63, 1st Sgt. Paroled as a Pvt., Charleston, W. Va., 5/22/65. Desc.: age 23, 5'11_", fair comp., dark hair and black eyes. NFR.

BAUGHMAN, WILLIAM C. (D.) - Pvt. Co. B. b. Nicholas Co., W. Va., 12/3/37. Age 23, farmhand, Webster Co., W. Va. 1860 Census. Prior service, Co. B, 3rd VSL. Enl. Frankfort, Greenbrier Co., W. Va., 3/7/63. Not stated if present or absent on muster-in roll dated 3/63. Employed as a courier, 8/1/63 - 8/31/63. Discharged as a farrier, 9/1/63. Age 43, farmer, Glade, Webster Co., W. Va. 1880 Census. d. 5/9/91.

BAUGHMAN, WILLIAM C. - Pvt. Co. C. b.c. 1840. Prior service, Co. D, 3rd VSL. Enl. Pocahontas Co., W. Va., 4/1/63. Ab. 12/31/63 - 8/31/64, detailed as a tanner in Bath Co., 9/1/63; has one horse. Ab. 9/1/64 - 10/31/64, detailed as a tanner in Bath Co., 9/1/63; $100 enl. bounty due. Paroled at Charleston, W. Va., 5/10/65. Desc.: age 25, 5'11", dark comp., dark hair, dark eyes and dark whiskers. NFR.

BAUGHMAN, WILLIAM D. - Pvt. Co. B. b. Nicholas Co.,W. Va., c. 1837. Age 23, farmhand, Webster Co., W. Va. 1860 Census. Prior service, Co. B, 3rd VSL. Enl. Frankfort, Greenbrier Co., W. Va., 3/7/63. Not stated if present or absent on muster-in roll dated 3/63. Age 43, farmer, Glade, Webster Co., W. Va. 1880 Census. NFR.

BAYNE, WILLIAM - Pvt. Co. G. Enl. Greenbrier Co., W. Va., 8/21/63. Ab. 9/1/64 - 10/31/64, on detached service; $50 enl. bounty due. NFR.

BEARD, CHARLES W. - Corp. Co. I. Thought to have served in Co. K, 3rd VSL. Enl. Pocahontas Co., W. Va., 2/1/63. Present on muster-in roll dated 3/63. Mustered into service, 3/19/63. [Probably Charles Woods Beard, listed below]. NFR.

BEARD, CHARLES WOODS - Pvt. Co. F. b. Locust Creek, Pocahontas Co., 9/6/27. Age 32, merchant, Edray, Pocahontas Co., W. Va. 1860 Census. Enl. Hillsboro, Pocahontas Co., W. Va., 9/1/63. Ab. 1/1/64 - 2/29/64, on detail. Ab. 9/1/64 - 10/31/64, wd. Bunker Hill, W. Va., 7/19/64, shoulder; enl. bounty due. Adm. Gen. Hosp., Winchester, 8/1/64. Paroled at Charleston, W. Va., 5/10/65. Desc.: age 37, 5'10", light comp., brown hair, blue eyes and brown whiskers. Post war farmer, and resident of the "Poage Homestead," Hillsboro, W. Va. Age 52, farmer, Little Levels, Pocahontas Co., W. Va. 1880 Census. d. Pocahontas Co., W. Va. 7/8/1902.

BEARD, JOHN JORDAN - 3rd Lt. Co. F. b. Greenbrier Co., W. Va., 4/21/35. Age 25, merchant, Academy, Pocahontas Co., W. Va. 1860 Census. Member Hillsboro Patrol, Pocahontas Co., W. Va., 5/61. Prior service, Co. F, 11th Va. Cav. Transf. to Co. F, 19th Va. Cav., 3/9/63. Also listed as prior service, McNeel's Co., 2nd VSL. Enl. Hillsboro, Pocahontas Co., W. Va., 3/9/63 (4/1/63). Not stated if present or absent on muster-in roll dated 3/63, Jr. 2nd Lt. Commanding Co. in Pocahontas Co., W. Va., 12/31/63. Present 1/1/64 - 2/29/64. Granted 20 days leave, 2/17/64. Ab. 9/1/64 - 10/31/64, wd. near Charles Town, W. Va., 8/21/64, and left in the hands of the enemy. Wd. desc. as fracture of inferior maxilla. Suffered hemorrhage's on 8/21/64 and 9/4/64. Treated by ligation of the common carotid artery, 9/4/64, by Confed. Surg. W. S. Love. Age listed as 28. Adm. USA Depot Field Hosp., Winchester, 9/19/64, vulnus sclopeticum, mouth. Date of injury also as 9/19/64 and 8/13/64. Transf. to another hosp. 11/16/64. Ab. 10/25/64, wd. and in enemy hands. Ab. 12/15/64, wd. 8/21/64, temporarily disabled. Post war resident of Huntersville, W. Va. Age 45, Clerk, Circuit Court, Huntersville, Pocahontas Co., W. Va. 1880 Census. d. Huntersville, W. Va., 4/11/98.

BEATHE, FELIX G. - Pvt. Co. K. b. Highland Co., c. 1845. Not on muster rolls. POW record shows his enl. as Highland Co., 11/63. Clothing issued 2/5/64, 4/30/64 and 6/17/64. Cpd. Beverly, W. Va., 10/29/64 Sent to Clarksburg, W. Va., then to Wheeling, 11/2/64. Confined at the Atheneum Prison. 11/2/64. Desc.: age 19, 5'4", fair comp., light hair and blue (gray) eyes. Occ. farmer, residing in Highland Co. Transf. to Camp Chase, 11/3/64. Confined at Camp Chase, 11/4/64. Took the oath of allegiance and was released, 6/12/65. Desc.: age 19, 5'4 1/2", fair comp., light comp., light hair and gray eyes, a resident of Highland Co. Moved west after the war. Listed in CSR also as Heath B. Felix. NFR.

BECK, JAMES - Pvt. Co. H. b.c. 1847. Thought to have served in Co. G, 3rd VSL. Not on muster rolls. Roll of Honor shows him as a member of this unit, and that he enl. 4/12/62. Wd. during war. Disc. 4/15/64, on account of wounds. Pension record shows service in Co. F. Post war resident of Martinsville, age 55 in 1902. NFR.

BECK, JOHN - Pvt. Co. D. b. Rockingham Co., NC, c. 1841. Not on muster rolls. POW record shows enl. as Highland Co., 1/15/65. Cpd. Upshur Co., W. Va., 4/1/65. Transf. to Clarksburg, W. Va. Confined in the guard house at Clarksburg, W. Va., 4/5/65. Desc.: age 24, 5'10_", fair comp., brown hair and dark eyes. Occ. farmer, residing in Rockingham Co., NC. Transf. to Cumberland, Md., 4/6/65. NFR.

BELCH, WILLIAM M. - Pvt. Co. D. Prior service, Co. C, 3rd VSL. Enl. Williamsburg, Greenbrier Co., W. Va., 3/8/63. Not stated if present or absent on muster-in roll dated 3/63. Served in Co. B, 20th Va. Cav. NFR.

BELKNAP, THOMAS - Pvt. Co. B. b.c. 1833. Prior service, Co. B, 3rd VSL. Enl. Frankfort, Greenbrier Co., W. Va., 3/9/63. Not stated if present or absent on muster-in roll dated 3/63. Ab. 11/1/63 - 2/29/64, cpd. 8/23/63. Cpd. Pocahontas Co., W. Va., 8/23/63. Confined at the Atheneum Prison, 8/30/63. Desc.: age 30, 6'2", dark comp., dark hair, mixed with gray and hazel eyes. Occ. farmer, residing in Braxton Co., W. Va. Transf. to Camp Chase, 8/31/63. Confined at Camp Chase, 9/1/63. Transf. to Rock Island, Ill., 1/14/64. Confined at Rock Island Prison, 1/17/64. Ab. 9/1/64 - 10/31/64, POW; $100 enl. bounty due. Transf. 3/2/65, to be exchanged. Exchanged at Dutch Gap. Listed himself as a member of Imboden's Brigade, and gave his post office as Gordonsville, Orange Co. Adm. Gen. Hosp. No. 9, 3/10/65. Transf. to Chimborazo Hosp., 3/11/65. Adm. Chimborazo Hosp. No. 2, 3/11/65, chronic diarrhoea. Adm. Gen. Hosp. No. 9, 3/16/65. Furloughed 3/18/65, 30 days. Post war resident of Braxton Co., W. Va. Age 45, farmer, Otter Dist., Braxton Co., W. Va. 1880 Census. NFR.

BELL, JOHN NICKSON CURRENCE "Squire" - Pvt. Co. I. b. 10/5/44. Age 15, farmer, Randolph Co., W. Va. 1860 Census. Post war rosters only, which show him as a resident of Randolph Co., W. Va. Served in Co. C, 20th Va. Cav. Member Gen. Pegram Camp, UCV, Valley Head, W. Va. Post war Justice of the Peace, Huttonsville Dist., Randolph Co., W. Va. Age 35, farmer, Huttonsville, Randolph Co., W. Va. 1880 Census. d. 10/26/1911, age c. 68 years. Bur. Kelley Cem., Kelley Farm, Randolph Co., W. Va.

BELL, JOSEPH - Pvt. Co. C. Only reference is a card in the CSR, "See Co. C, 19th Bn. Ga. Cav." NFR.

BELLKNAPP (BELKNAP), NORMAN - Pvt. Co. I. b.c. 1826. Enl. Huntersville, Pocahontas Co., W. Va., 8/15/63. Ab. 6/30/63 - 2/29/64, cpd. while on scout to Upshur Co., W. Va., 12/63; mounted; enl. bounty due. Cpd. Upshur Co., W. Va., 11/28/63. Transf. to Clarksburg, W. Va. Confined at the Atheneum Prison, 12/9/63. Desc.: age 37, 5'10", fair comp., dark hair, blue eyes and sandy whiskers. Occ. farmer, residing in Upshur Co., W. Va. Transf. to Camp Chase, 12/12/63. Confined at Camp Chase, 12/13/63. Transf. to Ft. Delaware, 2/29/64. Confined at Ft. Delaware, 3/2/64. Took the oath of allegiance and was released, 6/15/65, resident of Webster Co., W. Va. Age 53, farmer, Banks Dist., Upshur Co., W. Va. 1880 Census. NFR.

BELT, JASPER N. - Pvt. Co. A. b. Wirt Co., W. Va., c. 1843. Served in Co. A, 3rd VSL. Post war rosters only, which show him as a resident of Calhoun Co., W. Va. Age 27, farmer, Sheridan Dist., Calhoun Co., W. Va. 1870 Census. NFR.

BENNETT, CORNELIUS H. - Pvt. Co. D. b. Harrison Co., W. Va., c. 1841. Not on muster rolls. Enl. Highland Co., 5/63. Clothing issued 2/7/64, 4/21/64, 5/21/64 and 6/17/64. Deserted and surrendered at Clarksburg, W. Va., 3/11/65. Confined at the Atheneum Prison, 3/13/65. Desc.: age 24, 5'8_", fair comp., light hair and blue eyes. Occ. farmer, residing in Taylor Co., W. Va. Took the amnesty oath at Clarksburg, W. Va., and was sent North, 3/12/65. Age 38, farm laborer, North CH Dist., Taylor Co., W. Va. 1880 Census. NFR.

BENNETT (BARNETT), GRANVILLE - 1st Corp. Co. F. b.c. 1841. Prior service, McNeel's Co., 2nd VSL. Enl. Hillsboro, Pocahontas Co., W. Va., 3/9/63 (4/1/63). Not stated if present or absent on muster-in roll dated 3/63, 2nd Corp. Present 1/1/64 - 2/29/64. Clothing issued 7/64 and 8/64. Ab., 1st Corp, 9/1/64 - 10/31/64, AWOL since 9/22/64. Paroled at Charleston, W. Va., 5/11/65. Desc.: age 24, 5'6", light comp., light hair, blue eyes and light whiskers. Post war resident of Lewis Co., W. Va. NFR.

BENNETT (BARNETT), LEVI - Pvt. Co. F. b.c. 1844. Enl. Hillsboro, Pocahontas Co., W. Va., 4/17/63. Present 1/1/64 - 2/29/64. Clothing issued 7/65 and 8/64. Ab. 9/1/64 - 10/31/64, AWOL since 10/7/64; enl. bounty due. Paroled at Staunton, 6/1/65. Desc.: age 21, 5'5", fair comp., light hair and brown eyes. NFR.

BESTOR (BESTER, BESTON), JOHN ROLLIN Jr. - Pvt. Co. I. b. Baltimore, Md., c. 1842. Desc.: age ?, 5'8_", dark hair and dark eyes. Prior service, Co. B, 21st Va. Inf. (12 mo's.), mustered out 5/24/62, then Maj. D. B. Stewart's Partisan Rangers (as 1st Lt., 8 mo's.). Authorized by Maj. Stewart to raise a Co. of Cav. for Stewart's Battn., 6/13/62. Succeeded in raising a number of men for the Co. by 6/27/62. Not on muster rolls. Applied for a clerkship, 6/2/63, from Richmond, in Col. Walter H. S. Taylor's 2nd Auditor's Dept. Cpd. Baltimore, Md., 3/8/65. Confined at Ft. McHenry, 2/8/65, for safe keeping. Took the oath of allegiance and was released, 5/9/65, a resident of Baltimore, Md. Twin of Rollin John Bestor. d. Old Soldier's Home, Pikesville, Md., by 1894.

BESTOR (BESTER, BESTON), ROLLIN JOHN - Pvt. Co. I. b. Baltimore, Md., c. 1842. Desc.: age ?, 5'8_", dark hair and dark eyes. Prior service, Co. B, 21st Va. Inf. (12 mo's.), mustered out 5/24/62, then Maj. D. B. Stewart's Partisan Rangers. Not on muster rolls. Cpd. Baltimore, Md., 3/8/65. Confined at Ft. McHenry, 2/8/65, for safe keeping. Took the oath of allegiance and was released, 5/9/65, a resident of Baltimore, Md. Twin of John Rollin Bestor, Jr. NFR.

BEVERAGE, JOSIAH - Pvt. Co. F. b. 4/3/44. Age 16, farmer, Edray, Pocahontas Co., W. Va. 1860 Census. Prior service, McNeel's Co., 2nd VSL. Enl. Hillsboro, Pocahontas Co., W. Va., 3/9/63. Not stated if present or absent on muster-in roll dated 3/63. Joined Imboden's command before 4/1/63. Served in 2nd Co. D and Co. A, 62nd Va. Mtd. Inf. Post war resident of Highland Co. Desc. 1865: age ?, 6'2_", dark comp., dark hair and blue eyes. d. Highland Co., 2/17/1925. Bur. Doe Hill Cem., Highland Co.

BIBLE, WILLIAM F. - Pvt. Co. F. b.c. 1834. Age 26, farmer, Greenbank, Pocahontas Co., W. Va. 1860 Census. Enl. Hillsboro, Pocahontas Co., W. Va., 4/17/63. Ab. 1/1/64 - 2/29/64, in the hands of the enemy. Cpd. Pocahontas Co., W. Va., 8/22/63. Confined at the Atheneum Prison, 8/30/63. Desc.: age 28, 6'_", dark comp., dark hair and black eyes. Occ. farmer, residing in Pocahontas Co., W. Va. Transf. to Camp Chase, 8/31/63. Confined at Camp Chase, 9/1/63. Transf. to Rock Island, Ill., 1/14/64. Confined at Rock Island Prison, 1/17/64, barracks no. 53. Adm. Prison Hosp., 3/26/64, chronic pneumonia. DOD. Rock Island, Ill., 4/24/64, phthisis pulm. Bur. Rock Island, Ill., grave no. 1083. Ab. 9/1/64 - 10/31/64, cpd. 8/63; enl. bounty due.

BICKELL (BICKLE), GEORGE W. - Pvt. Co. K. b. Braxton Co., W. Va., c. 1840. Age 20, farmer, Webster Co., W. Va. 1860 Census. Prior service, Co. I, 3rd VSL. Enl. Frankfort, Greenbrier Co., W. Va., 3/20/63. Not stated if present or absent on muster-in roll dated 3/63. Cpd. Webster Co., W. Va., 1/13/64, charged with being a bushwhacker. Transf. to Clarksburg, W. Va., 1/22/64. Note in his file shows he was issued clothing 3/25/64. NFR.

BIRD, CHARLES W. - Pvt. Co. ?. b. Highland Co., c. 1840. Age 20, farmhand, Meadow Dale, Highland Co. 1860 Census. Post war rosters only, which show he was a member of Jackson's Cav. Post war resident of Highland Co. and Mo. NFR.

BIRD, JOHN WADE - Pvt. Co. I. b. Bath Co., 10/2/35. Age 24, farmhand, Meadow Dale, Highland Co. 1860 Census. Prior service, 2nd Co. B, 31st Va. Inf. Enl. Huntersville, Pocahontas Co., W. Va., 7/1/63. Ab. 6/30/63 - 2/29/64, sick; mounted. Ab. 2/29/64 - 8/31/64, return demanded by the 31st Va. Inf., dropped from rolls of the 19th Va. Cav. Desc.: age ?, 5'8", fair comp., dark hair and blue eyes. Post war farmer and resident of Highland Co. d. Monterey, Highland Co., 6/14/1914. Bur. Green Hill Methodist Church Cem., Highland Co.

BISHOP, MOSES L. - Pvt. Co. A. b.c. 1845. Prior service, Co. A, 3rd VSL. Enl. in Co. A, Williamsburg, Greenbrier Co., W. Va., 3/1/63. Not stated if present or absent on muster-in roll dated 3/63. Cpd. Jackson Co., W. Va., 11/3/63. Confined at the Atheneum Prison, 12/63. Desc.: age 19, 5'6_", dark comp., dark hair and dark eyes. Occ. farmer, residing in Roane Co., W. Va. Transf. to Camp Chase, 12/13/63. Confined at Camp Chase, 12/15/63, applied to take the oath of allegiance. DOD. Camp Chase, 4/7/65, pneumonia. Bur. 1/3 mile South of Camp Chase, grave No. 824 (1824).

BISHOP, MOSES L. - Pvt. Co. H. Enl. Frankfort, Greenbrier Co., W. Va., 3/19/63 in Co. H. Not stated if present or absent on muster-in roll dated 3/63. CSR shows him as a member of Co. F, and that he was confined at the guard house at Clarksburg, W. Va., 12/22/64 and was sent to Wheeling, W. Va. on 2/24/64. Post war resident of Nicholas Co., W. Va. NFR.

BLAND, WILLIAM JOHN - Surgeon, Jackson's Cav. Brigade. b. 11/10/16. Took part in the Red River Expedition, 1842. Practiced medicine at Weston, W. Va. until the fall of 1861. Appointed Asst. Surg., 7/4/61, accepted 7/22/61. Directed to report to Brig. Gen. R. S. Garnett. Appointed Surg., 11/16/61, accepted 1/8/62. Served as Surgeon, 31st Va. Inf. by 12/13/61. In charge of temporary hosp. at Port Republic, date not given, probably 1862. Served as a Delegate, Va. Gen. Assembly, from Lewis Co., W. Va., 1863. Ordered to report to Brig. Gen. A. G. Jenkins, 3/17/64, for assignment. Assigned to duty with Jackson's Cav. Brigade, 3/64. Served again in the legislature, 1/65. Age 63, physician, Weston, Lewis Co., W. Va. 1880 Census. Superintendent of W. Va. State Hosp., Weston, W. Va., 1881 - 1889. d. Lewis Co., W. Va., 2/18/97.

BLACK, GARLAND C. - Pvt. Co. I. b.c. 1831. Prior service, Co. F, 27th Va. Inf. Enl. Huntersville, Pocahontas Co., W. Va., 7/26/63. Ab. 6/30/63 - 2/29/64, deserted at Marlin's Bottom. Cpd. Pocahontas Co., W. Va., 11/5/63. Confined at the Atheneum Prison, 11/16/63. Desc.: age 32, 5'10_", florid comp., dark hair and gray eyes. Occ. farmer, residing in Rockbridge Co. Transf. to Camp Chase, 11/18/63. Confined at Camp Chase, 11/18/63. Adm. Chase USA Gen. Hosp., Camp Chase, 1/29/64, smallpox. Returned to prison 2/29/64. Ab. 2/29/64 - 8/31/64, cpd. near Marlin's Bottom, 11/4/63. Ab. 9/1/64 - 10/31/64, POW. Transf. to Ft. Delaware, 2/29/64. Confined at Ft. Delaware, 3/4/64 (3/2/64). Released by order of the Sec. of War, 12/3/64, took the oath of allegiance. Desc.: age ?, 6'1_", light comp., brown hair and gray eyes, a resident of Rockbridge Co. NFR.

BLACK, JOHN R. - Pvt. Co. I. b.c. 1840. Enl. Huntersville, Pocahontas Co., W. Va., 7/26/63. Ab. 6/30/63 - 2/29/64, deserted at Marlin's Bottom. Cpd. Pocahontas Co., W. Va., 11/6/63. Confined at the Atheneum Prison, 11/16/63. Desc.: age 23, 6'3/4", fair comp., fair hair and blue eyes. Occ. farmer, residing in Rockbridge Co. Transf. to Camp Chase, 11/18/63. Confined at Camp Chase, 11/18/63. Desired to take the oath of allegiance, 6/10/64, stating he was a conscript and had deserted. DOD. Camp Chase, 8/18/64, typhoid fever. Bur. 1/3 miles South of Camp Chase, grave no. 210.

BLAKE, JOHN JORDAN - Pvt. Capt. Pace's Co. b.c. 1837. Age 23, laborer, Mill Point, Pocahontas Co., W. Va. 1860 Census. Transf. to Co. F, 11th Va. Cav., 11/15/63, stating that he had served in Capt. Pace's Co., 19th Va. Cav. NFR.

BLANKINSHIP, G. W. - Pvt. Co. B. Prior service, Co. B, 3rd VSL. Enl. Frankfort, Greenbrier Co., W. Va., 3/7/63. Not stated if present or absent on muster-in roll dated 3/63. NFR.

BOBBETT (BOBBITT), JAMES H. - Pvt. Co. A. b.c. 1844. Prior service, Co. A, 22nd Va. Inf. History of 22nd Va. Inf. shows he transf. to Co. A, 19th Va. Cav., and was given up as a deserter. Enl. Frankfort, Greenbrier Co., W. Va., 3/1/63 (Williamsburg,

Greenbrier Co., W. Va., 1862). Not stated if present or absent on muster-in roll dated 3/63. Paroled at Lewisburg, W. Va., 4/25/65. Desc.: age 21, 5'9", fair comp., brown hair and hazel eyes, a farmer. NFR.

BODE (BODY, BODEY), LEWIS (LOUIS) - Pvt. Co. D. b.c. 1848. Prior service, Co. C, 3rd VSL. Enl. Williamsburg, Greenbrier Co., W. Va., 3/8/63. Not stated if present or absent on muster-in roll dated 3/63. Served in Co. B, 20th Va. Cav. Age 32, farmer, Southwest Dist., Doddridge Co., W. Va. 1880 Census. NFR.

BODKIN (BODKINS), CHARLES W. - Pvt. Co. D. b.c. 1844. Prior service, Co. C, 3rd VSL. Enl. Williamsburg, Greenbrier Co., W. Va., 3/8/63. Not stated if present or absent on muster-in roll dated 3/63. Served in Co. B, 20th Va. Cav. NFR.

BOGG (BOGGS), JAMES - Sgt. Co. H. Prior service, Co. G, 3rd VSL. Enl. Clay Co., W. Va., 4/1/63. Ab., Sgt., 9/1/64 - 10/31/64, AWOL. NFR.

BOGGS, ARCHIBALD - Pvt. Co. G. Prior service, Co. F, 3rd VSL. Enl. Frankfort, Greenbrier Co., W. Va., 3/12/63. Not stated if present or absent on muster-in roll dated 3/63. NFR.

BOGGS, CHARLES WESLEY - Pvt. Co. H. b. Braxton Co., W. Va., 1844. Prior service, Co. G, 3rd VSL. Enl. Frankfort, Greenbrier Co., W. Va., 3/19/63 (Clay Co., W. Va., 4/1/63). Not stated if present or absent on muster-in roll dated 3/63. Ab. 9/1/64 - 10/31/64, AWOL. NFR.

BOGGS, JOHN W. - Pvt. Co. C. b. Braxton Co., W. Va., 6/6/45. Prior service, Co. F, 20th Va. Cav. Not on muster rolls. d. Braxton Co., W. Va., 10/23/1906. Bur. Home Cem., Coon Creek, Braxton Co., W. Va.

BOGGS, LEVI L. - 3rd Sgt. Co. K. b. Lewis Co., W. Va., 6/4/32. Age 28, farmer, Gilmer Co., W. Va. 1860 Census. Prior service, Co. I, 3rd VSL and Co. D, 31st Va. Inf. Enl. Frankfort, Greenbrier Co., W. Va., 3/20/63. Not stated if present or absent on muster-in roll dated 3/63, 3rd Sgt. Age 50, farmer, Center Dist., Gilmer Co., W. Va. 1880 Census. NFR.

BOGGS, NORMAN - Pvt. Co. B. b. Nicholas Co., W. Va., c. 1818. Prior service, Va. Rangers and Co. B, 3rd VSL. Enl. Co. B, 3rd VSL, 9/30/62. Discharged at Frankfort, W. Va., 3/1/63. Desc.: age 45, 5'10", dark comp., gray hair and blue eyes, a farmer. Enl. Frankfort, Greenbrier Co., W. Va., 3/7/63. Not stated if present or absent on muster-in roll dated 3/63. Listed as Worman Boggs in CSR. NFR.

BOGGS, THADDEUS - Pvt. Co. H. b. Kanawha Co., W. Va., on Easter Sunday, 1835. Moved to what became Roane Co., W. Va., 1846. Prior service, Co. B, 34th Va. Inf. and 34th Va. Battn. Thought to have served in Co. G, 3rd VSL. Enl. Pocahontas Co., W. Va., 8/1/63 (also as 6/62). Clothing issued 3/1/64, 4/1/64 and 6/17/64, signed by x. Ab. 9/1/64 - 10/31/64, AWOL; $50 enl. bounty due. Cpd. Braxton Co., W. Va., 12/9/64, charged with being a horse thief, house burner and house and store robber. Sent to Clarksburg, W. Va., 12/13/64, then to Wheeling, W. Va., 12/15/64. Confined at the Atheneum Prison, 12/15/64. Desc.: age 29, 5'11", fair comp., light hair and hazel (gray) eyes. Occ. farmer, residing in Roane Co. (Braxton Co.), W. Va. Transf. to Camp Chase, 12/30/64. Confined at Camp Chase. Took the oath of allegiance and was released, 6/6/65. Post war farmer and resident of Linden, Roane Co., W. Va. Age 46, farmer, Smithfield Dist., Roane Co., W. Va. 1880 Census. NFR.

BOGGS, WALTER D. - Pvt. Co. H. b. Roane Co., W. Va., 8/25/47. Prior service, Co. G, 3rd VSL. Enl. Clay Co., W. Va., 4/1/63. Clothing issued 2/7/64, 3/8/64, 6/17/64, 7/64 and 8/64, signs by x. Ab. 9/1/64 - 10/31/64, AWOL; has a serviceable horse. Cpd. Braxton Co., W. Va., 12/9/64. Sent to Clarksburg, W. Va., 12/13/64, then to Wheeling, W. Va., 12/15/64. Confined at the Atheneum Prison, 12/15/64. Desc.: age 18, 5'7", fair comp., light hair and gray eyes. Occ. farmer, residing in Braxton Co., W. Va. Transf. to Camp Chase, 12/27/64. Confined at Camp Chase, 12/28/64, desires to take the oath of allegiance. Took the oath of allegiance and was released, 5/15/65. Desc.: age 18, 5'7", dark comp., dark hair and dark eyes, a resident of Roane Co., W. Va. Signs oath by x. Age 34, farmer, Smithfield Dist., Roane Co., W. Va. 1880 Census. NFR.

BOGGS, WILLIAM L. - Pvt. Co. H. Prior service, Co. G, 3rd VSL. Enl. Frankfort, Greenbrier Co., W. Va., 3/19/63 (6/23/63). Not stated if present or absent on muster-in roll dated 3/63. Served in Co. A, 47th Battn. Va. Cav., transf. to 19th Va. Cav. Clothing issued 4/1/64, 6/17/64, 7/64 and 8/64, signs by x. Ab. 9/1/64 - 10/31/64, AWOL. Cpd. Mt. Jackson (Harrisonburg), 9/23/64. Sent to Harpers Ferry, W. Va., then to Pt. Lookout, 10/1/64. Confined at Pt. Lookout, 10/4/64. Paroled 1/17/65 (signs by x), to be exchanged. Arrived at Bouleware's Wharf, James River, 1/21/65. Present on MR of paroled and exchanged prisoners, dated 1/26/65. NFR.

BOLIN, WILLIAM - Pvt. Co. A. Prior service, Co. A, 3rd VSL. Enl. Williamsburg, Greenbrier Co., W. Va., 3/1/63. Not stated if present or absent on muster-in roll dated 3/63. NFR.

BOOKER, JOHN - Pvt. Co. G. Prior service, Co. F, 3rd VSL. Enl. Frankfort, Greenbrier Co., W. Va., 3/12/63. Not stated if present or absent on muster-in roll dated 3/63. NFR.

BOOKER, JONATHAN G. - Pvt. Co. A. Prior service, Co. A, 3rd VSL. Enl. Williamsburg, Greenbrier Co., W. Va., 3/1/63. Not stated if present or absent on muster-in roll dated 3/63. Clothing issued 2/23/64. Post war resident of Greenbrier Co., W. Va. NFR.

BOONE, THOMAS - Pvt. Co. A. Served in Co. A, 3rd VSL. Post war rosters only for service in the 19th Va. Cav., which show he was a resident of Nicholas Co., W. Va. d. Bath Alum Springs, Bath Co., 1/9/63.

BOORAM, ISAAC A. - Pvt. Co. G. Prior service, Co. F, 3rd VSL. Enl. Frankfort, Greenbrier Co., W. Va., 3/12/63. Not stated if present or absent on muster-in roll dated 3/63. NFR.

BOSTICK, JAMES L. - Pvt. Co. G. Prior service, Co. F, 3rd VSL. Enl. Frankfort, Greenbrier Co., W. Va., 3/12/63. Not stated if present or absent on muster-in roll dated 3/63. Transf. to Co. F, 46th Battn. Va. Cav. NFR.

BOWEN, H. G. - Pvt. Co. C. Not on muster rolls. Cpd. Wirt Co., W. Va., 3/11/65, and was sent to Cumberland, Md. NFR.

BOWIN, WILLIAM - Pvt. Co. K. Prior service, Co. I, 3rd VSL. Enl. Frankfort, Greenbrier Co., W. Va., 3/20/63. Not stated if present or absent on muster-in roll dated 3/63. NFR.

BOWMAN, ADAM COLEMAN - 2nd Lt. Co. K. b. Randolph (Tucker) Co., W. Va., 5/1/39. Studied law and taught school. Resident of Barbour Co., W. Va. Arrested and confined at Wheeling, W. Va. Released on his oath and bond by 3/13/62. Prior service, Co. K, 31st Va. Inf. Post war autobiography states he recruited a co. and joined W. L. Jackson's command. Not on muster rolls. Paid as 2nd Lt., Co. K, 7/1/64 - 8/31/64. Promoted to Capt., Co. H. Paroled at Charleston, W. Va., 5/10/65. Desc.: age 26, 6', dark comp., dark hair, black eyes and dark whiskers. Post war resident of Barbour Co., W. Va. Age 40, Cove Dist., Barbour Co., W. Va. 1880 Census. Attorney, farmer, postmaster, gun store owner. Post war roster shows him as Capt., and as having been wd. twice during the war. d. 8/25/1909. Bur. New Hope Cem., Barbour Co., W. Va.

BOWMAN, JACOB W. - Pvt. Co. A. b.c. 1833. Not on muster rolls. Cpd. Winchester, 10/31/63. Confined at the Atheneum Prison, 11/29/63, said he was a conscript. Desc.: age 30, 5'8", light comp., gray hair and gray eyes, a resident of Strasburg, Shenandoah Co. Transf. to Camp Chase, 11/11/63. Confined at Camp Chase, 11/12/63. Transf. to Rock Island, Ill., 1/14/64. Confined at Rock Island Prison, 1/17/64. Transf. for exchange 3/20/65. Exchanged at Bouleware's Wharf, James River, 3/27/§5. NFR.

BOYER, LEONARD - Pvt. Co. ?. b.c. 1809. Prior service, Co. G, 31st Va. Inf. Thought to be in Jackson's Cav. Age 53, 6', in 1862. NFR.

BOYERS (BOWERS), JOHN E. - Pvt. Co. I: b.c. 1821. Age 39, laborer, Pocahontas Co., W. Va. 1860 Census. Enl. Huntersville, Pocahontas Co., W. Va., 9/23/63 (8/1/63). Present 6/30/63 - 2/29/64, has no horse; enl. bounty due. Present 2/29/64 - 8/31/64. Clothing issued 3/22/64 and 3rd Qr. 1864. Present 9/1/64 - 10/31/64, $100 enl. bounty due. Age 64(?), farmer, Huntersville, Pocahontas Co., W. Va. 1880 Census. NFR.

BRADY, JOHN N. (A.) - Pvt. Co. C. Prior service, Co. D, 3rd VSL. Enl. Frankfort, Greenbrier Co., W. Va, 3/15/63 (Pocahontas Co., W. Va., 4/1/63). Not stated if present or absent on muster-in roll dated 3/63. Present 1/1/63 - 4/1/63, had one horse. Cpd. Braxton Co. (Weston), W. Va., 5/12/63. Sent to Wheeling, W. Va., 5/19/63. Confined at the Atheneum Prison, 5/21/63. Desc.: age 18, 5'6_", florid comp., dark hair and gray eyes. Occ. farmer, residing in Lewis Co., W. Va. Transf. to Camp Chase, 5/21/63. Confined at Camp Chase, 5/22/63. Transf. to Johnson's Island, 6/14/63. Confined at Johnson's Island, 6/14/63. Transf. to Pt. Lookout, 11/3/63. Confined at Pt. Lookout, 11/4/63. Paroled until exchanged, 12/24/63. Exchanged at City Point, 12/28/63. Clothing issued 12/30/63, as a paroled and exchanged prisoner, and 2/25/64. Not stated if present or absent, 12/31/63 - 8/31/64, returned to camp; found not guilty of desertion; transf. to Co. A, 19th Va. Cav.; has one horse. Paroled at Staunton, 5/17/65, signs by x, as John A. Brady. Desc.: age 21, 5'10", dark comp., dark hair and blue eyes. Served in Co. E, 20th Va. Cav. Age 35, farmer, CH Dist., Lewis Co., W. Va. 1880 Census, listed as John A. Brady. NFR.

BRAGG, J. A. - Pvt. Co. K. Post war rosters only, which show him as a resident of Northview, W. Va. Bur. Northview Cem., Clarksburg, W. Va. [Could be James Bragg, Co. H.]

BRAGG, JAMES - 4th Corp. Co. H. b.c. 1841. Prior service, Co. G, 3rd VSL. Enl. Frankfort, Greenbrier Co., W. Va., 3/19/63. Not stated if present or absent on muster-in roll dated 3/63, 4th Corp. Clothing issued as Corp. 2/7/64; as a Pvt., 3/1/64, 4/1/64, 5/26/64 and 6/17/64. Paroled at Charleston, W. Va., 6/12/65, signs by x. Desc.: age 24, 5'6_", dark comp., brown hair, black eyes and black whiskers. Age 40, farmer, Glade, Webster Co., W. Va. 1880 Census. NFR.

BRANNON (BRANNAN), HENRY - Pvt. Co. A. b. Jackson Co., W. Va., 9/15/31. Age 28, farmer, Calhoun Co., W. Va. 1860 Census. Prior service, Co. A, 3rd VSL. Enl. Williamsburg, Greenbrier Co., W. Va., 3/1/63. Not stated if present or absent on muster-in roll dated 3/63. Deserted. Cpd. Calhoun Co., W. Va., 10/30/63. Confined at the Atheneum Prison, 11/20/63. Transf. to Camp Chase, 11/20/63. Confined at Camp Chase, 11/21/63. Desires to take the oath, 6/10/64. Statement dated Camp Chase, 1/25/65, lists his age as 33 and from Calhoun Co., W. Va. Says he went to the store of Absalom Knotts (a rebel recruiting officer), who tried to persuaded him to enl. in his company. Brannon refused and went home. Several days later he was taken by a guard of three men and sent to Monroe Co., W. Va. Deserted during the night of 10/30/63 and went home. Asks now that he be released. Released by order of the Sec. of War, 2/17/65, after taking the oath of allegiance. Petition submitted for his release. Desc.: age 33, 5'7", dark comp., black hair and blue eyes, a farmer. Resident of Calhoun Co., W. Va. Post war rosters show resident of Nicholas Co., W. Va. Post war roster shows he d. Columbus, O. and was bur. Camp Chase Confederate Cem. NFR.

BRANNON, JOHN Jr. - Sgt. Co. A. b. Jackson Co., W. Va., c. 1833. Age 27, farmer, Calhoun Co., W. Va. 1860 Census. Prior service, Co. A, 3rd VSL. Enl. Williamsburg, Greenbrier Co., W. Va., 3/1/63. Not stated if present or absent on muster-in roll dated 3/63. Deserted. Cpd. Calhoun Co., W. Va., 10/30/63. Confined at the Atheneum Prison, 11/20/63. Desc.: age 30, 5'10", dark comp., dark hair and hazel eyes. Occ. farmer, residing in Calhoun Co., W. Va. Transf. to Camp Chase, 11/20/63. Confined at Camp Chase, 11/21/63. Desires to take the oath of allegiance, 6/10/64. Took the oath of allegiance and was released by order of the Sec. of War, 2/17/65. Post war resident of Nicholas Co., W. Va. Age 46, farmer, Lee Dist., Calhoun Co., W. Va. 1880 Census. NFR.

BRANSFORD, THOMAS H. - Pvt. Co. ?. Post war rosters only, which show he was a resident of Greenbrier Co., W. Va., 6/1/1903. NFR.

BROOKHART, HENRY H. - Pvt. Co. C. Left home and joined the army at age 17 (1862). Prior service, Co. E, 20th Va. Cav. Enl. Pocahontas Co., W. Va., 7/31/63 (4/1/63). Present 12/31/63 - 8/31/64, had his own horse since 7/1/64. Wd. Droop Mtn., 11/6/63, shoulder. A comrade dismounted and put him on his horse and he rode 30 miles before getting his wds. dressed. On the retreat he sat down and would have been cpd. if not for the assistance. Clothing issued 2/2/64, 4/30/64 and 6/17/64, signs by x. Present 9/1/64 - 10/31/64, has one horse; $100 enl. bounty due. Post war resident of Wood Co., W. Va. "He was a fearless soldier and was at first despatch carrier in battle. He carried water to the fighting lines in canteens, but was in the line of battle when wounded. The horse on which he rode had seven bullets in him." Returned home, hungry, sick, half clad and with blistered feet, having walked all the way from Richmond. Was arrested and compelled to take the oath a few days before Lee's surrender. NFR.

BROOKS, ABRAM - Pvt. Co. K. Prior service, Co. I, 3rd VSL. Enl. Frankfort, Greenbrier Co., W. Va., 3/20/63. Not stated if present or absent on muster-in roll dated 3/63. NFR.

BROOKS, ANDREW T. - Pvt. Co. A. b. Pa. Resident of Calhoun Co., W. Va. Prior service, Co. A, 3rd VSL. Enl. Williamsburg, Greenbrier Co., W. Va., 3/1/63. Not stated if present or absent on muster-in roll dated 3/63. Employed as a laborer at Warm Springs, on extra duty, 1/1/64 - 3/31/64. Clothing issued 2/19/64, 2/23/64, 5/21/64 and 6/17/64. Cpd. Loudoun Co. (near Harpers Ferry), 7/16/64, and sent to Washington, DC, 7/20/64. Confined at the Old Capitol Prison, 7/20/64. Transf. to Elmira, NY, 7/23/64. Confined at Elmira Prison, 7/25/64. Desires to take the oath of allegiance, 9/3/64, states that he vol. 2/28/63, and has lived in Ohio, where he now wishes to go. DOD. Elmira, NY, 1/31/65, chronic diarrhoea. Bur. Woodlawn Cem., Elmira, NY, grave 1758 (1775).

BROOKS, GEORGE W. - Pvt. Co. B. Prior service, Co. B, 3rd VSL. Enl. Camp Miller, Pocahontas (Greenbrier) Co., W. Va., 3/9/63 (7/15/63). Present 11/1/63 - 2/29/64, enl. bounty due. Clothing issued 1st Qr. 1864, 2/11/64, 4/30/64 and 6/17/64. Present 9/1/64 - 10/31/64, $100 enl. bounty due. NFR.

BROOKS (BROOK), JOHN - Pvt. Co. K. b. Nicholas Co., W. Va., c. 1827. Age 33, farmer, Webster Co., W. Va. 1860 Census. Prior service, Co. I, 3rd VSL. Enl. Frankfort, Greenbrier Co., W. Va., 3/20/63. Not stated if present or absent on muster-in roll dated 3/63. Age 56, farmer, Holly Dist., Webster Co., W. Va. 1880 Census. NFR.

BROOKS, MILES P. - Pvt. Co. B. b. Braxton Co., W. Va., c. 1844. Enl. Camp Miller, Pocahontas (Greenbrier) Co., W. Va., 7/15/63. POW records shows he enl. Greenbrier Co., 9/64. Present 11/1/63 - 2/29/64. Clothing issued 1st Qr. 1864, 2/5/64, 4/30/64 and 6/17/64, signs by x. Present 9/1/64 - 10/31/64, $100 enl. bounty due. Cpd. Webster Co., W. Va., 2/23/65. Desc.: age 22, 5'6_", dark comp., black hair and black eyes, a resident of Braxton Co., W. Va. Sent to Clarksburg, W. Va. and Cumberland, Md, then to Camp Chase, 2/26/65. Confined at the Atheneum Prison, 2/28/65. Desc.: age 21, 5'8", dark comp., dark hair and hazel eyes. Occ. farmer, residing in Braxton Co., W. Va. Indicted for robbing a store and stealing horses. Transf. to Camp Chase, 3/1/65. Confined at Camp Chase, 3/2/65. Took the oath of allegiance and was released, 5/16/65. Age 38, farmer, Holly Dist., Webster Co., W. Va. 1880 Census. NFR.

BROWN, BALLARD - 4th Corp. Co. C. Resident of Jackson Co., W. Va. Prior service, Co. D, 3rd VSL. Enl. Frankfort, Greenbrier Co., W. Va., 3/15/63 (Pocahontas Co., W. Va., 4/1/63). Not stated if present or absent on muster-in roll dated 3/63. Present 1/1/63 - 4/1/63, had one horse. Ab., 4th Corp., 12/31/63 - 8/31/64, promoted 4th Corp. 2/1/64; has one horse; d. 5/1/64. d. Pocahontas Co., W. Va., 5/1/64, consumption. Brother of Henry B. Brown.

BROWN, HENRY B. - 1st Lt. Co. H. b.c. 1842. Resident of Jackson Co., W. Va. Not on muster rolls. Paroled at Charleston, W. Va., 5/10/65. Desc.: age 23, 5'7", dark comp., dark hair, blue eyes and dark whiskers. Age 37, farmer, Washington Dist., Jackson Co., W. Va. 1880 Census. Brother of Ballard Brown. NFR.

BROWN, JAMES A. - Pvt. Co. B. Prior service, Co. B, 3rd VSL. Enl. Frankfort, Greenbrier Co., W. Va., 3/7/63. Not stated if present or absent on muster-in roll dated 3/63. NFR.

BROWN, ROBERT S. - Pvt. Co. F. b. South River Dist., Augusta Co., c. 1825. Post war rosters show him as a resident of Washington, DC. Enl. Middlebrook, Augusta Co., 6/6/64. Present 9/1/64 - 10/31/64. Moved to Rockbridge Co., 1865, farmer. d. Buena Vista, 9/25/91, age 66. Bur. Timber Ridge Presbyterian Church Cem.

BRUFFY (BRUFFEY, BUFFEE), WILLIAM S. - 2nd Lt. Co. F. b.c. 1837 (1828). Age 32, farmer, Greenbank, Pocahontas Co., W. Va. 1860 Census. Prior service, McNeel's Co., 2nd VSL. Enl. Hillsboro, Pocahontas Co., W. Va., 3/9/63 (4/1/63). Not stated if present or absent on muster-in roll dated 3/63, 1st Sgt. Ab. 1/1/64 - 2/29/64, on leave. Clothing issued 2/6/64. Present 9/1/64 - 10/31/64, enl. bounty due. Promoted to 2nd Lt. Paroled at Charleston, W. Va., 5/10/65, as a 2nd Lt. Desc.: age 28(?), 5'7", fair comp., dark hair, blue eyes and dark whiskers. NFR.

BRUGH (BURGESS), ELIJAH C. - Pvt. Co. C. b.c. 1830. Prior service, Co. D, 3rd VSL. Enl. Frankfort, Greenbrier Co., W. Va., 3/15/63. Not stated if present or absent on muster-in roll dated 3/63. Post war roster shows he was detailed as Commissary Sgt. Cpd. Roane Co., W. Va., 10/27/63. Confined at the Atheneum Prison, 11/1/63. Desc.: age 33, 5'10", sallow comp., light hair and blue eyes. Occ. cooper, residing in Jackson Co., W. Va. Transf. to Camp Chase, 11/2/63. Confined at Camp Chase, 11/13/63. Transf. to Rock Island, Ill., 1/14/64. Confined at the Rock Island Prison, 1/17/64. Desires to take the oath of allegiance, 3/18/64, lives within Federal lines. DOD. Rock Island, Ill., 2/3/65, pneumonia. Bur. Rock Island, Ill., grave no. 1855.

BRUGH (BURGE), SAMUEL C. - Pvt. Co. C. Prior service, Co. D, 3rd VSL. Enl. Frankfort, Greenbrier Co., W. Va., 3/15/63. Not stated if present or absent on muster-in roll dated 3/63. Muster Roll for D, 3rd VSL, 1/1/63 - 4/1/63, shows that he was KIA. Prestonburg, Ky., 12/4/62, along with his horse. NFR.

BRUMAGE, ISAAC - Pvt. Co. C. b.c. 1835. Prior service, Co. C, 3rd VSL. Enl. Williamsburg, Greenbrier Co., W. Va., 3/8/63. Not stated if present or absent on muster-in roll dated 3/63. Cpd. Alleghany Co. (Pocahontas Co., W. Va.), 12/21/63. Confined at the Atheneum Prison, 12/31/63. Desc.: age 28, 6', fair comp., dark hair and blue eyes. Occ. farmer, residing in Marion Co., W. Va. Transf. to Camp Chase, 12/31/63. Confined at Camp Chase, 1/1/64. Transf. to Ft. Delaware, 3/14/64. Confined at Ft. Delaware, 3/17/64. Took the oath of allegiance and was released, 6/19/65, signs by x. Resident of Marion Co., W. Va. Age 44, farmer, Grant Dist., Marion Co., W. Va. 1880 Census. NFR.

BUCKNER, JAMES M. - Pvt. Co. G. Prior service, Co. F, 3rd VSL. Enl. Frankfort, Greenbrier Co., W. Va., 3/12/63 (4/1/63). Not stated if present or absent on muster-in roll dated 3/63. Clothing issued 5/26/64 and 6/17/64. Present 9/1/64 - 10/31/64, has a serviceable horse. NFR.

BUCKNER (BECKNER), SAMUEL P. - 4th Sgt. Co. E. b.c. 1841. Prior service, Co. E, 3rd VSL. Enl. Frankfort, Greenbrier Co., W. Va., 3/13/63 (4/1/63). Not stated if present or absent on muster-in roll dated 3/63, Pvt. Present, 4th Sgt., 10/31/63 - 10/31/64, had his own horse since 7/1/64. Clothing issued as 4th Sgt., 1/3/64, 4/30/64, 5/21/64 and 6/17/64. Paroled at Charleston, W. Va., 5/12/65. Desc.: age 24, 5'6", fair comp., light hair, blue eyes and sandy whiskers. NFR.

BUFFINGTON, CALVIN E. - Pvt. Co. G. Prior service, Co. F, 3rd VSL. Enl. Frankfort, Greenbrier Co., W. Va., 3/12/63 (4/1/63). Not stated if present or absent on muster-in roll dated 3/63. NFR.

BURDETT, JOHN J. - Pvt. Co. A. Resident of Greenbrier Co., W. Va. Arrested and confined by 3/15/62. Charged with having sent Union men into rebel custody. Prior service, Co. A, 3rd VSL. Post war rosters only for service in Co. A, 19th Va. Cav. NFR.

BURDETT, LEWIS P. - Pvt. Co. A. Prior service, Co. A, 3rd VSL. Post war rosters only for service in Co. A, 19th Va. Cav. NFR.

BURGE, LEVI - Pvt. Co. F. b.c. 1844. Prior service, Co. F, 46th Battn. Va. Cav. Not on muster rolls. Paroled at Charleston, W. Va., 5/11/65. Desc.: age 21, 5'10", light comp., black hair, blue eyes and light whiskers. Age 36, farmer, Ravenswood Dist. 2, Jackson Co., W. Va. 1880 Census. NFR.

BURGESS, HUGH Mc. - Pvt. Co. F. b.c. 1833. Prior service, McNeel's Co., 2nd VSL. Enl. Hillsboro, Pocahontas Co., W. Va., 3/9/63. Not stated if present or absent on muster-in roll dated 3/63. Transf. to Co. G, 19th Va. Cav., enl. Pocahontas Co., W. Va., 11/1/63. Employed as a carpenter 11/1/63 - 11/20/63, left sick in Pocahontas Co., W. Va., 11/20/63. Clothing issued 1st Qr. 1864. Employed as a carpenter 2/1/64 - 3/31/64, on extra duty at Warm Springs. Ab. 9/1/64 - 10/31/64, on detached service; $50 enl. bounty due. Age 47, saddler, Little Levels, Pocahontas Co., W. Va. 1880 Census. NFR.

BURK, JAMES M. - Pvt. Co. ?. Not on muster rolls. Served as a substitute for F. H. Cherryholmes. NFR.

BURNER, CHARLES G. - Pvt. Co. F. b. Pocahontas Co., W. Va., c. 1840. Age 21, farmer, Pocahontas Co., W. Va. 1860 Census. Prior service, McNeel's Co., 2nd VSL. Enl. Hillsboro, Pocahontas Co., W. Va., 3/9/63. Not stated if present or absent on muster-in roll dated 3/63. Served in Co. C, 20th Va. Cav. Age 40, farmer, Green Banks, Pocahontas Co., W. Va. 1880 Census. NFR.

BURNER, (BEEMER, BUNNER, BRENNER), JOHN E. - Pvt. Co. A. b.c. 1834. Prior service, Co. A, 3rd VSL. Enl. Williamsburg, Greenbrier Co., W. Va., 3/1/63. Not stated if present or absent on muster-in roll dated 3/63. Served in Co. F 20th Va. Cav. Returned to Co. A, 19th Va. Cav. Post war rosters show him as a resident of Calhoun Co., W. Va. Age 46, farm laborer, Green Banks Dist., Pocahontas Co., W. Va. 1880 Census. CSR listed as Beemer. NFR.

BURNS, GRANVILLE B. - Pvt. Co. H. Prior service, Co. G, 3rd VSL. Enl. Roane Co., W. Va., 4/1/63. Ab. 9/1/64 - 10/31/64, AWOL. NFR.

BURR, JAMES - Pvt. Co. I. b.c. 1832. Age 28, farmer, Academy, Pocahontas Co., W. Va. 1860 Census. Thought to have served in Co. K, 3rd VSL. Enl. Pocahontas Co., W. Va., 3/1/63. Present on muster-in roll dated 3/63. Mustered into service 3/19/63. NFR.

BURR, JOHN - Pvt. Co. F. b. 1826. Age 34, farmer, Dunmore, Pocahontas Co., W. Va. 1860 Census. Prior service, McNeel's Co., 2nd VSL and 2nd Co. I, 25th Va. Inf. Enl. Hillsboro, Pocahontas Co., W. Va., 3/9/63 (4/17/63). Not stated if present or absent on muster-in roll dated 3/63. Ab. 1/1/64 - 2/29/64, AWOL, not fit for duty. Ab. 9/1/64 - 10/31/64, AWOL. Apparently returned to 2nd Co. I, 25th Va. Inf. Age 54, farmer, Little Level Dist., Pocahontas Co., W. Va., 1880 census. NFR.

BURROWS (BUREUS) (?), WILLIAM H. - Pvt. Co. A. b. Randolph Co., W. Va., 8/19/25. Age 38 (?), Calhoun Co., W. Va. 1860 Census. Post war rosters only which show he was cpd. during the war, and was a resident of Calhoun Co., W. Va. Age 48, farmer, Center Township, Calhoun Co., W. Va. 1870 Census. d. 7/1/1903. Bur. Burrows Cem., Calhoun Co., W. Va.

BURTON, ALLEN - Pvt. Co. D. Prior service, Co. C, 3rd VSL. Enl. Williamsburg, Greenbrier Co., W. Va., 3/8/63. Not stated if present or absent on muster-in roll dated 3/63. Employed as a teamster 11/1/63 - 11/30/63 and 1/1/64 - 2/29/64. Served in Co. B, 20th Va. Cav. NFR.

BURTON, ELMORE B. - Pvt. Co. D. b. Harrison Co., W. Va., c. 1840. Age 20, farmer, Gilmer Co., W. Va. 1860 Census. Prior service, Co. C, 3rd VSL. Enl. Williamsburg, Greenbrier Co., W. Va., 3/8/63. Not stated if present or absent on muster-in roll dated 3/63. Served in Co. B, 20th Va. Cav. Age 40, farmer, Troy Dist., Gilmer Co., W. Va. 1880 Census. NFR.

BURTON, JAMES I. - Pvt. Co. D. b. Doddridge Co., W. Va., c. 1843. Prior service, Co. C, 3rd VSL. Enl. Williamsburg, Greenbrier Co., W. Va., 3/8/63. Not stated if present or absent on muster-in roll dated 3/63. Served in Co. B, 20th Va. Cav. Age 36, farmer, Troy Dist., Gilmer Co., W. Va. 1880 Census. NFR.

BUSH, ALFRED - Pvt. Co. E. b. Lewis Co., W. Va., c. 1844. Age 16, farmer, Gilmer Co., W Va. 1860 Census. Prior service, Co. E, 3rd VSL. Enl. Frankfort, Greenbrier Co., W. Va., 3/13/63 (4/1/63). Not stated if present or absent on muster-in roll dated 3/63. Present 10/31/63 - 10/31/64, had his own horse since 7/1/64. Clothing issued 3/1/64 and 5/21/64. Paroled at Charleston, W. Va., 5/11/65. Desc.: age 21, 5'10", fair comp., dark hair and dark eyes. Age 37, farmer, Troy Dist., Gilmer Co., W. Va. 1880 Census. NFR.

BUSH, DANIEL H. - Pvt. Co. I. Enl. Dunmore, Pocahontas Co., W. Va., 12/4/63. Present 6/30/63 - 2/29/64, has no horse; enl. bounty due. Present 2/29/64 - 8/31/64. Clothing issued 3/22/64 and 3rd Qr. 1864. Present 9/1/64 - 10/31/64. NFR.

BUSH, GEORGE A. - Pvt. Co. E. b. Lewis Co., W. Va., c. 1833 (1839). Age 21, farmer, Gilmer Co., W. Va. 1860 Census. Enl. Gilmer Co., W. Va., 10/8/64. Present 10/31/63 - 10/31/64, had his own horse since 10/8/64; enl. bounty due. Surrendered at Cornwallas, W. Va., 5/4/65. Paroled at Clarksburg, W. Va., 5/4/65, signs by x. Desc.: age 26, 5'9", dark comp., brown hair and hazel eyes. Occ. farmer, residing in Gilmer Co., W. Va. Brother of William R. Bush. NFR.

BUSH, GEORGE S. - 2nd Sgt. Co. E. b. Lewis Co., W. Va., 10/10/35. Moved to Gilmer Co., W. Va., 1855. Age 24, farmer, Gilmer Co., W. Va. 1860 Census. Prior service, Co. E, 3rd VSL. Enl. Frankfort, Greenbrier Co., W. Va., 3/13/63 (4/1/63). Enl. also as Pocahontas Co., W. Va., 9/62. Not stated if present or absent on muster-in roll dated 3/63. Ab., 2nd Sgt., 10/31/63 - 10/31/64, deserted. Clothing issued as 2nd Sgt., 3/1/64. Cpd. Glenville, W. Va., 9/19/64. Desc.: age 29, 5'7", dark hair and brown eyes. Occ. farmer, residing in Gilmer Co., W. Va. Took the oath of allegiance and was released, 10/8/64. Post war farmer and resident of Tannersville, Gilmer Co., W. Va. Age 44, farming, DeKalb Dist., Gilmer Co., W. Va. 1880 Census. NFR.

BUSH, HENRY F. - Pvt. Co. E. b. Lewis Co., W. Va., c. 1821. Age 39, farmer, Gilmer Co., W. Va. 1860 Census. Prior service, Co. E, 3rd VSL. Enl. Frankfort, Greenbrier Co., W. Va., 3/13/63 (4/1/63). Hosp. records show him as having enl. at Mill Point, Pocahontas Co., W. Va., 9/2/62, by Capt. George Dusky. Not stated if present or absent on muster-in roll dated 3/63. Present Hosp. MR, Warm Springs, 4/1/63 - 1/1/64, attached to hosp. 8/15/63 as a nurse. Clothing issued 3/1/64. Age 59, blacksmith, Union Dist., Jackson Co., W. Va. 1880 Census. NFR.

BUSH, JEHU - Pvt. Co. E. Prior service, Co. E, 3rd Va. State line. Enl. Frankfort, Greenbrier Co., W. Va., 3/13/63 (4/1/63). Not stated if present or absent on muster-in roll dated 3/63. Ab. 10/31/63 - 10/31/64, had his own horse since 7/1/64; cpd. 7/15/64. Clothing issued 3/1/64, 3/25/64, 4/30/64 and 6/17/64. Cpd. Leesburg, Loudoun Co. (near Harpers Ferry), 7/15/64. Transf. to Washington, DC, 7/64. Confined at the Old Capitol Prison, 7/17/64. Transf. to Elmira, NY, 7/23/64. Confined at Elmira Prison, 7/25/64. Desires to take the oath of allegiance, 9/30/64, says he gave himself up and wishes to go home to Gilmer Co., W. Va. Took the oath of allegiance and was released, 5/13/65. Desc.: age ?, 5'7_", fair comp., light hair and blue eyes, a resident of Gilmer Co., W. Va. NFR.

BUSH, SAMUEL L. - 4th Sgt. Co. E. b. Lewis Co., W. Va., c. 1843. Age 17, farmer, Gilmer Co., W. Va. 1860 Census. Prior service, Co. E, 3rd VSL. Enl. Frankfort, Greenbrier Co., W. Va., 3/13/63 (4/1/63). Not stated if present or absent on muster-in roll dated 3/63, 4th Sgt. Ab., Pvt., 10/31/63 - 10/31/64, had his own horse until 8/20/64; POW. Clothing issued 3/1/64, 4/30/64, 5/21/64 and 6/17/64. Cpd. Gilmer Co., W. Va., 9/11/64. Confined at the Atheneum Prison, 10/64. Desc.: age 22, 5'10", fair comp., red hair and blue eyes. Occ. farmer, residing in Gilmer Co., W. Va. Transf. to Camp Chase, 10/6/64. Confined at Camp Chase, 10/7/64, wishes to take the oath of allegiance. Age 37, farmer, DeKalb Dist., Gilmer Co., W. Va. 1880 Census. NFR.

BUSH, SILAS F. - Pvt. Co. E. b. Lewis Co., W. Va., c. 1834. Age 26, Gilmer Co., W. Va. 1860 Census. Prior service, Co. E, 3rd VSL. Enl. Frankfort, Greenbrier Co., W. Va., 3/13/63 (4/1/63). Not stated if present or absent on muster-in roll dated 3/63. NFR.

BUSH, W. A. - Pvt. Co. B. Post war rosters only. NFR.

BUSH, WILLIAM R. - Pvt. Co. E. b. Gilmer (Lewis) Co., W. Va., c. 1842. Age 18, farmer, Gilmer Co., W. Va. 1860 Census. Prior service, Co. E, 3rd VSL. Enl. Frankfort, Greenbrier Co., W. Va., 3/13/63 (4/1/63). POW records show him as enl. Falling Springs, 8/62. Not stated if present or absent on muster-in roll dated 3/63. Ab. 10/31/63 - 10/31/64, deserted. Clothing issued 3/1/64 and 6/17/64, signs by x. Surrendered at Beverly, W. Va., 8/20/64. Took the oath of allegiance and was released, 8/

64. Desc.: age 22, 5'6", dark comp., black hair and brown eyes. Occ. farmer, residing in Gilmer Co., W. Va. Brother of George A. Bush. Age 37, farmer, Troy Dist., Gilmer Co., W. Va. 1880 Census. NFR.

BUTCHER, WARWICK - Pvt. Co. B. b.c. 1819. Prior service, Co. B, 3rd VSL. Enl. Frankfort, Greenbrier Co., W. Va., 3/13/63 (4/1/63). Not stated if present or absent on muster-in roll dated 3/63. Deserted. Cpd. Nicholas Co., W. Va., 7/29/63. Confined at the Atheneum Prison, 9/16/63. Desc.: age 44, 5'10", florid comp., dark hair, blue eyes and dark whiskers. Occ. blacksmith, residing in Nicholas Co., W. Va. Transf. to Camp Chase, 9/17/63. Confined at Camp Chase, 9/18/63. Transf. to Rock Island, Ill., 1/14/64. Confined at Rock Island Prison, 1/17/64. DOD. Rock Island, Ill., 12/3/64, tuberculosis. Bur. Rock Island, Ill., grave no. 1637.

BUTLER, OLIVER Mc. - Pvt. Co. H. b.c. 1828. Resident of Clay Co., W. Va. Arrested and confined by 3/15/62, charged with being a thief and a bad man. Prior service, Co. G, 3rd VSL. Enl. Frankfort, Greenbrier Co., W. Va., 3/19/63. Not stated if present or absent on muster-in roll dated 3/63. Age 52, farmer, Otter Dist., Clay Co., W. Va. 1880 Census. NFR.

BUTT, H. - Pvt. Co. H. b.c. 1846. Enl. Lewisburg, W. Va., 1864. Not on muster rolls. Paroled at Lewisburg, W. Va., 4/25/65. Desc.: age 19, 5'5", dark comp., dark hair and dark eyes. NFR.

BUTTERWORTH, WILLIAM - Pvt. Co. G. Prior service, Co. F, 3rd VSL. Enl. Frankfort, Greenbrier Co., W. Va. 3/12/63. Not stated if present or absent on muster-in roll dated 3/63. NFR.

BUZZARD, JAMES ASBURY - Pvt. Co. F. b.c. 1844. Age 15, farmer, Pocahontas Co., W. Va. 1860 Census, listed as Joseph A. Buzzard. Prior service, McNeel's Co., 2nd VSL, listed as Joseph A. Buzzard. Enl. Hillsboro, Pocahontas Co., W. Va., 3/9/63. Not stated if present or absent on muster-in roll dated 3/63. Ab. 1/1/64 - 2/29/64, AWOL. Clothing issued 2/6/64. Present 9/1/64 - 10/31/64. Paroled at Charleston, W. Va., 5/10/65. Desc.: age 21, 5'7", fair comp., light hair, blue eyes and light whiskers. NFR.

BYERS, JOHN W. - Pvt. Co. I. b. Va., c. 1846. Age 14, farmhand, 4th Dist., Rockbridge Co. 1860 Census. Enl. Huntersville, Pocahontas Co., W. Va., 8/1/63. Present 6/30/63 - 2/29/64, has no horse; enl. bounty due. Present 2/29/64 - 8/31/64, on extra duty. Present 9/1/64 - 10/31/64, on extra duty; has one horse; $100 enl. bounty due. Age 25, wagon maker, Buffalo Dist., Rockbridge Co. 1870 Census. NFR.

CACKLEY, WILLIAM H. - Pvt. Co. F. b. Mill Point, Pocahontas Co., W. Va. 6/25/45. Age 15, student, Academy, Pocahontas Co., W. Va. 1860 Census. Enl. Hillsboro, Pocahontas Co., W. Va., 7/1/63. Obit. says 8/63. Present 1/1/64 - 2/29/64. Clothing issued 2/6/64. Present 9/1/64 - 10/31/64, enl. bounty due. Paroled at Charleston, W. Va., 5/10/65. Desc.: age 20, 5'10", light comp., dark hair and blue eyes. Post war merchant and deputy sheriff. Post war resident of Pocahontas and Greenbrier Co's., W. Va. Moved to Mo. in 1869. Taught school near Jamesport, Mo. Returned to W. Va. in 1870. Moved to Iowa after 1871. Returned to W. Va. c. 1873. Age 34, farmer, Green Banks, Pocahontas Co., W. Va. 1880 Census. Moved to Ronceverte, c. 1894, merchant and businessman. Post war resident of Fort Springs Dist., Greenbrier Co., W. Va. Member of David S. Creigh Camp, UCV, Lewisburg, W. Va. Brother-in-law of John S. Jackson. d. Ronceverte, W. Va., 9/2/1924, age 84 (?), of injuries received when struck by an automobile. 8/16/1924. Bur. Riverview Cem., Ronceverte, W. Va.

CACKLEY, WILLIAM J. - Pvt. Co. F. b. Pocahontas Co., W. Va., c. 1825. Age 35, farmer, Mill Point, Pocahontas Co., W. Va. 1860 Census. Enl. Hillsboro, Pocahontas Co., W. Va., 7/10/63. Ab. 1/1/64 - 2/29/64, sick. NFR.

CAIN (CANE), COMMODORE - Pvt. Co. A. b. Ritchie Co., W. Va., 7/11/46. Not on muster rolls. Enl. Sweet Springs, W. Va., 5/64. Clothing issued 6/17/64, signs by x. Cpd. Beverly, W. Va., 10/29/64. Sent to Clarksburg, W. Va., then to Wheeling, W. Va., 11/2/64. Confined at the Atheneum Prison, 11/64. Desc.: age 18, 5'11", fair comp., light hair and blue eyes. Occ. farmer, residing in Ritchie Co., W. Va. Transf. to Camp Chase, 11/29/64. Confined at Camp Chase, 11/30/64, desires to take the oath of allegiance. DOD. Camp Chase, 3/9/65, typhoid fever. Bur. 1/3 mile South of Camp Chase, grave no. 1604. Brother of John W. and Sciota Cain.

CAIN, HIRAM PRIBLE - Pvt. Co. A. b. Ritchie Co., W. Va., 2/8/46. Not on muster rolls. Deserted and surrendered at Clarksburg, W. Va., 5/13/65. Desc.: age 19, 6', florid comp., light hair and gray eyes. Occ. farmer, residing in Ritchie Co., W. Va. Took the oath of allegiance and was released 5/13/65. Post war resident of Ritchie Co., W. Va. Age 36, farmer, South Grant Dist., Ritchie Co., W. Va. 1880 Census. d. Cairo, Ritchie Co., W. Va., 12/5/1929. Bur. Ellefritz Cem., Petroleum, Ritchie Co., W. Va.

CAIN, JAMES T. - Pvt. Co. ?. b.c. 1847. Post war rosters only, which show he was a resident of Ritchie Co., W. Va. Age 33, farmer, South Grant Dist., Ritchie Co., W. Va. 1880 Census. Bur. Egypt Cem., Cairo, Ritchie Co., W. Va.

CAIN, JOHN W. - Pvt. Co. ?. Post war rosters only, which show he was a resident of Ritchie Co., W. Va. Bur. Jessie Cain Cem., Racy, Ritchie Co., W. Va.

CAIN, JOHN WILLIAM "Sud" - Pvt. Co. C. b. Rusk, Wood Co., W. Va., 2/28/40. Served in Co. D, 3rd VSL. Served in Co. H, 20th Va. Cav. Served in Lurty's Batty., exchanged for R. F. Watson, 19th Va. Cav., 3/25/64. Post war rosters only, which show he was a resident of Ritchie Co., W. Va. Brother of Commodore and Sciota Cain. Age 40, farmer, South Grant Dist., Ritchie Co., W. Va. 1880 Census. d. Petroleum, Ritchie Co., W. Va., 12/7/1920. Bur. Jesse Cain Cem., Rusk, Ritchie Co., W. Va.

CAIN, SCIOTA (SIOTHA) - Pvt. Co. ?. b.c 1842. Post war rosters only, which show he was a resident of Ritchie Co., W. Va. Age 38, farmer, South Grant Dist., Ritchie Co., W. Va. 1880 Census. Brother of Commodore and John W. Cain. NFR.

CALLISON, THOMAS FRANKLIN - Pvt. Co. F. b.c. 1845. Age 15, farmer, Academy, Pocahontas Co., W. Va. 1860 Census. Prior service, McNeel's Co., 2nd VSL. Enl. Hillsboro, Pocahontas Co., W. Va., 4/1/63. Present 1/1/64 - 2/29/64. Ab. 9/1/64 - 10/31/64, sick; enl. bounty due. Paroled at Charleston, W. Va., 5/10/65. Desc.: age 20, 5'10", light comp., brown hair, gray eyes and light whiskers. CSR lists him as Thomas E. Callison. Age 35, farmer, Little Levels, Pocahontas Co., W. Va. 1880 Census. NFR.

CAMP, F. M. - Pvt. Co. A. b.c. 1832. Not on muster rolls. Cpd. Preston Co., W. Va., 7/1/63. Confined at the Atheneum Prison, 7/2/63. Desc.: age 31, 6', dark comp., dark hair and dark eyes. Occ. farmer, residing in Monongahala Co., W. Va. Transf. to Camp Chase, 8/10/63. Confined at Camp Chase, 8/11/63. Took the oath of allegiance and was released, 6/15/64, by order of the Sec. of War. Age 48, farmer, Battelle Dist., Monongalia Co., W. Va. 1880 Census. NFR.

CAMPBELL, BENJAMIN F. - Pvt. Co. K. b. Gilmer Co., W. Va., c. 1847. Age 13, Gilmer Co., W. Va. 1860 Census. F Co. I, 3rd VSL. Enl. Frankfort, Greenbrier Co., W. Va., 3/20/63. Not stated if present or absent on muster-in roll o Wd./Cpd. Bulltown, W. Va., 10/13/63. Confined at Clarksburg, W. Va., and turned over to the Post Surgeon for treat 15/64. Confined at the Atheneum Prison, 2/9/64. Desc.: age 18, 5'6 1/2", light comp., light hair and blue eyes. Occ. black residing in Gilmer Co., W. Va. Transf. to Camp Chase, 3/4/64. Confined at Camp Chase, 3/5/64. Transf. to Ft. Delawai 14/64. Confined at Ft. Delaware, 3/17/64. Took the oath of allegiance and was released, 6/19/65. Desc.: age ?, 5'4", fair com, light hair and gray eyes, a resident of Gilmer Co., W. Va. Brother of Sida H., Perry C. and William H. Campbell. Post wa resident of Calhoun Co., W. Va. NFR.

CAMPBELL, ELIAS M. - Capt. Co. K. Post war rosters only. Served in Co. I, 3rd VSL. NFR.

CAMPBELL, GEORGE W. - 3rd Corp. Co. G. Prior service, Co. F, 3rd VSL. Enl. Frankfort, Greenbrier Co., W. Va., 3/12/63. Not stated if present or absent on muster-in roll dated 3/63, 3rd Corp. NFR.

CAMPBELL, JOHN CHAMBERS - 2nd Lt. Co. K. b. Clarksburg, W. Va., c. 1842. Also as having been b. Lewis Co., W. Va. Age 18, Gilmer Co., W. Va. 1860 Census. Not on muster rolls. Enl. Staunton, 4/62. 2nd Lt., at Camp Cameron, Bath Co., 11/27/63. Resigned 2/13/64. Cpd. Braxton Co., W. Va., 11/8/64. Sent to Clarksburg, W. Va., then to Wheeling, W. Va., 11/15/64. Confined at the Atheneum Prison, 11/64. Desc.: age 22, 5'11", fair comp., light hair and blue eyes. Occ. clerk, residing at Clarksburg, W. Va. Transf. to Camp Chase, 11/18/64. Confined at Camp Chase, 11/19/64. Took the oath of allegiance and was released, 5/10/65. Desc.: age 24, 5'11", fair comp., light hair and blue eyes, a resident of Harrison Co., W. Va. Post war resident of Spencer, W. Va. NFR.

CAMPBELL, JOHN H. - Pvt. Co. G. b. Ireland, c. 1829. Prior service, Co. F, 3rd VSL. Enl. Frankfort, Greenbrier Co., W. Va, 3/12/63. Not stated if present or absent on muster-in roll dated 3/63. Paroled at Charleston, W. Va., 3/20/63, to report every 10 days. Age 51, farmer, Ravenswood Dist. 2, Jackson Co., W. Va. 1880 Census. NFR.

CAMPBELL, JOHN P. - Pvt. Co. G. Prior service, Co. F, 3rd VSL. Enl. Frankfort, Greenbrier Co., W. Va, 3/12/63. Not stated if present or absent on muster-in roll dated 3/63. NFR.

CAMPBELL, PERRY COMMODORE - Pvt. Co. B. b. Rockbridge Co. (Wood Co., W. Va.), 1830 (1832, 1834). Age 26, farmer, Gilmer Co., W. Va. 1860 Census. Prior service, 3rd VSL. Cpd. Gilmer Co., W. Va., 10/18/62, at home. Confined at the Atheneum Prison, 10/62. Desc.: age 30, 5'10_", fresh comp., auburn hair and blue eyes. Occ. farmer, residing near Glenville, Gilmer Co., W. Va. Transf. to Camp Chase, 10/23/62. Confined at Camp Chase, 10/24/62. Transf. to Cairo, Ill., 11/20/62, to be exchanged. Exchanged near Vicksburg, Miss., 12/8/62. Enl. Frankfort, Greenbrier Co., W. Va., 3/7/63. Not stated if present or absent on muster-in roll dated 3/63. Post war rosters show he served 3 years, and spent five weeks at Camp Chase. Moved to Calhoun Co., W. Va., 1871 (1882). Age 48, keeps ferry, Center Dist., Calhoun Co., W. Va. 1880 Census. Post war ferryman and hotel keeper. Brother of William H., Sida H., and Benjamin Campbell. NFR.

CAMPBELL, SIDA (SILAS) H. - Capt. Co. K. b. Wood Co., W. Va., 1/33 (1835). Age 25, farmer, Gilmer Co., W. Va. 1860 Census. Prior service, Co. C, 25th Va. Inf. and Co. D, 31st Va. Inf. Age 29 (1862), 5'10", dark comp., black hair, black whiskers and blue eyes. Transf. to Co. K, 19th Cav., as Capt. Commanding Co. K, Marlin's Bottom, Pocahontas Co., W. Va., 10/2/63. Member of Board of Survey, 1/21/64, to condemn quartermaster and commissary stores. Wd. Centerville, W. Va., 9/14/64, supposed mortally, under the right eye, the ball passing out the back of his right ear. Was cared for in Burchtown. Resigned 10/12/64 (also as 8/14/63), had a disagreement with Lt. Col. W. P. Thompson. Resignation accepted 10/24/64. Paroled at Charleston, W. Va., 5/10/65. Desc.: age 30, 5'10", light comp., brown hair, blue eyes and brown whiskers. Age 46, farmer, Glenville, Gilmer Co., W. Va. 1880 Census. Brother of Benjamin, and William H. Campbell. d. 3/12/1910. Bur. Campbell Cem., Calhoun Co., W. Va.

CAMPBELL, WILLIAM H. - Pvt. Co. K. b. Glenville, Gilmer (Lewis) Co., W. Va., 1/27/44. Age 16, Gilmer Co., W. Va. 1860 Census. Post war rosters only, which show he was wd. during the war and that he served 4 years in Co. E, 31st Va. Inf. Transf. to Lurty's Betty., by Capt. S. H. Campbell, 1864. Post war farmer, blacksmith and lumber dealer, Eden, Calhoun Co., W. Va. Brother of Sida H., Benjamin and Perry C. Campbell. Age 36, farmer, Washington Dist., Calhoun Co., W. Va. 1880 Census. NFR.

CARPENTER, GEORGE HENRY - Capt. Co. H. b.c. 1843. Age 17, student, 1st Dist., Rockingham Co., 1860 census. Resident of Mt. Crawford. Prior service, Co. I, 1st Va. Cav. Attended VMI, 10/2/62. Resigned from VMI, 1/12/64. Enl. Co. H, 19th Va. Cav., as a Sgt., Pocahontas Co., W. Va., 8/1/63. Clothing issued as a Pvt., 3/1/64; as Sgt. 6/17/64. Promoted 2nd Lt., 6/64. Present 9/1/64 - 10/31/64, 2nd Lt., commanding Co. Promoted Capt. 10/64. Ab. 12/15/64, on leave by order of Gen. Jubal A. Early, on recruiting duty, still listed as 2nd Lt. Paroled at Staunton, 4/30/65, as Capt. Desc.: age 22, 5'9", dark comp., light hair and gray eyes, a resident of Rockingham Co. Post war MD, Cumberland, Md., 1910. d. after 1918. NFR.

CARPENTER, GEORGE H. - Pvt. Co. I. Not on muster rolls. Cpd. Gettysburg, Pa., 7/3/63. Confined at Ft. Delaware, then sent to Pt. Lookout. Confined at Pt. Lookout, 10/27/64. Paroled 2/13/65, to be exchanged. Exchanged at Coxes Landing, James River, 2/65. NFR.

CARPENTER, HUGH M. (H.) - Pvt. Co. F. b.c. 1825. Age 35, farmer, Dunmore, Pocahontas Co., W. Va. 1860 Census. Prior service, McNeel's Co., 2nd VSL. Enl. Hillsboro, Pocahontas Co., W. Va., 3/9/63. Not stated if present or absent on muster-in roll dated 3/63. Ab. 1/1/64 - 2/29/64, AWOL. Ab. 9/1/64 - 10/31/64, AWOL since 5/1/64. Age 55, farmer, Green Banks, Pocahontas Co., W. Va. 1880 Census. NFR.

CARPENTER, JACOB - Pvt. Co. B. b. 8/16/20. Prior service, Co. B, 3rd VSL. Enl. Frankfort, Greenbrier Co., W. Va., 3/7/63. Not stated if present or absent on muster-in roll dated 3/63. Post war rosters show service in Matthew Perrine's Co., Partisan Rangers. Post war resident of Webster Co., W. Va. Age 56, farmer, Glade, Webster Co., W. Va. 1880 Census. d. 4/7/1901. Bur. Erbacon Cem., Erbacon, Glade Dist., Webster Co., W. Va.

CARPENTER, JAMES - Pvt. Co. K. Prior service, Co. I, 3rd VSL. Enl. Frankfort, Greenbrier Co., W. Va., 3/20/63. Not stated if present or absent on muster-in roll dated 3/63. NFR.

CARPENTER, JAMES A. - Pvt. Co. A. Prior service, Co. A, 3rd VSL. Post war rosters only. NFR.

CARPENTER, JOHN JEHU (JAHUGH) - Pvt. Co. B. b. Braxton Co., W. Va., 1840. Prior service, 2nd Co. C., 25th Va. Inf. Transf. to Co. B, 19th Va. Cav., 2/29/64, in exchange for William F. Phillips. Clothing issued 3/21/64, 6/17/64 and 8/29/64, signs by x. Present 9/1/64 - 10/31/64, transf. from the 25th Va. Inf., 3/18/64; $100 enl. bounty due. Deserted. Surrendered at Bulltown, W. Va., 1/27/65. Sent to Clarksburg, W. Va., held in the guard house, 1/30/65. Desc.: age 24, 5'5", dark comp., dark hair and brown eyes. Occ. farmer, residing in Braxton Co., W. Va. Held waiting a petition for his release. Adm. USA Post Hosp.,

Clarksburg, W. Va., 2/10/65, febris intermittent. RTD. 2/13/65. Age 39, farmer, Holly Dist., Braxton Co., W. Va. 1880 census. Related to the Knight Family. d. by 1919. NFR.

CARPENTER, JOHN M. - Pvt. Co. K. Prior service, Co. I, 3rd VSL. Enl. Frankfort, Greenbrier Co., W. Va., 3/20/63. Not stated if present or absent on muster-in roll dated 3/63. NFR.

CARPENTER, SOLOMON - 2nd Corp. Co. H. Prior service, Co. G, 3rd VSL. Enl. Frankfort, Greenbrier Co., 3/19/63. Not stated if present or absent on muster-in roll dated 3/63, 2nd Corp. Clothing issued as a Pvt., 3/11/64. NFR.

CART, ELI T. - Pvt. Co. G. b.c. 1846. Prior service, Co. F, 3rd VSL. Enl. Frankfort, Greenbrier Co., W. Va., 3/12/63 (4/1/63). Not stated if present or absent on muster-in roll dated 3/63. Clothing issued 1st Qr. 1864, 4/30/64, 5/25/64 and 6/17/64, signs by x. Present 9/1/64 - 10/31/64, has a serviceable horse. Deserted. Surrendered at Charleston, W. Va., 3/65. Took the amnesty oath and was sent North, 3/17/65. Desc.: age 19, 5'5_", dark comp., black hair and dark eyes, a farmer. NFR.

CARTER, WILLIAM - Pvt. Co. C. Prior service, Co. D, 3rd VSL. Enl. Frankfort, Greenbrier Co., W. Va., 3/15/63. Not stated if present or absent on muster-in roll dated 3/63. Muster roll for Co. D, 3rd VSL shows he d. Jeffersonville, 12/15/62, and had one horse. NFR.

CASEBOLT, GEORGE M. - Pvt. Co. F. b.c. 1835. Age 25, farmer, Mt. Murphy, Pocahontas Co., W. Va. 1860 Census. Enl. Hillsboro, Pocahontas Co., W. Va., 7/15/63. Ab. 1/1/64 - 2/29/64, sick. NFR.

CASTO, GEORGE - Pvt. Co. ?. Post war source only, which states he, Balas C. DeWees and Squire W. W. Bailey joined Jackson's command in the fall of 1863. These men took part in the fight at Bulltown, W. Va., 10/13/63. NFR.

CASTO, MANLEY - Pvt. Co. A. Prior service, Co. A, 3rd VSL. Post war rosters only for Co. A, 19th Va. Cav. NFR.

CHANDLER, DAVID - Pvt. Co. C. Served in Co. D, 3rd VSL. Post war rosters only, which show he was a resident of Mineral Co., W. Va. NFR.

CHANNELL, JOHN C. (P.) Jr. - Pvt. Co. I. b. 7/22/34. Age 25, farmer, Randolph Co., W. Va. 1860 Census. Enl. Beverly, W. Va., 4/30/63. Prior service, Co. C, 20th Va. Cav. Present 6/30/63 - 2/29/64, transf. from Co. C, 20th Va. Cav., 7/1/63; mounted. Present 2/29/64 - 8/31/64. Ab. 9/1/64 - 10/31/64, cpd. Fisher's Hill, 9/23/64. Cpd. Strasburg, 9/23/64. Sent to Harpers Ferry, W. Va., then to Pt. Lookout, 9/30/64. Confined at Pt. Lookout, 10/3/64. Took the oath and was released by order of the President, 1/11/65. Post war resident of Randolph Co., W. Va. Age 45, farmer and miller, Mingo, Randolph Co., W. Va. 1880 Census. d. 10/25/1901. Bur. Snyder Cem., Randolph Co., W. Va.

CHENOWITH, WILLIAM C. - Pvt. Co. I. b. Randolph Co., W. Va., c. 1822. Enl. Huntersville, Pocahontas Co., W. Va., 10/24/63. Ab. 6/30/63 - 2/29/64, detailed to buy cattle; mounted; enl. bounty due. Ab. 2/29/64 - 8/31/64, detailed to buy stock; mounted; enl. bounty due. Ab. 9/1/64 - 10/31/64, detailed to buy cattle for Jackson's Brigade. Cpd. Crab Bottom, Highland Co., 12/17/64. Desc.: age 42, 5'8_", fair comp., light hair and blue eyes. Occ. Dealer in stock, residing in Clarksburg, W. Va. Sent to Clarksburg, W. Va., then to Wheeling, W. Va., 12/24/64. Confined at the Atheneum Prison, 12/24/64. Transf. to Camp Chase, 12/27/64. Confined at Camp Chase, 12/28/64, desires to take the oath of allegiance. Took the oath of allegiance and was released, 6/12/65. NFR.

CHERRYHOLMES, F. H. - Pvt. Co. ?. Not on muster rolls. Desc.: age 22, 5'8 3/4", fair comp., dark hair and brown eyes, a farmer, residing in Rockingham Co. Hired a substitute in the person of James M. Burk. NFR.

CHEWNING (TUNING), ALBERT B. "Al" - Pvt. Co. B. b. Nelson Co., 1833. Moved to Randolph Co., W. Va., by 1854. Enl. Frankfort, Greenbrier Co., W. Va., 3/7/63. Not stated if present or absent on muster-in roll dated 3/63. Clothing issued 3/24/64 as a member of Capt. A. J. Chewning's scouts. Wd. James Dyer's Farm, on the Gauley River, 3/3/65 (3/4/65), by the 10th W. Va. Inf. DOW. 3/3/65 (3/4/65), two hours after being wd. Place of death also listed as Webster Springs, Webster Co., W. Va. Bur. Dyer Cem., Beaver Run, Gauley River, Fork Lick Dist., Webster Co., W. Va. Brother-in-law of Andrew C. Riffle; brother of Andrew J. and Frederick Chewning. Had been involved in guerilla warfare. Listed as Capt. when KIA., as a member of an independent co. being formed for guerilla warfare.

CHEWNING (TUNING), A. G. - Pvt. Co. B. Prior service, Co. B, 3rd VSL. Enl. Frankfort, Greenbrier Co., W. Va., 3/7/63. Not stated if present or absent on muster-in roll dated 3/63. NFR.

CHEWNING (TUNING), ANDREW JACKSON "Jack" - Capt. Co. B. b. Nelson Co., 1835. Moved to Randolph Co., W. Va. by 1854, then to Braxton Co., W. Va. Blacksmith (farrier). Led a group of "brigands" in Webster Co., W. Va., 1861, which operated with the Moccasin Rangers. Not on muster rolls. Cpd. 5/62 along with Capt. John S. Spriggs. Confined at Camp Chase. Sent to Wheeling, W. Va., 6/62 for trial, probably as a guerilla. Exchanged 8/25/62. Attached to Jenkin's Brigade as scout, 6/12/63. Led a scout 11/1/63 - 11/23/63, 18 men, through Pocahontas, Webster and Braxton Co's., W. Va. Scouted for Gen. J. E. B. Stuart, 12/2/63 around Richmond. Listed as Capt., 12/18/63. Promoted to Capt. 2/21/65 for valor and skill. Asks permission to raise a co. of independent troops behind the enemy's lines, 2/21/65, stating he has a company of 73 men. Paroled at Charlottesville, 6/5/65. Occ. farrier. Changed his name to Jackson Dell, and was a school teacher in Braxton Co., W. Va. Brother of Albert B. and Frederick Chewning; brother-in-law of Andrew C. Riffle. d. Hacker Valley, near the Braxton and Webster Co. line, 1900. His death is reported to have occurred at the home of Clinton Newbank, 1896, and bur. near Corley. Bur. Robinson Cem., Braxton Co., W. Va.

CHEWNING (TUNING), FREDERICK G. "Fred" - Pvt. Co. B. b. 1840. Resident of Braxton Co., W. Va. Prior service, Co. B, 3rd VSL. Cpd., tried as a guerrilla, and was sentenced to death by 6/25/62 at Clarksburg, W. Va. Confined at Wheeling, W. Va., by 8/3/62. In service by 6/14/63, most likely as a scout. Prior service, 60th Va. Inf., and transf. as a Sgt. to the 21st (?) Va. Cav. Brother to Albert B. and Andrew J. Chewning. Had been involved in guerilla warfare. Listed as a Lt. when KIA. Post war source shows him as a member of this Co., and that he was Wd. near James Dyer's Farm, on the Gauley River 3/3/65 (3/4/65), by the 10th W. Va. Inf. DOW. near James Dyer's Farm, Gauley River, W. Va., 3/6/65. Also as Webster Springs, Webster Co., W. Va. Bur. Dyer Cem., Beaver Run, Gauley River, Fork Lick Dist., Webster Co., W. Va.

CHILDERS (CHILDRES), FRANCIS - Pvt. Co. A. Prior service, Co. A, 3rd VSL. Resident of Roane Co., W. Va. Arrested and confined by 3/15/62. Charged as being a violent secessionist. Prior service, Co. A, 3rd VSL. Enl. Williamsburg, Greenbrier Co., W. Va., 3/1/63. Not stated if present or absent on muster-in roll dated 3/63. Transf. to Co. K. Requested furlough at Montgomery White Sulphur Springs Hosp., 12/3/63, listed as Lt. Requested furlough at Montgomery White Sulphur Springs Hosp., 1/7/64, listed as Lt. Served in Co. E, 20th Va. Cav. and Co. D, 46th Battn. Va. Cav. NFR.

CHRESMORE (CHRISMORE), RUFUS E. - Pvt. Co. F. Prior service, McNeel's Co., 2nd VSL. Post war rosters only. NFR.

CHRISMAN, ISAAC L. - Pvt. Co. E. b.c. 1846. Enl. Gilmer Co., W. Va., 7/15/63. Present 10/31/63 - 10/31/64, had his own horse since 7/1/64. Clothing issued 3/1/64. Age 34, clerk in dry goods store, Glenville, Gilmer Co., W. Va. 1880 Census. NFR.

CHRISMAN, JOSEPH B. - Pvt. Co. E. b. Montgomery Co., c. 1843. Prior service, Co. E, 3rd VSL. Enl. Frankfort, Greenbrier Co., W. Va., 3/13/63 (4/1/63). Not stated if present or absent on muster-in roll dated 3/63. Present 10/31/63 - 10/31/64, had his own horse since 7/1/64. Clothing issued 3/1/64, 4/11/64, 6/17/64, 7/64 and 8/64. Cpd. Beverly, W. Va., 10/29/64. Sent to Clarksburg, W. Va., then to Wheeling, W. Va., 11/2/64. Desc.: age 21, 5'11", light comp., light hair and blue eyes. Occ. farmer, residing in Gilmer Co., W. Va. Confined at the Atheneum Prison, 11/2/64. Transf. to Camp Chase, 11/3/64. Confined at Camp Chase, 11/4/64. Took the oath of allegiance and was released, 6/12/65. Desc.: age 21, 5'10", florid comp., light hair and blue eyes, a resident of Gilmer Co., W. Va. NFR.

CLARK, SAMUEL T. - Pvt. Co. F. b.c. 1824. Age 36, tailor, Academy, Pocahontas Co., W. Va. 1860 Census. Member Hillsboro Patrol, Pocahontas Co., W. Va., 5/61. Prior service, McNeel's Co., 2nd VSL. Enl. Hillsboro, Pocahontas Co., W. Va., 3/9/63 (4/1/63). Not stated if present or absent on muster-in roll dated 3/63. Ab. 1/1/64 - 2/29/64, on leave. Present 9/1/64 - 10/31/64, enl. bounty due. Clothing issued 7/64 and 8/64. Paroled at Charleston, W. Va., 5/10/65. Desc.: age 40, 5'11", dark comp., brown hair, brown eyes and brown whiskers. Listed as Clarke on CSR, but signs his name without the "e". Age 55, farmer, Little Levels, Pocahontas Co., W. Va. 1880 Census. NFR.

CLARKE (CLARK), GEORGE L. - Pvt. Co. C. Served in Co. D, 3rd VSL. Enl. Frankfort, Greenbrier Co., W. Va., 3/15/63. Not stated if present or absent on muster-in roll dated 3/63. Present 1/1/63 - 4/1/63, had one horse. Served in Co. F, 46th Battn. Va. Cav. NFR.

CLARKE, JAMES H. - Pvt. Co. I. b.c. 1837. Age 24, laborer, N. Dist., Augusta Co. 1860 Census. Prior service, Co. C, 5th Va. Inf. Not on muster rolls. Cpd. Beverly, W. Va., 2/15/64. Confined at the Atheneum Prison, 2/21/64. Desc.: age 27, 5'8", fair comp., sandy hair and gray eyes. Occ. farmer, residing in Augusta Co. Took the oath of allegiance and was released, 2/22/64. Post war rosters show him in Co. F. Post war resident of Augusta Co. NFR.

CLARKE (CLARK), JOSEPH - Pvt. Co. C. Prior service, Co. D, 3rd VSL. Enl. Frankfort, Greenbrier Co., W. Va., 3/15/63. Not stated if present or absent on muster-in roll dated 3/63. Ab. 1/1/63 - 4/1/63, deserted 11/18/62; has one horse. NFR.

CLARY, JESSE - Pvt. Co. B. b.c. 1845. Not on muster rolls. Cpd. Pocahontas Co., W. Va., 8/29/63. Confined at the Atheneum Prison, 9/63. Desc.: age 19, 5'8", dark comp., dark hair and dark eyes. Transf. to Camp Chase, 9/63. Confined at Camp Chase, 9/8/63. Transf. to Rock Island, Ill., 1/22/64. Confined at Rock Island Prison, 1/24/64. Transf. for exchange 3/2/65. NFR.

CLAY, JOHN - Pvt. Co. B. Not on muster rolls. Cpd. Pocahontas Co., W. Va., 8/29/63. Confined at Camp Chase, wishes to take the oath of allegiance, and not be exchanged. States that he deserted and was a conscript. NFR.

CLEIRDENCE, JAMES - Pvt. Co. B. b.c. 1837. Not on muster rolls. Cpd. Beverly, W. Va., 3/21/64. Confined at the Atheneum Prison, 3/24/64. Desc.: age 27, 5'6", fair comp., dark hair and blue eyes. Occ. carpenter, residing in Jackson Co., W. Va. Took the oath of allegiance and was released, 3/25/64. NFR.

CLEMENS, JOSIAH - Pvt. Co. A. Served in Co. A, 3rd VSL. Post war rosters only. NFR.

CLIFTON, JOHN F. - Pvt. Co H. b. Braxton Co., W. Va., c. 1840. Age 20, farmhand, Webster Co., W. Va. 1860 Census. No enl. data. Not stated if present or absent on muster-in roll dated 3/63. Age 40, farmer, Holly Dist., Webster Co., W. Va. 1880 Census. NFR.

CLIFTON, ROBERT H. - Pvt. Co. B. b. Braxton Co., W. Va., c. 1842. Age 18, farmhand, Webster Co., W. Va. 1860 Census. Prior service, Co. B, 3rd VSL. Enl. Frankfort, Greenbrier Co., W. Va., 3/7/63. Not stated if present or absent on muster-in roll dated 3/63. Surrendered at Bulltown, W. Va., 5/7/65. Sent to Clarksburg, W. Va. Confined at Clarksburg, W. Va., 5/10/65. Desc.: age 24, 5'7_", fair comp., brown hair and blue eyes. Occ. farmer, residing in Webster Co., W. Va. Paroled for exchange, 5/11/65, signs by x. Age 38, farmer, Holly Dist., Webster Co., W. Va. 1880 Census. NFR.

COBERLY, ASBY (ASBURY) M. - 2nd Sgt. Co. K. Prior service, Co. I, 3rd VSL. Enl. Frankfort, Greenbrier Co., W. Va., 3/20/63. Not stated if present or absent on muster-in roll dated 3/63, 2nd Sgt. Clothing issued as a Pvt., 2/5/64, 4/30/64 and 6/17/64. NFR.

COBERLY, BRUSHROD W. - Pvt. Co. I. b.c. 1820. Prior service, Va. Mounted Rangers. Adm. Gen. Hosp. No. 3, 10/12/63, listed as Sgt. RTD. 10/23/62. Enl. Huntersville, Pocahontas Co., W. Va., 11/28/63. Ab. 6/30/63 - 2/29/64, on parole; mounted; enl. bounty due. Present 2/29/64 - 8/31/64. Clothing issued 6/17/64. Ab. 9/1/64 - 10/31/64, on horse detail; $100 enl. bounty due. Age 60, farm laborer, Dry Fork, Randolph Co., W. Va. 1880 Census. NFR.

COBERLY, WILLIAM HARRISON - Pvt. Co. I. b. 9/19/24. Age 35, farmer, Randolph Co., W. Va. 1860 Census. Post war rosters only, which show he was a resident of Randolph Co., W. Va. Served in Co. D, 20th Va. Cav. Sold land to help start the present-day town of Elkins, W. Va. Age 55, farmer, Green Dist., Randolph Co., W. Va. 1880 Census. d. 1/27/1904. Bur. Maplewood Cem., Randolph Co., W. Va.

COCHRAN, AARON - 3rd Sgt. Co. D. b. Taylor Co., W. Va., c. 1844. Age 16, farm laborer, Pruntytown, Taylor Co., W. Va. 1860 Census. Prior service, Co. C, 3rd VSL. Post war rosters show service in Co. A, 25th Va. Inf. Enl. Williamsburg, Greenbrier Co., W. Va., 3/8/63. Not stated if present or absent on muster-in roll dated 3/63, 3rd Sgt. Served in Co. B, 20th Va. Cav. Age 36, farmer, Booth Creek, Taylor Co., W. Va. 1880 Census. NFR.

COCHRAN, DAVID J. - Pvt. Co. H. b.c. 1828. Age 32, farmer, Pocahontas Co., W. Va. 1860 Census. Prior service, Co. G, 3rd VSL. Enl. Frankfort, Greenbrier Co., W. Va., 3/19/63. Not stated if present or absent on muster-in roll dated 3/63. NFR.

COCHRAN, DAVID - Pvt. Co. D. b. Taylor Co., W. Va., c. 1846. Prior service, Co. C, 3rd VSL. Enl. Williamsburg, Greenbrier Co., W. Va., 3/8/63. POW record shows his enl. as Alum Springs, 12/62. Not stated if present or absent on muster-in roll dated 3/63. Cpd. Clarksburg, W. Va., 8/4/64. Desc.: age 18, 5'11_", dark comp., dark hair and hazel eyes. Occ. farmer, residing in Taylor Co., W. Va. Took the oath of allegiance and was released, 8/10/64. Served in Co. B, 20th Va. Cav. NFR.

COCHRAN (COCHRANE), GEORGE W. A. "Big" - Pvt. Co. F. b.c. 1838 (1831). Age 29, farmer, Edray, Pocahontas Co., W. Va. 1860 Census. Prior service, McNeel's Co., 2nd VSL and Co. F, 11th Va. Cav. Enl. Hillsboro, Pocahontas Co., W. Va., 3/9/63 (4/17/63). Not stated if present or absent on muster-in roll dated 3/63. Present 1/1/64 - 2/29/64. Clothing issued 2/6/64. Ab. 9/1/64 - 10/31/64, AWOL since 9/22/64. Deserted. Surrendered at Charleston, W. Va., 3/65. Took the oath of allegiance and was sent North, 3/31/65. Desc.: age 27, 5'10", fair comp., dark hair and gray eyes. Occ. wagonmaker, residing in Greenbrier Co., W. Va. Post war resident of White Sulphur Dist., Greenbrier Co., W. Va. Member of David S. Creigh Camp, UCV, Lewisburg, W. Va. Post war resident of Hillsboro and Beard, W. Va., age 81 in 1924. d. 12/8/1927.

COCHRAN (COCHRANE), MORDICA THOMAS - Pvt. Co. F. b. Mt. Murphy, Pocahontas Co., W. Va., 1/21/31. Age 29, farmer, Pocahontas Co., W. Va. 1860 Census. Enl. Rockford, Harrison Co., W. Va., 5/3/63. Cpd. Pocahontas Co., W. Va., 12/21/63. Confined at the Atheneum Prison, 12/63. Desc.: age 32, 5'7 3/4", dark comp., dark hair and blue eyes. Transf. to Camp Chase, 12/64. Confined at Camp Chase, 1/1/64. Transf. to Ft. Delaware, 3/14/64. Confined at Ft. Delaware, 3/17/64. Ab. 1/1/64 - 2/29/64, in the hands of the enemy. DOD. Ft. Delaware, 6/18/64, acute dysentery. Ab. 9/1/64 - 10/31/64, cpd. 12/63; enl. bounty due. Bur. Finn's Pt. National Cem., NJ. Post war rosters show him in Co. I.

COCHRAN, PRESTON B. - 2nd Sgt. Co. H. Prior service, Co. G, 3rd VSL. Enl. Frankfort, Greenbrier Co., W. Va., 3/19/63 (Pocahontas Co., W. Va., 3/1/64). Not stated if present or absent on muster-in roll dated 3/63, 2nd Sgt. Ab. 9/1/64 - 10/31/64, AWOL. NFR.

COCHRAN, SAMUEL - Pvt. Co. I. Thought to have served in Co. K, 3rd VSL. Enl. Pocahontas Co., W. Va., 3/19/63. Present on muster-in roll dated 3/63. Mustered into service 3/19/63. NFR.

COCHRAN, SAMUEL B. - Pvt. Co. F. b. Pocahontas Co., W. Va., c. 1836. Age 24, farmer, Academy, Pocahontas Co., W. Va. 1860 Census. Prior service, McNeel's Co., 2nd VSL. Enl. Hillsboro, Pocahontas Co, W. Va., 3/9/63 (4/1/63). Not stated if present or absent on muster-in roll dated 3/63. Present 1/1/64 - 2/29/64. Ab. 9/1/64 - 10/31/64, AWOL since 10/20/64. NFR.

COCHRAN, WILLIAM C. - Pvt. Co. C. b. Pocahontas Co., W. Va., c. 1824. Age 36, farmer, Webster Co., W. Va. 1860 Census. Not on muster rolls. Cpd. Webster Co., W. Va., 12/31/63. Confined at the Atheneum Prison, 1/64. Desc.: age 40, 5'9", dark comp., dark hair and hazel eyes. Transf. to Camp Chase, 1/64. Confined at Camp Chase, 1/21/64. Transf. to Ft. Delaware, 3/14/64. Confined at Ft. Delaware, 3/17/64. DOD. Ft. Delaware, 6/18/64. Bur. Jersey Shore.

COFFMAN, JOHN W. - 1st Lt. Co. D. b. Harrison Co., W. Va., c. 1841. Resident of Harrison Co., W. Va. Prior service, Co. C, 3rd VSL. Cpd. and held at Wheeling, W. Va. and Sandusky, O., by 2/3/62. Released on his oath and bond by 2/8/62. Enl. Williamsburg, Greenbrier Co., W. Va., 3/8/63. POW record shows his enl. as Highland Co., 8/62. Not stated if present or absent on muster-in roll dated 3/63. 1st Lt., commanding Co., 10/22/63 - 12/10/63. Paid as 1st Lt., 1/1/64 - 8/31/64. Cpd. Upshur Co., W. Va. 4/5/65 (4/1/65). Sent to Clarksburg, W. Va., then to Cumberland, Md., 4/10/65. Desc.: age 24, 6'1", fair comp., dark hair and dark eyes. Occ. student, residing in Harrison Co., W. Va. Post war rosters show him as Capt. Post war farmer and resident of Harrison Co., W. Va. d. 11/?/1914. Bur. Elk View Cem., Clarksburg, W. Va.

COGAR, JOHN R. - Pvt. Co. B. b. Lewis Co., W. Va., c. 1821. Age 39, farmer, Webster Co., W. Va. 1860 Census. Prior service, Co. B, 3rd VSL. Enl. Frankfort, Greenbrier Co., W. Va., 3/7/63. Not stated if present or absent on muster-in roll dated 3/63. Age 59, farmer, Fork Lick, Webster Co., W. Va. 1880 Census. NFR.

COGAR, TOBIAS C. - Pvt. Co. B. b. Braxton Co., W. Va., c. 1846. Age 14, Webster Co., W. Va. 1860 Census. Enl. Greenbrier Co., W. Va., 9/1/63. Present 11/1/63 - 2/29/64, had his own horse until 2/1/64. Clothing issued 4/30/64 and 6/17/64, signs by x. Ab., 9/1/64 - 10/31/64, $100 enl. bounty due; wd. 8/31/64 and sent to hosp. Date of injury also as 8/26/64 and 7/17/64 at GS Ferry. Cpd. Winchester, 9/19/64. Adm. USA Depot Field Hosp., Winchester, 9/19/64, from the field, vulnus sclopeticum, compound fracture of skull. Removed bone fragments and dressed wd. Transf. 12/20/64. Adm. USA Gen. Hosp., West's Building, Baltimore, Md., from Winchester, 12/21/64, gunshot wd. to head, carrying away part of frontal bone. Adm. West Building, US Gen. Hosp., Baltimore, Md. Transf. to Ft. McHenry, 1/5/65. Transf. to Ft. McHenry Gen. Hosp., 1/5/65. Transf. to Pt. Lookout, 2/20/65. Evidently exchanged. Surrendered at Bulltown, W. Va., 5/9/65. Sent to Clarksburg, W. Va. Desc.: age 18, 5'6", fair comp., brown hair and hazel eyes. Occ. farmer, residing in Webster Co., W. Va. Paroled at Clarksburg, W. Va., to be exchanged, 5/12/65. Bur. Cogar Cem., Sugar Creek, Calhoun Co., W. Va. NFR.

COLLINS, JOHN W. - Pvt. Co. D. Prior service, Co. C, 3rd VSL. Enl. Williamsburg, Greenbrier Co., W. Va., 3/8/63. Not stated if present or absent on muster-in roll dated 3/63. Served in Co. B, 20th Va. Cav. NFR.

COLLINS, JOHN W. - Pvt. Co. H. b. Pike Co., Ky., c. 1836. Prior service, 3rd VSL. Enl. Pocahontas Co., W. Va., 6/1/63. POW record shows his enl. as Bulltown, W. Va., 10/62. Ab. 9/1/64 - 10/31/64, AWOL; enl. bounty due. Cpd. Webster Co., W. Va., 2/23/65. Sent to Clarksburg, W. Va., 2/26/65. Confined at Clarksburg, W. Va., 2/27/65. Desc.: age 29, 5'10", dark comp., black hair and hazel eyes. Occ. farmer, residing in Roane Co., W. Va. Transf. to Wheeling, W. Va., 2/28/65. Confined at the Atheneum Prison, 2/28/65. Desc.: age 29, 6', florid comp., dark hair and gray eyes. Transf. to Camp Chase, 3/1/65. Confined at Camp Chase, 3/2/65. Applied to take the oath of allegiance, 4/65, stating he was a conscript. Took the oath of allegiance and was released, 5/16/65. Desc.: age 33, 5'10_", dark comp., dark hair and gray eyes, a resident of Roane Co., W. Va. Card in his CSR shows him cpd. at Big Birch, Va., 4/24/65. NFR.

COLLINS, WILLIAM HUTCHISON - Pvt. Co. F. b. 3/23. Age 37, farmer, Greenbank, Pocahontas Co., W. Va. 1860 Census. Prior service, Co. B (G), 31st Va. Inf. Enl. Hillsboro, Pocahontas Co., W. Va., 7/20/63. Present 1/1/64 - 2/29/64. Fought against his brother Samuel, who was a member of the 10th W. Va. Inf., at Droop Mtn., 11/6/63. Clothing issued 2/6/64. Ab. 9/1/64 - 10/31/64, on detached service, attending horses; enl. bounty due. Paroled at Staunton, 5/19/65. Desc.: age 42, 6'2", dark comp., dark hair and blue eyes. Age 57, farmer, Green Banks, Pocahontas Co., W. Va. 1880 Census. d. 1904. Bur. Hosterman Cem.

COMPTON, JAMES M. - Pvt. Co. I. b.c. 1839. Not on muster rolls. Deserted. Surrendered at Charleston, W. Va., 3/65. Took the oath and was sent North, 3/30/65. Desc.: age 26, 5'11", dark comp., dark hair and hazel eyes, a farmer. NFR.

CONAWAY, L. D. - Pvt. Co. A. Not on muster rolls. Cpd. Beverly, W. Va., 7/5/63. Confined at Johnson's Island, 12/9/63. Note in his CSR states he came to Johnson's Island under the name of J. D. Duncan, with the assumed rank of Major. DOD. Johnson's Island, 1/15/64, consumption. Bur. Johnson's Island Confederate Cem., Sandusky, O., grave no. 105.

CONLEY (CONNOLLY, CONNELLY), THOMAS C. - Pvt. Co. E. b. Lewis Co., W. Va., c. 1834. Age 26, farmer, Calhoun Co., W. Va. 1860 Census. Prior service, Co. E, 3rd VSL. Enl. Frankfort, Greenbrier Co., W. Va., 3/13/63 (4/1/63). Not stated if present or absent on muster-in roll dated 3/63. Ab. 10/31/63 - 10/31/64, on horse detail, time expired. Employed as a teamster, 11/1/63 - 11/30/63, discharged 12/18/63. Clothing issued 3/1/64 and 6/17/64. Cpd. Calhoun Co., W. Va., 11/7/64 (10/29/64). Confined at the Atheneum Prison, 11/64. Desc.: age 31, 5'7_", dark comp., dark hair and black eyes. Occ. farmer, residing in Calhoun Co., W. Va. Transf. to Camp Chase, 11/29/64. Confined at Camp Chase, 11/30/64, desires to take the oath of allegiance. Statement at Camp Chase, 1/26/65, lists him as a resident of Calhoun Co., W. Va., age 33. Was arrested by the

110

Home Guards of Roane Co., W. Va., 10/29/64. States he was induced to enl. 9/1/62 for 12 months. At the expiration of his term, he was conscripted. Became sick 7/64 and was sent to a hosp. When well enough, he went to Pocahontas Co., W. Va., on sick leave, and was arrested while sick. Took the oath of allegiance and was released, 2/18/65. NFR.

CONLEY, WILLIAM - Pvt. Co. A. Served in Co. A, 3rd VSL. Post war rosters only, which show he was cpd. 1/28/63. NFR.

CONNOLLY (CONLEY), PERRY D. Sr. - Capt. Co. A. b. Kanawha (Lewis) Co., W. Va., 1837. Age 23, farmer, Calhoun Co., W. Va. 1860 Census. Desc. as "a large, powerful man, six feet three inches in height, agile and fleet of foot. He could walk eight miles an hour, keeping up this rapid pace for an indefinite period." Capt., Calhoun Co. Home Guards. Served in the 3rd VSL. Led the "outlaw" portion of the Moccasin Rangers. KIA. Webster Co., at the battle of Welch Glade, 1/2/62 (12/30/62). Badly wd., he continued to fight, until he was beaten to death by gunbutts. He was Capt of a partisan Co., the Moccasin Rangers, not a commissioned officer in the 19th Cav. Post war rosters list him as a member of Co. A, 19th Va. Cav. Bur. Bobbitt farm, near Cowen, W. Va. His brothers, Cornelius and James were US soldiers.

CONNELL, ROBERT - Pvt. Co. F. Post war rosters only. NFR.

CONRAD, JOHN - Pvt. Co. K. b. Lewis Co., W. Va., c. 1824. Age 36, farmer, Gilmer Co., W. Va. 1860 Census. Prior service, Co. I, 3rd VSL. Enl. Frankfort, Greenbrier Co., W. Va., 3/30/63. Not stated if present or absent on muster-in roll dated 3/63. NFR.

CONRAD, JOHN SUMMERFIELD - Pvt. Co. B. b. Braxton Co., W. Va., c. 1842. Grad. 1862 Columbia College, Washington, DC. Prior service, Co. B, 3rd VSL. Cpd. Braxton Co., W. Va., 6/23/62. Desc.: age 17, 5'7", dark comp., brown hair and black eyes. Confined at the Atheneum Prison by 8/3/62. Transf. to Camp Chase, 9/62. Confined at Camp Chase, 9/16/62. Exchanged. Enl. Frankfort, Greenbrier Co., W. Va., 3/9/63 (4/1/63). Not stated if present or absent on muster-in roll dated 3/63. Present 11/1/63 - 2/29/64, has one horse. Clothing issued 1st Qr. 1864, 2/11/64, 4/30/64 and 6/17/64, signs by x. Present 9/1/64 - 10/31/64, $100 enl. bounty due. Cpd. Braxton Co., W. Va., 11/8/64 (11/28/64), a horse thief and bushwhacker. Confined at the post guard house, Clarksburg, W. Va. Desc.: age 22, 5'7", dark comp., light hair and hazel eyes. Occ. farmer, residing in Braxton Co., W. Va. Transf. to Cumberland, Md., then to Camp Chase, 1/16/65. Confined at the Atheneum Prison, 1/14/65. Desc.: age 22, 5'5", fair comp., dark hair and hazel eyes. Transf. to Camp Chase, 1/16/65. Confined at Camp Chase, 1/17/65, desires to take the oath of allegiance. Took the oath of allegiance and was released, 6/13/65. Age 37, farm laborer, Kanawha Dist., Braxton Co., W. Va. 1880 Census. Post war professor at St. Dennis, Md. Alive 1891. NFR.

CONRAD, STANLEY - Pvt. Co. B. Post war rosters only, which show him as a resident of Braxton Co., W. Va. NFR.

CONWAY, ISAAC D. - Pvt. Co. E. b.c. 1828. Not on muster rolls. Cpd. Beverly, W. Va., 7/3/63. Confined at the Atheneum Prison, 7/8/63. Desc.: age 35, 6', dark comp., brown hair, blue eyes and dark whiskers. Occ. physician, residing in Wood Co., W. Va. Transf. to Camp Chase, 7/9/63. Confined at Camp Chase, 7/10/63. Transf. to Ft. Delaware, 7/14/63. Confined at Ft. Delaware, 7/63. NFR.

CONWAY, P. A. - Pvt. Co. B. Not on muster rolls. Adm. Chirnborazo Hosp. No. 3, 12/1/64, reason not stated. RTD. 1/7/65. NFR.

COOGER (COGER), SYLVESTER - Pvt. Co. K. Prior service, Co. I, 3rd VSL. Enl. Frankfort, Greenbrier Co., W. Va., 3/20/63. Not stated if present or absent on muster-in roll dated 3/63. NFR.

COOK, WILLIAM H. - Pvt. Co. C. b. Page Co., c. 1841. Prior service, Co. D, 3rd VSL. Enl. Frankfort, Greenbrier Co., W. Va., 3/15/63 (Pocahontas Co., W. Va., 4/1/63). Not stated if present or absent on muster-in roll dated 3/63. Present 1/1/63 - 4/1/63, had one horse. Ab. 12/31/63 - 8/31/64, AWOL since 7/20/64; has one horse. Clothing issued 2/2/64, 6/17/64 and 7/6/64. Ab. 9/1/64 - 10/31/64, AWOL since 7/20/64; has one horse. Cpd. Calhoun Co., W. Va., 12/11/64. Confined at the Atheneum Prison, 12/25/64. Desc.: age 23, 6'2", fair comp., light hair and gray eyes. Occ. farmer, residing in Jackson Co., W. Va. Transf. to Camp Chase, 12/27/64. Confined at Camp Chase, 12/28/64, desires to take the oath of allegiance. Took the oath of allegiance and was released, 5/15/65. Desc.: age 25, 6'2_", florid comp., dark hair and blue eyes. Post war resident of Kanawha Co., W. Va. Age 29 (1870). Age 39, farmer, Ravenswood Dist. 2, Jackson Co., W. Va. 1880 Census. NFR.

COON, GEORGE R. - 4th Corp. Co. D. Prior service, Co. C, 3rd VSL. Enl. Williamsburg, Greenbrier Co., W. Va., 3/8/63. Not stated if present or absent on muster-in roll dated 3/63, 4th Corp. Clothing issued as a Pvt., 2/7/64, 5/21/64, 6/17/64, 7/64 and 8/64, signs by x. NFR.

COON, WILLIAM - Pvt. Co. ?. b.c. 1834. Not on muster rolls. Cpd. Marion Co., W. Va., 6/29/64. Confined at the Atheneum Prison, 7/11/64. Desc.: age 30, 5'10_", fair comp., dark hair and hazel eyes. Occ. laborer, residing in Marion Co., W. Va. Transf. to Camp Chase, 7/14/64. Confined at Camp Chase, 7/64. Apparently exchanged. Cpd. Marion Co., W. Va., 12/24/64. Transf. to Camp Chase, 12/30/64. Sent to Cumberland, Md., then to Wheeling, W. Va. Confined at the Atheneum Prison, 12/24/64. Desc.: age 30, 5'10", fair comp., brown hair and gray eyes, a resident of Marion Co., W. Va. Took the oath of allegiance and was released, 6/26/65. NFR.

COON (KOON), WILLIAM W. - Pvt. Co. D. Prior service, Co. C, 3rd VSL. Enl. Williamsburg, Greenbrier Co., W. Va., 3/8/63. Not stated if present or absent on muster-in roll dated 3/63. Employed as a teamster 11/1/63 - 11/30/63, signs by x. Clothing issued 11/30/63, 2/7/64, 4/1/64 and 6/17/64. Clothing issued at Staunton, 7/29/64, while on his way to his command. Surrendered at Shepherdstown, W. Va., 8/3/64. Confined at the Old Capitol Prison, 8/8/64. Transf. to Elmira, NY, 8/12/64. Confined at Elmira Prison, 8/12/64. Desires to take the oath of allegiance, 9/15/64. Took the oath of allegiance and was released, 5/17/65. Desc.: age ?, 5'6_", dark comp., auburn hair and blue eyes, a resident of Farmington, W. Va. Signs oath by x. States he was conscripted 1/20/64 and remained at home near Shepherdstown, W. Va., on detached duty until 8/3/64, when he surrendered. Surrendered for protection to the Lt. Col. of the 14th Pa. Cav., for protection. NFR.

COOPER, CHARLES SLAVENS - 1st Corp. Co. E. b. Lewis Co., W. Va., 1844. Age 16, farmer, Gilmer Co., W. Va. 1860 Census. Prior service, Co. C, 3rd VSL. Enl. Frankfort, Greenbrier Co., W. Va., 3/13/63 (4/1/63). Not stated if present or absent on muster-in roll dated 3/63, 1st Corp. Ab., Pvt., 10/31/63 - 10/31/64, POW since 7/15/64; had his own horse since 7/15/64. Clothing issued 3/1/64, 5/26/64 and 6/17/64. Cpd. Loudoun Co., 7/15/64. Sent to Harpers Ferry, W. Va., then to Washington, DC, 7/64. Confined at the Old Capitol Prison, 7/17/64. Transf. to Elmira, NY, 7/23/64. Confined at Elmira Prison, 7/25/64. Paroled for exchange, 3/14/65. Exchanged at Bouleware's Wharf, James River, 3/18/65. Present on a MR of paroled and exchanged prisoners at Camp Lee, near Richmond, 3/20/65. Paroled at Charleston, W. Va., 5/11/65. Desc.: age 21, 5'10", dark comp., dark hair and gray eyes. Age 36, farmer, Troy Dist., Gilmer Co., W. Va. 1880 Census. Nephew of Joseph W. Cooper; brother of George W. Cooper; brother-in-law of Jacob S. Hall. d. 1921.

COOPER, GEORGE WILLIAM - 2nd Sgt. Co. E. b. Lewis Co., W. Va., 1840. Age 19, farmer, Gilmer Co., W. Va. 1860 Census. Prior service, Co. E, 3rd VSL. Enl. Frankfort, Greenbrier Co., W. Va., 3/13/63. Not stated if present or absent on muster-in roll dated 3/63, 2nd Sgt. Ab., Pvt., 10/31/63 - 10/31/64, had his own horse since 7/1/64; KIA. Waterford (Water Ville), Loudoun Co., 7/15/64, shot through the head. Clothing issued 3/1/64, 4/11/64, 4/30/64 and 6/17/64, signs by x. Nephew of Joseph W. Cooper; brother of Charles S. Cooper. Post war source shows he was KIA. Fisher's Hill, 9/64.

COOPER, JOSEPH WILLIAM - Pvt. Co. I. b. Cooper Run, near Greenbank, Pocahontas Co., W. Va., 4/18/23. Age 37, farmer, Pocahontas Co., W. Va. 1860 Census. May have served in the 60th Va. Inf. Thought to have served in Co. K, 3rd VSL. Enl. Huntersville, Pocahontas Co., W. Va., 3/18/63 (2/18/63). Present on muster-in roll dated 3/63. Mustered into service 3/19/63. Ab. 6/30/63 - 2/29/64, sick; does not have a horse. Present 2/29/64 - 8/31/64. Sent home 2/64, to recuperate from an illness. Ab. 9/1/64 - 10/31/64, cpd. Fisher's Hill, 9/23/64. Clothing issued 6/17/64. Cpd. Strasburg, 9/23/64. Sent to Harpers Ferry, W. Va., then to Pt. Lookout, 9/30/64. Confined at Pt. Lookout, 10/3/64. Paroled for exchange, 2/18/65. Exchanged at Bouleware's Wharf, James River, 2/65. Present on a MR of paroled and exchanged prisoners at Camp Lee, near Richmond, 2/28/65. Adm. Gen. Hosp. No. 9, 2/27/65. Furloughed 2/28/65, 30 days. Post war roster shows him as a member of Co. C. Post war resident of Greenbank, W. Va. Age 57, farmer, Green Banks, Pocahontas Co., W. Va. 1880 Census. Uncle of George W. and Charles S. Cooper. d. near Greenbank, Pocahontas Co., W. Va., 4/29/98. Bur. Warwick Cem., Greenbank, W. Va.

COOPER, WILLIAM - Pvt. Co. I. Not on muster rolls. Clothing issued 9/30/64. NFR.

CORBETT, MUSTOE HAMILTON - Pvt. Co. A. b. Highland Co., 10/8/42. Age 17, farmhand, Green Bank, Pocahontas Co., W. Va. 1860 Census. Prior service, 2nd Co. I, 25th Va. Inf. and 2nd Co. G, 18th Va. Cav. Not on muster rolls. Clothing issued 3/21/64 and 6/17/64. Surrendered at Huntersville, W. Va., 4/18/65. Desc.: age 22, 6 3/4", fair comp., fair hair and gray eyes. Occ. farmer, residing in Pocahontas Co., W. Va. Confined at Clarksburg, W. Va., 4/25/65. Took the oath of allegiance and was paroled until exchanged, 4/25/65. Post war resident of Mustoe, Highland Co. Post war farmer and resident of Mustoe, Va. and Pickney, W. Va. Age 38, farmer, Huntersville Dist., Pocahontas Co., W. Va. 1880 census. Age 57, farmer, Monterey Dist., Highland Co. 1900 census. Attended the Washington Confed. Reunion, 1917. d. Mustoe, 3/14/1926. Bur. Hamilton Church Cem., Highland Co.

CORLEY, ALLEN LEWIS - Pvt. Co. F. b. Randolph Co., W. Va., 7/3/26 (7/3/36). Moved to Braxton, 1858. Not on muster rolls. Cpd. Braxton Co., W. Va., 4/3/65 (4/1/65). Post war roster shows he was cpd. 3/65. Sent to Cumberland, Md., then to Wheeling, W. Va. Confined at the Atheneum Prison, 4/11/65. Desc.: age 39, 5'10", fair comp., dark hair and gray eyes. Occ. farmer, residing in Braxton Co., W. Va. Transf. to Camp Chase, 4/13/65. Confined at Camp Chase, 4/14/65. Took the oath of allegiance and was released, 5/15/65, a resident of Braxton Co., W. Va. Post war roster shows he served in the Commissary Dept., buying and driving cattle, until 3/65. Post war rosters list him as a member of Co. H. Post war farmer, grazier and lumberman, residing at Frametown, Braxton Co., W. Va. Age 52, farmer, Burch Dist., Braxton Co., W. Va. 1880 Census. d. Frametown, W. Va., 8/18/98.

COTTERAL (COTTRIL), MARSHALL R. - Pvt. Co. H. Prior service, Co. G, 3rd VSL. Enl. Frankfort, Greenbrier Co., W. Va., 3/19/63. Not stated if present or absent on muster-in roll dated 3/63. Clothing issued 2/7/64 and 3/11/64. Ab. 9/1/64 - 10/31/64, AWOL. NFR.

COTTERAL, SINETT J. - Pvt. Co. H. Prior service, Co. G, 3rd VSL. Enl. Frankfort, Greenbrier Co., W. Va., 3/19/63. Not stated if present or absent on muster-in roll dated 3/63. NFR.

COUGHREN, M. C. - Pvt. Co. A. b.c. 1830. Not on muster rolls. Cpd. Pocahontas Co., W. Va., 12/21/63. Confined at the Atheneum Prison, 12/31/63. Desc.: age 33, 5'7", dark comp., dark hair and blue eyes. Occ. farmer, residing in Pocahontas Co., W. Va. Transf. to Camp Chase 12/31/63. NFR.

COULTER, CHARLES - Pvt. Co. F. Prior service, McNeel's Co., VSL. Enl. Hillsboro, Pocahontas Co., W. Va., 3/9/63. Not stated if present or absent on muster-in roll dated 3/63. NFR.

COULTER, GEORGE J. - Pvt. Co. F. b.c. 1830. Age 30, farmer, Dunmore, Pocahontas Co., W. Va. 1860 Census. Post war rosters only. NFR.

COURTNEY, GEORGE W. - Pvt. Co. F. b.c. 1846. Age 14, Pocahontas Co., W. Va. 1860 Census. Enl. Staunton, 7/1/64. Ab. 9/1/64 - 10/31/64, on horse detail. NFR.

COX, G. WARREN - Pvt. Co. G./F&S QM Sgt. b.c. 1837. Enl. Pocahontas Co., W. Va., 9/8/63. Present, QM Sgt., F&S MR 9/1/63 - 10/31/63, appointed 9/15/63; has his own horse. Present, QM Sgt., F&S MR 11/1/63 - 12/31/63, has his own horse. Present, Pvt., 9/1/64 - 10/31/64, detailed in QM Dept.; has a serviceable horse. Paroled at Staunton, 5/1/65. Desc.: age 28, 5'10", light comp., brown hair and gray eyes, a resident of New Orleans, La. NFR.

COX, ROBERT GARLAND - Pvt. Co. A. b.c. 1844. Age 16, farmer, Randolph Co., W. Va. 1860 Census. Prior service, Co. F, 31st Va. Inf. Not on muster rolls. Cpd. Bath Co. (Pocahontas Co., W. Va.), 8/22/63. Confined at the Atheneum Prison, 9/6/63. Desc.: age 19, 6', light comp., brown hair and gray eyes. Occ. farmer, residing in Randolph Co., W. Va. Transf. to Camp Chase, 9/7/63. Confined at Camp Chase, 9/8/63. Transf. to Rock Island, Ill., 1/22/64. Confined at Rock Island Prison, Barracks 80, 1/24/64. Adm. USA Gen. Hosp., Rock Island, Ill., 10/9/64, inflamed liver. DOD. Rock Island, Ill., 10/14/64, pneumonia. Bur. Rock Island, Ill. CSR also lists him as Co. B.

CRACRAFT, GEORGE A. - Major/Surgeon. b. Pa., 1815. Prior service, Brig. Gen. A. G. Jenkin's Cav. Banished from Triadelphia, 1863, because of his Southern sympathies. Appointed surgeon 6/13/63. Present F&S MR 9/1/63 - 10/31/63. Paid for service 11/1/63 - 1/31/64. Father of William A. Cracraft, 20th Va. Cav. d. 4/88.

CRANFORD, ——— - Acting Adjutant. Not on muster rolls. Received "honorable mention" from Lt. Col. W. P. Thompson in his report of the battle of Droop Mtn., W. Va., 11/6/63. NFR.

CREEL, GEORGE - Pvt. Co. A. Prior service, Co. A, 3rd VSL. Post war rosters only. NFR.

CROPP, EDGAR V. - Pvt. Co. G. Prior service, Co. I, 3rd VSL. Enl. Frankfort, Greenbrier Co., W. Va., 3/12/63. Not stated if present or absent on muster-in roll dated 3/63. Clothing issued 3/1/64, 4/1/64 and 5/26/64. Drew a pension in Okla. NFR.

CROSS, SOLOMON H. - Pvt. Co. D. b.c. 1838. Enl. Pocahontas Co., W. Va., 6/21/63. Transf. to Co. C, 19th Va. Cav. Ab. 12/31/63 - 8/31/64, has one horse; cpd. 10/20/63, since vol. in Yankee army. Cpd. Jackson Co., W. Va., 10/22/63. Confined at the Atheneum Prison, 10/29/63. Desc.: age 24, 5'10 7/8", fair comp., light hair, blue eyes and dark sandy whiskers. Occ. farmer, residing in Jackson Co., W. Va. Transf. to 10/30/63. Confined at Camp Chase, 10/31/63. Isaac Cross, his brother, obtained his release by a petition signed by Union officers. Took the oath of allegiance and was released by order of the Sec. of War,

1/5/64. To avoid capture by CSA troops, he enl. in Co. K, 11th W. Va. Inf., with his brother John M. Cross. Age 42, farmer, Grant Dist., Jackson Co., W. Va. 1880 Census. NFR.

CUMMINGS, GIDEON M. (W.) - Pvt. Co. A. b.c. 1846. Post war rosters show service in 19th Va. Cav. Served in Co. F, 20th Va. Cav. DOD. Johnson's Island, O. Bur. Johnson's Island Confederate Cem.

CUMMINS, WILLIAM R. - Pvt. Co. K. Prior service, Co. I, 3rd VSL. Enl. Frankfort, Greenbrier Co., W. Va., 3/20/63. Not stated if present or absent on muster-in roll dated 3/63. NFR.

CUNNINGHAM, WILLIAM D. - Pvt. Co. D. Prior service, Co. C, 3rd VSL. Enl. Williamsburg, Greenbrier Co., W. Va., 3/8/63. Not stated if present or absent on muster-in roll dated 3/63. Furloughed 1/4/65. Served in Co. B, 20th Va. Cav. NFR.

CURNEY, GEORGE S. - Pvt. Co. D. b.c. 1847. Not on muster rolls. Enl. Pocahontas Co., W. Va., 5/63. Deserted. Surrendered at Clarksburg, W. Va., 8/6/64. Desc.: age 17, 5'7", dark comp., black hair and brown eyes. Occ. farmer, residing in Taylor Co., W. Va. Took the oath of allegiance and was released, 8/9/64. NFR.

CURRANCE (CURRENCE), ADAM C. - Pvt. Co. I. b.c. 1843. Age 18, farmer, Randolph Co., W. Va. 1860 Census. Enl. Beverly, W. Va., 4/30/63. Present 6/30/63 - 2/29/64, mounted. Present 2/29/64 - 8/31/64. Present 9/1/64 - 10/31/64, $100 enl. bounty due. Paroled at Charleston, W. Va., 5/10/65. Desc.: age 22, 5'10", fair comp., brown hair and blue eyes. Age 38, farmer, Mingo, Randolph Co., W. Va. 1880 Census. d. by 1916. Bur. Mill Creek Cem., Randolph Co., W. Va.

CURRENCE, JOHN - Pvt. Co. I. Post war rosters only. Most likely Jonathan H. Currence. NFR.

CURRENCE, JONATHAN H. - 2nd Corp. Co. I. b.c. 1834. Enl. Beverly, W. Va., 4/30/63. Present, 2nd Corp., mounted. Present 2/29/64 - 8/31/64. Clothing issued 7/64 and 8/64. Present 9/1/64 - 10/31/64, $100 enl. bounty due. Paroled at Mt. Sidney, 5/8/65. Desc.: age 31, 6', light comp., light hair and blue eyes. Post war rosters show him as Sgt. of couriers, Lomax's Div. Post war resident of Randolph Co., W. Va. Age 49, farmer, Middle Fork, Randolph Co., W. Va. 1880 Census. Served as constable of Huttonsville Dist., 7 years. Served as Mayor of Mill Creek, Randolph Co., W. Va. Attended Confederate Reunion, Randolph Co., W. Va., 1906. Cross of honor awarded, 1/20/1908. Attended Gettysburg Reunion, 1913. Resident of Mill Creek, W. Va., 1924. Bur. Crouch Cem., Randolph Co., W. Va.

CURRENCE, LABEN D. - Pvt. Co. I. b.c. 1829. Age 31, farmer, Randolph Co., W. Va. 1860 Census. Enl. Beverly, W. Va., 4/30/63. Ab. 6/30/63 - 2/29/64, recruited in enemy lines, not yet reported. NFR.

CURRY, BASIL - Pvt. Co. ?. Post war rosters only, which show he was a resident of Ritchie Co., W. Va. Brother of Elmer Curry. NFR.

CURRY, ELMER (ELMORE) - Pvt. Co. ?. Post war rosters only, which show he was a resident of Ritchie Co., W. Va. Brother of Basil Curry. NFR.

CURRY, JAMES C. - Pvt. Co. I. Resident of Ritchie Co., W. Va. Enl. Huntersville, Pocahontas Co., W. Va., 4/15/64. Present 2/29/64 - 8/31/64, mounted; enl. bounty due. Present 9/1/64 - 10/31/64. KIA. Gordonsville, no date. Post war rosters also list him as having been KIA. Appomattox. NFR.

CURRY, JOSEPH - Pvt. Co. ?. Post war rosters only, which show he was from Ritchie Co., W. Va. NFR.

CURRY, MILTON - Sgt. Co. D. b. Taylor Co., W. Va., 9/20/33. Not on muster rolls. Enl. Pocahontas Co., W. Va., 7/63. Clothing issued 1st Qr. 1864 and 7/10/64. Deserted. Surrendered at Grafton, W. Va., 3/11/65. Sent to Clarksburg, W. Va. Took the amnesty oath and was sent North, 3/12/65. Confined at the Atheneum Prison, 3/13/65. Desc.: age 31, 6', light comp., light hair and gray eyes. Occ. farmer, residing in Ritchie Co., W. Va. d. 5/25/1915. Bur. Harmony Grove Cem., Pruntytown, Taylor Co., W. Va.

CURRY, MORGAN - Pvt. Co. I. b. Hot Springs, Bath Co., 12/27/44. Age 14 (?), Bath CH, Bath Co. 1860 Census. Enl. Huntersville, Pocahontas Co., W. Va., 5/20/64. Present 2/29/64 - 8/31/64, mounted; enl. bounty due. Ab. 9/1/64 - 10/31/64, on horse detail. Post war farmer and resident of Edray, W. Va. Age 36, farm laborer, Huntersville, Pocahontas Co., W. Va. 1880 Census. d. Edray, Pocahontas Co., W. Va., 2/3/1926. Bur. Dunmore Cem., Pocahontas Co., W. Va.

CURTAIN, ANDREW - Pvt. Co. G. b.c. 1844. Not on muster rolls. Deserted. Surrendered at Charleston, W. Va., 3/6/65. Took the amnesty oath and was sent North, 3/6/65. Desc.: age 21, 6'1", dark comp., light hair and gray eyes, a farmer. NFR.

CUSTER, JAMES P. - Pvt. Co. A. Prior service, Co. A, 3rd VSL. Post war rosters only. NFR.

CUTLIP, DAVID H. - Pvt. Co. H. b. Nicholas Co., W. Va., c. 1848. Age 12, Webster Co., W. Va. 1860 Census. Prior service, Co. G, 3rd VSL. Enl. Frankfort, Greenbrier Co., W. Va., 3/19/63 (Pocahontas Co., W. Va., 8/1/63). Not stated if present or absent on muster-in roll dated 3/63. Ab. 9/1/64 - 10/31/64, AWOL. NFR.

CUTLIP, GEORGE - Pvt. Co. A. b.c. 1844. Not on muster rolls. Clothing issued 2/19/64, 2/23/64 and 5/21/64, signed by x. Adm. CSA Gen. Hosp., Charlottesville, 6/12/64, catarrhous. Transf. to a convalescent camp near Charlottesville, 6/18/64. Paroled at Charleston, W. Va., 5/10/65. Desc.: age 21, 5'6", dark comp., dark hair, blue eyes and dark whiskers. NFR.

CUTLIP, JACKSON - Pvt. Co. H. b. Nicholas Co., W. Va., c. 1828. Age 34 (?), farmer, Webster Co., W. Va. 1860 Census. Prior service, Co. G, 3rd VSL. Enl. Frankfort, Greenbrier Co., W. Va., 3/19/63 (Pocahontas Co., W. Va., 8/1/63). Not stated if present or absent on muster-in roll dated 3/63. Ab. 9/1/64 - 10/31/64, AWOL. Cpd. Webster Co., W. Va., 3/25/64. Confined at the Atheneum Prison, 4/22/64. Desc.: age 36, 6'1 1/2", florid comp., dark hair and blue eyes. Occ. farmer, residing in Braxton Co., W. Va. Transf. to Camp Chase, 5/6/64. Desires to take the oath of allegiance, 5/11/64. DOD. Camp Chase, 3/4/65, pneumonia. Bur. Camp Chase Confederate Cem., 1/3 mile South of Camp Chase, grave no. 1532.

CUTLIP, JOHN (JOHNSEY) F. - Pvt. Co. F. b.c. 1830. Age 30, farmhand, Pocahontas Co., W. Va. 1860 Census. Prior service, McNeel's Co., 2nd VSL. Adm. Staunton Gen. Hosp., 1/15/63, diphtheria. Present, Hosp. MR, Staunton Gen. Hosp., 3/63, nurse 3/18/63 - 3/31/63. DOD. Staunton, 6/13/63, pneumonia. Records show his unit as "Pocahontas Cavalry." Enl. Hillsboro, Pocahontas Co., W. Va., 3/9/63. Not stated if present or absent on muster-in roll dated 3/63. Age 51, farmer, Little Levels, Pocahontas Co., W. Va. 1880 Census. NFR.

CUTLIP, THOMAS - Pvt. Co. H. Prior service, Co. G, 3rd VSL. Enl. Frankfort, Greenbrier Co., W. Va., 3/19/63 (Pocahontas Co., W. Va., 8/1/63). Not stated if present or absent on muster-in roll dated 3/63. Ab. 9/1/64 - 10/31/64, AWOL. NFR.

CUTLIP, WILLIAM W. - Pvt. Co. K. b. Braxton Co., W. Va., c. 1846. Age 14, Webster Co., W. Va. 1860 Census. Prior service, Co. I, 3rd VSL. Enl. Frankfort, Greenbrier Co., W. Va., 3/20/63. Not stated if present or absent on muster-in roll dated 3/63. NFR.

DAILEY, WILLIAM A. - Pvt. Co. H. b.c. 1843. Prior service, Co. G, 3rd VSL. Not on muster rolls. Cpd. near Little Cacapon (Romney), W. Va., 3/17/63 (3/10/63). Desc.: age 20, 5'11", light comp., light hair and gray eyes. Confined at Ft. McHenry, 4/17/63. Paroled and sent to Ft. Monroe, on the way to City Point, to be exchanged, 4/19/63. NFR.

DAVIDSON, ISRAEL S. - Pvt. Co. E. b.c. 1844. Prior service, Co. E, 3rd VSL. Enl. Frankfort, Greenbrier Co., W. Va., 3/12/63 (4/1/63). Not stated if present or absent on muster-in roll dated 3/63. Present 10/31/63 - 10/31/64, had his own horse since 12/20/63. Clothing issued 3/1/64 and 6/17/64. Deserted. Surrendered at Clarksburg, W. Va., 3/65. Took the amnesty oath, 5/23/65 and was sent North. Desc.: age 20, 5'6", fair comp., fair hair and gray eyes. Occ. farmer, residing in Gilmer Co., W. Va. Age 26, farmer, Gilmer Co., W. Va. 1870 Census. Age 36, farming, DeKalb Dist., Gilmer Co., W. Va. 1880 Census. NFR.

DAVIS, EDWARD - Pvt. Co. C. Prior service, Co. D, 3rd VSL. Enl. Pocahontas Co., W. Va., 4/1/63. Served in Co. F, 20th Va. Cav. Transf. back to Co. C, 19th Va. Cav. Present 12/31/63 - 8/31/64, had his own horse since 7/1/64. Clothing issued 2/25/64, 4/30/64, 5/1/64 and 6/17/64. Ab. 9/1/64 - 10/31/64, went on horse detail for 16 days 9/1/64; wd. while going through enemy lines; absent yet; has one horse. Probably Edward Davis, Co. G, 20th Va. Cav. NFR.

DAVIS, JAMES C. - Pvt. Co. H. Not on muster rolls. Clothing issued 3/11/64. Transf. to Co. B, 46th Battn. Va. Cav., 3/1/64. NFR.

DAVIS, JOHN P. - Pvt. Co. H. Prior service, Co. G, 3rd VSL. Enl. Frankfort, Greenbrier Co., W. Va., 3/19/63 (Pocahontas Co., W. Va., 6/1/63). Not stated if present or absent on muster-in roll dated 3/63. Ab. 9/1/64 - 10/31/64, AWOL. NFR.

DAVIS, JOSEPH C. - Pvt. Co. K. Prior service, Co. I, 3rd VSL. Enl. Frankfort, Greenbrier Co., W. Va., 3/20/63. Not stated if present or absent on muster-in roll dated 3/63. Clothing issued 2/7/64. NFR.

DAVIS, OWEN V. B. - Pvt. Co. H. Prior service, Co. A, 3rd VSL. Enl. Frankfort, Greenbrier Co., W. Va., 3/19/63. Not stated if present or absent on muster-in roll dated 3/63. Post war rosters show him as being in Co. A, a resident of Nicholas Co., W. Va. KIA. Droop Mtn..

DAVIS, REYNOLDS (RUNNELS) - 1st Lt. Co. B. Resident of Braxton Co., W. Va. Prior service, Co. B and F&S, 3rd VSL. Enl. Frankfort, Greenbrier Co., W. Va., 4/1/63. Appraised horses with W. H. Justice, 8/22/63. Present, 1st Lt., 11/1/63 - 2/29/64, commanding co. Ab. 9/1/64 - 10/31/64, wd. Cedar Creek (Winchester) 9/19/64. DOW. Woodstock, 9/26/64. CSR listed as Runnels Davis.

DAVIS, SIMEON T. - Pvt. Co. H. Enl. Pocahontas Co., W. Va., 6/1/63. Ab. 9/1/64 - 10/31/64, AWOL. NFR.

DAVIS, WILLIAM H. - Pvt. Co. G. b. Rockingham Co., 6/11/16. Moved to Roane Co., W. Va. Prior service, Co. F, 3rd VSL. Enl. Frankfort, Greenbrier Co., W. Va., 3/12/63. Not stated if present or absent on muster-in roll dated 3/63. Post war source states he served two years. Age 65, milling, Geary Dist., Roane Co., W. Va. 1880 Census. d. Roane Co., W. Va., 1/25/81.

DEARING (DERING), GEORGE M. - Capt. Co. A. b.c. 1835. Resident of Hampshire Co., W. Va. Arrested and confined by 3/15/62. Charged as being a rebel mail carrier. Prior service, Co. A, 3rd VSL. Post war rosters only, which show he was Asst. QM., and a resident of Germantown, Md. Member Army and Navy Society, Md. Line Association. Entered Old Soldier's Home, Pikesville, Md., 6/23/89, age 54, from Montgomery Co., Md., a merchant. d. Germantown, Md., 3/11/1913 (4/8/94). Bur. Loudoun Park Cem., Baltimore, Md.

DEEM (DEAN), COMMODORE D. - Pvt. Co. b. Wirt Co., W. Va., c. 1843. Enl. Pocahontas Co., W. Va., 7/1/63. POW record shows enl. as Camp Miller, Pocahontas (Greenbrier) Co., W. Va., 8/63. Present 12/31/63 - 8/31/64, has one horse. Clothing issued 6/17/64, 7/64, 8/64 and 3rd Qr. 1864. Present 9/1/64 - 10/31/64, has one horse; $100 enl. bounty due. Cpd. Ritchie Co., W. Va., 2/11/65. Also listed as cpd. in Wirt Co. and Tucker Co., W. Va. Sent to Clarksburg, W. Va., Cumberland, Md., then to Wheeling, W. Va., 2/13/65. Confined at the Atheneum Prison, 2/15/65. Desc.: age 22, 5'10", light comp., brown hair and gray eyes. Occ. farmer, residing in Pocahontas Co., W. Va. Sent to Camp Chase, 2/21/65. Confined at Camp Chase, 2/22/65. Took the oath of allegiance and was released, 6/13/65. Desc.: age 21, 5'9", dark comp, dark hair and blue eyes, a resident of Ritchie Co., W. Va. Age 32, farmer, South Grant Dist., Ritchie Co., W. Va. 1880 Census. NFR.

DeLACEY, PACKINGHAM - Pvt. Co. A. Prior service, Co. A, 3rd VSL. Enl. Williamsburg, Greenbrier Co., W. Va., 3/1/63. Not stated if present or absent on muster-in roll dated 3/63. NFR.

DELANEY (DULANEY), JAMES - Pvt. Co. ?. Post war rosters, which show he was a resident of Ritchie Co., W. Va. NFR.

DELANEY (DULANEY), PATRICK - Pvt. Co. ?. Post war rosters only, which show he was a resident of Ritchie Co., W. Va. and that he was KIA. Standing Stone Creek. NFR.

DeMOSS, NATHANIEL - Pvt. Co. C. Gravestone shows service in this unit. Bur. DeMoss Cem., near the Ritchie - Wood Co., W. Va. line. NFR.

DENNISON, JOHN S. - Pvt. Co. D. Prior service, Co. C, 3rd VSL. Enl. Williamsburg, Greenbrier Co., W. Va., 3/8/63. Not stated if present or absent on muster-in roll dated 3/63. Served in Co. B, 20th Va. Cav. NFR.

DENT, CHARLES (CYRUS, SYRUS) M. - Pvt. Co. C. Prior service, Co. D, 3rd VSL. Enl. Frankfort, Greenbrier Co., W. Va., 3/15/63. Not stated if present or absent on muster-in roll dated 3/63. Ab. 1/1/63 - 4/1/63, deserted 9/20/62, had one horse. NFR.

DENT, CORNELIUS B. - Pvt. Co. C. b. Monongalia Co., W. Va., 3/24/43. Age 7, 1850 Wirt Co., W. Va. Census. Prior service, Co. D, 3rd VSL. Arrested and held at Wheeling, W. Va. Released on his oath by 3/13/62. Prior service, Co. D, 3rd VSL. Present, 3rd Corp., 1/1/63 - 4/1/63, had one horse. Post war rosters only for service in the 19th Va. Cav. Age 37, farmer, Burning Springs, Wirt Co., W. Va. 1880 Census. d. 7/24/1917. Bur. Wolverton Cem., Wirt Co., W. Va.

DENT, JAMES - Pvt. Co. A. b.c. 1819. Prior service, Co. A, 3rd VSL. Not on muster rolls. Cpd. Roane Co., W. Va., 5/18/63. Confined at the Atheneum Prison, 5/21/63. Desc.: age 44, 5'9", florid comp., dark hair and blue eyes. Occ. farmer, residing in Wirt Co., W. Va. Sent to Camp Chase, 5/25/63. Confined at Camp Chase, 5/26/63. Transf. to Johnson's Island, 6/14/63. Confined at Johnson's Island, 6/14/63. Transf. to Pt. Lookout, 11/3/63. Confined at Pt. Lookout, 11/4/63. DOD. Pt. Lookout, 11/20/63. Bur. Pt. Lookout, Md.

DENT, MARSHAL M. - Pvt. Co. C. b. 2/22/44. Prior service, Co. D, 3rd VSL. Enl. Frankfort, Greenbrier Co., W. Va., 3/15/63 (Pocahontas Co., W. Va., 4/1/63). POW records shows he enl. Wytheville, 8/62. Not stated if present or absent on muster-in roll dated 3/63. Present 1/1/63 - 4/1/63, had one horse. Cpd. Roane Co., W. Va., 5/19/63. Confined at the Atheneum Prison, 5/21/63. Desc.: age 19, 5'9_", fresh comp., sandy hair and gray eyes. Occ. farmer, residing in Wirt Co., W. Va. Sent to Camp Chase, 5/25/63. Confined at Camp Chase, 5/26/63. Transf. to Johnson's Island, 6/14/63. Confined at Johnson's Island, 6/14/63. Transf. to Pt. Lookout, 11/3/63. Confined at Pt. Lookout, 11/4/63. Ab. 12/31/63 - 8/31/64, cpd. 5/15/63; $50 enl. bounty due; has one horse. Ab. 9/1/64 - 10/31/64, cpd. 5/15/63; $100 enl. bounty due; has one horse. Exchanged 9/30/64. Adm. Chimborazo Hosp. No. 1, 10/7/64, diarrhoea. Furloughed 10/10/64, 60 days, to Washington Co. Present Hosp. MR, Chimborazo Hosp. No. 1, 10/10/64, paroled prisoner, sick. Clothing issued at Chimborazo Hosp. No. 1, 10/13/64. Paroled at Charleston, W. Va., 5/24/65. Desc.: age 21, 5'8_", sandy comp., red hair and gray eyes. Age 36, farmer, Elizabeth Dist., Wirt Co., W. Va. 1880 Census. d. 10/27/1902. Bur. Palestine Cem., Wirt Co., W. Va.

DENT, RICHARD M. - Pvt. Co. C. Prior service, Co. D, 3rd VSL. Enl. Frankfort, Greenbrier Co., W. Va., 3/15/63. Not stated if present or absent on muster-in roll dated 3/63. Present 1/1/63 - 4/1/63, had one horse. NFR.

DENT, WILLIAM B. - 4th Corp. Co. C. b. 7/22/42. Prior service, Co. D, 3rd VSL. Enl. Frankfort, Greenbrier Co., W. Va., 3/15/63. Not stated if present or absent on muster-in roll dated 3/63, 4th Corp. Present, 4th Corp., 1/1/63 - 4/1/63, had one horse. KIA. Elizabeth, Wirt Co., W. Va., 5/16/63. Bur. Palestine Cem., Wirt Co., W. Va.

DEPUE, DAVID - Pvt. Co. H. b.c. 1816. Enl. Roane Co., W. Va., 6/20/63. Ab. 9/1/64 - 10/31/64, AWOL. Age 64, farmer, Ravenswood Dist. 2, Jackson Co., W. Va. 1880 Census. NFR.

DEPUE, HENRY - Pvt. Co. H. b.c. 1841. Enl. Roane Co., W. Va., 6/20/63. Ab. 9/1/64 - 10/31/64, AWOL. Age 39, farmer, Spencer Dist., Roane Co., W. Va. NFR.

DEVER (DEVIER), JOHN - Pvt. Co. I. Prior service, Cc. B, 31st W. Va. Inf. Over 45 years of age, by 8/4/63. Enl. Huntersville, Pocahontas Co., W. Va., 4/27/64. Present 2/29/64 - 8/31/64, mounted; enl. bounty due. Clothing issued 6/17/64, 7/64 and 8/64. Ab. 9/1/64 - 10/31/64, AWOL since 10/30/64; $100 bond due. NFR.

DeWEES, BALAS CARR - Pvt. Co. ?. b. Jackson Co., W. Va., 8/25/28. Mexican War veteran. Post war source only, which state he, George Casto and Squire W. W. Bailey joined Jackson's command in the fall of 1863. These men took part in the fight at Bulltown, W. Va., 10/13/63. NFR.

DeWEES, DANIEL S. - Pvt. Co. K. b. on Swan Survey, mouth of Steer Run, Gilmer Co., W. Va., 3/11/21. Age 39, farmer, Braxton Co., W. Va. 1860 Census. Prior service, Co. I, 3rd VSL. Enl. Frankfort, Greenbrier Co., W. Va., 3/20/63. Not stated if present or absent on muster-in roll dated 3/63. Cpd. Webster Co., W. Va., 12/31/63. Confined at the Atheneum Prison, 1/16/64. Desc.: age 46, 6', dark comp., dark hair, hazel eyes and dark whiskers. Occ. farmer, residing in Braxton Co., W. Va. Sent to Camp Chase, 1/20/64. Confined at Camp Chase 1/20/64. Transf. to Ft. Delaware, 3/15/64. Confined at Ft. Delaware, 3/17/64. Paroled 9/14/64, to be exchanged. Transf. to Aiken's Landing, 9/18/64. Exchanged at Varina, Va., 9/22/64. Adm. Gen. Hosp. No. 9, 9/21/64. Transf. to Chimborazo Hosp., 9/22/64. Adm. Chimborazo Hosp. No. 5, 9/22/64, chronic diarrhoea, paroled prisoner. Furloughed 9/27/64, 35 days. Clothing issued at Chimborazo Hosp. No. 5, 9/27/64, signs by x. Pass issued at Chimborazo Hosp. No. 5, 9/30/64 to Bath Co. Treated for Hemorrhage, 10/18/64 - 10/22/64, Gordonsville Hosp. Listed as Dweese on CSR. Post war rosters list him as Co. C. Age 59, dry goods merchant, Troy Dist., Gilmer Co., W. Va. 1880 Census. Wrote "Recollections of a Lifetime" in 1904; Photograph in his book. NFR.

DILLEY (DILLY), ANDREW - Pvt. Co. F. b.c. 1823. Age 37, farmer, Huntersville, Pocahontas Co., W. Va. 1860 Census. Enl. Hillsboro, Pocahontas Co., W. Va., 9/11/63. Ab. 1/1/64 - 2/29/64, discharged. Age 58, farmer, Huntersville, Pocahontas Co., W. Va. 1880 Census. NFR.

DILLEY (DILLY), CLAYTON - Pvt. Co. F. b.c. 1839. Age 21, farmer, Huntersville, Pocahontas Co., W. Va. 1860 Census. Prior service, McNeel's Co., 2nd VSL. Enl. Hillsboro, Pocahontas Co., W. Va., 3/9/63 (4/1/63). Not stated if present or absent on muster-in roll dated 3/63. Ab. 1/1/64 - 2/29/64, discharged. Age 40, farm laborer, Huntersville, Pocahontas Co., W. Va. 1880 Census. NFR.

DILLEY (DILLY), JEREMIAH W. - Pvt. Co. F. b.c. 1833. Age 27, laborer, Frost, Pocahontas Co., W. Va. 1860 Census. Prior service, McNeel's Co., 2nd VSL. Enl. Hillsboro, Pocahontas Co., W. Va., 3/9/63. Not stated if present or absent on muster-in roll dated 3/63. Age 45, farmer, Huntersville, Pocahontas Co., W. Va. 1880 Census. NFR.

DILLEY (DILLY), THOMAS - Pvt. Co. I. b.c. 1825. Age 35, farmer, Huntersville, Pocahontas Co., W. Va. 1860 Census. Thought to have served in Co. K, 3rd VSL. Enl. Huntersville, Pocahontas Co., W. Va., 2/1/63 (3/18/63). Present on muster-in roll dated 3/63. Mustered into service 3/19/63. Present 6/30/63 - 2/29/64, mounted. Ab. 2/29/64 - 8/31/64, cpd. 6/1/64. Cpd. Buckhannon, W. Va., 5/24/64. Confined at the Atheneum Prison, 6/10/64. Desc.: age 40, 5'11", dark comp., dark hair and blue eyes. Occ. farmer, residing in Pocahontas Co., W. Va. Charged with being a rebel spy. Sent to Camp Chase, 6/16/64. Confined at Camp Chase, 6/17/64. Ab. 9/1/64 - 10/31/64, POW; $100 enl. bounty due. Paroled for exchange 3/2/65, did not go. DOD. Camp Chase, 4/25/65, chronic diarrhoea. Bur. Camp Chase Confederate Cem., grave 1916, 1/3 mile South of Camp Chase. Had two brothers in the 12th Miss. Inf. Listed as Dilly on CSR.

DIXON (DIXSON, DICKRSON), GEORGE W. - Pvt. Co. E. b. Monroe Co., W. Va., c. 1834. Age 26, farmer, Gilmer Co., W. Va. 1860 Census. Prior service, Co. E, 3rd VSL. Enl. Frankfort, Greenbrier Co., W. Va., 3/13/63 (4/1/63). Not stated if present or absent on muster-in roll dated 3/63. Present 10/31/63 - 10/31/64, fell behind on the march to Md. and cannot be found. Was foot footed when he fell behind. Reported to his camp 12/29/63 with papers showing he was under nurse all the time during his absence. Clothing issued 3/1/64 and 6/17/64. NFR.

DORMAN, HIRAM (HYRAM) - Pvt. Co. F. b.c. 1829. Age 31, Mill Point, Pocahontas Co., W. Va. 1860 Census. Prior service, McNeel's Co., 2nd VSL. Enl. Hillsboro, Pocahontas Co., W. Va., 3/9/63 (4/1/63). Not stated if present or absent on muster-in roll dated 3/63. Ab. 1/1/64 - 2/29/64, sick. Ab. 9/1/64 - 10/31/64, on horse detail; enl. bounty due. Paroled at Charleston, W. Va., 5/10/65, signs by x. Desc.: age 37, 5'10_", dark comp., dark hair, dark eyes and dark whiskers. Age 52, farmer, Edray, Pocahontas Co., W. Va. 1880 Census. NFR.

DORSON, RICHARD S. - Pvt. Co. H. Prior service, Co. G, 3rd VSL. Enl. Frankfort, Greenbrier Co., W. Va., 3/20/63 (Clay Co., W. Va., 4/1/63). Not stated if present or absent on muster-in roll dated 3/63. Ab. 9/1/64 - 10/31/64, AWOL. NFR.

DOUGLAS, JOSHUA - Pvt. Co. A. Served in Co. A, 3rd VSL. Post war rosters only. Consort of Nancy Hart, after Perry Connolly's death. Moved to Greenbrier Co., W. Va. NFR.

DOUGLAS, MARTIN VAN BUREN - 3rd Corp. Co. A. b. Roane Co., W. Va., 1840 (1835). Post war rosters only. Served in Co. A, 3rd VSL, and was wd. Arnoldsburg, W. Va., 5/6/62, crippled for life. Age 35, farmer, Washington Township, Calhoun Co., W. Va. 1870 Census. Age 47, farmer, Washington Dist., Calhoun Co., W. Va. 1880 Census. NFR.

DOWDY, WILLIAM B. - Corp. Co. I. b. Va., 1/18/39. Farmhand, Oakdale, Rockbridge Co. 1860 Census. Thought to have served in Co. K, 3rd VSL. Enl. Huntersville, Pocahontas Co., W. Va., 3/18/63 (2/1/63). Present on muster-in roll dated 3/63, Corp. Mustered into service 3/19/63. Ab., Pvt., 6/30/63 - 2/29/64, claims to have a discharge. Ab. 2/29/64 - 8/31/64, AWOL. Ab. 9/1/64 - 10/31/64, AWOL since 12/20/63. Exempt, Fancy Hill, 2/8/64, chronic bronchitis and phthisis. Desc.: age 23, 6', fair comp., dark hair and gray eyes. Occ. farmer. Post war resident of Rockbridge Co. Farmer, Natural Bridge Dist., Rockbridge Co. 1870 Census. d. Rockbridge Co., 1/7/1905. Bur. High Bridge Presbyterian Church Cem.

DOWNS, GEORGE - Major/Capt. Co. A. b. Monongalia Co., W. Va., 4/7/20. Age 39, miller, Calhoun Co., W. Va. 1860 Census. Prior service, Co. A, 3rd VSL. Cpd. Big Bend, W. Va., 7/2/62. Confined at Parkersburg and Camp Chase. Paroled and released. Commissioned Capt. of Rangers by Gov. John Letcher, 3/19/63, to rank from 7/15/61. Enl. Williamsburg, Greenbrier Co., W. Va., 3/1/63. Not stated if present or absent on muster-in roll dated 3/63, Capt. Appointed Capt. 3/1/63. Ab. sick 7/2/63. Mentioned for "brave bearing" by Col. W. L. Jackson at the battle of Droop Mtn., W. Va., 11/6/63. Commanding Reg't., 4/64. Was one of two men considered for promotion to Major, 2/64. Col. W. L. Jackson promoted him to Major at Warm Springs, 4/22/64, "on account of his qualifications, his marked gallantry on several occasions, his influence in the Regiment..." Appointed Major 6/28/64, to rank from 2/26/64. Accepted the appointment 8/18/64. His appointment was confirmed 1/5/65. Ab. F&S MR 9/1/64 - 10/31/64, wd. Lynchburg, 6/17/64. Applied for a furlough at Staunton, 7/9/64. Adm. Gen. Hosp. No. 1, Lynchburg, there on 7/14/64, RTD. Ab. 10/25/64, wd., now on 120 day leave. Ab. 12/15/64, wd. 6/19/64, no steps have been taken to replace him; absent by order of Gen. J. A. Early. Tried and imprisoned by a Federal court for leading a raid on the Post Office at Ripley, W. Va., 12/19/61. Post war resident of Calhoun Co., W. Va. Age 50, farmer, Center Township, Calhoun Co., W. Va. 1870 Census. Age 60, farmer, Lee Dist., Calhoun Co., W. Va. 1880 Census. Post war rosters list him as being a resident of Marion Co., W. Va. d. 3/18/99. Bur. Sturm Cem., Calhoun Co., W. Va.

DOWNS, JOHN S. - Pvt. Co. A. b. 1843. Not on muster rolls. Rode with James Hamilton from Marion Co., W. Va., to join the army. Paroled at Charleston, W. Va., 5/11/65. Desc.: age 21, 5'4", light comp., brown hair, gray eyes and light whiskers. Served in Co. K, 20th Va. Cav. Post war resident of Marion Co., W. Va. d. 1931.

DOYLE, GEORGE W. - Pvt. Co. I. b. Highland Co., c. 1832. Age 28, farmer, Wilsonville, Highland Co. 1860 Census. Enl. Huntersville, Pocahontas Co., W. Va., 3/1/64. Present 2/29/64 - 8/31/64, mounted; enl. bounty due. Clothing issued 7/64 and 8/64. Ab. 9/1/64 - 10/31/64, AWOL since 10/30/64. Post war rosters show service in Co. B, 31st Va. Inf. d. on Jackson River, Highland Co., 5/21/1904. Bur. Wesley Chapel.

DOYLE (DOYL), JACOB - Pvt. Co. I. b. Highland Co., c. 1835. Age 25, farmer, Wilsonville, Highland Co. 1860 Census. Prior service, Co. B, 31st Va. Inf. Enl. Huntersville, Pocahontas Co., W. Va., 8/15/63. Present 6/30/63 - 2/29/64, not mounted. Clothing issued 3/22/64. Listed as Doyl on CSR. Served in Co. G, 20th Va. Cav. DOD. Elmira Prison, 9/11/64. Bur. Woodlawn National Cem., grave no. 352 (512).

DOYLE, WILLIAM - Pvt. Co. I. b.c. 1829 (1833). Age 27, laborer, Elk, Pocahontas Co., W. Va. 1860 Census. Enl. Huntersville, Pocahontas Co., W. Va., 4/15/63. Ab. 6/30/63 - 2/29/64, sick at home; mounted. Ab. 2/29/64 - 8/31/64, AWOL. Ab. 9/1/64 - 10/31/64, AWOL since 7/20/74. Paroled at Charleston, W. Va., 5/10/65. Desc.: age 36, 5'5", light comp., brown hair, blue eyes and brown whiskers. Age 51, farmer, Edray, Pocahontas Co., W. Va. 1880 Census. NFR.

DRAGOO (DRAGGOO), EPHRAIM M. (W.) - Pvt. Co. D. b. Marion Co., W. Va., c. 1843 (1840). Prior service, Co. C, 3rd VSL. Enl. Williamsburg, Greenbrier Co., W. Va., 3/8/63. Not stated if present or absent on muster-in roll dated 3/63. Served in Co. B, 20th Va. Cav. Post war resident of Jackson Co., W. Va. Age 31 (1874). Post war pensioner and resident of Okla., 1915. NFR.

DRAKE, JAMES THOMAS - Sgt. Co. A. b. Ashbury Co., C., 5/6/26. Post war rosters show service in 19th Va. Cav., but not likely. Did serve in Co. A, 46th Battn. Va. Cav., which was attached to the 19th Va. Cav. in 1863. No muster rolls of 19th Va. Cav. Enl. Ritchie Co., W. Va., 7/11/63. Lost a horse, Wirt Co., W. Va., 10/27/63. Transf. to 46th Battn. Va. Cav. in 1864 (which became the 26th Va. Cav. in 1865). Post war farmer and resident of Lafayette Co., Mo. d. Lafayette Co., Smabar Township, Mo., 9/28/86.

DUCK, PERRY - Pvt. Co. ?. Post war rosters only, which shows service in Jackson's Cav. Brigade, and that he was a resident of Lewis Co., W. Va. NFR.

DULANEY, JAMES E. P. - 4th Corp. Co. K. Prior service, Co. I, 3rd VSL. Enl. Frankfort, Greenbrier Co., W. Va., 3/20/63. Not stated if present or absent on muster-in roll dated 3/63, 4th Corp. Clothing issued 5/26/64, 6/17/64 and 7/6/64. NFR.

DUNCAN, SYLVANUS (SYLVESTER) N. - 2nd Corp. Co. D. Prior service, Co. C, 3rd VSL. Enl. Williamsburg, Greenbrier Co., W. Va., 3/8/63. Not stated if present or absent on muster-in roll dated 3/63, 2nd Corp. Served in Co. B, 20th Va. Cav. NFR.

DUNLOP (DUNLAP), ROBERT BAILEY - Pvt. Co. ?. b. Augusta Co., 5/?/43. Age 16, laborer, N. Dist., Augusta Co. 1860 Census. Enrolled as a conscript at Camp Lee, near Richmond, 2/26/64. Assigned to the 19th Va. Cav., 2/29/64. Post war resident of Augusta Co. d. 12/19/1934.

DUNSMORE, ANDREW - Pvt. Co. G. Prior service, Co. F, 3rd VSL. Enl. Frankfort, Greenbrier Co., W. Va., 3/12/63. Not stated if present or absent on muster-in roll dated 3/63. NFR.

DUSKEY (DUSKY), DANIEL - Pvt. Co. A. b. Alleghany Co., Pa., 1809. Age 51, farmer, Calhoun Co., W. Va. 1860 Census. Capt. Co. C, 186th Va. Militia, 1857. Justice of the Peace, Calhoun Co., W. Va. Recruited and commanded one section (company) of the Moccasin Rangers. Cpd. Wirt Co., W. Va., 12/15/61, with 33 of his men. Confined at the Atheneum Prison, under heavy guard. Indicted for treason and turned over the US Marshal for the Western Dist. of Va. by 3/28/62. Tried by US Court in Western Va., 4/14/62, for robbing the Post Office at Ripley, W. Va.; convicted and sentenced to 4 years in prison. Imprisoned at Albany, NY, before 6/11/63. Released by Presidential pardon, 6/17/63. Returned to the Little Kanawha Valley. Not on muster rolls. Cpd. Webster Co., W. Va., 2/9/64. Sent to Cumberland, Md., then to Wheeling, W. Va. Confined at the Atheneum Prison, 2/21/64. Desc.: age 55, 5'7", fair comp., brown hair and gray eyes. Occ. farmer, residing in Calhoun Co., W. Va. Charged with being a bushwhacker. Escaped from military prison, 7/18/65. It is said he boasted that "he had a little graveyard of his own in which he buried a considerable number of Union men." Post war source lists him as Capt. Father of George Duskey. NFR.

DUSKEY (DUSKY), GEORGE W. - Pvt. Co. C. b. Lewis Co., W. Va., c. 1840. Age 20, Calhoun Co., W. Va. 1860 Census. Cpd. Wirt Co., W. Va., 12/15/61. Confined at the Atheneum Prison, under heavy guard. Pretended to be ill, and was sent to the Sprigg Hill Hosp., Wheeling, W. Va. While there he escaped with a few of his men, and returned to Calhoun Co., W. Va., and there reorganized the Moccasin Rangers. Prior service, Co. A, 3rd VSL. Enl. Pocahontas Co., W. Va., 4/1/63. Ab. 12/31/63 - 8/31/64, has one horse; cpd. Roane Co., W. Va., 6/20/63. Ab. 9/1/64 - 10/31/64, $100 enl. bounty due; cpd. 6/20/63. Was reported on 11/29/64 that Duskey and Lt. William A. Gandy were being held in solitary confinement at Wheeling, W. Va., and in irons. Ordered to be released from solitary confinement, and be sent to Ft. Monroe, for exchange, 1/21/65. Reported as being held in the Wheeling City Jail, which served as a State Prison, 1/25/65; Duskey being held by civil authorities, under indictment for treason and robbing the mail (Post Office at Ripley, W. Va.). Cpd. 2/2/65, no place stated (this is probably their release date from prison, and the time that the military took control of them again). Confined at Baltimore, Md., then sent to Camp Hamilton. Transportation to Ft. Monroe for Duskey and Lt. Gandy ordered 2/4/65. Confined at Camp Hamilton, Va., military prison, awaiting exchange, 2/6/65. Released 2/11/65. Post war rosters show service in Co. A. Duskey, apparently an officer at one point during the war, was not considered such by the US. Son of Daniel Duskey. NFR.

DYE, CUMMINS - Pvt. Co. G. Enl. Frankfort, Greenbrier Co., W. Va., 3/12/63 (4/1/63). Not stated if present or absent on muster-in roll dated 3/63. Clothing issued 3/1/64 and 6/17/64, signs by x. Adm. CSA Gen. Hosp., Charlottesville, 8/17/64, debility. Transf. to Lynchburg, 8/18/64. Present 9/1/64 - 10/31/64, has a serviceable horse. NFR.

EAGAN (EAGON), CHARLES W. - Pvt. Co. I/Asst. Surgeon. b.c. 1831. Prior service, Co. G, 14th Va. Cav. Enl. Rockbridge Co., 1/1/63. Present 2/29/64 - 8/31/64, transf. from Co. G, 14th Va. Cav., 4/12/64. Present 9/1/64 - 10/31/64, $100 enl. bounty due. Clothing issued 7/64 and 8/64. Petition submitted by residents of Pocahontas Co., W. Va., asking he be relieved of military duty, to practice medicine. Cpd. Huntersville, W. Va., 4/19/65 by Capt. Badger's Co., listed as Asst. Surgeon, 19th Va. Cav. Desc.: age 34, 5'9", fair comp., dark hair and blue eyes. Occ. physician, residing at Huntersville, W. Va. Confined at Clarksburg, W. Va., 4/25/65. Paroled at Clarksburg, W. Va., and released for exchange, 4/25/65. Listed as E. A. Eagon in 14th Va. Cav. Age 49, physician, Glenville, Gilmer Co., W. Va. 1880 Census. NFR.

EAGAN, FRANKLIN - Pvt. Co. I. Enl. Huntersville, Pocahontas Co., W. Va., 9/1/63. Ab. 6/30/63 - 2/29/64, AWOL 10 days; mounted. Clothing issued 3/22/64. NFR.

EAGLE, DAVID W. - Pvt. Co. C. b. Rockingham Co., c. 1836. Prior service, Co. D, 3rd VSL. Enl. Frankfort, Greenbrier Co., W. Va., 3/15/63 (Pocahontas Co., W. Va., 4/1/63). Not stated if present or absent on muster-in roll dated 3/63. Present 1/1/63 - 4/1/63, had one horse. Employed as a courier 11/1/63 - 11/30/63, returned to his Co. 12/1/63. Ab. 12/31/63 - 8/31/64, transf. to the 36th Battn. Va. Cav., 5/1/64; has one horse. Clothing issued 2/2/64 and 2/25/64. Post war resident of Jackson Co., W. Va. Age 29 (1865). NFR.

EARL (EARLE), ARCHIBALD F. - Pvt. Co. I. b.c. 1832. Age 28, farmer, Randolph Co., W. Va. 1860 Census. Served as a guide to Lt. David Poe and Imboden's forces in the attack on Beverly, W. Va., 4/24/63. Enl. Huntersville, Pocahontas Co., W. Va., 1/1/64. Ab. 6/30/63 - 2/29/64, recruited, did not have his name at time of last return; mounted; enl. bounty due. Present 2/29/64 - 8/31/64, mounted; enl. bounty due; on extra duty. Clothing issued 7/64 and 8/64. Present 9/1/64 - 10/31/64, on extra duty; $100 bond due. Paroled at Harrisonburg, 5/2/65. Desc.: age 32, 6', light comp., dark hair and hazel eyes, a resident of Hardy Co., W. Va. Post war resident of Randolph Co., W. Va. d. by 1916. NFR.

EDDY, DANIEL E. - Pvt. Co. ?. b. 8/6/28. Post war rosters only, which show him as a resident of Ritchie Co., W. Va. Served in Co. H, 20th Va. Cav. Age 49, farmer, Murphy Dist., Ritchie Co., W. Va. 1880 Census. d. Mellin, Ritchie Co., W. Va., 11/28/1918. Bur. Eddy-Welch Cem., Mellin, Ritchie Co., W. Va.

EDMISTON, ABRAM (ABRAHAM) J. - Pvt. Co. F. b.c. 1845. Age 15, farmer, Pocahontas Co., W. Va. 1860 Census. Enl. Hillsboro, Pocahontas Co., W. Va., 4/1/63. Ab. 1/1/64 - 2/29/64, sick. Present 9/1/64 - 10/31/64, enl. bounty due. Paroled at Charleston, W. Va., 5/10/65. Desc.: age 20, 6', dark comp., dark hair, blue eyes and dark whiskers. Brother of Richard M. Edmiston. NFR.

EDMISTON, RICHARD McN. - 4th Sgt. Co. F. b.c. 1843. Age 17, farmer, Academy, Pocahontas Co., W. Va. 1860 Census. Member Locust Creek Patrol, Pocahontas Co., W. Va., 5/61. Prior service, Co. F, 11th Va. Cav. Transf. to Co. F, 19th Va. Cav., 11/15/63. Enl. Hillsboro, Pocahontas Co., W. Va., 9/20/63. Ab., Pvt., 1/1/64 - 2/29/64, on leave. Ab., 4th Sgt., 9/1/64 - 10/31/64, on horse detail; enl. bounty due. Post war resident of Mo. Brother of Abram J. Edmiston. NFR.

EGON, MICHAEL - Pvt. Co. E. Enl. Frankfort, Greenbrier Co., W. Va., 3/13/63. Not stated if present or absent on muster-in roll dated 3/63. NFR.

ELESON (ELLYSON, ELLISON), JOHN - Pvt. Co. E. b. Harrison Co., W. Va., c. 1829. Age 31, farmer, Gilmer Co., W. Va. 1860 Census. Enl. Gilmer Co., W. Va., 10/8/64. Ab. 10/31/63 - 10/31/64, new recruit; on horse detail, time expired. Age 51, farmer, DeKalb Dist., Gilmer Co., W. Va. 1880 Census. NFR.

ELLIOTT, EDWARD (EDGAR) C. - Pvt. Co. C. b.c. 1836. Prior service, Co. D, 3rd VSL, listed as Edgar C. Elliott. Enl. Frankfort, Greenbrier Co., W. Va., 3/15/63. Not stated if present or absent on muster-in roll dated 3/63. Ab. 1/1/63 - 4/1/63, discharged and furnished a substitute in the person of Andrew J. McCalister; had one horse. Served in Co. D, 20th Va. Cav., listed as Edgar C. Elliott. CSR contains cards for Edgar C. Elliott, Co. A, 22nd [20th?] Va. Cav. or the 19th Va. Cav. These cards show: Cpd. Floyd Co., Ky., 9/9/63. Sent to Louisa, Ky., then to Cincinnati, 9/13/63. Sent to Kemper Barracks, Cincinnati, then to McLean Barracks, Cincinnati, 9/16/63. Confined at McLean Barracks, Cincinnati, 9/16/63. Took the oath of allegiance and was released, 9/26/63. NFR.

ELLIOTT, SOLOMON P. - Pvt. Co. C. Prior service, Co. D, 3rd VSL. Enl. Frankfort, Greenbrier Co., W. Va., 3/15/63 (Pocahontas Co., W. Va., 4/1/63). Not stated if present or absent on muster-in roll dated 3/63. Present 1/1/63 - 4/1/63, had one horse. Ab. 12/31/63 - 8/31/64, has one horse; promoted to Lt. in 20th Va. Cav., 4/1/64. Clothing issued 2/2/64 and 2/25/64. Served in Co. D, 20th Va. Cav. NFR.

ELLISON, SAMUEL W. - Pvt. Co. E. b. Harrison Co., W. Va., c. 1839. Age 21, farmer, Gilmer Co., W. Va. 1860 Census. Enl. Frankfort, Greenbrier Co., W. Va., 3/13/63. Not stated if present or absent on muster-in roll dated 3/63. NFR.

ELLYSON, FRANKLIN - Pvt. Co. A. Served in Co. A, 3rd VSL. Post war rosters only. NFR.

EMMETT, SAMUEL - Pvt. Co. C. Enl. Frankfort, Greenbrier Co., W. Va., 3/15/63. Not stated if present or absent on muster-in roll dated 3/63. NFR.

EMRICK, SAMUEL - Pvt. Co. C. b.c. 1845. Prior service, Co. D, 3rd VSL. Enl. Pocahontas Co., W. Va., 4/1/63. Present 1/1/63 - 4/1/63, had one horse. Cpd. Jackson Co., W. Va., 6/6/63. Confined at the Atheneum Prison, 6/12/63. Desc.: age 18, 5'10_", fair comp., light hair and blue eyes. Occ. farmer, residing in Wood Co., W. Va. Sent to Camp Chase, 6/15/63. Confined at Camp Chase, 6/16/63. Transf. to Johnson's Island, 6/20/63. Confined at Johnson's Island, 6/20/63. Transf. to Pt. Lookout, 11/3/64. Confined at Pt. Lookout, 11/4/63. Paroled for exchange 4/27/64, sent to City Point. Exchanged at city Point, 4/30/64. Adm. Chimborazo Hosp. No. 3, 5/1/64, chronic diarrhoea. Furloughed 5/6/64, 30 days. Clothing issued 6/17/64. Ab. 12/31/63 - 8/31/64, has one horse; transf. to the 17th Va. Cav., 7/1/64. NFR.

ERVIN (ERWIN), JAMES W. - Pvt. Co. E. b. Lewis Co., W. Va., c. 1846. Enl. Bath Co., 3/1/64. Present 10/31/63 - 10/31/64, had his own horse since 3/1/64; enl. bounty due. Clothing issued 5/21/64 and 6/17/64. Paroled at Charleston. W. Va., 6/13/65. Desc.: age 19, 5'10", fair comp., light hair and blue eyes. Post war resident of Charleston, Ark. Adjutant, A. S. Cabell Camp, UCV, Charleston, Ark. Living in 1907. NFR. "

ERVIN, WILLIAM EDWARD - Pvt. Co. F. b. Marlinton, Pocahontas Co., W. Va., 8/20/39. Age 20, farmer, Greenbank, Pocahontas Co., W. Va. 1860 Census. Prior service, McNeel's Co., 2nd VSL and Co. G, 31st Va. Inf. Enl. Hillsboro, Pocahontas Co., W. Va., 3/9/63 (4/1/63). Not stated if present or absent on muster-in roll dated 3/63. Present 1/1/64 - 2/29/64. Clothing issued 2/7/64 and 7/10/64. Present 9/1/64 - 10/31/64, enl. bounty due. Paroled at Charleston, W. Va., 5/10/65. Desc.: age 24, 6', light comp., light hair and gray eyes. Moved to near St. Louis, Mo., then to Buchanan Co., Mo. Fruit farmer. Post war resident of South St. Joseph, Mo. d. Buchanan Co., Mo., 12/29/1926. Bur. King Hill Cem., St. Joseph, Mo.

ERVINE, JAMES ARLIE - Pvt. Co. F. b.c. 1818. Age 42, farmer, Pocahontas Co., W. Va. 1860 Census. Post war rosters only, which also show service in Co. E. NFR.

ERVINE (ERVIN), JOHN V. - Pvt. Co. D. b. Highland Co., c. 1836. Age 24, carpenter, Mill Gap, Highland Co. 1860 Census. Prior service, Co. E, 31st Va. Inf. Transf. to Co. F, 11th Va. Cav., 10/29/63. Transf. to Co. D, 19th Va. Cav., 12/29/63. Transf. to Co. C, 46th Battn. Va. Cav., by 2/1/64. Alive 1919. NFR.

ERWIN, J. B. - Pvt. Co. E. Post war rosters only. Post war pensioner and resident of Franklin Co., Ark., 1913. NFR.

ESTEP, CORNELIUS - 1st Corp. Co. G. b.c. 1845. Enl. Frankfort, Greenbrier Co., W. Va., 3/12/63 (4/1/63). Not stated if present or absent on muster-in roll dated 3/63, Pvt. Clothing issued 4/30/64 and 7/10/64. Present, 1st Corp., 9/1/64 - 10/31/64, has a serviceable horse. Deserted. Surrendered at Charleston, W. Va., 3/65. Took the amnesty oath and was sent North, 3/18/65. Paroled at Charleston, W. Va., 3/18/65. Desc.: age 20, 5'11", fair comp., fair hair and hazel eyes. Occ. farmer, residing in Kanawha Co., W. Va. NFR.

EVERSON, THOMAS H. B. (E.) - Pvt. Co. D. b. 12/28/40. Enl. Williamsburg, Greenbrier Co., W. Va., 3/8/63. Not stated if present or absent on muster-in roll dated 3/63. Served in Co. B, 20th Va. Cav. d. 3/9/1908. Bur. Sturm Cem., Calhoun Co., W. Va.

EWING, JOHN - Pvt. Co. I. Enl. Huntersville, Pocahontas Co., W. Va., 1/25/64. Present 6/30/63 - 2/29/64, mounted; enl. bounty due. Clothing issued 3/22/64. NFR.

EXLINE (EXELINE), LABAN R. - Capt. Co. ?. Prior service, Co. A, 31st Va. Inf., where he lost an arm at Sharpsburg, Md., 9/17/62. Mentioned in Col. W. L. Jackson's report of the Battle of Droop Mtn., 11/6/63, as being attached to his command, and for his "brave bearing." It is not known if Exline was a member of the 19th or 20th Virginia Cavalry, or was a member of Jackson's staff. Resident of Monongalia Co., W. Va. NFR.

FABRAY (FABRA, FABRO), FRANKLIN - Pvt. Co. C. Prior service, Co. D, 3rd VSL. Enl. Pocahontas Co., W. Va., 4/1/63. Present 1/1/63 - 4/1/63, has one horse. Employed as a blacksmith, 11/1/63 - 11/30/63. Present 12/31/63 - 8/31/64, on detached service as blacksmith for this Brigade, 4/1/63; has one horse. Employed as a blacksmith at Warm Springs, 1/1/64 - 3/31/64. Clothing issued, 6/17/64. Ab. 9/1/64 - 10/31/64, has one horse; $100 enl. bounty due; on detached service as blacksmith for this Brigade, 4/1/63. NFR.

FACEMIRE, ANDREW S. (L.) - Pvt. Co. B. Enl. Frankfort, Greenbrier Co., W. Va., 3/7/63. Not stated if present or absent on muster-in roll dated 3/63. Surrendered at Bulltown, W. Va., 3/64. Confined at Clarksburg, W. Va., 3/4/64. Took the oath of allegiance and was released 3/5/64, by order of Col. N. Wilkerson. NFR.

FAINTER, WILLIAM F. - 4th Sgt. Co. I. b.c. 1827. Enl. Huntersville, Pocahontas Co., W. Va., 3/19/63 (3/18/63). Present on muster-in roll dated 3/63, Pvt. Mustered into service 3/19/63. Ab., 4th Sgt., 6/30/63 - 2/29/64, detailed to attend horses for Capt. Marshall's command; has his own horse. Ab. 2/29/64 - 8/31/64, wd. Lynchburg, 6/64; dropped as Sgt. 7/1/64, reduced to ranks. Clothing issued 3/22/64. Cpd. near Lynchburg, 6/18/64. Sent to Cumberland, Md., then to Wheeling, W. Va. Confined at the Atheneum Prison, 7/10/64, listed as Sgt. Desc.: age 37, 6', dark comp., dark hair and dark eyes. Occ. farmer, residing in Rockbridge Co. Transf. to Camp Chase, 7/11/64. Confined at Camp Chase, 7/12/64. Ab., Pvt., 9/1/64 - 10/31/64, wd. and POW. Paroled 3/2/65, to be exchanged and sent to City Point. Exchanged at Bouleware's & Coxes Wharves, James River, 3/65. NFR.

FALBY (FALSBY), JAMES MATH. - Pvt. Co. I. b. Rockbridge Co., c. 1843. Enl. Huntersville, Pocahontas Co., W. Va., 3/18/63. POW record shows he enl. at Lexington, 9/63. Ab. 6/30/63 - 2/29/64, mounted; enl. bounty due. Present 2/29/64 - 8/31/64, mounted; enl. bounty due. Ab. 9/1/64 - 10/31/64, detailed to go to Beverly, W. Va.; $100 bond due. Deserted. Surrendered at Beverly, W. Va., 11/29/64. Took the oath of allegiance and was released, 12/3/64. Desc.: age 21, 5'10", fair comp., light hair and blue eyes. Occ. farmer, residing in Rockbridge Co. Post war resident of Rockbridge Co. NFR.

FARLEY, ANDREW J. "Andy" - Sgt. Co. I. b.c. 1841. Enl. Huntersville, Pocahontas Co., W. Va., 4/10/63. Ab., Pvt., 6/30/63 - 2/29/64, detailed to attend horses for Capt. Marshall's command; has his own horse. Paroled at Staunton, 5/29/65, listed as Sgt. Desc.: age 24, 5'10", fair comp., dark hair and blue eyes. Post war resident of Giles Co. NFR.

FARLEY, WILLIAM - Pvt. Co. I. Enl. Huntersville, Pocahontas Co., W. Va., 4/10/63. Present 6/30/63 - 2/29/64, mounted. Ab. 2/29/64 - 8/31/64, transf. to Co. H, 19th Va. Cav. 6/1/64. Clothing issued, Co. H, 6/17/64, signs by x. Post war resident of Giles Co. NFR.

FARNSWORTH, J. J. - Pvt. Co. G. Enl. Wood Co., W. Va., 5/2/63. Not stated if present or absent on muster-in roll dated 8/63. Ab. 11/1/63 - 2/29/64, deserted 9/1/63. NFR.

FARROW, PERRY - Pvt. Co. G. b.c. 1835. Reference card only for service in the 19th Va. Cav. Served in Co. I, 18th Va. Cav. Desc.: age ?, 5'7", light comp., light hair and dark eyes, a millwright. NFR.

FARROW, WILLIAM H. - Pvt. Co. G. Enl. Wood Co., W. Va., 5/2/63 (5/12/63). Not stated if present or absent on muster-in roll dated 8/63. Present 11/1/63 - 2/29/64. Clothing issued 2/29/64. Present 7/1/64 - 8/31/64, had his own horse. Ab. 9/1/64 - 10/31/64·(dated 12/29/64), AWOL for 10 days. Cpd. Parkersburg, W. Va., 2/6/65. Charged with being a spy, 2/9/65. Confined at the Atheneum Prison, 3/6/65. Desc.: age 21, 5'8", fair comp., brown hair and gray eyes. Occ. tobacconist, residing in Parkersburg, W. Va. Transf. to Camp Chase, 3/28/65. Confined at Camp Chase, 3/29/65. Took the oath and was released, 3/29/65. Desc.: age 20(?), 5'9", florid comp., black hair and blue eyes, a resident of Wood Co., W. Va. NFR.

FERREL (FERRELL), ROBERT - Pvt. Co. H. b. Monongalia Co., W. Va., c. 1839. Age 21, Calhoun Co., W. Va. 1860 Census. Enl. Valley of Va., 10/1/64. Ab. 10/31/63 - 8/31/64, AWOL. Ab. 9/1/64 - 10/31/64 (dated 12/30/64), AWOL. Brother of Thomas F. Ferrell. NFR.

FERREL (FERRELL), ROBERT C. - Pvt. Co. E. b.c. 1833. Enl. Camp Miller, Pocahontas Co., W. Va., 10/1/63. Ab. 1/1/64 - 8/31/64 (dated 1/6/65), cpd. Upshur Co., 10/15/63. Ab. 9/1/64 - 10/31/64 (dated 12/29/64), cpd. Upshur Co., W. Va., 10/30/63; entitled to $100 bond. Deserter. Cpd. Buckhannon, W. Va., 10/20/63 (11/4/63). Confined at the Atheneum Prison, no date. Desc.: age 30, 5'6", fair comp., dark hair and blue eyes, a resident of Upshur Co., W. Va. Transf. to Camp Chase, 11/28/63. Confined at Camp Chase, 11/29/63. Desires to take the oath of allegiance 6/10/64. Took the oath of allegiance and was released, 10/11/64, ordered to report to the Gov. of W. Va. for orders. Desc.: age 30, 5'8", dark comp., dark hair and gray eyes. NFR.

FERRELL, HENRY ALLISON - 1st Sgt. Co. D. b. Monongalia Co., W. Va. Post war rosters show he enl. 9/10/62. Enl. Williamsburg, Greenbrier Co., W. Va., 3/8/63. Not stated if present or absent on muster-in roll dated 3/63, 1st Sgt. Served as Capt., Co. C, 46th Battn. Va. Cav. Post war roster shows service as "33rd Regiment." Post war resident of Freed, Calhoun Co., W. Va. Age 42, farmer, Sheridan Dist., Calhoun Co., W. Va. 1880 Census. d. Freed, Calhoun Co., W. Va., 1/1919. Bur. Freed Cem., Leading Creek.

FERRELL, LEWIS SKIDMORE - Pvt. Co. E. Enl. Camp Miller, Pocahontas Co., W. Va., 10/23/63. Ab. 1/1/64 - 8/31/64 (dated 1/6/65), wd.; entitled to $100 bond. Ab. 9/1/64 - 10/31/64 (dated 12/29/64), wd. near Beverly, W. Va., 7/1/63, since not able for service; entitled to $100 bond. Member Gen. Pegram Camp, UCV, Valley Head, W. Va. d. by 1915.

FERRELL, THOMAS F. - Pvt. Co. A. b. Lewis Co., W. Va., c. 1843. Age 17, farmer, Calhoun Co., W. Va. 1860 Census. Served in Co. A, 3rd VSL. Post war rosters only. Brother of Robert Ferrell. Age 36, farmer, Sherman Dist., Calhoun Co., W. Va. 1880 Census. NFR.

FERRELL, WILLIAM - Pvt. Co. F. Post war rosters only. Could be William Fuel, listed below. NFR.

FIELDS, WILLIAM R. - Pvt. Co. g. b.c. 1843. Enl. Greenbrier Co., W. Va., 5/22/63. Employed as a teamster, 11/1/63 - 11/30/63. Employed as a teamster at Warm Springs, 1/1/64 - 3/31/64. Clothing issued 1/16/64 and 6/17/64. Present 9/1/64 - 10/31/64, detailed wagoner. Paroled at Charleston, W. Va., 5/19/65. Desc.: age 22, 5'11", dark comp., brown hair and gray eyes. NFR.

FIGGENS, THOMAS B. - Pvt. Co. A. Prior service, Co. A, 3rd VSL. Enl. Williamsburg, Greenbrier Co., W. Va., 3/1/63. Not stated if present or absent on muster-in roll dated 3/63. Clothing issued, 2/19/64, 3/21/64 and 6/17/64, signs by x. NFR.

FINNEY (FEENEY, FINNY), WILLIAM A. - Pvt. Co. C. Prior service, Co. D, 3rd VSL. Enl. Frankfort, Greenbrier Co., W. Va., 3/15/63 (Pocahontas Co., W. Va., 4/1/63). Not stated if present or absent on muster-in roll dated 3/63. Present 1/1/63 - 4/1/63, on detached service in QM Dept., has one horse. Ab. 12/31/63 - 8/31/64, on detached service as courier since 4/1/63; has one horse. Employed as a courier 11/1/63 - 11/30/63. Employed as a courier at Warm Springs, 1/1/64 - 3/31/64, discharged and sent to his Co. Clothing issued 11/21/63, 2/23/64 and 6/17/64. Ab. 9/1/64 - 10/31/64, on detached service as courier since 4/1/63; has one horse; $100 enl. bounty due. NFR.

FISHER, ANDREW G. - Pvt. Co. E. b. Nicholas Co., W. Va., c. 1836. Age 24, farmer, Webster Co., W. Va. 1860 Census. Not on muster rolls. Surrendered at Bulltown, W. Va. Confined at Clarksburg, W. Va., 3/12/64. Age 44, farmer, Fork Lick, Webster Co., W. Va. 1880 Census. NFR.

FISHER, ASA L. - Pvt. Co. K. b. Lewis Co., W. Va., c. 1834. Age 26, farmhand, Webster Co., W. Va. 1860 Census. Enl. Frankfort, Greenbrier Co., W. Va., 3/20/63. Not stated if present or absent on muster-in roll dated 3/63. Present on a MR of Co. B, Ward's Battn. CS Prisoners, 7/64, listed as belonging to Co. F, 21st Va. Cav. Ward's Battn. was formed at Lynchburg, 6/11/64. The members of this unit were pardoned by Pres. Davis, 7/30/64, and ordered to return to their former units. Age 45, farmer, Holly Dist., Webster Co., W. Va. 1880 Census. Bur. Cutlip Cem., Right Fork of Holly River, Holly Dist., Webster Co., W. Va.

FISHER (FIGHER), JOHN A. - Sgt. Co. I. b.c. 1838. Enl. Huntersville, Pocahontas Co., W. Va., 5/22/63. Ab., 6/30/63 - 2/29/64, cpd. at Warm Springs, 8/25/63; mounted. Cpd. Bath Co., 8/25/63. Sent to Clarksburg, W. Va., then to Wheeling, W. Va. Confined at the Atheneum Prison, 9/6/63. Desc.: age 25, 6'1_", dark comp., dark hair and brown eyes. Occ. farmer, residing in Rockbridge Co. Transf. to Camp Chase, 9/7/63. Confined at Camp Chase, 9/8/63. Transf. to Rock Island, Ill., 1/22/64. Confined at Rock Island Prison, 1/24/64. Ab. 2/29/64 - 8/31/64, cpd. Jackson River, Bath Co., 8/25/63. Ab. 9/1/64 - 10/31/64, cpd. 1863; $100 enl. bond due. DOD. Rock Island, Ill., 2/25/64, variola. Bur. South of Prison Barracks, grave no. 610. POW records list him as Sgt., Co. G.

FISHER, LEWIS M. - Pvt. Co. K. Enl. Frankfort, Greenbrier Co., W. Va., 3/20/63. Not stated if present or absent on muster-in roll dated 3/63. Cpd. Webster Co., W. Va., 10/25/64. NFR.

FISHER, WILLIAM - Pvt. Co. B. Post war rosters only. NFR.

FISHER, WILLIAM T. - Pvt. Co. K. Enl. Sperryville, 11/20/63. Present 2/29/64 - 8/31/64, mounted; $50 enl. bounty due. NFR.

FITZGERALD, GEORGE - Pvt. Co. I. b.c. 1842. Enl. Camp Northwest, W. Va., 6/2/63, age 21. Not stated if present or absent on muster-in roll dated 5/5/63. NFR.

FITZGERALD, WILLIAM - Pvt. Co. I. b.c. 1841. Enl. Camp Northwest, W. Va., 6/2/63, age 22. Not stated if present or absent on muster-in roll dated 5/5/63. NFR.

FITZWATER, HENRY M. - Pvt. Co. H. Enl. Frankfort, Greenbrier Co., W. Va., 3/19/63. Not stated if present or absent on muster-in roll dated 3/63. NFR.

FITZWATER, JOHN - Pvt. Co. H. Enl. Frankfort, Greenbrier Co., W. Va., 3/19/63. Not stated if present or absent on muster-in roll dated 3/63. Clothing issued 3/2/64. NFR.

FITZWATER, P. J. - Pvt. Co. H. Enl. Frankfort, Greenbrier Co., W. Va., 3/19/63. Not stated if present or absent on muster-in roll dated 3/63. NFR.

FLEMING, DUNCAN - Pvt. Co. D. b.c. 1845. Not on muster rolls. Cpd. Gauley Bridge, Nicholas Co., W. Va., 5/28/63. Charged with being a conscript, CSA. Confined at the Atheneum Prison, 6/15/63. Desc.: age 18, 5'7", dark comp., brown hair and blue eyes. Occ. farmer, residing in Alleghany Co. Transf. to Camp Chase, 6/15/63. Confined at Camp Chase 6/16/63. Transf. to Johnson's Island, 6/20/63. Confined at Johnson's Island, 6/20/63. Took the oath of allegiance and was released, 6/10/65, signs by x. Desc.: age 20, 5'8_", dark comp., dark hair and gray eyes, a resident of Alleghany Co. NFR.

FLENNER (FLENER), JACOB F. (T.) - Pvt. Co. E. b.c. 1841. Enl. Gilmer Co., W. Va., 10/8/64. Present 10/31/63 - 10/31/64, enl. bounty due. Surrendered at Glenville, 5/14/65. Sent to Clarksburg, W. Va. Confined at Clarksburg, 5/17/65. Paroled at Clarksburg, W. Va., 5/17/65, to be exchanged, signs by x. Desc.: age 23, 5'9", fair comp., light hair and blue eyes. Occ. farmer, residing in Gilmer Co., W. Va. Age 29, farm laborer, Gilmer Co., W. Va. 1870 Census. NFR.

FLESHER, JAMES - Pvt. Co. D. b. Highland Co., c. 1846. Enl. Hightown, Highland Co., 4/1/64. POW record shows enl. as Bath Co., 6/64. Ab. 12/31/63 - 8/31/64 (dated 1/6/65), AWOL. Ab. 9/1/64 - 10/31/64, AWOL. Deserted. Reported at Clarksburg, W. Va., 11/21/64. Took the oath of allegiance and was released, 11/21/64. Desc.: age 18, 5'10", dark comp., dark hair and black eyes. Occ. farmer, residing in Highland Co. NFR.

FLETCHER, BENJAMIN E. - Pvt. Capt. Winter's Co. b.c. 1842. Not on muster rolls. Cpd. Harrison Co., W. Va., 5/5/63. Confined at the Atheneum Prison, 5/9/63. Desc.: age 21, 5'10", dark comp., black hair, blue eyes and sandy whiskers. Occ. farmer, residing in Marion Co., W. Va. Transf. to Camp Chase, 5/11/63. Confined at Camp Chase, 5/12/63. Transf. to Johnson's Island, 6/14/63. Confined at Johnson's Island, 6/14/63. Transf. to Pt. Lookout, 11/3/63. Confined at Pt. Lookout, 11/4/63. Took the oath of allegiance and was released, 4/11/64. Post war resident of Marion Co., W. Va. Age 38, farmer, Lincoln School Dist., Marion Co., W. Va. 1880 Census. NFR.

FLINN, BENJAMIN W. - 5th Sgt. Co. C. b.c. 1838. Enl. Randolph (Pocahontas) Co., W. Va., 5/5/63. Not stated if present or absent on muster-in roll dated 8/63, 5th Sgt. Ab., Pvt., 6/30/63 - 8/31/64 (dated 1/6/65), POW since 12/27/63; 6% bond due. Cpd. Pocahontas Co., W. Va., 12/26/63. Confined at the Atheneum Prison, 1/6/64. Desc.: age 26, 5'6_", fair comp., black hair and hazel eyes. Occ. farmer, residing in Preston Co., W. Va. Transf. to Camp Chase, 1/7/64. Confined at Camp Chase, 1/8/64. Transf. to Ft. Delaware, 3/14/64. Confined at Ft. Delaware, 3/17/64. Ab., Pvt., 9/1/64 - 10/31/64 (dated 12/30/64), POW since 12/27/63; 6% bond due. Took the oath of allegiance and was released, 6/20/65. Desc.: age ?, 5'6", fair comp., dark hair and blue eyes, a resident of Preston Co., W. Va. Age 43, furnace manager, Lyon Dist., Preston Co., W. Va. 1880 Census. NFR.

FLINN, JAMES T. - Pvt. Co. C. b. Fauquier Co., c. 1842. Enl. Pocahontas Co., W. Va., 5/14/63. Not stated if present or absent on muster-in roll dated 8/63. Present 6/30/63 - 8/31/64 (dated 1/6/65), 6% bond due. Ab. 9/1/64 - 10/31/64 (dated 12/30/64), on horse detail; 6% bond due. Clothing issued 9/2/64. Deserted. Reported at Clarksburg, W. Va., 12/31/64. Took the oath of allegiance and was released 1/3/65. Desc.: age 23, 5'10", fair comp., light hair and blue eyes. Occ. farmer, residing in Preston Co., W. Va. Age 38, farmer, Lyon Dist., Preston Co., W. Va. 1880 Census. NFR.

FLINN, WILLIAM T. - Pvt. Co. C. b. Fauquier Co., c. 1844. Enl. Pocahontas Co., W. Va., 5/14/63. Not stated if present or absent on muster-in roll dated 8/63. Ab. 6/30/63 - 8/31/64 (dated 1/6/65), POW since 12/27/63; 6% bond due. Deserted. Surrendered at Rowlesburg, W. Va., 8/24/64 (also as having been cpd. Rowlesburg, W. Va., 10/19/64, and sent to Camp Chase, 10/28/64). Desc.: age 20, 5'8", fair comp., dark hair and gray eyes. Occ. farmer, residing in Preston Co., W. Va. Confined at the Atheneum Prison, no date. Desc.: age 20, 5'8", light comp., dark hair and hazel eyes. Ab. 9/1/64 - 10/31/64 (dated 12/30/64), POW since 12/27/63; 6% bond due. Took the oath of allegiance and was released, 9/30/64. NFR.

FLINN, WILLOUGHBY - Pvt. Co. C. Enl. Pocahontas Co., W. Va., 5/18/63. Not stated if present or absent on muster-in roll dated 8/63. Ab. 6/30/63 - 8/31/64 (dated 1/6/65), on detached service; 6% bond due. Ab. 9/1/64 - 10/31/64 (dated 12/30/64), AWOL since 10/11/64; 6% bond due. NFR.

FLORENCE, WILLIAM E. - Pvt. Co. ?. Not on muster rolls. Paroled at Richmond, 4/21/65. NFR.

FLUKER (FLEEKER), WILLIAM - Pvt. Co. I. Not on muster rolls. Cpd. 3/10/65, no place given. Took the oath at New Creek, W. Va., and sent to Ohio, 3/12/65. Confined at the Atheneum Prison, 3/12/65, listed as a resident of Augusta Co. NFR.

FOLEY, ANDREW - Pvt. Co. I. b.c. 1836. Enl. Warm Springs, 4/21/63, age 27. Not stated if present or absent on muster-in roll dated 5/5/63. NFR.

FOLEY, JOHN MASON - Sgt. Co. G. b. Wood Co., W. Va., c. 1838. Enl. Wood Co., W. Va., 5/2/63 (Pocahontas Co., W. Va., 5/12/63, 6/2/63). Not stated if present or absent on muster-in roll dated 8/63, 4th Corp. Present, 2nd Corp., 11/1/63 - 2/29/64, had his own horse and equipment since 12/27/63. Present, 1st Corp., 7/1/64 - 8/31/64, has his own horse; entitled to bond. Present, 1st Corp., 9/1/64 - 10/31/64 (dated 12/29/64), entitled to $100 bond. Cpd. Parkersburg, Wood Co., W. Va., 4/4/65, listed as a Sgt. Confined at Clarksburg, W. Va., 4/5/65. Desc.: age 27, 5'11", fair comp., sandy hair and blue eyes. Occ. farmer, residing in Wood Co., W. Va. Transf. to Wheeling, W. Va., 4/6/65. Confined at the Atheneum Prison, 4/6/65. Desc.: age 27, 5'11", fair comp., light hair and blue eyes. Transf. to Camp Chase, 4/13/65. Confined at Camp Chase, 4/14/65, charged with being a guerrilla. Took the oath of allegiance and was released, 6/13/65. Desc.: age 28, 5'11", florid comp., light hair and blue eyes, a resident of Wood Co., W. Va. NFR.

FOLEY, PATRICK - Pvt. Co. B. b. Ireland, c. 1825. Age 35, laborer, Lewisburg, Greenbrier Co., W. Va. 1860 census. Enl. Greenbrier Co., W. Va., 1861. Prior service, 8th Va. Cav. and 2nd Co. A, 14th Va. Cav. Transf. to Co. B, 19th Va. Cav. Clothing issued 6/17/64, signs by x. Present 9/1/64 - 10/31/64, transf. from the 14th Va. Cav., 3/1/64; $100 enl. bounty due. Post war resident of Braxton Co., W. Va. NFR.

FORD, JOHN WILLIAM ANDREW - 1st Lt. Co. G. b. Lewisburg, W. Va., 1843. Enl. Wood Co., W. Va., 5/12/63. Not stated if present or absent, Pvt., 7/1/64 - 8/31/64, has his own horse; entitled to bond. Cpd. Washington, DC, 7/14/64. Confined at the Old Capitol Prison, 7/14/64. Transf. to Ft. Delaware, 7/22/64. Confined at Ft. Delaware, 7/23/64, listed as 1st Lt., ADC. Transf. to Hilton Head, SC, 8/20/64, listed as 3rd Lt., ADC. One of the "Immortal 600." Ab., Pvt., 9/1/64 - 10/31/64 (dated 12/29/64), cpd. Md., 7/13/64; entitled to bond. Confined at Ft. Pulaski, Ga., 10/21/64, still there 12/26/64. Transf. from Hilton Head, SC, to Ft. Delaware, 3/12/65. Took the oath of allegiance and was released, 6/17/65, listed as 1st Lt. Desc.: age ?, 5'6", light comp., light hair and blue eyes, a resident of Greenbrier Co., W. Va. CSR shows him as 1st Lt., Co. K, 20th Va. Cav. Post war pensioner and resident of Va., 1915. NFR.

FORD, WINSTON W. - Pvt. Co. I. b.c. 1842. Enl. Camp Northwest, W. Va., 7/3/63 (7/1/63), age 21. Also as having enl. Rockbridge Co., 9/4/63. Not stated if present or absent on muster- in roll dated 5/5/63. Ab. 11/1/63 - 8/31/64 (dated 1/6/65), POW. Deserted. Reported at Clarksburg, W. Va.; by 10/15/63 (11/63). Took the oath of allegiance and was sent North, 11/22/63. Desc.: age 22, 5'11", fair comp., dark hair and blue eyes, a resident of Rockingham Co. Ab. 11/1/63 - 10/31/64 (dated 12/31/64), POW. NFR.

FORMASH, W. P. - Pvt. Co. D. Post war rosters only, which show him as a resident of Babylon, W. Va. NFR.

FORSYTH, W. O. - Pvt. Co. C. Not on muster rolls. Cpd. Front Royal, 6/30/62 and held on the Steamer Coatzacoalcos. NFR.

FOSTER, D. C. - Pvt. Co. C. Enl. Pocahontas Co., W. Va., 3/19/63. Not stated if present or absent on muster-in roll dated 8/63. Ab. 6/30/63 - 8/31/64 (dated 1/6/65), deserted 9/1/63. NFR.

FOUGHT (FAUGHT), JAMES M. - Pvt. Co. K. b.c. 1834. Age 16, 1850 Wirt Co., W. Va. Census. Not on muster rolls. Clothing issued 4/30/64. Cpd. Wirt Co., W. Va., 3/8/65. Sent to Cumberland, Md., then to Wheeling, W. Va. Confined at the Atheneum Prison, 3/27/65. Desc.: age 31, 5'8", dark comp., black hair and hazel eyes. Occ. farmer, residing in Wirt Co., W. Va. Transf. to Camp Chase, 3/28/65. Confined at Camp Chase, 3/29/65. Took the oath of allegiance and was released, 6/13/65. Desc.: age 30, 5'7 3/4", dark comp., black hair and black eyes, a resident of Wirt Co., W. Va. NFR.

FOURD (FORD), LEWIS G. - Pvt. Co. K. b. Harrison Co., W. Va., c. 1844. Age 16, farmer, Gilmer Co., W. Va. 1860 Census. Enl. Frankfort, Greenbrier Co., W. Va., 3/20/63. Not stated if present or absent on muster-in roll dated 3/63. Clothing issued 2/5/64, 6/17/64, 7/64 and 8/64, signs by x. Paroled at Charleston, W. Va., 5/10/65, signs by x. Desc.: age 20, 5'9", fair comp., light hair and blue eyes. NFR.

FOWLER, CALVIN - Pvt. Co. B. Enl. Frankfort, Greenbrier Co., W. Va., 3/7/63. Not stated if present or absent on muster-in roll dated 3/63. NFR.

FOWLER, JOHN W. - Pvt. Co. F. b. Harrison Co., W. Va., c. 1842. Enl. Bulltown, Braxton Co., W. Va., 5/10/63. Not stated if present or absent on muster-in roll dated 7/20/63. Ab. 7/1/63 - 8/31/64 (dated 1/6/65), AWOL. Ab. 9/1/64 - 10/31/64 (dated 12/30/64), AWOL. Deserted. Reported at Clarksburg, W. Va., 11/7/64. Took the oath of allegiance and was released, 11/7/64. Desc : age 22, 5'9", fair comp., light hair and blue eyes. Occ. farmer, residing in Harrison Co., W. Va. NFR.

FOWLER, NATHAN - Pvt. Co. ?. b.c. 1836. Age 24, laborer, Randolph Co., W. Va. 1860 Census. Post war rosters only, which show him as a resident of Randolph Co., W. Va. d. by 1916. NFR.

FOWLER (FOULLER), REASON B. (K.) - Pvt. Co. D. Not on muster rolls. Clothing issued 1st Qr. 1864 and 2/7/64. Note dated 4/29/64 shows that exchanged places in the army with a soldier named Martin. Name listed on a MR of Co. B, Ward's Battn. CS Prisoners, 7/6/4, as having deserted since joining the battn. Ward's Battn. was formed at Lynchburg, 6/11/64. The members of this unit were pardoned by Pres. Davis, 7/30/64, and ordered to return to their former units. Note in file shows this entry cancelled. Reported to the Conscript Bureau, 12/2/64, as a deserter, to be found in Highland Co. Note made 1/65, shows he has gone to the public enemy. Post war rosters list him as a resident of Marion Co., W. Va. NFR.

FOWLER, SIMON - Pvt. Co. I. b.c. 1829. Age 31, laborer, Randolph Co., W. Va. 1860 Census. Enl. Beverly, W. Va., 4/30/64. Present 6/30/63 - 2/29/64, mounted. Ab. 2/29/64 - 8/31/64, AWOL since 6/1/64. Ab. 9/1/64 - 10/31/64, deserted 7/64. Post war resident of Randolph Co., W. Va. Age 50, farmer, Valley Bend, Randolph Co., W. Va. 1880 Census (listed as Fouler). d. by 1916. NFR.

FOX, JASPER LITTLETON - Pvt. Co. I. b. Highland Co. 4/27/46. Enl. Huntersville, Pocahontas Co., W. Va., 4/27/64. Present 2/29/64 - 8/31/64, mounted; pay and bounty due. from enl. Clothing issued 3/22/64, 6/17/64 and 7/10/64. Present 9/1/64 - 10/31/64. Paroled at Staunton, 6/1/65, signs parole as Littleton J. Fox. Desc.: age 19, 5'8", fair comp., light hair and blue eyes. Post war rosters show him as a resident of Highland Co. and Randolph Co., W. Va. d. Weston, Lewis Co., W. Va., 12/21/1931.

FRAME (FRAIM), MARSHALL - Pvt. Co. H. Enl. Calhoun Co., W. Va., 5/16/63. Also as Camp Northwest, W. Va., 6/1/63 (6/28/63). Not stated if present or absent on muster-in roll dated 8/63. Ab. 10/31/63 - 8/31/64, deserted 8/63. Ab. 9/1/64 - 10/31/64 (dated 12/30/64), deserted 6/63. NFR.

FRANKS, STEPHEN J. - Jr. 2nd Lt. Co. A. b.c. 1841. Grew up in Pa. Enl. Augusta Co., 12/25/62, age 23 (?). Elected 2nd Sgt. Not stated if present or absent on muster-in roll dated 8/63, 2nd Sgt. Present, 2nd Sgt., 10/31/63 - 8/31/64. Paroled at Staunton, 5/16/65, as Jr. 2nd Lt. Desc.: age 24, 5'10", dark comp., dark hair and blue eyes. Post war resident of Monongalia Co., W. Va. Post war rosters show him as 1st Sgt. "Bold and fearless, of quick thought." NFR.

FRAZIER, JAMES A. - Pvt. Co. I. b.c. 1841. Enl. Camp Northwest, W. Va., 7/19/63, age 22. Also as Pocahontas Co., W. Va., 7/5/63 and 8/10/63. Not stated if present or absent on muster-in roll dated 5/5/63. Ab. 11/1/63 - 8/31/64 (dated 1/6/65), POW. Ab. 11/1/63 - 10/31/64 (dated 12/31/64), POW. NFR.

FREEL (FRIEL), ISRAEL - Pvt. Co. C. b.c. 1844. Age 16, laborer, Pocahontas Co., W. Va. 1860 Census. Enl. Pocahontas Co., W. Va., 3/19/63. Not stated if present or absent on muster-in roll dated 8/63. Present 6/30/63 - 8/31/64 (dated 1/6/65), 6% bond due. Clothing issued 3/10/64. Ab. 9/1/64 - 10/31/64 (dated 12/30/64), on leave, horse detail; 6% bond due. Horse wd. Leetown, 9/?/64. Age 35, farmer, Edray, Pocahontas Co., W. Va. 1880 Census. NFR.

FRIEL, MONTGOMERY ALLEN - Pvt. Co. F. b. Pocahontas Co., W. Va., c. 1840. Age 20, laborer, Thorny Creek, Pocahontas Co., W. Va. 1860 census. Prior service, McNeel's Co., VSL. Enl. Hillsboro, Pocahontas Co., W. Va., 3/9/63. Not stated if present or absent on muster-in roll dated 3/63. Served in 2nd Co. I, 25th Va. Inf. and Co. D, 14th Va. Cav. Post war farmer and resident of Huntersville, W. Va. Age 40, farmer, Huntersville Dist., Pocahontas Co., W. Va. 1880 census. NFR.

FUEL, WILLIAM - Pvt. Co. F. Enl. Glade Hill, 9/20/63. Ab. 1/1/64 - 2/29/64, AWOL. Ab. 9/1/64 - 10/31/64, AWOL since 5/64. Could be William Ferrell, listed above. NFR.

FULKNER, B. - Sgt. Co. I. Not on muster rolls. Adm. Gen. Hosp. No. 9, 3/12/65. Sent to Chimborazo Hosp., 3/13/65. NFR.

FULL, LEWIS - 5th Sgt. Co. C. b.c. 1833. Prior service, Co. D, 3rd VSL. Enl. Frankfort, Greenbrier Co., W. Va., 3/15/63 (Pocahontas Co., W. Va., 4/1/63). Not stated if present or absent on muster-in roll dated 3/63, 5th Sgt. Present, 5th Sgt., 1/1/63 - 4/1/63, had one horse. Cpd. Ravenswood, Jackson Co., W. Va., 7/25/63. Adm. USA Gen. Hosp., Parkersburg, W. Va., 8/16/63, gunshot wd. Wd. by a conical ball in transverse direction through calf of legs, 5" from knee. Present Hosp. MR, USA Gen. Hosp., Parkersburg, W. Va., 7/1/63 - 8/31/63. Released 10/6/63(?). Confined at Clarksburg, W. Va., then sent to Wheeling, W. Va. Confined at the Atheneum Prison, 9/11/63. Desc.: age 30, 6'3", dark comp., dark hair and blue eyes. Occ. farmer, residing at Ravenswood, Jackson Co., W. Va. Transf. to Camp Chase, 9/14/63. Confined at Camp Chase, 9/15/63. Ab., Pvt., 12/31/63 - 8/31/64, has one horse; cpd. 8/3/63. Transf. to Rock Island, Ill., 1/22/64. Confined at Rock Island Prison, 1/24/64. Desires to take the oath of allegiance and not be exchanged, 3/18/64. Ab. 9/1/64 - 10/31/64, has one horse; cpd. 8/3/63; $100 enl. bounty due. Took the oath of allegiance and was released 5/25/65. Desc.: age 32, 6'3", dark comp., black hair and blue eyes, a resident of Ravenswood, Jackson Co., W. Va. Age 47, farmer, Ravenswood Dist. 1, Jackson Co., W. Va. 1880 Census. NFR.

FULL, ZEBEDEE E. - Pvt. Co. C. b.c. 1827. Prior service, Co. D, 3rd VSL. Enl. Frankfort, Greenbrier Co., W. Va., 3/15/63 (Pocahontas Co., W. Va., 4/1/63). Not stated if present or absent on muster-in roll dated 3/63. Present 1/1/63 - 4/1/63, has one horse. Present 12/31/63 - 8/31/64, has one horse. Present 9/1/64 - 10/31/64, has one horse; $100 enl. bounty due. Paroled at Staunton, 5/27/65, as a member of Co. E. Desc.: age 38, 5'9", light comp., dark hair and blue eyes. Age 52, farmer, Ravenswood Dist. 1, Jackson Co., W. Va. 1880 Census. NFR.

FURBEE (FERBEE), AARON - 3rd Corp. Co. A. b.c. 1835. Enl. Pocahontas Co., W. Va., 3/13/63 (3/23/63), age 26. Not stated if present or absent on muster-in roll dated 3/23/63, 3rd Corp. Ab., 3rd Corp., 10/31/63 - 8/31/64, AWOL since 6/64. Clothing issued 3rd Qr. 1864. Deserted. Surrendered at Wheeling, W. Va., 10/20/64. Confined at the Atheneum Prison. Took the amnesty oath and was released 10/20/64. Desc.: age 29, 5'6", dark comp., light hair and hazel eyes, a resident of Marion Co., W. Va. Post war resident of Marion Co., W. Va. "A good soldier." Age 45, farmer, Mannington Dist., Marion Co., W. Va. 1880 Census. NFR.

FURBEE (FERBEE), CALEB - Pvt. Co. A. b.c. 1842. Resident of Marion Co., W. Va. Enl. Augusta Co., 2/15/63, age 21. Not stated if present or absent on muster-in roll dated 2/15/63. Ab. 10/31/63 - 8/31/64, (listed as present); reported as KIA. Beverly, W. Va., 10/26/64. Wd./Cpd. Beverly, W. Va., 10/29/64. Adm. USA Gen. Hosp., Beverly, W. Va., 10/20/64, wd. right shoulder. Treated with simple dressing. DOW. Beverly, W. Va., 11/1/64. "A good soldier."

FURBEE (FERBEE), JACOB - Pvt. Co. A. b. Marion Co., W. Va., c. 1838. Enl. Pocahontas Co., W. Va., 3/12/63 (5/10/63), age 25. POW record shows enl. as Philippi, W. Va., 5/62. Not stated if present or absent on muster-in roll dated 3/12/63. Cpd. Grafton, W. Va., 5/17/63. Confined at Ft. McHenry. Paroled and sent to Ft. Monroe, 5/20/63, to be exchanged, signs by x. Present 10/31/63 - 8/31/64. Clothing issued 2/29/64 and 3rd Qr. 1864. Deserted. Surrendered at Mannington, W. Va., 2/3/65. Sent to Clarksburg, W. Va. Confined at Clarksburg, W. Va., 2/4/65. Took the amnesty oath and was sent North, 3/7/65. Desc.: age 27, 5'9", light comp., light hair and blue eyes. Occ. farmer, residing in Marion Co., W. Va. Held in Post Guard House, awaiting petition for his release. Confined at the Atheneum Prison, 3/7/65. Desc.: age 24(?), 5'9", fair comp., light hair and gray eyes. "A good soldier." NFR.

FURY (FURRY), THOMAS - Pvt. Co. G. b.c. 1823. Enl. Frankfort, Greenbrier Co., W. Va., 3/12/63. Not stated if present or absent on muster-in roll dated 3/63. Clothing issued 1st Qr. 1864. Paroled at Charleston, W. Va., 5/11/65. Desc.: age 42, 6', dark comp., dark hair, blue eyes and dark whiskers. NFR.

GAINER, SYLVESTER - Pvt. Co. A. b. Barbour Co., W. Va., c. 1844. Age 16, Calhoun Co., W. Va. 1860 Census. Served in Co. A. 3rd VSL. Post war rosters only. NFR.

GALFORD (GUILFORD), BROWN N. - Pvt. Co. I. b.c. 1843(?). Age 14, Pocahontas Co., W. Va. 1860 Census. Enl. Huntersville, Pocahontas Co., W. Va., 4/1/63. Present 6/30/63 - 2/29/64, mounted. Present 2/29/64 - 8/31/64, mounted. Clothing issued 7/64 and 8/64, signs by x. Ab. 9/1/64 - 10/31/64, wd. Fisher's Hill, 9/23/64; $100 bond due. Messmate of William Gragg. Age 37, farmer, Green Banks, Pocahontas Co., W. Va. 1880 Census. NFR.

GALFORD (GUILFORD), JAMES H. - Pvt. Co. F. b. Pocahontas Co., W. Va., c. 1838. Age 22, farmer, Pocahontas Co., W. Va. 1860 Census. Enl. Hillsboro, Pocahontas Co., W. Va., 8/17/63. Ab. 1/1/64 - 2/29/64, ordered on special duty, detached service. Clothing issued, 2/7/64. Present 9/1/64 - 10/31/64, enl. bounty due. Age 42, farmer, Edray, Pocahontas Co., W. Va. 1880 Census. NFR.

GALFORD (GUILFORD), JOHN F. - Pvt. Co. I. b.c. 1845. Age 15, laborer, Dunmore, Pocahontas Co., W. Va. 1860 Census. Enl. Huntersville, Pocahontas Co., W. Va., 3/19/63. Ab. by permission on muster-in roll dated 3/63. Mustered into service 3/19/63. NFR.

GALFORD (GUILFORD), THOMAS J. - Pvt. Co. I. b.c. 1845 (1847). Age 15, Dunmore, Pocahontas Co., W. Va. 1860 Census. Enl. Dunmore, W. Va., 9/15/63. Present 6/30/63 - 2/29/64, mounted; enl. bounty due. Present 2/29/64 - 8/31/64. Clothing issued 7/64 and 8/64. Present 9/1/64 - 10/31/64, $100 bond due. Paroled at Charleston, W. Va., 5/10/65. Desc.: age 20, 5'3", light comp., dark hair, blue eyes and light whiskers. Age 35, farmer, Green Banks, Pocahontas Co., W. Va. 1880 Census. NFR.

GALFORD, WILLIAM HENRY HARRISON - Pvt. Co. F. b Huntersville, Pocahontas Co., 5/26/42. Age 20(?), farmhand, Pocahontas Co., W. Va. 1860 Census. Enl. Hillsboro, Pocahontas Co., W. Va., 8/17/63. Wd. Droop Mtn., 11/6/63. Present 1/1/64 - 2/29/64. Clothing issued 2/7/64. Present 9/1/64 - 10/31/64. Paroled at Charleston, W. Va., 5/10/65. Desc.: age 23, 5'8", fair comp., light hair and blue eyes, wore a mustache. Post war rosters show he had a substitute, in the person of William Pugh. Post war resident of Upshur Co., W. Va. Moved to Bear Garden Run, Braxton Co., W. Va., 1868. Post war farmer at Salt Lick Bridge, Braxton Co., W. Va. Age 38, farmer, Kanawha Dist., Braxton Co., W. Va. 1880 Census. NFR.

GALLAHER, JOHN - Pvt. Co. G. Enl. Frankfort, Greenbrier Co., W. Va., 3/12/63. Not stated if present or absent on muster-in roll dated 3/63. NFR.

GAMMON, CYRUS S. - Pvt. Co. F. b.c. 1828. Prior service, 2nd Co. I, 25th Va. Inf. Enl. Hillsboro, Pocahontas Co., W. Va., 9/1/63. Present 1/1/64 - 2/29/64. Clothing issued 2/6/64. Ab. 9/1/64 - 10/31/64, AWOL since 9/23/64. Paroled at Charleston, W. Va., 5/10/65. Desc.: age 37, 6', dark comp., dark hair, blue eyes and dark whiskers. NFR.

GANDY (GANDER), WILLIAM A. - 2nd Lt. Co. C. b.c. 1840. Prior service, Co. D, 3rd VSL. Enl. Frankfort, Greenbrier Co., W. Va., 3/15/63 (Pocahontas Co., W. Va., 4/1/63). Not stated if present or absent on muster-in roll dated 3/63. Present 1/1/63 - 4/1/63, had one horse cpd. at Prestonburg, Ky. Ab. 12/31/63 - 8/31/64, promoted (elected) 2nd Lt. 2/15/64; cpd. 3/1/64; has one horse. Ab. 9/1/64 - 10/31/64, cpd. 3/1/64. Ab. 10/25/64, POW, six months. CSR shows that he DOD. Wheeling, W. Va., but he did not. It was reported 11/29/64 that Gandy and George Duskey were being held in solitary confinement at Wheeling, W. Va., and in irons. Ordered to be released 1/21/65, and be sent to Ft. Monroe, to be exchanged. It was reported on 1/25/65 that Gandy was not at Wheeling, but had been imprisoned for 10 years for horse stealing, by the Wood Co., W. Va. Court.

Gandy, however, was confined in the Wheeling City Jail, which served as a State Prison. Cpd., Lt., 2/2/65, place not given (this is probably his release date, and the time when the military took control of him again). Confined at Baltimore, then sent to Ft. Monroe. Transportation to Ft. Monroe for Gandy and George W. Dusky ordered 2/4/65. Confined at Camp Hamilton, Ft. Monroe, 2/3/65. Released 2/11/65, awaiting exchanged. Apparently exchanged. Deserted. Surrendered at Charleston, W. Va., 3/65, listed as Pvt. Desc.: age 25, 5'5", dark comp., fair hair and blue eyes. Occ. farmer, residing in Jackson Co., W. Va. Took the amnesty oath and was sent North, 3/25/65. NFR.

GARDNER, JAMES A. - Pvt. Co. B. b. Bath Co., c. 1842. Age 18, farmhand, Webster Co., W. Va. 1860 Census. Enl. Frankfort, Greenbrier Co., W. Va., 3/7/63. Not stated if present or absent on muster-in roll dated 3/63. Post war rosters show him as KIA. Post war rosters show he was from Braxton Co., W. Va. Brother of John L. Gardner. NFR.

GARDNER, JOHN L. - Pvt. Co. B. b. Alleghany Co., c. 1837. Age 23, farmhand, Webster Co., W. Va. 1860 Census. Enl. Frankfort, Greenbrier Co., W. Va., 3/7/63. Not stated if present or absent on muster-in roll dated 3/63. Post war rosters show him as KIA. Post war rosters show he was from Braxton Co., W. Va. Brother of James A. Gardner. NFR.

GARRISON, JACOB "Jack" - Pvt. Co. A. b.c. 1846. Not on muster rolls. Deserted. Surrendered at Parkersburg, W. Va., and took the oath of allegiance, 2/22/65. Arrested Wood Co., W. Va., 3/8/65, suspected of having been drafted in the US Army a few months ago, but preferred to join the rebel service. Sent to Clarksburg, W. Va., 3/12/65. Confined at the Atheneum Prison, 3/21/65. Desc.: age 19, 5'6", fair comp., light hair and blue eyes. Occ. farmer, residing in Wirt Co., W. Va. Sent to Camp Chase, 3/28/65. Confined at Camp Chase, 3/29/65. Took the oath of allegiance and was released, 6/13/65. Desc.: age 19, 5'6_", florid comp., dark hair and blue eyes. NFR.

GARVIN, LEWIS - Pvt. Co. K. b. Bath Co., c. 1839. Age 21, mechanic, Webster Co., W. Va. 1860 Census. Enl. Frankfort, Greenbrier Co., W. Va., 3/20/63. Not stated if present or absent on muster-in roll dated 3/63. Age 49, farmer, Holly Dist., Webster Co., W. Va. 1880 Census. NFR.

GAY, GEORGE V. - 2nd Lt. Co. I. b. Pocahontas Co., W. Va., c. 1835 (1841). Age 25, farmer, Edray, Pocahontas Co., W. Va. 1860 Census. Prior service, 1st Co. K and 2nd Co. D, 62nd Va. Mtd. Inf. Desc. 1862: age 26, 6', dark comp., black hair and hazel eyes. Occ. farmer, residing in Pocahontas Co., W. Va. Enl. Huntersville, Pocahontas Co., W. Va., 2/1/63 (3/18/63). Present on muster-in roll dated 3/63, Sr. 2nd Lt. Mustered into service 3/19/63. Present 6/30/63 - 2/29/64. Ab. 2/29/64 - 8/31/64, KIA in skirmish, 6/64. KIA. on Swago (New Mtn.), W. Va., 6/20/64, age 23.

GAY, JOSEPH C. - Pvt. Co. F. b.c. 1826. Age 34, farmer, Edray, Pocahontas Co., W. Va. 1860 Census. Prior service, 1st Lt., 2nd Co. D and Co. A, 62nd Va. Mtd. Inf. Desc. 1862: age ?, 6'1", dark comp., black hair and blue eyes. Occ. farmer, residing in Pocahontas Co., W. Va. Enl. Hillsboro, Pocahontas Co., W. Va., 4/1/64. Ab. 9/1/64 - 10/31/64, AWOL since 10/5/64. Served as Capt. of a Confederate Home Guard Co., in Pocahontas Co., W. Va. Post war rosters show service in Co. I. Age 53, farmer, Edray, Pocahontas Co., W. Va. 1880 Census. NFR.

GAY, LEVI - 1st Sgt. Co. I. b. 12/22/40. Age 19, farmer, Edray, Pocahontas Co., W. Va. 1860 Census. Enl. Huntersville, Pocahontas Co., W. Va., 3/18/63. Present 6/30/63 - 2/29/64, mounted. Clothing issued, Pvt., 3/22/64. Paroled at Charleston, W. Va., 5/10/65, listed as Sgt. Desc.: age 22, 6', light comp., dark hair, blue eyes and light whiskers. Post war rosters show service in Co. F, 31st W. Inf. Post war Sheriff, Pocahontas Co., W. Va. Age 39, farmer, Edray, Pocahontas Co., W. Va. 1880 Census. NFR.

GEORGE, HENRY J. - Pvt. Co. C. Resident of Roane Co., W. Va. Arrested and held at Wheeling, W. Va. Released on his oath by 3/13/62. Prior service, Co. D, 3rd VSL. Enl. Frankfort, Greenbrier Co., W. Va., 3/15/63 (Pocahontas Co., W. Va., 4/1/63). Not stated if present or absent on muster-in roll dated 3/63. Present 1/1/63 - 4/1/63, has one horse. Present 12/31/63 - 8/31/64, had his own horse since 7/1/64. Clothing issued 2/25/64, 4/30/64, 6/17/64, 7/64 and 8/64. Ab. 9/1/64 - 10/31/64, $100 enl. bounty due; detailed on scout under Capt. Hill; has one horse. Age 46, farmer, Reedy Dist., Roane Co., W. Va. 1880 Census. NFR.

GEORGE, WALTER - Pvt. Co. H. b. Pendleton Co., W. Va., c. 1826 (1829). Age 34, farmer, Calhoun Co., W. Va. 1860 Census. Enl. Frankfort, Greenbrier Co., W. Va., 3/19/63 (Pocahontas Co., W. Va., 4/1/63). Not stated if present or absent on muster-in roll dated 3/63. Deserted. Cpd. Calhoun (Roane) Co., W. Va., 11/1/63. Confined at the Atheneum Prison, 11/20/63. Desc.: age 34, 6'_", light comp., brown hair and blue eyes. Occ. farmer, residing in Roane Co., W. Va. Transf. to Camp Chase, 11/20/63. Confined at Camp Chase, 11/21/63. Desired to take the oath of allegiance, 6/10/64. Statement taken 1/26/65, lists him as age 42, a resident of Roane Co., W. Va. He states that on 9/7/62 a squad of men arrested him and took him to Greenbrier Co., W. Va., and assigned him to Co. H, 19th Va. Cav. He deserted 1/63 and was recaptured 40 miles away. Deserted again 10/27/63 and went home, where he surrendered. Says he never fired a gun in service and has always been opposed to the rebellion. Ab. 9/1/64 - 10/31/64, POW. Took the oath of allegiance and was released 2/17/65, by order of the Sec. of War. NFR.

GIBSON, GEORGE W. - 2nd Lt. Co. A. b. Bath Co., 11/30/40. Resident of Wirt Co., W. Va. Member of Daniel Duskey's section of the Moccasin Rangers. Cpd. Wirt Co., W. Va., 12/15/61. Prior service, Co. A, 3rd VSL. Cpd. 12/31/61 and imprisoned at Camp Chase. Enl. Williamsburg, Greenbrier Co., W. Va., 3/1/63. Not stated if present or absent on muster-in roll dated 3/63. 2nd Lt. by 1/1/64. Paroled at Charleston, W. Va., 5/11/65, listed as 2nd Lt. No desc. Post war resident of Calhoun Co., W. Va. d. Calhoun Co., W. Va., 8/11/1923. Bur. Gibson Cem., Calhoun Co., W. Va.

GIBSON, WILLIAM H. - Pvt. Co. B. b.c. 1836. Enl. Frankfort, Greenbrier Co., W. Va., 3/9/63. Not stated if present or absent on muster-in roll dated 3/63. Present 11/1/63 - 2/29/64, has one horse; detached as clerk for Col. W. L. Jackson at HQ. Clothing issued 1st Qr. 1864 and 10/14/64, while on the way to his command. Ab. 9/1/64 - 10/31/64, AWOL; not entitled to $100 enl. bounty. Paroled at Staunton, 5/12/65. Desc.: age 29, 5'10", fair comp., light hair and hazel eyes. NFR.

GIBSON, WILLIAM L. - Pvt. Co. I. b.c. 1821. Age 39, farmer, Pocahontas Co., W. Va. 1860 Census. Prior service, Co. E, 46th Battn. Va. Cav. Enl. Huntersville, Pocahontas Co., W. Va., 2/1/64. Ab. 2/29/64 - 8/31/64, elected Justice of the Peace, 5/64, relieved from duty 7/10/64; mounted; enl. bounty due; dropped from rolls. NFR.

GILBERT, WALKER - Pvt. Co. C. b.c. 1846. Not on muster rolls. Surrendered at Glenville, W. Va., 5/1/65. Sent to Clarksburg, W. Va. Confined at Clarksburg, W. Va., 5/65, charged with being a deserter. Desc.: age 19, 5'8", fair comp., dark hair and hazel eyes. Occ. farmer, residing in Wood Co., W. Va. Took the amnesty oath and was released, 5/3/65. NFR.

GILLESPIE, JONATHAN Y. - Pvt. Co. ?. b.c. 1842. Age 18, apprentice, Braxton Co., W. Va. 1860 Census. Not on muster rolls. Cpd. and sent to Camp Chase. Took the oath of allegiance and was released 5/13/65. Desc.: age ?, 5'11_", dark comp., dark hair and dark eyes, a resident of Braxton Co., W. Va. Signs oath by x. Age 37, farmer, Holly Dist., Braxton Co., W. Va. 1880 Census. NFR.

GILLESPIE (GILLASPIE), WILLIAM J. - Pvt. Co. F. b.c. 1841. Age 19, farmer, Pocahontas Co., W. Va. 1860 Census. Prior service, McNeel's Co., 2nd VSL. Enl. Hillsboro, Pocahontas Co., W. Va., 3/9/63. Not stated if present or absent on muster-in roll dated 3/63. Cpd. in a hosp., 4/3/65. Adm. Gen. Hosp., Petersburg, 4/15/65. Name appears on a list of POW's at Fair Ground Post Hosp., Petersburg. Paroled 5/5/65. Moved west after the war. Bur. Konantz Cem., Walsh, Colorado.

GILMORE, JAMES A. - Pvt. Co. I. Enl. Pocahontas Co., W. Va., 2/9/63. Ab., AWOL, on muster-in roll dated 3/63. NFR.

GILPIN, SQUIRE WALKER - Pvt. Co. C. Prior service, Co. D, 3rd VSL. Enl. Frankfort, Greenbrier Co., W. Va., 3/15/63 (Pocahontas Co., W. Va., 4/1/63). Not stated if present or absent on muster-in roll dated 3/63. Present 1/1/63 - 4/1/63, has one horse. Present 12/31/63 - 8/31/64. Clothing issued 2/25/64, 4/1/64, 4/30/64 and 8/13/64, signs by x. Ab. 9/1/64 - 10/31/64, $100 enl. bounty due; on horse detail 10/12/64 for 10 days; AWOL since expiration of time. NFR.

GINN, AHAS - Pvt. Co. B. Enl. Frankfort, Greenbrier Co., W. Va., 3/7/63. Not stated if present or absent on muster-in roll dated 3/63. NFR.

GINN, WILLIAM - Pvt. Co. B. Enl. Frankfort, Greenbrier Co., W. Va., 3/7/63. Not stated if present or absent on muster-in roll dated 3/63. NFR.

GITTINGS, JOHN GEORGE JACKSON - 1st Lt./Adjutant. b. 1835. VMI, class of 1856. Prior service, 1st Lt. and Adjutant, 31st Va. Inf. Resigned 5/26/63, accepted 6/27/63. Resigned because the post of adjutant is out of the line of promotion and he has served as such for two years. Acting Adjutant for Major D. B. Stewart's command at the Beverly, W. Va. fight, 7/2/63 - 7/3/73. Recommended as Adjutant of the 19th Va. Cav. by Col. W. L. Jackson, 10/4/63, stating Gittings has been in service since the beginning of the war and is a brave and accomplished officer, and is now with Jackson's command. Appointed Adjutant and 1st Lt., 19th Va. Cav., 10/23/63, to rank from 10/14/63, was confirmed 1/13/64. Present F&S MR 9/1/63 - 10/31/63. Present F&S MR 11/1/63 - 12/31/63. Serving as AAAG, Jackson's Brigade, 1/18/64, 3/10/64 & 3/20/64. Signs MR's of 46th and 47th Battn's. Va. Cav. as Inspecting & Mustering Officer, 8/31/64. Present F&S MR 9/1/64 - 10/31/64, sick. Recommended for Maj., 26th Va. Cav., by Maj. Gen. L. L. Lomax, 10/28/64. Col. W. L. Jackson wrote of Gittings, 12/19/64: "...in my opinion is a most gallant officer - a graduate of the Virginia Military Institute -, and who has served with distinction since the commencement of the war." According to David Poe, Gittings commanded a battn. during 12/64. Commanded the 26th Va. Cav., 1/10/65. Staff File listed as Gittings. Post war rosters show him as Maj. Wrote "Personal Recollections of Stonewall Jackson" in 1899. Post war doctor and resident of Clarksburg, W. Va. d. 1904. Bur. IOOF Cem., Clarksburg, W. Va.

GIVEN (GIVENS), SAMUEL FIELDS Jr. "Uncle Sam" - Pvt. Co. B. b. Nicholas Co., W. Va.. c. 1839 (on Elk River, Webster Co., W. Va., 8/15/36). Age 21, farmhand, Webster Co., W. Va. 1860 Census. Post war rosters only, which show he was a resident of Braxton Co., W. Va. Obit. shows he was wd. and discharged. Wrote several articles about his war experiences for the Braxton Co. newspaper after the war. Post war roster shows service, 40th Va. Cav. (error) Age 52, farmer, Glade, Webster Co., W. Va. 1880 Census. d. 1/4/1912. Bur. Walnut Grove Cem., Braxton Co., W. Va.

GIVEN (GIVENS), ROBERT E. - Pvt. Co. K. b c. 1821. Enl. Frankfort, Greenbrier Co., W. Va., 3/20/63. Not stated if present or absent on muster-in roll dated 3/63. Transf. to Co. B, 19th Va. Cav. Enl. Frankfort. Greenbrier Co., W. Va., 3/7/63. Not stated if present or absent on muster-in roll dated 3/63. Present 11/1/63 - 2/29/64, has one horse. Clothing issued 6/17/64 and 3rd Qr. 1864, signs by x. Ab. 9/1/64 - 10/31/64, $100 enl. bounty due; wd. Woodstock, 10/9/64, sent to hosp. Paroled at Staunton, 5/11/65. Age 44, 6'1", dark comp., dark hair and hazel eyes. Post war roster shows service, 40th Va. Cav. (error). Post war resident of Braxton Co., W. Va. NFR.

GLASKOCK (GLASSCOCK), CHARLES E. - 3rd Corp. Co. D. Enl. Williamsburg, Greenbrier Co., W. Va., 3/8/63. Not stated if present or absent on muster-in roll dated 3/63, 3rd Corp. Served in Co. B, 20th Va. Cav. DOD. Mt. Jackson, 7/31/64. Probably bur. at Mt. Jackson.

GLENN, SAMUEL - Pvt. Co. I. Enl. Huntersville, Pocahontas Co., W. Va., 4/1/63 (8/1/63). Present 6/30/63 - 2/29/64, does not have a horse; enl. bounty due. Present 2/29/64 - 8/31/64. Clothing issued 7/64 and 8/64, signs by x. Ab. 9/1/64 - 10/31/64, AWOL. Post war rosters show he was a volunteer from Rockbridge Co. NFR.

GLOVER, HENRY - Pvt. Co. A. b.c. 1846. Not on muster rolls. Cpd. Marion Co., W. Va., 6/30/63. Confined at the Atheneum Prison, 7/6/63. Desc.: age 17, 5'10", light comp., auburn hair and blue eyes. Occ. farmer, residing in Wetzel Co., W. Va. Transf. to Camp Chase, 8/10/63. Confined at Camp Chase, 8/11/63. Took the oath of allegiance and was released 2/22/64, by order of the Sec. of War. Desc.: age 18, 5'9_", light comp., light hair and gray eyes, a resident of Wetzel Co., W. Va. NFR.

GLOVER, LEVI - Pvt. Co. A. b c. 1840. Not on muster rolls. Cpd. Preston Co., W. Va., 7/1/63. Confined at the Atheneum Prison, 7/2/63. Desc.: age 23, 6'3", dark comp., black hair and green eyes. Occ. farmer, residing in Wetzel Co., W. Va. Transf. to Camp Chase, 8/8/63. Confined at Camp Chase, 8/11/63. Took the oath of allegiance and was released 2/22/64, by order of the Sec. of War. NFR.

GOFF, ALEXANDER B. - Pvt. Co. A. b.c. 1827. Prior service, Co. A, 3rd VSL and Co. A, 22nd Va. Inf. Not on muster rolls. Paroled at Charleston, W. Va., 5/10/65, listed as belonging to Co. A, 19th Va. Cav. Signs oath by x. Desc.: age 38, 6', dark comp., black hair and dark eyes. Post war resident of Calhoun and Ritchie Co., W. Va. Age 61 (?), farmer, Murphy Dist., Ritchie Co., W. Va. 1880 Census. NFR.

GOFF, GEORGE ALLEN - Pvt. Co. E. b. Lewis Co., W. Va., c. 1843. Age 17, farmer, Gilmer Co., W. Va. 1860 Census. Enl. Gilmer Co., W. Va., 5/15/63. Ab. 10/31/63 - 10/31/64, had his own horse since 7/1/64; cpd. 7/15/64; d. in prison. Clothing issued 3/1/64, 4/11/64, 4/30/64 and 5/26/64, signs by x. Cpd. Loudoun Co. (near Harpers Ferry, W. Va.), 7/15/64. Wd. foot, probably when cpd. Sent to Washington, DC, 7/64. Confined at the Old Capitol Prison, 7/17/64. Transf. to Elmira, NY, 7/23/64. Confined at Elmira Prison, 7/25/64. DOD. Elmira, NY, 8/7/64, pneumonia (gunshot wd. to foot). Bur. Woodlawn National Cem., Elmira, NY, grave no. 32 (12).

GOFF (GOUG, GOUGH), JACOB W. - Capt. Co. C. b.c. 1836. Age 14, 1850 Wirt Co., W. Va. Census. Prior service, Co. D, 3rd VSL, listed as Gough. Enl. Frankfort, Greenbrier Co., W. Va., 3/15/63 (Pocahontas Co., W. Va., 4/1/63). Not stated if present or absent on muster-in roll dated 3/63, 4th Sgt. Present, 4th Sgt., 1/1/63 - 4/1/63, had one horse. Promoted to 2nd Lt. Present 2nd Lt., 12/31/63 - 8/31/64, promoted to Capt., 2/1/64. Present Capt., 9/1/64 - 10/31/64. Post war resident of Wirt Co., W. Va. Age 44, farmer, Reedy Dist., Wirt Co., W. Va. 1880 Census. NFR.

GOFF, JAMES R. - Pvt. Co. E. Enl. Frankfort, Greenbrier Co., W. Va., 3/12/63 (4/1/63). Enl. shown on Hosp. MR as Mill Point, Pocahontas Co., W. Va., 9/2/62, by Capt. Duskey. Not stated if present or absent on muster-in roll dated 3/63. Present Hosp. MR, Warm Springs, 4/1/63 - 1/1/64, attached to hosp. 3/19/63 as Wagon Master. Ab. 10/31/63 - 10/31/64, DOD. Harrisonburg Hosp., 8/19/64; not mounted. Clothing issued 1st Qr. 1864, 3/1/64, 5/26/64, 6/17/64.

GOFF, THOMAS M. - Pvt. Co. B. b. Nicholas Co., W. Va., c. 1843. Age 17, farmhand, Webster Co., W. Va. 1860 Census. Prior service, Co. A, 3rd VSL. Enl. Frankfort, Greenbrier Co., W. Va., 3/7/63. Not stated if present or absent on muster-in roll dated 3/63. Served in Co. A, 46th Battn. Va. Cav. and Co. A, 26th Va. Cav. Post war resident of Webster Co., W. Va. Post war rosters show him as a member of Co. A, from Calhoun Co., W. Va. Age 37, farmer, Glade, Webster Co., W. Va. 1880 Census. NFR.

GOFF, WILLIAM H. - Pvt. Co. E. Enl. Gilmer Co., W. Va., 7/15/63. Ab. 10/31/63 - 10/31/64, deserted. Cpd. and took the oath of allegiance and was sent North, 11/22/63. NFR.

GOLDEN, ANDREW J. - Pvt. Co. D. b.c. 1836. Not on muster rolls. Cpd. Webster Co., W. Va., 5/16/64. Confined at the Atheneum Prison, 6/10/64. Desc.: age 28, 5'11", dark comp., dark hair and black eyes. Occ. farmer, residing in Webster Co., W. Va. Transf. to Camp Chase, 6/16/64. Confined at Camp Chase, 6/17/64. Paroled 3/2/65, to be exchanged at City Point, did not go. DOD. Camp Chase, 4/8/65, fever inter. Bur. Camp Chase Confederate Cem., 1/3 mile South of camp, grave no. 1831.

GORDON, WILLIAM H. - Pvt. Co. A. Not on muster rolls. Surrendered at Conrad's Ferry, Md. Paroled 5/5/65. NFR.

GRAN, HENRY H. - Pvt. Co. B. Enl. Frankfort, Greenbrier Co., W. Va., 3/7/63. Not stated if present or absent on muster-in roll dated 3/63. NFR.

GREANLEAF, GEORGE - Pvt. Co. E. Enl. Frankfort, Greenbrier Co., W. Va., 3/13/63 (4/1/63). Not stated if present or absent on muster-in roll dated 3/63. Ab. 10/31/63 - 10/31/64, on horse detail, time now expired. Clothing issued 3/1/64. 5/21/64 and 6/17/64. NFR.

GREATHOUSE, JAMES A. - Pvt. Co. D. b.c. 1846. Enl. Williamsburg, Greenbrier Co., W. Va., 3/8/63. Not stated if present or absent on muster-in roll dated 3/63. Served in Co. B, 20th Va. Cav. Age 34, farmer. Southwest Dist., Doddridge Co., W. Va. 1880 Census. NFR.

GREATHOUSE, JEHU - Pvt. Co. A. Prior service, Co. A, 3rd VSL. Enl. Williamsburg, Greenbrier Co., W. Va., 3/1/63. Not stated if present or absent on muster-in roll dated 3/63. NFR.

GREATHOUSE, JESSE - Pvt. Co. A. b. Jackson Co., W. Va., c. 1840. Age 20, farmer, Calhoun Co., W. Va. 1860 Census. Prior service, Co. A, 3rd VSL. Not on muster rolls. Clothing issued 2/2/64 and 2/19/64. Cpd. Roane Co., W. Va., 4/23/64. Confined at the Atheneum Prison, 5/2/64. Desc.: age 23, 6', fresh comp., light hair and blue eyes. Occ. farmer, residing in Roane Co., W. Va. Transf. to Camp Chase 5/10/64. Confined at Camp Chase 5/11/64. Adm. Chase USA Gen. Hosp., Camp Chase, 9/9/64, variola. RTD. 10/5/64, age 23, not vaccinated. Gave statement at Camp Chase, 1/25/65, listed as age 23, a resident of Calhoun Co., W. Va. Was arrested in Roane Co., W. Va. by the home guards, states that he enl. Webster Co., W. Va., 2/62 for 12 months. Took the oath of allegiance and was released by order of the Sec. of War, 2/17/65. Son of Samuel Greathouse. Cards filed in CSR of Jehu Greathouse. Age 40, farmer, Smithfield Dist., Roane Co., W. Va. 1880 Census. NFR.

GREATHOUSE, SAMUEL WILLIAM - Pvt. Co. A. b. Kanawha Co., W. Va., c. 1816 (1814). Age 44, farmer, Calhoun Co., W. Va. 1860 Census. Prior service, Co. A, 3rd VSL. Enl. Williamsburg, Greenbrier Co., W. Va., 3/1/63. Not stated if present or absent on muster-in roll dated 3/63. Deserted. Cpd. Webster Co., W. Va., 2/10/64. Confined at the Atheneum Prison, 2/21/64. Desc.: age 50, 5'9_", fair comp., dark hair and blue eyes. Occ. farmer, residing in Calhoun Co., W. Va. Transf. to Camp Chase, 3/4/64. Confined at Camp Chase, 3/5/64. Desired to take the oath of allegiance, 6/10/64. Gave statement at Camp Chase, 1/25/65: listed age 52, a resident of Calhoun Co., W. Va. Shown as a member of Co. A, Swann's Inf. Battn. Says he enl. 2/28/63 in Swann's Battn. under threats of violence. Desc. as "deplorably ignorant and easily misled." Took the oath of allegiance and was released by order of the Sec. of War, 2/17/65. Father of Jesse Greathouse. Age 66, work hand, Reedy Dist., Roane Co., W. Va. 1880 Census. NFR.

GREATHOUSE, WILLIAM W. - Pvt. Co. A. Served in Co. A, 3rd VSL. Post war rosters only. NFR.

GREEN, BENJAMIN WATTON (WALTON) - Pvt. Co. B. b.c. 1828. Enl. Frankfort, Greenbrier Co., W. Va., 3/7/63. Not stated if present or absent on muster-in roll dated 3/63. Cpd. Webster Co., W. Va., 5/16/64. Confined at the Atheneum Prison, 6/10/64. Desc.: age 36, 5'9", dark comp., dark hair and gray eyes. Occ. farmer, residing in Webster Co., W. Va. Transf. to Camp Chase 6/16/64. Confined at Camp Chase, 6/17/64. Adm. Chase USA Gen. Hosp., Camp Chase, 9/8/64, variola. Transf. to another hosp., 10/20/64, age 36, not vaccinated. Gave statement at Camp Chase, 2/6/65: listed as age 36, a resident of Webster Co., W. Va. Lists place of capture as Braxton Co., W. Va. Says he enl. 2/1/62 for 12 months and went home at the end of that term, and was arrested in Braxton Co., W. Va. Took the oath of allegiance and was released by order of the Sec. of War, 2/10/65. Desc.: age 36, 5'9", florid comp., black hair and gray eyes, a resident of Webster Co., W. Va. Post war resident of Webster Co., W. Va. Age 51, farmer, Glade, Webster Co., W. Va. 1880 Census, listed as Beniga. NFR.

GREEN, JOHN - Pvt. Co. K. b. Braxton Co., W. Va., c. 1844. Age 16, farmhand, Webster Co., W. Va. 1860 Census. Enl. Frankfort, Greenbrier Co., W. Va., 3/20/63. Not stated if present or absent on muster-in roll dated 3/63. Deserted. Surrendered in W. Va., 11/22/63 and was sent to Wheeling, W. Va. "Had a commission from Genl. J. E. B. Stuart to steal horses." Age 35, Holly Dist., Webster Co., W. Va. 1880 Census. NFR.

GREEN, ROBERT N. - Pvt. Co. I. b.c. 1833. Not on muster rolls. Paroled at Charleston, W. Va., 5/15/65. Desc.: age 32, 6', fair comp., light hair, blue eyes and light whiskers. NFR.

GREEN, ROBERT S. - Pvt. Co. B. b.c. 1844. Enl. Frankfort, Greenbrier Co., W. Va., 3/7/63. Not stated if present or absent on muster-in roll dated 3/63. Post war resident of Webster Co., W. Va. Age 36, farmer, Glade, Webster Co., W. Va. 1880 Census. NFR.

GREEN, WILLIAM - Pvt. Co. C. b.c. 1827. Prior service, Co. D, 3rd VSL. Enl. Frankfort, Greenbrier Co., W. Va., 3/15/63 (Pocahontas Co., W. Va., 4/1/63). Not stated if present or absent on muster-in roll dated 3/63. Present 1/1/63 - 4/1/63, has one horse. Ab. 12/31/63 - 8/31/64, has one horse; cpd. 10/25/63. Ab. 9/1/64 - 10/31/64, $100 enl. bounty due; has one horse; cpd. 10/25/63. Cpd. Roane Co., W. Va., 10/25/63. Confined at the Atheneum Prison, 10/29/63. Desc.: age 36, 5'9", florid comp., sandy hair, blue eyes and sandy whiskers. Occ. farmer, residing in Roane Co., W. Va. Transf. to Camp Chase, 10/30/63. Confined at Camp Chase, 10/31/63. Transf. to Rock Island, Ill., 1/22/64. Confined at Rock Island Prison, 1/24/64. Took the oath of allegiance and was released, 5/16/65. His residence was listed as Ripley, Jackson Co., W. Va. Age 53, farmer, Washington Dist., Jackson Co., W. Va. 1880 Census, listed as Greene. NFR.

GREENLEAF (GREENLEAVES), ALLEN A. - Pvt. Co. K. b. Lewis Co., W. Va., c. 1842. Age 18, farmer, Gilmer Co., W. Va. 1860 Census. Prior service, Co. D, 31st Va. Inf. Enl. Frankfort, Greenbrier Co., W. Va., 3/20/63. Not stated if present or absent on muster-in roll dated 3/63. Clothing issued 3/1/64. Post war resident of Gilmer Co., W. Va. Post war rosters show service in Co. B. Brother of Franklin, John W. and Samuel E. Greenleaf. NFR.

GREENLEAF (GREANLEAF, GREENLEAVES), FRANKLIN - Pvt. Co. E. b. Lewis Co., W. Va., c. 1841. Age 19, farmer, Gilmer Co., W. Va. 1860 Census. Prior service, Co. D, 31st Va. Inf. Enl. Frankfort, Greenbrier Co., W. Va., 3/13/63. Not stated if present or absent on muster-in roll dated 3/63. Clothing issued 3/1/64. Wartime deserter list show service in Co. B, 19th Va. Cav. Post war resident of Gilmer Co., W. Va. Brother of Allen A., John W. and Samuel E. Greenleaf. Age 44, farmer, Center Dist., Gilmer Co., W. Va. 1880 Census. NFR.

GREENLEAF (GREENLEAVES), JOHN W. - Pvt. Co. K. b. Gilmer Co., W. Va., c. 1845. Age 15, farmer, Gilmer Co., W. Va. 1860 Census. Enl. Frankfort, Greenbrier Co., W. Va., 3/20/63. Not stated if present or absent on muster-in roll dated 3/63. Clothing issued 1st Qr. 1864, 2/5/64, 3/25/64, 4/11/64 and 6/17/64, signs by x. Cpd. Gilmer Co., W. Va., 9/9/64 (also as having been cpd. at Glenville, W. Va., 5/23/64). Confined at the Atheneum Prison, 9/18/64. Desc.: age 16 (?), 5'5", fair comp., light hair and gray eyes. Occ. farmer, residing in Gilmer Co., W. Va. Transf. to Camp Chase, 10/6/64. Confined at Camp Chase, 10/7/64, desires to take the oath of allegiance. Desires to take the oath of allegiance, 12/6/64. Took the oath of allegiance and was released, 5/15/65. Desc.: age 20, 5'6", florid comp., dark hair and gray eyes, a resident of Gilmer Co., W. Va. Brother of Franklin, Allen A. and Samuel E. Greenleaf. NFR.

GREENLEAF (GREENLEAVES), SAMUEL E. - Pvt. Co. A. b. Gilmer Co., W. Va., c. 1848. Age 12, Gilmer Co., W. Va. 1860 Census. Not on muster rolls. Cpd. Beverly, W. Va., 10/29/64. Confined at Camp Chase. Took the oath of allegiance and was released, 5/15/65, signed by x. Desc.: age 17, 5'11", dark comp., black hair and dark eyes, a resident of Gilmer Co., W. Va. Brother of Franklin, Allen and John W. Greenleaf. Age 30(?), farmer, Center Dist., Gilmer Co., W. Va. 1880 Census. NFR.

GREGG (GRAGG, GROGG), WILLIAM E. - Pvt. Co. I. b. 1839. Enl. Huntersville, Pocahontas Co., W. Va., 3/1/64. Present 2/29/64 - 8/31/64, mounted; enl. bounty due. Clothing issued 7/64 and 8/64, signed by x. Ab. 9/1/64 - 10/31/64, on horse detail. Cpd. Ritchie Co., W. Va., 4/11/65. Desc.: age 26, 5'7", fair comp., dark hair and hazel eyes. Occ. farmer, residing in Ritchie Co., W. Va. Confined at the Post Guard House, Clarksburg, W. Va. Paroled at Clarksburg, W. Va., 4/24/65. Desc.: age 26, 5'7_", fair comp., dark hair and hazel eyes. Messmate with Brown N. Galford. Post war farmer and stonemason, residing near Durbin, W. Va. Age 34, Green Banks, Pocahontas Co., W. Va. 1880 Census. d. 7/22/1934.

GREGORY, JAMES M. - Pvt. Co. B. b. Braxton Co., W. Va., 8/13/38. Age 22, farmer and mechanic, Webster Co., W. Va. 1860 Census. Not on muster rolls. Cpd. Webster Co., W. Va., 1/1/64 (Hampshire Co., W. Va.), 11/4/63). Confined at the Atheneum Prison, 1/16/64. Desc.: age 26, 5'10", florid comp., brown hair and gray eyes. Occ. miller, residing in Webster Co., W. Va. Transf. to Camp Chase, 1/28/64. Confined at Camp Chase, 1/29/64. Transf. to Ft. Delaware, 3/14/64. Confined at Ft. Delaware, 3/17/64. Paroled 2/27/65, sent to City Point to be exchanged. Post war rosters show service in the 62nd Va. (Mtd.) Inf. Age 41, farmer, Fork Lick, Webster Co., W. Va. 1880 Census. d. 2/18/1923. Bur. Fairview Church Cem., Grassy Creek, Fork Lick Dist., Webster Co., W. Va.

GREGORY, MIFFLIN G. - Pvt. Co. C. b.c. 1842. Not on muster rolls. Deserted. Cpd. Clarksburg, W. Va., 9/10/63. Confined at Clarksburg, W. Va., 10/13/63 (10/7/63). Desc.: age 22 (21), 5'11", fair (dark) comp., brown hair and blue eyes, a resident of Upshur (Harrison) Co., W. Va. Charged that he took the oath of allegiance before joining the rebel army, held for examination. Took the oath of allegiance and sent to Wheeling, W. Va. Confined at the Atheneum Prison, 10/15/63. Desc.: age 21, 6', florid comp., dark hair and blue eyes. Occ. farmer, residing in Upshur Co., W. Va. Transf. to Camp Chase, 10/22/63. Confined at Camp Chase, 10/23/63. Transf. to Rock Island, Ill., 1/22/64. Confined at Rock Island Prison, 1/24/64. Enl. in the US Navy at Rock Island, Ill., sent to the naval rendezvous at Camp Douglas, Chicago, Ill., 1/25/64. Age 37, farmer, Union Dist., Upshur Co., W. Va. 1880 Census. NFR.

GRIFFIN, JAMES L. - Pvt. Co. K. b.c. 1830. Age 30, laborer, Pocahontas Co., W. Va. 1860 Census. Not on muster rolls. Clothing issued 2/23/64, 4/1/64, 4/30/64 and 6/17/64. Cpd. Loudoun Co. (near Harpers Ferry, W. Va.), 7/15/64. Sent to Harpers Ferry, W. Va., then to Washington, DC. Confined at the Old Capitol Prison, 7/17/64. Transf. to Elmira, NY, 7/23/64. Confined at Elmira Prison, 7/25/64. DOD. Elmira, NY, 9/18/64, typhoid pneumonia. Bur. Woodlawn National Cem., Elmira, NY, grave no. 346 (515).

GRIFFITH, JOHN P. - Pvt. Co. D. Enl. Williamsburg, Greenbrier Co., W. Va., 3/8/63. Not stated if present or absent on muster-in roll dated 3/63. NFR.

GREGGORY, LAWRENCE - Pvt. Co. H. Enl. Frankfort, Greenbrier Co., W. Va., 3/19/63. Not stated if present or absent on muster-in roll dated 3/63. NFR.

GUILY (GULLY), JOSEPH N. - Pvt. Co. B. Post war rosters only, which show him as a resident of Big Isaac, W. Va. Alive 1918, living at Miltus, Va. NFR.

GUM, B. FRANKLIN - 4th Sgt. Co. F. Post war rosters only. NFR.

GUM, ERVIN - Pvt. Co. I. Post war rosters only. NFR.

GUM, GEORGE - Pvt. Co. F. Post war rosters only. NFR.

GUM (GUMM), JAMES F. - Pvt. Co. F. b. Pocahontas Co., W. Va., c. 1838. Age 22, constable, Greenbank, Pocahontas Co., W. Va. 1860 Census. Prior service, McNeel's Co., VSL. and Co. G, 31st Va. Inf. Enl. Hillsboro, Pocahontas Co., W. Va., 3/9/63 (4/1/63). Not stated if present or absent on muster-in roll dated 3/63. Present 1/1/64 - 2/29/64. Clothing issued 2/7/64. Present 9/1/64 - 10/31/64, enl. bounty due. NFR.

GUM, JAMES HENRY - Pvt. Co. I. b.c. 1843. Age 17, farmer, Frost, Pocahontas Co., W. Va. 1860 Census. Prior service, Co. F, 31st Va. Inf. Enl. Huntersville, Pocahontas Co., W. Va., 2/8/64. Ab. 6/30/63 - 2/29/64, never reported to the co., dropped from the rolls. d. Portsmouth, 5/14/1926, age 82. Bur. Bedford City Cem.

GUM, JOHN E. - Pvt. Co. F. b.c. 1833. Age 27, farmer, Greenbank, Pocahontas Co., W. Va. 1860 Census. Prior service, McNeel's Co., VSL. Enl. Hillsboro, Pocahontas Co., W. Va., 3/9/63 (4/1/63). Not stated if present or absent on muster-in roll dated 3/63. Ab. 1/1/64 - 2/29/64, sick. Clothing issued 2/6/64. Ab. 9/1/64 - 10/31/64, sick. Enl. Co. I, 19th Va. Cav., Huntersville, Pocahontas Co., W. Va., 1/1/64. Not stated if present or absent 6/30/63 - 2/29/64, mounted; enl. bounty due. Present 2/29/64 - 8/31/64, acting 4th Sgt. since 7/1/64, promoted from Pvt. Present, 4th Sgt., 9/1/64 - 10/31/64, $100 bond due. Post war resident of Highland Co. and Greenbank, W. Va. Age 47, farm laborer, Green Banks, Pocahontas Co., W. Va. 1880 Census. Member Moffett Poague Camp, UCV, Pocahontas Co., W. Va. May have served in the 18th Va. Cav. d. near Arbovale, W. Va., 4/16/1924, age 94. Bur. Arbovale Cem., Pocahontas Co., W. Va.

GUM, McBRIDE - Pvt. Co. I. b.c. 1824. Age 36, farmer, Edray, Pocahontas Co., W. Va. 1860 Census. Enl. Huntersville, Pocahontas Co., W. Va., 3/18/63 (2/18/63). Present on muster-in roll dated 3/63. Mustered into service 3/19/63. Present 6/30/63 - 2/29/64, has no horse. Age 58, farmer, Edray, Pocahontas Co., W. Va. 1880 Census. NFR.

GUM, McBRIDE J. (of Jacob) - Pvt. Co. I. b.c. 1834. Age 26, farmer, Greenbank, Pocahontas Co., W. Va. 1860 Census. Enl. Huntersville, Pocahontas Co., W. Va., 2/1/63 (3/18/63). Present on muster-in roll dated 3/63. Mustered into service 3/19/63. Present 6/30/63 - 2/29/64, mounted. Present 2/29/64 - 8/31/64. Present 9/1/64 - 10/31/64, $100 bond due. Post war rosters show service in Co. F. Age 45, farmer, Green Banks, Pocahontas Co., W. Va. 1880 Census. NFR.

GWATHMEY, JOSEPH W. - Pvt. Co. ?. Post war rosters only. NFR.

GWIN (GUIN, GUINN), JOHN CLAYTON - Pvt. Co. I. b. 10/29/45. Enl. Huntersville, Pocahontas Co., W. Va., 12/4/63. Present 6/30/63 - 2/29/64, mounted; enl. bounty due. Present 2/29/64 - 8/31/64. Ab. 9/1/64 - 10/31/64, sick; $100 bond due. Paroled at Staunton, 6/1/65. Desc.: age 20, 5'11", fair comp., light hair and blue eyes. Post war rosters show he was wd. at Martinsburg, W. Va., during the war. Post war resident of Augusta and Bath Co. Married in Bath Co., 1878. d. Augusta Co., 11/14/1909. Bur. Mt. Tabor Lutheran Church Cem.

HALL, ANDREW J. - Pvt. Co. I. b. Rockbridge Co., c. 1833. Enl. Huntersville, Pocahontas Co., W. Va., 5/22/63. POW records show enl. as Rockbridge Co., 3/62. Present 6/30/63 - 2/29/64, mounted. Present 2/29/64 - 8/31/64. Ab. 9/1/64 - 10/31/64, cpd. Pocahontas Co., W. Va., 10/64. Deserted. Clothing issued 7/64 and 8/64. Cpd. Beverly, W. Va., 10/25/64. Sent to Clarksburg, W. Va. Desc.: age 31, 5'10", fair comp., light hair and gray eyes. Occ. farmer, residing in Rockbridge Co. Took the oath of allegiance and was released, 10/29/64. Post war rosters show him as a resident of Randolph Co., W. Va. NFR.

HALL, DAVID (DANIEL) L. - Pvt. Co. C. Prior service, Co. D, 3rd VSL. Enl. Frankfort, Greenbrier Co., W. Va., 3/15/63. Not stated if present or absent on muster-in roll dated 3/63. Present 1/1/63 - 4/1/63, has one horse. Post war rosters show service in Co. B. NFR.

HALL, JACOB - Pvt. Co. A. b.c. 1848. Not on muster rolls. Enl. Huntersville, Pocahontas Co., W. Va., 4/11/62. Clothing issued 2/19/64, 5/21/64, 5/26/64, 6/17/64, 7/64, 8/64, 10/31/64, 11/15/64, 11/29/64 and 12/2/64, signs by x. Present Hosp. MR, Robertson Hosp., dated 11/30/64. Appears on list of soldiers at Robertson Hosp., dated 12/9/64, showing that he was there 9/23/64, amputation of all toes from his right foot. Furloughed to New Market, 60 days. Paroled at Staunton, 5/27/65. Desc.: age 17, 5'10", fair comp., brown hair and brown eyes. NFR.

HALL, JACOB S. - 1st Corp. Co. E. b. 1839. Resident of Gilmer Co., W. Va. Enl. Frankfort, Greenbrier Co., W. Va., 3/13/63 (4/1/63). Not stated if present or absent on muster-in roll dated 3/63, Pvt. Ab., 1st Corp., 10/31/63 - 10/31/64, cpd. 7/15/64; had his own horse since 7/1/64. Clothing issued, 1st Corp., 3/1/64, 4/30/64 and 6/17/64. Cpd. Loudoun Co. (near Harpers Ferry, W. Va.), 7/15/64. Sent to Harpers Ferry, W. Va., then to Washington, DC. Confined at the Old Capitol Prison, 7/17/64. Transf. to Elmira, NY, 7/23/64. Confined at Elmira Prison, 7/25/64, barracks no. 3, ward 12. Took the oath of allegiance and was released, 7/3/65. Desc.: age ?, 5'10", dark comp., dark hair and blue eyes, a resident of West Point. Brother-in-law to Charles S. Cooper. Post war resident of Wayside, Monroe Co., W. Va. "He was an unreconstructed Confederate and cavalryman to the end." d. 12/77, killed when his horse slipped on an icy stream and fell with him. Bur. Greenbrier Baptist Church Cem., Alderson, W. Va.

HALL, MINOR S. - Pvt. Co. C. Enl. Frankfort, Greenbrier Co., W. Va., 3/15/63. Not stated if present or absent on muster-in roll dated 3/63. NFR.

HALL, NATHANIEL G. - Pvt. Co. G. b.c. 1823. Enl. Pocahontas Co., W. Va., 10/22/63. Present 9/1/64 - 10/31/64, has a serviceable horse. Clothing issued 3/1/64, 4/1/64 and 6/17/64. Clothing issued at Staunton, 9/1/64, on his way to his command. Paroled at Staunton, 5/19/65. Desc.: age 42, 5'10", fair comp., dark hair and black eyes. NFR.

HALL, ROBERT W. - Pvt. Co. E. Enl. Frankfort, Greenbrier Co., W. Va., 3/13/63 (4/1/63). Not stated if present or absent on muster-in roll dated 3/63. Ab. 10/31/64 - 10/31/64, gone to the enemy. Clothing issued 3/1/64 and 4/30/64. NFR.

HALL, THOMAS A. - Pvt. Co. C. Prior service, Co. D, 3rd VSL. Enl. Pocahontas Co., W. Va., 4/1/63. Present 1/1/63 - 4/1/63, has one horse. Ab. 12/31/63 - 8/31/64, deserted 1/5/64, while at Camp Cameron in Bath Co. NFR.

HAMILTON, CALVIN - Pvt. Co. I. b.c. 1845. Not on muster rolls. Cpd. Laurel Hill, W. Va., 7/1/63. Confined at the Atheneum Prison, 7/4/63. Desc.: age 18, 5'11_", dark comp., dark hair and dark eyes. Occ. farmer, residing in Marion Co., W. Va. Transf. to Camp Chase, 7/7/63. Confined at Camp Chase, 7/7/63. Transf. to Ft. Delaware, 7/14/63. Confined at Ft. Delaware, 7/20/63. Released by order of the Sec. of War, joined 1st Conn. Cav. Age 33, carpenter, Lincoln Dist., Marion Co., W. Va. 1880 Census. NFR.

HAMILTON, CHARLES B. - Pvt. Co. F. b.c. 1840. Age 20, laborer, Bath CH, Bath Co. 1860 Census. Enl. Hillsboro, Pocahontas Co., W. Va., 3/19/63 (4/1/63). Not stated if present or absent on muster-in roll dated 3/63. Present 1/1/64 - 2/29/64. Clothing issued 2/6/64. Ab. 9/1/64 - 10/31/64, AWOL since 7/1/64. Name appears on a MR of Co. A, Ward's Battn CS Prisoners, 7/64, deserted from battn., not known. Note in CSR shows that this entry was cancelled. Post war rosters show him as a resident of Bath Co. NFR.

HAMILTON, ELMOS W. - Pvt. Co. D. b. Marion Co., W. Va., c. 1843. Enl. Williamsburg, Greenbrier Co., W. Va., 3/8/63. Not stated if present or absent on muster-in roll dated 3/63. Served in Co. B, 20th Va. Cav. Post war resident of Marion Co., W. Va. Age 38, farmer, Lincoln Dist., Marion Co., W. Va. 1880 Census. NFR.

HAMILTON, GEORGE - Pvt. Co. ?. Pension record only. d. Albemarle Co., 1/10/1922.

HAMILTON, GEORGE J. - Pvt. Co. I. b. Highland Co., c. 1838. Age 22, farmer, Huntersville, Pocahontas Co., W. Va. 1860 Census. Enl. Huntersville, Pocahontas Co., W. Va., 2/1/63 (3/18/63). Present on muster-in roll dated 3/63. Mustered into service 3/19/63. Present 6/30/63 - 2/29/64, mounted. Present 2/29/64 - 8/31/64. Present 9/1/64 - 10/31/64, $100 bond due. Cpd. Huntersville, W. Va., 4/17/65, by Capt. Badger's Co., 8th Ohio Cav. Sent to Clarksburg, W. Va. Confined at Clarksburg, W. Va., 4/25/65. Desc.: age 29(?), 6'_", fair comp., fair hair and blue eyes. Occ. farmer, residing in Pocahontas Co., W. Va.

Paroled for exchange, 4/25/65, and released. Post war resident and pensioner of Okla. Moved to Florida. d. 1902. Bur. Mandarin Cem., Mandarin, Florida.

HAMILTON, JAMES D. - Pvt. Co. I. b.c. 1846. Age 13, Bath CH, Bath Co. 1860 Census. Enl. Huntersville, Pocahontas Co., W. Va., 6/1/64. Present 2/29/64 - 8/31/64, mounted; enl. bounty due. Ab. 9/1/64 - 10/31/64, absent without permission. Paroled at Staunton, 5/25/65. Desc.: age 19, 5'10", fair comp., light hair and black eyes. Post war rosters show him as a resident of Bath Co. NFR.

HAMILTON, JAMES M.- Pvt. Co. D. b.c. 1840. Enl. Williamsburg, Greenbrier Co., W. Va., 3/8/63. Not stated if present or absent on muster-in roll dated 3/63. Served in Co. B, 20th Va. Cav. Post war rosters show he rode with John S. Downs from Marion Co., W. Va. to join the army. Post war resident of Marion Co., W. Va. Age 40, farmer, Lincoln Dist., Marion Co., W. Va. 1880 Census. NFR.

HAMILTON, JOHN LUCIAN - Pvt. Co. G. b. South Buffalo Creek, Rockbridge Co., 2/29/48. Not on muster rolls. Pension record shows service in Co. G, 19th Va. Cav. Post war school teacher and IRS employee, residing at Vesuvius, 1900. Buffalo Dist., Rockbridge Co. 1910 Census. d. Chatham, 5/24/1926. Bur. Collierstown Presbyterian Church Cem.

HAMMER, GEORGE - Pvt. Co. I. Enl. Huntersville, Pocahontas Co., W. Va., 1/1/64. Not stated if present or absent, 6/30/63 - 2/29/64, enl. bounty due. Ab. 2/29/64 - 8/31/64, sick. Ab. 9/1/64 - 10/31/64, sick. NFR.

HAMMOND, S. R. - Pvt. Co. G. Enl. Frankfort, Greenbrier Co., W. Va., 3/12/63. Not stated if present or absent on muster-in roll dated 3/63. NFR.

HAMRICK (HAMBRICK), ARTHUR - Pvt. Co. K. b. Randolph Co., W. Va., c. 1840. Age 20, Webster Co., W. Va. 1860 Census. Enl. Frankfort, Greenbrier Co., W. Va., 3/20/63. Not stated if present or absent on muster-in roll dated 3/63. Brother of George Hamrick. Age 41, farmer, Glade, Webster Co., W. Va. 1880 Census, listed as Hambrick. NFR.

HAMRICK, ASA (ASE) - Pvt. Co. A. b. Lewis Co., W. Va., c. 1824 (1829). Age 31, farmer, Calhoun Co., W. Va. 1860 Census. Prior service, Co. A, 3rd VSL. Enl. Williamsburg, Greenbrier Co., W. Va., 3/1/63. Not stated if present or absent on muster-in roll dated 3/63. Clothing issued 2/19/64, 5/21/64 and 6/17/64. Post war rosters show him as a resident of Calhoun Co., W. Va. Age 46, farmer, Lee Township, Calhoun Co., W. Va. 1870 Census. May have served in Co. G, 10th W. Va. Inf.; MR for 8/18/62 shows that he was cpd. by guerrillas, 7/1/62. Later rolls show that he deserted at Glenville, W. Va., 7/1/62. NFR.

HAMRICK, CHRISTOPHER - Pvt. Co. B. b. Nicholas Co., W. Va., c. 1825. Age 35, farmer, Webster Co., W. Va. 1860 Census. Enl. Frankfort, Greenbrier Co., W. Va., 3/7/63. Not stated if present or absent on muster-in roll dated 3/63. Age 56, farmer, Fork Lick, Webster Co., W. Va. 1880 Census. NFR.

HAMRICK (HAMBRICK), GEORGE - Pvt. Co. K. b. Randolph Co., W. Va., c. 1846. Age 14, Webster Co., W. Va. 1860 Census. Enl. Frankfort, Greenbrier Co., W. Va., 3/20/63. Not stated if present or absent on muster-in roll dated 3/63. Brother to Arthur Hamrick. NFR.

HAMRICK (HAMBRICK), MARSHALL - Pvt. Co. D. b. Braxton Co., W. Va., c. 1843. Age 17, farmhand, Webster Co., W. Va. 1860 Census. Not on muster rolls. POW record shows enl. as Webster Co.. W. Va., 8/7/63. Cpd. Braxton Co., W. Va., 10/13/63. Wd. Bulltown, W. Va., 10/13/63, lower third of leg amputated. Adm. USA Post Hosp., Clarksburg, W. Va., 12/17/63, amputation of leg. Sent to Provost Marshall, 12/31/63. Operation performed by Surgeon Gammon. Confined at the Atheneum Prison, 12/31/63. Desc.: age 28(?), 5'11", dark comp., dark hair and hazel eyes. Occ. farmer, residing in Webster Co., W. Va. Transf. to Camp Chase, 1/4/64. Confined at Camp Chase, 1/5/64. Adm. Chase USA Gen. Hosp, Camp Chase, 1/30/64, smallpox. RTD. 2/21/64. Transf. to Ft. Delaware, 3/14/64. Confined at Ft. Delaware, 3/17/64. Paroled for exchange, 9/14/64. Exchanged at Varina, 9/22/64. Adm. Chimborazo Hosp. No. 5, 9/22/64, amputation of lower third of left leg, paroled prisoner. Present Hosp. MR, Chimborazo Hosp., 9/27/64. Clothing issued at Chimborazo Hosp., 9/27/64. Issued a pass to Bath Co., 9/30/64. Furloughed 9/27/64, 60 days. Adm. CSA Gen. Hosp., Charlottesville, 10/7/64, vulnus sclopeticum, amputation of left leg. Discharged from hosp. 4/18/65. Applied for an artificial limb while at Charlottesville, 10/8/64. Age 37, farmer, Fork Lick, Webster Co., W. Va. 1880 Census. NFR.

HANDSHAW, PERRY - Pvt. Co. H. Enl., Clay Co., W. Va., 5/1/63. Ab. 9/1/64 - 10/31/64, AWOL. NFR.

HANNAH, JOSEPH W. - 2nd Lt. Co. C. b.c. 1828. Age 32, constable, Pocahontas Co., W. Va. 1860 Census. Prior service, Co. D, 3rd VSL. Enl. Mill Point, Pocahontas Co., W. Va., 4/1/63. Present, 3rd Sgt., 1/1/63 - 4/1/63, had one horse. Ab., 2nd Sgt., 12/31/63 - 8/31/64, had one horse; promoted to 2nd Sgt., 2/15/64. Post war rosters show service in Co. A and that he was a resident of Calhoun Co., W. Va. Post war rosters show he was KIA. Winchester, 1863. d. 8/10/64.

HANNAH (HANNA), ROBERT A. - Pvt. Co. F. b.c. 1834. Age 26, trader, Huntersville, Pocahontas Co., W. Va. 1860 Census. Prior service, 2nd Co. I, 25th Va. Inf. and McNeel's Co., VSL. Enl. Hillsboro, Pocahontas Co., W. Va., 3/9/63. Not stated if present or absent on muster-in roll dated 3/63. Returned to 2nd Co. I, 25th Va. Inf. Moved west after the war. NFR.

HARDING, ALEXANDER W. - Pvt. Co. ?. Not on muster rolls. Cpd. Confined at Pt. Lookout. Took the oath of allegiance and was released 6/13/65. Desc.: age ?, 5'7", dark comp., brown hair and blue eyes, a resident of Amherst Co. NFR.

HARDWAY, DAVID - Pvt. Co. G. b.c. 1832. Enl. Frankfort, Greenbrier Co., W. Va., 3/12/63 (4/1/63). Not stated if present or absent on muster-in roll dated 3/63. Clothing issued 1st Qr. 1864, 5/26/64, 6/17/64 and 8/25/64. Present 9/1/64 - 10/31/64, has a serviceable horse. Paroled at Charleston, W. Va., 5/11/65. Desc.: age 33, 6', light comp., dark hair, blue eyes and light whiskers. NFR.

HARLER, THEOPHILUS K. - Pvt. Co. D. b. Tyler Co., W. Va., c. 1838. Not on muster rolls. POW records show his enl. as Richmond, 3/63. Deserted. Cpd. Philippi, W. Va., 3/7/65. Sent to Clarksburg, W. Va., where he took the amnesty oath and was sent to Wheeling, W. Va., 3/9/65. Confined at the Atheneum Prison, 3/11/65. Desc.: age 27, 5'10_", dark comp., dark hair and blue eyes. Occ. saddler, residing in Tyler Co., W. Va. NFR.

HARFORD, SAMUEL H. - Pvt. Co. D. Enl. Williamsburg, Greenbrier Co., W. Va., 3/8/63. Not stated if present or absent on muster-in roll dated 3/63. Clothing issued 1st Qr. 1864, 4/30/64 and 5/25/64. NFR.

HARLESS, A. - Pvt. Co. C. b.c. 1817. Not on muster rolls. Deserted. Took the amnesty oath at Clarksburg, W. Va., 4/11/65, and sent North. Desc.: age 48, 6'1", red comp., light hair and blue eyes, a farmer. NFR.

HARPER, EZEKIEL - Pvt. Co. A. b. 1823. Mexican War Veteran. Acted as a guide (scout) to Brig. Gen. R. S. Garnett, 7/61. Served as Capt. of a Co. of Rangers. An excellent woodsman and a good scout. Led a raid on Beverly, W. Va., 5/62. Served with Imboden's command. Not on muster rolls. Went home on a scout, 10/63. Cpd. Tucker Co., W. Va., 10/28/63. Confined in jail, St. George, Tucker Co., W. Va. Transf. to Rowlesburg, W. Va. the next day, then to Clarksburg and Wheeling, W. Va. Was chained to a post. Confined at the Atheneum Prison, 11/3/63. Desc.: age 39, 5'7", florid comp., dark hair and blue eyes, residing in Tucker Co., W. Va. Transf. to Camp Chase, 11/11/63. Confined at Camp Chase, 11/12/63. Transf. to Rock Island, Ill., 1/14/64. Confined at Rock Island Prison, 1/17/64. Exchanged 2/15/65 under the name of Allen Gibson, Pvt. Co. D, Kirkpatrick's Battn. Post war rosters show he was transf. to Pt. Lookout, and exchanged. Post war resident of Tucker Co., W. Va. d. 1892.

HARPER, FRANKLIN (FRANCIS) WILSON "Frank" - Pvt. Co. I. b. Huntersville, W. Va., 5/20/46. Enl. Huntersville, Pocahontas Co., W. Va., 4/24/64. Present 2/29/64 - 8/31/64, mounted; enl. bounty due. Ab. 9/1/64 - 10/31/64, sick. Paroled at Charleston, W. Va., 5/10/65. Desc.: age 19, 5'8", fair comp., dark hair and black eyes. Signs parole as Francis W. Harper. Post war farmer and resident of Hillsboro, W. Va. Member UCV. Age 34, farmer, Little Levels, Pocahontas Co., W. Va. 1880 Census. Age 78 in 1924. Brother of Preston M. Harper. d. Hillsboro, W. Va., 3/12/1927. Bur. Hillsboro, W. Va.

HARPER, JOHN T. - Pvt. Co. G. Enl. Frankfort, Greenbrier Co., W. Va., 3/12/63 (4/1/63). Not stated if present or absent on muster-in roll dated 3/63. Employed as forage master, 11/63. Employed as forage master at Warm Springs, 1/1/64 - 3/31/64. Clothing issued 5/21/64 and 3rd Qr. 1864. Present 9/1/64 - 10/31/64, has a serviceable horse; detailed in the QM Dept. Post war resident of White Sulphur Dist., Greenbrier Co., W. Va. Member of David S. Creigh Camp, UCV, Lewisburg, W. Va., 1895. NFR.

HARPER, PETER - Pvt. Co. I. b.c. 1840. Age 20, farmer, Huntersville, Pocahontas Co., W. Va. 1860 Census. Enl. Huntersville, Pocahontas Co., W.Va., 2/1/63 (3/18/63). Present on muster-in roll dated 3/63. Mustered into service 3/19/63. Present 6/30/63 - 2/29/64, sick; mounted. Ab. 2/29/64 - 8/31/64, sick. Clothing issued 3/22/64. Ab. 9/1/64 - 10/31/64, sick. Paroled at Staunton, 6/1/65. Desc.: age 25, 5'9", fair comp., light hair and blue eyes. Age 40, Huntersville, Pocahontas Co., W. Va. 1880 Census. NFR.

HARPER, PRESTON MOORE - Pvt. Co. I. b. 3/16/44. Age 16, farmer, Huntersville, Pocahontas Co., W. Va. 1860 Census. Enl. Huntersville, Pocahontas Co., W. Va., 2/1/63 (3/18/63). Present on muster-in roll dated 3/63. Mustered into service 3/19/63. Present 6/30/63 - 2/29/64, mounted. Present 2/29/64 - 8/31/64. Present 9/1/64 - 10/31/64, $100 bond due. Paroled at Charleston, W. Va., 5/10/65. Desc.: age 21, 5'10_", dark comp., black hair and black eyes. Brother of Franklin W. Harper. Age 36, farm laborer, Huntersville, Pocahontas Co., W. Va. 1880 Census. d. Marlinton, W. Va., 10/24/1913, age 69.

HARRIS, JOHN W. - Pvt. Co. ?. b.c. 1843. Post war rosters only, which show he was a member of Jackson's Cav. Brigade, and that he was a resident of Lewis Co., W. Va. Age 37, farmer, Skin Creek Dist., Lewis Co., W. Va. 1880 Census. NFR.

HARRIS, WILLIAM - 1st Lt. Co. A. b. Rockingham Co., 1828. Resident of Parkersburg, Wood Co., W. Va. Printer and type-setter, "Parkersburg News." Publisher of "Old Dominion." Recruited men for the Moccasin Rangers. Served as Capt. of his own company of the 3rd VSL. Post war rosters also show him as cpd. at Big Bend, 7/2/62, and that he rejoined his command. Commissioned Capt., 3/18/62. Sent a large amount of mail, medicine, stolen horses and other plunder to the Confederacy. Enl. Williamsburg, Greenbrier Co., W. Va., 3/1/63. Not stated if present or absent on muster-in roll dated 3/63, 1st Lt. Commanding Co., 7/2/63. On the evening of 7/3/63, he told his friends that he felt he would be killed in battle the next day. They tried to cheer him up, and poked fun at his premonition, but to no avail. So despondent was he that he would not remain with his company that night, but remained alone on the hillside. On the morning of 7/4/63, he gave a ring and some letters to Lieut. Logue, with the request that they be sent to Parkersburg, W. Va. Wd. right hand, little finger shot off. Wd. again, in the thigh, severing the artery, causing him to bleed to death. Was wd. the second time by his own men, which mistook him for a Union man. KIA. Beverly, W. Va., 7/4/63, while leading a charge. Name appears on a list of casualties of Maj. D. Boston Stewart's command at Beverly, W. Va., 7/2/63 - 7/9/63. Commanding Co. A at the time of his death. Post war rosters show his date of death as 6/29/63. Post war rosters show him as 2nd Lt. and Capt. "Well educated, generous, high minded and a pure patriot, he laid all upon the alter of his country."

HARRISON, JACOB W. - 3rd Sgt. Co. C. Enl. Frankfort, Greenbrier Co., W. Va., 3/15/63. Not stated if present or absent on muster-in roll dated 3/63, 3rd Sgt. NFR.

HARROLD (HEROLD), BENJAMIN F. - Pvt. Co. I. b.c. 1842. Age 18, farmer, Pocahontas Co., W. Va. 1860 Census. Enl. Huntersville, Pocahontas Co., W. Va., 3/19/63. Ab. by permission on muster-in roll dated 3/63. Served in 2nd Co. I, 25th W. Va. Inf. Brother of John A. Harrold. NFR.

HARROLD (HEROLD), JOHN ANDREW - Pvt. Co. I. b. 8/7/22. Enl. Huntersville, Pocahontas Co., W. Va., 7/15/63. Ab. 2/29/64 - 8/31/64, detailed with broken down horses. Ab. 9/1/64 - 10/31/64, wd. Paroled at Charleston, W. Va., 5/10/65. Desc.: age 43, 5'9", fair comp., brown hair, gray eyes and brown whiskers. d. 6/28/1902. Brother to Benjamin Harrold.

HARROLD (HEROLD), WASHINGTON L. - Pvt. Co. I. b. Pocahontas Co., W. Va., c. 1829. Farmer, age 26 (1855). Enl. Huntersville, Pocahontas Co., W. Va., 3/19/63. Ab. by permission on muster-in roll dated 3/63. Age 53, farmer, Huntersville, Pocahontas Co., W. Va. 1880 Census. NFR.

HARTMAN, PETER N. - Pvt. Co. F. b.c. 1845. Age 15, farmer, Greenbank, Pocahontas Co., W. Va. 1860 Census. Enl. Hillsboro, Pocahontas Co., W. Va., 8/9/63. Present 1/1/64 - 2/29/64. Present 9/1/64 - 10/31/64, enl. bounty due. Paroled at Charleston, W. Va., 5/10/65. Desc.: age 20, 5'8", dark comp., black hair, black eyes and brown whiskers. Moved west after the war. Brother William B. Hartman. NFR.

HARTMAN, WILLIAM B. - Pvt. Co. F. b.c. 1843. Age 17, farmer, Greenbank, Pocahontas Co., W. Va. 1860 Census. Enl. Hillsboro, Pocahontas Co., W. Va., 4/1/63. Present 1/1/64 - 2/29/64. Ab. 9/1/64 - 10/31/64, wd. Shepherdstown, W. Va., 8/25/64; enl. bounty due. Paroled at Charleston, W. Va., 5/10/65. Desc.: age 22, 5'8", light comp., brown hair, black eyes and light whiskers. Moved west after the war. Brother Peter N. Hartman. NFR.

HARVEY, LEWIS C. - Capt. and Asst. Surg. b.c. 1839. Not on muster rolls. Paid for service from 1/1/64 to 8/31/64. Granted 30 day leave, 2/6/64, listed as Asst. Surg. Cpd. Pocahontas Co., W. Va., 5/6/64. Confined at the Atheneum Prison, 5/16/64. Desc.: age 25, 5'9", fair comp., dark hair and gray eyes. Occ. surgeon, residing in Lawdness (?), Miss. Transf. to Camp Chase, 5/17/64. Confined at Camp Chase, 5/18/64. Transf. to Ft. Delaware, 8/15/64. Confined at Ft. Delaware, 8/17/64. Released unconditionally, 9/15/64. NFR.

HASKINS, JOSEPH - Pvt. Co. D. Not on muster rolls. Wartime letter shows he was KIA. New Market, 1864. NFR.

HAUGHT, GARRETT - Pvt. Co. A. b.c. 1845. Not on muster rolls. Cpd. Preston Co., W. Va. 7/1/63. Confined at the Atheneum Prison, 7/2/63. Desc.: age 18, 6', light comp., light hair and green eyes. Occ. farmer, residing in Monongahala Co., W. Va. Transf. to Camp Chase, 8/10/63. Confined at Camp Chase, 8/11/63. Took the oath of allegiance and was released 8/8/64 by order of the Sec. of War. Desc.: age 20, 6', light comp., light hair and gray eyes. NFR.

HAUGHT, SILAS - Pvt. Co. A. b.c. 1835. Not on muster rolls. Cpd. Preston Co., W. Va. 7/1/63. Confined at the Atheneum Prison, 7/2/63. Desc.: age 28, 5'11", florid comp., auburn hair and blue eyes. Occ. farmer, residing in Monongahala Co., W. Va. Transf. to Camp Chase, 8/10/63. Confined at Camp Chase, 8/11/63. Took the oath of allegiance and was released 8/8/64 by order of the Sec. of War. Desc.: age 30, 5'10", light comp., light hair and gray eyes. Age 46, farmer, Battelle Dist., Monongalia Co., W. Va. 1880 Census. NFR.

HAYS, JOHN E. - Pvt. Co. I. b.c. 1821. Not on muster rolls. Paroled at Charleston, W. Va. 5/10/65. Desc.: age 44, 6', light comp., gray hair, gray eyes and gray whiskers. NFR.

HAYS, PEREGRINE G. "Perry" - Pvt. Co. A. b. Harrison Co., W. Va., 10/7/19. Post war rosters only. Moved from Lewis Co., W. Va., to Gilmer Co., W. Va., then to Arnoldsburg, Calhoun Co., W. Va., c. 1840. Postmaster, Arnoldsburg, W. Va., 1849. Represented Gilmer and Wirt Co's., in the Va. House of Delegates, 1855-56. Partner with George W. Silcott in the mercantile and land business. Major, Va. Militia, on Gov. Wise's staff. Wealthiest man in Calhoun Co., W. Va., 1860. Served as Sheriff of Calhoun Co., W. Va., 1861. Helped organize the "Moccasin Rangers" in 1861, along with George W. Silcott. Became disgusted with the actions of the co., and returned to Arnoldsburg, W. Va. Capt. Daniel Duskey ordered his arrest for desertion. US forces arrested him, and he was confined at Camp Chase. Paroled, and went to Monroe Co., W. Va. There he served as a purchasing agent for the CS QM Dept. Despite his commission as Major, Hays enl. as a Pvt. in Capt. George Downs' Co. Enl. in Capt. George Down's Co., the Moccasin Rangers. Entered Spencer, W. Va. with George W. Silcott, under flag of truce and secured a cease fire for 8 days from Col. J. C. Rathbone, so Capt. Down's men could visit their homes unmolested. Commissioned as Major by Gov. John Letcher. Cpd. Big Bend, Calhoun Co., W. Va., 1862. Confined at Camp Chase. Paroled for exchange. Served in the W. Va. Legislature, 1866 and 1877. Age 51, farmer, Lee Township, Calhoun Co., W. Va. 1870 Census. Age 59, farmer, Glenville, Gilmer Co., W. Va. 1880 Census. d. 1/6/1905. Bur. Glenville, Gilmer Co., W. Va.

HEATER, CALVIN - Pvt. Co. B. b. 1/4/31 (1/4/34). Prior service, 22nd Va. Inf. Gave himself up in Gilmer Co., W. Va., 6/12/62. Confined at the Atheneum Prison, then sent to Camp Chase, 6/30/62. Desc.: age 30, 6'_", dark comp., brown hair, dark eyes and light mustache and beard. Paroled for exchange 8/25/62, sent to Vicksburg, Miss. Exchanged near Vicksburg, Miss., 9/11/62. States he volunteered in the 22nd Va. Inf., came home on furlough, tired of service, and gave himself up. Enl. Frankfort, Greenbrier Co., W. Va., 3/7/63. Not stated if present or absent on muster-in roll dated 3/63. Cpd. Glenville (also as Braxton Co.), W. Va., 5/23/64. Confined at the Atheneum Prison, Desc.: age 33, 5'8", dark comp., dark hair and brown eyes. Occ. farmer, residing in Braxton Co., W. Va. Transf. to Camp Chase, 10/6/64. Confined at Camp Chase, 10/7/64, desires to take the oath of allegiance. Took the oath of allegiance and was released, 6/13/65. Desc.: age 33, 6'1", dark comp., dark hair and dark eyes, a resident of Braxton Co., W. Va. Age 49, farmer, Salt Lick Dist., Braxton Co., W. Va. 1880 Census. Brother of Perry Heater; 1st Cousin of Elijah Heater. d. 1905. Bur. Burnsville, Braxton Co., W. Va. Stone in Spring Run Cem., Petroleum, Ritchie Co., W. Va. for him and his wife.

HEATER, ELIJAH - Pvt. Co. B. b. Braxton Co., W. Va., 1834. From Gilmer Co., W. Va. Prior service, Co. D, 31st Va. Inf. and 22nd Va. Inf. Age 26 (1861). Gave himself up in Gilmer Co., W. Va., 6/12/62. Confined at the Atheneum Prison, then sent to Camp Chase, 6/30/62. Desc.: age 25, 6', light comp., brown hair, blue eyes and light mustache. Paroled for exchange 8/25/62, sent to Vicksburg, Miss. Exchanged near Vicksburg, Miss., 9/11/62. States he volunteered in the 22nd Va. Inf., came home on furlough, tired of service, and gave himself up. Enl. Frankfort, Greenbrier Co., W. Va., 3/7/63. Not stated if present or absent on muster-in roll dated 3/63. Cpd. Droop Mtn., Pocahontas Co., W. Va., 11/6/63. Confined at the Atheneum Prison, 11/16/63. Desc.: age 24, 6'4", fair comp., sandy hair and blue eyes. Occ. farmer, residing in Gilmer Co., W. Va. Transf. to Camp Chase, 11/18/63. Confined at Camp Chase, 11/18/63. Transf. to Ft. Delaware, 2/29/64. Confined at Ft. Delaware, 3/4/64 (3/2/64). Took the oath of allegiance and was released 6/15/65, signs by x. Desc.: age ?, 6', dark comp., dark hair and blue eyes, a resident of Gilmer Co., W. Va. Post war rosters show his residence as Braxton Co., W. Va. Age 41, farmer, Salt Lick Dist., Braxton Co., W. Va. 1880 Census. 1st Cousin to Calvin and Perry Heater. NFR.

HEATER, KELLER (KELLEY, KELIS) R. - 3rd Sgt. Co. B. b.c. 1835. Age 25, farmer, Braxton Co., W. Va. 1860 Census. Prior service, 1st Co. I and 2nd Co. G, 62nd Va. Mtd. Inf. Enl. Pocahontas Co., W. Va., 8/20/63. Clothing issued 3/21/64, 5/21/64 and 6/17/64. Present, 3rd Sgt., 9/1/64 - 10/31/64, promoted to 3rd Sgt. 7/1/64; transf. from 62nd Va. Mtd. Inf.; $100 enl. bounty due. Surrendered at Bulltown, W. Va., 5/1/65. Confined at Clarksburg, W. Va., 5/3/65. Desc.: age 30, 5'10", dark comp., brown hair and black eyes. Occ. farmer, residing in Braxton Co., W. Va. Paroled at Clarksburg, W. Va., 5/3/65, to be exchanged, and released. NFR.

HEATER, PERRY - Pvt. Co. B. b. Braxton Co., W. Va., c. 1842. Age 18, Braxton Co., W. Va. 1860 Census. Enl. Frankfort, Greenbrier Co., W. Va., 3/7/63 (3/9/63). POW records show his enl. as Pocahontas Co., W. Va., 12/61. Not stated if present or absent on muster-in roll dated 3/63. Present 11/1/63 - 2/29/64, has one horse. Clothing issued 6/17/64, signs by x. Present 9/1/64 - 10/31/64. $100 enl. bounty due. Cpd. near Buckhannon, W. Va., 2/17/65. Sent to Clarksburg, W. Va., then to Wheeling, W. Va., 2/22/65. Confined at the Atheneum Prison, 2/22/65. Desc.: age 20, 6', fair comp., brown hair and dark eyes. Occ. farmer, residing in Braxton Co., W. Va. Transf. to Camp Chase, 2/24/65. Confined at Camp Chase, 2/25/65. Took the oath of allegiance and was released, 6/13/65. Desc.: age 21, 6'1", dark comp., dark hair and brown eyes, a resident of Braxton Co., W. Va. Brother of Calvin Heater; 1st Cousin of Elijah Heater. NFR.

HEATER, PETER - Pvt. Co. B. Post war rosters only, which show he was a resident of Braxton Co., W. Va. NFR.

HEATER, THOMAS B. - Pvt. Co. A. b.c. 1830. Resident of Gilmer Co., W. Va. Arrested and confined by 3/15/62. Charged with being a bushwhacker. Prior service, Co. A, 3rd VSL. Enl. Williamsburg, Greenbrier Co., W. Va., 3/1/63. Not stated if present or absent on muster-in roll dated 3/63. Cpd. Calhoun Co., W. Va., 12/12/64. Confined at the Atheneum Prison, 12/23/64. Desc.: age 34, 5'11", dark comp., brown hair and blue eyes. Occ. farmer, residing in Calhoun Co., W. Va. Transf. to Camp Chase, 12/27/64. Confined at Camp Chase, 12/28/64, desires to take the oath of allegiance. Took the oath of allegiance and was released, 6/12/65, signs by x. Desc.: age 34, 5'11", light comp., dark hair and blue eyes, a resident of Calhoun Co., W. Va. NFR.

HEAVENER (HEVENER), WILLIAM - Pvt. Co. I. Post war rosters only, which show him as a resident of Highland Co. NFR.

HEAVNER (HEVENER, HEFFNER), GEORGE WASHINGTON - Pvt. Co. I. b. Highland Co., 12/18/31. Age 28, farmer, New Hamden, Highland Co. 1860 Census. Prior service, Co. E, 31st Va. Inf. Enl. Huntersville, Pocahontas Co., W. Va., 1/1/64.

Not stated if present or absent 6/30/63 - 2/29/64, mounted; enl. bounty due. Ab. 2/29/64 - 8/31/64, detailed as farmer, 9/16/64; mounted; enl. bounty due. Officially transf. to Co. I, 19th Va. Cav., 2/27/65, being unable to perform inf. duty. Post war resident of Hightown, Highland Co. d. Hightown, 1/10/1918.

HECKERT (HACKERT), ADAM A. - Pvt. Co. A. Prior service, Co. A, 3rd VSL. Enl. Williamsburg, Greenbrier Co., W. Va., 3/1/63. Not stated if present or absent on muster-in roll dated 3/63. Post war resident of Calhoun Co., W. Va. NFR.

HECKERT (HACKERT), HENRY H. (W.) - Pvt. Co. A. Prior service, Co. A, 3rd VSL. Enl. Williamsburg, Greenbrier Co., W. Va., 3/1/63. Not stated if present or absent on muster-in roll dated 3/63. Clothing issued 2/2/64 and 3/21/64. Post war resident of Calhoun Co., W. Va. NFR.

HECKERT, JOHN S. - Pvt. Co. E. b. Gilmer Co., W. Va., c. 1833. Age 27, house carpenter, Gilmer Co., W. Va. 1860 Census. Enl. Bath Co., 1/1/64. Present 10/31/63 - 10/31/64, enl. bounty due. Clothing issued 3/1/64, 4/21/64 and 6/17/64. Paroled at Charleston, W. Va., 5/11/65. Desc.: age 33, 5'7", dark comp., brown hair, black eyes and brown whiskers. Age 40(?), farmer, Troy, Gilmer Co., W. Va. 1880 Census. NFR.

HEFNER, JAMES - Pvt. Co. A. Served in Co. A, 3rd VSL. Post war rosters only. NFR.

HEFNER, JOHN W. - Pvt. Co. A. b. Greenbrier Co., W. Va., c. 1833 (1837). Age 23, farmer, Calhoun Co., W. Va. 1860 Census. Prior service, Co. A, 3rd VSL. Not on muster rolls. Paid on 10/18/64 for service from 11/1/62 - 2/28/63. Clothing issued 2/18/64. Clothing issued at Staunton Gen. Hosp., 10/18/64. Paroled at Charleston, W. Va., 5/11/65. Desc.: age 32, 5'11", dark comp., black hair, blue eyes and black whiskers. Post war resident of Calhoun Co., W. Va. NFR.

HEFNER (HEAVENER, HEVENER), SAMUEL C. - Pvt. Co. F. b. Broadway, Rockingham Co., 9/8/43. Age 16, farm hand, Pocahontas Co., W. Va. 1860 Census. Enl. Hillsboro, Pocahontas Co., W. Va., 9/10/63. Present 1/1/64 - 2/29/64. Present 9/1/64 - 10/31/64, enl. bounty due. Paroled at Charleston, W. Va., 5/10/65. Desc.: age 21, 5'5", fair comp., black hair and blue eyes. Post war farmer and resident of Hosterman, W. Va. Age 36, farmer, Green Banks, Pocahontas Co., W. Va. 1880 Census. Age 79 in 1924. d. Hosterman, W. Va., 6/21/1926. Bur. Hosterman, W. Va.

HEFNER (HEAVENER, HEVENER), URIAH - Pvt. Co. F. b. near Hightown, Highland Co., 5/20/22. Age 38, farmer, Pocahontas Co., W. Va. 1860 Census. Enl. Hillsboro, Pocahontas Co., W. Va., 10/1/63. Present 1/1/64 - 2/29/64. Ab. 9/1/64 - 10/31/64, on detached service, attending horses; enl. bounty due. Listed as a deserter in Highland Co., tending horses, 12/2/64. Order for his arrest issued, which was endorsed on 2/10/65 that he was Sheriff of Pocahontas Co., W. Va., and is exempt from service. Age 58, farmer, Green Banks, Pocahontas Co., W. Va. 1880 Census. d. near Arbovale, Green Bank Dist., Pocahontas Co., W. Va., 5/8/1912, age 89 years, 11 months and 18 days.

HEFFNER (HEFNER), JAMES - Pvt. Co. B. b.c. 1825. Post war rosters only, which show him as a resident of Braxton Co., W. Va. Age 55, farmer, Salt Lick Dist., Braxton Co., W. Va. 1880 Census. NFR.

HELMES, MATHEW - Pvt. Co. I. Not on muster rolls. Cpd. Loudoun Co., 7/16/64. Confined at Elmira Prison. DOD. Elmira, NY, 1/18/65, pneumonia. Bur. Woodlawn National Cem., Elmira, NY.

HENDERSHOTT, JOHN - Pvt. Co. C. b.c. 1832. Enl. Pocahontas Co., W. Va., 5/10/63. Ab. 12/31/63 - 8/31/64, cpd. 10/13/63; has one horse. Cpd. Bulltown, Braxton Co., W. Va., 10/13/63. Confined at the Atheneum Prison, 10/20/63. Desc.: age 31, 5'10", fair comp., light hair and blue eyes, a resident of Wood Co., W. Va. Transf. to Camp Chase, 10/22/63. Confined at Camp Chase, 10/23/64. Transf. to Rock Island, Ill., 1/22/64. Confined at Rock Island Prison, 1/24/64. Desired to take the oath of allegiance 3/18/64, "will be loyal." Ab. 9/1/64 - 10/31/64, $100 enl. bounty due; cpd. 10/13/63; has one horse. Took the oath of allegiance and was released 5/20/65, a resident of Wood Co., W. Va. Reference jacket shows service in Co. B, 20th Va. Cav. Post war resident of Wood Co., W. Va. NFR.

HENRY, JUDSON - Pvt. Co. C. From Wood Co., W. Va. Prior service, Co. D, 3rd VSL. Enl. Frankfort, Greenbrier Co., W. Va., 3/15/63. Not stated if present or absent on muster-in roll dated 3/63. Ab. 1/1/63 - 4/1/63, d. 2/10/63, had one horse.

HERTZOG, W. T. - Surg. Not on muster rolls. Wartime letter of Seth Slocum mentions him as "our" physician, 2/27/64. Cpd. Beverly, W. Va., 10/29/64. Cared for the wd. prisoners there. Served in the 46th Battn. Va. Cav. NFR.

HETER, HENRY H. - Pvt. Co. K. Enl. Frankfort, Greenbrier Co., W. Va., 3/20/63. Not stated if present or absent on muster-in roll dated 3/63. NFR.

HEVENER, G. H. - Pvt. Co. I. Post war rosters only. Could be George Washington Heavner. NFR.

HEVENER (HEAVENER), LEVI - Pvt. Co. I. b. 1833. Age 26, farmer, Randolph Co., W. Va. 1860 Census. Prior service, Co. F, 31st Va. Inf. Transf. to Co. I, 19th Va. Cav., 2/27/65, being unable to perform inf. service. Not on muster rolls. Paroled at Staunton, 5/25/65. Desc.: age 30, 6', fair comp., light hair and blue eyes. Post war resident of Mingo, Randolph Co., W. Va. Age 45, farmer, Mingo, Randolph Co., W. Va. 1880 Census. d. Mingo, W. Va., 2/1/1905. Bur. Heavener Cem., Monterville, Randolph Co., W. Va.

HEWITT, JOSEPH M. (N.) - Pvt. Co. E. b. Ritchie Co., W. Va., c. 1835. Age 25, farmer, Gilmer Co., W. Va. 1860 Census. Enl. Gilmer Co., W. Va., 10/8/64. Ab. 10/31/63 - 10/31/64, new recruit; on horse detail, time now expired. NFR.

HEWITT, LEVI - 2nd Lt. Co. E. b. Preston Co., W. Va., c. 1840. Age 20, Gilmer Co., W. Va. 1860 Census. Enl. Frankfort, Greenbrier Co., W. Va., 3/13/63. Not stated if present or absent on muster-in roll dated 3/63, Pvt. Present, Sgt., 10/31/63 - 10/31/64, had his own horse since 7/1/64. Clothing issued as 3rd Sgt., 1st Qr. 1864, 3/1/64 and 6/17/64. Paroled at Charleston, W. Va., 5/11/65, listed as 2nd Lt. Desc.: age 24, 5'5", dark comp., black hair and black eyes. Brother of Rosewell G. Hewitt. NFR.

HEWITT, ROSWELL G. - 3rd Corp. Co. E. b. Preston Co., W. Va., c. 1838. Age 22, farmer, Gilmer Co., W. Va. 1860 Census. Enl. Frankfort, Greenbrier Co., W. Va., 3/13/63. Not stated if present or absent on muster-in roll dated 3/63, 4th Corp. Present 10/31/63 - 10/31/64, had his own horse since 7/1/64. Clothing issued as 3rd Corp., 3/1/64, 4/30/64, 6/17/64 and 3rd Qr. 1864. Paroled at Charleston, W. Va., 5/11/65. Desc.: age 27, 5'9_", dark comp., dark hair, dark eyes and dark whiskers. Brother of Levi Hewitt. Age 42, laborer, Center Dist., Gilmer Co., W. Va. 1880 Census. NFR.

HIBBS (HEBBS, HAIBBS), PETER - Pvt. Co. A. b.c. 1837. Not on muster rolls. Cpd. Preston Co., W. Va. 7/1/63. Confined at the Atheneum Prison, 7/2/63. Desc.: age 26, 5'8_", fresh comp., dark hair and blue eyes. Occ. farmer, residing in Wetzel Co., W. Va. Transf. to Camp Chase, 8/10/63. Confined at Camp Chase, 8/11/63. Took the oath of allegiance and was released 1/30/64 by order of the Sec. of War. NFR.

HIGGINBOTHAM, ANDREW - Pvt. Co. G. Enl. Frankfort, Greenbrier Co., W. Va., 3/12/63. Not stated if present or absent on muster-in roll dated 3/63. NFR.

HIGGINS, CHARLES - Pvt. Co. D. b.c. 1829. Not on muster rolls. Cpd. Beverly, W. Va., 2/10/64. Confined at the Atheneum Prison, 2/21/64. Desc.: age 35, 5'6 3/4", fresh comp., light hair and blue eyes. Occ. farmer, residing in Rockbridge Co. Took the oath of allegiance and was released 2/22/64. NFR.

HIGHRY, JOSEPH L. - Pvt. Co. A. Enl. Williamsburg, Greenbrier Co., W. Va., 3/1/63. Not stated if present or absent on muster-in roll dated 3/63. NFR.

HILL, RICHARD V. - Pvt. Co. F. b. Pocahontas Co., W. Va., c. 1830. Age 30, clerk, Academy, Pocahontas Co., W. Va. 1860 Census. Member Hillsboro Patrol, Pocahontas Co., W. Va., 5/61. Enl. Hillsboro, Pocahontas Co., W. Va., 3/9/63. Not stated if present or absent on muster-in roll dated 3/63. NFR.

HINDMAN, ——— - Pvt. Co. G. Enl. Frankfort, Greenbrier Co., W. Va., 3/12/63. Not stated if present or absent on muster-in roll dated 3/63. NFR.

HINEMAN, LAFAYETTE - Pvt. Co. C. Prior service, Co. D, 3rd VSL. Enl. Frankfort, Greenbrier Co., W. Va., 3/15/63. Not stated if present or absent on muster-in roll dated 3/63. Ab. 1/1/63 - 4/1/63, deserted 1/63; had one horse. NFR.

HINEMAN, SAMUEL B. - Pvt. Co. C. Prior service, Co. D, 3rd VSL. Enl. Frankfort, Greenbrier Co., W. Va., 3/15/63. Not stated if present or absent on muster-in roll dated 3/63. Ab. 1/1/63 - 6/30/63, deserted 8/2/62; had one horse. NFR.

HINES, MATHEW B. (W.) - Pvt. Co. B. b.c. 1829. Age 31, farmer, Braxton Co., W. Va. 1860 Census. Enl. Frankfort, Greenbrier Co., W. Va., 3/7/63. Not stated if present or absent on muster-in roll dated 3/63. Post war rosters show he was a resident of Braxton Co., W. Va. and was KIA during the war. NFR.

HINKLE, ABRAHAM - Pvt. Co. H. b.c. 1847. Enl. Nicholas Co., W. Va., 4/31/63. Clothing issued 1st Qr. 1864, 5/25/64 and 6/17/64, signs by x. Present 9/1/64 - 10/31/64, has a serviceable horse. Age 33, farming, Hamilton Dist., Nicholas Co., W. Va. 1880 Census. NFR.

HINKLE, JOHN - Pvt. Co. H. Enl. Frankfort, Greenbrier Co., W. Va., 3/19/63 (Pocahontas Co., W. Va., 4/1/63). Not stated if present or absent on muster-in roll dated 3/63. Ab. 9/1/64 - 10/31/64, AWOL. NFR.

HINKLE, WILLIAM - Pvt. Co. H. Enl. Frankfort, Greenbrier Co., W. Va., 3/19/63 (Pocahontas Co., W. Va., 4/1/63). Not stated if present or absent on muster-in roll dated 3/63. Employed as a teamster 11/63. Employed as a teamster at Warm Springs, 1/1/64 - 3/31/64. Clothing issued 11/30/63, 12/29/63 (as a teamster), 1/17/64 and 6/17/64, signs by x. Cpd. Loudoun Co. (near Harpers Ferry, W. Va.), 7/15/64. Sent to Harpers Ferry, W. Va., then to Washington, DC. Confined at the Old Capitol Prison, 7/17/64. Transf. to Elmira, NY, 7/23/64. Confined at Elmira Prison, 7/25/64. Ab. 9/1/64 - 10/31/64, POW. Desires to take the oath of allegiance, 9/30/64, says he volunteered 9/62 and has a sister in Ohio, where he now wishes to go. DOD. Elmira, NY, 11/21/64 (11/22/64), chronic diarrhoea. Bur. Woodlawn National Cem., Elmira, NY, grave no. 917 (937).

HINTY, CHARLES F. (T.) - Pvt. Co. E. b. Glenville, W. Va., c. 1846. Age 14, Gilmer Co., W. Va. 1860 Census. Enl. Bath Co., 3/1/64. Present 10/31/63 - 10/31/64, had his own horse since 7/1/64; enl. bounty due. Clothing issued 6/17/64 and 7/10/64, signs by x. Brother of William H. Hinty. NFR.

HINTY, WILLIAM HENRY JR. - Jr. 2nd Lt. Co. E. b. Bath Co., 1842. Age 18, cabinet maker, Gilmer Co., W. Va 1860 Census. Prior service, Co. B, 52nd Va. Inf. and 2nd Rockbridge Arty. Elected 2nd Lt., Co. E, 19th Va. Cav., 7/6/64, and transf. Not on muster rolls. Paid as Jr. 2nd Lt. for service from 3/2/64 - 6/30/64. Submitted his resignation 9/17/64, feeling he was not suited for the position. Resignation accepted 11/24/64. Age 27, carpenter, South River Dist., Rockbridge Co. 1870 census. Post war wagonmaker and mechanic. Brother of Charles F. Hinty. d. East Lexington, 3/27/96. Bur. Stonewall Jackson Cem., Lexington.

HOGSHEAD, SAMUEL McC. - Pvt. Co. ?. b. Pocahontas Co., W. Va., c. 1838. Age 21 in 1862, farmer and merchant. Listed on post war rosters as being from Rockbridge Co. Post war rosters only, which show he was wd. Madison CH. DOW. 6/2/65, age 27.

HOKE, C. C. - Pvt. Co. G. Enl. Frankfort, Greenbrier Co., W. Va., 3/12/63. Not stated if present or absent on muster-in roll dated 3/63. NFR.

HOKE, HENRY - Pvt. Co. G. Enl. Frankfort, Greenbrier Co., W. Va., 3/12/63. Not stated if present or absent on muster-in roll dated 3/63. NFR.

HOLBERT, JOHN K. - Pvt. Co. D. b.c. 1838. Enl. Williamsburg, Greenbrier Co., W. Va., 3/8/63. Not stated if present or absent on muster-in roll dated 3/63. Clothing issued 6/17/64. Post war resident of Marion Co., W. Va. Age 42, farmer, Grant Dist., Marion Co., W. Va. 1880 Census. NFR.

HOLBERT, REUBEN E. 3rd Sgt. Co. E. b. Lewis Co., W. Va., c. 1839. Age 21, Gilmer Co., W. Va. 1860 Census. Enl. Frankfort, Greenbrier Co., W. Va., 3/13/63. Not stated if present or absent on muster-in roll dated 3/63, 3rd Sgt. Clothing issued 3/1/64. NFR.

HOLCOMB, WILLIAM HENRY - Pvt. Co. I. b. Bath Co., c. 1841. Age 19, farmhand, Webster Co., W. Va. 1860 Census. Prior service, Capt. John S. Sprigg's Company VSL. Not on muster rolls. Present on a MR of paroled and exchanged prisoners at Camp Lee, near Richmond, 3/28/65. Enl. shown as Huntersville, W. Va, 8/16/63. Post war rosters show he was from Webster Co., W. Va., and d. in prison (error). Age 38, farmer, Glade, Webster Co., W. Va. 1880 Census. d. Webster Co., W. Va., 1880's. Bur. Holcomb Cem., near Erbacon, Webster Co., W. Va.

HOLSAPPLE, JAMES P. - Pvt. Co. G. Enl. Frankfort, Greenbrier Co., W. Va., 3/12/63. Not stated if present or absent on muster-in roll dated 3/63. NFR.

HOLSAPPLE, JAMES V. - Pvt. Co. G. Enl. Frankfort, Greenbrier Co., W. Va., 3/12/63. Not stated if present or absent on muster-in roll dated 3/63. NFR.

HOLT (HALT), WALTER (WALKER) - Pvt. Co. K. b.c. 1846. Not on muster rolls. Cpd. Slains Cross Roads, 3/23/63. Confined at Ft. McHenry, 4/17/63. Transf. to Ft. Monroe, 4/19/63. Desc.: age 17, 5'5", light comp., light hair and blue eyes. NFR.

HOOKER, JAMES D. - Pvt. Co. K. b. Bath Co., c. 1847. Not on muster rolls. POW records show his enl. as Augusta Co., 2/61 (so on roll). Clothing issued 2/6/64, 4/30/64, 5/25/64 and 6/17/64, signs by x. Cpd. Beverly, W. Va., 10/29/64. Sent to Clarksburg, W. Va. Confined at Clarksburg, W. Va., 11/1/64. Sent to Wheeling, W. Va., 11/2/64. Confined at the Atheneum Prison, 11/

2/64. Desc.: age 17, 5'7", fair comp., dark hair and brown eyes. Occ. farmer, residing in Barbour Co., W. Va. Transf. to Camp Chase, 11/22/64. Confined at Camp Chase, 11/23/64, desires to take the oath of allegiance. DOD. Camp Chase, 3/26/65 (3/25/65), chronic diarrhoea. Bur. Camp Chase Confederate Cem., 1/3 mile South of Camp Chase, grave no. 1755.

HOOVER, J. M. - Pvt. Co. A. b.c. 1836. Not on muster rolls. Cpd. Pocahontas Co., W. Va., 12/21/63. Confined at the Atheneum Prison, 12/31/63. Desc.: age 27, 5'10", dark comp., black hair and gray eyes. Occ. farmer, residing in Braxton Co., W. Va. Transf. to Camp Chase, 12/31/63. Confined at Camp Chase, 1/1/64. Desires to take the oath of allegiance, 6/10/64, says he is a conscript and deserter. Took the oath of allegiance and was released, 5/13/65. Desc.: age ?, 5'9", dark comp., dark hair and hazel eyes, a resident of Braxton Co., W. Va. Age 43, farmer, Salt Lick Dist., Braxton Co., W. Va. 1880 Census. NFR.

HOSEY (HOSIE), ARCHIBALD L. - Pvt. Co. B. b.c. 1835. Enl. Frankfort, Greenbrier Co., W. Va., 3/7/63. Not stated if present or absent on muster-in roll dated 3/63. Enl. in Co. K, Frankfort, Greenbrier Co., W. Va., 3/20/63. Not stated if present or absent on muster-in roll dated 3/63. Age 45, farmer, Holly Dist., Braxton Co., W. Va. 1880 Census. NFR.

HOSTETTER (HOSTETLER), WILLIAM - 1st Lt. Co. C. Prior service, Co. D, 3rd VSL. Enl. Frankfort, Greenbrier Co., W. Va., 3/15/63 (Mill Point, Pocahontas Co., W. Va., 4/1/63). Not stated if present or absent on muster-in roll dated 3/63, 3rd Lt. Present, 3rd Lt., 1/1/63 - 4/1/63, had 2 horses. Ab., 1st Lt., 12/31/63 - 8/31/64, resigned and was relieved of duty, 2/1/64. Submitted resignation 1/22/64, stating "the Company are much dissatisfied with me..." Post war rosters show him as having served in Co. G, 20th Va. Cav., and as a resident of Wood Co., W. Va. NFR.

HOUCHINS (HONCHIN), JOHN - 1st Lt. Co. A. Prior service, Co. A, 3rd VSL. Elected 1st Lt., 2/14/62. Enl. Williamsburg, Greenbrier Co., W. Va., 3/1/53. Not stated if present or absent on muster-in roll dated 3/63, Pvt. Post war rosters show him as a resident of Calhoun Co., W. Va. NFR.

HOUSEMAN, J. G. - Pvt. Co. E. Post war rosters only, which show he was a member of the John L. Mirick Camp, UCV, in Mo. d. Carrollton, Mo., 5/2/99.

HOWELL, JEREMIAH B. - 1st Lt. Co. K. Enl. Frankfort, Greenbrier Co., W. Va., 3/20/63. Not stated if present or absent on muster-in roll dated 3/63, 2nd Lt. Deserted. Surrendered as 1st Lt., Bulltown, W. Va., 3/8/64. Confined at the Post Guard House, Clarksburg, 3/12/64. NFR.

HOWELL, MARSHALL W. - Pvt. Co. K. Enl. Frankfort, Greenbrier Co., W. Va., 3/20/63. Not stated if present or absent on muster-in roll dated 3/63. Served in Co. B, 46th Battn. Va. Cav. NFR.

HUBBARD, J. - Pvt. Co. A. Not on muster rolls. Adm. Jackson Hosp., 3/6/65, debilitas. Furloughed 3/8/65, 30 days. NFR.

HUDKINS (HUDKINS), BAZWELL (BASIL, BASWELL) - Pvt. Co. C. Reference jacket in CSR only, which shows service in Co. H, 20th Va. Cav. NFR.

HULL, JOSEPH W. - 2nd Corp. Co. F. b.c. 1845. Enl. Hillsboro, Pocahontas Co., W. Va., 8/9/63. Present 1/1/64 - 2/29/64. Clothing issued 2/6/64, 7/64 and 8/64. Present, 2nd Corp., 9/1/64 - 10/31/64, enl. bounty due. Paroled at Charleston, W. Va., 5/10/65. Desc.: age 20, 5'10", light comp., dark hair and blue eyes. NFR.

HUMPHRIES, MATHEW - Pvt. Co. F. Post war rosters only. NFR.

HUNTLEY, ROBERT JEFFERSON - Pvt. Co. H. b. Fluvanna Co., c. 1844. Enl. Pocahontas Co., W. Va., 6/1/63. Clothing issued 2/7/64, 3/7/64, 5/25/64 and 6/17/64, signs by x. Ab. 9/1/64 - 10/31/64, on horse detail. Age 26, farmer, South River Dist., Rockbridge Co. 1870 Census. Laborer, Verona, 1901. Member Stonewall Jackson Camp, UCV, Staunton, 1916, age 72. d. Staunton, 8/29/1930, age 84. Bur. Emmanuel Episcopal Church, Verona.

HUNTLEY, THOMAS W. - Pvt. Co. H. b. Fluvanna Co., c. 1847. Enl. Pocahontas Co., W. Va., 11/16/63. Ab. 9/1/64 - 10/31/64, AWOL. Paroled at Staunton, 5/17/65. Desc.: age 18, 5'8", dark comp., dark hair and black eyes. Post war rosters show service in Co. K. Post war locomotive engineer, residing at Staunton. Alive 1908, age 61. NFR.

HURDMAN (HARDMAN), WILLIAM L. - Pvt. Co. E. Enl. Frankfort, Greenbrier Co., W. Va., 3/13/63. Not stated if present or absent on muster-in roll dated 3/63. Deserted and surrendered. Took the oath of allegiance 12/25/63. NFR.

HUTCHINSON, NATHANIEL (NATHAN) M. - Pvt. Co. B. b.c. 1825. Age 35, Braxton Co., W. Va. 1860 Census. Enl. Frankfort, Greenbrier Co., W. Va., 3/7/63 (3/9/63). Not stated if present or absent on muster-in roll dated 3/63. Ab. 11/1/63 - 2/29/64, sick since 1863. Ab. 9/1/64 - 10/31/64, sick; $100 enl. bounty due. Post war resident of Braxton Co., W. Va. Age 54, works on farm, Holly Dist., Braxton Co., W. Va. 1880 Census. NFR.

HYDE, THOMAS - Pvt. Co. I. Enl. Huntersville, Pocahontas Co., W. Va., 2/10/64. Ab. 6/30/63 - 2/29/64, mounted; enl. bounty due; dropped from rolls, no reason given. NFR.

HYSAM (HYMAN), BENJAMIN F. - Pvt. Co. ?. Post war rosters only, which show he was a resident of Ritchie Co., W. Va. 1890 Union Census marked him as a Confederate. NFR.

ICE, GEORGE M. - Pvt. Co. D. Not on muster rolls. Clothing issued 3/13/64. Age 43, farmer, Mannington Dist., Marion Co., W. Va. 1880 Census. NFR.

ICE, JACOB T. - Pvt. Co. A. b.c. 1840. Not on muster rolls. Cpd. Preston Co., W. Va. 7/1/63. Confined at the Atheneum Prison, 7/2/63. Desc.: age 23, 6', light comp., brown hair and dark eyes. Occ. farmer, residing in Marion Co., W. Va. Transf. to Camp Chase, 8/10/63. Confined at Camp Chase, 8/11/63. Took the oath of allegiance and was released 1/14/64, by order of the Sec. of War. Desc.: age 23, 6', light comp., dark hair, hazel eyes and dark whiskers. NFR.

IRVINE (ERVINE), GEORGE R. - Pvt. Co. I. b.c. 1846. Age 15, laborer, Pocahontas Co., W. Va. 1860 Census. Not on muster rolls. Paroled at Charleston, W. Va., 5/10/65, signs by x. Desc.: age 19, 5', dark comp., dark hair, blue eyes and a dark mustache. Age 37, farmer, Edray, Pocahontas Co., W. Va. 1880 Census. NFR.

ISENHART, GEORGE W. - Pvt. Co. E. b. Lewis Co., W. Va., c. 1843. Age 17, farmer, Gilmer Co., W. Va. 1860 Census. Enl. Frankfort, Greenbrier Co., W. Va., 3/12/63 (4/1/63). Not stated if present or absent on muster-in roll dated 3/63. Clothing issued 3/1/64 and 6/17/64, signs by x. Present 10/31/63 - 10/31/64, had his own horse since 7/1/64. Deserted. Surrendered at Glenville, W. Va., 3/1/65. Sent to Clarksburg, W. Va. Desc.: age 22, 6'1", dark comp., black hair and gray eyes. Occ. farmer, residing in Gilmer Co., W. Va. Took the amnesty oath and was released, 5/3/65. Age 37, farmer, Troy, Gilmer Co., W. Va. 1880 Census. NFR.

JACKSON, EDWARD - Pvt. Co. A. b. Lewis Co., W. Va., 7/25/40. Age 19, Calhoun Co., W. Va. 1860 Census. Prior service, Co. A, 3rd VSL. Enl. Williamsburg, Greenbrier Co., W. Va., 3/1/63. Not stated if present or absent on muster-in roll dated 3/63. Clothing issued 2/19/64. Adm. CSA Gen. Hosp., Charlottesville, 6/12/64, acute rheumatism. RTD. 6/18/64. Served also in Co. F, 20th Va. Cav. Post war roster shows him as a resident of Pocahontas Co., W. Va. Age 39, farmer, Center Dist., Calhoun Co., W. Va. 1880 Census. d. 12/18/1918. Bur. Nobe Cem., Calhoun Co., W. Va.

JACKSON, GEORGE W. - Pvt. Co. F. b.c. 1843 (1845). Age 15, laborer, Greenbank, Pocahontas Co., W. Va. 1860 Census. Prior service, McNeel's Co., VSL and Co. G, 31st Va. Inf. Enl. Hillsboro, Pocahontas Co., W. Va., 3/9/63 (4/1/63). Not stated if present or absent on muster-in roll dated 3/63. Ab. 1/1/64 - 2/29/64, on detached service. Clothing issued 2/6/64. Ab. 9/1/64 - 10/31/64, wd. 8/64; enl. bounty due. Paroled at Charleston, W. Va., 5/10/65. Desc.: age 19, 5'7", sandy comp., red hair and blue eyes. Post war resident of Pocahontas Co., W. Va. and Rutland, O. d. Rutland, O., 4/2/1923, age c. 80. Capt. McNeel said of him: "No braver or better man ever walked the sod..."

JACKSON, JOHN S. - Pvt. Co. F. b. 3/12/43. Age 17, farmer, Dunmore, Pocahontas Co., W. Va. 1860 Census. Prior service, McNeel's Co., VSL. Enl. Hillsboro, Pocahontas Co., W. Va., 3/9/63 (4/1/63). Not stated if present or absent on muster-in roll dated 3/63. Present 1/1/64 - 2/29/64. Clothing issued, 2/7/64. Present 9/1/64 - 10/31/64, enl. bounty due. Paroled at Charleston, W. Va., 5/10/65. Desc.: age 22, 5'9", light comp., light hair and blue eyes. Age 36, Asst. on farm, Green Banks, Pocahontas Co., W. Va. 1880 Census. Member Camp Creigh, UCV, Lewisburg, W. Va. Post war resident of Ronceverte, W. Va. d. Ronceverte, W. Va., 3/13/1922, age 79. Brother-in-law of W. H. Cackley.

JACKSON, WILLIAM LOWTHER "Mudwall" or "Bill" - Col. b. Clarksburg, W. Va., 2/3/25. Orphaned at age 10. Self educated. Resident of Ritchie and Wood Co., W. Va. Admitted to the bar, 1847. Commonwealth Attorney, Wood Co., W. Va. Member Virginia House of Delegates, 2 terms (1851 and 1853). Served as Va. 2nd Auditor, 2 terms. Supt. State Library Fund. Candidate for Lt. Gov., 1854 and 1858, serving one term, under Gov. Henry A. Wise. Resigned to serve as Judge, 19th Judicial Dist., at Parkersburg, W. Va., 1860. Adjourned court in Harrisville, Ritchie Co., W. Va. and left to join the Confederate Army. Resigned as judge 1861, to enter the Confederate Army, as a private soldier. Prior service, Lt. Col., Va. Vols., and Col., 31st Va. Inf. Declined re-election as Col., 31st Va. Inf. Served as Vol. Aide-de-Camp to his 2nd cousin, Maj. Gen. Thomas J. Jackson, 6/4/62 - 9/5/62. T. S. Haymond recommends the appointment of Jackson to Brig. Gen., 1/3/63. Jackson is referred to as Judge Jackson. Officers of the 25th Va. Inf., at Warm Springs, recommended Jackson for promotion to Brig. Gen., 1/9/63. Charles W. Russell recommended Jackson to command the VSL troops when they were turned over to the CS Gov't., 3/3/63. Formed the 19th Va. Cav., 4/11/63 (5/1/63). Appointed Col., 6/5/63, confirmed by election, to date from 4/11/63. Accepted appointment 6/8/63. Commanding post at Warm Springs, 4/13/63. Present F&S MR 9/1/63 - 10/31/63, Inspector and Mustering Officer. Present F&S MR 11/1/63 - 12/31/63, Inspector and Mustering Officer. Commanding Brigade, 3/31/64. Ab. F&S MR 9/1/64 - 10/31/64, wd. 8/13/64. Wd. Cedar Creek, 8/13/64. Wartime newspaper shows he was wd. at Shepherdstown, W. Va., 8/25/64, in the thigh. The account stated that while Jackson was returning his pistol to its holster, it accidentally discharged and the ball struck him in the leg. Arrived at Staunton, 8/31/64. Ab. 10/25/64, wd., now on leave. Recommended for promotion to Brig. Gen. by Maj. Gen. L. L. Lomax, 10/28/64, "for valuable service." Gen. Jubal A. Early also recommended his appointment to Brig. Gen. Gen. R. E. Lee approved the recommendation, 11/18/64, "I believe Col. Jackson to be a brave efficient officer...." Appointed Brig. Gen., 1/12/65, confirmed the same day, to date from 12/19/64. Assigned to command Brig. Gen. H. B. Davidson's old brigade, 1/20/65. Accepted appointment 2/3/65. Paroled at Brownsville, Tx., 7/26/65. Had blue eyes, and weighed 200 lbs., 6' tall, dark red hair and whiskers. "He had unusually fine shoulders, head and face." Went to Mexico for a period of time. Returned to W. Va., found he could not practice law because of his service to the Confederacy. Moved to Louisville, Ky. and opened a law office there 1/1/66. Appointed judge, 9th District, an office he held until his death (17 years). d. Louisville, Ky., 3/24/90. Bur. Cave Hill Cem., Louisville, Ky. "He was a lawyer of marked ability and a gentleman in the highest and fullest sense of the term."

JAMES, SAMUEL - Pvt. Co. F. b.c. 1826. Not on muster rolls. Deserter. Surrendered at Charleston, W. Va., 3/65. Took the Amnesty oath and was sent North, 3/13/65. Desc.: age 39, 5'8", dark comp., dark hair and dark eyes. Occ. farmer, residing in Braxton Co., W. Va. Age 54, farmer, Burch Dist., Braxton Co., W. Va. 1880 Census. NFR.

JAMISON, PIERCE L. - Pvt. Co. D. b.c. 1840. Enl. Williamsburg, Greenbrier Co., W. Va., 3/8/63. Not stated if present or absent on muster-in roll dated 3/63. Served in Co. A, 20th Va. Cav. Post war resident of Monongalia Co., W. Va. "A good soldier." NFR.

JARRETT, BURDETT - 3rd Sgt. Co. G. b.c. 1844. Enl. Frankfort, Greenbrier Co., W. Va., 3/12/63 (4/1/63). Not stated if present or absent on muster-in roll dated 3/63, 3rd Sgt. Clothing issued, 3/1/64, 4/30/64, 6/17/64 and 7/10/64, signs by x. Present, Pvt, 9/1/64 - 10/31/64, has a serviceable horse. Deserted. Surrendered at Charleston, W. Va., 2/65. Took the Amnesty oath and was sent North, 2/11/65. Desc.: age 21, 5'7", dark comp., dark hair and brown eyes. Occ. farmer, residing in Kanawha Co., W. Va. NFR.

JARRETT, MARCUS V. "Mark" - 1st Lt. Co. G. b.c. 1835. Enl. Frankfort, Greenbrier Co., W. Va., 3/12/63 (4/1/63). Not stated if present or absent on muster-in roll dated 3/63, 1st Sgt., listed as Mark Jarrett. Also appears on roll dated 3/63 as Marcus V. Jarrett, 3rd Lt. Paid as a 2nd Lt. in 1/64. Present, 1st Lt., 9/1/64 - 10/31/64. Paroled at Charleston, W. Va., 5/10/64. Desc.: age 30, 5'8", dark comp, dark hair, black eyes and a mustache. NFR.

JARRETT, STATON - Pvt. Co. G. b.c. 1847. Enl. Frankfort, Greenbrier Co., W. Va., 3/12/63 (4/1/63). Not stated if present or absent on muster-in roll dated 3/63. Clothing issued, 3/1/64, 5/26/64 and 6/17/64, signs by x. Present 9/1/64 - 10/31/64, has a serviceable horse. Deserted. Surrendered at Charleston, W. Va., 2/65. Took the Amnesty oath and was sent North, 2/11/65. Desc.: age 18, 5'8", dark comp., dark hair and gray eyes. Occ. farmer, residing in Kanawha Co., W. Va. NFR.

JARVIS, JOHN H. - Pvt. Co. H. Enl. Pocahontas Co., W. Va., 11/1/63. Clothing issued 3/9/64. Ab. 9/1/64 - 10/31/64, AWOL; $50 enl. bounty due. NFR.

JENKINS, JOHN J. - Corp. Co. B. Not on muster rolls. Cpd. Webster Co., W. Va., 1/17/65. Sent to Cumberland, Md., then to Wheeling, W. Va. and Camp Chase. Confined at Camp Chase, 4/14/65, supposed to be a horse thief. NFR.

JENKINS, P. E. - Pvt. Co. I. Enl. Huntersville, Pocahontas Co., W. Va., 5/22/63. Ab. 6/30/63 - 2/29/64, deserted 12/12/63. NFR.

JOHNS, WILLIAM LEWIS - Pvt. Co. C. b. Lewis Co., W. Va., 1841. Age 18, Jackson Co., W. Va. 1860 Census. Prior service, Co. D, 3rd VSL. Enl. Frankfort, Greenbrier Co., W. Va., 3/15/63 (Pocahontas Co., W. Va., 4/1/63). Post war rosters show he enl. 10/1/62. Not stated if present or absent on muster-in roll dated 3/63. Present 12/31/63 - 8/31/64, has one horse. Clothing issued 2/2/64 and 6/17/64. Present 9/1/64 - 10/31/64, has one horse; $100 enl. bounty due. Cpd. Jackson Co., W. Va., 3/

12/65. Confined at Clarksburg, W. Va., 3/15/65. Desc.: age 24, 6', fair comp., dark hair and blue eyes. Occ. farmer, Jackson Co., W. Va. Transf. to Wheeling, W. Va., 3/16/65. Confined at the Atheneum Prison, 3/16/65. Transf. to Camp Chase, 3/28/65. Confined at Camp Chase, 3/29/65. Took the oath of allegiance and was released, 6/13/65. Desc.: age 24, 6', dark comp., dark hair and gray eyes, a resident of Jackson Co., W. Va. Post war rosters show service in Co. D. Age 39, farmer, Washington Dist., Jackson Co., W. Va. 1800 Census. Post war resident of Kentuck, Jackson Co., W. Va., 1890. d. Kentuck, W. Va., 1916. Bur. Poling Cem., Kentuck, Jackson Co., W. Va.

JOHNSON, JASPE (JASPER) - Pvt. Co. B. Enl. Frankfort, Greenbrier Co., W. Va., 3/9/63. Ab. 11/1/63 - 2/29/64, shot to death with musketry, by order of Gen. Court Martial, 3/15/64. Post war history states that Johnson was cpd. by US Forces and enl. in the US service. He then deserted and rejoined the 19th Va. Cav. Becoming tired of the service, he deserted again and determined to remain at home. He was arrested by US Forces, tried and sentenced to be shot. He escaped and returned to the CSA Forces. Col. W. L. Jackson had him tried by court martial and he was shot to death at Camp Cameron, Bath Co., for having twice deserted his army. His comrades thought that Johnson was young and a victim of circumstances, and should not be shot. They arranged for his escape, but Johnson refused to run, saying that if the Federals caught him, he would be shot. NFR.

JOHNSON, JASPER N. - Jr. 2nd Lt. Co. K. Enl. Frankfort, Greenbrier Co., W. Va., 3/20/63. Not stated if present or absent on muster-in roll dated 3/63, Jr. 2nd Lt. Clothing issued 2/11/64 and 3/1/64. NFR.

JOHNSON, WILLIAM E. - Pvt. Co. I. b.c. 1833. Age 27, farmer, Pocahontas Co., W. Va. 1860 Census. Enl. Huntersville, Pocahontas Co., W. Va., 6/10/63. Ab. 6/30/63 - 2/29/64, deserted 11/63. Served later in a Confederate Home Guard Co., formed in Pocahontas Co., W. Va. Post war resident of Pocahontas Co. Age 47, farmer, Edray, Pocahontas Co., W. Va. 1880 Census. NFR.

JOHNSON, WILLIAM N. - Capt. Co. A. Post war rosters only, which show he was a member of this unit. NFR.

JONES, ANDREW J. - Pvt. Co. D. b. 9/16/35. Enl. Williamsburg, Greenbrier Co., W. Va., 3/8/63. Not stated if present or absent on muster-in roll dated 3/63. Cpd. 3/63, place not stated. Confined at Camp Chase. Paroled at Camp Chase, 5/13/63, to be exchanged. Exchanged at City Point, 5/17/63. Adm. Hosp., Camp Lee, near Richmond, 5/20/63, diarrhoea. RTD. 5/28/63. Rejoined Jackson's command, 6/1/63, attached himself to Co. B, 20th Va. Cav. Acting as courier at Beverly, W. Va., 7/3/63. Served in Co. B, 20th Va. Cav. Post war resident of Monongalia Co., W. Va. Age 44, farmer, Clinton Dist., Monongalia Co., W. Va. 1880 Census. d. 10/7/1900. Bur. Pisgah Cem., Monongalia Co., W. Va.

JONES, DAVID A. - Pvt. (Musician) Co. E. b. Alleghany Co., Md., c. 1844. Age 16, farmer, Gilmer Co., W. Va. 1860 Census. Enl. Frankfort, Greenbrier Co., W. Va., 3/12/63 (4/1/63). Not stated if present or absent on muster-in roll dated 3/63. Ab. 10/31/63 - 10/31/64, d. Staunton Hosp., 7/11/64 (so on roll). Clothing issued 3/1/64 and 5/21/64. DOD. Staunton Gen. Hosp., 10/18/64. NFR.

JONES, WILLIAM D. - Pvt. Co. K. Enl. Frankfort, Greenbrier Co., W. Va., 3/20/63. Not stated if present or absent on muster-in roll dated 3/63. NFR.

JOP, M. A. - Capt. Co. G. Not on muster rolls. Wd. Gettysburg, Pa., 7/63, right lung. Cpd. Gettysburg, Pa., 7/63. Adm. to US Hosp. at Gettysburg. NFR.

JORDAN, JAMES A. - Pvt. Co. K. b.c. 1845. Not on muster rolls. Clothing issued, 4/30/64 and 6/17/64. Paroled at Staunton, 5/25/65. Desc.: age 20, 5'7", fair comp., dark hair and blue eyes. NFR.

JOSEPH, MOSES W. - Pvt. Co. A. Post war rosters only which show him as a resident of Greenbrier Co., W. Va. NFR.

JUSTICE, ALEX - Corp. Co. G. Enl. Frankfort, Greenbrier Co., W. Va., 4/1/63. Clothing issued 8/31/64. Present 9/1/64 - 10/31/64, has a serviceable horse. NFR.

JUSTICE, WILLIAM H. - Capt. Co. G. b. Pike Co., Ky., c. 11/8/33. Moved to what became Roane Co., W. Va. in 1856. Prior service, Co. E, 22nd Va. Inf. Enl. Frankfort, Greenbrier Co., W. Va., 4/1/63. Not stated if present or absent on muster-in roll dated 3/63, 2nd Lt. Appraised horses with Rennals Davis, 8/22/63. Promoted to 1st Lt. by 1/64. Promoted to Capt. Ab. 9/1/64 - 10/31/64, wd.; was badly wd. at Frederick City, Md., brought out and when nearly well went home through the lines, was cpd. on his return. Applied for a furlough at Staunton Gen. Hosp., 9/4/64, 45 days. Cpd. Braxton Co., W. Va., 10/7/64. Ab. 10/25/64, wd. and in hands of the enemy. Confined at the Atheneum Prison, 11/64. Desc.: age 31, 5'10", dark comp., dark hair and gray eyes. Occ. farmer, residing in Roane Co. Transf. to Camp Chase, 11/9/64. Confined at Camp Chase, 11/10/64. Wished to take the oath of allegiance, 11/64. Ab. 12/15/64, POW since 10/64. Paroled and sent to Pt. Lookout, to be exchanged, 2/17/64. Adm. Gen. Hosp. No. 9, 2/28/65, paroled prisoner. Transf. to Camp Lee, 3/1/65. Post war farmer, merchant and postmaster, Left Hand, Roane Co., W. Va. Served a four year term as assessor, secretary of the board of education and justice of the peace. Age 46, farming, Geary Dist., Roane Co., W. Va. 1880 Census. NFR.

KARTNER, ANDREW - Pvt. Co. G. Enl. Frankfort, Greenbrier Co., W. Va., 3/12/63 (4/1/63). Not stated if present or absent on muster-in roll dated 3/63. Present 9/1/64 - 10/31/64, has a serviceable horse. NFR.

KEARNS (KERNS), ELISHA - Pvt. Co. A. b.c. 1841. Prior service, Co. A, 3rd VSL. Cpd. Braxton Co., W. Va., 7/2/62 (also as Clay Co., W. Va., 7/25/62). Confined at the Atheneum Prison, 8/9/62. Desc.: age 21, 5'11", dark comp., dark hair and blue eyes. Occ. farmer, residing in Taylor Co., W. Va. Transf. to Camp Chase, 8/12/62. Confined at Camp Chase, 8/12/62. Exchanged at Vicksburg, Miss., 12/6/62. Enl. Williamsburg, Greenbrier Co., W. Va., 3/1/63. Not stated if present or absent on muster-in roll dated 3/63. Clothing issued 2/19/64, 4/11/64 and 6/17/64, signs by x. Served in Co. F, 20th Va. Cav., listed as Kerns. Post war rosters show him as a resident of Calhoun Co., W. Va. NFR.

KEASY (KEESEY), JAMES B. - Pvt. Co. I. Enl. Huntersville, Pocahontas Co., W. Va., 1/1/64. Not stated if present or absent 6/30/63 - 2/29/64, mounted; enl. bounty due; recruit. Served in Co. A, 46th Battn. Va. Cav. NFR.

KEENER, NATHANIEL - Pvt. Co. B. Enl. Frankfort, Greenbrier Co., W. Va., 3/7/63. Not stated if present or absent on muster-in roll dated 3/63. DOD. Montgomery Springs Hosp., 4/5/63, pneumonia. NFR.

KEER, GEORGE - Pvt. Co. I. Enl. Huntersville, Pocahontas Co., W. Va., 3/19/63. Present on muster-in roll dated 3/63. Mustered into service 3/19/63. Could be George Kerr. NFR.

KEISTER, GEORGE - Pvt. Co. C. Enl. Frankfort, Greenbrier Co., W. Va., 3/15/63. Not stated if present or absent on muster-in roll dated 3/63. NFR.

KEISTER, JACOB C. - 1st Lt. Co. C. b.c. 1831. Prior service, Co. D, 3rd VSL. Enl. Frankfort, Greenbrier Co., W. Va., 3/15/63. Not stated if present or absent on muster-in roll dated 3/63. Present, 1st Lt., 1/1/63 - 4/1/63, had 2 horses. Transf. to Lurty's Batty. and Co. A, 46th Battn. Va. Cav. NFR.

KEITH (KEETH), ANDREW J. - Pvt. Co. E. b. Lewis Co., W. Va., c. 1830. Age 30, farmer, Gilmer Co., W. Va. 1860 Census. Enl. Gilmer Co., W. Va., 10/8/64. Ab. 10/31/63 - 10/31/64, new recruit; on horse detail; time now expired. Age 50, farmer, Glenville, Gilmer Co., W. Va. 1880 Census. NFR.

KEITH, ROBERT M. - Pvt. Co. K. b. Lewis Co., W. Va., c. 1834 (1830). Age 30, farmer, Gilmer Co., W. Va. 1860 Census. Arrested and confined by 3/15/62. Charged as being a secessionist and bushwhacker. Not on muster rolls. Paroled at Charleston, W. Va., 5/10/65. Desc.: age 31, 6'2", fair comp., light hair, blue eyes and light whiskers. NFR.

KELLISON, CHARLES W. - Pvt. Co. F. b.c. 1844. Age 16, laborer, Pocahontas Co., W. Va. 1860 Census. Prior service, McNeel's Co., 2nd VSL. Enl. Hillsboro, Pocahontas Co., W. Va., 3/9/63 (4/1/63). Not stated if present or absent on muster-in roll dated 3/63. Present 1/1/64 - 2/29/64. Clothing issued 2/6/64. Ab. 9/1/64 - 10/31/64, enl. bounty due; cpd. 4/28/64. Cpd. Pocahontas Co., W. Va., 4/28/64. Confined at the Atheneum Prison, 5/12/64. Desc.: age 20, 6'2", fair comp., dark hair and dark eyes. Occ. farmer, residing in Pocahontas Co., W. Va. Transf. to Camp Chase, 5/13/64. Confined at Camp Chase, 5/14/64. Paroled and sent to City Point, 2/25/65, to be exchanged. Exchanged. Adm. Jackson Hosp., 3/7/65, debilitas. Furloughed 3/8/65, 30 days. Paroled at Charleston, W. Va., 5/11/65. Desc.: age 21, 6'2", dark comp., black hair and dark eyes. Post war resident of Augusta Co. Age 36, laborer, Little Levels, Pocahontas Co., W. Va. 1880 Census. NFR.

KELLISON, JOSEPH ALLEN - Pvt. Co. F. b.c. 1845. Age 15, laborer, Pocahontas Co., W. Va. 1860 Census. Enl. Hillsboro, Pocahontas Co., W. Va., 6/7/63. Present 1/1/64 - 2/29/64. Clothing issued 2/6/64 and 7/10/64. Ab. 9/1/64 - 10/31/64, on horse detail; enl. bounty due. Paroled at Charleston, W. Va., 5/11/65. Desc.: age 20, 5'11", dark comp., dark hair and dark eyes. NFR.

KELLISON, SAMUEL C. - Pvt. Co. F. b.c. 1834 (1837). Age 23, farmer, Mt. Murphy, Pocahontas Co., W. Va. 1860 Census. Post war rosters only. Age 46, farmer, Little Levels, Pocahontas Co., W. Va. 1880 Census. d. Droop Mountain, Greenbrier Co., W. Va., 1/17/1910, age 76.

KELLY (KELLEY), JAMES - Pvt. Co. A. b. Randolph Co., W. Va., c. 1823 (1825). Age 35, farmer, Calhoun Co., W. Va. 1860 Census. Prior service, Co. A, 3rd VSL. Enl. Williamsburg, Greenbrier Co., W. Va., 3/1/63. Not stated if present or absent on muster-in roll dated 3/63. Surrendered at Clarksburg, W. Va., 5/5/65, and was paroled for exchange. Desc.: age 43, 5'7", fair comp., dark hair and hazel eyes. Occ. farmer, residing in Calhoun Co., W. Va. Served in Co. F, 20th Va. Cav. Age 47, farmer, Sherman Township, Calhoun Co., W. Va. 1870 Census. Age 55, farmer, Sherman Dist., Calhoun Co., W. Va. 1880 Census. NFR.

KEMAR, H. - Pvt. Co. ?. Not on muster rolls. Gravestone only record, which shows he d. 8/64. Bur. Stonewall Cem., Winchester. NFR.

KENNEY (KINNEY), JOHN - Pvt. Co. I. b. Ireland, c. 1825. Age 35, Randolph Co., W. Va. 1860 Census. Enl. Beverly, Randolph Co., W. Va., 4/30/63. Present 6/30/63 - 2/29/64, mounted. Ab. 2/29/64 - 8/31/64, wd. near Sweet Springs, W. Va., 6/23/64. Clothing issued 3/22/64. Ab. 9/1/64 - 10/31/64, wd.; $100 bond due. Post war resident of Randolph Co., W. Va. d. by 1916. Bur. Wamsley Cem., Randolph Co., W. Va.

KERNS, BENJAMIN - Pvt. Co. K. b. Lewis Co., W. Va., c. 1837. Age 23, Gilmer Co., W. Va. 1860 Census. Enl. Frankfort, Greenbrier Co., W. Va., 3/20/63. Not stated if present or absent on muster-in roll dated 3/63. NFR.

KERNS, JOSEPH - Pvt. Co. K. b. Randolph Co., W. Va., c. 1825. Age 35, farmer, Gilmer Co., W. Va. 1860 Census. Enl. Frankfort, Greenbrier Co., W. Va., 3/20/63. Not stated if present or absent on muster-in roll dated 3/63. NFR.

KERR (CAR), ANDREW W. - Pvt. Co. F. b.c. 1828. Age 32, farmer, Greenbank, Pocahontas Co., W. Va., 1860 Census. Prior service, McNeel's Co., 2nd VSL. Enl. Hillsboro, Pocahontas Co., W. Va., 3/9/63 (4/1/63). Not stated if present or absent on muster-in roll dated 3/63. Ab. 1/1/64 - 2/29/64, sick. Ab. 9/1/64 - 10/31/64, sick; enl. bounty due. Paroled at Charleston, W. Va., 5/10/65. Desc.: age 37, 5'9", light comp., dark hair, dark eyes and light whiskers. Age 52, blacksmith, Green Banks, Pocahontas Co., W. Va. 1880 Census. NFR.

KERR, DAVID B. - Pvt. Co. F. b. Greenbank, Pocahontas Co., W. Va., 12/15/44. Enl. Hillsboro, Pocahontas Co., W. Va., 9/10/63. Present 1/1/64 - 2/29/64. Clothing issued 2/6/64. Ab. 9/1/64 - 10/31/64, AWOL since 9/22/64. Twin brother of James D. Kerr. d. 1875.

KERR, GEORGE - Pvt. Co. F. b. Pocahontas Co., W. Va., 1829. Age 30, farmer, Pocahontas Co., W. Va. 1860 Census. Prior service, Co. G, 31st Va. Inf. and McNeel's Co., 2nd VSL. Enl. Hillsboro, Pocahontas Co., W. Va., 3/9/63 (4/1/63). Not stated if present or absent on muster-in roll dated 3/63. Present 1/1/64 - 2/29/64. Ab. 9/1/64 - 10/31/64, sick. Age 51, farmer, Green Banks Dist., Pocahontas Co., W. Va. 1880 Census. Could be same person as George Keer. d. 1896.

KERR, JACOB THORNTON - Pvt. Co. F. b. 1822. Age 38, farmer, Greenbank, Pocahontas Co., W. Va. 1860 Census. Enl. Hillsboro, Pocahontas Co., W. Va., 8/19/63. Present 1/1/64 - 2/29/64. Ab. 9/1/64 - 10/31/64, enl. bounty due; discharged 9/1/64, reason not given. Age 56, farmer, Green Banks Dist., Pocahontas Co., W. Va. 1880 Census. d. 1898.

KERR, JAMES DANIEL - Pvt. Co. F. b. Greenbank, Pocahontas Co., W. Va., 12/15/44. Age 15, laborer, Pocahontas Co., W. Va. 1860 Census. Enl. Hillsboro, Pocahontas Co., W. Va., 9/10/63. Present 1/1/64 - 2/29/64. Clothing issued 2/6/64. Ab. 9/1/64 - 10/31/64, AWOL since 9/20/64. Post war farmer and resident of Boyer, W. Va. Member of the Moffett Poague Camp, UCV, Pocahontas Co., W. Va. Twin brother of David B. Kerr. Age 35, farmer, Green Banks, Pocahontas Co., W. Va. 1880 Census. d. Boyer, W. Va., 6/4/1931. Bur. Boyer, W. Va.

KERSHNER (KEISHNER), ROYAL PARIS - Sgt. Co. K. b. Greenbrier Co., W. Va., 6/26/40. Prior service, Co. A and K, 14th Va. Cav. Not on muster rolls. Clothing issued as Sgt., Co. K, 2/5/64, 2/23/64, 4/30/64 and 6/17/64. Desc. 1865: age ?, 5'6", dark comp., dark hair and dark eyes. Occ. harness maker. Post war resident of Greenbrier and Pocahontas Co's., W. Va. Age 44(?), saddler, Little Levels, Pocahontas Co., W. Va. 1880 Census. d. 5/10/1918. Bur. Whiting Cem., on Droop Mountain, Pocahontas Co., W. Va.

KESSLER, JOSEPH R. - Capt. Co. C./Major. Prior service, Co. D, 3rd VSL. Wd. near Prestonburg, Ky., 12/4 - 5/62. Enl. Frankfort, Greenbrier Co., W. Va., 3/15/63. Not stated if present or absent on muster-in roll dated 3/63, Capt. Appointed Capt. 3/15/63. Present, Capt., 1/1/63 - 4/1/63, has 2 horses. Appointed Major, 6/5/63, to be confirmed by election, to rank from 4/11/63. Accepted appointment 6/21/63. Present, Major, F&S MR 9/1/63 - 10/31/63. Present, Major F&S MR 11/1/63 - 12/31/63. Received "honorable mention" from Lt. Col. W. P. Thompson in his report of the battle of Droop Mountain, W. Va., 11/6/63. Superintended election of Co. Officers, 46th Battn. Va. Cav., at Camp Cameron, Bath Co., 2/11/64. Appointed (elected) Lt. Col., 46th Battn. Va. Cav., 2/26/64. Appointed Lt. Col., 26th Va. Cav., 1/65. NFR.

KIDWELL, CHARLES HEZEKIAH - Pvt. Co. C. Enl. Pocahontas Co., W. Va., 9/16/63. Employed as a courier 11/63. Present 12/31/63 - 8/31/64, has one horse. Employed as a courier at Warm Springs, 1/1/64 - 3/31/64. Clothing issued 1/17/64, detailed as courier; 5/26/64 and 6/17/64. Ab. 9/1/64 - 10/31/64, has one horse; $100 enl. bounty due; AWOL since 10/25/64. NFR.

KIGER (KIZER), HUGH - Pvt. Co. A. Served in Co. A, 3rd VSL. Post war rosters only. NFR.

KILLINGSBURGER, EUGENUS - Pvt. Co. I. b.c. 1847. Not on muster rolls. Surrendered at Buckhannon, W. Va., 5/14/65. Confined at Clarksburg, W. Va., 5/16/65. Paroled for exchange, 5/17/65. Desc.: age 18, 5'8", dark comp., light hair and blue eyes. Occ. farmer, residing in Randolph Co., W. Va. NFR.

KINCADE, W. A. - Pvt. Co. G. Not on muster rolls. Deserted. Reported at Clarksburg, W. Va., 10/14/63. Took the oath of allegiance and was sent North, via Wheeling, W. Va. Listed his residence as Alleghany Co. NFR.

KINCAID, ANTHONY BURGER - Pvt. Co. F. b. near Lewisburg, W. Va., 8/20/46. Student, Lewisburg PO, Greenbrier Co., W. Va. 1860 census. Served in Co. K, 14th Va. Cav. Desc. 1865: age ?, 5'10", fair comp., light hair and blue eyes. Post war rosters and reference jacket only for service in the 19th Va. Cav. Post war farmer and resident of Greenbrier Co., W. Va. Farmer, Williamsburg Dist., Greenbrier Co., W. Va. 1870 census. Moved to Hot Springs, Bath Co. Cedar Creek Dist., Bath Co. 1910 census. Alive 1915. NFR.

KINCAID, LEWIS B. - Pvt. Co. B. Enl. Strasburg, 7/29/64. Present 9/1/64 - 10/31/64, not entitled to $100 enl. bounty. NFR.

KINCAID, S. BROWN - Pvt. Co. B. b. 1847. Post war rosters only, which show he enl. 4/64 and served until 4/65. Post war resident of Williamsville, Bath Co. NFR.

KINCAID, SAMUEL C. - Pvt. Co. I. b.c. 1823. Age 37, farmer, Frost, Pocahontas Co., W. Va. 1860 Census. Enl. Huntersville, Pocahontas Co., W. Va., 3/22/63. Ab. 6/30/63 - 2/29/64, relieved by Enrolling Officer as a shoemaker. Ab. 2/29/64 - 8/31/64, detailed by Enrolling Officer as a shoemaker. Ab. 9/1/64 - 10/31/64, without permission. Age 58, farmer, Huntersville, Pocahontas Co., W. Va. 1880 Census. NFR.

KINDLE, HENRY H. - Pvt. Co. D. Not on muster rolls. Clothing issued 1st Qr. 1864. Cpd., date and place unknown. Confined at Camp Morton, Indianapolis, Ind., 6/21/64. Took the oath of allegiance and was released 2/20/65. Desc.: age ?, 5'9 3/4", dark comp., brown hair and brown eyes, a resident of Marion Co., W. Va. NFR.

KING, J. W. - Pvt. Co. I. Not on muster rolls. Cpd. Shelbyville, Tenn., 6/27/63. Sent to Camp Chase, then to Ft. Delaware. Confined at Ft. Delaware, 7/14/63. NFR.

KING, ROBERT H. - Pvt. Co. I. Not on muster rolls. Cpd. Shelbyville, Tenn., 6/27/63. Sent to Camp Chase, then to Ft. Delaware. Confined at Ft. Delaware, 7/14/63. NFR.

KINNISON (KENNISON), NATHANIEL C. B. - Pvt. Co. F. b.c. 1843. Age 17, farmer, Academy, Pocahontas Co., W. Va. 1860 Census. Post war rosters only for Co. F, 19th Va. Cav. Served in Co. D, 14th Va. Cav. Brother of William E. Kinnison. NFR.

KINNISON (KENNISON), WILLIAM E. - Pvt. Co. I. b.c. 1844. Enl. Huntersville, Pocahontas Co., W. Va., 2/15/63 (3/18/63). Present on muster-in roll dated 3/63. Mustered into service 3/19/63. Present 6/30/63 - 2/29/64, mounted. Present 2/29/64 - 4/30/64. Clothing issued 6/17/64. Present 9/1/64 - 10/31/64, $100 Bond due. Paroled at Charleston, W. Va., 5/10/65. Desc.: age 21, 5'5", dark comp., dark hair, blue eyes and brown whiskers. Post war rosters show service in Co. F. NFR.

KITTLE, IRA C. - Pvt. Co. ?. b.c. 1820. Age 40, blacksmith, Randolph Co., W. Va. 1860 Census. Post war rosters only, which show he was a resident of Randolph Co., W. Va. Age 59, farmer, Huttonsville, Randolph Co., W. Va. 1880 Census. NFR.

KIZER (KEISER, KISER), JOHN - 2nd Corp. Co. C. Prior service, Co. D, 3rd VSL. Enl. Frankfort, Greenbrier Co., W. Va., 3/15/63 (Pocahontas Co., W. Va., 4/1/63). Not stated if present or absent on muster-in roll dated 3/63, Pvt. Present, Pvt., 1/1/63 - 4/1/63, has one horse. Present 12/31/63 - 8/31/64, had his own horse since 7/1/64; Promoted to Corp. 2/1/64. Clothing issued 2/25/64, 4/30/64, 6/17/64, 7/64 and 8/64. Present 9/1/64 - 10/31/64, has one horse; $100 enl. bounty due. Served in Co. E, 20th Va. Cav. NFR.

KIZER (KISER, KEISER), WILLIAM - Pvt. Co. C. Prior service, Co. D, 3rd VSL. Enl. Frankfort, Greenbrier Co., W. Va., 3/15/63 (Pocahontas Co., W. Va., 4/1/63). Not stated if present or absent on muster-in roll dated 3/63. Present 1/1/63 - 4/1/63, has one horse. Present 12/31/63 - 8/31/64, has one horse. Clothing issued 2/25/64, 4/30/64 and 6/17/64. Present 9/1/64 - 10/31/64, has one horse; $100 enl. bounty due. Served in Co. E, 20th Va. Cav. Post war resident of Wood Co., W. Va. NFR.

KNAPP, JOHN J. - Pvt. Co. H. b.c. 1847. Not on muster rolls. Mustered into service at Frankfort, Greenbrier Co., W. Va., 1865. Paroled at Lewisburg, W. Va., 4/27/65. Desc.: age 18, 5'10", fair comp., brown hair and blue eyes, a farmer. NFR.

KNAPP, THOMAS F. "Tom" - Pvt. Co. I. b.c. 1845. Age 15, laborer, Pocahontas Co., W. Va. 1860 Census. Enl. Huntersville, Pocahontas Co., W. Va., 1/4/63 (3/18/63). Present on muster-in roll dated 3/63. Mustered into service 3/19/63. Present 6/30/63 - 2/29/64, mounted. Ab. 2/29/64 - 8/31/64, cpd. near Marlin's Bottom, 4/64. Clothing issued 3/22/64. Ab. 9/1/64 - 10/31/64, POW; $100 Bond due. Cpd. Pocahontas Co., W. Va., 5/6/64 (4/64). Confined at the Atheneum Prison, 5/16/64. Desc.: age 19, 5'6", fair comp., light hair and blue eyes. Occ. farmer, residing in Pocahontas Co., W. Va. Transf. to Camp Chase, 5/17/64. Confined at Camp Chase, 5/18/64. Paroled and sent to City Point, 2/25/65, to be exchanged. Exchanged. Adm. Jackson Hosp., 3/7/65, debilitas. Furloughed 3/8/65, 30 days. NFR.

KNIGHT, H. B. - Pvt. Co. B. Enl. Frankfort, Greenbrier Co., W. Va., 3/7/63. Not stated if present or absent on muster-in roll dated 3/63. Most likely this is Hudson D. Knight. NFR.

KNIGHT, HUDSON D. - Pvt. Co. K. b.c. 1833. Age 27, farmer, Braxton Co., W. Va. 1860 Census. Enl. Frankfort, Greenbrier Co., W. Va., 3/20/63. Not stated if present or absent on muster-in roll dated 3/63. Surrendered at Bulltown, W. Va. and sent to Clarksburg, W. Va., listed as a member of Co. G. Confined at Clarksburg, W. Va., 3/4/64. Took the oath of allegiance and was released by order of Col. N. Wilkerson, 3/5/64. Post war rosters show service in Co. B, and list him as Judson D. Knight. Post war resident of Braxton Co., W. Va. Age 52, farmer, Holly Dist., Braxton Co., W. Va. 1880 Census. Most likely same as H. B. Knight. Uncle of James Francis, Orville Sheldon and John Wesley Knight. NFR.

KNIGHT, JAMES FRANCIS - Pvt. Co. B. b.c. 1843. Age 17, Braxton Co., W. Va. 1860 Census. Enl. Frankfort, Greenbrier Co., W. Va., 3/7/63 (3/9/63). Not stated if present or absent on muster-in roll dated 3/63. Present 11/1/63 - 2/29/64. Clothing issued 2/11/64, 2/23/64, 6/17/64 and 3rd Qr. 64, signs by x. Present 9/1/64 - 10/31/64, $100 enl. bounty due. Surrendered in Braxton Co., W. Va., 4/20/65. Confined at Clarksburg, W. Va., 4/24/65. Desc.: age 22, 6' 3/4", fair comp., fair hair and blue eyes. Occ. farmer, residing in Braxton Co., W. Va. Paroled for exchange and released, 4/24/65, signs by x. Age 46, farmer, Holly Dist., Braxton Co., W. Va. 1880 Census. Brother of Orville Sheldon and John Wesley Knight; nephew of Hudson D. Knight. NFR.

KNIGHT, JOHN WESLEY - 4th Corp. Co. B. b. Braxton Co., W. Va., c. 1842. POW record shows his enl. as Lewisburg, W. Va., 3/62. Enl. Frankfort, Greenbrier Co., W. Va., 3/7/63 (3/9/63). Not stated if present or absent on muster-in roll dated 3/63, Pvt. Present, 4th Corp., 11/1/63 - 2/29/64. Clothing issued 2/11/64 and 4/30/64, signs by x. Present, 4th Corp., 9/1/64 - 10/31/64, $100 enl. bounty due. Deserted. Cpd. Bulltown, W. Va., 11/15/64. Confined at Clarksburg, W. Va. Desc.: age 23, 5'9", fair comp., light hair and gray eyes. Occ. farmer, residing in Braxton Co., W. Va. Took the oath of allegiance and was released, 11/20/64. Arrested 2/14/65 and sent to Wheeling, W. Va. Confined at the Atheneum Prison, 5/5/65. Desc.: age 23, 5'8_", florid comp., brown hair and gray eyes, a resident of Braxton Co., W. Va. Took the oath of allegiance and was released, 5/9/65. Age 37, farmer, Holly Dist., Braxton Co., W. Va. 1880 Census. Brother of Francis and Sheldon Knight; nephew of Hudson D. Knight. NFR.

KNIGHT, ORVILLE SHELDON (SHELTON) - Pvt. Co. B. b. Braxton Co., W. Va., c. 1840. POW record shows his enl. as Greenbrier Co., W. Va., 3/62. Enl. Frankfort, Greenbrier Co., W. Va., 3/7/63 (3/9/63). Not stated if present or absent on muster-in roll dated 3/63. Present 11/1/63 - 2/29/64. Clothing issued 2/11/64, 4/30/64 and 6/17/64, signs by x. Ab. 9/1/64 - 10/31/64, on detached service; $100 enl. bounty due. Cpd. Braxton Co., W. Va., 10/24/64. Confined at Clarksburg, W. Va. Desc.: age 24, 6', fair comp., light hair and gray eyes. Occ. farmer, residing in Braxton Co., W. Va. Sent to Wheeling, W. Va., 11/5/64. Confined at the Atheneum Prison, 11/6/64. Desc.: age 24, 6', fair comp., light hair and gray eyes. Occ. farmer, residing in Braxton Co., W. Va. Transf. to Camp Chase, 11/29/64. Confined at Camp Chase, 11/30/64, desires to take the oath of allegiance. Took the oath of allegiance and was released, 5/15/65, signs by x. Desc.: age 25, 6', dark comp., dark hair and dark eyes. Age 43, farmer, Holly Dist., Braxton Co., W. Va. 1880 Census, listed as Shelton O. Knight. Brother of James Francis and John Wesley Knight; nephew of Hudson Q. Knight. d. Braxton Co., W. Va., 1905.

KNOTTS, ABEL W. - 1st Corp. Co. D. Enl. Williamsburg, Greenbrier Co., W. Va., 3/8/63. Not stated if present or absent on muster-in roll dated 3/63, 1st Corp. NFR.

KOVALOSKY (COVELESKI), EDWARD A. - Sgt. Co. C. b. England, c. 1840. Prior service, Co. D, 3rd VSL. Enl. Frankfort, Greenbrier Co., W. Va., 3/15/63 (Pocahontas Co., W. Va., 4/1/63). Not stated if present or absent on muster-in roll dated 3/63. Present, Pvt., 1/1/63 - 4/1/63, has one horse. Present, 3rd Sgt., 12/31/63 - 8/31/64. Clothing issued 2/2/64, 4/30/64, 6/17/64, 7/64 and 8/64. Ab. 9/1/64 - 10/31/64, $100 enl. bounty due; wd. Fisher's Hill, 9/22/64: was due from hosp., 10/1/64; AWOL since 10/1/64; has one horse. Clothing issued while at Liberty Gen. Hosp., 9/30/64. Served in Co. G, 20th Va. Cav., listed as Covalosky. Age 40, clerk in sewing machine office, Parkersburg, Wood Co., W. Va. 1880 Census. NFR.

KREMER (KRAMER), HENRY - Pvt. Co. I. Enl. Huntersville, Pocahontas Co., W. Va., 1/1/64. Ab. 6/30/63 - 2/29/64, mounted; enl. bounty due; KIA near Strasburg, 8/1/64. Bur. Stonewall Cem., Winchester. Post war rosters shows him as being KIA. at New Market or Winchester.

KUFFMAN, J. C. - Pvt. Co. B. b.c. 1840. Not on muster rolls. Paroled at Staunton, 5/1/65. Desc.: age 25, 5'10", light comp., dark hair and hazel eyes. NFR.

KYLE, GEORGE H. - Pvt. Co. ?. b. 12/15/36. Farmer, N. Dist., Augusta Co. 1860 Census. Prior service, Co. I, 14th Va. Cav. Not on muster rolls. Enrolled as a Conscript at Camp Lee, near Richmond, 2/26/64. Assigned to the 19th Va. Cav., 2/19/64. Served in Co. G, 18th Va. Cav. Desc.: age ?, 5'5", fair comp., light hair and blue eyes. Post war resident of Augusta Co. d. 2/3/85. Bur. Mossy Creek Presbyterian (old) Cem., Augusta Co.

KYLE, ST. CLAIR M. - Pvt. Co. F. b. Va., c. 1843. Age 17, student, N. Dist., Augusta Co. 1860 Census. Prior service, Co. C, 5th Va. Inf. Not on muster rolls. Cpd. Beverly, W. Va., 2/15/64. Confined at the Atheneum Prison, 2/21/64. Desc.: age 22, 5'11_", dark comp., dark hair and gray eyes. Occ. farmer, residing in Augusta Co. Took the oath of allegiance and was released, 2/22/64. Post war resident of Augusta Co. NFR.

LACKEY, JAMES SHAFER - Pvt. Co. D. b. Rockbridge Co., 10/1/47. Age 12, Kerr's Creek Dist., Rockbridge Co. 1860 Census. Not on muster rolls. Enl. 3/25/65, place not stated, age 16. Desc.: age 16, 5'9", fair comp., dark hair and blue eyes, a farmer. Moved to Arkansas in 1873. Post war merchant. d. Fayetteville, Ark., 3/27/1912.

LAKE, JAMES P. - 2nd Sgt. Co. B. b.c. 1837. Age 23, farmer, Braxton Co., W. Va. 1860 Census. Prior service, Co. A, 3rd VSL. Enl. Frankfort, Greenbrier Co., W. Va., 5/1/63 (Greenbrier Co., W. Va., 3/9/63). Present, Pvt., 11/1/63 - 2/29/64, has one horse. Employed as a courier 11/63. Employed as a courier at Warm Springs, 1/1/64 - 3/31/64. Clothing issued 2/11/64, 6/17/64 and 3rd Qr. 1864. Present, 2nd Sgt., 9/1/64 - 10/31/64, promoted to 2nd Sgt. 7/1/64; $100 enl. bounty due. Cpd. Addison, Webster Co., W. Va., 3/19/65. Sent to Cumberland, Md., then to Wheeling, W. Va. Confined at the Atheneum Prison, 3/25/65. Desc.: age 27, 5'8", fair comp., dark hair and dark eyes. Occ. farmer, residing in Braxton Co., W. Va. Transf. to Camp Chase, 3/28/65. Confined at Camp Chase, 3/29/65. Took the oath of allegiance and was released, 5/16/65. Desc.: age 27, 5'9", dark comp., dark hair and dark eyes, a resident of Braxton Co., W. Va. Bur. Spring Hill Cem., Huntington, W. Va.

LAKE, WILLIAM E. - Lt. Co. ?. Mentioned in Major D. B. Stewart's report of the fight at Beverly, W. Va., 7/2/63 - 7/3/63. Post war rosters show he was a resident of Ritchie Co., W. Va. Served in Co. C, 46th Battn. Va. Cav. NFR.

LAMBERT, RICHARD J. - Pvt. Co. I. b.c. 1834. Age 26, farmer, Randolph Co., W. Va. 1860 Census. Enl. Beverly, Randolph Co., W. Va., 4/30/63. Ab. 6/30/63 - 2/29/64, deserted 5/63 and joined the Yanks. Dropped from the rolls. NFR.

LANDERS, JOHN - Pvt. Co. I. Enl. Huntersville, Pocahontas Co., W. Va., 3/19/63. Present on muster-in roll dated 3/63. Mustered into service 3/19/63. NFR.

LAUGH, HEZEKIAH - Pvt. Co. A. b.c. 1841. Not on muster rolls. Cpd. Preston Co., W. Va., 7/1/63. Confined at the Atheneum Prison, 7/2/63. Desc.: age 22, 5'9_", light comp., light hair and blue eyes. Occ. farmer, residing in Monongahala Co., W. Va. Transf. to Camp Chase, 8/8/63. Confined at Camp Chase, 8/11/63. Took the oath and was released 12/29/63, by order of the Sec. of War. NFR.

LEE, H. F. - Pvt. Co. C. Enl. Frankfort, Greenbrier Co., W. Va., 3/15/63. Not stated if present or absent on muster-in roll dated 3/63. NFR.

LEE, JOHN B. - Pvt. Co. C. b. Wirt (Wood) Co., W. Va., 8/10/25. Age 24, miller, 1850 Wirt Co., W. Va. Census. Magistrate, 1856. Prior service, Co. D, 3rd VSL. Enl. Frankfort, Greenbrier Co., W. Va., 3/15/63 (Pocahontas Co., W. Va., 4/1/63). Not stated if present or absent on muster-in roll dated 3/63. Present 1/1/63 - 4/1/63, has one horse. In service 7/1/63 to 8/12/63. Disc. 8/12/63, being a Capt. in the 46th Battn. Va. Cav. Desc.: age 40, 5'10", light comp., black hair and blue eyes, a miller. Served in Co. F, 46th Battn. Va. Cav. Post war rosters show service in Co. B, 17th Va. Cav. Magistrate, 1880. Post war farmer, Reedy Ripple, Wirt Co., W. Va. Age 54, farmer, Elizabeth Dist., Wirt Co., W. Va. 1880 Census. NFR.

LEE, WILLIAM B. - Pvt. Co. C. b.c. 1833. Prior service, Co. D, 3rd VSL. Enl. Frankfort, Greenbrier Co., W. Va., 3/15/63. Not stated if present or absent on muster-in roll dated 3/63. Present 1/1/63 - 4/1/63, has one horse. Cpd. Alleghany Co., W. Va., 12/19/63. Confined at the Atheneum Prison, 12/31/63. Desc.: age 30, 5'9", fair comp., light hair and blue eyes. Occ. farmer, residing in Right Co. (?) [Wirt Co., W. Va.] Transf. to Camp Chase, 12/31/63. Confined at Camp Chase, 1/1/64. Desired to take the oath of allegiance, 6/10/64. DOD. Camp Chase, 9/13/64, typhoid fever. Bur. Camp Chase Confederate Cem., 1/3 mile South of Camp Chase, grave no. 239. Could be William Lee, Co. F, 46th Battn. Va. Cav.

LEESON (LEASON), JOHN Jr. - Pvt. Co. A. b. Monongalia Co., W. Va., c. 1834. Age 26, farmer, Calhoun Co., W. Va. 1860 Census. Prior service, Co. A, 3rd VSL. Enl. Williamsburg, Greenbrier Co., W. Va., 3/1/63. Not stated if present or absent on muster-in roll dated 3/63. Clothing issued 4/11/64. Served in Co. F, 20th Va. Cav. Age 35, farmer, Sheridan Township, Calhoun Co., W. Va. 1870 Census. Age 46, farmer, Sheridan Dist., Calhoun Co., W. Va. 1880 Census. [Could be John Seeson, CSA, Bur. United Brethern Cem., Pennsboro, Ritchie Co., W. Va.] NFR.

LEESON (LEASON), NATHANIEL G. - Pvt. Co. A. b. Monongalia Co., W. Va., c. 1830. Age 30, farmer, Calhoun Co., W. Va. 1860 Census. Prior service, Co. A, 3rd VSL. Enl. Williamsburg, Greenbrier Co., W. Va., 3/1/63. Not stated if present or absent on muster-in roll dated 3/63. Cpd. Alleghany Co., 8/25/63. Confined at the Atheneum Prison, 9/6/63. Desc.: age 22(?), 6'1", fair comp., red hair and blue eyes. Occ. farmer, residing in Calhoun Co., W. Va. Transf. to Camp Chase, 9/7/63. Confined at Camp Chase, 9/8/63. Transf. to Rock Island, Ill., 1/22/64. Confined at Rock Island Prison, 1/24/64. Took the oath of allegiance and was released 6/16/65. Desc.: age 25, 5'11_", fair comp., sandy hair and blue eyes, a resident of Big Bend, Calhoun Co., W. Va. Served in Co. F, 20th Va. Cav. Age 40, farmer, Sheridan Township, Calhoun Co., W. Va. 1870 Census. Age 47(?), farmer, Sheridan Dist., Calhoun Co., W. Va. 1880 Census. NFR.

LEESON, W. G. - Pvt. Co. A. Not on muster rolls. Deserted. Confined at Clarksburg, W. Va., 10/14/63, then sent North, via Wheeling, W. Va. Resident of Calhoun Co., W. Va. NFR.

LEGARD, CHARLES C. - Pvt. Co. I. Hired as a substitute for Samuel A. Montgomery, 9/62. Enl. Huntersville, Pocahontas Co., W. Va., 9/16/63. Ab. 6/30/63 - 2/29/64, detailed to gather some men AWOL; enl. bounty due; mounted. Present 2/29/64 - 8/31/64. Ab. 9/1/64 - 10/31/64, AWOL; $100 Bond due. Post war resident of Rockbridge Co. NFR.

LEGG, FRANKLIN - Pvt. Co. F. In service (VSL) by 6/1/62. Was taken prisoner along with Rich Lewis by John Hannah (citizen), 6/1/62. Enl. Hillsboro, Pocahontas Co., W. Va., 9/14/63. Present 1/1/64 - 2/29/64. Clothing issued 2/6/64. NFR.

LEHEW (LEAHN), ANDREW J. - Pvt. Co. C. b.c. 1839. Prior service, Co. D, 3rd VSL. Enl. Frankfort, Greenbrier Co., W. Va., 3/15/63 (Pocahontas Co., W. Va., 4/1/63). Not stated if present or absent on muster-in roll dated 3/63. Present 1/1/63 - 4/1/63, had one horse. Ab. 12/31/63 - 8/31/64, deserted 1/15/64 in Bath Co. Clothing issued 2/2/64. Cpd. Beverly, W. Va., 3/21/64. Confined at the Atheneum Prison, 3/24/64. Desc.: age 25, 5'9", fair comp., light hair and blue eyes. Occ. farmer, residing in Jackson Co., W. Va. Took the oath of allegiance and was released, 3/25/64. NFR.

LEMLEY, ELIAS S. - Pvt. Co. A. b.c. 1841. Not on muster rolls. Cpd. Preston Co., W. Va., 7/1/63. Confined at the Atheneum Prison, 7/2/63. Desc.: age 22, 5'9", light comp., auburn hair and blue eyes. Occ. farmer, residing in Monongahala Co., W. Va. Transf. to Camp Chase, 8/10/63. Confined at Camp Chase, 8/11/63. Took the oath and was released 1/14/64, by order of the Sec. of War. Age 39, farmer, Battelle Sub Dist., Monongalia Co., W. Va. 1880 Census, listed as Elihu S. Lemley. NFR.

LEMLEY, SAMUEL - Pvt. Co. A. b.c. 1843. Not on muster rolls. Cpd. Preston Co., W. Va., 7/1/63. Confined at the Atheneum Prison, 7/2/63. Desc.: age 20, 5'8", dark hair, dark hair and black eyes. Occ. farmer, residing in Wetzel Co., W. Va. Transf. to Camp Chase, 8/10/63. Confined at Camp Chase, 8/11/63, prison no. 2. Shot by Pvt. Moody, Co. C, 88th Ohio Vol. Inf., a sentinel, 9 p.m., 9/17/63. Pvt. Moody gave Lemley the order to halt three times, then fired at him. Lemley had ran behind a sink, within ten feet of the fence around the prison, which was forbidden. Lemley was wd. in the side, and either walked or was carried to the prison hosp., where his wd. was treated. The musket of the sentinel was loaded with "buck and ball," which is one round ball and three buckshot. The ball passed through is right arm, fracturing the humerus, then entered the body at the seventh rib, passed out at left inguinal region. Two of the three buckshot lodged in his arm, while the third passed through the arm, leaving a contused spot on his side. Treated with a simple dressing. d. Camp Chase, 1 a.m., 9/18/63. Bur. Camp Chase Confederate Cem., Columbus, O., grave no. 23. Served in Co. C, 46th Battn. Va. Cav.

LEMON, CHARLES NEWTON - Pvt. Co. A. b. MacFarland, Ritchie Co., W. Va., 12/4/43. Not on muster rolls. Clothing issued 2/19/64, 4/30/64 and 7/6/64. Deserted. Reported at Parkersburg, W. Va., 5/7/65. Sent to Clarksburg, W. Va., and confined there 5/9/65. Desc.: age 21, 5'8", fair comp., black hair and dark eyes. Occ. farmer, residing in Ritchie Co., W. Va. Took the amnesty oath and was released, 5/9/65. Brother of Frederick J. and Phillip J. Lemon. Age 36, carpenter, Murphy Dist., Ritchie Co., W. Va. 1880 Census. d. MacFarland, Ritchie Co., W. Va., 1/7/1930. Bur. Lemon Cem., MacFarland, Ritchie Co., W. Va.

LEMON, ELISHA - Pvt. Co. A. Served in Co. A, 3rd VSL. Post war rosters only. Post war resident of Pocahontas Co., W. Va. NFR.

LEMON, FREDERICK JOHN - Pvt. Co. A. b. Ritchie Co., W. Va., 2/24/44. Not on muster rolls. Deserted. Reported at Parkersburg, W. Va., 5/7/65. Sent to Clarksburg, W. Va., and confined there 5/9/65. Desc.: age 19, 5'9", fair comp., light hair and blue eyes. Occ. farmer, residing in Ritchie Co., W. Va. Took the amnesty oath and was released, 5/9/65. Brother of Charles N. and Phillip J. Lemon. Age 34, farmer, Murphy Dist., Ritchie Co., W. Va. 1880 Census. d. MacFarland, Ritchie Co., W. Va., 9/15/1928. Bur. Lemon Cem., MacFarland, Ritchie Co., W. Va.

- LEMON, PHILIP J. - Pvt. Co. A. b. 5/1/1837. Prior service, Co. A, 3rd VSL. Not on muster rolls. Clothing issued 2/19/64 and 5/26/64. Deserted. Reported at Parkersburg, W. Va., 5/7/65. Sent to Clarksburg, W. Va., and confined there 5/9/65. Desc.: age 27, 5'9", fair comp., red hair and blue eyes. Occ. farmer, residing in Ritchie Co., W. Va. Took the amnesty oath and was released, 5/9/65. Brother of Charles N. and Frederick J. Lemon. Age 42, farmer, Murphy Dist., Ritchie Co., W. Va. 1880 Census. Bur. Lemon Cem., MacFarland, Ritchie Co., W. Va.

LEONARD (LENARD), JOHN W. - Pvt. Co. D. b. Marion Co., W. Va., 8/10/36. Not on muster rolls. POW record shows enl. as Pocahontas Co., W. Va., 5/63. Clothing issued, 1st Qr. 1864, 4/1/64, 5/21/64, 6/17/64, 7/64 and 8/64. Deserted. Reported at Fairmont, W. Va. and sent to Clarksburg, W. Va. 11/1/64. Desc.: age 28, 5'7", dark comp., dark hair and blue eyes. Occ. farmer, residing in Ritchie Co., W. Va. Took the oath of allegiance and was released, 11/12/64. Age 43, farmer, South Grant Dist., Ritchie Co., W. Va. 1880 Census. d. Lost Run, Ritchie Co., W. Va., 6/8/1903. Bur. Victory Ridge Cem., Harrisville, W. Va.

LEVY (LEROY), AARON R. - Pvt. Co. ? Post war rosters only. NFR.

LEWIS, ASBURY - Capt. Co. ?. b. Harrison Co., W. Va., c. 1842 (1840). Prior service, Co. C, 31st Va. Inf. Age 18, a farmer, 1861. Post war rosters only, which show he was promoted to Capt. and transf. to the 19th Va. Cav. Served in Co. F, 20th Va. Cav. Post war farmer and resident of the Jesse Run Community, Smithfield Dist. and Spencer, W. Va. Post war farmer and trader. Moved to Spencer, Roane Co., W. Va., 1880, farmer. Alive 1913. NFR.

LEWIS, CHRISTIE (CHRISTOPHER) M. - Pvt. Co. F. b.c. 1845. Age 14, Pocahontas Co., W. Va. 1860 Census. Enl. Hillsboro, Pocahontas Co., W. Va., 8/1/63. Ab. 1/1/64 - 2/29/64, discharged, reason not given. Paroled at Charleston, W. Va., 5/10/65, signs by x. Desc.: age 20, 5'7", fair comp., dark hair and gray eyes. Age 34, farmer, Little Levels, Pocahontas Co., W. Va. 1880 Census. NFR.

LEWIS, EDWARD J. J. - Pvt. Co. I. Enl. Huntersville, Pocahontas Co., W. Va., 3/19/63. Present on muster-in roll dated 3/63. Mustered into service 3/19/63. Served in Co. C, 20th Va. Cav. NFR.

LEWIS, HEZEKIAH - Pvt. Co. C. Prior service, Co. D, 3rd VSL. Enl. Frankfort, Greenbrier Co., W. Va., 3/15/63. Not stated if present or absent on muster-in roll dated 3/63. Present 1/1/63 - 4/1/63, has one horse. NFR.

LIGHTNER, ANTHONY M. - Pvt. Co. I. b. Hightown, Pendleton Co., W. Va., 10/18/36. Age 24, farmhand, Mill Gap, Highland Co. 1860 Census. Prior service, Co. E, 31st Va. Inf. and Co. E, 46th Battn. Va. Cav. Enl. Huntersville, Pocahontas Co., W. Va., 2/4/64. Ab. 6/30/63 - 2/29/64, on furlough; mounted; enl. bounty due. Ab. 2/29/64 - 8/31/64, sick; mounted; enl. bounty due. Ab. 9/1/64 - 10/31/64, sick. Paroled at Charleston, W. Va., 5/10/65. Desc.: age 28, 5'8", dark comp., dark hair, black eyes and dark whiskers. Awarded Cross of Honor. Post war farmer and resident of Valley Center, Highland Co. d. Blue Grass (Valley Center), 6/12/1916, age 79 years, 7 months and 24 days. Bur. Bird Farm Cem., near Monterey, Highland Co.

LIGON (LIGGON), JOHN - Asst. Surg./Pvt. Co. F. b. Nelson Co., c. 1834. Grad. medical school, Philadelphia, Pa. Enl. Warm Springs, Bath Co., Present, Pvt., 1/1/64 - 2/29/64, enl. bounty due. Ab. 1/1/64 - 10/31/64, on leave; enl. bounty due. Ab., Asst. Surg., F&S MR 9/1/64 - 10/31/64, on leave. Appointed Asst. Surg. 1/28/65, to rank from 10/28/64. Confirmed 1/28/64. Assigned to duty 11/2/64. Paroled at Charleston, W. Va., 5/11/65. No desc. Post war rosters show service as Co. I. Post war doctor and resident of Pocahontas Co., W. Va. Age 36, physician, Lincoln Township, Pocahontas Co., W. Va. 1870 Census. Age 46, physician, Edray, Pocahontas Co., W. Va. 1880 Census. Member of Moffett Poage Camp, UCV, Marlinton, W. Va. d. Clover Lick, Pocahontas Co., W. Va., 3/29/1911 (4/2/1911), age c. 77. Bur. Clover Lick Cem., Pocahontas Co., W. Va.

LILLY (LILLEY), DAVID H. - Pvt. Co. ?. b.c. 1825. Age 35, lawyer, Randolph Co., W. Va. 1860 Census. Post war rosters only, which show him as a resident of Randolph Co., W. Va. Wartime document shows him as AAQM for Major John B. Lady's detachment of Cav., 6/28/64. Attended Confederate Reunion, Randolph Co., W. Va., 1906, claimed to be a member of the 19th Va. Cav. Served in Co. D, 20th Va. Cav. Post war roster shows him as a resident of Rockbridge Co., and that he served in the 27th Battn. Va. Cav. d. by 1916. NFR.

LINDSAY (LINDSEY), JAMES HARVEY - Pvt. Co. F. b. Bath Co., 1825. Age 35, farmer, Dunmore, Pocahontas Co., W. Va. 1860 Census. Enl. Hillsboro, Pocahontas Co., W. Va., 6/13/63. Post war rosters show he was mustered into service 2/19/64. Ab. 1/1/64 - 2/29/64, on special duty, detached service. Clothing issued 2/6/64. Ab. 9/1/64 - 10/31/64, wd. Berry's Ford or Ashby's Gap, 7/19/64; enl. bounty due. A. Pocahontas Co., W. Va., 1876. One of seven brothers which served in the Confederate Army.

LINDSEY (LINDSAY), THOMAS G. - Pvt. Co. ?. b. Pocahontas Co., W. Va., 1834. Age 27, farmhand, Thorny Creek, Pocahontas Co., W. Va. 1860 Census. Post war rosters only, which show he was a resident of Randolph Co., W. Va. Age 47, farmer, Green Banks, Pocahontas Co., W. Va. 1880 Census. d. Randolph Co., W. Va., 1900.

LINT, EDWARD - Pvt. Co. A. Enl. Williamsburg, Greenbrier Co., W. Va., 3/1/63. Not stated if present or absent on muster-in roll dated 3/63. NFR.

LITTLE, JOHN S. (L.) - Pvt. Co. A. Not on muster rolls. Clothing issued, 4/30/64, 5/21/64 and 6/17/64, signs by x. d. Staunton Gen. Hosp., 7/12/64.

LITTLEPAGE, JOHN CALHOUN - Pvt. Co. G. b. King William Co., 10/13/46. Enl. Frankfort, Greenbrier Co., W. Va., 3/12/63 (4/1/63). Not stated if present or absent on muster-in roll dated 3/63. Employed as a courier 10/1/63 - 12/31/63. Clothing issued 3/14/64. Ab. 9/1/64 - 10/31/64, AWOL. Paroled at Charleston, W. Va., 5/20/65. Desc.: age 19, 5'10", fair comp., red hair and dark hair. Post war rosters show service in Co. H. Grad. VMI, 1870. Post war employee of the US Treasury Dept., Auditor of War Dept. d. 10/27/1933. Bur. Arlington Cem.

LOCKHART, JOHN - Pvt. Co. C. b.c. 1815. Enl. Frankfort, Greenbrier Co., W. Va., 3/15/63. Not stated if present or absent on muster-in roll dated 3/63. Age 65, farmer, Grant Dist., Jackson Co., W. Va. 1880 Census. NFR.

LOCKHART, SAMUEL - Pvt. Co. C. Prior service, Co. D, 3rd VSL. Enl. Frankfort, Greenbrier Co., W. Va., 3/15/63. Present 1/1/63 - 4/1/63, had one horse. Present 12/31/63 - 8/31/64, has one horse; $100 enl. bounty due. Clothing issued, 2/2/64, 6/17/64, 7/64 and 8/64. Present 9/1/64 - 10/31/64, has one horse. Adm. CSA Gen. Hosp., Charlottesville, 11/10/64, acute diarrhoea. RTD. 12/28/64. NFR.

LOCKRIDGE, JAMES T. - Pvt. Co. F. b.c. 1822. Age 38, farmer, Huntersville, Pocahontas Co., W. Va. 1860 Census. Enl. Martinsburg, W. Va., 8/10/64. Ab. 9/1/64 - 10/31/64, AWOL since 10/1/64. Post war rosters show service in Co. I. Age 59, farmer, Huntersville, Pocahontas Co., W. Va. 1880 Census. NFR.

LOCKREY (LOCKERY), JAMES - Pvt. Co. F. b.c. 1825. Enl. Mt. Jackson, 10/11/64. Present 9/1/64 - 10/31/64. Paroled at Charleston, W. Va. 5/31/65. Desc.: age 40, 5'7", fair comp., black hair, hazel eyes and dark whiskers. Post war resident of Weston, W. Va. NFR.

LOGAN, JAMES A. - Pvt. Co. I. b.c. 1844. Age 16, farmer, Randolph Co., W. Va. 1860 Census. Prior service, Co. I, 4th VSL and Co. G, 31st Va. Inf. Enl. Beverly, Randolph Co., W. Va., 4/30/63. Present 6/30/63 - 2/29/64, mounted. Present 2/29/64 - 8/31/64. Clothing issued 3/22/64. Present 9/1/64 - 10/31/64, $100 bond due. Paroled at Charleston, W. Va., 5/10/65. Desc.: age 22, 5'6", light comp., brown hair and black eyes. Post war resident of Randolph Co., W. Va. Age 36, farmer, Mingo, Randolph Co., W. Va. 1880 Census. Attended Confederate Reunion, Randolph Co., W. Va., 1906. Member Gen. Pegram Camp, UCV, Valley Head, Randolph Co., W. Va. Attended Gettysburg Reunion, 1913. Resident of Belington, W. Va., 1916. NFR.

LOGAN, JOHN W. - Pvt. Co. ?. b.c. 1818. Age 42, farmer, Randolph Co., W. Va. 1860 Census. Post war rosters only, which show he was a resident of Randolph Co., W. Va. d. by 1916. NFR.

LOGAN, THOMAS - Pvt. Co. ?. Post war rosters only, which show he was a resident of Randolph Co., W. Va. d. by 1916. NFR.

LONG, JAMES M. - Pvt. Co. I. b.c. 1842. Enl. Huntersville, Pocahontas Co., W. Va., 9/6/64. Ab. 6/30/63 - 2/29/64, cpd. Droop Mtn., W. Va., 11/6/63; mounted; enl. bounty due. Confined at the Atheneum Prison, 11/16/63. Desc.: age 21, 5'9 1/2", fair comp., sandy hair and blue eyes. Occ. farmer, residing in Rockbridge Co. Transf. to Camp Chase, 11/18/63. Confined at Camp Chase, 11/18/63. Transf. to Ft. Delaware, 2/29/64. Confined at Ft. Delaware, 3/4/64 (3/2/64). Took the oath of allegiance and was released, 6/14/65. Desc.: age ?, 5'7", fair comp., light hair and gray eyes, a resident of Calhoun Co., W. Va. NFR.

LONG, JOHN E. - Pvt. Co. A. Post war rosters only, which show he served three years, and was a resident of Bedford Co. Wd. during the war and cpd. Confined at Camp Chase, where he d. Bur. Camp Chase Confederate Cem., Columbus, O.

LONG, JOHN H. - Pvt. Co. A. b.c. 1845. Not on muster rolls. Post war pensioner and resident of Lowly, Bedford Co. Alive 1901, age 56. NFR.

LONG, JOHN W. - Pvt. Co. I. b.c. 1839. Age 21, laborer, Greenbank, Pocahontas Co., W. Va. 1860 Census. Enl. Huntersville, Pocahontas Co., W. Va., 7/25/63 (1/10/64). Ab. 6/30/63 - 2/29/64, at home sick; mounted; enl. bounty due. Ab. 2/29/64 - 8/31/64, sick. Ab. 9/1/64 - 10/31/64, AWOL. NFR.

LONG, PERRY - Pvt. Co. ?. Prior service, Co. K, 31st Va. Inf. History of 31st Va. Inf. shows service in 19th Va. Cav. Post war rosters only. [Could be O. H. Perry Long, from Randolph Co., W. Va.] NFR.

LONGUE (LOGUE), LEWIS - Capt. Co. A. b. 1832. Prior service, Co. A, 3rd VSL. Enl. Williamsburg, Greenbrier Co., W. Va., 3/1/63. Not stated if present or absent on muster-in roll dated 3/63, Jr. 2nd Lt. Paid as 1st Lt., 1/64. Granted 15 days leave, 2/17/64. Ab. 12/15/64, AWOL since 12/1/64, no steps taken to have him dropped. Paroled at Charleston, W. Va., 5/12/65, as Capt. Desc.: age 32, 5'9", fair comp., brown hair and gray eyes. Post war rosters show him as a resident of Calhoun Co. and Ritchie Co., W. Va. d. 1907. Bur. Confederate Cem., Peewee Valley, Oldham Co., Ky.

LORENTZ, JACOB - Pvt. Co. F. Post war rosters only. Served in Co. B, 46th Battn. Va. Cav. NFR.

LOUGH, WASHINGTON - Pvt. Co. K. Enl. Frankfort, Greenbrier Co., W. Va., 3/20/63. Not stated if present or absent on muster-in roll dated 3/63. NFR.

LOUKIN, AMBROSE - Pvt. Co. B. Not on muster rolls. Paroled at Charleston, W. Va., 5/10/65. No desc. NFR.

LOURY (LOWRY), JAMES ROBERT - Pvt. Co. F. b. Stafford Co., c. 1847. Age 15(?), farmer, Pocahontas Co., W. Va. 1860 Census. Enl. Hillsboro, Pocahontas Co., W. Va., 12/1/63. Ab. 1/1/64 - 2/29/64, on leave. Present 9/1/64 - 10/31/64. Cpd. Huntersville, W. Va., 4/18/65 by Capt. Badger's Co., 8th Ohio Cav. Confined at Clarksburg, W. Va., 4/25/65. Desc.: age 19, 5'8 3/4", fair comp., dark hair and blue eyes. Occ. farmer, residing in Pocahontas Co., W. Va. Paroled for exchange and released, 4/25/65. Paroled at Charleston, W. Va., 4/25/65. Desc.: age 18, 5'8 3/4", fair comp., dark hair and blue eyes. NFR.

LOVELL, BENJAMIN F. - Pvt. Co. D. Enl. Williamsburg, Greenbrier Co., W. Va., 3/8/63. Not stated if present or absent on muster-in roll dated 3/63. Served in Co. B, 20th Va. Cav. Returned to the 19th Va. Cav., 4/64. NFR.

LOW, JOHN - Pvt. Co. H. Enl. Roane Co., W. Va., 3/1/64. Ab. 9/1/64 - 10/31/64, AWOL. NFR.

LOWE, CALVIN C. (E.) - Pvt. Co. G. b. Russel Co., 1/27/34. Moved to Kanawha Co., W. Va., 1855. Enl. Frankfort, Greenbrier Co., W. Va., 3/12/63. Not stated if present or absent on muster-in roll dated 3/63. Post war roster shows he was held POW at Charleston for about ten days. Post war rosters show service in Co. C. Post war farmer and resident of Junction Palace, Kanawha Co., W. Va. NFR.

LOWERS, ABRAHAM (ABRAM) - Pvt. Co. A. b. Kanawha Co., W. Va., c. 1839. Age 21, farmer, Calhoun Co., W. Va. 1860 Census. Prior service, Co. A, 3rd VSL. Reported AWOL on last roll; he was a POW at the time, escaped and rejoined his co. Enl. Williamsburg, Greenbrier Co., W. Va., 3/1/63. Not stated if present or absent on muster-in roll dated 3/63. Age 41, farmer, Washington Dist., Calhoun Co., W. Va. 1880 Census. NFR.

LOWERS, HENRY - Pvt. Co. C. b. Lewis Co., W. Va., c. 1814. Age 46, farmer, Calhoun Co., W. Va. 1860 Census. Prior service, Co. D, 3rd VSL. Enl. Frankfort, Greenbrier Co., W. Va., 3/15/63 (Pocahontas Co., W. Va., 4/1/63). Not stated if present or absent on muster-in roll dated 3/63. Present 1/1/63 - 4/1/63, has one horse. Present 12/31/63 - 8/31/64, had his own horse since 7/1/64. Clothing issued 2/25/64 and 6/17/64. Wd. Bunker Hill, W. Va., 7/19/64. RTD. 10/64. Present 9/1/64 - 10/31/64, has one horse; $100 enl. bounty due. Ab., 2/2/65, leave of absence. Post war roster shows service in Co. A. Age 69, farmer, Washington Dist., Calhoun Co., W. Va. 1880 Census. Brother of William Lowers, cousin of Thomas Lowers. Bur. Minnora Cem., Calhoun Co. W. Va.

LOWERS, JOHN W. - Pvt. Co. A. Post war rosters only. NFR.

LOWERS, M. J. - Pvt. Co. C. Enl. Frankfort, Greenbrier Co., W. Va., 3/15/63. Not stated if present or absent on muster-in roll dated 3/63. NFR.

LOWERS, THOMAS J. - Pvt. Co. C. b.c. 1843. Prior service, Co. D, 3rd VSL. Enl. Pocahontas Co., W. Va., 4/1/63. Present 1/1/63 - 4/1/63, has one horse. Present 12/31/63 - 8/31/64, has one horse. Clothing issued, 2/25/64, 4/11/64, 5/1/64 and 6/17/64, signs by x. Present 9/1/64 - 10/31/64, has one horse; $100 enl. bounty due. Cpd. Parkersburg, W. Va., 4/21/65. Confined at Clarksburg, W. Va., 4/22/65. Desc.: age 22, 5'11", fair comp., black hair and blue eyes. Occ. farmer, residing in Wood Co., W. Va. Paroled for exchange and released, 4/24/65. Post war resident of Wood Co., W. Va. Cousin of Henry and William Lowers. NFR.

LOWERS, WILLIAM H. - Pvt. Co. A. b. Kanawha (Wood) Co., W. Va., 2/23/43. Age 18, farmer, Calhoun Co., W. Va. 1860 Census. Prior service, Co. D, 3rd VSL. Enl. Frankfort, Greenbrier Co., W. Va., 3/15/63 (Pocahontas Co., W. Va., 4/1/63). Not stated if present or absent on muster-in roll dated 3/63. Present 1/1/63 - 4/1/63, has one horse. Present 12/31/63 - 8/31/64, had his own horse since 7/1/64. Clothing issued, 4/25/64 and 6/17/64. Present 9/1/64 - 10/31/64, has one horse; enl. bounty due. Cpd. Parkersburg, W. Va., 4/21/65. Confined at Clarksburg, W. Va., 4/22/65. Desc.: age 21, 5'10_", fair comp., black hair and brown eyes. Occ. farmer, residing in Wood Co., W. Va. Paroled for exchange and released, 4/24/65. "He was a good soldier and a good citizen." Brother of Henry Lowers, cousin of Thomas Lowers. NFR.

LOWTHER, JOHN - Capt. Co. ?. Post war rosters only, which show he was wd. at Low Gap, Va. and DOW. Resident of Wirt Co., W. Va. NFR.

LOX, J. L. - Pvt. Co. ?. Post war rosters only. Bur. Peterson Cem., Brilliant, W. Va. NFR.

LURTY, GEORGE WASHINGTON - Pvt. Co. B. Wartime list of deserters, dated 8/12/63, shows he served in Co. C, 31st Va. Inf. and is now with Col. W. L. Jackson's command. Served in Lurty's Batty., transf. to Co. B, 19th Va. Cav. NFR.

LURTY, WARREN SEYMOUR - 1st Lt. and Adjutant. b. Clarksburg, W. Va., 5/18/39. A cousin of Maj. Gen. Thomas J. Jackson. Prior service, Staunton Arty. and the 6th Va. Cav. Appointed Adjutant, 37th Battn. Va. Cav. and 19th Va. Cav. Not on muster rolls. Appointed 1st Lt. and Adjutant, 5/2/63. Resigned 10/13/63. Served as AAG, Brig. Gen. William L. Jackson's staff. Organized a battery of artillery, in which he served as Capt., 1/8/63. Desc. 1865: age ?, 5'9", sallow comp., dark hair and blue eyes, a resident of Harrison Co., W. Va. Served as US Marshall, Okla. Post war lawyer and resident of Harrisonburg, 1884 - 1901. Served as US Dist. Atty. for Western Va., 10 years. d. Harrisonburg, 2/1/1906. Bur. Woodbine Cem., Harrisonburg.

LUZADER (LUZADDERS), JOHN W. - Pvt. Co. K. b. Gilmer Co., W. Va., 1/16/46. Age 13, Gilmer Co., W. Va. 1860 Census. Not on muster rolls. Clothing issued, 2/5/64, 2/23/64, 4/1/64, 4/30/64 and 6/17/64. Paroled at Charleston, W. Va., 5/10/65. Desc.: age 18, 5'8", dark comp., dark hair and black eyes, signs by x. Post war resident of Ritchie Co., W. Va. Brother of William H. Luzader. Age 33, farmer, Clay Dist., Ritchie Co., W. Va. 1880 Census. Bur. Smith Cem. No. 2, near Middlebourne, Tyler Co., W. Va.

LUZADER (LUZZADER, LUZADDERS), WILLIAM H. - Pvt. Co. K. b. Lewis Co., W. Va., c. 1844. Age 16, farmer, Gilmer Co., W. Va. 1860 Census. Prior service, D, 10th W. Va. Inf. (US). Deserted to the enemy (CSA), 6/5/63, at Philippi, W. Va. Not on muster rolls. Clothing issued 4/30/64 and 6/17/64. Brother of John W. Luzader. NFR.

LYLE, JOHN NEWTON - Adjutant. Wartime letter, dated 12/1/63, shows him as AAAG, Jackson's Brigade. Post war rosters show he was appointed Adjutant, 19th Va. Cav., 1/65. NFR.

LYNCH, ADAM G. - Pvt. Co. H. b. Nicholas Co., W. Va., c. 1827. Age 33, farmer, Webster Co., W. Va. 1860 Census. Enl. Webster Co., W. Va., 8/1/63. Ab. 9/1/64 - 10/31/64, AWOL. NFR.

LYNCH, ANDREW W. - Pvt. Co. G. Enl. Frankfort, Greenbrier Co., W. Va., 3/12/63. Not stated if present or absent on muster-in roll dated 3/63. NFR.

LYNCH, BENJAMIN - Pvt. Co. ?. b. Lewis Co., W. Va., c. 1830. Age 30, farmer, Gilmer Co., W. Va. 1860 Census. Prior service, Co. D, 31st Va. Inf. Post war rosters only for service in the 19th Va. Cav. NFR.

LYNCH, JOHN M. - Pvt. Co. H. b. Nicholas Co., W. Va., c. 1845. Age 15, farmhand, Webster Co., W. Va. 1860 Census. Enl. Frankfort, Greenbrier Co., W. Va., 3/19/63. Not stated if present or absent on muster-in roll dated 3/63. Served in Co. A, 46th Battn. Va. Cav. Brother of William Lynch. NFR.

LYNCH, WILLIAM R. - Pvt. Co. H. b. Nicholas Co., W. Va., c. 1840. Age 20, farmer, Webster Co., W. Va. 1860 Census. Enl. Frankfort, Greenbrier Co., W. Va., 3/19/63. Not stated if present or absent on muster-in roll dated 3/63. Cpd. Webster Co., W. Va., 1/1/64. Confined at the Atheneum Prison, 1/6/64. Desc.: age 25, 5'8", florid comp., sandy hair and gray eyes. Occ. farmer, residing in Webster Co., W. Va. Transf. to Camp Chase, 1/20/64. Confined at Camp Chase, 1/21/64. Transf. to Ft. Delaware, 3/14/64. Confined at Ft. Delaware, 3/17/64. Took the oath of allegiance and was released, 6/7/65. Desc.: age ?, 5'7", ruddy comp., brown hair and blue eyes, a resident of Webster Co., W. Va. Brother of John M. Lynch. NFR.

LYNN, DAVID - Capt. Co. F. b. 12/30/37. Post war rosters only, which show he was a resident of Md. Served in the 18th Va. Cav. Post war resident of Cumberland, Md. Post war merchant, Hyattsville, Md. d. Hyattsville, Md., 12/28/1904.

LYONS, ELIJAH - Pvt. Co. H. b.c. 1840. Enl. Frankfort, Greenbrier Co., W. Va., 3/19/63 (Webster Co., W. Va., 8/1/63). Not stated if present or absent on muster-in roll dated 3/63. Ab. 9/1/64 - 10/31/64, AWOL. Cpd. Big Birch, Webster Co., W. Va., 3/2/65. Sent to Cumberland, Md., then to Wheeling, W. Va. Confined at the Atheneum Prison, 3/11/65. Desc.: age 25, 5'7", fair comp., light hair and blue eyes. Occ. farmer, residing in Webster Co., W. Va. Transf. to Camp Chase, 3/16/65. Confined at Camp Chase, 3/17/65. Applied for oath of allegiance, 4/65, stating he was a conscript. Took the oath of allegiance and was released, 5/16/65, signs by x. Desc.: age 25, 5'7", dark comp., dark hair and blue eyes, a resident of Calhoun Co., W. Va. NFR.

McALISTER (McCALISTER), ANDREW C. (J.) - Pvt. Co. C. Prior service, Co. D, 3rd VSL. Enl. Pocahontas Co., W. Va., 4/1/63. Present 1/1/63 - 4/1/63, substitute for Edgar C. Elliott; no horse. Present 12/31/63 - 8/31/64, has one horse. Clothing issued, 4/30/64, 6/17/64 and 4th Qr. 1864. Present 9/1/64 - 10/31/64, has one horse. NFR.

McALPIN (McCALPIN), JAMES WILLIAM - Pvt. Co. I. b.c. 1827. Age 31, farmer, Pocahontas Co., W. Va. 1860 Census. Enl. Huntersville, Pocahontas Co., W. Va., 2/1/63 (3/18/63). Present on muster-in roll dated 3/63. Mustered into service 3/19/63. Present 6/30/63 - 2/29/64, Acting Commissary for Capt. Marshall's detachment, 1/1/64; mounted. Ab. 2/29/64 - 8/31/64, cpd. 2/15/64. Cpd. Clover Creek, Pocahontas Co., W. Va., 2/16/64. Confined at the Atheneum Prison, 2/21/64. Desc.: age 37, 5'11_", fair comp., auburn hair, gray eyes and dark whiskers. Occ. farmer, residing in Pocahontas Co., W. Va. Transf. to Camp Chase, 2/22/64, wishes to be exchanged. Confined at Camp Chase, 2/23/64. Transf. to Ft. Delaware, 3/14/64. Confined at Ft. Delaware, 3/17/64. Ab. 9/1/64 - 10/31/64, POW; $100 bond due. Took the oath of allegiance and was released, 6/7/65. Also as James H. McCalpin on CSR. Age 54, farmer, Green Banks, Pocahontas Co., W. Va. 1880 Census. NFR.

McATEE, HARRISON H. - Pvt. Co. I. b.c. 1821. Age 39, tailor, Randolph Co., W. Va. 1860 Census. Enl. Huntersville, Pocahontas Co., W. Va., 2/1/63. Present on muster-in roll dated 3/63. Mustered into service 3/19/63. Father of William McAtee. NFR.

McATEE, WILLIAM - Pvt. Co. I. b.c. 1845. Age 15, tailor, Randolph Co., W. Va. 1860 Census. Enl. Huntersville, Pocahontas Co., W. Va., 3/19/63 (3/18/63). Present on muster-in roll dated 3/63. Mustered into service 3/19/63. Present 6/30/63 - 2/29/64, sick; mounted. Present 2/29/64 - 8/31/64, wd. Fisher's Hill, 9/22/64. Present 9/1/64 - 10/31/64, $100 Bond due. Post war resident of Randolph Co., W. Va. Son of Harrison H. McAtee. Living in 1916. NFR.

McAVOY, JAMES - 3rd Sgt. Co. B. b. Bath Co., 4/11/15. Age 44, farmer, Webster Co., W. Va. 1860 Census. Post war rosters show service in Matthew Perrine's Co., Partisan Rangers. Enl. Frankfort, Greenbrier Co., W. Va., 3/7/63 (Braxton Co., W. Va., 4/1/63). Not stated if present or absent on muster-in roll dated 3/63, Pvt. Clothing issued as 3rd Sgt., 2/7/64, 3/1/64 and 6/17/64. Present 9/1/64 - 10/31/64, has a serviceable horse. Was issued a pass in 1864 by Capt. John S. Spriggs. Post war resident of Webster Co., W. Va. d. Webster Co., W. Va., 4/16/78. Bur. Handschumacher Cem., Upper Glade, Glade Dist., Webster Co., W. Va.

McCALLISTER, JOHN - Pvt. Co. F. b.c. 1839. Enl. Hillsboro, Pocahontas Co., W. Va., 3/15/64. Ab. 9/1/64 - 10/31/64, wd. Winchester, 9/19/64; enl. bounty due. Paroled at Charleston, W. Va., 5/10/65. Desc.: age 26, 5'8", light comp., brown hair, blue eyes and light whiskers. NFR.

McCANN, JAMES MUNROE - Capt. Co. ?. b. Bridgeport, Harrison Co., W. Va., c. 1843. Prior service, Co. C, 31st Va. Inf. and Co. B, 17th Va. Cav. Requested authority to raise a Co. Transf. to the 19th Va. Cav. as a Captain. Postwar farmer and animal breeder. Member Staunton Camp UCV, age 62 (1905). NFR.

McCARTNEY (McCARTY) GEORGE DEXTER "Dee" - Pvt. Co. F. b. Lewis Co., W. Va. 12/17/37. Enl. Hillsboro, Pocahontas Co., W. Va., 4/1/63. Present 1/1/64 - 2/29/64. Clothing issued 2/6/64. Ab. 9/1/64 - 10/31/64, AWOL since 10/8/64; enl. bounty due. Deserted. Surrendered at Bulltown, W. Va., 3/9/65. Sent to Clarksburg, W. Va. Confined at Clarksburg and paroled for exchange and released, 5/12/65. Desc.: age 28, 5'9", fair comp., black hair and hazel eyes. Occ. farmer, residing in Webster Co., W. Va. Post war farmer and resident of Replete, Webster Co., W. Va. Brother in US service. Age 43, farmer, Hacker Valley, Webster Co., W. Va. 1880 Census. NFR.

McCARTY, ANDREW J. - Pvt. Co. I. b.c. 1847. Age 12, Pocahontas Co., W. Va. 1860 Census. Enl. Huntersville, Pocahontas Co., W. Va., 3/18/64. Present 2/29/64 - 8/31/64, mounted; enl. bounty due. Present 9/1/64 - 10/31/64. Clothing issued, 3rd Qr. 1864, signs by x. Paroled at Charleston, W. Va., 5/12/65, signs by x. Desc.: age 18, 5'4", light comp., light hair and gray eyes. NFR.

McCLARY, JAMES - Pvt. Co. C. Enl. Frankfort, Greenbrier Co., W. Va., 5/15/63. Ab. 12/31/63 - 8/31/64, missing while on a scout since 9/1/63; has one horse. Ab. 9/1/64 - 10/31/64, missing while on a scout since 9/1/63; $100 enl. bounty due. Post war rosters show service in the 20th Va. Cav. NFR. [Could be James McCleary]

McCLEARY, JAMES - Pvt. Co. B. b.c. 1844. Not on muster rolls. Cpd. Pocahontas Co., W. Va., 8/29/63. Confined at the Atheneum Prison, 9/6/63. Desc.: age 19, 5'8", dark comp., dark hair and dark eyes. Occ. soldier, residing in Wood Co., W. Va. Transf. to Camp Chase, 9/7/63. NFR. [Could be James McClary]

McCLINTIC (McCLINTOCK), H. D. - Pvt. Co. I. Enl. Huntersville, Pocahontas Co., W. Va., 3/19/63 (3/18/63). Present on muster-in roll dated 3/63. Mustered into service 3/19/63. Present 6/30/63 - 2/29/64, detailed as assistant Provost Marshal of Bath Co., by 7/24/63. Ab. 2/29/64 - 8/31/64, assistant Provost Marshal of Bath Co. NFR.

McCLINTIC, JOHN S. - Sgt. Co. I. Enl. Huntersville, Pocahontas Co., W. Va., 3/19/63. Present on muster-in roll dated 3/63, Sgt. Mustered into service 3/19/63. NFR.

McCLINTIC, WILLIAM HUNTER - Pvt. Co. I. b. Bath Co., 8/8/25. Age 34, farmer, Mill Point, Pocahontas Co., W. Va. 1860 Census. Member Mill Point Patrol, Pocahontas Co., W. Va., 5/61. Enl. Huntersville, Pocahontas Co., W. Va., 2/1/63 (3/18/63). Present on muster-in roll dated 3/63. Mustered into service 3/19/63. Present 6/30/63 - 2/29/64, mounted. Ab. 2/29/64 - 8/31/64, detailed in charge of broken down horses of the Brigade. Ab. 9/1/64 - 10/31/64, Detailed in charge of broken down horses of the Brigade; $100 Bond due. Paroled at Charleston, W. Va., 5/10/65. Desc.: age 40, 5'10", dark comp., dark hair, dark eyes and dark whiskers. Post war farmer and stock raiser, residing in Pocahontas Co., W. Va. d. Pocahontas Co., W. Va., 1/20/92.

McCLUNG, CHARLES HENRY "Charley" - 1st Sgt. Co. C. b. Greenbank (Greenbrier Co.), W. Va., 4/30/41. Farmhand. Prior service, Co. D, 3rd VSL. Enl. Frankfort, Greenbrier Co., W. Va., 3/15/63 (Mill Point, Pocahontas Co., W. Va., 4/1/63). Not stated if present or absent on muster-in roll dated 3/63. Present, Pvt., 1/1/63 - 4/1/63, had one horse. Present, 3rd Corp., 12/31/63 - 8/31/64, promoted to 1st Sgt., 2/1/64; has one horse. Clothing issued 2/25/64 and 6/17/64. Present, 1st Sgt., 9/1/64 - 10/31/64, has one horse. Cpd. Fayette Co., W. Va., 1/20/65. Sent to Cumberland, Md., then to Wheeling, W. Va. Confined at the Atheneum Prison, 2/10/65. Desc.: age 23, 5'11_", fair comp., dark hair and gray eyes. Occ. farmer, residing in Greenbrier Co., W. Va. Transf. to Camp Chase, 2/13/65. Confined at Camp Chase, 2/14/65. Took the oath of allegiance and was released, 5/16/65. Desc.: age 23, 5'11", dark comp., light hair and blue eyes. Post war rosters show him as Adjutant. Post war foreman, C&O RR, merchant and Sheriff 1877 - 1881, residing in Fayette Co., W. Va. Moved to Meadow View, Washington Co., merchant and Deputy Sheriff, 1890. d. Glade Spring, 3/6/1911. Bur. Emory Cem., Emory.

McCLUNG, HENRY H. - Pvt. Co. C. Prior service, Co. D, 3rd VSL. Enl. Frankfort, Greenbrier Co., W. Va., 3/15/63. Not stated if present or absent on muster-in roll dated 3/63. Present 1/1/63 - 4/1/63, has one horse. NFR.

McCLUNG, MADISON (MADDISON) - Sgt. Co. C. Prior service, Co. D, 3rd VSL. Enl. Frankfort, Greenbrier Co., W. Va., 3/15/63 (Mill Point, Pocahontas Co., W. Va., 4/1/63). Not stated if present or absent on muster-in roll dated 3/63, Pvt. Present, Pvt., 1/1/63 - 4/1/63, had one horse. Not stated if present or absent 12/31/63 - 8/31/64, 1st Sgt., went to the ranks, 2/1/64; has one horse. Clothing issued 4/11/64 and 4/30/64. Ab. 9/1/64 - 10/31/64, AWOL since 10/1/64; has one horse. NFR.

McCLUNG, S. K. - Pvt. Co. A. b.c. 1839. Not on muster rolls. Paroled at Lewisburg, W. Va., 4/27/65. Desc.: age 26, 5'9", ruddy comp., black hair and hazel eyes. NFR.

McCOMB, JAMES PRICE - Pvt. Co. F. b.c. 1826 (1833). Age 35, Stone Mason, Pocahontas Co., W. Va. 1860 Census. Enl. Hillsboro, Pocahontas Co., W. Va., 3/9/63. Not stated if present or absent on muster-in roll dated 3/63. Surrendered at Clarksburg, W. Va., 5/16/65. Desc.: age 32(?), 5'7_", dark comp., black hair and gray eyes. Occ. farmer, residing in Lewis Co., W. Va. Paroled for exchange and released, 5/17/65. Age 54, brick mason, Huntersville, Pocahontas Co., W. Va. 1880 Census. NFR.

McCOMB, WILLIAM W. - Pvt. Co. F. b.c. 1826. Age 32, farmer, Pocahontas Co., W. Va. 1860 Census. Prior service, McNeel's Co., 2nd VSL. Enl. Hillsboro, Pocahontas Co., W. Va., 3/9/63 (4/1/63). Not stated if present or absent on muster-in roll dated 3/63. Ab. 1/1/64 - 2/29/64, sick. Ab. 9/1/64 - 10/31/64, AWOL since 6/16/64. Age 54, farmer, Huntersville, Pocahontas Co., W. Va. 1880 Census. NFR.

McCORD, AARON P. - Pvt. Co. B. Enl. Frankfort, Greenbrier Co., W. Va., 3/7/63 (3/9/63). Not stated if present or absent on muster-in roll dated 3/63. Present 11/1/63 - 2/29/64, has one horse. Employed as a courier 11/19/63 - 11/30/63. Clothing issued, 4/1/64 and 6/17/64, signs by x. Present 9/1/64 - 10/31/64, $100 enl. bounty due. NFR.

McCOY, GEORGE WASHINGTON - Pvt. Co. F. b. 1/15/30. Age 31, farmer, Academy, Pocahontas Co., W. Va. 1860 Census. Member Locust Creek Patrol, Pocahontas Co., W. Va., 5/61. Prior service, McNeel's Co., 2nd VSL. Enl. Hillsboro, Pocahontas Co., W. Va., 3/9/63 (4/1/63). Not stated if present or absent on muster-in roll dated 3/63. Ab. 1/1/64 - 2/29/64, sick. Present 9/1/64 - 10/31/64. Paroled at Charleston, W. Va., 5/10/65. Desc.: age 36, 6', light comp., dark hair, gray eyes and dark whiskers. Age 50, farmer, Little Levels, Pocahontas Co., W. Va. 1880 Census. d. 12/19/87. Brother of Noah D. and W. O. McCoy.

McCOY, NOAH DAVIS Sr. - Pvt. Co. F. b. Beard, W. Va., 7/14/43 (7/14/44). Age 15, laborer, Pocahontas Co., W. Va. 1860 Census. Enl. Hillsboro, Pocahontas Co., W. Va., 4/1/63. Present 1/1/64 - 2/29/64, enl. bounty due. Present 9/1/64 - 10/31/64, enl. bounty due. Paroled at Charleston, W. Va., 5/10/65, signs by x. Desc.: age 20, 6', dark comp., brown hair and blue eyes. Post war farmer and resident of Beard (near Droop Mtn.), W. Va. Age 34, farmer, Little Levels, Pocahontas Co., W. Va. 1880 Census. Age 79, 1924. Member Moffett Poague Camp, UCV, Pocahontas Co., W. Va. Brother of George W. and W. O. McCoy. d. Beard, W. Va., 5/1/1932. Bur. Beard, W. Va.

McCOY, WILLIAM O. Jr. - Pvt. Co. F. b. Pocahontas Co., W. Va., 10/5/33. Age 26, farmer, Mt. Murphy, Pocahontas Co., W. Va. 1860 Census. Enl. Hillsboro, Pocahontas Co., W. Va., 3/9/63 (4/1/63). Not stated if present or absent on muster-in roll dated 3/63. Ab. 1/1/64 - 2/29/64, sick. Ab. 9/1/64 - 10/31/64, sick. Brother of George W. and Noah D. McCoy. Age 47, farmer, Little Levels, Pocahontas Co., W. Va. 1880 Census. NFR.

McCRAY, JOSEPH - Pvt. Co. B. b. Lewis Co., W. Va., c. 1837. Age 23, farmhand, Webster Co., W. Va. 1860 Census. Enl. Frankfort, Greenbrier Co., W. Va., 8/9/63. Ab. 11/1/63 - 2/29/64, cpd. 8/20/63, supposed dead. Cpd. Pocahontas Co., W. Va., 8/23/63. Confined at the Atheneum Prison, 8/20/63. Desc.: age 25, 5'11_", dark comp., black hair and brown eyes. Occ. farmer, residing in Webster Co., W. Va. Transf. to Camp Chase, 8/31/63. Confined at Camp Chase, 9/1/63. Transf. to Rock Island, Ill., 1/4/64. Confined at Rock Island Prison, 1/64. Ab. 9/1/64 - 10/31/64, POW since 8/16/63; $100 enl. bounty due. Took the oath of allegiance and was released 6/16/65. Desc.: age 28, 5'10", dark comp., black hair and hazel eyes, a resident of Frenchton, Upshur Co., W. Va. Post war rosters show residence as Braxton Co., W. Va. NFR.

McCULLOCH, JOHN - Pvt. Co. C. Prior service, Co. D, 3rd VSL. Enl. Frankfort, Greenbrier Co., W. Va., 3/15/63. Not stated if present or absent on muster-in roll dated 3/63. Muster roll for Co. D, 3rd VSL shows he d. Salem, 3/25/63, and had one horse. NFR.

McCUNE, DANIEL W. - Pvt. Co. A. b. Lewis Co., W. Va., c. 1834. Age 26, Calhoun Co., W. Va. 1860 Census. Prior service, Co. A, 3rd VSL. Enl. Williamsburg, Greenbrier Co., W. Va., 3/1/63. Not stated if present or absent on muster-in roll dated 3/63. Not stated if present or absent on Hosp. MR, Warm Springs, 4/1/63 - 1/1/64, attached to hosp. as a nurse since 11/1/63; his enl. shown as Calhoun Co., W. Va., 5/6/61. Served in Lurty's Battery. Brother of John H., Paulson B. and Timothy McCune. d. Calhoun Co., W. Va., 1910.

McCUNE, FALSER - Pvt. Cunningham's Cav. b.c. 1847. Cards included in CSR of Paulser B. McCune. Cpd. Braxton Co., W. Va., 9/17/63. Confined at the Atheneum Prison, 10/2/63. Desc.: age 16, 5'10_", florid comp., dark hair and blue eyes. Occ. farmer, residing in Braxton Co., W. Va. Charged with being a bushwhacker. Transf. to Camp Chase, 10/6/63. Confined at Camp Chase, 10/6/63. Transf. to Rock Island, Ill., 1/14/64. Confined at Rock Island Prison, 1/17/64. Transf. for exchange and d. on Str. New York, 2/20/65.

McCUNE, JOHN H. - Pvt. Co. A. b. Lewis Co., W. Va., c. 1838. Age 22, Calhoun Co., W. Va. 1860 Census. Post war rosters only, which show he was KIA. 10/62, and was a resident of Calhoun Co., W. Va. Brother of Daniel W., Paulson B. and Timothy McCune.

McCUNE, PAULSON (FAULSER, PAULCER) B. - Pvt. Co. A. b. Lewis Co., W. Va., c. 1832. Age 28, Calhoun Co., W. Va. 1860 Census. Prior service, Co. A, 3rd VSL. Enl. Williamsburg, Greenbrier Co., W. Va., 3/1/63. Not stated if present or absent on muster-in roll dated 3/63. Clothing issued, 1/17/64 and 4/30/64. Served in Co. F, 20th Va. Cav. Paroled at Charleston, W. Va., 5/11/65. Desc.: age 32, 5'10", light comp., dark hair, blue eyes and light whiskers. Post war resident of Calhoun Co., W. Va. Age 37, farm laborer, Lee Township, Calhoun Co., W. Va. 1870 Census. Age 49, farmer, Lee Dist., Calhoun Co., W. Va. 1880 Census. Brother of Daniel W. and Paulson B. McCune. Bur. McCune Cem., near Hur, Calhoun Co., W. Va.

McCUNE, TIMOTHY - Pvt. Co. A. b. Calhoun Co., W. Va., 11/11/38. Prior service, Co. A, 3rd VSL. Enl. Williamsburg, Greenbrier Co., W. Va., 3/1/63. Not stated if present or absent on muster-in roll dated 3/63. Also as having enl. in Co. E at Frankfort, Greenbrier Co., W. Va., 3/13/63. Not stated if present or absent on muster-in roll dated 3/63. Also as having enl. in Co. H at Frankfort, Greenbrier Co., W. Va., 3/19/63. Not stated if present or absent on muster-in roll dated 3/63. Served in Lurty's Batty., transf. from 3rd VSL by Geo. Downs, 10/1/63. Served in Co. F, 20th Va. Cav. Surrendered at Appomattox CH, 4/9/65. Name does not appear on Appomattox Parole list. Post war rosters show his enl. 12/61. Brother of Daniel W., John H. and Paulson B. McCune. Post war miller and resident of Lee Dist., Richardson, Calhoun Co., W. Va. Age 31, farmer, Lee Township, Calhoun Co., W. Va. 1870 Census. Age 42, farmer, Lee Dist., Calhoun Co., W. Va. 1880 Census. May be bur. in the Wright Cem., Calhoun Co., W. Va.

McCUTCHEON, JOHN B. - Pvt. Co. I. b.c. 1832. Age 28, farmer, Huntersville, Pocahontas Co., W. Va. 1860 Census. Enl. Huntersville, Pocahontas Co., W. Va., 9/10/63. Present 6/30/63 - 2/29/64, sick; mounted; enl. bounty due. Present 2/29/64 - 8/31/64. Present 9/1/64 - 10/31/64, $100 bond due. Paroled at Charleston, W. Va., 5/10/65, signs by x. Desc.: age 32, 5'5", dark comp., dark hair and blue eyes. Post war resident of Greenbrier Co., W. Va. Age 47, farmer, Green Banks, Pocahontas Co., W. Va. 1880 Census. NFR.

McCUTCHEON, SAMUEL H. (M.) - Sgt. Co. I. b. Pocahontas Co., W. Va., c. 1828. Age 32, farmer, Huntersville, Pocahontas Co., W. Va. 1860 Census. Enl. Huntersville, Pocahontas Co., W. Va., 2/1/63 (3/18/63). Present on muster-in roll dated 3/63, Sgt.

Mustered into service 3/19/63. Ab., Pvt., 6/30/63 - 2/29/64, taken prisoner 8/25/63; mounted. Cpd. Bath Co., 8/24/63. Confined at the Atheneum Prison, 9/6/63. Desc.: age 35, 6', dark comp., dark hair and blue eyes. Occ. farmer, residing in Pocahontas Co., W. Va. Transf. to Camp Chase, 9/7/63. Confined at Camp Chase, 9/8/63. Transf. to Johnson's Island, 9/13/63. Confined at Johnson's Island, 9/14/63. Ab. 2/29/64 - 8/31/64, taken prisoner 8/25/63; mounted. Ab. 9/1/64 - 10/31/64, POW; $100 bond due. Desires to take the oath of allegiance, 9/30/64, stating he was conscripted 12/1/62. Was kept under Provost Guard until 3/63, when he was given a choice of joining the army or be taken to Richmond. He wishes to get out of prison and go home. Does not wish to join either side and does not care which side succeeds. Desires to take the amnesty oath, 3/1/65, stating he was conscripted into the provost guard of Pocahontas Co. and desires to take the oath and get out of prison and remain North. Does not wish to be exchanged or be connected with the Southern Confederacy in any shape. Took the amnesty oath and was released, 5/13/65. Desc.: age 36, 6', fair comp., dark hair and gray eyes, a resident of Dunmore, W. Va. d. Pocahontas Co., W. Va., 7/2/69, age 41.

McDANIEL, JOHN - Pvt. Co. I. Enl. Huntersville, Pocahontas Co., W. Va., 4/2/64. Ab. 2/29/64 - 8/31/64, MIA since 8/64, supposed cpd.; mounted; enl. bounty due. Ab. 9/1/64 - 10/31/64, POW. NFR.

McDEVITT (McDIVET), JOHN - Pvt. Co. F. b. Ireland, c., 1816. Laborer, age 42 (1858). Prior service, McNeel's Co., 2nd VSL. Enl. Hillsboro, Pocahontas Co., W. Va., 3/9/63 (4/1/63). Not stated if present or absent on muster-in roll dated 3/63. Present 1/1/64 - 2/29/64. NFR.

McDONAHUE, JAMES - Pvt. Co. B. b.c. 1827. Not on muster rolls. Name appears on a register of the Federal Provost Marshal's Office, 4th Dist., Richmond, not dated. Desc.: age 38, 5'5", dark comp., dark hair and blue eyes, a peddler. NFR.

McDONALD, A. H. - Pvt. Co. E. Enl. Frankfort, Greenbrier Co., W. Va., 3/12/63 (4/1/63). Not stated if present or absent on muster-in roll dated 3/63. NFR.

McDOUGAL, JOHN N. - Pvt. Co. H. b.c. 1841. Not on muster rolls. Cpd. Parkersburg, W. Va., 4/65. Confined at the Post Guard House, Clarksburg, W. Va. Desc.: age 24, 5'11", fair comp., brown hair and blue eyes. Occ. farmer, residing in Wood Co., W. Va. Paroled 4/22/65, signs by x. NFR.

McELWAINE, GEORGE - Pvt. Co. B. b. 4/17/40. Enl. Frankfort, Greenbrier Co., W. Va., 3/7/63. Not stated if present or absent on muster-in roll dated 3/63. Post war rosters show service in Matthew Perrine's Co., Partisan Rangers. Post war resident of Webster Co., W. Va. Age 41, farmer, Glade, Webster Co., W. Va. 1880 Census. 9/18/99. Bur. McElwain Cem., Wainville, Glade Dist., Webster Co., W. Va.

McELWAIN, HENRY HARRISON "Dick" - 3rd Corp. Co. B. b.c. 1841. Age 19, Braxton Co., W. Va. 1860 Census. Enl. Frankfort, Greenbrier Co., W. Va., 3/7/63. Not stated if present or absent on muster-in roll dated 3/63, 3rd Corp. Cpd. and confined at Camp Chase. Felix Skidmore, Sycamore Dale, Harrison Co., W. Va. sent a petition to Camp Chase, 1/13/64, asking for his release. The petition stated he was a resident of Braxton Co., W. Va., and was being held as a citizen prisoner. Statement given by McElwain at Camp Chase, 1/17/65, shows him as being 23 years old and a resident of Braxton Co., W. Va. He was arrested in Webster Co., W. Va., 2/10/64 (so in statement) and confined at Camp Chase, 3/5/64. He was charged with having been in the rebel service. States in 1/62 Capt. Spriggs Co. came to Sutton, and he returned to Braxton Co. with them and enl. for 12 months. At the end of the term, he was threatened with conscription and deserted and went home, where he remained until taken prisoner. Took the oath of allegiance and was released, 1/23/65. Age 39, farmer, Holly Dist., Braxton Co., W. Va. 1880 Census. NFR.

McELWAINE (McELWAIN), LEWIS - Pvt. Co. B. b. Nicholas Co., W. Va., c. 1832. Age 28, farmer, Webster Co., W. Va. 1860 Census. Enl. Frankfort, Greenbrier Co., W. Va., 3/7/63. Not stated if present or absent on muster-in roll dated 3/63. Cpd. Webster Co., W. Va., 2/10/64. Confined at the Atheneum Prison, 5/12/64. Desc.: age 31, 6'2", dark comp., dark hair and blue eyes. Occ. farmer, residing in Webster Co., W. Va. Desired to take the oath of allegiance, 6/10/64. Transf. to Camp Chase, 8/30/64. Confined at Camp Chase, 8/64. Paroled 5/11/65. Post war resident of Webster Co., W. Va. Age 48, farmer, Glade, Webster Co., W. Va. 1880 Census. NFR.

McELWAINE, V. B. - Sgt. Co. B. Enl. Frankfort, Greenbrier Co., W. Va., 3/7/63. Not stated if present or absent on muster-in roll dated 3/63, Sgt. NFR.

McELWEE (McWEE), BUDD D. - Pvt. Co. K. b. Huntersville, Pocahontas Co., W. Va., 8/12/41. Prior service, 1st Co. G, 25th Va. Inf. and Co. F, 11th Va. Cav. Desc. 1861: age 20, 5'6", dark comp., black hair and blue eyes. Occ. carpenter. Enl. Frankfort, Greenbrier Co., W. Va., 3/20/63. Not stated if present or absent on muster-in roll dated 3/63. Deserted, took the oath of allegiance and was sent North, 11/22/63. Served in Co. D & H, 77th Ohio Vol. Inf., 2/23/64 - 3/8/66. US pensioner. Was a union man, and wished to remain at home, but could not. Was forced into Confederate service, went with the intention of deserting. McElwee said that he volunteered to avoid conscription. If he had told anyone how he felt, he would have been killed. Post war resident of Dunmore, Pocahontas Co., W. Va. Age 35, Green Banks, Pocahontas Co., W. Va. 1880 Census, listed as McElever. d. Dunmore, W. Va., 12/30/1923.

McGINNIS, WILLIAM L. - 2nd Lt. Co. K. b. Harrison Co., W. Va., c. 1843. Age 17, farmer, Gilmer Co., W. Va. 1860 Census. Enl. Frankfort, Greenbrier Co., W. Va., 3/20/63. Not stated if present or absent on muster-in roll dated 3/63, Pvt. Enl. in Co. G, Frankfort, Greenbrier Co., W. Va., 4/1/63. Clothing issued 5/1/64 and 6/17/64. Present, 4th Sgt., 9/1/64 - 10/31/64, has a serviceable horse. Paroled at Charleston, W. Va., 5/11/65, listed as 2nd Lt. Desc.: age 22, 5'5", light comp., dark hair, gray eyes and light whiskers. Adm. Lee Camp Soldiers Home, 11/1/1922, age 79. d. Richmond, 1/10/1929. Bur. Hollywood Cem., Richmond.

McGLAUGHLIN (McLAUGHLIN), ANDREW MATHEWS - 2nd Sgt. Co. I. b. Lightner (near Huntersville), Pocahontas Co., W. Va., 12/1/44. Age 15, farmer, Huntersville, Pocahontas Co., W. Va. 1860 Census. Enl. Huntersville, Pocahontas Co., W. Va., 3/18/63 (3/1/63). Post war roster shows he enl. 10/62. Present on muster-in roll dated 3/63, Pvt. Mustered into service 3/19/63. Ab., 3rd Sgt., 6/30/63 - 2/29/64, detailed to attend horses for Capt. Marshall's command; mounted. Present, 2nd Sgt., 2/29/64 - 8/31/64. Clothing issued 3/22/64 and 9/30/64. Present 9/1/64 - 10/31/64, $100 bond due. Post war rosters show him as Orderly (1st) Sgt., and promoted to 1st Lt. Post war farmer and stock raiser, Marlinton, W. Va. Age 35, farmer, Edray, Pocahontas Co., W. Va. 1880 Census. d. 3/8/1913. Bur. Clifton Cem., Greenbrier Co., W. Va. Brother of George H., John C. and Harper McGlaughlin.

McGLAUGHLIN, DAVID - Pvt. Co. F. b.c. 1821. Age 39, farmer, Dunmore, Pocahontas Co., W. Va. 1860 Census. Enl. Hillsboro, Pocahontas Co., W. Va., 8/19/63. Present 1/1/64 - 2/29/64. Clothing issued 2/7/64 and 6/17/64. Ab. 9/1/64 - 10/31/64, on detached service; enl. bounty due. Age 58, farmer, Green Banks, Pocahontas Co., W. Va. 1880 Census. NFR.

McGLAUGHLIN (McLAUGHLIN), GEORGE DALLAS - Pvt. Co. F. b. 1846. Age 13, Pocahontas Co., W. Va. 1860 Census. Prior service, McNeel's Co., 2nd VSL. Enl. Hillsboro, Pocahontas Co., W. Va., 3/9/63 (8/15/63). Not stated if present or absent on muster-in roll dated 3/63. Clothing issued 2/6/64. Ab. 9/1/64 - 10/31/64, AWOL since 9/22/64. Post war resident of Stony Bottom. Age 33, Green Banks, Pocahontas Co., W. Va. 1880 Census. d. 1926.

McGLAUGHLIN (McLAUGHLIN), GEORGE HENRY - Pvt. Co. I. b. Pocahontas Co., W. Va., 10/1/44. Age 18, farmer, Academy PO, Pocahontas Co., W. Va. 1860 census. Prior service, Co. I and D, 14th Va. Cav. Transf. to Co. I, 19th Va. Cav., 9/18/63. Enl. Huntersville, Pocahontas Co., W. Va., no date given. Present 6/30/63 - 2/29/64, transf. from Co. D, 14th Va. Cav., 9/18/63; mounted. Clothing issued 3/22/64 and 6/17/64. Ab. 2/29/64 - 8/31/64, missing since 7/22/64. Ab. 9/1/64 - 10/31/64, POW; $100 bond due. Age 38, farmer, Green Banks, Pocahontas Co., W. Va. 1880 Census. d. Marlinton, W. Va., 10/2/1910. Bur. Old McGlaughlin Cem., near Marlinton Cem. "A brave Confederate soldier." Brother of Andrew M., John C., and Harper McGlaughlin.

McGLAUGHLIN (McLAUGHLIN), HARPER - Pvt. Co. I. b.c. 1847. Age 13, Pocahontas Co., W. Va. 1860 Census. Enl. Huntersville, Pocahontas Co., W. Va., 4/1/64. Present 2/29/64 - 8/31/64, mounted; enl. bounty due. Present 9/1/64 - 10/31/64. Age 32, farmer, Edray, Pocahontas Co., W. Va. 1880 Census. Post war resident of Hot Springs, Bath Co. Age 63, Cedar Creek Dist., Bath Co. 1910 Census. Bur. Warm Springs Cem., Warm Springs, Bath Co. Brother of Andrew M., John C. and George H. McGlaughlin.

McGLAUGHLIN (McLAUGHLIN), JOHN M. - Pvt. Co. F. Enl. Hillsboro, Pocahontas Co., W. Va., 8/15/63. Ab. 1/1/64 - 2/29/64, on special duty, detached service. Post war rosters show he DOD. Camp Chase. NFR.

McGLEASON, ——— Lt. Co. ?. Post war rosters only. NFR.

McINTIRE, CHARLES - Pvt. Co. D. b.c. 1837. Enl. Williamsburg, Greenbrier Co., W. Va., 3/8/63. Not stated if present or absent on muster-in roll dated 3/63. Clothing issued 3/1/64. Paroled at Staunton, 5/10/65. Desc.: age 28, 5'10", dark comp., dark hair and hazel eyes. NFR.

McINTIRE, THOMAS B. - Pvt. Co. D. Enl. Williamsburg, Greenbrier Co., W. Va., 3/8/63. Not stated if present or absent on muster-in roll dated 3/63. Transf. to Co. B, 20th Va. Cav. KIA. Droop Mtn., W. Va., 11/6/63.

McKEEVER, ALLEN F. - Pvt. Co. F. b.c. 1842. Age 18, farmhand, Academy, Pocahontas Co., W. Va. 1860 Census. Prior service, McNeel's Co., 2nd VSL. Enl. Hillsboro, Pocahontas Co., W. Va., 3/9/63. Not stated if present or absent on muster-in roll dated 3/63. NFR.

McKEEVER, FRANKLIN "Frank" - Pvt. Co. F. Prior service, McNeel's Co., 2nd VSL. Enl. Hillsboro, Pocahontas Co., W. Va., 3/9/63. Not stated if present or absent on muster-in roll dated 3/63. NFR.

McKINDLE, H. - Pvt. Co. D. Not on muster rolls. Name appears on a list of POW's under guard at Staunton, 6/8/64, and sent to Wheeling, W. Va. NFR.

McLAUGHLIN, JOHN C. - Pvt. Co. I. b.c. 1839. Age 21, teacher, Academy, Pocahontas Co., W. Va. 1860 Census. Post war rosters only. Age 41, deputy clerk of court, Huntersville, Pocahontas Co., W. Va. 1880 Census. Brother of Andrew M., Harper and George H. McLaughlin. NFR.

McLAUGHLIN (McGLAUGHLIN), JOHN M. - 3rd Lt. Co. H. b.c. 1835. Cpd. Pocahontas Co., W. Va., 7/5/62. Desc.: age 27, 5'8_", fair comp., red hair, blue eyes and red whiskers. Occ. farmer, residing in Pocahontas Co., W. Va. Charged with being a guerrilla. Exchanged. Enl. Frankfort, Greenbrier Co., W. Va., 3/19/63 (Clay Co., W. Va., 4/1/63). Not stated if present or absent on muster-in roll dated 3/63, 3rd Sgt. Listed as 3rd Lt., Lady's Battn. Va. Cav. (20th Va. Cav.), 1863. Cpd. Clay Co., W. Va., 4/2/63. Confined at Camp Chase, 5/13/63. Transf. to City Point, to be exchanged. Arrived at City Point, 5/17/63. Exchanged 5/23/63. Ab., 3rd Lt., 9/1/64 - 10/31/64, lost a leg in the Woodstock fight, 10/5/64. Ab. 10/25/64, wd. and in hosp., no steps taken to have him retired. DOW. Bur. Lutheran Church (Massanutton) Cem., Woodstock.

McLAUGHLIN, WILLIAM - Pvt. Co. H. Enl. Frankfort, Greenbrier Co., W. Va., 3/19/63. Not stated if present or absent on muster-in roll dated 3/63. Wd. 4/1/63 (4/22/63), place not given. DOW. 4/23/63. "Age not 20 years. A fine and promising youth. A brave soldier and true patriot." Post war rosters show he was from Rockbridge Co.

McMILLIN, JAMES K. - Pvt. Co. B. Served in Co. D, 3rd VSL, enl. by 6/1/62. On furlough 12/1/62. Enl. Frankfort, Greenbrier Co., W. Va., 3/7/63. Not stated if present or absent on muster-in roll dated 3/63. Appears on Muster Roll of Co. D, 3rd VSL, 1/1/63 - 4/1/63, as having deserted and joined the Yankees; no horse. Paroled at Charleston, W. Va., 5/10/65. Desc.: age 24, 6', dark comp., brown hair, black eyes and brown whiskers. Post war resident of Braxton Co., W. Va. Resident of Nicholas Co., W. Va., 1880. NFR.

McMILLIN (McMILLION), JOSEPH - Pvt. Co. B. Post war rosters only, which show he was a resident of Braxton Co., W. Va. Resident of Nicholas Co., W. Va., 1880. NFR.

McNEEL, ANDREW GATEWOOD - Pvt. Co. F. b. Pocahontas Co., W. Va., 1/20/39. Age 21, farmer, Mill Point, Pocahontas Co., W. Va. 1860 Census. Prior service, Capt., Little Levels Cav. (disbanded fall 1861) and Co. F, 11th Va. Cav. Listed as having served in Co. D, 14th Va. Cav. Transf. to Co. F, 19th Va. Cav., c. 11/1/63. Enl. Hillsboro, Pocahontas Co., W. Va., 11/1/63. Present 1/1/64 - 2/29/64. Present 9/1/64 - 10/31/64. Paroled at Charleston, W. Va., 5/10/65. Desc.: age 26, 6'2", light comp., dark hair, hazel eyes and black whiskers. Moved west following the war. Brother of John A. and George S. McNeel. d. 10/14/87.

McNEEL, GEORGE SEE - Pvt. Co. F. b. Pocahontas Co., W. Va., 8/6/35. Age 24, farmer, Mill Point, Pocahontas Co., W. Va. 1860 Census. Enl. Hillsboro, Pocahontas Co., W. Va., 9/1/63. Ab. 1/1/64 - 2/29/64, sick. Present 9/1/64 - 10/31/64. Paroled at Charleston, W. Va., 5/10/65. Desc.: age 29, 6'3", dark comp., black hair, dark gray eyes and black whiskers. Post war rosters show him as belonging to Gen. R. E. Lee's personal bodyguard, and lists his rank as Col. Brother of A. G. and J. A. McNeel. Age 44, farmer, Little Levels, Pocahontas Co., W. Va. 1880 Census. d. 12/26/1903.

McNEEL (McNEIL), JOHN ADAM - Pvt. Co. F. b. Pocahontas Co., W. Va., 10/4/45. Age 14, Mill Point, Pocahontas Co., W. Va. 1860 Census. Enl. Hillsboro, Pocahontas Co., W. Va., 9/14/63. Had a horse, 15_ hands high, 5 years old, with a star on its forehead. Wd. Droop Mtn., W. Va., 11/6/63, leg and ankle crushed. Ab. 1/1/64 - 2/29/64, sick. Ab. 9/1/64 - 10/31/64, wd. since 11/3/63; enl. bounty due. Wd. Greenbank, W. Va., 11/3/63. Retired 12/6/64. Post war rosters show service in McNeil's Rangers (probably his brother's co.). Cross of Honor awarded, 6/2/1905. Age 35, farmer, Edray, Pocahontas Co., W. Va. 1880 Census. Moved to New Monmouth area of Rockbridge Co., 1892, farmer. Member Lee-Jackson Camp, UCV, Lexington.

Newspaper writer, Lexington Dist., Rockbridge Co. 1910 Census. Brother of A. G. and G. S. McNeel. d. New Monmouth, Rockbridge Co., 3/14/1916. Bur. New Monmouth Presbyterian Church Cem.

McNEEL, MATTHEW JOHN (JOHN MATTHEW) - 2nd Lt. Co. F. b. 10/10/44. Age 15, farmer, Mill Point, Pocahontas Co., W. Va. 1860 Census. Prior service, McNeel's Co., 2nd VSL. Enl. Hillsboro, Pocahontas Co., W. Va., 3/9/63 (4/1/63). Not stated if present or absent on muster-in roll dated 3/63, 4th Sgt. Present, 4th Sgt., 1/1/64 - 2/29/64. Clothing issued, 7/10/64. Present, 3rd Sgt., 9/1/64 - 10/31/64, enl. bounty due. Paroled at Charleston, W. Va., 5/10/65, listed as 2nd Lt. Desc.: age 20, 5'11", light comp., light hair, blue eyes and light whiskers. Post war farmer and resident of Seebert, Pocahontas Co., W. Va. Age 35, farmer, Little Levels, Pocahontas Co., W. Va. 1880 Census. Served as Sheriff of Pocahontas Co., 1889 - 90. Member W. Va. House of Delegates, 1897 - 98. Member of county court. Elected President of Bank of Marlinton, 1899. Member of Pocahontas Co. Camp UCV, 1924. Last Confederate Veteran in Pocahontas Co., W. Va. Post war rosters show him as a member of Co. K. d. Pocahontas Co., W. Va., 1/6/1938.

McNEEL, WILLIAM LAMB - Capt. Co. F. b. near Hillsboro, Pocahontas Co., W. Va., 10/13/25 (7/13/25). Age 34, farmer, Mill Point, Pocahontas Co., W. Va. 1860 Census. Prior service, McNeil's Co., 2nd VSL. Enl. Hillsboro, Pocahontas Co., W. Va., 3/9/63 (4/1/63). Appointed Capt., 3/9/63. Not stated if present or absent on muster-in roll dated 3/63, Capt. Ab. 1/1/64 - 2/29/64, on leave as member of Va. House of Delegates, served two terms. Was one of two men considered for promotion to Major, 2/64. Wished to raise a battn., but had delayed it due to other duties. Col. W. L. Jackson offered his assistance 2/64, in helping McNeel form the battn., should he gain permission to do so. Commanding Reg't., 7/31/64. Present 9/1/64 - 10/31/64, commanding Reg't. Submitted his resignation, 11/8/64, as he had been elected to the House of Delegates. Endorsed by Lt. Col. W. P. Thompson, "[Capt. McNeel] has proved himself a competent, efficient and gallant officer." Resignation not accepted, and 30 day leave granted by Gen. R. E. Lee. Ab. 12/15/64, on leave since 11/20/64. Paroled at Charleston, W. Va., 5/11/65. No desc. During the war, Capt. McNeel took the battle flag from the color bearer, who was wd., keeping it from being cpd. Post war farmer and stock raiser, residing at Academy (Hillsboro), Pocahontas Co., W. Va. Served as Sheriff of Pocahontas Co., W. Va., 1872 - 1876. Age 54, farmer, Little Levels, Pocahontas Co., W. Va. 1880 Census. Member W. Va. Senate, 1880 - 1883. d. Hillsboro, W. Va., 10/8/99 (10/13/99).

McPHERSON, SAMUEL - Pvt. Co. E. b. Harrison Co., W. Va., c. 1835. Age 25, farmer, Gilmer Co., W. Va. 1860 Census. Enl. Frankfort, Greenbrier Co., W. Va., 3/12/63 (4/1/63). Not stated if present or absent on muster-in roll dated 3/63. Not stated if present or absent on Hosp. MR, Warm Springs, 4/1/63 - 1/1/64, attached to hosp. 3/18/63 as a cook; sent back to his Co., 8/1/63; enl. shown as Mill Point, Pocahontas Co., W. Va., 9/2/62. Present 10/31/63 - 10/31/64, dismounted, driving an ambulance for the Reg't. Clothing issued 3/1/64, 4/30/64 and 6/17/64, signs by x. NFR.

McQUAIN (McQUEEN), THOMAS - 1st Sgt. Co. H. Enl. Frankfort, Greenbrier Co., W Va., 3/19/63 (Clay Co., W. Va., 4/1/63). Not stated if present or absent on muster-in roll dated 3/63, 1st Sgt. Cpd. Sweet Springs (Alleghany Co.), 12/15/63. Confined at the Atheneum Prison, confined as Sgt. Desc.: age 24, 5'11_", sandy comp., dark hair and gray eyes. Occ. farmer, residing in Roane Co., W. Va. Transf. to Camp Chase, 12/31/63. Confined at Camp Chase, 1/1/64. Transf. to Ft. Delaware, 3/14/64. Confined at Ft. Delaware, 3/17/64. Ab., Pvt., 9/1/64 - 10/31/64, POW since 12/15/63. DOD. Ft. Delaware, 7/22/64, typhoid mal. fever. Bur. Finn's Point National Cem., Jersey Shore.

MACE, COBENHOUR - Pvt. Co. D. Enl. Williamsburg, Greenbrier Co., W. Va., 3/8/63. Not stated if present or absent on muster-in roll dated 3/63. NFR.

MACE, PETER P. - Pvt. Co. A. b.c. 1842. Prior service, Co. A, 3rd VSL. Enl. Williamsburg, Greenbrier Co., W. Va., 3/1/63. Not stated if present or absent on muster-in roll dated 3/63. Clothing issued 4/30/64 and 6/17/64, signs by x. Post war resident of Nicholas Co., W. Va. Age 28, farmer, Lee Township, Calhoun Co., W. Va. 1870 Census. Bur. Mace Cem., Calhoun Co., W. Va.

MACMANAWAY (McMANAMA), WILLIAM - 1st. Sgt. Co. C. Enl. Frankfort, Greenbrier Co., W. Va., 3/15/63. Not stated if present or absent on muster-in roll dated 3/63, 1st Sgt. Served in Co. F, 46th Battn. Va. Cav. d. 12/63.

MALCOM (MALCOLB, MALCOMB), JOHN - Pvt. Co. C. b.c. 1837. Prior service, Co. D, 3rd VSL. Enl. Pocahontas Co., W. Va., 4/1/63. Present 1/1/63 - 4/1/63, has one horse. Ab. 12/31/63 - 8/31/64, has one horse; cpd. by the enemy 5/3/63, and has since died. Cpd. Harrison Co., W. Va., 5/5/63. Confined at the Atheneum Prison 5/9/63. Disc.: age 26, 5'10", dark comp., dark hair, gray eyes and dark whiskers. Occ. farmer, residing in Wirt Co., W. Va. Transf. to Camp Chase, 5/11/63. Confined at Camp Chase, 5/12/63. Transf. to Johnson's Island, 6/14/63. Confined at Johnson's Island, 6/14/63. Transf. to Pt. Lookout, 10/30/63. Confined at Pt. Lookout, 11/4/63. DOD. Pt. Lookout, 3/12/64, rheumatism. Bur. Pt. Lookout, Md. Post war rosters show service in Co. A.

MALCOMB, F. L. - Pvt. Co. I. Enl. Pocahontas Co., W. Va., 3/19/63. Ab. on muster-in roll dated 3/63, by permission. Mustered into service 3/19/63. NFR.

MALCOMB, WILLIAM B. - Pvt. Co. I. Enl. Pocahontas Co., W. Va., 3/19/63. Ab. on muster-in roll dated 3/63, by permission. Mustered into service 3/19/63. Paroled at Staunton, 5/9/65. Desc.: age 18, 5'8", fair comp., brown hair and black eyes. NFR.

MALONY, THOMAS - Pvt. Co. G. Enl. Frankfort, Greenbrier Co., W. Va., 3/12/63. Not stated if present or absent on muster-in roll dated 3/63. NFR.

MANLEY, JOHN H. Jr. - Pvt. Co. I. b.c. 1847. Age 13, Randolph Co., W. Va. 1860 Census. Enl. Beverly, Randolph Co., W. Va., 4/30/63. Present 6/30/63 - 2/29/64, mounted. Present 2/29/64 - 8/31/64. Present 9/1/64 - 10/31/64, $100 enl. bounty due. Post war rosters show him as being from Marion Co., Greenbrier Co., Randolph Co., W. Va. and Mo. Age 32, farmer, Grant Dist., Marion Co., W. Va. 1880 Census. d. Bird's Point, Mo. by 1916.

MANN, ROBERT E. - Pvt. Co. I. b.c. 1829. Enl. Huntersville, Pocahontas Co., W. Va., 3/1/63 (3/18/63). Not stated if present or absent on muster-in roll dated 3/63. Mustered into service 3/19/63. Ab. 6/30/63 - 2/29/64, detailed to feed cattle for Gov't.; mounted. Ab. 2/29/64 - 8/31/64, AWOL. Ab. 9/1/64 - 10/31/64, AWOL. Age 51, works on farm, Little Levels, Pocahontas Co., W. Va. 1880 Census. NFR.

MANN, WILLIAM H. - Pvt. Co. G. Enl. Greenbrier Co., W. Va., 12/10/63. Clothing issued 4/30/64 and 6/17/64. Ab. 9/1/64 - 10/31/64, wd.; has a serviceable horse. Clothing issued while at the Staunton Hosp., 10/14/64. NFR.

MARISON, JAMES - Pvt. Co. I. Enl. Beverly, Randolph Co., W. Va., 4/30/63. Ab. 6/30/63 - 2/29/64, KIA. Droop Mtn., 11/6/63; mounted; dropped from rolls.

MARKS, EMANUEL - Pvt. Co. C. Not on muster rolls. Deserted. Took the oath of allegiance and was released, 12/25/63. NFR.

MARKS, EZEKIEL T. - Pvt. Co. K. b. Lewis Co., W. Va., c. 1843. Age 17, farmer, Gilmer Co., W. Va. 1860 Census. Prior service, Norris' Co., 3rd VSL. Enl. Frankfort, Greenbrier Co., W. Va., 3/20/63. Not stated if present or absent on muster-in roll dated 3/63. Arrested in Gilmer Co., W. Va., 1/27/?? (year not given, probably 1865). Desc.: age 19, 5'11", dark comp., brown hair and brown eyes, a farmer. Age 36, farmer, Center Dist., Gilmer Co., W. Va. 1880 Census. NFR.

MARKS, JOHN - Pvt. Co. A. b. Lewis Co., W. Va., c. 1838. Age 22, Calhoun Co., W. Va. 1860 Census. Also listed as being a resident of Gilmer Co., W. Va. Arrested and confined by 3/15/62. Charged with destroying Union men's property. Prior service, Co. A, 3rd VSL. Enl. Williamsburg, Greenbrier Co., W. Va., 3/1/63. Not stated if present or absent on muster-in roll dated 3/63. NFR.

MARKS, LEMUEL - 3rd Corp. Co. E. b.c. 1823. Resident of Gilmer Co., W. Va. Farmer, age 38 (1861). Prior service, Co. D, 31st Va. Inf. Enl. Frankfort, Greenbrier Co., W. Va., 3/13/63. Not stated if present or absent on muster-rolls dated 3/63, 3rd Corp. Returned to the 31st Va. Inf. by 4/20/64. Wartime deserter list shows service in Co. B, 19th Va. Cav. NFR.

MARKS, MARSHALL - 1st Corp. Co. K. b. Lewis Co., W. Va., c. 1844. Age 16, laborer, Gilmer Co., W. Va. 1860 Census. Prior service, Co. D, 31st Va. Inf. Enl. Frankfort, Greenbrier Co., W. Va., 3/20/63. Not stated if present or absent on muster-in roll dated 3/63. Wartime deserter list show service in Co. B, 19th Va. Cav. Post war resident of Gilmer Co., W. Va. NFR.

MARKS, MARTIN M. - Pvt. Co. K. Not on muster rolls. Clothing issued 2/5/64, 2/23/64, 4/30/64 and 6/17/64. [Could be Marshall Marks] NFR.

MARLOW (MARLOWE), ANDREW J. - Pvt. Co. C. Resident of Wood Co., W. Va. Prior service, Co. D, 3rd VSL. and Co. C, 2nd Va. Inf. (not listed in history). Enl. Frankfort, Greenbrier Co., W. Va., 3/15/63 (Pocahontas Co., W. Va., 4/1/63). Not stated if present or absent on muster-in roll dated 3/63. Ab. 1/1/63 - 4/1/63, sick in Wytheville; has one horse. Ab. 12/31/63 - 8/31/64, deserted 8/1/64. Clothing issued 2/25/64. Post war account shows he was promoted to Major, 19th Va. Cav., 5/23/63. Scout and spy. Recruited men on several trips to Columbus, Ohio, 10/64 and 11/64. Surrendered at Columbus, after the end of the war. Post war resident of Columbus, O. NFR.

MARLOW, LEVI - 4th Sgt. Co. C. b.c. 1834. Prior service, Co. D, 3rd VSL. Enl. Frankfort, Greenbrier Co., W. Va., 3/15/63 (Mill Point, Pocahontas Co., W. Va., 4/1/63). Not stated if present or absent on muster-in roll dated 3/63, Pvt. Present 1/1/63 - 4/1/63, has one horse. Ab., 4th Sgt., 12/31/63 - 8/31/64, cpd. 3/1/64, has since taken the oath to the Yankee Gov't. Deserted. Cpd. Jackson Co., W. Va., 3/29/64. Confined at the Atheneum Prison, 4/4/64. Desc.: age 30, 5'8", fair comp., dark hair and blue eyes. Occ. farmer, residing in Wood Co., W. Va. Transf. to Camp Chase, 5/10/64. Confined at Camp Chase 5/11/64. Desires to take the oath of allegiance, 6/10/64. Took the oath and was released, 10/4/64. Post war resident of Wood Co., W. Va. NFR.

MARSHALL, JOHN R. - Pvt. Co. I. b.c. 1846. Not on muster rolls. Cpd. Huntersville, Pocahontas Co., W. Va., 4/17/65, by Capt. Badger's Co., 8th Ohio Cav. Confined at Clarksburg, W. Va., 4/25/65. Desc.: age 19, 5'9", fair comp., light hair and blue eyes. Occ. farmer, residing in Pocahontas Co., W. Va. Paroled for exchange and released, 4/25/65. Age 35, works at saw mill, Edray, Pocahontas Co., W. Va. 1880 Census. NFR.

MARSHALL, JACOB WILLIAMSON - Capt. Co. I. b. Cairo, Ritchie Co., W. Va., 4/6/30. Prewar resident of Cairo, W. Va. Moved to Marlin's Bottom, Pocahontas Co., W. Va., 1848, where he was a merchant. Moved to Mingo, Randolph Co., W. Va. Age 30, merchant, Randolph Co., W. Va. 1860 Census. Served as a scout and guide on Gen. R. E. Lee's Staff. Acting as Provost Marshall, Pocahontas and Randolph Co's, W. Va., 4/26/62. Authorized to raise troops under Col. W. L. Jackson, 1862. Led 30 men on detached service for 16 days, 8/12/62, apparently under the command of Col. John D. Imboden, 1st Va. Partisan Rangers. Enl. Huntersville, Pocahontas Co., W. Va., 2/1/63 (3/18/63). Ab. on muster-in roll dated 3/63, sick. Mustered into service 3/19/63. Appointed Captain, 3/19/63. Serving as Provost Marshall for Pocahontas Co., W. Va., 4/5/63, stationed at "Camp Harrold". Ab. 6/30/63 - 2/29/64, on furlough. Assigned to duty as Provost Marshall for Pocahontas, Bath & Randolph Co's., 6/28/63. Mentioned for "distinguished conduct" at Beverly, 7/63, by W. L. Jackson in his report. Jackson added: "I was much indebted throughout the Captain Marshall on account of his thorough knowledge of the country, personal bravery, and excellent judgement." Assigned to duty, 7/16/63. Acting as Provost Marshall of Pocahontas, Bath and Randolph Counties, 7/18/63. Lt. Col. W. P. Thompson said of Marshall in his report of Droop Mtn., W. Va., 11/6/63: "distinguished himself for his coolness and calm disregard of danger." Sold 103,044 pounds of hay to the CS Gov't., was paid $3,091.32. House burned by Union troops, 12/63, because it was a "harboring place of guerrillas..." Present 2/29/64 - 8/31/64. Present 9/1/64 - 10/31/64. Name appears on F&S MR 9/1/64 - 10/31/64 as commanding the Reg't., and as Inspecting and Mustering Officer. Post war source shows he was wd. through the right lung during the war, from which he never fully recovered. Post war rosters show him as Lt. Col., and that he was prom. to Col. by the end of the war, but did not serve as such. Post war merchant and hotel operator at Mingo, Randolph Co., W. Va. Age 50, farmer, Mingo, Randolph Co., W. Va. 1880 Census. Deputy Collector, US Internal Revenue, 1885. d. Mingo, W. Va., 5/11/99. "He is said to have been in battle, cool, daring and resourceful..."

MARTIN, BENJAMIN K. - Pvt. Co. D. b.c. 1844. Not on muster rolls. Clothing issued 2/7/64, 4/1/64, 5/21/64, 6/17/64, 7/6/64, 7/64 and 8/64. Paroled at Clarksburg, W. Va., 4/30/65. Desc.: age 21, 5'11", fair comp., light hair and blue eyes. NFR.

MARTIN, DAVID - Pvt. Co. D. b. Marion Co., W. Va., c. 1839. Resident of Gauley Mount, W. Va. Arrested and confined at Wheeling, W. Va. Released on his oath by 3/13/62. Enl. Williamsburg, Greenbrier Co., W. Va., 3/8/63. Not stated if present or absent on muster-in roll dated 3/63. Served in Co. B, 20th Va. Cav. Post war resident of Marion Co., W. Va. NFR.

MARTIN, EZEKIEL - 1st Lt. Co. D. Enl. Williamsburg, Greenbrier Co., W. Va., 3/8/63. Not stated if present or absent on muster-in roll dated 3/63, 1st Lt. Served in Co. B, 20th Va. Cav. Post war resident of Marion Co., W. Va. NFR.

MARTIN, GEORGE - Pvt. Co. A. b. Marion Co., W. Va., c. 1837. Age 23, carpenter, Calhoun Co., W. Va. 1860 Census. Post war rosters only. NFR.

MARTIN, HENRY - Pvt. Co. D. Not on muster rolls. Wartime letter dated 3/11/64 shows him as a member of this unit. "He came up on furlow and swaped places with one of our company." NFR.

MARTIN, JAMES R. - Corp. Co. H. Enl. Frankfort, Greenbrier Co., W. Va., 3/19/63 (Clay Co., W. Va., 5/1/63). Not stated if present or absent on muster-in roll dated 3/63. Ab. 9/1/64 - 10/31/64, AWOL. Shot himself through the toe by 9/10/64. NFR.

MARTIN, JASPER - Pvt. Co. D. b. Harrison Co., W. Va., c. 1835. Not on muster rolls. POW record shows his enl. as Barbour Co., W. Va., 6/63. Present 2/27/64. Clothing issued 4/1/64. Deserted. Surrendered at Paw Paw, W. Va., 2/65. Confined at Clarksburg, W. Va., 3/25/65. Desc.: age 28, 5'7", fair comp., light hair and blue eyes. Occ. farmer, residing in Marion Co., W. Va. Took the amnesty oath and was sent North, 3/30/65. Age 43, farmer, Grant Dist., Marion Co., W. Va. 1880 Census. NFR.

MARTIN, JOHN J. - Pvt. Co. D. b.c. 1843. Not on muster rolls. Paroled at Clarksburg, W. Va., 4/30/65. Age 37, farmer, Grant Dist., Marion Co., W. Va. 1880 Census. NFR.

MARTIN, JOSEPH - Pvt. Co. G. b.c. 1814. Prior service, Co. A, 3rd VSL. Cpd. Calhoun Co., W. Va., 10/24/62. Desc.: age 49, 5'9", dark comp., black hair and dark eyes. Confined at the Atheneum Prison, 10/28/62. Desc.: age 49, 5'9", dark comp., black hair and dark eyes. Occ. farmer, residing in Calhoun Co., W. Va. Transf. to Camp Chase, 11/1/62. Confined at Camp Chase, 11/2/62. Transf. to Cairo, Ill., 11/20/62. Exchanged. Enl. Frankfort, Greenbrier Co., W. Va., 3/12/63. Not stated if present or absent on muster-in roll dated 3/63. Enl. in Co. A, Williamsburg, Greenbrier Co., W. Va., 3/1/63. Not stated if present or absent on muster-in roll dated 3/63. Clothing issued as a member of Co. A, 2/19/64 and 6/17/64. Paroled at Charleston, W. Va., 5/11/65. Desc.: age 52, 5'10", dark comp., dark hair and dark eyes. Served in the 20th Va. Cav. Age 56, farm laborer, Center Township, Calhoun Co., W. Va 1870 Census. Age 64, farmer, Center Dist., Calhoun Co., W. Va. 1880 Census. NFR.

MARTIN, JOSHUA H. - Pvt. Co. A. b. Marion Co., W. Va., c. 1842. Age 18, Calhoun Co., W. Va. 1860 Census. Prior service, Co. A, 3rd VSL. Enl. Williamsburg, Greenbrier Co., W. Va., 3/1/63. POW record shows his enl. as Calhoun Co., W. Va., 7/62. Not stated if present or absent on muster-in roll dated 3/63. Deserted. Took the oath of allegiance 12/5/63. Apparently returned to duty. Present 2/27/64. Clothing issued 5/21/64 and 6/17/64. Cpd. Beverly, W. Va., 10/29/64. Sent to Clarksburg, W. Va., then to Wheeling, W. Va., 11/2/64. Desc.: age 19, 5'10", dark comp., dark hair and hazel eyes. Occ. farmer, residing in Calhoun Co., W. Va. Confined at the Atheneum Prison, 11/2/64. Transf. to Camp Chase, 11/22/64. Confined at Camp Chase, 11/23/64. Took the oath of allegiance and was released, 5/15/65. Desc.: age 20, 5'10", florid comp., dark hair and dark eyes, a resident of Calhoun Co., W. Va. Age 38, farmer, Center Dist., Calhoun Co., W. Va. 1880 Census. NFR.

MARTIN, JOSHUA R. - Pvt. Co. D. b. Harrison Co., W. Va., c. 1824. Not on muster rolls. POW record shows his enl. as Highland Co., 8/63. Clothing issued, 5/25/64. Cpd. Crab Bottom, Highland Co., 12/17/64. Confined at the Atheneum Prison, 12/24/64. Desc.: age 40, 5'7", dark comp., dark hair and dark eyes. Occ. farmer, residing in Marion Co., W. Va. Transf. to Camp Chase, 12/27/64. Confined at Camp Chase, 12/28/64, desires to take the oath of allegiance. Took the oath of allegiance and was released, 6/12/65. Desc.: age 41, 5'6 3/4", fair comp., dark hair and brown eyes, a resident of Marion Co., W. Va. NFR.

MARTIN, WILLIAM F. - Pvt. Co. D. b.c. 1835. Enl. Williamsburg, Greenbrier Co., W. Va., 3/8/63. Not stated if present or absent on muster-in roll dated 3/63. Served in Co. B, 20th Va. Cav. Post war resident of Marion Co., W. Va. Age 44, farmer, Lincoln Dist., Marion Co., W. Va. 1880 Census. NFR.

MASON, JOHNSON (JOHN) - Pvt. Co. D. b.c. 1841. Enl. Williamsburg, Greenbrier Co., W. Va., 3/8/63. Not stated if present or absent on muster-in roll dated 3/63. Clothing issued 2/7/64, 4/1/64, 5/1/64, 6/1/64, 7/64 and 8/64. Cpd. Marion Co., W. Va., 3/13/65. Confined at Clarksburg, W. Va. Desc.: age 24, 6', dark comp., dark hair and black eyes. Occ. farmer, residing in Marion Co., W. Va. Adm. USA Post Hosp., Clarksburg, W. Va., 4/21/65, gunshot wd. RTD. 4/25/65. Took the oath of allegiance and was released, 4/25/65. NFR.

MATHEWS (MATTHEWS), CHARLES R. - Pvt. Co. I. Age 21, Clerk, Pocahontas Co., W. Va. 1860 Census. Enl. Huntersville, Pocahontas Co., W. Va., 3/19/63 (3/18/63). Present on muster-in roll dated 3/63. Mustered into service 3/19/63. Present 6/30/63 - 2/29/64, acting adjutant for Capt. Marshall's detachment; mounted. Clothing issued, 3/22/64. Present 2/29/64 - 8/31/64, detailed with horses. Present 9/1/64 - 10/31/64, on detached service. d. by 1916. NFR.

MATHEWS, WILLIAM H. - Pvt. Co. B. Enl. Frankfort, Greenbrier Co., W. Va., 3/9/63. Not stated if present or absent on muster-in roll dated 3/63. Present 11/1/63 - 2/29/64, has one horse. Clothing issued, 1st Qr. 1864 and 4/30/64. Ab. 9/1/64 - 10/31/64, on leave; $100 enl. bounty due. Post war resident of Braxton Co., W. Va. NFR.

MAUZY, GEORGE W. - Pvt. Co. I. b. 1845. Enl. Huntersville, Pocahontas Co., W. Va., 1/1/64. POW record shows his enl. as Pocahontas Co., W. Va., 2/64. Not stated if present or absent 6/30/63 - 2/29/64, mounted; enl. bounty due. Ab. 2/29/64 - 8/31/64, AWOL since 9/23/64. Present 9/1/64 - 10/31/64, mounted; enl. bounty due. Deserted. Reported at Beverly, W. Va., 12/28/64. Desc.: age 18, 5'8", fair comp., brown hair and hazel eyes. Occ. farmer, residing in Highland Co. Took the oath of allegiance and was released, 12/24/64. Post war resident of New Hampden, Highland Co. Member S. B. Gibbons Camp, UCV, Harrisonburg. d. 1941. Bur. Union Chapel Methodist Church Cem., Highland Co.

MAY, GEORGE B. - Pvt. Co. E. b. Pocahontas Co., W. Va., c. 1842. Age 18, Calhoun Co., W. Va. 1860 Census. Enl. Frankfort, Greenbrier Co., W. Va., 3/12/63 (4/1/63). Not stated if present or absent on muster-in roll dated 3/63. Ab. 10/31/63 - 10/31/64, on horse detail, time now expired. Clothing issued, 3/1/64, 4/30/64 and 6/17/64, signs by x. Cpd. Calhoun Co., W. Va., 10/27/64 (11/3/64). Confined at the Atheneum Prison, 11/64. Desc.: age 22, 5'7", fair comp., brown hair and gray eyes. Occ. farmer, residing in Calhoun Co., W. Va. Transf. to Camp Chase, 11/29/64. Confined at Camp Chase, 11/30/64. Took the oath of allegiance and was released, 6/12/65. Desc.: age 22, 5'7_", fair comp., dark hair and gray eyes, a resident of Calhoun Co., W. Va. Age 38, farmer, Washington Dist., Calhoun Co., W. Va. 1880 Census. Brother of William J. May. NFR.

MAY, JOHN - Pvt. Co. B. Enl. Frankfort, Greenbrier Co., W. Va., 3/7/63. Not stated if present or absent on muster-in roll dated 3/63. Present 11/1/63 - 2/29/64, has one horse. Clothing issued 2/1/64 and 3/1/64. Ab. 9/1/64 - 10/31/64, detailed as nurse in the hosp.; $100 enl. bounty due. Cpd. near Petersburg, 10/27/64. Sent to City Point, then to Pt. Lookout. Confined at Pt. Lookout, 10/31/64. Paroled for exchange, 2/13/65. Exchanged at Coxes Landing, James River, 2/14-15/65. Post war resident of Braxton Co., W. Va. NFR.

MAY, JOHN R. - Pvt. Co. E. b. Pocahontas Co., W. Va., c. 1833. Age 27, farmer, Calhoun Co., W. Va. 1860 Census. Enl. Frankfort, Greenbrier Co., W. Va., 3/13/63 (4/1/63). Not stated if present or absent on muster-in roll dated 3/63. Ab. 10/31/63 - 10/31/64, cpd. 7/15/64; had his own horse until 7/1/64. Cpd. Loudoun Co. (near Harpers Ferry, W. Va.), 7/15/64. Sent to Harpers Ferry, W. Va., then to Washington, DC. Confined at the Old Capitol Prison, 7/17/64. Transf. to Elmira, NY, 7/23/64. Confined at Elmira Prison, 7/25/64. Desired to take the oath of allegiance, 9/30/64, says he has family in Calhoun Co., W. Va., and wishes to go there. DOD. Elmira Prison, 11/29/64, pneumonia. Bur. Woodlawn National Cem., Elmira, NY, grave no. 904 (1005).

MAY, ROBERT S. - Pvt. Co. E. b. Pocahontas Co., W. Va., c. 1837. Age 23, farmer, Calhoun Co., W. Va. 1860 Census. Enl. Frankfort, Greenbrier Co., W. Va., 3/12/63 (4/1/63). Not stated if present or absent on muster-in roll dated 3/63. Ab. 10/31/63 - 10/31/64, on horse detail, time now expired. Clothing issued 3/1/64 and 6/17/64. Cpd. Calhoun Co., W. Va. 10/27/64. Confined at the Atheneum Prison, 11/64. Desc.: age 28, 5'6", fair comp., black hair and blue eyes. Occ. farmer, residing in Calhoun Co., W. Va. Transf. to Camp Chase, 11/29/64. Confined at Camp Chase, 11/30/64, desires to take the oath of allegiance. DOD. 3/7/65 (3/18/65), pneumonia. Bur. Camp Chase Confederate Cem., 1/3 mile South of Camp Chase, grave no. 1700.

MAY, SYLVESTER - Pvt. Co. B. b.c. 1844. Enl. Frankfort, Greenbrier Co., W. Va., 3/9/63. Not stated if present or absent on muster-in roll dated 3/63. Clothing issued 3/21/64 and 6/17/64, signs by x. Ab. 9/1/64 - 10/31/64, AWOL; not entitled to $100 enl. bounty. Paroled at Mt. Jackson, 4/21/65. Desc.: age 21, 5'8", dark comp., brown hair and gray eyes. Post war rosters show service in the 20th Va. Cav. NFR.

MAY, WILLIAM J. - Pvt. Co. E. b. Pocahontas Co., W. Va., c. 1841. Age 19, Calhoun Co., W. Va. 1860 Census. Enl. Frankfort, Greenbrier Co., W. Va., 3/12/63 (4/1/63). Not stated if present or absent on muster-in roll dated 3/63. Ab. 10/31/63 - 10/31/64, cpd. 7/15/64; had his own horse since 7/1/64. Clothing issued 3/1/64 and 6/17/64, signs by x. Cpd. Loudoun Co. (near Harpers Ferry, W. Va.), 7/15/64. Sent to Harpers Ferry, W. Va., then to Washington, DC. Confined at the Old Capitol Prison, 7/17/64. Transf. to Elmira, NY, 7/23/64. Confined at Elmira Prison, 7/25/64. Desired to take the oath of allegiance, 9/30/64, and remain in the North. Took the oath of allegiance and was released, 5/15/65. Desc.: age ?, 5'7", dark comp., auburn hair and gray eyes, a resident of Clarksburg, W. Va., signs by x. Age 41, farmer, Washington Dist., Calhoun Co., W. Va. 1880 Census. Brother of George B. May. NFR.

MAYO, GEORGE W. - 4th Sgt. Co. A. Prior service, Co. A, 3rd VSL. Enl. Williamsburg, Greenbrier Co., W. Va., 3/1/63. Not stated if present or absent on muster-in roll dated 3/63, 4th Sgt. Clothing issued as a Pvt., 5/26/64 and 6/17/64. NFR.

MAZE (MAYS), ALFRED - Pvt. Co. A. Post war rosters only, which show he was a member of this unit. Bur. Maze Cem., Calhoun Co., W. Va. NFR.

MAZE (MAIZE, MAYS), GEORGE WASHINGTON - Pvt. Co. A. b. Greenbrier Co., W. Va., c. 1842. Age 18, Calhoun Co., W. Va. 1860 Census. Served in Co. A, 3rd VSL. Post war rosters only. Post war member of W. Va. Legislature. Age 38, farmer, Sheridan Dist., Calhoun Co., W. Va. 1880 Census. d. 1/18/1923. Bur. Maze Cem., Calhoun Co., W. Va.

MAZE (MAYS), JOSEPH - Pvt. Co. A. b. Lewis Co., W. Va., c. 1838. Age 22, Calhoun Co., W. Va. 1860 Census. Served in Co. A, 3rd VSL. Post war rosters only. NFR.

MAZE (MAYS), THOMAS S. - Pvt. Co. A. b. Harrison Co., W. Va., c. 1816 (1814). Age 46, farmer, Calhoun Co., W. Va. 1860 Census. Served in Co. A, 3rd VSL. Post war rosters only. Age 54, farmer, Sheridan Township, Calhoun Co., W. Va. 1870 Census. NFR.

MELLEHAN, JOHN P. - Pvt. Co. H. b.c. 1845. Enl. Clay Co., W. Va., 5/1/63. Ab. 9/1/64 - 10/31/64, AWOL. Cpd. Clay Co., W. Va., 5/12/64. Confined at the Atheneum Prison, 6/10/64. Desc.: age 19, 5'8", light comp., brown hair and hazel eyes. Occ. farmer, residing in Clay Co., W. Va. Transf. to Camp Chase, 6/11/64. Confined at Camp Chase, 6/13/64, charged with being a bushwhacker and robber. Gave a statement 1/26/65, which listed him as age 20, a resident of Braxton Co., W. Va. Says he was arrested 5/62 by Capt. O'Brien (VSL) with a guard of 5 or 6 men, taken to Bath Co., and assigned to Co. H. Deserted on the night of 4/28/64, escaping the vigilance of the pickets in the dark and walked 100 miles home. Cpd. within 10 miles of his home. Took the oath of allegiance and was released by order of the Sec. of War, 2/8/65. NFR.

MERRILL, JOHN - Pvt. Co. A. Served in Co. A, 3rd VSL. Post war rosters only. NFR.

MERRITT, ERASMUS - Pvt. Co. ?. Post war rosters only, which show he was a resident of Ritchie Co., W. Va. NFR.

MERRITT, WILLIAM - Pvt. Co. ?. Post war rosters only, which show he was a resident of Ritchie Co., W. Va. NFR.

METZ, SAMUEL - Pvt. Co. A. b.c. 1843. Not on muster rolls. Deserted. Cpd. Prestonburg, Preston Co., W. Va., 7/1/63. Confined at the Atheneum Prison, 7/2/63. Desc.: age 20, 5'8_", light comp., brown hair and hazel eyes. Occ. farmer, residing in Marion Co., W. Va. Transf. to Camp Chase, 8/?/63. Confined at Camp Chase, 8/11/63. Desires to take the oath of allegiance, 6/10/64. Took the oath of allegiance and was released, 5/16/65. Desc.: age 22, 5'7", dark comp., dark hair and dark eyes. Age 35, works on farm, Mannington Dist., Marion Co., W. Va. 1880 Census. NFR.

MICHAEL, JOSEPH T. (S.) - Pvt. Co. A. b.c. 1844. Not on muster rolls. Cpd. Preston Co., W. Va., 7/1/63. Confined at the Atheneum Prison, 7/2/63. Desc.: age 19, 5'10", florid comp., black hair and brown eyes. Occ. farmer, residing in Wetzel Co., W. Va. Transf. to Camp Chase, 8/?/63. Confined at Camp Chase, 8/10/63. Desires to take the oath of allegiance, 6/10/64. Took the oath of allegiance and was released by order of the Sec. of War, 4/5/65. NFR.

MICK, FRANCIS MARION - Sgt. Co. K. b.c. 1844. Resident of Upshur Co., W. Va. Not on muster rolls. Paroled as a Sgt., Charleston, W. Va., 5/12/65. Desc.: age 21, 5'10", fair comp., light hair and gray eyes. Post war resident of Buckhannon, W. Va. Bur. Mick Hill Cem., Upshur Co., W. Va.

MIDDLETON, SAMUEL - Pvt. Co. ?. Post war rosters only, which show he was a resident of Ritchie Co., W. Va. Served in the 20th Va. Cav. NFR.

MILES (MYLES), SAMUEL - Pvt. Co. F. b.c. 1823. Enl. Hillsboro, Pocahontas Co., W. Va., 9/3/63. Present 1/1/64 - 2/29/64. Ab. 9/1/64 - 10/31/64, AWOL since 6/10/64. Paroled at Charleston, W. Va., 5/11/65. Desc.: age 42, 5'11", dark comp., dark hair, black eyes and dark whiskers. Post war resident of White Sulphur Dist., Greenbrier Co., W. Va. Member David S. Creigh Camp, UCV, Lewisburg, W. Va., 1895. NFR.

MILLER, CHARLES T. - Pvt. Co. C. b.c. 1839. Not on muster rolls. Deserter. Reported to US Forces, 1/5/64. Took the oath of allegiance and was sent North, via New Creek. Desc.: age 25, 5'8", dark comp., brown hair and black eyes. Occ. blacksmith, residing in Albemarle Co. NFR.

MILLER, GEORGE H. - 1st Lt. Co. G. Prior service, Co. H & K, 22nd Va. Inf. Transf. to Jackson's Reg't., promoted to 1st Lt., 3/26/62 (?). Enl. Frankfort, Greenbrier Co., W. Va., 3/12/63. Not stated if present or absent on muster-in roll dated 3/63, 1st Lt. Submitted his resignation 7/16/63, unconditional. Resignation accepted 7/31/63. NFR.

MILLER, SAMUEL E. - Pvt. Co. E. Enl. Frankfort, Greenbrier Co., W. Va., 3/13/63. Not stated if present or absent on muster-in roll dated 3/63. NFR.

MILLER, WILLIAM J. - Pvt. Co. F. b.c. 1841. Age 19, farmer, Huntersville, Pocahontas Co., W. Va. Prior service, McNeel's Co., 2nd VSL. Enl. Hillsboro, Pocahontas Co., W. Va., 3/9/63. Not stated if present or absent on muster-in roll dated 3/63. Cpd. Beverly, W. Va., 1/20/64. Confined at the Atheneum Prison, 2/1/64. Desc.: age 22, 5'11 3/4", florid comp., dark hair and blue eyes. Occ. farmer, residing in Pocahontas Co., W. Va. Took the oath of allegiance and was released, 2/2/64. Age 38, carpenter, Huntersville, Pocahontas Co., W. Va. 1880 Census. NFR.

MILLINS, JOSHUA - Pvt. Co. I. b.c. 1836. Not on muster rolls. Deserted. Reported at Clarksburg, W. Va., 10/24/63. Took the oath of allegiance and was sent North via New Creek, W. Va. Desc.: age 27, 6', light comp., light hair and blue eyes. Occ. farmer, residing in Hawkins, Tenn. NFR.

MILLS, SAMUEL - Pvt. Co. F. Post war rosters only. NFR.

MINTER, CLAUDIUS W. - Capt. Co. E. b. Clarksburg, Harrison Co., W. Va., 1838. Age 22, town sergeant, Gilmer Co., W. Va. 1860 Census. Prior service in a co. called Va. Volunteers, raised in Gilmer Co., W. Va., and in "Secret Service" until 8/62, then served in Co. E, 3rd VSL. Enl. Frankfort, Greenbrier Co., W. Va., 3/13/63. Not stated if present or absent on muster-in roll dated 3/63, 1st Lt. Commanding Co., 7/2/63. Present, 1st Lt., 10/31/63 - 10/31/64. Mentioned for his "brave bearing" at the battle of Droop Mtn., W. Va., 11/6/63, by Col. W. L. Jackson. Detailed for duty on a Gen. Court Martial, Warm Springs, Bath Co., 2/25/64. Ab. 10/25/64, sick in hosp., 15 days. Adm. Gen. Hosp., Harrisonburg, 10/64 and transf. to another hosp. Adm. Charity Hosp., Gordonsville, 1/65 and transf. to another hosp., listed as 1st Lt. Promoted to Capt., 3/65. Paroled as a Capt., Staunton, 5/19/65. Desc.: age 26, 6', fair comp., light hair and blue eyes. Moved from W. Va. to Paris, Ky., remained there 10 years. Moved to Kansas City, Mo., 1880. Commander, Kansas City Camp, UCV. Brother of Maxwell M. and George B. Minter. d. Mo., 1934.

MINTER, GEORGE B. - Pvt. Co. E. b. Harrison Co., W. Va., c. 1846. Age 14, Gilmer Co., W. Va. 1860 Census. Enl. Bath Co., 3/1/64. Present 10/31/63 - 10/31/64; enl. bounty due; had his own horse since 3/1/64. Clothing issued 5/21/64 and 6/17/64. Brother of Claudius W. and Maxwell M. Minter. NFR.

MINTER, MAXWELL MARTIN - Sgt. Major/Pvt. Co. E. b. Harrison Co., W. Va., c. 1841. Age 19, Gilmer Co., W. Va. 1860 Census. Prior service, Co. A, 3rd VSL. Enl. Frankfort, Greenbrier Co., W. Va., 3/13/63 (4/1/63). Not stated if present or absent on muster-in roll dated 3/63, Pvt. Present F&S MR 9/1/63 - 10/31/63, appointed Sgt. Major, 4/1/63; has his own horse. Present F&S MR 11/1/63 - 12/31/63, has his own horse. Received "honorable mention" from Lt. Col. W. P. Thompson in his report of the battle of Droop Mtn., W. Va., 11/6/63. Clothing issued, 3/1/64, 5/21/64 and 6/17/64. Ab. F&S MR 9/1/64 - 10/31/64, on leave; $100 bond due. Paroled at Charleston, W. Va., 5/11/65. Desc.: age 24, 5'6", light comp., light hair, gray eyes and light whiskers. Brother of Claudius W. and George B. Minter. NFR.

MITCHELL, ALEXANDER J. - Pvt. Co. A. Not on muster rolls. Wd. 12/15/63, place not stated. Present on Hosp. MR, Staunton, 12/31/63, which shows he was enl. at Salem, 8/15/63. Attached to hosp. 12/21/63, wd., is improving. Applied for a furlough from Liberty Hosp., 3/8/64. Clothing issued 4/21/64, 7/64 and 8/64. NFR.

MITCHELL, F. R. - Pvt. Co. B. Not on muster rolls. Wd. Winchester, 9/19/64. Adm. USA Depot Field Hosp., Winchester, 9/19/64, vulnus sclopeticum, chest, through lung. DOW. Winchester, 9/23/64.

MITCHELL, RICHARD H. - Pvt. Co. I. b. Ireland, c. 1816. Age 44, laborer, Pocahontas Co., W. Va. 1860 Census. Enl. Huntersville, Pocahontas Co., W. Va., 6/9/63. Ab. 6/30/63 - 2/29/64, got a furlough 12/11/63, 40 days, has not reported. Ordered to remain on duty, 1/22/64. NFR.

MOLAHAN, P. B. - Pvt. Co. H. Not on muster rolls. Clothing issued 3/9/64. NFR.

MONROE, ASA A. - Pvt. Co. A. b. 4/11/31. Prior service, Co. A, 3rd VSL. Enl. Williamsburg, Greenbrier Co., W. Va., 3/1/63. Not stated if present or absent on muster-in roll dated 3/63. Clothing issued 2/2/64 and 6/17/64. Post war rosters show he was a US soldier. Age 39, farmer, Sheridan Township, Calhoun Co., W. Va. 1870 Census. d. 1/21/99. Bur. Sixteen Cem., near Industry, Calhoun Co., W. Va.

MONROE, JAMES - Pvt. Co. A. Served in Co. A, 3rd VSL. Post war rosters only. Served in Co. F, 46th Battn. Va. Cav. NFR.

MONROE, JOHN N. (J.) - Pvt. Co. G. Enl. White Sulphur Springs, Greenbrier Co., W. Va., 8/21/63. Clothing issued 2/11/64, 4/11/64, 4/30/64, 6/17/64 and 8/13/64. Present 9/1/64 - 10/31/64, has a serviceable horse. Paroled at Lewisburg, W. Va., 4/27/65. Desc.: age 20, 5'9", light comp., light hair and dark eyes, a driver by occupation. Virginia pensioner, 1922. NFR.

MONROE, THOMAS - Pvt. Co. A. Served in Co. A, 3rd VSL. Post war rosters only, which show he was from Calhoun Co., W. Va. Served in Co. F, 46th Battn. Va. Cav. Bur. Nebo Cem., Wirt Co., W. Va.

MONTGOMERY, HENRY - Pvt. Co. ?. b.c. 1837. Not on muster rolls. Cpd. Beverly, W. Va., 3/9/64. Confined at the Atheneum Prison, 3/24/64. Desc.: age 27, 5'8", fair comp., black hair and blue eyes, a resident of Botetourt Co. Took the oath of allegiance and was released, 3/25/64. NFR.

MONTGOMERY, SAMUEL A. - Pvt. Co. C. b. Va., c. 10/9/20. Farmer, 4th Dist., Rockbridge Co. 1860 Census. Not on muster rolls. Hired Charles C. Legard as a substitute, 9/62. Detailed 12/21/64. Farmer, Buffalo Dist., Rockbridge Co. 1870 Census. d. near Collierstown, 5/28/96. Bur. Oxford Presbyterian Church Cem.

MONTGOMERY, WILLIAM J. - Sgt. Co. ?. b.c. 1837. Not on muster rolls. Cpd. Beverly, W. Va., 3/9/64. Confined at the Atheneum Prison, 3/24/64. Desc.: age 27, 5'11", fair comp., black hair and dark eyes. Occ. farmer, residing in Botetourt Co., W. Va. Took the oath of allegiance and was released, 3/25/64. NFR.

MOON, J. M. - Pvt. Co. C. Not on muster rolls. Wd., date and place not known. Adm. Gen. Hosp. No. 9, 5/12/64. Transf. to Chimborazo Hosp., 5/13/64. Adm. Chimborazo Hosp. No. 4, 5/14/64, gunshot wd., side and arm. Furloughed 9/2/64. NFR.

MOORE, AMERICA - Pvt. Co. I. Post war rosters only, which show he was a resident of Randolph Co., W. Va. [Could be James A. Moore.] NFR.

MOORE, JACOB S. - Pvt. Co. F. b.c. 1841. Post war rosters only. Post war farmer and resident of Pocahontas Co., W. Va. Age 38, farmer, Edray, Pocahontas Co., W. Va. 1880 Census. d. Pocahontas Co., W. Va., 12/9/1909, age 68.

MOORE, JAMES A. - Pvt. Co. I. b.c. 1832. Age 28, farmer, Randolph Co., W. Va. 1860 Census. Enl. Huntersville, Pocahontas Co., W. Va., 4/30/63. Ab. 6/30/63 - 2/29/64, mounted; detailed to attend horses for Capt. Marshall's command. Present 2/29/64 - 8/31/64. Clothing issued 3/22/64. Ab. 9/1/64 - 10/31/64, detailed to procure a fresh horse; $100 bond due. Paroled at Charleston, W. Va., 5/11/65. Desc.: age 34, 5'7", light comp., light hair, blue eyes and light whiskers. Post war resident of Randolph Co., W. Va. [Could be same as America Moore.] NFR.

MOORE, JOHN - Pvt. Co. H. b.c. 1848. Not on muster rolls. Surrendered at Ravenswood, W. Va., 5/13/65. Confined at Clarksburg, W. Va. Paroled for exchange and was released, 5/20/65, signs by x. Desc.: age 17, 5'7", dark comp., fair hair and black eyes. Occ. farmer, residing in Jackson Co., W. Va. Age 33, laborer, Grant Dist., Jackson Co., W. Va. 1880 Census. NFR.

MOORE, JOHN - Pvt. Co. A. Post war rosters only, which show he was from Calhoun Co., W. Va. Cpd. 10/14/62. d. in hands of enemy. NFR.

MOORE, JONATHAN - Pvt. Co. A. b. Randolph Co., W. Va., 3/18/38. Prior service, Co. A, 3rd VSL. Enl. Williamsburg, Greenbrier Co., W. Va., 3/1/63. Not stated if present or absent on muster-in roll dated 3/63. Cpd. Calhoun Co., W. Va., 11/1/63. Wd., probably at time of capture. Confined at the Atheneum Prison, 11/20/63. Desc.: age 25, 6', light comp., brown hair and hazel eyes. Occ. farmer, residing in Calhoun Co., W. Va. Transf. to Camp Chase, 11/20/63. Confined at Camp Chase, 11/21/63. Took the oath of allegiance and was released, 5/13/65. Desc.: age ?, 6', florid comp., dark hair and gray eyes, a resident of Roane Co., W. Va. Post war farmer and resident of Hamilin, Lincoln Co., W. Va. NFR.

MOORE, MACK - Pvt. Co. I. Post war rosters only, which show he was a resident of Randolph Co., W. Va. Attended Confederate Reunion, Randolph Co., W. Va., claimed to have served in the 19th Va. Cav. NFR.

MOORE, SAMUEL A. - Pvt. Co. B. Prior service, Co. A, 3rd VSL. Enl. Camp Cameron, Bath Co., 2/20/63. Ab. 11/1/63 - 2/29/64. NFR.

MOORE, SAMUEL A. - Pvt. Co. I. b. Randolph Co., W. Va., c. 1835. Age 25, farmer, Randolph Co., W. Va. 1860 Census. Enl. Beverly, Randolph Co., W. Va., 4/30/63. Present 6/30/63 - 2/29/64, mounted. Present 2/29/64 - 8/31/64. Clothing issued 3/22/64. Present 9/1/64 - 10/31/64, $100 bond due. Paroled at Charleston, W. Va., 5/11/65. Desc.: age 31, 5'4", light comp., light hair, blue eyes and light whiskers. Post war resident of Randolph Co., W. Va. and Wilmington, Fluvanna Co., Va. Age 73 in 1909. NFR.

MOORE, THOMAS M. - Pvt. Co. I. b. 5/8/35. Enl. Beverly, Randolph Co., W. Va., 4/30/63. Present 6/30/63 - 2/29/64, mounted. Ab. 2/29/64 - 8/31/64, AWOL. Ab. 9/1/64 - 10/31/64, AWOL. Paroled at Charleston, W. Va., 5/11/65. Desc.: age 30, 5'8", fair comp., light hair, blue eyes and sandy whiskers. Post war resident of Randolph Co., W. Va. Age 45, farmer, Mingo, Randolph Co., W. Va. 1880 Census. Member of Gen. Pegram Camp, UCV, Valley Head, W. Va. d. 2/22/1912. Bur. Mingo Cem., Randolph Co., W. Va.

MOORE, WILLIAM ALLEN "Pat" - 3rd Sgt. Co. I. b. 1/1/33. Age 26, store clerk, Randolph Co., W. Va. 1860 Census. Enl. Beverly, Randolph Co., W. Va., 4/30/63. Also as enl. Huntersville. Ab., Pvt., 6/30/63 - 2/29/64, mounted; detailed to attend horses of Capt. Marshall's command. Present 2/29/64 - 8/31/64, appointed 3rd Sgt., 6/1/64. Ab. 9/1/64 - 10/31/64, cpd. Fisher's Hill, 9/23/64; $100 bond due. Cpd. Harrisonburg, 9/25/64. Sent to Harpers Ferry, W. Va., then to Pt. Lookout, 10/1/64. Confined at Pt. Lookout, 10/4/64. Paroled for exchange, 10/30/64. Exchanged at Venus Point, Savannah River, 11/15/64. Post war rosters show him as 1st Sgt. Post war resident of Randolph Co., W. Va. Member of Gen. Pegram Camp, UCV, Valley Head, W. Va. Awarded Cross of Honor. Resident of Huttonsville, W. Va., 1916. d. 5/5/1917. Bur. Brick Church Cem., Randolph Co., W. Va.

MOREHEAD, NATHANIEL - Pvt. Co. C. Enl. Pocahontas Co., W. Va., 5/15/63. Present 12/31/63 - 8/31/64, has one horse. Clothing issued 4/30/64. Present 9/1/64 - 10/31/64, has one horse; $100 enl. bounty due. Paroled at Charleston, W. Va., 5/10/65, signs by x. Desc.: age 23, 5', fair comp., dark hair and blue eyes. NFR.

MORGAN, EDWARD (EDWIN) L. - Pvt. Co. A. b.c. 1832. Prior service, Co. A, 31st Va. Inf. Not on muster rolls. Cpd. Farmington (Riceville and Marion Co.), W. Va., 11/5/63 (11/3/63 and 11/4/63). Confined at the Atheneum Prison, 11/12/63. Desc.: age 31, 5'9", light comp., dark hair and gray eyes. Occ. farmer, residing in Marion Co., W. Va. Transf. to Camp Chase, 12/13/63. Confined at Camp Chase, 12/15/63. Took the oath of allegiance and was released, 5/15/65. Desc.: age ?, 5'8", florid comp., dark hair and hazel eyes, a resident of Marion Co., W. Va. Age 47, farmer, Paw Paw Dist., Marion Co., W. Va. 1880 Census. NFR.

MORGAN, JAMES W. - 2nd Lt. Co. A. Prior service, Co. A, 3rd VSL. Enl. Williamsburg, Greenbrier Co., W. Va., 3/1/63. Not stated if present or absent on muster-in roll dated 3/63, Sr. 2nd Lt. Clothing issued at Marlin's Bottom, 10/2/63. Mentioned for his "brave bearing" at the battle of Droop Mtn., W. Va., 11/6/63, by Col. W. L. Jackson. KIA. Droop Mtn., W. Va., 11/6/63. Post war rosters show him as 2nd Sgt.

MORGAN, STEPHEN E. - Pvt. Co. F. b.c. 1838. Resident of Marion Co., W. Va. Prior service, Major, 19th Va. Militia. Post war rosters only. Served as adjutant of Gitting's Battn., 12/64. Served in Co. K, 20th Va. Cav. Adm. Lee Camp Soldiers Home, 1/8/1919, age 81. d. Richmond, 2/25/1926. Bur. Family Section, Hollywood Cem., Richmond. "A brave soldier and gentleman."

MORRIS, EMANUEL M. - Pvt. Co. G. Enl. Frankfort, Greenbrier Co., W. Va., 3/12/63 (4/1/63). Not stated if present or absent on muster-in roll dated 3/63. Clothing issued, 1st Qr. 1864 and 7/10/64. Present 9/1/64 - 10/31/64, has a serviceable horse. NFR.

MORRISON, JAMES H. - Pvt. Co. F. b.c. 1843. Age 17, laborer, Mt. Murphy, Pocahontas Co., W. Va. 1860 Census. Prior service, McNeel's, 2nd VSL. Enl. Hillsboro, Pocahontas Co., W. Va., 3/9/63 (4/1/63). Not stated if present or absent on muster-in roll dated 3/63. Ab. 1/1/64 - 2/29/64, sick. Ab. 9/1/64 - 10/31/64, AWOL since 6/17/64. KIA. Droop Mtn., 11/6/63. Post war rosters show service in Co. I, and that he was a resident of Randolph Co., W. Va.

MORROW, DAVID M. - Pvt. Co. D. b. Pa., c. 1838. Enl. Camp Northwest, Pocahontas Co., W. Va. Not on muster rolls. Clothing issued 2/7/64, 5/1/64, 5/25/64 and 7/10/64. Cpd. Randolph (Harrison) Co., W. Va., 3/1/65. Confined in the Post Guard House, Clarksburg, W. Va., 3/9/65. Desc.: age 27, 5'11", fair comp., light hair and blue eyes. Occ. farmer, residing in Harrison Co., W. Va. Transf. to Wheeling, W. Va. Confined at the Atheneum Prison, 4/24/65. Took the oath of allegiance at Cumberland, Md. NFR.

MORTIMORE, CHARLES - 1st Lt. Co. ?. b.c. 1836. Not on muster rolls. Cpd. Lewis Co., W. Va., 7/7/63. Confined at the Atheneum Prison, 7/9/63. Desc.: age 27, 5'11", fair comp., dark hair and blue eyes. Occ. merchant, residing in New Orleans, La. Sent to Pittsburgh, Pa., 7/13/63. NFR.

MORTON, JOHN - Pvt. Co. A. Post war rosters only. NFR.

MORTON, ROBERT - 1st Lt. Co. B. b. Pendleton Co., W. Va., c. 1822. Age 37, farmer, Webster Co., W. Va. 1860 Census. Enl. Frankfort, Greenbrier Co., W. Va., 3/7/63. Not stated if present or absent on muster-in roll dated 3/63, 1st Lt. Post war rosters show service in Co. A. Post war resident of Webster Co., W. Va. Age 58, farmer, Glade, Webster Co., W. Va. 1880 Census. NFR.

MORTON, THOMAS C. - Pvt. Co. B. Enl. Frankfort, Greenbrier Co., W. Va., 3/7/63. Not stated if present or absent on muster-in roll dated 3/63. NFR.

MOSBY, C. A. - Pvt. Co. K. Post war rosters only, which show he was a resident of Buckhannon, W. Va. NFR.

MOSS, OWEN C. - Pvt. Co. K. Enl. Frankfort, Greenbrier Co., W. Va., 3/20/63. Not stated if present or absent on muster-in roll dated 3/63. NFR.

MULLEN, WILLIAM - Pvt. Co. F. Post war rosters only. NFR.

MULLINS (MULLIN, MULLENS, MULLEN), MARSHALL "Marsh" - Pvt. Co. H. b. Russell Co., Ky., c. 1839 (1841). Age 19, farmhand, Webster Co., W. Va. 1860 Census. Enl. Frankfort, Greenbrier Co., W. Va., 3/19/63. Not stated if present or absent on muster-in roll dated 3/63. Enl. in Co. C, Bath Co., 2/1/64. Ab. 12/31/63 - 8/31/64, deserted 8/1/64. Clothing issued, 2/7/64, 3/4/64, 4/30/64, 5/1/64 and 6/17/64, signs by x. Surrendered at Buckhannon, W. Va., 5/15/65. Confined at Clarksburg, W. Va., 5/19/65. Desc.: age 24, 5'8", fair comp., light hair and blue eyes. Occ. farmer, residing in Nicholas Co., W. Va. Paroled for exchange and released, 5/20/65. Age 38, farmer, Huttonsville, Randolph Co., W. Va. 1880 Census. d. Mill Creek, Randolph Co., W. Va., 2/16/1909, age 70, dropsy. Bur. Rich Mtn. Cem., Randolph Co., W. Va. Son of Samuel Mullins.

MULLINS (MULLIN, MULLEN), SAMUEL - Pvt. Co. H. b. Pike Co., Ky., c. 1817. Age 43, farmer, Webster Co., W. Va. 1860 Census. Enl. Frankfort, Greenbrier Co., W. Va., 3/19/63 (Webster Co., W. Va., 8/1/63). Not stated if present or absent on muster-in roll dated 3/63. Ab. 9/1/64 - 10/31/64, AWOL. Father of Marshall Mullins. NFR.

MURPHY, P. G. - Pvt. Co. H. Enl. Frankfort, Greenbrier Co., W. Va., 3/19/63. Not stated if present or absent on muster-in roll dated 3/63. NFR.

MURPHY (MURPHEY), THOMAS - Pvt. Co. F. Prior service, McNeel's Co., 2nd VSL. Enl. Hillsboro, Pocahontas Co., W. Va., 3/9/63 (4/1/63). Not stated if present or absent on muster-in roll dated 3/63. Present 1/1/64 - 2/29/64. Clothing issued 2/6/64. Ab. 9/1/64 - 10/31/64, wd. Woodstock, 10/8/64; enl. bounty due. Post war rosters show he was from Webster Co., W. Va. DOW. Bur. Lutheran Church (Massanutton) Cem., Woodstock.

MURTIN (MARTIN), WILLIAM G. - 4th Sgt. Co. H. Enl. Frankfort, Greenbrier Co., W. Va., 3/19/63. Not stated if present or absent on muster-in roll dated 3/63, 4th Sgt. NFR.

MYERS, BENJAMIN - Pvt. Co. E. Not on muster rolls. Paroled at Charleston, W. Va., 5/11/65. No desc. NFR.

MYERS, JOHN J. - Pvt. Co. G. b.c. 1844. Enl. Frankfort, Greenbrier Co., W. Va., 3/12/63 (4/1/63). Not stated if present or absent on muster-in roll dated 3/63. Clothing issued 3/1/64 and 7/10/64, signs by x. Present 9/1/64 - 10/31/64, has a serviceable horse. Paroled at Charleston, W. Va., 5/10/65, signs by x. Desc.: age 21, 6', dark comp., dark hair and gray eyes. NFR.

NESMITH, WILLIAM H. - Pvt. Co. G. Enl. Pocahontas Co., W. Va., 12/1/63. Clothing issued 1/16/64 and 6/17/64. Present 9/1/64 - 10/31/64, has a serviceable horse; detailed to the Commissary Dept. Post war rosters show service in Co. D, 20th Va. Cav. Post war resident of Mo. Bur. Confederate Memorial Cem., Higginsville, Mo.

NEWCOMB, GEORGE W. - Pvt. Co. A. Prior service, Co. A, 3rd VSL. Enl. Williamsburg, Greenbrier Co., W. Va., 3/1/63. Not stated if present or absent on muster-in roll dated 3/63. Transf. to Lurty's Batty., from 3rd VSL by Geo. Downs, 10/1/63. NFR.

NEWMAN, JAMES C. - Pvt. Co. I. b. Highland Co., c. 1842. Age 18, teacher, New Hampden, Highland Co. 1860 Census. Enl. Huntersville, Pocahontas Co., W. Va., 1/1/64. Not stated if present or absent 6/30/63 - 2/29/64, mounted; enl. bounty due. Ab. 2/29/64 - 8/31/64, detailed as enrolling officer of Highland Co. Ab. 9/1/64 - 10/31/64, AWOL since 7/15/64. NFR.

NOE, SAMUEL - 3rd Sgt. Co. G. b. Roane (Kanawha) Co., W. Va., 5/21/36. Age 24, farmer, Gilmer Co., W. Va. 1860 Census. Prior service, Co. E, 22nd Va. Inf. Enl. Greenbrier Co., W. Va., 4/1/64. Clothing issued 2/7/64 as 4th Sgt., 3/7/64, 6/17/64 and 7/6/64. Ab., 3rd Sgt., 9/1/64 - 10/31/64, on leave; has a serviceable horse. Wd. Bunker Hill, 9/64, badly. Cpd. Roane Co., W. Va., 10/6/64 (Clay Co., W. Va., 9/27/64). Confined at the Atheneum Prison. Desc.: age 26, 5'8", dark comp., brown hair and blue eyes. Occ. farmer, residing in Roane Co., W. Va. Transf. to Camp Chase, 10/28/64. Confined at Camp Chase, 10/29/64, charge with being a horsethief and robber. Took the oath of allegiance and was released, 6/11/65. Desc.: age 27, 5'8", florid comp., light hair and blue eyes, a resident of Roane Co., W. Va. Served in Co. I, 20th Va. Cav. Wd. several other times, slightly. Post war rosters show service in the 14th Va. Cav. Post war source states he was cpd. four times, and escaped three times. Age 42, famrer, Geary Dist., Roane Co., W. Va. 1880 Census. Post war farmer and resident of Newton, Roane Co., W. Va., 1884. Served as school trustee, 2 years. NFR.

NORMAN, HENRY H. - Pvt. Co. E. b. Randolph Co., W. Va., c. 1842. Age 18, farmer, Gilmer Co., W. Va. 1860 Census. Enl. Frankfort, Greenbrier Co., W. Va., 3/13/63. Not stated if present or absent on muster-in roll dated 3/63. NFR.

NORMAN (NORMMAN), THOMAS S. - Pvt. Co. E. b. Monongalia Co., W. Va., c. 1833. Age 27, farmer, Gilmer Co., W. Va. 1860 Census. Enl. Frankfort, Greenbrier Co., W. Va., 3/13/63. Not stated if present or absent on muster-in roll dated 3/63. NFR.

NORRIS, EDWARD - Capt. Co. K. b.c. 1837. Enl. Frankfort, Greenbrier Co., W. Va., 3/20/63. Appointed Capt. 3/20/63. Not stated if present or absent on muster-in roll dated 3/63, Capt., commanding co. Wd. Bulltown, Braxton Co., W. Va., 10/13/63, left elbow, cared for at the home of John Lorentz. Resigned at Staunton, 6/28/64. Resignation accepted 8/2/64. Examined by a medical board 3/6/65, listed as "late 1st Lt. Co. K," suffering from vulnus sclopeticum of the left elbow. Has anchylosis of elbow joint, permanently unfit for field service. Found able to perform any light duty not requiring the use of his left arm. Post war rosters show him as 1st Lt. NFR.

NORRIS, WILLIAM P. - 1st Lt. Co. K. b. Lewis Co., W. Va., c. 1830. Age 30, farmer, Gilmer Co., W. Va. 1860 Census. Enl. Frankfort, Greenbrier Co., W. Va., 3/20/63. Not stated if present or absent on muster-in roll dated 3/63, 1st Lt. Enl. Alleghany Co., 5/1/64 in Co. E. Present, Pvt., 10/31/63 - 10/31/64, had his own horse since 5/1/64. NFR.

NOTTINGHAM, JACOB J. - Pvt. Co. H. Enl. Frankfort, Greenbrier Co., W. Va., 3/19/63. Not stated if present or absent on muster-in roll dated 3/63. NFR.

NUTTER (NUTLER), ALBERT - Pvt. Co. A. Prior service, Co. A, 3rd VSL. Enl. Williamsburg, Greenbrier Co., W. Va., 3/1/63. Not stated if present or absent on muster-in roll dated 3/63. NFR.

NUTTER, CHARLES C. - Pvt. Co. D. b.c. 1837. Age 24, farmer, Harrison Co., W. Va. 1860 Census. Prior service, Co. C, 31st Va. Inf. Enl. Williamsburg, Greenbrier Co., W. Va., 3/8/63. Not stated if present or absent on muster-in roll dated 3/63. Post war rosters show service in Co. A and in Co. B; that he was from Braxton Co., W. Va., and was KIA. NFR.

NUTTER (NUTHER), JOSEPH - Pvt. Co. A. Prior service, Co. A, 3rd VSL. Not on muster rolls. Deserted. Reported to US forces, 1/5/64. Took the oath of allegiance and was sent North. NFR.

NUTTER (NUTLER), LEVI - Pvt. Co. A. b. Kanawha Co., W. Va., 1825. Age 35, farmer, Calhoun Co., W. Va. 1860 Census. Prior service, Co. A, 3rd VSL. Enl. Williamsburg, Greenbrier Co., W. Va., 3/1/63. Not stated if present or absent on muster-in roll dated 3/63. Post war rosters show he enl. 12/6/62. Age 55, farmer, Lee Dist., Calhoun Co., W. Va. 1880 Census. d. 1912. Bur. Ball Cem., near Rocksdale, Calhoun Co., W. Va.

O'BRYAN (O'BRIEN, O'BRYEN, O'BRION), JOHN M. - Pvt. Co. A. Prior service, Co. A, 3rd VSL. Enl. Williamsburg, Greenbrier Co., W. Va., 3/1/63. Not stated if present or absent on muster-in roll dated 3/63. Enl. in Co. H, Frankfort, Greenbrier Co., W. Va., 3/19/63. Not stated if present or absent on muster-in roll dated 3/63. Served in Co. F, 20th Va. Cav. NFR.

O'BRYAN (O'BRIEN), MILES - Pvt. Co. A. Prior service, Co. A, 3rd VSL. Enl. Williamsburg, Greenbrier Co., W. Va., 3/1/63. Not stated if present or absent on muster-in roll dated 3/63. Enl. in Co. H, Frankfort, Greenbrier Co., W. Va., 3/19/63. Not stated if present or absent on muster-in roll dated 3/63. Served in Co. F, 20th Va. Cav. NFR.

O'BRYAN (O'BRIEN), WILLIAM P. - Capt. Co. H. b. Braxton Co., W. Va., 3/14/34. Moved to Roane Co., W. Va. before 1856. Prior service, Co. E, 22nd Va. Inf. and 3rd VSL. Resident of Roane Co., W. Va. Left 22nd Va. Inf. to raise a Co., 9/16/62. Transf. to Co. H, 19th Va. Cav., 4/1/63. Enl. Frankfort, Greenbrier Co., W. Va., 3/19/63 (Clay Co., W. Va., 4/1/61). Appointed Capt., 3/19/63. Not stated if present or absent on muster-in roll dated 3/63, Capt., commanding Co. Mentioned for gallantry in Col. W. L. Jackson's report, 12/63. Had a horse KIA, 1863, in W. Va. Present 9/1/64 - 10/31/64, in arrest for insubordination. Ab. 12/15/64, AWOL since 10/20/64, no steps taken to have him dropped. Dropped from the rolls 2/8/65 (12/1/64). Cpd. Roane Co., W. Va., 3/11/65 (Clay Co., W. Va., 3/4/65). Sent to Cumberland, Md., then to Wheeling, W. Va. Confined at the Atheneum Prison, 3/27/65. Desc.: age 31, 6'1_", dark comp., black hair and blue eyes. Occ. farmer, residing in Roane Co., W. Va. Transf. to Camp Chase, 3/28/65. Confined at Camp Chase, 3/29/65. Took the oath of allegiance and was released 5/11/65. Desc.: age ?, 5'11", dark comp., dark hair and gray eyes, a resident of Newton, Roane Co., W. Va. Served as school trustee for two years. Post war farmer, Newton, Roane Co., W. Va. Age 46, working on farm, Geary Dist., Roane Co., W. Va. 1880 Census. Thought to be bur. in Roane Co., W. Va. Cem., now covered by I-64. NFR.

OGDEN, NELSON G. - Pvt. Co. A. b.c. 1842. Not on muster rolls. Cpd. Preston Co. (Cheat Mtn.), W. Va., 7/1/63. Confined at the Atheneum Prison, 7/2/63. Desc.: age 21, 5'11 3/4", light comp., light hair and dark eyes. Occ. farmer, residing in Harrison Co., W. Va. Transf. to Camp Chase, 8/8/63. Confined at Camp Chase, 8/11/63. Took the oath of allegiance and was released 5/11/65. Desc.: age ?, 5'11", fair comp., light hair and dark eyes, a resident of Harrison Co., W. Va. NFR.

O'TOOLE, PATRICK L. - Pvt. Co. A. b. Wicklow, Ireland, 1841. Came to Charlottesville, 1861. Not on muster rolls. "Gen. Rosser presented him a horse for distinguished gallantry." Liveryman, age 28, Staunton 1870 Census. d. 11/16/74, age 33 years and 2 months. Bur. Thornrose Cem., Staunton. There is a Patrick O'Toole listed in the 19th Va. Inf. book.

OVERHOLT, WILLIAM H. "Bill" - Pvt. Co. F. b. Rockingham Co., c. 1841. Soldier, age 22 (1863), residing in Pocahontas Co., W. Va. Enl. Hillsboro, Pocahontas Co., W. Va., 3/16/64. Present 9/1/64 - 10/31/64, detailed as hosp. steward; enl. bounty due. Paroled at Charleston, W. Va., 5/10/65. Desc.: age 23, 5'10", light comp., light hair, blue eyes and light whiskers. Age 38, dry goods merchant, Little Levels, Pocahontas Co., W. Va. 1880 Census. Post war resident of White Sulphur Dist., Greenbrier Co., W. Va. Member of David S. Criegh Camp, UCV, Lewisburg, W. Va., 1895. NFR.

OYLER, J. M. - Pvt. Co. I. Enl. Huntersville, Pocahontas Co., W. Va., 5/22/63. Present 6/30/63 - 2/29/64, acting Commissary Officer until 1/1/64; mounted; promoted to 1st Lt., Capt. Apperson's Co., 47th Battn. Va. Cav. Served in the 47th Battn. Va. Cav. NFR.

PAGE, JOHN C. - Pvt. Co. I. b. 3/13/40. Prior service, Co. E, 31st Va. Inf. Enl. Huntersville, Pocahontas Co., W. Va., 1/1/64. Not stated if present or absent 6/30/63 - 2/29/64, mounted; enl. bounty due. Present 2/29/64 - 8/31/64, mounted; enl. bounty due. Clothing issued 7/10/64. Present 9/1/64 - 10/31/64. Wd. Bunker Hill, 9/64. Post war resident of Naples, W. Va. d. 1/29/1934. Bur. Fairview Methodist Church Cem., Highland Co.

PAINTER, GEORGE WASHINGTON - Pvt. Co. I. b. 10/10/39 (1838). Post war rosters only. Age 40, miller and carpenter, Mingo, Randolph Co., W. Va. 1880 Census. Commander, Gen. Pegram Camp, UCV, Valley Head, Randolph Co., W. Va. Attended Gettysburg Reunion, 1913. d. Valley Head, Randolph Co., W. Va., 4/3/1914 (4/13/1914), age 75 years, 6 months and 3 days. Bur. Ware Ridge Cem., Randolph Co., W. Va.

PAINTER, WILLIAM - Pvt. Co. I. Post war rosters only, which show he was from Randolph Co., W. Va. NFR.

PALMER, JAMES K. - Pvt. Co. C. Prior service, Co. D, 3rd VSL. Enl. Frankfort, Greenbrier Co., W. Va., 3/15/63. Not stated if present or absent on muster-in roll dated 3/63. Post war resident of Wood Co., W. Va. Muster roll for Co. D, 3rd VSL, 1/1/63 - 4/1/63, shows that he d. Frankfort, 3/19/63, and had one horse. NFR.

PARISH (PARRISH), RICHARD A. (E.) - Pvt. Co. A. b. Marion Co., W. Va., 1845. Not on muster rolls. Surrendered at Parkersburg, W. Va. and took the oath of allegiance, 2/22/65. Sent to Clarksburg, W. Va. Arrested several days later, suspected of having been drafted into the US Army, but preferred the rebel service. Cpd. Oil Works, Wood Co., W. Va., 3/8/65. Confined at the Atheneum Prison, 3/21/65. Desc.: age 19, 5'7", fair comp., light hair and blue eyes. Occ. farmer, residing in Wirt Co., W. Va. Transf. to Camp Chase, 3/28/65. Confined at Camp Chase, 3/29/65. Took the oath of allegiance and released, 5/16/65. Desc.: age 20, 5'8", light comp., light hair and blue eyes, a resident of Wirt Co., W. Va. Also known as Robert E. Parrish. d. 1912. Bur. Hereford Cem.

PARRISH, WILLIAM E. - Pvt. Co. A. b. Marion Co., W. Va., 1847. Post war source only. d. 1931. Bur. Hereford Cem.

PARKINS, JOHN T. - Pvt. Co. C. b.c. 1842. Prior service, Co. D, 3rd VSL. Enl. Frankfort, Greenbrier Co., W. Va., 3/15/63. Not stated if present or absent on muster-in roll dated 3/63. Deserted. Reported at Clarksburg, W. Va., 10/25/63. Took the oath of allegiance and was sent North, 10/25/63. Desc.: age 21, 5'8_", fair comp., brown hair and gray eyes. Occ. farmer, residing in Greenbrier Co., W. Va. NFR.

PARSONS, WILLIAM L. - Pvt. Co. C. Resident of Roane Co., W. Va. Arrested and confined at Wheeling, W. Va. Released on his oath by 3/13/62. Prior service, Co. D (Moccasin Rangers), 3rd VSL. Enl. Frankfort, Greenbrier Co., W. Va., 3/15/63. Not stated if present or absent on muster-in roll dated 3/63. Ab. 1/1/63 - 4/1/63, deserted 10/62. Served in Co. F, 20th Va. Cav. NFR.

PATTON, JOHN S. - 4th Sgt. Co. D. Enl. Williamsburg, Greenbrier Co., W. Va., 3/8/63. Not stated if present or absent on muster-in roll dated 3/63, 4th Sgt. Served in Co. B, 20th Va. Cav. NFR.

PATTON, ZACHARIAH H. - Pvt. Co. D. b. Gilmer Co., W. Va., c. 1843. Enl. Williamsburg, Greenbrier Co., W. Va., 3/8/63. Not stated if present or absent on muster-in roll dated 3/63. Served in Co. B, 20th Va. Cav. NFR.

PAYNE, FRANCIS N. (M.) "Frank" - Pvt. Co. K. b. Ky., c. 1839. Age 21, farmhand, Webster Co., W. Va. 1860 Census. Enl. Frankfort, Greenbrier Co., W. Va., 3/20/63. Not stated if present or absent on muster-in roll dated 3/63. Brother of George W. Payne. Age 40, farmer, Fork Lick, Webster Co., W. Va. 1880 Census. NFR.

PAYNE, GEORGE W. - Pvt. Co. K. b. Ky., c. 1843. Age 17, farmhand, Webster Co., W. Va. 1860 Census. Enl. Frankfort, Greenbrier Co., W. Va., 3/20/63. Not stated if present or absent on muster-in roll dated 3/63. Brother of Francis N. Payne. NFR.

PAYNE, JAMES W. - Pvt. Co. K. Enl. Frankfort, Greenbrier Co., W. Va., 3/20/63. Not stated if present or absent on muster-in roll dated 3/63. NFR.

PAYNE, WILLIAM HANK - Pvt. Co. F. b. Rockingham Co., c. 1836. Moved to Pocahontas Co., W. Va., 1858. Age 24, farmhand, Mill Point, Pocahontas Co., W. Va. 1860 Census. Prior service, McNeel's Co., 2nd VSL. Enl. Hillsboro, Pocahontas Co., W. Va., 3/9/63 (4/1/63). Not stated if present or absent on muster-in roll dated 3/63. Present 1/1/64 - 2/29/64. Clothing issued, 1/17/64. Ab. 9/1/64 - 10/31/64, AWOL since 10/8/64; enl. bounty due. Paroled at Charleston, W. Va., 5/10/65. Desc.: age 30, 5'8", light comp., light hair, blue eyes and a mustache. Post war farmer and resident of Pocahontas Co., W. Va. Age 43, carpenter, Little Levels, Pocahontas Co., W. Va. 1880 Census. d. Seebert (near Academy), W. Va., 11/3/1912, age 78. Bur. Oak Grove Cem., Pocahontas Co., W. Va.

PEAK, JOHN - Pvt. Co. D. Not on muster rolls. Cpd. 4/23/65, place not given. Confined at the Atheneum Prison, 4/24/65. No. Desc. Resident of Rockingham Co. Took the oath of allegiance at Cumberland, Md. NFR.

PEATE (PEYATT, PEATT), GEORGE - Pvt. Co. C. b.c. 1834. Prior service, Co. D, 3rd VSL. Enl. Frankfort, Greenbrier Co., W. Va., 3/15/63 (Pocahontas Co., W. Va., 4/1/63). Not stated if present or absent on muster-in roll dated 3/63. Present 1/1/63 - 4/1/63, has one horse. Ab. 12/31/63 - 8/31/64, deserted 2/3/64; had one horse. Cpd. Beverly, W. Va., 1/18/64. Confined at the Atheneum Prison, 2/1/64, listed as a member of Co. D. Desc.: age 30, 5'9", dark comp., dark hair and blue eyes. Occ. farmer, residing in Roane Co., W. Va. Took the oath of allegiance and was released, 2/2/64. Served in Co. E, 20th Va. Cav. NFR.

PEATE (PEATT), JOHN - Pvt. Co. C. b.c. 1841. Prior service, Co. D, 3rd VSL. Enl. Frankfort, Greenbrier Co., W. Va., 3/15/63 (Pocahontas Co., W. Va., 4/1/63). Not stated if present or absent on muster-in roll dated 3/63. Present 1/1/63 - 4/1/63, has one horse. Ab. 12/31/63 - 8/31/64, deserted 2/3/64; had one horse. Cpd. Beverly, W. Va., 1/18/64. Confined at the Atheneum Prison, 2/1/64, listed as a member of Co. D. Desc.: age 23, 5'11_", florid comp., sandy hair and blue eyes. Occ. farmer, residing in Nicholas Co., W. Va.. Took the oath of allegiance and was released, 2/2/64. Served in Co. E, 20th Va. Cav. NFR.

PENNYBACKER, HIRAM H. - Pvt. Co. C. b. 1844. Not on muster rolls. Reference jacket only, which shows service in the 20th Va. Cav. d. 1923. Bur. IOOF Cem., Parkersburg, W. Va.

PERDEU, D. L. - Pvt. Co. D. Not on muster rolls. Taken prisoner and confined at Camp Chase. DOD. Camp Chase, 5/23/64. Bur. Camp Chase Confederate Cem., grave no. 165. Note in file says "See Citizens." NFR.

PERKINS, ADAM - Pvt. Co. B. Enl. Frankfort, Greenbrier Co., W. Va., 3/9/63. Present 11/1/63 - 2/29/64, had one horse until 2/1/64. Employed as a courier 11/1/63 - 11/13/63, sent to his company; signs by x. Clothing issued 2/11/64, 4/30/64 and 6/17/64, signs by x. Ab. 9/1/64 - 10/31/64, on detached service; $100 enl. bounty due. Cpd. Blue Ridge Gap, 9/25/64 (Port Republic, 9/26/64). Sent to Harpers Ferry, W. Va., then to Pt. Lookout, 10/10/64. Confined at Pt. Lookout, 10/12/64. Paroled for exchange and sent to Aiken's Landing, 3/17/65. Exchanged at Boulewares Wharf, 3/19/65. Present on a MR of paroled and exchanged prisoners at Camp Lee, near Richmond, dated 3/19/65. Enl. listed as Braxton Co., W. Va., 5/63. NFR.

PERKINS, ALEX. J. - Pvt. Co. F. Enl. Hillsboro, Pocahontas Co., W. Va., 6/8/63. Ab. 1/1/64 - 2/29/64, sick. Ab. 9/1/64 - 10/31/64, wd. 8/63, place not stated. NFR.

PERRIN (PERRINE), SHADRACH C. - Pvt. Co. K. b. Braxton Co., W. Va., c. 1842. Age 18, farmhand, Webster Co., W. Va. 1860 Census. Prior service, Co. G, 25th Va. Inf. Enl. Frankfort, Greenbrier Co., W. Va., 3/20/63. Not stated if present or absent on muster-in roll dated 3/63. Age 35, farmer, Holly Dist., Webster Co., W. Va. 1880 Census. Bur. Benjamin Cogar Cem., Guardian, Holly Dist., Webster Co., W. Va.

PERRINE (PRINE, PERINE), HENRY R. - Pvt. Co. B. b.c. 1839. Age 21, Braxton Co., W. Va. 1860 Census. Enl. Frankfort, Greenbrier Co., W. Va., 3/7/63. Not stated if present or absent on muster-in roll dated 3/63. Present 11/1/63 - 2/29/64, had one horse. Clothing issued 2/11/64 and 6/17/64, signs by x. Present 9/1/64 - 10/31/64, $100 enl. bounty due. Paroled at Charleston, W. Va., 5/8/65, signs by x. Desc.: age 26, 5'6", dark comp., dark hair, gray eyes and dark whiskers. Post war resident of Braxton Co., W. Va. Age 43, farmer, Holly Dist., Braxton Co., W. Va. 1880 Census. NFR.

PERRINE (PRINE, PERINE), ROBERT G. (E.) - Pvt. Co. B. b.c. 1841. Age 19, Braxton Co., W. Va. 1860 Census. Enl. Frankfort, Greenbrier Co., W. Va., 3/7/63 (3/9/63). Not stated if present or absent on muster-in roll dated 3/63. Present 11/1/63 - 2/29/64, has one horse. Present 9/1/64 - 10/31/64, $100 enl. bounty due. Surrendered at Bulltown, W. Va., 5/7/65. Confined at Clarksburg, W. Va., 5/10/65. Paroled for exchange and was released, 5/11/65. Desc.: age 20, 5'7_", fair comp., light hair and blue eyes. Occ. farmer, residing in Braxton Co., W. Va. Age 37, farmer, Holly Dist., Braxton Co., W. Va. 1880 Census. NFR.

PERRINE (PRINA, PRINE, PERINE), SAMUEL - Pvt. Co. B. Enl. Frankfort, Greenbrier Co., W. Va., 3/7/63. Not stated if present or absent on muster-in roll dated 3/63. Age 39, farmer, Otter Dist., Braxton Co., W. Va. 1880 Census. NFR.

PERRINE (PRINE), W. H. - Pvt. Co. B. Enl. Frankfort, Greenbrier Co., W. Va., 3/7/63. Not stated if present or absent on muster-in roll dated 3/63. CSR listed as Prine. NFR.

PERRINE (PERINE), WILLIAM J. - 2nd Sgt. Co. B. b.c. 1840. Enl. Frankfort, Greenbrier Co., W. Va., 3/7/63. Not stated if present or absent on muster-in roll dated 3/63, 2nd Sgt. Clothing issued, 4/1/64 and 6/17/64, listed as Pvt., signs by x. Post war resident of Braxton Co., W. Va. NFR.

PERRINE (PRINE), WILLIAM L. - Pvt. Co. B. b.c. 1841. Age 20, Braxton Co., W. Va. 1860 Census. Enl. Frankfort, Greenbrier Co., W. Va., 3/7/63. Not stated if present or absent on muster-in roll dated 3/63. Present 11/1/63 - 2/29/64, has one horse. Clothing issued 2/11/64 and 9/25/64. Present 9/1/64 - 10/31/64, $100 enl. bounty due. Paroled at Charleston, W. Va., 5/8/65, signs by x. Desc.: age 24, 6', dark comp., dark hair, dark eyes and dark whiskers. CSR listed as Prine. Post war resident of Braxton Co., W. Va. NFR.

PERRY, JOHN W. - Pvt. Co. H. b.c. 1847. Not on muster rolls. Took care of horses for the 8th Va. Cav., along with another man, 9/16/62 - 10/22/62. Paroled at Charleston, W. Va., 5/10/65. Desc.: age 18, 5', fair comp., black hair and blue eyes. NFR.

PERRY, WILLIAM T. (F.) - Pvt. Co. I. b. Greenbrier Co., W. Va., c. 1836. Age 24, farmer, Dunmore, Pocahontas Co., W. Va. 1860 Census. Enl. Huntersville, Pocahontas Co., W. Va., 2/1/63 (3/18/63). Present on muster-in roll dated 3/63. Mustered into service 3/19/63. Present 6/30/63 - 2/29/64, mounted. Present 2/29/64 - 8/31/64. Clothing issued, 7/10/64. Present 9/1/64 - 10/31/64, $100 bond due. Paroled at Charleston, W. Va., 5/10/65. Desc.: age 29, 5'6", light comp., light hair, blue eyes and light whiskers. Age 43, farmer, Huntersville, Pocahontas Co., W. Va. 1880 Census. NFR.

PHARES, ANDREW M. J. - Pvt. Co. K. Enl. Frankfort. Greenbrier Co., W. Va., 3/20/63. Not stated if present or absent on muster-in roll dated 3/63. NFR.

PHARES, JAMES H. H. - Pvt. Co. K. Enl. Frankfort, Greenbrier Co., W. Va., 3/20/63. Not stated if present or absent on muster-in roll dated 3/63. NFR.

PHILLIPS, DANIEL MARTIN VAN BUREN - Pvt. Co. A. b. Cairo, Ritchie Co., W. Va., 5/30/43. Not on muster rolls. POW records show he enl. Calhoun Co., W. Va., 5/63. Clothing issued, 2/19/64, 5/1/64 and 6/17/64, signs by x. Wd. Beverly, W. Va., 10/29/64, left leg. Cpd. Beverly, W. Va., 10/29/64. Adm. USA Post Hosp., Beverly, W. Va., 10/29/64, listed as having been wd. in the bowels, mortally. Simple dressing applied. Transf. to Grafton, W. Va., 11/10/64. Sent to Clarksburg, W. Va. instead. Adm. USA Post Hosp., Clarksburg, W. Va., 11/12/64, gunshot wd. Transf. to Grafton Gen. Hosp., 12/4/64. Desc.: age 21, 6', fair comp., light hair and blue eyes. Occ. farmer, residing in Ritchie Co., W. Va. Adm. USA Gen. Hosp., Grafton, W. Va., 12/4/64, gunshot wd., upper third, inner side of left leg, tibia injured by spencer rifle; cold water dressing. Turned over to Post Commander, Grafton, W. Va., 2/8/65. Transf. to Wheeling, W. Va. Confined at the Atheneum Prison, 2/9/65. Desc.: age 21, 5'9", fair comp., brown hair and gray eyes. Occ. farmer, residing in Ritchie Co., W. Va. Transf. to Camp Chase, 2/13/65. Confined at Camp Chase, 2/14/65. Took the oath of allegiance and was released, 5/16/65, signs by x. Desc.: age 22, 5'10", light comp., light hair and blue eyes, a resident of Ritchie Co., W. Va. Age 38, farmer, Murphy Dist., Ritchie Co., W. Va. 1880 Census. d. Smithville, Ritchie Co., W. Va., 6/28/1917. Bur. Phillips Cem., Cedar Grove, Ritchie Co., W. Va.

PHILLIPS (PHILIPS), GEORGE W. - 3rd Corp. Co. F. b.c. 1840. Age 20, laborer, Huntersville, Pocahontas Co., W. Va. 1860 Census. Prior service, McNeel's Co., 3rd VSL and Co. G, 31st Va. Inf. History of the 31st Va. Inf. shows he transf. to the 19th Va. Cav., 2/24/64. Enl. Hillsboro, Pocahontas Co., W. Va., 3/9/63 (4/1/63). Not stated if present or absent on muster-in roll dated 3/63, Pvt. Present, 3rd Corp., 1/1/64 - 2/29/64. Court martialed 3/17/64, for illegal transf. Sentence remitted 4/7/64. Cpd. Pocahontas Co., W. Va., 4/28/64. Confined at the Atheneum Prison, 5/12/64. Desc.: age 21, 5'9_", dark comp., dark hair and dark eyes. Occ. farmer, residing in Pocahontas Co., W. Va. Transf. to Camp Chase, 5/13/64. Confined at Camp Chase, 5/14/64. Ab. 9/1/64 - 10/31/64, cpd. 4/28/64; enl. bounty due. Paroled for exchange and sent to City Point, 2/25/65. Exchanged. Adm. Jackson Hosp., 3/6/65, debilitas. Furloughed 3/8/65, 30 days. Paroled at Staunton, 5/29/65. Desc.: age 24, 5'9", fair comp., dark hair and hazel eyes. Post war resident of Pocahontas Co. Age 38, works on farm, Green Banks, Pocahontas Co., W. Va. 1880 Census. d. by 1910. Bur. near Norton, W. Va.

PHILLIPS, WILLIAM F. - Pvt. Co. B. Enl. Frankfort, Greenbrier Co., W. Va., 1/7/63. Present 11/1/63 - 2/29/64, has one horse. Transf. to Co. C, 25th Va. Inf., 2/29/64, in exchange for John Jehu Carpenter. Paroled at Richmond, 4/21/65. NFR.

PIERCE, JOHN - Pvt. Co. B. b.c. 1842. Enl. Frankfort, Greenbrier Co., W. Va., 7/11/63. Ab. 11/1/63 - 2/29/64, deserted 11/15/63. Cpd. Beverly, W. Va., 1/15/64. Confined at the Atheneum Prison, 2/1/64. Desc.: age 22, 5'7 3/4", florid comp., dark hair and gray eyes. Occ. farmer, residing in Pocahontas Co., W. Va. Took the oath of allegiance and was released, 2/2/64. Ab. 9/1/64 - 10/31/64, not entitled to $100 enl. bounty; deserted Camp Cameron, Bath Co., 3/1/64. NFR.

PIERCY (PEARCY), ALBERT F. - Pvt. Co. D. b. Doddridge Co., W. Va., c. 1844. Enl. Williamsburg, Greenbrier Co., W. Va., 3/8/63. Not stated if present or absent on muster-in roll dated 3/63. Served in Co. B, 20th Va. Cav. Age 36, farmer, New Milton, Harrison Co., W. Va. 1880 Census. NFR.

PILES (PYLES), JACOB, Jr. - Pvt. Co. I. b. Pocahontas Co., W. Va., c. 1830. Age 30, laborer, Mill Point, Pocahontas Co., W. Va. 1860 Census. Enl. Huntersville, Pocahontas Co., W. Va., 3/19/63. Ab. on muster-in roll dated 3/63, AWOL. Deserted. Cpd. Beverly, W. Va., 8/19/63. Desc.: age 33, 5'9_", dark comp., brown hair and dark eyes. Occ. farmer, residing in Pocahontas Co., W. Va. Transf. to Camp Chase, 8/31/63. Confined at Camp Chase, 9/1/63. Took the oath of allegiance and was released, 1/13/64, not exchanged. Post war rosters show service in Co. F. NFR.

PILES (PYLES), JOHN - Pvt. Co. F. b.c. 1836. Age 24, laborer, Huntersville, Pocahontas Co., W. Va. 1860 Census. Prior service, 2nd Co. I, 25th Va. Inf. Enl. Hillsboro, Pocahontas Co., W. Va., 8/1/63. Ab. 1/1/64 - 2/29/64, sick. Clothing issued 2/6/64. Age 46, farmer, Little Level Dist., Pocahontas Co., W. Va. 1880 census. NFR.

PLECKER, WILLIAM - 4th Corp. Co. I. Enl. Huntersville, Pocahontas Co., W. Va., 10/22/63. Present, 4th Corp., 6/30/63 - 2/29/64, mounted; enl. bounty due. NFR.

POAGE (POAGUE), GEORGE WASHINGTON Jr. "Wash" - 4th Corp. Co. I. b. Pocahontas Co., W. Va., 4/14/19. Graduated Hillsboro Academy, Hillsboro, Pocahontas Co., W. Va. Age 41, farmer, Mill Point, Pocahontas Co., W. Va. 1860 Census. Enl. Huntersville, Pocahontas Co., W. Va., 3/19/63 (3/18/63). Present on muster-in roll dated 3/63. Mustered into service 3/19/63. Present 6/30/63 - 2/29/64, mounted; enl. bounty due. Present, 4th Corp., 2/29/64 - 8/31/64, appointed 4th Corp., 7/1/64. Clothing issued, 3/22/64. Ab. 9/1/64 - 10/31/64, sick; $100 bond due. Paroled at Charleston, W. Va., 5/10/65. Desc.: age 46, 6', dark comp., dark hair, dark eyes and dark whiskers. Post war farmer and resident of Huntersville, W. Va. d. Walker, Mo., 1/15/98.

POAGE, WILLIAM ANTHONY - 1st Corp. Co. F. b. Pocahontas Co., W. Va., c. 1840. Age 20, farmer, Edray, Pocahontas Co., W. Va. 1860 Census. Enl. Hillsboro, Pocahontas Co., W. Va., 3/9/63 (4/1/63). Not stated if present or absent on muster-in roll dated 3/63, 1st Corp. Present, 1st Corp. Present, 1/1/64 - 2/29/64. Ab. 9/1/64 - 10/31/64, KIA. Danville, 7/25/64; enl. bounty due. Post war source shows he was KIA. Valley of Va., 7/25/64, age 24.

POLLARD, GEORGE BRAXTON - Pvt. Co. F. b. 2/22/35. Prior service, McNeel's Co., 2nd VSL. Enl. Hillsboro, Pocahontas Co., W. Va., 3/9/63 (4/1/63). Not stated if present or absent on muster-in roll dated 3/63. Present 1/1/64 - 2/29/64. Clothing issued 7/15/64 and 12/2/74. Ab. 9/1/64 - 10/31/64, wd. Gap Mountain, 5/13/64; enl. bounty due. Adm. Gen. Hosp. No. 9, 8/2/64, sent to Pvt. Qrs. 8/3/64. Furloughed at Gen. Hosp. No. 9, 8/17/64, 60 days, vulnus sclopeticum, right side of neck; residence listed as Rockbridge Baths. Adm. Gen. Hosp. No. 9, 11/2/64. Furloughed 11/2/64, 60 days; residence listed as Richmond. Adm. Chimborazo Hosp. No. 2, vulnus sclopeticum, right shoulder, 1/30/65. Deserted 2/28/65. Adm. Gen. Hosp. No. 9, 3/14/65. Adm. Gen. Hosp. No. 9, 3/15/65, certificate of disability issued, retired. Disabled 5/13/64, vulnus sclopeticum, ball in left side, inf. maxillary exiting near spine, right arm paralyzed. Ordered to report to Enrolling Officer, New Kent Co. Listed as a member of Davis' Battn., Mosby's Rangers. Detailed 3/25/65. Paroled Salisbury, NC, 5/1/65. d. 1882.

POMEROY, EVANS MORGAN - 2nd Corp. Co. C. b. near Morgantown, W. Va., 10/31/37. Worked on his father's farm at Fairmont, W. Va. and ran a ferry. Moved to Wirt Co., W. Va., 1853, where he farmed and carried oil on a boat. Prior service, Co. D, 3rd VSL. Dispatch bearer for Henry A. Wise; John B. Floyd and W. L. Jackson. Enl. Frankfort, Greenbrier Co., W. Va., 3/15/63 (Pocahontas Co., W. Va., 4/1/63). Not stated if present or absent on muster-in roll dated 3/63, 2nd Corp. Present, 2nd Corp., 1/1/63 - 4/1/63, had one horse. Present, Pvt., 12/31/63 - 8/31/64, had one horse. Clothing issued 4/30/64 and 6/17/64. Present 9/1/64 - 10/31/64, had one horse. Cpd. Wirt Co., W. Va., 3/8/65. Post war rosters show cpd. 2/9/65. Sent to Cumberland, Md., then to Wheeling, W. Va. Confined at the Atheneum Prison, 3/27/65. Desc.: age 28, 5'10", light comp., brown hair and blue eyes. Occ. farmer, residing in Wirt Co., W. Va. Transf. to Camp Chase, 3/28/65. Confined at Camp Chase, 3/29/65. Took the oath of allegiance and was released, 6/13/65. Desc.: age 28, 5'8", florid comp., dark hair and blue eyes, a resident of Wirt Co., W. Va. Released 6/17/65. Returned to Wirt Co., W. Va. and farmed. Mason, 1870, at Spencer, W. Va. Superintendent of county farm, 1871, served four years. Hotel business, 1876 - 1883, Elizabeth, W. Va., running the "Old Virginia House." Age 42, landlord, Elizabeth Dist., Wirt Co., W. Va. 1880 Census. Returned to farming until 1893, when he retired. d. Elizabeth, Wirt Co., W. Va., 2/4/1912.

POMEROY, FRANCIS D. - 1st Lt. Co. C. b. Marion Co., W. Va., 4/22/42. Resident of Wirt Co., W. Va. since 1859. Prior service, Co. D, 3rd VSL. Enl. Frankfort, Greenbrier Co., W. Va., 3/15/63 (Pocahontas Co., W. Va., 4/1/63). Not stated if present or absent on muster-in roll dated 3/63, 2nd Sgt. Present, 2nd Sgt., 1/1/63 - 4/1/63, had one horse. Promoted Jr. 2nd Lt. Present, Jr. 2nd Lt., 12/31/63 - 8/31/64, promoted to 1st Lt., 2/1/64. Wd. Bunker Hill, Berkeley Co., W. Va., 9/64. Present 9/1/64 - 10/31/64. Commanding Co. 11/24/63. Ab. 12/15/64, on leave. Cpd. Roane Co., W. Va., 3/11/65. Sent to Cumberland, Md., then to Wheeling, W. Va. Confined at the Atheneum Prison, 3/27/65. Desc.: age 23, 5'10". fair comp., dark hair and gray eyes. Occ. farmer, residing in Wirt Co., W. Va. Transf. to Camp Chase, 3/28/65. Confined at Camp Chase, 3/29/65, charged with being a guerrilla. Took the oath of allegiance and was released, 6/14/65. Desc.: age 23, 5'9", fair comp., black hair and gray eyes, a resident of Wirt Co., W. Va. Post war farmer and resident of Elizabeth Dist., Wirt Co. Age 38, farmer, Elizabeth Dist., Wirt Co., W. Va. 1880 Census. d. 1917. Bur. Palestine Cem., Wirt Co., W. Va.

POMPHREY, JOHN - Pvt. Co. F. Post war rosters only. NFR.

POWELL, JOHN F. - Pvt. Co. K. b. Taylor Co., W. Va., c. 1846. Age 14, Gilmer Co., W. Va. 1860 Census. Not on muster rolls. Clothing issued 6/17/64. Cpd. Leesburg, Loudoun Co. (near Harpers Ferry, W. Va.), 7/15/64. Sent to Harpers Ferry, W. Va., then to Washington, DC. Confined at the Old Capitol Prison, 7/17/64. Transf. to Elmira, NY, 7/23/64. Confined at Elmira Prison, 7/25/64. Wished to take the oath of allegiance, 9/30/64, says he vol. 5/19/63, and is a resident of Gilmer Co., W. Va., and wishes to go there. Took the oath of allegiance and was released, 5/15/65. Desc.: age ?, 5'9", fair comp., light hair and blue eyes, a resident of Clarksburg, W. Va. Age 34, farmer, Glenville, Gilmer Co., W. Va. 1880 Census. NFR.

PREBBLE, H. J. - Pvt. Co. ?. Post war rosters only, which show he was a resident of Ritchie Co., W. Va. NFR.

PRICE, G. B. - Pvt. Co. G. Not on muster rolls. Adm. CSA Gen. Hosp., Charlottesville, 8/17/64, feb. int. quo. Transf. to Lynchburg, 9/27/64. [Could be John B. Price, below.] NFR.

PRICE, JAMES HENRY - Pvt. Co. F. b. 1834. Age 25, farmer, Edray, Pocahontas Co., W. Va. 1860 Census. Prior service, McNeel's Co., 2nd VSL. Enl. Hillsboro, Pocahontas Co., W. Va., 4/1/63. Present 1/1/64 - 2/29/64. Clothing issued 2/6/64. Ab. 9/1/64 - 10/31/64, cpd. 4/28/64; enl. bounty due. Cpd. Pocahontas Co., W. Va., 4/28/64. Confined at the Atheneum Prison, 5/12/64. Desc.: age 30, 5'8", dark comp., black hair and blue eyes. Occ. farmer, residing in Pocahontas Co., W. Va. Transf. to Camp Chase, 5/13/64. Confined at Camp Chase, 5/14/64. Paroled and sent to City Point, 2/25/65, to be exchanged. Exchanged. Adm. Jackson Hosp., 3/6/65, debilitas. Furloughed 3/8/65, 30 days. Paroled at Charleston, W. Va., 5/10/65. Desc.: age 31, 5'8", light comp., dark hair, blue eyes and dark whiskers. Brother of John C. and Josiah W. Price. Age 46, farmer, Edray, Pocahontas Co., W. Va. 1880 Census. d. 1899 (1898).

PRICE, JOHN B. - Pvt. Co. G. b.c. 1842. Enl. Frankfort, Greenbrier Co., W. Va., 3/12/63 (4/1/63). Not stated if present or absent on muster-in roll dated 3/63. Clothing issued 1st Qr. 1864, 4/30/64, 5/1/64 and 6/17/64, signs by x. Present 9/1/64 - 10/31/64, has a serviceable horse. Paroled at Charleston, W. Va., 5/10/65. Desc.: age 23, 5'4", dark comp., dark hair and black eyes. [Could be G. B. Price, above.] NFR.

PRICE, JOHN CALVIN - 2nd Sgt. Co. F. b. Marlinton, W. Va., 1840. Age 19, farmer, Edray, Pocahontas Co., W. Va. 1860 Census. Prior service, McNeel's Co., 2nd VSL. Enl. Hillsboro, Pocahontas Co., W. Va., 3/9/63 (4/1/63). Not stated if present or absent on muster-in roll dated 3/63, 3rd Sgt. Ab., 3rd Sgt., 1/1/64 - 2/29/64, on detail. Present, 2nd Sgt., 9/1/64 - 10/31/64, enl. bounty due. Wd. Marlin's Bottom (Marlinton), W. Va., while at home on furlough, as he was trying to escape by swimming the Greenbrier River. Paroled at Charleston, W. Va., 5/10/65. Desc.: age 24, 5'10", dark comp., black hair, gray eyes and dark mustache. Post war farmer and resident of Dunmore, W. Va. Brother of James H. and Josiah W. Price. Age 39, farmer, Edray, Pocahontas Co., W. Va. 1880 Census. d. Pocahontas Co., W. Va. 9/20/1915, age 75. Bur. Clover Lick Cem., Pocahontas Co., W. Va.

PRICE, JOSIAH WOODS - 1st Lt. Co. F. b. Va., 2/19/36. Age 24, farmer, Edray, Pocahontas Co., W. Va. 1860 Census. Grad. Washington College, Lexington, 1861. Prior service, McNeel's Co., 2nd VSL and Co. F, 11th Va. Cav. Transf. to Co. F, 19th Va. Cav., 1/21/63 and promoted to 2nd Lt. Enl. Hillsboro, Pocahontas Co., W. Va., 3/9/63 (4/1/63). Not stated if present or absent on muster-in roll dated 3/63, Sr. 2nd Lt. Present, 2nd Lt., 1/1/64 - 2/29/64, commanding Co. Present, 2nd Lt., 9/1/64 - 10/31/64, commanding Co. Adm. CSA Gen. Hosp., Charlottesville, 1/4/65, chronic diarrhoea. Transf. to Staunton, 1/5/65. Paroled at Charleston, W. Va., 5/10/65, as 1st Lt. Desc.: age 29, 5'8", fair comp., light hair, blue eyes and light whiskers. Brother of James H. and John C. Price. Post war farmer and teacher, Clover Lick, Pocahontas Co., W. Va. Resident of Marlinton, W. Va., 1912. d. Pocahontas Co., W. Va., 3/5/1918 (3/6/1918), age 82 years, 16 days. Bur. Atla Price Cem., Marlinton, W. Va.

PRICE, SQUIRE B. - Pvt. Co. G. b.c. 1842. Enl. Frankfort, Greenbrier Co., W. Va., 3/12/63 (4/1/63). Not stated if present or absent on muster-in roll dated 3/63. Clothing issued 1st Qr. 1864, 5/25/64, 6/17/64 and 7/10/64, signs by x. Present 9/1/64 - 10/31/64, has a serviceable horse. Deserted. Surrendered at Charleston, W. Va. Took the amnesty oath and was sent North, 2/11/

65. Desc.: age 23, 5'8", dark comp., dark hair and blue eyes. Occ. farmer, residing in Kanawha Co., W. Va. d. 11/9/1914. Bur. Springhill Cem., Charleston, W. Va.

PRITT, WILLIAM - Pvt. Co. D. Not on muster rolls. In Gordonsville Hosp., 1/14/65 - 1/25/65, chronic rheumatism. NFR.

PRITT, WILLIAM PARKER (S.) - Pvt. Co. B. b. Beverly, 10/23/22. Cpd. Greenbrier Co., W. Va., 8/62, charged with being a bushwhacker. Desc.: age 36, 5'10", dark comp., dark hair and hazel eyes. Sent to Gallipolis Ohio, then to Camp Chase. Confined at Camp Chase, 9/18/62. Transf. to Johnson's Island by 9/16/62. Transf. to Vicksburg, Miss., 11/22/62, to be exchanged. Exchanged at Vicksburg, Miss., 12/8/62. Enl. Frankfort, Greenbrier Co., W. Va., 3/9/63. Not stated if present or absent on muster-in roll dated 3/63. Cpd. Highland Co. (Randolph Co., W. Va.), 8/16/63, deserter. Confined at the Atheneum Prison, 8/30/63. Desc.: age 36, 6' 3/4", florid comp., dark hair and blue eyes. Occ. farmer, residing in Pocahontas Co., W. Va. Transf. to Camp Chase, 8/31/63. Confined at Camp Chase, 9/1/63. Took the oath of allegiance and was released, 1/13/64. Rejoined his command, 2/64. Present 11/1/63 - 2/29/64, has one horse; detailed with his horse since 11/63; enl. shown as 1/1/64. Clothing issued 1st Qr. 1864. Ab. 9/1/64 - 10/31/64, on detached service; $100 enl. bounty due. Surrendered at Bulltown, W. Va., 5/9/65. Confined at Clarksburg, W. Va. Paroled for exchange 5/12/65, and released. Desc.: age 43, 5'10", dark comp., black hair and hazel eyes. Occ. farmer, residing in Upshur Co., W. Va. Age 56, farmer, Banks Dist., Upshur Co., W. Va. 1880 Census. d. Pritt Mtn., Upshur Co., W. Va., 3/29/95.

PROCTOR, RICHARD - Pvt. Co. G. Enl. Frankfort, Greenbrier Co., W. Va., 3/12/63. Not stated if present or absent on muster-in roll dated 3/63. Clothing issued 3/1/64 and 3rd Qr. 1864, signs by x. NFR.

PROPST, ADAM M. Jr. - 3rd Corp. Co. I. b.c. 1844. Enl. Beverly, Randolph Co., W. Va., 4/25/63. Present, 3rd Corp., 6/30/63 - 2/29/64. Ab. 2/29/64 - 8/31/64, cpd. near Staunton, 6/4/64. Cpd. near Lexington, 6/11/64 (Augusta Co., 6/10/64). Sent to Cumberland, Md., then to Wheeling, W. Va., 6/17/64. Confined at the Atheneum Prison, 7/1/64. Desc.: age 20, 5'8", florid comp., dark hair and dark eyes. Occ. farmer, residing in Randolph Co., W. Va. Transf. to Camp Chase, 7/2/64. Confined at Camp Chase, 7/3/64. Adm. Chase USA Gen. Hosp., Camp Chase, 8/13/64, variola, never vaccinated; age 21. DOD. Camp Chase, 8/22/64, smallpox. Ab. 9/1/64 - 10/31/64, cpd. Augusta Co., 5/12/64; $100 bond due. Bur. Camp Chase Confederate Cem., 1/3 mile S. of Camp Chase, grave no. 216.

PROPST, E. - Pvt. Co. I. Enl. Huntersville, Pocahontas Co., W. Va., 1/1/64. Ab. 6/30/63 - 2/29/64, dropped from rolls, never reported to Co.; mounted; enl. bounty due. Ab. 2/29/64 - 8/31/64, deserted and dropped from the rolls. NFR.

PROPST (PROPTS, PROPS), NOAH W. - Pvt. Co. H. Resident of Nicholas Co., W. Va. Arrested and confined by 3/15/62. Charged with being a bushwhacker. Prior service, Co. A, 3rd VSL. Enl. Frankfort, Greenbrier Co., W. Va., 3/19/63. Not stated if present or absent on muster-in roll dated 3/63. NFR.

PROVINCE (PROVINE), DAVID - Pvt. Co. D. b.c. 1846. Enl. Bath Co., 4/63. Not on muster rolls. Clothing issued, 5/25/64, 6/17/64, 7/64 and 8/64. Cpd. Upshur Co., W. Va., 4/1/65. Confined at Clarksburg, W. Va., 4/5/65. Desc.: age 19, 5'9_", fair comp., fair hair and blue eyes. Occ. farmer, residing in Marion Co., W. Va. Sent to Cumberland, Md., 4/6/65. Post war resident of Marion Co., W. Va. NFR.

PUFFENBARGER, JAMES - Pvt. Co. F. Post war rosters only, which show he was KIA. Fisher's Hill, 9/22/64. NFR.

PUFFENBARGER, JONAS - Pvt. Co. F. Prior service, McNeel's Co., 2nd VSL. Enl. Hillsboro, Pocahontas Co., W. Va., 3/9/63 (4/1/63). Not stated if present or absent on muster-in roll dated 3/63. Present 1/1/64 - 2/29/64. Clothing issued 2/6/64. Present 9/1/64 - 10/31/64, enl. bounty due. Post war rosters show service in Co. A, 62nd Va. Mtd. Inf. NFR.

PUFFENBARGER, JOSEPH - Pvt. Co. F. Post war rosters only. NFR.

PUGH, KERTIS (CURTIS) - Pvt. Co. F. Post war rosters only. NFR.

PUGH, LELBURN (LILBURN) C. - Pvt. Co. F. b.c. 1830. Age 30, laborer, Mill Point, Pocahontas Co., W. Va. 1860 Census. Prior service, McNeel's Co., 2nd VSL. Enl. Hillsboro, Pocahontas Co., W. Va., 3/9/63 (4/1/63). Not stated if present or absent on muster-in roll dated 3/63. Ab. 1/1/64 - 2/29/64, sick. Clothing issued 2/6/64. Ab. 9/1/64 - 10/31/64, AWOL since 10/5/64. Cpd. Braxton Co., W. Va., 4/8/65 (4/23/65). Confined at Clarksburg, W. Va., then sent to Cumberland, Md., 4/11/65. Desc.: age 36, 5'10", dark comp., black hair and brown eyes. Occ. farmer, residing in Pocahontas Co., W. Va. Confined at the Atheneum Prison, 4/24/65. Took the oath of allegiance at Cumberland, Md. Resident of Upshur Co., W. Va. NFR.

PUGH, LORENTZ - Pvt. Co. F. Post war rosters only. NFR.

PUGH, WILLIAM - Pvt. Co. F. Post war rosters only, which show he was a substitute for William H. H. Galford. Cpd. and sent to Camp Chase. NFR.

PUGH, WILSON L. - Pvt. Co. F. b.c. 1846 (1844). Age 16, carpenter, Randolph Co., W. Va., 1860 Census. Enl. Hillsboro, Pocahontas Co., W. Va., 1/1/64(?). Cpd. Greenbank, Pocahontas Co., W. Va., 11/3/63. Confined at the Atheneum Prison, 11/16/63. Desc.: age 17, 5'9 3/4", fair comp., fair hair and brown eyes. Occ. farmer, residing in Randolph Co., W. Va. Transf. to Camp Chase, 11/18/63. Confined at Camp Chase, 11/18/63. Ab. 1/1/64 - 2/29/64, in the hands of the enemy. Transf. to Ft. Delaware, 2/29/64. Confined at Ft. Delaware, 3/4/64 (3/2/64). Ab. 9/1/64 - 10/31/64, cpd. 11/3/63; enl. bounty due. Took the oath of allegiance and was released, 6/20/65. Desc.: age ?, 5'6", light comp., dark hair and dark eyes, a resident of Randolph Co., W. Va. Age 36, farm laborer, Green Banks, Pocahontas Co., W. Va. 1880 Census. d. c. 1887, age 41.

PULLINS (PULLIN), ADAM M. - 2nd Sgt. Co. F. b. Pendleton Co., W. Va., c. 1835. Age 25, merchant, Mt. Murphy, Pocahontas Co., W. Va. 1860 Census. Member Locust Creek Patrol, Pocahontas Co., W. Va., 5/61. Prior service, McNeel's Co., 2nd VSL. Enl. Hillsboro, Pocahontas Co., W. Va., 3/9/63 (4/1/63). Not stated if present or absent on muster-in roll dated 3/63, 2nd Sgt. Detailed as acting QM Sgt., for a detachment of the 19th Va. Cav., 4/17/63 - 9/20/63. Ab., Pvt., 1/1/64 - 2/29/64, on leave. Clothing issued 2/7/64. Ab. 9/1/64 - 10/31/64, on horse detail. Paroled at Charleston, W. Va., 5/10/65. Desc.: age 31, 5'6", dark comp., dark hair, gray eyes and dark whiskers. Age 48, farmer, Little Levels, Pocahontas Co., W. Va. 1880 Census. NFR.

PUTNAM, JEREMIAH "Jerry" - Pvt. Co. K. b. Fauquier Co., c. 1838. Age 22, farmer, Gilmer Co., W. Va. 1860 Census. Enl. Frankfort, Greenbrier Co., W. Va., 3/20/63. Not stated if present or absent on muster-in roll dated 3/63. Enl. in Co. B, Frankfort, Greenbrier Co., W. Va., 3/9/63. Present 11/1/63 - 2/29/64. Employed as a teamster 11/1/63 - 11/30/63, signs by x. Employed as a teamster at Warm Springs, 1/1/64 - 2/16/64, discharged and sent to his Co., signs by x. Clothing issued 11/20/63, 12/29/63, detailed; 1/17/64, detailed teamster; 5/26/64 and 6/17/64, signs by x. Ab. 9/1/64 - 10/31/64, POW since 7/15/64; $100 enl. bounty due.

PUTNAM, JOSEPH B. - Pvt. Co. E. b. Fauquier Co., c. 1843. Age 17, farmer, Gilmer Co., W. Va. 1860 Census. Enl. Frankfort, Greenbrier Co., W. Va., 3/13/63 (4/1/63). Not stated if present or absent on muster-in roll dated 3/63. Present 10/31/63 - 10/31/64, had his own horse since 7/1/64. Clothing issued, 3/1/64, 4/21/64 and 6/17/64, signs by x. Adm. CSA Gen. Hosp., Charlottesville, 9/1/64, pneumonia. RTD. 9/23/64. Deserted. Took the amnesty oath at Charleston, W. Va., and was sent North, 3/22/65. Desc.: age 20, 6'1", fair comp., fair hair and blue eyes, a farmer. NFR.

PUTNAM, SAMUEL - Pvt. Co. ?. Not on muster rolls. Served in Co. B, 46th Battn. Va. Cav. Was AWOL, and surrendered at Beverly, W. Va., 9/24/64, and listed as a member of the 19th Va. Cav. Sent to Wheeling, W. Va. Took the amnesty oath and was released, 9/30/64. Desc.: age 27, 5'7", light comp., dark hair and gray eyes. Occ. farmer, residing in Bath Co. NFR.

RADER, WALLACE - Pvt. Co. A. Served in Co. A, 3rd VSL. Post war rosters only. NFR.

RAFFERTY, PATRICK "Pat" - Pvt. Co. A. b. Latram, Ireland, c. 1822. Age 38, farmer, Calhoun Co., W. Va. 1860 Census. Prior service, Co. A, 3rd VSL. Enl. Williamsburg, Greenbrier Co., W. Va., 3/1/63. Not stated if present or absent on muster-in roll dated 3/63. Clothing issued 3/21/64. Paroled at Charleston, W. Va., 5/11/65., Desc.: age 43, 5'10", dark comp., black hair, gray eyes and brown whiskers. Post war roster shows he was cpd. during the war by Capt. Simpson's detachment, a few miles east of Grantsville, W. Va. Age 50, farmer, Sherman Township, Calhoun Co., W. Va. 1870 Census. NFR.

RAINER, W. V. - Pvt. Co. B. Enl. Frankfort, Greenbrier Co., W. Va., 3/7/63. Not stated if present or absent on muster-in roll dated 3/63. NFR.

RAINS (RAINES), THOMAS - Pvt. Co. C. Prior service, Co. D, 3rd VSL. Enl. Frankfort, Greenbrier Co., W. Va., 3/15/63. Not stated if present or absent on muster-in roll dated 3/63. Present 1/1/63 - 4/1/63, has one horse. NFR.

RALES, TOBIAS - Pvt. Co. ?. Not on muster rolls. Reported at Washington, DC, 5/15/65 from Pt. Lookout. Transportation furnished to Clarksburg, W. Va. NFR.

RAMSEY, SAMUEL J. - Pvt. Co. F. b.c. 1820. Age 40, laborer, Elk, Pocahontas Co., W. Va. 1860 Census. Post war rosters only. NFR.

RANDOLPH, WILLIAM J. - Pvt. Co. F. Enl. Hillsboro, Pocahontas Co., W. Va., 8/1/63. Ab. 1/1/64 - 2/29/64, on leave. Clothing issued 2/6/64, 7/64 and 8/64. Ab. 9/1/64 - 10/31/64, AWOL since 10/25/64. NFR.

RANKIN, GEORGE WASHINGTON - Pvt. Co. F. b. Va., c. 1822. Age 37, farmer, Mill Point, Pocahontas Co., W. Va. 1860 Census. Member Locust Creek Patrol, Pocahontas Co., W. Va., 5/61. Prior service, Co. D, 14th Va. Cav. Transf. to Co. F, 19th Va. Cav. after 10/31/64. Paroled at Charleston, W. Va., 5/10/65. Desc.: age 43, 5'10", brown comp., black hair, gray eyes and black whiskers. Post war resident of Pocahontas Co., W. Va. Age 57, farmer, Little Levels, Pocahontas Co., W. Va. 1880 Census. d. Pocahontas Co., W. Va., 1/15/90. Bur. McNeel Cem., Hillsboro, W. Va.

RANKIN, ROBERT D. (B.) - Pvt. Co. F. b. Pocahontas Co., W. Va., c. 1845. Age 15, farmer, Mill Point, Pocahontas Co., W. Va. 1860 Census. Enl. Hillsboro, Pocahontas Co., W. Va., 6/10/63. Cpd. Pocahontas Co., W. Va., 12/19/63. Confined at the Atheneum Prison, 12/31/63. Desc.: age 19, 5'11", fair comp., light hair and blue eyes. Occ. farmer, residing in Pocahontas Co., W. Va. Transf. to Camp Chase, 12/31/63. Confined at Camp Chase, 1/1/64. Ab. 1/1/64 - 2/29/64, in the hands of the enemy. Transf. to Ft. Delaware, 3/14/64. Confined at Ft. Delaware, 3/17/64. Ab. 9/1/64 - 10/31/64, cpd. 12/63; enl. bounty due. DOD. Ft. Delaware, 9/28/64, typhoid fever. Bur. Jersey Shore. Post war source shows he d. at Camp Chase, 9/25/64, age 19.

RATCLIFF (RATLIFF), JAMES O. - Pvt. Co. I. b.c. 1833. Age 27, farmer, Edray, Pocahontas Co., W. Va. 1860 Census. Enl. Huntersville, Pocahontas Co., W. Va., 2/1/63 (3/18/63). Present on muster-in roll dated 3/63. Mustered into service 3/19/63. Present 6/30/63 - 2/29/64, mounted. Ab. 2/29/64 - 8/31/64, wd., date and place not stated, arm amputated. Ab. 9/1/64 - 10/31/64, wd., arm off; $100 bond due. Age 52, farmer, Edray, Pocahontas Co., W. Va. 1880 Census. NFR.

RATCLIFF, JOHN N. - Pvt. Co. A. b.c. 1841. Prior service, Co. A, 3rd VSL. Enl. Williamsburg, Greenbrier Co., W. Va., 3/1/63. Not stated if present or absent on muster-in roll dated 3/63. Clothing issued 2/19/64. Served in Co. F, 20th Va. Cav. Paroled at Staunton, 6/1/65. Desc.: age 24, 5'10", dark comp., dark hair and dark eyes. Age 39, farmer, Edray, Pocahontas Co., W. Va. 1880 Census. NFR.

RATCLIFF, LEONARD - Pvt. Co. E. Enl. Lewis Co., W. Va., 5/15/63. Clothing issued 3/1/64, 5/21/64 and 6/17/64. Ab. 10/31/63 - 10/31/64, killed while on detail to procure a fresh horse, date not stated. NFR.

RATCLIFF (RATLIFF), WILLIAM A. - Pvt. Co. I. b. Pocahontas Co., W. Va., c. 1835. Age 25, farmer, Edray, Pocahontas Co., W. Va. 1860 Census. Enl. Huntersville, Pocahontas Co., W. Va., 3/20/63. Ab. 6/30/63 - 2/29/64, sick; does not have a horse. Ab. 2/29/64 - 8/31/64, AWOL since 4/64. Ab. 9/1/64 - 10/31/64, AWOL since 1/64. Age 48, farmer, Edray, Pocahontas Co., W. Va. 1880 Census. NFR.

RATCLIFFE, JAMES - Pvt. Co. K. Enl. Frankfort, Greenbrier Co., W. Va., 3/20/63. Not stated if present or absent on muster-in roll dated 3/63. NFR.

READ, A. S. - Pvt. Co. I. Enl. Huntersville, Pocahontas Co., W. Va., 3/22/63. Ab. 6/30/63 - 2/29/64, deserted 10/63. NFR.

RECTOR, BENJAMIN - Pvt. Co. ?. Not on muster rolls. Wartime letter dated 2/27/64 described him as being as "fat as a pig." NFR.

REED, JOHN B. - Pvt. Co. C. b.c. 1844. Prior service, Co. D, 3rd VSL. Enl. Frankfort, Greenbrier Co., W. Va., 3/15/63 (Pocahontas Co., W. Va., 4/1/63). POW. record shows his enl. as Roane Co., W. Va., 8/62. Not stated if present or absent on muster-in roll dated 3/63. Present 1/1/63 - 4/1/63, has one horse. Present 12/31/63 - 8/31/64, had his own horse since 7/1/64. Clothing issued 2/2/64, 5/26/64 and 6/17/64. Ab. 9/1/64 - 10/31/64, $100 enl. bounty due; cpd. Fisher's Hill, 9/23/64; had one horse. Cpd. Strasburg, 9/23/64. Sent to Harpers Ferry, W. Va., then to Pt. Lookout. Confined at Pt. Lookout, 10/3/64. Paroled 3/17/65, to be exchanged. Transf. to Aiken's Landing. Exchanged at Boulware's Wharf, 3/19/65. Present on a MR of Paroled and Exchanged Prisoners at Camp Lee, near Richmond, 3/19/65. Paroled at Charleston, W. Va., 5/10/65. Desc.: age 21, 6', dark comp., black hair and blue eyes. NFR.

REED, JOHN WESLEY - Pvt. Co. B. b. Spring Hill, Augusta Co., 8/10/36. Not on muster rolls. Cpd., date and place not given. Confined at Camp Chase. Transf. to Ft. Delaware. Confined at Ft. Delaware, 3/2/64. Took the oath of allegiance and was released, 6/15/65. Desc.: age ?, 5'9", light comp., light hair and blue eyes, a resident of Augusta Co. Post war farmer and merchant, Mustoe, Highland Co. d. 12/18/1900. Bur. Stoney Run Church Cem.

:apt. Co. C. Prior service, Co. D, 3rd VSL. Enl. Frankfort, Greenbrier Co., W. Va., 3/15/63 (Mill Point, Va., 4/1/63). Not stated if present or absent on muster-in roll dated 3/63,˚2nd Lt. Present, 2nd Lt., 1/1/ rses. Ab., Capt., 12/31/63 - 8/31/64, resigned and relieved of duty, 2/1/64. Resignation submitted 1/6/ . W. L. Jackson remarked that Reeder was "not competent to command the company [because of] his ecognition." Reeder said he was an officer in the 8th (W.) Va. Regiment (US) at the beginning of the war.

o. F. Not on muster rolls. Cpd. Smith Co., Tenn., 8/22/63, stated he was a conscript and deserter. Sent to shed to take to oath of allegiance and not be exchanged. Transf. to Rock Island, Ill., 1/22/64. NFR.

REID, JAMES n. . . Co. E. b. Harrison Co., W. Va., c. 1838. Enl. Frankfort, Greenbrier Co., W. Va., 3/12/63. POW record shows enl. as Pocahontas Co., W. Va., 7/63. Not stated if present or absent on muster-in roll dated 3/63. Transf. to Co. C. Cpd. Alleghany Co., 12/19/63. Confined at the Atheneum Prison, 12/31/63. Desc.: age 25, 6', dark comp., black hair and hazel eyes. Occ. farmer, residing in Lewis Co., W. Va. Transf. to Camp Chase, 12/31/63. Confined at Camp Chase, 1/1/64. Transf. to Ft. Delaware, 3/14/64. Confined at Ft. Delaware, 3/17/64. Paroled 9/28/64, until exchanged. Sent to Aiken's Landing, 9/30/ 64. Exchanged at Varina, Va., 10/5/64, signs by x. Adm. Chimborazo Hosp. No. 3, 10/7/64, chronic diarrhoea. Furloughed 10/15/64, 40 days. Passport issued to Bath Co., 10/14/64. Clothing issued at Chimborazo Hosp., 10/15/64. Reported at Clarksburg, W, Va., 1/26/65. Took the oath of allegiance and was released, 1/30/65. Desc.: age 26, 6', dark comp., black hair and dark eyes. Occ. farmer, residing in Lewis Co., W. Va. NFR.

REID, MADISON - Pvt. Co. G. Enl. Frankfort, Greenbrier Co., W. Va., 3/12/63. Not stated if present or absent on muster-in roll dated 3/63. NFR.

REID, THORNTON - Pvt. Co. G. Enl. Frankfort, Greenbrier Co., W. Va., 3/12/63. Not stated if present or absent on muster-in roll dated 3/63. NFR.

RENNELS (REYNOLDS), JACOB - Pvt. Co. H. b.c. 1845. Enl. Roane Co., W. Va., 3/19/63. Ab. 9/1/64 - 10/31/64, AWOL; not mounted; enl. bounty due. Age 35, farmer, Spencer Dist., Roane Co., W. Va. 1880 Census. NFR.

REYNOLDS, DALLAS - Pvt. Co. K. Post war roster only, which show he was a resident of Carroll Co. NFR.

REYNOLDS, JAMES D. - Pvt. Co. I. Enl. Huntersville, Pocahontas Co., W. Va., 9/16/63. Ab. 6/30/63 - 2/29/64, at home sick; mounted; enl. bounty due. Clothing issued 2/5/64, 5/26/64 and 10/24/64, while on the way to his command. Adm. CSA Gen. Hosp., Charlottesville, 3/2/65, scrofula. Transf. to Lynchburg, 4/7/65. NFR.

RHODES, ERASMUS - Pvt. Co. I. b. 1826. Enl. Huntersville, Pocahontas Co., W. Va., 1/1/64. Not stated if present or absent, 6/30/63 - 2/29/64, new recruit. Ab. 2/29/64 - 8/31/64, AWOL. Ab. 9/1/64 - 10/31/64, sick. Age 55, farmer, Collins Settlement, Lewis Co., W. Va. 1880 Census. d. Roanoke, Lewis Co., W. Va., 1900.

RHODES, LYMAN P. - Pvt. Co. C. Enl. Pocahontas Co., W. Va., 6/30/63. Ab. 12/31/63 - 8/31/64, cpd. 7/16/64; has one horse. Clothing issued 2/25/64 and 6/17/64. Cpd. Loudoun Co. (near Harpers Ferry, W. Va.), 7/16/64. Sent to Harpers Ferry, W. Va., then to Washington, DC. Confined at the Old Capitol Prison, 7/20/64. Transf. to Elmira, NY, 7/23/64. Confined at Elmira Prison, 7/25/64. Ab. 9/1/64 - 10/31/64, $100 enl. bounty due; cpd. 7/16/64; had one horse. Took the oath of allegiance and was released, 6/14/65. Desc.: age ?, 5'8", florid comp., auburn hair and hazel eyes, a resident of New England Landing, Va. NFR.

RIBLET (RIBBET), GEORGE JOHN - Pvt. Co. D. b. Fayette Co., Pa., c. 1829. Not on muster rolls. POW record shows his enl. as Highland Co., 7/63. Clothing issued 2/7/64, 6/17/64, 7/64 and 8/64. Detailed to work in the blacksmith shop, 2/27/64. Deserted and reported at Beverly, W. Va., 1/12/65. Sent to Clarksburg, W. Va. Confined at Clarksburg, W. Va., 1/16/65. Desc.: age 36, 5'10", dark comp., brown hair and blue eyes. Occ. blacksmith, residing in Marion Co., W. Va. Took the oath of allegiance and was released. Brother of Windel Riblet. NFR.

RIBLET, WINDEL - Pvt. Co. ?. Not on muster rolls. Wartime document shows he was in service on 2/27/64. Brother of George Riblet. NFR.

RICE, A. W. - Pvt. Co. A. Not on muster rolls. Cpd. Preston Co., W. Va., 7/1/63. Sent to Wheeling, W. Va., then to Camp Chase. Confined at Camp Chase, 8/11/63. Took the oath and was released by order of the Sec. of War, 4/19/64. Had a dark sorrel horse, 14_ hands high, valued at $1,933.33 1/3, 2/14/65: May have served as a Sgt. in the 47th Battn. Va. Cav., taken prisoner and held at Baltimore, Md. NFR.

RICHARDS, NELSON Jr. - Pvt. Co. A. b. Harrison Co., W. Va., c. 1835 (1833). Age 29, farmer, Calhoun Co., W. Va. 1860 Census. Enl. Williamsburg, Greenbrier Co., W. Va., 3/1/63. Not stated if present or absent on muster-in roll dated 3/63. Cpd. Parkersburg, W. Va., 1/17/65. Confined at the Atheneum Prison, 1/22/65. Desc.: age 30, 5'8", dark comp., black hair and brown eyes. Occ. farmer, residing in Calhoun Co., W. Va. Transf. to Camp Chase, 1/28/65. Age 37, farmer, Center Township, Calhoun Co., W. Va. 1870 Census. NFR.

RICHARDS, WILLIAM (1st) - Pvt. Co. B. b.c. 1829. Not on muster rolls. Cpd. Bulltown, W. Va., 5/20/65, a deserter. Confined at Clarksburg, W. Va., 5/21/65. Desc.: age 36, 6', dark comp., dark hair and brown eyes. Occ. farmer, residing in Nicholas Co., W. Va. Took the amnesty oath and was released, 5/22/65. NFR.

RICHARDS, WILLIAM (2nd) - Pvt. Co. B. b.c. 1809. Not on muster rolls. Cpd. Bulltown, W. Va., 5/20/65, a deserter. Confined at Clarksburg, W. Va., 5/21/65. Desc.: age 56, 6', dark comp., dark hair and brown eyes. Occ. farmer, residing in Braxton Co., W. Va. Took the amnesty oath and was released, 5/22/65. NFR.

RIDDEL, BENJAMIN F. - Pvt. Co. A. b. Lewis Co., W. Va., c. 1839. Age 22, Calhoun Co., W. Va. 1860 Census. Not on muster rolls. Clothing issued 4/21/64 and 6/17/64. Surrendered at Cornwallas, W. Va., 5/2/65. Confined at Clarksburg, W. Va., 5/4/ 65. Desc.: age 26, 6, fair comp., light hair and hazel eyes. Occ. farmer, residing in Calhoun Co., W. Va. Paroled 5/4/65, to be exchanged, and released. Was shot at by William Wiant's Co., Gilmer Co. Home Guards (US), and killed his horse. Was later wd. and hid under a rock near Richardson, W. Va., and was cared for by a lady named Townsend. The bullet was never removed from his body. Age 31, farmer, Sheridan Township, Calhoun Co., W. Va. 1870 Census. Age 41, physician and surgeon, Sheridan Dist., Calhoun Co., W. Va. 1880 Census. Bur. Wright Cem., Calhoun Co., W. Va.

RIDER, ALEXANDREA (ALEXANDRE) W. - Pvt. Co. I. b.c. 1806. Enl. Huntersville, Pocahontas Co., W. Va., 3/19/63. Present on muster-in roll dated 3/63. Mustered into service 3/19/63. Age 74, farmer, Huntersville, Pocahontas Co., W. Va. 1880 Census. NFR.

RIDER, HEZEKIAH H. - Pvt. Co. F. b. Highland Co., c. 1836. Age 24, farmer, Huntersville, Pocahontas Co., W. Va. 1860 Census. Prior service, McNeel's Co., 2nd VSL. Enl. Hillsboro, Pocahontas Co., W. Va., 3/9/63 (4/1/63). Not stated if present or absent on muster-in roll dated 3/63. Ab. 1/1/64 - 2/29/64, on leave. Clothing issued 2/6/64. Ab. 9/1/64 - 10/31/64, AWOL since 9/15/64. NFR.

RIDER, JAMES R. T. (J.) - Pvt. Co. F. b.c. 1846. Enl. Hillsboro, Pocahontas Co., W. Va., 2/28/64. Ab. 1/1/64 - 2/29/64, on leave. Age 34, farmer, Huntersville, Pocahontas Co., W. Va. 1880 Census. NFR.

RIDER, JAMES W. (F.) - Pvt. Co. I. b. Bath Co., Oct. 1838. Age 23, laborer, Traveler's Repose, Pocahontas Co., W. Va. 1860 Census. Prior service, Co. I, 31st Va. Inf. History of the 31st Va. Inf. shows he transf. illegally to the 19th Va. Cav., at Winchester, 5/31/62. Enl. Huntersville, Pocahontas Co., W. Va., 3/19/63 (3/18/63). Present on muster-in roll dated 3/63. Mustered into service 3/19/63. Present 6/30/63 - 2/29/64, mounted. Evidently returned to the infantry, as he was paroled as a member of Co. I, 31st Va. Inf. Post war rosters indicate service in the 18th Va. Cav., does not appear in history. Post war farmer and resident of Dunmore, Pocahontas Co., W. Va. Age 42, farmer, Huntersville, Pocahontas Co., W. Va. 1880 Census. d. Dunmore, Pocahontas Co., W. Va., 4/1/1932. Bur. Warwick Cem., Pocahontas Co., W. Va.

RIFFE, DAVID CAMPBELL - Pvt. Co. A. b. James River, Williamsburg Dist., Greenbrier Co., 1/19/34. Not on muster rolls. Cpd. during the war and was confined at Camp Chase. Post war resident of Williamsburg Dist., Greenbrier Co., W. Va. Member of David S. Creigh Camp, UCV, Lewisburg, W. Va., 1895. Served as justice of the peace. Listed as Campbell B. Riffe on 6/1/1903 roster of Confed. Veterans living in Greenbrier Co., W. Va. d. Sunlight, Williamsburg Dist., Greenbrier Co., W. Va., 10/7/1909, effects of a stroke, age 75 years, 8 months and 18 days. Bur. Methodist E. Church, Williamsburg, Greenbrier Co., W. Va. "He was a kindly gentleman, well liked by all who knew him..."

RIFFLE, ANTHONY - Pvt. Co. A. b.c. 1842. Age 18, Braxton Co., W. Va. 1860 Census. Served in Co. A, 3rd VSL. Post war rosters only, which show he deserted 2/1/63. NFR.

RIFFLE, BENJAMIN - Pvt. Co. B. b.c. 1831. Enl. Frankfort, Greenbrier Co., W. Va., 3/7/63 (3/9/63). Not stated if present or absent on muster-in roll dated 3/63. Present 11/1/63 - 2/29/64, detailed as wagon driver since enl. Clothing issued 11/20/63, 12/29/63 (detailed), 12/30/63 (detailed) and 6/17/64, signs by x. Employed as a teamster 11/1/63 - 11/30/63. Employed as a teamster at Warm Springs, 1/1/64 - 3/31/64, signs by x. Ab. 9/1/64 - 10/31/64, $100 enl. bounty due; detailed in QM Dept. Paroled at Charleston, W. Va., 5/10/65. Desc.: age 34, 5'11, dark comp., black hair, black eyes and brown whiskers. Post war resident of Braxton Co., W. Va. Age 50, farmer, Salt Lick Dist., Braxton Co., W. Va. 1880 Census. Brother of Isaac Riffle. NFR.

RIFFLE, EDWARD R. - 1st Corp. Co. B. b. Braxton Co., W. Va., c. 1837. Age 23, farmer, Braxton Co., W. Va. 1860 Census. Prior service, Spriggs' Co., 3rd VSL. Cpd. Braxton Co., W. Va., 6/8/62. Confined at the Atheneum Prison, 6/18/62. Desc.: age 23, 5'11_", dark comp., brown hair and brown eyes. Occ. farmer, residing in Braxton Co., W. Va. Transf. to Camp Chase, 6/25/62. Enl. Frankfort, Greenbrier Co., W. Va., 3/9/63. POW record shows his enl. as Pocahontas Co., W. Va., 3/63. Not stated if present or absent on muster-in roll dated 3/63. Present, 1st Corp., 11/1/63 - 2/29/64, had his own horse. Clothing issued 4/21/64 and 6/17/64. Ab., 1st Corp., 9/1/64 - 10/31/64, deserted 8/18/64. Reported at Beverly, W. Va., 10/25/64. Confined at Clarksburg, W. Va., where he took the oath of allegiance and was released, 10/29/64. Desc.: age 28, 6', fair comp., light hair and brown eyes. Occ. farmer, residing in Braxton Co., W. Va. Age 45, farmer, Salt Lick Dist., Braxton Co., W. Va. 1880 Census. NFR.

RIFFLE, ISAAC - Pvt. Co. A. b.c. 1833. Served in Co. A, 3rd VSL. Post war rosters only, which show he deserted 2/1/63. Age 47, farmer, Kanawha Dist., Braxton Co., W. Va. 1880 Census. Brother of Benjamin Riffle. NFR.

RIGHT (WRIGHT), GEORGE W. - 2nd Corp. Co. K. b. Kanawha Co., W. Va., c. 1823. Age 37, farmer, Calhoun Co., W. Va. 1860 Census. Enl. Frankfort, Greenbrier Co., W. Va., 3/20/63. Not stated if present or absent on muster-in roll dated 3/63, 2nd Corp. NFR.

RIGHTER, JOHN - Capt. Co. D. b. 1829. Enl. Williamsburg, Greenbrier Co., W. Va., 3/8/63. Appointed Capt., 3/9/63. Not stated if present or absent on muster-in roll dated 3/63, Capt., commanding co. Mentioned for "distinguished conduct" at Beverly, 7/63, by Col. W. L. Jackson in his report. Rumored to be in Harrison Co., W. Va., recruiting, 3/64, and has gathered about 80 men. Ab. 10/25/64, POW, for the last 14 months. Confined at Wheeling, W. Va., 11/8/64, rumored to have been turned over to W. Va. Civil Authorities and is being treated cruelly. Ab. 12/15/64, POW, since 4/64. Cpd. Harrison Co., W. Va., 4/3/65. Sent to Cumberland, Md., then to Wheeling, W. Va. Confined at the Atheneum Prison, 4/5/65. Desc.: age 35, 5'8", dark comp., black hair and dark eyes. Occ. farmer, residing in Marion Co., W. Va. Escaped 7/18/65, charge with being a spy. Paroled at Clarksburg, W. Va., 8/8/65. Desc.: age 37, 5'8", dark comp., black hair and dark eyes. Post war rosters show him as a resident of Marion Co., W. Va. d. Marion Co., W. Va., 1911. Bur. Righter Family Plot, n. Shinnston, W. Va. Also as being bur. Martin Cem., Grant Dist., Marion Co., W. Va.

RIGHTER, PETER B. - Pvt. Co. D. "...well to do farmer and grazier, lived in a handsome residence on Coon's Run about four miles from Shinnston just over the Marion County line." His home was used as a headquarters for those favoring secession. His home and outbuildings were burned 6/22/61. Prior service, VSL. Cpd. Marion Co., W. Va., 5/5/62. Confined at the Atheneum Prison, 5/6/62. Transf. to Camp Chase, 6/15/62. Confined at Camp Chase, 6/25/62, "Bad Secesh & guerrilla leader." Desc.: age 56, 5'10", ruddy comp., gray hair, blue eyes and gray whiskers. Occ. farmer, residing in Marion Co., W. Va. Paroled for exchange and sent to Vicksburg, Miss. Arrived at Vicksburg, Miss., 9/11/62. Exchanged at Aiken's Landing, 11/16/62 (note in file shows his name cancelled). Enl. Williamsburg, Greenbrier Co., W. Va., 3/8/63. Not stated if present or absent on muster-in roll dated 3/63. Post war resident of Marion Co., W. Va. NFR.

RILEY, JONATHAN GORDON - Capt. Co. D. Prior service, Imboden's Brigade. Enl. Williamsburg, Greenbrier Co., W. Va., 3/8/63. States on 1/24/64 that he had been with Jackson's command since 9/63. Not stated if present or absent on muster-in roll dated 3/63, Pvt. Appointed Capt., 4/11/63, to rank from 2/26/63. Accepted the appointment 4/19/63. Authorized to raise a co. within enemy lines, 4/11/63. Wd. Bulltown, Braxton Co., W. Va., 10/13/63, left leg and left hand. Lost the forefinger of his left hand, amputated at the first knuckle joint near the hand. The remaining fingers are drawn down into his hand and he is unable to raise them. Authorization to raise a co. expired by limitation (SO No. 4, AIGO, 1/64). Has the commission of a Capt. and belongs to Co. D, but has not been present since last fall. Stated on 1/24/64 that he does not wish to remain in the active field of service, but does not wish to leave the service entirely. Recommended by members of the Va. Legislature for the position of traveling agent for the Gov't. as an Ordnance Officer, 1/29/64. Col. W. L. Jackson likewise recommended him for a position out of the field, and wrote "He is intelligent and trustworthy." Ab. 2/64, wd. on leave at Staunton and Churchville. Assigned to duty in the Ordnance Dept., 3/11/64, being disabled for field service. "He is a great soldier." In Richmond 3/28/64 - 4/30/64. NFR.

ROACH, SAMUEL J. (D.) - Pvt. Co. D and E. Not on muster rolls. Prior service, Luenburg Cav., deserted. Arrested by Maj. Lady's command, and sent to Staunton, 6/14/63, for sealing. Sent to Richmond, 6/17/63, to be confined in Castle Thunder. Adm. Gen. Hosp. No. 13, 6/19/63, epilepsy, listed as a member of Co. E. Transf. to Castle Thunder, 6/22/63. Post Office listed as Pleasant Grove. Adm. Gen. Hosp. No. 13, 6/27/63, hysteria, listed as a member of Co. D. Transf. to Castle Thunder, 7/7/63. Served in Co. K, 20th Va. Cav. NFR.

ROADS, GEORGE W. - Pvt. Co. E. Enl. Gilmer Co., W. Va., 10/8/64. Ab. 10/31/63 - 10/31/64, enl. bounty due; new recruit, on horse detail, time now expired. Wd., date and place not stated. Adm. CSA Gen. Hosp., Charlottesville, 4/22/65, vulnus sclopeticum. Paroled at Farmville, 4/27/65, as a member of Co. A. Name appears on a list of POW's at US Hosp., Farmville, 4/65 - 6/15/65. Adm. US Hosp., Farmville, 5/11/65, vulnus sclopeticum, right shoulder joint. DOW. Farmville, 6/3/65. Bur. Hosp. Cem., Farmville.

ROBERTS, ANDREW J. - Pvt. Co. A. Served in Co. A, 3rd VSL. Post war rosters only, which show he deserted 12/20/62, gone to Ohio. NFR.

ROBERTS, JOHN E. - Pvt. Co. A. Prior service, Co. A, 3rd VSL. Enl. Williamsburg, Greenbrier Co., W. Va., 3/1/63. Not stated if present or absent on muster-in roll dated 3/63. Transf. to Lurty's Batty., from the 3rd VSL by Capt. Downs, 10/1/63. Served in Co. F, 20th Va. Cav. d. Columbus, O. Bur. Camp Chase Confederate Cem.

ROBERTS, WILLIAM H. (J.) - Pvt. Co. A. b.c. 1841. Prior service, Co. A, 3rd VSL. Deserted 12/20/62, gone to Ohio. Not on muster rolls. Cpd. Preston Co., W. Va., 7/1/63. Confined at the Atheneum Prison, 7/2/63. Desc.: age 22, 5'10", dark comp., black hair and blue eyes. Occ. farmer, residing in Greenbrier Co., W. Va. Transf. to Camp Chase, 8/8/63. Confined at Camp Chase, 8/11/63. Desired to take the oath of allegiance, 6/10/64. Took the oath and was released by order of the Sec. of War, 4/19/65. NFR.

ROBERTSON, GEORGE W. - 2nd Lt. Co. G. b.c. 1844. Enl. Frankfort, Greenbrier Co., W. Va., 3/12/63 (4/1/63). Not stated if present or absent on muster-in roll dated 3/63, 2nd Sgt. Clothing issued, 3/1/64, 7/64 and 8/64. Present, 3rd Lt., 9/1/64 - 10/31/64. Wd. Rappahannock, 12/5/64. In Harrisonburg Gen. Hosp., 12/64. Ab. 12/15/64, wd. Adm. Depot Field Hosp., Winchester, 5/15/64, gunshot wd., right leg, minnie ball. Transf. to Gen. Hosp., 5/29/65. Cpd. Crab Bottom, Highland Co., Md., 5/30/65, gunshot wd., right leg, pistol bullet. Treated by simple dressing. Transf. to Gen. Hosp., 6/5/65, age 21. Paroled at Staunton, 5/10/65, as a 2nd Lt. Desc.: age 21, 5'10", light comp., red hair and blue eyes. NFR.

ROBERTSON, JOHN S. - Pvt. Co. E. b. Dinwiddie Co., c. 1834. Age 26, blacksmith, Gilmer Co., W. Va. 1860 Census. Enl. Gilmer Co., W. Va., 6/15/63. Wd. Beverly, W. Va., 7/63, arm, while on a raid with Maj. D. Boston Stewart. Present 10/31/63 - 10/31/64, not mounted; wagoner for the brigade. Clothing issued 3/1/64, 4/11/64, 6/17/64, 7/6/64 and 3rd Qr. 1864. NFR.

ROBINSON, D. H. - Pvt. Co. E. Enl. Frankfort, Greenbrier Co., W. Va., 3/12/63. Not stated if present or absent on muster-in roll dated 3/63. NFR.

ROBINSON, JAMES - Pvt. Co. C. Prior service, Co. D, 3rd VSL. Enl. Frankfort, Greenbrier Co., W. Va., 3/15/63. Not stated if present or absent on muster-in roll dated 3/63. Ab. 1/1/63 - 4/1/63, deserted 9/18/62. NFR.

ROBINSON, JOHN H. - Pvt. Co. A. Served in Co. A, 3rd VSL. Post war rosters only, which show he was cpd. 12/24/62. NFR.

ROBINSON, MARSHALL - Pvt. Co. H. No enl. data listed. Probably enl. Frankfort, Greenbrier Co., W. Va., 3/19/63. Not stated if present or absent on muster-in roll dated 3/63. NFR.

ROBINSON, SMITH D. (D. SMITH) - Pvt. Co. D. b. Barbour Co., W. Va., c. 1835. POW records show him as enl. Taylor Co., 5/61. Resident of Taylor Co., W. Va. Cpd., date and place not stated. Confined at the Atheneum Prison, 4/11/62. Transf. to Camp Chase, 5/5/62. Exchanged. Enl. Williamsburg, Greenbrier Co., W. Va., 3/8/63. Not stated if present or absent on muster-in roll dated 3/63. Clothing issued, 2/7/64, 4/1/64 and 6/17/64. Cpd. Crab Bottom, Highland Co., 12/17/64 (12/18/64). Sent to Clarksburg, W. Va. Confined at Clarksburg, W. Va. Desc.: age 29, 6', dark comp., brown hair and gray eyes. Occ. brickmason, residing in Barbour Co., W. Va. Transf. to Wheeling, W. Va., 12/24/64. Confined at the Atheneum Prison, 12/25/64. Desc.: age 28, 6', fair comp., dark hair and gray eyes. Occ. brickmason, residing in Barbour Co., W. Va. Transf. to Camp Chase, 12/27/64. Confined at Camp Chase, 12/28/64, desires to take the oath of allegiance. Took the oath of allegiance and was released, 6/12/65. Desc.: age 28, 5'11_", fair comp., dark hair and gray eyes. Post war rosters show service in the 25th Va. Inf. Age 43, farmer, Philippi, Barbour Co., W. Va. 1880 Census. NFR.

ROBISON, ANDREW D. - Pvt. Co. D. b. Va., c. 1843. Age 17, farmhand, Collierstown, Rockbridge Co. 1860 Census. Not on muster rolls. Cpd. Beverly, W. Va., 2/14/64. Confined at the Atheneum Prison, 2/21/64. Desc.: age 21, 5'9", florid comp., dark hair and blue eyes. Occ. farmer, residing in Rockbridge Co. Took the oath of allegiance and was released, 2/22/64. NFR.

ROCKE, FLOYD G. - Capt. AQM. Prior service, AQM, 3rd VSL. Appointed Capt. and AQM, 5/28/63, to rank from 5/2/63. This appointment was confirmed 2/17/64. Present F&S MR 9/1/63 - 10/31/63. Ab. F&S MR 11/1/63 - 12/31/63, on sick leave. Mentioned as AQM of 19th and 20th Va. Cav., 12/10/63. Still with the 19th Va. Cav. as AQM, 3/31/64. Recommended to be assigned as AQM for Jackson's Brigade, 9/16/64, by Col. W. L. Jackson. Ab. F&S MR 9/1/64 - 10/31/64, acting QM for Jackson's Cav. Brigade. Performing duty as Brigade AQM, 11/7/64. NFR.

ROCKMAN, J. W. - Pvt. Co. I. Not on muster rolls. Adm. Gen. Hosp. No. 9, 10/6/64. Sent to Camp Lee, 10/7/64. NFR.

RODGERS (ROGERS), JAMES S. (L.) Jr. - Pvt. Co. F. b. 1/1/31. Age 29, farmer, Mill Point, Pocahontas Co., W. Va. 1860 Census. Prior service, McNeel's Co., 2nd VSL. Enl. Hillsboro, Pocahontas Co., W. Va., 3/9/63. Not stated if present or absent on muster-in roll dated 3/63. Age 49, farmer, Edray, Pocahontas Co., W. Va. 1880 Census. NFR.

ROGERS (ROGGERS), CHARLES L. - Pvt. Co. K. b.c. 1832. Resident of Braxton Co., W. Va. Arrested and confined by 3/15/62. Charged with being a secessionist and rebel aider. Enl. Frankfort, Greenbrier Co., W. Va., 3/20/63. Not stated if present or absent on muster-in roll dated 3/63. Clothing issued 3/25/64, as a member of Capt. A. J. Chewning's Scouts. Paroled at Charleston, W. Va., 5/10/65, as a member of Co. H. Desc.: age 28, 6', light comp., brown hair, blue eyes and sandy whiskers. Age 47, farmer, Otter Dist., Braxton Co., W. Va. 1880 Census. NFR.

ROGERS, JAMES - Corp. Co. H. b.c. 1845. Enl. Frankfort, Greenbrier Co., W. Va., 3/19/63 (Clay Co., W. Va., 4/1/63). Not stated if present or absent on muster-in roll dated 3/63. Clothing issued, 3/1/64, 6/17/64, 7/64 and 8/64, signed by x. Present, Corp., 9/1/64 - 10/31/64, has a serviceable horse. Paroled at Charleston, W. Va., 5/9/65. Desc.: age 20, 5'9", fair comp., dark hair and dark eyes. Age 36, farmer, Henry Dist., Clay Co., W. Va. 1880 Census. NFR.

ROGERS, JARED - Pvt. Co. D. b.c. 1830. Enl. Williamsburg, Greenbrier Co., W. Va., 3/8/63. Not stated if present or absent on muster-in roll dated 3/63. Employed as a teamster 11/1/63 - 11/30/63. Employed as a teamster at Warm Springs, 1/1/64 - 2/29/64. Served in Co. A, 20th Va. Cav. Age 51, farmer, Fetterman, Taylor Co., W. Va. 1880 Census, listed as Jarret Rogers. Post war resident of Taylor Co., W. Va., over age 80 in 1911. NFR.

ROGERS, JOHN - Pvt. Co. A. Not on muster rolls. Post war rosters show he was from Calhoun Co., W. Va. d. Columbus, O. Bur. Camp Chase Confederate Cem. NFR.

ROGERS, JOSEPH W. - Pvt. Co. H. b. Braxton Co., W. Va., c. 1837. Age 23, farmer, Gilmer Co., W. Va. 1860 Census. Enl. Frankfort, Greenbrier Co., W. Va., 3/19/63. Not stated if present or absent on muster-in roll dated 3/63. Served in Co. I, 20th Va. Cav. NFR.

ROGERS, ROBERT MARION - Pvt. Co. A. Prior service, Co. A, 3rd VSL. Enl. Williamsburg, Greenbrier Co., W. Va., 3/1/63. Not stated if present or absent on muster-in roll dated 3/63. Served in Co. H, 20th Va. Cav. Brother in US service. NFR.

ROGERS, WILLIAM - Pvt. Co. B and K. Enl. Frankfort, Greenbrier Co., W. Va., 3/7/63. Not stated if present or absent on muster-in roll dated 3/63. Enl. in Co. K, at Frankfort, Greenbrier Co., W. Va., 3/20/63. Not stated if present or absent on muster-in roll dated 3/63. NFR.

ROLLINS, GEORGE - Pvt. Co. H. Enl. Frankfort, Greenbrier Co., W. Va., 3/19/63 (Clay Co., W. Va., 5/1/63). Not stated if present or absent on muster-in roll dated 3/63. Clothing issued 3/4/64. Ab. 9/1/64 - 10/31/64, AWOL. NFR.

ROLLINS, HARRISON C. - Pvt. Co. A. Prior service, Co. A, 3rd VSL. Cpd., tried as a guerrilla, and was sentenced to death at Clarksburg, W. Va., by 6/25/62. Told Federals he was John S. Spriggs. Confined at Wheeling, W. Va. 8/3/62. Enl. Williamsburg, Greenbrier Co., W. Va., 3/1/63. Not stated if present or absent on muster-in roll dated 3/63. Post war resident of Greenbrier Co., W. Va. NFR.

ROLLINS, HENRY - Pvt. Co. H. b.c. 1846. Enl. Clay Co., W. Va., 5/1/63. Clothing issued 3/5/64 and 6/17/64. Present 9/1/64 - 10/31/64. Paroled 5/9/65, signs by x. Desc.: age 19, 5'9", light comp., brown hair and black eyes. Paroled again at Charleston, 7/15/65, signs by x. Desc.: age 19, 5'7", light comp., dark hair and blue eyes, a resident of Clay Co., W. Va. NFR.

ROLLINS, MOSES - Pvt. Co. ?. Post war rosters only, which show he was from Ritchie Co., W. Va. Brother of William and Wilson Rollins. Served in Co. H, 20th Va. Cav. Age 37, laborer, West Union Dist., Ritchie Co., W. Va. 1880 Census. NFR.

ROLLINS, WILLIAM - Pvt. Co. ?. Post war rosters only, which show he was from Ritchie Co., W. Va. Brother of Moses and Wilson Rollins. Post war rosters show service in Co. H, 20th Va. Cav. Age 34, farm laborer, Clay Dist., Ritchie Co., W. Va. 1880 Census. NFR.

ROLLINS, WILSON - Pvt. Co. ?. Post war rosters only, which show he was from Ritchie Co., W. Va. Post war rosters show service Co. H, 20th Va. Cav. Brother of Moses and William Rollins. Age 39, farmer, North Grant Dist., Ritchie Co., W. Va. 1880 Census. Bur. Victory Ridge Cem., Harrisville, Ritchie Co., W. Va.

ROMAINE (ROMINE), MATHEW M. "Mack" - Pvt. Co. H. b.c. 1845. Not on muster rolls. Cpd. Greenbrier Co., W. Va., 3/28/65 (4/4/65; Kanawha Co., 4/3/65). Sent to Cumberland, Md., then to Wheeling, W. Va. Confined at the Atheneum Prison, 4/11/65. Desc.: age 20, 5'7", dark comp., brown hair and gray eyes. Occ. farmer, residing in Wood Co., W. Va. Transf. to Camp Chase, 4/13/65. Confined at Camp Chase, 4/15/65. Took the oath of allegiance and was released, 6/13/65. Desc.: age 20, 5'9 3/4", dark comp., light hair and gray eyes, a resident of Wood Co., W. Va. Post war resident of Wood Co., W. Va. and Randolph Co., Ark., where he drew a pension. d. Randolph Co., Ark., 11/26/1924.

ROSE, TOBIAS - Pvt. Co. C. b.c. 1846. Not on muster rolls. Also listed as being in Co. F. Cpd. Webster Co., W. Va., 2/8/64 (1/8/64). Confined at the Atheneum Prison, 2/21/64. Desc.: age 18, 5'7", fair comp., dark hair and blue eyes. Occ. farmer, residing in Webster Co., W. Va. Transf. to Camp Chase, 3/4/64. Confined at Camp Chase, 3/5/64. Transf. to Pt. Lookout, 3/26/65, to be exchanged. Confined at Pt. Lookout, 3/31/65. Age 33, farmer, Fork Lick, Webster Co., W. Va. 1880 Census. NFR.

ROSENCRANZ, LEONIDAS - Pvt. Co. K. Enl. Frankfort, Greenbrier Co., W. Va., 3/20/63. Not stated if present or absent on muster-in roll dated 3/63. NFR.

ROSS, HENRY F. - Pvt. Co. H. Enl. Bath Co., 2/1/63 (2/1/64?). Clothing issued, 6/17/64, 7/64 and 8/64. Ab. 9/1/64 - 10/31/64, wd.(date and place not given), now in hosp.; $50 enl. bounty due. DOD. Hosp., 1/25/65, erysip. super. NFR.

ROUZEE (ROUSY), EDWARD - Pvt. Co. F. Enl. Hightown, Highland Co., 3/18/64. Present 9/1/64 - 10/31/64, enl. bounty due; Acting Ass't. Surgeon. Post war doctor and resident of Hanover Co. NFR.

ROWSIE, LEM - Pvt. Co. F. Post war rosters only. NFR.

ROWAN (ROAN), HEZEKIAH Z. - Pvt. Co. C. Prior service, Co. D, 3rd VSL. Enl. Frankfort, Greenbrier Co., W. Va., 3/15/63 (Pocahontas Co., W. Va., 4/1/63). Not stated if present or absent on muster-in roll dated 3/63. Present 1/1/63 - 4/1/63, has one horse. Horse KIA. Droop Mtn., W. Va., 11/6/63, was paid $500. Present 12/31/63 - 8/31/64, has one horse. Clothing issued 2/2/64, 2/25/64 and 6/17/64. Ab. 9/1/64 - 10/31/64, $100 enl. bounty due; detailed with horses in Bath Co. since 7/25/64, reported 11/4/64; has one horse. Cpd. Wirt Co., W. Va., 3/11/65. Sent to Cumberland, Md., then to Wheeling, W. Va. Confined at the Atheneum Prison, 3/27/65. Desc.: age 22, 5'5", light comp., fair hair and hazel eyes. Occ. farmer, residing in Wirt Co., W. Va. Transf. to Camp Chase, 3/28/65. Confined at Camp Chase, 3/29/65, charged with being a guerilla. Took the oath of allegiance and was released, 6/13/65. Desc.: age 22, 5'6", florid comp., dark hair and hazel eyes, a resident of Wirt Co., W. Va. Served in Co. F, 20th Va. Cav. NFR.

RUCKMAN, CHARLES B. - Pvt. Co. F. b.c. 1838. Member Mill Point Patrol, Pocahontas Co., W. Va., 5/61. Prior service, Co. G, 31st Va. Inf. and McNeel's Co., 2nd VSL. Left the 31st 11/5/62. Enl. Hillsboro, Pocahontas Co., W. Va., 3/9/63 (4/1/63). Not stated if present or absent on muster-in roll dated 3/63. Cpd. Pocahontas Co., W. Va., 12/12/63. Confined at the Atheneum Prison, 12/24/63. Desc.: age 25, 5'11", fair comp., gray hair and light eyes. Occ. Schoolteacher, residing in Pocahontas Co., W. Va. Transf. to Camp Chase, 12/26/63. Confined at Camp Chase, 12/27/63. Ab. 1/1/64 - 2/29/64, in the hands of the enemy. Transf. to Ft. Delaware, 3/14/64. Confined at Ft. Delaware, 3/17/64. Ab. 9/1/64 - 10/31/64, cpd. 12/12/63; enl. bounty due. Took the oath of allegiance and was released, 6/22/65. Desc.: age ?, 5'11", fair comp., brown hair and brown eyes, a resident of Pocahontas Co., W. Va. d. Ft. McHenry, Md. by 7/7/65. Bur. Loudon Park Cem., Confederate Section, Baltimore, Md. Brother of J. W. Ruckman.

RUCKMAN, JAMES WATTS - Pvt. Co. F. b. Pendleton (Pocahontas) Co., W. Va., c. 1826. Age 34, farmer, Mill Point, Pocahontas Co., W. Va. 1860 Census. Member Mill Point Patrol, Pocahontas Co., W. Va., 5/61. Enl. Hillsboro, Pocahontas Co., W. Va., 7/1/63. Cpd. Pocahontas Co., W. Va., 12/11/63. Confined at the Atheneum Prison, 12/24/63. Desc.: age 38, 6', dark comp., black hair and hazel eyes. Occ. farmer, residing in Pocahontas Co., W. Va. Transf. to Camp Chase, 12/26/63. Confined at Camp Chase, 12/27/63. Ab. 1/1/64 - 2/29/64, in the hands of the enemy. Transf. to Ft. Delaware, 3/14/64. Confined at Ft. Delaware, 3/17/64. Ab. 9/1/64 - 10/31/64, cpd. 12/11/63; enl. bounty due. Paroled for exchange 9/28/64. Sent to Aiken's Landing, 9/30/64. Exchanged at Varina, 10/5/64. Clothing issued 10/12/64, as a paroled prisoner, listed as a member of Co. I. Post war rosters show him as a Corp. Age 56, farmer, Little Levels, Pocahontas Co., W. Va. 1880 Census. d. Camp Lee Post Hosp., near Richmond, 10/16/64 (10/17/64), chronic diarrhoea, age 42. Bur. Hollywood Cem., Richmond, grave V-264. Moved to the Ruckman Cem. Brother of Charles B. Ruckman.

RUCKMAN, SIDNEY B. - Pvt. Co. F. b.c. 1835. Age 25, farmer, Academy, Pocahontas Co., W. Va. 1860 Census. Member Mill Point Patrol, Pocahontas Co., W. Va., 5/61. Prior service, Co. G, 31st Va. Inf. Enl. Hillsboro, Pocahontas Co., W. Va., 7/1/63. Present 1/1/64 - 2/29/64. Clothing issued 2/6/64. Present 9/1/64 - 10/31/64, enl. bounty due. Paroled at Staunton, 5/1/65. Desc.: age 28, 6', light comp.; light hair and gray eyes, a resident of Pocahontas Co., W. Va. NFR.

RUCKMAN, WILLIAM - Pvt. Co. C. Not on muster rolls. Cpd. Romney, W. Va., 3/10/63 (3/9/63). Held at Mechanicsburg Gap until 4/14/63. Desc.: age 19, 5'5", light comp., light hair and brown eyes. Confined at Ft. McHenry, 4/17/63. Transf. to Ft. Monroe, 4/19/63, and confined there the same day. Paroled 4/19/63, to be exchanged, and sent to City Point. NFR.

RUFFNER, HENRY DANIEL - Capt. Co. G. b. 8/15/34. Age 24, farm manager, Charleston, W. Va. 1860 Census. Prior service, Co. H, 22nd Va. inf. Enl. Frankfort, Greenbrier Co., W. Va., 3/12/63. Not stated if present or absent on muster-in roll dated 3/63, Capt., commanding Co. Appointed Capt. 3/12/63. Received "honorable mention" from Lt. Col. W. P. Thompson in his report of the battle of Droop Mtn., W. Va., 11/6/63. Detailed for duty on a Gen. Court Martial, Warm Springs, Bath Co., 2/25/64. Promoted (elected) to Major, 46th Battn. Va. Cav., 2/26/64. Served as Major of 26th Va. Cav., 1/65. Was 5'11" tall. Paroled at Charleston, W. Va., 5/10/65. Post war rosters show him as Col. Post war silver mine operator in Colo. Post war resident of Charleston, W. Va. d. Rosebud, Fla., 7/25/1925. Bur. Spring Hill Cem., Charleston, W. Va. Last member of Co. H, 22nd Va. Inf. to die.

RUFFNER, SAMUEL L. - 2nd Lt. Co. G. Resident of Illinois before the war, and came east to join the Confederacy. Enl. Frankfort, Greenbrier Co., W. Va., 3/12/63 (4/1/63). Not stated if present or absent on muster-in roll dated 3/63, Pvt. Recruiting Officer, Lexington, Rockbridge Co., 1/64, listed as Lt. 2nd Lt. by 2/64. Detailed for duty on a Gen. Court Martial, Warm Springs, Bath Co., 2/25/64, listed as a Lt. Adm. Gen. Hosp. No. 3, Lynchburg, 7/64. RTD 7/64. Present, 2nd Lt., 9/1/64 - 10/31/64. Resigned 1/14/65, feels that he is not fit to be an officer. NFR.

RUSH, WILLIAM P. - Pvt. Co. I. Enl. Huntersville, Pocahontas Co., W. Va., 2/1/64. Present 6/30/63 - 2/29/64, mounted; enl. bounty due. Ab. 2/29/64 - 8/31/64, sick. NFR.

RUTLEDGE, JOHN A. - Pvt. Co. I. Not on muster rolls. Employed as a teamster at Warm Springs, 1/1/64 - 3/31/64. Clothing issued 1/16/64, 2/7/64, and 5/1/64, signs by x. Cpd. Union, W. Va., 5/16/64. Confined at the Atheneum Prison, 5/25/64. No desc. Transf. to Camp Chase, 5/26/64. Confined at Camp Chase, 5/26/64. DOD. Camp Chase, 11/30/64, smallpox. Bur. Camp Chase Confederate Cem., grave no. 535.

SAMPSON, HARRISON - Pvt. Co. G. Enl. Frankfort, Greenbrier Co., W. Va., 3/12/63. Not stated if present or absent on muster-in roll dated 3/63. NFR.

SAVILLE, GEORGE - Pvt. Co. C. Not on muster rolls. Reference jacket only, which shows service in the 19th Va. Cav. and the 18th Va. Cav. Arrested in Hampshire Co., W. Va., 3/24/6? (year not given), listed as Co. C, 19th Va. Cav. Desc.: age 20, 5'7 3/4", dark comp., brown hair and gray eyes. Occ. farmer, residing in Hampshire Co., W. Va. NFR.

SAYRE, CHARLES - Pvt. Co. H. b.c. 1844. Not on muster rolls. Paroled at Charleston, W. Va., 5/22/65. Desc.: age 21, 5'8", dark comp., brown hair and gray eyes. NFR.

SAYRE, H. J. - Sgt. Co. H. b.c. 1843. Not on muster rolls. Paroled at Charleston, W. Va., 5/17/65. Desc.: age 22, 5'10", fair comp., brown hair and gray eyes. NFR.

SCHOOLCRAFT, E. P. - Pvt. Co. G. Enl. Frankfort, Greenbrier Co., W. Va., 3/12/63. Not stated if present or absent on muster-in roll dated 3/63. Clothing issued 2/11/64. Post war resident of Searcy Co., Ark., where he drew a pension. d. Searcy Co., Ark., 2/2/1922.

SCHOOLCRAFT, JAMES A. - Pvt. Co. G. Enl. Greenbrier Co., W. Va., 4/1/63. Employed as a courier 11/1/63 - 11/30/63, signs by x. Employed as a courier at Warm Springs, 1/1/64 - 3/31/64. Clothing issued 3/1/64 and 6/17/64, signs by x. Ab. 9/1/64 - 10/31/64, in hosp. sick. NFR.

SCHOOLCRAFT, JAMES H. - Pvt. Co. G. b.c. 1843. Enl. Frankfort, Greenbrier Co., W. Va., 3/12/63 (4/1/63). Not stated if present or absent on muster-in roll dated 3/63. Clothing issued, 4/21/64 and 7/10/64, signs by x. Ab. 9/1/64 - 10/31/64, wd. (date and place not given); has a serviceable horse. Paroled at Charleston, W. Va., 5/29/65, signs by x. Desc.: age 22, 5'8", fair comp., black hair and black eyes. NFR.

SCHOONOOVA (SCHOONOVER), BENJAMIN - Pvt. Co. ?. Post war source only, which states he was KIA. Bulltown, W. Va., 10/13/63, and was from the Sand Fork of the Little Kanawha River. Name appears on post war roster of Co. I, 17th Va. Cav.

SCOTT, WILLIAM - Pvt. Co. D. b.c. 1833. Not on muster rolls. Cpd. Camp Piatt, 11/1/63. Sent to Charleston, W. Va., then to Camp Chase. Confined at Camp Chase, 5/21/63. Desc.: age 30, 6'1", light comp., brown hair and blue eyes. Took the oath of allegiance and was released, 3/19/64. NFR.

SCYOC, ABEL - 3rd Corp. Co. C. b.c. 1844. Prior service, Co. D, 3rd VSL. Enl. Frankfort, Greenbrier Co., W. Va., 3/15/63 (Pocahontas Co., W. Va., 4/1/63). Not stated if present or absent on muster-in roll dated 3/63. Present 1/1/63 - 4/1/63, has one horse. Present 12/31/63 - 8/31/64, promoted to Corp., 2/1/64; has one horse. Clothing issued 4/21/64 and 6/17/64. Present, 3rd Corp, 9/1/64 - 10/31/64, $100 enl. bounty due; has one horse. Deserted. Surrendered at Charleston, W. Va., 3/65. Took the amnesty oath and was sent North, 3/25/65. Desc.: age 21, 5'8", fair comp., dark hair and blue eyes. Occ. farmer, residing in Jackson Co., W. Va. NFR.

SCYOC, WILLIAM H. - Pvt. Co. C. Enl. Jefferson Co., W. Va., 7/1/64. Present 12/31/63 - 8/31/64, not mounted. DOD. 9/1/64, place not stated. NFR.

SEAMON (SEAMAN), DAVID W. - Pvt. Co. C. Prior service, Co. D, 3rd VSL. Enl. Frankfort, Greenbrier Co., W. Va., 3/15/63 (Pocahontas Co., W. Va., 4/1/63). Not stated if present or absent on muster-in roll dated 3/63. Present 1/1/63 - 4/1/63, has one horse. Employed as a blacksmith 11/11/63 - 11/30/63. Present 12/31/63 - 8/31/64, has one horse; on daily duty as blacksmith for the Reg't. Employed as a blacksmith at Warm Springs, 1/1/64 - 3/31/64. Clothing issued 1/17/64 (detailed blacksmith), 4/30/64 and 7/6/64. Present 9/1/64 - 10/31/64, $100 enl. bounty due; on daily duty as blacksmith for the Reg't.; has one horse. NFR.

SEARS, JOHN - Pvt. Co. A. Post war rosters only, which show he was from Greenbrier Co., W. Va. NFR.

SEITZ, EMANUEL (MANUEL) - Pvt. Co. C. Enl. Pocahontas Co., W. Va., 5/15/63. Present 12/31/63 - 8/31/64, has one horse. Clothing issued 2/25/64, 4/30/64, 5/26/64, 6/17/64, 7/64 and 8/64. Present 9/1/64 - 10/31/64, $100 enl. bounty due; has one horse. Post war resident of Wood Co., W. Va. NFR.

SEVY, AARON R. - Pvt. Co. A. b.c. 1846. Not on muster rolls. POW record shows he enl. at Warm Springs, in 1863. Paroled at Lewisburg, W. Va., 4/27/65. Desc.: age 19, 5'8", fair comp., sandy hair and blue eyes, a miller. NFR.

SHAFER (SHAVER), JOHN - Pvt. Co. C. Prior service, Co. D, 3rd VSL. Enl. Frankfort, Greenbrier Co., W. Va., 3/15/63. Not stated if present or absent on muster-in roll dated 3/63. Ab. 1/1/63 - 4/1/63, deserted 3/18/63; has one horse. NFR.

SHARER, OCTAVUS - Pvt. Co. D. b.c. 1849. Not on muster rolls. Paroled at Clarksburg, W. Va., 4/30/65, signs by x. Desc.: age 16, 5'8", fair comp., dark hair and blue eyes. NFR.

SHARP, ANDREW - Pvt. Co. F. b.c. 1819. Age 41, farmer, Huntersville, Pocahontas Co., W. Va. 1860 Census. Post war rosters only. Age 61, farmer, Huntersville, Pocahontas Co., W. Va. 1880 Census. NFR.

SHARP, GEORGE B. - Pvt. Co. A. b. Pocahontas Co., W. Va., c. 1833. Age 27, farmer, Thorny Creek, Pocahontas Co., W. Va. 1860 Census. Resident of Knapps Creek, Pocahontas Co., W. Va. Prior service, 2nd Co. I, 25th Va. Inf. Enl. Huntersville, Pocahontas Co., W. Va., 2/1/63 (3/18/63). Ab. on muster-in roll dated 3/63, AWOL. Ab. 6/30/63 - 2/29/64, DOD. Camp Chase by 11/1/63; not mounted; deserter. Cpd. Warm Springs, Bath Co., 8/26/63 (8/24/63). Confined at the Atheneum Prison, 9/6/63. Desc.: age 30, 6' 3 _", florid comp., red hair and blue eyes. Occ. farmer, residing in Pocahontas Co., W. Va. Transf. to Camp Chase, 9/7/63. Confined at Camp Chase, 9/8/63. DOD. Camp Chase, 9/28/63. Bur. Camp Chase Confederate Cem.

SHARP, HENRY D. - Pvt. Co. F. b. Pocahontas Co., W. Va., 7/4/31. Farmer, age 24 (1855). Post war rosters only, which show he was KIA. on the Elk River (no date), Pocahontas Co., W. Va. Post war farmer and resident of Pocahontas Co., W. Va. d. Driscol, W. Va., 2/20/1910, age 78. Age 48, farmer, Huntersville, Pocahontas Co., W. Va. 1880 Census. NFR.

SHARP, JAMES L. (S.) - Pvt. Co. F. b. Pocahontas Co., W. Va., c. 1820. Age 40, farmer, Mill Point, Pocahontas Co., W. Va. 1860 Census. Enl. Hillsboro, Pocahontas Co., W. Va., 9/1/63. Ab. 1/1/64 - 2/29/64, sick. Ab. 9/1/64 - 10/31/64, cpd. 9/64; enl. bounty due. Cpd. Pocahontas Co., W. Va., 9/21/64. Confined at the Atheneum Prison, 10/64. Desc.: age 44, 5'8", sallow comp., light hair and blue eyes. Occ. farmer, residing in Pocahontas Co., W. Va. Transf. to Camp Chase, 10/6/64. Confined at Camp Chase, 10/7/64, desires to take the oath of allegiance. DOD. Camp Chase, 12/9/64. Bur. Camp Chase Confederate Cem., grave no. 735 (725).

SHARP, LINDSAY (LANDSAY) H. - Pvt. Co. I. b.c. 1826. Age 34, farmer, Thorny Creek, Pocahontas Co., W. Va. 1860 Census. Enl. Huntersville, Pocahontas Co., W. Va., 1/21/64. Ab. 6/30/63 - 2/29/64, on furlough; not mounted; enl. bounty due. Ab. 2/29/64 - 8/31/64, sick. Ab. 9/1/64 - 10/31/64, AWOL since 8/8/64. Age 53, farmer, Huntersville, Pocahontas Co., W. Va. 1880 Census. NFR.

SHARP, THORNTON F. - Pvt. Co. D. b. Harrison Co., W. Va., c. 1827. Enl. Williamsburg, Greenbrier Co., W. Va., 3/8/63. Not stated if present or absent on muster-in roll dated 3/63. Served in Co. B, 20th Va. Cav. Post war resident of Marion Co., W. Va. Age 53, farmer, Lincoln School Dist., Marion Co., W. Va. 1880 Census. NFR.

SHEETS, HENRY - Pvt. Co. I. b. Pocahontas Co., W. Va., 3/12/30. Age 29, farmer, Greenbank, Pocahontas Co., W. Va. 1860 Census. Prior service, Co. G, 31st Va. Inf. Enl. Huntersville, Pocahontas Co., W. Va., 2/9/63 (3/18/63). Present on muster-in roll dated 3/63. Mustered into service 3/19/63. Ab. 6/30/63 - 2/29/64, at home sick; mounted. Post war farmer and resident of Pocahontas Co., W. Va. Hauled freight from Staunton to Pocahontas Co., W. Va. Brother of William R. Sheets. Age 49, farmer, Green Banks, Pocahontas Co., W. Va. 1880 Census. d. Pocahontas Co., W. Va., 1/28/1906, age 76.

SHEETS, WILLIAM R. - Pvt. Co. F. b.c. 1844. Age 16, farmer, Greenbank, Pocahontas Co., W. Va. 1860 Census. Prior service, Co. F, 62nd Va. Mtd. Inf. Enl. Hillsboro, Pocahontas Co., W. Va., 4/1/63. Present 1/1/64 - 2/29/64. Present 9/1/64 - 10/31/64, enl. bounty due. Brother of Henry Sheets. Age 36, farmer, Green Banks, Pocahontas Co., W. Va. 1880 Census. NFR.

SHELTON, JAMES K. POLK - Pvt. Co. A. b. Bath Co., c. 1844. Age 15, laborer, Bath CH, Bath Co. 1860 Census. Not on muster rolls. POW record shows he enl. in Bath Co., 12/62. Cpd. Beverly, W. Va., 10/5/64. Confined at Clarksburg, W. Va. Desc.: age 20, 5'7", dark comp., dark hair and black eyes. Occ. farmer, residing in Bath Co. Took the oath of allegiance and was released, 10/8/64. NFR.

SHIFLET (SHIFFLET, SHIFLETT), NIMROD - Pvt. Co. C. b. 3/22/44 (1846). Age 14, Randolph Co., W. Va. 1860 Census. Enl. Pocahontas Co., W. Va., 4/15/63. Ab. 12/31/63 - 8/31/64, wd. near Charles Town, W. Va., 8/21/64; now at a hosp.; has one horse. Clothing issued, 2/25/64, 4/30/64 and 6/17/64, signs by x. Ab. 9/1/64 - 10/31/64, wd. near Charles Town, W. Va., 8/21/64; now at a hosp.; has one horse; enl. bounty due. Wd. Winchester, 9/19/64 (Charles Town, W. Va., 8/25/64). Cpd. Winchester, 9/19/64. Adm. USA Depot Field Hosp., Winchester, 9/19/64, vulnus sclopeticum, through right lung. Simple dressing applied. Transf. to other hosp., 10/17/64. Adm. USA Gen. Hosp., West's Building, Baltimore, 10/19/64. Wd. left chest, lung, by minnie ball. Wd. Charles Town, W. Va., 8/25/64. Sent to Gen. Hosp., Pt. Lookout, 10/27/64. Confined at Pt. Lookout, 10/29/64. Paroled at Pt. Lookout, 10/28/64. Exchanged at Venus Point, Savannah River, 11/15/64. Adm. Gen. Hosp. No. 9, 11/24/64. Furloughed 11/25/64, 30 days. Clothing issued as a paroled prisoner, 11/24/64, signs by x. Paroled at Charleston, W. Va., 5/10/65, signs by x. Desc.: age 18, 5', fair comp., light hair and blue eyes. Post war rosters show service in the 20th Va. Cav. Post war resident of Randolph Co., W. Va. Attended Confederate Reunion, Randolph Co., W. Va., 1906. Attended Gettysburg Reunion, 1913. Resident of Montross, W. Va., 1916. d. 9/25/1917. Bur. Baptist Church Cem., Montross, W. Va.

SHIFFLETT, SAMUEL McDOWELL - Pvt. Co. I. b.c. 1841. Prior service, Co. C, 5th Va. Inf. Age 21 (1861). Not on muster rolls. Cpd. Beverly, W. Va., 2/13/64. Confined at the Atheneum Prison, 2/21/64. Desc.: age 23, 5'11 3/4", fair comp., fair hair and blue eyes. Occ. farmer, residing in Augusta Co. Took the oath of allegiance and was released, 2/22/64. Post war rosters show service in Co. F. d. 8/8/1928. Bur. Summit Chapel of the Brethren, Augusta Co.

SHIFLET, SIMEON - Pvt. Co. I. b.c. 1849. Age 11, Randolph Co., W. Va. 1860 Census. Not on muster rolls. Surrendered at Buckhannon, W. Va., 5/14/65. Confined at Clarksburg, W. Va., 5/16/65. Desc.: age 16, 5'8", fair comp., light hair and blue eyes. Occ. farmer, residing in Randolph Co., W. Va. Paroled for exchange and was released, 5/17/65. NFR.

SHINABERRY (SHINEBERRY), JACOB W. - Pvt. Co. F and Co. I. b.c. 1829. Age 31, farmer, Dunmore, Pocahontas Co., W. Va. 1860 Census. Prior service, McNeel's Co., 2nd VSL. Enl. Hillsboro, Pocahontas Co., W. Va., 2/1/63 (4/1/63). Ab. on muster in roll of Co. I, dated 3/63, absent by permission. Present in Co. F, 1/1/64 - 2/29/64. Clothing issued, 2/6/64. Ab. 9/1/64 - 10/31/64, cpd. 4/28/64; enl. bounty due. Cpd. Pocahontas Co., W. Va., 4/28/64. Confined at the Atheneum Prison, 5/12/64. Desc.: age 36, 5'8", fair comp., light hair and blue eyes. Occ. farmer, residing in Pocahontas Co., W. Va. Transf. to Camp Chase, 5/13/64. Confined at Camp Chase, 5/14/64. Paroled and sent to City Point, 2/25/65, to be exchanged. Exchanged. Adm. Jackson Hosp., 3/6/65, debilitas. Furloughed 3/8/65, 30 days. Served in Co. E, 20th Va. Cav. Age 53, farmer, Edray, Pocahontas Co., W. Va. 1880 Census. NFR.

SHISLER (SCHISLER), JAMES W. - 4th Corp. Co. F. b.c. 1839. Age 21, clerk, Mt. Murphy, Pocahontas Co., W. Va. 1860 Census. Member Locust Creek Patrol, Pocahontas Co., W. Va., 5/61. Prior service, McNeel's Co., 2nd VSL. Enl. Hillsboro, Pocahontas Co., W. Va., 3/9/63 (4/1/63). Not stated if present or absent on muster-in roll dated 3/63, 4th Corp. Present, Pvt., 1/1/64 - 2/29/64. Clothing issued 2/6/64. Present 9/1/64 - 10/31/64. Paroled at Charleston, W. Va., 5/10/65. Desc.: age 26, 5', light comp., light hair and blue eyes. Post war resident of White Sulphur Dist., Greenbrier Co., W. Va. Member David S. Creigh Camp, UCV, Lewisburg, W. Va., 1895. NFR.

SHOCK, ALBERT - Pvt. Co. K. b. Gilmer Co., W. Va., c. 1846. Age 14, Gilmer Co., W. Va. 1860 Census. Not on muster rolls. Clothing issued 3/21/64, 5/26/64, 6/17/64, 7/64 and 8/64. Paroled at Charleston, W. Va., 5/11/65. Desc.: age 19, 5'9", fair comp., black hair and dark eyes. Post war resident of Calhoun Co., W. Va. NFR.

SHORT, NATHANIAL A. - Pvt. Co. D. b.c. 1846. Not on muster rolls. Cpd. Webster Co. (Pocahontas Co.), W. Va., 2/19/64. Confined at the Atheneum Prison, 2/21/64. Desc.: age 19, 5'4", dark comp., dark hair and black eyes. Occ. farmer, residing in Webster Co., W. Va. Transf. to Camp Chase, 3/4/64. Confined at Camp Chase, 3/5/64. Transf. to Ft. Delaware, 3/14/64. Confined at Ft. Delaware, 3/17/64. Took the oath of allegiance and was released, 6/7/65. Desc.: age ?, 5'2_", ruddy comp., brown hair and hazel eyes, a resident of Webster Co., W. Va. NFR.

SHOWALTER, N. K. - Pvt. Co. A. b.c. 1841. Not on muster rolls. Cpd. Preston Co., W. Va., 7/1/63. Confined at the Atheneum Prison, 7/2/63. Desc.: age 22, 6'_", light comp., red hair and gray eyes. Occ. farmer, residing in Monongahala Co., W. Va. Transf. to Camp Chase, 8/8/63. Confined at Camp Chase, 8/11/63. Took the oath of allegiance and was released, 1/14/64. NFR.

SHOWALTER, SAMUEL H. - Pvt. Co. A. b.c. 1837. Not on muster rolls. Cpd. Preston Co., W. Va., 7/1/63. Confined at the Atheneum Prison, 7/2/63. Desc.: age 26, 6'_", light comp., red hair and gray eyes. Occ. farmer, residing in Monongahala Co., W. Va. Transf. to Camp Chase, 9/14/63. Confined at Camp Chase, 9/15/63, charge with being a horse thief. Took the oath of allegiance and was released 2/13/64, by order of the Sec. of War. NFR.

SHRADER, JAMES C. - Pvt. Co. K and B. b.c. 1844. Age 16, Braxton Co., W. Va. 1860 Census. Enl. Frankfort, Greenbrier Co., W. Va., 3/20/63, in Co. K. Not stated if present or absent on muster-in roll dated 3/63. Enl. Frankfort, Greenbrier Co., W. Va., 3/9/63, in Co. B. Present 11/1/63 - 2/29/64, had one horse until 2/1/64. Clothing issued 2/11/64, 5/26/64 and 6/17/64, signs by x. Present 9/1/64 - 10/31/64, $100 enl. bounty due. Paroled at Charleston, W. Va., 5/10/65. Desc.: age 20, 5'10", fair comp., light hair and blue eyes. Listed as a deserter, taking the oath of allegiance 5/30/65, signs by x. Desc.: age 20, 5'9", fair comp., light hair and blue eyes. Occ. farmer, residing in Braxton Co., W. Va. NFR.

SHRADER, JONES C. - Pvt. Co. K. Enl. Frankfort, Greenbrier Co., W. Va., 3/20/63. Not stated if present or absent on muster-in roll dated 3/63. NFR.

SHULL, JOHN - Pvt. Co. A. b.c. 1820. Not on muster rolls. Cpd. Preston Co., W. Va., 7/1/63. Confined at the Atheneum Prison. No desc. Transf. to Camp Chase. Confined at Camp Chase, 8/11/63. Took the oath of allegiance and was released, 1/14/64, by order of the Sec. of War. Age 50, farmhand, 3rd Dist., Augusta Co. 1870 Census. d. Augusta Co., 8/23/1900, age 80. Bur. St. Michael's Church Cem.

SILCOTT, GEORGE W. - Pvt. Co. G. Capt. ACS. b. Fauquier Co., 11/29/30. Age 29, Clerk of Court, Calhoun Co., W. Va. 1860 Census. Capt. of prewar militia. Partner of Peregrine Hays in the mercantile and land business. Helped Peregrine Hays organize the "Moccasin Rangers." Became disgusted with the way the co. was acting, and returned to Arnoldsburg. Capt. Daniel Dusky ordered his arrest as a deserter. US forces arrested him, and he was confined at Camp Chase. Paroled and returned to Calhoun Co., W. Va. Prior service, Co. A, 3rd VSL. Entered Spencer, W. Va. with P. Hays under flag of truce and secured a cease fire from Col. J. C. Rathbone for 8 days so Down's men could visit their homes unmolested. Enl. Frankfort, Greenbrier Co., W. Va., 3/12/63 (Bath Co., 3/1/64). Not stated if present or absent on muster-in roll dated 3/63, Pvt. Ab. F&S MR 9/1/64 - 10/31/64, QM Sgt., on leave; $100 bond due. Acting Assistant Adjutant Gen., Jackson's Cavalry Brigade, 4/30/65. Paroled at Staunton, 5/1/65, as Capt., ACS. Desc.: age 34, 5'7_", fair comp., brown hair and hazel eyes, a resident of Calhoun Co., W. Va. Post war roster shows he was commissioned as a Capt. by Gov. John Letcher. Post war Co. Clerk, Calhoun Co., W. Va. Age 50, clerk of court, Center Dist., Calhoun Co., W. Va. 1880 Census. d. 5/6/1903. Bur. Bethlehem Cem., Calhoun Co., W. Va.

SILVIUS (SILVER), GEORGE - Pvt. Co. K. Not on muster rolls. Deserted. Reported at Gettysburg, Pa. Sent to Ft. Delaware, 7/20/64, desires to take oath. At Chambersburg, Pa., 7/22/64. Confined at Ft. Delaware, 7/?/64, from Washington, DC. Took the oath of allegiance and was released, 6/21/65, signs by x. Desc.: age ?, 5'8", dark comp., dark hair and dark eyes, a resident of Greenbrier Co., W. Va. NFR.

SIMES, GRANVILLE W. - Pvt. Co. C. b.c. 1838. Prior service, Co. D, 3rd VSL. Enl. Frankfort, Greenbrier Co., W. Va., 3/15/63. Not stated if present or absent on muster-in roll dated 3/63. Ab. 1/1/63 - 4/1/63, deserted 3/15/63; has one horse. Cpd. Clay Co., W. Va., 7/22/63. Confined at the Atheneum Prison, 8/16/63. Desc.: age 25, 6'1_", florid comp., sandy hair and gray eyes. Occ. farmer, residing in Roane Co., W. Va. Transf. to Camp Chase, 8/17/63. Confined at Camp Chase, 8/18/63. Transf. to Ft. Delaware, 2/29/64. Confined at Ft. Delaware, 3/4/64 (3/2/64). Took the oath of allegiance and was released, 6/21/65, signs by x. Desc.: age ?, 6', dark comp., dark hair and dark eyes, a resident of Jackson Co., W. Va. NFR.

SIMMONS, ADAM - Pvt. Co. I. b.c. 1832. Post war rosters only, which show he was a resident of Randolph Co., W. Va. Age 48, farmer, Middle Fork, Randolph Co., W. Va. 1880 Census. NFR.

SIMMONS, ANANIAS - Pvt. Co. E. b. 1841. Prior service, 3rd VSL. Enl. Frankfort, Greenbrier Co., W. Va., 3/12/63 (4/1/63). Not stated if present or absent on muster-in roll dated 3/63. Present 10/31/63 - 10/31/64, had his own horse since 10/20/63. Clothing issued, 3/1/64, 3/22/64 and 6/17/64. Cpd. Ritchie Co., W. Va., 4/11/65. Confined at Ciarksburg, W. Va. Desc.: age 23, 5'9", fair comp., dark hair and gray eyes. Occ. farmer, residing in Ritchie Co., W. Va. Paroled 4/22/65. Age 39, farmer, Sherman Dist., Calhoun Co., W. Va. 1880 Census. Post war resident of Sherman Dist., Calhoun Co., W. Va., age 68 in 1910. Post war roster lists him as a resident of Lewis Co., W. Va. d. 8/26/1913. Bur. Pleasant Hill Cem., Pleasant Hill, Calhoun Co., W. Va.

SIMMONS, HEZEKIAH H. - Pvt. Co. F. b.c. 1827. Age 33, farmer, Greenbank, Pocahontas Co., W. Va. 1860 Census. Prior service, McNeel's Co., 2nd VSL. Enl. Hillsboro, Pocahontas Co., W. Va., 3/9/63 (4/1/63). Not stated if present or absent on muster-in roll dated 3/63. Ab. 1/1/64 - 2/29/64, sick. Ab. 9/1/64 - 10/31/64, AWOL. NFR.

SIMMONS, JACOB - 3rd (Jr. 2nd) Lt. Co. I. b.c. 1833. Age 27, Academy, Pocahontas Co., W. Va. 1860 Census. Prior service, Co. G, 31st Va. Inf. Enl. Huntersville, Pocahontas Co., W. Va., 2/1/63 (3/18/63). Present on muster-in roll dated 3/63, Jr. 2nd Lt. Mustered into service 3/19/63. Ab. 6/30/63 - 2/29/64, on furlough. Present 2/29/64 - 8/31/64. Present 9/1/64 - 10/31/64. Ab. 12/15/64, AWOL since 12/12/64, no steps taken to have his name dropped from the rolls. Age 45, farmer, Edray, Pocahontas Co., W. Va. 1880 Census. Post war member of Moffett Poage Camp, UCV, Marlinton, W. Va. Alive 1897. NFR.

SIMMONS (SIMONDS), JAMES M. - Pvt. Co. C. Prior service, Co. D, 3rd VSL. Enl. Frankfort, Greenbrier Co., W. Va., 3/15/63. Not stated if present or absent on muster-in roll dated 3/63. Ab. 1/1/63 - 4/1/63, deserted 1/63; has one horse. NFR.

SIMMONS, JESSE W. - Pvt. Co. I. b.c. 1831. Age 29, farmer, Randolph Co., W. Va. 1860 Census. Enl. Beverly, Randolph Co., W. Va., 4/30/63. Ab. 6/30/63 - 2/29/64, new recruit, not yet reported. Reported 3/64; enl. bounty due; not mounted. Present 2/29/64 - 8/31/64. Clothing issued 3/22/64, 7/64 and 8/64, signs by x. Present 9/1/64 - 10/31/64, $100 bond due. Surrendered at Buckhannon, W. Va., 5/11/65. Confined at Clarksburg, W. Va., 5/14/65. Paroled for exchange and was released, 5/15/65. Desc.: age 34, 5'10", fair comp., dark hair and blue eyes. Occ. farmer, residing in Randolph Co., W. Va. Post war resident of Randolph Co., W. Va. Age 49, farmer, Mingo, Randolph Co., W. Va. 1880 Census. Member Gen. Pegram Camp, UCV, Valley Head, W. Va. Attended Confederate Reunion, Randolph Co., W. Va., 1906. Awarded Cross of Honor. Resident of Valley Head, W. Va., 1916. d.c. 1920. Bur. Simmons Cem., Valley Head, W. Va.

SIMMONS, JOHN - Pvt. Co. I. b. Pocahontas (Pendleton) Co., W. Va., c. 1831. Farmer, age 24 (1855). Age 30, farmer, Pocahontas Co., W. Va. 1860 Census, listed as Simons. Enl. Huntersville, Pocahontas Co., W. Va., 2/1/63 (3/18/63). Ab. on muster-in roll dated 3/63, absent by permission. Mustered into service 3/19/63. Ab. 6/30/63 - 2/29/64, relieved by enrolling officer to make shoes. Ab. 2/29/64 - 8/31/64, detailed by Capt. F. G. Rocke as a shoemaker. Ab. 9/1/64 - 10/31/64, AWOL since 9/10/64. Post war farmer and resident of Pocahontas Co., W. Va. Age 49, farmer, Edray, Pocahontas Co., W. Va. 1880 Census. d. Edray, Pocahontas Co., W. Va., 10/20/91, age 60.

SIMMONS, JONAS S. - Pvt. Co. I. b. 1842. Age 17, farmer, Randolph Co., W. Va. 1860 Census. Enl. Beverly, Randolph Co., W. Va., 4/30/63. Present 6/30/63 - 2/29/64, sick; mounted. Present 2/29/64 - 8/31/64. Clothing issued 7/64 and 8/64. Ab. 9/1/64 - 10/31/64, wd. (date and place not stated), now at a Lynchburg Hosp.; $100 bond due. Paroled at Charleston, W. Va., 5/10/65, signs by x. Desc.: age 21, 5'10", fair comp., light hair and blue eyes. Post war resident of Randolph Co., W. Va. Age 36, farmer, Mingo, Randolph Co., W. Va. 1880 Census. d. 9/19/84. Bur. Holly Bush Road Cem., Mingo, Randolph Co., W. Va.

SIMMONS, JOSEPH - Pvt. Co. ?. b.c. 1840. Age 20, Academy, Pocahontas Co., W. Va. 1860 Census. Post war rosters only, which show him as a resident of Randolph Co., W. Va. d. by 1916. NFR.

SIMMONS, THOMAS - Pvt. Co. C. Prior service, Co. D, 3rd VSL. Enl. Frankfort, Greenbrier Co., W. Va., 3/15/63. Not stated if present or absent on muster-in roll dated 3/63. Ab. 1/1/63 - 4/1/63, deserted 1/63; has one horse. NFR.

SIMPSON (SAMPSON), HARVEY G. - 1st Lt. Co. H. b.c. 1834. Prior service, Co. A, 3rd VSL. Enl. Frankfort, Greenbrier Co., W. Va., 3/19/63 (Clay Co., W. Va., 4/1/64). Not stated if present or absent on muster-in roll dated 3/63, 1st Lt. Ab. 9/1/64 - 10/31/64, AWOL since 8/5/64. Ab. 10/25/64, AWOL for 67 days, recommended to be dropped. Lt. Col. W. P. Thompson asked that Simpson be dropped from the rolls, 11/27/64, due to prolonged AWOL. Simpson left the Co. at Sharpsburg, Md., 7/6/64 or 7/7/64, came back for a short time, then went to Western Va. Ab. 12/25/64, AWOL since 7/6/64, recommended to be dropped. Dropped from the rolls, 12/29/64 (1/3/65). Deserter. Desc. 12/31/64: age 29, 5'7_", sandy comp., light hair and blue eyes, a farmer. Post war rosters show him as 1st Sgt., Co. A. NFR.

SIMPSON, THOMAS - Pvt. Co. C. b.c. 1838. Not on muster rolls. Cpd. Highland Co., 8/22/63. Confined at the Atheneum Prison, 8/30/63. Desc.: age 25, 5'10_", florid comp., dark hair and blue eyes. Occ. farmer, a resident of England. Transf. to Camp Chase, 8/31/63. Confined at Camp Chase, 9/1/63. Transf. to Rock Island, Ill., 1/22/64, desires to take the oath of allegiance and not be exchanged. Says he is a conscript and a deserter. Confined at Rock Island Prison, 1/24/64. Enl. US Navy. Sent to the Naval rendezvous at Camp Douglas, Chicago, Ill., 1/25/64. NFR.

SIMS, EDWARD J. - Pvt. Co. C. Prior service, Co. D, 3rd VSL. Enl. Frankfort, Greenbrier Co., W. Va., 3/15/63 (Pocahontas Co., W. Va., 5/15/63). Not stated if present or absent on muster-in roll dated 3/63. Present 1/1/63 - 4/1/63, has one horse. Employed as a teamster 11/1/63 - 11/30/63. Present 12/31/63 - 8/31/64, on daily duty as blacksmith; has one horse. Employed as a teamster at Warm Springs, 1/1/64 - 2/29/64, transf. Clothing issued, 11/22/63, 1/7/64 (detailed as blacksmith), 6/17/64 and 7/6/64, signs by x. Present 9/1/64 - 10/31/64, on daily duty as blacksmith; has one horse; $100 enl. bounty due. NFR.

SIMS (SIMMS), GEORGE W. - Pvt. Co. C. b.c. 1843. Age 17, laborer, Frost, Pocahontas Co., W. Va. 1860 Census. Prior service, Co. D, 3rd VSL. Enl. Frankfort, Greenbrier Co., W. Va., 3/15/63 (Pocahontas Co., W. Va., 4/1/63). Not stated if present or absent on muster-in roll dated 3/63. Present 1/1/63 - 4/1/63, has one horse. Present 12/31/63 - 8/31/64, has one horse. Present 9/1/64 - 10/31/64, has one horse; $100 enl. bounty due. Served in Co. F, 20th Va. Cav. NFR.

SINGER, CALVERT - Pvt. Co. ?. Not on muster rolls. Cpd., place and date not stated. Confined at Pt. Lookout. Transf. to Washington, DC. Transportation furnished from Washington, DC to Harrison Co., W. Va., 5/16/65. NFR.

SIPLE (SIPLES), GEORGE W. - 1st Lt. Co. F. b. Augusta Co., c. 1829. Resident of Highland Co., 1855, farmer, age 25. Age 31, farmer, Greenbank, Pocahontas Co., W. Va. 1860 Census. Prior service, Co. G, 31st 1/2a. Inf. and McNeel's Co., 2nd VSL. Enl. Hillsboro, Pocahontas Co., W. Va., 3/9/63. Not stated if present or absent on muster-in roll dated 3/63, 1st Lt.

Commanding detachment at Dunmore, Pocahontas Co., W. Va., 11/3/63. Cpd. Pocahontas Co., W. Va., 12/12/63. Confined at the Atheneum Prison, 12/24/63. Desc.: age 34, 6'1_", dark comp., dark hair and blue eyes. Occ. farmer, residing in Pocahontas Co., W. Va. Transf. to Camp Chase, 12/26/63. Confined at Camp Chase, 12/27/63. Ab. 1/1/64 - 2/29/64, prisoner in the hands of the enemy. Transf. to Ft. Delaware, 3/25/64. Confined at Ft. Delaware, 3/27/64. Ab. 9/1/64 - 10/31/64, cpd. 12/12/63. Ab. 10/25/64, POW. Ab. 12/15/64, POW since 12/19/64. Took the oath of allegiance and was released, 6/12/65. Desc.: age ?, 6'1", dark comp., dark hair and blue eyes, a resident of Pocahontas Co., W. Va. Post war farmer, residing in Pocahontas Co., W. Va. Age 51, farmer, Green Banks, Pocahontas Co., W. Va. 1880 Census. d. Greenbank, W. Va., 2/23/1908, age 77.

SLANKER, DeWITT CLINTON - Pvt. Co. I. b.c. 1834. Age 26, merchant, Academy, Pocahontas Co., W. Va. 1860 Census. Enl. Huntersville, Pocahontas Co., W. Va., 3/1/63. Ab. on muster-in roll dated 3/63, on leave. Age 48, farmer, Edray, Pocahontas Co., W. Va. 1880 Census, listed as Slunker. NFR.

SLAVEN (SLAVIN), JOHN RANDOLPH - Pvt. Co. F. b.c. 1830. Age 30, farmer, Huntersville, Pocahontas Co., W. Va. 1860 Census. Prior service, McNeel's Co., 2nd VSL. Enl. Hillsboro, Pocahontas Co., W. Va., 3/9/63 (4/1/63). Not stated if present or absent on muster-in roll dated 3/63. Present 1/1/64 - 2/29/64. Ab. 9/1/64 - 10/31/64, AWOL since 9/22/64. Post war resident of Huntersville, W. Va. Brother of L. L. Slaven. Age 49, farmer, Green Banks, Pocahontas Co., W. Va. 1880 Census. NFR.

SLAVEN (SLAVIN), LANCELOT LOCKRIDGE "Lanty" - 2nd Sgt. Co. F. b. Pocahontas Co., W. Va., c. 1834. Age 26, farmer, Traveler's Repose, Pocahontas Co., W. Va. 1860 Census. Prior service, McNeel's Co., 2nd VSL. Enl. Hillsboro, Pocahontas Co., W. Va., 3/9/63 (4/1/63). Not stated if present or absent on muster-in roll dated 3/63, 2nd Sgt. Present 1/1/64 - 2/29/64. Clothing issued 2/7/64, listed as a Pvt. Ab., Pvt., 9/1/64 - 10/31/64, AWOL since 9/22/64. Post war resident of Back Alleghany, W. Va. Brother of J. R. Slaven. CSR listed as Santy L. Slaven. NFR.

SLICER, JOSEPH SAMUEL - Capt. Co. ?. b. 10/6/39. Post war rosters only. d. 8/8/98. Bur. Longwood Cem., Bedford Co.

SLIDER, JOSEPH - Pvt. Co. H and Co. A. b. Tyler Co., W. Va., 6/10/43. Age 16, Calhoun Co., W. Va. 1860 Census. Prior service, Co. A, 3rd VSL. Enl. Frankfort, Greenbrier Co., W. Va., 3/19/63, in Co. H. Not stated if present or absent on muster-in roll dated 3/63. Enl. Williamsburg, Greenbrier Co., W. Va., 3/1/63, in Co. A. Not stated if present or absent on muster-in roll dated 3/63. Clothing issued, 4/1/64, 4/30/64, 6/17/64, 7/64 and 8/64, signs by x. Cpd. Parkersburg, W. Va., no date. Sent to Clarksburg, W. Va., by 4/20/65. Confined at Clarksburg, W. Va., 4/22/65. Desc.: age 21, 5'11", florid comp., brown hair and gray eyes. Occ. farmer, residing in Calhoun Co., W. Va. Age 27, farmer, Lee Township, Calhoun Co., W. Va. 1870 Census. Age 37, farmer, Lee Dist., Calhoun Co., W. Va. 1880 Census. d. 5/31/1914. Bur. Slider Cem., Calhoun Co., W. Va.

SLOCUM, SETH - Pvt. Co. D. b. Harrison Co., W. Va., c. 1840. Not on muster rolls. POW record shows he enl. Barbour Co., W. Va., 6/63. Wartime letters support this claim. Helped take care of horses captured from the Yankees 9/63. Ab. in Rockbridge Co. for two months. Weighed 160 lbs. 2/13/64, which he says is 15 lbs. heavier than when he enl. Had trouble with rheumatism during the winter of 1863 - 1864. Exempted from duty for several days, 2/64, by Dr. Hertzag. Expects to be detailed to work in shoe shop, 2/27/64. Detailed to make shoes 2/28/64. Writes 3/11/64 that he "has been busy ever since and I have not got the company neared shoed yet." Clothing issued, 2/7/64, 4/1/64, 5/21/64; 6/17/64, 7/64 and 8/64, signs by x. Cpd. Clarksburg, W. Va., 3/29/65. Desc.: age 25, 5'10", fair comp., dark hair and blue eyes. Occ. Shoemaker, residing in Harrison Co., W. Va. Took the amnesty oath and was sent north, 3/30/65. NFR.

SMALL, JAMES - Pvt. Co. C. b. Rockingham Co., c. 1833. Prior service, Co. D, 3rd VSL. Enl. Frankfort, Greenbrier Co., W. Va., 3/15/63 (Pocahontas Co., W. Va., 4/1/63). Not stated if present or absent on muster-in roll dated 3/63. Present 1/1/63 - 4/1/63, has one horse. Ab. 12/31/63 - 8/31/64, sent to hosp., 11/1/63, got a furlough and went home. Clothing issued, 4/30/64 and 5/26/64. Ab. 9/1/64 - 10/31/64, AWOL since 7/16/64. Cpd. Pond Creek, Jackson Co., W. Va., 8/18/64. Sent to Clarksburg, W. Va. Desc.: age 31, 5'6", dark comp., dark hair and black eyes. Occ. farmer, residing in Jackson Co., W. Va. Confined at the Atheneum Prison, 9/12/64. Desc.: age 31, 5'7_", fair comp., light hair and hazel eyes. Occ. farmer, residing in Jackson Co., W. Va. Transf. to Camp Chase, 9/15/64. Confined at Camp Chase, 9/17/64. DOD. Camp Chase, 5/23/65, typhoid fever. Bur. Camp Chase Confederate Cem., grave no. 1994.

SMALL, THOMAS F. - Pvt. Co. C. b. Rockingham Co., NC, c. 1842. Prior service, Co. D, 3rd VSL. Enl. Frankfort, Greenbrier Co., W. Va., 3/15/63 (Pocahontas Co., W. Va., 4/1/63). POW record shows his enl. as Wythe Co., 8/62. Not stated if present or absent on muster-in roll dated 3/63. Present 1/1/63 - 4/1/63, has one horse. Present 12/31/63 - 8/31/64, has one horse. Clothing issued, 2/25/64 and 6/17/64. Ab. 9/1/64 - 10/31/64, enl. bounty due; missing while on scout with Capt. Hill; horse cpd. 10/1/64. Cpd. Beverly, W. Va., 10/29/64. Sent to Clarksburg, W. Va., then to Wheeling, W. Va., 11/2/64. Desc.: age 22, 5'6", dark comp., dark hair and brown eyes. Occ. farmer, residing in Jackson Co., W. Va. Confined at the Atheneum Prison, no date. Desc.: age 22, 5'6", dark comp., blond hair and black eyes. Occ. farmer, residing in Jackson Co., W. Va. Transf. to Camp Chase, 11/29/64. Confined at Camp Chase, 11/30/64, desires to take the oath of allegiance. Took the oath of allegiance and was released, 6/12/65. Desc.: age 23, 5'6_", fair comp., dark hair and brown eyes, a resident of Jackson Co., W. Va. Age 37, farmer, Grant Dist., Jackson Co., W. Va. 1880 Census. NFR.

SMARR, JESSE V. - Pvt. Co. A. b. Lewis Co., W. Va., c. 1843. Age 17, Calhoun Co., W. Va. 1860 Census. Prior service, Co. A, 3rd VSL. Enl. Williamsburg, Greenbrier Co., W. Va., 3/1/63. Not stated if present or absent on muster-in roll dated 3/63. NFR.

SMITH, ALEXANDER - Pvt. Co. C. b.c. 1841. Prior service, Co. D, 3rd VSL. Enl. Frankfort, Greenbrier Co., W. Va., 3/15/63 (Pocahontas Co., W. Va., 4/1/63). Not stated if present or absent on muster-in roll dated 3/63. Present 1/1/63 - 4/1/63, has one horse. Ab. 12/31/63 - 8/31/64, wd. 8/28/64, now in Staunton Gen. Hosp.; has one horse. Clothing issued 2/25/64 and 6/17/64, signs by x. Ab. 9/1/64 - 10/31/64, wd. 8/28/64, now in Staunton Gen. Hosp.; has one horse; $100 enl. bounty due. Served in Co. F, 20th Va. Cav. Paroled at Charleston, W. Va., 5/10/65, signs by x. Desc.: age 24, 6'1", dark comp., black hair and black eyes. NFR.

SMITH, AMOS G. - Pvt. Co. A. b. Lewis Co., W. Va., c. 1839. Age 21, farmer, Calhoun Co., W. Va. 1860 Census. Prior service, Co. A, 3rd VSL. Enl. Williamsburg, Greenbrier Co., W. Va., 3/1/63. Not stated if present or absent on muster-in roll dated 3/63. Transf. to Lurty's Batty., from the 3rd VSL, by Capt. Downs, 10/1/63. Brother of Joshua Smith. NFR.

SMITH, BARNES N. - Pvt. Co. A. b. Ritchie Co., W. Va., c. 1848. Age 12, Calhoun Co., W. Va. 1860 Census. Served in Co. A, 3rd VSL. Post war rosters only, which show he was wd. in Webster Co., W. Va., 6/11/63. Post war resident of Calhoun Co., W. Va. Age 23, farmer, Washington Township, Calhoun Co., W. Va. 1870 Census. Brother of Henry B. Smith. NFR.

SMITH, BENJAMIN M. - Capt. Co. ?. b.c. 1834. Prior service, Co. C, 31st Va. Inf. Age 27, farmer, 1861. Post war rosters only. NFR.

SMITH, DANIEL PERKINS - Pvt. Co. ?. b. 1820. Post war rosters only. d. 1894. Bur. Evergreen Cem., Jacksonville, Fla.

SMITH, FELIX - Pvt. Co. B and Co. K. b. Harrison (Braxton) Co., W. Va., c. 1828. Age 32, Braxton Co., W. Va. 1860 Census. Enl. Frankfort, Greenbrier Co., W. Va., 3/7/63, in Co. B. POW record shows he enl. in Bath Co., 8/62). Not stated if present or absent on muster-in roll dated 3/63. Transf. to Co. K. Clothing issued, as a member of Co. K, 1st Qr. 1864, 4/30/64 and 6/17/64. Cpd. Webster (Braxton) Co., W. Va., 12/23/64. Sent to Cumberland, Md., then to Clarksburg, W. Va. and to Wheeling, W. Va., 12/28/64. Confined at the Atheneum Prison, 12/28/64. Desc.: age 35, 5'4", light comp., fair hair and hazel eyes. Occ. farmer, residing in Braxton Co., W. Va. Took the oath of allegiance and was released, 6/26/65. CSR shows that he was transf. to Camp Chase, 12/30/64, no other cards for his confinement there. Age 52, farmer, Otter Dist., Braxton Co., W. Va. 1880 Census. Post war resident of Gilmer Co., W. Va. Adm. Lee Camp Soldier's Home, Richmond, 6/8/1906, age 77. d. Richmond, 5/13/1908, age 78. Bur. Hollywood Cem., Richmond.

SMITH, FRANK - Pvt. Co. G. Enl. Frankfort, Greenbrier Co., W. Va., 3/12/63. Not stated if present or absent on muster-in roll dated 3/63. NFR.

SMITH, HENRY B. - Pvt. Co. B. b. Lewis Co., W. Va., c. 1843. Age 17, Calhoun Co., W. Va. 1860 Census. Enl. Frankfort, Greenbrier Co., W. Va., 3/7/63. Not stated if present or absent on muster-in roll dated 3/63. Brother of Barnes N. Smith. NFR.

SMITH, JAMES E. - Pvt. Co. A. Served in Co. A, 3rd VSL. Also listed as belonging to Co. D, 3rd VSL. Post war rosters only for service in 19th Va. Cav. Present 1/1/63 - 4/1/63, has one horse. Transf. to Co. D, 46th Battn. Va. Cav. KIA. Little Sandy, Jackson Co., W. Va., 9/1/64.

SMITH, JAMES L. (A.) - Pvt. Co. A. b.c. 1827. Prior service, Co. A, 3rd VSL. Enl. Williamsburg, Greenbrier Co., W. Va., 3/1/63. Clothing issued 2/2/64 and 4/30/64. Not stated if present or absent on muster-in roll dated 3/63. Cpd. Roane (Calhoun) Co., W. Va., 3/2/65. Sent to Cumberland, Md., then to Wheeling, W. Va. Confined at the Atheneum Prison, 3/11/65. Desc.: age 37, 5'8", fair comp., light hair and blue eyes. Occ. farmer, residing in Ritchie Co., W. Va. Transf. to Camp Chase, 3/27/65. Confined at Camp Chase, 3/27/65. Took the oath of allegiance and was released, 6/13/65. Desc.: age 38, 5'7_", dark comp., black hair and blue eyes, a resident of Ritchie Co., W. Va. NFR.

SMITH, JASPER N. - Pvt. Co. D. Enl. Williamsburg, Greenbrier Co., W. Va., 3/8/63. Not stated if present or absent on muster-in roll dated 3/63. Served in Co. E, 20th Va. Cav. Post war resident of Marion Co., W. Va. Age 38, farmer, Grant Dist., Monongalia Co., W. Va. 1880 Census. NFR.

SMITH, JESSE - Pvt. Co. B. Post war rosters only, which show he was a resident of Braxton Co., W. Va. NFR.

SMITH, JOHN F. - Pvt. Co. A. Enl. Williamsburg, Greenbrier Co., W. Va., 3/1/63. Not stated if present or absent on muster-in roll dated 3/63. NFR.

SMITH, JOSHUA - 4th Corp. Co. A. b. Lewis Co., W. Va., c. 1844. Age 16, Calhoun Co., W. Va. 1860 Census. Prior service, Co. A, 3rd VSL. Post war rosters show he was on detached duty 12/20/62. Enl. Williamsburg, Greenbrier Co., W. Va., 3/1/63. Not stated if present or absent on muster-in roll dated 3/63. Transf. to Lurty's Batty., from the 3rd VSL, by Capt. Downs, 10/1/63. Brother of Amos G. Smith. NFR.

SMITH, KINZA (KINSEY) - Pvt. Co. C. b.c. 1838. Enl. Pocahontas Co., W. Va., 3/15/63. Present 12/31/63 - 8/31/64, has one horse. Clothing issued 2/2/64. Present 9/1/64 - 10/31/64, has one horse; $100 enl. bounty due. Deserted. Surrendered at Charleston, W. Va., 3/25/65. Took the amnesty oath and was sent North, signs by x. Desc.: age 27, 5'6", fair comp., fair hair and blue eyes. Occ. farmer, residing in Wood Co., W. Va. Post war resident of Wood Co., W. Va. NFR.

SMITH, MIRABAN L. - 2nd Sgt. Co. D. Enl. Williamsburg, Greenbrier Co., W. Va., 3/8/63. Not stated if present or absent on muster-in roll dated 3/63, 2nd Sgt. NFR.

SMITH, ROBERT G. - Pvt. Co. F. b.c. 1838. Age 22, laborer, Mt. Murphy, Pocahontas Co., W. Va. 1860 Census. Clerk, age 24 (1861). Prior service, Co. C, 31st Va. Inf. and McNeel's Co., 2nd VSL. Age 24, clerk, 1861. Enl. Hillsboro, Pocahontas Co., W. Va., 3/9/63. Not stated if present or absent on muster-in roll dated 3/63. Post war laborer and resident of Pocahontas Co., W. Va. d. Pocahontas Co., W. Va., 8/7/1905, age 67.

SMITH, SAMUEL S. - Pvt. Co. A. b. Harrison Co., W. Va., c. 1826 (1817). Age 34, farmer, Calhoun Co., W. Va. 1860 Census. Prior service, Co. A, 3rd VSL. Cpd. Calhoun Co., W. Va., 10/24/62. Confined at the Atheneum Prison, 10/28/62. Desc.: age 44, 5'8", dark comp., bald, blue eyes. Occ. farmer, residing in Calhoun Co., W. Va. Charge with being a volunteer in the CS Army. Transf. to Camp Chase, 11/1/62. Confined at Camp Chase, 11/2/62. Transf. to Cairo, Ill., 11/20/62. Exchanged. Enl. Williamsburg, Greenbrier Co., W. Va., 3/1/63. Not stated if present or absent on muster-in roll dated 3/63. Served in Co. B, 46th Battn. Va. Cav. NFR.

SMITH, SAMUEL K. - Pvt. Co. E. Enl. Frankfort, Greenbrier Co., W. Va., 3/12/63 (4/1/63). Not stated if present or absent on muster-in roll dated 3/63. NFR.

SMITH, THOMAS J. - Pvt. Co. A. b. Harrison Co., W. Va., c. 1837. Age 23, farmer, Calhoun Co., W. Va. 1860 Census. Enl. Williamsburg, Greenbrier Co., W. Va., 3/1/63. Not stated if present or absent on muster-in roll dated 3/63. Deserted. Took the oath of allegiance 12/25/63 and gave his bond. Age 49(?), farmer, Lee Dist., Calhoun Co., W. Va. 1880 Census. NFR.

SMITH, WILLIAM - Pvt. Co. E. Enl. Bath Co., 3/1/64. Ab. 10/31/63 - 10/31/64, on horse detail, time now expired; had his own horse since 7/1/64; enl. bounty due. Clothing issued 6/17/64, signs by x. NFR.

SMITH, WILLIAM J. - Pvt. Co. A. b. Lewis Co., W. Va., c. 1841. Age 19, Calhoun Co., W. Va. 1860 Census. Prior service, Co. A, 3rd VSL. Enl. Williamsburg, Greenbrier Co., W. Va., 3/1/63. Not stated if present or absent on muster-in roll dated 3/63. Deserted. Took the oath of allegiance 12/25/63 and gave his bond. NFR.

SMITHERMAN, DAVID - 2nd Sgt. Co. C. b. 1830. Prior service, Co. D, 3rd VSL. Enl. Frankfort, Greenbrier Co., W. Va., 3/15/63 (Mill Point, Pocahontas Co., W. Va., 4/1/63). Not stated if present or absent on muster-in roll dated 3/63, 1st Corp. Present, 1st Corp., 1/1/63 - 4/1/63, had one horse. Present, 1st Corp., 12/31/63 - 8/31/64, has one horse; promoted to 2nd Sgt., 2/15/64. Clothing issued, 2/2/64 and 6/17/64. Present, 2nd Sgt., 9/1/64 - 10/31/64, has one horse; $100 enl. bounty due. Post war resident of Wood Co., W. Va. and Mo. d. Mo., 1910. Bur. Higginsville Confederate Cem., Higginsville, Mo.

SMOOT, THOMAS S. - Pvt. Co. D. Enl. Williamsburg, Greenbrier Co., W. Va., 3/8/63. Not stated if present or absent on muster-in roll dated 3/63. Clothing issued, 2/7/64. NFR.

SNYDER, JACOB - Pvt. Co. K. Not on muster rolls. Transf. to Lurty's Batty., by Capt. Campbell, 11/1/63. NFR.

SNIDER (SNYDER), JOHN K. - Pvt. Co. ?. b.c. 1835. Tailor, age 26 (1861). Prior service, Co. D, 31st Va. Inf. Not on muster rolls. Transf. to the 19th Va. Cav. by 10/31/63. Returned to the 31st Va. Inf. by 2/28/65. NFR.

SNIDER (SNYDER), SAMUEL B. - Corp. Co. K. b. Gilmer (Lewis) Co., W. Va., c. 1845. Age 15, farmer, Gilmer Co., W. Va. 1860 Census. Not on muster rolls. POW record shows his enl. as Pocahontas Co., W. Va., 7/63. Clothing issued, 2/5/64, 2/23/64 (as a Corp.), 4/30/64, 6/17/64 and 3rd Qr. 1864, signs by x. Deserted. Reported to Clarksburg, W. Va., 12/5/64. Desc.: age 19, 5'7", dark comp., light hair and blue eyes. Occ. farmer, residing in Gilmer Co., W. Va. Took the oath of allegiance and was released, 12/6/64. Post war resident of Clarksburg, Harrison Co., W. Va. NFR.

SNYDER (SNIDER), DAVID - Pvt. Co. I. b. Highland Co., c. 1823. Age 37, farmer, New Hamden, Highland Co. 1860 Census. Enl. Huntersville, Pocahontas Co., W. Va., 1/1/64. Not stated if present or absent, 6/30/63 - 2/29/64, new recruit; enl. bounty due; mounted. Ab. 2/29/64 - 8/31/64, detailed as a farmer. NFR.

SNYDER, SAMUEL - Pvt. Co. I. b. Pendleton Co., W. Va., c. 1844. Enl. Huntersville, Pocahontas Co., W. Va., 1/1/64. Not stated if present or absent, 6/30/63 - 2/29/64, new recruit; enl. bounty due; mounted. Present 2/29/64 - 8/31/64, mounted; enl. bounty due. Ab. 9/1/64 - 10/31/64, AWOL. Deserted. Reported (Cpd.) at Beverly, W. Va., 12/28/64. Desc.: age 20, 5'10", fair comp., light hair and blue eyes. Occ. farmer, residing in Highland Co. Confined at Clarksburg, W. Va. Took the oath of allegiance and was released, 12/31/64. NFR.

SNYDER, WILLIAM - Pvt. Co. F. Post war rosters only. NFR.

SONAKER, ANDREW - Pvt. Co. H. Enl. Frankfort, Greenbrier Co., W. Va., 3/19/63. Not stated if present or absent on muster-in roll dated 3/63. NFR.

SOMMERS, S. M. - AQM. Prior service Co. C, 31st Va. Inf. History of the 31st Va. Inf. shows he was promoted to Capt. and AQM, and was transf. to the 19th Va. Cav. Not on muster rolls of the 19th Va. Cav. NFR.

SPENCER, ALLEN W. - Pvt. Co. C. Prior service, Co. D, 3rd VSL. Enl. Frankfort, Greenbrier Co., W. Va., 3/15/63 (Pocahontas Co., W. Va., 4/1/63). Not stated if present or absent on muster-in roll dated 3/63. Present 1/1/63 - 4/1/63, has one horse. Present 12/31/63 - 8/31/64, has one horse. Clothing issued, 2/2/64, 7/64 and 8/64. Ab. 9/1/64 - 10/31/64, deserted 10/15/64; has one horse; enl. bounty due. NFR.

SPENCER, CRAWFORD - Pvt. Co. C. Prior service, Co. D, 3rd VSL. Enl. Frankfort, Greenbrier Co., W. Va., 3/15/63. Not stated if present or absent on muster-in roll dated 3/63. Ab. 1/1/63 - 4/1/63, transf. to O'Brien's Co., 2/20/63. NFR.

SPENCER, ELIAS C. - Pvt. Co. H. Enl. Frankfort, Greenbrier Co., W. Va., 3/19/63. Not stated if present or absent on muster-in roll dated 3/63. NFR.

SPENCER, EVANDER - Pvt. Co. C and Co. H. Prior service, Co. D, 3rd VSL. Enl. Frankfort, Greenbrier Co., W. Va., 3/15/63 in Co. C, 19th Va. Cav. Enl. Frankfort, Greenbrier Co., W. Va., 3/19/63, in Co. H, 19th Va. Cav. Not stated if present or absent on muster-in roll dated 3/63. Ab. 1/1/63 - 4/1/63, on muster roll of Co. D, 3rd VSL, transf. to O'Brien's Co., 2/20/63. NFR.

SPENCER, ROBERT - Pvt. Co. D. Enl. Williamsburg, Greenbrier Co., W. Va., 3/8/63. Not stated if present or absent on muster-in roll dated 3/63. NFR.

SPRIGGS (SPRIGG), JAMES D. - 2nd Lt. Co. B. b.c. 1840. Age 20, farmer, Braxton Co., W. Va. 1860 Census. In service (State Line) by 6/1/62. Was shot at by John Hannah, on or about 6/1/62. Enl. Frankfort, Greenbrier Co., W. Va., 3/7/63 (3/9/63). Not stated if present or absent on muster-in roll dated 3/63, Pvt. Cpd. Pocahontas Co., W. Va., 8/23/63. Confined at the Atheneum Prison, 8/30/63. Desc.: age 23, 5'·1_", fair comp., dark hair and dark eyes. Occ. farmer, residing in Braxton Co., W. Va. Transf. to Camp Chase, 8/31/63. Confined at Camp Chase, 9/1/63. Ab., 2nd Lt., 11/1/63 - 2/29/64, cpd. 8/25/63. Desires to take the oath of allegiance, 6/10/64. Ab. 9/1/64 - 10/31/64, POW since 8/16/63. Ab. 12/15/64, POW since 8/21/63. Took the oath of allegiance and was released, 6/11/65. Desc.: age 25, 5'10_", fair comp., dark hair and blue eyes, a resident of Braxton Co., W. Va. CSR also lists him as a Sgt. Post war resident of Salt Lick Bridge, W. Va. Age 40, boot & shoemaker, Holly Dist., Braxton Co.. W. Va. 1880 Census, listed as James R. Spriggs. NFR.

SPRIGGS, JOHN S. - Capt. Co. B. b.c. 1833. Age 27, farmer, Braxton Co., W. Va. 1860 Census. Prior service, Co. B, 3rd VSL. Was in service with a company of cavalry in late 1861, operating out of Braxton Co., W. Va., with the Moccasin Rangers. Cpd. Callaghan's (Braxton or Greenbrier Co., W. Va.), 5/15/62, listed as being "a noted character." Charged as being a bushwhacker, not in the regular service. According to Federal documents, was to be hanged. Gov. John Letcher intervened, 5/27/62, stating Spriggs was a regularly commissioned officer of the Virginia Forces. Transf. to Camp Chase, 5/30/62. President Lincoln ordered an investigation in his case by 6/20/62. Transf. to Johnson's Island, 7/3/62. Confined at Johnson's Island, 7/3/62. Transf. to Vicksburg, Miss., 11/22/62, to be exchanged. Exchanged at Vicksburg, Miss., 12/8/62. Enl. Frankfort, Greenbrier Co., W. Va., 3/9/63. Appointed Capt., 3/7/63. Not stated if present or absent on muster-in roll dated 3/63, Capt., commanding co. Mentioned for "distinguished conduct" at Beverly, 7/63 by Col. W. L. Jackson in his report. Not stated if present or absent, 11/1/63 - 2/29/64, commanding co. Mentioned for gallantry in Col. W. L. Jackson's report, 12/63. Commanding a detachment of the 19th Va. Cav., 12/63 - 1/64, on the Cow Pasture River, foraging 275 horses, by order of Col. W. L. Jackson. Commanding a detachment of the 19th Va. Cav., 2/64 - 4/64, at Doe Hill, Highland Co., foraging 62 horses, by order of Col. W. L. Jackson. Ab. 9/1/64 - 10/31/64, AWOL since 10/1/64. Ab. 10/25/64, AWOL, 10 days, no steps taken to have him dropped, has sent in his resignation. Ab. 12/15/64, AWOL since 11/1/64, no steps taken to have him dropped. Dropped from the rolls, 2/8/65. Joined an independent command, raised by A. B. Chewning, for service in northwest Va. (W. Va.). Wd. James Dyer's Farm, Gauley River, W. Va., 3/4/65, at the same time that A. B. Chewning and Frederick Chewning were killed. Paroled at Charleston, W. Va., 5/10/65. Desc.: age 32, 5'11", fair comp., light hair, gray eyes and sandy whiskers. Age 47, farms & visits west, Holly Dist., Braxton Co., W. Va. 1880 Census. "...a splendid specimen of manhood; tall, erect and of pleasing manner, a superb horseman, a dashing cavalier." NFR.

SPRINGTON (SPRINGSTON), JOSEPH BENTON - Pvt. Co. E. b. Lewis Co.. W. Va., c. 1839. Age 21, farmer, Gilmer Co., W. Va. 1860 Census. Enl. Gilmer Co., W. Va., 10/2/64. Present 10/31/63 - 10/31/64, enl. bounty due; had his own horse since enl. Paroled at Charleston, W. Va., 5/11/65. Desc.: age 26, 5'6", light comp., brown hair, gray eyes and brown whiskers. Age 41, farmer, Troy, Gilmer Co., W. Va. 1880 Census. NFR.

SQUIRES, FRANKLIN F. - 4th Sgt. Co. K and Co. B. b.c. 1842. Age 18, farmer, Braxton Co., W. Va. 1860 Census. Enl. Frankfort, Greenbrier Co., W. Va., 3/20/63, in Co. K. Not stated if present or absent on muster-in roll dated 3/63. Enl. Frankfort,

Greenbrier Co., W. Va., 3/7/63 (3/9/63), in Co. B. Not stated if present or absent on muster-in roll dated 3/63. Present 11/1/63 - 2/29/64, has his own horse. Clothing issued 2/6/64, 2/23/64 and 6/17/64. Present 9/1/64 - 10/31/64, $100 enl. bounty due; was 4th Sgt., 3/9/64 - 7/1/64. Paroled at Charleston, W. Va., 5/10/65. Desc.: age 22, 5'10", dark comp., dark hair, black eyes and dark whiskers. Age 38, farmer, Salt Lick Dist., Braxton Co., W. Va. 1880 Census. NFR.

SQUIRES, J. LEE - Pvt. Co. B. b.c. 1835. Age 25, hotel keeper, Pocahontas Co., W. Va. 1860 Census. Enl. Frankfort, Greenbrier Co., W. Va., 10/1/63. Present 11/1/63 - 2/29/64, has one horse. Clothing issued 2/6/64. Ab. 9/1/64 - 10/31/64, $100 enl. bounty due; AWOL since 10/8/64. NFR.

SQUIRES, JAMES W. - 1st Sgt. Co. B. b.o. 1829. Age 31, farmer, Braxton Co., W. Va. 1860 Census. Enl. Frankfort, Greenbrier Co., W. Va., 3/17/63. Ab., 1st Sgt., 11/1/63 - 2/29/64, cpd. & KIA. by the enemy, 1/21/64. Post war rosters show him as being a Lt.

SQUIRES, L. W. - Pvt. Co. B. Post war rosters only, which show he was a resident of Greenbrier Co., W..Va., 6/1/63. NFR.

ST. JOHN, —— - Pvt. Co. ?. Post war recollections only, which show he was from Lewis Co., W. Va. NFR.

STAICHER (STACHER, STARTCHER), JOHN - Pvt. Co. C. b.c. 1844. Enl. Frankfort, Greenbrier Co., W. Va., 3/15/63 (Pocahontas Co., W. Va., 4/1/63). Not stated if present or absent on muster-in roll dated 3/63. Present 12/31/63 - 8/31/64, has one horse. Present 9/1/64 - 10/31/64, has one horse; enl. bounty due. Paroled 4/22/65, no place given. Desc.: age 21, 5'9", fair comp., yellow hair and blue eyes. Served in Co. F, 20th Va. Cav. NFR.

STALLMAN, ALFRED - Pvt. Co. A. b. Lewis Co., W. Va., c. 1841. Age 19, Calhoun Co., W. Va. 1860 Census. Served in Co. A, 3rd VSL. Post war rosters only. Brother of William Stallman. NFR.

STALLMAN, WILLIAM - Pvt. Co. A. b. Gilmer (Lewis) Co., W. Va., c. 1843. Age 17, Calhoun Co., W. Va. 1860 Census. Prior service, Co. A, 3rd VSL. Enl. Williamsburg, Greenbrier Co., W. Va., 3/1/63. POW records show his enl. as Greenbrier Co., W. Va., 5/61. Not stated if present or absent on muster-in roll dated 3/63. Clothing issued, 3/21/64, 5/25/64 and 6/17/64. Cpd. Beverly, W. Va., 10/29/64. Sent to Clarksburg, W. Va., then to Wheeling, W. Va., 11/2/64. Confined at the Atheneum Prison, 11/?/64. Desc.: age 22, 5'4", fair comp., light hair and brown eyes. Occ. farmer, residing in Calhoun Co., W. Va. Transf. to Camp Chase, 11/29/64. Confined at Camp Chase. 11/30/64, desires to take the oath of allegiance. Took the oath of allegiance and was released, 5/15/65. Desc.: age 23, florid comp., dark hair and hazel eyes, a resident of Calhoun Co., W. Va. Served in Co. F, 20th Va. Cav. Brother of Alfred Stallman. NFR.

STALNAKER, ADAM C. - Pvt. Co. ?. Prior service, Co. D, 31st Va. Inf. Post war rosters only. Post war resident of Elkins, W. Va. Age 44, farmer, Valley Bend, Randolph Co., W. Va. 1880 Census. Attended Gettysburg Reunion, 1913. d. by 1916. NFR.

STALNAKER, NELSON C. - 1st Lt. Co. E. b.c. 1832. Enl. Frankfort, Greenbrier Co., W. Va., 3/13/63. Not stated if present or absent on muster-in roll dated 3/63, listed as Pvt. and 3rd Lt. Present, Lt., 10/31/63 - 10/31/64. Paid as a 2nd Lt. 1/1/64 - 8/31/64. Granted 15 days leave, 2/27/64. Paroled at Charleston, W. Va., 5/11/65, listed as 1st Lt. Desc.: age 33, 5'6", light comp., light hair, blue eyes and light whiskers. NFR.

STALNAKER, NUTEN (NEWTON) C. - Pvt. Co. I. b. Randolph Co., W. Va., c. 1839. Age 21, farmer, Gilmer Co., W. Va. 1860 Census. Prior service, Co. D, 31st Va. Inf. Enl. Huntersville, Pocahontas Co., W. Va., 3/19/63. Present on muster-in roll dated 3/63. Mustered into service 3/19/63. Age 41, farmer, DeKalb Dist., Gilmer Co., W. Va. 1880 Census. Returned to Co. D, 31st Va. Inf. NFR.

STALNAKER, STANFORD - Sgt. Co. E. b. Randolph Co., W. Va., c. 1842. Age 18, farmer, Gilmer Co., W. Va. 1860 Census. Enl. Frankfort, Greenbrier Co., W. Va., 3/13/63 (Pocahontas Co., W. Va., 4/1/63). Not stated if present or absent on muster-in roll dated 3/63, Pvt. Present, Sgt., 10/31/63 - 10/31/64, had his own horse since 7/1/64. Clothing issued, 3/1/64 (listed as a musician), 3/25/64, 4/1/64, 5/21/64, 7/64 and 8/64. NFR.

STALNAKER, WILLIAM W. - Pvt. Co. E. b.c. 1840. No enl. data. Present 10/31/63 - 10/31/64, had his own horse from 7/1/64 - 7/15/64; horse cpd. in battle. Clothing issued 5/21/64, 6/17/64 and 7/6/64. Cpd. Loudoun Co. (near Harpers Ferry, W. Va.), 7/15/64. Sent to Harpers Ferry, W. Va., then to Washington, DC. Confined at the Old Capitol Prison, 7/17/64. Transf. to Elmira, NY, 7/23/64. Confined at Elmira Prison, 7/25/64. Paroled 10/11/64 to be exchanged. Confined at Pt. Lookout, 10/14/64, on his way to be exchanged. Exchanged at Venus Point, Savannah River, Ga., 10/29/64. Paroled at Charleston, W. Va., 5/11/65. Desc.: age 25, 5'9", fair comp., dark hair, gray eyes and a mustache. NFR.

STANLEY, BARKER (BARCUS) - Pvt. Co. H and Co. K. Prior service, Co. A, 3rd VSL. Enl. Frankfort, Greenbrier Co., W. Va., 3/19/63, in Co. H. Not stated if present or absent on muster-in roll dated 3/63. Enl. Frankfort, Greenbrier Co., W. Va., 3/20/63, in Co. K. Not stated if present or absent on muster-in roll dated 3/63. Clothing issued 1/16/64, 3/1/64 and 9/2/64, signs by x. Employed as a courier, 11/1/63 - 11/30/63. Employed as a courier at Warm Springs, 1/1/64 - 3/31/64. Post war resident of Ritchie Co., W. Va. NFR.

STANLEY, JACKSON - Pvt. Co. A. b.c. 1847. See Co. D, 46th Battn. Va. Cav. Not on muster rolls. Cpd. Roane Co., W. Va., 10/29/63. Confined at the Atheneum Prison, 11/12/63. Desc.: age 16, 5'5", light comp., sandy hair and hazel eyes. Occ. farmer, residing in Jackson Co., W. Va. Transf. to Camp Chase, 11/13/63. Confined at Camp Chase, 11/15/63. Desires to take the oath of allegiance, a boy of 17. Took the oath and was released, 12/3/64, by order of the President. Special conditions: he was to remain in Ohio during the war. Desc.: age 17, 5'4", light comp., light hair and gray eyes, a resident of Jackson Co., W. Va. Age 35, farmer, Ravenswood Dist. 2, Jackson Co., W. Va. 1880 Census. NFR.

STANLEY, JOSEPH WILSON - Pvt. Co. A. b. Wood Co., W. Va., 6/1/34 (1840). Not on muster rolls. Clothing issued 5/26/64 and 6/17/64. Paroled at Charleston, W. Va., 5/11/65. Desc.: age 25, 5'10", light comp., light hair, blue eyes and light whiskers. Post war resident of Ritchie Co., W. Va. Age 47, farmer, South Grant Dist., Ritchie Co., W. Va. 1880 Census. d. Petroleum, Ritchie Co., W. Va., 10/9/1917. Bur. Mason Cem., Racy, Ritchie Co., W. Va.

STANLEY, WILLIAM B. - Pvt. Co. ?. Post war rosters only, which show he was a resident of Ritchie Co., W. Va. NFR.

STARCHER, ALFRED - Pvt. Co. A. b. Jackson Co., W. Va., c. 1834. Age 26, farmer, Calhoun Co., W. Va. 1860 Census. Served in Co. A, 3rd VSL and Co. F, 46th Battn. Va. Cav. Post war rosters only. NFR.

STARCHER, HENRY - Pvt. Co. A. b. Webster Co., W. Va., 1834. Served in Co. A, 3rd VSL. Post war rosters only, which show service from 1861 to 1865. d. 3/16/1915. Bur. Gibson Cem., Calhoun Co., W. Va.

STARCHER, HEZEKIAH (HESSKIA) H. - Pvt. Co. A and Co. H. b. Jackson Co., W. Va., 2/25/40. Age 18(?), Calhoun Co., W. Va. 1860 Census. Prior service, Co. A, 3rd VSL. Enl. Williamsburg, Greenbrier Co., W. Va., 3/1/63, in Co. A. Not stated if present or absent on muster-in roll dated 3/63. Enl. Frankfort, Greenbrier Co., W. Va., 3/19/63, in Co. H. Not stated if present or absent on muster-in roll dated 3/63. Clothing issued, as a member of Co. A, 2/23/64, 4/1/64, 4/30/64, 6/17/64 and 7/6/64, signs by x. Age 29, farmer, Lee Township, Calhoun Co., W. Va. 1870 Census. Age 40, farmer, Lee Dist., Calhoun Co., W. Va. 1880 Census. d. 10/1/1919. Bur. Gibson Cem., Calhoun Co., W. Va.

STARCHER, ISAAC Jr. - Pvt. Co. A. b. Kanawha Co., W. Va., 6/2/42. Age 18, Calhoun Co., W. Va. 1860 Census. Prior service, Co. A, 3rd VSL. Enl. Williamsburg, Greenbrier Co., W. Va., 3/1/63. Not stated if present or absent on muster-in roll dated 3/63. Clothing issued, 2/19/64, 4/30/64, 6/17/64 and 7/6/64. Cpd. Parkersburg, W. Va., no date given. Sent to Clarksburg, W. Va., and confined in the post guard house. Paroled 4/22/65. Desc.: age 23, 6'_", fair comp., fair hair and blue eyes. Occ. farmer, residing in Calhoun Co., W. Va. Age 29, farmer, Lee Township, Calhoun Co., W. Va. 1870 Census. Age 38, farmer, Lee Dist., Calhoun Co., W. Va. 1880 Census. d. 10/5/1930. Bur. Hur Cem., Calhoun Co., W. Va.

STARCHER, JACOB P. - 3rd Corp. Co. A. b. Jackson Co., W. Va., c. 1844. Age 16, Calhoun Co., W. Va. 1860 Census. Prior service, Co. A, 3rd VSL. Enl. Williamsburg, Greenbrier Co., W. Va., 3/1/63. Not stated if present or absent on muster-in roll dated 3/63, 3rd Corp. Clothing issued as a Pvt., 3/21/64 and 6/17/64, signs by x. Post war rosters show he was at'Gettysburg, Pa. Post war resident of Calhoun Co., W. Va. Moved to the mouth of Big Run of the Gauley River, Webster Co., W. Va., 1870's. d. Webster Co., W. Va. Bur. unmarked grave, Sand Run Cem., Bolair, Fork Lick Dist., Webster Co., W. Va.

STARCHER, JEHU (JEHUE, JAHUE) - Sgt. Co. A. b. Kanawha Co., W. Va., 9/20/45. Age 16, Calhoun Co., W. Va. 1860 Census. Not on muster rolls. Clothing issued, 2/19/64, 4/30/64, 5/21/64 and 6/17/64, signs by x. Cpd. Parkersburg, W. Va., no date given; listed as a Sgt. Confined in the post guard house, Clarksburg, W. Va. Paroled 4/22/65. Desc.: age 26(?), 5'9_", fair comp., yellow hair and blue eyes. Occ. farmer, residing in Calhoun Co., W. Va. Brother of Peter and Thomas Starcher. d. 8/14/74. Bur. Gibson Cem., Calhoun Co., W. Va.

STARCHER, JOHN C. - 1st Corp. Co. A and Co. C. b.c. 1837. Prior service, Co. A, 3rd VSL. Also listed as belonging to Co. D, 3rd VSL. Enl. Williamsburg, Greenbrier Co., W. Va., 3/1/63. Not stated if present or absent on muster-in roll dated 3/63, 1st Corp. Present, Pvt., Muster Roll of Co. D, 3rd VSL, 1/1/63 - 4/1/63, has one horse. Clothing issued, 6/17/64 and 7/10/64, signs by x. Paroled at Charleston, W. Va., 6/8/65, listed as a member of Co. C. Desc.: age 28, 5'7", fair comp., dark hair and black eyes. NFR.

STARCHER, JOSIAH P. - Pvt. Co. A. b. 8/6/30. Post war rosters only, which show he enl. 12/6/62. d. 5/21/1915. Bur. Wayne Cem., Calhoun Co., W. Va.

STARCHER, PETER - Pvt. Co. A. b. Calhoun (Kanawha) Co., W. Va., c. 1841. Age 19, Calhoun Co., W. Va. 1860 Census. Prior service, Co. A, 3rd VSL. Enl. Williamsburg, Greenbrier Co., W. Va., 3/1/63. Not stated if present or absent on muster-in roll dated 3/63. Employed as a laborer at Warm Springs, 1/15/64 - 2/29/64, signs by x. Clothing issued, 3/21/64 and 6/17/64, signs by x. Cpd. Arnoldsburg, Calhoun Co., W. Va., 10/30/64. Sent to Cumberland, Md., then to Wheeling, W. Va., 11/2/64. Desc.: age 22, 5'10", fair comp., light hair and blue eyes. Occ. farmer, residing in Calhoun Co., W. Va. Confined at the Atheneum Prison, 11/?/64. Desc.: age 22, 5'10", light comp., light hair and blue eyes. Occ. farmer, residing in Calhoun Co., W. Va. Transf. to Champ Chase, 11/29/64. Confined at Camp Chase, 11/30/64, desires to take the oath of allegiance. Gave a statement at Camp Chase, 1/30/65, listed as being 22 years of age, a resident of Calhoun Co., W. Va. Says he enl. 6/62 for 12 months, to avoid conscription. At the expiration of his term of enl., he was not permitted to go home or be discharged. He was detailed to procure horses while in the Valley of Va., his being disabled. He went home with the intention of deserting. Took the oath of allegiance and was released, 2/18/65, by order of the Sec. of War. Age 28, farm laborer, Lee Township, Calhoun Co., W. Va. 1870 Census. Age 38, farmer, Lee Dist., Calhoun Co., W. Va. 1880 Census. Brother of Jehu and Thomas Starcher. d. near Bolair, W. Va., 9/12/96. Bur. Webster Co., W. Va.

STARCHER, PHILIP - Pvt. Co. A. b. Jackson Co., W. Va., c. 1832 (1836). Age 24, farmer, Calhoun Co., W. Va. 1860 Census. Arrested and confined at Wheeling, W. Va. Released on his oath and bond by 3/13/62. Prior service, Co. A, 3rd VSL. Enl. Williamsburg, Greenbrier Co., W. Va., 3/1/63. Not stated if present or absent on muster-in roll dated 3/63. Cpd. Roane Co., W. Va., 1/17/64. Confined at the Atheneum Prison, 2/1/64. Desc.: age 32, 6', dark comp., dark hair and hazel eyes. Occ. farmer, residing in Calhoun Co., W. Va. Transf. to Cumberland, Md., 4/27/64. Clothing issued, 4/30/64, 5/21/64, 6/17/64, 7/64 and 8/64, signs by x. Age 34, farmer, Lee Township, Calhoun Co., W. Va. 1870 Census. Age 46, farmer, Lee Dist., Calhoun Co., W. Va. 1880 Census. Post war rosters show him as a US soldier. NFR.

STARCHER, THOMAS - Pvt. Co. A. b. Kanawha Co., W. Va., c. 1832 (1835). Age 25, Calhoun Co., W. Va. 1860 Census. Prior service, Co. A, 3rd VSL. Enl. Williamsburg, Greenbrier Co., W. Va., 3/1/63. Not stated if present or absent on muster-in roll dated 3/63. Employed as a laborer at Warm Springs, 1/15/64 - 2/29/64, signs by x. Clothing issued, 4/21/64 and 6/17/64, signs by x. Believed to have been KIA. Brother of Jehu and Peter Starcher. NFR.

STARK, WILLIAM B. - 1st Sgt. Co. G. b.c. 1844. Enl. Greenbrier Co., W. Va., 7/1/63. Not stated if present or absent on muster-in roll dated 3/63. Clothing issued, 1st Qr. 1864, 4/30/64, 6/17/64 and 7/10/64. Ab. 9/1/64 - 10/31/64,, on horse detail; has serviceable horse. Deserted. Took the amnesty oath and was sent North, 3/6/65. Desc.: age 21, 5'6", dark comp., light hair and brown eyes. Occ. farmer, residing in Kanawha Co., W. Va. NFR.

STEPHENS (STEVENS), HENRY W. - Pvt. Co. A. b. Pa., c. 1839. Not on muster rolls. Cpd. Preston Co., W. Va., 7/1/63. Confined at the Atheneum Prison, 7/2/63. Desc.: age 24, 5'11", light comp., light hair and gray eyes. Occ. blacksmith, residing in Marion Co., W. Va. Transf. to Camp Chase. Confined at Camp Chase, 8/11/63. Took the oath of allegiance and was released, 2/22/65, by order of the Sec. of War. Desc.: age 26, 5'11_", light comp., dark hair and gray eyes, a resident of Marion Co., W. Va. Age 41, farmer, Mannington Sub Dist., Marion Co., W. Va. 1880 Census. NFR.

STEWARD, JOHN - Pvt. Co. H. b.c. 1847. Not on muster rolls. POW record shows his enl. as Union, W. Va., 8/21/64. Paroled at Lewisburg, W. Va., 4/25/65. Desc.: age 18, 5'1_", dark comp., light hair and brown eyes, a farmer. NFR.

STEWART, ELLSWORTH - Pvt. Co. D. Enl. Williamsburg, Greenbrier Co., W. Va., 3/8/63. Not stated if present or absent on muster-in roll dated 3/63. NFR.

STEWART, ROBERT W. - Pvt. Co. E. Not on muster rolls. Cpd. Highland Co., 8/20/63. Confined at the Atheneum Prison, 8/30/63. Desc.: age 25, 5'9", florid comp., brown hair and dark eyes. Occ. farmer, residing in Highland Co. Transf. to Camp Chase, 8/31/63. Confined at Camp Chase, 9/1/63. DOD. Camp Chase, 10/5/63. Bur. Camp Chase Confederate Cem., grave no. 37. CSR lists him as a member of Co. C.

STONESTREET, ANDREW B. - 1st Corp. Co. B. b.c. 1828. Age 32, farmer, Braxton Co., W. Va. 1860 Census. Enl. Frankfort, Greenbrier Co., W. Va., 3/7/63 (3/9/63). Not stated if present or absent on muster-in roll dated 3/63, 1st Corp. Present, Pvt., 11/1/63 - 2/29/64, has one horse; detailed as butcher. Clothing issued 11/30/63, 6/17/64 and 3rd Qr. 1864, signed by x. Ab. 9/1/64 - 10/31/64, $100 enl. bounty due; detailed in Commissary Dept., 4/11/63. Paroled at Charleston, W. Va., 5/10/65. Desc.: age 36, 5'11", fair comp., brown hair, blue eyes and a light mustache. Post war resident of Braxton Co., W. Va. Age 51, farmer, Otter Dist., Braxton Co., W. Va. 1880 Census. NFR.

STOUT, JOSIAH B. S. - Pvt. Co. E. b. Harrison Co., W. Va., c. 1838. Age 22, farmer, Gilmer Co., W. Va. 1860 Census. Prior service, 3rd VSL. Enl. Frankfort, Greenbrier Co., W. Va., 3/13/63. Not stated if present or absent on muster-in roll dated 3/63. Cpd. Gilmer Co., W. Va., 2/9/63. Confined at the Atheneum Prison, 2/?/63. Desc.: age 26, 5'11", sallow comp., dark hair, brown eyes and sandy whiskers. Occ. farmer, residing in Gilmer Co., W. Va. Transf. to Camp Chase, 2/20/63. Confined at Camp Chase, 2/21/63. Took the oath of allegiance and was released, 3/26/63. NFR.

STOUT, JOHNSON - Pvt. Co. K. b. Braxton Co., W. Va., c. 1840. Age 20, Braxton Co., W. Va. 1860 Census. Not on muster rolls. POW record shows he enl. Greenbrier Co., W. Va., 3/62. Cpd. while at home in Buckhannon, W. Va. (Braxton Co., W. Va.), 9/12/62. Sent to Cincinnati, then to Wheeling, W. Va., 9/23/62. Confined at Camp Chase, from Wheeling, W. Va., 9/24/64. Desc.: age 22, 5'11", fair comp., light hair and gray eyes. Listed as being a guerilla, a member of the 8th Va. Cav. and the Partisan Rangers. Sent to Vicksburg, Miss., to be exchanged. Exchanged at Vicksburg, 12/8/62. Clothing issued, 2/23/64, 4/30/64, 6/17/64 and 9/30/64. Cpd. near Bulltown, 10/30/64 (10/31/64). Confined at Clarksburg, W. Va. Desc.: age 25, 5'10", fair comp., light hair and blue eyes. Occ. farmer, residing in Braxton Co., W. Va. Sent to Wheeling, W. Va., 11/5/64. Confined at the Atheneum Prison, 11/?/64. Transf. to Camp Chase, 11/29/64. Confined at Camp Chase, 11/30/64, desires to take the oath of allegiance. Took the oath of allegiance and was released, 5/15/65. Desc.: age 25, 5'11_", florid comp., dark hair and blue eyes. Age 41, farmer, Otter Dist., Braxton Co., W. Va. 1880 Census. NFR.

STOUT, MICHAEL - Sgt. Co. K. b.c. 1831. Age 29, farmer, Braxton Co., W. Va. 1860 Census. Enl. Frankfort, Greenbrier Co., W. Va., 3/20/63 (4/1/63). Not stated if present or absent on muster-in roll dated 3/63. Not stated if present or absent on Hosp. MR, Warm Springs, 4/1/63 - 1/1/64. Attached to hosp. 4/1/63 as a nurse. Sent to his Co. 5/4/63. Clothing issued, 3/21/64 and 6/17/64, listed as Sgt. Cpd. Loudoun Co. (near Harpers Ferry, W. Va.), 7/15/64. Sent to Harpers Ferry, W. Va., then to Washington, DC. Confined at the Old Capitol Prison, 7/17/64. Transf. to Elmira, NY, 7/23/64. Confined at Elmira Prison, 7/25/64. Took the oath of allegiance and was released, 6/16/65. Desc.: age ?, 5'10_", fair comp., light hair and gray eyes, a resident of Clarksburg, W. Va. NFR.

STRUP, JOSEPH - Pvt. Co. B. Enl. Frankfort, Greenbrier Co., W. Va., 3/7/63. Not stated if present or absent on muster-in roll dated 3/63. NFR.

STUART, JAMES W. - Pvt. Co. C. Enl. Frankfort, Greenbrier Co., W. Va., 3/15/63. Not stated if present or absent on muster-in roll dated 3/63. NFR.

STUART, W. B. - Pvt. Co. ?. b.c. 1850. Post war rosters only, which show he enl. 7/64 and served until 4/65. Post war resident of Highland Co. NFR.

STULL, GEORGE W. - Pvt. Co. G. b.c. 1829. Enl. Greenbrier Co., W. Va., 4/1/63. Employed as a blacksmith, 11/1/63 - 11/30/63. Employed as a blacksmith at Warm Springs, 1/1/64 - 1/30/64, discharged 1/31/64 and sent to his Co. Clothing issued, 3/1/64, 4/1/64 and 4/30/64. Ab. 9/1/64 - 10/31/64, wd. (date and place not given); has a serviceable horse. Paroled at Charleston, W. Va., 6/6/65. Desc.: age 36, 5'3", light comp., dark hair, gray eyes and brown whiskers. NFR.

STULTING (STUTLING, STULLING), NICHOLAS - Pvt. Co. F. b.c. 1821. Member Hillsboro Patrol, Pocahontas Co., W. Va., 5/61. Age 34, tailor, Pocahontas Co., W. Va. 1860 Census. Prior service, McNeel's Co., 2nd VSL. Enl. Hillsboro, Pocahontas Co., W. Va., 3/9/63 (4/1/63). Not stated if present or absent on muster-in roll dated 3/63. Present 1/1/64 - 2/29/64. Present 9/1/64 - 10/31/64, enl. bounty due. Paroled at Charleston, W. Va., 5/10/65. Desc.: age 44, 5'6", dark comp., brown hair, hazel eyes and brown whiskers. CSR listed as Stulling. Age 54, brick mason, Little Levels, Pocahontas Co., W. Va. 1880 Census. NFR.

STUMP, ALLEN - Pvt. Co. B and Co. A. b.c. 1841. Enl. Frankfort, Greenbrier Co., W. Va., 3/7/63, in Co. B. Not stated if present or absent on muster-in roll dated 3/63. Enl. Williamsburg, Greenbrier Co., W. Va., 3/1/63, in Co. A. Not stated if present or absent on muster-in roll dated 3/63. Employed as a teamster, 11/1/63 - 11/30/63. Employed as a teamster at Warm Springs, 1/1/64 - 3/31/64. Clothing issued 11/20/63, 1/16/64, 1/17/64 (teamster), 5/26/64 and 6/17/64, signs by x. Paroled at Charleston, W. Va., 5/11/65, as a member of Co. A. Desc.: age 24, 6'1", fair comp., brown hair, gray eyes and a mustache. NFR.

STUMP, GEORGE G. - Pvt. Co. A. b. 4/18/44. Prior service, Co. A, 3rd VSL. Not on muster rolls. Clothing issued 2/23/64 and 6/17/64, signs by x. Cpd. Roane Co., W. Va., 3/1/65 (Calhoun Co., W. Va., 3/2/65). Confined at the Atheneum Prison, 3/11/65. Desc.: age 20, 5'9", fair comp., light hair and blue eyes. Occ. farmer, residing in Calhoun Co., W. Va. Transf. to Camp Chase, 3/16/65. Confined at Camp Chase, 3/17/65. Took the oath of allegiance and was released, 6/13/65. Desc.: age 21, 5'9", florid comp., light hair and hazel eyes, a resident of Calhoun Co., W. Va. Brother of Joseph B. Stump. Age 35, farmer, Lee Dist., Calhoun Co., W. Va. 1880 Census. d. 12/30/1927. Bur. Dry Hill Cem., Roane Co., W. Va.

STUMP, HENRY - Pvt. Co. A. b.c. 1842. Not on muster rolls. Cpd. Preston Co., W. Va., 7/1/63. Confined at the Atheneum Prison, 7/2/63. Desc.: age 21, 5'4", dark comp., black hair and hazel eyes. Occ. farmer, residing in Preston Co., W. Va. Transf. to Camp Chase, 8/8/63. Confined at Camp Chase, 8/11/63. Took the oath of allegiance and was released, 1/15/65, by order of the Sec. of War. Desc.: age 21, 5'4", light comp., dark hair and hazel eyes, a resident of Wetzel Co., W. Va., signs by x. NFR.

STUMP, JOSEPH B. - Pvt. Co. E. Enl. Frankfort, Greenbrier Co., W. Va., 3/12/63. Not stated if present or absent on muster-in roll dated 3/63. Post war rosters show he d. while a POW, of smallpox. Brother of George Stump.

STURM, ASBURY P. (B.) - Pvt. Co. D. Not on muster rolls. POW record shows he enl. Richmond, 3/63. Clothing issued 4/11/64. Cpd. Marion Co., W. Va., 8/2/64. Confined at the Atheneum Prison, 8/4/64. Desc.: age 36, 6'1_", dark comp., dark brown hair and dark eyes. Occ. farmer, residing in Harrison Co., W. Va. Transf. to Camp Chase, 8/6/64. Confined at Camp Chase, 8/8/64. Transf. to Ft. Delaware. Confined at Ft. Delaware, 2/29/64. Paroled 9/30/64, sent to Aiken's Landing, to be exchanged. Exchanged at Varina, Va., 10/5/64. Present, MR of Paroled Prisoners at Camp Lee, near Richmond, 11/22/64. Clothing issued 11/24/64 as a paroled prisoner. Paroled at Staunton, 5/10/65. Desc.: age 37, 6', light comp., dark hair and hazel eyes. Took the amnesty oath at Clarksburg, W. Va., 9/15/65. Post war resident of Calhoun Co., W. Va. NFR.

STURMS, ———— - Lt. Co. ?. Mentioned in Brig. Gen. John D. Imboden's report of the Jones - Imboden raid into Western Virginia, April - May 1863, as being a member of the 19th Va. Cav., and commanding a detachment of that reg't. sent to burn bridges. NFR.

SUMERS, GEORGE - Pvt. Co. F. Enl. Hillsboro, Pocahontas Co., W. Va., 3/9/63. Not stated if present or absent on muster-in roll dated 3/63. NFR.

SUMMERS, ANDREW J. - Corp. Co. H. b.c. 1844. Enl. Clay Co., W. Va., 4/1/63. Clothing issued 3/1/64, 4/1/64 and 8/13/64. Ab., Corp., 9/1/64 - 10/31/64, AWOL. Age 36, farmer, Henry Dist., Clay Co., W. Va. 1880 Census. NFR.

SUMPTER, JOHN W. - Pvt. Co. E. b. Giles Co., c. 1845. Age 15, farmer, Gilmer Co., W. Va. 1860 Census. Enl. Frankfort, Greenbrier Co., W. Va., 3/13/63 (4/1/63). Not stated if present or absent on muster-in roll dated 3/63. Ab. 10/31/63 - 10/31/64, POW. Broke a leg at Bulltown, W. Va. 10/13/63, and was cared for at the home of Moses Cunningham. Cpd. Bulltown, 10/16/63 (10/13/63), turned over to post surgeon at Clarksburg, W. Va. for treatment. Was wd. in the right shoulder when cpd. Confined at the Atheneum Prison, no date. Desc.: age 18, 5'4", fair comp., light hair and blue eyes. Occ. farmer, residing in Gilmer Co., W. Va. Transf. to Camp Chase, 3/4/64, listed as a member of Co. B. Confined at Camp Chase, 3/5/64. Adm. Chase USA Gen. Hosp., 4/26/64, RTD. 5/4/64. Paroled and sent to City Point, Va., 2/25/65, to be exchanged. Landed at Dutch Gap, 3/12/65(?). Adm. Gen. Hosp. No. 9, 3/9/65. Transf. to Chimborazo Hosp., 3/10/65. Adm. Chimborazo Hosp. No. 2, 3/10/65, vulnus sclopeticum, right shoulder. Furloughed 3/17/65, 30 days, to Wytheville, Wythe Co. NFR.

SUTTON, GEORGE MCN. - Pvt. Co. F. b.c. 1845. Age 15, farmer, Pocahontas Co., W. Va. 1860 Census. Prior service, McNeel's Co., 2nd VSL. Enl. Hillsboro, Pocahontas Co., W. Va., 3/9/63 (4/1/63). Not stated if present or absent on muster-in roll dated 3/63. Present 1/1/64 - 2/29/64. Ab. 9/1/64 - 10/31/64, AWOL since 9/22/64. Paroled at Charleston, W. Va., 5/10/65. Desc.: age 20, 5'10", fair comp., light hair, blue eyes and light whiskers. Brother of Samuel J. Sutton. NFR.

SUTTON, SAMUEL J. - Pvt. Co. F. b.c. 1842. Age 18, farmer, Greenbank, Pocahontas Co., W. Va. 1860 Census. Prior service, Co. G, 31st Va. Inf. Post war rosters only, which show he was from Highland Co. Age 38, Green Banks, Pocahontas Co., W. Va. 1880 Census. Brother of George M. Sutton. NFR.

SWECKER, WILLIAM A. - Pvt. Co. I. b.c. 1839. Age 21, farmer, Randolph Co., W. Va. 1860 Census. Post war rosters only, which show he was a resident of Randolph Co., W. Va. Age 41, farmer, Edray, Pocahontas Co., W. Va. 1880 Census. Member of Gen. Pegram Camp, UCV, Valley Head, W. Va. d.c. 1920. NFR.

SWOOPE, BOLLING ROBERTSON - Pvt. Co. A. b.c. 1842. Scholar, age 20, 1862. Prior service, Co. L, 5th Va. Inf. Enrolled as a conscript at Camp Lee, near Richmond, 1/31/64. Assigned to Co. A, 19th Va. Cav., 3/18/64. Transf. to Lurty's Batty., 4/1/64. NFR.

SWORD, NATHAN - 2nd Sgt. Co. G. b.c. 1839. POW record shows his enl. as Charles Town, W. Va., 9/1/62 in Capt. John S. Swann's Co., 26th Battn. Va. Inf. Enl. Frankfort, Greenbrier Co., W. Va., 3/12/63 (4/1/63). Not stated if present or absent on muster-in roll dated 3/63, 1st Corp. Cpd. Buckhannon, W. Va., 5/11/63 (5/12/63). Confined at Clarksburg, W. Va., 5/26/63. Confined at the Atheneum Prison, 5/27/63. Desc.: age 24, 5'9", florid comp., dark hair and dark eyes. Occ. farmer, residing in Harrison Co., W. Va. Transf. to Camp Chase, 5/?/63. Confined at Camp Chase, 5/30/63. Transf. to Johnson's Island, 6/14/63. Confined at Johnson's Island, 6/14/63. Transf. to Pt. Lookout, 10/30/63. Confined at Pt. Lookout, 11/4/63. Ab., 2nd Sgt., 9/1/64 - 10/31/64, POW since 4/63; $50 enl. bounty due. Paroled 9/18/64 and sent to Aiken's Landing, to be exchanged. Exchanged at Varina, Va., 9/22/64. Adm. Gen. Hosp. No. 9, 9/29/64, sick. Furloughed 9/29/64, 40 days. Adm. Chimborazo Hosp., 9/?/64, residence listed as Smith, Va. Present on a Hosp. MR of paroled prisoners at Chimborazo Hosp. No. 5, 9/27/64; adm. 9/23/64, debility. Furloughed 9/27/64, 40 days. Clothing issued at Chimborazo Hosp., 9/28/65. Paroled at Charleston, W. Va., 5/15/65. Desc.: age 26, 5'10", fair comp., brown hair and black eyes. CSR also lists him as a member of Co. F. NFR.

SYME, CHAPMAN J. - Pvt. Co. G. Employed as a courier, 11/1/63 - 11/30/63. Paid for service between 11/1/63 - 4/30/64. Enl. Bath Co., 2/1/64. Employed as a clerk, Signal Corps, Breckinridge's Div., 4/25/64 - 7/31/64. Ab. 9/1/64 - 10/31/64, on detached service in the Signal Corps. Paid 9/30/64 for service between 5/1/64 - 8/31/64. On extra duty as Signal Operator, 8/1/64 - 9/30/64, Breckinridge's Div. NFR.

TACY (TACEY, TRACY), JOHN A. - Sgt. Co. I. b. 10/13/30. Enl. Huntersville, Pocahontas Co., W. Va., 2/1/63 (3/18/63). Present on muster-in roll dated 3/63, Sgt. Mustered into service 3/19/63. Ab., Pvt., 6/30/63 - 2/29/64, detailed to attend horses of Capt. Marshall's command; mounted. Present 2/29/64 - 8/31/64. Present 9/1/64 - 10/31/64, $100 bond due. Paroled at Charleston, W. Va., 5/10/65, signs by x. Desc.: age 33(?), 5'6", dark comp., dark hair, gray eyes and dark whiskers. Post war resident of Randolph Co., W. Va. Age 49, farmer, Huttonsville, Randolph Co., W. Va. 1880 Census. Bur. Wells Cem., Randolph Co., W. Va.

TANNER, ELIJAH - Pvt. Co. H. Resident of Clay Co., W. Va. Arrested and confined at Wheeling, W. Va. Released on his oath and bond to live in O., by 3/13/62. Enl. Bath Co., 12/1/63. Clothing issued, 2/7/64 and 3/6/64. Ab. 9/1/64 - 10/31/64, AWOL; $50 enl. bounty due. NFR.

TANNER, GEORGE W. - Pvt. Co. A. b. Jackson Co., W. Va., c. 1834. Age 26, farmer, Calhoun Co., W. Va. 1860 Census. Post war roster only, which shows service in Daniel Duskey's section of the "Moccasin Rangers." NFR.

TANNER, JOSHUA - Pvt. Co. A. b. Calhoun Co., W. Va., c. 1842. Resident of Clay (Calhoun) Co., W. Va. Arrested and confined at Wheeling, W. Va. Released on his oath and bond to live in O., by 3/13/62. Prior service, 3rd VSL. Cpd. 12/6/62, place not stated. Confined at the Atheneum Prison. Not on muster rolls. POW record shows he enl. Greenbrier Co., W. Va., 10/63. Cpd. Webster Co., W. Va., 2/23/65 (2/22/65). Confined at Clarksburg, W. Va., 2/27/65. Desc.: age 23, 5'9", dark comp., light hair and blue eyes. Occ. farmer, residing in Webster Co., W. Va. Transf. to Wheeling, W. Va., 2/28/65. Confined at the Atheneum Prison, 2/28/65. Desc.: age 23, 5'9", fair comp., light hair and gray eyes, a resident of Roane Co., W. Va. Transf. to Camp Chase, 3/1/65. Confined at Camp Chase, 3/2/65. Joined US service, 3/20/65 and was sent to Chicago, Ill. NFR.

TANNER, LORENZO D. - Pvt. Co. A. Served in Co. A, 3rd VSL. Post war rosters only. NFR.

TANNER, THOMAS - Pvt. Co. A. Prior service, Co. A, 3rd VSL. Enl. Williamsburg, Greenbrier Co., W. Va., 3/1/63. Not stated if present or absent on muster-in roll dated 3/63. Clothing issued, 2/19/64, 2/23/64, 4/11/64, 4/30/64, 6/17/64 and 7/6/64, signs by x. NFR.

TAYLOR, ANDREW N. - Pvt. Co. I. b.c. 1846. Post war rosters only, which show he was a resident of Cass, Pocahontas Co., W. Va. Age 33, farmer, Edray, Pocahontas Co., W. Va. 1880 Census. Member of Moffett Poage Camp, UCV, Marlinton, W. Va. d. Cass, W. Va., 7/6/1927, age 81.

TAYLOR, CHARLES - 2nd Corp. Co. G. Enl. Frankfort, Greenbrier Co., W. Va., 3/12/63 (4/1/63). Not stated if present or absent on muster-in roll dated 3/63, Pvt. Clothing issued, 2/11/64, 4/30/64 and 6/17/64. Present, 2nd Corp., 9/1/64 - 10/31/64, has a servicable horse. NFR.

TAYLOR, GEORGE W. (of Daniel) - Pvt. Co. F. b.c. 1842. Enl. Dunmore, Pocahontas Co., W. Va., 2/15/64. Present 1/1/64 - 2/29/64. Cpd. Pocahontas Co., W. Va., 4/28/64. Confined at the Atheneum Prison, 5/12/64. Desc.: age 22, 5'9_", fair comp., dark hair and brown eyes. Occ. farmer, residing in Rockingham Co. Transf. to Camp Chase, 5/13/64. Confined at Camp Chase, 5/14/64. Ab. 9/1/64 - 10/31/64, cpd. 4/28/64; enl. bounty due. Paroled 2/25/65 and sent to City Point, to be exchanged. Exchanged. Adm. Jackson Hosp., 3/7/65, debilitas. Furloughed 3/8/65, 30 days. NFR.

TAYLOR, HENRY - Pvt. Co. I. b.c. 1847. Age 13, Pocahontas Co., W. Va. 1860 Census. Enl. Huntersville, Pocahontas Co., W. Va., 3/19/63 (3/18/63). Present on muster-in roll dated 3/63. Mustered into service 3/19/63. Ab. 6/30/63 - 2/29/64, not yet 18, given permission to remain at home. Post war resident of White Sulphur Dist., Greenbrier Co., W. Va. Member David S. Creigh Camp, UCV, Lewisburg, W. Va., 1895. NFR.

TAYLOR, LEVI J. - Pvt. Co. A. b. Gilmer Co., W. Va., c. 1845. Age 15, Calhoun Co., W. Va. 1860 Census. Prior service, Co. A, 3rd VSL. Enl. Williamsburg, Greenbrier Co., W. Va., 3/1/63. Not stated if present or absent on muster-in roll dated 3/63. CSR filed as Lin J. Taylor. NFR.

TAYLOR, THOMAS B. C. - Pvt. Co. I. b. Randolph Co., W. Va., c. 1835. Enl. Huntersville, Pocahontas Co., W. Va., 3/19/63. Present on muster-in roll dated 3/63. Mustered into service 3/19/63. Post war resident of Pocahontas Co., W. Va. NFR.

TAYLOR, WILLIAM SMITH - Pvt. Co. F. b. Harrisonburg, 6/9/38. Farmer, age 23, Harrison Co., W. Va. (1861). Prior service, McNeel's Co., 2nd VSL. and Co. C, 31st Va. Inf. Enl. Hillsboro, Pocahontas Co., W. Va., 3/9/63 (4/1/63). Not stated if present or absent on muster-in roll dated 3/63. Employed as a wagonmaster, 11/1/63 - 11/30/63. Present 1/1/64 - 2/29/64. Employed as a teamster at Warm Springs, 1/1/64 - 2/29/64. Present 9/1/64 - 10/31/64, enl. bounty due. Post war resident of Pocahontas, Harrison and Nicholas Co's., W. Va. d. Nicholas Co., W. Va., 4/14/1924. Bur. Taylor Family Cem., Nicholas Co., W. Va.

TAYLOR, WILLIAM W. - Pvt. Co. B. Post war rosters only, which show he was from Braxton Co., W. Va., and that he d. in service. NFR.

TENNANT, ALPHEUS "Alf" - Pvt. Co. A. b.c. 1840 (1842). Prior service, Co. A, 3rd VSL. Not on muster rolls, reference jacket only. Reference jacket shows enlistment in Co. A, 20th Va. Cav. Postwar rosters show he was cpd. and RTD. 7/10/63. Served in Lurty's Batty. Paroled as a member of Co. A, 19th Va. Cav., 5/23/65 at Rock Island Prison, Ill. Desc.: age 25, 5'8", fair comp., dark hair and blue eyes, a resident of Petroleum, Ritchie Co., W. Va. Believed to be bur. Dry Ridge Cem., Petroleum, Ritchie Co., W. Va.

THART (THARP), ZACHARIAH - Pvt. Co. K. Enl. Frankfort, Greenbrier Co., W. Va., 3/20/63. Not stated if present or absent on muster-in roll dated 3/63. Could be Zachariah Tharp. Served in Co. F, 46th Battn. Va. Cav. NFR.

THAYER (THAYEY), MORTIMER - Pvt. Co. B. b.c. 1846. Enl. Frankfort, Greenbrier Co., W. Va., 4/1/63. Present 11/1/63 - 2/29/64. Employed as a teamster, 11/15/63 - 11/30/63. returned to his Co., 11/16/63. Employed as a teamster at Warm Springs, 1/1/64 - 3/17/64, discharged and sent to his Co. Clothing issued, 1/17/64 (teamster), 4/11/64, 4/21/64 and 6/17/64, signs by x. Ab. 9/1/64 - 10/31/64, detailed in QM Dept. as teamster; $100 enl. bounty due. Paroled at Charleston, W. Va., 5/12/65, signs by x. Desc.: age 19, 5'8", fair comp., brown hair and gray eyes. NFR.

THOMAS, JOHN D. (B.) - Pvt. Co. I. b. Greenbrier Co., W. Va., c. 1834. Resident of Greenbrier Co., W. Va., 1856, age 21, a blacksmith. Age 26, laborer, Huntersville, Pocahontas Co., W. Va. 1860 Census. Prior service, Co. G, 31st Va. Inf. Enl. Huntersville, Pocahontas Co., W. Va., 2/1/63 (3/18/63). Present on muster-in roll dated 3/63. Mustered into service 3/19/63. Present 6/30/63 - 2/29/64, mounted. Ab. 2/29/64 - 8/31/64, transf. back to the 31st Va. Inf., 8/1/64. NFR.

THOMPSON, ALLEN R. - Sgt. Co. B. b.c. 1831. Enl. Frankfort, Greenbrier Co., W. Va., 3/7/63. Not stated if present or absent on muster-in roll dated 3/63, Pvt. Cpd. Pocahontas Co., W. Va., 12/20/63, listed as a Sgt., Co. K. Confined at the Atheneum Prison, 12/31/63. Desc.: age 32, 5'10", fair comp., dark hair, gray eyes and dark whiskers. Occ. blacksmith, residing in Pocahontas Co., W. Va. Transf. to Camp Chase, 12/31/63. Confined at Camp Chase, 1/1/64. Transf. to Ft. Delaware, 3/14/64. Confined at Ft. Delaware, 3/17/64. Paroled 10/30/64, to be exchanged. Exchanged at Venus Pt., Savannah River, 11/15/64. Adm. Ocmulgee Hosp., Macon, Ga., 11/15/64; residence listed as Pocahontas Co., W. Va. Transf. 11/18/64. Clothing issued 11/27/64 at Hood Hosp., Cuthbert, Ga. Paroled at Charleston, W. Va., 5/10/65, listed as a deserter, Sgt., Co. K. Desc.: age 34, 5'9 3/4", florid comp., dark hair and gray eyes. Occ. blacksmith, residing in Putnam Co., W. Va. Took the oath of allegiance, 5/31/65. NFR.

THOMPSON, S. P. - Pvt. Co. ?. Post war rosters only. NFR.

THOMPSON, WILLIAM - 4th Sgt. Co. G. Enl. Frankfort, Greenbrier Co., W. Va., 3/12/63. Not stated if present or absent on muster-in roll dated 3/63, 4th Sgt. Clothing issued, 3/1/64, listed as a Pvt. Clothing issued 4/30/64, listed as a member of Co. K. NFR.

THOMPSON, WILLIAM H. - Pvt. Co. G. b.c. 1843. Enl. Frankfort, Greenbrier Co., W. Va., 4/1/63. Clothing issued, 5/25/64, listed as a member of Co. D. Ab. 9/1/64 - 10/31/64, sick. Paroled at Charleston, W. Va., 6/22/65, as a member of Co. G. Desc.: age 22, 6', dark comp., dark hair and dark eyes. NFR.

THOMPSON, WILLIAM J. - Asst. Surg. Resident of Marion Co., W. Va. Hired by Col. W. L. Jackson as Asst. Surg., 4/3/63. Appointed Asst. Surg., 9/8/63. Present F&S MR 9/1/63 - 10/31/63. Present F&S MR 11/1/63 - 12/31/63. In charge of the Brigade Hosp., Warm Springs, 1/1/64 - 3/31/64. NFR.

THOMPSON, WILLIAM P. - Col. b. Wheeling, W. Va., 1/7/37. Resident of Wheeling, W. Va. Graduate of Jefferson College, in Pa. Lawyer, Fairmont, W. Va., 1857 - 1861. Age 24 (1861). Formed a Co. at Fairmont, W. Va., 5/17/61. Prior service, Co. A, 31st Va. Inf. and Major, 25th Va. Inf. Dropped as Major, 25th Va. Inf., 5/1/62. Appointed Lt. Col., 19th Va. Cav., 6/15/63, to rank from 4/11/63. Present F&S MR 9/1/63 - 10/31/63. Present F&S MR 11/1/63 - 12/31/63. Reported KIA. at Droop Mtn., W. Va., 11/6/63, but was not. Commanding Reg't. 11/6/63. Commanding Reg't. 1/64 - 3/64. Detailed as Pres., of a Gen. Court Martial, Warm Springs, Bath Co., 2/25/64. Relieved of duty on Gen. Court Martial, 3/4/64. Ab. on sick furlough, 7/31/64. Ab., F&S MR 9/1/64 - 10/31/64, on furlough. Commanding Brigade 10/4/64. Ab. 12/15/64, sick since 12/23/63. Adm. Charity Hosp.,

175

Gordonsville, 12/64. Transf. to Staunton Gen. Hosp. by 12/31/64. Member of the Va. Legislature, 1863 - 1864. Commanding Jackson's Brigade, 4/30/65, signing himself as Col. Paroled at Staunton, 5/20/65, as Col. Desc.: age 27, 6', light comp., light hair and gray eyes. Post war lawyer and resident of Chicago, Ill. In the Oil business, vice president of Standard Oil, Cleveland, O. Resigned 1887. Railroad director, New York City, 1890. Post war millionaire lead industrialist, said to be worth 20 million dollars. d. Brookdale, NJ, 2/3/96.

THORN, ALBERT G. - Pvt. Co. C. b. Jackson Co., W. Va., c. 1842. Enl. Jackson Co., W. Va., 10/1/64 (Greenbrier Co., W. Va., 9/64). Present 9/1/64 - 10/31/64, has one horse; $50 enl. bounty due. Cpd. Jackson Co., W. Va., 2/19/65. Confined at Clarksburg, W. Va., 2/21/65. Desc.: age 23, 5'9", fair comp., brown hair and blue eyes. Occ. farmer, residing in Jackson Co., W. Va. Transf. to Wheeling, W. Va., 2/22/65. Confined at the Atheneum Prison, 2/22/65. Transf. to Camp Chase, 2/24/65. Confined at Camp Chase, 2/25/65. Took the oath of allegiance and was released, 6/13/65. Desc.: age 24, 5'9_", florid comp., dark hair and blue eyes, a resident of Jackson Co., W. Va. NFR.

THORNBURG, JOHN S. - 1st Lt. Co. ?. b. 1826. Prior service, Co. E, 8th Va. Cav. Commissary Officer at Millboro, 4/13/63. Recommended by Col. W. L. Jackson, 6/6/63 for appointment as 1st Lt. and Drillmaster. Jackson said Thornburg had been authorized to raise a Co., but Jackson needed him as Acting Commissary and he lost the chance to raise his Co. "He is an efficient officer..." Appointed 1st Lt. and Drillmaster, 6/8/63, ordered to report to Col. W. L. Jackson. Resigned 10/5/63, approved 10/27/63. Post war resident of Cabell Co., W. Va. d. 1903. Bur. Spring Hill Cem., Huntington, W. Va.

THRASHER, ISAAC - 3rd Sgt. Co. B. b.c. 1839. Enl. Frankfort, Greenbrier Co., W. Va., 3/7/63 (3/9/63). Not stated if present or absent on muster-in roll dated 3/63, 3rd Sgt. Present, Pvt., 11/1/63 - 2/29/64, has one horse. Clothing issued, 2/11/64. Present 9/1/64 - 10/31/64, $100 enl. bounty due. Paroled at Charleston, W. Va., 5/8/65. Desc.: age 26, 5'8", fair comp., light hair, gray eyes and sandy whiskers. NFR.

TIBBS, EUGENIUS - 1st Sgt. Co. A. b.c. 1828 (1827). Prior service, Co. A, 3rd VSL. Enl. Williamsburg, Greenbrier Co., W. Va., 3/1/63. Not stated if present or absent on muster-in roll dated 3/63, 1st Sgt. Commanding a detachment of unorganized recruits, 7/2/63. Deserted, listed as a Pvt. Confined at Charleston, W. Va., 5/30/65. Took the amnesty oath and was released, 5/30/65. Desc.: age 37, 5'7_", fair comp., dark hair, dark eyes and sandy whiskers. Occ. farmer, residing in Ritchie Co., W. Va. Documents in his CSR show he was elected to the Va. House of Delegates from Pleasants and Ritchie Co's., W. Va., and that he resigned 8/63. Wished to raise a Co. of rangers, 2/26/65, was granted authority to do so. It is not known if he ever raised the Co. Post war source states he was a Capt. in the CS Secret Service, but the war ended before he could be called to active service. Post war resident and deputy sheriff, Ritchie Co., W. Va. Moved to South Dakota. Brother of Francis M. Tibbs. d. South Dakota.

TIBBS, FRANCIS MARION - 2nd Corp. Co. A. b.c. 1840. Prior service, Co. A, 3rd VSL. Enl. Williamsburg, Greenbrier Co., W. Va., 3/1/63. Not stated if present or absent on muster-in roll dated 3/63, 2nd Corp. Cpd. Wirt Co., W. Va., 1/23/64. Confined at the Atheneum Prison, 2/1/64. Desc.: age 24, 5'9", florid comp., sandy hair and blue eyes. Occ. farmer, residing in Ritchie Co., W. Va. To be held until further orders. Transf. to Camp Chase, 3/3/64. Confined at Camp Chase, 3/4/64. Transf. to Ft. Delaware, 3/14/64. Confined at Ft. Delaware, 3/17/64. Took the oath of allegiance and was released, 6/21/65. Desc.: age ?, 5'9", fair comp., red hair and gray eyes, a resident of Ritchie Co., W. Va. Post war resident of Paris, Mo. Brother of Eugenius Tibbs. Bur. Paris, Monroe Co., Mo.

TOLER (TOLLER), JOHN W. - Pvt. Co. B. Enl. Frankfort, Greenbrier Co., W. Va., 3/7/63 (3/9/63). Not stated if present or absent on muster-in roll dated 3/63. Present 11/1/63 - 2/29/64, had his own horse since 1/1/64. Present 9/1/64 - 10/31/64, $100 enl. bounty due. Paroled at Staunton, 5/11/65. Desc.: age 33, 6'_", fair comp., sandy hair and blue eyes. NFR.

TOLLEY, EDWARD C. - Pvt. Co. B. b. Augusta Co., c. 1843. POW record shows enl. as Augusta Co., 3/62. Not on muster rolls. Deserted. Reported at Beverly, W. Va., 10/26/64. Confined at Clarksburg, W. Va., 10/29/64. Took the oath of allegiance and was released, 10/29/64. Desc.: age 21, 5'10", fair comp., light hair and gray eyes. Occ. farmer, residing in Augusta Co. NFR.

TOMBLIN, JAMES P. - Pvt. Co. K. b. Albemarle Co., c. 1844. POW record shows enl. as Buckhannon Co., W. Va., 5/63. Not on muster rolls. Clothing issued, 2/5/64, 4/21/64, 5/1/64, 7/64 and 8/64. Cpd. near Buckhannon, Upshur Co., W. Va., 2/17/65. Confined at Clarksburg, W. Va., 2/20/65. Desc.: age 20, 5'11", fair comp., dark hair and black eyes. Occ. farmer, residing in Upshur Co., W. Va. Sent to Wheeling, W. Va., 2/22/65. Confined at the Atheneum Prison, 2/22/65. Transf. to Camp Chase, 2/24/65. Confined at Camp Chase, 2/25/65. Took the oath of allegiance and was released, 6/13/65. Desc.: age 21, 5'10", fair comp., dark hair and brown eyes, a resident of Upshur Co., W. Va. NFR.

TOMBLINSON (THOMBLINSON), DAVID - Corp. Co. H. b.c. 1848. Enl. Frankfort, Greenbrier Co., W. Va., 3/19/63 (Clay Co., W. Va., 4/1/63). Not stated if present or absent on muster-in roll dated 3/63. Clothing issued, 2/7/64, 3/1/64, 4/11/64 and 6/17/64, signs by x. Present, Corp., 9/1/64 - 10/31/64, has a servicable horse. Deserted. Paroled at Charleston, W. Va., 12/2/64. Desc.: age 16, 5'6", fair comp., dark hair and gray eyes, a farmer. NFR.

TONKIN, AMBROSE - Pvt. Co. B. b.c. 1839. Enl. Frankfort, Greenbrier Co., W. Va., 3/7/63 (3/9/63). Not stated if present or absent on muster-in roll dated 3/63. Present 11/1/63 - 2/29/64, has one horse. Clothing issued 4/30/64, 6/17/64 and 7/10/64. Present 9/1/64 - 10/31/64, $100 enl. bounty due. Paroled at Charleston, W. Va., 5/10/65. Desc.: age 26, 6', light comp., dark hair, gray eyes and light whiskers. NFR.

TONKIN, JOHN J. (I.) - 3rd Corp. Co. B. b. Lewis Co., W. Va., c. 1843. Enl. Frankfort, Greenbrier Co., W. Va., 3/7/63 (3/9/63). Not stated if present or absent on muster-in roll dated 3/63, Pvt. Present, 3rd Corp., 11/1/63 - 2/29/64, has his own horse. Clothing issued, 1st Qr. 1864, 4/21/64, 5/1/64 and 6/17/64, signs by x. Present 9/1/64 - 10/31/64, $100 enl. bounty due. Cpd. Webster Co., W. Va., 1/19/65. Confined at Clarksburg, W. Va., 1/23/65. Desc.: age 22, 5'10", fair comp., light hair and blue eyes. Occ. farmer, residing in Braxton Co., W. Va. Sent to Wheeling, W. Va., 1/24/65. Confined at the Atheneum Prison, 1/24/65. Transf. to Camp Chase, 4/13/65. Transf. to USA Post Hosp., Camp Chase, 7/11/65. DOD. Camp Chase, 7/20/65, pneumonia. Bur. Camp Chase Confederate Cem.

TOWNSEND, ALBERT - Pvt. Co. A. b. Kanawha Co., W. Va., c. 1842. Age 18, serving, Calhoun Co., W. Va. 1860 Census. Prior service, Co. A, 3rd VSL. Enl. Williamsburg, Greenbrier Co., W. Va., 3/1/63. Not stated if present or absent on muster-in roll dated 3/63. Clothing issued, 2/5/64, 2/19/64, 6/17/64 and 8/25/64, signs by x. NFR.

TOWNSEND, ALBERT A. - 3rd Corp. Co. K. b. Lewis Co., W. Va., c. 1843. Age 17, farmer, Gilmer Co., W. Va. 1860 Census. Enl. Frankfort, Greenbrier Co., W. Va., 3/20/63. Not stated if present or absent on muster-in roll dated 3/63, 3rd Corp. NFR.

TOWNSEND (TOWNSEN), JAMES Jr. - Pvt. Co. F. b.c. 1827. Age 33, laborer, Dunmore, Pocahontas Co., W. Va. 1860 Census. Prior service, McNeel's Co., 2nd VSL. Enl. Hillsboro, Pocahontas Co., W. Va., 3/9/63. Not stated if present or absent on muster-in roll dated 3/63. NFR.

TOWNSEND, LEVI N. - Pvt. Co. K. Enl. Frankfort, Greenbrier Co., W. Va., 3/20/63. Not stated if present or absent on muster-in roll dated 3/63, 3rd Corp. NFR.

TRACY, JAMES A. - Pvt. Co. F. b.c. 1845. Age 15, laborer, Greenbank, Pocahontas Co., W. Va. 1860 Census. Prior service, Co. G, 31st Va. Inf. Transf. to Co. F, 19th VA. Cav., 9/11/63. Enl. Hillsboro, Pocahontas Co., W. Va., 9/11/63. Not stated if present or absent 1/1/64 - 2/29/64, transf. to Co. G, 31st Va. Inf., 2/24/64. DOD. Elmira Prison, 3/17/65, chronic diarrhoea. Bur. Woodlawn National Cem., grave 1427 (1533).

TRACY, JOHN J. - Pvt. Co. F. Prior service, McNeel's Co., 2nd VSL. Enl. Hillsboro, Pocahontas Co., W. Va., 3/9/63. Not stated if present or absent on muster-in roll dated 3/63. NFR.

TRACY, JOHN P. - Pvt. Co. H. No enl. data. Not stated if present or absent on muster-in roll dated 3/63. NFR.

TRICKETT, MICHAEL E. - Pvt. Co. D. b.c. 1828. Enl. Williamsburg, Greenbrier Co., W. Va., 3/8/63. Not stated if present or absent on muster-in roll dated 3/63. Served in Co. A, 20th Va. Cav. DOD. Camp Chase, 9/10/64 (10/20/64), typhoid fever. Bur. Camp Chase Confederate Cem., grave no. 236.

TRIPPETT, CALEB - Pvt. Co. A. b. Monongalia Co., W. Va., c. 1845. Age 15, Calhoun Co., W. Va. 1860 Census. Prior service, Co. A, 3rd VSL. Age 16, Calhoun Co., W. Va. 1860 Census. Enl. Williamsburg, Greenbrier Co., W. Va., 3/1/63. Not stated if present or absent on muster-in roll dated 3/63. Clothing issued 2/19/64 and 4/30/64. Brother of Philip, son of Franklin. NFR.

TRIPPETT, FRANKLIN - Pvt. Co. A. b. Monongalia Co., W. Va., c. 1809. Age 51, farmer, Calhoun Co., W. Va. 1860 Census. Served in Co. A, 3rd VSL. Post war rosters only. Post war rosters show he enl. 6/15/61, and was discharged in 1864. Father of Philip and Caleb. Calhoun Co. History shows that he had 3 sons in the 19th Va. Cav., but does not name them. NFR.

TRIPPETT, PHILIP - 2nd Lt. Co. A. b. Monongalia Co., W. Va., 12/28/38. Moved to Calhoun Co., 12/1853. Age 21, Calhoun Co., W. Va. 1860 Census. Enl. 6/15/61. Prior service, Co. A, 3rd VSL, 1st Corp. Deserted at Lewisburg, W. Va., 2/15/63. Transf. to Co. A, 19th Va. Cav. Promoted to 2nd Lt., 1863. Paid for service 1/1/64 - 8/31/64 as Jr. 2nd Lt. Ab. 10/25/64, AWOL for 33 days, no steps taken to have him dropped from the rolls. Dropped as 2nd Lt., Co. A, 1/3/65. Post war farmer, Sheridan Dist., Big Bend, Calhoun Co., W. Va. Age 31, farmer, Sheridan Township, Calhoun Co., W. Va. 1870 Census. d. Calhoun Co., W. Va., 1/28/1922. Bur. Barr Cem., Sheridan Dist., Calhoun Co., W. Va. Son of Franklin, brother of Caleb.

TROTTER, A. S. - Pvt. Co. H. b.c. 1848. Not on muster rolls. Paroled at Charleston, W. Va., 5/22/65. Desc.: age 17, 5'5", light comp., brown hair and gray eyes. NFR.

TRUMAN, ROBERT - Pvt. Co. K. b. Gilmer Co., W. Va., c. 1849. Age 11, Calhoun Co., W. Va. 1860 Census. Enl. Frankfort, Greenbrier Co., W. Va., 3/20/63. Not stated if present or absent on muster-in roll dated 3/63. NFR.

TRUMAN, SHEDRICK - Pvt. Co. H. b. O., c. 1853. Enl. Roane Co., W. Va., 4/18/63. Ab. 9/1/64 - 10/31/64, AWOL; not mounted; enl. bounty due. Age 27, farmer, Spencer Dist., Roane Co., W. Va. 1880 Census, listed as Shadric Truman. NFR.

TUCKER, BENJAMIN F. - Pvt. Co. D. b. Marion Co., W. Va., c. 1844. Enl. Williamsburg, Greenbrier Co., W. Va., 3/8/63. POW record shows enl. as Highland Co., 8/62. Not stated if present or absent on muster-in roll dated 3/63. Clothing issued 6/17/64. Cpd. Upshur Co., W. Va., 4/1/65. Confined at Clarksburg, W. Va., 4/5/65. Desc.: age 21, 5'11_", fair comp., brown hair and blue eyes. Occ. farmer, residing in Marion Co., W. Va. Transf. to Cumberland, Md., 4/6/65. Post war resident of Marion Co., W. Va. NFR.

TUCKER, CHRISTOPHER B. - Pvt. Co. H. b.c. 1845. Prior service, Co. K, 11th W. Va. Inf. Age 18 in 1863. Deserted to CSA. Enl. Clay Co., W. Va., 5/14/63. Ab. 9/1/64 - 10/31/64, AWOL; not mounted; enl. bounty due. Post war resident of Angerona, Jackson Co., W. Va. NFR.

TUCKER, ETHAN W. - Pvt. Co. D. Prior service, Co. C, 46th Battn. Va. Cav. Not on muster rolls. Clothing issued 4/1/64 and 6/17/64. Cpd., date and place not known. Adm. USA Post Hosp., Clarksburg, W. Va., 11/17/64, inflamation of throat. RTD. 12/24/64. NFR.

TUCKER, JACOB - Pvt. Co. D. b. Harrison Co., W. Va., c. 1827. Age 33, farmer, Pruntytown, Taylor Co., W. Va. 1860 census. Prior service, Hansbrough's Co., 9th Battn. Va. Inf. and Co. A, 25th Va. Inf. Requested permission to raise a Co. for Col. W. L. Jackson's command, 4/28/63, permission refused. Not on muster rolls. POW record shows his enl. as Pruntytown, W. Va., 5/61. Cpd. Barbour Co., W. Va., 1/3/65. Confined at Clarksburg, W. Va., 1/4/65. Desc.: age 36, 5'11", fair comp., light hair and blue eyes. Occ. farmer, residing in Taylor Co., W. Va. Transf. to Wheeling, W. Va. Confined at the Atheneum Prison, 1/14/65. Transf. to Camp Chase, 1/16/65. Confined at Camp Chase, 1/17/65, supposed spy. Took the oath of allegiance and was released, 6/13/65. Desc.: age 36, 5'10_", fair comp., light hair and blue eyes, a resident of Taylor Co., W. Va. NFR.

TUCKER, JAMES M. - Pvt. Co. A. Post war rosters only, which show he was a resident of Calhoun Co., W. Va. NFR.

TUCKER, JOHN J. - Corp. Co. B. Not on muster rolls. Cpd. Webster Co., W. Va., 1/17/65. NFR.

TUCKER, JOHN N. - Pvt. Co. D. Prior service, Co. C, 46th Battn. Va. Cav. Not on muster rolls. Clothing issued, 6/17/64. Could be John Nathan Tucker. NFR.

TUCKER, NATHAN - Pvt. Co. D. b.c. 1837. Enl. Williamsburg, Greenbrier Co., W. Va., 3/8/63. Not stated if present or absent on muster-in roll dated 3/63. Cpd. Beverly, W. Va., 1/9/64, gave himself up, wishes to take the oath of allegiance. Confined at the Atheneum Prison, 1/16/64. Desc.: age 27, 5'10", florid comp., dark hair and dark eyes. Occ. farmer, residing in Marion Co., W. Va. Transf. to Camp Chase, 1/20/64. Confined at Camp Chase, 1/21/64. Desires to take the oath of allegiance, 6/10/64, deserter. Joined the US Navy, 7/21/64. Age 44, farmer, Mannington Dist., Marion Co., W. Va. 1880 Census. NFR.

TUCKER, WESLEY - Pvt. Co. B. b. Taylor Co., W. Va., c. 1838. Not on muster rolls. POW record shows enl. as Crab Bottom, Highland Co., 7/63. Cpd. Taylor Co., W. Va., 10/28/64. Confined at Clarksburg, W. Va. Desc.: age 26, 5'9", fair comp., dark hair and brown eyes. Occ. farmer, residing in Taylor Co., W. Va. NFR.

TURNER, EMMETT C. - Pvt. Co. A. Served in Co. A, 3rd VSL. Roll for 2/28/63 shows he deserted and joined the Confederate service. Post war rosters only. NFR.

TURNER, ROBERT LEWIS - 2nd Corp. Co. G. Enl. Frankfort, Greenbrier Co., W. Va., 3/12/63. Not stated if present or absent on muster-in roll dated 3/63, 2nd Corp. Clothing issued, 3/1/64, 4/30/64 and 6/17/64. Post war resident of Okla. Pensioner, 1915. NFR.

TUTWILER, EDWARD H. - Pvt. Co. H. Enl. Bath Co., 2/1/64. Clothing issued 3/12/64 and 6/17/64. Present 9/1/64 - 10/31/64, has a servicable horse; $50 enl. bounty due; on detached duty. NFR.

TYLER, JAMES (JOHN) E. - Pvt. Co. F. b.c. 1845. Age 15, laborer, Pocahontas Co., W. Va. 1860 Census. Prior service, McNeel's Co., 2nd VSL. Enl. Hillsboro, Pocahontas Co., W. Va., 3/9/63. Not stated if present or absent on muster-in roll dated 3/63. Cpd. Beverly, W. Va., 1/15/64. Confined at the Atheneum Prison, 2/1/64. Desc.: age 19, 6', dark comp., dark hair and dark eyes. Occ. farmer, residing in Pocahontas Co., W. Va. Took the oath of allegiance and was released, 2/2/64. NFR.

UMPHREYS (HUMPHREYS), MADISON - Pvt. Co. F. Post war rosters only. NFR.

UNDERWOOD, MICHAEL M. - Pvt. Co. I. b.c. 1822. Age 38, farmer, Mill Point, Pocahontas Co., W. Va. 1860 Census. Enl. Huntersville, Pocahontas Co., W. Va., 3/22/63. Ab. 6/30/63 - 2/29/64, at home sick. Age 51, farmer, Huntersville, Pocahontas Co., W. Va. 1880 Census. NFR.

UTTER, BRYANT - Pvt. Co. C. b.c. 1840. Age 10, 1850 Wirt Co., W. Va. Census. Prior service, Co. D, 3rd VSL. Enl. Frankfort, Greenbrier Co., W. Va., 3/15/63 (Pocahontas Co., W. Va., 4/1/63). Not stated if present or absent on muster-in roll dated 3/63. Present 1/1/63 - 4/1/63, has one horse. Not stated if present or absent, 12/31/63 - 8/31/64, wd. near Winchester, 7/20/64; was absent sick and deserted; has one horse. Clothing issued 2/25/64, 4/30/64 and 6/17/64, signs by x. Served in Co. F, 20th Va. Cav. Brother of Marion and Samuel Utter. NFR.

UTTER, MARION - Pvt. Co. C. b.c. 1838. Age 12, 1850 Wirt Co., W. Va. Census. Prior service, Co. D, 3rd VSL. Enl. Frankfort, Greenbrier Co., W. Va., 3/15/63 (Pocahontas Co., W. Va., 4/1/63). POW record shows enl. as Wirt Co., W. Va., 10/62. Not stated if present or absent on muster-in roll dated 3/63. Present 1/1/63 - 4/1/63, has one horse. Present 12/31/63 - 8/31/64, had his own horse since 7/1/64. Clothing issued, 2/25/64. Ab. 9/1/64 - 10/31/64, sick; furloughed since 9/15/64; has one horse. Wd. Fisher's Hill, 9/22/64, left leg. Cpd. Fisher's Hill, 9/22/64 (9/27/64). Adm. Sheridan Depot Field Hosp., Winchester, 10/6/64, wd. left leg. Sent to Gen. Hosp., Martinsburg, W. Va., 10/12/64. Adm. USA Gen. Hosp., West's Building, Baltimore, Md., 10/13/64, gunshot wd. to left leg, near the ankle by round ball. Simple dressing applied. Age 24, doing well. Sent to Pt. Lookout, Gen. Hosp., 10/27/64. Confined at Pt. Lookout, 10/29/64. Paroled 10/30/64, to be exchanged, signs by x. Exchanged at Venus Point, Savannah River, Ga., 11/15/64. Present on MR of paroled and exchanged prisoners at Camp Lee, near Richmond, 12/1/64. Clothing issued as a paroled prisoner, 12/1/64, signs by x. Served in Co. F, 20th Va. Cav. Brother of Bryant and Samuel Utter. NFR.

UTTER, SAMUEL - Pvt. Co. C. b.c. 1846. Age 4, 1850 Wirt Co., W. Va. Census. Enl. Alleghany Co., 5/1/64. Present 12/31/63 - 8/31/64, has one horse; $50 enl. bounty due. Clothing issued 4/30/64 and 6/17/64, signs by x. Adm. Gen. Hosp., Winchester, 7/26/64, rubeola. Adm. Gen. Hosp., Winchester, 8/2/64, debilitas. RTD. 8/3/64, transf. to Dr. Hagy. Present 9/1/64 - 10/31/64, has one horse. Deserted. Took the amnesty oath at Charleston, W. Va., 4/25/65, and was sent North. Desc.: age 15, 5'8", dark comp., dark hair and dark eyes. Occ. farmer, residing in Wirt Co., W. Va. Brother of Bryant and Marion Utter. NFR.

VANCE, HENRY L. - Pvt. Co. G. Enl. Pocahontas Co., W. Va., 7/1/63. Ab. 9/1/64 - 10/31/64, POW. Employed as a teamster, 11/1/63 - 11/30/63, signs by x. Employed as a teamster at Warm Springs, 1/1/64 - 2/29/64, signs by x. Clothing issued, 11/20/63, 1/16/64, 5/1/64, 5/25/64 and 6/17/64, signs by x. Cpd. Loudoun Co. (near Harpers Ferry, W. Va.), 7/16/64. Sent to Harpers Ferry, W. Va., then to Washington, DC. Confined at the Old Capitol Prison, 7/20/64. Transf. to Elmira, NY, 7/23/64. Confined at Elmira Prison, 7/25/64. Took the oath of allegiance and was released 6/14/65. Desc.: age ?, 5'8 3/4", dark comp., dark hair and hazel eyes, a resident of Staunton. Drew a Va. Pension, 1915.

VANDAE (VANDALL), WILLIAM F. - Pvt. Co. C. Prior service, Co. D, 3rd VSL. Enl. Frankfort, Greenbrier Co., W. Va., 3/15/63. Not stated if present or absent on muster-in roll dated 3/63. Ab. 1/1/63 - 4/1/63, deserted 3/15/63; has one horse. Served in Co. D, 46th Battn. Va. Cav. NFR.

VANDINE, ISAIAH (JOSIAH) - Pvt. Co. C. Enl. Pocahontas Co., W. Va., 7/1/63. Present 12/31/63 - 8/31/64, has one horse. Clothing issued, 4/30/64, 7/64 and 8/64. Ab. 9/1/64 - 10/31/64, has one horse; deserted 9/22/64. NFR.

Van REENAN (Van RENEN, Van RENAN, VANRENAN), JOHN - Pvt. Co. F. b.c. 1841. Age 19, laborer, Huntersville, Pocahontas Co., W. Va. 1860 Census. Prior service, McNeel's Co., 2nd VSL. Enl. Hillsboro, Pocahontas Co., W. Va., 3/9/63 (4/1/63). Not stated if present or absent on muster-in roll dated 3/63. Present 1/1/64 - 2/29/64. Present 9/1/64 - 10/31/64, enl. bounty due. Paroled at Charleston, W. Va., 5/11/65. Desc.: age 22, 5'9", light comp., light hair, blue eyes and light whiskers. NFR.

VARNER (VARNEY), JACOB - Pvt. Co. A. Not on muster rolls. Resident of Jackson Co., W. Va. Cpd. Wirt Co., W. Va., 12/15/61. Confined at the Atheneum Prison, under heavy guard. Tried by a US Court in Western Va., 4/14/62, for robbing the post office at Ripley, W. Va.; convicted and sentenced to three years in prison. Confined at Albany, NY, before 6/63. Released 6/4/63, by Presidential Pardon, dated 6/1/63. Post war rosters show him as a member of Daniel Duskey's section of the "Moccasin Rangers." Post war resident of Calhoun Co., W. Va. NFR.

VARNER, JOHN W. - Corp. Co. I. b.c. 1842. Age 18, laborer, Pocahontas Co., W. Va. 1860 Census. Enl. Huntersville, Pocahontas Co., W. Va., 2/1/64 (3/18/63). Present on muster-in roll dated 3/63, Corp. Mustered into service 3/19/63. Ab., Pvt., 6/30/63 - 2/29/64, detailed to feed horses for Capt. Marshall's Co.; mounted. Present 2/29/64 - 8/31/64, wd. Flint Stone Creek, Md., 8/1/64. Ab. 9/1/64 - 10/31/64, wd; $100 bond due. Age 39, farmer, Edray, Pocahontas Co., W. Va. 1880 Census. Post war resident of Randolph Co., W. Va. Member of Gen. Pegram Camp, UCV, Valley Head, W. Va. d. by 1915. NFR.

VASS, ED C. - Pvt. Co. G. Enl. Frankfort, Greenbrier Co., W. Va., 3/12/63. Not stated if present or absent on muster-in roll dated 3/63. NFR.

VERNAY, BENJAMIN - Pvt. Co. B. Enl. Frankfort, Greenbrier Co., W. Va., 3/7/63. Not stated if present or absent on muster-in roll dated 3/63. NFR.

VIARS (VIAZZ), MATTHEW - Pvt. Co. A. Served in Co. A, 3rd VSL. Post war rosters only. NFR.

VICKERS, FRANCIS MARION - Pvt. Co. G. b. Kanawha Co., W. Va., c. 1843. Enl. Pocahontas Co., W. Va., 8/8/63. Wd. Droop Mtn., 11/6/63, right arm, amputated at shoulder joint. Clothing issued 4/30/64. Ab. 9/1/64 - 10/31/64, lost arm at Droop Mtn., 11/6/63. Adm. CSA Gen. Hosp., Charlottesville, 6/16/64, vulnus sclopeticum, right arm; transf. 6/26/64. At Columbia, SC, Gen. Hosp., 7/27/64. Clothing issued at Gen. Hosp. No. 1, Columbia, SC, 7/28/64. Adm. CSA Gen. Hosp., Charlottesville, 11/1/64, vulnus sclopeticum, right arm amputated. Clothing issued at Staunton Gen. Hosp., 12/13/64. Adm. CSA Gen. Hosp., Charlottesville, 1/17/65, vulnus sclopeticum, right arm amputated. Retired 1/19/65 because of gunshot. Desc.: age 22, 5'8", fair comp., dark hair and hazel eyes. Applied for retirement, 1/20/65(?), from Charlottesville. Adm. Gen. Hosp. No. 9, 1/21/65, retired. NFR.

VIERS, MATHESON (MADISON) - Pvt. Co. B. b.c. 1843. Enl. Frankfort, Greenbrier Co., W. Va., 6/14/63. Ab. 11/1/63 - 2/29/64, deserted 11/4/63. Ab. 9/1/64 - 10/31/64, deserted 11/5/63; not entitled to $100 enl. bounty. Cpd. Webster Co., W. Va., 3/2/65. Confined at the Atheneum Prison, 3/11/65. Desc.: age 22, 5'7", dark comp., black hair and black eyes. Occ. farmer, residing at Franklin, W. Va. Transf. to Camp Chase, 3/16/65. Confined at Camp Chase, 3/17/65. Took the oath of allegiance and was released, 6/13/65. Desc.: age 22, 5'7", dark comp., black hair and black eyes, a resident of Webster Co., W. Va. NFR.

VINCENT, ———— - Lt. Co. ?. Mentioned in Brig. Gen. John D. Imboden's report of the Jones - Imboden Raid into Western Virginia, 4-5/63, as having been "lost." Bur. Frenchton Cem., Upshur Co., W. Va.

VINCENT, EDWARD FLETCHER - Pvt. Co. B. b. Marion Co., W. Va., 5/14/25. Prewar farmer. Prior service, Co. A, 31st Va. Inf. Transf. to Co. B, 20th Va. Cav., 8/1/63. Enl. Highland Co., 4/1/63. Present, QM Sgt., FS MR. Not on muster rolls. Clothing issued as a member of Co. B, 19th Va. Cav., 2/7/64. Served in Co. B, 20th Va. Cav. Post war member of Staunton Camp UCV, age 81 in 1906. d. Shutterlee Mill Road, Augusta Co., 7/11/1914 (7/10/1914).

VINCENT, ISAAC T. - Pvt. Co. D. Enl. Williamsburg, Greenbrier Co., W. Va., 3/8/63. Not stated if present or absent on muster-in roll dated 3/63. NFR.

WADE, HENRY H. - Pvt. Co. I. b.c. 1841. Enl. Huntersville, Pocahontas Co., W. Va., 5/22/63. Ab. 6/30/63 - 2/29/64, cpd. Droop Mtn., 11/6/63. Cpd. Droop Mtn., Pocahontas Co., W. Va., 11/6/63. Confined at the Atheneum Prison, 11/16/63. Desc.: age 22, 6'2", dark comp., dark hair and dark eyes. Occ. farmer, residing in Rockbridge Co. Transf. to Camp Chase, 11/18/63. Confined at Camp Chase, 11/18/63. Transf. to Ft. Delaware, 2/29/64. Confined at Ft. Delaware, 3/4/64 (3/2/64). Ab. 2/29/64 - 8/31/64, cpd. Droop Mtn., 11/6/63. Ab. 9/1/64 - 10/31/64, cpd. Droop Mtn., 11/6/63; $100 bond due. Took the oath of allegiance and was released, 6/7/65. Desc.: age ?, 5'10", dark comp., black hair and hazel eyes, a resident of Rockbridge Co. NFR.

WADE, THOMAS SMITH - Chaplain. b. Highland Co., 8/5/38. Methodist Minister, licensed 8/58. Appointed Chaplain 4/15/63. Present F&S MR 9/1/63 - 10/31/63. Ab. F&S MR 11/1/63 - 12/31/63, leave. Ab. F&S MR 9/1/64 - 10/31/64, AWOL. Postwar minister and resident of Clarksburg and Wood Co., W. Va. Bur. IOOF Cem., Clarksburg, W. Va.

WAGNER (WAGGONER), SAMUEL - Pvt. Co. C. Prior service, Co. D, 3rd VSL. Enl. Frankfort, Greenbrier Co., W. Va., 3/15/63. Not stated if present or absent on muster-in roll dated 3/63. Muster roll for Co. D, 3rd VSL, 1/1/63 - 4/1/63, shows that he d. Wytheville, 3/1/63, and had one horse. NFR.

WAGONER (WAGGONER), ISAAC S. - Pvt. Co. I. b. Highland Co., c. 1831. Age 29, farmhand, Monterey, Highland Co. 1860 Census. Enl. Huntersville, Pocahontas Co., W. Va., 1/1/64. POW record shows enl. as Pocahontas Co., W. Va., 6/63. Not stated if present or absent 6/30/63 - 2/29/64, new recruit; mounted; enl. bounty due. Present 2/29/64 - 8/31/64, enl. bounty due. Ab. 9/1/64 - 10/31/64, AWOL. Deserter. Reported at Beverly, W. Va., 12/31/64. Confined at Clarksburg, W. Va., 1/3/65. Took the oath of allegiance and was released, 1/3/65. Desc.: age 34, 5'8", fair comp., light hair and blue eyes. Occ. farmer, residing in Highland Co. NFR.

WALKER, ROBERT W. - Pvt. Co. E. b. Botetourt Co., c. 1830. Age 30, farmer, Gilmer Co., W. Va. 1860 Census. Enl. Frankfort, Greenbrier Co., W. Va., 3/13/63 (4/1/63). Not stated if present or absent on muster-in roll dated 3/63. Present 10/31/63 - 10/31/64, had his own horse since 7/1/64; wagon master. Employed as a wagon master, 11/1/63 - 11/30/63. Employed as a wagon master at Warm Springs, 1/1/64 - 2/29/64. Clothing issued, 1/16/64, 1/17/64 (detailed wagon master); 3/1/64, 5/1/64, 5/21/64, 5/26/64, 6/17/64 and 3rd Qr. 1864. Paroled at Charleston, W. Va., 5/11/65. Desc.: age 37, 5'10", fair comp., dark hair, blue eyes and light whiskers. NFR.

WALKER, WILLIAM E. - Pvt. Co. H. b.c. 1846. Not on muster rolls. Cpd. Beverly, W. Va., 2/10/64. Confined at the Atheneum Prison, 2/21/64. Desc.: age 18, 5'10", fair comp., dark hair and gray eyes. Occ. mechanic, residing in NC. Took the oath of allegiance and was released, 2/22/64. NFR.

WALTON, JOSEPH FRANKLIN - Pvt. Co. F. b.c. 1825. Age 35, farmer, Pocahontas Co., W. Va. 1860 Census. Member Locust Creek Patrol, Pocahontas Co., W. Va., 5/61. Prior service, McNeel's Co., 2nd VSL. Enl. Hillsboro, Pocahontas Co., W. Va., 3/9/63 (9/11/63). Not stated if present or absent on muster-in roll dated 3/63. Present 1/1/64 - 2/29/64. Present 9/1/64 - 10/31/64, enl. bounty due. Paroled at Charleston, W. Va., 5/10/65. Desc.: age 40, 5'5", dark comp., dark hair, gray eyes and dark hair. Age 55, farmer, Little Levels, Pocahontas Co., W. Va. 1880 Census. NFR.

WAMSLEY, ADAM H. - 1st Sgt. Co. I. b. Randolph Co., W. Va., 10/12/38. Age 22, farmer, Randolph Co., W. Va. 1860 Census. Enl. Beverly, W. Va., 4/25/63. Present, Pvt., 6/30/63 - 2/29/64, mounted. Present, Pvt., 2/29/64 - 8/31/64, detailed to care for the wd. Present 9/1/64 - 10/31/64, $100 bond due. Paroled at Charleston, W. Va., 5/10/65, listed as 1st Sgt. Desc.: age 26, 6', light comp., light hair, blue eyes and light whiskers. Post war resident of Randolph Co., W. Va. Brother of George F. and Samuel Wamsley. Age 41, farmer, Valley Bend, Randolph Co., W. Va. 1880 Census. d. 8/12/1903.

WAMSLEY, G. B. - Pvt. Co. I. Enl. Beverly, W. Va., 4/25/63. Present 9/1/64 - 10/31/64, detailed for blacksmith in Co.; $100 bond due. NFR.

WAMSLEY, GEORGE F. - Pvt. Co. I. b. 8/10/45. Age 15, farmer, Randolph Co., W. Va. 1860 Census. Enl. Camp Northwest, Pocahontas Co., W. Va., 4/12/63. Present 6/30/63 - 2/29/64, mounted. Ab. 2/29/64 - 8/31/64, POW. Clothing issued 3/22/64. Cpd. Randolph Co., W. Va., 3/26/64. Confined at the Atheneum Prison, 4/5/64. Desc.: age 19, 5'11", fair comp., light hair and dark eyes. Occ. farmer, residing in Randolph Co., W. Va. Transf. to Camp Chase, 4/8/64. Confined at Camp Chase, 4/9/64. Ab. 9/1/64 - 10/31/64, POW; $100 bond due. Took the oath of allegiance and was released, 8/26/64, by order of the Sec. of War. Andrew M. Wamsley, posted a bond of $500 as surety. Desc.: age 19, 5'6", light comp., dark hair and gray eyes, a resident of Randolph Co., W. Va. Post war resident of Randolph Co., W. Va. Brother of Adam and Samuel Wamsley. Age 34, Valley Bend, Randolph Co., W. Va. 1880 Census. d. 2/21/81. Bur. Huttonsville, W. Va.

WAMSLEY, JACOB SEE - Capt. Co. D. b. Randolph Co., W. Va., 9/4/23. Age 36, farmer, Randolph Co., W. Va. 1860 Census. Enl. Huntersville, Pocahontas Co., W. Va., 2/1/63 (3/18/63). Asst. Provost Marshall, Pocahontas Co., W. Va., 2/63. Present on muster-in roll dated 3/63, 1st Lt., commanding Co. Mustered into service 3/19/63. Present 6/30/63 - 2/29/64, commanding Co. Mentioned for "distinguished conduct" at Beverly, W. Va., 7/63, by Col. W. L. Jackson in his report. Mentioned for "good conduct" in Maj. D. B. Stewart's report also, who reports him as being a member of Capt. J. W. Marshall's Co. Present 2/29/64 - 8/31/64, commanding Co. Present 9/1/64 - 10/31/64, commanding Co. Paroled at Charleston, W. Va., 5/10/65, as Capt. Desc.: age 41, 6'1", dark comp., black hair, black eyes and dark whiskers. Obit. shows service in Co. I. Post war resident of Randolph Co., W. Va. Age 56, farmer, Huttonsville, Randolph Co., W. Va. 1880 Census. Member of the Randolph Co. Court, 1882-1888. Also listed as being a resident of Pocahontas Co., W. Va. d. Huttonsville (near Elk Water), W. Va., 4/22/1898, after a lingering illness. Bur. Old Brick Church Cem., Huttonsville, W. Va.

WAMSLEY, RANDOLPH J. - Pvt. Co. I. Enl. Huntersville, Pocahontas Co., W. Va., 3/19/63. Present on muster-in roll dated 3/63. Mustered into service 3/19/63. Acted as a guide for Maj. D. B. Stewart in the Beverly, W. Va. fight, 7/2/63 - 7/3/63. KIA. near Beverly, W. Va., 7/3/63. Bur. Holly Bush Road Cem., Mingo, Randolph Co., W. Va.

WAMSLEY, SAMUEL B. Jr. - Pvt. Co. I. b. 1/28/40. Age 20, farmer, Randolph Co., W. Va. 1860 Census. Enl. Beverly, W. Va., 4/25/63. Present 6/30/63 - 2/29/64, sick; mounted. Present 2/29/64 - 8/31/64. Paroled at Charleston, W. Va., 5/10/65. Desc.: age 25, 5'9", fair comp., brown hair and blue eyes. Post war rosters show him as being from Tucker Co., W. Va., and that he was a member of Co. D. Post war rosters show him as a farmer, residing at Horse Shoe, Tucker Co., W. Va. Brother of Adam H. and George F. Wamsley. Attended Confederate Reunion, Randolph Co., W. Va., 1906. Resident of Ft. Cobb, Okla., 1916. d. 7/28/1930.

WANLESS, STEPHEN H. - Pvt. Co. I. b.c. 1834. Age 26, farmer, Huntersville, Pocahontas Co., W. Va. 1860 Census. Post war rosters only. Age 47, farmer, Huntersville, Pocahontas Co., W. Va. 1880 Census. NFR.

WARD, ADAM S. - Pvt. Co. I. b. 6/7/42. Age 19, farmer, Randolph Co., W. Va. 1860 Census. Attended Huttonsville Academy, 1861. Prior service, Co. F, 31st Va. Inf. History of the 31st Va. Inf. shows he transf. to the 19th Va. Cav., 4/22/64. Enl. Beverly, W. Va., 4/30/63. Present 2/29/64 - 8/31/64, transf. from the 31st Va. Inf. Present 9/1/64 - 10/31/64, $100 bond due. Also listed as being a member of Co. A, 19th Va. Cav. Post war resident of Randolph Co., W. Va. and Shamrock, Mo. (1916). Brother of Jacob G. and Rennix S. Ward. Age 38, farmer, Mingo, Randolph Co., W. Va. 1880 Census. d. 3/29/1919.

WARD, ANDREW - Pvt. Co. I. Post war rosters only, which show he was a resident of Randolph Co., W. Va. NFR.

WARD, ELIHU B. - Pvt. Co. I. b. 4/11/38. Age 22, farmer, Randolph Co., W. Va. 1860 Census. Enl. Beverly, W. Va., 4/30/63. Ab. 6/30/63 - 2/29/64, detailed to feed horses for Capt. Marshall's Co. Present 2/29/64 - 8/31/64, wd. Winchester, 9/20/64. Present 9/1/64 - 10/31/64, $100 bond due. Paroled at Charleston, W. Va., 5/10/65. Desc.:age 26, 5'9", fair comp., dark hair, blue eyes and a mustache. Post war resident of Randolph Co., W. Va. Age 42, farmer, Huttonsville, Randolph Co., W. Va. 1880 Census. Attended Confederate Reunion, Randolph Co., W. Va., 1906. Awarded Cross of Honor. Member Gen. Pegram Camp, UCV, Valley Head, W. Va. d. Huttonsville, W. Va., 11/13/1909. Bur. Brick Church Cem., Huttonsville, W. Va.

WARD, GEORGE W. - Pvt. Co. I. b. 5/4/35. Age 25, farmer, Randolph Co., W. Va. 1860 Census. Enl. Dunmore, Pocahontas Co., W. Va., 12/26/63. Ab. 6/30/63 - 2/29/64, by permission; mounted; enl. bounty due. Ab. 2/29/64 - 8/31/64, mounted; enl. bounty due; POW. Clothing issued, 3/22/64. Cpd. Randolph Co., W. Va., 3/26/64. Confined at the Atheneum Prison, 4/5/64. Desc.: age 28, 5'8_", florid comp., black hair and gray eyes. Occ. farmer, residing in Randolph Co., W. Va. Transf. to Camp Chase, 6/25/64. Confined at Camp Chase, 6/26/64, took the oath of allegiance in 1861, then joined the rebels. Ab. 9/1/64 - 10/31/64, $100 bond due; POW. Took the oath of allegiance and was released, 1/8/65. Desc.: age 29, 5'9", dark comp., dark hair and gray eyes, a resident of Randolph Co., W. Va. Post war resident of Randolph Co., W. Va. d. 5/17/77. Bur. Brick Church Cem., Huttonsville, W. Va.

WARD, JACOB G. - 2nd Lt. Co. I. b.c. 1844. Age 16, farmer, Randolph Co., W. Va. 1860 Census. Enl. Huntersville, Pocahontas Co., W. Va., 4/12/63. Present, Pvt., 6/30/63 - 2/29/64, mounted. Present 2/29/64 - 8/31/64, appointed 1st Sgt., 6/1/64. Clothing issued 3/22/64. Present 9/1/64 - 10/31/64, $100 bond due. Promoted to 2nd Lt. Paroled at Mt. Sidney, 5/8/65, as a 2nd Lt. Desc.: age 21, 6'_", fair comp., black hair and hazel eyes. Post war resident of Randolph Co., W. Va. and Springfield, Colo. Brother of Adam S. and Rennix S. Ward. Age 36, farmer, Huttonsville, Randolph Co., W. Va. 1880 Census. d. by 1916. Bur. Springfield Cem., Springfield, Colo.

WARD, JAMES R. - Pvt. Co. H. Enl. Frankfort, Greenbrier Co., W. Va., 3/19/63 (Clay Co., W. Va., 5/14/63). Not stated if present or absent on muster-in roll dated 3/63. Ab. 9/1/64 - 10/31/64, AWOL. NFR.

WARD, LEE M. - Sgt. Co. I. b.c. 1846 (1844). Age 16, farmer, Randolph Co., W. Va. 1860 Census. Enl. Huntersville, Pocahontas Co., W. Va., 4/12/63. Present 6/30/63 - 2/29/64, mounted. Present 2/29/64 - 8/31/64. Present 9/1/64 - 10/31/64, $100 bond due. Paroled at Charleston, W. Va., 5/10/65, as a Sgt. Desc.: age 19, 5'8", fair comp., light hair and blue eyes. Post war resident of Randolph Co., W. Va. Age 35, farmer, Huttonsville, Randolph Co., W. Va. 1880 Census. Attended Confederate Reunion, Randolph Co., W. Va., 1906. Awarded Cross of Honor. Resident of Huttonsville, W. Va., 1916. d. 10/30/1916. Bur. Brick Church Cem., Huttonsville, W. Va.

WARD, RENICK (RENNICK) S. - Pvt. Co. I. b.c. 1846. Age 14, Randolph Co., W. Va. 1860 Census. Enl. Huntersville, Pocahontas Co., W. Va., 3/18/63. Present 6/30/63 - 2/29/64, mounted. Ab. 2/29/64 - 8/31/64, wd. Flint Stone Creek, Md., 8/1/64. Ab. 9/1/64 - 10/31/64, wd.; $100 bond due. Clothing issued, 9/30/64. Paroled at Charleston, W. Va., 5/10/65. Desc.: age 19, 6'3", fair comp., light hair and blue eyes. Post war resident of Randolph Co., W. Va. Brother of Adam S. and Jacob G. Ward. Age 34, farmer, Huttonsville, Randolph Co., W. Va. 1880 Census. d. by 1916. NFR.

WARD, ROBERT S. M. - Pvt. Co. I. Pension record and gravestone only. d. Bath Co., 12/26/1927. Bur. Jones Cem., Bath Co.

WARE, ALLEN B. - Pvt. Co. ?. b. 6/20/30. Age 30, farmer, Randolph Co., W. Va. 1860 Census. Post war rosters only, which show he was a resident of Randolph Co., W. Va. Age 49, farmer, Mingo, Randolph Co., W. Va. 1880 Census. d. 11/19/95. Bur. Ware Cem., Ware School, Randolph Co., W. Va.

WARE, BENJAMIN T. - Pvt. Co. ?. b.c. 1843. Post war rosters only, which show he was a resident of Randolph Co., W. Va. Age 37, farmer, Mingo, Randolph Co., W. Va. 1880 Census. Member Gen. Pegram Camp, UCV, Valley Head, Randolph Co., W. Va. Attended Gettysburg Reunion, 1913. d. by 1916. NFR.

WARE, CHRISTIAN B. - Pvt. Co. B. b. Braxton Co., W. Va., c. 1838. Age 22, farmer, Webster Co., W. Va. 1860 Census. Enl. Frankfort, Greenbrier Co., W. Va., 3/7/63. Not stated if present or absent on muster-in roll dated 3/63. NFR.

WARE, GEORGE W. M. Jr. - Pvt. Co. H. b. 1838. Age 22, farmer, Randolph Co., W. Va. 1860 Census. Post war rosters only, w show he was a resident of Randolph Co., W. Va. Age 42, farmer, Mingo, Randolph Co., W. Va. 1880 Census. d. 1925. Ware Cem., Ware Ridge School, Randolph Co., W. Va.

WARE, JOHN ADOLPHUS - Pvt. Co. I. Post war rosters only, which show he was a resident of Randolph Co., W. Va. d. by 1910. NFR.

WARE, JOHN H. - Capt. Co. ?. Post war rosters only. NFR.

WARFIELD, THOMAS - Pvt. Co. I. Enl. Huntersville, Pocahontas Co., W. Va., 1/25/64. Present 2/29/64 - 8/31/64. Clothing issued 3/22/64. Ab. 9/1/64 - 10/31/64, prisoner. No POW records. NFR.

WARNER, ADAM - Pvt. Co. A. b.c. 1842. Prior service, Co. A, 3rd VSL. Enl. Williamsburg, Greenbrier Co., W. Va., 3/1/63. Not stated if present or absent on muster-in roll dated 3/63. Clothing issued, 3/21/64 and 6/17/64, signed by x. Deserted. Reported at Clarksburg, W. Va., took the oath of allegiance and was released, 4/14/65. Desc.: age 23, 5'8", dark comp., brown hair and blue eyes. Occ. farmer, residing in Braxton Co., W. Va. NFR.

WARNER, JOHN - Pvt. Co. C. b. Lewis Co., W. Va., c. 1844. Prior service, Co. D, 3rd VSL. Enl. Frankfort, Greenbrier Co., W. Va., 3/15/63 (Pocahontas Co., W. Va., 4/1/63). POW record shows his enl. as Jackson Co., W. Va., 8/62. Not stated if present or absent on muster-in roll dated 3/63. Present 1/1/63 - 4/1/63, has one horse. Present 12/31/63 - 8/31/64, charged $60 for a musket; has one horse. Clothing issued 2/26/64, 4/21/64, 6/17/64, 7/10/64 and 11/26/64, signs by x. Present 9/1/64 - 10/31/64, has one horse. Cpd. Jackson Co., W. Va., 3/12/65. Confined at Clarksburg, W. Va., 3/15/65. Desc.: age 20, 6'3", fair comp., light hair and blue eyes. Occ. farmer, residing in Jackson Co., W. Va. Sent to Wheeling, W. Va., 3/16/65. Confined at the Atheneum Prison, 3/16/65. Desc.: age 21, 6'3", fair comp., dark hair and blue eyes. Transf. to Camp Chase, 3/28/65. Confined at Camp Chase, 3/29/65. Took the oath of allegiance and was released, 6/13/65. Desc.: age 20, 6'2", florid comp., dark hair and blue eyes, a resident of Jackson Co., W. Va. Served in Co. F, 20th Va. Cav. NFR.

WARTH (WORTH), CHARLES - Pvt. Co. C. b. Jackson Co., W. Va., c. 1846. Enl. Jackson Co., W. Va., 10/1/64 (Greenbrier Co., W. Va., 11/64). Present 9/1/64 - 10/31/64, $50 enl. bounty due; has one horse. Deserted. Cpd. Ravenswood, W. Va., 3/14/65. Confined at Clarksburg, W. Va., 3/16/65. Desc.: age 19, 5'9", dark comp., black hair and black eyes. Occ. farmer, residing in Jackson Co., W. Va. Took the amnesty oath and was released, 4/14/65 (4/22/65). Desc.: age 19, 5'7", dark comp., black hair and black eyes. NFR.

WARWICK, WILLIAM F. - Pvt. Co. F. b.c. 1823. Age 37, farmer, Pocahontas Co., W. Va. 1860 Census. Enl. Hillsboro, Pocahontas Co., W. Va., 8/19/63. Present 1/1/64 - 2/29/64. Clothing issued, 2/7/64. Ab. 9/1/64 - 10/31/64, AWOL since 5/64. NFR.

WATERS, HIRAM - Pvt. Co. C. Enl. Maryland, 7/15/64. Present 12/31/63 - 8/31/64, has one horse; enl. bounty due. Clothing issued 7/10/64 (?). Ab. 9/1/64 - 10/31/64, went on scout with Capt Hill, now missing; $50 enl. bounty due; horse KIA. 10/9/64. Wd. Beverly, W. Va., 10/29/64. Adm. USA Gen. Hosp., Beverly, W. Va., 10/29/64, wd. bowels, mortally; simple dressing applied. DOW. Beverly, W. Va., 11/1/64.

WATKINS, DAVID G. - Pvt. Co. K. Post war rosters only, which show he was a resident of Buckhannon, W. Va. NFR.

WATKINS, JEREMAIH "Jerry" - Pvt. Co. C. Prior service, Co. D, 3rd VSL. Enl. Pocahontas Co., W. Va., 4/1/63. Present 1/1/63 - 4/1/63, has one horse. Ab. 12/31/63 - 8/31/64, cpd. 7/15/64. Clothing issued, 6/17/64, signs by x. Cpd. Germantown, Md., 7/10/64. Confined at the Old Capitol Prison, 7/10/64. Transf. to Elmira, NY, 7/23/64. Confined at Elmira Prison, 7/25/64. Ab. 9/1/64 - 10/31/64, cpd.; $100 enl. bounty due; has one horse. Desires to take the oath of allegiance, 9/15/64, says he volunteered 8/20/63 and now desires to become a loyal citizen of the US. Took the oath of allegiance and was released, 5/29/65. Desc.: age ?, 5'7_", dark comp., gray hair and hazel eyes, a resident of Ravenswood, W. Va. NFR.

WATSON, JOHN A. - Pvt. Co. F. b.c. 1846. Not on muster rolls. Paroled at Charleston, W. Va., 5/10/65. Desc.: age 19, 6'2", fair comp., black hair, blue eyes and light whiskers. Post war resident of Marion Co., W. Va. NFR.

WATSON, JOSEPH E. - Pvt. Co. C. Not on muster rolls. Adm. Gen. Hosp. No. 9, 10/2/64. Transf. to Chimborazo Hosp., 10/3/64. Adm. Chimborazo Hosp. No. 3, 10/5/64, febris intermittent. Sent to Castle Thunder, 11/19/64. Adm. Gen. Hosp. No. 13, 11/15/64. RTD. 11/22/64. NFR.

WATSON, ROBERT F. - Sgt. Co. K. b.c. 1843. Prior service, Lurty's Batty. Transf. to Co. K, 19th Va, Cav., in exchange for John W. Cain, 3/25/64. Not on muster rolls. Clothing issued, 4/30/64, 5/1/64, 6/17/64, 8/25/64 and 4th Qr. 1864. Paroled at Charleston, W. Va., 5/10/65. Desc.: age 22, 5'8", dark comp., black hair and black eyes. NFR.

WAUGH, BEVERLY H. - Pvt. Co. F. b.c. 1822. Age 38, farmer, Huntersville, Pocahontas Co., W. Va. 1860 Census. Enl. Hillsboro, Pocahontas Co., W. Va., 9/11/63. Ab. 1/1/64 - 2/29/64, sick. Ab. 9/1/64 - 10/31/64, AWOL since 3/1/64. Paroled at Charleston, W. Va., 5/10/65. Desc.: age 43, 5'10", dark comp., dark hair and hazel eyes. Age 58, farmer, Little Levels, Pocahontas Co., W. Va. 1880 Census. NFR.

WAYBRIGHT, ANDREW JENKINS "Andy" - Pvt. Co. I. b. Highland Co., c. 1832 (1828). Prior service, Co. C, 14th Va. Cav. Not on muster rolls. POW record shows he enl. Highland Co., 3/62. Deserter. Reported at Beverly, W. Va., 12/31/64. Confined at Clarksburg, W. Va. Took the oath of allegiance and was released, 1/3/65. Desc.: age 33, 5'11", dark comp., dark hair and blue eyes. Occ. farmer, residing in Highland Co. d. Highland Co., 1905. Bur. Blue Grass Cem.

WAYNE (WAIN), HENRY M. - Pvt. Co. A. b. Gilmer Co., W. Va., c. 1845. Age 15, Calhoun Co., W. Va. 1860 Census. Not on muster rolls. Cpd. Calhoun Co., W. Va., 11/1/63. Confined at the Atheneum Prison, 11/20/63. Desc.: age 19, 6', light comp., brown hair and blue eyes. Occ. farmer, residing in Calhoun Co., W. Va. Transf. to Camp Chase, 11/20/63. Confined at Camp Chase, 11/21/63. Adm. Chase USA Gen. Hosp., Camp Chase, 3/12/64, smallpox, age 19. RTD. 3/27/64. Desires to take the oath of allegiance, 6/10/64, says he is a deserter. DOD. Camp Chase, 8/16/64, typhoid fever. Bur. Camp Chase Confederate Cem., grave no. 207.

WEAVER, EUGENIUS - Pvt. Co. E. b.c. 1843. Enl. Frankfort, Greenbrier Co., W. Va., 3/12/63 (4/1/63). Not stated if present or absent on muster-in roll dated 3/63. Present 10/31/63 - 10/31/64, had his own horse since 7/1/64. Clothing issued 3/1/64, 4/30/64 and 6/17/64. Deserted. Surrendered at Charleston, W. Va., 3/?/65. Took the oath of allegiance and was sent North, 3/22/65. Desc.: age 22, 5'6", dark comp., dark hair and dark eyes. Occ. farmer, residing in Gilmer Co., W. Va. Age 37, farmer, DeKalb Dist., Gilmer Co., W. Va. 1880 Census. NFR.

WEBB, BENJAMIN H. - Pvt. Co. A. b. Ritchie Co., W. Va., c. 1847. Age 13, Calhoun Co., W. Va. 1860 Census. Not on muster rolls. Wd. Lynchburg, 6/17/64. Served in Co. F, 46th Battn. Va. Cav. Post war lawyer and resident of Charleston, W. Va., 1911. NFR.

WEBB, JAMES - Pvt. Co. H. Enl. Roane Co., W. Va., 6/20/63. Ab. 9/1/64 - 10/31/64, AWOL. NFR.

WEES (WEESE), ARTHUR B. - Pvt. Co. B. Enl. Frankfort, Greenbrier Co., W. Va., 3/7/63. Not stated if present or absent on muster-in roll dated 3/63. Post war resident of Webster Co., W. Va. NFR.

WEESE, LEWIS - Pvt. Co. B. b. 1842. Post war rosters only, which show he was from Webster Co., W. Va. and was KIA. Post war roster shows him as Lt. Served in Co. A, 46th Battn. Va. Cav. KIA. Bulltown, W. Va., 10/13/63. Bur. Weese Cem., Weese Mtn., Right Fork Holly River, Holly Dist., Webster Co., W. Va. No marker, but tradition says he is there.

WEESE, SIMON - Pvt. Co. K. b. Pendleton Co., W. Va., c. 1824. Age 36, farmer, Webster Co., W. Va. 1860 Census. Enl. Frankfort, Greenbrier Co., W. Va., 3/20/63. Not stated if present or absent on muster-in roll dated 3/63. NFR.

WEITZEL, JOHN - Pvt. Co. C. Enl. Frankfort, Greenbrier Co., W. Va., 3/15/63. Not stated if present or absent on muster-in roll dated 3/63. NFR.

WELCH (WELSH), SQUIRE B. - 2nd Lt. Co. D. Enl. Williamsburg, Greenbrier Co., W. Va., 3/8/63, Pvt. Not stated if present or absent on muster-in roll dated 3/63. Promoted to 2nd Lt. Ab. 10/25/64, 2nd Lt., sent on a scout by Lt. Col. W. P. Thompson. Ab. 12/15/64, 2nd Lt., AWOL since 12/12/64, no steps yet taken to have him dropped. Dropped as 2nd Lt., 2/8/65. NFR.

WELLS, ALLEN L. - Pvt. Co. ?. Post war source only, which states he was wd. at Bulltown, W. Va., 10/13/63, and DOW on the retreat. Bur. Big Run, 3 miles from Bulltown, W. Va.

WEST, CHARLES N. - Pvt. Co. D. b.c. 1834. Enl. Williamsburg, Greenbrier Co., W. Va., 3/8/63. Not stated if present or absent on muster-in roll dated 3/63. Ab. on detached service, went to Monongalia and Marion Co's. by order of Col. W. L. Jackson, with one man, 3/10/63 - 4/29/63. Served in Co. B, 20th Va. Cav. and Co. C, 46th Battn. Va. Cav. Age 46, farmer, Paw Paw Dist., Marion Co., W. Va. 1880 Census. NFR.

WEST, MARCELLUS I. - 2nd Lt. Co. H. Enl. Frankfort, Greenbrier Co., W. Va., 3/19/63. Not stated if present or absent on muster-in roll dated 3/63, 2nd Lt. Paid as a 2nd Lt., 6/63. Post war rosters show he was KIA. Sharpsburg, Md. NFR.

WESTFALL, GEORGE A. - Pvt. Co. B. b.c. 1835. Enl. Frankfort, Greenbrier Co., W. Va., 3/7/63 (3/9/63). Not stated if present or absent on muster-in roll dated 3/63. Deserted. Ab. 11/1/63 - 2/29/64, deserted 6/15/63. Took the oath of allegiance and gave bond, 12/25/63. Ab. 9/1/64 - 10/31/64, deserted 7/63; not entitled to $100 enl. bounty. Post war resident of Braxton Co., W. Va. Age 45, works on farm, Holly Dist., Braxton Co., W. Va. 1880 Census. NFR.

WESTFALL, HIRAM W. - Pvt. Co. B. b. Braxton Co., W. Va., c. 1839. Enl. Frankfort, Greenbrier Co., W. Va., 3/7/63 (3/9/63). POW record shows enl. as Greenbrier Co., 3/61. Not stated if present or absent on muster-in roll dated 3/63. Present 11/1/63 - 2/29/64, had his own horse since 7/1/64. clothing issued, 2/11/64, 4/21/64, 5/26/64 and 6/17/64. Ab. 9/1/64 - 10/31/64, $100 enl. bounty due; POW since 9/25/64. Cpd. Braxton Co., W. Va., 10/25/64. Confined at Clarksburg, W. Va. Desc.: age 25, 6', fair comp., black hair and black eyes. Occ. farmer, residing in Braxton Co., W. Va. Sent to Wheeling, W. Va., 10/31/64. Confined at the Atheneum Prison, no date. Transf. to Camp Chase, 11/3/64. Confined at Camp Chase, 11/4/64. Took the oath of allegiance and was released, 6/12/65. Desc.: age 25, 6', dark comp., black hair and black eyes, a resident of Braxton Co., W. Va. Post war resident of Braxton Co., W. Va. Age 42, farmer, Otter Dist., Braxton Co., W. Va. 1880 Census. NFR.

WESTFALL, JACOB - Pvt. Co. C. Prior service, Co. D, 3rd VSL. Enl. Frankfort, Greenbrier Co., W. Va., 3/15/63 (Pocahontas Co., W. Va., 4/1/63). Not stated if present or absent on muster-in roll dated 3/63. Present 1/1/63 - 4/1/63, has one horse. Ab. 12/31/63 - 8/31/64, cpd. 10/20/63; has one horse. Ab. 9/1/64 - 10/31/64, $100 enl. bounty due; cpd. 10/20/63 (place not stated); has one horse. Took the oath of allegiance and was released, 12/5/63, gave bond. NFR.

WESTFALL, JACOB E. - 1st Sgt. Co. B. b.c. 1841. Enl. Frankfort, Greenbrier Co., W. Va., 3/7/63 (3/9/63). Not stated if present or absent on muster-in roll dated 3/63, 4th Corp. Present, 3rd Sgt., 11/1/63 - 2/29/64, has his own horse. Clothing issued, 2/11/64, 4/21/64, 5/25/64 and 6/17/64. Served as 1st Sgt., 3/15/64 - 7/1/64. Present, Pvt., 9/1/64 - 10/31/64, $100 enl. bounty due; on detached service. Deserted to enemy lines, 4/27/65. Confined at Clarksburg, W. Va., 5/5/65. Paroled at Clarksburg, W. Va., 5/5/64, signs by x. Desc.: age 24, 5'9", dark comp., black hair and black eyes. Post war resident of Braxton Co., W. Va. Age 39, farmer, Otter Dist., Braxton Co., W. Va. 1880 Census. NFR.

WESTFALL, JAMES - Sgt. Co. A. Not on muster rolls. Deserted. Cpd. Beverly, W. Va., 10/4/63 (10/8/63). Confined at Clarksburg, W. Va., 10/13/63. Desc.: age 26, 5'10", a resident of Braxton Co., W. Va.; held for examination. Confined at the Atheneum Prison, 10/20/63. Desc.: age 26, 5'10", fair comp., light hair and gray eyes, a resident of Braxton Co., W. Va. Transf. to Camp Chase, 10/22/63. Confined at Camp Chase, 10/23/63. Transf. to Rock Island, Ill., 1/22/64(?). Confined at Rock Island Prison, 1/17/64, listed as Sgt. DOD. Rock Island, Ill., 6/18/64, phthisis pulmonalis. Bur. Rock Island, Ill., grave 1253.

WESTFALL (WESTPHAL), JAMES H. - Pvt. Co. B. b.c. 1838. Age 22, Randolph Co., W. Va. 1860 Census. Enl. Frankfort, Greenbrier Co., W. Va., 3/7/63 (3/9/63). Not stated if present or absent on muster-in roll dated 3/63. Not stated if present or absent, 11/1/63 - 2/29/64, left sick on a raid within the enemy lines, 4/63. Ab. 9/1/64 - 10/31/64, $100 enl. bounty due; left sick on a raid within enemy lines, 4/63; POW since 4/63. Post war resident of Braxton Co., W. Va. NFR.

WESTFALL, PERRY - Pvt. Co. H. b.c. 1840. Enl. Roane Co., W. Va., 6/20/63. Ab. 9/1/64 - 10/31/64, AWOL. Age 40, farmer, Spencer Dist., Roane Co., W. Va. 1880 Census. NFR.

WHEAT, QUINCEY A. - Pvt. Co. F. b. Alexandria, c. 1842. Prior service, 26th Battn. Va. Inf. and Co. A, 35th Battn. Va. Cav. Enl. Hillsboro, Pocahontas Co., W. Va., 1/12/64. POW record shows his enl. as Laurel Hill, 1861. Ab. 1/1/64 - 2/29/64, on leave. Ab. 9/1/64 - 10/31/64, sick. Treated for bronchitis chronic, 10/23/64, at Gordonsville Hosp. Paroled at Lewisburg, W. Va., 4/27/65. Desc.: age 22, 5'5", light comp., light hair and blue eyes, a student. NFR.

WHITE, ALEXANDER - Pvt. Co. E. b.c. 1847. Enl. Bath Co., 4/1/64. Clothing issued, 4/30/64 and 6/17/64, signs by x. Ab. 10/31/63 - 10/31/64, deserted. Surrendered at Charleston, W. Va. Took the amnesty oath and was sent North, 3/25/65, signs by x. Desc.: age 18, 5'5", dark comp., fair hair and gray eyes. Occ. farmer, residing in Roane Co., W. Va. NFR.

WHITE, ARTHUR V. - Pvt. Co. E. b.c. 1843. Enl. Frankfort, Greenbrier Co., W. Va., 3/13/63 (4/1/63). Not stated if present or absent on muster-in roll dated 3/63. Present 10/31/63 - 10/31/64, had his own horse since 7/1/64. Employed as a teamster 11/1/63 - 11/30/63. Employed as a teamster at Warm Springs, 1/1/64 - 2/1/64, returned to his Co. Clothing issued, 11/30/63, 12/29/

63 (detailed), 1/16/64, 1/17/64 (detailed teamster), 3/1/64, 4/30/64, 6/17/64, 7/64 and 8/64. Deserted. Surrendered at Charleston, W. Va. Took the amnesty oath and was sent North, 3/25/65. Desc.: age 22, 5'7", fair comp., fair hair and gray eyes. Occ. farmer, residing in Roane Co., W. Va. Age 37, farming, Geary Dist., Roane Co., W. Va. 1880 Census. NFR.

WHITE, JOHN - Pvt. Co. E. Enl. Frankfort, Greenbrier Co., W. Va., 3/13/63 (4/1/63). POW record shows his enl. as Greenbrier Co., 3/15/63. Not stated if present or absent on muster-in roll dated 3/63. Ab. 10/31/63 - 10/31/63, enl. bounty due; had his own horse since 7/1/64; POW. Clothing issued 3/1/64. Cpd. Loudoun Co. (near Harpers Ferry, W. Va.), 7/15/64. Sent to Harpers Ferry, W. Va. and then to Washington, DC. Confined at the Old Capitol Prison, 7/17/64. Transf. to Elmira, NY, 7/23/64. Confined at Elmira Prison, 7/25/64. Paroled 2/9/65 (2/13/65) and sent to the James River, via Pt. Lookout, to be exchanged. Exchanged at Boulware & Cox Wharf, James River, 2/20/65 - 2/21/65. Adm. Gen. Hosp. No. 9, 2/20/65. Transf. to Chimborazo Hosp., 2/22/65. Adm. Chimborazo Hosp. No. 4, 2/22/65, chronic diarrhoea and debilitias. Present, Hosp. MR, Chimborazo Hosp. No. 4, paroled prisoner, 2/25/65. Transf. to Chimborazo Hosp. No. 2, 3/6/65. Adm. Chimborazo Hosp. No. 2, 3/6/65, chronic diarrhoea. CSR shows he was adm. Chimborazo Hosp. No. 1, 3/65. Furloughed to Lynchburg, Campbell Co., 3/16/65 (3/19/65). DOD. Lynchburg, 3/23/65, variola.

WHITE, N. J. - Pvt. Co. A. Not on muster rolls. Adm. Jackson Hosp., 4/8/65. Sent to the Provost Marshall, 4/14/65. NFR.

WHITE, WEADON (WEEDEN) - Pvt. Co. E. b. Lewis Co., W. Va., c. 1834. Age 26, farmer, Gilmer Co., W. Va. 1860 Census. Enl. Gilmer Co., W. Va., 10/8/64. Ab. 10/31/63 - 10/31/64, new recruit on horse detail, time now expired; enl. bounty due. Age 46, farmer, Center Dist., Gilmer Co., W. Va. 1880 Census. NFR.

WHITE, WELLINGTON J. - 2nd Corp. Co. E. b. Lewis Co., W. Va., c. 1841. Age 19, farmer, Gilmer Co., W. Va. 1860 Census. Prior service, Co. D, 31st Va. Inf. Enl. Frankfort, Greenbrier Co., W. Va., 3/13/63. Not stated if present or absent on muster-in roll dated 3/63, 2nd Corp. Clothing issued as 4th Corp., 3/1/64. Wartime deserter roll and CSR show service in Co. B, 19th Va. Cav. Transf. back to the 31st Va. Inf. by 4/20/64. Post war resident of Gilmer Co., W. Va. NFR.

WHITEHEAD, JOHN (Alias FRANCIS) - Pvt. Co. C. Prior service, Co. D, 3rd VSL. Enl. Frankfort, Greenbrier Co., W. Va., 3/15/63. Not stated if present or absent on muster-in roll dated 3/63. Ab. 1/1/63 - 4/1/63, deserted 10/62; had one horse. NFR.

WHITMAN (WHITEMAN), MICHAEL - Pvt. Co. C. b.c. 1841. Prior service, Co. D, 3rd VSL. Enl. Frankfort, Greenbrier Co., W. Va., 3/15/63 (Pocahontas Co., W. Va., 4/1/63). Not stated if present or absent on muster-in roll dated 3/63. Present 1/1/63 - 4/1/63, has one horse. Present 12/31/63 - 8/31/64, has one horse. Clothing issued, 2/25/64, 5/26/64, 6/17/64, 7/64 and 8/64. Present 9/1/64 - 10/31/64, has one horse. Paroled at Charleston, W. Va., 5/10/65. Desc.: age 24, 6', light comp., dark hair and blue eyes. NFR.

WIGGEL (WIGGLE), JOHN - 1st Corp. Co. C. Prior service, Co. D, 3rd VSL. Enl. Mill Point, Pocahontas Co., W. Va., 4/1/63. Present 1/1/63 - 4/1/63, has one horse. Present, 2nd Corp., 12/31/63 - 8/31/64, has one horse. Present, 1st Corp., 9/1/64 - 10/31/64, has one horse; $100 enl. bounty due. NFR.

WILCOX, ELIUD W. - Pvt. Co. D. b.c. 1842. Not on muster rolls. Cpd. Alleghany Co., 12/23/63. Confined at Wheeling, W. Va. Confined at Camp Chase, 1/1/64. Desc.: age 22, 6'2", fair comp., dark hair and blue eyes. Desires to take the oath of allegiance 6/10/64 and 10/64. Took the oath of allegiance and was released, 5/13/65, signs by x. Desc.: age ?, 6'2", dark comp., black hair and dark eyes, a resident of Marion Co., W. Va. Age 39, farmer, Lincoln Dist., Marion Co., W. Va. 1880 Census. NFR.

WILEY, MARCELLUS FRANKLIN - Pvt. Co. I. b. Monterey (on Jackson River), 3/14/47. Enl. Huntersville, Pocahontas Co., W. Va., 5/4/64. Present 2/29/64 - 8/31/64, mounted; enl. bounty due. Clothing issued 7/64 and 8/64. Present 9/1/64 - 10/31/64. Paroled at Staunton, 6/1/65. Desc.: age 18, 5'10", fair comp., dark hair and black eyes. Post war rosters show him as a member of Co. G. Post war resident of Bolar, Highland Co. Member S. B. Gibbons Camp, UCV, Harrisonburg, 1896. Attended the dedication of the Confederate Monument at Warm Springs, June 20, 1923. d. 2/13/1936. Bur. Old Stony Run Cem., Highland Co.

WILFONG, DAVID - Pvt. Co. F. b. Pendleton Co., W. Va., c. 1823. Age 37, farmer, Traveler's Repose, Pocahontas Co., W. Va. 1860 Census. Enl. Hillsboro, Pocahontas Co., W. Va., 10/3/63. Ab. 1/1/64 - 2/29/64, sick. Ab. 9/1/64 - 10/31/64, sick; enl. bounty due. Age 57, farmer, Green Banks, Pocahontas Co., W. Va. 1880 Census. NFR.

WILFONG, HENRY - Pvt. Co. F. b. Bath Co., c. 1828. Resident of Highland Co., 1855, farmer, age 27. Age 32, farmer, Dunmore, Pocahontas Co., W. Va. 1860 Census. Prior service, Co. G, 31st Va. Inf. Enl. Hillsboro, Pocahontas Co., W. Va., 6/25/63. Ab. 1/1/64 - 2/29/64, on leave. Clothing issued 2/6/64. Ab. 9/1/64 - 10/31/64, AWOL since 9/5/64. Age 52, farm laborer, Green Banks, Pocahontas Co., W. Va. 1880 Census. NFR.

WILFONG, JOHN E. - Pvt. Co. F. b.c. 1835. Age 25, farmer, Traveler's Repose, Pocahontas Co., W. Va. 1860 Census. Prior service, McNeel's Co., 2nd VSL. Enl. Hillsboro, Pocahontas Co., W. Va., 3/9/63 (4/1/63). Not stated if present or absent on muster-in roll dated 3/63. Ab. 1/1/64 - 2/29/64, on leave. Clothing issued 2/6/64. Present 9/1/64 - 10/31/64, enl. bounty due. Paroled at Staunton, 5/29/65. Desc.: age 30, 5'7", fair comp., dark hair and gray eyes. NFR.

WILKESON, ALFRED J. - Pvt. Co. F. Enl. Hillsboro, Pocahontas Co., W. Va., 9/14/63. Present 1/1/64 - 2/29/64. Present 9/1/64 - 10/31/64, enl. bounty due. NFR.

WILLIAMS, EDWARD R. - Pvt. Co. H and Co. A. b.c. 1832. Age 18, 1850 Braxton Co., W. Va. Census. Enl. Frankfort, Greenbrier Co., W. Va., 3/19/63, in Co. H. Not stated if present or absent on muster-in roll dated 3/63. Enl. Williamsburg, Greenbrier Co., W. Va., 3/1/63, in Co. A. Not stated if present or absent on muster-in roll dated 3/63. Employed as a teamster 11/1/63 - 11/30/63. Employed as a teamster at Warm Springs, 1/1/64 - 2/29/64. Clothing issued, 11/22/63, 12/20/63 (detailed), 6/17/64 and 9/30/64. Cpd. Webster Co., W. Va., 3/2/65, listed as a member of Co. A. Sent to Cumberland, Md., then to Wheeling, W. Va. Confined at the Atheneum Prison, 3/11/65. Desc.: age 33, 5'11", fair comp., black hair and blue eyes. Occ. farmer, residing in Lewis Co., W. Va. Transf. to Camp Chase, 3/16/65. Confined at Camp Chase, 3/17/65. Took the oath of allegiance and was released, 6/13/65. Desc.: age 35, 5'10", florid comp., dark hair and blue eyes, a resident of Jacksonville, Lewis Co., W. Va. A post war statement made by Williams states that the was cpd. at Lewisburg, W. Va. He was held at Camp Chase until 6/14/65, "being the last Confederate soldier to leave Camp Chase." NFR.

WILLIAMS, ELI - Pvt. Co. D. b. Pa., c. 1832. Not on muster rolls. Cpd. Alleghany Co., 12/23/63. Confined at the Atheneum Prison, 12/31/63. Desc.: age 32, 6'2", fair comp., dark hair and blue eyes. Occ. farmer, residing in Marion Co., W. Va. Transf. to Camp Chase, 12/31/63. Age 36, farming, Fairmont Dist., Marion Co., W. Va. 1880 Census. NFR.

WILLIAMS, HANSON O. - Pvt. Co. B. b.c. 1837. Post war rosters only, which show he was a resident of Braxton Co., W. Va. NFR.

WILLIAMS, HUGH - Pvt. Co. B. b. Greenbrier Co., W. Va., 1801. Age 49, Braxton Co., W. Va. 1850 Census. Moved to Braxton Co., W. Va., 1805. Post war source and family history only for service. d. Braxton Co., W. Va., 1865.

WILLIAMS, HUGH (HENRY) J. - 2nd Corp. Co. A and Co. B. b. 1838. Age 12, Braxton Co., W. Va. 1850 Census. Prior service, Co. A, 3rd VSL. Enl. Williamsburg, Greenbrier Co., W. Va., 3/1/63, in Co. A. Not stated if present or absent on muster-in roll dated 3/63. Enl. Frankfort, Greenbrier Co., W. Va., 3/7/63, in Co. B. Ab., 2nd Corp., 11/1/63 - 2/29/64, cpd. 2/11/64. Cpd. Braxton Co., W. Va., 2/14/64. Confined at Clarksburg, W. Va., 2/21/64. Transf. to Wheeling, W. Va. Confined at the Atheneum Prison, 2/23/64. Desc.: age 24, 5'11_", fair comp., dark hair and black eyes. Occ. farmer, residing in Braxton Co., W. Va. Transf. to Camp Chase, 3/4/64. Confined at Camp Chase, 3/5/64. Transf. to Ft. Delaware, 3/14/64. Confined at Ft. Delaware, 3/17/64. Ab., 2nd Corp., 9/1/64 - 10/31/64, $100 enl. bounty due; POW. Took the oath of allegiance and was released, 6/21/65, signs by x. Age ?, 5'10", ruddy comp., dark hair and brown eyes, a resident of Braxton Co., W. Va. Post war resident of Braxton Co., W. Va. Age 42, farmer, Holly Dist., Braxton Co., W. Va. 1880 Census. Son of Richard Williams, brother of William H. Williams. NFR.

WILLIAMS, J. - Pvt. Co. F. Not on muster rolls. Cpd. Mt. Jackson, 3/5/65. Sent to Harpers Ferry, W. Va., then to Ft. Delaware, 3/9/65. Also as having been confined at Ft. Delaware from Waynesboro. NFR.

WILLIAMS, JAMES - Pvt. Co. I. b. Ky., c. 1846. Enl. Huntersville, Pocahontas Co., W. Va., 12/1/63. POW record shows his enl. as Pocahontas Co., 10/61. Present 6/30/63 - 2/29/64, mounted; enl. bounty due. Present 2/29/64 - 8/31/64. Clothing issued 3/22/64. Ab. 9/1/64 - 10/31/64, on detached duty; $100 bond due. Cpd. Beverly, W. Va., 10/29/64. Sent to Clarksburg, W. Va., then to Wheeling, W. Va., 11/2/64. Confined at the Atheneum Prison, 11/2/64. Desc.: age 18, 5'9", dark comp., dark hair and dark eyes. Occ. farmer, residing in Giles Co. Transf. to Camp Chase, 11/3/64. Confined at Camp Chase, 11/4/64. DOD. Camp Chase, 3/15/65, pneumonia. Bur. Camp Chase Confederate Cem., grave no. 1673. Post war rosters show service in Co. F.

WILLIAMS, JAMES E. - Pvt. Co. B. b.c. 1841. Enl. Frankfort, Greenbrier Co., W. Va., 3/7/63 (3/9/63). Not stated if present or absent on muster-in roll dated 3/63. Not stated if present or absent 11/1/63 - 2/29/64. Cpd. Braxton Co., W. Va., 2/14/64. Confined at Clarksburg, W. Va., 2/21/64. Sent to Wheeling, W. Va. Confined at the Atheneum Prison, 2/23/64. Desc.: age 23, 5'8_", fair comp., sorrel hair and blue eyes. Occ. farmer, residing in Braxton Co., W. Va. Transf. to Camp Chase, 3/4/64. Confined at Camp Chase, 3/5/64. Transf. to Ft. Delaware, 3/14/64. Confined at Ft. Delaware, 3/17/64. Ab. 9/1/64 - 10/31/64, $100 enl. bounty due; POW since 2/14/64. Took the oath of allegiance and was released, 6/7/65. Desc.: age ?, 5'7", sallow comp., brown hair and blue eyes, a resident of Braxton Co., W. Va. Post war resident of Braxton Co., W. Va. Age 40, farmer, Holly Dist., Braxton Co., W. Va. 1880 Census. NFR.

WILLIAMS, JAMES T. - Pvt. Co. A. b.c. 1835. Not on muster rolls. Paroled at Charleston, W. Va., 5/11/65. Desc.: age 30, 5'10", dark comp., brown hair, black eyes and brown hair. NFR.

WILLIAMS, JOHN - Pvt. Co. D. Post war rosters only, which show he was cpd. and confined at Camp Chase, where he DOD. Bur. Camp Chase Confederate Cem.

WILLIAMS, JOHN J. - Sr. 2nd Lt. Co. B. b.c. 1830. Enl. Frankfort, Greenbrier Co., W. Va., 3/7/63 (3/9/63). Not stated if present or absent on muster-in roll dated 3/63. Present, Jr. 2nd Lt., 11/1/63 - 2/29/64, commanding Co. Ab. on detached duty with 14 men in Monroe Co., W. Va., 11/10/63 - 11/24/63. Present 9/1/64 - 10/31/64. Paroled at Charleston, W. Va., 5/10/65. Desc.: age 35, 5'5_", fair comp., light hair, dark eyes and a mustache. Post war rosters show him as 3rd Lt. Post war resident of Braxton Co., W. Va. NFR.

WILLIAMS, JOSEPH - Pvt. Co. I. Enl. Huntersville, Pocahontas Co., W. Va., 8/15/63. Present 6/30/63 - 2/29/64, mounted; enl. bounty due. Present 2/29/64 - 8/31/64. Present 9/1/64 - 10/31/64. NFR.

WILLIAMS, RENICK H. - Pvt. Co. F. b.c. 1846. Enl. Hillsboro, Pocahontas Co., W. Va., 9/14/63. Ab. 1/1/64 - 2/29/64, sick. Clothing issued, 2/6/64. Ab. 9/1/64 - 10/31/64, AWOL since 3/1/64. Paroled at Charleston, W. Va., 5/11/65. Desc.: age 19, 5'5", dark comp., dark hair and black eyes. NFR.

WILLIAMS, RICHARD - Pvt. Co. B. b.c. 1810. Age 40, Braxton Co. 1850 Census. Enl. Frankfort, Greenbrier Co., W. Va., 3/7/63 (3/9/63). POW record shows he enl. Webster Co., W. Va., 4/62. Not stated if present or absent on muster-in roll dated 3/63. Not stated if present or absent 11/1/63 - 2/29/64. Cpd. Braxton Co., W. Va., 2/14/64. Sent to Clarksburg, W. Va. Confined at Clarksburg, W. Va., 2/21/64, then sent to Wheeling, W. Va. Confined at the Atheneum Prison, 2/23/64. Desc.: age 54, 5'10_", fair comp., black hair and black eyes. Occ. farmer, residing in Braxton Co., W. Va. Transf. to Camp Chase, 3/4/64. Confined at Camp Chase, 3/5/64. Transf. to Ft. Delaware, 3/14/64. Confined at Ft. Delaware, 3/17/64. Ab. 9/1/64 - 10/31/64, $100 enl. bounty due; POW since 2/14/64. Paroled 9/28/64, until exchanged, signs by x. Sent to Aiken's Landing, 9/30/64. Exchanged at Varina, Va., 10/5/64. Clothing issued, paroled prisoner, 10/11/64. Present on a MR of paroled and exchanged prisoners at Camp Lee, near Richmond, 10/12/64. Adm. Gen. Hosp. No. 9, 10/12/64. Furloughed 10/13/64, 30 days. Paroled at Clarksburg, W. Va., 5/22/65, listed as a deserter. Desc.: age 56, 6', dark comp., dark hair and brown eyes, a resident of Nicholas Co., W. Va. Father of Hugh J. and William H. Williams. NFR.

WILLIAMS, RICHARDSON - Pvt. Co. B. Enl. Frankfort, Greenbrier Co., W. Va., 3/7/63. Ab. 11/1/63 - 2/29/64, transf. to Co. A, 19th Va. Cav., 11/1/63. NFR.

WILLIAMS, ROBERT - Pvt. Co. I. Enl. Huntersville, Pocahontas Co., W. Va., 10/20/63. Ab. 6/30/63 - 2/29/64, got furlough 1/10/64, 20 days; has no horse; enl. bounty due. NFR.

WILLIAMS, WILLIAM H. - Pvt. Co. B. b. 1844. Enl. Frankfort, Greenbrier Co., W. Va., 3/7/63 (3/9/63). Not stated if present or absent on muster-in roll dated 3/63. Cpd. Pocahontas Co., W. Va., 8/21/63. Confined at the Atheneum Prison, 8/30/63. Desc.: age 19, 5'7_", florid comp., dark hair and dark eyes. Occ. farmer, residing in Braxton Co., W. Va. Transf. to Camp Chase, 8/31/63. Confined at Camp Chase, 9/1/63. Ab. 11/1/63 - 2/29/64, cpd. 8/26/63. Transf. to Rock Island, Ill., 1/14/64. Confined at Rock Island Prison, 1/17/64. Ab. 9/1/64 - 10/31/64, $100 enl. bounty due; POW since 2/14/64(?). Took the oath of allegiance and was released, 6/16/65, signs by x. Desc.: age 20, 5'5", light comp., auburn hair and hazel eyes, a resident of Suttonsville, Braxton Co., W. Va. Age 35, farmer, Holly Dist., Braxton Co., W. Va. 1880 Census. Son of Richard Williams, brother of Hugh J. Williams. NFR.

WILMOTH, DAVID J. - Pvt. Co. ?. Post war rosters only, which show he was a resident of Randolph Co., W. Va. NFR.

WILMOTH, GEORGE W. - Corp. Co. E. b.c. 1840. Age 20, laborer, Randolph Co., W. Va. 1860 Census. Enl. Gilmer Co., W. Va., 5/15/63. Present, Corp., 10/31/63 - 10/31/64, had his own horse 7/1/64 - 9/3/64; horse broke down. Clothing issued 3/1/64,

4/30/64, 6/17/64 and 7/10/64. Paroled at Charleston, W. Va., 5/11/65. Desc.: age 26, 6'2", light comp., brown hair, brown eyes and red whiskers. Age 45, farmer, New Interest, Randolph Co., W. Va. 1880 Census. NFR.

WILMOTH, JACOB - Pvt. Co. ?. Post war rosters only, which show he was a resident of Randolph Co., W. Va. Resident of Belington, W. Va., 1916. Bur. Mill Creek Cem., Randolph Co., W. Va.

WILMOTH (WILMOUTH), SAMUEL C. (J.) - 2nd Sgt. Co. I. b. Randolph Co., W. Va., 2/24/26 (1833). Age 27, farmer, residing in Randolph Co., W. Va., 1857. Enl. Huntersville, Pocahontas Co., W. Va;, 2/1/63 (3/18/63). Present on muster-in roll dated 3/63, Corp. Mustered into service 3/19/63. Present, 2nd Sgt., 6/30/63 - 2/29/64, mounted. Present, Pvt., 2/29/64 - 8/31/64, was 2nd Sgt. to 6/13/64, reduced to ranks. Clothing issued, 3/22/64. Ab. 9/1/64 - 10/31/64, on detail to procure a fresh horse; $100 bond due. Surrendered at Clarksburg, W. Va., 4/26/65. Paroled 4/28/65, to be exchanged and was released. Desc.: age 38, 5'9", dark comp., black hair and blue eyes. Occ. farmer, residing in Pocahontas Co., W. Va. d. 6/6/1900. Bur. Israel Cem., Kerens, W. Va.

WILMOTH, WILLIAM L. - Pvt. Co. I. b. 2/25/22. Age 37, farmer, Greenbank, Pocahontas Co., W. Va. 1860 Census. Enl. Huntersville, Pocahontas Co., W. Va., 2/1/63 (3/18/63). Present on muster-in roll dated 3/63. Mustered into service 3/19/63. Present 6/30/63 - 2/29/64, mounted; enl. bounty due. Present 2/29/64 - 8/31/64. Ab. 9/1/64 - 10/31/64, POW. Cpd. Winchester, 9/19/64. Sent to Harpers Ferry, W. Va., then to Pt. Lookout, 11/18/64. Took the oath of allegiance and was released, 2/14/65. Post war rosters show service in Co. F, 19th Va. Cav. Age 56, Green Banks, Pocahontas Co., W. Va. 1880 Census. d. 1/1910 (1919).

WILSON, ALEXANDER DAVIDSON - Pvt. Co. I. b. Rockbridge Co., c. 1834 (1831, 1836). Age 24, farmer, 4th Dist., Rockbridge Co. 1860 Census. Prior service, VSL. Enl. Huntersville, Pocahontas Co., W. Va., 5/22/63 (Rockbridge Co., 5/63). Ab. 6/30/63 - 2/29/64, went home without permission 12/12/63, not yet reported; mounted. Ab. 2/29/64 - 8/31/64, AWOL. Ab. 9/1/64 - 10/31/64, AWOL. Cpd. Beverly, W. Va., 11/29/64. Confined at Clarksburg, W. Va. Desc.: age 33, 6'3", fair comp., dark hair and blue eyes. Occ. farmer, residing in Rockbridge Co. Took the oath of allegiance and was released, 12/3/64. Post war resident of Rockbridge Co. Age 36, farmer, Buffalo Dist., 1870 Census. Bur. Oxford Presbyterian Church Cem.

WILSON, CALINDER (CALDER) H. (L.) - Pvt. Co. E. b. Monongalia Co., W. Va., c. 1838. Age 22, farmer, Gilmer Co., W. Va. 1860 Census. Enl. Gilmer Co., W. Va.. 10/8/64. Ab. 10/31/63 - 10/31/64, on horse detail, time now expired; enl. bounty due; new recruit. Brother of Obediah Wilson. Age 43, farmer, Center Dist., Gilmer Co., W. Va. 1880 Census. NFR.

WILSON, DANIEL - Pvt. Co. C. b.c. 1841. Prior service, Co. D, 3rd VSL. Enl. Frankfort, Greenbrier Co., W. Va., 3/15/63 (Pocahontas Co., W. Va., 5/1/63). Not stated if present or absent on muster-in roll dated 3/63. Present 1/1/63 - 4/1/63, has one horse. Cpd. near Bellville, 8/5/63, bushwhacker. Wd. when cpd. Adm. USA Gen. Hosp., Parkersburg, W. Va., 8/9/63, gunshot wd. Present on Hosp. MR, USA Gen. Hosp., Parkersburg, W. Va., 7/1/63 - 8/31/63. Not stated if present or absent on Hosp. MR., USA Gen. Hosp., Parkersburg, W. Va., 9/1/63 - 12/31/63. Released from hosp., 2/5/64. Confined at the Atheneum Prison, 2/6/64. Desc.: age 23, 5'6", sallow comp., light hair and blue eyes. Occ. farmer, residing in Jackson Co., W. Va. Transf. to Camp Chase, 2/6/64. Confined at Camp Chase, 2/7/64. Transf. to Ft. Delaware, 3/14/64. Confined at Ft. Delaware, 3/17/64. Ab. 9/1/64 - 10/31/64, $100 enl. bounty due; has one horse; cpd. 8/15/63. Took the oath of allegiance and was released, 6/21/65, signs by x. Desc.: age ?, 5'7", sallow comp., light hair and blue eyes, a resident of Wood Co., W. Va. NFR.

WILSON, GEORGE - Pvt. Co. ?. Post war rosters only, which show he was from Wood Co., W. Va. NFR.

WILSON, GEORGE R. - Pvt. Co. A. b. Monongalia Co., W. Va., c. 1811. Age 49, farmer, Calhoun Co., W. Va. 1860 Census. Not on muster rolls. Cpd. near Grafton, W. Va., 5/17/63. Confined at Ft. McHenry. Paroled and sent to Ft. Monroe, 5/20/63. Employed as a blacksmith 11/1/63 - 11/30/63. Employed as a blacksmith at Warm Springs, 1/1/64 - 2/29/64. Clothing issued 2/7/64. NFR.

WILSON, GRANVILLE P. - Pvt. Co. B. b.c. 1832. Post war rosters only, which show he was a resident of Braxton Co., W. Va. NFR.

WILSON, J. A. - Pvt. Co. ?. Not on muster rolls. Enrolled as a conscript at Camp Lee, near Richmond, 1/31/64. Assigned to the 19th Va. Cav., 3/18/64. NFR.

WILSON, J. W. - Pvt. Co. B. Post war rosters only. Member James F. Preston Camp, UCV, Christiansburg, 1893. NFR.

WILSON, J. W. - Pvt. Co. H. b.c. 1840. Not on muster rolls. Paroled at Staunton, 5/22/65. Desc.: age 25, 6'1", light comp., light hair and blue eyes. NFR.

WILSON, JAMES - Pvt. Co. A. Not on muster rolls. Clothing issued 5/21/64 and 6/17/64, signs by x. NFR.

WILSON, JAMES C. - Pvt. Co. A. b. Jackson Co., W. Va., 1842. Age 19, Calhoun Co., W. Va. 1860 Census. Enl. Prior service, Co. A, 3rd VSL. Williamsburg, Greenbrier Co., W. Va., 3/1/63. Not stated if present or absent on muster-in roll dated 3/63. Deserter. Took the oath of allegiance and gave his bond, 12/5/63. Post war rosters show him as 3rd Sgt. Brother of Joseph, Robert and William C. Wilson. Age 37, farmer, Center Dist., Calhoun Co., W. Va. 1880 Census. d. 1/11/1929. Bur. Nobe Cem., Calhoun Co., W. Va.

WILSON, JAMES M. - Pvt. Co. G. Enl. Frankfort, Greenbrier Co., W. Va., 3/12/63. Not stated if present or absent on muster-in roll dated 3/63. Clothing issued 3rd Qr. 1864. NFR.

WILSON, JAMES W. - Pvt. Co. A. b.c. 1830. Age 30, farmer, Braxton Co., W. Va. 1860 Census. Not on muster rolls. Cpd. Braxton Co., W. Va., 7/2/63. Confined at the Atheneum Prison, 7/9/63. Desc.: age 33, 6', dark comp., black hair and dark eyes. Occ. farmer, residing in Braxton Co., W. Va. Transf. to Camp Chase, 7/10/63. Confined at Camp Chase, 7/11/63. Transf. to Ft. Delaware, 7/14/63. Confined at Ft. Delaware, 7/20/63. Took the oath of allegiance and was released, 6/21/65, signs by x. Desc.: age ?, 6', dark comp., dark hair and dark eyes, a resident of Braxton Co., W. Va. NFR.

WILSON, JOSEPH - Pvt. Co. A. b. Jackson Co., W. Va., c. 1843. Age 17, Calhoun Co., W. Va. 1860 Census. Served in Co. A, 3rd VSL. Arrested and confined by 3/15/62. To be released for Joseph Durkin, of Hampshire Co., W. Va. Post war rosters only. Brother of James C., Robert and William C. Wilson. Age 36, farmer, Center Dist., Calhoun Co., W. Va. 1880 Census. NFR.

WILSON, OBEDIAH - 2nd Corp. Co. E. b. Monongalia Co., W. Va., c. 1842. Age 18, farmer, Gilmer Co., W. Va. 1860 Census. Enl. Gilmer Co., W. Va., 7/15/63. Ab., 2nd Corp., 10/31/63 - 10/31/64, had his own horse since 7/1/64; cpd. 7/15/64. Clothing issued 3/1/64, 4/30/64, 5/26/64 and 6/17/64. Cpd. near Hillsboro, Loudoun Co. (near Harpers Ferry, W. Va.), 7/15/64. Sent to Harpers Ferry, W. Va., then to Washington, DC. Confined at the Old Capitol Prison, 7/17/64. Transf. to Elmira, NY, 7/23/64. Confined at Elmira Prison, 7/25/64. Desires to take the oath of allegiance 9/15/64, says he volunteered 7/20/63, and now wishes to become a loyal citizen of the US. DOD. Elmira, NY, 3/23/65, variola. Bur. Woodlawn National Cem., Elmira, NY., grave no. 2432. Brother of Calder H. Wilson.

WILSON, RILEY - Pvt. Co. C. b.c. 1836. Prior service, Co. D, 3rd VSL. Enl. Frankfort, Greenbrier Co., W. Va., 3/15/63 (Pocahontas Co., W. Va., 4/1/63). Not stated if present or absent on muster-in roll dated 3/63. Present 1/1/63 - 4/1/63, has one horse. Cpd. Jackson Co., W. Va., 9/27/63. Confined at the Atheneum Prison, 10/1/63. Desc.: age 27, 5'9", dark comp., brown hair and gray eyes, a farmer. Transf. to Camp Chase, 10/6/63. Confined at Camp Chase, 10/6/63. Ab. 12/31/63 - 8/31/64, has one horse; cpd. 9/25/63. Transf. to Rock Island, Ill., 1/14/64. Confined at Rock Island Prison, 1/17/64. Ab. 9/1/64 - 10/31/64, $100 enl. bounty due; has one horse; cpd. 9/25/63. Took the oath of allegiance and was released, 5/25/65. Residence listed as Belleville, Wood Co., W. Va. Post war sketch states he was wd. by William Logston, Captain of home guards, and recovered. Post war resident of Wood Co., W. Va. Age 44, sawyer, Grant Dist., Jackson Co., W. Va. 1800 Census. Post war pensioner, Baxter Co., Ark. d. Baxter Co., Ark., 1/11/1916.

WILSON, ROBERT - Pvt. Co. A. b. Marion (Monongalia) Co., W. Va., 9/15/39. Age 21, Calhoun Co., W. Va. 1860 Census. Prior service, Co. A, 3rd VSL. Enl. Williamsburg, Greenbrier Co., W. Va., 3/1/63. Not stated if present or absent on muster-in roll dated 3/63. Served in Co. H, 20th Va. Cav. Brother of James C., Joseph and William C. Wilson. Age 40, farmer, Center Dist., Calhoun Co., W. Va. 1880 Census. d. 4/26/1916. Bur. Broomstick Cem., Calhoun Co., W. Va.

WILSON, SAMUEL - Pvt. Co. C. Enl. Pocahontas Co., W. Va., 5/1/63. Ab. 12/31/63 - 8/31/64, has one horse; cpd. 8/15/63, place not given. No POW records. NFR.

WILSON, WILLIAM - Pvt. Co. B. Enl. Highland Co., 3/1/64. Ab. 9/1/64 - 10/31/64, $100 enl. bounty due; detailed as nurse in hosp. at Woodstock. NFR.

WILSON (WILLSON), WILLIAM C. - Pvt. Co. A. b. Monongalia (Roane) Co., W. Va., 2/17/37. Age 24, Calhoun Co., W. Va. Prior service, Co. A, 3rd VSL. Enl. Williamsburg, Greenbrier Co., W. Va., 3/1/63. Not stated if present or absent on muster-in roll dated 3/63. Served in Co. H, 20th Va. Cav. Brother of James C., Joseph and Robert Wilson. Age 43, farmer, Sheridan Dist., Calhoun Co., W. Va. 1880 Census. d. 9/19/1908. Bur. Prosperity-Saunders Cem., Calhoun Co., W. Va.

WILSON, WILLIAM G. - Pvt. Co. B. Enl. Frankfort, Greenbrier Co., W. Va., 3/7/63 (3/9/63). Not stated if present or absent on muster-in roll dated 3/63. Present 11/1/63 - 2/29/64, has one horse. Clothing issued 4/21/64, 6/17/64 and 3rd Qr. 1864. Ab. 9/1/64 - 10/31/64, on leave; $100 enl. bounty due. Paroled at Richmond, 4/25/65. NFR.

WINES, RICHARD W. (M.) - Pvt. Co. A. Prior service, Co. A, 3rd VSL. Enl. Williamsburg, Greenbrier Co., W. Va., 3/1/63. Not stated if present or absent on muster-in roll dated 3/63. Wd. Beverly, W. Va., 7/63, side, slight. CSR. listed as Richard W. Wine. NFR.

WISE, FRANCIS M. - Pvt. Co. C. b.c. 1845. Enl. Jackson Co., W. Va., 10/1/64. Present 9/1/64 - 10/31/64, has one horse; $50 enl. bounty due. Age 35, laborer, Grant Dist., Jackson Co., W. Va. 1880 Census. NFR.

WISE, GEORGE W. - Pvt. Co. C. b. Marshall Co., W. Va., 3/12/41. Age 19, Sandyville, Jackson Co., W. Va. 1860 Census. Prior service, Co. D, 3rd VSL. Enl. Frankfort, Greenbrier Co., W. Va., 3/15/63 (Pocahontas Co., W. Va., 4/1/63). Not stated if present or absent on muster-in roll dated 3/63. Present 1/1/63 - 4/1/63, has one horse. Employed as a blacksmith, 11/1/63 - 11/30/63. Present 12/31/63 - 8/31/64, has one horse; blacksmith for the Co. Employed as a blacksmith at Warm Springs, 1/1/64 - 2/29/64. Clothing issued, 11/20/63, 1/16/64, 1/17/64 (detailed as teamster), 5/1/64, 7/6/64 and 2nd Qr. 1864, signs by x. Present 9/1/64 - 10/31/64, $100 enl. bounty due; blacksmith for the Co.; has one horse. Post war roster shows he was mustered out 1/64. Post war farmer and resident of Grant Dist., Jackson Co., W. Va., 1883. Also ran a saw-mill and was a blacksmith. Age 39, blacksmith, Grant Dist., Jackson Co., W. Va. 1880 Census. NFR.

WISEMAN (WISMAN), JOSIAH - Pvt. Co. D. Enl. Williamsburg, Greenbrier Co., W. Va., 3/8/63. Not stated if present or absent on muster-in roll dated 3/63. Cpd. Preston Co., W. Va., 7/1/63. Confined at the Atheneum Prison, 7/2/63. Desc.: age 35, 6'1_", dark comp., dark hair and gray eyes, a resident of Monongahala Co., W. Va. Transf. to Camp Chase, 8/10/63. Confined at Camp Chase, 8/11/63. Transf. to Ft. Delaware, 3/14/64. Confined at Ft. Delaware, 3/17/64. Took the oath of allegiance and was released, 6/21/64. Desc.: age ?, 6', dark comp., dark hair and dark eyes, a resident of Monongahala Co., W. Va. Served in Co. C, 46th Battn. Va. Cav. NFR.

WOFTER (WOOFTER), CALVIN - 1st Sgt. Co. E. b. Lewis Co., W. Va., c. 1841. Age 19, farmer, Gilmer Co., W. Va. 1860 Census. Enl. Frankfort, Greenbrier Co., W. Va., 3/13/63 (4/1/63). Not stated if present or absent on muster-in roll dated 3/63, 1st Sgt. Ab. 10/31/63 - 10/31/64, had his own horse since 12/20/63; POW. Clothing issued, 3/1/64, 6/17/64, 7/64 and 8/64. Cpd. Strasburg, 9/23/64. Sent to Harpers Ferry, W. Va., then to Pt. Lookout, 9/30/64. Confined at Pt. Lookout, 10/3/64. Paroled 3/17/65 and sent to Aiken's Landing, to be exchanged. Landed at Dutch Gap, 3/18/65. Exchanged at Boulware's Wharf, 3/19/65. Adm. Chimborazo Hosp. No. 1, 3/65. Furloughed to Lexington, Rockbridge Co., 3/?/65. Adm. Gen. Hosp. No 9, 3/19/65. Transf. to Chimborazo Hosp., 3/20/65. Adm. Chimborazo Hosp. No. 2, 3/20/65, rheumatism. Furloughed 3/25/65, 30 days. Age 39, farmer, Troy Dist., Gilmer Co., W. Va. 1880 Census. NFR.

WOLF, ELMORE T. - Jr. 2nd Lt. Co. E. Enl. Frankfort, Greenbrier Co., W. Va., 3/13/63. Not stated if present or absent on muster-in roll dated 3/63, listed as Pvt. and 2nd Lt. Clothing issued 10/21/63. Deserted and remained absent for 30 days by 2/8/64. Dropped from rolls as 2nd Lt., 2/24/64. NFR.

WOLF, LOYD (LLOYD) C. - Pvt. Co. E. b. Harrison Co., W. Va., c. 1832. Age 28, farmer, Gilmer Co., W. Va. 1860 Census. Enl. Frankfort, Greenbrier Co., W. Va., 3/13/63 (4/1/63). Not stated if present or absent on muster-in roll dated 3/63. Ab. 10/31/63 - 10/31/64, deserted. Took the oath of allegiance and gave his bond, 12/25/63. NFR.

WOLF, ROBERT T. - Pvt. Co. G. b.c. 1837. Enl. Frankfort, Greenbrier Co., W. Va., 3/12/63. Not stated if present or absent on muster-in roll dated 3/63. Clothing issued 3/1/64, 4/11/64, 4/30/64, 6/17/64 and 7/10/64, signs by x. Deserted. Surrendered. Took the oath of allegiance at Charleston, W. Va., and was sent North, 4/20/65. Desc.: age 28, 5'6", fair comp., fair hair and gray eyes. Occ. carpenter, residing in Kanawha Co., W. Va. d. 9/9/1912.

WOLFE (WOLF), GRANDISON NORMAN - Pvt. Co. E. b. Fauquier Co. (Harrison Co., W. Va.), 2/9/41. Moved to near Glenville, W. Va., c. 1851, attended school. Age 19, farmer, Gilmer Co., W. Va. 1860 Census. Says he was forced into the war. US forced him to take the "death warrant oath" not to aid or abet the South. Joined Capt. Duskey's Co., VSL, 4/62. Enl. Frankfort, Greenbrier Co., W. Va., 3/13/63 (4/1/63). Not stated if present or absent on muster-in roll dated 3/63. Ab. 10/31/63 - 10/31/64, deserted. Clothing issued, 3/1/64 and 6/17/64. Became ill 7/64 and was sent to the hosp. at Winchester, where he remained until the close of the war. Walked home. Surrendered to a citizen and was confined at Clarksburg, 8/23/64. Desc.: age 23, 5'7", dark comp., black hair and hazel eyes. Occ. farmer, residing in Gilmer Co., W. Va. Post war resident of Mt. Zion, W. Va., 1 year; Wentzville, Mo., 5 years; returned to Harrisville, W. Va. Employed by the Pennsboro & Harrisville RR and farmed. Age 39, farmer, West Union Dist., Ritchie Co., W. Va. 1880 Census. Worked until he was c. 80 years of age. Married 5 times, last time when he was 83 years old. His wife left him after 9 months. Has 45 grandchildren; 25 great- grandchildren and one great-great-grandchild. Alive 1930, resident of Ellenboro, W. Va. d. Harrisville, Ritchie Co., W. Va., 5/13/1937. Bur. Harrisville IOOF Cem., Ritchie Co., W. Va.

WOOD, DAVIS M. - Pvt. Co. I. b.c. 1836. Age 24, farmer, Randolph Co., W. Va. 1860 Census. Enl. Beverly, W. Va., 4/30/63. Ab. 6/30/63 - 2/29/64, detailed to feed horses for Capt. Marshall's Co.; mounted. Present 2/29/64 - 8/31/64. Clothing issued 7/64 and 8/64. Present 9/1/64 - 10/31/64, $100 bond due. Post war resident of Randolph Co., W. Va. d. by 1916. NFR.

WOOD (WOODS), HENRY T. (C.) - Pvt. Co. I. Enl. Elk Mtn., W. Va., 8/1/63. Clothing issued 11/20/63 and 6/17/64. Ab. 2/29/64 - 8/31/64, sick; mounted; enl. bounty due. Ab. 9/1/64 - 10/31/64, AWOL. Post war resident of Botetourt Co. NFR.

WOOD, JOHN M. - Pvt. Co. I. b. Randolph Co., W. Va., 5/7/31. Age 29, farmer, Randolph Co., W. Va. 1860 Census. Enl. Beverly, W. Va., 4/30/63. Present 6/30/63 - 2/29/64, sick; mounted. Ab. 2/29/64 - 8/31/64, discharged 5/1/64, disability; dropped from rolls. Desc.: age 32, 5'10", fair comp., light hair and blue eyes. Examined at Warm Springs, Bath Co., 3/7/64, found to be suffering from chronic bronchitis. Clothing issued 3/1/64. Post war resident of Randolph Co., W. Va. Age 49, farmer, Mingo, Randolph Co., W. Va. 1880 Census. d. 6/27/1905. Bur. Wood Cem., Mingo, W. Va.

WOOD, S. C. - Pvt. Co. I. Enl. Huntersville, Pocahontas Co., W. Va., 8/1/63. Ab. 6/30/63 - 2/29/64, mounted; enl. bounty due; cpd. Bath Co., 12/16/63. NFR.

WOOD, THOMAS EMERSON - Pvt. Co. I. b.c. 1805. Age 55, farmer, Randolph Co., W. Va. 1860 Census. Scout for Gen. W. W. Loring, 1861, called "most noted scout". Enl. Huntersville, Pocahontas Co., W. Va., 2/1/63 (3/18/63). Ab. on muster-in roll dated 3/63, wd. in an engagement sometime since. Mustered into service 3/19/63. Ab. 6/30/63 - 2/29/64, at home sick, wd.; mounted. Wd. Droop Mtn., W. Va., 11/6/63, through body, thought to be mortal. Ab. 2/29/64 - 8/31/64, wd. Ab. 9/1/64 - 10/31/64, wd.; $100 bond due. Post war farmer and resident of Randolph Co., W. Va. Age 74, farmer and shoemaker, Mingo, Randolph Co., W. Va. 1880 Census. d. 1883. Bur. Holly Bush Road Cem., Mingo, Randolph Co., W. Va.

WOOD, WILLIAM - Pvt. Co. ?. Post war rosters only, which show he was from Randolph Co., W. Va., and DOD. in a hospital. NFR.

WOOD, WILLIAM D. - Pvt. Co. B. b. Augusta Co., c. 1841. Not on muster rolls. POW record shows enl. as Augusta Co., 6/63. Deserted. Reported at Beverly, W. Va., 10/28/64. Confined at Clarksburg, W. Va. Took the oath of allegiance and was released, 10/29/64. Desc.: age 23, 5'11", dark comp., dark hair and gray eyes. Occ. farmer, residing in Augusta Co. NFR.

WOODDELL, ADAM ARBOGAST - Pvt. Co. F. b. Pocahontas Co., W. Va., c. 1840. Age 20, farmer, Greenbank, Pocahontas Co., W. Va. 1860 Census. Prior service, McNeel's Co., 2nd VSL. Enl. Hillsboro, Pocahontas Co., W. Va., 3/9/63. Not stated if present or absent on muster-in roll dated 3/63. Served in Co. A, 62nd Va. Mtd. Inf. Brother of Preston W. H. Wooddell. Age 40, Green Banks, Pocahontas Co., W. Va. 1880 Census. NFR.

WOODDELL, JACOB SLAVEN - Pvt. Co. F. b. 1829. Age 31, farmer, Greenbank, Pocahontas Co., W. Va. 1860 Census. Prior service, McNeel's Co., 2nd VSL. Enl. Hillsboro, Pocahontas Co., W. Va., 3/9/63 (4/1/63). Not stated if present or absent on muster-in roll dated 3/63. Ab. 1/1/64 - 2/29/64, sick; his substitute was cpd. 11/1/63. Ab. 9/1/64 - 10/31/64, sick. Post war farmer and resident of Pocahontas Co., W. Va. Age 50, farmer, Green Banks, Pocahontas Co., W. Va. 1880 Census. d. 1900. Bur. Oak Flats Cem., near Greenbank, Pocahontas Co., W. Va.

WOODDELL (WOODLE), JOHN B. - Pvt. Co. I. b.c. 1833. Age 27, farmer, Greenbank, Pocahontas Co., W. Va. 1860 Census. Enl. Huntersville, Pocahontas Co., W. Va., 3/1/63. Present on muster-in roll dated 3/63. Mustered into service 3/19/63. NFR.

WOODDELL, PRESTON W. H. - 4th Corp. Co. F. b.c. 1833. Age 27, farmer, Greenbank, Pocahontas Co., W. Va. 1860 Census. Enl. Hillsboro, Pocahontas Co., W. Va., 4/1/63. Present, 4th Corp. 1/1/64 - 2/29/64. Clothing issued 2/7/64. Ab. 9/1/64 - 10/31/64, wd./cpd. Fisher's Hill (Winchester), 9/22/64; enl. bounty due. Adm. Sheridan Depot Field Hosp., Winchester, 9/24/64, vulnus sclopeticum, right thigh. Transf. to Gen. Hosp., Martinsburg, W. Va., 10/12/64. Adm. USA Depot Field Hosp., Winchester, 10/19/64, compound fracture of upper third of thigh, leg amputated by Surg. W. S. Love, PACS. DOW. Winchester, 11/8/64, exhaustion, age 25. Brother of Adam A. Wooddell. CSR listed as W. P. H. Wooddell.

WOODS, WILLIAM J. - Pvt. Co. B. b. Nicholas Co., W. Va., 9/28/25. Age 34, farmer, Webster Co., W. Va. 1860 Census. Prior service, 3rd VSL. Enl. Frankfort, Greenbrier Co., W. Va., 3/7/63. Not stated if present or absent on muster-in roll dated 3/63. Age 54, farmer, Glade, Webster Co., W. Va. 1880 Census. d. 4/22/1914. Bur. Woods Cem., Welch Glade, Glade Dist., Webster Co., W. Va.

WOODYARD, ELIAS - Pvt. Co. E. b. Harrison Co., W. Va., c. 1829. Age 31, farmer, Gilmer Co., W. Va. 1860 Census. Enl. Gilmer Co., W. Va., 10/8/64. Ab. 10/31/63 - 10/31/64, new recruit, on horse detail, term now expired; enl. bounty due. Age 52, blacksmith, Glenville, Gilmer Co., W. Va. 1880 Census. NFR.

WOOFTER, JONATHAN - Pvt. Co. E. Enl. Frankfort, Greenbrier Co., W. Va., 4/1/63. Present 10/31/63 - 10/31/64, had his own horse since 12/20/63. Clothing issued 2/6/64, 3/1/64 and 6/17/64. NFR.

WRIGHT, ANDREW JACKSON - Pvt. Co. A. b. Lewis Co., W. Va., c. 1842. Age 18, Calhoun Co., W. Va. 1860 Census. Prior service, Co. A, 3rd VSL. Enl. Williamsburg, Greenbrier Co., W. Va., 3/1/63. Not stated if present or absent on muster-in roll dated 3/63. Clothing issued 5/21/64. Age 39, farmer, Sheridan Dist., Calhoun Co., W. Va. 1880 Census. NFR.

WRIGHT, R. S. - Pvt. Co. B. Not on muster rolls. Employed as a clerk in Gen. W. H. F. Lee's Division, 9/1/64 - 9/30/64. NFR.

WRIGHT, RICHARD - Pvt. Co. C. b.c. 1843. Not on muster rolls. Cpd. Gilmer Co., W. Va., 9/20/63. Confined at the Atheneum Prison, 10/2/63, charged as a bushwhacker. Desc.: age 20, 6_", florid comp., dark hair and dark eyes. Occ. farmer, residing in Gilmer Co., W. Va. Transf. to Camp Chase, 10/6/63. Confined at Camp Chase, 10/6/63. Transf. to Rock Island, Ill., 1/14/64. Confined at Rock Island Prison, 1/17/64, barracks 55. DOD. Prison Hosp., Rock Island, Ill., 2/21/64, typhoid fever. Bur. Rock Island, Ill., south of the prison barracks, grave no. 578.

WYERS, BENJAMIN F. - Pvt. Co. E. b. Lewis Co., W. Va., c. 1839. Age 21, farmer, Gilmer Co., W. Va. 1860 Census. Enl. Frankfort, Greenbrier Co., W. Va., 3/12/63 (4/1/63). Not stated if present or absent on muster-in roll dated 3/63. Ab. 10/31/63 - 10/31/64, on horse detail, time expired. Clothing issued, 3/1/64 and 5/21/64. Paroled at Charleston, W. Va., 5/11/65, signs by x.

Desc.: age 25, 6', dark comp., auburn hair and black eyes. Age 40, farmer, DeKalb Dist., Gilmer Co., W. Va. 1880 Census. NFR.

WYNE (WINE, WINES), JACKSON - Pvt. Co. B. b. Braxton Co., W. Va., c. 1841. Age 19, Braxton Co., W. Va. 1860 Census. Enl. Pocahontas Co., W. Va., 9/63. Ab. 9/1/64 - 10/31/64, deserted 11/5/63, not entitled to $100 enl. bounty. Cpd. near Bulltown, Braxton Co., W. Va., 11/5/64. Confined at Clarksburg, W. Va. Desc.: age 23, 6', fair comp., light hair and gray eyes. Occ. farmer, residing in Braxton Co., W. Va. Sent to Wheeling, W. Va., 11/7/64. Confined at the Atheneum Prison, 11/7/64. Desc.: age 23, 6', fair comp., dark hair and gray eyes. Transf. to Camp Chase, 11/29/64. Confined at Camp Chase, 11/30/64, desires to take the oath of allegiance. DOD. Camp Chase, 1/30/65, variola. Bur. Camp Chase Confederate Cem., grave no. 983. Post war rosters show service in Co. C.

WYNE (WINES), JOHN PEYTON - Pvt. Co. B. b. Braxton Co., W. Va., c. 1845. Enl. Pocahontas Co., W. Va., 9/?/63. Ab. 9/1/64 - 10/31/64, deserted 11/5/63, not entitled to $100 enl. bounty. Cpd. near Bulltown, Braxton Co., W. Va., 11/5/64. Confined at Clarksburg, W. Va. Desc.: age 19, 5'11", fair comp., light hair and blue eyes. Occ. farmer, residing in Braxton Co., W. Va. Sent to Wheeling, W. Va., 11/7/64. Confined at the Atheneum Prison, 11/7/64. Desc.: age 19, 5'10", fair comp., dark hair and blue eyes. Transf. to Camp Chase, 11/29/64. Confined at Camp Chase, 11/30/64, desires to take the oath of allegiance. DOD. Camp Chase, 2/9/65, diarrhoea. Bur. Camp Chase Confederate Cem., grave no. 1137. Post war rosters show service in Co. C.

WYNE, WILLIAM - Pvt. Co. B. Enl. Pocahontas Co., W. Va., 9/?/63. Ab. 9/1/64 - 10/31/64, deserted 11/5/63; not entitled to $100 enl. bounty. NFR.

WYNN, JAMES A. - Pvt. Co. C. Prior service, Co. C, 1st Md. Cav. Post war rosters only, which show he was a resident of Baltimore, Md. Member (1894) Society of the CSA Army & Navy of Md. NFR.

YEAGER, PETER DILLEY - Pvt. Co. F. b. Pocahontas Co., W. Va., 1831. Age 29, farmer, Traveler's Repose, Pocahontas Co., W. Va. 1860 Census. Enl. Hillsboro, Pocahontas Co., W. Va., 4/1/63. Ab. 1/1/64 - 2/29/64, in the hands of the enemy. Deserted. Cpd. Beverly, W. Va., 10/4/63. Confined at Clarksburg, W. Va., 10/12/63. Desc.: age 33, 5'8", a resident of Pocahontas Co., W. Va.; held for examination. Confined at the Atheneum Prison, 10/20/63. Desc.: age 33, 5'8", fair comp., brown hair and hazel eyes, a resident of Pocahontas Co., W. Va. Transf. to Camp Chase, 10/22/63. Confined at Camp Chase, 10/23/63. Transf. to Rock Island, Ill., 1/14/64. Confined at Rock Island Prison, 1/24/64. Ab. 9/1/64 - 10/31/64, enl. bounty due; cpd. 8/63. Took the oath of allegiance and was released, 6/16/65. Desc.: age 30(?), 5'8", fresh comp., dark hair and hazel eyes, a resident of Greenbank, Pocahontas Co., W. Va. Post war farmer and hotel owner. Age 49, farmer, Green Banks, Pocahontas Co., W. Va. 1880 Census. Member of Pocahontas Co. Board of Education, 24 years. Postmaster, Traveler's Repose (Bartow), W. Va., 52 years. Served in Co. E, 20th Va. Cav. NFR.

YERKEY, THOMAS F. - Pvt. Co. K. b. Gilmer Co., W. Va., c. 1849. Age 11, Gilmer Co., W. Va. 1860 Census. Not on muster rolls. POW record shows his enl. as Gilmer Co., W. Va., 5/62. Clothing issued 2/5/64, 4/30/64 and 6/17/64, signs by x. Deserted. Reported at Clarksburg, W. Va., 12/5/64. Desc.: age 15, 5'6", fair comp., light hair and hazel eyes. Occ. farmer, residing in Gilmer Co., W. Va. Took the oath of allegiance and was released, 12/5/64. Age 31, farmer, Glenville, Gilmer Co., W. Va. 1880 Census. NFR.

YOUNG, DAVID - Pvt. Co. B. b.c. 1832. Enl. Frankfort, Greenbrier Co., W. Va., 3/7/63 (3/9/63). Not stated if present or absent on muster-in roll dated 3/63. Transf. to Co. H. Enl. shown as Braxton Co., W. Va., 4/18/63. Ab. 9/1/64 - 10/31/64, AWOL, not mounted; enl. bounty due. Age 48, farmer, Burch Dist., Braxton Co., W. Va. 1880 Census. NFR.

YOUNG, DAVID H. - Pvt. Co. B. b. O., c. 1830. Enl. Pocahontas Co., W. Va., 4/1/63. Ab. 12/31/63 - 8/31/64, cpd. 10/20/63. Ab. 9/1/64 - 10/31/64, $100 enl. bounty due; cpd. 10/20/63. Post war resident of Wood Co., W. Va. Age 50, farmer, Ripley Dist. 1, Jackson Co., W. Va. 1880 Census. NFR.

YOUNG, JESSE J. - Pvt. Co. G. b.c. 1831. Enl. Frankfort, Greenbrier Co., W. Va., 3/12/63 (4/1/63). POW record shows enl. as Alleghany Co., 1862 in Swann's Co. Employed as a wagon master, 11/1/63 - 11/30/63. Employed as a wagon master at Warm Springs, 1/1/64 - 2/26/64, discharged and sent to his Co. Not stated if present or absent on muster-in roll dated 3/63. Clothing issued 11/21/63, 1/16/64, 3/1/64 (wagon master), 4/30/64, 6/17/64 and 3rd Qr. 1864. Present 9/1/64 - 10/31/64, has a serviceable horse; detailed as wagoner. Adm. CSA Gen. Hosp., Charlottesville, 12/24/64, febris int. tert. RTD. 12/29/64. Paroled at Lewisburg, W. Va., 4/27/65. Desc.: age 34, 5'10", light comp., dark hair and hazel eyes, a farmer. NFR.

ZANE, EDMUND P. - Lt. and Adjutant. Not on muster rolls. Paid as adjutant 2/1/64 - 5/30/64. Detailed as Judge Advocate of a Gen. Court Martial, Warm Springs, Bath Co., 2/2564. Relieved of duty on Gen. Court Martial, 3/4/64. Ab. 10/25/64, wd.; on leave, 15 days. Ab. 12/15/64, wd. since 10/19/64. Wd. Cedar Creek, 10/19/64. Adm. Gen. Hosp. No. 1, Danville, 11/9/64, vulnus sclopeticum, left arm. Furloughed 11/10/64, 40 days. Took the oath of allegiance at Danville, 5/8/65 (5/25/65). NFR.

ZIMMERMAN, WILLIAM - Pvt. Co. ?. Post war rosters only, which show he was a resident of Blue Sulphur Dist., Greenbrier Co., W. Va. Member of David S. Creigh Camp, UCV, Lewisburg, W. Va., 1895. Living 6/1/1903. NFR.

20th Virginia Cavalry

AGNER, DAVID V. - Pvt. Co. K. b. Rockbridge Co., 3/19/1841. Cooper, Natural Bridge Dist., Rockbridge Co. 1860 Census. Prior service, Co. K, 11th Va. Inf. Enl. Camp Marlin's Bottom, W. Va., 8/27/63. Ab. 7/1/63 - 11/1/63 (dated 1/6/64), deserted, taking his gun with him. Arrested and returned to Co. K, 11th Va. Inf. Pardoned by Sec. of War, 11/10/64. Farmhand, Buffalo Dist., Rockbridge Co. 1870 Census. d. near Brushy Hill, 8/25/1910. Bur. Stonewall Jackson Cem., Lexington.

AILSTOCK, ABNER - Pvt. Co. K. b.c. 1839. Enl. Camp Northwest, W. Va., 7/21/63, age 24. Not stated if present or absent on muster roll dated 7/21/63. NFR.

AILSTOCK, ABSALOM - Pvt. Co. K. b. Rockbridge Co., c. 1837. Age 24 (1861). Prior service, Co. G, 58th Va. Inf. Enl. Camp Northwest, W. Va., 7/2/63. Ab. muster roll dated 7/21/63, claimed by another command. Returned to Co. G, 58th Va. Inf. by 11/14/63. Tried for desertion and fined 2 months pay. Entered Old Soldiers Home, Richmond, from Bath Co., 3/26/1909, age 72. d. Richmond, 12/31/1909, age 73. Bur. Hollywood Cem., Richmond.

AILSTOCK, MARSHALL - Pvt. Co. K. b.c. 1843. Enl. Camp Northwest, W. Va., 6/3/63, age 20. Not stated if present or absent on muster roll dated 7/21/63. Present 7/1/63 - 11/1/63 (dated 1/6/64), substitute; had his own horse from enl. to 8/25/63. Present 11/1/63 - 2/29/64, substitute. Present 2/29/64 - 8/31/64, substitute; had his own horse since enl. Clothing issued, 2/29/64. In Gordonsville Hosp., 1/17/65 - 1/24/65, rheumatism. NFR.

AILSTOCK (ARLSTOCK), ROBERT - Pvt. Co. K. b.c. 1845. Prior service, Co. F, 11th Va. Cav. Enl. Camp Northwest, W. Va. (Warm Springs), 7/18/63, age 18. Not stated if present or absent on muster-in roll dated 7/21/63. Present 7/1/63 - 11/1/63 (dated 1/6/64), had his own horse from enl. to 11/6/63; lost Sharps rifle. Present 11/1/63 - 2/29/64, horse KIA Droop Mtn., 11/6/63; lost cartridge box and strap. Had his own horse from 7/1/63. Present 2/29/64 - 8/31/64, mounted; $100 enl. bounty due. Wd. by 12/20/64, neck. Adm. CSA Gen. Hosp., Charlottesville, 12/20/64, vulnus sclopeticum, neck. RTD. 1/2/65. NFR.

AILSTOCK, WILLIAM - Pvt. Co. K. b.c. 1845. Enl. Camp Northwest, W. Va., 5/1/63, age 18. Not stated if present or absent on muster-in roll dated 7/21/63. NFR.

ALBOTT (ALBERT, ALBERTS, ABBOTT), JOHN R. - 3rd Sgt. Co. G. b.c. 1812. Resident of Parkersburg, W. Va. Thrown into prison because of his southern sympathies. Held at Camp Chase for a while, then sent to Richmond. In Richmond, he was arrested by the CS as a suspected spy, and held in Libby Prison. Released on petition of citizens of Parkersburg, W. Va., and returned home. Enl. Wood Co., W. Va., 3/19/63. Not stated if present or absent on muster roll dated 8/1/63, 2nd Corp. Present, 4th Sgt., 11/1/63 - 2/29/64, had his own horse and equipment since 12/21/63. Clothing issued 2/29/64. Present, 3rd Sgt., 7/1/64 - 8/31/64, has his own horse; bond due. Ab. 9/1/64 - 10/31/64, (dated 12/29/64), on detached service; $100 bond due. Cpd. Parkersburg, W. Va., 4/16/65. Confined at Clarksburg, W. Va., by 4/20/65. Desc.: age 53, 5'10", dark comp., dark hair and brown eyes. Occ. shoemaker, residing in Wood Co., W. Va. Paroled at Clarksburg, W. Va., 4/22/65. Name appears on post war rosters as Alberts. NFR.

ALEXANDER, OTHO - Capt. Co. K. b. Rockbridge Co., c. 1835. Brickmason. Prior service, Co. L, 4th Va. Inf. Disc. for disability, 3/62. Enl. Montgomery Co., 12/10/62. Not stated if present or absent on muster-in roll dated 7/21/63, commanding Co. Elected Capt. 7/22/63. Present 7/1/63 - 11/1/63 (dated 1/6/64), promoted to Capt. 7/21/63; had his own horse since enl. Present 11/1/63 - 2/29/64. Ab. 2/29/64 - 8/31/64, resigned 4/16/64, accepted 5/2/64. Submitted his resignation at Camp Cameron, Bath Co., 4/16/64, wishes to join "his own state troops" from Mo. Col. W. L. Jackson wrote that Alexander lacked the qualities to command the Co. d. Greenbrier Co., W. Va., 11/65, age 30.

ALFORD, JAMES A. - Pvt. Co. D. Enl. Oakland Depot, Alleghany Co., 4/1/64. Ab. 12/31/63 - 8/31/64 (dated 1/6/65), AWOL since 7/64. Ab. 9/1/64 - 10/31/64, AWOL. Bur. Shiloh Cem., Barbour Co., W. Va. NFR.

ALTON, THOMAS - Pvt. Co. B. Enl. Camp Northwest, W. Va., 6/15/63 (Marion Co., W. Va., 2/17/63). Not stated if present or absent on muster-in roll dated 7/25/63. Present 11/1/63 - 8/31/64 (dated 1/6/65). Present 9/1/64 - 10/31/64 (dated 12/30/64). Post war resident of Marion Co., W. Va. NFR.

AMMONS (AMMON, AMONS), ALPHEUS - Pvt. Co. A. b.c. 1841. Resident of Marion (Monongalia) Co., W. Va. Enl. Pocahontas Co., W. Va., 6/10/63, age 22. Mustered into service, 6/10/63. Not stated if present or absent on muster-in roll dated 6/10/63. Present 7/1/63 - 9/1/63. Ab. 10/31/63 - 8/31/64, KIA. 9/25/64. Probably KIA near Piedmont. Clothing issued 2/29/64 and 3/64.

AMMONS (AMMON, AMONS), REZIN (REASON, RESIN) - Pvt. Co. A. b. Monongalia Co., W. Va., c. 1839. Resident of Monongalia (Marion) Co., W. Va. Enl. Pocahontas Co., W. Va., 6/10/63, age 24. Mustered into service, 6/10/63. Not stated if present or absent on muster-in roll dated 6/10/63. Present 7/1/63 - 9/1/63. Present 10/31/63 - 8/31/64. Clothing issued 8/17/64. Deserted. Cpd. Taylor Co., W. Va., 10/24/64. Confined at Clarksburg, W. Va., 10/?/64. Desc.: age 24, 5'7", light comp., light hair and gray eyes. Occ. farmer, residing in Monongalia Co., W. Va. Sent to Wheeling, W. Va., 10/31/64. Confined at the Atheneum Prison, then sent to Camp Chase, 11/3/64. Confined at Camp Chase, 11/4/64, wished to take the oath of allegiance. Gave a statement at Camp Chase, 1/15/65, age 25. Says he remained in the army until 10/10/64 or 10/12/64, then started home from New Market, Shenandoah Co. and surrendered in Taylor Co., W. Va. Took the oath of allegiance and was released, 1/17/65, by order of the Sec. of War. Age 41, farmer, Battelle Sub Dist., Monongalia Co., W. Va. 1880 Census. NFR.

AMMONS, T. B. - Pvt. Co. ?. Not on muster rolls. A wartime voting list for the 16th Confed. Congressional Dist. lists him as a member of this unit in 1863. NFR.

AMMONS (AMMON, ALMOND), ZIMRI (ZEMRI) F. - Pvt. Co. A. b. Marion Co., W. Va., c. 1846. Resident of Marion (Monongalia) Co., W. Va. Enl. Lynchburg, 6/20/63. Ab. 10/31/63 - 8/31/64, deserted 9/15/64. Cpd. Beverly, W. Va., 9/28/64, sent to Clarksburg, W. Va. Confined at Clarksburg, W. Va. Desc.: age 18, 5'5", dark comp., dark hair and gray eyes. Occ. farmer,

189

on Co., W. Va. Took the oath of allegiance and was released, 10/5/64, sent to Ohio. Post war resident of Marion Age 33, carpenter, Paw Paw Dist., Marion Co., W. Va. 1880 Census. NFR.

3. - Pvt. Co. A. b.c. 1843. Resident of Monongalia Co., W. Va. Enl. Pocahontas Co., W. Va., 3/20/63, age 20. into service, 3/20/63. Not stated if present or absent on muster-in roll dated 3/20/63. Present 7/1/63 - 9/1/63. Ab. - 8/31/64, cpd. Droop Mtn., Pocahontas Co., W. Va., 11/6/63. Confined at the Atheneum Prison, 11/16/63. Desc.: 5'10", florid comp., sandy hair and gray eyes. Occ. farmer, residing in Marion Co., W. Va. Transf. to Camp Chase, 63. Confined at Camp Chase, 11/18/63. Desired to take the oath of allegiance, 6/10/64. Took the oath of allegiance /as released, 5/27/65, by order of the Sec. of War. Age 37, merchant, Paw Paw Dist., Marion Co., W. Va. 1880 Census.

AMOS, VAN C. - Pvt. Co. A. b.c. 1843. Resident of Monongalia Co., W. Va. Enl. Pocahontas Co., W. Va., 6/10/63, age 20. Not stated if present or absent on muster-in roll dated 6/10/63. Present 7/1/63 - 9/1/63. Present 10/31/63 - 8/31/64, AWOL for 10 days. Cpd. Marion Co., W. Va., 2/29/64. Confined at the Atheneum Prison, 3/1/64. Desc.: age 21, 5'8+", fair comp., black hair and black eyes. Occ. farmer, residing in Marion Co., W. Va. Turned over to civil authorities and sent to Monongalia Co., 4/12/64. Clothing issued 9/4/64. Paroled at Staunton, 5/1/65. NFR.

ANDERSON, EVANS G. (ERVAN S.) - 1st Sgt. Co. K. b.c. 1840. Enl. Lewisburg, W. Va., 4/1/63, age 22. Not stated if present or absent on muster-in roll dated 7/21/63, 2nd Sgt. Present, 2nd Sgt., 7/1/63 - 11/1/63 (dated 1/6/64), promoted to 2nd Sgt., 7/21/63. Present, 1st Sgt., 11/1/63 - 2/29/64, promoted to 1st Sgt., 1/1/64. Present 2/29/64 - 8/31/64, had his own horse since 5/1/64; $100 enl. bounty due. Clothing issued 2/29/64. Cpd. Parkersburg, W. Va., 4/20/65. Confined at Clarksburg, W. Va. Paroled 4/22/65, to be exchanged and was released. Desc.: age 25, 5'4+", fair comp., light hair and blue eyes. Occ. farmer, residing in Rockbridge Co. NFR.

ANDERSON, GEORGE A. - Pvt. Co. D. b. Loudoun Co., c. 1846. Enl. Philippi, W. Va., 10/4/63 (10/1/63). POW record shows enl. as Highland Co., 11/63. Present 7/1/63 - 1/1/64 (dated 1/1/64), enl. bounty due; has no horse. Ab. 12/31/63 - 8/31/64 (dated 1/6/65), AWOL since 7/64. Clothing issued 2/29/64. Ab. 9/1/64 - 10/31/64, AWOL. Reported at Parkersburg, W. Va., 11/3/64. Confined at Clarksburg, W. Va. Took the oath of allegiance and was released, 11/3/64. Desc.: age 18, 5'8", light comp., light hair and blue eyes. Occ. farmer, residing in Barbour Co., W. Va. NFR.

ANDERSON, JEFFERSON - Pvt. Co. D. b. Loudoun Co., c. 1814. Enl. Camp Miller, 9/4/63. POW record shows enl. as Highland Co., 8/63. Present 7/1/63 - 1/1/64 (dated 1/1/64), has his own horse; enl. bounty due. Ab. 12/31/63 - 8/31/64 (dated 1/6/65), AWOL since 7/64. Ab. 9/1/64 - 10/31/64, AWOL. Reported at Clarksburg, W. Va., 11/5/64. Took the oath of allegiance and was released, 11/5/64. Desc.: age 50, 5'5", fair comp., light hair and blue eyes. Occ. farmer, residing in Barbour Co., W. Va. NFR.

ARBOGAST (ARBOGHAST), SILAS - Pvt. Co. C. b.c. 1844. Age 16, farmer, Randolph Co., W. Va. 1860 Census. Enl. Randolph Co., W. Va., 4/28/63. Not stated if present or absent on muster-in roll dated 8/63. Present 6/30/63 - 8/31/64 (dated 1/6/65). Clothing issued 3/10/64. Ab. 9/1/64 - 10/31/64 (dated 12/30/64), AWOL. Surrendered at Buckhannon, W. Va., 3/11/65. Sent to Clarksburg, W. Va. Paroled for exchange 5/15/65 and was released. Desc.: age 21, 5'6", fair comp., fair hair and blue eyes. Occ. farmer, residing in Randolph Co., W. Va. NFR.

ARMENTROUT, CHARLES E. - Pvt. Co. K. b. Augusta Co., c. 1840. Age 20, laborer, N. Dist., Augusta Co. 1860 Census. Not on muster rolls. Served in Co. F, 19th Va. Cav. Wartime letter from Col. W. L. Jackson, dated 5/4/64, states he was a member of Capt. Alexander's Co. (K), and that he was a deserter from another command. Thought to have been a post war resident of Rockbridge Co. NFR.

ARMSTRONG, JEFFERSON - Pvt. Co. E. b. Barbour Co., W. Va., c. 1839. Enl. Bulltown, W. Va., 3/10/63. Not stated if present or absent on muster-in roll dated 7/18/63. Present 1/1/64 - 8/31/64 (dated 1/6/65). Present 9/1/64 - 10/31/64 (dated 12/29/64), $100 bond due. Reported at Philippi, W. Va., 10/12/64. Sent to Clarksburg, W. Va. Took the oath of allegiance and was released, 10/14/64. Desc.: age 25, 5'8", light comp., light hair and gray eyes. Occ. farmer, residing in Harrison Co., W. Va. NFR.

ARNETT, JONATHAN T. - 2nd Lt. Co. B. b.c. 1844. Enl. Clay Hill, 4/15/63 (1/4/63). Not stated if present or absent, Jr. 2nd Lt., on muster-in roll dated 7/25/63. Present, 2nd Lt., 11/1/63 - 8/31/64 (dated 1/6/65), promoted (elected) 2nd Lt. 8/15/63. Detailed for duty on a Gen. Court Martial, Warm Springs, Bath Co., 2/25/64. Present, 2nd Lt., 9/1/64 - 10/31/64 (dated 12/30/64). Ab. 10/25/64, sick in hosp. for 6 days. Ab. 12/15/64, sick since 10/?/64. Paroled at Staunton, 5/22/65. Desc.: age 21, 6', fair comp., light hair and hazel eyes. Post war resident of Marion Co., W. Va. NFR.

ARNETT, THOMAS CALVIN - Pvt. Co. B. b.c. 1833. Prior service, Co. D, 19th Va. Cav. Enl. Williamsburg, Greenbrier Co., W. Va., 3/17/63. Not stated if present or absent on muster-in roll dated 7/25/63. Ab. 11/1/63 - 8/31/64 (dated 1/6/65), deserted 10/63. Ab. 9/1/64 - 10/31/64 (dated 12/30/64), deserted 10/63. Post war resident of Monongalia Co., W. Va. Age 46, carpenter, Clay Dist., Monongalia Co., W. Va. 1880 Census, listed as Calvin. NFR.

ARNETT, WILLIAM WILEY - Capt. Co. B and Colonel. b. Marion Co., W. Va., 10/23/39. Attended Fairmont Academy. Grad. Alleghany College, Meadowville, Pa., 1860, lawyer. Gov. John Letcher recommended him for Lt. Col. of Va. Vol's., 5/22/61. Confirmed by the State Advisory Council. Prior service, Co. A, 31st Va. Inf. Claimed to have been Lt. Col. of 8th Va. (Battn.) Inf. and 23rd Va. Inf. Applied for leave of absence until his resignation as Lt. Col., Va. Vol's. is accepted, 8/24/61. Resignation accepted 9/6/61. Enl. Clay Hill, 4/15/63. Present at Beverly, W. Va., 7/63. Not stated if present or absent on muster-in roll dated 7/25/63, Capt., commanding Co. Nominated by David Poe for the position of Colonel. Elected Colonel, 8/14/63. Appointed Colonel 10/7/63, confirmed by election, to rank from 8/14/63. Accepted appointment 10/21/63. Present FS MR 1/1/64 - 8/31/64 (dated 1/6/65). Granted 20 day leave, 2/13/64. Paroled at Staunton, 5/17/65. Desc.: age 23(?), 6', fair comp., dark hair and black eyes. Post war lawyer. Represented Marion Co., W. Va. in the Va. Legislature, 1861 - 1865. Post war lawyer and resident of Berryville. Moved to St. Louis, Mo., 1872. Moved to Wheeling, W. Va., 1875 - 1890. d. Wheeling, W. Va., 2/15/1902.

ASHFORD, CLAIBORN - 1st Corp. Co. C. b.c. 1840. Post war roster shows service in the 19th Va. Cav. Enl. Randolph Co., W. Va., 5/5/63. Not stated if present or absent on muster-in roll dated 8/63. Present, 1st Corp., 6/30/63 - 8/31/63 (dated 1/6/65). Present, 1st Corp., 9/1/64 - 10/31/64 (dated 12/30/64). Clothing issued 10/15/64, while on his way to his command. Paroled at Charleston, W. Va., 5/10/65, as a Pvt. Desc.: age 25, 5'8", fair comp., dark hair, blue eyes and dark whiskers. Age 41, Green Banks Dist., Pocahontas Co., W. Va. 1880 Census. Post war resident of Greenbank, Pocahontas Co., W. Va., 1916. NFR.

ATKINSON, JAMES K. (A.) - 3rd Corp. Co. G. Enl. Wood Co., W. Va., 6/24/63. Not stated if present or absent, Pvt., on muster-in roll dated 8/63. Present, 4th Corp., 11/1/63 - 2/29/64, has his own horse and equipment. Clothing issued 2/29/64. Not stated if present or absent, 3rd Corp., 7/1/64 - 8/31/64. Ab., 3rd Corp., 9/1/64 - 10/31/64 (dated 12/29/64), deserted 10/1/64. Post war resident of Wood Co., W. Va. Age 37, farm laborer, Steele Dist., Wood Co., W. Va. 1880 Census. NFR.

AUSTIN, SAMUEL HUNTER (HENRY) - Asst. Surgeon. b. near Tinkling Springs, Augusta Co., 3/18/40. Resident of West Milford, Harrison Co., W. Va., 1843. Attended VMI, 1856-60. Studied medicine under his father, Dr. A. M. Austin. Attended Winchester Medical College (Dr. McGuire), 2 years, 1860-61. Attended lectures at the Medical College of Va. Prior service, Jackson Rifles, 36th Va. Inf. and transf. to Co. B, 22nd Va. Inf. Also as having served in the 19th Va. Cav. Enl. in the 20th Va. Cav., spring 1863. Acting Assistant Surgeon, White Sulphur Springs Hosp., W. Va. In 20th Va. Cav., spring 1864. Moved to Greenbrier Co., W. Va., 1865. Grad. Medical College of Va., 3/1866. Post grad. courses at Philadelphia, Pa. US examining surgeon, Lewisburg, W. Va., 1881, 6 years. Served as Commissioner of Schools, 4 years. Chairman, Democratic Executive Committee. Surgeon-Major, 2nd W. Va. National Guard. Post war MD, residing at Lewisburg, W. Va., 1894. Member David S. Creigh Camp, UCV, Lewisburg, W. Va. d. Charleston, W. Va., 11/16/1926. Bur. Old Stone Church Cem., Lewisburg, W. Va.

AYERS, STEPHEN W. - Pvt. Co. I. b.c. 1843. Enl. Camp Northwest, W. Va., 6/25/63, age 20. Not stated if present or absent on muster-in roll dated 5/5/63. NFR.

AYRES, JAMES JORDAN - Sgt. Co. K. b. Rockbridge Co., 11/17/41. Carpenter's apprentice, Kerr's Creek Dist., Rockbridge Co. 1860 Census. Prior service, 1st Rockbridge Arty., and Co. C, 5th Va. Inf. Enl. Camp Northwest, W. Va., 6/3/63, age 20. POW record shows his enl. as Lexington, 4/61. Not stated if present or absent, Pvt., on muster-in roll dated 7/21/63. Present, 4th Corp., 7/1/63 - 11/1/63 (dated 1/6/64), promoted to 4th Corp., 8/1/63; lost Mississippi Rifle. Present, 3rd Corp., 11/1/63 - 2/29/64, promoted to 3rd Corp., 1/1/64; had his own horse since 5/1/64. Clothing issued 2/29/64. Ab., 2/29/64 - 8/31/64, sick. Reported at Clarksburg, W. Va., 12/14/64, listed as Sgt. Took the oath of allegiance and was released, 12/14/64. Desc.: age 21, 5'10", fair comp., light hair and blue eyes. Occ. carpenter, residing in Rockbridge Co. Member Lee-Jackson Camp, UCV, Lexington. d. near Denmark, 1914. Bur. Greenhill Cem., Beuna Vista, Rockbridge Co. Brother of Napoleon B. Ayres.

AYRES, NAPOLEON BONAPARTE - Pvt. Co. I. b. Rockbridge Co., c. 1843. Age 18, carpenter, Kerr's Creek Dist., Rockbridge Co. 1860 Census. Prior service, Capt. Archibald Graham's Co., Va. Light (1st Rockbridge) Arty. Enl. Camp Northwest, W. Va., 6/25/63, age 20. POW record shows enl. as Lexington, 7/61. Not stated if present or absent on muster-in roll dated 5/5/63. Cpd. Beverly, W. Va., 10/13/64. Sent to Clarksburg, W. Va., and was confined. Took the oath of allegiance and was released, 10/17/64. Desc.: age 23, 5'8", fair comp., light hair and blue eyes. Occ. farmer, residing in Bath Co. Brother of James J. Ayres. Entered Old Soldier's Home, Richmond, 3/27/1924, age 84. d. Richmond, 12/28/1926. Bur. Hollywood Cem., Richmond.

AYRES, SAMUEL ROGERS - 3rd Sgt. Co. K. b. Rockbridge Co., 7/4/45. Prior service, 1st Rockbridge Arty., Cutshaw's Batty., and Carpenter's Batty. Enl. Camp Northwest, W. Va., 5/1/63, age 18. Not stated if present or absent, 4th Sgt., on muster-in roll dated 7/21/63. Present, 4th Sgt., 7/1/63 - 11/1/63 (dated 1/6/64), promoted to 4th Sgt., 7/21/63; had his own horse from 9/17/63 - 11/1/63. Ab., 3rd Sgt., 11/1/63 - 2/29/64, promoted to 3rd Sgt., 1/64; claimed by another command. Clothing issued 2/29/64. Ab., listed as Pvt. and 3rd Sgt., 2/29/64 - 8/31/64, claimed by another command. Returned to Carpenter's Batty., 6/10/64. Moved to Indiana, 1870. d. Franklin, Ind., 4/22/1927. Bur. Franklin, Ind.

AYRES, WILLIAM C. - Pvt. Co. H. Enl. Camp Northwest, W. Va., 7/1/63 (6/28/63). Not stated if present or absent on muster-in roll dated 8/63. Ab. 10/31/63 - 8/31/64, deserted 7/1/63. Ab. 9/1/64 - 10/31/64 (dated 12/30/64), deserted 7/1/63. Served in Mason's Arty., Staunton. Post war pensioner, Rockbridge Co., 1924. NFR.

BAILEY, JAMES D. T. - 3rd Sgt. Co. E. Enl. Bulltown, W. Va., 5/10/63. Not stated if present or absent, 3rd Sgt., on muster-in roll dated 7/18/63. Ab., 4th Sgt., 1/1/64 - 8/31/64 (dated 1/6/65), cpd. Frederick Co., Md., 7/10/64. Clothing issued 1/17/64, detailed as carpenter. Employed at Warm Springs, 1/1/64 - 3/31/64, as a carpenter. Cpd. Frederick Co., Md. (near Harpers Ferry, W. Va.), 7/10/64. Sent to Harpers Ferry, W. Va., then to Washington, DC. Confined at the Old Capitol Prison, 7/17/64. Transf. to Elmira, NY, 7/23/64. Confined at Elmira Prison, 7/25/64. Ab., 4th Sgt., 9/1/64 - 10/31/64 (dated 12/29/64), cpd. Md., 7/10/64; $100 bond due. Desired to take the oath of allegiance, 9/30/64; says he volunteered 5/10/63, to work as a shoemaker. Was permitted to do so for only a year, then deserted and gave up at Frederick Co., Md. Does not wish to be exchanged. DOD. Elmira, NY, 12/9/64, pneumonia. Bur. Woodlawn Cem., Elmira, NY, grave No. 1163 (1118).

BAILEY, MINTER X. - Pvt. Co. E. b. Lewis Co., W. Va., c. 1834. Enl. Bulltown, W. Va., 5/10/63. Not stated if present or absent on muster-in roll dated 7/18/63. Present 1/1/64 - 8/31/64 (dated 1/6/65). Employed as a carpenter at Warm Springs, 1/1/64 - 3/31/64. Clothing issued 6/17/64, detailed as carpenter. Present 9/1/64 - 10/31/64 (dated 12/29/64), $100 bond due. Deserted. Reported at Clarksburg, W. Va., 11/5/64. Took the oath of allegiance and was released 11/5/64. Desc.: age 30, 5'9", fair comp., light hair and blue eyes. Occ. carpenter, residing in Harrison Co., W. Va. NFR.

BALL, EMERY MADISON - 1st Lt. Co. H. b. Lewis (Calhoun) Co., W. Va., c. 1843 (1841). Age 17, farmer, Calhoun Co., W. Va. 1860 Census. Prior service, Co. A, 19th Va. Cav. Enl. Camp Northwest, W. Va., 6/1/63. Elected 1st Lt., 6/4/63. Not stated if present or absent, 1st Lt., on muster-in roll dated 8/63. Ab., 1st Lt., 10/31/63 - 8/31/64, in arrest. Commanding Co. H, 10/2/63. Ab., 1st Lt., 9/1/64 - 10/31/64 (dated 12/30/64), in arrest. Ab. 12/15/64, POW since 10/13/63. Deserted. Reported to US forces, 12/25/64, took the oath of allegiance and gave his bond. Age 27, farmer, Center Dist., Calhoun Co., W. Va. 1870 Census. Age 39, farmer, Center Dist., Calhoun Co., W. Va. 1880 Census. d. 1918. Bur. Sand Ridge Cem., W. Va.

BALL, WILLIAM H. - Pvt. Co. A. b.c. 1841. Enl. Pocahontas (Randolph) Co., W. Va., 7/3/63, age 22. Not stated if present or absent on muster-in roll, 7/3/63. Present 7/1/63 - 9/1/63. Present 10/31/63 - 8/31/64. Clothing issued 4/21/64, detached in hosp. Adm. Gen. Hosp. No. 9, 8/21/64, cause not stated. Furloughed 8/21/64, 30 days. Adm. CSA Gen. Hosp., Charlottesville, 9/18/64, debilitas. Transf. to another hosp., 9/25/64. Post war resident of Taylor Co., W. Va. NFR.

BANE, ANDREW - Pvt. Co. K. Enl. Camp Marlin's Bottom, W. Va., 10/13/63. Ab. 7/1/63 - 11/1/63 (dated 1/6/64), deserted; lost Mississippi Rifle. NFR.

BARB, PETER B. - Pvt. Co. ?. Post war rosters only, which show he was in service by 9/12/63, and was a resident of Upshur Co., W. Va. Served in Co. B, 46th Battn. Va. Cav. NFR.

BARKER, DAVID - Pvt. Co. B. Prior service, Co. D, 19th Va. Cav. Enl. Williamsburg, Greenbrier Co., W. Va., 3/17/63. Not stated if present or absent on muster-in roll dated 7/25/63. Ab. 11/1/63 - 8/31/64 (dated 1/6/65), POW, in hands of the enemy. Ab. 9/1/64 - 10/31/64 (dated 12/30/64), POW since 3/63. NFR.

BARKER (BAKER), EDGAR L. - Pvt. Co. A. b. 4/3/42. Enl. Monongalia Co., W. Va., 8/1/64. Present 10/31/63 - 8/31/64, entitled to $50 enl. bounty. Post war resident of Monongalia Co., W. Va. Post war rosters show he was wd. during the war, and has not been able to walk since. Age 38, no occ., Grant Dist., Monongalia Co., W. Va. 1880 Census. d. 6/21/1918. Bur. Barker Cem., Monongalia Co., W. Va.

BARKER (BAKER), FRANKLIN - 2nd Corp. Co. H and Co. G. b.c. 1843. Enl. Calhoun Co., W. Va., 5/14/63 in Co. H. Not stated if present or absent, 2nd Corp., on muster-in roll dated 8/63. Enl. Wood Co., W. Va., 5/9/63 (6/18/63) in Co. G. Not stated if present or absent, Pvt., on muster-in roll dated 8/63. Ab. 11/1/63 - 2/29/64, deserted 11/6/63. Cpd. by Home Guards, St. Mary's, Pleasants Co., W. Va., 11/23/63. Confined at the Atheneum Prison, 11/25/63. Desc.: age 20, 5'10", fair comp., fair hair and gray eyes. Occ. farmer, residing in Pleasants Co., W. Va. Transf. to Camp Chase, 2/10/64. Confined at Camp Chase, 2/11/64. Desires to take the oath of allegiance, 6/10/64, says he was a conscript. Ab. 7/1/64 - 8/31/64, cpd. 11/5/63. Ab. 9/1/64 - 10/31/64 (dated 12/29/64), cpd. 11/6/63. Took the oath of allegiance and was released, 5/15/65. Desc.: age ?, 5'9", florid comp., dark hair and blue eyes, a resident of Pleasants Co., W. Va. NFR.

BARKER (BAKER), GEORGE - Pvt. Co. H and G. b.c. 1845. Enl. Calhoun Co., W. Va., 5/14/63, in Co. H. Not stated if present or absent on muster-in roll dated 8/63. Enl. Wood Co., W. Va., 5/9/63 (6/18/63), in Co. G. Not stated if present or absent on muster-in roll dated 8/63. Ab. 11/1/63 - 2/29/64, deserted to the enemy, 11/6/63. Cpd. by Home Guards in Pleasants Co., W. Va., 11/23/63. Confined at the Atheneum Prison, 11/25/63. Desc.: age 18, 5'7"+, fair comp., auburn hair and gray eyes. Occ. farmer, residing in Pleasants Co., W. Va. Transf. to Camp Chase, 2/10/64. Confined at Camp Chase, 2/11/64. Desired to take the oath of allegiance, 6/10/64, says he was a conscript. Ab. 7/1/64 - 8/31/64, cpd. 11/5/63. Ab. 9/1/64 - 10/31/64 (dated 12/29/64), cpd. 11/6/63. Enl. in US service, 3/20/65 and was sent to Chicago, Ill. NFR.

BARKER, ZADOCK (ZANE) - Pvt. Co. B. b.c. 1831. Enl. Hightown, 11/17/62 (11/6/62). POW record shows enl. as Highland Co., 10/61. Not stated if present or absent on muster-in roll dated 7/25/63. Present 11/1/63 - 8/31/64 (dated 1/6/65), cpd. Beverly, W. Va., 10/64. Clothing issued 3/31/64 and 8/31/64. Present 9/1/64 - 10/31/64 (dated 12/30/64). Cpd. Beverly, W. Va., 10/29/64. Sent to Clarksburg, W. Va., then to Wheeling, W. Va. Desc.: age 33, 5'6", dark comp., black hair and brown eyes. Occ. boatman, residing in Taylor Co., W. Va. Confined at the Atheneum Prison, 11/2/64. Desc.: age 33, 5'5", dark comp., dark hair and dark eyes. Occ. raftsman, residing in Taylor Co., W. Va. Transf. to Camp Chase, 11/3/64. Confined at Camp Chase, 11/4/64. Took the oath of allegiance and was released, 6/12/65, signs by x. Desc.: age 34, 5'6", dark comp., dark hair and black eyes, a resident of Taylor Co., W. Va. NFR.

BARTLETT, THOMAS H. W. - Pvt. Co. B. b. Harrison Co., W. Va., c. 1826. Enl. Camp Northwest, W. Va., 7/7/63 (6/20/63). Not stated if present or absent on muster-in roll dated 7/25/63. Ab. 11/1/63 - 8/31/64 (dated 1/6/65), deserted. Clothing issued 3/31/64. Clothing issued at Staunton, 7/29/64, while on his way to his command. Ab. 9/1/64 - 10/31/64 (dated 12/30/64), deserted 9/64. Reported at Buckhannon, W. Va., 9/27/64. Sent to Clarksburg, W. Va. Took the oath of allegiance and was released, 10/10/64, sent to Ohio. Desc.: age 38, 5'9", light comp., dark hair and brown eyes. Occ. merchant, residing in Marion Co., W. Va. NFR.

BARTON, JAMES - Pvt. Co. A. Post war rosters only. Could be James Batson. NFR.

BASSELL (BASSEL), JOHN Y. (1st) - Pvt. Co. A. b.c. 1846. Enl. Upshur Co., W. Va., 4/30/63, age 17. Not stated if present or absent on muster-in roll dated 4/30/63. Present 7/1/63 - 9/1/63, detailed as orderly for Col. W. L. Jackson since enl. Ab. 10/31/63 8/31/64, wd. Droop Mtn., 11/6/63, very bad wd. Post war resident of Upshur Co., W. Va. This is most likely the same man as is listed below. NFR.

BASSELL (BASSEL), JOHN Y. (2nd) - Pvt. Co. E. b.c. 1847. Enl. Bulltown, W. Va., 5/10/63. Not stated if present or absent on muster roll dated 7/18/63. Ab. 1/1/64 - 8/31/64 (dated 1/6/65), wd.; entitled to $100 bond. Adm. CSA Gen. Hosp., Charlottesville, 4/29/64, vulnus sclopeticum, old. RTD. 9/5/64. Ab. 9/1/64 - 10/31/64 (dated 12/29/64), wd. Droop Mtn., 11/6/63, very bad wd.; $100 bond due. Wd. while fighting at the side of Capt. John W. Young. "a youth scarce sixteen." This is most likely the same man as above. NFR.

BATSON, JAMES - Pvt. Co. A. b.c. 1838. Enl. Marion Co., W. Va., 5/12/63 by Sgt. Youst (Yost), age 25. Not stated if present or absent on muster-in roll dated 5/12/63. Ab. 7/1/63 - 9/1/63, not reported for duty. Ab. 10/31/63 - 8/31/64, never reported for duty. NFR.

BEALL, JOHN T. - Pvt. Co. A. b.c. 1845. Enl. Highland Co., 5/4/63, age 18. Not stated if present or absent on muster-in roll dated 5/25/63. Present 7/1/63 - 9/1/63. Ab. 10/31/63 - 8/31/64, cpd. 9/23/64, listed as being present. Cpd. Harrisonburg, 9/25/64 (9/26/64). Sent to Harpers Ferry, W. Va., then to Pt. Lookout. Confined at Pt. Lookout, 10/4/64. Took the oath of allegiance and was released, 5/12/65. Occ. farmer, residing in Monongalia Co., W. Va. Post war resident of Monongalia (Marion) Co., W. Va. Age 55(?), farmer, Morgan Dist., Monongalia Co., W. Va. 1880 Census. NFR.

BEAN (BEEN), JOHN - 3rd Sgt. Co. D. b. Barbour Co., W. Va., c. 1833. Enl. Weston, W. Va., 5/1/63. POW record shows enl. as Pocahontas Co., W. Va., 5/63. Not stated if present or absent, 3rd Sgt., on muster roll dated 8/63. Present, Pvt., 7/1/63 - 1/1/64 (dated 1/1/64), has his own horse. Present 12/31/63 - 8/31/64 (dated 1/6/65). Present 9/1/64 - 10/31/64, entitled to $100 enl. bounty. Surrendered at Clarksburg, W. Va., 3/18/65. Took the amnesty oath and was sent North, 3/23/65. Desc.: age 32, 5'11", dark comp., sandy hair and dark eyes. Occ. farmer, residing in Barbour Co., W. Va. NFR.

BEAN, WESTLEY - Pvt. Co. D. Enl. Weston, W. Va., 5/1/63. Not stated if present or absent on muster-in roll dated 8/63. NFR.

BELCH, WILLIAM M. - Pvt. Co. B. Prior service, Co. D, 19th Va. Cav. Enl. Williamsburg, Greenbrier Co., W. Va., 3/17/63. Not stated if present or absent on muster roll dated 7/25/63. Ab. 11/1/63 - 8/31/64 (dated 1/6/65), AWOL. Ab. 9/1/64 - 10/31/64 (dated 12/30/64), AWOL. NFR.

BELL, EDWARD - Pvt. Co. A. Post war rosters only, which show he was a resident of Monongalia Co., W. Va. NFR.

BELL, GEORGE - Pvt. Co. K. b.c. 1845. Enl. Warm Springs, Bath Co., 4/1/63, age 18. Not stated if present or absent on muster roll dated 7/21/63. Present 7/1/63 - 11/1/63 (dated 1/6/64), lost a sharps rifle and cartridge box. Present 11/1/63 - 2/29/64, had his own horse since 7/1/64. Clothing issued 2/29/64. Present 2/29/64 - 8/31/64. NFR.

BELL, JAMES L. - Pvt. Co. C. b. Augusta Co., c. 1840. Enl. Pocahontas (Randolph) Co., W. Va., 5/14/63. POW record shows his enl. as Pocahontas Co., W. Va., 6/62. Not stated if present or absent on muster roll dated 8/63. Present 6/30/63 - 8/31/64 (dated 1/6/65). Clothing issued 3/10/64. Ab. 9/1/64 - 10/31/64 (dated 12/30/64), AWOL. Deserted. Reported at Beverly, W. Va., 12/17/64. Sent to Clarksburg, W. Va. Took the oath of allegiance and was released, 12/22/64. Desc.: age 24, 6' 3/4", fair comp., dark hair and black eyes. Occ. farmer, residing in Preston Co., W. Va. Age 40, farmer, Reno Dist., Preston Co., W. Va. 1880 Census. NFR.

BELL, JOHN NICKSON CURRENCE "Squire" - Pvt. Co. C. b. 10/5/44. Age 15, farmer, Randolph Co., W. Va. 1860 Census. Enl. Randolph Co., W. Va., 4/28/63 (4/23/63). Not stated if present or absent on muster roll dated 8/63. Present 6/30/63 - 8/31/64 (dated 1/6/65), 6% bond due. Ab. 9/1/64 - 10/31/64 (dated 12/30/64), sick; 6% bond due. Post war resident of Randolph Co., W. Va. Post war rosters show service in Co. I, 19th Va. Cav. Age 35, farmer, Huttonsville, Randolph Co., W. Va. 1880 Census. Attended Confederate Reunion, Randolph Co., W. Va., 1906. Post war Justice of the Peace, Huttonsville Dist., Randolph Co., W. Va. d. 10/26/1911, c. 68 years. Bur. Kelley Cem., on the Kelley Farm, Randolph Co., W. Va.

BEN, WILLIAM - Pvt. Co. ?. Post war rosters only, which show he was in service by 9/12/63, and was a resident of Barbour Co., W. Va. NFR.

BENNETT, JOHN - Pvt. Co. C. b. Randolph Co., W. Va., c. 1844 (1841). Enl. Beverly, Randolph Co., W. Va., 5/5/63. Not stated if present or absent on muster-in roll dated 8/63. Ab. 6/30/63 - 8/31/64 (dated 1/6/65), AWOL since 6/1/64. Clothing issued 3/10/64. Ab. 9/1/64 - 10/31/64 (dated 12/30/64), deserted 6/1/64. Reported at Beverly, W. Va., 11/10/64. Sent to Clarksburg, W. Va. Took the oath of allegiance and was released, 11/13/64. Desc.: age 20, 5'11", fair comp., light hair and gray eyes. Occ. blacksmith, residing in Randolph Co., W. Va. Age 39, blacksmith, Huttonsville, Randolph Co., W. Va. 1880 Census. Bur. Crouch Cem., Randolph Co., W. Va. NFR.

BENNETT, NORVAL S. - Pvt. Co. A. b.c. 1840. Enl. Marion Co., W. Va., by Sgt. Yost, 4/6/63 (4/12/63), age 23. Not stated if present or absent on muster-in roll dated 4/6/63. Ab. 7/1/63 - 9/1/63, not reported for duty. Ab. 10/31/63 - 8/31/64, never reported for duty. NFR.

BENNETT, THOMAS T. (L.) - Pvt. Co. A. b.c. 1843. Enl. Pocahontas Co., W. Va., 3/28/63, age 20. Not stated if present or absent on muster-in roll dated 3/28/63. Ab. 7/1/63 - 9/1/63, deserted 5/6/63. Ab. 10/31/63 - 8/31/64, deserted 5/6/63. NFR.

BENNETT, VEAL - Pvt. Co. ?. Post war rosters only, which show he was in service by 9/12/63, and was a resident of Marion Co., W. Va. NFR.

BENNETT, WILLIAM M. - Pvt. Co. ?. Post war rosters only, which show he was in service by 9/12/63, and was a resident of Upshur Co., W. Va. NFR.

BENNINGTON, NIMROD - Pvt. Co. H. Enl. Camp Northwest, W. Va., 6/14/63. Not stated if present or absent on muster-in roll dated 8/63. NFR.

BENSON, JAMES H. - Pvt. Co. A. b.c. 1827. Prior service, Co. B, 31st Va. Inf. Employed in Highland Co. Niter Caves. Enl. Augusta Co., 2/18/63, age 36. Not stated if present or absent on muster-in roll dated 2/18/63. Ab. 7/1/63 - 9/1/63, detailed to work in niter cave since enl. Ab. 10/31/63 - 8/31/64, detailed in niter works. Employed at Kirkpatrick's Niter Works, Bath Co., 9/1/63 - 12/31/63. Returned to Co. B, 31st Va. Inf., by 11/20/63. Post war resident of Highland Co. NFR.

BENSON, WADE HAMPSON (HAMPTON) - Pvt. Co. G. b.c. 1841. Enl. Wood Co., W. Va., 7/1/63. Not stated if present or absent on muster-in roll dated 8/63. Ab. 11/1/63 - 2/29/64, supposed cpd. 11/6/63. Cpd. Pocahontas Co., W. Va., 11/6/63, listed as a deserter. Sent to Wheeling, W. Va., then to Camp Chase. Confined at Camp Chase, 11/18/63. Desc.: age 22, 5'11", dark comp., auburn hair and blue eyes. Ab. 7/1/63 - 8/31/64, cpd. 11/6/63. Ab. 9/1/64 - 10/31/64 (dated 12/29/64), cpd. 11/6/63. Applied to take the oath of allegiance, 11/64. Gave a statement 1/10/65: age 22, resident of Doddridge Co., W. Va. Says he volunteered 7/8/62. "Volunteered from a conviction that the rebel cause was a just one and was deceived by misrepresentation." Took the oath of allegiance to the US and W. Va., and was released, 1/17/65, ordered to report to Gov. Bowman. Desc.: age 23, 5'11", dark comp., dark hair and gray eyes. Most likely same as Wade Hampson, Co. G, 20th Va. Cav. NFR.

BENSON, WILLIAM C. - Pvt. Co. H and Co. G. Enl. Calhoun Co., W. Va., 5/14/63 in Co. H. Not stated if present or absent on muster-in roll dated 8/63. Enl. Wood Co., W. Va., 5/9/63 (6/18/63), in Co. G. Not stated if present or absent on muster-in roll dated 8/63. Present 11/1/63 - 2/29/64. Clothing issued 2/29/64. Not stated if present or absent 7/1/64 - 8/31/64. Ab. 9/1/64 - 10/31/64 (dated 12/29/64), MIA Piedmont, 9/25/64; supposed cpd.; entitled to $100 enl. bounty. NFR.

BENSON, WILLIAM H. - Pvt. Co. D. Enl. Weston, W. Va., 5/1/63. Not stated if present or absent on muster-in roll dated 8/63. Ab. 7/1/63 - 1/1/64 (dated 1/1/64), POW. Broke a leg at Bulltown, W. Va., 10/13/63, cared for at the home of P. B. Berry. Cpd. near Bulltown, W. Va. Ab. 12/31/63 - 8/31/64 (dated 1/6/65), POW. Ab. 9/1/64 - 10/31/64, wd. and in hands of the enemy. Post war minister. NFR.

BERSH, G. N. - Pvt. Co. G. Not on muster rolls. Paroled at Staunton, 5/11/65. No desc. NFR.

BEVERIDGE, JOHN M. - Pvt. Co. I. Enl. Camp Cameron, Bath Co., 9/3/64. Ab. 11/1/63 - 8/31/64 (dated 1/6/65), deserted. NFR.

BICKEL (BECKEL, BICKLE), LEWIS PHILLIPP - 2nd Corp. Co. G. b.c. 1843. Enl. Wood Co., W. Va., 5/2/63 (5/12/63). Not stated if present or absent, Pvt., on muster-in roll dated 8/63. Present, 3rd Corp., 11/1/63 - 2/29/64. Clothing issued 2/29/64. Not stated if present or absent, 2nd Corp., 7/1/64 - 8/31/64, has is own horse; entitled to enl. bounty. Ab. 9/1/64 - 10/31/64 (dated 12/29/64), in hosp., leg amputated 9/19/64; $100 enl. bounty due. Wd. Winchester, 9/19/64, left thigh, by shell. Operated on by Surg. Sawers, 9/20/64, lower third of left thigh amputated. Applied for an artificial limb 2/11/65, listed his residence as Montgomery White Sulphur Springs. Paroled at Charleston, W. Va., 5/22/65. Desc.: age 22, 5'5", fair comp., brown hair and hazel eyes. Post war resident of Wood Co., W. Va. NFR.

BIRD, SAMUEL R. - Pvt. Co. C. b. Va., c. 1844. Prior service, Co. E, 31st Va. Inf. Enl. Pocahontas Co., W. Va., 6/12/63. POW record shows enl. as Monterey, 5/62. Not stated if present or absent on muster roll dated 8/63. Deserted. Gave himself up at Beverly, W. Va., 7/15/64. Sent to Clarksburg, W. Va. Took the oath of allegiance and was released, 7/18/64. Desc.: age 20, 5'11", fair comp., light hair and gray eyes. Occ. farmer, residing in Highland Co. CSR listed as Samuel Birard. NFR.

BIRD (BYRD), JAMES M. - Pvt. Co. A. Reference envelope and letter addressed to him, showing service in Co. A, 20th Va. Cav. Cpd. and confined at Ft. Delaware, by 11/18/64. Served in Co. C, 46th Battn. Va. Cav. NFR.

BIRD, R. A. - Pvt. Co. C. Enl. Highland Co., 6/12/63. Ab. 6/30/63 - 8/31/64 (dated 1/6/65), deserted 6/1/64. NFR.

BISHOP, MOSES L. - Pvt. Co. F. Enl. Camp Northwest, W. Va., 7/19/63. Also as having enl. at Camp Miller. Not stated if present or absent on muster-in roll dated 7/20/63. Ab. 7/1/63 - 8/31/64 (dated 1/6/65), transf. to Co. A, 19th Va. Cav. Ab. 9/1/64 10/31/64 (dated 12/30/64), transf. to Co. A, 19th Va. Cav. NFR.

BITTLE, SPENCE - Pvt. Co. ?. Post war rosters only. NFR.

BLACK, FRANCES J. - 1st Sgt. Co. I and Sgt. Major. Enl. Warm Springs, Bath Co., 4/20/63 (Staunton, 5/10/63). Not stated if present or absent on muster-in roll dated 5/5/63, 1st Sgt. Clothing issued 2/29/64. Ab., Sgt. Major, FS MR 1/1/64 - 8/31/64 (dated 1/6/65), deserted. NFR.

BLACK, HENRY ARMENTROUT - Pvt. Co. K.*b. Rockbridge Co., 5/17/43. POW record shows he was b. Amherst Co. Farmhand, Kerr's Creek Dist., Rockbridge Co. 1860 census. Exempt 3/62, gen. debility. Prior service, Co. I, 12th Va. Cav. Enl. Camp Northwest, Pocahontas Co., W. Va., 6/1/63, in Co. K, 20th Va. Cav. Present 7/1/63 - 11/1/63 (dated 1/6/64), had his own horse from 9/20/63 - 11/12/63. Present 11/1/63 - 2/29/64, horse d. 11/12/63. Ab. 2/29/64 - 8/31/64, reported to have gone to the Yankees. Clothing issued 2/29/64 and 3/23/64. Reported at Beverly, W. Va., 10/18/64. Sent to Clarksburg, W. Va. Took the oath of allegiance and was released, 10/23/64. Desc.: age 21, 5'4" (5'11"), light comp., light hair and gray eyes. Occ. farmer, residing in Rockbridge Co. Farmer, Demark, Rockbridge Co. 1910 census. d. Rockbridge Co., 9/3/1914. Bur. Harbarger Cem., Rt. 621, Kerr's Creek.

BLACK, J. L. - Pvt. Co. K. Not on muster rolls. Wartime letter from Col. W. L. Jackson mentions that he was a member of Capt. Alexander's Co. (K), and was claimed as a deserter from another command. NFR.

BLACKWOOD, RICHARD A. (E.) - Pvt. Co. C. Enl. Pocahontas Co., W. Va., 5/14/63. Not stated if present or absent on muster-in roll dated 8/63. Ab. 6/30/63 - 8/31/64 (dated 1/6/65), POW since 12/23/63; d. 10/64; 6% bond due. Cpd. Preston Co., W. Va., 4/16/64. Confined at the Atheneum Prison, 5/16/64. Desc.: age 19, 5'7", fair comp., dark hair and gray eyes. Occ. farmer, residing in Preston Co., W. Va. Transf. to Camp Chase, 5/17/64. Confined at Camp Chase, 5/18/64. Ab. 9/1/64 - 10/31/64 (dated 12/30/64), POW since 12/27/64; 6% bond due. DOD. Camp Chase, 9/15/64, diarrhoea. Bur. Camp Chase Confederate Cem., grave no. 245.

BLAIN, ABNER W. - 3rd Corp. Cq. I. b.c. 1828. Enl. Camp Northwest, Pocahontas Co., W. Va., 6/18/63 (6/1/63, 3/20/63) by J. H. Cammack, age 35. Not stated if present or absent on muster-in roll dated 5/5/63, Pvt. Ab., 3rd Corp., 11/1/63 - 8/31/64 (dated 1/6/65), POW. Ab., Pvt., 11/1/63 - 10/31/64 (dated 12/31/64), POW. Cpd. Harrisonburg, 9/27/64. Sent to Harpers Ferry, W. Va., then to Pt. Lookout, 10/1/64. Confined at Pt. Lookout, 10/4/64. Adm. POW Camp Hosp., Pt. Lookout, 2/6/65, congestive chill. DOD. Pt. Lookout, 2/8/65 (2/9/65), congestive intermittent fever. Bur. POW graveyard, Pt. Lookout.

BLAIR, GEORGE - Pvt. Co. F. Enl. Camp Clover Lick, 7/11/63 (Bulltown, W. Va., 5/10/63). Not stated if present or absent on muster-in roll dated 7/20/63. Ab. 7/1/63 - 8/31/64 (dated 1/6/65), POW since 5/13/63; entitled to enl. bounty. Ab. 9/1/64 - 10/31/64 (dated 12/30/64), since 5/13/63. NFR.

BLAIR, MATHEW A. - Pvt. Co. D. and Surgeon. Enl. Camp Scott, 8/1/63. Present, Pvt., 7/1/63 - 1/1/64 (dated 1/1/64), entitled to enl. bounty; appointed Surgeon, 9/15/63; has own horse. Present, Surgeon, FS MR 1/1/64 - 8/31/64 (dated 1/6/65), commissioned 8/14/63. NFR.

BLAIR, SAMUEL S. - Pvt. Co. A (F). b.c. 1839. Not on muster rolls. Cpd. Clarksburg, Harrison Co., W. Va., 8/14/63 by Addison Campbell. Confined at the Atheneum Prison, 8/22/63. Desc.: age 24, 6'4+", light comp., light hair and dark eyes. Occ. farmer, residing in Harrison Co., W. Va. Transf. to Camp Chase, 1/28/64. Confined at Camp Chase, 1/29/64. Transf. to Ft. Delaware, 3/14/64. Confined at Ft. Delaware, 3/17/64. Paroled 9/14/64, signs by x, and sent to Aiken's Landing 9/18/64, to be exchanged. Exchanged at Varina, 9/22/64. Adm. Chimborazo Hosp. No. 3, 9/22/64, debility. Furloughed 10/1/64, 40 days. Post war resident of Mt. Clare, W. Va. Age 40, farmer, Elk Dist., Harrison Co., W. Va. 1880 Census. Bur. Mt. Clare Cem., Clarksburg, W. Va.

BLAKE, EBENEZER - Pvt. Co. K. Enl. Camp Marlin's Bottom, W. Va., 9/22/63. Ab. 7/1/63 - 11/1/63 (dated 1/6/64), AWOL. Ab. 11/1/63 - 2/29/64, claimed by another command. Ab. 2/29/64 - 8/31/64, claimed by another command. NFR.

BLOSSER, HENRY - Pvt. Co. F. Enl. Camp Clover Lick, 7/11/63. Not stated if present or absent on muster-in roll dated 7/20/63. Ab. 7/1/63 - 8/31/64 (dated 1/6/65), transf. to Co. C, 19th Va. Cav. Ab. 9/1/64 - 10/31/64 (dated 12/30/64), transf. to Co. C, 19th Va. Cav. NFR.

BODE (BODY, BODEY), LOUIS (LEWIS) - Pvt. Co. B. b.c. 1841. Prior service, Co. D, 19th Va. Cav. Enl. Williamsburg, Greenbrier Co., W. Va., 3/17/63. Not stated if present or absent on muster-in roll dated 7/25/63. Present 11/1/63 - 8/31/64 (dated 1/6/65), POW since 9/64. Clothing issued 3/31/64. Ab. 9/1/64 - 10/31/64 (dated 12/30/64), POW since 9/64. Cpd. Charles Town, W. Va., 9/8/64. Confined at the Atheneum Prison, 9/12/64. Desc.: age 23, 5'4", dark comp., dark hair and gray eyes. Occ. farmer, residing in Doddridge Co., W. Va. Transf. to Camp Chase, 9/15/64. Confined at Camp Chase, 9/17/64. Took the oath of allegiance and was released, 6/11/65. Desc.: age 23, 5'4+", fair comp., dark hair and blue eyes, a resident of Doddridge Co., W. Va. Age 32(?), farmer, Southwest Dist., Doddridge Co., W. Va. 1880 Census. NFR.

BODKIN, ELI - Pvt. Co. K. b.c. 1839. Enl. Camp Northwest, W. Va., 6/3/63, age 24. Not stated if present or absent on muster-in roll dated 7/21/63. Ab. 7/1/63 - 11/1/63 (dated 1/6/64), AWOL. Ab. 11/1/63 - 2/29/64, AWOL. Ab. 2/29/64 - 8/31/64, AWOL. NFR.

BODKINS (BODKIN, BATKINS), CHARLES W. - Pvt. Co. B. b.c. 1844. Prior service, Co. D, 19th Va. Cav. Enl. Williamsburg, Greenbrier Co., W. Va., 3/17/63. Not stated if present or absent on muster-in roll dated 7/25/63. Present 11/1/63 - 8/31/64 (dated 1/6/65). Clothing issued 3/31/64 and 8/31/64. Present 9/1/64 - 10/31/64 (dated 12/30/64), entitled to $100 enl. bounty. Clothing issued 11/14/64, while on his way to his command. Paroled at Staunton, 5/25/65, signs by x. Desc.: age 21, 5'9", dark comp., brown hair and blue eyes. NFR.

BOER (BOOR), EDWARD "Ed" - Pvt. Co. B. Post war rosters only, which show he was from Monongalia (Marion) Co., W. Va. NFR.

BOER, THOMAS C. (E. or W.) - Pvt. Co. B. b. Marion Co., W. Va., c. 1843. Enl. Marion Co., W. Va., 2/17/63. Not stated if present or absent on muster-in roll dated 7/25/63. Present 11/1/63 8/31/64 (dated 1/6/65). Clothing issued 3/31/64. Present 9/1/64 10/31/64 (dated 12/30/64). Cpd. Marion Co., W. Va., 11/8/64. Sent to Clarksburg, W. Va., and confined, 11/10/64. Desc.:

age 21, 5'8+", sandy (fair) comp., light hair and gray eyes. Occ. farmer, residing in Marion Co., W. Va. Transf. to Wheeling, W. Va., 11/11/64. Confined at the Atheneum Prison, 11/11/64. Transf. to Camp Chase, 11/18/64. Confined at Camp Chase, 11/19/64. Paroled 5/2/65 and was sent to New Orleans, La., to be exchanged. Exchanged at Vicksburg, Miss., 5/12/65. NFR.

BOGAN, SAMUEL WASHINGTON PERRY - Pvt. Co. C. b. 4/9/46. Age 14, Bath CH, Bath Co. 1860 Census. Enl. Pocahontas Co., W. Va., 4/10/64 (4/9/64). Ab. 6/30/63 - 8/31/64 (dated 1/6/65), sick; enl. bounty due. Cpd. Lexington, 6/11/64, retaken immediately. Present 9/1/64 - 10/31/64 (dated 12/30/64). Paroled at Staunton, 5/20/65. Desc.: age 19, light comp., dark hair and blue eyes. Post war rosters show he enl. 5/61. Post war resident of Warm Springs, Bath Co. Age 64, Warm Springs, Bath Co. 1910 Census. d. Rocky Ridge, Bath Co., 8/7/1910.

BOGGESS, ALBERT - Pvt. Co. E. Enl. Camp Clover Lick, 7/15/63 (7/10/63). Not stated if present or absent on muster-in roll dated 7/18/63. Deserted. Gave himself up at Spencer, Roane Co., W. Va., 4/21/63 (so on roll). Confined at the Atheneum Prison, 5/5/63. Desc.: age 28, 6'1", fair comp., light hair and gray eyes. Occ. school teacher, residing in Harrison Co., W. Va. Transf. to Camp Chase, 5/7/63, "been in rebel service." Exchanged. Transf. to Lurty's Batty., 9/63. NFR.

BOGGS, JOHN W. - Pvt. Co. F. b. Braxton Co., W. Va., 6/6/45. Enl. Camp Clover Lick, 7/11/63 (Camp Miller, 7/17/63). Not stated if present or absent on muster-in roll dated 7/20/63. Ab. 7/1/63 - 8/31/64 (dated 1/6/65), transf. to Co. C, 19th Va. Cav. Ab. 9/1/64 - 10/31/64 (dated 12/30/64), transf. to Co. C, 19th Va. Cav. Age 36, farming, Otter Dist., Braxton Co., W. Va. 1880 Census. d. 10/23/1906. Bur. Home Cem., Coon Creek, Braxton Co., W. Va.

BOGGS (BAGGS), WILLIAM W. - 1st Lt. Co. I. b.c. 1837. Enl. Warm Springs, 4/1/63 (4/17/63), age 26. Not stated if present or absent on muster-in roll dated 5/5/63, 1st Lt. Elected 1st Lt., 5/4/63. Present at Beverly, W. Va., 7/63, commanding the co. Ab., 1st Lt., 11/1/63 - 8/31/64 (dated 1/6/65), POW. Received "honorable mention" from Lt. Col. W. P. Thompson in his report of the battle of Droop Mtn., W. Va., 11/6/63. Commanding Co., 12/63 and 3/64. Ab. 11/1/63 - 10/31/64 (dated 12/31/64), POW. Detailed as Judge Advocate on a Gen. Court Martial, Warm Springs, Bath Co., 3/4/65. Cpd. Loudoun Co., 7/15/64 (7/16/64). Sent to Harpers Ferry, W. Va., then to Washington, DC. Confined at the Old Capitol Prison, 7/20/64. Transf. to Ft. Delaware, 7/22/64. Confined at Ft. Delaware, 7/23/64. Sent to Hilton Head, SC, 8/20/64, as one of the "Immortal 600." Confined at Ft. Pulaski, Ga., 10/21/64. Ab. 10/25/64, POW for 120 days. Ab. 12/15/64, POW since 7/16/64. At Ft. Pulaski, Ga., 12/26/64. Returned to Ft. Delaware, 3/12/65, from Hilton Head, SC. Took the oath of allegiance and was released, 6/10/65. Desc.: age ?, 5'7", ruddy comp., dark hair and gray eyes, a resident of Wheeling, W. Va. Post war resident of Wheeling, W. Va. NFR.

BOND, ALEXANDER C. - Pvt. Co. H. Enl. Camp Northwest, W. Va., 7/1/63. Not stated if present or absent on muster-in roll dated 8/63. Transf. to Lurty's Batty., then to Co. A, 46th Battn. Va. Cav. NFR.

BONNER (BONER), SAMPSON (SAMUEL) S. - Pvt. Co. D. b. Bath Co., 1/9/1848. Enl. Barbour Co., W. Va., 4/1/64. POW record shows enl. as Crab Bottom, 5/64. Not stated if present or absent 12/31/63 - 8/31/64 (dated 1/6/65). Ab. 9/1/64 - 10/31/64, POW. Cpd. Harrisonburg, 9/25/64. Adm. Sheridan Depot Field Hosp., Winchester, 10/9/64, debility. Sent to Gen. Hosp., 10/12/64, via Martinsburg, W. Va. Adm. USA Gen. Hosp., West's Building, Baltimore, 10/13/64, convalescing from febris intermittent. Sent to Pt. Lookout, 10/25/64, well. Confined at Pt. Lookout, 10/26/64. Paroled 10/30/64, signs by x, to be exchanged. Exchanged at Venus Pt., Savannah River, Ga., 11/15/64. Present on a MR of paroled and exchanged prisoners at Camp Lee, near Richmond, 10/31/64 (dated 11/29/64). Clothing issued 11/29/64, signs by x, a paroled prisoner. Deserted. Reported at Beverly, W. Va., 12/17/64. Sent to Clarksburg, W. Va. Took the oath of allegiance and was released, 12/22/64. Desc.: age 16, 5'4", dark comp., dark hair and blue eyes. Occ. farmer, residing in Barbour Co., W. Va. Age 32, farmer, East Barker Dist., Barbour Co., W. Va. 1880 Census. Attended Confederate Reunion, Randolph Co., W. Va., 1906, claimed as a member of Lady's Reg't. Member Gen. Pegram Camp, UCV, Valley Head, W. Va. Attended Gettysburg Reunion, 1913. d. 1/2/1929. Bur. Beverly Cem., Beverly, W. Va.

BOONE, ANDERSON - Pvt. Co. I. b.c. 1823. Enl. Camp Northwest, W. Va., age 40. Not stated if present or absent on muster-in roll dated 5/5/63. NFR.

BOONE, JOHN - Pvt. Co. I. b.c. 1820. Enl. Lewisburg, W. Va., 3/10/63, age 43. Not stated if present or absent on muster-in roll dated 5/5/63. NFR.

BOOTHE, SIMON G. - Pvt. Co. A. b. Wetzel Co., W. Va., c. 1846. Enl. Wetzel Co., W. Va., 2/13/64 by Oliver Haines. POW record shows enl. as Richmond, 4/63. Ab. 10/31/63 - 8/31/64, cpd. 10/20/64; entitled to $50 enl. bounty. Wd./Cpd. Beverly, W. Va., 10/29/64. Adm. USA Post Hosp., Beverly, 10/29/64, wd. left shoulder, slight; simple dressing applied; sent to Grafton, W. Va., 11/10/64. Adm. USA Post Hosp., Clarksburg, W. Va., 11/12/64, gunshot wd. Sent to Provost Marshall, 12/2/64. Desc.: age 18, 5'8", fair comp., dark hair and blue eyes. Occ. farmer, residing in Wetzel Co., W. Va. Confined at the Atheneum Prison, 12/64. Transf. to Camp Chase, 12/13/64. Confined at Camp Chase, 12/15/64, desires to take the oath of allegiance. Gave a statement at Camp Chase, 4/26/65, says he was persuaded to enl. about 1/64. Took the oath of allegiance and was released, 6/12/65. Desc.: age 19, 5'9", fair comp., light hair and blue eyes, a resident of Wetzel Co., W. Va. NFR.

BOYCE (BOYER), EBBERT - Pvt. Co. A. b. Taylor Co., W. Va., c. 1841. Enl. Pocahontas Co., W. Va., 7/3/63, age 22. POW record shows enl. as Alleghany Co., 7/63. Not stated if present or absent on muster-in roll dated 7/3/63. Present 7/1/63 - 9/1/63. Present 10/31/63 - 8/31/64. Deserted. Reported at Grafton, W. Va., 11/21/64. Sent to Clarksburg, W. Va. Took the oath of allegiance and was released, 11/22/64. Desc.: age 23, 6', fair comp., light hair and blue eyes. Occ. farmer, residing in Taylor Co., W. Va. Post war resident of Taylor Co., W. Va. NFR.

BRACKEY, HANLON - Pvt. Co. C. b.c. 1831. Not on muster rolls. Deserted. Surrendered 4/65. Took the amnesty oath and was sent North. Desc.: age 34, 5'8", dark comp., fair hair and gray eyes, a farmer. NFR.

BRADFORD, THOMAS A. - Pvt. Co. D. b.c. 1827. Enl. Warm Springs, 3/1/64. Present 12/31/63 - 8/31/64 (dated 1/6/65), enl. bounty due. Employed as a Forage Agent, 3/1/64 - 3/31/64. Employed as an Agent, 5/1/64 - 5/31/64 and 7/1/64 - 8/31/64, procuring supplies, tax in kind; employed in the "Ord. Res.", prior to his enlistment; application has been made to Gen. R. E. Lee for his detail. Ab. 9/1/64 - 10/31/64, entitled to $100 enl. bounty; absent on detached service. Employed as a clerk, "Ord. Res.," 10/64. Paroled at Staunton, 5/11/65. Desc.: age 38, 6'1+", dark comp., dark hair and hazel eyes. NFR.

BRADY, JOHN N. (A.) - Pvt. Co. E. Enl. Camp Clover Lick, 7/17/63. Not stated if present or absent on muster-in roll dated 7/18/63. Served in Co. C, 19th Va. Cav. Age 35, farmer, CH Dist., Lewis Co., W. Va. 1880 Census, listed as John A. Brady. NFR.

BRADY, WILLIAM H. - Pvt. Co. A. b.c. 1838. Age 22, laborer, Randolph Co., W. Va. 1860 Census. Not on muster rolls. Paroled at Staunton, 5/27/65. Desc.: age 27, 5'11", fair comp., dark hair and blue eyes. Served in Co. A, 46th Battn. Va. Cav. Post war resident of Randolph Co., W. Va. Member of Gen. Pegram Camp, UCV, Valley Head, W. Va. Attended Gettysburg Reunion, 1913. NFR.

BRIDWELL, JAMES H. - 1st Corp. Co. H. Enl. Camp Northwest, W. Va., 6/1/63. Not stated if present or absent, Pvt., on muster-in roll dated 8/63. Ab., 4th Corp., 10/31/63 - 8/31/64, in hands of the enemy since 10/63. Ab., 1st Corp., 9/1/64 - 10/31/64 (dated 12/30/64), POW since 10/63. Deserted. Took the oath of allegiance and gave bond, 12/25/63. NFR.

BRITTON, E. - Pvt. Co. C. Not on muster rolls. Cpd. Woodstock, 10/20/63. Sent to Harpers Ferry, W. Va., then to Pt. Lookout. Confined at Pt. Lookout, 11/1/64. Paroled 3/28/65, signs by x, and sent to Aiken's Landing, to be exchanged. Exchanged at Boulware's Wharf, 3/20/65. NFR.

BROOKHART, HENRY H. - Pvt. Co. E. Left home and joined the army when but 17 years of age (1862). Enl. Camp Clover Lick, 7/17/63. Not stated if present or absent on muster-in roll dated 7/18/63. Served in Co. C, 19th Va. Cav. Post war resident of Wood Co., W. Va. NFR.

BROWN, FERDINAND H. - Pvt. Co. I. b.c. 1839. Enl. Camp Northwest, W. Va., 3/10/63, age 24. Not stated if present or absent on muster-in roll dated 5/5/63. NFR.

BROWN, THOMAS M. - Pvt. Co. I. b.c. 1837. Enl. Camp Northwest, W. Va., 6/23/63, age 26. Not stated if present or absent on muster-in roll dated 5/5/63. NFR.

BROWN, WILLIAM - Pvt. Co. I. b.c. 1848. Not on muster rolls. Adm. Jackson Hosp., 7/31/65. Took the amnesty oath, 8/4/65, age 17. Occ. farmer, residing at Little Hampton. NFR.

BRYANT, JOHN H. - Pvt. Co. I. b. Va., c. 1835. Age 25, laborer, Kerr's Creek Dist., Rockbridge Co. 1860 census. May have served in Co. I, 4th Va. Inf. Enl. Warm Springs, 4/20/63, age 20. Not stated if present or absent on muster-in roll dated 5/5/63. Clothing issued 2/29/64. Age 35, farmhand, Kerr's Creek, Rockbridge Co. 1870 census. Age 73, farmhand, Kerr's Creek Dist., Rockbridge Co. 1910 census. d. Rockbridge Alum Springs, 6/28/1924, age 86. Bur. Forbus Cem., Bratton's Run.

BUCKLEY, EDMUND - Pvt. Co. K. b.c. 1839. Enl. Warm Springs, 4/1/63, age 24. Not stated if present or absent on muster-in roll dated 7/21/63. Ab. 7/1/63 - 11/1/63 (dated 1/6/64), deserted. NFR.

BUNCUTTER, WILLIAM C. - Pvt. Co. C. b.c. 1845. Enl. Pocahontas Co., 5/14/63. Not stated if present or absent on muster-in roll dated 8/63. Ab. 6/30/63 - 8/31/64 (dated 1/6/65), POW since 12/27/63; 6% bond due. Cpd. Pocahontas Co., W. Va., 12/26/63. Confined at the Atheneum Prison, 1/6/64. Desc.: age 19, 5'9", fair comp. fair hair and brown eyes. Occ. farmer, residing in Preston Co., W. Va. Transf. to Camp Chase, 1/7/64. Confined at Camp Chase, 1/8/64. Transf. to Ft. Delaware, 3/14/64. Confined at Ft. Delaware, 3/17/64. Ab. 9/1/64 - 10/31/64 (dated 12/30/64), POW since 12/27/63; 6% bond due. Took the oath of allegiance and was released, 6/19/65. Desc.: age ?, 5'9", dark comp., brown hair and brown eyes, a resident of Preston Co., W. Va. Age 35, farming, Union Dist., Preston Co., W. Va. 1880 Census. NFR.

BURCHER, HENRY - Pvt. Co. ?. b. Lewis Co., W. Va. Post war source only, which shows he was wd. Fisher's Hill, 9/22/64 and taken prisoner. Confined in a prison, from which he escaped. NFR.

BURKE, CHARLES - Pvt. Co. I. b.c. 1843. Enl. Camp Northwest, W. Va., 6/1/63, age 20. Not stated if present or absent on muster-in roll dated 5/5/63. NFR.

BURNER, CHARLES G. - Pvt. Co. C. b.c. 1840. Age 21, farmer, Pocahontas Co., W. Va. 1860 Census. Prior service, Co. F, 19th Va. Cav. Enl. Pocahontas Co., W. Va., 6/19/63. Not stated if present or absent on muster-in roll dated 8/63. Present 6/30/63 - 8/31/64 (dated 1/6/65). Ab. 9/1/64 - 10/31/64 (dated 12/30/64). AWOL. Age 40, farmer, Green Banks Dist., Pocahontas Co., W. Va. 1880 Census. Brother Lee Burner. NFR.

BURNER, JOHN E. - Pvt. Co. F. b.c. 1834. Prior service, Co. A, 19th Va. Cav. Enl. Camp Northwest, W. Va. (also as Camp Miller), 7/19/63. Not stated if present or absent on muster-in roll dated 7/20/63. Ab. 7/1/63 - 8/31/64 (dated 1/6/65), transf. to Co. A, 19th Va. Cav. Ab. 9/1/64 - 10/31/64 (dated 12/30/64), transf. to Co. A, 19th Va. Cav. CSR in 20th Va. Cav. listed as John P. Burner. Age 46, farm laborer, Green Banks Dist., Pocahontas Co., W. Va. 1880 Census. NFR.

BURNER, LEE - 3rd Corp. Co. C. b.c. 1837. Age 23, farmer, Pocahontas Co., W. Va. 1860 Census. Arrested and confined at Wheeling, W. Va. Released on his oath and bond by 3/13/62. Enl. Pocahontas Co., W. Va., 4/1/63. Not stated if present or absent, 3rd Corp., on muster-in roll dated 8/63. Present, 3rd Corp., 6/30/63 - 8/31/64 (dated 1/6/65), 6% bond due. Ab., 3rd Corp., 9/1/64 - 10/31/64 (dated 12/30/64), 6% bond due; AWOL since 10/4/64. Age 43, farmer, Green Banks Dist., Pocahontas Co., W. Va. 1880 Census. Brother Charles G. Burner. NFR.

BURNS, DAVID B. - 2nd Lt. Co. A. b.c. 1843. Enl. Highland Co., 10/15/62, age 19. Appointed Jr. 2nd Lt., 4/15/63. Not stated if present or absent on muster-in roll dated 10/15/62, Jr. 2nd Lt. Present, 2nd Lt., 7/1/63 - 9/1/63, promoted 2nd Lt., 8/14/63. Elected (appointed) 2nd Lt., 8/14/63. Present, 2nd Lt., 10/31/63 - 8/31/64. Commanding Co. A, 10/63. Wd. Droop Mtn., W. Va., 11/6/63, hand. Sent on a scout to Barbour Co., W. Va., with 7 men, 5/64. Ab. 12/15/64, on leave by order of Gen. J. A. Early, collecting absentees, since 12/17/64. Paroled at Staunton, 5/22/65. Desc.: age 21, 6', dark comp., dark hair and brown eyes. "A youth from near Fairmont, Marion Co., W. Va." A gallant officer. Brother of John M. and Gideon M. Burns. Moved to Braxton Co., 1866, with his brothers. Post war resident of Fla. Age 41, lumberman, Salt Lick Dist., Braxton Co., W. Va. 1880 Census. NFR.

BURNS, GIDEON M. - Pvt. Co. A. b.c. 1846. Not on muster rolls. Paroled at Staunton, 5/22/65. Desc.: age 19, 5'6", fair comp., black hair and black eyes. Post war resident of Marion Co., W. Va. Moved to Braxton Co., W. Va., 1866, with his brothers. Brother of David B. and John M. Burns. Age 34, lumberman, Salt Lick Dist., Braxton Co., W. Va. 1880 Census. NFR.

BURNS, JOHN MILLER - Capt. Co. A and Capt./AQM. b. Hampshire Co., W. Va., 6/10/34. Prior service, Co. A, 31st Va. Inf. Capt. commanding Co. A, 20th Va. Cav., 7/63 and 10/63. Served as Capt., Co. C, 46th Battn. Va. Cav. Recommended for AQM, 20th Va. Cav., by Col. W. W. Arnett. Appointed AQM, 9/7/63; appointment marked revoked. Appointed AQM, 10/6/63 (10/27/63). Present FS MR 1/1/64 8/31/64 (dated 1/6/65), Capt. and AQM. Paroled at Staunton, 5/22/65, listed as Capt. Co. A. Desc.: age 30, 6', dark comp., dark hair and black eyes. Served also in the 46th Battn. Va. Cav. Moved to Braxton Co., W. Va., 1866, with his brothers. Established Burnsville, Braxton Co., W. Va. Post war lumber business, Salt Lick Dist., Braxton Co., W. Va. Brother of David B. and Gideon M. Burns. d. Braxton Co. W. Va., 7/20/77.

BURTON, ALLEN - Pvt. Co. B. Prior service, Co. D, 19th Va. Cav. Enl. Williamsburg, Greenbrier Co., W. Va., 3/17/63. Not stated if present or absent on muster-in roll dated 7/25/63. Present 11/1/63 - 8/31/64 (dated 1/6/65). Clothing issued, 12/20/63 (detailed), 1/17/64 (detailed teamster) and 3/31/64. Employed as a teamster at Warm Springs, 1/1/64 - 2/29/64. Present 9/1/64 - 10/31/64 (dated 12/30/64), entitled to $100 bond. NFR.

BURTON, ELMORE B. - Pvt. Co. B. b. Harrison Co., W. Va., c. 1840. Age 20, farmer, Gilmer Co., W. Va. 1860 Census. Prior service, Co. D, 19th Va. Cav. Enl. Williamsburg, Greenbrier Co., W. Va., 3/17/63. Not stated if present or absent on muster-in roll dated 7/25/63. Present 11/1/63 - 8/31/64 (dated 1/6/65), sick from wd., unfit for duty. Ab. 9/1/64 - 10/31/64 (dated 12/30/64), sick from wd.; entitled to $100 bond. Clothing issued 11/11/64, on his way to his command. Age 40, farmer, Troy Dist., Gilmer Co., W. Va. 1880 Census. NFR.

BURTON, JAMES I. - Pvt. Co. B. b. Doddridge Co., W. Va., c. 1843. Prior service, Co. D, 19th Va. Cav. Enl. Williamsburg, Greenbrier Co., W. Va., 3/17/63. Not stated if present or absent on muster-in roll dated 7/25/63. Present 11/1/63 - 8/31/64 (dated 1/6/65). Clothing issued 3/31/64. Present 9/1/64 - 10/31/64 (dated 12/30/64), entitled to $100 bond. Clothing issued 11/11/64, while on the way to his command. Deserted. Reported at Glenville, W. Va., 12/22/64. Sent to Clarksburg, W. Va. Took the oath of allegiance and was released, 12/27/64. Desc.: age 21, 5'7", light comp., light hair and blue eyes. Occ. farmer, residing in Gilmer Co., W. Va. Age 36, farmer, Troy Dist., Gilmer Co., W. Va. 1880 Census. NFR.

BUSSEY, DAVID - Pvt. Co. A. Post war rosters only, which show he was a resident of Monongalia Co., W. Va. NFR.

BUSSEY, EDWARD - Pvt. Co. E. b.c. 1843. Enl. Harrison Co., W. Va., 5/6/63 (5/4/63), by John L. Bussey. Arrested Harrison Co., W. Va., 5/5/63, by a citizen, while on his way to join Col. W. L. Jackson at or near Weston, W. Va. Confined at the Atheneum Prison, 5/9/63. Desc.: age 20, 5'8", fresh comp., sandy hair and gray eyes. Occ. farmer, residing in Harrison Co., W. Va. Transf. to Camp Chase, 5/11/63, charged with recruiting for the rebels. Not stated if present or absent on muster-in roll dated 7/18/63. Ab. 1/1/64 - 8/31/64 (dated 1/6/65), cpd. Harrison Co., W. Va., 5/7/63. Ab. 9/1/64 - 10/31/64 (dated 12/29/64), cpd. Harrison Co., W. Va., 5/6/63. Age 37, farmer, Union Dist., Harrison Co., W. Va. 1880 Census. NFR.

BUSSEY, JAMES K. (T.) - Pvt. Co. E. b.c. 1845. Enl. Harrison Co., W. Va., 5/4/63 (5/6/63), by John L. Bussey. Arrested Buffalo Creek, Harrison Co., W. Va., 5/4/63, by a citizen, while on his way to join Col. W. L. Jackson at or near Weston, W. Va. Confined at the Atheneum Prison, 5/9/63. Desc.: age 18, 5'7,", dark comp., dark hair and dark eyes. Occ. farmer, residing in Harrison Co., W. Va. Transf. to Camp Chase, 5/11/63, charged with recruiting for the rebels. Not stated if present or absent on muster-in roll dated 7/18/63. Ab. 1/1/64 - 8/31/64 (dated 1/6/65), cpd. Harrison Co., W. Va., 5/7/63. Ab. 9/1/64 - 10/31/64 (dated 12/29/64), cpd. Harrison Co., W. Va., 5/6/63. Age 35, farmer, Ten Mile Dist., Harrison Co., W. Va. 1880 Census. NFR.

BUSSEY, JOHN L. - 1st Sgt. Co. E. Resident of Harrison Co., W. Va. Enl. Bulltown, W. Va., 5/10/63. Serving as recruiting officer for Capt. John W. Young, 5/63, in Harrison Co., W. Va. Not stated if present or absent, 1st Sgt., on muster-in roll dated 7/18/63. Deserted. Took the oath of allegiance and gave his bond, 11/22/63. Ab., 1st Sgt., 1/1/64 - 8/31/64 (dated 1/6/65), AWOL since 11/1/63. Ab., Pvt., 9/1/64 - 10/31/64 (dated 12/29/64), AWOL since 11/1/63. NFR.

BUTLER, OLIVER W. - Pvt. Co. I. b.c. 1827. Enl. Lewisburg, W. Va., 3/20/63 (4/1/63), age 36. Enl. also as Camp Northwest, W. Va., 5/63. Not stated if present or absent on muster-in roll dated 5/5/63. Ab. 11/1/63 - 8/31/64 (dated 1/6/65), on horse detail. Clothing issued 2/29/64. Ab. 11/1/63 - 10/31/64 (dated 12/31/64), POW. NFR.

BUZARD (BUZZARD), JOHN M. - Pvt. Co. C. b.c. 1830. Age 34, laborer, Pocahontas Co., W. Va. 1860 Census. Enl. Pocahontas Co., W. Va., 3/19/63. Not stated if present or absent on muster-in roll dated 8/63. Ab. 6/30/63 - 8/31/64 (dated 1/6/65), in Castle Thunder. Ab. 9/1/64 - 10/31/64 (dated 12/30/64), in Castle Thunder, Richmond. Age 50, farmer, Huntersville, Pocahontas Co., W. Va. 1880 Census. NFR.

CADE, BAYLIS - Pvt. Co. ?. Post war recollections only, which show he was from Barbour (Braxton) Co., W. Va. Prior service, Co. G, 11th Va. Cav. Post war rosters show service in Co. Co. G, 25th Va. Inf. Enl. early 1864. Served in Co. C, 46th Battn. Va. Cav. Post war professor in a Southeastern Va. High School. Post war Baptist minister, Richmond. "Held his place like a man." NFR.

CAIN, HARRISON - Pvt. Co. H. Enl. Camp Northwest, W. Va., 6/12/63. Not stated if present or absent on muster-in roll dated 8/63. Transf. to Lurty's Batty., 11/1/63. NFR.

CAIN, JOHN WILLIAM "Sud" - 1st Sgt. Co. H. b. Rusk, Wood Co., W. Va., 2/28/40. Enl. Camp Northwest, W. Va., 7/1/63 (6/28/63). Not stated if present or absent, Pvt., on muster-in roll dated 8/63. Present, 1st Sgt., 10/31/63 - 8/31/64, promoted 1st Sgt., 6/1/64; has one horse since 7/1/64. Clothing issued 2/29/64. Present, Pvt., 9/1/64 - 10/31/64 (dated 12/30/64), entitled to $100 bond. Paroled at Staunton, 5/12/65, as a Sgt. Desc.: age 25, 5'11", fair comp., dark hair and hazel eyes. Served in Lurty's Batty., exchanged with R. F. Watson, 19th Va. Cav., 3/25/64. Post war rosters show service in Co. C, 19th Va. Cav. Age 40, farmer, South Grant Dist., Ritchie Co., W. Va. 1880 Census. d. Petroleum, Ritchie Co., W. Va., 12/7/1920. Bur. Jessie Cain Cem., Racy, Ritchie Co., W. Va.

CAIN, RUFUS P. - 1st Sgt. Co. H. Enl. Camp Northwest, W. Va., 6/1/63 (Calhoun Co., W. Va., 5/8/63). Not stated if present or absent, Orderly Sgt., on muster-in roll dated 8/63. Ab., 1st Sgt., 10/31/63 - 8/31/64, KIA. Lynchburg, 6/17/64. Clothing issued 2/29/64. Not stated if present or absent, 1st Sgt., 9/1/64 - 10/31/64 (dated 12/30/64).

CALLIHAN, SALATHAEL M. - Pvt. Co. D. b.c. 1841. Enl. Weston, W. Va., 5/1/63. Not stated if present or absent on muster-in roll dated 8/63. Ab. 7/1/63 - 1/1/64 (dated 1/1/64), POW. Cpd. Highland Co., 8/20/63. Confined at the Atheneum Prison, 8/20/63. Desc.: age 22, 5'11 3/4", florid comp., dark hair and dark eyes. Occ. carpenter, residing in Barbour Co., W. Va. Transf. to Camp Chase, 8/31/63. Confined at Camp Chase, 9/1/63. Transf. to Rock Island, Ill., 1/14/64. Confined at Rock Island Prison, 1/17/64. Ab. 12/31/63 - 8/31/64 (dated 1/6/65), POW. Ab. 9/1/64 - 10/31/64, POW. Transf. to City Point, 2/25/65, to be exchanged. Exchanged as Samuel H. Lansdill. Adm. Jackson Hosp., 3/6/65, debilitas. Furloughed 3/8/65, 30 days. NFR.

CAMMACK, JOHN HENRY - Pvt. Co. I. b. Dayton, Rockingham Co., 12/22/43. Moved to Amherst Co., then to Harrison Co., W. Va., 1859. Prior service, Co. C, 31st Va. Inf. Age 17, farmer in 1861. Transf. to 20th Cav., 4/63. Enl. Warm Springs, 5/1/63, age 20. Not stated if present or absent on muster-in roll dated 5/5/63. Elected 2nd Lt. Served only a few days in this position. A young man from Monroe Co., W. Va., wished the position, and it was given to him. Sent to Richmond by Col. Arnett, 7/63, to open a recruiting office. Remained there 5 or 6 weeks. Spent a week in Rockingham Co. Detailed to catch deserters, 1863, along with Lt. Steve Rice. Detailed to go on a scout into Harrison Co., W. Va., late 9/63, with nine men (one of which was Henry Caton), gone 35 days. Rode a mare. Became sick with a fever while at home on the scout. Went to Richmond, 11/63. Became sick, 12/63. Enl. Co. C, 10th Va. Arty., with the understanding that he would return to the Cav. in the spring of 1864. When time came for him to leave, the Capt. would not allow it. Returned to the 20th Va. Cav., 12/23/64. Capt. Barlow requested his return; Col. Arnett refused. Guard, Libby Prison, 1865. Paroled at Columbia, 5/65. Post war cigar maker, residing at Staunton and Lexington. Moved to Williamstown, W. Va., 1868, cigar maker. Moved to Marietta, O., then back to Williamstown, W. Va. Bought an interest in a steamboat, 1875. Served as a clerk on the Little Kanawha River. Moved back to Marietta, O. several years later, cigar business. Moved to Huntington, W. Va., 1878, clothing business. Went into the real estate and insurance business in 1890. Member of Camp Garnett Camp UCV, Huntington, W. Va. d. Huntington, W. Va., 5/6/1920, 6 pm. Bur. Spring Hill Cem., Huntington, W. Va. Wrote "Personal Recollections of Private John Henry Cammack."

CAMP, ANDREW (ADAM) J. - Pvt. Co. A. b.c. 1840. Enl. Monongalia Co., W. Va., 8/17/64. Present 10/31/63 - 8/31/64, entitled to $50 enl. bounty. Cpd. Barbour Co., W. Va., 4/5/65. Sent to Clarksburg, W. Va. Confined at Clarksburg, W. Va. Paroled at Clarksburg, W. Va., 4/22/65, signs by x. Desc.: age 25, 5'10", dark comp., dark hair, hazel eyes and dark whiskers. Occ. farmer, residing in Monongalia Co., W. Va. Post war resident of Monongalia Co., W. Va. Age 50(?), farmer, Grant Dist., Monongalia Co., W. Va. 1880 Census. NFR.

CAMP, DAVID M. - Capt. Co. A. b. 4/8/33. Enl. Highland Co., 10/8/62, age 29. Not stated if present or absent, 1st Lt., on muster-in roll dated 10/8/62. Cpd. Highland Co., 11/7/62 (11/8/62), listed as a Pvt., Co. A, Stewart's Battn. Confined at the Atheneum Prison, 11/18/62. Desc.: age 29, 5'10,", fresh comp., sandy hair and gray eyes. Occ. farmer, residing in Monongalia Co., W. Va. Transf. to Camp Chase, 11/19/62. Confined at Camp Chase, 11/20/62. Paroled and sent to Cairo, Ill., 11/20/62, to be exchanged. Exchanged. Appointed 1st Lt., 4/15/63. Present, 1st Lt., 7/1/63 - 9/1/63, promoted Capt., 8/14/63. Elected Capt. 8/14/63. Not stated if present or absent, Capt., 10/31/63 - 8/31/64. At the battle of Droop Mtn., W. Va., 11/6/63, his blanket was nearly shot off him, having 8 or 10 holes shot in it. Mentioned for "brave bearing" by Col. W. L. Jackson in his report of the battle of Droop Mtn., W. Va., 11/6/63. Detailed for duty on a Gen. Court Martial, Warm Springs, Bath Co., 2/25/64. Detailed on a scout in the mountains, 7/64. Ab. 10/25/64, recruiting by order of Gen. J. A. Early, 40 days; was to return in 30 days. Detailed to take 10 men and impress horses in Augusta Co., 3/65. Paroled at Staunton, 5/22/65. Desc.: age 30, 5'11', fair comp., light hair and blue eyes. Post war resident of Monongalia Co., W. Va. "d. a respected citizen. A brave and consistent officer and man." d. 4/25/98. Bur. Burnt Meeting House Cem., Monongalia Co., W. Va.

CAMP, JACKSON - Pvt. Co. A. Post war rosters only. NFR.

CAMP, LOVEBERRY (LONEBERRY) B. - Pvt. Co. A. b. 4/8/25. Enl. Highland Co., 6/7/63 (Pocahontas Co., W. Va., 7/20/63). Present 7/1/63 - 9/1/63. Present 10/31/63 - 8/31/64. Paroled at Staunton, 5/22/65. Desc.: age 40, 5'11", dark comp., gray hair and gray eyes. Post war resident of Monongalia (Marion) Co., W. Va. d. 5/27/66. Bur. Burnt Meeting House Cem., Monongalia Co., W. Va.

CAMP, ULYSSES S. - Pvt. Co. A. b. 10/10/27. Enl. Monongalia Co., W. Va., 8/17/64. Present 10/31/63 - 8/31/64, entitled to $100 bond. Surrendered at Beverly, W. Va., 5/15/65. Sent to Clarksburg, W. Va. Confined at Clarksburg, W. Va., 5/16/65. Paroled 5/16/65 for exchange and was released. Desc.: age 38, 5'7+", dark comp., dark hair and blue eyes. Occ. farmer, residing in Monongalia Co., W. Va. Post war resident of Monongalia Co., W. Va. Age 52, farmer, Grant Dist., Monongalia Co., W. Va. 1880 Census. d. 6/18/1903. Bur. East Oak Grove Cem., Monongalia Co., W. Va.

CAMPBELL, CHARLES T. - Pvt. Co. E. b. 1847. Enl. Staunton, Augusta Co., 5/1/64. Present 1/1/64 - 8/31/64 (dated 1/6/65). Present 9/1/64 - 10/31/64 (dated 12/29/64), entitled to $100 bond. Paroled at Staunton, 5/25/65. Desc.: age 18, 5'11", dark comp., black hair and black eyes. NFR.

CAMPBELL, HENRY KIDWELL - Pvt. Co. A. b.c. 1844. Enl. Pocahontas Co., W. Va., 4/6/63, age 19. Not stated if present or absent on muster-in roll dated 4/6/63. Present 7/1/63 - 9/1/63. Ab. 10/31/63 - 8/31/64, cpd. 5/28/64. Clothing issued 2/29/64. Cpd. Lewisburg (Sulphur Springs), W. Va., 6/2/64. Confined at Camp Morton, Indianapolis, Ind., 6/21/64. Took the oath of allegiance and was released, 5/20/65, signs by x. Desc.: age ?, 5'11", florid comp., sandy hair and blue eyes, a resident of Mannington, W. Va. Post war resident of Marion Co., W. Va. NFR.

CAMPBELL, JAMES S. - Pvt. Co. A. b.c. 1844. Enl. Pocahontas Co., W. Va., 5/12/63, age 19. Not stated if present or absent on muster-in roll dated 5/12/63. Cpd. Grafton, W. Va., 5/17/63. Confined at Ft. McHenry, Md. Paroled and sent to Ft. Monroe, 5/20/63, to be exchanged. Exchanged. Present 7/1/63 - 9/1/63. Present 10/31/63 - 8/31/64. Clothing issued 2/29/64 and 9/4/64. Deserted. Surrendered at Mannington, W. Va., 2/11/65. Took the oath of allegiance at Clarksburg, W. Va., and was sent North, 2/11/65. Confined at the Atheneum Prison, 2/12/65. Desc.: age 20, 5'8", fair comp., fair hair and gray eyes. Occ. farmer, residing in Marion Co., W. Va. Post war resident of Marion Co., W. Va. NFR.

CAMPBELL, JOHN - Pvt. Co. A. b.c. 1840. Resident of Glover's Gap, Wetzel Co., W. Va. Enl. Pocahontas Co., W. Va., 4/6/63, age 23. Not stated if present or absent on muster-in roll dated 4/6/63. Present 7/1/63 - 9/1/63. Present 10/31/63 - 8/31/64. Detailed to guard prisoners, 12/63. Clothing issued 2/29/64. Paroled at Staunton, 5/23/65. Desc.: age 24, 6', fair comp., dark hair and hazel eyes. Post war resident of Marion Co., W. Va. NFR.

CAMPBELL, JOSEPH - Pvt. Co. K. b.c. 1839. Enl. Warm Springs, 4/1/63, age 24. Not stated if present or absent on muster-in roll dated 7/21/63. Ab. 7/1/63 - 11/1/63 (dated 1/6/64), AWOL. NFR.

CAMPBELL, KIDWELL "Kidd" - Pvt. Co. ?. Post war rosters only, which show he was detailed to guard prisoners, 12/63. Post war resident of Wetzel Co., W. Va. NFR.

CAMPBELL, OSCAR JAMES - Pvt. Co. A. b. 12/9/47. Not on muster rolls. Paroled at Staunton, 5/23/65. Desc.: age 17, 5'6", fair comp., light hair and blue eyes. Post war rosters show he was in service for 16 days. Post war rosters show service in Co. E. Post war doctor and resident of Highland Co. Member of S. B. Gibbons Camp, UCV, Harrisonburg, 1896. Age 51, farmer, Monterey Dist., Highland Co. 1900 Census. d. Monterey, 2/8/1935. Bur. Monterey Cem., Highland Co.

CAMPBELL, WILLIAM A. - Pvt. Co. A. b. 1847. Not on muster rolls. Post war rosters show he enl. 2/65. Paroled at Staunton, 5/23/65. Desc.: age 17, 5'8", fair comp., light hair and blue eyes. Awarded Cross of Honor, 8/3/1912, in Rockingham Co. Post war resident of Franklin, W. Va. d. 1917. Bur. Cedar Hill Cem., Pendleton Co., W. Va.

CANNON, JAMES A. - Pvt. Co. E. b. Culpeper Co., c. 1838. Enl. Bulltown, Braxton Co., W. Va., 5/10/63. Not stated if present or absent on muster-in roll dated 7/18/63. Present 1/1/64 - 8/31/64 (dated 1/6/65). Adm. CSA Gen. Hosp., Charlottesville, 6/12/64, debility. RTD. 6/18/64. Present 9/1/64 - 10/31/64 (dated 12/29/64), entitled to $100 bond. Cpd. Beverly, W. Va., 10/29/64. Sent to Clarksburg, W. Va., then to Wheeling, W. Va., 11/2/64. Desc.: age 26, 5'9", sandy comp., auburn hair and brown eyes. Occ. farmer, residing in Harrison Co. - W. Va. Confined at the Atheneum Prison, 11/2/64. Desc.: age 26, 5'9", light comp., sandy hair and blue eyes. Transf. to Camp Chase, 11/22/64. Confined at Camp Chase, 11/23/64, desires to take the oath of allegiance. Took the oath of allegiance and was released, 5/15/65. Desc.: age 28, 5'9", florid comp., dark hair and dark eyes, a resident of Harrison Co., W. Va. NFR.

CARDER, RANDOLPH - Pvt. Co. E. Enl. Bulltown, Braxton Co., W. Va., 5/10/63. Not stated if present or absent on muster-in roll dated 7/18/63. Ab. 1/1/64 - 8/31/64 (dated 1/6/65), AWOL since 8/1/63. Ab. 9/1/64 - 10/31/64 (dated 12/29/64), AWOL since 9/1/63. NFR.

CARDER, THOMAS J. - 4th Corp. Co. E. Enl. Bulltown, Braxton Co., W. Va., 5/10/63. Not stated if present or absent on muster-in roll dated 7/18/63, 4th Corp. Ab., 4th Corp., 1/1/64 - 8/31/64 (dated 1/6/65), AWOL since 8/1/63. Ab., 4th Corp., 9/1/64 - 10/31/64 (dated 12/29/64), AWOL since 9/1/63. NFR.

CARTER, BUCK - Pvt. Co. ?. Post war rosters only, which show he was a resident of Barbour Co., W. Va. and that he carried a Spencer Rifle during the war. NFR.

CARTER, C. B. - 2nd Sgt. Co. B. Enl. Hightown, Highland Co., 4/15/63 (11/6/62). Not stated if present or absent on muster-in roll dated 7/25/63, 2nd Sgt. Present, 2nd Sgt., 11/1/63 - 8/31/64 (dated 1/6/65), AWOL 9/14/64. Clothing issued 2/29/64. Ab., 2nd Sgt., 9/1/64 - 10/31/64 (dated 12/30/64), AWOL since 9/14/64. NFR.

CARTER, W. E. - Pvt. Co. K. Enl. Camp Cameron, Bath Co., 2/15/64, by Z. B. Vess. Ab. 11/1/63 - 2/29/64, claimed by another command. Ab. 2/29/64 - 8/31/64, claimed by another command. Clothing issued 3/23/64. NFR.

CARY, WILLIAM - Pvt. Co. I. Enl. Lewisburg, W. Va., 3/20/63, age 35. Not stated if present or absent on muster-in roll dated 5/5/63. NFR.

CASH, JAMES A. - Pvt. Co. K. b.c. 1843. Enl. Camp Northwest, W. Va., 6/25/63, age 20. Not stated if present or absent on muster-in roll dated 7/21/63. Ab. 7/1/63 - 11/1/63 (dated 1/6/64), substitute; deserted. Present 11/1/63 - 2/29/64, had his own horse since enlistment. Present 2/29/64 - 8/31/64, had his own horse since enlistment. NFR.

CASH, JOSEPH BENJAMIN - Pvt. Co. K. b. Augusta Co., 3/4/44. Shoemaker, Rapps Mill, Rockbridge Co. 1860 Census. Prior service, Co. E, 52nd Va. Inf. Enl. Camp Northwest, W. Va., 6/21/63 (6/25/63), age 18. Not stated if present or absent on muster-in roll dated 7/21/63. Ab. 7/1/63 - 11/1/63 (dated 1/6/64), AWOL. Returned to Co. E, 52nd Va. Inf., 2/29/64. d. Natural Bridge, Rockbridge Co., 11/19/1915. Bur. Natural Bridge Baptist Church Cem.

CASH, SAMUEL - Pvt. Co. K. Enl. Camp Northwest, W. Va., 7/1/63. Not stated if present or absent on muster-in roll dated 7/21/63. Ab. 7/1/63 - 11/1/63 (dated 1/6/64), AWOL. NFR.

CASTO, WINFIELD T. - Pvt. Co. D. Enl. Camp Pisgah, Bath Co., 1/1/64. Present 7/1/63 - 1/1/64 (dated 1/1/64). Ab. 12/31/63 - 8/31/64 (dated 1/6/65), AWOL since 11/64. Ab. 9/1/64 - 10/31/64, AWOL. NFR.

CASTOR (CASTEN), VINCENT - 2nd Lt. Co. F. b.c. 1827. Resident of Harrison Co., W. Va. Enl. Bulltown, Braxton Co., W. Va., 5/10/63. Elected Bvt. 2nd Lt., 5/10/63. Not stated if present or absent on muster-in roll dated 7/20/63, Bvt. 2nd Lt. Present, Bvt. 2nd Lt., 7/1/63 - 8/31/64 (dated 1/6/65). Present, Bvt. 2nd Lt., 9/1/64 - 10/31/64 (dated 12/30/64). Ab. 10/25/64, wd., now in hosp., 36 days. Surrendered at Clarksburg, W. Va., 5/15/65. Paroled for exchange and was released, 5/15/65. Desc.: age 38, 5'10+", fair comp., light hair and blue eyes. Occ. farmer, residing in Harrison Co., W. Va. NFR.

CATON, HENRY - Pvt. Co. ?. b. 2/23/45. From Wheeling, W. Va., moved to Texas and served in the Rangers and the 1st Texas Cav. Was in Mexico City, 1861. Detailed to go with John H. Cammack on a scout into Harrison Co., W. Va. A good woodsman. Furloughed after the scout and went to Wheeling, W. Va. Cpd. Wheeling, W. Va. "He was a gallant gentleman and as good a soldier as I [John H. Cammack] ever saw." Served in Co. A, 47th Battn. Va. Cav. Name appears on post war roster as a member of Co. K, 62nd Va. Mtd. Inf. d. 3/23/1929. Bur. Mt. Zion Cem., Pendleton Co., W. Va.

CEASE, E. A. - Pvt. Co. C. Enl. Pocahontas Co., W. Va., 6/1/64. Ab. 6/30/63 - 8/31/64 (dated 1/6/65), on leave; enl. bounty due. Ab. 9/1/64 - 10/31/64 (dated 12/30/64), AWOL. NFR.

CEASE, V. A. - Pvt. Co. C. Enl. Pocahontas Co., W. Va., 12/1/63. Present 6/30/63 - 8/31/64 (dated 1/6/65), 6% bond due. Present 9/1/64 - 10/31/64 (dated 12/30/64), 6% bond due. NFR.

CHANELL, JOHN P. - Pvt. Co. C. b. 7/22/34. Age 25, farmer, Randolph Co., W. Va. 1860 Census. Enl. Randolph Co., W. Va., 4/26/63. Not stated if present or absent on muster-in roll dated 8/63. Ab. 6/30/63 - 8/31/64 (dated 1/6/65), transf. to Co. I, 19th Va. Cav., 7/1/63, listed as John C. Channell. Age 45, farmer and miller, Mingo, Randolph Co., W. Va. 1880 Census. d. 10/25/1901. Bur. Snyder Cem., Randolph Co., W. Va.

CHENOWITH, JACOB - Pvt. Co. C. b. 3/9/39. Age 21, farmer, Randolph Co., W. Va. 1860 Census. Enl. Randolph (Pocahontas) Co., W. Va., 7/21/63 (8/1/63). Not stated if present or absent on muster-in roll dated 8/63. Ab. 6/30/63 - 8/31/64 (dated 1/6/65), transf. to Co. ?, 21st Va. Cav., 9/12/63. Post war resident of Randolph Co., W. Va. d. 9/25/1920. Bur. Chenoweth Cem., Randolph Co., W. Va.

CHEWNING, THOMAS A. - Pvt. Co. E. b.c. 1847. Age 13, Cleek's Mill, Bath Co. 1860 Census. Enl. Williamsville, Bath Co., 1/1/64 by Thomas Drummond. Ab. 1/1/64 - 8/31/64 (dated 1/6/65), AWOL since 6/25/64. Ab. 9/1/64 - 10/31/64 (dated 12/29/64), AWOL since 7/1/64. NFR.

CHILDERS (CHILDRESS), FRANCIS M. - Pvt. Co. E. Enl. Camp Clover Lick, 7/17/63. Not stated if present or absent on muster-in roll dated 7/18/63. Served also in Co. A, 19th Va. Cav. and Co. D, 46th Battn. Va. Cav. NFR.

CHRISMORE, RUFUS (RUFFUS) - Pvt. Co. I. b.c. 1821. Enl. Lewisburg, W. Va., 3/20/63, age 42. Not stated if present or absent on muster-in roll dated 5/5/63. NFR.

CLAIR, S. S. - Pvt. Co. F. Post war resident of Mt. Clare, Pleasants Co., W. Va. NFR.

CLANCY, _____ - Lt. Co. ?. Not on muster rolls. The only reference to this man is in Maj. J. B. Lady's report of the fight at Beverly, W. Va., 7/3/63. NFR.

CLANCEY, JOHN - Pvt. Co. K. b.c. 1841. Enl. Warm Springs (Camp Northwest, W. Va.), 6/3/62 (4/25/63), age 22. Not stated if present or absent on muster-in roll dated 7/21/63. Ab. 7/1/63 - 11/1/63 (dated 1/6/64), cpd. by the enemy. Ab. 11/1/63 - 2/29/64, cpd. near Bulltown, W. Va., 8/6/63. Ab. 2/29/64 - 8/31/64, cpd. 8/1/63 by enemy near Bulltown, W. Va. No POW records. NFR.

CLARK, GEORGE MILLER - Pvt. Co. B. b. Monongalia Co., W. Va., c. 1843. Enl. Marion Co., W. Va., 3/27/63 (3/23/63). POW record shows enl. as Bath Co., 4/63. Not stated if present or absent on muster-in roll dated 7/25/63. Present 11/1/63 - 8/31/64 (dated 1/6/65), AWOL since 9/14/64. Clothing issued 3/31/64. Ab. 9/1/64 10/31/64 (dated 12/30/64), AWOL since 9/

14/64. Cpd. Marion Co., W. Va., 3/11/65 (3/10/65). Sent to Cumberland, Md., then to Clarksburg, W. Va. Transf. to Wheeling, W. Va., 3/13/65. Confined at the Atheneum Prison, 3/13/65. Desc.: age 22, 5'10", fair comp., light hair and blue eyes. Occ. farmer, residing in Monongalia Co., W. Va. Transf. to Camp Chase, 3/13/65. Confined at Camp Chase, 3/14/65. Took the oath of allegiance and was released, 6/13/65. Desc.: age 22, 5'10", fair comp., light hair and blue eyes, a resident of Monongalia Co., W. Va. Post war resident of Monongalia Co., W. Va. Age 37, farmer, Battelle Sub Dist., Monongalia Co., W. Va. 1880 Census. NFR.

CLARK, JOHN - Pvt. Co. I. Enl. Alleghany Co., 4/1/64. Ab. 11/1/63 - 8/31/64 (dated 1/6/65), on detached service. NFR.

CLARK, M. C. - Pvt. Co. I. Not on muster rolls. Arrested 4/8/65 and sent to Clarksburg, W. Va. Took the oath of allegiance and was sent to Wheeling, W. Va. Confined at the Atheneum Prison, 4/10/65. Post war resident of Botetourt Co. NFR.

CLARKE, WILLIAM M. - Pvt. Co. I. Enl. Camp Cameron, Bath Co., 2/1/64. Present 11/1/63 - 8/31/64 (dated 1/6/65), detailed as wagoner. Clothing issued 3rd Qr. 1864. Arrested 4/8/65 and sent to Clarksburg, W. Va. Took the oath of allegiance and was sent to Wheeling, W. Va. Confined at the Atheneum Prison, 4/10/65. Post war resident of Botetourt Co. NFR.

CLAYTON, EDWARD B. - Pvt. Co. A. b. Marion Co., W. Va., c. 1843. Not on muster rolls. POW record shows he enl. Marion Co., W. Va., 8/64. Cpd. Grafton, W. Va., 3/23/65. Sent to Clarksburg, W. Va. Confined at Clarksburg, W. Va., 3/25/65. Sent to Wheeling, W. Va. Confined at the Atheneum Prison, 3/30/65. Desc.: age 22, 5'9+", dark comp., black hair and black eyes. Occ. farmer, residing in Marion Co., W. Va. Took the oath of allegiance and was released, 6/26/65. Age 35, farm laborer, Lincoln Dist., Marion Co., W. Va. 1880 Census, listed as Edwin B. Clayton. NFR.

CLAYTON, JASPER - 4th Sgt. Co. B. b.c. 1835. Enl. Marion Co., W. Va., c. 4/15/63 (2/17/63). Not stated if present or absent on muster-in roll dated 7/25/63, 4th Sgt. Present, 4th Sgt., 11/1/63 - 8/31/64 (dated 1/6/65). Clothing issued 3/31/64. Present, 4th Sgt., 9/1/64 - 10/31/64 (dated 12/30/64). Paroled at Winchester, 5/10/65. Desc.: age 30, 5'2", ruddy comp., dark hair and gray eyes. Post war resident of Marion Co., W. Va. Age 45, farmer, Lincoln Dist., Marion Co., W. Va. 1880 Census. NFR.

CLEEK (CLICK), JACOB - Pvt. Co. D. b.c. 1828. Age 32, farmer, Hot Springs, Bath Co. 1860 Census. Prior service, Co. E, 46th Battn. Va. Cav. Enl. Camp Pisgah, 1/1/64. Present 12/31/63 - 8/31/64 (dated 1/6/65). Ab. 9/1/64 - 10/31/64, AWOL; not entitled to enl. bounty. d. Hively, Bath Co., by 1903. NFR.

CLELLAN (CLELLAND), DANIEL S. - Pvt. Co. A. Enl. Lewis (Pocahontas) Co., W. Va., 5/3/63. Not stated if present or absent on muster-in roll dated 5/3/63. Present 7/1/63 - 9/1/63, detailed Blacksmith, 5/21/63. Ab. 10/31/63 - 8/31/64, deserted. NFR.

COBERLY, WILLIAM HARRISON - Pvt. Co. D. b. 9/19/24. Age 35, farmer, Randolph Co., W. Va. 1860 Census. Enl. Camp Northwest, W. Va., 6/1/63. Present 7/1/63 - 1/1/64 (dated 1/1/64), entitled to enl. bounty. Ab. 12/31/63 - 8/31/64 (dated 1/6/65), AWOL since 9/64. Ab. 9/1/64 - 10/31/64, on detached service; entitled to $100 enl. bounty. Post war rosters show he served in Co. I, 19th Va. Cav. Post war resident of Randolph Co., W. Va. CSR listed as Coverly and Cuberly. Sold land to help start the present-day town of Elkins, W. Va. Age 55, farmer, Green Dist., Randolph Co., W. Va. 1880 Census. d. 1/27/1904. Bur. Maplewood Cem., Randolph Co., W. Va.

COCHRAN, AARON - Pvt. Co. B. b. Taylor Co., W. Va., c. 1844. Age 16, farm laborer, Pruntytown, Taylor Co., W. Va. 1860 Census. Prior service, Co. D, 19th Va. Cav. Enl. Williamsburg, Greenbrier Co., W. Va., 3/17/63. POW record shows enl. as Highland Co., 8/62. Not stated if present or absent on muster-in roll dated 7/25/63. Present 11/1/63 - 8/31/64 (dated 1/6/65). Ab. 9/1/64 - 10/31/64 (dated 12/30/64), AWOL. Deserted. Reported at Clarksburg, W. Va., 10/25/64. Desc.: age 20, 5'11", light comp., light hair and blue eyes. Occ. farmer, residing in Taylor Co., W. Va. Took the oath of allegiance and was released, 10/25/64. Age 36, farmer, Booth Creek, Taylor Co., W. Va. 1880 Census. NFR.

COCHRAN, DAVID - Pvt. Co. B. b. Taylor Co., W. Va., c. 1846. Prior service, Co. D, 19th Va. Cav. Enl. Williamsburg, Greenbrier Co., W. Va., 3/17/63. Not stated if present or absent on muster-in roll dated 7/25/63. Ab. 11/1/63 - 8/31/64 (dated 1/6/65), AWOL since 5/15/63. Ab. 9/1/64 - 10/31/64 (dated 12/30/64), AWOL since 5/15/63. NFR.

COCHRAN, JOSEPH - Pvt. Co. ?. Not on muster rolls. Reference jacket only, which shows service in Co. B, 46th Battn. Va. Cav. NFR.

COFFINDAFFER (COFFENDAFFER), SMITH - Pvt. Co. E. Enl. Harrison Co., W. Va., 5/4/63, by John L. Bussey. Not stated if present or absent on muster-in roll dated 7/18/63. Taken prisoner, 5/63, while on the way to join Col. W. L. Jackson, at or near Weston, W. Va. Confined at Camp Chase, as a political prisoner. NFR.

COLLINS, BENJAMIN J. - Pvt. Co. H. b.c. 1843. Enl. Camp Northwest, W. Va., 7/1/63 (6/25/63, 6/28/63). Not stated if present or absent on muster-in roll dated 8/63. Ab. 10/31/63 - 8/31/64, deserted 8/63. Ab. 9/1/64 - 10/31/64 (dated 12/30/64), deserted 7/63. Deserted. Reported at Clarksburg, W. Va., 10/14/63. Desc.: age 20, 5'8", a resident of Ritchie Co., W. Va. Took the oath of allegiance and was sent North. Age 40, farmer, Clay Dist., Ritchie Co., W. Va. 1880 Census. NFR.

COLLINS, CREED - Pvt. Co. ?. b. 12/14/42. Not on muster rolls. Reference jacket only, which shows service in Co. A, 46th Battn. Va. Cav. Age 36, dry goods merchant, Clay Dist., Ritchie Co., W. Va. 1880 Census. d. Pennsboro, Ritchie Co., W. Va., 4/23/1909. Bur. Pennsboro Masonic Cem., Pennsboro, Ritchie Co., W. Va.

COLLINS, DANIEL - Pvt. Co. H. b. 1836. Enl. Camp Northwest, W. Va., 6/14/63 (6/25/63, 6/28/63). Not stated if present or absent on muster-in roll dated 8/63. Ab. 10/31/63 - 8/31/64, deserted 8/63. Ab. 9/1/64 - 10/31/64 (dated 12/30/64), deserted 7/63. Deserted. Reported at Clarksburg, W. Va., 10/14/63. Desc.: age 27, 5'7", resident of Ritchie Co., W. Va. Took the oath of allegiance and was sent North. Post war resident of Ritchie Co., W. Va. Age 43, farmer, Murphy Dist., Ritchie Co., W. Va. 1880 Census. d. 4/11/1910. Bur. Six Cem., Cairo, Ritchie Co., W. Va.

COLLINS, JOHN W. - Pvt. Co. B. Prior service, Co. D, 19th Va. Cav. Enl. Williamsburg, Greenbrier Co., W. Va., 3/17/63. Not stated if present or absent on muster-in roll dated 7/25/63. NFR.

COLLINS, JOHN W. - Pvt. Co. K. b.c. 1827. Enl. Camp Northwest, W. Va., 6/3/63 (4/63), age 36. Not stated if present or absent on muster-in roll dated 7/21/63. Ab. 7/1/63 - 11/1/63 (dated 1/6/64), AWOL. Ab. 11/1/63 - 2/29/64, AWOL. Ab. 2/29/64 - 8/31/64, AWOL. Post war resident of Wood Co., W. Va. NFR.

COMBS (COOMBS, COOMS), VAN B. - Pvt. Co. A. b.c. 1837. Resident of Monongalia (Marion Co., W. Va. Enl. Highland Co., 10/8/62, age 25. Not stated if present or absent on muster-in roll dated 10/8/62. Ab. 7/1/63 - 9/1/63, d. in hosp., 4/26/63.

COMPTON, WILLIAM B. - Pvt. Co. B. Enl. Nelson Co., 6/13/64. Present 11/1/63 - 8/31/64 (dated 1/6/65), entitled to enl. bounty. Present 9/1/64 - 10/31/64 (dated 12/30/64), entitled to $100 bond and enl. bounty. NFR.

CONAWAY, ISAAC D. - Pvt. Co. B. Enl. Braxton Co., W. Va., 5/17/63. Not stated if present or absent on muster-in roll dated 7/25/63. Ab. 11/1/63 - 8/31/64 (dated 1/6/65), prisoner in hands of the enemy. Ab. 9/1/64 - 10/31/64 (dated 12/30/64), POW. No POW records. NFR.

CONAWAY, JACOB H. - Pvt. Co. B. Enl. Braxton Co., W. Va., 5/17/63. Not stated if present or absent on muster-in roll dated 7/25/63. Ab. 11/1/63 - 8/31/64 (dated 1/6/65), AWOL. Ab. 9/1/64 - 10/31/64 (dated 12/30/64), AWOL since 10/63. NFR.

CONAWAY (CONWAY), J. RUFUS - Pvt. Co. A. Enl. Highland Co., 3/10/64. Present 10/31/63 - 8/31/64, entitled to $50 enl. bounty. Post war resident of Marion Co., W. Va. NFR.

CONRAD, ———— - Pvt. Co. ?. Post war rosters only, which show he deserted. NFR.

COONTZ (KOONTZ), JAMES - Pvt. Co. D. b. Barbour Co., W. Va., c. 1846. Enl. Oakland Depot, 4/1/64. Also as having enl. at Crab Bottom, Highland Co., 7/64. Present 12/31/63 - 8/31/64 (dated 1/6/65). Ab. 9/1/64 - 10/31/64, AWOL. Cpd. Beverly, W. Va., 10/29/64. Sent to Clarksburg, W. Va., then to Wheeling, W. Va., 11/2/64. Desc.: age 18, 5'9", fair comp., light hair and gray eyes. Occ. farmer, residing in Barbour Co., W. Va. Confined at the Atheneum Prison, 11/2/64. Desc.: age 18, 5'9", fair comp., brown hair and hazel eyes. Transf. to Camp Chase, 11/22/64. Confined at Camp Chase, 11/23/64, desires to take the oath of allegiance. Enl. in US service, 4/22/65. NFR.

COONTZ (KOONTZ), JAMES C. - Pvt. Co. D. b.c. 1849. Not on muster rolls. Surrendered at Philippi, W. Va., 5/1/65. Sent to Clarksburg, W. Va. Confined at Clarksburg, W. Va., 5/3/65. Desc.: age 16, 5'5", dark comp., dark hair and blue eyes. Occ. farmer, residing in Barbour Co., W. Va. Paroled for exchange and released, 5/4/65. NFR.

COONTZ (KOONTZ), JOHN - Pvt. Co. D. b. Barbour Co., W. Va., c. 1847. Enl. Barbour Co., W. Va., 4/1/64 (Crab Bottom, Highland Co., 5/64). Not stated if present or absent, 12/31/63 - 8/31/64 (dated 1/6/65). Ab. 9/1/64 - 10/31/64, POW. Cpd. Beverly, W. Va., 10/29/64. Sent to Clarksburg, W. Va. Confined at Clarksburg, W. Va., then sent to Wheeling, W. Va., 11/2/64. Desc.: age 17, 5'7", fair comp., light hair and gray eyes. Occ. farmer, residing in Barbour Co., W. Va. Confined at the Atheneum Prison, 11/2/64. Desc.: age 17, 5'7", fair comp., dark hair and gray eyes. Transf. to Camp Chase, 11/3/64. Confined at Camp Chase, 11/4/64. NFR.

CORAGAN (COLLIGAN, CARRIGAN, CORRIGAN, CURIGAN), JAMES H. "Jimmie" - Pvt. Co. C. b. Newtown, Irons, Ireland, 3/25/28 (3/26/37). Prior service, Co. C, 22nd Va. Inf. Enl. Pocahontas Co., W. Va., 3/19/63. Ab. 6/30/63 - 8/31/64 (dated 1/6/65), on detached service; 6% bond due; enl. bounty due. Ab. 9/1/64 - 10/31/64 (dated 12/30/64), on detached service; 6% bond due. Paroled at Staunton, 5/26/65. Desc.: age 26, 5'6", dark comp., black hair and blue eyes. Post war rosters list unit as Capt. Hutton's Mounted Infantry, and state he was a British subject at the time he enl. Post war resident of Vanderpool, Highland Co. Age 60(?), farmer, Monterey Dist., Highland Co. 1900 Census. d. Jackson River (Vanderpool), Highland Co., 6/22/1905 (6/22/1915, 6/23/1915). Bur. Houlihan Family Cem., Highland Co.

CORDER, EDWARD M. - Capt. Co. D. b. 12/27/32. Resident of Philippi, Barbour Co., W. Va. Prior service, Capt. W. K. Jenkins' Cav. Co., 1st Co. B, 62nd Va. Mtd. Inf. and Co. I, 14th Va. Cav. Detailed to recruit in Northwest Virginia, 2/14/63. No enl. data. Not stated if present or absent on muster-in roll dated 8/63, Capt. commanding Co. Elected (appointed) Capt. 6/1/63. Present, Capt., 7/1/63 - 1/1/64 (dated 1/1/64), elected Capt. 5/3/63. Ab. 12/31/63 8/31/64 (dated 1/6/65), elected Capt. 5/3/63; KIA. 9/19/64. Granted 20 days leave, 2/17/64. Ab. 9/1/64 - 10/31/64, elected Capt. 5/3/63; KIA. 3rd Battle of Winchester, 9/19/64.

CORDER, WILLIAM ERVIN (ERWIN) - Pvt. Co. D. b. 2/12/45. Resident of Philippi, Barbour Co., W. Va. Enl. Grass Land, 5/1/63. Not stated if present or absent on muster-in roll dated 8/63. Post war resident of Barbour Co., W. Va. d. 1936.

CORDER, WILSON PATTON - Pvt. Co. D. b. 7/15/43. Resident of Philippi, Barbour Co., W. Va. Enl. Grass Land, 5/1/63. Not stated if present or absent on muster-in roll dated 8/63. Post war resident of Philippi, W. Va. d. 3/26/1931.

CORNELL, WILLIAM PERRY - Pvt. Co. G. Enl. Wood Co., W. Va., 5/2/63 (6/13/63, 6/18/63). Not stated if present or absent on muster-in roll dated 8/63. Present 11/1/63 - 2/29/64. Clothing issued 2/29/64. Not stated if present or absent, 7/1/64 - 8/31/64, had his own horse; entitled to bond. Ab. 9/1/64 - 12/29/64, wd. Shepherdstown, W. Va., 8/25/64, now in hosp.; entitled to $100 bond. Clothing issued 12/12/64, Staunton Gen. Hosp. d. Sperryville, 1/2/1930.

CORTER (CORDER), PAGE G. - Pvt. Co. D. Enl. Grass Land, 5/1/63. Not stated if present or absent on muster-in roll dated 8/63. NFR.

COUGHLIN, JOHN - Pvt. Co. A. b.c. 1845. Enl. Pocahontas Co., W. Va., 4/4/63, age 18. Not stated if present or absent on muster-in roll dated 4/4/63. Present 7/1/63 - 9/1/63. Ab. 10/31/63 - 8/31/64, deserted 9/63. Cpd. Wetzel Co., W. Va., 10/26/63. Confined at the Atheneum Prison, 10/27/63. Desc.: age 17, 5'7", florid comp., dark hair and blue eyes. Occ. farmer, residing in Wetzel Co., W. Va. Took the oath of allegiance and was released, 10/28/63. Post war resident of Marion Co., W. Va. NFR.

COURTNEY, JOHN A. - Pvt. Co. C. b.c. 1837. Age 23, laborer, Randolph Co., W. Va. 1860 Census. Enl. Randolph Co., W. Va., 4/29/63 (4/27/63). Not stated if present or absent on muster-in roll dated 8/63. Ab. 6/30/63 - 8/31/64 (dated 1/6/65), deserted 9/63. Cpd. Beverly, W. Va., 1/20/64. Confined at the Atheneum Prison, 2/1/64. Desc.: age 24, 5'9", florid comp., dark hair and dark eyes. Occ. farmer, residing in Randolph Co., W. Va. Took the oath of allegiance and was released, 2/2/64. Age 43, Huttonsville, Randolph Co., W. Va. 1880 Census. NFR.

COVELASKIE, (COVESESKI, KOVALOSKY), EDWARD - Pvt. Co. G. b. England, c. 1840. Served in Co. C, 19th Va. Cav., listed as Kovalosky. Post war rosters only, which show he was a resident of Wood Co., W. Va. Age 40, clerk in sewing machine office, Parkersburg, Wood Co., W. Va. 1880 Census. NFR.

COWELL, ELIAS - Pvt. Co. B. b. Greene Co., Pa., c. 1842. Enl. Marion Co., W. Va., 2/1/64, by H. P. Wilson. Present 11/1/63 8/31/64 (dated 1/6/65), entitled to enl. bounty. Ab. 9/1/64 - 10/31/64 (dated 12/30/64), POW since 10/64. Clothing issued 9/2/64. Cpd. Beverly, W. Va., 10/29/64. Sent to Clarksburg, W. Va., then to Wheeling, W. Va., 11/2/64. Desc.: age 22, 5'11", fair comp., light hair and hazel eyes. Occ. farmer, residing in Greene Co., Pa. Confined at the Atheneum Prison, 11/2/64. Desc.: age 22, 5'11", fair comp., light hair and gray eyes. Occ. farmer, residing in Marion Co., W. Va. Transf. to Camp Chase, 11/3/64. Confined at Camp Chase, 11/4/64. DOD. Camp Chase, 4/14/65, pneumonia. Bur. Camp Chase Confederate Cem., grave no. 1861.

CRACRAFT, WILLIAM ALLEN - 3rd (Bvt. 2nd) Lt. Co. I. b. Claysville, Pa., 2/23/44. Moved to Triadelphia, Ohio Co., W. Va., 1848. Educated at West Alexander, Pa. Prior service, Co. G, 27th Va. Inf. Disc. 9/30/62. Post war account says he joined the cav.

service in Richmond, 1862. Detailed to Rockbridge Co., on recruiting duty. Formed 2 co's. in Rockbridge and adjoining co's. for Maj. J. B. Lady's Battn. (47th Battn. Cav.). Enl. Warm Springs, 4/1/63 (4/17/63), age 18. Elected Jr. 2nd Lt., 5/4/63. Not stated if present or absent, 3rd Lt., on muster-in roll dated 5/5/63. Ab., Jr. 2nd Lt., 11/1/63 - 8/31/64 (dated 1/6/65), on sick furlough. Present 11/1/63 - 10/31/64 (dated 12/31/64). Seriously injured at Fisher's Hill, 9/22/64, explosion of shell, suffered hearing loss the rest of his life. Furloughed for 3 weeks. Ab. 10/25/64, on sick leave, 30 days. Was absent on a scout with 30 men at the time of the surrender, 4/9/65. Cpd. Parkersburg, W. Va., 4/21/65. Sent to Clarksburg, W. Va. Confined at Clarksburg, W. Va., 4/21/65. Desc.: age 20, 5'8,", fair comp., light hair and gray eyes. Occ. student, residing in Ohio Co., W. Va. Paroled for exchange, 4/24/65, and was released. Also as having been paroled at Charleston, W. Va., and Clarksburg, W. Va., as a Pvt., 4/22/65. Paroled again at Staunton, having lost the other parole. Remained in Staunton until 6/65, then returned to Triadelphia, W. Va. Studied medicine. Attended UVa., 1866-1867. Practiced medicine at Triadelphia, 4 years. Moved to Elm Grove, W. Va. Document in his file shows he was a former resident of Lexington, Ky., and was going to Winchester. Post war rosters show he was a resident of Wheeling, W. Va. Post war resident of Elm Grove, Ohio Co., W. Va. Served as Co. Physician, 1872 - 1893. Appointed Physician for Home for the Aged, 1892. Appointed Chief Surgeon, W. Va. Div., UCV, 1897. Son of Dr. George A. Cracraft, 19th Va. Cav. NFR.

CRAIG, J. A. - Pvt. Co. C. Post war rosters only, which show he served for one year and was a resident of Montgomery Co. NFR.

CROUCH, ABRAHAM - Pvt. Co. C. b. 1832. Age 27, farmer, Randolph Co., W. Va. 1860 Census. Enl. Randolph Co., W. Va., 4/28/63. Not stated if present or absent on muster-in roll dated 8/63. Age 48, farmer, Huttonsville, Randolph Co., W. Va. 1880 Census. d. 1901.

CROUCH, ANDREW C. "Buck" - Sgt. Co. C. b.c. 1843. Enl. Randolph Co., W. Va., 4/28/63 (4/4/63). Not stated if present or absent on muster-in roll dated 8/63, 4th Corp. Present, 4th Corp., 6/30/63 - 8/31/64 (dated 1/6/65), 6% bond due. Present, 4th Corp., 9/1/64 - 10/31/64 (dated 12/30/64), 6% bond due. Paroled at Charleston, W. Va., 5/10/65, listed as a Sgt. Desc.: age 22, 6'1", fair comp., dark hair, blue eyes and dark whiskers. Post war resident of Randolph Co., W. Va. Age 39, farmer, Huttonsville, Randolph Co., W. Va. 1880 Census. Attended Confederate Reunion, Randolph Co., W. Va., 1906. Member Gen. Pegram Camp, UCV, Valley Head, W. Va. Attended Gettysburg Reunion, 1913. Resident of Huttonsville, W. Va., 1916. NFR.

CRAWFORD, ROBERT A. - Pvt. Co. D. Enl. Camp Scott, 8/19/63 (8/1/63). Present 7/1/63 - 1/1/64 (dated 1/1/64), entitled to enl. bounty. Ab. 12/31/63 - 8/31/64 (dated 1/6/65), d. Highland Co., 4/10/64. Ordered to report for duty, 2/10/64. Ab. 9/1/64 - 10/31/64, deceased. d. Highland Co., 4/10/64.

CRIST, HECTAR CROSON - Pvt. Co. I. b. Rockbridge Co., 1834. Age 26, farmer, Kerr's Creek Dist., Rockbridge Co. 1860 Census. Prior service, Co. G, 58th Va. Inf. Enl. Camp Morton, Rockbridge Co., 9/10/63. Ab. 11/1/63 - 8/31/64 (dated 1/6/65), deserted. Ab. 11/1/63 - 10/31/64 (dated 12/31/64), claimed by another command. Returned by 11/14/63 to Co. G, 58th Va. Inf. Age 34, farmhand, Kerr's Creek Dist., Rockbridge Co. 1870 Census. Moved to Greene Co., Ill., 1878. d. Greene Co., Ill., c. 1880. Bur. Oaklawn Cem., Greenfield, Ill.

CROUSEHRON, JOHN W. - Pvt. Co. K. b.c. 1845. Enl. Camp Northwest, W. Va., 6/18/63 (4/18/63, 6/1/63), by J. H. Cammack. Not stated if present or absent on muster-in roll dated 7/21/63. Ab. 7/1/63 - 11/1/63 (dated 1/6/64), AWOL. Ab. 11/1/63 - 2/29/64, transf. to Capt. Heiskell's Co. (I.), 1/10/64. Ab. 2/29/64 - 8/31/64, transf. to Co. I, 20th Va. Cav. Enl. shown on rolls of Co. I as Rockbridge Co., 9/4/63. Ab., Co. I, 11/1/63 - 8/31/64 (dated 1/6/65), wd. Ab. 11/1/63 - 10/31/64 (dated 12/31/64), wd. Lynchburg, 6/17/64, and not reported for duty. Paroled at Staunton, 5/19/65. Desc.: age 20, 5'5", fair comp., light hair and gray eyes. NFR.

CUMMINGS (CUMINGS, CUMMINS), GIDEON M. - Pvt. Co. F. b.c. 1846. Enl. Camp Clover Lick, 7/11/63 (Bulltown, W. Va., 5/10/63). Not stated if present or absent on muster-in roll dated 7/20/63. Cpd. Jane Lew, Lewis Co., W. Va., 5/5/63, listed as being a member of the 19th Va. Cav. Confined at the Atheneum Prison, 5/9/63. Desc.: age 17, 5'6,", fresh comp., light hair and blue eyes. Occ. farmer, residing in Harrison Co., W. Va. Transf. to Camp Chase, 5/11/63. Confined at Camp Chase, 5/12/63. Transf. to Johnson's Island, 6/14/63. Confined at Johnson's Island, 6/14/63, block 8. Ab. 7/1/63 - 8/31/64 (dated 1/6/65), cpd. by the enemy in Harrison Co., W. Va., d. since in Camp Chase. Ab. 9/1/64 - 10/31/64 (dated 12/30/64), cpd. 5/13/63 and since d. in prison. DOD. Johnson's Island, O., 7/14/63, rubeola and pneumonia. Bur. Johnson's Island Cem.

CUMMINGS, WILLIAM - 3rd Sgt. Co. F. Enl. Bulltown, Braxton Co., W. Va., 5/10/63. Not stated if present or absent on muster-in roll dated 7/20/63, 3rd Sgt. Present, 3rd Sgt., 7/1/63 - 8/31/64 (dated 1/6/65), has his own horse; entitled to enl. bounty. Present, 3rd Sgt., 9/1/64 - 10/31/64 (dated 12/30/64), entitled to enl. bounty. Paroled at Charleston, W. Va., 5/12/65. Desc.: age 38, 5'7", dark comp., dark hair, dark eyes and dark whiskers. NFR.

CUNNINGHAM, BENJAMIN - Pvt. Co. B. b.c. 1815. Enl. Camp Northwest, W. Va., 6/10/63. Not stated if present or absent on muster-in roll dated 7/25/63. Ab. 11/1/63 - 8/31/64 (dated 1/6/65), POW, marked on former roll as AWOL. Cpd. Farmington, W. Va., 11/5/63. Confined at the Atheneum Prison, 11/12/63. Desc.: age 47, 5'7", florid comp., sandy hair and gray eyes. Occ. farmer, residing in Marion Co., W. Va. Ab. 9/1/64 - 10/31/64 (dated 12/30/64), POW, marked on former roll as AWOL. Cpd. Farmington (Marion Co.), W. Va., 10/4/64 (11/5/63). Confined at the Atheneum Prison. Transf. to Camp Chase, 1/16/65. Confined at Camp Chase, 1/17/65, desires to take the oath of allegiance. Took the oath of allegiance and was released, 5/15/65, signs by x. Desc.: age 48, 5'7", dark comp., dark hair and dark eyes. Age 65, farmer, Fairmont Dist., Marion Co., W. Va. 1880 Census. NFR.

CUNNINGHAM, EOFF H. - 1st Lt. Co. B. b.c. 1835. Not on muster rolls. Cpd. Covington, Alleghany Co., 12/20/63 (9/19/63), listed as 1st Lt. Confined at the Atheneum Prison, 12/31/63. Desc.: age 28, 5'7", florid comp., dark hair and blue eyes, a resident of Ohio Co., W. Va. Transf. to Camp Chase, 1/4/64. Confined at Camp Chase, 1/5/64. Transf. to Ft. Delaware, 3/25/64. Confined at Ft. Delaware, 3/27/64. Took the oath of allegiance and was released, 5/10/65. Desc.: age ?, 5'5+", dark comp., brown hair and gray eyes, a resident of Ohio Co., W. Va. Listed also as 2nd Lt. NFR.

CUNNINGHAM, FRANCIS M. - Pvt. Co. B. b. Marion Co., W. Va., c. 1842. Not on muster rolls. POW record shows his enl. as Pocahontas Co., W. Va., 10/63. Cpd. Beverly, W. Va., 10/29/64. Sent to Clarksburg, W. Va., then to Wheeling, 11/2/64. Desc.: age 22, 5'11", fair comp., dark hair and blue eyes. Occ. farmer, residing in Marion Co., W. Va. Confined at the Atheneum Prison, 11/2/64. Desc.: age 22, 6', fair comp., dark hair and blue eyes. Transf. to Camp Chase, 11/29/64. Confined at Camp Chase, 11/30/64. Applied to take the oath of allegiance, 12/64. Took the oath of allegiance and was released, 5/15/65. Desc.: age 22, 5'11+", dark comp., dark hair and blue eyes, a resident of Marion Co., W. Va. NFR.

CUNNINGHAM, JAMES L. - Pvt. Co. D. Not on muster rolls. Reference jacket only, which shows service in the 46th Battn. Va. Cav. NFR.

CUNNINGHAM, STEPHEN R. - Pvt. Co. H. b. Ritchie Co., W. Va., c. 1835. Enl. Calhoun Co., W. Va., 5/14/63 (5/8/63); (Camp Northwest, W. Va., 5/63 or 6/28/63). Not stated if present or absent on muster-in roll dated 8/63. Present 10/31/63 - 8/31/64. Clothing issued 1st Qr. 1864. Adm. CSA Gen. Hosp., Charlottesville, 8/17/64, ascites. Transf. to Lynchburg, 8/18/64. Ab. 9/1/64 - 10/31/64 (dated 12/30/64), on leave. Clothing issued 11/24/64. Deserted. Reported at Ellenboro, W. Va., 12/26/64. Took the oath of allegiance and was released at Ellenboro, W. Va., 12/26/64. Desc.: age 30, 5'9", dark comp., dark hair and brown eyes. Occ. farmer, residing in Ritchie Co., W. Va. Age 46, farmer, West Union Dist., Ritchie Co., W. Va. 1880 Census. NFR.

CUNNINGHAM, WILLIAM D. - Pvt. Co. B. Prior service, Co. D, 19th Va. Cav. Enl. Williamsburg, Greenbrier Co., W. Va., 3/17/63. Not stated if present or absent on muster-in roll dated 7/25/63. Enl. Campbell Co., 5/25/64, in Co. C, 20th Va. Cav. Ab. 6/30/63 - 8/31/64 (dated 1/6/65), AWOL. NFR.

CUNNINGHAM, WILLIAM I. - Ass't. Surgeon. Not on muster rolls. Appointed Ass't. Surgeon, 8/14/63. Transf. to Lynchburg Hosp., 5/64. NFR.

CURRY, ALEXANDER - Pvt. Co. C. b. Bath Co., c. 1832 (1837). Age 23, laborer, Bath CH, Bath Co. 1860 Census. Enl. Pocahontas Co., W. Va., 3/19/63. POW record shows enl. as Pocahontas Co., 8/62. Not stated if present or absent on muster-in roll dated 8/63. Ab. 6/30/63 - 8/31/64 (dated 1/6/65), deserted 3/10/64. Deserted. Reported at Beverly, W. Va., 11/7/64. Sent to Clarksburg, W. Va. Took the oath of allegiance and was released, 11/10/64. Desc.: age 32, 6'1", fair comp., dark hair and gray eyes. Occ. farmer, residing in Bath Co. NFR.

CURRY, PETER L. - Pvt. Co. C. Enl. Pocahontas Co., W. Va., 3/19/63. Not stated if present or absent on muster-in roll dated 8/63. Ab. 6/30/63 - 8/31/64 (dated 1/6/65), claimed by Co. K, 32nd Va. Inf., 3/1/64. This is probably an error, as his name does not appear in the roster of the 32nd Va. Inf. NFR.

CURTIS, JOHN - Pvt. Co. F. Enl. Camp Clover Lick, 7/11/63 (Bulltown, W. Va., 5/10/63). Not stated if present or absent on muster-in roll dated 7/20/63. Ab. 7/1/63 - 8/31/64 (dated 1/6/65), deserted 5/13/64. Ab. 9/1/64 - 10/31/64 (dated 12/30/64), deserted 5/13/63. NFR.

DANIELS, ANDREW JACKSON "Jack" - Pvt. Co. D. b.c. 1840. Enl. Weston, W. Va., 5/1/63. Not stated if present or absent on muster-in roll dated 8/63. Ab. 7/1/63 - 1/1/64 (dated 1/1/64), prisoner. Cpd. Barbour Co., W. Va., 7/18/63. Confined at the Atheneum Prison, 7/22/63. Desc.: age 23, 5'11", dark comp., dark hair, dark eyes and dark whiskers. Occ. farmer, residing in Barbour Co., W. Va. Transf. to Camp Chase, 7/23/63. Confined at Camp Chase, 7/24/63. Ab. 12/31/63 - 8/31/64 (dated 1/6/65), prisoner. Transf. to Ft. Delaware, 2/29/64. Confined at Ft. Delaware, 3/4/64 (3/2/64). Ab. 9/1/64 - 10/31/64, POW. Took the oath of allegiance and was released, 5/8/65. Desc.: age ?, 5'11", dark comp., brown hair and gray eyes, a resident of Barbour Co., W. Va. Bur. Heavener Cem., Buckhannon, W. Va.

DANIELS, JOHN H. - 3rd Corp. Co. D. b.c. 1845. Enl. Weston, W. Va., 5/1/63. Not stated if present or absent on muster-in roll dated 8/63, 3rd Corp. Ab., Pvt., 7/1/63 - 1/1/64 (dated 1/1/64), prisoner. Cpd. Highland Co., 8/20/63. Confined at the Atheneum Prison, 8/30/63. Desc.: age 18, 5'8 3/4", dark comp., black hair and black eyes. Occ. farmer, residing in Barbour Co., W. Va. Transf. to Camp Chase, 8/31/63. Confined at Camp Chase, 9/1/63. Ab. 12/31/63 - 8/31/64 (dated 1/6/65), prisoner. Transf. to Rock Island, Ill., 1/14/64. Confined at Rock Island Prison, 1/17/64. Ab. 9/1/64 - 10/31/64, POW. Transf. for exchange 2/15/65. Exchanged. Adm. Howard's Grove Gen. Hosp., 3/3/65 (3/4/65). Transf. to Gen. Hosp. No. 9, 3/6/65(?). Adm. Gen. Hosp. No. 9, 3/5/65. Transf. to Chimborazo Hosp., 3/6/65. Adm. Chimborazo Hosp. No. 2, 3/7/65, catarrh. Furloughed 3/16/65, 60 days. Paroled at Staunton, 5/10/65. Desc.: age 20, 5'8", dark comp., black hair and black eyes. Age 34, farmer, Philippi, Barbour Co., W. Va. 1880 Census. NFR.

DANIELS, WILLIAM W. - 1st Lt. Co. D. No enl. data. Not stated if present or absent on muster-in roll dated 8/63, 1st Lt. Present, 1st Lt., 7/1/63 - 1/1/64 (dated 1/1/64), elected 1st Lt., 6/1/63. Present, 1st Lt., 12/31/63 - 8/31/64 (dated 1/6/65), commanding Co. Present, 1st Lt., 9/1/64 - 10/31/64, commanding Co. On furlough, 9/63. Wd., date and place not stated. Ab. 10/25/64, wd., now on leave, 30 days. NFR.

DAVIS, EDWARD - Pvt. Co. F. Prior service, Co. C, 19th Va. Cav. Enl. Camp Clover Lick (Camp Miller), 7/17/63. Not stated if present or absent on muster-in roll dated 7/20/63. Ab. 7/1/63 - 8/31/64 (dated 1/6/65), transf. to Co. C, 19th Va. Cav. Ab. 9/1/64 10/31/64 (dated 12/30/64), transf. to Co. C, 19th Va. Cav. NFR.

DAVIS, EDWARD "EDDIE" - Pvt. Co. G. Enl. Wood Co., W. Va., 5/2/63. Not stated if present or absent on muster-in roll dated 8/63. Was wd. in some manner on his way south to join the army. Cpd. Winchester. He lost his hat and coat. That night, he went to a lady's house and asked for something to wear. He was given a Union artillery blouse and cap. Thus dressed, he walked out of the camp, and made his escape. Rejoined his command a mile and a half away. Post war resident of Wood Co., W. Va. Most likely the same as Edward Davis, Co. F, listed above, and in Co. C, 19th Va. Cav. "He was very brave, there was no better soldier." NFR.

DAVIS, GEORGE A. - Pvt. Co. F. b. Harrison Co., W. Va., c. 1840. Resident of Harrison Co., W. Va. Arrested and confined at Wheeling, W. Va. and Sandusky, O., by 2/3/62. Released on his oath and bond by 2/8/62. Enl. Bulltown, Braxton Co., 5/10/63. Not stated if present or absent on muster-in roll dated 7/20/63. Ab. 7/1/63 - 8/31/64 (dated 1/6/65), prisoner; entitled to enl. bounty. Ab. 9/1/64 - 10/31/64 (dated 12/30/64), prisoner since 10/28/64. Cpd. Beverly, W. Va., 10/29/64. Sent to Clarksburg, W. Va. Confined at Clarksburg, W. Va. Desc.: age 24, 6'2", fair comp., dark hair and blue eyes. Occ. farmer, residing in Harrison Co., W. Va. Transf. to Wheeling, W. Va., 11/2/64. Confined at the Atheneum Prison, 11/2/64. Desc.: age 24, 6'2", fair comp., dark hair and gray eyes. Transf. to Camp Chase, 11/22/64. Confined at Camp Chase, 11/23/64, desires to take the oath of allegiance. DOD. Camp Chase, 1/23/65, erysipelas. Bur. Camp Chase Confederate Cem., grave no. 850.

DAVIS, HARVEY (HARRY, HENRY) S. - Pvt. Co. D. b. Highland Co., c. 1826. Age 34, farmhand, McDowell, Highland Co. 1860 Census. Prior service, Co. I, 14th Va. Cav. Not on muster rolls. Employed at Moyer's Cave Niter Works, 2/63. Employed at Moyer's Cave and Kirkpatrick's Cave Niter Works, 3/63 - 7/64. Paroled at Staunton, 5/25/65. Desc.: age 39, 6', fair comp., dark hair and hazel eyes. Occ. farmer. NFR.

DAVIS, JOHN W. - 3rd (Bvt. 2nd) Lt. Co. E. Enl. Bulltown, Braxton Co., W. Va., 5/10/63. Elected Bvt. 2nd Lt., 5/10/63. Not stated if present or absent on muster-in roll dated 7/18/63, 2nd Lt. Ab., 2nd Lt., 1/1/64 - 8/31/64 (dated 1/6/65), cpd. Frederick Co., Md., 7/10/64. Cpd. Harpers Ferry, W. Va., 7/10/64. Sent to Washington, DC. Confined at the Old Capitol Prison, 7/17/64. Transf. to Ft. Delaware, 7/22/64. Confined at Ft. Delaware, 7/23/64. Sent to Hilton Head, SC, 8/20/64, as one of the "Immortal 600." Confined at Ft. Pulaski, Ga. Ab., 2nd Lt., 9/1/64 - 10/31/64 (dated 12/29/64), cpd. in Md., 7/10/64. Ab. 10/25/64, POW, 100 days. Transf. to Hilton Head, SC, 11/19/64. Ab. 12/15/64, POW since 7/12/64. Asked to take the oath of allegiance at Hilton Head, SC, 3/6/65, and was allowed to do so. Post war resident of Clarksburg, W. Va. NFR.

DAVIS, JOSEPH - Pvt. Co. K. b.c. 1837. Enl. Camp Northwest, W. Va. (Warm Springs), 5/10/63, age 26. Not stated if present or absent on muster-in roll dated 7/21/63. Ab. 7/1/63 - 11/1/63 (dated 1/6/64), POW. Ab. 11/1/63 - 2/29/64, POW, cpd. Beverly, W. Va., 7/3/63. Ab. 2/29/64 - 8/31/64, POW, cpd. Beverly, W. Va., 7/3/63. No POW records. NFR.

DAVIS, SQUIRE W. C. - Pvt. Co. A. b.c. 1845. Enl. Pocahontas Co., W. Va., 5/12/63, age 18. Not stated if present or absent on muster-in roll dated 5/12/63. Cpd. Grafton, W. Va., 5/17/63, listed as a member of Co. B, 19th Va. Cav. Confined at Ft. Monroe, Md. Paroled and sent to Ft. Monroe, 5/20/63, to be exchanged. Exchanged. Present 7/1/63 - 9/1/63. Ab. 10/31/63 - 8/31/64, d. Highland Co., 5/64. Clothing issued 2/29/64.

DAVIS, WILLIAM J. - 4th Corp. Co. F. b.c. 1841. Resident of Harrison Co., W. Va. Enl. Bulltown, W. Va., 5/10/63. Not stated if present or absent on muster-in roll dated 7/20/63, Corp. Ab., 4th Corp., 7/1/63 - 8/31/64 (dated 1/6/65), POW since 12/18/63; entitled to enl. bounty. Cpd. Alleghany Co., 12/20/63. Confined at the Atheneum Prison, 12/31/63. Desc.: age 22, 6', fair comp., black hair and blue eyes. Occ. farmer, residing in Harrison Co., W. Va. Transf. to Camp Chase, 12/31/63. Confined at Camp Chase, 1/1/64. Transf. to Ft. Delaware, 3/14/64. Confined at Ft. Delaware, 3/17/64. Ab., 4th Corp., 9/1/64 - 10/31/64 (dated 12/30/64), prisoner since 12/18/64. Took the oath of allegiance and was released, 6/20/65, signs by x. Desc.: age ?, 5'10", sallow comp., dark hair and gray eyes, a resident of Harrison Co., W. Va. NFR.

DAWSON, WILLIAM D. - Pvt. Co. A. b.c. 1845. Enl. Pocahontas Co., W. Va., 5/9/63, age 18. Not stated if present or absent on muster-in roll dated 5/9/63. Present 7/1/63 - 9/1/63. Present 10/31/63 - 8/31/64. Clothing issued 2/29/64. Paroled at Staunton, 5/23/65. Desc.: age 19, 5'9", dark comp., black hair and gray eyes. Post war resident of Marion Co., W. Va. NFR.

DEARTH (DARTH, DIRTH), JOHN W. - Sgt. Co. H and Co. G. b. Monroe Co., W. Va., c. 1837. Enl. Calhoun Co., W. Va., 5/14/63 in Co. H. POW record shows enl. as Camp Northwest, W. Va., 5/63. Not stated if present or absent on muster-in roll dated 8/63, Pvt. Enl. Wood Co., W. Va., 5/9/63 (6/18/63), in Co. G. Not stated if present or absent on muster-in roll dated 8/63, 3rd Corp. Present, 1st Corp., 11/1/63 - 2/29/64. Clothing issued 2/29/64. Not stated if present or absent, 4th Sgt., 7/1/64 - 8/31/64, has his own horse; entitled to bond. Ab., 4th Sgt., 9/1/64 - 10/31/64 (dated 12/29/64), MIA Piedmont, 9/25/64, supposed to be cpd; entitled to $100 bond. Cpd. Pleasants Co., W. Va., 2/14/65. Sent to Cumberland, Md., then to Clarksburg, W. Va. Confined at Clarksburg, W. Va. Desc.: age 27, 5'10", dark comp., black hair and blue eyes. Occ. farmer, residing in Pleasants Co., W. Va. Transf. to Wheeling, W. Va. Confined at the Atheneum Prison, 2/20/65. Desc.: age 27, 5'10", fair comp., dark hair and black eyes. Transf. to Camp Chase, 2/21/65. Confined at Camp Chase, 2/22/65. Took the oath of allegiance and was released, 6/13/65. Desc.: age 27, 5'10", dark comp., dark hair and black eyes, a resident of Pleasants Co., W. Va. NFR.

DENMAN, STEVE - Pvt. Co. ?. Post war rosters only, which show he was wd. Leetown, W. Va., 8/28/64, hand. Post war Baptist minister. NFR.

DENNISON, ANDREW JACKSON - Pvt. Co. I. b.c. 1833. Enl. Camp Northwest, W. Va., 7/11/63 (6/15/63), age 30 (Bath Co., 7/30/63). Not stated if present or absent on muster-in roll dated 5/5/63. Ab. 11/1/63 - 8/31/64 (dated 1/6/65), POW. Clothing issued 2/29/64. Ab. 11/1/63 - 10/31/64 (dated 12/31/64), POW. Cpd. Goshen, 6/5/64. Confined at Camp Morton, Indianapolis, Ind., 6/21/64. DOD. Camp Morton, Indianapolis, Ind., 1/25/65, inflammation of the lungs. Bur. Greenlawn Cem., Indianapolis, Ind., grave no. 1310.

DENNISON, JOHN S. - Pvt. Co. B. Prior service, Co. D, 19th Va. Cav. Enl. Williamsburg, Greenbrier Co., W. Va., 3/17/63. Not stated if present or absent on muster-in roll dated 7/25/63. Present 11/1/63 - 8/31/64 (dated 1/6/65). Clothing issued 3/21/64. Present 9/1/64 - 10/31/64 (dated 12/30/64), entitled to $100 bond. Furloughed 2/15/65 to Greenbrier Co., W. Va., 20 days. Desc.: age ?, 5'10", fair comp., auburn hair and blue eyes. NFR.

DENNISON, SALATHIEL L. - Pvt. Co. B. Enl. Camp Northwest, W. Va., 3/17/63 (6/1/63). Not stated if present or absent on muster-in roll dated 7/25/63. Ab. 11/1/63 - 8/31/64 (dated 1/6/65), prisoner in the hands of the enemy, marked on former rolls as AWOL. Ab. 9/1/64 - 10/31/64 (dated 12/30/64), POW, marked on former rolls as AWOL. No POW records. NFR.

DENT, _____ - Pvt. Co. ?. Not on muster rolls. The only reference to this man appears in Major John B. Lady's report of the fight at Beverly, W. Va., 7/2/63. KIA. by Jacob Simmons, a noted Yankee bushwhacker and spy. Major Lady said Dent was: "a gallant soldier." NFR.

DEVER, SAMUEL G. - 2nd Corp. Co. C. b. 9/1/44 (1846). Enl. Pocahontas Co, W. Va. (Highland Co.), 6/25/63. Not stated if present or absent on muster-in roll dated 8/63, Pvt. Present 6/30/64 - 8/31/64 (dated 1/6/65). Present, 2nd Corp., 9/1/64 - 10/31/64 (dated 12/30/64). Paroled at Staunton, 5/24/65. Desc.: age 20, 6', fair comp., brown hair and blue eyes. Post war rosters show he was wd. at Shepherdstown, W. Va., 8/25/64, and was a POW at Camp Chase during the war. Post war resident of Mill Gap, Highland Co. Member S. B. Gibbons Camp, UCV, Harrisonburg, 1905. d. Staunton, 12/5/1921. Bur. Green Hill Methodist Church Cem., Highland Co.

DeWITT, JOHN H. - Pvt. Co. D. b. Alleghany Co., Md., 4/1/44. Age 16, shoemaker, Randolph Co., W. Va. 1860 Census. Enl. Camp Scott, 8/1/63 (Highland Co., 5/63). Present 7/1/63 - 1/1/64 (dated 1/1/64), entitled to enl. bounty; has no horse. Ab. 12/31/63 - 8/31/64 (dated 1/6/65), prisoner. Ab. 9/1/64 - 10/31/64 (dated 12/30/64), POW. Wd./Cpd. Beverly, W. Va., 10/29/64, left knee. Adm. USA Gen. Hosp., Beverly, W. Va., 10/29/64, wd., left thigh, flesh; simple dressing applied. Sent to US Hosp., Grafton, W. Va., 12/10/64(?). Adm. USA Gen. Hosp., Grafton, W. Va., 12/7/64, gunshot wd., left knee, with fracture of patella, by carbine ball; age 20; turned over to post commander, Grafton, 2/8/65. Sent to Wheeling, W. Va. Confined at the Atheneum Prison. Desc.: age 21, 5'10", dark comp., light hair and blue eyes. Occ. shoemaker, residing in Randolph Co., W. Va. Transf. to Camp Chase, 2/13/65. Confined at Camp Chase, 2/14/65. Took the oath of allegiance and was released, 6/12/65. Desc.: age 21, 5'7+", fair comp., light hair and gray eyes. Post war resident of Randolph Co., W. Va. Age 36, boltmaker, Beverly, Randolph Co., W. Va. 1880 Census, listed as DeWatt. Attended Confederate Reunion, Randolph Co., W. Va., 1906. Attended Gettysburg Reunion, 1913. Resident of Beverly, W. Va., 1916. d. 8/11/1917. Bur. Beverly Cem., Beverly, W. Va.

DEILWORTH (DILWORTH), F. SYLVESTER - Pvt. Co. H. Enl. Camp Northwest, W. Va., 7/1/63. Not stated if present or absent on muster-in roll dated 8/63. Transf. to Lurty's Batty., by Capt. Hayhurst, 11/1/63. NFR.

DIX (DICK), D. D. (DARLEY, DAILEY, DAVID D.) - Pvt. Co. C. b. Upshur Co., W. Va., c. 1848. Enl. Pocahontas Co., W. Va., 5/18/63. POW record shows enl. as Huttonsville, W. Va., 5/63. Not stated if present or absent on muster-in roll dated 8/63. Present 6/30/63 - 8/31/64 (dated 1/6/65), 6% bond due. Ab. 9/1/64 - 10/31/64 (dated 12/30/64), AWOL since 10/10/64; 6% bond due. Clothing issued 3rd Qr. 1864. Cpd. Huttonsville (Beverly), Randolph Co., W. Va., 2/16/65 (2/15/65). Confined at Clarksburg, W. Va., 2/18/65. Desc.: age 17, 5'7", fair comp., light hair and blue eyes. Occ. farmer, residing in Upshur Co., W. Va. Sent to Wheeling, W. Va. Confined at the Atheneum Prison, 2/20/65. Desc.: age 17, 5'6", fair comp., light hair and gray eyes. Transf. to Camp Chase, 2/21/65. Confined at Camp Chase, 2/22/65. Transf. to Pt. Lookout, 3/26/65, to be exchanged. Confined at Pt. Lookout, 3/31/65. Was not exchanged because he was sick. Took the oath of allegiance and was released, 6/4/65. NFR.

DOBBS, THOMAS E. - Pvt. Co. K. b.c. 1841. Enl. Warm Springs, 4/1/63, age 22. Not stated if present or absent on muster-in roll dated 7/21/63. Ab. 7/1/63 - 11/1/63 (dated 1/6/64), AWOL. NFR.

DODD (DODDS), JOHN - Pvt. Co. K. b.c. 1818. Age 42, farmer, Webster Co., W. Va. 1860 Census. Enl. Camp Cameron, Bath Co., 3/30/63. Ab. 11/1/63 - 2/29/64, deserted. Ab. 2/29/64 - 8/31/64, deserted. NFR.

DONALD, ANGUS - Pvt. Co. K. Not on muster rolls. Cpd. Greenbrier Co., W. Va., 11/7/63. Confined at the Atheneum Prison, 11/16/63. Desc.: age 26, 5'8 3/4", florid comp., sandy hair and gray eyes. Occ. laborer, residing in Cordo Parish, La. Transf. to Camp Chase, 11/18/63. NFR.

DOTSON, MARION D. - 4th Sgt. Co. H and Co. G. Enl. Calhoun Co., W. Va., 5/14/63, in Co. H. Not stated if present or absent on muster-in roll dated 8/63, 4th Sgt. Enl. Wood Co., W. Va., 5/9/63 (6/18/63), in Co. G. Not stated if present or absent on muster-in roll dated 8/63, Pvt. Present 11/1/63 - 2/29/64. Clothing issued 2/29/64 and 8/25/64, signs by x. Present 7/1/64 - 8/31/64, has his own horse. Ab. 9/1/64 - 10/31/64 (dated 12/29/64), AWOL for 10 days. Surrendered at Parkersburg, W. Va., 4/25/65. Sent to Clarksburg, W. Va. Confined at Clarksburg, W. Va., 4/26/65. Took the oath of allegiance and was released, 4/28/65. Desc.: age 22, 5'8", fair comp., light hair and blue eyes. Occ. farmer, residing in Pleasants Co., W. Va. NFR.

DOTSON, MARTIN L. - Pvt. Co. H. and Co. G. Enl. Calhoun Co., W. Va., 5/14/63, in Co. H. Not stated if present or absent on muster-in roll dated 8/63. Enl. Wood Co., W. Va., 5/9/63 (6/18/63), in Co. G. Not stated if present or absent on muster-in roll dated 8/63. Present 11/1/63 - 2/29/64, had his own horse since 12/21/63. Clothing issued 2/29/64. Present 7/1/64 - 8/31/64, has his own horse; entitled to bond. Present 9/1/64 - 10/31/64 (dated 12/29/64), entitled to $100 bond. NFR.

DOUGHERTY (DAUGHERTY), JACOB - 3rd Sgt. Co. H. b. 6/27/29. Enl. Camp Northwest, W. Va., 7/1/63 (6/2/63, 6/29/63). Not stated if present or absent on muster-in roll dated 8/63, Pvt. Present, Pvt., 10/31/63 - 8/31/64. Ab., 3rd Sgt., 9/1/64 - 10/31/64 (dated 12/30/64), prisoner in hands of enemy, cpd. 9/64. Cpd. Ritchie Co., W. Va., 9/6/64 (Charles Town, W. Va., 9/8/64). Confined at the Atheneum Prison, 9/12/64. Desc.: age 33, 5'9+", light comp., dark hair and blue eyes. Occ. farmer, residing in Ritchie Co., W. Va. Transf. to Camp Chase, 9/15/64. Confined at Camp Chase, 9/17/64. Took the oath of allegiance and was released, 6/11/65. Desc.: age 35, 5'9+", fair comp., light hair and blue eyes, a resident of Ritchie Co., W. Va. Brother's George and Wesley, were US Soldiers. Post war farmer and resident of Ritchie Co., W. Va. Age 51, farmer, Murphy Dist., Ritchie Co., W. Va. 1880 Census. d. 5/15/1908. Bur. Reeves Cem., Goffs, Ritchie Co., W. Va.

DOUGLASS, IRVING - 4th Corp. Co. D. Enl. Weston, W. Va., 5/1/63. Not stated if present or absent on muster-in roll dated 8/63, Pvt. Present, 4th Corp., 7/1/63 - 1/1/64 (dated 1/1/64), has his own horse. Present, 4th Corp., 12/31/63 - 8/31/64 (dated 1/6/65). Clothing issued 2/29/64. Present, 4th Corp., 9/1/64 - 10/31/64, entitled to $100 enl. bounty. NFR.

DOWD (DOUD), J. E. O. - Pvt. Co. A. b.c. 1830. Enl. Marion Co., W. Va., 3/23/63, age 33, by Sgt. Yost (Youst). Not stated if present or absent on muster-in roll dated 8/63. Ab. 7/1/63 - 9/1/63, not reported for duty. Ab. 10/31/63 - 8/31/64, never reported for duty. NFR.

DOWNS, JOHN S. - 5th Sgt. Co. K. b.c. 1833 (1843). Enl. Warm Springs, 4/1/63, age 30. Not stated if present or absent on muster-in roll dated 8/63, 5th Sgt. Present, 5th Sgt., 7/1/63 - 11/1/63 (dated 1/6/64), promoted 5th Sgt. 7/21/63. Served in Co. A, 19th Va. Cav. Post war resident of Marion Co., W. Va. d. 1931.

DOYLE (DOYL), JACOB - Pvt. Co. ?. b. Highland Co., c. 1835. Age 25, farmer, Wilsonville, Highland Co. 1860 Census. Prior service, 2nd Co. B, 31st Va. Inf. and Co. I, 19th Va. Cav. Transf. to 20th Va. Cav. Not on muster rolls. Returned to 31st Inf. by 2/28/64. DOD. Elmira Prison, 9/11/64. Bur. Woodlawn National Cem., grave no. 352 (512).

DRAGGOO, EPHRAIM M. (W.) - Pvt. Co. B. b. Marion Co., W. Va., c. 1840 (1843). Prior service, Co. D, 19th Va. Cav. Enl. Williamsburg, Greenbrier Co., W. Va., 3/17/63. Not stated if present or absent on muster-in roll dated 7/25/63. Present 11/1/63 8/31/64 (dated 1/6/65). Present 9/1/64 - 10/31/64 (dated 12/30/64), entitled to $100 bond. Took the amnesty oath at Clarksburg, W. Va., 4/14/65. Desc.: age 25, 5'10", fair comp., dark hair and gray eyes. Occ. farmer, residing in Marion Co., W. Va. Post war resident of Jackson Co., W. Va. Age 31 (1874). Post war pensioner and resident of Okla., 1915. NFR.

DRUMMOND, STEPHEN - 1st Lt. Co. E. b.c. 1843. Enl. Bulltown, Braxton Co., W. Va., 5/10/63 (Camp Miller, 5/13/63 and Summersville, W. Va., 5/13/63). Not stated if present or absent on muster-in roll dated 7/18/63, 4th Sgt. Commanding Co., late 1863. Present, 3rd Sgt., 1/1/64 - 8/31/64 (dated 1/6/65), entitled to $100 bond. Ab., 3rd Sgt., 9/1/64 - 10/31/64 (dated 12/29/64), absent because of wd. 9/20/64 - 12/6/64; entitled to $100 bond. Wd. Winchester, 9/19/64. Paroled at Staunton, 5/17/65, as 1st Lt. Desc.: age 22, 5'10", dark comp., black hair and black eyes. NFR.

DRUMMOND, SYLVESTER - Pvt. Co. E. Enl. Camp Miller, 5/25/63 (5/15/63, 5/20/63). Not stated if present or absent on muster-in roll dated 7/18/63. Ab. 1/1/64 - 8/31/64 (dated 1/6/65), MIA since 6/20/64, supposed to be a prisoner. Ab. 9/1/64 - 10/31/64 (dated 12/29/64), MIA since 6/25/64, supposed to be a prisoner. Gave himself up at Paw Paw, W. Va., 7/19/64. NFR.

DRUMMOND, THOMAS - Pvt. Co. E. Enl. Camp Miller, 5/25/63 (5/15/63, 5/20/63). Not stated if present or absent on muster-in roll dated 7/18/63. Present 1/1/64 - 8/31/64 (dated 1/6/65), entitled to $100 bond. Present 9/1/64 - 10/31/64 (dated 12/29/64), entitled to $100 bond. Post war minister. Bur. Randolph Co., W. Va. NFR.

DUDLEY, E. A. - Pvt. Co. A. b.c. 1829. Not on muster rolls. Paroled at Staunton, 5/19/65. Desc.: age 36, 5'5+", fair comp., brown hair and blue eyes. NFR.

DUNCAN, _____ - Capt. Co. ?. Not on muster rolls. Only reference to this man is in Major John B. Lady's report of the fight at Beverly, W. Va., 7/2/63 - 7/3/63. NFR.

DUNCAN, ALEXANDER - Pvt. Co. K. b.c. 1839. Enl. Warm Springs, 4/1/63 (4/20/63), age 24. Not stated if present or absent on muster-in roll dated 7/21/63. Present, 7/1/63 - 11/1/63 (dated 1/6/64), transf. to Capt. Heiskell's Co. (Co. I), 20th Va. Cav., 7/21/63. Ab., Co. I, 11/1/63 - 8/31/64 (dated 1/6/65), POW. Ab. 11/1/63 - 10/31/64 (dated 12/31/64), POW. Cpd. Lewisburg, W. Va., 11/7/63. Confined at the Atheneum Prison, 11/20/63. Desc.: age 23, 5'5", light comp., dark hair and hazel eyes. Occ. cooper, residing in New Orleans, La. Transf. to Camp Chase, 11/20/63. Confined at Camp Chase, 11/21/63. Transf. to Ft. Delaware, 2/29/64. Confined at Ft. Delaware, 3/4/64 (3/2/64). NFR.

DUNCAN, SYLVESTER (SYLVANUS) N. - Pvt. Co. B. Prior service, Co. D, 19th Va. Cav. Enl. Williamsburg, Greenbrier Co., W. Va., 3/17/63. Not stated if present or absent on muster-in roll dated 7/25/63. Present 11/1/63 - 8/31/64 (dated 1/6/65). Clothing issued 3/31/64. Present 9/1/64 - 10/31/64 (dated 12/30/64), entitled to $100 bond. NFR.

EAGLE, JOHN A. - Pvt. Co. D. Enl. Hightown, 7/15/63. Not stated if present or absent on muster-in roll dated 8/63. NFR.

EDDY, DANIEL E. - Pvt. Co. H. b. 8/6/28. Enl. Camp Northwest, W. Va., 7/1/63 (6/28/63, 6/29/63). Not stated if present or absent on muster-in roll dated 8/63. Present 10/31/63 - 8/31/64. Clothing issued 2/29/64. Present 9/1/64 - 10/31/64 (dated 12/30/64). Had red hair and beard, which led to his being called "Red Horse." Post war rosters show service in the 19th Va. Cav. Age 49, farmer, Murphy Dist., Ritchie Co., W. Va. 1880 Census. d. Mellin, Ritchie Co., W. Va., 11/28/1918. Bur. Eddy- Welch Cem., Mellin, Ritchie Co., W. Va.

EDMUNDS, WILLIAM - 4th Sgt. Co. I. b.c. 1835. Enl. Camp Northwest, W. Va., 5/15/63, age 28. Not stated if present or absent on muster-in roll dated 5/5/63, 1st Corp. Ab., Pvt., 11/1/63 - 8/31/64 (dated 1/6/65), POW. Ab., 4th Sgt., 11/1/63 - 10/31/64 (dated 12/31/64), POW. No POW records. NFR.

ELLIOTT, EDWARD (EDGAR) C. - Pvt. Co. D. b.c. 1836. Prior service, Co. C, 19th Va. Cav. Enl. Barbour Co., W. Va., 4/1/64. Present 12/31/63 - 8/31/64 (dated 1/6/65). Ab. 9/1/64 - 10/31/64, AWOL; not entitled to enl. bounty. Paroled at Staunton, 5/10/65. Desc.: age 29, 5'9", fair comp., dark hair and hazel eyes. NFR.

ELLIOTT, SOLOMON P. - Bvt. 2nd Lt. Co. D. Prior service, Co. C, 19th Va. Cav. No enl. data. Ah , Bvt. 2nd Lt., 12/31/63 - 8/31/64 (dated 1/6/65), absent sick; elected 2nd Lt., 5/20/64. Ab., Bvt. (Jr.) 2nd Lt., 9/1/64 - 10/31/64, elected 5/20/64, recommended for retirement. Adm. Gen. Hosp., Harrisonburg, 10/63. Granted a leave of absence, 11/19/64. Ab. 12/15/64, sick since 11/10/64, recommended to be retired. NFR.

ELLIOTT, TRUMAN THEODORE - Pvt. Co. D. b. 1844. Enl. Barbour Co., W. Va., 4/1/64. Present 12/31/63 - 8/31/64 (dated 1/6/65). Present 9/1/64 - 10/31/64, entitled to $100 enl. bounty. Post war farmer and resident of Belington, W. Va. Elected Sheriff, 1892. NFR.

ENGLAND, JOHN - Pvt. Co. D. b. Pocahontas Co., W. Va., c. 1842. Enl. Oakland Depot, Alleghany Co., 4/1/64. POW record shows enl. as Alleghany Co., 5/64. Not stated if present or absent, 12/31/63 - 8/31/64 (dated 1/6/65). Deserted. Reported at Beverly, W. Va., 8/22/64. Sent to Clarksburg, W. Va. Took the oath of allegiance and was released 8/21/64. Desc.: age 22, 5'8", fair comp., dark hair and blue eyes. Occ. farmer, residing in Barbour Co., W. Va. Ab. 9/1/64 - 10/31/64, AWOL. Paroled at Richmond, 4/21/65. NFR.

ENTSMINGER, DAVID E. - Pvt. Co. K. b. Rockbridge Co., 9/4/39 (1836). Exempt, Rockbridge Co., 3/13/62, general debility. Enl. Warm Springs, 4/20/63, age 27 (Camp Northwest, W. Va., 7/1/63 and 7/20/63). Not stated if present or absent on muster-in roll for Co. K, dated 7/21/63. Ab. 7/1/63 - 11/1/63 (dated 1/6/64), AWOL. Ab. 11/1/63 - 2/29/64, AWOL. Ab. 2/29/64 - 8/31/64, AWOL. Enl. in Co. I, 20th Va. Cav., Rockbridge Co., 8/10/63 (11/5/63). Ab. 11/1/63 - 8/31/64 (dated 1/6/65), in Niter Bureau. Ab. 11/1/63 - 10/31/64 (dated 12/31/64), deserted. Served in Co. E, 46th Battn. Va. Cav. d. Rockbridge Co., 8/3/67. Bur. Collierstown Presbyterian Church Cem.

ERVINE (ERVIN), WILLIAM M. - Pvt. Co. K and Co. C. b. Highland Co., c. 1835 (1839). Age 25, farmer, Wilsonville, Highland Co. 1860 Census. Prior service, Co. G (D), 31st Va. Inf. Thought to have joined the 20th Va. Cav. 9/15/62, or went AWOL. Enl. Camp Northwest, W. Va., 6/18/63, age 24. Not stated if present or absent on muster-in roll dated 7/21/63. Enl. in Co. C, Pocahontas Co., W. Va., 3/19/63. Not stated if present or absent muster-in roll dated 8/63. Ab. 6/30/63 - 8/31/64 (dated 1/6/65), deserted 9/1/63. Post war resident of Highland Co. and Pocahontas Co., W. Va. NFR.

EVANS, DUDLEY - Lt. Col./Capt. Co. A. b. Morgantown, W. Va., 1/27/38. Graduated Washington & Jefferson College, 1859. School teacher, residing in Monongalia Co., W. Va. Desires appointment as a clerk in the Gov't., 7/24/61. Prior service, Co. I, 1st Va. Inf., substitute for Clement C. Tinsley. Discharged 8/1/62. Served in the Va. Legislature, 1862. Served as Capt. Co. A, Maj. D. B. Stewart's Va. Cav. Cpd. Highland Co., 11/8/62. Confined at the Atheneum Prison, 11/18/62. Desc.: age 24, 5'10", florid comp., black hair and hazel eyes. Occ. school teacher, residing in Morgantown, W. Va. Transf. to Camp Chase, 11/19/62. Confined at Camp Chase, 11/20/62. Transf. to Cairo, Ill., 11/21/62, to be exchanged. Exchanged at Vicksburg, Miss., 12/8/62. No enl. data. Elected (appointed) Capt. Co. A, 20th Va. Cav., 4/15/63, age 25. Not stated if present or absent on muster-in roll dated 8/63. Not stated if present or absent 7/1/63 - 9/1/63, promoted to Lt. Col., 8/14/63. Present at Beverly, W. Va., 7/63. Elected Lt. Col., 8/14/63 (appointed 10/7/63, confirmed by election, to rank from 8/14/63; accepted 10/8/63). Present, Lt. Col., FS MR 1/1/64 - 8/31/64 (dated 1/6/65), elected 8/14/63. Resigned 11/4/64, as a member of the Va. Legislature. Resignation accepted 11/23/63 (11/22/64). Listed as being 5'10" tall. Served in the Va. Legislature. Post war roster (1894) lists him as a member of the Society of the CSA Army and Navy of Md. Post war businessman, Chicago, Ill. Post war agent for Wells Fargo Express in Oregon. President of Wells Fargo Express Company, New York City, 1902 - 1910. Was president of the Co. when he died. M. P. H. Potts says "he was a nice man and we all loved him, but he was cowardly..." Attended the Culpeper reunion. Post war rosters show him as Lt. d. New York City, 3/27/1910, age 72.

EVANS, JOHN - 3rd Sgt. Co. K. b.c. 1839. Enl. Camp Northwest, W. Va., 5/10/63, age 24. Not stated if present or absent on muster-in roll dated 7/21/63, 2nd Corp. Present, 1st Corp., 7/1/63 - 11/1/63 (dated 1/6/64), promoted to 1st Corp., 8/1/63. Present, 4th Sgt., 11/1/63 - 2/29/64, promoted to 4th Sgt.; had his own horse since 12/19/64. Present, 3rd Sgt., 2/29/64 - 8/31/64, mounted; $100 enl. bounty due. Clothing issued 3/23/64 and 8/25/64. NFR.

EVERSON, THOMAS H. B. - Pvt. Co. B. b. 12/28/40. Prior service, Co. D, 19th Va. Cav. Enl. Williamsburg, Greenbrier Co., W. Va., 3/17/63. Not stated if present or absent on muster-in roll dated 7/25/63. Present 11/1/63 - 8/31/64 (dated 1/6/65). Clothing issued 3/31/64. Present 9/1/64 - 10/31/64 (dated 12/30/64), entitled to $100 bond. d. 3/9/1908. Bur. Sturm Cem., Calhoun Co., W. Va.

206

FARNSWORTH, JAMES J. - Pvt. Co. G. Enl. Wood Co., W. Va., 5/2/63. Not stated if present or absent on muster-in roll dated 8/63. Ab. 11/1/63 - 2/29/64, deserted 9/1/63. Age 38, farmer, Walker Dist., Wood Co., W. Va. 1880 Census. NFR.

FARROW, WILLIAM H. - Pvt. Co. G. b.c. 1844. Enl. Wood Co., W. Va., 5/2/63 (5/12/63). Not stated if present or absent on muster-in roll dated 8/63. Present 11/1/63 - 2/29/64. Clothing issued 2/29/64. Present 7/1/64 - 8/31/64, had his own horse. Ab. 9/1/64 - 10/31/64 (dated 12/29/64), AWOL for 10 days. Cpd. Parkersburg, W. Va., 2/6/65. Charged with being a spy, 2/9/65. Confined at the Atheneum Prison, 3/6/65. Desc.: age 21, 5'8", fair comp., brown hair and gray eyes. Occ. tobacconist, residing in Parkersburg, W. Va. Transf. to Camp Chase, 3/28/65. Confined at Camp Chase, 3/29/65. Took the oath and was released, 3/29/65. Desc.: age 20(?), 5'9", florid comp., black hair and blue eyes, a resident of Wood Co., W. Va. Post war resident of Wood Co., W. Va. Post war rosters list him as a scout. NFR.

FERREL, ROBERT - Pvt. Co. H. Enl. Valley of Va., 10/1/64. Ab. 10/31/63 - 8/31/64, AWOL. Ab. 9/1/64 - 10/31/64 (dated 12/30/64), AWOL. NFR.

FERREL (FERRELL), ROBERT C. - Pvt. Co. E. b.c. 1833. Enl. Camp Miller, 10/1/63. Ab. 1/1/64 - 8/31/64 (dated 1/6/65), cpd. Upshur Co., 10/15/63. Ab. 9/1/64 - 10/31/64 (dated 12/29/64), cpd. Upshur Co., W. Va., 10/30/63; entitled to $100 bond. Deserter. Cpd. Buckhannon, W. Va., 10/20/63 (11/4/63). Confined at the Atheneum Prison, no date. Desc.: age 30, 5'6", fair comp., dark hair and blue eyes, a resident of Upshur Co., W. Va. Transf. to Camp Chase, 11/28/63. Confined at Camp Chase, 11/29/63. Desires to take the oath of allegiance 6/10/64. Took the oath of allegiance and was released, 10/11/64, ordered to report to the Gov. of W. Va. for orders. Desc.: age 30, 5'8", dark comp., dark hair and gray eyes. NFR.

FERRELL, HIRAM - Pvt. Co. ?. b.c. 1848. Post war rosters only, which show he was from Calhoun Co., W. Va. Age 32, farmer, Sheridan Dist., Calhoun Co., W. Va. 1880 Census. NFR.

FERRELL, LEWIS SKIDMORE - Pvt. Co. E. Cpd. and confined at Sandusky, O., by 2/3/62. Released by 2/8/62. Enl. Camp Miller, 10/23/63. Ab. 1/1/64 - 8/31/64 (dated 1/6/65), wd.; entitled to $100 bond. Ab. 9/1/64 - 10/31/64 (dated 12/29/64), wd. near Beverly, W. Va., 7/1/63, since not able for service; entitled to $100 bond. NFR.

FERRELL, S. G. - Pvt. Co. E. Post war rosters only. d. between by 1915. Member Gen. Pegram Camp, UCV, Valley Head, W. Va. Most likely Lewis S. Ferrell.

FISHER, WILLIAM - Pvt. Co. B. Post war rosters only. NFR.

FISHER, WILLIAM R. - Pvt. Co. A. b. 1840. Gravestone shows service in Co. A, 20th Va. Cav. Post war resident of Monongalia Co., W. Va. d. 3/17/1917. Bur. Wisman Cem., Monongalia Co., W. Va.

FISHER, WILLIAM T. - Pvt. Co. K. Enl. Sperryville, 11/20/63. Present 2/29/64 - 8/31/64, mounted; $50 enl. bounty due. NFR.

FITZGERALD, GEORGE - Pvt. Co. I. b.c. 1842. Enl. Camp Northwest, W. Va., 6/2/63, age 21. Not stated if present or absent on muster-in roll dated 5/5/63. NFR.

FITZGERALD, WILLIAM - Pvt. Co. I. b.c. 1841. Enl. Camp Northwest, W. Va., 6/2/63, age 22. Not stated if present or absent on muster-in roll dated 5/5/63. NFR.

FLEISHER (FLESHER), JAMES - Pvt. Co. D. b. Highland Co., 1846. Enl. Hightown, Highland Co., 4/1/64. POW record shows enl. as Bath Co., 6/64. Ab. 12/31/63 - 8/31/64 (dated 1/6/65), AWOL. Ab. 9/1/64 - 10/31/64, AWOL. Deserted. Reported at Clarksburg, W. Va., 11/21/64. Took the oath of allegiance and was released, 11/21/64. Desc.: age 18, 5'10", dark comp., dark hair and black eyes. Occ. farmer, residing in Highland Co. d. 1919. Bur. Monterey Cem., Highland Co.

FLINN, BENJAMIN W. - 5th Sgt. Co. C. b.c. 1838. Enl. Randolph (Pocahontas) Co., W. Va., 5/5/63. Not stated if present or absent on muster-in roll dated 8/63, 5th Sgt. Ab., Pvt., 6/30/63 - 8/31/64 (dated 1/6/65), POW since 12/27/63; 6% bond due. Cpd. Pocahontas Co., W. Va., 12/26/63. Confined at the Atheneum Prison, 1/6/64. Desc.: age 26, 5'6+", fair comp., black hair and hazel eyes. Occ. farmer, residing in Preston Co., W. Va. Transf. to Camp Chase, 1/7/64. Confined at Camp Chase, 1/8/64. Transf. to Ft. Delaware, 3/14/64. Confined at Ft. Delaware, 3/17/64. Ab., Pvt., 9/1/64 - 10/31/64 (dated 12/30/64), POW since 12/27/63; 6% bond due. Took the oath of allegiance and was released, 6/20/65. Desc.: age ?, 5'6", fair comp., dark hair and blue eyes, a resident of Preston Co., W. Va. Age 43, furnace manager, Lyon Dist., Preston Co., W. Va. 1880 Census. NFR.

FLINN, JAMES T. - Pvt. Co. C. b. Fauquier Co., c. 1842. Enl. Pocahontas Co., W. Va., 5/14/63. Not stated if present or absent on muster-in roll dated 8/63. Present 6/30/63 - 8/31/64 (dated 1/6/65), 6% bond due. Ab. 9/1/64 - 10/31/64 (dated 12/30/64), on horse detail; 6% bond due. Clothing issued 9/2/64. Deserted. Reported at Clarksburg, W. Va., 12/31/64. Took the oath of allegiance and was released 1/3/65. Desc.: age 23, 5'10", fair comp., light hair and blue eyes. Occ. farmer, residing in Preston Co., W. Va. Age 38, farmer, Lyon Dist., Preston Co., W. Va. 1880 Census. NFR.

FLINN, WILLIAM T. - Pvt. Co. C. b. Fauquier Co. c. 1844. Enl. Pocahontas Co., W. Va., 5/14/63. Not stated if present or absent on muster-in roll dated 8/63. Ab. 6/30/63 - 8/31/64 (dated 1/6/65), POW since 12/27/63; 6% bond due. Deserted. Surrendered at Rowlesburg, W. Va., 8/24/64 (cpd. Rowlesburg, W. Va., 10/19/64, and sent to Camp Chase, 10/28/64). Desc.: age 20, 5'8", fair comp., dark hair and gray eyes. Occ. farmer, residing in Preston Co., W. Va. Confined at the Atheneum Prison, no date. Desc.: age 20, 5'8", light comp., dark hair and hazel eyes. Ab. 9/1/64 - 10/31/64 (dated 12/30/64), POW since 12/27/63; 6% bond due. Took the oath of allegiance and was released, 9/30/64. NFR.

FLINN, WILLOUGHBY - Pvt. Co. C. Enl. Pocahontas Co., W. Va., 5/18/63. Not stated if present or absent on muster-in roll dated 8/63. Ab. 6/30/63 - 8/31/64 (dated 1/6/65), on detached service; 6% bond due. Ab. 9/1/64 - 10/31/64 (dated 12/30/64), AWOL since 10/11/64; 6% bond due. NFR.

FLORENCE, WILLIAM E. - Pvt. Co. ?. Not on muster rolls. Paroled at Richmond, 4/21/65. NFR.

FOLEY, ANDREW - Pvt. Co. I. b.c. 1836. Enl. Warm Springs, 4/21/63, age 27. Not stated if present or absent on muster-in roll dated 5/5/63. NFR.

FOLEY, JOHN MASON - Sgt. Co. G. b. Wood Co., W. Va., c. 1838. Enl. Wood Co., W. Va., 5/2/63 (Pocahontas Co., W. Va., 5/12/63, age 2/6/63). Not stated if present or absent on muster-in roll dated 8/63, 4th Corp. Wd. Bulltown, W. Va., 10/13/63. Present, 2nd Corp., 11/1/63 - 2/29/64, had his own horse and equipment since 12/27/63. Clothing issued 2/29/64. Present, 1st Corp., 7/1/64 - 8/31/64, has his own horse; entitled to bond. Present, 1st Corp., 9/1/64 - 10/31/64 (dated 12/29/64), entitled to $100 bond. Cpd. Parkersburg, Wood Co., W. Va., 4/4/65, listed as a Sgt. Confined at Clarksburg, W. Va., 4/5/65. Desc.:

207

age 27, 5'11", fair comp., sandy hair and blue eyes. Occ. farmer, residing in Wood Co., W. Va. Transf. to Wheeling, W. Va., 4/6/65. Confined at the Atheneum Prison, 4/6/65. Desc.: age 27, 5'11", fair comp., light hair and blue eyes. Transf. to Camp Chase, 4/13/65. Confined at Camp Chase, 4/14/65, charged with being a guerrilla. Took the oath of allegiance and was released, 6/13/65. Desc.: age 28, 5'11", florid comp., light hair and blue eyes, a resident of Wood Co., W. Va. Postwar resident of Wood Co., W. Va. Age 42, farmer, Outside Parkersburg, Wood Co., W. Va. 1880 Census. NFR.

FORD, JAMES WILLIAM ANDREW - 1st Lt. Co. G. b. Lewisburg, Greenbrier Co., W. Va., 1843. Educated at Custer's Academy, Greenbrier Co., W. Va. Prior service, Co. E, 27th Va. Inf. Post war sketch states that he was discharged from the 27th Va. Inf. and returned to Greenbrier Co., W. Va., where he raised a company of cavalry. Enl. Wood Co., W. Va., 5/12/63. Served as recruiting officer in the Valley of Va., 1/64 - 2/64. Not stated if present or absent, Pvt., 7/1/64 - 8/31/64, has his own horse; entitled to bond. Cpd. Washington, DC (near Rockville, Md.), 7/14/64. Confined at the Old Capitol Prison, 7/14/64. Transf. to Ft. Delaware, 7/22/64. Confined at Ft. Delaware, 7/23/64 at 5 pm, listed as 1st Lt., ADC. Transf. to Hilton Head, SC, 8/20/64, on the steamer Crescent, listed as 3rd Lt., ADC. One of the "Immortal 600." Ab., Pvt., 9/1/64 - 10/31/64 (dated 12/29/64), cpd. Md., 7/13/64; entitled to bond. Arrived at Hilton Head, SC, 8/24/64. Landed at Morris Island, SC, 9/7/64. Transf. to Ft. Pulaski, Ga., 10/21/64. Confined at Ft. Pulaski, Ga., 10/23/64, still there 12/26/64. Transf. from Hilton Head, SC, to Ft. Delaware, 3/12/65. Took the oath of allegiance and was released, 6/17/65, listed as 1st Lt. Desc.: age ?, 5'6", light comp., light hair and blue eyes, a resident of Greenbrier Co., W. Va. CSR shows him as 1st Lt., Co. K, 20th Va. Cav. Post war rosters show him as being a member of the 19th Va. Cav. A highly respected citizen of Lewisburg, W. Va. Post war merchant, Lewisburg, W. Va. Organized a militia company in Greenbrier Co., W. Va., 1888. Post war colonel, 2nd W. Va. Inf. (National Guard), 1889. Post war pensioner and resident of Va., 1915. NFR.

FORD, WINSTON W. - Pvt. Co. I. b.c. 1842. Prior service, Co. E, 27th Va. Inf. Enl. Camp Northwest, W. Va., 7/3/63 (7/1/63), age 21 (Rockbridge Co.), 9/4/63). Not stated if present or absent on muster-in roll dated 5/5/63. Ab. 11/1/63 - 8/31/64 (dated 1/6/65), POW. Deserted. Reported at Clarksburg, W. Va., by 10/15/63 (11/63). Took the oath of allegiance and was sent North, 11/22/63. Desc.: age 22, 5'11", fair comp., dark hair and blue eyes, a resident of Rockingham Co. Ab. 11/1/63 - 10/31/64 (dated 12/31/64), POW. NFR.

FORMASH (FORNASH), W. P. - 2nd Lt. Co. D. Post war rosters only, which show him as a 2nd Lt., and as a resident of Babylon, W. Va. NFR.

FORSYTH, W. O. - Pvt. Co. C. Not on muster rolls. Cpd. Front Royal, 6/30/62 and held on the Steamer Coatzacoalcos. This card is obviously misfiled, as the 20th Va. Cav. did not exist in 1862. NFR.

FOSTER, D. C. - Pvt. Co. C. Enl. Pocahontas Co., W. Va., 3/19/63. Not stated if present or absent on muster-in roll dated 8/63. Ab. 6/30/63 - 8/31/64 (dated 1/6/65), deserted 9/1/63. NFR.

FOWLER, JOHN W. - Pvt. Co. F. b. Harrison Co., W. Va., c. 1842. Resident of Harrison Co., W. Va. Enl. Bulltown, Braxton Co., W. Va., 5/10/63. Not stated if present or absent on muster-in roll dated 7/20/63. Ab. 7/1/63 - 8/31/64 (dated 1/6/65), AWOL. Ab. 9/1/64 - 10/31/64 (dated 12/30/64), AWOL. Deserted. Reported at Clarksburg, W. Va., 11/7/64. Took the oath of allegiance and was released, 11/7/64. Desc.: age 22, 5'9", fair comp., light hair and blue eyes. Occ. farmer, residing in Harrison Co., W. Va. NFR.

FRAME (FRAIM), MARSHALL - Pvt. Co. H. Enl. Calhoun Co., W. Va., 5/16/63. Also as Camp Northwest, W. Va., 6/1/63 (6/28/63). Not stated if present or absent on muster-in roll dated 8/63. Ab. 10/31/63 - 8/31/64, deserted 8/63. Ab. 9/1/64 - 10/31/64 (dated 12/30/64), deserted 6/63. NFR.

FRANKS, STEPHEN J. - Jr. 2nd Lt. Co. A. b.c. 1841. Grew up in Pa. Enl. Augusta Co., 12/25/62, age 23(?). Elected 2nd Sgt. Not stated if present or absent on muster-in roll dated 8/63, 2nd Sgt. Present, 2nd Sgt., 7/1/63 - 9/1/63. Present, 2nd Sgt., 10/31/63 - 8/31/64. Paroled at Staunton, 5/16/65, as Jr. 2nd Lt. Desc.: age 24, 5'10", dark comp., dark hair and blue eyes. Post war resident of Monongalia Co., W. Va. Post war rosters show him as 1st Sgt. "Bold and fearless, of quick thought." NFR.

FRAZIER, JAMES A. - Pvt. Co. I. b.c. 1841. Enl. Camp Northwest, W. Va., 7/19/63, age 22 (Pocahontas Co., W. Va., 7/5/63 and 8/10/63). Not stated if present or absent on muster-in roll dated 5/5/63. Ab. 11/1/63 - 8/31/64 (dated 1/6/65), POW. Ab. 11/1/63 - 10/31/64 (dated 12/31/64), POW. No POW records. NFR.

FREEL (FRIEL), ISRAEL - Pvt. Co. C. b.c. 1844. Age 16, laborer, Edray, Pocahontas Co., W. Va. 1860 Census. Enl. Pocahontas Co., W. Va., 3/19/63. Not stated if present or absent on muster-in roll dated 8/63. Present 6/30/63 - 8/31/64 (dated 1/6/65), 6% bond due. Clothing issued 3/10/64. Ab. 9/1/64 - 10/31/64 (dated 12/30/64), on leave, horse detail; 6% bond due. Horse wd. in knee, Leetown, 8/28/64. Age 35, farmer, Edray, Pocahontas Co., W. Va. 1880 Census. NFR.

FRIEL, WILLIAM T. - Pvt. Co. C. b. 1/3/43. Post war rosters show he was cpd. on the Gatewood Farm (Mountain Grove), Bath Co., on the hill between Back Creek and the Jackson River. Was sent to Camp Chase, where it is reported he DOD. Gravestone in W. Va. shows he d. 4/24/80. Bur. Conrad Cem., Valley Head, Randolph Co., W. Va.

FULWILDER, JAMES W. - Pvt. Co. K. b. Va., c. 1846. Age 14, Rockbridge Baths, Rockbridge Co. 1860 census. Enl. Camp Northwest, W. Va., 6/26/63, age 18. Not stated if present or absent on muster-in roll dated 7/21/63. Ab. 7/1/63 - 11/1/63 (dated 1/6/64), KIA. Droop Mtn., 11/6/63. Ab. 11/1/63 - 2/29/64, KIA. Droop Mtn., 11/6/63. Ab. 2/29/64 - 8/31/64, KIA. Droop Mtn., 11/6/63.

FURBEE (FERBEE), AARON - 3rd Corp. Co. A. b.c. 1835. Enl. Pocahontas Co., W. Va., 3/23/63, age 26. Not stated if present or absent on muster-in roll dated 3/23/63, 3rd Corp. Present, 3rd Corp., 7/1/63 - 9/1/63. Ab., 3rd Corp., 10/31/63 - 8/31/64, AWOL since 6/64. Clothing issued 3rd Qr. 1864. Deserted. Surrendered at Wheeling, W. Va., 10/20/64. Confined at the Atheneum Prison. Took the amnesty oath and was released 10/20/64. Desc.: age 29, 5'6", dark comp., light hair and hazel eyes, a resident of Marion Co., W. Va. Post war resident of Marion Co., W. Va. "A good soldier." Age 45, farmer, Mannington Dist., Marion Co., W. Va. 1880 Census. NFR.

FURBEE (FERBEE), CALEB - Pvt. Co. A. b.c. 1842. Resident of Marion Co., W. Va. Enl. Augusta Co., 2/15/63, age 21. Not stated if present or absent on muster-in roll dated 2/15/63. Present 7/1/63 - 9/1/63. Ab. 10/31/63 - 8/31/64, (listed as present); reported as KIA. Beverly, W. Va., 10/26/64. Wd./Cpd. Beverly, W. Va., 10/29/64. Adm. USA Gen. Hosp., Beverly, W. Va., 10/20/64, wd. right shoulder. Treated with simple dressing. DOW. Beverly, W. Va., 11/1/64. "A good soldier."

FURBEE (FERBEE), JACOB - Pvt. Co. A. b. Marion Co., W. Va., c. 1838. Enl. Pocahontas Co., W. Va., 5/12/63, age 25. POW record shows enl. as Philippi, W. Va., 5/62. Not stated if present or absent on muster-in roll dated 5/12/63. Cpd. Grafton,

W. Va., 5/17/63. Confined at Ft. McHenry. Paroled and sent to Ft. Monroe, 5/20/63, to be exchanged, signs by x. Present 7/1/63 - 9/1/63. Present 10/31/63 - 8/31/64. Clothing issued 2/29/64 and 3rd Qr. 1864. Deserted. Surrendered at Mannington, W. Va., 2/3/65. Sent to Clarksburg, W. Va. Confined at Clarksburg, W. Va., 2/4/65. Took the amnesty oath and was sent North, 3/7/65. Desc.: age 27, 5'9", light comp., light hair and blue eyes. Occ. farmer, residing in Marion Co., W. Va. Held in Post Guard House, awaiting petition for his release. Confined at the Atheneum Prison, 3/7/65. Desc.: age 24(?), 5'9", fair comp., light hair and gray eyes. "A good soldier." Post war resident of Marion Co., W. Va. NFR.

GAINER, SYLVESTER - 3rd Sgt. Co. H. b.c. 1844. Prior service, Co. A, Maj. D. B. Stewart's Battn. (called 1st Va. Reg't.) Va. Cav. Cpd. Calhoun Co., W. Va., 11/27/62 (9/15/62). Confined at the Atheneum Prison, 12/4/62. Desc.: age 18, 5'6 3/4", sallow comp., auburn hair and blue eyes. Occ. farmer, residing in Calhoun Co., W. Va. Transf. to Camp Chase, 12/6/62. Confined at Camp Chase, 12/7/62. Paroled at Alton, Ill., and sent to City Point, to be exchanged, 4/1/63. Exchanged City Point, 4/8/63. Enl. Camp Northwest, W. Va., 6/1/63 (6/2/63). Also as having enl. in Greenbrier Co., W. Va., 3/1/63. Not stated if present or absent on muster-in roll dated 8/63, Pvt. Ab., 3rd Sgt., 10/31/63 - 8/31/64, in hands of enemy since 10/63. Deserted. Took the oath of allegiance and gave bond, 12/25/63. Ab., 4th Sgt., 9/1/64 - 10/31/64 (dated 12/30/64), prisoner, in hands of enemy, cpd. 10/63. NFR.

GALFORD, THOMAS - Pvt. Co. C. b. Pocahontas Co., W. Va., c. 1820. Enl. Pocahontas Co., W. Va., 7/1/63. Also as having enl. in Highland Co., 8/20/63. POW record shows enl. as Pocahontas Co., W. Va., 5/61. Ab. 6/30/63 - 8/31/64 (dated 1/6/65), on detached service; transf. to Co. G, 18th Va. Cav. Ab. 9/1/64 - 10/31/64 (dated 12/30/64), sick. Post war rosters show he was detailed to go to Alleghany Mtn., fall 1864.Deserted. Reported at Buckhannon, W. Va., 1/20/65. Sent to Clarksburg, W. Va. Confined at Clarksburg, W. Va., 1/22/65. Took the amnesty oath and was released, 1/22/65. Desc.: age 45, 5'9", dark comp., brown hair and brown eyes. Occ. farmer, residing in Lewis Co., W. Va. NFR.

GALL, ANDREW J. - Pvt. Co. D. b. Pendleton Co., W. Va., 1829. Enl. Camp Scott, 7/20/63. Not stated if present or absent on muster-in roll dated 8/63. Present 7/1/63 - 1/1/64 (dated 1/1/64), entitled to enl. bounty; had his own horse. Present 12/31/63 - 8/31/64 (dated 1/6/65). Clothing issued 2/29/64. Present 9/1/64 - 10/31/64. Post war farmer and resident of Stewart's Run, Barbour Co., W. Va. Age 50, farmer, Elk, Barbour Co., W. Va. 1880 Census. NFR.

GALL, BURTON M. "Bert" - Pvt. Co. D. Enl. Camp Pisgah, Bath Co., 12/1/63. Present 7/1/63 - 1/1/64 (dated 1/1/64), entitled to enl. bounty; had his own horse. Present 12/31/63 - 8/31/64 (dated 1/6/65). Clothing issued 2/29/64. Present 9/1/64 - 10/31/64, entitled to $100 bond. Post war resident of Barbour Co., W. Va. Age 43, farmer, Elk, Barbour Co., W. Va. 1880 Census, listed as Bertin M. Gall. NFR.

GALL, LAFAYETTE E. - Pvt. Co. D. Enl. Spaw Lick, 5/1/63. Not stated if present or absent on muster-in roll dated 8/63. NFR.

GALLAGHER, JOHN - Pvt. Co. I. Enl. Strasburg, 8/15/64. Ab. 11/1/63 - 8/31/64 (dated 1/6/65), on horse detail. NFR.

GARRISON, GEORGE - Pvt. Co. A. Post war rosters only, which show he was a resident of Monongalia Co., W. Va. NFR.

GARVIS (JARVIS), WILLIAM - Pvt. Co. A. Post war rosters only, which show he was a resident of Monongalia Co., W. Va. NFR.

GASTON, DAVISSON - Pvt. Co. E. Enl. Bulltown, Braxton Co., W. Va., 5/10/63. Not stated if present or absent on muster-in roll dated 7/18/63. NFR.

GASTON, JAMES W. - Pvt. Co. E. b. 1838. Enl. Bulltown, Braxton Co., W. Va., 5/10/63. Not stated if present or absent on muster-in roll dated 7/18/63. Ab. 1/1/64 - 8/31/64 (dated 1/6/65), sick in Staunton Gen. Hosp.; entitled to $100 bond. Ab. 9/1/64 - 10/31/64 (dated 12/29/64), sick in Staunton Gen. Hosp.; entitled to $100 bond. Adm. CSA Gen. Hosp., Charlottesville, 9/26/64, debility. Transf. to Lynchburg, 9/27/64. Post war resident of Lost Creek, W. Va. d. 1921. Bur. Lost Creek Cem.

GAWTHROP, JOSEPH L. W. - Pvt. Co. A. b.c. 1842. Enl. Pocahontas Co., W. Va., 4/18/63. Not stated if present or absent on muster-in roll dated 4/18/63. Present 7/1/63 - 9/1/63. Post war merchant and resident of Upshur Co., W. Va. "A brave man who rather than surrender, left his bed barefoot and had his toes froze off." NFR.

GAY, HAMILTON B. - Pvt. Co. G. b.c. 1842. Age 18, farmer, Mill Point, Pocahontas Co., W. Va. 1860 Census. Post war rosters only. Age 38, works on farm, Edray, Pocahontas Co., W. Va. 1880 Census. NFR.

GENTRY, ANDREW S. - Pvt. Co. C. b.c. 1838. Age 22, laborer, Randolph Co., W. Va. 1860 Census. Enl. Randolph (Pocahontas) Co., W. Va., 5/5/63. Not stated if present or absent on muster-in roll dated 8/63. Ab. 6/30/63 - 8/31/64 (dated 1/6/65), POW since 11/4/63; 6% bond due. Cpd. Philippi, W. Va., 11/6/63. Confined at the Atheneum Prison, 11/16/63. Desc.: age 25, 6'4", fair comp., light hair and brown eyes. Occ. farmer, residing in Randolph Co., W. Va. Transf. to Camp Chase, 11/18/63. Confined at Camp Chase, 11/18/63. Desires to take the oath of allegiance, 6/10/64, listed as a deserter. Ab. 9/1/64 - 10/31/64 (dated 12/30/64), POW since 11/4/63; 6% bond due. Enl. in the US Navy, 7/20/64 (7/21/64), and was released. d. by 8/7/1916. NFR.

GENTRY, ISAAC S. - 1st Sgt. Co. C. b. Green Co., W. Va., c. 1835. Enl. Randolph Co., W. Va., 5/14/63. POW record shows enl. as Green, W. Va., 4/61. Not stated if present or absent on muster- in roll dated 8/63, 2nd Sgt. Ab., 2nd Sgt., 6/30/63 - 8/31/64 (dated 1/6/65), sick. Clothing issued 3/10/64, 3/20/64 and 3rd Qr. 1864. Ab., 2nd Sgt., 9/1/64 - 10/31/64 (dated 12/30/64), AWOL. Deserted. Reported at Philippi, W. Va., 2/4/65. Confined at Clarksburg, W. Va., 2/5/65. Took the amnesty oath and was sent to Ohio, 2/9/65, listed as 1st Sgt. Desc.: age 30, 6', fair comp., light hair and blue eyes. Occ. mechanic, residing in W. Va. Post war pensioner and resident of Okla., 1915. Cards in the CSR shows name as Jacob S. Gentry. Resident of Avard, Okla., 1916. NFR.

GIBSON, GEORGE W. - Pvt. Co. E. Resident of Wirt Co., W. Va. Arrested and confined by 3/15/62. Charged with being a secessionist. Enl. Winchester, 8/15/64 (8/1/64). Ab. 1/1/64 - 8/31/64 (dated 1/6/65), AWOL since 8/25/64. Ab. 9/1/64 - 10/31/64 (dated 12/29/64), AWOL since 8/10/64). NFR.

GIGER (GEIGER, GUIGER), GODFREY - Pvt. Co. C. b.c. 1849. Enl. Pocahontas Co., W. Va., 4/1/64. Ab. 6/30/63 - 8/31/64 (dated 1/6/65), transf. to Co. A, 62nd Va. Inf. (Mounted), 4/10/64. Age 31, farmer, Edray, Pocahontas Co., W. Va. 1880 Census. NFR.

GILMORE (GILMER), WILLIAM B. (E.) - Pvt. Co. K. b.c. 1843. Enl. Camp Northwest, W. Va., 5/10/63, age 20. Not stated if present or absent on muster-in roll dated 7/21/63. Ab. 7/1/63 - 11/1/63 (dated 1/6/64), POW, cpd. Droop Mtn., 11/6/63; lost Sharps Rifle. Ab. 11/1/63 - 2/29/64, cpd. Droop Mtn., 11/6/63. Cpd. Lewisburg, W. Va., 11/7/63. Confined at the Atheneum Prison,

11/20/63. Desc.: age 20, 5'6", light comp., black hair and hazel eyes. Occ. sailor, residing in Richmond. Transf. to Camp Chase, 11/20/63. Confined at Camp Chase, 11/21/63. Ab. 2/29/64 - 8/31/64, cpd. Droop Mtn., 11/6/63. Desires to take the oath of allegiance, 6/10/64. Enl. in the US Navy, 7/21/64, but did not go as he was sick in the hosp. Took the oath of allegiance and was released 5/13/65. Desc.: age ?, 5'6", dark comp., black hair and black eyes, a resident of New York City, NY. NFR.

GILPIN, WALKER - Pvt. Co. G. Post war rosters only, which show he was a resident of Wood Co., W. Va. NFR.

GINGER, JAMES P. - Pvt. Co. K. b.c. 1836. Prior service, Co. G, 11th Va. Cav. Enl. Camp Northwest, W. Va., 6/2/63, age 27. Not stated if present or absent on muster-in roll dated 7/21/63. Ab. 7/1/63 - 11/1/63 (dated 1/6/64), claimed by another command. Post war resident of Bath Co. Age 42, farm laborer, Little Level, Pocahontas Co., W. Va. 1880 Census. Bur. Ruckman-Gilmor Cem., Mill Gap, Highland Co.

GISINGER, ADAM M. (W.) - Pvt. Co. A. b. Va., c. 1847. Age 14, 6th Dist., Rockbridge Co. 1860 Census. Not on muster rolls. Cpd. near Lexington, 6/11/64. Confined at the Atheneum Prison, 7/1/64. Desc.: age 17, 5'10", florid comp., dark hair and blue eyes. Occ. miller, residing in Rockbridge Co. Transf. to Camp Chase, 7/2/64. Confined at Camp Chase, 7/3/64. Was to be exchanged, 3/2/65, but had DOD. Camp Chase, 2/22/65, pneumonia. Bur. Camp Chase Confederate Cem., grave no. 1388. NFR.

GLASSCOCK (GLASKOCK), CHARLES E. - Pvt. Co. B. Prior service, Co. D, 19th Va. Cav. Enl. Williamsburg, Greenbrier Co., W. Va., 3/17/63. Not stated if present or absent on muster-in roll dated 7/25/63. Ab. 11/1/63 - 8/31/64 (dated 1/6/65), DOD. Mt. Jackson, 7/31/64. Probably bur. at Mt. Jackson. Clothing issued 3/31/64. Post war rosters show service in 26th Battn. Va. Inf.

GLOVER, LEONARD - Pvt. Co. B. Enl. Hightown, Highland Co., 10/19/62 (11/6/62). Not stated if present or absent on muster-in roll dated 7/25/63. Present 11/1/63 - 8/31/64 (dated 1/6/65). Clothing issued 3/31/64. Present 9/1/64 - 10/31/64 (dated 12/30/64), entitled to $100 bond. Post war resident of Marion Co., W. Va. NFR.

GOFF, CLAUDIUS "Claude" - Pvt. Co. C. b.c. 1833. Enl. Pocahontas Co., W. Va., 9/1/63. Present 6/30/63 - 8/31/64 (dated 1/6/65), enl. bounty due. Present 9/1/64 - 10/31/64 (dated 12/30/64). Paroled at Staunton, 5/15/65. Desc.: age 32, 5'7", light comp., black hair and blue eyes. Post war resident of Randolph Co., W. Va. Age 47, lawyer, Beverly, Randolph Co., W. Va. 1880 Census. d. by 1916. Bur. in Randolph Co., W. Va. NFR.

GOFF, JOHN W. - Pvt. Co. H. Enl. Camp Northwest, W. Va., 7/1/63 (6/28/63). Not stated if present or absent on muster-in roll dated 8/63. Present 10/31/63 - 8/31/64, has one horse since 11/1/63. Clothing issued 2/29/64. Present 9/1/64 - 10/31/64 (dated 12/30/64), entitled to $100 bond. NFR.

GOFF, MARSELIUS A. - Pvt. Co. H. Enl. Camp Northwest, W. Va., 7/1/63 (6/28/63). Not stated if present or absent on muster-in roll dated 8/63. Ab. 10/31/63 - 8/31/64, in hands of enemy since 8/63. Not stated if present or absent, 9/1/64 - 10/31/64 (dated 12/30/64). NFR.

GOFF, PHILIP - Corp. Co. H. b. 6/20/39. Enl. Camp Northwest, W. Va., 7/1/63 (6/28/63). Not stated if present or absent on muster-in roll dated 8/63. Ab. 10/31/63 - 8/31/64, in hands of the enemy since 10/63. Ab. 9/1/64 - 10/31/64 (dated 12/30/64), prisoner in hands of the enemy since 8/63. No POW records. Age 41, farmer, Murphy Dist., Ritchie Co., W. Va. 1880 Census. d. 7/14/1913. Bur. Bethany Cem., Goff's, Ritchie Co., W. Va.

GOLDFISH, HENRY L. - Pvt. Co. I. b.c. 1842. Enl. Lewisburg, W. Va., 4/20/63, age 21. Not stated if present or absent on muster-in roll dated 5/5/63. NFR.

GOLDEN, L. B. - Pvt. Co. H. b.c. 1840. Not on muster rolls. Reference jacket only, which shows service in Co. B, 46th Battn. Va. Cav. DOD. Camp Chase. Bur. Camp Chase Confederate Cem. Post war rosters show service in Co. K, 20th Va. Cav.

GOLDEN, WILLIAM HENRY - Pvt. Co. H. b.c. 1844. Not on muster rolls. Reference jacket only, which shows service in Co. B, 46th Battn. Va. Cav. NFR.

GOLDRICK, MICHAEL E. - Pvt. Co. I. b. New Orleans, La., c. 1838. Not on muster rolls. POW record shows enl. as New Orleans, La., 4/61. Deserted. Reported at Beverly, W. Va., 11/10/64. Sent to Clarksburg, W. Va. Took the oath of allegiance and was released, 11/13/64. Desc.: age 26, 5'9", fair comp., light hair and gray eyes. Occ. printer, residing in New Orleans, La. NFR.

GOODBAR, GEORGE - Pvt. Co. K. b. Upper Kerr's Creek, Rockbridge Co., 4/15/36. Farmer, Collierstown, Rockbridge Co. 1860 Census. Prior service, Co. E, 27th Va. Inf. Enl. Camp Northwest, W. Va., 7/16/63, age 27(?). Not stated if present or absent on muster-in roll dated 7/16/63. Ab. 7/1/63 - 11/1/63 (dated 1/6/64), AWOL. Farmhand, Buffalo Dist., Rockbridge Co. 1870 Census. Farmer, Collierstown, 1884. d. Collierstown, 6/24/1907. Bur. Collierstown Presby. Ch. Cem.

GOODBAR, JOHN MARION - Pvt. Co. I. b. Rockbridge Co., c. 1844. Enl. Camp Northwest, W. Va., 7/16/63, age 19. Also as having enl. at Camp Martin, 9/10/64 and in Rockbridge Co., 9/4/64. POW record shows enl. as Rockbridge Co., 9/63. Not stated if present or absent on muster-in roll dated 5/5/63. Ab. 11/1/63 - 8/31/64 (dated 1/6/65), AWOL. Clothing issued 2/29/64. Ab. 11/1/63 - 10/31/64 (dated 12/31/64), AWOL. Cpd. Beverly, W. Va., 10/18/64. Sent to Clarksburg, W. Va. Took the oath of allegiance and was released, 10/23/64. Desc.: age 20, 5'8", fair comp., light hair and hazel eyes. Occ. farmer, residing in Rockbridge Co. NFR.

GOODBAR, WILLIAM HARVEY - Pvt. Co. I. b. Rockbridge Co., c. 1843. Age 17, farmhand, Collierstown, Rockbridge Co. 1860 Census. Enl. Camp Northwest, W. Va., 7/16/63, age 20. Also as having enl. at Camp Martin, 9/10/64 and in Rockbridge Co., 9/4/64. Not stated if present or absent on muster-in roll dated 5/5/63. Ab. 11/1/63 - 8/31/64 (dated 1/6/65), at home sick. Ab. 11/1/63 - 10/31/64 (dated 12/31/64), sick. Age 27, farmhand, Buffalo Dist., Rockbridge Co. 1870 Census. Farmer, Kerr's Creek Moved to Cass Co., Mo., 1874. d. Cass Co., Mo., 1924. Bur. Fulton Cem., Mo.

GOODWIN, JAMES C. - Pvt. Co. D. Enl. Hightown, Highland Co., 1/20/64 (1/2/64). Present 7/1/63 - 1/1/64 (dated 1/1/64), entitled to enl. bounty. Ab. 12/31/63 - 8/31/64 (dated 1/6/65), on detached service; entitled to enl. bounty. Ab. 9/1/64 - 10/31/64, on detached service. NFR.

GORDON, WILLIAM F. Jr. - Capt. Co. E. Prior service, Co. B, 17th Va. Cav. Not on muster rolls. Paroled at Charlottesville, 5/17/65, as a member of Co. E, 20th Va. Cav. Residence listed as Harrison Co., W. Va. NFR.

GOUGH, BENJAMIN - Pvt. Co. G. Not on muster rolls. Entered the Old Soldier's Home, Pikesville, Md., 2/7/??, age 57, from St. Mary's Co., Md., a MD. NFR.

GOULD, DEXTER - Pvt. Co. D. b. Upshur Co., W. Va., c. 1841. Resident of Upshur Co., W. Va. Enl. Weston, W. Va., 5/1/63. POW record shows enl. as Pocahontas Co., W. Va. Not stated if present or absent on muster-in roll dated 8/63. Present 7/1/63 - 1/1/64 (dated 1/1/64), has his own horse. Ab. 12/31/63 - 8/31/64 (dated 1/6/65), prisoner. Clothing issued 2/29/64. Ab. 9/1/64 - 10/31/64, POW. Wd./Cpl. Beverly, W. Va., 10/29/64. Adm. USA Post Hosp., Beverly, W. Va., 10/29/64, wd., left wrist and hand. Treated by simple dressing. Sent to Clarksburg, W. Va., 11/21/64. Confined at Clarksburg, W. Va., 1/9/65. Desc.: age 24, 5'7", dark comp., brown hair and hazel eyes. Occ. farmer, residing in Upshur Co., W. Va. Transf. to Wheeling, W. Va., 1/10/65. Confined at the Atheneum Prison, 1/11/65. Desc.: age 24, 5'7+", fair comp., brown hair and hazel eyes. Transf. to Camp Chase, 1/16/65. Confined at Camp Chase, 1/17/65. Transf. to Pt. Lookout, 3/26/65, to be exchanged. Confined at Pt. Lookout, 3/31/65. Took the oath of allegiance and was released, 6/4/65. Age 40, farmer, Buckhannon, Upshur Co., W. Va. 1880 Census. NFR.

GREATHOUSE, ALEXANDER W. - Pvt. Co. D. b.c. 1843. Enl. Weston, W. Va., 5/1/63. Not stated if present or absent on muster-in roll dated 8/63. Present 7/1/63 - 1/1/64 (dated 1/1/64), had his own horse. Present 12/31/63 -.8/31/64 (dated 1/6/65). Clothing issued 2/29/64. Present 9/1/64 - 10/31/64, entitled to $100 enl. bounty. Paroled at Staunton, 5/19/65, signs by x. Desc.: age 22, 5'4", light comp., light hair and blue eyes. NFR.

GREATHOUSE, JAMES A. - Pvt. Co. B. b.c. 1846. Prior service, Co. D, 19th Va. Cav. Enl. Williamsburg, Greenbrier Co., W. Va., 3/17/63. Not stated if present or absent on muster-in roll dated 7/25/63. Ab. 11/1/63 - 8/31/64 (dated 1/6/65), prisoner since 9/64; unfit for duty, sick. Clothing issued 3/31/64. Ab. 9/1/64 - 10/31/64 (dated 12/30/64), POW since 9/64. Cpd. Charleston, W. Va., 9/8/64. Confined at the Atheneum Prison, 9/12/64. Desc.: age 23, 5'8", fair comp., dark hair and gray eyes. Occ. farmer, residing in Doddridge Co., W. Va. Transf. to Camp Chase, 9/15/64. Confined at Camp Chase, 9/17/64. Took the oath of allegiance and was released, 6/11/65. Desc.: age 20(?), 5'8+", fair comp., dark hair and hazel eyes, a resident of Doddridge Co., W. Va. Age 34, farmer, Southwest Dist., Doddridge Co., W. Va. 1880 Census. NFR.

GREGG (GRAGG), JACOB - Pvt. Co. H. b.c. 1830. Took the oath of allegiance before joining the rebel service. Enl. Camp Northwest, W. Va., 7/1/63 (6/28/63). Not stated if present or absent on muster-in roll dated 8/63. Ab. 10/31/63 - 8/31/64, in hands of enemy since 10/63. Deserted. Cpd. Ritchie Co., W. Va., 10/13/63 (10/12/63). Confined at the Atheneum Prison, 10/24/63. Desc.: age 35, 5'5", fair comp., dark hair, gray eyes and dark whiskers. Occ. farmer, residing in Ritchie Co., W. Va. Transf. to Camp Chase, 10/26/63. Confined at Camp Chase, 10/27/63. Transf. to Rock Island, Ill., 1/22/64. Confined at Rock Island Prison, 1/?/64. Desires to take the oath of allegiance, 3/18/64, wishes to go home. Ab. 9/1/64 - 10/31/64 (dated 12/30/64), cpd. 10/63. Took the oath of allegiance and was released, 2/16/65. Desc.: age 35, 5'4", dark comp., black hair and dark eyes, a resident of Boone Creek, W. Va. Cpd. Ritchie Co., W. Va., 2/16/65. Confined at the Atheneum Prison, 4/6/65. NFR.

GREGORY, WILLIAM H. - Pvt. Co. D. b. Nicholas Co., W. Va., c. 1849. Age 11, Webster Co., W. Va. 1860 Census. Enl. Hightown, Highland Co., 6/27/63. Not stated if present or absent on muster- in roll dated 8/63. Ab. 7/1/63 - 1/1/64 (dated 1/1/64), AWOL since 8/63. Ab. 12/31/63 - 8/31/64 (dated 1/6/65), AWOL since 8/63. Ab. 9/1/64 - 10/31/64, AWOL. Age 32, farmer, Fork Lick, Webster Co., W. Va. 1880 Census. NFR.

GROGG, JOHN - Pvt. Co. ?. b. Highland Co., c. 1844. Age 16, farmhand, New Hamden, Highland Co. 1860 Census. Post war rosters only, which show he was a resident of Highland Co. Prior service, Co. E (D), 31st Va. Inf. NFR.

GULLEY, JOSEPH N. B. - Pvt. Co. E. b.c. 1846. Enl. Bulltown, W. Va., 5/10/63. Not stated if present or absent on muster-in roll dated 7/18/63. Present 1/1/64 - 8/31/64 (dated 1/6/65), entitled to $100 bond. Present 9/1/64 - 10/31/64 (dated 12/29/64), entitled to $100 bond. Cpd. Upshur Co., W. Va., 4/8/65. Sent to Clarksburg, W. Va. Paroled at Clarksburg, W. Va., 4/22/65. Desc.: age 19, 5'9", fair comp., auburn hair and gray eyes. Occ. farmer, residing in Upshur Co., W. Va. NFR.

GUM, AARON DeKALB - Pvt. Co. C. b. Highland Co., 1/10/39. Age 21, farmhand, Hightown, Highland Co. 1860 Census. Prior service, 25th Va. Inf. Enl. Pocahontas Co., W. Va., 6/1/63. Also as having enl. in Highland Co. POW record shows he enl. in Pocahontas Co., W. Va., 5/62. Not stated if present or absent on muster-in roll dated 8/63. Present 6/30/63 - 8/31/64 (dated 1/6/65), 6% bond due. Clothing issued 3/10/64. Ab. 9/1/64 - 10/31/64 (dated 12/30/64), on detached service by order of Gen. Jubal A. Early; 6% bond due. Deserted. Reported at Beverly, W. Va., 11/7/64. Sent to Clarksburg, W. Va. Took the oath of allegiance and was released, 11/10/64. Desc.: age 26, 5'9", fair comp., dark hair and hazel eyes. Occ. farmer, residing in Highland Co. Post war rosters show unit as Capt. Hutton's Mounted Inf. Member S. B. Gibbons Camp, UCV, Harrisonburg, 1896. Age 61, farmer, Blue Grass Dist., Highland Co. 1900 Census. d. Meadowdale, Highland Co., 3/5/1921. Bur. Wade Family Cem., Highland Co.

GUM, WILLIAM WASHINGTON - Pvt. Co. C. b. Highland Co., c. 1840 (1842). Age 20, farmhand, Meadow Dale, Highland Co. 1860 Census. Prior service, Co. F, 25th Va. Inf. Enl. Pocahontas Co., W. Va., 6/1/63. Also as having enl. Highland Co. Not stated if present or absent on muster-in roll dated 8/63. Ab. 6/30/63 - 8/31/64 (dated 1/6/65), on detached service. Clothing issued 3/10/64. Present 9/1/64 - 10/31/64 (dated 12/30/64). Paroled at Staunton, 5/24/65. Desc.: age 23, 5'5", fair comp., fair hair and blue eyes. d. Back Creek, Highland Co., 11/3/1916, heart trouble.

GUY, PETER - Pvt. Co. I and Co. K. b.c. 1840. Enl. Camp Northwest, W. Va., 6/17/63, age 23, in Co. I. Not stated if present or absent on muster-in roll dated 5/5/63. Enl. Camp Northwest, W. Va., 6/18/63 in Co. K. Not stated if present or absent on muster-in roll dated 7/21/63. NFR.

HAINS (HAINES), OLIVER P. - Pvt. Co. A. b.c. 1830. Enl. Pocahontas Co, W. Va., 3/19/63, age 33. Not stated if present or absent on muster-in roll dated 3/19/63. Present 7/1/63 - 9/1/63. Ab. 10/31/63 - 8/31/64, AWOL since 10/1/64. NFR.

HALL, ALLEN S. - 4th Sgt. Co. A. b. Ritchie Co., W. Va., c. 1845. Resident of near New Martinsville. Enl. Richmond, 2/1/63, age 19. POW record shows enl. Richmond, 1/62. Not stated if present or absent on muster-in roll dated 2/1/63, 2nd Corp. Present, 2nd Corp., 7/1/63 - 9/1/63. Present, 2nd Corp., 10/31/63 8/31/64. Detailed to guard prisoners, 12/63. Cpd. Barbour Co., W. Va., 2/12/65 (2/11/65), by a citizen, listed as 4th Sgt. Confined at Clarksburg, W. Va., 2/12/65. Desc.: age 21, 5'4", fair comp., light hair and brown eyes. Occ. farmer, residing in Ritchie Co., W. Va. Transf. to Wheeling, W. Va. Confined at the Atheneum Prison, 2/20/65. Desc.: age 21, 5'4", fair comp., light hair and gray eyes. Transf. to Camp Chase, 2/21/65. Confined at Camp Chase, 2/22/65. Took the oath of allegiance and was released, 6/13/65. Desc.: age 22, 5'6", florid comp., dark hair and hazel eyes, a resident of Henrico Co. Post war rosters show he was a resident of Wetzel Co., W. Va. Moved west after the war, where he lost his life in the Rocky Mtn's. Post war source states he may have served in the US Cav. after the war. d. between 1880 and 1890, Ft. Sill, Indian Territory (Okla.).

HALL (HALE), ANDREW A. - Pvt. Co. A. Enl. Bath Co., 3/27/63. Present 7/1/63 - 9/1/63. Probably Andrew H. Hale, below. NFR.

HALL, ANDREW H. - Pvt. Co. A. Post war rosters only, which show he was a resident of Barbour Co., W. Va. Probably Andrew A. Hall, above. NFR.

HALL, ANDREW JACKSON - Pvt. Co. B. b. Monongalia Co., W. Va., c. 1836. Enl. Hightown, Highland Co., 11/4/62. POW record shows enl. as Highland Co., 10/62. Not stated if present or absent on muster-in roll dated 7/25/63. Present 11/1/63 - 8/31/64 (dated 1/6/65), prisoner. Clothing issued 2/29/64 and 3/31/64. Present 9/1/64 - 10/31/64 (dated 12/30/64), entitled to $100 bond. Cpd. Taylor Co., W. Va., 10/24/64 (Cairo, W. Va., 10/17/64). Sent to Clarksburg, W. Va. Desc.: age 28, 5'10", light comp., dark hair and gray eyes. Occ. farmer, residing in Monongalia Co., W. Va. Transf. to Wheeling, W. Va., 10/31/64. Confined at the Atheneum Prison, 10/31/64. Transf. to Camp Chase, 11/22/64. Confined at Camp Chase, 11/23/64, desires to take the oath of allegiance. Took the oath of allegiance and was released, 5/15/65, signs by x. Desc.: age 30, 5'10+" dark comp., dark hair and hazel eyes, a resident of Marion Co., W. Va. NFR.

HALL, WILLIAM - Pvt. Co. D. b. Barbour Co., W. Va., c. 1826. Enl. Weston, W. Va., 5/1/63. POW record shows enl. as Bath Co., 5/63. Not stated if present or absent on muster-in roll dated 8/63. Present 7/1/63 - 1/1/64 (dated 1/1/64), has his own horse. Ab. 12/31/63 - 8/31/64 (dated 1/6/65), AWOL since 9/24/64. Clothing issued 2/29/64. Ab. 9/1/64 - 10/31/64, AWOL. Cpd. Philippi, W. Va,, 10/18/64. Sent to Clarksburg, W. Va. Desc.: age 38, 5'8", light comp., light hair and blue eyes. Occ. farmer, residing in Barbour Co., W. Va. Adm. USA Post Hosp., Clarksburg, W. Va., 10/28/64, rheumatism. Released to Provost Marshall, 12/4/64. Age 53, farmer, Union Dist., Barbour Co., W. Va. 1880 Census. NFR.

HAMILTON, ELMOS W. - 3rd Sgt. Co. B. b. Marion Co., W. Va., c. 1843. Prior service, Co. D, 19th Va. Cav. Enl. Williamsburg, Greenbrier Co., W. Va., 3/17/63. Enl. also as Marion Co., W. Va., 4/15/63. POW record shows his enl. as Highland Co., 8/62. Not stated if present or absent on muster-in roll dated 7/25/63, 3rd Sgt. Ab., 3rd Sgt., 11/1/63 - 8/31/64 (dated 1/6/65), AWOL. Clothing issued 3/31/64. Ab., 3rd Sgt., 9/1/64 - 10/31/64 (dated 12/30/64), AWOL. Cpd. Barrackville, W. Va., 9/27/64. Sent to Clarksburg, W. Va. Took the oath of allegiance and was released, 10/5/64. Desc.: age 22, 5'8", dark comp., dark hair and brown eyes. Occ. farmer, residing in Marion Co., W. Va. Age 38, farmer, Lincoln Dist., Marion Co., W. Va. 1880 Census, listed as Elmas W. Hamilton. NFR.

HAMILTON, GEORGE D. - Pvt. Co. I. b. Bath Co., 2/24/44. Age 16, Bath CH, Bath Co., 1860 Census. Resident of Back Creek, Bath Co. Enl. Camp Northwest, W. Va., 5/20/63, age 19. Not stated if present or absent on muster-in roll dated 5/5/63. Post war rosters and gravestone show service in Co. F, 11th Va. Cav. K. accidentally near Fairview (Bath Alum), Bath Co., 12/23/63 (12/24/63), shot through head. Was riding alone, when the strap holding the gun of a soldier who was marching close by, broke. The gun struck the ground and discharged, the ball passing through his head. Had a pass to go to his home the next day. Bur. George Cleek Cem., Bath Co.

HAMILTON, HENRY (HARVEY) - Pvt. Co. K. b.c. 1845. Enl. Camp Northwest, W. Va., 6/21/63 (6/18/63), age 18. Not stated if present or absent on muster-in roll dated 7/21/63. Ab. 7/1/63 - 11/1/63 (dated 1/6/64), AWOL. Ab. 11/1/63 - 2/29/64, AWOL. Ab. 2/29/64 - 8/31/64, AWOL. NFR.

HAMILTON, JAMES M. - 1st Corp. Co. B. b.c. 1840. Prior service, Co. D, 19th Va. Cav. Enl. Williamsburg, Greenbrier Co., W. Va., 3/17/63 (4/15/63). Not stated if present or absent on muster-in roll dated 7/25/63, 1st Corp. Ab., 1st Corp., 11/1/63 - 8/31/64 (dated 1/6/65), prisoner in hands of enemy. Cpd. Farmington, Marion Co., W. Va., 11/5/63. Confined at the Atheneum Prison, 11/12/63. Desc.: age 23, 5'9", fair comp., dark hair and blue eyes. Occ. farmer, residing in Marion Co., W. Va. Transf. to Camp Chase, 1/16/64. Confined at Camp Chase, 1/17/64, desires to take the oath of allegiance. Ab., 1st Corp., 9/1/64 - 10/31/64 (dated 12/30/64), POW since 10/63. Took the oath of allegiance and was released, 5/15/65. Desc.: age 23, 5'9", dark comp., dark hair and hazel eyes, a resident of Marion Co., W. Va. Post war rosters show he rode with John S. Downs from Marion Co., W. Va. to join the army. Age 40, farmer, Lincoln Dist., Marion Co., W. Va. 1880 Census. NFR.

HAMILTON, JOHN GIVEN (GWIN) - Pvt. Co. C. b. Highland Co., c. 1839. Age 21, farmhand, Wilsonville, Highland Co. 1860 Census. Enl. Highland Co., 1/1/64 (7/1/64). Ab. 6/30/63 - 8/31/64 (dated 1/6/65), sick. Ab. 9/1/64 - 10/31/64 (dated 12/30/64), sick. Paroled at Staunton, 6/1/65. Desc.: age 25, 5'5", fair comp., dark hair and dark eyes. Post war rosters show him as a member of Hutton's Inf. Post war resident of Vanderpool, Highland Co. Bur. Hamilton Church Cem., Highland Co.

HAMILTON, ZACHARIAH - Pvt. Co. K. Enl. Camp Marlin's Bottom, W. Va., 9/17/63. Present 7/1/63 - 11/1/63 (dated 1/6/64), lost Sharps Rifle. Present 11/1/63 - 2/29/64. Clothing issued 2/29/64. Ab. 2/29/64 - 8/31/64, deserted. NFR.

HAMPSON, WADE - Pvt. Co. G. b.c. 1841. Not on muster rolls. Cpd. Pocahontas Co., W. Va., 11/6/63. Confined at the Atheneum Prison, 11/16/63. Desc.: age 22, 5'11+", florid comp., auburn hair and blue eyes. Occ. farmer, residing in Doddridge Co., W. Va. Transf. to Camp Chase, 11/18/63. Most likely Wade Hampson Benson. NFR.

HARDING, JOSEPH FRENCH - Major. Co. C. b. Ellicott Mills, Anne Arundel Co., Md., 11/8/38 (11/9/38). Moved to Randolph Co., W. Va. Age 21, student, Randolph Co., W. Va. 1860 Census. Attended Huttonsville Academy. Prior service, Co. F, 31st Va. Inf. Transf. to Co. C, 20th Va. Cav. late 1863, promoted to 3rd Lt. Enl. Randolph Co., W. Va., 4/1/64. Present, 3rd Lt., 6/30/63 - 8/31/64 (dated 1/6/65). Promoted (elected) to Jr. 2nd Lt., 4/1/64. Present, 3rd Lt., 9/1/64 - 10/31/64 (dated 12/30/64). Promoted (elected) to 2nd Lt., 9/2/64. Ab. 12/15/64, sick since 10/7/64. Rode a black horse during the fall of 1864. Post war rosters show him as Major. Said to have fired the last shot of the war, at Knapp's Creek, W. Va., 4/18/65, in an engagement with Capt. Joseph Badger, 8th Ohio Cav. Horse KIA, while Harding escaped. Tried to go west after the surrender and continue to fight. Wrote his own parole, 4/23/65. Wd. several times during the war. Post war source shows he was promoted to Maj., and to be Col. at the end of the war. Helped write the 1872 Constitution of W. Va. Member of the West Va. Legislature, from Randolph and Tucker Co's, 1885 and 1897. Member Constitutional Convention, W. Va., 1873 (1872). Age 41, Sheriff, New Interest, Randolph Co., W. Va. 1880 Census, place of birth shown as Iowa. Sheriff of Randolph Co., 1877 - 1881. Post war resident of Beverly, then moved to "The Retreat", in Elkins, W. Va. Admitted to the bar, Elkins, Randolph Co., 1885. Awarded Cross of Honor. d. North Boundary Ave., Elkins, W. Va., 2/15/1919. Bur. Beverly Cem., Beverly, W. Va. Also as having been bur. in Maplewood Cem., Randolph Co., W. Va.

HARDY, W. E. - Pvt. Co. K. Enl. Camp Cameron, Bath Co., 3/1/63. Ab. 11/1/63 - 2/29/64, discharged, under age; lost Sharps Rifle and Accoutrements; paid for. Ab. 2/29/64 - 8/31/64, discharged, under age. NFR.

HAROLD (HEROLD), CHARLES B. - Pvt. Co. C. b.c. 1841. Age 19, farmer, Mill Point, Pocahontas Co., W. Va. 1860 Census. Prior service, Co. I, 25th Va. Inf. Enl. Pocahontas Co., W. Va., 3/19/63. Not stated if present or absent on muster-in roll dated 8/63. Ab. 6/30/63 - 8/31/64 (dated 1/6/65), claimed and returned to Co. I, 25th Va. Inf., 4/1/64. Clothing issued 3/10/64. Moved south after the war. NFR.

HARRIS, ALPHEUS E. - Pvt. Co. E. Enl. Sommerville [Summersville], W. Va., 3/13/63. Not stated if present or absent muster-in roll dated 7/18/63. Present 1/1/64 - 8/31/64 (dated 1/6/65), entitled to $100 bond. Present 9/1/64 - 10/31/64 (dated 12/29/64), entitled to $100 bond. NFR.

HARRIS, ELLIS (ELIAS) - Pvt. Co. A. b.c. 1837. Enl. Upshur Co., W. Va., 5/2/63, age 26. Also as having enl. in Pocahontas Co., W. Va., 5/28/63. Not stated if present or absent on muster-in roll dated 5/2/63. Ab. 7/1/63 - 9/1/63, deserted 5/6/63. Ab. 10/31/63 - 8/31/64, deserted 5/18/63. NFR.

HARRIS, JAMES H. - Pvt. Co. D. b.c. 1833. Enl. Luray, 10/20/64. Present 12/31/63 - 8/31/64 (dated 1/6/65). Present 9/1/64 - 10/31/64. Paroled at Staunton, 5/1/65. Desc.: age 32, 5'7", florid comp., light hair and gray eyes, a resident of Augusta Co. NFR.

HARRIS, JOHN W. - Pvt. Co. E. Enl. Sommerville [Summersville], W. Va., 5/13/63. Not stated if present or absent on muster-in roll dated 7/18/63. NFR.

HARRIS, JUNIUS HASKINS - Pvt. Co. C. b. 1842. Post war rosters only. d. 1910.

HARRIS, OLIVER - Pvt. Co. A. Post war rosters only. NFR.

HARRIS, THOMAS W. - Pvt. Co. H. Enl. Camp Northwest, W. Va., 7/1/63. Not stated if present or absent on muster-in roll dated 8/63. Transf. to Lurty's Batty. by Capt. Hayhurst, 11/1/63. NFR.

HARRISON, ROBERT R. - Pvt. Co. G. b. Ky. Enl. in CS service in Ky., was cpd. and escaped. Came to Belleville Bottom, Wood Co., W. Va. Made his way south a year later with Allen and Preston Harwood. Enl. Wood Co., W. Va., 6/24/63. Not stated if present or absent on muster-in roll dated 8/63. Present 11/1/63 - 2/29/64, had his own horse since 12/21/63. Clothing issued 2/29/64, signs by x. Present 7/1/64 - 8/31/64, has his own horse; entitled to bond. Present 9/1/64 - 10/31/64 (dated 12/29/64), entitled to $100 bond. Post war rosters show he was mortally wd. near the close of the war. DOW. Wood Co., W. Va., 5/?/65. "He was a stalwart man, six feet tall, brave and daring, and could be depended upon in hazardous undertakings where he was often sent. He fought with conspicuous bravery to the close of the war, and when the company disbanded in Highland Co., and they started for home, a squad of home guards "bushwhacked" them in Wi:t County, firing upon them, and he was mortally wounded. He was brought to the residence of Mrs. [Gassaway] Harwood, where he died...." Bur. Harwood Cem., overlooking the Ohio River. "He said if he "could only have fallen in battle, what an honor it would have been."

HART, JOHN J. - Pvt. Co. I. b.c. 1826. Enl. Camp Northwest, W. Va., 3/1/63, age 37. Also as having enl. in Rockbridge Co., 4/4/63. Not stated if present or absent on muster-in roll dated 5/5/63. Ab. 11/1/63 - 8/31/64 (dated 1/6/65), deserted. NFR.

HARTMAN, AUSTIN J. - Pvt. Co. D. b. Upshur Co., W. Va., c. 1846. Enl. Camp Pisgah, Bath Co., 2/1/64. POW record shows enl. as Highland Co., 2/64. Present 7/1/63 - 1/1/64 (dated 1/1/64), entitled to bounty. Ab. 12/31/63 - 8/31/64 (dated 1/6/65), prisoner. Ab. 9/1/64 - 10/31/64, POW. Cpd. Beverly, W. Va., 10/29/64. Confined at Clarksburg, W. Va. Desc.: age 18, 6', fair comp., light hair and brown eyes. Occ. farmer, residing in Barbour Co., W. Va. Transf. to Wheeling, W. Va., 11/2/64. Confined at the Atheneum Prison, 11/2/64. Desc.: age 18, 6', fair comp., brown hair and brown eyes. Transf. to Camp Chase, 11/3/64. Confined at Camp Chase, 11/4/64. Took the oath of allegiance and was released, 6/12/65. Desc.: age 19, 6', dark comp., dark hair and black eyes, a resident of Barbour Co., W. Va. Age 34, farmer, Union Dist., Barbour Co., W. Va. 1880 Census. NFR.

HARVEY, JOHN M. (W.) - 2nd Corp. Co. D. b. Harrison Co., W. Va., c. 1843. Enl. Weston, W. Va., 5/1/63. POW record shows enl. as Pocahontas Co., W. Va., 5/63. Not stated if present or absent on muster-in roll dated 8/63, Pvt. Present, 2nd Corp., 7/1/63 - 1/1/64 (dated 1/1/64), had his own horse. Ab., 2nd Corp., 12/31/63 8/31/64 (dated 1/6/65), AWOL since 11/1/64. Clothing issued 2/29/64. Ab., 2nd Corp., 9/1/64 - 10/31/64, AWOL. Deserted. Reported at Philippi, W. Va., 10/24/64. Confined at Clarksburg, W. Va. Took the oath of allegiance and was released, 10/28/64. Desc.: age 21, 6', light comp., light hair and hazel eyes. Occ. farmer, residing in Barbour Co., W. Va. Post war rosters show him as a Sgt., residing at Weston, W. Va. Age 36, works on farm, Union Dist., Barbour Co., W. Va. 1880 Census. NFR.

HARVEY, MARSHALL T. (P.) - Pvt. Co. D. b.c. 1844. Enl. Weston, W. Va., 5/1/63. Not stated if present or absent on muster-in roll dated 8/63. Ab. 7/1/63 - 1/1/64 (dated 1/1/64), prisoner. Cpd. Barbour Co., W. Va., 7/18/63. Confined at the Atheneum Prison, 7/22/63. Desc.: age 19, 6'2", dark comp., dark hair and dark eyes. Occ. farmer, residing in Barbour Co., W. Va. Transf. to Camp Chase, 7/23/63. Confined at Camp Chase, 7/24/63. Ab. 12/31/63 - 8/31/64 (dated 1/6/65), prisoner. Transf. to Ft. Delaware, 2/29/64. Confined at Ft. Delaware, 3/4/64 (3/2/64). Ab. 9/1/64 - 10/31/64, POW. Took the oath of allegiance and was released, 5/8/65. Desc.: age ?, 6', light comp., dark hair and hazel eyes, a resident of Barbour Co., W. Va. NFR.

HARWOOD, JOHN ALLEN - 1st Lt. Co. G. Resident of Wood Co., W. Va. Arrested and confined at Wheeling, W. Va. and Sandusky, O. by 2/3/62. Released on his oath by 2/8/62. Made his way south to join the army, with his brother Preston and R. R. Harrison. Enl. Wood Co., W. Va., 5/12/63. Elected 1st Lt., 5/12/63. Not stated if present or absent on muster-in roll dated 8/63, 1st Lt. Not stated if present or absent 11/1/63 - 2/29/64, dropped from rolls by Special Order No. 501, 12/19/63. Col. W. W. Arnett requested Harwood be dropped from the rolls, 12/3/63, stating that he had absented himself from Camp Marlin's Bottom, W. Va., since 9/2/63, without consent. Brother of Preston Harwood. Post war resident of Wood Co., W. Va. NFR.

HARWOOD, PRESTON - Pvt. Co. G. Post war rosters only. Made his way south with his brother and R. R. Harrison to join the army. Brother of John Allen Harwood. NFR.

HAWKINS, JEREMIAH "Jerry" - Pvt. Co. A. b.c. 1838. Enl. Pocahontas Co., W. Va., 6/25/63, age 25. Not stated if present or absent on muster-in roll dated 6/25/63. Present 7/1/63 - 9/1/63. Present 10/31/63 - 8/31/64. Clothing issued 2/29/64 and during the 4th Qr. 1864, while he was on his way to join his command. Horse KIA. near Madison CH, 12/21/64, throwing Hawkins into a fence corner. Hawkins pulled a wd. Yankee Major out of the road, keeping him from being ran over. When the Yankees fell back, Hawkins was released and allowed to return to his command. Post war resident of Marion Co., W. Va. Age 42, farm hand, Mannington Dist., Marion Co., W. Va. 1880 Census. Alive 1905. NFR.

HAWKINS, JOHN - Pvt. Co. G. Enl. Wood Co., W. Va., 5/2/63 (6/18/63). Not stated if present or absent on muster-in roll dated 8/63. Present 11/1/63 - 2/29/64, had his own horse since 12/21/63. Clothing issued 2/29/64. Not stated if present or absent 7/1/64 - 8/31/64, has his own horse; entitled to bond. Present 9/1/64 - 10/31/64 (dated 12/29/64), entitled to $100 bond. NFR.

HAYHURST, CALDER - 1st Corp. Co. H. Enl. Calhoun Co., W. Va., 4/4/63 (4/8/63). Not stated if present or absent on muster-in roll dated 8/63, 1st Corp. Present, Pvt., 10/31/63 - 8/31/64, had one horse from 11/8/63 till 2/1/64. Present 9/1/64 - 10/31/64 (dated 12/30/64). NFR.

HAYHURST, JOSEPH - Capt. Co. H. b.c. 1828. Enl. Calhoun Co., W. Va., 5/14/63. Elected (appointed) Capt., 6/4/63. Present at Beverly, W. Va., 7/63. Not stated if present or absent on muster- in roll dated 8/63. Present 10/31/63 - 8/31/64. Commanding a detachment of cav. near Covington, 6/26/64 - 7/3/64. Present 9/1/64 - 10/31/64 (dated 12/30/64), entitled to $100 bond. Ab. 10/25/64, 150 days, in charge of horses. Post war resident of Calhoun Co., W. Va. Age 52, farming, Sheridan Dist., Calhoun Co., W. Va. 1880 Census. NFR.

HAYS, JAMES H. - Pvt. Co. D. Post war rosters only, which show he served 3 years, and was a resident of Amherst Co. NFR.

HEARLSTON, WILLIAM J. - Pvt. Co. G. Enl. Wood Co., 8/1/64. Also as Missouri, 10/1/64. Present 7/1/64 - 8/31/64, $50 enl. bounty due. Present 9/1/64 - 10/31/64 (dated 12/29/64), $50 enl. bounty due. NFR.

HEINER, E. S. - Pvt. Co. B. Enl. Buchannon, W. Va., 5/4/63. Not stated if present or absent on muster-in roll dated 7/25/63. Could be E. S. Hiner, Co. C, 46th Battn. Va. Cav. ÑFR.

HEISKEL, HENRY LEE - Capt. Co. I. b.c. 1839. Enl. Winchester, 5/17/62, age 23. Also as Warm Springs, 4/17/63. Not stated if present or absent on muster-in roll dated 5/5/63, Capt. Elected (appointed) Capt., 5/4/63. Present, Capt., 11/1/63 - 8/31/64 (dated 1/6/65). Present, Capt., 11/1/63 - 10/31/64 (dated 12/31/64). Ab. on sick furlough, 11/63. Ab. in Staunton Gen. Hosp., 12/63. Col. W. W. Arnett requested Heiskel's name be dropped, 12/31/63. Col. W. L. Jackson requested that Heiskel's name not be dropped, 1/14/64, as he as returned to duty and has requested a court of inquiry. No record of inquiry. Dropped for prolonged absence without leave, 2/24/64. Maj. John B. Lady, wrote 3/1/64, that Heiskel was "an officer of intelligence and capacity..."; and had been absent sick, and not AWOL. A petition signed by the officers and men of Co. I, requested that his position be restored. Order to drop him was revoked, 3/23/64. Post war resident of Harrison Co., W. Va. Entered the Old Soldier's Home, Pikesville, Md., 2/7/93, age 52, from Baltimore, Md., a merchant. d. Pikesville, Md., 4/12/1900.

HELMICK, DANIEL G. - Bvt. 2nd Lt. Co. B. Resident of Harrison Co., W. Va. Enl. Camp Harlan, 4/15/63. Not stated if present or absent on muster-in roll dated 7/25/63, Pvt. Transf. to Co. E. Not stated if present or absent on muster-in roll dated 7/18/63, Bvt. 2nd Lt. Elected Jr. 2nd Lt., 5/10/63. Deserted. Took the amnesty oath and gave his bond, 11/22/63. Col. W. W. Arnett requested Helmick be dropped from the rolls, 12/31/63, having been AWOL for 3 months in enemy country and has taken the oath of allegiance. Dropped from the rolls, 2/25/64. NFR.

HELMICK, ISRAEL M. - Pvt. Co. E. b.c. 1831. Enl. Bulltown, W. Va., 5/10/63. Not stated if present or absent on muster-in roll dated 7/18/63. Present 1/1/64 - 8/31/64 (dated 1/6/65), entitled to $100 bond. Clothing issued 1/17/64 (detailed blacksmith), 6/20/64 and 3rd Qr. 1864. Employed as a blacksmith at Warm Springs, 1/64 and 3/64. Ab. 9/1/64 - 10/31/64 (dated 12/29/64), on detached service as Brigade Blacksmith; entitled to $100 bond. Paroled at Charleston, W. Va., 5/10/65. Desc.: age 34, 5'9", light comp., brown hair, black eyes and brown whiskers. NFR.

HENDERSHOT, JOHN - Pvt. Co. B. Not on muster rolls. Reference jacket only, which shows service in Co. C, 19th Va. Cav. Post war resident of Wood Co., W. Va. NFR.

HENKLE (HINKLE), HENRY C. - Pvt. Co. E. b.c. 1843. Enl. Bulltown, W. Va., 5/10/63. Not stated if present or absent on muster-in roll dated 7/18/63. Present 1/1/64 - 8/31/64 (dated 1/6/65), entitled to $100 bond. Present 9/1/64 - 10/31/64 (dated 12/29/64), entitled to $100 bond. Paroled at Staunton, 5/19/65. Desc.: age 22, 6'2", light comp., sandy hair and gray eyes. NFR.

HENRY, JAMES H. - Pvt. Co. B. Enl. Hightown, Highland Co., 10/8/62. Not stated if present or absent on muster-in roll dated 7/25/63. NFR.

HERRON (HERON), JOHN - Pvt. Co. ?. b. 8/23/37. Age 22, farmer, Randolph Co., W. Va. 1860 Census. Post war rosters only, which show him as a resident of Randolph Co., W. Va. Attended Confederate Reunion, Randolph Co., W. Va., 1906, claimed to be a member of the 20th Va. Cav. Resident of Huttonsville, W. Va., 1916. d. 5/26/1925. Bur. Brick Church Cem., Huttonsville, W. Va.

HERTZOG (HERTZHOG), WILLIAM T. (L.) - Pvt. Co. A. b.c. 1837. Enl. Pocahontas Co., W. Va., 5/28/63, age 26. Not stated if present or absent on muster-in roll dated 8/63. Present 7/1/63 - 9/1/63, detailed. Served as Surgeon, 46th Battn. Va. Cav. Post war resident of Taylor Co., W. Va. NFR.

HIBBS, JASON - Pvt. Co. A. b.c. 1841. Resident of Marion Co., W. Va. Enl. Pocahontas (Marion) Co., W. Va., 5/9/63, age 22. Not stated if present or absent on muster-in roll dated 5/9/63. Cpd. near Grafton, W. Va., 5/17/63. Confined at Ft. McHenry. Paroled and sent to Ft. Monroe, 5/20/63, signs by x. Exchanged. Present 7/1/63 - 9/1/63. Ab. 10/31/63 - 8/31/64, KIA. Rockville, Md., 7/13/64. Clothing issued 2/29/64. Post war rosters show he was KIA. Darkesville, W. Va., 7/64.

HICKMAN, JAMES M. - 3rd Sgt. Co. D. Enl. Weston, W. Va., 5/1/63 (5/2/63). Not stated if present or absent on muster-in roll dated 8/63, Pvt. Present, 2nd Sgt., 7/1/63 - 1/1/64 (dated 1/1/64), appointed 2nd Sgt., 7/1/63; has his own horse. Present 12/31/63 - 8/31/64 (dated 1/6/65). Present 9/1/64 - 10/31/64, entitled to $100 bond. NFR.

HICKMAN, JAMES S. - Pvt. Co. B. b. Barbour Co., W. Va., c. 1827. Enl. Camp Northwest, Pocahontas Co., W. Va., 7/17/63. Not stated if present or absent on muster-in roll dated 7/25/63. Present 11/1/63 - 8/31/64 (dated 1/6/65), sick from wd., reported for duty. Wd., date and place not stated. Ab. 9/1/64 - 10/31/64 (dated 12/30/64), sick from wd. Deserted. Reported at Clarksburg, W. Va., 3/22/65. Confined at Clarksburg, W. Va. Took the amnesty oath and was sent North, 3/23/65. Desc.: age 38, 5'10", fair comp., red hair and blue eyes. Occ. farmer, residing in Doddridge Co., W. Va. NFR.

HICKMAN, JOHN S. - Bvt. 2nd Lt. Co. D. b.c. 1839. Resident of Barbour Co., W. Va. No enl. data. Not stated if present or absent on muster-in roll dated 8/63, Bvt. 2nd Lt. Present 7/1/63 - 1/1/64 (dated 1/1/64), elected Jr. 2nd Lt., 6/1/63. Appointed AQM, 20th Va. Cav., 8/14/63, appointment revoked. Resigned 12/24/64 (1/27/64). Enl. Weston, W. Va., 3/1/64, as a Pvt. Present, Pvt., 12/31/63 - 8/31/64 (dated 1/6/65), entitled to enl. bounty. Present 9/1/64 - 10/31/64, entitled to enl. bounty. Paroled at Staunton, 5/25/65. Desc.: age 26, 5'5", fair comp., brown hair and gray eyes. NFR.

HICKMAN, LEWIS - 2nd Lt. Co. D. b. Harrison (Barbour) Co., W. Va., 4/17/39. Resident of Barbour Co., W. Va. Enl. 1863. Not stated if present or absent on muster-in roll dated 8/63, 2nd Lt. Elected 2nd Lt., 6/1/63. Present, 2nd Lt., 7/1/63 - 1/1/64 (dated 1/1/64), elected 2nd Lt., 5/3/63. Present, 2nd Lt., 12/31/63 - 8/31/64 (dated 1/6/65). Present, 2nd Lt., 9/1/64 - 10/31/64. Post war rosters show him as a Capt. Moved to Rockbridge Co., 1866. Farmer, Kerr's Creek, 1880. Cattle dealer, Denmark, 1887. Member Lee-Jackson Camp, UCV, Lexington. d. Kerr's Creek, 4/12/1916. Bur. New Monmouth Presbyterian Church Cem.

HICKMAN, THOMAS - Pvt. Co. D. Resident of Barbour Co., W. Va. Enl. Weston, W. Va., 5/1/63. Not stated if present or absent on muster-in roll dated 8/63. Present 7/1/63 - 1/1/64 (dated 1/1/64). Clothing issued 2/29/64. Ab. 12/31/63 - 8/31/64 (dated 1/6/65), drowned 5/14/64. Ab. 9/1/64 - 10/31/64, deceased.

HICKOK (HICKOCK), JOHN J. - Pvt. Co. D. b.c. 1847. Enl. Hightown, Highland Co., 3/1/64. Present 12/31/63 - 8/31/64 (dated 1/6/65), enl. bounty due. Present 9/1/64 - 10/31/64, entitled to $100 bond. Paroled at Staunton, 5/25/65. Desc.: age 18, 5'10", fair comp., red hair and dark eyes. Member Camp 435, UCV, in Ga. d. Richmond, by 5/10/1907. NFR.

HIGGS, JACOB - Pvt. Co. A. Post war rosters only, which show he was KIA. Darkesville, W. Va., 7/64. NFR.

HILKEY, PHILIP H. - Pvt. Co. D. Enl. Weston, W. Va., 5/1/63. Not stated if present or absent on muster-in roll dated 8/63. Transf. to the 17th Va. Cav. in exchange for C. L. Norman. NFR.

HILL, ISAAC - Pvt. Co. B. Enl. Camp Northwest, W. Va., 7/1/63. Present 11/1/63 - 8/31/64 (dated 1/6/65). Clothing issued 3/31/64. Present 9/1/64 - 10/31/64 (dated 12/30/64), entitled to $100 bond. Post war rosters show he enl. in 1862 and served until the close of the war. NFR.

HILL, W. E. - Rank ?, Co. ?. Not on muster rolls. Recommended for promotion to Maj., 20th Va. Cav., 11/30/64, by Brig. Gen. H. B. Davidson, for "valor and skill." NFR.

HILLARY, WILLIAM H. - Pvt. Co. D. Enl. Camp Miller, 9/1/63. Present 7/1/63 - 1/1/64 (dated 1/1/64), entitled to enl. bounty. Ab. 12/31/63 - 8/31/64 (dated 1/6/65), prisoner. Cpd. Sharpsburg, Md., 8/4/64 (8/5/64). Sent to Washington, DC. Confined at the Old Capitol Prison, 8/8/64. Transf. to Elmira, NY, 8/12/64. Confined at Elmira Prison, 8/12/64. Ab. 9/1/64 - 10/31/64, POW. Took the oath of allegiance and was released 7/11/65. Desc.: age ?, 5'11", fair comp., light hair and gray eyes, a resident of Staunton. Post war rosters show service in Co. C. Bur. Heavener Cem., Buckhannon, W. Va.

HILT, JOHN - Pvt. Co. K. Enl. Camp Cameron, Bath Co., 2/10/64, by W. T. Jennings. Ab. 11/1/63 - 2/29/64, deserted 4/12/64. Clothing issued 2/29/64. Ab. 2/29/64 - 8/31/64, deserted 4/12/64. NFR.

HINEGARDEN, JOSEPH ADAM B. - 4th Corp. Co. I. b.c. 1844. Enl. Camp Northwest, W. Va., 6/25/63 (7/2/63), (Warm Springs, 4/20/63), age 19. Not stated if present or absent on muster-in roll dated 5/5/63, Pvt. Present, 4th Corp., 11/1/63 - 8/31/64 (dated 1/6/65), promoted to 4th Corp., 2/1/64. Clothing issued 2/29/64. Present, 4th Corp., 11/1/63 - 10/31/64 (dated 12/31/64), promoted 4th Corp., 4/1/64. Paroled at Staunton, 5/26/65, signs by x. Desc.: age 19 (?), 6', dark comp., brown hair and gray eyes. NFR.

HINER, WILLIAM B. - Pvt. Co. C. b. 6/20/46. Enl. Highland Co., 6/29/63. Not stated if present or absent on muster-in roll dated 8/63. Ab. 6/30/63 - 8/31/64 (dated 1/6/65), transf. to Co. G, 18th Va. Cav. CSR in 18th Va. Cav. filed as U. B. Hiner. Post war farmer and resident of Highland Co. d. 3/13/1915. Bur. Hiner Family Cem., Highland Co.

HINER, WILLIAM H. - Pvt. Co. C. b. Highland Co., 6/20/46. Enl. Pocahontas Co., W. Va., 4/1/64 (4/15/64). Present 6/30/63 - 8/31/64 (dated 1/6/65), enl. bounty due. Present 9/1/64 - 10/31/64 (dated 12/30/64), on horse detail by order of Gen. Jubal A. Early. Post war rosters show he was wd. at Smithfield and at Winchester (Bunker Hill, W. Va.). Post war farmer and resident of Mill Gap, Highland Co. d. Mill Gap, Highland Co., 3/13/1915, age 69, Bright's disease. Bur. Hiner Family Cem., Highland Co.

HINES, JOSEPH C. - Pvt. Co. C. b.c. 1835. Not on muster rolls. Deserted. Surrendered, took the oath of allegiance and was sent North, 4/9/65. Desc.: age 30, 5'9", dark comp., dark hair and gray eyes, a farmer. NFR.

HINKLE (HENKLE), ADAM - Pvt. Co. I. b. Va., c. 1839. Age 21, farmer, Kerr's Creek Dist., Rockbridge Co. 1860 Census. Prior service, Co. G, 58th Va. Inf. Age 22, 1861. Enl. Camp Cameron, Bath Co., 12/10/63. Ab. 11/1/63 - 8/31/64 (dated 1/6/65), AWOL. Pension application shows wd. Droop Mtn., 11/6/63. Clothing issued 2/29/64. Age 35, farmhand, Kerr's Creek, Rockbridge Co. 1870 Census. d. Alphin, 5/4/1903, age 66. CSR filed as Adam Hinkee.

HINKLE (HENKLE), ANDREW P. - Pvt. Co. K. b. Va., c. 1844. Age 16, laborer, Kerr's Creek Dist., 1860 Rockbridge Co. Census. Enl. Camp Northwest, W. Va., 6/18/63, age 19. Not stated if present or absent on muster-in roll dated 7/21/63. Present 7/1/63 11/1/63 (dated 1/6/64). Ab. 11/1/63 - 2/29/64, deserted. Clothing issued 2/29/64. Ab. 2/29/64 - 8/31/64, deserted. Post war rosters show service in Co. I. Age 26, farmhand, Kerr's Creek, 1870 Rockbridge Co. Census. Shingle maker. Age 63, farmer, Rockbridge Alum Springs, 1902. Resident of Kerr's Creek, 1905. d. Kerr's Creek, 1/6/1922.

HINTON (HENTON), JOHN - Pvt. Co. K. Enl. Camp Northwest, W. Va., 6/18/63. Ab. 7/1/63 - 11/1/63 (dated 1/6/64), AWOL. Ab. 11/1/63 - 2/29/64, AWOL. Ab. 2/29/64 - 8/31/64, AWOL. NFR.

HODGE, ROBERT - Pvt. Co. A. Service shown as Maj. Lady's Cav. Battn. b. Edinburgh, Scotland, c. 1845. Not on muster rolls. Enl. Richmond, 8/18/63, age 18 years and 4 months, signs by x. Desc.: age 18 years and 4 months, 4'10", light comp., brown hair and black eyes, a laborer. NFR.

HOGSETT, HENRY L. V. - Pvt. Co. C. b. Va., c. 1848. Not on muster rolls. Enl. Lexington, 11/29/64. Desc.: age 16, 5'4", fair comp., light hair and blue eyes, a farmer. Farmhand, Lexington Dist., 1870 Rockbridge Co. Census. May have refuged from Pocahontas Co., W. Va. NFR.

HOGSETT, SAMUEL - Pvt. Co. C. Enl. Pocahontas Co., W. Va., 7/16/63 (7/1/63). Not stated if present or absent on muster-in roll dated 8/63. Present 6/30/63 - 8/31/64 (dated 1/6/65), mounted; enl. bounty due. Present 9/1/64 - 10/31/64 (dated 12/30/64). NFR.

HOGSHEAD, ———— - Lt. Co. ?. Post war rosters only, which show he was KIA. near Madison CH, 12/21/64. NFR.

HOLDEN, HEZEKIAH - Pvt. Co. F. b. Harrison Co., W. Va., 5/20/41. Prior service, Co. C, 31st Va. Inf. Deserted by 8/12/63. Had permission to raise a co. 3/63, but has not raised the co., "nor is he likely to raise one"; he is now with Col. W. L. Jackson. Enl. Camp Clover Lick, 7/11/63. Also as Camp Miller, 7/16/63. Not stated if present or absent on muster-in roll dated 7/20/63. Ab. 7/1/63 - 8/31/64 (dated 1/6/65), transf. to Capt. William P. Cooper's Co., 31st Va. Inf. Ab. 9/1/64 - 10/31/64 (dated 12/30/64), transf. to Capt. Cooper's Co., 31st Va. Inf. Returned to Co. C, 31st Va. Inf. by 4/30/64. KIA. near Winchester, 9/19/64.

HOLDEN, JOHN B. - Pvt. Co. D. b.c. 1841. Enl. Weston, W. Va., 5/1/63. Also as Barbour Co., W. Va., 5/63. Not stated if present or absent on muster-in roll dated 8/63. Present 7/1/63 - 1/1/64 (dated 1/1/64), has his own horse. Ab. 12/31/63 - 8/31/64 (dated 1/6/65), prisoner. Clothing issued 2/29/64. Ab. 9/1/64 - 10/31/64, POW. Cpd. Strasburg, 9/23/64. Sent to Harpers Ferry, W. Va., then to Pt. Lookout. Confined at Pt. Lookout, 10/3/64. Paroled and sent to Aiken's Landing, 3/17/65, to be exchanged. Exchanged at Boulware's Wharf, 3/19/65. Present on a MR of Paroled and Exchanged Prisoners at Camp Lee, near Richmond, 3/19/65. Deserted. Reported at Clarksburg, W. Va., 5/1/65, and was confined. Took the oath of allegiance and was released, 5/1/65. Desc.: age 23, 5'8", fair comp., fair hair and black eyes. Occ. farmer, residing in Barbour Co., W. Va. Age 39, farmer, Elk, Barbour Co., W. Va. 1880 Census. NFR.

HOLLAND, N. B. - 1st Lt. Co. K. Enl. Lewisburg, W. Va., 2/15/63. Not stated if present or absent on muster-in roll dated 7/21/63, 1st Lt. Elected (appointed) 1st Lt., 7/22/63. Ab., 1st Lt., 7/1/63 - 11/1/63 (dated 1/6/64), Promoted 1st Lt., 7/21/63; KIA. Droop Mtn., 11/6/63.

HOLLEN (HOLLAND), LEVI T. (I.) - Pvt. Co. D. b. Barbour Co., W. Va., c. 1827. Enl. Hightown, Highland Co., 7/15/63. Not stated if present or absent on muster-in roll dated 8/63. Present 7/1/63 1/1/64 (dated 1/1/64), entitled to enl. bounty; has his own horse. Ab. 12/31/63 - 8/31/64 (dated 1/6/65), prisoner. Ab. 9/1/64 - 10/31/64, POW. Cpd. Beverly, W. Va., 10/29/64. Sent to Clarksburg, W. Va., then to Wheeling, W. Va., 11/2/64. Desc.: age 37, 6'2", fair comp., light hair and blue eyes. Occ. farmer, residing in Barbour Co., W. Va. Confined at the Atheneum Prison, 11/2/64. Desc.: age 37, 6'2+", light comp., light hair and blue eyes. Occ. millwright, residing in Barbour Co., W. Va. Transf. to Camp Chase, 11/3/64. Confined at Camp Chase, 11/4/64. Took the oath of allegiance and was released, 6/12/65. Desc.: age 37, 6'3,", fair comp., light hair and blue eyes, a resident of Barbour Co., W. Va. Age 52, carpenter, East Barker Dist., Barbour Co., W. Va. 1880 Census. NFR.

HOOTER, J. - Pvt. Co. K. Post war rosters only. Cpd. and confined at Camp Chase. DOD. Camp Chase. Bur. Camp Chase Confederate Cem.

HORNER, JACOB D. - Pvt. Co. A. b.c. 1844. Enl. Marion Co., W. Va., 5/9/63, by Sgt. Youst (Yost). Present 10/31/63 - 8/31/64. Clothing issued 2/29/64 and 3/?/64. Paroled at Staunton, 5/25/65, signs by x. Desc.: age 21, 5'6", fair comp., dark hair and gray eyes. Age 38, Railroad laborer, Mannington Dist., Marion Co., W. Va. 1880 Census. NFR.

HOSTETTER, WILLIAM - Lt. Co. G. Post war rosters only, which show he was a resident of Wood Co., W. Va. Served in Co. C, 19th Va. Cav. NFR.

HUDKINS, BASIL (BASWELL, BAZWELL) - Pvt. Co. H. Enl. Calhoun Co., W. Va., 5/14/63. Not stated if present or absent on muster-in roll dated 8/63. Ab. 10/31/63 - 8/31/64, deserted 8/63. Adm. Gen. Hosp. No. 9, 8/5/63. Transf. to Chimborazo Hosp., 8/6/63, listed as Co. C, 19th Va. Cav. Ab. 9/1/64 - 10/31/64 (dated 12/30/64), deserted 9/63. Reference jacket in CSR shows service in Co. C, 19th Va. Cav. NFR.

HUDKINS, JOHN M. - Pvt. Co. D. Resident of Barbour Co., W. Va. Enl. Weston, W. Va., 5/1/63. Not stated if present or absent on muster-in roll dated 8/63. Ab. 7/1/63 - 1/1/64 (dated 1/1/64), prisoner. Cpd. Barbour Co., W. Va., 10/20/63 (9/27/63). Listed as a deserter, having taken the oath of allegiance before joining the Southern Army. Confined at the Atheneum Prison, 10/24/63. Desc.: age 20, 5'9+", fair comp., dark hair and hazel eyes. Occ. farmer, residing in Barbour Co., W. Va. Transf. to Camp Chase, 10/26/63. Confined at Camp Chase, 10/27/63. Ab. 12/31/63 - 8/31/64 (dated 1/6/65), prisoner. Transf. to Rock Island, Ill., 1/22/64. Confined at Rock Island Prison, 1/?/64. Desires to take the oath of allegiance, 3/18/64, wishes to go home. Ab. 9/1/64 - 10/31/64, POW. DOD. Rock Island, Ill., 3/18/64 (3/19/64), bronchitis. Bur. Rock Island, Ill., grave no. 852.

HUFFMAN, D. H. - Pvt. Co. G. b.c. 1832. Not on muster rolls. Paroled at Staunton, 5/11/65. Desc.: age 33, 5'5", fair comp., dark hair and gray eyes. NFR.

HUFFMAN, J. S. - Pvt. Co. A. Post war rosters only. NFR.

HUGHES, WILLIAM CALVIN - 1st Corp. Co. I. b.c. 1843. Enl. Warm Springs, Bath Co., 4/20/63 (4/1/63), age 20. Not stated if present or absent on muster-in roll dated 5/5/63, 2nd Corp. Cpd. Beverly, W. Va., 7/5/63, as a member of Co. D, Lady's Battn. Confined at the Atheneum Prison, 7/8/63. Desc.: age 21, 5'9", fresh comp., sandy hair and hazel eyes. Occ. farmer, residing in Albemarle Co. Transf. to Camp Chase, 7/9/63. Confined at Camp Chase, 7/10/63. Transf. to Ft. Delaware, 7/14/63. Apparently exchanged. Ab., 1st Corp., 11/1/63 - 8/31/64 (dated 1/6/65), claimed by another command. Clothing issued 2/29/64. Ab., 1st Corp., 11/1/63 - 10/31/64 (dated 12/31/64), claimed by another command. NFR.

HULL, ANDREW A. - Pvt. Co. A. b. Highland Co., c. 1846. Enl. Bath Co., 3/27/63, age 17. POW record shows enl. as Highland Co., 3/62. Not stated if present or absent on muster-in roll dated 3/27/63. Ab. 10/31/63 - 8/31/64, AWOL. Deserted. Clothing issued, 3/64. Cpd. Beverly, W. Va., 10/18/64. Confined at Clarksburg, W. Va. Took the oath of allegiance and was released, 10/23/64. Desc.: age 20, 5'9", fair comp., light hair and brown eyes. Occ. farmer, residing in Highland Co. Served in Co. E, 20th Va. Cav. Cpd. and sent to Clarksburg, W. Va. Took the oath of allegiance and was sent to Wheeling, W. Va., 3/28/65. Confined at the Atheneum Prison, 3/29/65. Post war resident of Highland Co. NFR.

HULL, JACOB W. - Pvt. Co. D. b. Highland Co., c. 1846. Enl. Highland Co., 3/63. Not on muster rolls. Cpd. Beverly, W. Va., 10/18/64. Confined at Clarksburg, W. Va. Took the oath of allegiance and was released, 10/23/64. Desc.: age 18, 5'11", light comp., light hair and brown eyes. Occ. farmer, residing in Highland Co. NFR.

HULL, JOHN McKEE - Pvt. Co. K. Enl. Camp Marlin's Bottom, W. Va., 10/6/63. Present 7/1/63 - 11/1/63 (dated 1/6/64), had his own horse since enl. Not stated if present or absent, 11/1/63 - 2/29/64, conscripted. Not stated if present or absent, 2/29/64 - 8/31/64, conscripted. NFR.

HULL, MORGAN - Pvt. Co. D. Enl. Camp Miller, 8/16/63. Ab. 7/1/63 - 1/1/64 (dated 1/1/64), AWOL since 9/64. Ab. 12/31/63 - 8/31/64 (dated 1/6/65), AWOL since 9/1/64. Ab. 9/1/64 - 10/31/64, AWOL. NFR.

HULL, WELCOME H. - Pvt. Co. D. b. 5/7/46. Post war rosters only, which show he was a resident of Crawford, W. Va. d. 9/29/99. Bur. Hedgesville Cem., Berkeley Co., W. Va.

HULL, WILLIAM HARVEY - Pvt. Co. D. b. Highland Co., c. 1840. Enl. Camp Pisgah, Bath Co., 6/20/63 (6/29/63). POW record shows enl. as Highland Co., 6/63. Present 7/1/63 - 1/1/64 (dated 1/1/64), entitled to enl. bounty. Employed at Kirkpatrick's Cave Niter Works, Bath Co., 7/63 - 2/64. Ab. 12/31/63 - 8/31/64 (dated 1/6/65), prisoner. Ab. 9/1/64 - 10/31/64, prisoner. Cpd. Beverly, W. Va., 10/29/64. Sent to Clarksburg, W. Va., then to Wheeling, W. Va., 11/2/64. Desc.: age 24, 5'7", fair comp., light hair and black eyes. Occ. farmer, residing in Upshur Co., W. Va. Confined at the Atheneum Prison, 11/2/64. Desc.: age 27, 5'7", fair comp., light hair and hazel eyes. Transf. to Camp Chase, 11/22/64. Confined at Camp Chase, 11/23/64, desires to take the oath of allegiance. Gave a statement to the US, 2/27/65; says he volunteered 8/63 at the niter works in Bath Co. Most of the workers were cpd. by Gen. W. W. Averell, and he escaped to Highland Co. Took the oath of allegiance and was released, 3/29/65, ordered to report to the Gov. of W. Va. d. Upshur Co., W. Va., 9/27/1924, age 84 years, 7 months and 5 days.

HUMPHREY, JAMES P. - Pvt. Co. I. Enl. Rockbridge Co., 4/10/64. Ab. 11/1/63 - 10/31/64 (dated 12/31/64), deserted. NFR.

HUNDLEY, CALVIN G. - Pvt. Co. F. b.c. 1817. Not on muster rolls. Enl. Lewisburg, W. Va., 1863. Paroled at Lewisburg, W. Va., 4/25/65. Desc.: age 48, 5'7", dark comp., dark hair and blue eyes. NFR.

HUNT, JOHN B. (W.) - 2nd Lt. Co. I. b.c. 1839. Enl. Lewisburg, W. Va., 4/15/63. Elected 2nd Lt., 5/4/63. Not stated if present or absent on muster-in roll dated 5/5/63, 2nd Lt., age 27(?). Present at Beverly, W. Va., 7/63. Present, 2nd Lt., 11/1/63 - 8/31/64 (dated 1/6/65), commanding Co. Furloughed by Gen. Sam Jones, 12/63. Present, 2nd Lt., 11/1/63 - 10/31/64 (dated 12/31/64), commanding Co. Detailed for duty on a Gen. Court Martial, Warm Springs, Bath Co., 2/25/64. Present 12/26/64. Cpd. Parkersburg, W. Va., 4/20/65. Confined at Clarksburg, W. Va., 4/21/65. Desc.: age 26, 5'11", fair comp., brown hair and blue eyes. Occ. clerk, residing in Rockbridge Co. Paroled and was released, 4/22/65, to be exchanged. NFR.

HUNTON, JOHN - Pvt. Co. K. b.c. 1845. Enl. Camp Northwest, W. Va., 6/18/63, age 18. Not stated if present or absent on muster-in roll dated 7/21/63. NFR.

HUPMAN (HAPMAN, HUPPMAN), HENRY - Pvt. Co. C. Enl. Pocahontas Co., W. Va., 6/1/63. Not stated if present or absent on muster-in roll dated 8/63. Ab. 6/30/63 - 8/31/64 (dated 1/6/65), POW since 11/12/63; enl. bounty due; 6% bond due. Cpd. Bath Co., 11/10/63. Confined at the Atheneum Prison, 11/18/63. Desc.: age 24, 5'7+", florid comp., black hair and dark eyes. Occ. farmer, residing in Augusta Co. Transf. to Camp Chase, 11/19/63. Confined at Camp Chase, 11/20/63. Shot by sentinel at 9 p.m., 12/15/63, while lying in bed, struck in right arm. Bled profusely for nearly a half hour before his friends could get permission to light a candle for 15 minutes and stop the bleeding. Was taken to the hosp. The ball entered his forearm, slightly fracturing the olecranon process of the ulna, passed through the elbow joint, up the arm into his shoulder, where it became lost. A large artery was severed in his arm, the bullet lodged near the head of the humerus. DOW. Camp Chase, 4 p.m., 12/18/63 (12/19/63). Bur. Camp Chase Confederate Cem. Ab. 9/1/64 - 10/31/64 (dated 12/30/64), POW since 11/12/63; 6% bond due. Post war rosters show him as being from Md.

HUPMAN, JAMES S. - Pvt. Co. A. b.c. 24. Enl. Augusta Co., 2/18/63, age 39. Not stated if present or absent on muster-in roll dated 2/18/63. Ab. 7/1/63 - 8/31/64 (dated 1/6/65), detailed to work in niter cave. Ab. 10/31/63 - 8/31/64, detailed to work at the niter works. Employed at Kirkpatrick's Cave Niter Works, 9/63 - 7/64. NFR.

HURRY, JAMES H. - Pvt. Co. C. b. 3/7/42. Post war rosters only. Served in Co. C, 46th Battn. Va. Cav. and the 26th Va. Cav. d. Bridgeport, W. Va., 10/1923.

HUTTON, ELIHU (ELISHA, ELEHEW) - Capt. Co. C and Lt. Col. b. on Riffles Creek, Randolph Co., W. Va., 12/31/37. Schooled by private tutors and attended Huttonsville Academy. Age 22, farmer, Randolph Co., W. Va. 1860 Census. Scouted for Gen. R. E. Lee at Elkwater, 1861. Prior service, Va. Militia. Desires authorization to raise a Co. in the Northwestern part of the state, 3/17/63. Enl. Randolph Co., W. Va., 4/23/63 (4/16/63). Elected Capt., 4/16/63. Present on muster-in roll dated 8/63, Capt. commanding Co. Present, Capt., 6/30/63 - 8/31/64 (dated 1/6/65). Mentioned for "distinguished conduct" at Beverly, 7/63 by Col. W. L. Jackson in his report. Received "honorable mention" from Lt. Col. W. P. Thompson in his report of the battle of Droop Mtn., W. Va., 11/6/63. Present, Capt., 9/1/63 - 10/31/64 (dated 12/30/64). Wd. Smithfield, 8/28/64, severe. Wd. Leetown, 8/28/64, ear. Recommended for Maj. 1/12/65. Appointed Major 2/23/65, confirmed the same day, to rank from 11/22/64. Promoted to Lt. Col. Paroled at Charleston, W. Va., 5/10/65, as Lt. Col. Desc.: age 27, 5'8", dark comp., dark hair, black eyes, a mustache and beard. Post war source shows he was promoted to Col. at the end of the war for "meritorious service." Post war farmer and resident of Randolph Co., W. Va. Served in W. Va. Legislature, 1877 - 1879. Age 42, farmer, Huttonsville, Randolph Co., W. Va. 1880 Census. Awarded Cross of Honor. Owned a large tract of land in Randolph Co., W. Va. Brother of Eugene Hutton. Planned to attend the Gettysburg Reunion, 1913. J. near Huttonsville, W. Va., 4/19/1916. Bur. Old Brick Presbyterian Church Cem., Huttonsville, W. Va.

HUTTON, EUGENIUS (EUGENE) - 2nd Lt. Co. C. b. Huttonsville, Randolph Co., W. Va., 3/19/40. Age 20, farmer, Randolph Co., W. Va. 1860 Census. Prior service, Co. F, 31st Va. Inf. Attended Huttonsville Academy, 1861. Transf. to Co. C, 20th Va. Cav. No enl. data. Elected Jr. 2nd Lt., 4/16/63. Not stated if present or absent on muster-in roll dated 8/63, Jr. 2nd Lt. Present, 2nd Lt., 6/30/63 - 8/31/64 (dated 1/6/65). Promoted to 2nd Lt., 2/1/64. Ab., 2nd Lt., 9/1/64 - 10/31/64 (dated 12/30/64), KIA. Bunker Hill, W. Va., near Winchester, 9/3/64, shot through the heart, while eating his breakfast. Bur. Stephen's City Cem. Body moved to the Old Brick Church Cem., Huttonsville, by Joseph F. Harding and Elihu Hutton, and buried on 10/9/1905. "...always cheerful, kind to comrades, ready for duty and took gallant part in every important action...He was a brave and intrepid soldier..." Brother of Elihu Hutton.

HYMAN, JOHN ALEXANDER - 5th Sgt. Co. I. b.c. 1828. Enl. Warm Springs, 4/25/63 (4/1/63, 4/20/63), age 35. Not stated if present or absent on muster-in roll dated 5/5/63, 5th Sgt. Ab., Pvt., 11/1/63 - 8/31/64 (dated 1/6/65), sick. Clothing issued 2/29/64, signs by x. Present, Pvt., 11/1/63 - 10/31/64 (dated 12/31/64). NFR.

ICE, ALVIN (ALVA) NEWTON "Nute" - Pvt. Co. B. Enl. Marion Co., W. Va., 10/10/63. Present 11/1/63 - 8/31/64 (dated 1/6/65). Clothing issued 3/31/64. Present 9/1/64 - 10/31/64 (dated 12/30/64), entitled to $100 bond. Rode a mare, fall 1864. NFR.

IRVIN, JESSE - 3rd Corp. Co. I. b.c. 1847. Enl. Camp Northwest, W. Va., 6/20/63, age 16 by George Minter. Not stated if present or absent on muster-in roll dated 5/5/63, 3rd Corp. NFR.

IRVIN (ERVINE), WILLIAM Mc. - Pvt. Co. K. b. Bath (Rockbridge) Co., 12/22/36. Age 25, farmer, Wilsonville, Highland Co. 1860 Census. Prior service, 2nd Co. F, 25th Va. Inf. (listed as Ervine); Co. E, 31st Va. Inf. and Co. E, 27th Va. Inf. Enl. Camp Northwest, W. Va., 7/10/63. POW record shows he enl. in Pocahontas Co., W. Va., 2/63. Ab. 7/1/63 - 11/1/63 (dated 1/6/64), AWOL. Ab. 11/1/63 - 2/29/64, transf. to Co. I, 20th Va. Cav., 1/10/64. Clothing issued 2/29/64, signs by x. Ab. 2/29/64 - 8/31/64, transf. to Co. I, 20th Va. Cav., 10/10/64. Enl. in Co. I, 20th Va. Cav. at Camp Martin, 9/15/64 (also as Rockbridge Co., 4/64). Ab., Co. I, 11/1/63 - 8/31/64 (dated 1/6/65), deserted. Not stated if present or absent, 11/1/63 - 10/31/64 (dated 12/31/64). Deserted. Reported at Beverly, W. Va., 11/7/64. Confined at Clarksburg, W. Va. Took the oath of allegiance and was released, 11/8/64. Desc.: age 27, 5'10", fair comp., light hair and gray eyes. Occ. farmer, residing in Highland Co. Member Bath Co. Camp, UCV, 1894. Post war farmer, residing at Marmion, Rockbridge Co., 1900. Retired, Buffalo Dist., Rockbridge Co. 1910 Census. Post war rosters show service in 19th Va. Cav. d. on Tod Run, 7/14/1913. Bur. Irvine Family Cem.

IRVINE, B. FRANK - Pvt. Co. I. Enl. Camp Northwest, W. Va., 9/15/64 (Rockbridge Co., 4/10/64). Ab. 11/1/63 - 8/31/64 (dated 1/6/65), on detached service. Clothing issued 2/29/64. Ab. 11/1/63 - 10/31/64 (dated 12/31/64), on detached service. NFR.

IRVINE, ROBERT W. - Pvt. Co. I. b.c. 1829. Conscripted in Rockbridge Co., 2/16/64. Desc.: age 33, 5'11", fair comp., light hair, and brown eyes. Occ. farmer, residing at Monmouth, Rockbridge Co. Enl. Camp Northwest, W. Va., 9/15/64 (Rockbridge Co., 8/4/64). Ab. 11/1/63 - 8/31/64 (dated 1/6/65), on horse detail. Present 11/1/63 - 10/31/64 (dated 12/31/64). Farmhand, Kerr's Creek Dist., Rockbridge Co. 1870 Census. d. 1903.

ISNER, EUGENUS (EUGENE) - Pvt. Co. C. b.c. 1839. Age 21, farmer, Randolph Co., W. Va. 1860 Census. Enl. Randolph (Pocahontas) Co., W. Va., 5/14/63. Not stated if present or absent on muster-in roll dated 8/63. Ab. 6/30/63 - 8/31/64 (dated 1/6/65), on leave. Present 9/1/64 - 10/31/64 (dated 12/30/64). Paroled at Charleston, W. Va., 5/10/65, signs by x. Desc.: age 26, 5'1", dark comp., black hair, black eyes and black whiskers. Awarded Cross of Honor. Post war resident of Beverly, Randolph Co., W. Va. "One of the most highly respected citizens of Randolph Co., W. Va." Awarded Cross of Honor. Age 50, works on farm, Edray, Pocahontas Co., W. Va. 1880 Census. Attended Confederate Reunion, Randolph Co., W. Va., 1906. Attended Gettysburg Reunion, 1913. Resident of Beverly, W. Va., 1924. d. Elkins, W. Va., 6/18/1929, age 92, while visiting his son. Bur. Randolph Co., W. Va.

JACKSON, EDWARD - Pvt. Co. F. b. Lewis Co., W. Va., 7/25/40. Age 19, Calhoun Co., W. Va. 1860 Census. Enl. Camp Northwest, W. Va., 7/19/63. Not stated if present or absent on muster-in roll dated 7/20/63. Ab. 7/1/63 - 8/31/64 (dated 1/6/65), transf. to Co. A, 19th Va. Cav. Ab. 9/1/64 - 10/31/64 (dated 12/30/64), transf. to Co. A, 19th Va. Cav. Post war roster shows him as a resident of Pocahontas Co., W. Va. Age 39, farmer, Center Dist., Calhoun Co., W. Va. 1880 Census. d. 12/18/1918. Bur. Nobe Cem., Calhoun Co., W. Va.

JACKSON, JOHN - 2nd Corp. Co. I. b.c. 1833. Enl. Warm Springs, 4/10/63, age 30. Not stated if present or absent on muster-in roll dated 5/5/63, 4th Corp. Ab., 2nd Corp., 11/1/63 - 8/31/64 (dated 1/6/65), wd. Droop Mtn., 11/6/63. Ab. 11/1/63 - 10/31/64 (dated 12/31/64), wd. Droop Mtn., 11/6/63 and not reported for duty. NFR.

JACKSON, W. J. - Pvt. Co. ?. Not on muster rolls. Listed as a Pvt. in Hutton's Cav. Enl. Philadelphia(?), 2/1/64. Adm. Lee Hosp., Lauderdale, Miss., 4/12/64. Present on Hosp. MR, 3/1/64 - 4/30/64 (dated 4/30/64). NFR.

JAMES, A. L. - Pvt. Co. H. Not on muster rolls. Wartime document shows him as a member of this co., 7/8/64. NFR.

JAMES, ASHBELL F. - Pvt. Co. F. Enl. Camp Clover Lick, 7/11/63 (Camp Miller, 7/17/63). Not stated if present or absent on muster-in roll dated 7/20/63. Ab. 7/1/63 - 8/31/64 (dated 1/6/65), sick; entitled to enl. bounty. Ab. 9/1/64 - 10/31/64 (dated 12/30/64), sick; entitled to enl. bounty. Clothing issued at Staunton Gen. Hosp., 10/31/64. NFR

JAMES, EPHRAIM - Pvt. Co. E. Post war rosters only, which show he was a resident of Wood Co., W. Va. Served in Co. H, 11th W. Va. Inf., and deserted to CS service, 10/25/62. NFR.

JAMES, JOSEPH - Pvt. Co. G. b.c. 1837. Not on muster rolls. Cpd. Parkersburg, W. Va., 4/65. Confined at Clarksburg, W. Va., by 4/20/65. Paroled and released at Clarksburg, W. Va., 4/22/65. Desc.: age 28, 5'11", fair comp., brown hair and blue eyes. Occ. cooper, residing in Wood Co., W. Va. NFR.

JAMES, THORTON B. - 2nd Sgt. Co. G. Enl. Wood Co., W. Va., 5/2/63 (5/12/63). Not stated if present or absent on muster-in roll dated 8/63, 3rd Sgt. Present, 2nd Sgt., 11/1/63 - 2/29/64, had his own horse and equipment since 12/21/63. Clothing issued 2/29/64. Present, Pvt., 7/1/64 - 8/31/64, had his own horse since 12/19/63; entitled to bond. Ab., Pvt., 9/1/64 - 10/31/64 (dated 12/29/64), on leave; entitled to $100 bond. Post war resident of Wood Co., W. Va. NFR.

JAMES, W. F. - Pvt. Co. K. Not on muster rolls. Paroled at Greensboro, NC, 5/3/65. No desc. NFR.

JAMISON, HARRISON - Pvt Co. F. Enl. Bulltown, W. Va., 5/10/63 (Camp Clover Lick, 7/11/63). Not stated if present or absent on muster-in roll dated 7/20/63. Ab. 7/1/63 - 8/31/64 (dated 1/6/65), taken prisoner 5/13/63. Ab. 9/1/64 - 10/31/64 (dated 12/30/64), taken prisoner 5/13/63. No POW records. NFR.

JAMISON, JOHN W. - Pvt. Co. A. b. 1843. Enl. Monongalia Co., W. Va., 4/1/64. Present 10/31/63 - 8/31/64, entitled to $50 enl. bounty. Post war rosters show he was disc. 1865. Post war resident of Monongalia Co., W. Va. Age 36, farmer, Grant Dist., Monongalia Co., W. Va. 1880 Census. d. 5/30/1912. Bur. Zoar Cem., Monongalia Co., W. Va.

JAMISON, PIERCE L. - 4th Sgt. Co. A. b.c. 1840. Enl. Highland Co., 10/16/62, age 22. Not stated if present or absent on muster-in roll dated 10/16/62, 4th Sgt. Present, 4th Sgt., 7/1/63 9/1/63. Ab., 4th Sgt., 10/31/63 - 8/31/64, cpd. 2/14/64. Cpd. Marion Co., W. Va., 2/29/64. Confined at the Atheneum Prison, 3/1/64. Desc.: age 23, 5'7", fair comp., dark hair and gray eyes. Occ. farmer, residing in Monongalia Co., W. Va. Took the oath and was released, 6/6/65. Served in Co. D, 19th Va. Cav. Post war resident of Monongalia Co., W. Va. "A good soldier." NFR.

JEFFERSON, LON - Pvt. Co. E. Post war rosters only. Could be Jefferson Lan. NFR.

JENKINS, AMAZIAH (AMOZIAH) - 2nd Corp. Co. F. Enl. Bulltown, W. Va., 5/10/63. Not stated if present or absent on muster-in roll dated 7/20/63, Corp. Ab., 2nd Corp., 7/1/63 - 8/31/64 (dated 1/6/65), prisoner since 7/10/63; entitled to enl. bounty. Cpd. Weston, Lewis Co., W. Va., 7/11/63 (8/11/63). Confined at the Atheneum Prison, 8/17/63. Desc.: age 27, 6'1+", sallow comp., dark hair and blue eyes. Occ. farmer, residing in Harrison Co., W. Va. Transf. to Camp Chase, 8/24/63. Confined at Camp Chase, 8/25/63. Transf. to Ft. Delaware, 2/29/64. Confined at Ft. Delaware, 3/4/64 (3/2/64). Ab., 2nd Corp., 9/1/64 - 10/31/64 (dated 12/30/64), prisoner since 7/10/63. Took the oath of allegiance and was released, 5/8/65 (5/10/65). Desc.: age ?, 5'11", dark comp., dark hair and blue eyes, a resident of Harrison Co., W. Va. Age 43, farmer, Elk Dist., Harrison Co., W. Va. 1880 Census. NFR.

JENKINS, PHILLIP E. - Corp. Co. A. b.c. 1837. Not on muster rolls. Cpd. Beverly, W. Va., 12/13/63. Confined at the Atheneum Prison, 12/24/63. Desc.: age 26, 5'9 3/4", dark comp., dark hair and blue eyes. Occ. farmer, residing in Rockbridge Co. Transf. to Camp Chase, 12/26/63. Confined at Camp Chase, 12/27/63. Desires to take the oath of allegiance, 6/10/64. Took the oath of allegiance and was released, 11/29/64, by order of the Commissary Gen. of Prisoners. Desc.: age ?, 5'8+", light comp., dark hair and brown eyes. NFR.

JENNINGS, WALTER T. (J.) - 4th Sgt. Co. K. Enl. Fluvanna Co., 7/25/63. Present 7/1/63 - 11/1/63 (dated 1/6/64), promoted 4th Sgt., 8/27/63. Present 11/1/63 - 2/29/64, refused to serve as Sgt., reduced to the ranks 1/1/64; had his own horse since 7/1/64. Present 2/29/64 - 8/31/64, had his own horse since 5/1/64; $100 enl. bounty due. Clothing issued 2/29/64 and 3/23/64. NFR.

JETT, WESTLEY (WESLEY) JR. - Pvt. Co. D. Resident of Barbour Co., W. Va. Enl. Weston, W. Va., 5/1/63. Not stated if present or absent on muster-in roll dated 8/63. Present 7/1/63 - 1/1/64 (dated 1/1/64). Ab. 12/31/63 - 8/31/64 (dated 1/6/65), prisoner. Cpd. Piedmont, 6/5/64. Confined at Camp Morton, Indianapolis, Ind., 6/21/64. Ab. 9/1/64 - 10/31/64, POW. Paroled and sent to City Point, via Baltimore, to be exchanged, 3/4/65, signs by x. Exchanged at Boulware's & Cox's Wharf, James River, 3/12/65. Adm. Gen. Hosp. No. 9, 3/12/65. Transf. to Chimborazo Hosp., 3/13/65. Adm. Chimborazo Hosp. No. 2, 3/13/65, chronic diarrhoea. DOD. Chimborazo Hosp. No. 2, 3/20/65. Post war source shows he d. Camp Chase.

JOHNSON, AMOS N. - Pvt. Co. H. b. Ind., 5/17/42. Enl. Camp Northwest, W. Va., 7/1/63. Not stated if present or absent on muster-in roll dated 8/63. Transf. to Lurty's Batty. by Capt. Hayhurst, 11/1/63, listed as a resident of Alleghany Co., Md. Brother of William H. Johnson. Age 36, farmer, West Union Dist., Ritchie Co., W. Va. 1880 Census. d. Ritchie Co., W. Va., 1923. Bur. Pine Grove Cem., Berea, Ritchie Co., W. Va.

JOHNSON, G. W. - Pvt. Co. C. Enl. Pocahontas Co., W. Va., 4/1/63. Not stated if present or absent on muster-in roll dated 8/63. Present 6/30/63 - 8/31/64 (dated 1/6/65), 6% bond due. Clothing issued 3/10/64. Ab. 9/1/64 - 10/31/64 (dated 12/30/64), MIA since Fisher's Hill, 9/23/64; 6% bond due. NFR.

JOHNSON, GEORGE W. - Pvt. Co. I. b.c. 1832. Enl. Camp Northwest, W. Va., 7/1/63 (Rockbridge Co., 9/1/63). Ab. 11/1/63 - 8/31/64 (dated 1/6/65), deserted. Ab. 11/1/63 - 10/31/64 (dated 12/31/64), POW. d. Rockbridge Co., 1/12/65, age 33. Bur. Stonewall Jackson Cem., Lexington.

JOHNSON, RICHARD M. "Dick" - 1st Sgt. Co. D. b. Harrison Co., W. Va., c. 1843. Resident of Bridgeport, Harrison Co., W. Va. Enl. Weston, W. Va., 5/1/63. Not stated if present or absent on muster-in roll dated 8/63, 1st Sgt. Present, 1st Sgt., 7/1/63 - 1/1/64 (dated 1/1/64), had his own horse. Ab., Pvt., 12/31/63 - 8/31/64 (dated 1/6/65), transf. to Co. E, 20th Va. Cav., 4/18/64. Clothing issued, Co. D, 2/29/64. Ab., Pvt., 9/1/64 - 10/31/64, transf. to Co. E, 20th Va. Cav., 4/18/64. Present in Company E, 1/1/64 - 8/31/64 (dated 1/6/65), transf. by Capt. Corder, 5/1/64; entitled to $100 bond. Present 9/1/64 - 10/31/64 (dated 12/29/64), entitled to $100 bond. Wd./Cpd. Beverly, W. Va., 10/29/64. Post war rosters show he was wd. 11/27/64. Adm. USA Gen. Hosp., Beverly, W. Va., 10/29/64, flesh wd. to left arm. Treated by simple dressing. Transf. to Clarksburg, W. Va., 11/10/64. Admitted to USA Post Hosp., Clarksburg, W. Va., 11/12/64, gunshot wd. Transf. to Gen. Hosp., Grafton, 12/4/64. Desc.: age 21, 5'8", dark comp., black hair and dark eyes. Occ. soldier, residing in Harrison Co., W. Va. Adm. USA Gen. Hosp., Grafton, W. Va., 12/4/64, gunshot wd., flesh, lower third, left arm, nerves injured. Wd. by carbine ball at Beverly, W. Va., 10/29/64. Treated by cold water dressing. Released to Provost Marshall, 2/8/65. Confined at the Atheneum Prison, 2/9/65. Desc.: age 21, 5'8", light comp., light hair and black eyes, a resident of Augusta Co. Transf. to Camp Chase, 2/13/65. Confined at Camp Chase, 2/14/65. DOD. Camp Chase, 3/16/65, pneumonia. Bur. Camp Chase Confederate Cem., grave no. 1677. Post war rosters show burial at Bridgeport Cem., Bridgeport, W. Va. Post war rosters show him as a member of Brig. Gen. W. L. Jackson's staff.

JOHNSON, T. C. - Sgt. Major./Pvt. Co. C. Enl. Pocahontas Co., W. Va., 4/1/63. Not stated if present or absent on muster-in roll dated 8/63, Pvt. Present, Pvt., 6/30/63 - 8/31/64 (dated 1/6/65), 6% bond due. Present, Sgt. Major, 9/1/64 - 10/31/64 (dated 12/30/64), promoted to Sgt. Major, 9/1/64; 6% bond due. NFR.

JOHNSON, WILLIAM - Pvt. Co. H. Enl. Camp Northwest, W. Va., 7/1/63. Not stated if present or absent on muster-in roll dated 8/63. NFR.

JOHNSON, WILLIAM H. - Pvt. Co. A. Post war rosters only, which show he was a resident of Ritchie Co., W. Va. Served in Lurty's Batty., Co. A, 46th Battn. Va. Cav. and Co. A, 26th Va. Cav. Brother of Amos N. Johnson. NFR.

JOHNSON, WILLIAM H. - Pvt. Co. K. b.c. 1845. Enl. Warm Springs, 4/1/63, age 18. POW record shows enl. as Richmond, 4/62. Not stated if present or absent on muster-in roll dated 7/21/63. Present 7/1/63 - 11/1/63 (dated 1/6/64), lost Mississippi Rifle. Ab. 11/1/63 - 2/29/64, deserted 3/24/64. Clothing issued 2/29/64. Ab. 2/29/64 - 8/31/64, cpd. in Md., 7/29/64. Deserter. Gave himself up at Wearerton(?), Md., 8/7/64. Sent to Harpers Ferry, W. Va. Desc.: age 21, 5'3+", florid comp., light hair and hazel eyes, a resident of Richmond. Wished to take the oath of allegiance, 8/17/64. Confined at the Old Capitol Prison, 8/18/64. Took the oath of allegiance and was released, 8/18/64. Transportation furnished to Philadelphia, Pa. NFR.

JOHNSON, WILLIAM M. - Pvt. Co. D. Enl. Weston, W. Va., 5/1/63. Not stated if present or absent on muster-in roll dated 8/63. Present 7/1/63 - 1/1/64 (dated 1/1/64), no horse. Present 12/31/63 - 8/31/64 (dated 1/6/65). Ab. 9/1/64 - 10/31/64, sick; entitled to $100 bond. Clothing issued 8/3/64 and 11/28/64. NFR.

JONES, ANDREW J. - Pvt. Co. B. b. 9/16/35. Prior service, Co. D, 19th Va. Cav. Enl. Williamsburg, Greenbrier Co., W. Va., 3/17/63. Acting as courier at Beverly, W. Va., 7/3/63. Not stated if present or absent on muster-in roll dated 7/25/63. Present 11/1/63 - 8/31/64 (dated 1/6/65). Clothing issued 3/31/64. Present 9/1/64 - 10/31/64 (dated 12/30/64), entitled to $100 bond. Became ill, 8/30/64. Surg. Certificate issued 9/1/64. On furlough 10/64. Paroled at Clarksburg, W. Va., 7/28/65. Desc.: age 29, 6'2", light comp., dark hair and gray eyes, a farmer. Post war rosters show him as a Sgt. Post war resident of Monongalia Co., W. Va. Age 44, farmer, Clinton Dist., Monongalia Co., W. Va. 1880 Census. d. 10/7/1900. Bur. Pisgah Cem., Monongalia Co., W. Va.

JONES, HENRY FRANK (FRANK H.) - 1st Sgt. Co. B. b. Marion Co., W. Va., c. 1842. Enl. Marion Co., W. Va., 4/15/63 (2/7/63). POW record shows enl. as Monongalia Co., W. Va., 2/63. Not stated if present or absent on muster-in roll dated 7/25/63, 1st Sgt. Present, 1st Sgt., 11/1/63 - 8/31/64 (dated 1/6/65), AWOL 9/14/64. Clothing issued 3/31/64. Ab., 1st Sgt., 9/1/64 - 10/31/64 (dated 12/30/64), AWOL since 9/14/64. Cpd. Monongalia Co., W. Va., 3/22/65. Confined at Clarksburg, W. Va., 3/25/65. Desc.: age 23, 5'10", fair comp., dark hair and gray eyes. Occ. farmer, residing in Marion Co., W. Va. Post war rosters show him as a resident of Monongalia Co., W. Va. Age 37, farmer, Paw Paw Dist., Marion Co., W. Va. 1880 Census. NFR.

JONES, J. M. - Pvt. Co. I. Enl. Warm Springs, 4/1/63. Ab. 11/1/63 - 8/31/64 (dated 1/6/65), deserted. NFR.

JONES, JAMES H. - Pvt. Co. I. b.c. 1841. Enl. Camp Northwest, W. Va., 3/10/63, age 22. Not stated if present or absent on muster-in roll dated 5/5/63. NFR.

JONES, WESLEY (WILL) C. - Pvt. Co. C. Resident of Marion Co., W. Va. Arrested and confined by 3/15/62. Charged with being a secessionist. Enl. Pocahontas Co., W. Va., 4/16/63. Not stated if present or absent on muster-in roll dated 8/63. Ab. 6/30/63 - 8/31/64 (dated 1/6/65), sick since 4/15/64. Clothing issued 3/10/64 and 4/21/64, while sick in a hosp. Ab. 9/1/64 - 10/31/64 (dated 12/30/64), sick; 6% bond due. Cpd. as a vidette, Piedmont, 6/5/64. Confined at Camp Morton, Indianapolis, Ind., 6/21/64. Paroled and sent to Pt. Lookout, via Baltimore, to be exchanged, 3/18/65. Was not exchanged. Confined at Pt. Lookout. Took the oath of allegiance and was released, 6/14/65. Desc.: age ?, 5'9,:, light comp., brown hair and blue

219

eyes, a resident of Campbell Co. Adm. Jackson Hosp. Transf. to another hosp., 9/6/65. CSR shows him as having been exchanged at Boulware's Wharf, and that he was adm. in Gen. Hosp. No. 9, 3/26/65, furloughed 60 days, 3/27/65. CSR also shows him as having been adm. in Chimborazo Hosp. No. 4, 3/27/65, dementia. NFR.

JONES, WILLIAM A. - Pvt. Co. I. b.c. 1844. Enl. Warm Springs, 4/10/63 (4/1/63), age 19 (Monroe Co., W. Va., 10/10/63). Not stated if present or absent on muster-in roll dated 5/5/63. Ab. 11/1/63 - 8/31/64 (dated 1/6/65), listed as KIA (error). Ab. 11/1/63 - 10/31/64 (dated 12/31/64), listed as KIA (error). Cpd. Berryville, 8/11/64. Sent to Washington, DC. Confined at the Old Capitol Prison, 8/17/64. Transf. to Elmira, NY, 8/28/64. Confined at Elmira Prison, 8/29/64. Paroled and sent to the James River, 2/25/65, to be exchanged. Post war rosters show service in Co. F. NFR.

JONES, WILLIAM E. - Pvt. Co. E. b. Highland Co., c. 1846. Enl. Doe Hill, Highland Co., 2/15/64. POW record shows enl. as Highland Co., 3/63. Present 1/1/64 - 8/31/64 (dated 1/6/65), entitled to $100 bond. Present 9/1/64 - 10/31/64 (dated 12/29/64), entitled to $100 bond. Cpd. Beverly, W. Va., 10/29/64. Confined at Clarksburg, W. Va. Desc.: age 18, 5'10", fair comp., light hair and blue eyes. Occ. farmer, residing in Highland Co. Transf. to Wheeling, W. Va., 11/2/64. Confined at the Atheneum Prison, 11/2/64. Desc.: age 19, 5'9+", light comp., dark hair and blue eyes. Transf. to Camp Chase, 11/3/64. Confined at Camp Chase, 11/4/64. DOD. Camp Chase, 2/25/64, pneumonia. Bur. Camp Chase Confederate Cem., grave no. 1438.

JONES, WILLIAM H. - Pvt. Co. E. Enl. Camp Miller, 6/8/63 (5/20/63, 5/25/63). Not stated if present or absent on muster-in roll dated 7/18/63. Present 1/1/64 - 8/31/64 (dated 1/6/65), entitled to $100 bond. Present 9/1/64 - 10/31/64 (dated 12/29/64), entitled to $100 bond. NFR.

KEARN, BRICE - Lt. Co. ?. Not on muster rolls. Wartime diary shows he was cpd. by Averell's forces, 8/63. Exchanged on Valley Mountain, 9/12/63. Jackson's command had cpd. a Capt., a Sgt. and a Pvt., which they exhanged for Kearn and another Lt. Was sworn to reveal nothing he saw while in captivity. "A boy of Fairmont." NFR.

KEITH, GEORGE H. - Pvt. Co. D. Post war rosters only, which show he served 3 years and was a resident of Amherst Co. NFR.

KELLY, FRANCIS (FRANK) - Pvt. Co. K. b.c. 1836. Resident of Roane Co., W. Va. Arrested and confined at Camp Chase, by 3/15/62. Charged as being a secessionist and bushwhacker. Prior service, Co. D, 5th Ga. Inf. Transf. to Va. Army, 6/62. Enl. Warm Springs, 4/1/63, age 27. Not stated if present or absent on muster-in roll dated 7/21/63. Ab. 7/1/63 - 11/1/63 (dated 1/6/64), sent to Richmond to be tried for desertion. Drew a Ga. Pension, 1915. NFR.

KELLEY (KELLY), ISAAC - Pvt. Co. A. b. Marion Co., W. Va., c. 1842. Enl. Augusta Co., 2/15/63, age 21. POW record shows enl. as Highland Co., 2/63. Not stated if present or absent on muster-in roll dated 2/15/63. Present 7/1/63 - 9/1/63. Ab. 10/31/63 - 8/31/64, cpd. 10/26/64. Clothing issued 2/29/64 and 3/64. Cpd. Beverly, W. Va., 10/29/64. Confined at Clarksburg, W. Va. Desc.: age 23, 6'1", fair comp., dark hair and gray eyes. Occ. farmer, residing in Marion Co., W. Va. Transf. to Wheeling, W. Va., 11/2/64. Confined at the Atheneum Prison, 11/2/64. Desc.: age 23, 6'2", fair comp., auburn hair and gray eyes. Transf. to Camp Chase, 11/3/64. Confined at Camp Chase, 11/4/64. Took the oath of allegiance and was released, 6/12/65. Desc.: age 24, 6'+", dark comp., dark hair and gray eyes. Post war resident of Marion Co., W. Va. d. by 1911. NFR.

KELLY, JAMES - Pvt. Co. F. b. Randolph Co., W. Va., c. 1823 (1825). Age 35, farmer, Calhoun Co., W. Va. 1860 Census. Enl. Camp Northwest, W. Va. (Camp Miller), 7/19/63. Not stated if present or absent on muster-in roll dated 7/20/63. Ab. 7/1/63 - 8/31/64 (dated 1/6/65), transf. to Co. A, 19th Va. Cav. Ab. 9/1/64 10/31/64 (dated 12/30/64), transf. to Co. A, 19th Va. Cav. Age 47, farmer, Sherman Township, Calhoun Co., W. Va. 1870 Census. Age 55, farmer, Sherman Dist., Calhoun Co., W. Va. 1880 Census. NFR.

KELLY (KELLEY), JESSE - Pvt. Co. C. b.c. 1845. Enl. Randolph Co., W. Va., 5/1/63. Not stated if present or absent on muster-in roll dated 8/63. Ab. 6/30/63 - 8/31/64 (dated 1/6/65), whereabouts not known since enl. Age 35, farmer, New Interest, Randolph Co., W. Va. 1880 Census, name listed as Kelley. NFR.

KENT, JOHN T. - Pvt. Co. D. b.c. 1843. Resident of Barbour Co., W. Va. Enl. Weston, W. Va., 5/1/63. Not stated if present or absent on muster-in roll dated 8/63. Present 7/1/63 - 1/1/64 (dated 1/1/64). Clothing issued 2/29/64. Ab. 12/31/63 - 8/31/64 (dated 1/6/65), transf. to Capt. Hill's Co., 62nd Va. (Mtd.) Inf., 3/64. Ab. 9/1/64 - 10/31/64 (dated 1/6/65), transf. to Capt. Hill's Co., 62nd Va. (Mtd.) Inf., 3/64. Age 37, carpenter, Elk, Barbour Co., W. Va. 1880 Census. NFR.

KERNS (KEARNS), ELISHA - Pvt. Co. F. Enl. Camp Northwest, W. Va., (Camp Miller), 7/19/63. Not stated if present or absent on muster-in roll dated 7/20/63. Ab. 7/1/63 - 8/31/64 (dated 1/6/65), transf. to Co. A, 19th Va. Cav. Ab. 9/1/64 - 10/31/64 (dated 12/30/64), transf. to Co. A, 19th Va. Cav. Post war rosters show him as a resident of Calhoun Co., W. Va. NFR.

KERSH, GEORGE P. - Pvt. Co. G. b. Va., 2/17/24. Farmer, N. Dist., Augusta Co. 1860 Census. Not on muster rolls. Paroled at Staunton, 5/11/65. Desc.: age 42, 5'8", dark comp., dark hair and blue eyes. d. Augusta Co., 8/30/93. Bur. St. Michael's Church Cem., Augusta Co. NFR.

KIBLER, D. JOHN - 5th Sgt. Co. G. b.c. 1842. Enl. Wood Co., W. Va., 5/2/63. Not stated if present or absent on muster-in roll dated 8/63, 5th Sgt. Ab. 11/1/63 - 2/29/64, deserted 9/1/63. Post war resident of Wood Co., W. Va. Age 38, farmer, Clay Dist., Wood Co., W. Va. 1880 Census. NFR.

KIDWELL, HESS - Pvt. Co. G. Post war rosters only, which show he was a resident of Wood Co., W. Va. NFR.

KIDWELL, J. T. - Capt. Co. C. Not on muster rolls. Paroled at Winchester, 4/17/65. No desc. NFR.

KIDWELL, JOHN H. - Pvt. Co. A. b.c. 1848. Enl. Marion Co., W. Va., 7/22/64. Present 10/31/63 - 8/31/64. Age 32, sewing machine agent, Mannington Dist., Marion Co., W. Va. 1880 Census. NFR.

KIFTER, JACKSON - Pvt. Co. G. b.c. 1843. Not on muster rolls. Deserted. Took the oath of allegiance at Clarksburg, W. Va., 10/14/63, and was sent North. Desc.: age 20, 5'7", fair comp., light hair and blue eyes, a resident of Wood Co., W. Va. NFR.

KILLINGSWORTH, JOHN W. - Pvt. Co. G. b.c. 1843. Age 17, farmer, Randolph Co., W. Va. 1860 Census. Post war rosters only, which show him as a resident of Randolph Co., W. Va. Resident of Trubade, W. Va., 1916. NFR.

KINCADE (KINKAID), JOHN - Pvt. Co. D. Enl. New Hampton, Highland Co., 3/1/64. Present 12/31/63 - 8/31/64 (dated 1/6/65), enl. bounty due. Ab. 9/1/64 - 10/31/64, AWOL, not entitled to enl. bounty. NFR.

KING (KAING), MARION - Pvt. Co. G. b.c. 1842. Enl. Wood Co., W. Va., 5/2/63. Not stated if present or absent on muster-in roll dated 8/63. Present 11/1/63 - 2/29/64. Clothing issued 2/29/64, signs by x. Present 7/1/64 - 8/31/64, had his own horse since 12/19/63; entitled to bond. Ab. 9/1/64 - 10/31/64 (dated 12/29/64), on leave; entitled to $100 bond. Age 38, farm laborer, Steele Dist., Wood Co., W. Va. 1880 Census. NFR.

KING, MELVILLE - Pvt. Co. G. Post war rosters only, which show he was a resident of Wood Co., W. Va. NFR.

KIRKPATRICK, JOHN - Pvt. Co. C. b. Highland Co., c. 1816. Age 44, carpenter, Wilsonville, Highland Co. 1860 Census. Enl. Highland Co., 7/1/64. Ab. 6/30/63 - 8/31/64 (dated 1/6/65), sick; enl. bounty due. Ab. 9/1/64 - 10/31/64 (dated 12/30/64), sick. NFR.

KISER (KIZER), JOHN - Pvt. Co. E. Enl, Camp Clover Lick, 7/17/63. Not stated if present or absent on muster-in roll dated 7/18/63. Served in Co. C, 19th Va. Cav. NFR.

KISER (KEISER, KIZER), WILLIAM - Pvt. Co. E. Enl. Camp Clover Lick, 7/17/63. Not stated if present or absent on muster-in roll dated 7/18/63. Served in Co. C, 19th Va. Cav. Post war resident of Wood Co., W. Va. NFR.

KITTLE, MORGAN - Pvt. Co. ?. b. 5/17/35. Age 25, blacksmith, Randolph Co., W. Va. 1860 Census. Post war rosters only, which show him as a resident of Randolph Co., W. Va. Age 45, farmer, Green Dist., Randolph Co., W. Va. 1880 Census. d. 4/17/88. Bur. Baptist Cem., Arnold Hill, Randolph Co., W. Va.

KITTLE, MOSES - Pvt. Co. E. b. Randolph Co., W. Va., 7/9/42. Enl. Camp Clover Lick, 7/11/63. Not stated if present or absent on muster-in roll dated 7/18/63. Served in the 26th Va. Cav. Post war farmer and resident of Sandyville, Jackson Co., W. Va. d. Sandyville, Jackson Co., W. Va., 12/25/1927. Bur. "Center Valley", Wirt Co., W. Va.

KNICK, JOSEPH - Pvt. Co. I. b.c. 1840. Enl. Warm Springs, 4/21/63, age 23. Not stated if present or absent on muster-in roll dated 5/5/63. NFR.

KNISLEY (KNISELEY), GEORGE W. - Pvt. Co. E. Enl. Bulltown, W. Va., 5/10/63. Not stated if present or absent on muster-in roll dated 7/18/63. Present 1/1/64 - 8/31/64 (dated 1/6/65), entitled to $100 bond. Present 9/1/64 - 10/31/64 (dated 12/29/64), entitled to $100 bond. NFR.

KNISLEY (KNISELEY), HOLDRIDGE M. (H. C.) - Pvt. Co. D. Enl. Hightown, Highland Co., 7/15/63. Not stated if present or absent on muster-in roll dated 8/63. Present 7/1/63 - 1/1/64 (dated 1/1/64), had his own horse; entitled to enl. bounty. Present 12/31/63 - 8/31/64 (dated 1/6/65). Clothing issued 2/29/64. Present 9/1/64 - 10/31/64, entitled to $100 enl. bounty. NFR.

KNISLEY (KNISELEY), LAFAYETTE M. - 1st Sgt. Co. D. Enl. Huntersville, W. Va., 6/1/63 (Weston, W. Va., 5/1/63 or 5/2/63). Not stated if present or absent on muster-in roll dated 8/63, 1st Sgt. Present, 1st Sgt., 7/1/63 - 1/1/64 (dated 1/1/64), appointed 1st Sgt., 7/1/63. Present 12/31/63 - 8/31/64 (dated 1/6/65). Clothing issued 2/29/64. Ab. 9/1/64 - 10/31/64, sick; entitled to $100 enl. bounty. NFR.

LACEY, JOHN - Pvt. Co. ?. Post war rosters only, which show he was in service by 9/12/63, and was a resident of Upshur Co., W. Va. NFR.

LADY, JOHN BUFORD - Major. b. Washington Co., Pa., 9/29/40. Moved to Wheeling, W. Va., nail cutter. Prior service, Shriver Greys, Co. G, 27th Va. Inf., 1st Lt., Co. D, 36th Battn. Va. Cav., and 14th Va. Cav. Wd. 1st Manassas, 7/21/61. Cpd. Kernstown, 3/23/62. Elected 1st Lt., Co. D, 36th Battn. Va. Cav., 12/10/62. Resigned 4/4/63, to raise a Battn. within enemy lines for service in Col. W. L. Jackson's brigade. Requested leave, but was denied. Ordered to report to Col. W. L. Jackson, 4/6/63. Hon. Charles W. Russell, House of Representatives requested that Lady's resignation not be accepted, 4/10/63, stating it was submitted by error. Raised two companies, by authority granted him by the Sec. of War. Elected Maj., 20th Va. Cav., 7/29/63. Appcinted Maj. 8/14/63, confirmed by election, to rank from 8/14/63. Mentioned for gallantry in Col. W. L. Jackson's report, 12/63. Present, Maj., FS MR 1/1/64 - 8/31/64 (dated 1/6/65). Detailed for duty on a Gen. Court Martial, Warm Springs, Bath Co., 2/25/64. Commanding a detachment of Cav. in Alleghany Co., 6/28/64. Recommended for Lt. Col., 11/18/64, by Brig. Gen. H. B. Davidson, who said Lady was "a gallant and meritorious officer..." Transf. to 47th Battn. Va. Cav., as Maj. Commanding 26th Va. Cav., 11/64. Appointed Lt. Col., 1/12/65, confirmed the same day, to rank from 11/22/64. Paroled at Staunton, 5/16/65 as Col. Desc.: age 25, 5'9+", fair comp., dark hair and gray eyes. Took the oath of allegiance 5/22/65. Farmer, Lexington Dist., Rockbridge Co. 1870 Census. Member Va. Legislature. "A brave and energetic officer, in service since the beginning of the war." d. near Lexington, 6/15/83, "of lead poisoning from a ball received when wounded in battle."

LAKE, ISAAC MILTON - Pvt. Co. A. b. Taylor Co., W. Va., c. 1839. Enl. Augusta Co. (Lewis Co., W. Va.), 3/16/63 (3/1/63), age 24. Not stated if present or absent on muster-in roll dated 3/16/63. Present 7/1/63 - 9/1/63. Present 10/31/63 - 8/31/64, was AWOL 9/1/64 - 10/20/64. Employed as a laborer at Warm Springs, 1/10/64 - 2/21/64, discharged and sent back to his Co. Clothing issued 2/29/64. Left behind enemy lines, summer 1864, for 10 days. Cpd. Randolph Co., W. Va., 3/8/65. Confined at Clarksburg, W. Va., 3/14/65. Desc.: age 26, 5'7", fair comp., light hair and blue eyes. Occ. farmer, residing in Taylor Co., W. Va. Transf. to Wheeling, W. Va., 3/15/65. Confined at the Atheneum Prison, 3/15/65. Desc.: age 26, 5'7", florid comp., dark hair and blue eyes. Transf. to Camp Chase, 3/16/65. Confined at Camp Chase, 3/17/65. Paroled and sent to New Orleans, La., 5/2/65, to be exchanged. Exchanged at Vicksburg, Miss., 5/12/65. Post war resident of Taylor Co., W. Va. NFR.

LAMB, CYRUS MORRISON - Pvt. Co. K. b. 2/19/37. Farmhand, 4th Dist., Rockbridge Co. 1860 Census. Prior service, Co. I, 4th Va. Inf. Enl. Camp Marlin's Bottom, Pocahontas Co., W. Va., 9/22/63. Ab. 7/1/63 - 11/1/63 (dated 1/6/64), POW, cpd. Droop Mtn., 11/6/63. Ab. 11/1/63 - 2/29/64, cpd. Droop Mtn., 11/6/63. Confined at the Atheneum Prison, 11/18/63. Desc.: age 26, 5'10 3/4", florid comp., dark hair and dark eyes. Occ. farmer, residing in Rockbridge Co. Transf. to Camp Chase, 11/19/63. Confined at Camp Chase, 11/20/63. Transf. to Ft. Delaware, 2/29/64. Confined at Ft. Delaware, 3/4/64 (3/2/64). Ab. 2/29/64 - 8/31/64, cpd. Droop Mtn., 11/6/63. Took the oath of allegiance and was released, 6/20/65. Desc.: age ?, 5'10", dark comp., dark hair and dark eyes, a resident of Rockbridge Co. Farmhand, Kerr's Creek Dist., Rockbridge Co. 1870 Census. d. Kerr's Creek, 11/24/99. Bur. McKee Cem., Rt. 631, Rockbridge Co.

LAN (LON, LAW, LANG), JEFFERSON - Pvt. Co. E. Post war resident of Jane Lew, W. Va. Could be Lon Jefferson. NFR.

LANCE (LANTZ), GEORGE WASHINGTON - Pvt. Co. D. b. Hamburg, Shenandoah Co., 6/18/28. Post war rosters show service in Co. C, 7th Va. Cav. Enl. Camp Scott, 8/9/63. Ab. 7/1/63 - 1/1/64 (dated 1/1/64), prisoner. Ab. 12/31/63 - 8/31/64 (dated 1/6/65), prisoner. Ab. 9/1/64 - 10/31/64, POW. No POW records. d. Mt. Jackson, 8/19/1904. Bur. Lantz-Bowman Cem., near Edinburg.

LANCE (LANSE), JOHN - Pvt. Co. D. Enl. Hightown, Highland Co., 6/27/63. Not stated if present or absent on muster-in roll dated 8/63. Ab. 7/1/63 - 1/1/64 (dated 1/1/64), AWOL since 9/63. Ab. 12/31/63 - 8/31/64 (dated 1/6/65), AWOL since 9/63. Ab. 9/1/64 10/31/64, AWOL. NFR.

LANCE (LANSE), WILLIAM J. - Pvt. Co. D. Enl. Hightown, Highland Co., 6/27/63. Not stated if present or absent on muster- in roll dated 8/63. Ab. 7/1/63 - 1/1/64 (dated 1/1/64), AWOL since 9/63. Ab. 12/31/63 - 8/31/64 (dated 1/6/65), AWOL since 9/63. Ab. 9/1/64 - 10/31/64, AWOL. NFR.

LANHAM, MANUEL (MANLEY) - Pvt. Co. E. Post war rosters only, which show he enl. 6/5/61 and was disc. 6/65. Bur. IOOF Cem., Clarksburg, W. Va.

LANKFORD, JAMES H. - Pvt. Co. K. b.c 1840. Enl. Warm Springs, 3/1/63, age 23. Enl. also as Lewisburg, W. Va. Not stated if present or absent on muster-in roll dated 7/21/63. Ab. 7/1/63 - 11/1/63 (dated 1/6/64), AWOL. Ab. 11/1/63 - 2/29/64, AWOL. Ab. 2/29/64 - 8/31/64, AWOL. NFR.

LASURE, FRANKLIN - Pvt. Co. C. Enl. Randolph Co., W. Va., 5/5/63. Not stated if present or absent muster-in roll dated 8/63. Ab. 6/30/63 - 8/31/64 (dated 1/6/65), whereabouts unknown since enl. NFR.

LAW (LANE), WILLIAM J. - Orderly (1st) Sgt. Co. E. b.c 1846. Enl. Bulltown, W. Va., 5/10/63. Not stated if present or absent on muster-in roll dated 8/63. Present 1st Corp. on 7/18/63, 1st Corp. Present 1st Corp., 1/1/64 8/31/64 (dated 1/6/65), entitled to $100 bond. Ab. 1st Corp., 9/1/64 - 10/31/64 (dated 12/29/64), sick in Staunton Gen. Hosp.; entitled to $100 bond. Clothing issued 11/9/64, on the way to his command. Paroled at Staunton, 5/9/65, as Orderly Sgt. Desc.: age 19, 6', fair comp., light hair and blue eyes. Took the amnesty oath at Clarksburg, W. Va., 9/11/65. NFR.

LEACHMAN, JERRY M. - Pvt. Co. G and Chaplain. b. Wood Co., W. Va., 3/14/27. Enl. Wood Co., W. Va., 6/24/63, in Co. G. Not stated if present or absent on muster-in roll dated 8/63. Present 11/1/63 - 2/29/64, appointed Chaplain, 8/15/63. Appointed Chaplain 9/7/63, to rank from 8/14/63. Present, Chaplain, FS MR 1/1/64 - 8/31/64 (dated 1/6/65). "In many of their marches he carried the flag. He not only preached, but fought and worked." Held a large number of meetings at Bath CH, where he had scores of converts and baptized a great many. "He was held in high esteem by all who knew him; a zealous leader of the Baptist denomination, he preached throughout West Virginia for twenty-five years." Post war minister, and resident of Wood Co., W. Va. Brother of John R. Leachman. d. 5/13/81, of a cold contracted while holding a revival service.

LEACHMAN; JOHN R. - Pvt. Co. G. b. Wood Co., W. Va., 8/17/32. Enl. Wood Co., W. Va., 6/24/63. Not stated if present or absent on muster-in roll dated 8/63. Present 11/1/63 - 2/29/64, has his own horse and equipment. Present 7/1/64 - 8/31/64, has his own horse; entitled to bond. Ab. 9/1/64 - 10/31/64 (dated 12/29/64), on leave; entitled to $100 bond. Paroled at Staunton, 5/23/65. Desc.: age 32, 6', fair comp., dark hair and gray eyes. Post war sketch states he enl. at Camp Northwest, on the Greenbrier River. Post war resident of Wood Co., W. Va. Age 47, farmer, Harris Dist., Wood Co., W. Va. 1880 Census. Member A. G. Jenkins Camp, UCV, Wood Co., W. Va. Brother of Jerry M. Leachman. Bur. Mt. Olivet Cem., Parkersburg, W. Va.

LEASON (LEESON), JOHN Jr. - Pvt. Co. F. b. Monongalia Co., W. Va., c. 1834. Age 26, farmer, Calhoun Co., W. Va. 1860 Census. Enl. Camp Northwest, W. Va. (Camp Miller), 7/19/63. Not stated if present or absent on muster-in roll dated 7/20/63. Ab. 7/1/63 - 8/31/64 (dated 1/6/65), transf. to Co. A, 19th Va. Cav. Ab. 9/1/64 10/31/64 (dated 12/30/64), transf. to Co. A, 19th Va. Cav. Age 35, farmer, Sheridan Township, Calhoun Co., W. Va. 1870 Census. Age 46, farmer, Sheridan Dist., Calhoun Co., W. Va. 1880 Census. Bur. United Brethern Cem., Pennsboro, Ritchie Co., W. Va., listed as John Seeson.

LEACH (LEECH), JAMES RODGERS - Pvt. Co. K. b. Collierstown, 4/27/45. Enl. Enl. Camp Marlin's Bottom, Pocahontas Co., W. Va., 8/27/63. Present 7/1/63 - 11/1/63 (dated 1/6/64), had his own horse since enl.; lost a Danville Rifle. Present 11/1/63 - 2/29/64, had his own horse since enl. Present 2/29/64 - 8/31/64, had his own horse since enl.; $100 enl. bounty due. Clothing issued 2/29/64 and 3/23/64. Post war roster shows he enl. 10/6/62. Post war farmer and resident of Collierstown, Rockbridge Co. d. Collierstown, 1/18/99. Bur. Collierstown Presbyterian Church Cem.

LEEPER, JOSEPH A. "Joe" - Jr. 2nd Lt. Co. B. b. Marion Co., W. Va., c. 1838. Prior service, Co. A, 31st Va. Inf. Enl. Fairmont, W. Va., 5/17/61. Present, Jr. 2nd Lt., 11/1/63 - 8/31/64 (dated 1/6/65), elected Jr. 2nd Lt., 9/4/63. Ab. 9/1/64 - 10/31/64 (dated 12/30/64), on detached service; elected Jr. 2nd Lt., 9/4/63. Ab. 10/25/64, in charge of horses, 90 days. Post war resident of Marion Co., W. Va. Age 43, farmer, Grant Dist., Marion Co., W. Va. 1880 Census. NFR.

LEESON, NATHANIEL G. - Pvt. Co. F. b. Monongalia Co., W. Va., c. 1841 (1830). Age 30, farmer, Calhoun Co., W. Va. 1860 Census. Prior service, Va. State Line. Enl. Camp Northwest, W. Va. (Camp Miller), 7/19/63. Not stated if present or absent on muster-in roll dated 7/20/63. Ab. 7/1/63 - 8/31/64 (dated 1/6/65), transf. to Co. A, 19th Va. Cav. Ab. 9/1/64 - 10/31/64 (dated 12/30/64), transf. to Co. A, 19th Va. Cav. Age 40, farmer, Sheridan Township, Calhoun Co., W. Va. 1870 Census. Age 47, farmer, Sheridan Dist., Calhoun Co., W. Va. 1880 Census. NFR.

LEECHMAN, THOMAS - Pvt. Co. I. b.c 1838. Enl. Lewisburg, W. Va., 4/25/63, age 25. Not stated if present or absent on muster-in roll dated 5/5/63. NFR.

LEWIS, ASBURY - Capt. Co. F. b. Harrison Co., W. Va., c. 1841 (1840). Age 18 (1861). Resident of Lewis Co., W. Va. Prior service, Co. C, 31st Va. Inf. Enl. Bulltown, W. Va., 5/10/63. Elected Capt., 5/10/63. Present on muster-in roll dated 7/20/63, signs roll. Present 7/1/63 - 8/31/64 (dated 1/6/65). Mentioned for his "brave bearing" at the battle of Droop Mtn., W. Va., 11/6/63, by Col. W. L. Jackson. Present 9/1/64 - 10/31/64 (dated 12/30/64). Member of Examining board, Jackson's Brigade, 10/27/64. Commanding Reg't., fall 1864. Horse Wd. Bunker Hill, 1864. Paroled at Charleston, W. Va., 5/10/65. Desc.: age 25, 5'9", fair comp., light hair and blue eyes. Post war farmer and trader. Moved to Spencer, Roane Co., W. Va., 1880, farmer. Alive 1913. NFR.

LEWIS, EDWARD J. J. - Pvt. Co. C. Prior service, Co. I, 19th Va. Cav. Enl. Pocahontas Co., W. Va., 6/30/63 (7/1/63, 7/12/63). Not stated if present or absent on muster-in roll dated 8/63. Ab. 6/30/63 - 8/31/64 (dated 1/6/65), deserted and gone to the enemy, 6/1/64. Ab. 9/1/64 - 10/31/64 (dated 12/30/64), deserted 6/1/64. NFR.

LEWIS, GEORGE W. - Pvt. Co. E. Enl. Harrison Co., W. Va., 5/6/63, by John L. Bussey. Ab. 1/1/64 - 8/31/64 (dated 1/6/65), cpd. Harrison Co., W. Va., 5/7/63. Ab. 9/1/64 - 10/31/64 (dated 12/29/64), cpd. Harrison Co., W. Va., 5/6/63. No POW records. NFR.

LEWIS, JAMES - Pvt. Co. E. Enl. Harrison Co., W. Va., 5/4/63, by John L. Bussey. Not stated if present or absent on muster-in roll dated 7/18/63. Was taken prisoner, 5/63, while on the way to join Col. W. L. Jackson, at or near Weston, W. Va. Confined at Camp Chase, as a political prisoner. NFR.

LEWIS, JOHN H. - 1st Lt. Co. B. Enl. Hightown, Highland Co., 4/15/63 (11/6/62). Not stated if present or absent on muster-in roll dated 7/25/63, 2nd Lt. Elected 1st Lt., 8/14/63. Present, 1st Lt., 11/1/63 - 8/31/64 (dated 1/6/65), promoted 1st Lt., 8/15/63. Mentioned for his "brave bearing" at the battle of Droop Mtn., W. Va., 11/6/63, by Col. W. L. Jackson, and received "honorable mention" from Lt. Col. W. P. Thompson in his report. Detailed on a scout in the mountains, 7/64. Granted a leave of absence 8/64 in the Dept. of Richmond. Ab., 1st Lt., 9/1/64 - 10/31/64 (dated 12/30/64), on detached service. Ab. 10/25/64, on recruiting duty by order of Gen. J. A. Early, 40 days, was to have returned in 30 days. Ab. 12/15/64, wd. since 12/7/64. Adm. Charity Hosp., Gordonsville, by 12/31/64. Applied for leave of absence at Staunton, 1/13/65, approved. Post war rosters show Co. A. Post war resident of Marion Co., W. Va. NFR.

LIGGOTT (LEGGETT), AUGUSTUS C. - 2nd Lt. Co. K. Enl. Warm Springs (Lewisburg, W. Va.), 2/16/63. Not stated if present or absent on muster-in roll dated 7/21/63, 3rd Lt. Elected Jr. 2nd Lt., 7/22/63. Ab., 3rd Lt., 7/1/63 - 11/1/63 (dated 1/6/64), promoted to 3rd Lt.; absent in hosp., wd. Droop Mtn., 11/6/63. Ab., 2nd Lt., 11/1/63 - 2/29/64, promoted 2nd Lt., 1/1/64; absent sick. Ab., 2nd Lt., 2/29/64 - 8/31/64, retired 4/22/64, due to wd. Ab. 10/25/64, wd., 11 months. NFR.

LILEY (LILLY), R. ALLISON - Pvt. Co. D. b.c. 1831. Enl. New Hampton, Highland Co., 4/1/64. Present 12/31/63 - 8/31/64 (dated 1/6/65). Present 9/1/64 - 10/31/64, entitled to $100 enl. bounty. Clothing issued at Montgomery Springs Gen. Hosp., 9/30/64. Clothing issued 11/13/64, on the way to his command. Paroled at Staunton, 5/24/65. Desc.: age 34, 5'11", light comp., light hair and gray eyes. NFR.

LILLEY (LILLY), DAVID H. - Pvt. Co. D. b.c. 1825. Age 35, lawyer, Randolph Co., W. Va. 1860 Census. Employed in the Ordnance Dept. at Bath Alum Springs, Bath Co., 10/63. Enl. Hightown, Highland Co., 3/1/64. Not stated if present or absent 12/31/63 - 8/31/64 (dated 1/6/65). Listed as AAQM for a detachment of Cav. under Maj. John B. Lady, 6/28/64. Ab. 9/1/64 - 10/31/64, AWOL. Surrendered at Beverly, W. Va., 5/15/65. Confined at Clarksburg, W. Va., 5/16/65. Paroled for exchanged and released, 5/16/65. Desc.: age 42, 6', fair comp., dark hair and blue eyes. Occ. lawyer, residing in Randolph Co., W. Va. Post war rosters show that he served as an aide to Col. Arnett, and that he was wd. in the hand at Darkesville, W. Va., 1864. Post war rosters shows he was a resident of Rockbridge Co., and that he served in the 27th Battn. Va. Cav. Served in the 19th Va. Cav. d. by 1916. NFR.

LIPSCOMB, FLAVIOUS J. - Pvt. Co. D. b.c. 1841. Enl. Weston, W. Va., 5/1/63. Not stated if present or absent on muster-in roll dated 8/63. Present 7/1/63 - 1/1/64 (dated 1/1/64), had his own horse. Present 12/31/63 - 8/31/64 (dated 1/6/65). Clothing issued 11/20/63, 12/22/63 (detailed) and 1/17/64, signs by x. Employed as a teamster at Warm Springs, 1/1/64 - 2/16/64, discharged and sent to his Co. Ab. 9/1/64 - 10/31/64, on detached service; entitled to $100 enl. bounty. Paroled at Staunton, 5/25/65, signs by x. Desc.: age 24, 5'4", dark comp., dark hair and brown eyes. NFR.

LOAN, J. W. - Pvt. Co. K. b.c. 1846. Age 14, Cleek's Mill, Bath Co. 1860 Census. Enl. Camp Cameron, Bath Co., 2/20/64. Present 11/1/63 - 2/29/64. Ab. 2/29/64 - 8/31/64, AWOL. Arrested 4/8/65. Took the oath of allegiance at Clarksburg, W. Va. Confined at the Atheneum Prison, 4/10/65. No desc., a resident of Bath Co. NFR.

LOCKE, ABIAH - 2nd Sgt. Co. H and Co. G. Enl. Calhoun Co., W. Va., 5/14/63 in Co. H. Not stated if present or absent on muster-in roll dated 8/63, Pvt. Enl. Wood Co., W. Va., 5/9/63 in Co. G. Not stated if present or absent on muster-in roll dated 8/63, 2nd Sgt. Ab. 11/1/63 - 2/29/64, deserted 9/63. NFR.

LOCKRIDGE, EDWARD FRANKLIN - Pvt. Co. ?. b. Augusta Co., c. 1822. Age 38, farmer, 6th Dist. Rockbridge Co. 1860 Census. Prior service, Co. G, 27th Va. Inf. Disc. 1863. Desc.: age 46, 6', fair comp., dark hair and brown eyes. Post war rosters only. d. near Raphine, 7/10/94, age 72. Bur. New Providence Presbyterian Church Cem.

LONG, P. H. - Pvt. Co. C. Enl. Randolph (Pocahontas) Co., W. Va., 5/2/63. Not stated if present or absent on muster-in roll dated 8/63. Ab. 6/30/63 - 8/31/64 (dated 1/6/65), deserted 9/1/63. NFR.

LOUDERMILK, WILLIAM - Pvt. Co. K. b.c. 1831. Enl. Lewisburg, W. Va., 5/1/63, age 32. Not stated if present or absent on muster-in roll dated 7/21/63. Ab. 7/1/63 - 11/1/63 (dated 1/6/64), AWOL. Ab. 11/1/63 - 2/29/64, AWOL. Ab. 2/29/64 - 8/31/64, AWOL. NFR.

LOVELL, BENJAMIN F. - 3rd Corp. Co. B. Prior service, Co. D, 19th Va. Cav. Enl. Williamsburg, Greenbrier Co., W. Va., 3/17/63 (4/15/63). Not stated if present or absent on muster-in roll dated 7/25/63, 4th Corp. Ab., 3rd Corp., 11/1/63 - 8/31/64 (dated 1/6/65), returned to his original Co. in the 19th Va. Cav., 4/64. (CSR shows 17th Va. Cav.) Ab. 9/1/64 - 10/31/64 (dated 12/30/64), taken back to his original Co. in 19th Va. Cav. NFR.

LOW (LOWE), ALEXANDER A. - Pvt. Co. G. b.c. 1839. Enl. Wood Co., W. Va., 6/24/63. Not stated if present or absent on muster-in roll dated 8/63. Ab. 11/1/63 - 2/29/64, had his own horse and equipment; cpd. Droop Mtn., W. Va., 11/6/63. Cpd. Pocahontas Co., W. Va., 11/6/63. Confined at the Atheneum Prison, 11/16/63. Desc.: age 24, 5'9+", florid comp., black hair and gray eyes. Occ. farmer, residing in Wood Co., W. Va. Transf. to Camp Chase, 11/18/63. Confined at Camp Chase, 11/18/63. Transf. to Ft. Delaware, 2/29/64. Confined at Ft. Delaware, 3/4/64. Ab. 7/1/64 - 8/31/64, cpd. by the enemy 11/4/63. Ab. 9/1/64 - 10/31/64 (dated 12/29/64), cpd. 11/6/63. Paroled and sent to City Point, 2/27/65, to be exchanged. Landed at Dutch Gap, 3/3/65. Adm. Chimborazo Hosp. No. 5, 3/4/65, chronic diarrhoea. Adm. Chimborazo Hosp. No. 1, 3/7/65. Furloughed 3/11/65, 30 days. Post Office listed as Christiansburg, Montgomery Co. Post war resident of Wood Co., W. Va. NFR.

LOW (LOWE), JOHN P. (B.) - Pvt. Co. G. Enl. Wood Co., W. Va., 6/24/63. Not stated if present or absent on muster-in roll dated 8/63. Present 11/1/63 - 2/29/64. Clothing issued 2/29/64. Not stated if present or absent 7/1/64 - 8/31/64, entitled to bond. Ab. 9/1/64 - 10/31/64 (dated 12/29/64), on detached service; entitled to $100 bond. Post war resident of Wood Co., W. Va. NFR.

LOW, NATHANIEL (NATHAN) P. (B.) - Pvt. Co. G. Enl. Wood Co., W. Va., 6/24/63 (6/18/63). Not stated if present or absent on muster-in roll dated 8/63. Present 11/1/63 - 2/29/64. Clothing issued 2/29/64. Not stated if present or absent 7/1/64 - 8/31/64, has his own horse; entitled to bond. Ab. 9/1/64 - 10/31/64 (dated 12/29/64), on detached service; entitled to $100 bond. Age 44, farmer, Steele Dist., Wood Co., W. Va. 1880 Census. NFR.

LOWEN, JOHN WILLIAM - Pvt. Co. A. b. Albemarle Co., c. 5/43. Prior service, Co. G, 25th Va. Inf. Pension record only, which shows he was a farmer, residing at Covington. Age 65 (1908). d. Clifton Forge, 5/13/1935.

LOWERS, HENRY - Pvt. Co. G. Post war rosters only, which show he was a resident of Wood Co., W. Va. Age 46, farmer, Harris Dist., Wood Co., W. Va. 1880 Census. NFR.

LOWMAN, WILLIAM C. - 1st Corp. Co. K. b.c. 1840. Enl. Camp Northwest, W. Va., 6/1/63, age 23. Not stated if present or absent on muster-in roll dated 7/21/63. 4th Corp. Present, 3rd Corp., 7/1/63 - 11/1/63 (dated 1/6/64), promoted to 3rd Corp., 8/1/63; had his own horse from enl. to 8/25/63. Present, 2nd Corp., 11/1/63 - 2/29/64, promoted to 2nd Corp., 1/1/64. Ab., 1st Corp., 2/29/64 - 8/31/64, POW, cpd. near Lexington, 6/9/64. Cpd. near Lexington, 6/11/64 (Augusta Co., 6/10/64). Confined at the Atheneum Prison, 7/1/64. Desc.: age 21(?), 5'6", fair comp., dark hair and blue eyes. Occ. miller, residing in Rockbridge Co. Transf. to Camp Chase, 7/2/64. Confined at Camp Chase, 7/3/64. Paroled and sent to City Point, 3/2/65, to be exchanged. Exchanged at Boulware's & Cox's Wharf, James River, 3/65. NFR.

LUCAS (LUCAIS), ABRAHAM F. - Pvt. Co. H and Co. G. b. Pa., 8/12/40. Enl. Calhoun Co., W. Va., 5/14/63 in Co. H. Not stated if present or absent on muster-in roll dated 8/63. Enl. Wood Co., W. Va., 5/9/63 in Co. G. Not stated if present or absent on muster-in roll dated 8/63. Present 11/1/63 - 2/29/64, had his own horse since 12/21/63. Clothing issued 2/29/64. Not stated if present or absent 7/1/64 - 8/31/64, had his own horse; entitled to bond. Ab. 9/1/64 - 10/31/64 (dated 12/29/64), in hosp.; entitled to $100 bond. Post war resident of Ritchie Co., W. Va. d. W. Va., 1/27/1905. Bur. Fairmont Ridge Cem., Cornwallis, Ritchie Co., W. Va.

LUCAS, D. C. - Pvt. Co. C. Enl. Pocahontas Co., W. Va., 7/16/63 (7/10/63). Ab. 6/30/63 - 8/31/64 (dated 1/6/65), on detached service; enl. bounty due. Present 9/1/64 - 10/31/64 (dated 12/30/64). Could be Robert C. Lucas. NFR.

LUCAS, ROBERT C. - Pvt. Co. C. b.c. 1825. Not on muster rolls. Paroled at Charleston, W. Va., 5/10/65. Desc.: age 40, 5'9", dark comp., dark hair, blue eyes and dark whiskers. Could be D. C. Lucas. NFR.

LURTY, ROBERT DEXTER - 1st Lt. Co. E. No enl. data. Not stated if present or absent on muster-in roll dated 7/18/63, 1st Lt. Elected 1st Lt., 5/10/63. Resignation submitted from Camp Miller, 10/8/63. Resigned because he was elected 1st Lt. in Lurty's Batty. Resignation accepted, effective 9/11/63 (10/8/63). Cpd. Beverly, W. Va., 10/29/64. NFR.

LYNCH, WILLIAM L. - Pvt. Co. I. b.c 1839. Resident of Lewis Co., W. Va. Arrested and held at Wheeling, W. Va. Released on his oath by 3/13/62. Enl. Camp Northwest, W. Va., 6/10/63, age 24. Not stated if present or absent on muster-in roll dated 5/5/63. NFR.

LYONS, ENOS - Pvt. Co. C. b. Ireland, c. 1843. Prior service, Co. I, 25th Va. Inf. Enl. Pocahontas Co., W. Va., 3/19/63. Not stated if present or absent on muster-in roll dated 8/63. Ab. 6/30/63 - 8/31/64 (dated 1/6/65), claimed and returned to Co. I, 25th Va. Inf., 1/64. Post war resident of Huntersville, W. Va. NFR.

McCABE (McKABE), WILLIAM - Pvt. Co. K. b.c. 1842. Enl. Warm Springs, 4/1/63, age 21. Not stated if present or absent on muster-in roll dated 7/21/63. Ab. 7/1/63 - 11/1/63 (dated 1/6/64), AWOL. NFR.

McCALLY, JOHN - Pvt. Co. C. Enl. Pocahontas Co., W. Va., 9/10/63. Ab. 6/30/63 - 8/31/64 (dated 1/6/65), deserted 6/21/64. NFR.

McCARTNEY, GEORGE D. - Pvt. Co. E. Resident of Clarksburg, W. Va. Arrested and confined at Wheeling, W. Va. Released on his oath and bond by 3/13/62. Enl. Camp Clover Lick, 7/11/63. Not stated if present or absent on muster-in roll dated 7/18/63. NFR.

McCARTY, PATRICK S. - Pvt. Co. D. b.c. 1836. Enl. Camp Willy (Wiley), 8/16/63. Present 7/1/63 - 1/1/64 (dated 1/1/64), entitled to enl. bounty; had his own horse. Not stated if present or absent 12/31/63 - 8/31/64 (dated 1/6/65). Present 9/1/64 - 10/31/64, entitled to $100 enl. bounty. Paroled at Staunton, 5/18/65. Desc.: age 29, 6', dark comp., dark hair and dark eyes. Murdered Kerr's Creek Bridge, 2 miles East of Lexington, after the war. Bur. Harrisonburg.

McCLARY, ISAAC - Pvt. Co. G. Enl. Wood Co., W. Va., 5/2/63. Not stated if present or absent on muster-in roll dated 8/63. NFR.

McCLARY, JAMES - Pvt. Co. ?. Post war rosters only, which show service in the 20th Va. Cav. Served in Co. C, 19th Va. Cav. NFR.

McCLARY, JESSE - Pvt. Co. F. Enl. Camp Clover Lick (Camp Miller), 7/17/63. Not stated if present or absent on muster-in roll dated 7/20/63. Ab. 7/1/63 - 8/31/64 (dated 1/6/65), transf. to Co. A, 19th Va. Cav. Ab. 9/1/64 - 10/31/64 (dated 12/30/64), transf. to Co. A, 19th Va. Cav. NFR.

McCUNE, MICHAEL - Pvt. Co. I. Enl. Camp Marlin's Bottom, Pocahontas Co., W. Va., 9/10/63. Ab. 11/1/63 - 8/31/64 (dated 1/6/65), POW. No POW records. NFR.

McCUNE, PALSER B. - Pvt. Co. F. b. Lewis Co., W. Va., c. 1832. Age 28, Calhoun Co., W. Va. 1860 Census. Enl. Camp Northwest, W. Va. (Camp Miller), 7/19/63. Not stated if present or absent on muster-in roll dated 7/20/63. Ab. 7/1/63 - 8/31/64 (dated 1/6/65), transf. to Co. A, 19th Va. Cav. Ab. 9/1/64 - 10/31/64 (dated 12/30/64), transf. to Co. A, 19th Va. Cav. Post war resident of Calhoun Co., W. Va. Age 37, farm laborer, Lee Township, Calhoun Co., W. Va. 1870 Census. Age 49, farmer, Lee Dist., Calhoun Co., W. Va. 1880 Census. Bur. McCune Cem., near Hur, Calhoun Co., W. Va.

McCUNE, THOMAS - Pvt. Co. I. Enl. Pocahontas Co., W. Va., 9/10/63. Ab. 11/1/63 - 8/31/64 (dated 1/6/65), POW. No POW record. NFR.

McCUNE, TIMOTHY - Pvt. Co. F. b. Calhoun Co., W. Va., 11/11/38. Prior service, 3rd VSL. Enl. Camp Northwest, W. Va., 7/19/63. Not stated if present or absent on muster-in roll dated 7/20/63. Ab. 7/1/63 - 8/31/64 (dated 1/6/65), transf. to Co. A, 19th Va. Cav. Ab. 9/1/64 - 10/31/64 (dated 12/30/64), transf. to Co. A, 19th Va. Cav. Served in Lurty's Batty. Brother of Paulson B. McCune. Post war miller and resident of Lee Dist., Richardson, Calhoun Co., W. Va. Age 31, farmer, Lee Township, Calhoun Co., W. Va. 1870 Census. Age 42, farmer, Lee Dist., Calhoun Co., W. Va. 1880 Census. May be bur. in the Wright Cem., Calhoun Co., W. Va.

McCUTCHEON, JUDSON ODELL - Pvt. Co. I. b. Augusta Co., 9/18/36. Clerk and Teacher, 1st Dist., Augusta Co. 1860 Census. Prior service, Co. D, 5th Va. Inf. Enl. Camp Northwest, W. Va., 6/3/63 (1/9/63), age 27. Also as Augusta Co., 4/6/63. Not stated if present or absent on muster-in roll dated 5/5/63. Present 11/1/63 - 8/31/64 (dated 1/6/65), acting Ordnance Sgt. for Reg't. Clothing issued 3/29/64. Ab. 11/1/64 - 10/31/64 (dated 12/31/64), on detached service. Paroled at Staunton, 5/15/65. Desc.: age 28(?), 5'10+", light comp., light hair and brown eyes. Farmer, Rivershead Dist., Augusta Co. 1870 Census. Post war clerk, and resident of Middlebrook, Augusta Co , 1893. d. Goshen, Rockbridge Co., 4/26/1902. Bur. Shemariah Church Cem., near Middlebrook, Augusta Co.

McCUTCHEON, WILLIAM - Pvt. Co. A. Post war rosters only, which show he was cpd. in Bath Co., 8/?/63, while acting as a courier. DOD. Camp Chase. Bur. Camp Chase Confederate Cem.

McDIFFET, PETER - Pvt. Co. A. b.c. 1839. Enl. Marion Co., W. Va., 3/25/63. Not stated if present or absent on muster-in roll dated 8/63. Ab. 10/31/63 - 8/31/64, never reported for duty. Age 41, farm hand, Mannington Dist., Marion Co., W. Va. 1880 Census. NFR.

McDIFFET, REMUS - Pvt. Co. A. Post war rosters only. NFR.

McDONALD, WILLIAM - Pvt. Co. D. b. Frederick Co., c. 1846. Not on muster rolls. POW record shows enl. in Frederick Co., 7/64. Cpd. Beverly, W. Va., 10/29/64. Confined at Clarksburg, W. Va. Desc.: age 18, 5'11", dark comp., dark hair and black eyes. Occ. laborer, residing in Frederick Co. Transf. to Wheeling, W. Va., 11/2/64. Confined at the Atheneum Prison, 11/2/64. Desc.: age 18, 5'10", dark comp., dark hair and dark eyes. Occ. farmer, residing in Frederick Co. Transf. to Camp Chase, 11/3/64. Confined at Camp Chase, 11/4/64. Paroled 5/2/65, sent to New Orleans, La., to be exchanged. Exchanged at Vicksburg, Miss., 5/12/65. NFR.

McERVIN, WILLIAM - Pvt. Co. ?. Prior service, Co. E, 31st Va. Inf. Post war rosters show service in the 20th Va. Cav. Post war resident of Highland Co. NFR.

McGLAUGHLIN, EVAN (EWING, EWEN, EWAN) A. - Pvt. Co. C. b. 6/15/46. Enl. Pocahontas Co., W. Va., 4/1/64. Present 6/30/63 - 8/31/64 (dated 1/6/65), enl. bounty due. Paroled at Staunton, 6/1/65. Desc.: age 19, 5'11", fair comp., dark hair and blue eyes. Post war resident of Highland Co. d. 4/4/1911. Bur. McGlaughlin Cem., Highland Co.

McGOLDRICH (McGOLDRICK), MICHAEL E. - Pvt. Co. I. Enl. Camp Northwest, W. Va., 5/25/63. Also as Warm Springs, Bath Co., 4/1/64 and 4/6/64. Not stated if present or absent on muster-in roll dated 5/5/63. Ab. 11/1/63 - 8/31/64 (dated 1/6/65), wd. Wd. Droop Mtn., W. Va., 11/6/63, three places and cpd. Present 11/1/63 - 10/31/64 (dated 12/31/64). Clothing issued 2/29/64. No POW records. NFR.

McGUFFIN, JAMES - Major. b. Bath Co., 1839. Prior service, Co. F, 11th Va. Cav. Post war rosters show he enl. 4/61, and became a Lt., then Capt. and Major. Post war rosters only for service in the 20th Va. Cav. Served in Co. E, 46th Battn. Va. Cav. Took the oath of allegiance, Bath Co., 4/9/66. Post war farmer and resident of Bath Co. Bur. Stoney Run Ch. Cem.

McINTIRE (McENTIRE), THOMAS B. - Pvt. Co. B. Prior service, Co. D, 19th Va. Cav. Enl. Williamsburg, Greenbrier Co., W. Va., 3/17/63. Not stated if present or absent on muster-in roll dated 7/25/63. Ab. 11/1/63 - 8/31/64 (dated 1/6/65), KIA. Droop Mtn., W. Va., 11/6/63.

McKEE, WILLIAM M. - Pvt. Co. I. b.c. 1845. Enl. Camp Northwest, W. Va., 6/15/63, age 18 in Co. I. Not stated if present or absent on muster-in roll dated 5/5/63. Transf. to Co. K, 20th Va. Cav. Enl. in Co. K at Camp Northwest, W. Va., 7/21/63. Present 7/1/63 - 11/1/63 (dated 1/6/64), transf. from Co. I, 20th Va. Cav., 7/21/63; lost Mississippi Rifle. Ab. 11/1/63 - 2/29/64, AWOL. Ab. 2/29/64 - 8/31/64, AWOL. NFR.

McKINNEY (McKENNEY, McKINLEY), JOHN R. - 1st Corp. Co. F. b.c. 1829. Resident of Harrison Co., W. Va. Enl. Bulltown, W. Va., 5/10/63. Not stated if present or absent on muster-in roll dated 7/20/63, Corp. Ab., 1st Corp., 7/1/63 - 8/31/63 (dated 1/6/65), prisoner since 12/18/63; entitled to enl. bounty. Cpd. Alleghany Co., 12/19/63. Confined at the Atheneum Prison, 12/31/63. Desc.: age 34, 5'8", fair comp., dark hair and gray eyes. Occ. farmer, residing in Harrison Co., W. Va. Transf. to Camp Chase, 12/31/63. Confined at Camp Chase, 1/1/64. Listed as a deserter, wishing to take the oath of allegiance, 6/10/64. Ab. 9/1/64 - 10/31/64 (dated 12/30/64), prisoner since 12/18/63. DOD. Camp Chase, 11/27/64, pneumonia (small pox). Bur. Camp Chase Confederate Cem., grave no. 525.

McKINNEY (McKENNEY), JOSEPH - Pvt. Co. F. b.c. 1829. Enl. Bulltown, W. Va., 5/10/63. Not stated if present or absent on muster-in roll dated 7/20/63. Ab. 7/1/63 - 8/31/63 (dated 1/6/65), prisoner since 12/18/63; entitled to enl. bounty. Cpd. Covington, Alleghany Co., 12/20/63. Confined at the Atheneum Prison, 12/31/63. Desc.: age 34, 6'2", dark comp., dark hair and hazel eyes. Occ. farmer, residing in Harrison Co., W. Va. Transf. to Camp Chase, 12/31/63. Confined at Camp Chase, 1/1/64. Listed as a deserter, wishing to take the oath of allegiance, 6/10/64. Ab. 9/1/64 - 10/31/64 (dated 12/30/64), prisoner since 12/18/63; entitled to enl. bounty. Took the oath of allegiance and was released, 5/13/65. Desc.: age ?, 6'2", dark comp., dark hair and hazel eyes, a resident of Barbour Co., W. Va. NFR.

McLAUGHLIN, JAMES HICKMAN - 1st Lt. Co. C. Prior service, Co. I, 25th Va. Inf. Enl. Randolph Co., W. Va., 4/16/63. Appointed 1st Lt., 4/16/63, confirmed by election. Not stated if present or absent on muster-in roll dated 8/63, 1st Lt. Ab., 1st Lt., 6/30/63 8/31/63 (dated 1/6/65), wd. Winchester, 9/19/63 (Shepherdstown, W. Va., 8/25/64 or 8/26/64). Ab., 1st Lt., 9/1/64 - 10/31/64 (dated 12/30/64), wd. and DOW. in hands of enemy, 9/64 or 10/64. Adm. USA Depot Field Hosp., Winchester, 9/19/64, gunshot wd., comp. fracture of tibia and fibia. Treated with a splint. DOD. Winchester, 9/23/64 (9/17/64), icterus and dysentery. Card in CSR shows him as being absent 10/25/64, wd. and on leave, 60 days.

McMULLAN (McMILLAN, McMILLIN), SAMUEL J. - 2nd Corp. Co. E. Enl. Bulltown, W. Va., 5/10/63. Not stated if present or absent on muster-in roll dated 7/18/63, 3rd Corp. Present, 2nd Corp., 1/1/64 8/31/64 (dated 1/6/65). Present, 2nd Corp., 9/1/64 - 10/31/64 (dated 12/29/64), entitled to $100 bond. Served in the 23rd Va. Cav. Paroled at Staunton, 5/24/65. NFR.

McNEIL, ANGUS - Pvt. Co. K. b.c. 1833. Enl. Camp Northwest, W. Va., 5/10/63, age 30. Not stated if present or absent on muster-in roll dated 7/21/63. Ab. 7/1/63 - 11/1/63 (dated 1/6/64), POW cpd. Droop Mtn., 11/6/63; had his own horse since 9/22/63. Ab. 11/1/63 - 2/29/64, cpd. Droop Mtn., 11/6/63. Ab. 2/29/64 - 8/31/64, cpd. Droop Mtn., 11/6/63. NFR.

McQUAIN, ARCHIBALD - Pvt. Co. I. b.c. 1839. Enl. Lewisburg, W. Va., 4/20/63, age 24. Not stated if present or absent on muster-in roll dated 5/5/63. NFR.

McRAY (McCRAY), ROBERT S. - Pvt. Co. C. b.c. 1829. Resident of Webster Co., W. Va. Arrested and confined at Wheeling, W. Va. Released on his oath by 3/13/62. Enl. Pocahontas Co., W. Va., 8/6/63. Ab. 6/30/63 - 8/31/64 (dated 1/6/65), taken prisoner 11/12/63; enl. bounty due; 6% bond due. Cpd. Bath Co., 11/10/63. Confined at the Atheneum Prison, 11/18/63. Desc.: age 34, 5'9+", florid comp., dark hair and blue eyes. Occ. farmer, residing in Webster Co., W. Va. Transf. to Camp Chase, 11/19/63. Confined at Camp Chase, 11/20/63. Transf. to Ft. Delaware, 3/14/64. Confined at Ft. Delaware, 3/17/64. Ab. 9/1/64 - 10/31/64 (dated 12/30/64), POW since 6/1/63; 6% bond due. Paroled and sent to City Point, 2/27/65, to be exchanged. Exchanged at Dutch Gap, 3/3/65. Adm. Chimborazo Hosp. No. 2, 3/4/65, catarrh; furloughed 3/17/65, 60 days. CSR shows he was adm. Chimborazo Hosp. No. 1, as a paroled prisoner and was furloughed to Warm Springs, Bath Co. NFR.

McVANEY, GEORGE W. - Pvt. Co. D. b.c. 1841. Enl. Hightown, Highland Co., 7/27/63. Not stated if present or absent on muster-in roll dated 8/63. Ab. 7/1/63 - 1/1/64 (dated 1/1/64), AWOL since 8/63. Deserted. Reported to Jacob Strager, citizen. Took the oath of allegiance and was sent North by 10/13/63. Desc.: age 22, 5'8", fair comp., light hair and blue eyes. Ab. 12/31/63 - 8/31/64 (dated 1/6/65), AWOL since 8/63. Ab. 9/1/64 - 10/31/64, AWOL. NFR.

McVICKER, STEWERT (STEPHEN, STEENROD) - Pvt. Co. B. b. Marion Co., W. Va., c. 1841. Arrested and confined at Wheeling, W. Va. Released on his oath by 3/13/62. Enl. Upshur Co., W. Va., 4/28/63. POW record shows enl. as Highland Co., 4/63. Not stated if present or absent on muster-in roll dated 7/25/63. Present 11/1/63 - 8/31/64 (dated 1/6/65). Clothing issued 3/31/64. Present 9/1/64 - 10/31/64 (dated 12/30/64), entitled to $100 bond. Cpd. Farmington, Marion Co., W. Va., 12/27/64. Confined at Clarksburg, W. Va. Desc.: age 23, 5'8", fair comp., dark hair and blue eyes. Occ. farmer, residing in Marion Co., W. Va. Transf. to Wheeling, W. Va., 1/2/65. Confined at the Atheneum Prison, 1/2/65. Transf. to Camp Chase, 1/16/65. Confined at Camp Chase, 1/17/65. Eñl. in US service, 3/20/65, and was sent to Chicago, Ill. CSR filed as Steenrod McVicker. NFR.

MAIZE, F. J. - Pvt. Co. H. Enl. Camp Northwest, W. Va., 7/1/63. Not stated if present or absent on muster-in roll dated 8/63. NFR.

MALCOMB, F. M. - Pvt. Co. C. Resident of Braxton Co., W. Va. Arrested and confined at Wheeling, W. Va. Released on his oath and bond by 3/13/62. Enl. Pocahontas Co., W. Va., 3/19/63. Not stated if present or absent on muster-in roll dated 8/63. Present 6/30/63 8/31/64 (dated 1/6/65). Clothing issued 3/10/64. Ab. 9/1/64 - 10/31/64 (dated 12/30/64), wd. 10/1/64 (probably Bridgewater, 10/2/64). NFR.

MALCOMB, WILLIAM C. - Pvt. Co. C. b.c. 1830. Enl. Pocahontas Co., W. Va., 3/21/63 (3/19/63). Not stated if present or absent on muster-in roll dated 8/63. Ab. 6/30/63 - 8/31/64 (dated 1/6/65), AWOL since 7/1/64. Ab. 9/1/64 - 10/31/64 (dated 12/30/64), AWOL. Age 50, farmer, Huntersville, Pocahontas Co., W. Va. 1880 Census. NFR.

MALONE, NUTTER W. - Pvt. Co. G. Enl. Wood Co., W. Va., 5/2/63. Not stated if present or absent on muster-in roll dated 8/63. Present 11/1/63 - 2/29/64, detailed as carpenter. Employed as carpenter at Warm Springs, 1/1/64 - 3/31/64. Present 7/1/64 - 8/31/64, detailed as carpenter since 12/24/63; entitled to bond as enl. bounty. Clothing issued 12/30/63 (detailed), 1/16/64, 3/1/64 and 3rd Qr. 1864. Present 9/1/64 - 10/31/64 (dated 12/29/64), detailed as carpenter, 12/24/63; has no horse; entitled to $100 bond. NFR.

MALONEY, JAMES B. - Pvt. Co. H. Enl. Camp Northwest, W. Va., 6/1/63 (Calhoun Co., W. Va., 5/8/63). Not stated if present or absent on muster-in roll dated 8/63. Ab. 10/31/63 - 8/31/64, in hands of enemy. Ab. 9/1/64 - 10/31/64 (dated 12/30/64), prisoner, cpd. 10/63. Deserted. Took the oath of allegiance and gave bond, 12/5/63. No POW records. NFR.

MAPHUS, G. B. - Pvt. Co. C. Enl. Pocahontas Co., W. Va., 4/1/64. Ab. 6/30/63 - 8/31/64 (dated 1/6/65), deserted 6/27/64. Ab. 9/1/64 - 10/31/64 (dated 12/30/64), deserted 6/27/64. NFR.

MARPLE, ADDISON - Pvt. Co. D. b.c. 1836. Enl. Hightown, Highland Co., 7/27/63. Not stated if present or absent on muster-in roll dated 8/63. Ab. 7/1/63 - 1/1/64 (dated 1/1/64), AWOL since 8/63. Ab. 12/31/63 - 8/31/64 (dated 1/6/65), AWOL since 8/63. Ab. 9/1/64 - 10/31/64, AWOL. Deserted. Reported to Joseph Strager (citizen). Took the oath of allegiance and was sent North, 10/13/63. Desc.: age 27, 5'9", fair comp., light hair and gray eyes, a resident of Upshur Co., W. Va. Age 44, farmer, Warren Dist., Upshur Co., W. Va. 1880 Census. NFR.

MARPLE, ALBINAS R. - Pvt. Co. D. b.c. 1834. Enl. Hightown, Highland Co., 7/27/63. Not stated if present or absent on muster-in roll dated 8/63. Ab. 7/1/63 - 1/1/64 (dated 1/1/64), AWOL since 8/63. Ab. 12/31/63 - 8/31/64 (dated 1/6/65), AWOL since 8/63. Ab. 9/1/64 - 10/31/64, AWOL. Deserted. Reported to Joseph Strager (citizen). Took the oath of allegiance and was sent North, 10/13/63. Desc.: age 29, 5'4", fair comp., black hair and gray eyes, a resident of Upshur Co., W. Va. Age 46, farmer, Warren Dist., Upshur Co., W. Va. 1880 Census. d. Upshur Co., W. Va., 9/27/1908, age 74 years, 7 months and 23 days.

MARSH, THOMAS - Pvt. Co. K. b c. 1838. Enl. Camp Northwest, W. Va., 6/10/63, age 25. Not stated if present or absent on muster-in roll dated 7/21/63. Ab. 7/1/63 - 11/1/63 (dated 1/6/64), AWOL. NFR.

MARSHALL, JAMES M. - Pvt. Co. E. b.c. 1847. Enl. Williamsville, Bath Co. 1/1/64. Ab. 1/1/64 - 8/31/64 (dated 1/6/65), sick in Staunton Gen. Hosp.; entitled to $100 bond. Ab. 9/1/64 - 10/31/64 (dated 12/29/64), sick in Staunton Gen. Hosp.; entitled to $100 bond. Paroled at Staunton, 5/23/65. Desc.: age 18, 5'10", fair comp., light hair and blue eyes. NFR.

MARSHALL, WILLIAM T. L. - Pvt. Co. E. b.c. 1846. Enl. Doe Hill, Highland Co. (Bath Co.), 2/1/64. Present 1/1/64 - 8/31/64 (dated 1/6/65), entitled to $100 bond. Present 9/1/64 - 10/31/64 (dated 12/29/64), entitled to $100 bond. Paroled at Staunton, 5/24/65. Desc.: age 19, 5'6", dark comp., black hair and blue eyes. NFR.

MARTIN, BLACKBURN K. - Pvt. Co. B. b.c. 1844. Prior service, Co. E, 62nd Va. Mtd. Inf. No enl. data. Present 11/1/63 - 8/31/64 (dated 1/6/65), transf. from Co. E, 62nd Va. Mtd. Inf., 6/12/64. Not stated if present or absent 9/1/64 - 10/31/64 (dated 12/30/64), transf. from Co. E, 62nd Va. Mtd. Inf. Post war resident of Marion Co., W. Va. Age 36, farmer, Grant Dist., Marion Co., W. Va. 1880 Census. NFR.

MARTIN, CHARLEY - Pvt. Co. ?. Post war rosters only. NFR.

MARTIN, DAVID - Pvt. Co. B. b. Marion Co., W. Va., c. 1839. Resident of Gauley Mount, W. Va. Prior service, Co. D, 19th Va. Cav. Enl. Williamsburg, Greenbrier Co., W. Va., 3/17/63. POW record shows enl. as Highland Co., 8/62. Not stated if present or absent on muster-in roll dated 7/20/63. Present 11/1/63 - 8/31/64 (dated 1/6/65). Ab. 9/1/64 - 10/31/64 (dated 12/30/64), sent to hosp. 9/64. Clothing issued at Liberty Gen. Hosp., 7/7/64. Clothing issued 9/2/64. Cpd. Randolph Co., W. Va., 3/1/65. Confined at Clarksburg, W. Va., 3/9/65. Desc.: age 26, 6'1", fair comp., black hair and brown eyes. Occ. farmer, residing in Marion Co., W. Va. Apparently released. Arrested 4/23/65. Confined at the Atheneum Prison, 4/24/65. Took the oath of allegiance at Cumberland, Md. Post war resident of Marion Co., W. Va. NFR.

MARTIN, EZEKIEL - Capt. Co. B. Prior service, Co. D, 19th Va. Cav. Enl. Williamsburg, Greenbrier Co., W. Va., 4/15/63. Not stated if present or absent on muster-in roll dated 7/25/63. Appointed Capt., 8/14/63, confirmed by election. Present, Capt., 11/1/63 - 8/31/64 (dated 1/6/65), promoted to Capt., 8/15/63. Mentioned for his "brave bearing" at the battle of Droop Mtn., W. Va., 11/6/63, by Col. W. L. Jackson. Wd. Droop Mtn., W. Va., 11/6/63, twice. Present, Capt., 9/1/64 - 10/31/64 (dated 12/30/64), promoted to Capt., 8/15/63. Present for duty in Highland Co., 2/15/65. Shown as 1st Lt. by records of the AIGO, 3/31/65. Post war rosters show he was discharged in 1865. Post war resident of Marion Co., W. Va. NFR.

MARTIN, JESSE THORNTON - 5th Sgt. Co. B. b.c. 1832. Enl. Camp Harold, 4/15/63. Not stated if present or absent on muster-in roll dated 7/25/63, 5th Sgt. Ab., 5th Sgt., 11/1/63 - 8/31/64 (dated 1/6/65), taken prisoner 6/2/64. Clothing issued 3/31/64. Cpd. Covington, 6/2/64. Confined at Camp Morton, Indianapolis, Ind., 6/21/64. Ab., 5th Sgt., 9/1/64 - 10/31/64 (dated 12/30/64), POW since 6/2/64. Took the oath of allegiance and was released, 2/20/65. Desc.: age ?, 5'7+", light comp., brown hair and gray eyes, a resident of Marion Co., W. Va. Age 48, farmer, Lincoln School Dist., Marion Co., W. Va. 1880 Census. NFR.

MARTIN, JOSEPH J. - Pvt. Co. F. Enl. Camp Northwest, W. Va. (Camp Miller), 7/19/63. Not stated if present or absent on muster-in roll dated 7/20/63. Ab. 7/1/63 - 8/31/64 (dated 1/6/65), transf. to Co. A, 19th Va. Cav. Ab. 9/1/64 - 10/31/64 (dated 12/30/64), transf. to Co. A, 19th Va. Cav. Paroled Farmville, 4/65, as a member of Co. F, 20th Va. Cav. NFR.

MARTIN, WILLIAM F. - Pvt. Co. B. b.c. 1835. Prior service, Co. D, 19th Va. Cav. Enl. Williamsburg, Greenbrier Co., W. Va., 3/17/63. Not stated if present or absent on muster-in roll dated 7/25/63. Present 11/1/63 - 8/31/64 (dated 1/6/65). Clothing issued 3/31/64. Present 9/1/64 - 10/31/64 (dated 12/30/64). Took the amnesty oath and was released, 4/14/65. Desc.: age 30, 5'10", fair comp., dark hair and gray eyes. Occ. farmer, residing in Marion Co., W. Va. Age 44, farmer, Lincoln School Dist., Marion Co., W. Va. 1880 Census. NFR.

MARTINS, J. - Capt. Co. B. Not on muster rolls. Ab. 10/25/64, AWOL 37 days; sent by Col. T. J. Berry after deserters with no time limit to return. NFR.

MASTERS, ANDREW M. - Pvt. Co. C. b. Pendleton Co., W. Va., 10/25/25. Age 33(?), carpenter, McDowell, Highland Co. 1860 Census. Enl. Pocahontas Co., W. Va., 8/19/64 (Highland Co.). POW record shows enl. as Highland Co., 5/61. Ab. 6/30/63 - 8/31/64 (dated 1/6/65), AWOL; enl. bounty due. Ab. 9/1/64 - 10/31/64 (dated 12/30/64), KIA. Beverly, W. Va., 10/26/64 (error). Cpd. Beverly, W. Va., 10/29/64. Confined at Clarksburg, W. Va. Desc.: age 40, 5'8", fair comp., light hair and blue eyes. Occ. farmer, residing in Highland Co. Transf. to Wheeling, W. Va., 11/2/64. Confined at the Atheneum Prison, 11/2/64. Desc.: age 40, 5'8+", dark comp., auburn hair and gray eyes. Occ. carpenter, residing in Highland Co. Transf. to Camp Chase, 11/3/64. Confined at Camp Chase, 11/4/64. Took the oath of allegiance and was released, 6/12/65. Desc.: age 40, 5'8+", dark comp., dark hair and blue eyes, a resident of Highland Co. d. Highland Co., 4/5/1911. Bur. McDowell Presby. Ch. Cem., Highland Co.

MASTON, WILLIAM - Pvt. Co. K. b.c. 1842. Enl. Warm Springs, 4/1/63. Not stated if present or absent on muster-in roll dated 7/21/63. Ab. 7/1/63 - 11/1/63 (dated 1/6/64), deserted, taking his gun with him. Ab. 11/1/63 - 2/29/64, deserted, taking his gun and accouterments with him. Ab. 2/29/64 - 8/31/64, deserted, taking his gun with him. NFR.

MATHANY, JOHN - Pvt. Co. D. Enl. Elk, W. Va., 5/1/63. Not stated if present or absent on muster-in roll dated 8/63. NFR.

MATHINY, REUBEN - Pvt. Co. K. Enl. Camp Northwest, W. Va., 6/6/63. Ab. 7/1/63 - 11/1/63 (dated 1/6/64), detailed for the battery. Present 11/1/63 - 2/29/64. Present 2/29/64 - 8/31/64, had his own horse since 8/15/63; $100 enl. bounty due. Clothing issued 3/23/64. NFR.

MATTHEWS (MATHEWS), JOHN M. (W.) - Pvt. Co. B. Enl. Clay Hill, 12/9/62. Not stated if present or absent on muster-in roll dated 7/25/63. Present 11/1/63 - 8/31/64 (dated 1/6/65). Clothing issued 3/31/64. Present 9/1/64 - 10/31/64 (dated 12/30/64). Member of Washington, DC Camp, UCV. d. Washington, DC, 12/1/1909. Bur. Section 16, Arlington National Cem., Arlington.

MAURICE, FRANCIS - Pvt. Co. K. b.c. 1836. Enl. Warm Springs, 4/20/63 (4/10/63), age 27. Not stated if present or absent on muster-in roll dated 7/21/63. Ab. 7/1/63 - 11/1/63 (dated 1/6/64), AWOL. NFR.

MAYBERRY, WILLIAM HENRY - Pvt. Co. G. Enl. Wood Co., W. Va., 6/24/63. Not stated if present or absent muster-in roll dated 8/63. Present 11/1/63 - 2/29/64, had his own horse and equipment to 11/4/63, cpd. by the enemy. Clothing issued 2/29/64. Present 7/1/64 - 8/31/64, had his own horse; entitled to bond. Present 9/1/64 - 10/31/64 (dated 12/29/64), entitled to $100 bond. Cpd. Parkersburg, W. Va., 4/21/65. Confined at Clarksburg, W. Va. Paroled for exchange and was released, 4/24/65. Desc.: 20, 5'7+", fair comp., light hair and blue eyes. Occ. farmer, residing in Wood Co., W. Va. Post war resident of Wood Co., W. Va. Age 35, clerk in store, Parkersburg, Wood Co., W. Va. 1880 Census. NFR.

MAY, SYLVESTER - Pvt. Co. ?. b.c. 1844. Post war rosters only. Served in Co. B, 19th Va. Cav. NFR.

MAYS, PIERCE - Pvt. Co. ?. Not on muster rolls. Cpd.(date and place not stated), confined in prison. Reported to the Provost Marshal General, Washington, DC, 6/30/65. Transportation furnished to Parkersburg, W. Va. NFR.

MAZINGO, GEORGE - Pvt. Co. K. b. Va., c. 1842. Enl. Camp Marlin's Bottom, Pocahontas Co., W. Va., 11/5/63. Ab. 7/1/63 - 11/1/63 (dated 1/6/64), detailed at hosp. Present 11/1/63 - 2/29/64, detailed at hosp. Ab. 2/29/64 - 8/31/64, missing. Age 28, carpenter, South River Dist., Rockbridge Co. 1870 Census. NFR.

MERRITT, WILLIAM - Pvt. Co. I and Co. K. b.c. 1837. Enl. in Co. I, Camp Northwest, W. Va., 7/19/63, age 24. Not stated if present or absent on muster-in roll dated 5/5/63. Enl. in Co. K, Camp Northwest, W. Va., 7/19/63, age 26. Not stated if present or absent on muster-in roll dated 7/21/63. Ab. 7/1/63 - 11/1/63 (dated 1/6/64), AWOL. NFR.

METZ (METTS), DANIEL - Pvt. Co. A. b.c. 1844. Enl. Pocahontas Co., W. Va., 6/21/63, age 19. Not stated if present or absent on muster-in roll dated 6/21/63. Present 7/1/63 - 9/1/63. Present 10/31/63 - 8/31/64. Clothing issued 2/29/64 and 3rd Qr. 1864. Surrendered at Clarksburg, W. Va., 5/25/65. Paroled and released for exchange, 5/25/65. Desc.: age 20, 5'9+", fair comp., light hair and blue eyes. Occ. farmer, residing in Marion Co., W. Va. NFR.

METZ, LEMUEL (LEAMECH, LAMECH, LARNECK) - Pvt. Co. A. b. Marion Co., W. Va., c. 1841. Resident of Glovers Gap, Wetzel Co., W. Va. Enl. Lewis Co., W. Va., 5/4/63, age 22. POW record shows enl. as Highland Co. Not stated if present or absent on muster-in roll dated 5/4/63. Present 7/1/63 - 9/1/63. Present 10/31/63 - 8/31/64. Detailed to guard prisoners, 12/63. Clothing issued 2/29/64. Cpd. Beverly, W. Va., 10/29/64. Confined at Clarksburg, W. Va. Desc.: age 23, 5'10", dark comp., light hair and hazel eyes. Occ. farmer, residing in Marion Co., W. Va. Transf. to Wheeling, W. Va., and confined at the Atheneum Prison, 11/2/64. Desc.: age 22, 5'10", dark comp., dark hair and gray eyes. Transf. to Camp Chase, 11/3/64. Confined at Camp Chase, 11/4/64. Took the oath of allegiance and was released, 6/12/65. Desc.: age 21, 5'9,", fair comp., light hair and gray eyes, a resident of Marion Co., W. Va. Post war resident of Marion Co., W. Va. Age 40, farmer, Mannington Dist., Marion Co., W. Va. 1880 Census. NFR.

MICHAEL (MITCHIE), FESTUS J. - Pvt. Co. A. b.c. 1843. Enl. Marion Co., W. Va., 3/30/63, age 20. Not stated if present or absent on muster-in roll dated 3/3/0/63. Ab. 10/31/63 - 8/31/64, never reported for duty. Age 37, farmer, Paw Paw Dist., Marion Co., W. Va. 1880 Census. NFR.

MICHAEL, REMUS J. - Pvt. Co. A. b.c. 1842. Enl. Marion Co., W. Va., 3/30/63, age 21. Not stated if present or absent on muster-in roll dated 3/3/0/63. Ab. 10/31/63 - 8/31/64, never reported for duty. Age 38, farmer, Paw Dist., Marion Co., W. Va. 1880 Census. NFR.

MIDDLETON, GEORGE ARCHIBALD - Pvt. Co. H. b. 7/5/31. Farm hand, Ritchie Co., W. Va. 1860 Census. Enl. Camp Northwest, W. Va., 7/1/63. Not stated if present or absent on muster-in roll dated 8/63. Transf. to Lurty's Batty., 11/1/63. Post war roster shows him as a resident of Ritchie Co., W. Va. Post war resident of Calhoun Co., W. Va. d. Calhoun Co., 1890. Bur. Big Spring Baptist Cem., Big Spring, Calhoun Co., W. Va. Brother of Samuel Middleton.

MIDDLETON, SAMUEL - Pvt. Co. ?. Post war rosters only, which show he was a resident of Ritchie Co., W. Va. May have served in the 19th Va. Cav. Brother of George Archibald Middleton. NFR.

MIDKIFF, WILLIAM - Pvt. Co. C. Not on muster rolls. d. 2/3/63. Bur. US National Cem., Baltimore, next to Loudoun Park Cem. NFR.

MILBURN, JOHN - Pvt. Co. G. Enl. Wood Co., W. Va., 6/24/63. Not stated if present or absent on muster-in roll dated 8/63. Present 11/1/63 - 2/29/64, had his own horse and equipment. Ab. 7/1/64 - 8/31/64, deserted 1/15/64. Ab. 9/1/64 - 10/31/64 (dated 12/29/64), deserted 1/15/64. NFR.

MILLER, SAMUEL - Pvt. Co. E. Enl. Harrison Co., W. Va., 5/4/63 by John L. Bussey. Not stated if present or absent on muster-in roll dated 7/18/63. Taken prisoner, 5/63, while on the way to join Col. W. L. Jackson, at or near Weston, W. Va. Confined at Camp Chase, as a political prisoner. NFR.

MILLS, WILLIAM - Pvt. Co. G. b.c. 1825. Enl. Wood Co., W. Va., 6/24/63. Not stated if present or absent on muster-in roll dated 8/63. Ab. 11/1/63 - 2/29/64, deserted 9/1/63. Deserted. Confined at Clarksburg, W. Va., 10/5/63. Desc.: age 39, 5'10", a resident of Wood Co., W. Va.; held for examination. Took the oath of allegiance and was sent North, 10/5/63. Desc.: age 38, 5'10", dark comp., dark hair and blue eyes, a resident of Wood Co., W. Va. NFR.

MILTON, JOHN L. - Pvt. Co. I. b.c. 1825. Not on muster rolls. Cpd. Beverly, W. Va., 1/29/64. Confined at the Atheneum Prison, 2/21/64. Desc.: age 39, 6'2", florid comp., black hair and blue eyes. Occ. farmer, residing in Rockbridge Co. Released to Provost Marshal upon taking the oath of allegiance, 2/22/64. NFR.

MINTER, GEORGE W. - 2nd Sgt. Co. I. b.c. 1836. Enl. Camp Northwest, W. Va., 5/10/63, age 27. Not stated if present or absent on muster-in roll dated 5/5/63, 2nd Sgt. NFR.

MITCHELL, ARTHUR P. - Pvt. Co. G. Enl. Wood Co., W. Va., 6/24/63. Not stated if present or absent on muster-in roll dated 8/63. Ab. 11/1/63 - 2/29/64, deserted 9/15/63. Post war resident of Wood Co., W. Va. NFR.

MITCHELL, GEORGE - Pvt. Co. K. b.c. 1839. Enl. Camp Northwest, W. Va., 6/10/63. age 24. Not stated if present or absent on muster-in roll dated 7/21/63. Ab. 7/1/63 - 11/1/63 (dated 1/6/64), AWOL. Ab. 11/1/63 - 2/29/64, AWOL. Ab. 2/29/64 - 8/31/64, AWOL. NFR.

MITCHELL, JOSEPH S. - Capt. Co. G. b.c. 1836. Enl. Wood Co., W. Va., 6/24/63. Not stated if present or absent on muster-in roll dated 8/63, 1st Sgt. Present, 1st Sgt., 11/1/63 - 2/29/64, had his own horse and equipment. Clothing issued 2/29/64. Present, 1st Sgt., 7/1/64 - 8/31/64, had his own horse; entitled to bond. Present, 1st Sgt., 9/1/64 - 10/31/64 (dated 12/29/64), entitled to $100 bond. Paroled at Staunton, 5/22/65, listed as Capt. Desc.: age 29, 5'8+", dark comp., dark hair and dark eyes. Post war resident of Wood Co., W. Va. NFR.

MITCHELL, THOMAS - Pvt. Co. C. b. Ireland, c. 1843. Enl. Pocahontas Co., W. Va., 2/1/64. Present 6/30/63 - 8/31/64 (dated 1/6/65), enl. bounty due; 6% bond due. Clothing issued 3/10/64. Present 9/1/64 - 10/31/64 (dated 12/30/64), 6% bond due. Paroled at Staunton, 5/1/65, signs by x. Desc.: age 22, 6'2", fair comp., dark hair and dark eyes, a resident of Augusta Co. Post war resident of Highland and Augusta Co's. d. near Mint Springs, 10/15/99, age 56. Bur. Thornrose Cem., Staunton. "A gallant soldier."

MOORE, A. S. - Pvt. Co. I. Enl. Oakhill, Page Co., 10/1/64. Ab. 11/1/63 - 8/31/64 (dated 1/6/65), absent on horse detail. Present 11/1/63 - 10/31/64 (dated 12/31/64). NFR.

MOORE, CHARLES L. - Pvt. Co. C. b.c. 1846. Prior service, Co. G, 31st Va. Inf. Enl. Pocahontas Co., W. Va., 9/12/63. Ab. 6/30/63 - 8/31/64 (dated 1/6/65), claimed by and returned to Co. G, 31st Va. Inf., 4/1/64. Clothing issued 3/10/64. Desc. 1865: age 19, 5'11", light comp., dark hair and blue eyes. CSR listed as Moor, and shows 37th Va. Inf., which is an error. Attended Beverly Confed. Reunion, 5/30/1908. Age 36, farmer, Huntersville, Pocahontas Co., W. Va. 1880 Census. Post war resident of Pocahontas Co., W. Va., 1910. NFR.

MOORE, RICHARD - Pvt. Co. G. Enl. Wood Co., W. Va., 6/24/63. Not stated if present or absent on muster-in roll dated 8/63. Ab. 11/1/63 - 2/29/64, deserted 9/15/63. NFR.

MOORE, THOMAS M. - Pvt. Co. I. b. 5/8/35. Post war rosters only. Age 45, farmer, Mingo, Randolph Co., W. Va. 1880 Census. Member of Gen. Pegram Camp, UCV, Valley Head, W. Va. d. 2/22/1912. Bur. Mingo Cem., Randolph Co., W. Va.

MORGAN, CHARLES R. "Charlie" - Pvt. Co. B. Resident of Marion Co., W. Va. Enl. Clay Hill, 3/3/63. Not stated if present or absent on muster-in roll dated 7/25/63. Present 11/1/63 - 8/31/64 (dated 1/6/65). Clothing issued 3/31/64. Present 9/1/64 - 10/31/64 (dated 12/30/64), entitled to $100 bond. "A brave, intelligent man." Wartime diary indicates he had a knowlege of geology. NFR.

MORGAN, JOHN - Pvt. Co. A. Post war rosters only, which show he was from Marion Co., W. Va., and that he was wd. at Darkesville, W. Va., 7/64. Lt. David Poe carried him to a nearby farm house, where he DOW. two days later.

MORGAN, STEPHEN E. - Capt. Co. K. b.c. 1838. Resident of Marion Co., W. Va. Prior service, Major, 19th Va. Militia. Not on muster rolls. Col. W. W. Arnett recommended that Morgan be promoted from Pvt. to Capt., for extraordinary valor and skill, 12/18/64. Appointed Capt. 3/2/65, confirmed 3/2/65, to rank from 2/18/65, for valor and skill. Paroled at Charlottesville, 5/16/65. Post war rosters show he was Capt./Adjutant of Major John G. Gittings Battn., 12/64. Post war rosters also show service in Co. F, 19th Va. Cav. Adm. Lee Camp Soldiers Home, 1/8/1919, age 81. d. Richmond, 2/25/1926. Bur. Family Section, Hollywood Cem., Richmond. "A brave soldier and gentleman."

MORGAN, ULYSSES - Lt. Co. A. Post war rosters only, which show he was KIA. at Droop Mtn., W. Va., 11/6/63. "A brave, gallant soldier."

MORRIS, DAVID MILLER - Pvt. Co. I. b. Pocahontas Co., W. Va., 2/26/47 (Kerr's Creek, Rockbridge Co.). Age 14, 5th Dist., Rockbridge Co. 1860 Census. Enl. Rockbridge Jr. Reserves, 4/64. Desc.: age 17, 5'11", fair comp., brown hair and brown eyes. Enl. Camp Northwest, W. Va., 7/18/63, age 17 (Oakland Depot, Alleghany Co., 4/1/64 and Pocahontas Co., W. Va., 10/10/63). Not stated if present or absent on muster-in roll dated 5/5/63. Ab. 11/1/63 - 8/31/64 (dated 1/6/65), on horse detail; $50 enl. bounty due. Ab. 11/1/63 - 10/31/64 (dated 12/31/64), on horse detail. Occ. farmer, residing at Kerr's Creek, Rockbridge Co. Farmhand, Buffalo Dist., Rockbridge Co. 1870 Census. d. Hayslett's Creek, Rockbridge Co., 6/20/1909. Bur. Collierstown Presbyterian Church Cem.

MORRIS, FRANK - Pvt. Co. I. Enl. Warm Springs, 4/20/63 (Marlin's Bottom, Pocahontas Co., W. Va., 9/15/63 and Pocahontas Co., W. Va., 10/10/63). Not stated if present or absent on muster-in roll dated 5/5/63. Ab. 11/1/63 - 8/31/64 (dated 1/6/65), claimed by another command. Ab. 11/1/63 - 10/31/64 (dated 12/31/64), claimed by another command. NFR.

MORRIS, JAMES - Pvt. Co. I. b.c. 1844. Enl. Camp Northwest, W. Va., 7/1/63, age 19. Not stated if present or absent on muster-in roll dated 5/5/63. NFR.

MORRIS, TILFORD B. - Pvt. Co. I. b. Rockbridge Co., 1844. Post war rosters show service in Co. G, 58th Va. Inf. Enl. Warm Springs, 4/20/63, age 18 (Warm Springs, 4/1/64 and Pocahontas Co., W. Va., 9/10/63). Not stated if present or absent on muster-in roll dated 5/5/63. Ab. 11/1/63 - 8/31/64 (dated 1/6/65), claimed by another command. Ab. 11/1/63 - 10/31/64 (dated 12/31/64), claimed by another command. Farmhand, Buffalo Dist., Rockbridge 1870 and 1880 Census. NFR.

MORRIS, WILLIAM TAYLOR "Bill" - Pvt. Co. I. b. Rockbridge Co., 8/29/46. Age 13, Kerr's Creek, Rockbridge Co. 1860 Census. Enl. Rockbridge Jr. Reserves, 4/64. Desc.: age 17, 5'8", fair comp., light hair and blue eyes. Occ. farmer, residing at Kerr's Creek, Rockbridge Co. Enl. Oakland Depot, Alleghany Co., 5/1/64 (Pocahontas Co., W. Va., 10/10/63). Present 11/1/63 - 8/31/64 (dated 1/6/65), $50 enl. bounty due. Present 11/1/63 - 10/31/64 (dated 12/31/64). Farmhand, Kerr's Creek, Rockbridge Co. 1870 Census. Post war farmer. Drew a pension, listed as Morrison. d. Waterloo Hollow, Rockbridge Co., 9/19/1917. Bur. Morris Cem., near his home, on Rt. 629, Rockbridge Co.

MORRISON, W. T. - Pvt. Co. ?. Post war rosters only, which show he was a resident of Rockbridge Co. Could be William T. Morris, above. NFR.

MORRISON (MORRESTON), WILLIAM COLUMBUS (COLUMBIA) - Pvt. Co. D. b. Barbour Co., W. Va., c. 1846. Post war rosters show him as a resident of Harrison Co., W. Va. Enl. Gnatty Creek (Weston, W. Va.,), 5/1/63. POW record shows enl. as Pocahontas Co., W. Va. Not stated if present or absent on muster-in roll dated 8/63. Present 7/1/63 - 1/1/64 (dated 1/1/64), had his own horse. Ab. 12/31/63 - 8/31/64 (dated 1/6/65), prisoner. Clothing issued 2/29/64. Ab. 9/1/64 - 10/31/64, POW. Cpd. Beverly, W. Va., 10/29/64. Confined at Clarksburg, W. Va. Desc.: age 18, 5'7", fair comp., light hair and gray eyes. Occ. farmer, residing in Barbour Co., W. Va. Transf. to Wheeling, W. Va., and confined at the Atheneum Prison, 11/2/64. Transf. to Camp Chase, 11/22/64. Confined at Camp Chase, 11/23/64, desires to take the oath of allegiance. DOD. Camp Chase, 3/18/65, pneumonia. Bur. Camp Chase Confederate Cem., grave no. 1706.

MORRISON, WILLIAM McK. - Pvt. Co. D. b.c. 1818. Enl. Huntersville, W. Va., 6/1/63 (Weston, W. Va., 5/1/63). Not stated if present or absent on muster-in roll dated 8/63. Present 7/1/63 1/1/64 (dated 1/1/64). Present 12/31/63 - 8/31/64 (dated 1/6/65). Ab. 9/1/64 - 10/31/64, on detached service; entitled to $100 enl. bounty. Paroled at Staunton, 5/14/65. Desc.: age 47, 5'7", dark comp., dark hair and gray eyes. NFR.

MORTON, ED - Pvt. Co. A. b.c. 1830. Enl. Augusta Co., 2/27/63, age 33. Not stated if present or absent on muster-in roll dated 2/27/63. Ab. 10/31/63 - 8/31/64, never reported for duty. NFR.

MURPHY, JOHN F. - Pvt. Co. K. b. Va., c. 1843. Age 17, apprentice shoemaker, Collierstown, Rockbridge Co. 1860 Census. Enl. Warm Springs, 4/1/63, age 20. Not stated if present or absent on muster-in roll dated 7/21/63. Present 7/1/63 - 11/1/63 (dated 1/6/64). Present 11/1/63 - 2/29/64, had his own horse since 12/19/63. Ab. 2/29/64 - 8/31/64, AWOL. Clothing issued 2/29/64. Paroled at Staunton, 5/23/65. Desc.: age 25, 5'8", fair comp., black hair and brown eyes. NFR.

MURPHY, M. - Lt. Co. I. Not on muster rolls. Ab. 10/25/64, in hosp. sick, 6 days. NFR.

MURPHY, MARTIN T. - 2nd Lt. Co. K. b.c. 1841. Enl. Warm Springs, 4/1/63, age 22. Not stated if present or absent on muster-in roll dated 7/21/63, 1st Sgt. Present 7/1/63 - 11/1/63 (dated 1/6/64), promoted 1st Sgt., 7/21/63. Present, 3rd Lt., 11/1/63 - 2/29/64, promoted from 1st Sgt. to 3rd Lt., 1/1/64. Present, 3rd Lt., 2/29/64 - 8/31/64, promoted from 1st Sgt. to 3rd Lt., 1/1/64; commanding Co. Promoted Sr. 2nd Lt., 3/64. NFR.

MURPHY, MICHAEL - Pvt. Co. D. b.c. 1819. Enl. Hightown, Highland Co., 7/27/63. Not stated if present or absent on muster-in roll dated 8/63. Ab. 7/1/63 - 1/1/64 (dated 1/1/64), prisoner since 8/63. Cpd. Upshur Co., W. Va., 8/26/63. Confined at the Atheneum Prison, 8/30/63. Desc.: age 44, 5'8+", dark comp., dark hair and dark eyes. Occ. farmer, residing in Upshur Co., W. Va. Transf. to Camp Chase, 8/31/63. Confined at Camp Chase, 9/1/63. Ab. 12/31/63 - 8/31/64 (dated 1/6/65), prisoner. Transf. to Rock Island, Ill., 1/14/64. Confined at Rock Island Prison, 1/17/64. Ab. 9/1/64 - 10/31/64, POW. Took the oath of allegiance and was released, 4/21/65. Desc.: age ?, 5'8", dark comp., black hair and hazel eyes, a resident of Buckhannon, W. Va. NFR.

MURRAY, WILLIAM J. - 2nd Sgt. Co. K. b.c. 1845. Enl. Camp Northwest, W. Va., 6/18/63, age 18. Not stated if present or absent on muster-in roll dated 7/21/63, 3rd Sgt. Present, 3rd Sgt., 7/1/63 - 11/1/63 (dated 1/6/64), reduced to the ranks 8/27/63; had his own horse from 9/1/63 - 11/6/63. Present, 2nd Sgt., 11/1/63 - 2/29/64, reinstated by order of Col. Comdg., 1/1/64; had his own horse since 5/1/64; lost bands and breech screw of musket. Ab., 2nd Sgt., 2/29/64 - 8/31/64, wd. Winchester; $100 enl. bounty due. Adm. Gen. Hosp., Winchester, 8/2/64, debilitas. RTD. 8/5/64. Adm. CSA Gen. Hosp., Charlottesville, 9/27/64, vulnus sclopeticum, head. Furloughed 10/5/64. Adm. CSA Gen. Hosp., Charlottesville, 11/6/64, vulnus sclopeticum, fractured cranium, right front. Clothing issued 11/17/64. Surrendered at Lynchburg, 4/14/65. NFR.

MUSGRAVE (MUSGRAVES), JAMES - Pvt. Co. ?. Post war rosters only, which show he was a resident of Ritchie Co., W. Va. Brother of Jonathan Musgrave. NFR.

MUSGRAVE (MUSGRAVES), JONATHAN - Pvt. Co. D or K. Not on muster rolls. Reference jacket shows service in Co. A, 46th Battn. Va. Cav. POW record shows he was a member of Capt. Jarvis' Co., 20th Va. Cav. (Capt. Jarvis' Co. was at this time attached to the 20th Va. Cav., as the 46th Battn. had not yet been formed). Cpd. Standing Stone, Wirt Co., W. Va., 10/26/63. Desc.: age 28, 5'10", light comp., black hair, gray eyes and brown whiskers. Occ. farmer, residing in Ritchie Co., W. Va. Wd. in the knee by pistol shot from Lt. Frost, 11th W. Va. Inf. Served in Co. A, 46th Battn. Va. Cav. Brother of James Musgrave. NFR.

MUTERSPAUGH (MOODASPAUGH, MUTERSPAW, MUDESPAUGH), LEONARD "Lind" - Pvt. Co. K. b.c. 1846. Enl. Camp Marlin's Bottom, Pocahontas Co., W. Va., 10/13/63. Present 7/1/63 - 11/1/63 (dated 1/6/64), lost a Mississippi Rifle. Present 11/1/63 - 2/29/64. Clothing issued 2/29/64. Ab. 2/29/64 - 8/31/64, sick. Sentenced to be shot for desertion, but was later released. Post war resident of Rockbridge Co. Age 64, farmhand, Lexington Dist., Rockbridge Co. 1910 census. NFR.

NEAL, JOHN DEXTER - Capt. Co. G. b. Parkersburg, W. Va., 1836. Age 24 (1861). Prior service, Co. I, 31st Va. Inf. Detached and sent to Parkersburg, W. Va. Organized Co. G, 20th Va. Cav. in Wood Co., W. Va. Enl. Wood Co., W. Va., 5/12/63. Appointed Capt., 5/12/63, confirmed by election. Not stated if present or absent on muster-in roll dated 8/63, Capt. Present 11/1/63 - 2/29/64, had his own horse and equipment. Present 7/1/64 8/31/64, had his own horse. Present 9/1/64 - 10/31/64 (dated 12/29/64). Resigned 2/4/65, document illegible. Paroled at Charleston, W. Va., 5/5/65. Desc.: age 24, 5'6", fair comp., light hair, hazel eyes and light whiskers. Post war resident of Lexington, and Houston, Tx. Drew a Tx. Pension. Age 41, farmer, Williams Dist., Wood Co., W. Va. 1880 Census. Brother of Paul Neal. d. Houston, Tx., 7/19/1914, age 67. Bur. Hollywood Cem., Houston, Tx.

NEAL, PAUL - 3rd Lt. Co. G. b. Parkersburg, W. Va., 8/8/32. Attended Parkersburg Institute and Prof. John C. Nash's school. Entered VMI, 1849. Grad. Jefferson (Washington & Jefferson) College, Canonsburg, Pa. Prewar hardware business, Parkersburg, W. Va. Commissioned Capt., Co. A, 113th Va. Militia, 1858. Had typhoid fever during the fall of 1861, sick for about 3 months. Displayed the 1st CSA flag in Parkersburg, W. Va. Recruited Co. G, 20th Va. Cav. Served as CSA recruiting officer at Parkersburg, W. Va., 1861. Drillmaster. Cpd. Ravenswood, W. Va., 1861, tried and sent to Camp Chase. Exchanged. Enl. Wood Co., W. Va., 5/12/63. Elected Jr. 2nd (3rd) Lt., 5/12/63. Not stated if present or absent on muster-in roll dated 8/63, 3rd Lt. Present, 3rd Lt., 11/1/63 - 2/29/64, had his own equipment since 12/21/63. Present, Jr. 2nd Lt., 7/1/64 - 8/31/64, had his own horse. Ab., Jr. 2nd Lt., 9/1/64 - 10/31/64 (dated 12/29/64), on leave. Cpd. Parkersburg, W. Va., by 4/20/65. Confined at Clarksburg, W. Va. Desc.: age 32, 5'8+", fair comp., red hair and black eyes. Occ. tobacconist, residing in Greenbrier Co., W. Va. Card in his CSR shows he resigned 11/3/63. Post war resident of Wood Co., W. Va. Age 47, farmer, Harris Dist., Wood Co., W. Va. 1880 Census. Brother of John D. Neal. d. 12/21/1919.

NEALE, THOMAS - Pvt. Co. G. Enl. Wood Co., W. Va., 5/12/63. Not stated if present or absent on muster-in roll dated 8/63. Present 7/1/64 - 8/31/64, had his own horse. Post war resident of Wood Co., W. Va. NFR.

NEPTUNE, AMOS - Pvt. Co. B. Enl. Marion Co., W. Va., 10/10/63. Present 11/1/63 - 8/31/64 (dated 1/6/65). Clothing issued, 3/31/64. Present 9/1/64 - 10/31/64 (dated 12/30/64), entitled to $100 bond. NFR.

NESMITH, WILLIAM H. - Pvt. Co. D. b. 1835. Post war rosters only for service in the 20th Va. Cav. Served in Co. G, 19th Va. Cav. Post war resident of Mo. d. 1916. Bur. Confederate Memorial Cem., Higginsville, Mo.

NICELY (KNISELY), JAMES A. K. - Pvt. Co. K. Enl. Camp Marlin's Bottom, Pocahontas Co., W. Va., 8/27/63 (8/1/63). Ab. 7/1/63 - 11/1/63 (dated 1/6/64), deserted, taking his gun with him. Post war resident of Rockbridge Co. NFR.

NICELY, JOHN - Pvt. Co. K. b. Va., c. 1845. Age 15, farmhand, N. Dist., Augusta Co. 1860 Census. Enl. Camp Marlin's Bottom, Pocahontas Co., W. Va., 8/27/63. Ab. 7/1/63 - 11/1/63 (dated 1/6/64), claimed by another command. Listed as being a deserter from another command, 5/4/64. NFR.

NICELY, JOHN A. - Pvt. Co. K. Enl. Bath Alum Springs, Bath Co., 8/22/63. Present 7/1/63 - 11/1/63 (dated 1/6/64), had his own horse since enl. Present 11/1/63 - 2/29/64, had his own horse since enl.; detailed as wagoner. Clothing issued 2/6/64, 3/1/64 and 3rd Qr. 1864, signs by x. Employed as a laborer at Warm Springs, 1/1/64 - 3/31/64. Present 2/29/64 - 8/31/64, detailed as teamster; had his own horse since enl.; $100 enl. bounty due. NFR.

NICHOLS, JAMES - Pvt. Co. K. b.c. 1840. Enl. Warm Springs, 4/21/63, age 23. Not stated if present or absent on muster-in roll dated 7/21/63. Ab. 7/1/63 - 11/1/63 (dated 1/6/64), AWOL. NFR.

NEICE, MARTIN - Pvt. Co. I. b.c. 1838. Enl. Camp Northwest, W. Va., 6/2/63, age 25. Not stated if present or absent on muster-in roll dated 5/5/63. NFR.

NOE, SAMUEL - Pvt. Co. I. b. Roane (Kanáwha) Co., W. Va., 5/21/36. Age 24, farmer, Gilmer Co., W. Va. 1860 Census. Enl. Lewisburg, W. Va., 4/20/63, age 23. Not stated if present or absent on muster-in roll dated 5/5/63. Served in Co. G, 19th Va. Cav. Age 42, farmer, Geary Dist., Roane Co., W. Va. 1880 Census. Post war farmer and resident of Newton, Roane Co., W. Va., 1884. Served as school trustee, 2 years. NFR.

NORMAN, CLEMENT L. - Pvt. Co. D. Prior service, 17th Va. Cav. Enl. Warm Springs, 10/1/63. Hosp. MR shows enl. as Weston, W. Va., 8/29/62. Not stated if present or absent on Hosp. MR, Warm Springs, 4/1/63 - 1/1/64; attached to hosp. 11/1/63 as a nurse. Present 7/1/63 - 1/1/64 (dated 1/1/64), exchanged for P. H. Hilkey; had his own horse. Present 12/31/63 - 8/31/64 (dated 1/6/65), exchanged for P. H. Hilkey. Present 9/1/64 - 10/31/64, entitled to $100 enl. bounty. Took the amnesty oath at Clarksburg, W. Va., 8/30/65. NFR.

NOSS, FRITZ - Pvt. Co. I. Enl. Marlin's, Pocahontas Co., W. Va., 9/1/63. Ab. 11/1/63 - 8/31/64 (dated 1/6/65), POW. No POW records. NFR.

NOSS, ROBERT - Pvt. Co. I. Enl. Pocahontas Co., W. Va., 4/4/63. Ab. 11/1/63 - 8/31/64 (dated 1/6/65), POW. No POW records. NFR.

NOSS, WILLIAM - Pvt. Co. I. b.c. 1840. Not on muster rolls. Listed as a deserter and shown as having been cpd. in Bath Co., 8/24/63. Took the oath and was sent North, via Wheeling, W. Va. Confined at the Atheneum Prison, 9/6/63. Desc.: age 23, 5'8+", dark comp., dark hair and black eyes. Occ. clerk, residing in Henrico Co. Transf. to Camp Chase, 9/7/63. Confined at Camp Chase, 9/8/63. Took the oath of allegiance and was released by order of the Sec. of War, 10/29/63. NFR.

OAKES, WILLIAM R. - Pvt. Co. D. Prior service, Co. B, 31st Va. Inf. Enl. Hightown, Highland Co., 7/15/63. Not stated if present or absent on muster-in roll dated 8/63. Returned to Co. B, 31st Va. Inf. by 2/64. KIA. Dabney's Mills, Hatcher's Run, 4/7/65.

O'BRIEN (O'BRYAN, O'BRYEN, O'BRION), JOHN M. - Pvt. Co. F. Enl. Camp Northwest (Camp Clover Lick and Camp Miller), W. Va., 7/19/63. Not stated if present or absent on muster-in roll dated 7/20/63. Ab. 7/1/63 - 8/31/64 (dated 1/6/65), transf. to Co. A, 19th Va. Cav. Ab. 9/1/64 - 10/31/64 (dated 12/30/64), transf. to Co. A, 19th Va. Cav. NFR.

O'BRIEN, MILES - Pvt. Co. F. Enl. Camp Northwest (Camp Clover Lick and Camp Miller), W. Va., 7/19/63. Not stated if present or absent on muster-in roll dated 7/20/63. Ab. 7/1/63 - 8/31/64 (dated 1/6/65), transf. to Co. A, 19th Va. Cav. Clothing issued at Liberty Gen. Hosp., 8/3/64, signs by x. Ab. 9/1/64 - 10/31/64 (dated 12/30/64), transf. to Co. A, 19th Va. Cav. NFR.

OLDAKER, JOHN - Pvt. Co. F. Enl. Bulltown, W. Va., 5/10/63 (Camp Clover Lick, 7/11/63. Not stated if present or absent on muster-in roll dated 7/20/63. Ab. 7/1/63 - 8/31/64 (dated 1/6/65), deserted 5/13/63. Ab. 9/1/64 - 10/31/64 (dated 12/30/64), deserted 5/13/63. NFR.

OPIE, HIEROME LINDSAY, Jr. - 1st Lt. and Drillmaster. b. Va. 1837. Resident of Staunton. Grad. UVa., 1857, lawyer. Age 23, N. Dist., Augusta Co. 1860 Census. Prior service, Staunton Arty., and Co. D, 6th Va. Cav. Capt. (afterwards Brig. Gen.) John D. Imboden wrote on 3/20/62 "his estate of some $40,000 was all at Wheeling. The Yankees have it all." Not on muster rolls. Appointed drill master, with rank of Lt., 11/3/63, on staff of Col. W. L. Jackson. Furloughed 1/64. Paroled 6/64 because of wds. by Brig. Gen. Duffie. Cpd. Fisher's Hill, 9/22/64, 1st Lt. Sent to Harpers Ferry, W. Va., then to Ft. Delaware, 9/25/64. Confined at Ft. Delaware, 9/27/64. Ab. 12/25/64, POW since 9/22/64. Farmer, age 33, Mt. Sidney, Augusta Co. 1870 Census. Lawyer, Covington, Ky. d. Covington, Ky., 5/25/92.

ORNDORFF, PHINEAS M. - Pvt. Co. A. b. Pendleton Co., W. Va., c. 1834. Age 25, laborer, 1st Dist. Augusta Co. 1860 Census. Prior service, Co. D, 25th Va. Inf. Enl. Augusta Co., 1/26/63, age 29. Not stated if present or absent on muster-in roll dated 1/26/63. Ab. 10/31/63 - 8/31/64, never reported for duty. Post war resident of Highland and Augusta Co's. d. Augusta Co., c. 1872.

OVERFIELD, JOHN - Pvt. Co. D. Enl. Elk, W. Va., 5/1/63. Not stated if present or absent on muster-in roll dated 8/63. NFR.

PAE [POE], WILLIAM E. - Sgt. Co. I. b.c. 1836. Cards in CSR also show service as Co. A and Co. G. Not on muster rolls. Cpd. Lewisburg, W. Va., 11/7/63, listed as Co. I. Confined at the Atheneum Prison, 11/20/63. Desc.: age 27, 5'4+", light comp., dark hair and blue eyes. Occ. slater, residing in Richmond. Transf. to Camp Chase, 11/20/63. Confined at Camp Chase, 11/21/63. Transf. to Ft. Delaware, 2/29/64. Confined at Ft. Delaware, 3/4/64. Took the Amnesty oath, 5/4/65. Listed as being age 18, a baker residing on Main Street in Richmond, between Madison and Monroe Streets. NFR.

PAINE (PAIN), THOMAS F. - Pvt. Co. D. b.c. 1830. Enl. Camp Northwest, W. Va., 8/9/63. Present 7/1/63 - 1/1/64 (dated 1/1/64), entitled to enl. bounty; had his own horse. Present 12/31/63 - 8/31/64 (dated 1/6/65). Present 9/1/64 - 10/31/64, entitled to $100 enl. bounty. Paroled at Staunton, 5/22/65. Desc.: age 35, 6', fair comp., dark hair and blue eyes. NFR.

PAINE, WILLIAM - Pvt. Co. E. Enl. Camp Clover Lick, 7/11/63. Not stated if present or absent on muster-in roll dated 7/18/63. NFR.

PARKER, JOHN M. - Pvt. Co. F. b. Bedford Co., 8/30/40. Prewar farmer. Prior service, Co. C, 42nd Va. Inf. Desc. 1862: age ?, 5'10", florid comp., dark hair and dark eyes. History of 42nd Va. Inf. shows service in Co. F, 20th Va. Cav. Post war farmer and deputy sheriff, Bedford Co. NFR.

PARSONS, WILLIAM L. - Pvt. Co. F. Resident of Roane Co., W. Va. Enl. Camp Clover Lick (Camp Miller), 7/17/63. Not stated if present or absent on muster-in roll dated 7/20/63. Ab. 7/1/63 - 8/31/64 (dated 1/6/65), transf. to Co. C, 19th Va. Cav. Ab. 9/1/64 10/31/64 (dated 12/30/64), transf. to Co. C, 19th Va. Cav. NFR.

PATTERSON, ROBERT - Pvt. Co. H. Enl. Calhoun Co., W. Va., 5/14/63. Not stated if present or absent on muster-in roll dated 8/63. Could be Robert H. Patterson, below. NFR.

PATTERSON, ROBERT (RICHARD) HENRY - Pvt. Co. G. b. 1842. Enl. Wood Co., W. Va., 5/9/63 (6/18/63, 6/24/63). Not stated if present or absent on muster-in roll dated 8/63. Present 11/1/63 - 2/29/64. Clothing issued 2/29/64 and 8/31/64. Not stated if present or absent 7/1/64 - 8/31/64, had his own horse; entitled to bond. Ab. 9/1/64 - 10/31/64 (dated 12/29/64), on detached service; entitled to $100 bond. Post war roster shows he was taken prisoner at some point, and paroled in 1865. d. 1931. Bur. Mt. Olivet Cem., Parkersburg, W. Va. Could be Robert Patterson, above.

PATTON (PATTEN), JOHN S. - 3rd Corp. Co. B. Prior service, Co. D, 19th Va. Cav. Enl. Williamsburg, Greenbrier Co., W. Va., 4/15/63. Not stated if present or absent on muster-in roll dated 7/25/63, 3rd Corp. NFR.

PATTON, ZACHARIAH H. - Pvt. Co. B. b. Gilmer Co., W. Va., c. 1843. Prior service, Co. D, 19th Va. Cav. Enl. Williamsburg, Greenbrier Co., W. Va., 3/17/63. Not stated if present or absent on muster-in roll dated 1/6/65), sick from wd., date and place of injury not given. Clothing issued 3/31/64. Ab. 9/1/64 - 10/31/64 (dated 12/30/64), sick from wd. Deserted. Reported at Glenville, W. Va., 12/22/64. Confined at Clarksburg, W. Va. Took the oath of allegiance and was released, 12/24/64. Desc.: age 21, 5'9", light comp., dark hair and black eyes. Occ. farmer, residing in Gilmer Co., W. Va. NFR.

PAUGH, WILSON M. - Pvt. Co. D. Resident of Barbour Co., W. Va. Prior service, Capt. W. K. Jenkins' Cav. Co. Enl. Weston, W. Va., 5/1/63. Not stated if present or absent on muster-in roll dated 8/63. Present 7/1/63 - 1/1/64 (dated 1/1/64), detailed as orderly for Col. W. W. Arnett; had his own horse. Present 12/31/63 8/31/64 (dated 1/6/65). Present 9/1/64 - 10/31/64, entitled to $100 enl. bounty. NFR.

PEACO, GEORGE W. - Pvt. Co. D. b. Staunton, 11/6/38. Carpenter, 1st Dist., Augusta Co. 1860 Census. Prior service, Staunton Arty. Enl. Camp Pisgah, Bath Co., 1/1/64. Present 7/1/63 1/1/64 (dated 1/1/64), entitled to enl. bounty. Present 12/31/63 8/31/64 (dated 1/6/65). Present 9/1/64 - 10/31/64, entitled to $100 enl. bounty. Paroled at Staunton, 5/12/65. Desc.: age 31, height ?, fair comp., light hair and black eyes. Carpenter, Staunton, 1870 Census. Member Stonewall Jackson Camp, UCV, Staunton. d. Staunton, 6/28/1909. Bur. Thornrose Cem., Staunton.

PEARCY (PIERCY), ALBERT F. - Pvt. Co. B. b. Doddridge Co., W. Va., c. 1844. Prior service, Co. D, 19th Va. Cav. Enl. Williamsburg, Greenbrier Co., W. Va., 3/17/63. Not stated if present or absent on muster-in roll dated 7/25/63. Present 11/1/63 8/31/64 (dated 1/6/65), AWOL since 9/27/64. Clothing issued 3/31/64. Ab. 9/1/64 - 10/31/64 (dated 12/30/64), AWOL since 9/64. Deserted. Reported at Clarksburg, W. Va., 11/23/64. Took the oath of allegiance and was released, 11/24/64. Desc.: age 20, 5'7", fair comp., light hair and blue eyes. Occ. farmer, residing in Doddridge Co., W. Va. Age 36, farmer, New Milton, Harrison Co., W. Va. 1880 Census. NFR.

PEARL, MATHEW - Pvt. Co. G. Post war rosters only, which show he was a resident of Wood Co., W. Va. NFR.

PEASE, FRANKLIN G. - Pvt. Co. G. Enl. Wood Co., W. Va., 6/14/63. Not stated if present or absent on muster-in roll dated 8/63. Present 11/1/63 - 2/29/64, had his own horse and equipment since 12/21/63. Clothing issued 2/29/64. Not stated if present or absent 7/1/64 - 8/31/64, had his own horse. Ab. 9/1/64 - 10/31/64 (dated 12/29/64), on detached service; entitled to $100 bond. Post war roster shows his name as Francis, and that he was a resident of Wood Co., W. Va. Age 38, farmer, Harris Dist., Wood Co., W. Va. 1880 Census. NFR.

PECK, SOLOMON C. - Pvt. Co. C. b.c. 1835. Age 25, farmer, Randolph Co., W. Va. 1860 Census. Enl. Randolph Co., W. Va., 4/28/63. Not stated if present or absent on muster-in roll dated 8/63. Ab. 6/30/63 - 8/31/64 (dated 1/6/65), DOD. 1/2/64, diphtheria. d. in a hospital.

PENNYBACKER, BENJAMIN R. - Pvt. Co. G. b. Belleville, W. Va., 10/41. Post war rosters only, which show he was a resident of Wood Co., W. Va. Served also in Ashby's (Co. B, 7th Va.) Cav. Post war sketch shows service in Co. F, 17th Va. Cav. Paroled and returned to Belleville, Wood Co., W. Va. Lived in Huntington, W. Va. for a few years, then returned to Belleville, W. Va. d. Covington, Ky., 2/4/1909, while visiting that place. Bur. Belleville Cem., Belleville, W. Va.

PENNYBACKER, BENJAMIN YANCEY - Pvt. Co. G. b. Wood Co., W. Va., 5/29/44. Enl. Wood Co., W. Va., 6/24/63. Not stated if present or absent on muster-in roll dated 8/63. Present 11/1/63 - 2/29/64. Clothing issued 2/29/64. Not stated if present or absent 7/1/64 - 8/31/64, had his own horse since 5/12/64; entitled to bond. Ab. 9/1/64 - 10/31/64 (dated 12/29/64), cpd. 9/24/64. Cpd. Winchester, 9/19/64. Sent to Harpers Ferry, W. Va., then to Pt. Lookout, 9/24/64. Confined at Pt. Lookout, 9/27/64. Made to chop wood with other prisoners. While chopping wood one day he and some of his comrades made an attempt to escape. He went about a mile he was captured and returned to the prison. A ball and chain was fastened to his leg for three months. Took the oath of allegiance and was released, 6/6/65. When released he was suffering from scurvy and weak from starvation. Reported at Washington, DC, 6/19/65, transportation furnished to Parkersburg, W. Va. Post war rosters show he was cpd. Fisher's Hill, 9/22/64, after fighting desperately to make his escape. He had been left by the command on picket with instructions to stay until relieved. He remained at the post of duty until surrounded by the Federals. In trying to escape from them, he attempted to make his horse to leap a stone fence, in the act of jumping, his enemies fired and killed the horse and as he fell the brave confederate sprang from his back and ran. He was overtaken and captured. Some of the soldiers wanted to shoot him after he was captured as he had killed two of their number shooting one of them in the face. Their commander said that he was too brave a soldier to be killed. Post war resident of Wood Co., W. Va. Post war farmer and resident of Belleville, W. Va. Cousin of Hiram H. Pennybacker. NFR.

PENNYBACKER, HIRAM H. - Pvt. Co. G. b. Wocd Co., W. Va., 4/12/44. Educated at Belleville, W. Va. Enl. Wood Co., W. Va., 6/24/63. Not stated if present or absent on muster-in roll dated 8/63. Present 11/1/63 - 2/29/64, had his own horse and equipment. Clothing issued 2/29/64. Present 7/1/64 - 8/31/64, had his own horse; entitled to bond. At the battle of Lynchburg (6/17/64), when the battle was at its height, the soldiers were almost famished for water, Lieut. Pennybacker and his cousin B. Y. Pennybacker, volunteered to bring water from a well where the bullets were flying thickest and raining so fast, the well curb was cut to pieces. They managed to save a piece of rope with which they drew water and filled fifteen canteens that they had brought. On returning from the perilous mission, they were warmly commended for their brave act. Present 9/1/64 - 10/31/64 (dated 12/29/64), entitled to bond. Clothing issued 4th Qr. 1864, while on the way to his command. Cpd. Parkersburg, W. Va., 4/21/65. Confined at Clarksburg, W. Va., 4/22/65. Paroled and released for exchange, 4/24/65. Desc.: age 21, 5'10", dark comp., black hair and blue eyes. Occ. farmer, residing in Wood Co., W. Va. Grave marker and post war roster shows him as a Lt. Reference jacket show service in Co. C, 19th Va. Cav. d. 1923. Bur. IOOF Cem., Parkersburg, W. Va.

PENNYBACKER, JOHN BIRD - 2nd Lt. Co. G. b. W. Va., c. 1840. Prior service, Co. A, 36th Va. Inf. Enl. Wood Co., W. Va., 5/12/63. Elected 2nd Lt., 5/12/63. Not stated if present or absent on muster-in roll dated 8/63, 2nd Lt. Ab., 2nd Lt., 11/1/63 2/29/64, resignation was accepted, 11/10/63. Submitted his resignation, 10/21/63 from Marlin's Bottom, Pocahontas Co., W. Va., stating the Co. was dissatisfied with him and he resigned for the benefit of it. Post war resident of Wood Co., W. Va. Adm. Lee Camp Soldier's Home, Richmond, 10/27/1908, age 68. d. Richmond, 11/15/1913, age 73. Bur. Hollywood Cem., Richmond.

PENNYBACKER, JOHN M. - Pvt. Co. G / Capt. ACS. b.c. 1836. Enl. Wood Co., W. Va., 6/24/63, as a Pvt. in Co. G. Not stated if present or absent on muster-in roll dated 8/63. Present 11/1/63 - 2/29/64, had his own horse and equipment; appointed Commissary Sgt., 9/15/63. Clothing issued 2/29/64. Not stated if present or absent 7/1/64 - 8/31/64, had his own horse; entitled to bond. Present 9/1/64 - 10/31/64 (dated 12/29/64), detailed as Commissary 8/15/63; entitled to $100 bond. Cpd. Wirt Co., W. Va., 11/9/64, listed as Capt., ACS. Confined at the Atheneum Prison, 11/64. Desc.: age 28, 5'6", fair comp., light hair and gray eyes. Occ. merchant, residing in Wood Co., W. Va. Transf. to Camp Chase, 11/18/64. Confined at Camp Chase, 11/19/64. Paroled 2/17/65 and sent to Pt. Lookout for exchange. Post war resident of Wood Co., W. Va. NFR.

PENNYBACKER, WILLIAM H. - Pvt. Co. G. Enl. Wood Co., W. Va., 6/24/63. Not stated if present or absent on muster-in roll dated 8/63. Present 11/1/63 - 2/29/64, had his own horse and equipment. Present 7/1/64 - 8/31/64, had his own horse; entitled to bond. Present 9/1/64 - 10/31/64 (dated 12/29/64), entitled to $100 bond. Surrendered at Parkersburg, W. Va., 5/4/65. Confined at Clarksburg, W. Va., 5/5/65. Paroled and released, to be exchanged, 5/5/65. Desc.: age 24, 5'11", fair comp., fair hair and blue eyes. Occ. farmer, residing in Wood Co., W. Va. Post war resident of Wood Co., W. Va. NFR.

PENNYBAKER (PENNYBACKER), ALBERT D. - Pvt. Co. G. b. Broadway, Rockingham Co., c. 1844. Age 16, merchant's clerk, Rockingham Co. 1860 Census. Prior service, Co. H, 7th Va. Cav. Not on muster rolls for 20th Va. Cav. Cpd. Parkersburg, W. Va., 4/21/65. Confined at Clarksburg, W. Va., 4/22/65. Paroled and released, to be exchanged, 4/24/65. Desc.: age 21, 6', dark comp., black hair and brown eyes. Occ. farmer, residing in Rockingham Co. Adm. Lee Camp Soldier's Home, Richmond, 9/30/1926, age 84. d. Richmond, 10/8/1928, age 85. Bur. Hollywood Cem., Richmond. Family in Tenn.

PERKINS, ALEXANDER - Pvt. Co. E. Enl. Camp Clover Lick, 7/11/63. Not stated if present or absent on muster-in roll dated 7/18/63. NFR.

PEYATT (PEATE), GEORGE - Pvt. Co. E. b.c. 1834. Enl. Camp Clover Lick, 7/17/63. Not stated if present or absent on muster-in roll dated 7/18/63. Served in Co. C, 19th Va. Cav., listed as Peate. NFR.

PEYATT (PEATE), JOHN - Pvt. Co. E. b.c. 1841. Enl. Camp Clover Lick, 7/17/63. Not stated if present or absent on muster-in roll dated 7/18/63. Served in Co. C, 19th Va. Cav., listed as Peate. NFR.

PHILLIPS, GEORGE W. - Pvt. Co. C. b. Barbour Co., W. Va., c. 1847. Enl. Pocahontas (Randolph) Co., W. Va., 6/9/63. POW record shows enl. as Pocahontas Co., 6/62. Not stated if present or absent on muster-in roll dated 8/63. Present 6/30/63

- 8/31/64 (dated 1/6/65), 6% bond due. Adm. Gen. Hosp. No. 9, 11/12/63, sent to Chimborazo Hosp., 11/13/64, listed as G. C. Phillips, Co. G, 19th Va. Cav. Ab. 9/1/64 - 10/31/64 (dated 12/30/64), AWOL since 10/5/64; 6% bond due. Deserted. Surrendered at Philippi, W. Va., 2/9/65. Confined at Clarksburg, W. Va., 2/10/65. Desc.: age 18, 5'9", fair comp., light hair and gray eyes. Occ. farmer, residing in Philippi, Barbour Co., W. Va. Took the amnesty oath and was sent North. Confined at the Atheneum Prison, 3/7/65. Desc.: age 18, 5'8", fair comp., light hair and gray eyes. Occ. farmer, residing in Barbour Co., W. Va. d. by 1916. NFR.

PHILLIPS, SAMUEL - Pvt. Co. C. b.c. 1841. Resident of Tucker Co., W. Va. Arrested and confined by 3/15/62. Charged with being a rebel mail carrier and horsethief. Not on muster rolls. Paroled at Staunton, 5/5/65. Desc.: age 24, 5'11+", dark comp., dark hair and dark eyes. NFR.

PHILLIPS, W. A. - Pvt. Co. C. Enl. Pocahontas (Randolph) Co., W. Va., 6/9/63. Not stated if present or absent on muster-in roll dated 8/63. Ab. 6/30/63 - 8/31/64 (dated 1/6/65), deserted 3/1/64. NFR.

PHILLIPS, WILLIAM H. - Pvt. Co. G. b. Va., c. 1845. Age 15, laborer, 1st Dist., Augusta Co. 1860 Census. Not on muster rolls. Cpd. near Lynchburg, 6/18/64. Sent to Cumberland, Md., then to Wheeling, W. Va. NFR.

PINER, GEORGE - Pvt. Co. K. b.c. 1840. Enl. Camp Northwest, W. Va., 6/14/63, age 23. Not stated if present or absent on muster-in roll dated 7/21/63. Ab. 7/1/63 - 11/1/63 (dated 1/6/64), AWOL. NFR.

PLOTT (PLATT), ALFRED ABRAM - Pvt. Co. K. b. Rockbridge Co., 1/?/40. Age 18, farmhand, Beard's Store, Rockbridge Co. 1860 Census. Enl. Camp Northwest, W. Va., 7/13/63, age 18. Not stated if present or absent on muster-in roll dated 7/21/63. Ab. 7/1/63 - 11/1/63 (dated 1/6/64), POW cpd. Droop Mtn., 11/6/63. Cpd. Greenbrier Co., W. Va., 11/10/63. Confined at the Atheneum Prison, 11/18/63. Desc.: age 19, 5'9", dark comp., black hair and dark eyes. Occ. farmer, residing in Rockbridge Co. Ab. 11/1/63 - 2/29/64, cpd. Droop Mtn., 11/6/63. Transf. to Camp Chase, 11/19/63. Confined at Camp Chase, 11/20/63. Ab. 2/29/64 - 8/31/64, cpd. Droop Mtn., 11/6/63. Transf. to Ft. Delaware, 2/29/64. Confined at Ft. Delaware, 3/4/64 (3/2/64). Took the oath of allegiance and was released, 6/20/65. Desc.: age ?, 5'6", ruddy comp., dark hair and blue eyes, a resident of Rockbridge Co. Post war farmer and resident of Kerr's Creek, age 66 in 1908. Drew a Confederate Pension. d. Kerr's Creek, Rockbridge Co., 4/5/1917. Bur. New Monmouth Presbyterian Church Cem.

PLOTT, JOSEPH N. - Pvt. Co. K. b. Rockbridge Co., 1/28/35. Farmhand, Beard's Store, Rockbridge Co. 1860 Census. Prior service, Cc. G, 58th Va. Inf. Enl. Camp Northwest, W. Va., 7/16/63 (7/15/63), age 25. Not stated if present or absent on muster-in roll dated 7/21/63. Ab. 7/1/63 - 11/1/63 (dated 1/6/64), claimed by another command. Returned to Co. G, 58th Va. Inf. by 8/1/63. Farmhand, Walker's Creek Dist., Rockbridge Co. 1870 Census. Brother of William M. Plott. d. Rockbridge Co., 11/27/1905. Bur. Bratton's Run or the Pines Cem., on Rt. 780, near California Furnace, Rockbridge Co.

PLOTT, WILLIAM M. - Pvt. Co. K. b. Rockbridge Co., c. 1833. Age 27, farmhand, Beard's Store, Rockbridge Co. 1860 Census. Enl. Camp Northwest, W. Va., 7/16/63, age 21(?). Not stated if present or absent on muster-in roll dated 7/21/63. Present 7/1/63 - 11/1/63 (dated 1/6/64). Deserted to the enemy, Beverly, W. Va., 7/31/64. Took the oath of allegiance and was released, 8/4/64. Age 32, farmhand, Walker's Creek Dist., Rockbridge Co. 1870 Census. Brother of Joseph N. Plott. d. Denmark, Rockbridge Co., 10/23/91. Bur. Bethel ARP Church Cem., Kerr's Creek, Rockbridge Co.

POE, DAVID - 1st Lt. Co. A. b.c. 1837. Prewar resident of Taylor Co., W. Va. Prior service, Co. A, 9th Battn. Va. Inf. and Co. A, 25th Va. Inf. Poe says he left the infantry service in the spring of 1862, due to poor health and a desire to join the cavalry. He was given authority to recruit troops in Northwest Virginia, and was accompanied by Davis Toothman on the first trip. Poe made several trips and soon had recruited Co. A, 20th Va. Cav. and Co. B, 20th Va. Cav. Enl. Augusta Co., 1/3/63, age 26. Not stated if present or absent on muster-in roll dated 1/3/63, 2nd Lt. Appointed 2nd Lt., 4/15/63. Horse fell with him in the attack on Beverly, W. Va., 4/24/63. Horse died from injuries, 4/25/63. Present, 2nd Lt., 7/1/63 - 9/1/63, promoted to 1st Lt., 8/14/63. Appointed 1st Lt., 8/14/63, confirmed by election. Commanding post at Millboro Springs, 8/63. Not stated if present or absent, 1st Lt., 10/31/63 - 8/31/64. Struck on the shoulder blade by a carbine at the Island Ford Bridge, Alleghany Co., 12/19/63, disabled a short time. Detailed to guard prisoners, 12/63. Detailed for duty on a Gen. Court Martial, Warm Springs, Bath Co., 2/25/64. Sent on a scout 5/64 with 17 men to Barbour Co., W. Va. Detailed on a scout in the mountains, 7/64. Ab. 10/25/64, on recruiting duty by order of Gen. J. A. Early, 40 days, was to have returned in 30 days. Ordered to appear before an examining board, 11/24/64, regarding his qualifications as an officer. Examined 12/20/64 on tactics, army regulations, outpost duty and orders. Poe was found to fully qualified. Requested authority to raise an independent Co. within enemy lines, to operate there, 1/18/65. This document shows he acted as a scout in Western Va. since the beginning of the war. Col. W. W. Arnett recommended that he be granted the authority to raise a Co., 2/6/65. Dudly Evans and J. A. Robinson, members of the Va. House of Delegates, recommend that he be given authority to raise a Co., 3/8/65. They call him "a brave soldier and efficient officer." Paroled at Staunton, 5/7/65. Desc.: age 26(?), 6', fair comp., dark hair and gray eyes. Post war resident of Upshur Co., W. Va. Wrote "Personal Reminiscences of the Civil War." d. Upshur Co., W. Va., 5/9/1915, age 68. Bur. Heavener Cem., Buckhannon, Upshur Co., W. Va.

POE, JAMES LEMUEL - Pvt. Co. A. Post war rosters only, which show he was a resident of Taylor Co., W. Va. CSR shows reference card for "James L. Poe" and states cards are filed with Lemuel S. Poe. Clothing issued 3/?/64 to James L. Poe. "One of those soldiers who could be trusted whether on a hazardous post as a signal officer, or in the thick of battle." Post war businessman, residing at Ravenswood, W. Va. Could be Lemuel S. Poe. NFR.

POE, LEMUEL S. - Pvt. Co. A. b.c. 1843. Enl. Highland Co., 4/23/63, age 20. Not stated if present or absent on muster-in roll dated 8/63. Present 7/1/63 - 9/1/63. Present 10/31/63 - 8/31/64, AWOL since 10/10/64. Deserted. Reported at Clarksburg, W. Va., 5/19/65. Took the amnesty oath and was released, 5/19/65. Desc.: age 21(?), 5'8", florid comp., dark hair and gray eyes. Occ. farmer, residing in Nicholas Co., W. Va. Could be James Lemuel Poe. NFR.

POLING, NATHIANIEL - Pvt. Co. A. b.c. 1833. Enl. Bath Co., 4/8/63, age 30. Not stated if present or absent on muster-in roll dated 4/8/63. Present 10/31/63 - 8/31/64, detailed in shoe factory. Paroled at Harrisonburg, 5/2/65. Desc.: age 32, 5'11", fair comp., black hair and dark eyes, a resident of Barbour Co., W. Va. Post war resident of Barbour Co., W. Va. NFR.

POST, ABRAHAM - Pvt. Co. D. Enl. Hightown, Highland Co., 6/27/63. Not stated if present or absent on muster-in roll dated 8/63. Present 7/1/63 - 1/1/64 (dated 1/1/64). Not stated if present or absent 12/31/63 - 8/31/64 (dated 1/6/65). Clothing issued 2/6/64. Ab. 9/1/64 - 10/31/64, on detached service; entitled to $100 enl. bounty. NFR.

POST, GEORGE W. - 4th Sgt. Co. D. Enl. Hightown, Highland Co., 6/27/63. Not stated if present or absent on muster-in roll dated 8/63. Ab., 4th Sgt., 7/1/63 - 1/1/64 (dated 1/1/64), appointed 4th Sgt., 7/1/63; prisoner. Cpd. Highland Co., 12/12/63. Ab., 4th Sgt., 12/31/63 - 8/31/64 (dated 1/6/65), prisoner. Confined at the Atheneum Prison, 1/19/64. Desc.: age 24, 5'11", fair comp., fair hair, blue eyes and light whiskers. Occ. farmer, residing in Barbour Co., W. Va. Transf. to Camp Chase, 1/20/64. Confined at Camp Chase, 1/21/64. Desired to take the oath of allegiance 6/10/64, listed as a deserter. Ab. 9/1/64 - 10/31/64, prisoner in hands of enemy. Took the oath of allegiance and was released, 1/20/65. Desc.: age ?, 5'11", light comp., light hair and gray eyes. Occ. farmer, residing in Barbour Co., W. Va. Age 39, farmer, Union Dist., Barbour Co., W. Va. 1880 Census. NFR.

POST, STEPHEN - Pvt. Co. D. Resident of Upshur Co., W. Va. Enl. Hightown, Highland Co., 6/27/63. Not stated if present or absent on muster-in roll dated 8/63. Ab. 7/1/63 - 1/1/64 (dated 1/1/64), prisoner. Deserted. Arrested at Clarksburg, W. Va., 9/21/63. Took the oath of allegiance at Clarksburg, W. Va., 10/7/63, and was sent North to Wheeling, W. Va. Confined at the Atheneum Prison, 10/15/63. Desc.: age 33, 6'1", florid (dark) comp., black (dark) hair and black (dark) eyes. Occ. farmer, residing in Upshur Co., W. Va. Transf. to Camp Chase, 10/22/63. Confined at Camp Chase, 10/23/63, listed as a deserter; had taken the oath of allegiance before joining the Southern Army; violated his parole. Ab. 12/31/63 - 8/31/64 (dated 1/6/65), prisoner. Transf. to Rock Island, Ill., 1/22/64. Confined at Rock Island Prison, 1/24/64. Desires to take the oath of allegiance, 3/18/64, wishes to be loyal. Took the oath of allegiance and was released, 8/5/64. Desc.: age 34, 6'1", florid comp., black hair and black eyes, a resident of Upshur Co., W. Va. Ab. 9/1/64 - 10/31/64, POW. NFR.

POTTS, MATHIAS PORTER HAMILTON "Ham" - Pvt. Co. C. b.c. 1846. Age 14, Randolph Co., W. Va. 1860 Census. Enl. Bath Co., 11/1/63. Potts, in his reminiscences of the war, says he volunteered 3/15/64, age 16 years. 10 months, and received a 30 day furlough at that time. He wrote that "he was too young to keep out [of the war]" in 1863." Present 6/30/63 - 8/31/64 (dated 1/6/65), enl. bounty due; 6% bond due. Present 9/1/64 - 10/31/64 (dated 12/30/64), 6% bond due. Paroled at Staunton, 6/1/65. Desc.: age 18, 5'11, dark comp., dark hair and blue eyes. Post war farmer and minister, residing in Mingo Dist., Randolph Co. and Clarksburg, W. Va. Hotel keeper, Elkins, W. Va. Age 34, farm laborer, Mingo, Randolph Co., W. Va. 1880 Census. Attended Confederate Reunion, Randolph Co., W. Va., 1906. Moved to near Grand Bay (Palm Bay), Ala., 11/3/1911, farmer. Served with honor and distinction. Resident of Bayou La Batre, Ala., 1916. Wrote " A Boy Scout of the Confederacy," his recollections of the war, in 1923. CSR listed as Hamilton Potts. NFR.

PRIBBLE, H. JOHN - Pvt. Co. H. b. Wood Co., W. Va., c. 1828. Enl. Camp Northwest, W. Va., 7/1/63. Not stated if present or absent on muster-in roll dated 8/63. Transf. to Lurty's Batty., 11/1/63. NFR.

PRICE, ALBERT - Pvt. Co. D. b. Barbour Co., W. Va., c. 1846. Enl. Barbour Co., W. Va., 4/1/64. POW record shows enl. as Highland Co., 5/63. Not stated if present or absent 12/31/63 - 8/31/64 (dated 1/6/65). Ab. 9/1/64 - 10/31/64, POW. Cpd. Beverly, W. Va., 10/29/64. Confined at Clarksburg, W. Va. Desc.: age 18, 6', fair comp., light hair and blue eyes. Occ. soldier, residing in Barbour Co., W. Va. Transf. to Wheeling, W. Va., 11/2/64. Confined at the Atheneum Prison, 11/2/64. Desc.: age 18, 6', fair comp., light hair and blue eyes. Occ. farmer, residing in Barbour Co., W. Va. Transf. to Camp Chase, 11/22/64. Confined at Camp Chase, 11/23/64, desires to take the oath of allegiance. Took the oath of allegiance and was released, 6/12/65. Desc.: age 19, 6'+". fair comp., light hair and blue eyes, a resident of Barbour Co., W. Va. Age 33, farmer, East Barker Dist., Barbour Co., W. Va. 1880 Census. NFR.

PRICE, DAVID W. - 3rd Sgt. Co. I. b. Washington Co.. c. 1844. Enl. Camp Northwest, W. Va., 6/1/64 (Warm Springs, 4/30/64). POW record shows enl. as Washington Co., 4/61. Ab., 4th Sgt., 11/1/63 8/31/64 (dated 1/6/65), AWOL. Clothing issued 2/29/64, signs by x. Ab., 3rd Sgt., 11/1/63 - 10/31/64 (dated 12/30/64), AWOL. Cpd. Beverly, W. Va., 10/18/64. Confined at Clarksburg, W. Va. Desc.: age 20, 5'10", fair comp., dark hair and gray eyes. Occ. farmer, residing in Washington Co. Took the oath of allegiance and was released, 10/23/64. NFR.

PRICE. JOHN B. - Pvt. Co. B. Enl. Weston, W. Va., 5/5/63. Not stated if present or absent on muster-in roll dated 7/25/63. Ab. 11/1/63 - 8/31/64 (dated 1/6/65), KIA. Droop Mtn., 11/6/63.

PRICE, SOLOMON - 4th Corp. Co. B. b.c. 1845. Enl. Camp Northwest, W. Va., 8/5/63. Ab., 4th Corp., 11/1/63 - 8/31/64 (dated 1/6/65), transf. to Co. A, 20th Va. Cav., 4/64. Present in Co. A, Pvt., 10/31/63 - 8/31/64. Clothing issued 3/31/64. Paroled at Staunton, 5/23/65. Desc.: age 20, 5'11", dark comp., dark hair and dark eyes. NFR.

PRINCE, R. O. D. - Pvt. Co. G. Enl. Wood Co., W. Va.. 5/2/63 (5/12/63). Not stated if present or absent on muster-in roll dated 8/63. Present 11/1/63 - 2/29/64. Clothing issued 1st Qr. 1864. Present 7/1/64 - 8/31/64, had his own horse; entitled to bond. Present 9/1/64 - 10/31/64 (dated 12/29/64), entitled to $100 bond. Post war roster shows him as Lt. Post war resident of Wood Co., W. Va. Age 39, farmer, Clay Dist., Wood Co., W. Va. 1880 Census. NFR.

PRINCE, SAMUEL HAYS - Pvt. Co. G. b.c. 1846. Enl. Wood Co., W. Va., 5/2/63 (5/12/63). Not stated if present or absent on muster-in roll dated 8/63. Present 11/1/63 - 2/29/64. Clothing issued 2/29/64. Present 7/1/64 - 8/31/64, had his own horse; entitled to bond. Present 9/1/64 - 10/31/64 (dated 12/29/64), entitled to $100 bond. Paroled at Charleston, W. Va., 5/17/65. Desc.: age 19, 6'+", dark comp., brown hair, blue eyes and brown whiskers. Post war resident of Wood Co., W. Va. NFR.

PRINCE (PIERCE), WILLIAM H. - Pvt. Co. G. b.c. 1839. Enl. Wood Co., W. Va., 5/2/63 (5/12/63). Not stated if present or absent on muster-in roll dated 8/63. Present 11/1/63 - 2/29/64. Clothing issued 2/29/64. Ab. 7/1/64 - 8/31/64, sick; entitled to bond. Clothing issued 8/15/64. Ab. 9/1/64 - 10/31/64 (dated 12/29/64), sick; entitled to $100 bond. Cpd. Parkersburg, W. Va., 4/?/65. Confined at Clarksburg, W. Va., by 4/20/65. Paroled and released, to be exchanged, 4/22/65. Desc.: age 26, 6', fair comp., light hair and blue eyes. Occ. SB Engineer, residing in Wood Co., W. Va. NFR.

PRITCHARD, F. A. - Jr. 2nd Lt. Co. A. b.c. 1841. Prewar resident of Pa. and Marion Co., W. Va. Enl. Augusta (Highland) Co., 12/25/62, age 21. Not stated if present or absent on muster- in roll dated 12/25/62, 1st Sgt. Present, 1st Sgt., 7/1/63 - 9/1/63, promoted to 2nd Lt., 8/14/63. Elected Jr. 2nd Lt., 8/14/63. Ab., Jr. 2nd Lt., 10/31/63 - 8/31/64, KIA. Winchester, 9/19/64. Member of board of survey, 1/21/64, to condemn quartermaster and commissary stores. Adm. USA Depot Field Hosp., Winchester, 9/19/64, vulnus sclopeticum. DOW. Winchester, 9/21/64. Ab. 10/25/64, wd., POW, 36 days. "Was nearly always present, bold and fearless, of quick thought." His broque was such that it was hard to tell which army he belonged to.

PRITT, DRAPER - Pvt. Co. C. b.c. 1838. Age 22, farmer, Randolph Co., W. Va. 1860 Census. Enl. Randolph (Pocahontas) Co., W. Va., 5/1/63. Not stated if present or absent on muster-in roll dated 8/63. Ab. 6/30/63 - 8/31/64 (dated 1/6/65), sick since 6/1/64. Clothing issued 3/10/64. Ab. 9/1/64 - 10/31/64 (dated 12/30/64), sick. Post war resident of Randolph Co., W. Va. d. by 1916. NFR.

PROCTOR, ALBERT - Pvt. Co. F. Enl. Bulltown, W. Va., 5/10/63 (Camp Clover Lick, 7/11/63). Not stated if present or absent on muster-in roll dated 7/20/63. Ab. 7/1/63 - 8/31/64 (dated 1/6/65), taken prisoner and since DOD. in Camp Chase. Ab. 9/1/64 - 10/31/64 (dated 12/30/64), cpd. 5/13/63, and since DOD. Camp Chase. NFR.

PROFFETT, P. H. - Pvt. Co. D. Post war rosters only, which show he served 3 years, and was a resident of Amherst Co. NFR.

QUEEN, ANDREW J. - 1st Lt. Co. F. b.c. 1829. Enl. Bulltown, W. Va., 5/10/63. Elected 1st Lt., 5/10/63. Not stated if present or absent muster-in roll dated 7/20/63, 1st Lt. Ab. 7/1/63 - 8/31/64 (dated 1/6/65), in arrest or confinement. Cpd. Alleghany Co., 12/19/63 (12/18/63). Confined at the Atheneum Prison, 12/31/63. Desc.: age 34, 6'1", dark comp., dark hair and gray eyes. Occ. farmer, residing in Lewis Co., W. Va. Transf. to Camp Chase, 12/31/63. Confined at Camp Chase, 1/1/64. Transf. to Ft. Delaware, 3/25/64. Confined at Ft. Delaware, 3/27/64. Present (error) 9/1/64 - 10/31/64 (dated 12/30/64). Ab. 10/25/64, POW for 10 months. Took the oath of allegiance and was released, 6/12/65. Desc.: age ?, 6', light comp., dark hair and gray eyes, a resident of Lewis Co., W. Va. Age 37, dry goods grocer, Hackers Creek, Lewis Co., W. Va. 1880 Census. NFR.

QUEEN, ASA (ASSEY) - Pvt. Co. F. b.c. 1842. Enl. Bulltown, W. Va., 5/10/63. Not stated if present or absent on muster-in roll dated 7/20/63. Ab. 7/1/63 - 8/31/64 (dated 1/6/65), prisoner since 12/18/63; entitled to enl. bounty. Cpd. Allegheny Co., 12/20/63, listed as a deserter. Confined at the Atheneum Prison, 12/31/63. Desc.: age 21, 5'7", fair comp., sandy hair and black eyes. Occ. farmer, residing in Harrison Co., W. Va. Transf. to Camp Chase, 12/31/63. Confined at Camp Chase, 1/1/64. Ab. 9/1/64 - 10/31/64 (dated 12/30/64), prisoner since 12/18/63; entitled to enl. bounty. Took the oath of allegiance and was released, 1/16/65, by order of the Sec. of War. NFR.

QUEEN, CHARLES W. - Corp. Co. F. Enl. Bulltown, W. Va., 5/10/63. Not stated if present or absent on muster-in roll dated 7/20/63, Corp. Present, Pvt., 7/1/63 - 8/31/64 (dated 1/6/65), detailed as a wagoner since 8/1/63; entitled to enl. bounty. Clothing issued 11/22/63 and 12/20/63 (detailed), signs by x. Employed as a teamster at Warm Springs 1/1/64 - 2/29/64, sent back to his Co. Present 9/1/64 - 10/31/64 (dated 12/30/64), entitled to enl. bounty. NFR.

QUEEN, CLARK W. - Pvt. Co. F. b. Harrison Co., 1842. Prewar farmer, and resident of Barbour Co., W. Va. Prior service, Co. C, 31st Va. Inf. Enl. Bulltown, W. Va., 5/10/63. Not stated if present or absent on muster-in roll dated 7/20/63. Ab. 7/1/63 - 8/31/64 (dated 1/6/65), claimed as a member of Co. C, 31st Va. Inf. and taken, 3/1/64 (detailed teamster). Employed as a teamster at Warm Springs, 1/1/64 - 1/27/64, disc. and sent to his Co. Ab. 9/1/64 - 10/31/64 (dated 12/30/64), claimed as a member of Co. C, 31st Va. Inf. and taken, 3/1/64. Age 38, farmer, Elk Dist., Harrison Co., W. Va. 1880 Census. d. Lost Creek, W. Va., 1929. Bur. Johnstown, W. Va. Cem.

QUEEN, ELIAS B. - Pvt. Co. ?. b. 3/15/40. Age 20, farmer, 1860 Census. Prior service, Co. C, 31st Va. Inf. Post war rosters show he joined the 20th Va. Cav. NFR.

QUEEN, GEORGE W. - 2nd Sgt. Co. F. b.c. 1833. Enl. Bulltown, W. Va., 5/10/63. Not stated if present or absent on muster-in roll dated 7/20/63, 2nd Sgt. Ab., 2nd Sgt., 7/1/63 - 8/31/64 (dated 1/6/65), d. in prison. Cpd. Alleghany Co., 12/20/63. Confined at the Atheneum Prison, 12/31/63. Desc.: age 30, 6'1", dark comp., black hair and blue eyes. Occ. carpenter, residing in Lewis Co., W. Va. Transf. to Camp Chase, 12/31/63. Confined at Camp Chase, 1/1/64. Ab., 2nd Sgt., 9/1/64 - 10/31/64 (dated 12/30/64), d. in prison. DOD. Camp Chase, 4/7/64 (8/7/64), constpio. Bur. Camp Chase Confederate Cem., grave no. 129.

QUEEN, JAMES B. - Pvt. Co. F. Enl. Bulltown, W. Va., 5/10/63 (Camp Clover Lick, 7/11/63). Not stated if present or absent on muster-in roll dated 7/20/63. Ab. 7/1/63 - 8/31/64 (dated 1/6/65), POW since 5/13/63. Ab. 9/1/64 - 10/31/64 (dated 12/30/64), POW since 5/13/63, since died. No POW records. NFR.

QUEEN, JOHN W. - Pvt. Co. F. Enl. Bulltown, W. Va., 5/10/63 (Camp Clover Lick, 7/11/63). Not stated if present or absent on muster-in roll dated 7/20/63. Ab. 7/1/63 - 8/31/64 (dated 1/6/65), POW since 5/13/63. Ab. 9/1/64 - 10/31/64 (dated 12/30/64), POW since 5/13/63. No POW records. NFR.

QUEEN, PETER - 4th Sgt. Co. F. b.c. 1837. Resident of Barbour Co., W. Va. Enl. Bulltown, W. Va., 5/10/63. Not stated if present or absent on muster-in roll dated 7/20/63, 4th Sgt. Present, 4th Sgt., 7/1/63 - 8/31/64 (dated 1/6/65), had his own horse; entitled to enl. bounty. Present, 4th Sgt., 9/1/64 - 10/31/64 (dated 12/30/64), entitled to enl. bounty. Age 43, carpenter, Elk Dist., Harrison Co., W. Va. 1880 Census. NFR.

QUEEN, RIZIN (ROSEN) P. - 3rd Corp. Co. F. b.c. 1837. Resident of Barbour Co., W. Va. Enl. Bulltown, W. Va., 5/10/63. Not stated if present or absent on muster-in roll dated 7/20/63, Pvt. Ab., 3rd Corp., 7/1/63 - 8/31/64 (dated 1/6/65), POW since 12/18/63; entitled to enl. bounty. Cpd. Alleghany Co., 12/20/63. Confined at the Atheneum Prison, 12/31/63. Desc.: age 26, 6', dark comp., dark hair and gray eyes. Occ. farmer, residing in Harrison Co., W. Va. Transf. to Camp Chase, 12/31/63. Confined at Camp Chase, 1/1/64. Desires to take the oath of allegiance, 6/10/64, listed as a deserter. Ab., 3rd Corp., 9/1/64 - 10/31/64 (dated 12/30/64), prisoner since 12/18/63. Took the oath of allegiance and was released, 1/16/64, by order of the Sec. of War. NFR.

QUEEN, WILSON - Pvt. Co. F. b.c. 1831. Enl. Bulltown, W. Va., 5/10/63. Not stated if present or absent on muster-in roll dated 7/20/63. Present 7/1/63 - 8/31/64 (dated 1/6/65), had his own horse. Present 9/1/64 - 10/31/64 (dated 12/30/64), entitled to enl. bounty. Took the amnesty oath at Clarksburg, W. Va., 9/1/65, a resident of Harrison Co., W. Va. Age 49, physician, Elk Dist., Harrison Co., W. Va. 1880 Census. NFR.

RADCLIFF, ANDREW - Pvt. Co. D. b.c. 1809. Enl. Weston, W. Va., 5/1/63. Not stated if present or absent on muster-in roll dated 8/63. Present 7/1/63 - 1/1/64 (dated 1/1/64), does not have a horse. Not stated if present or absent 12/31/63 - 8/31/64 (dated 1/6/65). Ab. 9/1/64 - 10/31/64, member House of Delegates. Paroled at Staunton, 5/10/65. Desc.: age 56, 6', fair comp., gray hair and dark eyes. NFR.

RADCLIFF, JOHN C. - Pvt. Co. D. b.c. 1811. Enl. Weston, W. Va., 5/1/63. Not stated if present or absent on muster-in roll dated 8/63. Present 7/1/63 - 1/1/64 (dated 1/1/64). Not stated if present or absent 12/31/63 - 8/31/64 (dated 1/6/65). Ab. 9/1/64 - 10/31/64, on detached service; entitled to $100 enl. bounty. Paroled at Staunton, 5/10/65. Desc.: age 54, 5'9", fair comp., gray hair and dark eyes. NFR.

RADCLIFF, JOHN M. - 2nd Sgt. Co. D. b. Harrison Co., W. Va., c. 1843. Enl. Weston (Bulltown), W. Va., 5/1/63. Not stated if present or absent on muster-in roll dated 8/63, 2nd Corp. Present, 2nd Sgt., 7/1/63 - 1/1/64 (dated 1/1/64), appointed 2nd Sgt., 7/1/63; had his own horse. Ab. 12/31/63 - 8/31/64 (dated 1/6/65), AWOL since 10/5/64. Clothing issued 2/29/64. Ab., 2nd Sgt., 9/1/64 - 10/31/64, AWOL. Reported at Weston, W. Va., 12/3/64. Confined at Clarksburg, W. Va. Took the oath of allegiance and was released, 12/5/64. Desc.: age 22, 5'7", fair comp., dark hair and black eyes. Occ. farmer, residing in Barbour Co., W. Va. NFR.

RADCLIFF (RATCLIFF), JOHN N. - Pvt. Co. F. b.c. 1841. Enl. Camp Northwest, W. Va. (Camp Miller), 7/19/63. Not stated if present or absent on muster-in roll dated 7/20/63. Ab. 7/1/63 - 8/31/64 (dated 1/6/65), transf. to Co. A, 19th Va. Cav., listed

235

as Ratcliff. Ab. 9/1/64 - 10/31/64 (dated 12/30/64), transf. to Co. A, 19th Va. Cav. Age 39, farmer, Edray, Pocahontas Co., W. Va. 1880 Census. NFR.

RADER, BENJAMIN T. - Pvt. Co. C. Enl. Pocahontas Co., W. Va., 1/12/64. Ab. 6/30/63 - 8/31/64 (dated 1/6/65), on detached service; enl. bounty due; 6% bond due. Clothing issued 3/10/64. Ab. 9/1/64 - 10/31/64 (dated 12/30/64), AWOL since 9/64. Nephew of Claude G. Rader. NFR.

RADER, CLAUDE (CLAUDIUS) GOFF "Squire" - 1st Sgt. Co. C. b. Randolph Co., W. Va., 1/22/44. Age 16, laborer, Randolph Co., W. Va. 1860 Census. Also as having been b. in Nelson Co. Farmer, age 17 (1861). Prior service, Co. E, 31st Va. Inf. Enl. Randolph Co., W. Va., 4/23/63. Not stated if present or absent on muster-in roll dated 8/63, 1st Sgt. Ab., 1st Sgt., 6/30/63 - 8/31/64 (dated 1/6/65), prisoner since 12/27/63; 6% bond due. Cpd. Pocahontas Co., W. Va., 12/23/63 (12/25/63). Confined at the Atheneum Prison, 1/6/64. Desc.: age 22, 5'7", dark comp., dark hair and gray eyes. Occ. merchant, residing in Randolph Co., W. Va. Transf. to Camp Chase, 1/7/64. Confined at Camp Chase, 1/8/64. Transf. to Ft. Delaware, 3/14/64, shot a Union Lt. named Simmons. Confined at Ft. Delaware, 3/17/64. Ab., 1st Sgt., 9/1/64 - 10/31/64 (dated 12/30/64), prisoner since 12/27/63; 6% bond due. Took the oath of allegiance and was released, 6/21/65. Desc.: age ?, 5'7", light comp., dark hair and blue eyes, a resident of Randolph Co., W. Va. Post war rosters show him as Capt. Post war resident of Mill Creek, Randolph Co. Farmer, carpenter, merchant, notary public and real estate speculator. Ran a freight line between Randolph Co., W. Va., and Staunton. Age 37, farm worker, Huttonsville, Randolph Co., W. Va. 1880 Census. Moved to Cameron Co., Tx., 1919. Returned to Randolph Co., W. Va. Awarded Cross of Honor. Resident of Huff, W. Va., 1916. d. Mill Creek, W. Va., 11/7/1922, respiratory complications. Bur. Currence Cem. (Mill Creek Cem.), Mill Creek, W. Va. Brother of William Rader, uncle of Benjamin T. Rader.

RADER, WILLIAM M. - Pvt. Co. C. Enl. Pocahontas Co., W. Va., 6/15/63 (5/6/63, 5/16/63). Not stated if present or absent on muster-in roll dated 8/63. Ab. 6/30/63 - 8/31/64 (dated 1/6/65), on detached service. Clothing issued 3/10/64. Ab. 9/1/64 - 10/31/64 (dated 12/30/64), AWOL since 9/64. Brother of Claude G. Rader. NFR.

RAMSEY, JOHN R. - Pvt. Co. K. b. Va., c. 1841. Enl. Camp Northwest, W. Va., 6/2/63, age 22. Not stated if present or absent on muster-in roll dated 7/21/63. Ab. 7/1/63 - 11/1/63 (dated 1/6/64), AWOL. Age 29, iron worker, Staunton, 1870 Census. d. near Staunton, 11/22/1922, age 82. Bur. Thornrose Cem., Staunton.

RAMSEY, WILLIAM BERKELEY - Pvt. Co. K. b. Va., 3/17/46. Student, N. Dist., Augusta Co. 1860 Census. Enl. Camp Northwest, W. Va., 6/2/63, age 18. Not stated if present or absent on muster- in roll dated 7/21/63. Ab. 7/1/63 - 11/1/63 (dated 1/6/64), AWOL. Ab. 11/1/63 - 2/29/64, AWOL. Ab. 2/29/64 - 8/31/64, AWOL. Age 25, farmhand, South River Dist., Augusta Co. 1870 Census. Machinist. d. near Staunton, 5/9/1902. Bur. Zion Lutheran Church Cem.

RATLIFF (RATCLIFFE, RATCLIFF), A. P. S. - Sr. 2nd Lt. Co. C. b.c. 1830. Elected 2nd Lt., 4/16/63. Not stated if present or absent on muster-in roll dated 8/63, 2nd Lt. Submitted his resignation from Camp Northwest, W. Va., 1/6/64 due to bad health, being unable to discharge the duties of the office. Resignation accepted, 2/1/64. Post war rosters show he resigned 1/27/64. Enl. Bath Co., 2/1/64 (3/1/64), as a Pvt. Granted 15 day leave, 2/6/64. Requested permission to raise a co. for Col. W. L. Jackson's command, 3/64. Present, Pvt., 6/30/63 - 8/31/64 (dated 1/6/65), enl. bounty due. Ab. 9/1/64 - 10/31/64 (dated 12/30/64), on horse detail. Reported at Clarksburg, W. Va., 5/17/65, listed as a deserter. Confined at Clarksburg, W. Va. Desc.: age 35, 5'10", dark comp., dark hair and hazel eyes. Occ. farmer, residing in Harrison Co., W. Va. Took the amnesty oath and was released, 5/19/65. NFR.

RAY, JOSEPH - Pvt. Co. I. b.c. 1844. Enl. Camp Northwest, W. Va., 6/18/63 (6/1/63, 7/63), age 19. Not stated if present or absent on muster-in roll dated 5/5/63. Ab. 11/1/63 - 8/31/64 (dated 1/6/65), deserted. Ab. 11/1/63 - 10/31/64 (dated 12/31/64), on horse detail. NFR.

RAY, WILLIAM T. (H.) - Pvt. Co. I. Enl. Oakhill, 10/1/64 (10/11/64). Ab. 11/1/63 - 8/31/64 (dated 1/6/65), on horse detail. Present 11/1/63 - 10/31/64 (dated 12/31/64). NFR.

REED, ALEX - Pvt. Co. H. Enl. Calhoun Co., W. Va., 5/14/63. Not stated if present or absent on muster-in roll dated 8/63. NFR.

REED, JAMES W. D. - Pvt. Co. D. Enl. Hightown, Highland Co., 6/27/63 (6/1/63). Not stated if present or absent on muster-in roll dated 8/63. Present 7/1/63 - 1/1/64 (dated 1/1/64), had his own horse. Present 12/31/63 - 8/31/64 (dated 1/6/65). Clothing issued 2/29/64. Present 9/1/64 - 10/31/64, entitled to $100 enl. bounty. NFR.

REED, JOHN - Pvt. Co. F. Resident of Barbour Co., W. Va. Enl. Camp Clover Lick (Camp Miller), 7/17/63. Not stated if present or absent on muster-in roll dated 7/20/63. Ab. 7/1/63 - 8/31/64 (dated 1/6/65), transf. to Co. A, 19th Va. Cav. Ab. 9/1/64 10/31/64 (dated 12/30/64), transf. to Co. A, 19th Va. Cav. NFR.

REED, JOHN W. - Pvt. Co. D. Enl. Hightown, Highland Co., 6/27/63 (6/1/63). Not stated if present or absent on muster-in roll dated 8/63. Present 7/1/63 - 1/1/64 (dated 1/1/64), had his own horse. Present 12/31/63 - 8/31/64 (dated 1/6/65). Present 9/1/64 - 10/31/64, entitled to $100 enl. bounty. NFR.

REED, THOMAS - Pvt. Co. F and 3rd Lt. Co. E. b.c. 1838. Prior service, Co. C, 31st Va. Inf. Enl. Bulltown, W. Va., 5/10/63, in Co. F (Camp Miller, 6/10/63). Not stated if present or absent on muster-in roll dated 7/20/63, 1st Sgt. Present, 1st Sgt., 7/1/63 - 8/31/64 (dated 1/6/65), had his own horse; entitled to enl. bounty. Present, 1st Sgt., 9/1/64 - 10/31/64 (dated 12/30/64), entitled to enl. bounty. Elected 3rd Lt. and transf. to Co. E. 20th Va. Cav. Paroled at Charleston, W. Va., 5/10/65, as 3rd Lt., Co. E. Desc.: age 27, 5'9", fair comp., dark hair, gray eyes and a mustache. Post war farmer. Member Staunton UCV, age 67 as of 12/1905. NFR.

REED, VINCENT A. - Pvt. Co. H. Enl. Calhoun Co., W. Va., 5/8/63 (5/4/63). Present 10/31/63 - 8/31/64, had his own horse from 11/1/63 to 2/64. Clothing issued 2/29/54. Ab. 9/1/64 - 10/31/64 (dated 12/30/64), wd. (date and place not stated), now in hosp.; entitled to $100 bond. NFR.

REMLY (REMLEY, RAMLY), CONRAD - Pvt. Co. A. b.c. 1823. Enl. Pocahontas Co., w. Va., 6/21/63 (6/23/63), age 40. Not stated if present or absent on muster-in roll dated 6/21/63. Present 7/1/63 - 8/31/63. Present 10/31/63 - 8/31/64. "Went home and gave up before the end of the war." Post war resident of Marion Co., W. Va. NFR.

REX, JOHN S. - Pvt. Co. B. Enl. Upshur Co., W. Va., 6/28/63 (4/28/63). Not stated if present or absent on muster-in roll dated 7/25/63. Present 11/1/63 - 8/31/64 (dated 1/6/65), transf. to Co. A, 31st Va. Inf., 10/64. Ab. 9/1/64 - 10/31/64 (dated 12/30/64), transf. to Co. A, 31st Va. Inf., 10/64. NFR.

REXRODE, SOLOMON Jr. - Pvt. Co. I. b. Highland Co., c. 1843. Age 17, farmhand, Monterey, Highland Co. 1860 Census. Prior service, Co. E, 31st Va. Inf. Post war rosters only, which show he was a member of Co. I, 20th Va. Cav. Post war resident of Highland Co. d. by 1911. NFR.

REXRODE, WILLIAM J. - Pvt. Co. ?. b. Pendleton Co., W. Va., c. 1836. Age 24, New Hampden, Highland Co. 1860 Census. Prior service, Co. E, 31st Va. Inf. Transf. to 20th Cav. 6/1/63, unauthorized. Not on muster rolls. Returned to 31st Va. Inf. before 4/9/65. Post war resident of Highland Co. d. by 1911. NFR.

REYNOLDS, JOHN - Pvt. Co. I. b.c. 1838. Not on muster rolls. Cpd. Beverly, W. Va., 1/24/64. Confined at the Atheneum Prison, 2/21/64. Desc.: age 26, 6'1", fair comp., black hair and black eyes. Occ. farmer, residing in Rockbridge Co. Took the oath of allegiance and was released to the Provost Marshal, 2/22/64. NFR.

REYNOLDS, JOSEPH - Pvt. Co. G. Enl. Wood Co., W. Va., 5/9/63 (6/18/63). Not stated if present or absent on muster-in roll dated 8/63. Present 11/1/63 - 2/29/64. Clothing issued 2/29/64. Not stated if present or absent 7/1/64 - 8/31/64, had his own horse; entitled to bond. Present 9/1/64 - 10/31/64 (dated 12/29/64), entitled to $100 bond. NFR.

REYNOLDS, JOSEPH - Pvt. Co. H. Enl. Calhoun Co., W. Va., 5/14/63. Not stated if present or absent on muster-in roll dated 8/63. NFR.

REYNOLDS, LEWIS F. C. - Pvt. Co. I. b. Va., c. 1825. Age 35, overseer, 7th Dist., Rockbridge Co. 1860 Census. Prior service, Co. H, 4th Va. Inf. Enl. Camp Northwest, W. Va., 6/15/63 (Rockbridge Co., 4/1/64). Ab. 11/1/63 - 8/31/64 (dated 1/6/65), sick at home. Present 11/1/63 - 10/31/64 (dated 12/31/64). NFR.

RIBLET, JOHN S. - Pvt. Co. D. b. Harrison Co., W. Va., 6/17/33. Enl. Hightown, Highland Co., 6/27/63 (6/1/63). Not stated if present or absent on muster-in roll dated 8/63. Ab. 7/1/63 - 1/1/64 (dated 1/1/64), AWOL since 12/63. Clothing issued 11/22/63. Ab. 12/31/63 - 8/31/64 (dated 1/6/65), AWOL since 12/63. Ab. 9/1/64 - 10/31/64, AWOL. Post war notary public and minister, residing at Jarvisville, Harrison Co., W. Va. Age 47, blacksmith, Union Dist., Harrison Co., W. Va. 1880 Census. NFR.

RICE, ALBERT - Pvt. Co. D. Post war rosters only, which show he was a resident of Cumberland, Md. Bur. Loudoun Park Cem., Baltimore, Md. NFR.

RICE, STEVE W. (J.) - 1st Lt. Co. K. b.c. 1841. Enl. Warm Springs, 4/1/63. Not stated if present or absent on muster-in roll dated 7/21/63, 2nd Lt. Elected 2nd Lt. 7/22/63. Ab., 2nd Lt., 7/1/63 - 11/1/63 (dated 1/6/64), promoted 2nd Lt., 7/21/63; now on leave. Detailed to catch deserters, 1863, along with John H. Cammack. Present, 1st Lt., 11/1/63 - 2/29/64, promoted from 2nd Lt. to 1st Lt., 1/1/64, vacancy caused by death of Lt. Holland. Mentioned for his "brave bearing" at the battle of Droop Mtn., W. Va., 11/6/63, by Col. W. L. Jackson. Ab. 1/64, on leave of absence at Staunton. Ab. 1/12/64, 1st Lt. Ab., 1st Lt., 2/29/64 - 8/31/64, in arrest without leave. Deserted 8/64, recommended to be dropped. Ab. 10/25/64, AWOL for 3 months. Ab. 12/15/64, AWOL since 8/1/64, recommended to be dropped from rolls. Dropped from rolls 1/3/65 (1/6/65). Paroled at Staunton, 5/10/65. Desc.: age 24, 5'8", fair comp., light hair and blue eyes. NFR.

RICHARDS, GEORGE W. - Pvt. Co. E. Enl. Harrison Co., W. Va., 5/4/63 (5/6/63), by John L. Bussey. Not stated if present or absent on muster-in roll dated 7/18/63. Ab. 1/1/64 - 8/31/64 (dated 1/6/65), cpd. Harrison Co., W. Va., 5/7/63, while on the way to join Col. W. L. Jackson, at or near Weston, W. Va. Ab. 9/1/64 - 10/31/64 (dated 12/29/64), cpd. Harrison Co., W. Va., 5/6/63. Confined at Camp Chase, as a political prisoner. NFR.

RICHARDSON, RUFUS E. - Pvt. Co. B. Enl. Marion Co., W. Va., 2/1/64. Present 11/1/63 - 8/31/64 (dated 1/6/65), entitled to enl. bounty; AWOL since 9/14/64. Ab. 9/1/64 - 10/31/64 (dated 12/30/64), AWOL 9/14/64. NFR.

RIDER, THOMAS - Pvt. Co. C. b.c. 1846. Enl. Pocahontas Co., 7/21/63. Ab. 6/30/63 - 8/31/64 (dated 1/6/65), deserted 5/20/64. Clothing issued 3/20/64, signs by x. Ab. 9/1/64 - 10/31/64 (dated 12/30/64), deserted 5/1/64. Paroled at Staunton, 6/5/65, signs by x. Desc.: age 19, 5'9", dark comp., light hair and blue eyes. NFR.

RIFFLE, ANDREW CROUCH - Pvt. Co. C. b. Randolph Co., W. Va., 2/2/38. Age 22, laborer, Randolph Co., W. Va. 1860 Census. Enl. Pocahontas Co., W. Va., 4/8/63. Not stated if present or absent on muster-in roll dated 8/63. Ab. 6/30/63 - 8/31/64 (dated 1/6/65), POW since 12/27/63; 6% bond due. Cpd. Pocahontas Co., W. Va., 12/26/63. Confined at the Atheneum Prison, 1/6/64. Desc.: age 25, 5'9", fair comp., fair hair and gray eyes. Occ. farmer, residing in Randolph Co., W. Va. Transf. to Camp Chase, 1/7/64. Confined at Camp Chase, 1/8/64. Transf. to Ft. Delaware, 3/14/64. Confined at Ft. Delaware, 3/17/64. Ab. 9/1/64 - 10/31/64 (dated 12/30/64), POW since 12/27/63; 6% bond due. Took the oath of allegiance and was released, 6/21/65. Desc.: age ?, 5'6", ruddy comp., dark hair and gray eyes, a resident of Randolph Co., W. Va. Age 41, farmer, Huttonsville, Randolph Co., W. Va. 1880 Census. Brother-in-law of Albert B. and Andrew J. Chewning. d. 9/22/1922. Bur. Brick Church Cem., Huttonsville, Randolph Co., W. Va.

RIFFLE, GRANDVILLE W. - Pvt. Co. C. b.c. 1846. Enl. Randolph Co., W. Va., 5/1/63 (4/28/63). Not stated if present or absent on muster-in roll dated 8/63. Ab. 6/30/63 - 8/31/64 (dated 1/6/65), POW since 12/27/63; 6% bond due. Cpd. Pocahontas Co., W. Va., 12/26/63. Confined at the Atheneum Prison, 1/6/64. Desc.: age 17, 5'8", fair comp., fair hair and gray eyes. Occ. farmer, residing in Braxton Co., W. Va. Transf. to Camp Chase, 1/7/64. Confined at Camp Chase, 1/8/64. Transf. to Ft. Delaware, 3/14/64. Confined at Ft. Delaware, 3/17/64. Ab. 9/1/64 - 10/31/64 (dated 12/30/64), POW since 12/27/63; 6% bond due. DOD. Ft. Delaware, 6/15/64, chronic diarrhoea. Bur. Jersey Shore.

RIGGLE (RUGGLES), JOSEPH - Pvt. Co. A. b.c. 1845. Not on muster rolls. Paroled at Staunton, 5/25/65. Desc.: age 20, 6', dark comp., dark hair and blue eyes. NFR.

RILEY, WILLIAM - Pvt. Co. I. b. Va., c. 1830. Age 30, farmer, 5th Dist., Rockbridge Co. 1860 Census. Enl. Camp Northwest, W. Va., 6/1/63 (Rockbridge Co., 9/8/63). Ab. 11/1/63 - 8/31/64 (dated 1/6/65), wd., place and date not given. Ab. 11/1/63 10/31/64 (dated 12/31/64), AWOL. NFR.

RINEHART (RHINEHART), ELI - Pvt. Co. F. b.c. 1835. Enl. Camp Clover Lick, 7/11/63. Not stated if present or absent on muster-in roll dated 7/20/63. Not stated if present or absent 7/1/63 - 8/31/64 (dated 1/6/65), had his own horse; entitled to enl. bounty. Adm. CSA Gen. Hosp., Charlottesville, 6/10/64, febris remiten. RTD. 6/14/64. Adm. Gen. Hosp., Winchester, 8/1/64, febris continua. Transf. to Gen. Hosp., 8/3/64. Not stated if present or absent 9/1/64 - 10/31/64 (dated 12/30/64), entitled to enl. bounty. Surrendered at Clarksburg, W. Va., 4/25/65. Confined at Clarksburg, W. Va. Paroled for exchange and was released, 4/26/65. Desc.: age 30, 5'6", fair comp., light hair and blue eyes. Occ. farmer, residing in Lewis Co., W. Va. Post war rosters show he was from Harrison Co., W. Va., and that the Yankees were after him, so he enl. in the Southern Army. Age 47, farmer, Hackers Creek, Lewis Co., W. Va. 1880 Census. NFR.

RITCHIE (RICHIE), GEORGE H. - 2nd Sgt. Co. I. b.c. 1828. Enl. Camp Northwest, W. Va., 5/15/63, age 35 (Warm Springs, 9/8/63). Not stated if present or absent on muster-in roll dated 5/5/63, 3rd Sgt. Present, 2nd Sgt., 11/1/63 - 8/31/64 (dated 1/6/65), acting as Reg'tl. Ordnance Sgt. Clothing issued 2/29/64. Ab. 11/1/63 - 10/31/64 (dated 12/31/64), on detached service. NFR.

ROBERTS, G. A. - Pvt. Co. G. Enl. Wood Co., W. Va., 5/2/63. Not stated if present or absent on muster-in roll dated 8/63. Ab. 11/1/63 - 2/29/64, deserted 11/6/63. NFR.

ROBERTS, JAMES - Pvt. Co. F. Enl. Camp Northwest, W. Va., 7/19/63 (Camp Miller and Camp Clover Lick). Not stated if preset or absent on muster-in roll dated 7/20/63. Ab. 7/1/63 - 8/31/64 (dated 1/6/65), transf. to Co. A, 19th Va. Cav. Ab. 9/1/64 - 10/31/64 (dated 12/30/64), transf. to Co. A, 19th Va. Cav. NFR.

ROBERTS, JOHN E. - Pvt. Co. F. Enl. Camp Northwest, W. Va., 7/19/63 (Camp Miller and Camp Clover Lick). Not stated if preset or absent on muster-in roll dated 7/20/63. Ab. 7/1/63 - 8/31/64 (dated 1/6/65), transf. to Co. A, 19th Va. Cav. Ab. 9/1/64 - 10/31/64 (dated 12/30/64), transf. to Co. A, 19th Va. Cav. Served in Lurty's Batty. d. Columbus, O. Bur. Camp Chase Confederate Cem.

ROBERTSON, JAMES M. - Pvt. Co. C. b. Highland Co., c. 1848. Enl. Pocahontas Co., W. Va., 4/25/64. POW record shows enl. as Highland Co., 5/64. Ab. 6/30/63 - 8/31/64 (dated 1/6/65), AWOL; enl. bounty due. Ab. 9/1/64 - 10/31/64 (dated 12/30/64), AWOL since 9/64. Cpd. Beverly, W. Va., 12/28/64. Confined at Clarksburg, W. Va. Took the oath of allegiance and was released, 12/31/64. Desc.: age 16, 5'7", fair comp., light hair and gray eyes. Occ. farmer, residing in Highland Co. NFR.

ROBINSON, DAVID - 1st Corp. Co. K. b.c. 1828. Enl. Warm Springs, 4/1/63, age 35. Not stated if present or absent on muster-in roll dated 7/21/63, 1st Corp. Ab., Pvt., 7/1/63 - 1/1/64 (dated 1/6/64), reduced in ranks 8/1/63; lost Merrill Rifle; KIA. Droop Mtn., 11/6/63. Ab. 11/1/63 - 2/29/64, KIA. Droop Mtn. Ab. 2/29/64 - 8/31/64, KIA. Droop Mtn., 11/6/63.

ROBINSON, ELAM C. - 2nd Sgt. Co. D. b.c. 1841. Enl. Weston, W. Va., 5/1/63. Not stated if present or absent on muster-in roll dated 8/63, 2nd Sgt. Ab., Pvt., 7/1/63 - 1/1/64 (dated 1/1/64), prisoner in Camp Chase. Cpd. Clarksburg, W. Va., 9/28/63, deserter. Confined at Clarksburg, W. Va. Desc.: age 22, 5'5", fair comp., light hair and gray eyes. Occ. farmer, residing in Upshur Co., W. Va. Had taken the oath of allegiance before enl. in the Southern Army; sent to Wheeling, W. Va. Confined at the Atheneum Prison, 10/9/63. Desc.: age 22, 5'8", florid comp., sandy hair and gray eyes. Transf. to Camp Chase, 10/22/63. Confined at Camp Chase, 10/23/63, deserter, violated his parole. Ab. 12/31/63 8/31/64 (dated 1/6/65), prisoner. Transf. to Rock Island, Ill., 1/22/64. Confined at Rock Island Prison, 1/24/64. Desires to take the oath of allegiance and be loyal, 3/18/64. Took the oath of allegiance and was released, 8/5/64. Desc.: age 23, 5'7", fair comp., light hair and gray eyes, a resident of Upshur Co., W. Va. Ab. 9/1/64 - 10/31/64, POW. NFR.

ROBINSON, GEORGE W. - 1st Corp. Co. D. b. Upshur Co., W. Va., c. 1844. Enl. Weston, W. Va., 5/1/63. POW record shows enl. as Pocahontas Co., W. Va., 5/63. Not stated if present or absent on muster-in roll dated 8/63, 1st Crop. Present, Pvt., 7/1/63 - 1/1/64 (dated 1/1/64). Ab. 12/31/63 - 8/31/64 (dated 1/6/65), AWOL since 12/63. Ab. 9/1/64 - 10/31/64, AWOL. Cpd. Beverly, W. Va., 10/2/64. Confined at Clarksburg, W. Va. Took the oath and was released, 10/6/64. Desc.: age 20, 6'2", fair comp., light hair and gray eyes. Occ. farmer, residing in Upshur Co., W. Va. NFR.

ROBINSON, JOHN - Pvt. Co. I. b. England, c. 1844. Age 16, miller, Randolph Co., W. Va. 1860 Census. Enl. Camp Cameron, Bath Co., 12/1/63 (Rockbridge Co., 9/5/64). Ab. 11/1/63 - 8/31/64 (dated 1/6/65), on horse detail. Clothing issued, 2/29/64. Present 11/1/63 - 10/31/64 (dated 12/31/64). Arrested 4/2/65. Took the oath of allegiance at Clarksburg, W. Va. and sent to Wheeling, W. Va. Confined at the Atheneum Prison, 4/14/65. NFR.

ROBINSON (ROBERTSON), RICHARD "Bunk" - Pvt. Co. I. b.c. 1842. Enl. Marlin's Bottom, Pocahontas Co., W. Va., 9/1/63 (Rockingham Co., 9/5/63). Ab. 11/1/63 - 8/31/64 (dated 1/6/65), POW. Ab. 11/1/63 - 10/31/64 (dated 12/31/64), POW. Cpd. Lewisburg, W. Ba., 11/7/63. Confined at the Atheneum Prison, 11/20/63. Desc.: age 21, 5'6", dark comp., black hair and hazel eyes. Occ. farmer, residing in Rockingham Co. Transf. to Camp Chase, 11/20/63. Confined at Camp Chase, 11/21/63. Transf. to Ft. Delaware, 2/29/64. Confined at Ft. Delaware, 3/4/64 (3/2/64). Took the oath of allegiance and was released, 6/15/65. Desc.: age ?, 5'6", dark comp., dark hair and dark eyes, a resident of Rockingham Co. NFR.

ROCHE (ROACH), SAMUEL D. (J.) - Pvt. Co. K. b.c. 1845. Prior service, Luenburg Cav., deserted. Enl. Warm Springs, 4/1/63, age 18. Not stated if present or absent on muster-in roll dated 7/21/63. Ab. 7/1/63 - 11/1/63 (dated 1/6/64), AWOL. Arrested by Maj. Lady's command, and sent to Staunton, 6/14/63, for sealing. Sent to Richmond, 6/17/63, to be confined in Castle Thunder. Adm. Gen. Hosp. No. 13, 6/19/63, epilepsy, listed as a member of Co. E. Transf. to Castle Thunder, 6/22/63. Post Office listed as Pleasant Grove. Adm. Gen. Hosp. No. 13, 6/27/63, hysteria, listed as a member of Co. D. Transf. to Castle Thunder, 7/7/63. Served in Co's. D and E, 19th Va. Cav. NFR.

ROCKE, FLOYD G. - Capt. AQM. Served as AQM, 19th Va. Cav. Wartime letter, dated 12/10/63, lists him as AQM for the 19th and 20th Va. Cav. NFR.

ROGERS, JAMES - Pvt. Co. I. b.c. 1843. Enl. Lewisburg, W. Va., 3/20/63, age 20 (Charleston, W. Va., 6/1/61). Not stated if present or absent on muster-in roll dated 5/5/63. NFR.

ROGERS, JAMES MADISON - Jr. 2nd Lt. Co. H. b. Lewis Co., W. Va., c. 1835 (1837). Age 24, Calhoun Co., W. Va. 1860 Census. Prior service, Co. G, 10th Va. Cav. Listed as having been promoted to Bvt. (3rd) 2nd Lt., 19th Va. Cav., 5/29/63. Enl. Camp Northwest, W. Va., 6/1/63. Elected Jr. 2nd Lt., 6/4/63. Not stated if present or absent on muster-in roll dated 8/63, Jr. 2nd Lt. Present, Jr. 2nd Lt., 10/31/63. Present 9/1/64 - 10/31/64 (dated 12/30/64), entitled to $100 bond. Ab. 10/25/64, sick in hosp., 7 days. Post war source shows he was in 72 battles and was wd. 3 times. Post war resident of Calhoun Co., W. Va. NFR.

ROGERS (RODGERS), JARED - Pvt. Co. A. b.c. 1830. Prior service, Co. D, 19th Va. Cav. Enl. Pocahontas Co., W. Va., 4/14/63, age 33. Not stated if present or absent on muster-in roll dated 4/14/63. RTD from fulough to Taylor Co., W. Va., 10/23/63. Ab. 10/31/63 - 8/31/64, cpd. 7/16/64. Employed as a teamster at Warm Springs, 1/1/64 - 3/31/64. Clothing issued 11/20/63 and 1/16/64. Cpd. Snickers Gap, Loudoun Co., near Harper's Ferry, W. Va., 7/16/64. Sent to Harpers Ferry, W. Va., then to Washington, DC, 7/20/64. Confined at the Old Capitol Prison, 7/20/64. Transf. to Elmira, NY, 7/23/64. Confined at Elmira Prison, 7/25/64. Desires to take the oath of allegiance, 9/30/64, stating he volunteered 9/10/62 and now wishes to go some friends in Taylor Co., W. Va. Took the oath of allegiance and was released, 5/29/65. Desc.: age ?, 5'10+", dark comp., dark hair and blue eyes, a resident of Grafton, W. Va. Post war rosters show he was cpd. while on detached duty. Age 51, farmer, Fetterman, Taylor Co., W. Va. 1880 Census, listed as Jarret Rogers. Post war resident of Taylor Co., W. Va., over age 80 in 1911. NFR.

ROGERS, JOHN W. - Pvt. Co. I. Enl. Camp Northwest, W. Va., 6/1/63. Ab. 11/1/63 - 8/31/64 (dated 1/6/65), discharged, reason not stated. NFR.

ROGERS, JOSEPH W. - Pvt. Co. I. b.c. 1837. b. Braxton Co., W. Va., c. 1837. Age 23, farmer, Gilmer Co., W. Va. 1860 Census. Enl. Lewisburg, W. Va., 3/20/63, age 26. Not stated if present or absent on muster-in roll dated 5/5/63. Served in Co. H, 19th Va. Cav. NFR.

ROGERS, ROBERT MARION - Pvt. Co. H. Prior service, Co. A, 19th Va. Cav. Enl. Camp Northwest, W. Va., 6/1/63 (Greenbrier Co., W. Va., 3/1/63). Not stated if present or absent on muster-in roll dated 8/63. Present 10/31/63 - 8/31/64, had his own horse since 11/1/63. Clothing issued 2/29/64. Present 9/1/64 - 10/31/64 (dated 12/30/64), entitled to $100 bond. Post war rosters show he was wd. during the war by a spent ball, and was unfit for service for some time. Same post war roster shows service as Co. H, 20th Va. Inf. (error). Brother in US service. NFR.

ROLLER, JARRED - Pvt. Co. A. Enl. Pocahontas Co., W. Va., 3/1/63. Present 7/1/63 - 9/1/63, detailed as wagoner. NFR.

ROLLINS, HARRISON COLUMBUS - Pvt. Co. E. Prior service, Co. A, 3rd VSL. Cpd., date and place not stated. Tried as a guerrilla, and was sentenced to death at Clarksburg, W. Va., by 6/25/62. Told Federal authorities he was John S. Spriggs. Confined at Wheeling, W. Va., 8/3/62. Served in Co. A, 19th Va. Cav. Enl. Camp Clover Lick, 7/17/63. Not stated if present or absent on muster-in roll dated 7/18/63. Served in Co. D, 46th Battn. Va. Cav. Post war resident of Greenbrier Co., W. Va. NFR.

ROLLINS, MOSES - 1st Corp. Co. H. Enl. Calhoun Co., W. Va., 4/4/63 (4/7/63). Not stated if present or absent on muster-in roll dated 8/63, 4th Corp. Ab., 1st Corp., 10/31/63 - 8/31/64, in hands of enemy since 10/63. Took the oath of allegiance and gave his bond by 11/22/63. Ab. 9/1/64 - 10/31/64 (dated 12/30/64), in hands of enemy since 10/63. Post war rosters show service in the 19th Va. Cav. Brother of William and Wilson Rollins. Post war resident of Ritchie Co., W. Va. Age 37, laborer, West Union Dist., Ritchie Co., W. Va. 1880 Census. No POW records. NFR.

ROLLINS, WILLIAM - Pvt. Co. H. Enl. Calhoun Co., W. Va., 5/14/63 (5/8/63). Not stated if present or absent on muster-in roll dated 8/63. Ab. 10/31/63 - 8/31/64, in hands of enemy; had his own horse since 7/1/64. Took the oath of allegiance and gave his bond by 11/22/63. Ab. 9/1/64 - 10/31/64 (dated 12/30/64), prisoner, cpd. 10/63. Post war rosters show service in the 19th Va. Cav. Brother of Moses and Wilson Rollins. Post war resident of Ritchie Co., W. Va. Age 34, farm laborer, Clay Dist., Ritchie Co., W. Va. 1880 Census. No POW records. NFR.

ROLLINS, WILSON - 2nd Corp. Co. H. b.c. 1841. Enl. Calhoun Co., W. Va., 5/14/63 (5/10/63). Not stated if present or absent on muster-in roll dated 8/63, 3rd Corp. Ab., 2nd Corp., 10/31/63 - 8/31/64, in hands of enemy since 10/63. Took the oath of allegiance and gave his bond by 11/22/63. Ab., 2nd Corp., 9/1/64 - 10/31/64 (dated 12/30/64), prisoner in hands of enemy since 10/63. Brother of Moses and William Rollins. Post war resident of Ritchie Co., W. Va. Age 39, farmer, North Grant Dist., Ritchie Co., W. Va. 1880 Census. No POW records. Bur. Victory Ridge Cem., Harrisville, Ritchie Co., W. Va.

ROSS, JOHN M. - Pvt. Co. A. b. Richmond, c. 3/47. Not on muster rolls. Enl. Richmond, 8/18/63, age 16 years and 5 months, signed enl. document by x. Desc.: age 16 years and 5 months, 5'4", dark comp., light hair and blue eyes. Occ. marketman, residing in Richmond. Service listed as Maj. Lady's Cavalry Battn. NFR.

ROUDABUSH, DAVID BIDDLE "Bittle" - Pvt. Co. C. b. Bath Co., c. 1845. Age 15, Cleek's Mill, Bath Co. 1860 Census. Enl. Bath Co., 11/1/63. Present 6/30/63 - 8/31/64 (dated 1/6/65), enl. bounty due; 6% bond due. Present 9/1/64 - 10/31/64 (dated 12/30/64), 6% bond due. Paroled at Staunton, 5/27/65. Desc.: age 20, 5'6", dark comp., dark hair and brown eyes. Post war farmer, and resident of Harrisonburg. Age 79 in 1924. d. Harrisonburg, 6/14/1926.

ROW (ROM), JOHN W. - Pvt. Co. D. b.c. 1841. Enl. Camp Scott, 8/12/63. Present 7/1/63 - 1/1/64 (dated 1/1/64), entitled to enl. bounty. Ab. 12/31/63 - 8/31/64 (dated 1/6/65), AWOL since 12/63. Cpd. Beverly, W. Va., 2/16/64. Confined at the Atheneum Prison, 2/21/64. Desc.: age 23, 6'1", florid comp., dark hair and blue eyes. Occ. farmer, residing in Highland Co. Took the oath of allegiance and was released to the Provost Marshal, 2/22/64. Ab. 9/1/64 - 10/31/64, AWOL. NFR.

ROWE (ROUGH), ALPHEUS E. - Pvt. Co. I. b.c. 1846. Enl. Camp Northwest, W. Va., 6/25/63, age 17. Not stated if present or absent on muster-in roll dated 5/5/63. Cpd. Beverly, W. Va., 2/13/64. Confined at the Atheneum Prison, 2/21/64. Desc.: age 18, 5'11+", fresh comp., light hair and blue eyes. Occ. farmer, residing in Preston Co., W. Va. Took the oath and was released, 2/22/64. Served in Co. C, 46th Battn. Va. Cav. Age 30, ore miner, Lyon Dist., Preston Co., W. Va. 1880 Census. NFR.

ROWEN (ROAN), HEZEKIAH Z. - Pvt. Co. F. Enl. Camp Clover Lick (Camp Miller), 7/17/63. Not stated if present or absent on muster-in roll dated 7/20/63. Ab. 7/1/63 - 8/31/64 (dated 1/6/65), transf. to Co. A, 19th Va. Cav. Ab. 9/1/64 - 10/31/64 (dated 12/30/64), transf. to Co. A, 19th Va. Cav. Served in Co. C, 19th Va. Cav. instead of Co. A. NFR.

ROWSEY, HENRY - Pvt. Co. K. b. 4/9/49. Enl. Camp Northwest, W. Va., 8/1/63. Ab. 7/1/63 - 11/1/64 (dated 1/6/64), disc., under age. d. Rockbridge Co., 1/19/1924. Bur. House Mtn. Cem., on Rt. 641, Rockbridge Co.

RUCKMAN, MOSES - Pvt. Co. G. b.c. 1838. Enl. Wood Co., W. Va., 5/2/63. Not stated if present or absent on muster-in roll dated 8/63. Ab. 11/1/63 - 2/29/64, deserted 9/1/63. Cpd. Nathington Creek, W. Va., 5/19/64. Confined at the Atheneum Prison, 5/27/64. Desc.: age 26, 5'10", light comp., light brown hair and blue eyes, a resident of Parkersburg, W. Va. Took the oath of allegiance and was released to the Provost Marshal, 5/27/64. NFR.

RUCKMAN (RUCHMAN), SAMUEL - Pvt. Co. G. b.c. 1827. Enl. Wood Co., W. Va., 5/1/63 (6/18/63). Present 11/1/63 - 2/29/64, had his own horse since 1/1/64; detailed as butcher. Clothing issued 2/29/64. Present 7/1/64 - 8/31/64, had his own horse; detailed as butcher; entitled to bond. Present 9/1/64 - 10/31/64 (dated 12/29/64), detailed as Brigade Butcher; entitled to $100 bond. Paroled at Charleston, W. Va., 5/10/65. Desc.: age 38, 5'9", light comp., dark hair, blue eyes and sandy whiskers. Signed parole as a member of the 19th Va. Cav. Post war resident of Wood Co., W. Va. NFR.

RUCKMAN, THOMAS - Pvt. Co. G. Enl. Wood Co., W. Va., 5/2/63 (6/18/63). Not stated if present or absent on muster-in roll dated 8/63. Present 11/1/63 - 2/29/64. Ab. 7/1/64 - 8/31/64, had his own horse. Ab. 9/1/64 - 10/31/64 (dated 12/29/64), on detached service; entitled to $100 bond. NFR.

RUMMELL (RUMMEL), D. BLACKMAN - Pvt. Co. C. b.c. 1842. Age 18, farmer, Randolph Co., W. Va. 1860 Census. Enl. Pocahontas Co., W. Va., 8/12/63. Ab. 6/30/63 - 8/31/64 (dated 1/6/65), absent 8/1/63; enl. bounty due. Cpd. Pocahontas Co., W. Va., 11/6/63. Confined at the Atheneum Prison, 11/16/63. Desc.: age 21, 5'6+", dark comp., black hair and blue eyes. Occ. saddler, residing in Randolph Co., W. Va. Transf. to Camp Chase, 11/18/63. Confined at

Camp Chase, 11/18/63. Transf. to Ft. Delaware, 2/29/64. Confined at Ft. Delaware, 3/4/64 (3/2/64). Ab. 9/1/64 - 10/31/64 (dated 12/30/64), POW since 11/6/63; 6% bond due. Took the oath of allegiance and was released, 6/21/65. Desc.: age ?, 5'5", sallow comp., dark hair and blue eyes, a resident of Randolph Co., W. Va. NFR.

RUTMAN, SAMUEL - Pvt. Co. G. Post war rosters only, which show he was from Wood Co., W. Va. Could be Samuel Putnam or more likely Samuel Ruckman.

SALSBERRY (SOLSBERRY, SAULSBERRY, SALISBURY), JACOB S. "Jake" Pvt. Co. C. b.c. 1840. Age 20, farmer, Randolph Co., W. Va. 1860 Census. Prewar resident of Beverly, W. Va. Enl. Randolph Co., W. Va., 5/5/63. Not stated if present or absent on muster-in roll dated 8/63. Ab. 6/30/63 - 8/31/64 (dated 1/6/65), wd. 7/20/64; DOW. 7/24/64; 6% bond due. Ab. 9/1/64 - 10/31/64 (dated 12/30/64), wd. 7/20/64; DOW. 7/24/64; 6% bond due. Wd. near Winchester, 7/20/64. DOW. 7/24/64. Post war rosters show him as being KIA at Winchester, and that he DOW. 7/21/64 (7/26/64). Bur. Stonewall Cem., Winchester.

SALISBURY, SHELDON C. (T.) - 3rd Sgt. Co. C. b.c. 1843. Age 17, farmer, Randolph Co., W. Va. 1860 Census. Enl. Randolph Co., W. Va., 5/5/63. Not stated if present or absent on muster-in roll dated 8/63, 3rd Sgt. Ab., 3rd Sgt., 6/30/63 - 8/31/64 (dated 1/6/65), Cpd. Pocahontas Co., W. Va., 12/26/63. Confined at the Atheneum Prison, 1/6/64. Desc.: age 21, 6'1", dark comp., dark hair, gray eyes and sandy whiskers. Occ. farmer, residing in Randolph Co., W. Va. Transf. to Camp Chase, 1/7/64. Confined at Camp Chase, 1/8/64. Transf. to Ft. Delaware, 3/14/64. Confined at Ft. Delaware, 3/17/64. Ab., 3rd Sgt., 9/1/64 - 10/31/64 (dated 12/30/64), POW since 12/27/63; 6% bond due. Took the oath of allegiance and was released, 1/10/65. Desc.: age ?, height ?, light comp., brown hair and gray eyes, a resident of Randolph Co., W. Va. Post war resident of Randolph Co., W.Va. Alive 1916. NFR.

SARGENT (SARGEANT, SERGEANT), JACOB - Pvt. Co. D. b. Barbour Co., W. Va., c. 1843. Resident of Barbour Co., W. Va. Enl. Hightown, Highland Co., 6/27/63. Not stated if present or absent on muster-in roll dated 8/63. Present 7/1/63 - 1/1/64 (dated 1/1/64). Clothing issued 2/29/64 and 8/13/64. Ab. 12/31/63 - 8/31/64 (dated 1/6/65), AWOL. Reported at Buckhannon, W. Va., 8/23/64. Confined at Clarksburg, W. Va. Desc.: age 21, 5'8", red comp., light hair and blue eyes. Occ. farmer, residing in Barbour Co., W. Va. Ab. 9/1/64 - 10/31/64, (dated 12/30/64), AWOL. NFR.

SEIVER, SAMUEL F. - Pvt. Co. D. b. Highland Co., c. 1846. Resident of New Hampden, Highland Co. Enl. New Hampden, Highland Co., 3/11/64. POW record shows enl. as Highland Co., 4/64. Not stated if present or absent 12/31/63 - 8/31/64 (dated 1/6/65). Ab. 9/1/64 - 10/31/64, POW. Cpd. Beverly, W. Va., 10/29/64. Sent to Clarksburg, W. Va. Confined at Clarksburg, W. Va. Desc.: age 18, 5'7", fair comp., light hair and gray eyes. Occ. farmer, residing in Highland Co. Transf. to Wheeling, W. Va., 11/2/64. Confined at the Atheneum Prison, 11/2/64. Transf. to Camp Chase, 11/3/64. Confined at Camp Chase, 11/4/64. Took the oath of allegiance and was released, 6/12/65. Desc.: age 18, 5'8+", florid comp., light hair and gray eyes, a resident of Highland Co. Post war rosters show him as a member of the 19th Va. Cav. Moved to Nebraska. NFR.

SHANNON, MARTIN B. - Pvt. Co. C. b. Ireland, c. 1844. Age 16, farmer, Randolph Co., W. Va. 1860 Census. Enl. Randolph (Pocahontas) Co., W. Va., 7/5/63 (7/1/63). Not stated if present or absent on muster-in roll dated 8/63. Ab. 6/30/63 - 8/31/64 (dated 1/6/65), POW since 12/27/63; enl. bounty due; 6% bond due. Cpd. Pocahontas Co., W. Va., 12/26/63. Confined at the Atheneum Prison, 1/6/64. Desc.: age 19, 5'7", fair comp., fair hair and gray eyes. Occ. farmer, residing in Randolph Co., W. Va. Transf. to Camp Chase, 1/7/64. Confined at Camp Chase, 1/8/64. Transf. to Ft. Delaware, 3/14/64. Confined at Ft. Delaware, 3/17/64. Ab. 9/1/64 - 10/31/64 (dated 12/30/64), POW since 12/27/63; 6% bond due. Took the oath of allegiance and was released, 6/21/65. Desc.: age ?, 5'7", fair comp., dark hair and blue eyes, a resident of Randolph Co., W. Va. Resident of Mill Creek, W. Va., 1916, and Adolph, W. Va., 1924. Bur. Randolph Co., W. Va. NFR.

SHARP, MINOR S. - Pvt. Co. D. b.c. 1848. Enl. Oakland Depot, Alleghany Co., 4/1/64. Ab. 12/31/63 - 8/31/64 (dated 1/6/65), prisoner. Cpd. Frederick, Md. (near Harpers Ferry, W. Va.), 7/10/64. Sent to Washington, DC. Confined at the Old Capitol Prison, 7/17/64. Transf. to Elmira, NY, 7/23/64. Confined at Elmira Prison, 7/25/64. Ab. 9/1/64 - 10/31/64, AWOL. Desires to take the oath of allegiance, 10/31/64; says he is only 16 years of age, was conscripted and deserted; now wishes to remain in the North. Took the oath of allegiance and was released, 5/29/65. Desc.: age ?, 5'8+", fair comp., dark hair and hazel eyes, a resident of Webster Co., W. Va. NFR.

SHARP (THARPE), THORNTON F. - 2nd Corp. Co. B. b. Harrison Co., W. Va., c. 1827. Prior service, Co. D, 19th Va. Cav. Enl. Williamsburg, Greenbrier Co., W. Va., 4/15/63 (3/17/63). POW record shows enl. as Greenbrier Co., W. Va., 5/62. Not stated if present or absent on muster-in roll dated 7/25/63, 2nd Corp. Present, 2nd Corp., 11/1/63 - 8/31/64 (dated 1/6/65), taken prisoner at Beverly, W. Va., 10/64. Clothing issued 8/31/64. Ab., 2nd Corp., 9/1/64 - 10/31/64 (dated 12/30/64), POW since 10/64. Cpd. Beverly, W. Va., 10/29/64. Confined at Clarksburg, W. Va. Desc.: age 37, 5'8", fair comp., auburn hair and blue eyes. Occ. farmer, residing in Marion Co., W. Va. Transf. to Wheeling, W. Va., 11/2/64. Confined at the Atheneum Prison, 11/2/64. Desc.: age 37, 5'7+", fair comp., red hair and gray eyes. Transf. to Camp Chase, 11/3/64. Confined at Camp Chase, 11/4/64. Took the oath of allegiance and was released, 6/12/65. Desc.: age 37, 5'7+", florid comp., red hair and blue eyes, a resident of Marion Co., W. Va. Age 53, farmer, Lincoln School Dist., Marion Co., W. Va. 1880 Census. NFR.

SHARPE (SHARP), MORRIS - Pvt. Co. I. b.c. 1828. Enl. Warm Springs, 4/21/63, age 35. Not stated if present or absent on muster-in roll dated 5/5/63. Clothing issued 1/17/64 (detailed as teamster) and 2/29/64. Employed as a teamster at Warm Springs, 1/1/64 - 2/29/64, transf. Age 52, farm laborer, Huntersville, Pocahontas Co., W. Va. 1880 Census. NFR.

SHAVER, JOHN RIFFLE - Pvt. Co. A. b. Marion Co., W. Va., c. 1842. Enl. Pocahontas Co., W. Va., 4/6/63 (4/15/63), age 21. POW record shows enl. as Pocahontas Co., W. Va., 4/61. Not stated if present or absent on muster-in roll dated 4/6/63. Present 7/1/63 - 9/1/63. Present 10/31/63 - 8/31/64. Clothing issued 2/29/64. Surrendered at Mannington, W. Va., 2/8/65. Confined at Clarksburg, W. Va., 2/8/65. Desc.: age 22, 6'+". dark comp., black hair and black eyes. Occ. farmer, residing in Marion Co., W. Va. Took the oath of allegiance and was sent North, 2/12/65. Confined at the Atheneum Prison, 2/12/65. Desc.: age 22, 6', fair comp., dark hair and hazel eyes. Post war resident of Marion Co., W. Va. Age 38, farmer, Mannington Dist., Marion Co., W. Va. 1880 Census. NFR.

SHAY, GEORGE S. - Pvt. Co. A. b.c. 1836. Grew up near Morgantown, W. Va. Was a Jayhawker in Ks. before the war. No enl. data. Present 10/31/63 - 8/31/64. Wd. Bunker Hill, W. Va., 9/64, in the hips. Granted a furlough, 9/7/64. Paroled at Staunton, 5/1/65. Desc.: age 29, 5'11", fair comp., brown hair and blue eyes, a resident of W. Va. Post war resident of Monongalia Co., W. Va. NFR.

SHEAR (SHREVE), JOHN - Pvt. Co. A. Post war rosters only. NFR.

SHEETS, WILLIAM - Pvt. Co. E. Enl. Camp Clover Lick, 7/11/63. Not stated if present or absent on muster-in roll dated 7/18/63. NFR.

SHIFLETT, NIMROD - Pvt. Co. ?. b. 3/22/44 (1846). Age 14, Randolph Co., W. Va. 1860 Census. Post war rosters only, which show he was a resident of Randolph Co., W. Va. Served in Co. C, 19th Va. Cav. Resident of Montross, W. Va., 1916. d. 9/25/1917. Bur. Baptist Church Cem., Montross, W. Va.

SHINABURY (SHINCBURY), JACOB - Pvt. Co. E. Enl. Camp Clover Lick, 7/11/63. Not stated if present or absent on muster-in roll dated 7/18/63. Served in Co. F, 19th Va. Cav. NFR.

SHREVE, JACOB B. - Pvt. Co. H. b. Pleasants Co., W. Va., c. 1840. Enl. Calhoun Co., W. Va., 5/14/63, in Co. H. Not stated if present or absent on muster-in roll dated 8/63. Enl. Wood Co., W. Va., 5/9/63 (6/18/63), in Co. G. POW record shows enl. as Pocahontas Co., W. Va., 5/63. Not stated if present or absent on muster-in roll dated 8/63. Present 11/1/63 - 2/29/64. Clothing issued 2/29/64. Present 7/1/64 - 8/31/64, had his own horse; entitled to bond. Present 9/1/64 - 10/31/64 (dated 12/29/64), entitled to $100 bond. Cpd. Pleasants Co., W. Va., 2/14/65. Confined at Clarksburg, W. Va., 2/19/65. Desc.: age 25, 5'8", fair comp., light hair and blue eyes. Occ. shoemaker, residing in Pleasants Co., W. Va. Transf. to Wheeling, W. Va. Confined at the Atheneum Prison, 2/20/65. Desc.: age 25, 5'8", florid comp., sandy hair and gray eyes. Transf. to Camp Chase, 2/21/65. Confined at Camp Chase, 2/22/65. Took the oath of allegiance and was released, 6/13/65. Desc.: age 25, 5'8+", fair comp., light hair and blue eyes, a resident of Pleasants Co., W. Va. NFR.

SHREVE (SHEAR, SHREEVES), JAMES S. (L.) - Pvt. Co. A. b. Pendleton Co., W. Va., c. 1826. Age 34, farmhand, Williamsville PO, Highland Co. 1860 Census. Enl. Highland Co., 2/26/63, age 37. Not stated if present or absent on muster-in roll dated 2/26/63. Post war resident of Highland or Augusta Co. NFR.

SIMMONS, ALF - Pvt. Co. ?. Post war rosters only. NFR.

SIMMONS, H. H. - Pvt. Co. E. Enl. Camp Clover Lick, 7/11/63. Not stated if present or absent on muster-in roll dated 7/18/63. Clothing issued 2/6/64, as a member of Co. F, 19th Va. Cav. NFR.

SIMS (SIMMS), GEORGE W. - Pvt. Co. F. b.c. 1843. Age 17, laborer, Frost, Pocahontas Co., W. Va. 1860 Census. Enl. Camp Clover Lick, 7/11/63 (Camp Miller, 7/17/63). Not stated if present or absent on muster-in roll dated 7/20/63. Ab. 7/1/63 - 8/31/64 (dated 1/6/65), transf. to Co. C, 19th Va. Cav. Ab. 9/1/64 - 10/31/64 (dated 12/30/64), transf. to Co. C, 19th Va. Cav. NFR.

SITES, EMANUEL - Pvt. Co. F. Enl. Camp Clover Lick (Camp Miller), 7/17/63. Not stated if present or absent on muster-in roll dated 7/20/63. Ab. 7/1/63 - 8/31/64 (dated 1/6/65), transf. to Co. C, 19th Va. Cav. Ab. 9/1/64 - 10/31/64 (dated 12/30/64), transf. to Co. C, 19th Va. Cav. NFR.

SITES, MANLEY - Pvt. Co. G. Enl. Wood Co., W. Va., 5/2/63. Not stated if present or absent on muster-in roll dated 8/63. NFR.

SKERIN, JOHN - Pvt. Co. I. b.c. 1837. Enl. Camp Northwest, W. Va., age 26. Not stated if present or absent on muster-in roll dated 5/5/63. NFR.

SLAVEN, STUART CRAWFORD - Pvt. Co. A. b. 6/24/24. Enl. Highland Co., 3/30/63, age 39 (Pocahontas Co., W. Va). Not stated if present or absent on muster-in roll dated 3/30/63. Ab. 10/31/63 8/31/64, AWOL since 7/1/64. Cpd. Highland Co., 4/19/65 by Capt. Badger's Co., 8th Ohio Cav. Confined at Clarksburg, W. Va., 4/25/65. Desc.: age 41, 5'8", fair comp., dark hair and blue eyes. Occ. farmer, residing in Highland Co. Paroled at Clarksburg, W. Va., to be exchanged and was released, 4/25/65. Post war rosters show he was cpd. twice during the war. Post war resident of Highland Co. d. 3/7/1907. Bur. Slaven Family Cem., Highland Co.

SMITH, ALEXANDER - Pvt. Co. F. b.c. 1841. Enl. Camp Clover Lick (Camp Miller), 7/17/63. Not stated if present or absent on muster-in roll dated 7/20/63. Ab. 7/1/63 - 8/31/64 (dated 1/6/65), transf. to Co. C, 19th Va. Cav. Ab. 9/1/64 - 10/31/64 (dated 12/30/64), transf. to Co. C, 19th Va. Cav. NFR.

SMITH, ANDREW J. - Sgt. Co. E. b.c. 1842. Enl. Bulltown, W. Va., 5/10/63. Not stated if present or absent on muster-in roll dated 7/18/63, 2nd Corp. Present, Pvt., 1/1/64 - 8/31/64 (dated 1/6/65), entitled to $100 bond. Present, Pvt., 9/1/64 - 10/31/64 (dated 12/29/64), entitled to $100 bond. Paroled at Staunton, 5/19/65, listed as a Sgt. Desc.: age 23, 6', light comp., light hair and blue eyes. Post war resident of Jane Lew, W. Va. NFR.

SMITH, BENJAMIN M. - Pvt. Co. B. / F&S Adjutant. b.c. 1834. Prewar farmer, age 27 in 1861. Prior service, Co. C, 31st Va. Inf. Transf. to Capt. Arnett's Co. (Co. A, 20th Va. Cav.), 5/27/63, by order of Brig. Gen. J. D. Imboden. Enl. Clarksburg, W. Va., 5/21/61, by Capt. Turner. Not stated if present or absent on muster-in roll of Co. B, 20th Va. cav., dated 7/25/63, Pvt. Appointed Adjutant, 20th Va. Cav., 8/14/63. Present, Adjutant, FS MR 1/1/64 - 8/31/64 (dated 1/6/65). Paroled at Staunton, 5/19/64. Desc.: age 31, 5'10", fair comp., dark hair and dark eyes. Post war rosters show him as a Capt., 19th Va. Cav. NFR.

SMITH, EDWARD J. - Pvt. Co. D. Enl. Camp Miller, 10/1/63. Present 7/1/63 - 1/1/64 (dated 1/1/64), entitled to enl. bounty. Present 12/31/63 - 8/31/64 (dated 1/6/65), entitled to enl. bounty. Present 9/1/64 - 10/31/64, entitled to $100 enl. bounty. NFR.

SMITH, G. W. - Pvt. Co. A. Enl. Pocahontas Co., W. Va., 1863. Present 7/1/63 - 9/1/63. Post war resident of Monongalia Co., W. Va. Age 35, house painter, Morgantown, Monongalia Co., W. Va. 1880 Census. NFR.

SMITH, HARVEY - Pvt. Co. G. b.c. 1837. Enl. Wood Co., W. Va., 6/24/63. Not stated if present or absent on muster-in roll dated 8/63. Ab. 11/1/63 - 2/29/64, deserted 9/1/64. Gave a $1,000 bond and was allowed to remain at home by 10/5/63. Desc.: age 26, 5'7+", a resident of Wood Co., W. Va. NFR.

SMITH, JASPER N. - Pvt. Co. B. b.c. 1842. Prior service, Co. D, 19th Va. Cav. Enl. Williamsburg, Greenbrier Co., W. Va., 3/17/63. Not stated if present or absent on muster-in roll dated 7/25/63. Present 11/1/63 - 8/31/64 (dated 1/6/65), taken prisoner at Woodstock, 10/9/64. Clothing issued 3/31/64. Ab. 9/1/64 - 10/31/64 (dated 12/30/64), taken prisoner at Woodstock, 10/9/64. Cpd. Woodstock, 10/8/64 (10/9/64). Sent to Harpers Ferry, W. Va., then to Pt. Lookout. Confined at Pt. Lookout, 10/20/64. Took the oath of allegiance and was released, 5/14/65. Occ. farmer, residing in Monongalia Co., W. Va. Reported at the Provost Marshal's office, Washington, DC, 5/16/65 and transportation provided to Fairmont, W. Va. Post war resident of Marion Co., W. Va. Age 38, farmer, Grant Dist., Monongalia Co., W. Va. 1880 Census. NFR.

SMITH, JOHN L. - Pvt. Co. B. b. Green Co., c. 1841. Enl. Camp Northwest, W. Va., 8/19/63. POW record shows enl. as Highland Co., 8/63. Present 11/1/63 - 8/31/64 (dated 1/6/65). Clothing issued, 3/31/64. Present 9/1/64 - 10/31/64 (dated 12/30/64), entitled to $100 bond. Cpd. Marion Co., W. Va., 3/10/65. Confined at Clarksburg, W. Va., 3/13/65. Desc.: age 24, 5'9", fair comp., light hair and blue eyes. Occ. farmer, residing in Marion Co., W. Va. Transf. to Wheeling, W. Va. Confined at the Atheneum Prison, 3/13/64. Desc.: age 24, 5'9", florid comp., light hair and blue eyes. Transf. to Camp Chase, 3/16/65. Confined at Camp Chase, 3/17/65. Paroled at Camp Chase, 5/2/65, and sent to New Orleans, La., to be exchanged. Exchanged at Vicksburg, Miss., 5/12/65. Age 40, farmer, Lincoln School Dist., Marion Co., W. Va. 1880 Census. NFR.

SMITH, MARTIN V. - Pvt. Co. C. b. 6/16/44. Post war rosters only. Post war resident of Valley Center, Highland Co. d. near Valley Center, Highland Co., 1/26/1923. Bur. Abijah Matheny Family Cem., Highland Co.

SMITH, MORGAN W. (H.) - Pvt. Co. A. b.c. 1839. Enl. Pocahontas Co., W. Va., 3/24/63, age 24. Not stated if present or absent on muster-in roll dated 3/24/63. Cpd. Marion Co., W. Va., 5/1/63. Confined at the Atheneum Prison, 5/6/63. Desc.: age 25, 5'10+", florid comp., dark hair and gray eyes. Occ. farmer, residing in Wetzel Co., W. Va. Transf. to Camp Chase, 5/7/63. Confined at Camp Chase, 5/8/63. Paroled at Camp Chase, 5/13/63, and sent to City Point, to be exchanged. Arrived at City Point, 5/17/63. Declared exchanged, 5/23/63. Present 10/31/63 - 8/31/64. Clothing issued 2/29/64. Post war resident of Wetzel Co., W. Va. NFR.

SMITH, PERRY G - Pvt. Co. F. Enl. Bulltown, W. Va., 5/10/63 (Camp Clover Lick, 7/11/63). Not stated if present or absent on muster-in roll dated 7/20/63. Ab. 7/1/63 - 8/31/64 (dated 1/6/65), prisoner since 5/13/63. Ab. 9/1/64 - 10/31/64 (dated 12/30/64), prisoner since 5/13/63. No POW records. NFR.

SMITH, ROBERT G. - Pvt. Co. E. Enl. Camp Clover Lick, 7/11/63. Not stated if present or absent on muster-in roll dated 7/18/63. NFR.

SMITH, ROBERT J. - Capt. Co. E. b.c. 1837. Prior service, Co. C, 31st Va. Inf. Prewar clerk, age 24 in 1861. Enl. Clarksburg, W. Va., 5/21/63, by Capt. Turner. History of 31st Va. Inf. states he "may have" transf. to the 19th Va. Cav., 1863. Enl. in Co. E, 20th Va. Cav. at Camp Northwest, W. Va., 6/1/63. Not stated if present or absent on muster-in roll dated 7/18/63, Pvt. Present, Pvt., 1/1/64 - 8/31/64 (dated 1/6/65), transf. by Capt. Cooper, 6/1/63 to Co. E, 20th Va. Cav.; entitled to $100 bond. Present, Pvt., 9/1/64 - 10/31/64 (dated 12/29/64), entitled to $100 bond. Paroled at Staunton, 5/24/65, listed as a Capt. Desc.: age 27, 5'11", fair comp., dark hair and dark eyes. NFR.

SMITH, SAMUEL (LEMUEL) - Pvt. Co. H. b.c. 1833. Enl. Camp Northwest, W. Va., 7/1/63 (6/27/63). Not stated if present or absent on muster-in roll dated 8/63. Ab. 10/31/63 - 8/31/64, in hands of enemy. Cpd. Ritchie Co., W. Va., 10/12/63. Confined at the Atheneum Prison, 10/24/63. Desc.: age 30, 5'7+", fair comp., sandy hair, blue eyes and sandy whiskers. Occ. farmer, residing in Ritchie Co., W. Va. Transf. to Camp Chase, 10/26/63. Confined at Camp Chase, 10/27/63, listed as a deserter. Transf. to Rock Island, Ill., 1/22/64. Confined at Rock Island Prison, 1/64. Desired to take the oath of allegiance, 3/18/64, stating he had been coerced and had surrendered. Ab. 9/1/64 - 10/31/64 (dated 12/30/64), prisoner, cpd. 10/63. DOD. Rock Island, Ill., 5/9/64, chronic diarrhoea. Bur. Rock Island, Ill., grave no. 1134.

SMITH, S. P. - Pvt. Co. B. Not on muster rolls. Cpd. Woodstock, 10/9/64. Sent to Harpers Ferry, W. Va., then to Pt. Lookout, 10/13/64. NFR.

SMITH, WASHINGTON W. - Pvt. Co. D or Co. B. b. Monongalia Co., W. Va., c. 1846. Not on muster rolls. POW record shows he enl. in Highland Co., 9/64. Cpd. Taylor Co., W. Va., 10/24/64, listed as a member of Co. D. Confined at Clarksburg, W. Va. Desc.: age 18, 5'8", fair comp., light hair and gray eyes. Occ. farmer, residing in Monongalia Co., W. Va. Transf. to Wheeling, W. Va., 10/31/64. Confined at the Atheneum Prison, 10/31/64, listed as a member of Co. E. Transf. to Camp Chase, 11/22/64. Confined at Camp Chase, 11/23/64, desires to take the oath of allegiance. Applied to take the oath of allegiance, 12/64. Gave a statement at Camp Chase, 2/6/65, stating he deserted. Took the oath of allegiance and was released, 2/18/65. Post war resident of Marion Co., W. Va. Age 34, farmer, Paw Paw Dist., Marion Co., W. Va. 1880 Census. NFR.

SNODGRASS, JOHN H. - Pvt. Co. A. b.c. 1841. Enl. Pocahontas Co., W. Va., 4/6/63, age 22. Not stated if present or absent on muster-in roll dated 4/6/63. Present 7/1/63 - 9/1/63. Present 10/31/63 - 8/31/64. Clothing issued 2/29/64. Post war resident of Marion Co., W. Va. Age 40, farmer, Mannington Dist., Marion Co., W. Va. 1880 Census. NFR.

SNODGRASS, SILAS N. - Pvt. Co. H. Enl. Camp Northwest, W. Va., 7/1/63 (6/27/63). Not stated if present or absent on muster-in roll dated 8/63. Present 10/31/63 - 8/31/64. Present 9/1/64 - 10/31/64 (dated 12/30/64), entitled to $100 bond. NFR.

SNYDER, ADDISON - Pvt. Co. ?. b. Randolph Co., W. Va., c. 1838. Age 22, farmer, Webster Co., W. Va. 1860 Census. Post war rosters only, which show he was a resident of Randolph Co., W. Va. Age 43, farmer, Mingo, Randolph Co., W. Va. 1880 Census. Bur. Randolph Co., W. Va. NFR.

SNYDER (SNIDER), JEREMIAH E. - Pvt. Co. F. Post war rosters only, which show he enl. 1863 and was disc. in 1865. Post war resident of Calhoun Co., W. Va. Age 49, physician, Murphy Dist., Ritchie Co., W. Va. 1880 Census. Bur. King Knob Cem., Mahone, Ritchie Co., W. Va.

SNYDER, S. S. - Pvt. Co. K. Enl. Camp Cameron, Bath Co., 3/10/64 (3/1/64). Ab. 11/1/63 - 2/29/64, deserted 3/24/64. Ab. 2/29/64 - 8/31/64, deserted 3/24/64. Clothing issued 3/23/64. NFR.

SOMERVILLE (SUMMERVILLE), ROBERT R. - Pvt. Co. G. b. Jackson Co., W. Va., c. 1846. Enl. Wood Co., W. Va., 6/24/63. POW record shows enl. as Highland Co., 5/64. Not stated if present or absent 7/1/64 - 8/31/64, $50 enl. bounty due. Clothing issued 8/13/64, listed as a member of Co. A. Present 9/1/64 - 10/31/64 (dated 12/29/64), $50 enl. bounty due; entitled to $100 bond. Cpd. Beverly, W. Va., 10/29/64. Confined at Clarksburg, W. Va. Desc.: age 18, 5'8", fair comp., light hair and blue eyes. Occ. farmer, residing in Jackson Co., W. Va. Transf. to Wheeling, W. Va., 11/2/64. Confined at the Atheneum Prison, 11/2/64. Transf. to Camp Chase, 11/29/64. Confined at Camp Chase, 11/30/64, desires to take the oath of allegiance. Took the oath of allegiance and was released, 5/15/65. Desc.: age 19, 5'9", dark comp., dark hair and blue eyes, a resident of Wood Co., W. Va. Age 34, farmer, Ravenswood Dist. 1, Jackson Co., W. Va. 1880 Census. NFR.

SPENCER, GEORGE - Pvt. Co. ?. Post war rosters only, which show he was in service by 9/12/63, and was a resident of Harrison Co., W. Va. NFR.

SPOHN (SPON), MILFORD - 1st Sgt. Co. I. b. Frederick Co., Md., c. 1843. Resident of Md. Enl. Richmond, 8/28/63. Desc.: age 20, 5'9", fair comp., light hair and blue eyes. Enl. Camp Northwest, W. Va., 9/15/63 (Greenbrier Bridge, 8/30/63). Ab., 1st Sgt., 11/1/63 - 8/31/64 (dated 1/6/65), on horse detail. Present, 1st Sgt., 11/1/63 - 10/31/64 (dated 12/31/64). Clothing issued 2/29/64. NFR.

SPROUSE, LEWIS M. - Pvt. Co. C. Enl. Pocahontas Co., W. Va., 10/16/63. Ab. 6/30/63 - 8/31/64 (dated 1/6/65), deserted 1/1/64. NFR.

STAGG (STAG), JAMES J. - Pvt. Co. G. b.c. 1833. Enl. Wood Co., W. Va., 5/2/63. Not stated if present or absent on muster-in roll dated 8/63. Ab. 11/1/63 - 2/29/64, deserted 9/1/63. Deserter, reported to US Forces by 10/14/63. and confined at Clarksburg, W. Va., for examination. Desc.: age 30, 5'11", a resident of Wood Co., W. Va. Post war resident of Wood Co., W. Va. Age 46, farmer, Clay Dist., Wood Co., W. Va. 1880 Census. NFR.

STAGG (STAG), JERRY P. - Pvt. Co. G. Enl. Wood Co., W. Va., 5/2/63. Not stated if present or absent on muster-in roll dated 8/63. Ab. 11/1/63 - 2/29/64, deserted 9/1/63. Post war resident of Wood Co., W. Va. Age 45, farmer, Clay Dist., Wood Co., W. Va. 1880 Census. NFR.

STALLMAN, WILLIAM - Pvt. Co. F. b. Gilmer (Lewis) Co., W. Va., c. 1843. Age 17, Calhoun Co., W. Va. 1860 Census. Enl. Camp Northwest (Camp Miller), W. Va., 7/19/63. Not stated if present or absent on muster-in roll dated 7/20/63. Ab. 7/1/63 - 8/31/64 (dated 1/6/65), transf. to Co. A, 19th Va. Cav. Ab. 9/1/64 - 10/31/64 (dated 12/30/64), transf. to Co. A, 19th Va. Cav. NFR.

STALNAKER, ADAM - 4th Sgt. Co. C. b.c. 1838. Age 22, laborer, Randolph Co., W. Va. 1860 Census. Enl. Randolph Co., W. Va., 5/8/63. Not stated if present or absent on muster-in roll dated 8/63, 4th Sgt. Ab., 4th Sgt., 6/30/63 - 8/31/64 (dated 1/6/65), POW since 12/27/63; 6% bond due. Cpd. Randolph Co., W. Va., 7/3/63. Confined at Ft. Delaware. Paroled at Ft. Delaware, 9/28/64, until exchanged, signs by x. Transf. to Aiken's Landing, 9/30/64, to be exchanged. Exchanged at Varina, 10/5/64. Adm. Gen. Hosp. No. 9, 10/6/64. Transf. to Chimborazo Hosp., 10/7/64. Adm. Chimborazo Hosp. No. 3, 10/7/64, sick, debilitas. Clothing issued, Chimborazo Hosp. No. 3, 10/13/64. Passport issued to Randolph Co., W. Va., 10/14/64. Ab., 4th Sgt., 9/1/64 - 10/31/64 (dated 12/30/64), sick; 6% bond due. Paroled at Clarksburg, W. Va., 4/29/65, as a Pvt. Desc.: age 28, 5'7+", dark comp., black hair and dark eyes. Post war resident of Randolph Co., W. Va. Age 44(?), farmer, Valley Bend, Randolph Co., W. Va. 1880 Census. d. by 1916. Bur. Randolph Co., W. Va.

STALLNAKER, D. - Pvt. Co. E. Post war rosters only, which chow he was cpd. Loudoun Co., 7/15/64. Confined in a prison, then transf. for exchange, 10/11/64. NFR.

STALNAKER, NEWTON C. - 2nd Corp. Co. C. Prior service, Co. D, 31st Va. Inf. Enl. Pocahontas Co., W. Va., 3/29/63. Not stated if present or absent on muster-in roll dated 8/63, 2nd Corp. Ab., 2nd Corp., 6/30/63 - 8/31/64 (dated 1/6/65), claimed and returned to Co. D, 31st Va. Inf., 4/1/64. NFR.

STANDIFORD (STANDEFORD), B. F. - Pvt. Co. G. Enl. Wood Co., W. Va., 7/1/63 (6/18/63). Present 11/1/63 - 2/29/64. Clothing issued 2/29/64. Not stated if present or absent 7/1/64 - 8/31/64, has his own horse; entitled to bond. Ab. 9/1/64 - 10/31/64 (dated 12/29/64), sick in hosp.; entitled to $100 bond. Cpd. Front Royal (near Ninevah), 11/12/64. Sent to Harpers Ferry, W. Va., then to Pt. Lookout. Confined at Pt. Lookout, 11/18/64. Took the oath of allegiance and was released, 5/14/65. Occ. farmer, residing in W. Va. Reported at the Provost Marshal General's Office, Washington, DC, 5/16/65. Transportation furnished him to Wood Co., W. Va. NFR.

STANLEY, DANIEL A. - Pvt. Co. H. b.c. 1837. Enl. Camp Northwest, W. Va., 6/1/63 (6/27/63, 6/28/63). Not stated if present or absent on muster-in roll dated 8/63. Deserted, and reported to US forces at Clarksburg, W. Va., by 10/15/63. Desc.: age 26, 6', fair comp., light hair and gray eyes, a resident of Ritchie Co., W. Va. Was sent North. Ab. 10/31/63 - 8/31/64, deserted 8/63. Ab. 9/1/64 - 10/31/64 (dated 12/30/64), deserted 8/63. Post war resident of Ritchie Co., W. Va. NFR.

STANLEY, JOHN T. - Pvt. Co. H. Enl. Camp Northwest, W. Va., 7/1/63 (6/27/63). Not stated if present or absent on muster-in roll dated 8/63. Present 10/31/63 - 8/31/64, had his own horse since 11/1/63. Clothing issued 2/29/64. Present 9/1/64 - 10/31/64 (dated 12/30/64). Age 51, farm laborer, South Grant Dist., Ritchie Co., W. Va. 1880 Census. Bur. Pribble Cem., Cisco, Ritchie Co., W. Va.

STACHER (STAICHER, STARTCHER), JOHN - Pvt. Co. F. b.c. 1844. Enl. Camp Clover Lick (Camp Miller), 7/17/63. Not stated if present or absent on muster-in roll dated 7/20/63. Ab. 7/1/63 - 8/31/64 (dated 1/6/65), transf. to Co. C, 19th Va. Cav. Ab. 9/1/64 10/31/64 (dated 12/30/64), transf. to Co. C, 19th Va. Cav. NFR.

STEEL (STEELE), THOMAS H. (M.) - Pvt. Co. A. b.c. 1844. Enl. Upshur (Pocahontas) Co., W. Va., 5/2/63, age 19. Not stated if present or absent on muster-in roll dated 5/2/63. Ab. 7/1/63 - 9/1/63, deserted 5/6/63. Ab. 10/31/63 - 8/31/64, deserted 5/3/63. Cpd. Monongalia Co., W. Va., 5/15/63 Confined at the Atheneum Prison, 5/22/63. Desc.: age 19, 6', dark comp., light hair and blue eyes, a resident of Monongalia Co., W. Va. "Has been with the rebels one week on trial." Transf. to Camp Chase, 5/25/63. Took the oath of allegiance and was released, 6/25/63, signs by x. Desc.: age 19, 6', light comp., brown hair and blue eyes. Post war resident of Monongalia Co., W. Va. NFR.

STENNETT, JOSEPH - Pvt. Co. I. b.c. 1841. Enl. Camp Northwest, W. Va., 6/2/63, age 22. Not stated if present or absent on muster-in roll dated 5/5/63. NFR.

STINNETT, REUBEN - Pvt. Co. I. b.c. 1845. Enl. Camp Northwest, W. Va., 6/2/63, age 18. Not stated if present or absent on muster-in roll dated 5/5/63. NFR.

STINNETT, WILLIAM - Pvt. Co. I. b.c. 1846. Enl. Camp Northwest, W. Va., 6/2/63, age 17. Not stated if present or absent on muster-in roll dated 5/5/63. NFR.

STEPHENS, GEORGE M. - Pvt. Co. E. Post war rosters only, which show he was cpd. Edwards Ferry, 7/14/64. Confined in prison and transf. for exchange, 3/2/65. NFR.

STEPHENS, WILLIAM T. - Pvt. Co. E. Post war rosters only, which show he was cpd. Edwards Ferry, 7/14/64. Confined in prison, took the oath of allegiance and was released 5/29/65. NFR.

STEWART, DAVID BOSTON - Major/Pvt. Co. A. b. 11/4/1826. Attended Kingwood Academy and Monongalia Academy, studied engineering. Farmer, residing in Monongalia Co., W. Va. Commissioned Major, 5/10/61, to rank from 5/9/61. Reported to Col. G. A. Porterfield, at Grafton, W. Va., 5/61. Detached on recruiting duty by Porterfield. Was at Rich Mtn., 7/11/61, and assisted in guiding the portion of Pegram's troops that escaped from Camp Garnett. Assigned to the 44th Va. Inf., summer 1861. Assigned by Gen. R. E. Lee to the 48th Va. Inf., by 10/31/61. Was not reelected 4/12/62, dropped from the rolls. Requested permission to raise a Battn. of Partisan Rangers, 5/6/62. Commissioned Maj., Partisan Rangers. Authorized by the Sec. of War to raise a Battn. of Partisan Rangers, 5/21/62. Had his HQ at Staunton, 6/13/62. Made arrangements to provision the recruits brought in by Lt. David Poe and others. While raising the Battn., was cpd. Highland Co., 8/7/62. Confined at Beverly, W. Va., 8/10/62. Confined at the Atheneum Prison, 8/14/62. Transf. to Camp Chase, 8/16/62. Confined at Camp Chase, 8/16/62. Held for recruiting a guerrilla band and for being "a dangerous man." Transf. to Vicksburg, Miss., 8/25/62, to be exchanged. Arrived Vicksburg, Miss., 9/11/62. Desc.: age ?, 5'8+", fair comp., dark hair, black eyes and dark whiskers. At Richmond, paroled prisoner, 9/25/62. Declared exchanged 11/10/62. Commanded a detachment of men during the fight at Beverly, W. Va., 7/2/63 - 7/3/63. Horse wd. Beverly, W. Va., 7/3/63. Requested authority from Pres. Jeff Davis, 3/25/64, to raise a Battn. of cavalry in northwest Va., and for the return of the co. he had given to the 20th Va. Cav. Col. Arnett refused to release the co., 4/22/64. Served as a aide on Brig. Gen. W. L. Jackson's staff. Member Virginia Legislature, 1863 - 1864. Member Military Committee and took part in the evacuation of Richmond, 4/2/65. Took the oath of allegiance, Richmond, 5/26/65. Age 53, farmer, Grant Dist., Monongalia Co., W. Va. 1880 Census. Post war resident of Monongalia Co., W. Va., where he farmed until his retirement in 1897. Moved to Morgantown, W. Va. d. Morgantown, Monongalia Co., 3/21/1915.

STEWART, ELSWORTH (ELLSWORTH) - Pvt. Co. A. Post war rosters only, which show he was a resident of Monongalia Co., W. Va. Served in the 19th Va. Cav. NFR.

STEWART, JAMES E. (A.) - Pvt. Co. A. b.c. 1840. Enl. Highland Co., 10/16/62, age 22. Not stated if present or absent on muster-in roll dated 10/16/62. Present 7/1/63 - 9/1/63. Present 10/31/63 - 8/31/64. NFR.

STEWART, WILLIAM CLARKE - Pvt. Co. A. b. Morgantown, W. Va., 10/14/44. Enl. Monongalia Co., W. Va., 8/1/64. Present 10/31/63 - 8/31/64, $50 enl. bounty due. Paroled at Appomattox CH, 4/10/65. Name does not appear on the Appomattox Parole Roster. Post war drayage owner, and resident of Vasalia, Calif. d. Porterville, Calif., 4/16/1922.

STINCHCOMB, THOMAS - 2nd Sgt. Co. G. Resident of Parkersburg, W. Va. Enl. while "a mere youth." Went south in company with John P. Woodyard. Enl. Wood Co., W. Va., 6/24/63. Not stated if present or absent on muster-in roll dated 8/63, 1st Corp. Present, 2nd Sgt., 11/1/63 - 2/29/64, had his own horse and equipment since 12/21/63. Clothing issued 2/29/64. Present, 2nd Sgt., 7/1/64 - 8/31/64, had his own horse; entitled to bond. Present, 2nd Sgt., 9/1/64 - 10/31/64 (dated 12/29/64), entitled to $100 bond. Post war sketch states he was wd. at Antietam, but recovered. Went to Mexico after the surrender at Appomattox. Came to Tx. a few years later. "He was a gallant soldier, never shirking his duty, was popular with the soldiers as well as with all with whom he came in contact. "Poor Tom Stinchcomb" said one of his boyhood companions upon learning of his death, "He was the brightest and brainest of our set and many a good time we had together." d. Mt. Pleasant, Tx., at age 43.

STOCKWELL, _____ - Pvt. Co. ?. Post war recollections only, which state he had a brother in US service, and was present at the capture of his brother in 5/64. NFR.

STOUT, HEZEKIAH - Pvt. Co. F. b.c. 1843. Enl. Bulltown, W. Va., 5/10/63. Not stated if present or absent on muster-in roll dated 7/20/63. Ab. 7/1/63 - 8/31/64 (dated 1/6/65), deserted 10/1/63. Cpd. and confined at Clarksburg, W. Va., by 10/15/63. Desc.: age 20, 5'9", fair comp., light hair and hazel eyes, a resident of Upshur Co., W. Va. Was sent North. Ab. 9/1/64 - 10/31/64 (dated 12/30/64), deserted 10/1/63. NFR.

STOUT (STONE), JOHN S. - Pvt. Co. D. b.c. 1845. Enl. Hightown, Highland Co., 6/27/63. Not stated if present or absent on muster-in roll dated 8/63. Ab. 7/1/63 - 1/1/64 (dated 1/1/64), prisoner. Cpd. Bath Co., 8/25/63 (8/24/63). Sent to Clarksburg, W. Va., then North, via Wheeling, W. Va. Confined at the Atheneum Prison, 9/6/63. Desc.: age 18, 5'8", dark comp., brown hair and brown eyes. Occ. farmer, residing in Upshur Co., W. Va. Transf. to Camp Chase, 9/7/63. Confined at Camp Chase, 9/8/63. Ab. 12/31/63 - 8/31/64 (dated 1/6/65), prisoner. Transf. to Rock Island, Ill., 1/22/64. Confined at Rock Island Prison, 1/24/64. Ab. 9/1/64 - 10/31/64, POW. Enl. in US service, 10/13/64, to serve on the frontier. NFR

STOUT, MICHAEL - Pvt. Co. K. Post war rosters only, which show he was cpd. Loudoun Co., 7/15/64. Confined in prison. Took the oath of allegiance and was released, 6/16/65. NFR.

STRAIGHT, AMOS F. - Pvt. Co. A. Enl. Pocahontas Co., W. Va., 11/22/63. Present 10/31/63 - 8/31/64, $50 enl. bounty due. Clothing issued, 2/29/64. Post war resident of Marion Co., W. Va. NFR.

STRAIGHT, WILLIAM G. - Pvt. Co. B. Enl. Marion Co., W. Va., 2/17/63. Not stated if present or absent on muster-in roll dated 7/25/63. Ab. 11/1/63 - 8/31/64 (dated 1/6/65), KIA. Droop Mtn., W. Va., 11/16/63. Post war roster shows him as Sgt., Capt. Downs Co., 19th Va. Cav., and that he was wd. not KIA.

STRAIGHT, WILLIAM LEBBUSS - Sgt. Co. A. b. 9/24/38. Enl. after Brig. Gen. W. E. Jones passed through Fairmont, 4/63. Enl. Lewis Co., W. Va., 5/4/63, age 23(?). Not stated if present or absent on muster-in roll dated 5/4/63, 1st Corp. Present, 1st Corp., 7/1/63 - 9/1/63. Ab., 5th Sgt., 10/31/63 - 8/31/64, cpd. 8/28/64. Wd. Droop Mtn., W. Va., 11/6/63. Clothing issued 2/29/64. Clothing issued at Staunton, 7/29/64, while on the way to his command. Cpd. Smithfield, 8/28/64. Sent to Harpers Ferry, W. Va., then to Camp Chase. Confined at Camp Chase, 9/2/64. Transf. to Pt. Lookout, 3/26/65, to be exchanged, but was not. Confined at Pt. Lookout, 3/31/65. Took the oath of allegiance and was released 6/3/65. Post war rosters show him as a Corp., Co. A. Post war resident of Marion Co., W. Va. Age 40, farmer, Fairmont Dist., Marion Co., W. Va. 1880 Census. d. Fairmont, W. Va., 10/24/1913. "One of the best soldiers."

STURM, CHARLES WESLEY - Pvt. Co. B. b. 10/5/39. Enl. Camp Northwest, W. Va., 5/14/63. Not stated if present or absent on muster-in roll dated 7/25/63. Present 11/1/63 - 8/31/64 (dated 1/6/65). Present 9/1/64 - 10/31/64 (dated 12/30/64), entitled to $100 bond. Post war rosters show he was paroled 4/10/65. Post war resident of Calhoun Co., W. Va. d. Littleton, W. Va., 6/18/1918.

STUTTING, NICHOLAS - Pvt. Co. E. Enl. Camp Clover Lick, 7/11/63. Not stated if present or absent on muster-in roll dated 7/18/63. NFR.

SULLIVAN, JAMES E. - Pvt. Co. E. Enl. Bulltown, W. Va., 5/10/63 (5/1/63). Not stated if present or absent on muster-in roll dated 7/18/63. Gave himself up at Clarksburg, W. Va., 8/8/63. Confined at the Atheneum Prison, 8/9/63. Desc.: age 33, 6'+", dark comp., dark hair and dark eyes. Occ. farmer, residing in Harrison Co., W. Va. Transf. to Camp Chase, 8/11/63. Confined at Camp Chase, 8/12/63. Ab. 1/1/64 - 8/31/64 (dated 1/6/65), cpd. Harrison Co., W. Va., 8/1/63. Took the oath of allegiance and was released, 1/14/64 (1/15/64), stating he was a conscript and had deserted. Was ordered to report to Gov. Bowman. Desc.: age 33, 6', light comp., black hair, black eyes and dark whiskers. Ab. 9/1/64 - 10/31/64 (dated 12/29/64), cpd. Harrison Co., W. Va., 9/1/63. NFR.

SUMMERS, C. P. - Capt. Co. D. b.c. 1837. Enl. Camp Pisgah, Bath Co., 2/1/64. Present, Pvt., 12/31/63 - 8/31/64 (dated 1/6/65), entitled to enl. bounty. Paroled at Staunton, 5/25/65, listed as Capt. Desc.: age 28, 6', fair comp., black hair and gray eyes. NFR.

SUTTON, GEORGE - Pvt. Co. E. Enl. Camp Clover Lick, 7/11/63. Not stated if present or absent on muster-in roll dated 7/18/63. NFR.

SWAIN, JAMES - Pvt. Co. G. Enl. Wood Co., W. Va., 6/25/63. Not stated if present or absent on muster-in roll dated 8/63. Ab. 11/1/63 - 2/29/64, deserted 9/1/63. NFR.

SWANS (SWANE), JOHN - Pvt. Co. K. b.c. 1840. Not on muster rolls. POW record shows he enl. at Richmond, 5/63. Deserted. Gave himself up at Halltown, 10/4/64. Sent to Harpers Ferry, W. Va., then to Washington, DC, 10/7/64. Took the oath of allegiance and was released, 10/8/64. Desc.: age 24, 5'10", florid comp., dark hair and blue eyes, a resident of Richmond. Transportation furnished him to Philadelphia, 10/8/64. NFR.

SWOPE (SWOOPE), JOHN H. - Pvt. Co. E. b. 1846. Enl. Williamsville, Bath Co., 7/15/64 (Highland Co.) Present 1/1/64 - 8/31/64 (dated 1/6/65), entitled to enl. bounty. Present 9/1/64 - 10/31/64 (dated 12/29/64), entitled to $100 bond. Paroled at Staunton, 6/7/65. Desc.: age 18, 5'9", fair comp., light hair and black eyes. Post war rosters show service in Co. A. Post war farmer. d. Martha Jefferson Hospital, Charlottesville, 6/26/1916, age 69. Bur. near Williamsville, Bath Co.

TALBOTT (TOLBERT, TALBERT), DAVID T. - Pvt. Co. D. b.c. 1827. Enl. Hightown, Highland Co., 6/27/63. Not stated if present or absent on muster-in roll dated 8/63. Present 7/1/63 - 1/1/64 (dated 1/1/64), detailed as a teamster for the 20th Va. Reg't.; has no horse. Employed as a teamster at Warm Springs, 1/1/64 - 2/29/64. Clothing issued 1/17/64 (detailed teamster). Present 12/31/63 - 8/31/64 (dated 1/6/65). Ab. 9/1/64 - 10/31/64, on detached service; entitled to $100 enl. bounty. Clothing issued 11/11/64, while on the way to join his command. Paroled at Staunton, 5/15/65. Desc.: age 38, 5'6", dark comp., light hair and gray eyes. NFR.

TAYLOR, ANDREW - Pvt. Co. C. b. 3/13/35. Age 25, farmer, Randolph Co., W. Va. 1860 Census. Enl. Pocahontas Co., W. Va., 3/26/64 (3/1/64). Ab. 6/30/63 - 8/31/64 (dated 1/6/65), on leave; enl. bounty due. Ab. 9/1/64 - 10/31/64 (dated 12/30/64), sick. Post war resident of Randolph Co., W. Va. Age 45, farmer, Green Dist., Randolph Co., W. Va. 1880 Census. d. 2/7/1912.

TAYLOR, CURTIS - Pvt. Co. C. b.c. 1838. Age 22, farmer, Randolph Co., W. Va. 1860 Census. Post war rosters only, which show he was a scout. Post war resident of Randolph Co., W. Va. d. by 1916. NFR.

TAYLOR, HENRY S. - Pvt. Co. C. b.c. 1848. Not on muster rolls. Paroled at Charleston, W. Va., 5/10/65, signs by x. Desc.: age 17, 6', light comp., light hair and blue eyes. NFR.

TAYLOR, LEVI - Pvt. Co. H. Enl. Camp Northwest, W. Va., 6/1/63 (Greenbrier Co., W. Va., 3/1/63 or Calhoun Co., W. Va., 4/1/63). Not stated if present or absent on muster-in roll dated 8/63. Ab. 10/31/63 - 8/31/64, in hands of enemy. Deserted and surrendered, taking the oath of allegiance and gave his bond, by 12/5/63. Ab. 9/1/64 - 10/31/64 (dated 12/30/64), prisoner, cpd. 10/63. NFR.

TAYLOR, T. C. - Pvt. Co. C. Enl. Pocahontas Co., W. Va., 3/21/63 (Randolph Co., W. Va., 3/19/63). Not stated if present or absent on muster-in roll dated 8/63. Ab. 6/30/63 - 8/31/64 (dated 1/6/65), sick. Ab. 9/1/64 - 10/31/64 (dated 12/30/64), AWOL. NFR.

TAYLOR, WILLIAM S. - Pvt. Co. E. Enl. Camp Clover Lick, 7/11/63. Not stated if present or absent on muster-in roll dated 7/18/63. NFR.

TEFFT, WILLIAM - Pvt. Co. G. Post war rosters only, which show he was a resident of Wood Co., W. Va. NFR.

TENNANT, ALPHEUS "Alf" - Pvt. Co. A. b.c. 1840 (1842). Prior service, Co. A, 3rd VSL. Not on muster rolls. Reference jacket only, which shows service in Co. A, 19th Va. Cav. and Lurty's Battery. Enl. Lurty's Batty., 10/1/63. Cpd. Braxton Co., W. Va., 10/13/63, listed as a member of Co. A, 20th Va. Cav. Sent to Wheeling, W. Va. Confined at the Atheneum Prison, 10/20/63. Desc.: age 26, 5'8", fair comp., brown hair and blue eyes, a resident of Ritchie Co., W. Va. Transf. to Camp Chase, 10/22/63. Confined at Camp Chase, 10/23/63. Desc.: age 26, 5'8", fair comp., brown hair and blue eyes. Transf. to Rock Island, Ill., 1/14/64. Confined at Rock Island Prison, 1/24/64. Paroled at Rock Island Prison, 5/23/65, listed as a member of Co. A, 19th Va. Cav. Desc.: age 25, 5'8", fair comp., dark hair and blue eyes, a resident of Petroleum, Ritchie Co., W. Va. Believed to be bur. Dry Ridge Cem., Petroleum, Ritchie Co., W. Va.

TENNANT, ANDREW - Pvt. Co. B. b. Monongalia Co., W. Va., c. 1839. Enl. Marion (Monongalia) Co., W. Va., 2/17/63. POW record shows enl. as Marion Co., W. Va., 2/63. Not stated if present or absent on muster-in roll dated 7/25/63. Present 11/1/63 - 8/31/64 (dated 1/6/65). Present 9/1/64 - 10/31/64 (dated 12/30/64). Cpd. Monongalia Co., W. Va., 3/22/65. Confined at Clarksburg, W. Va., 3/25/65. Desc.: age 26, 5'10", fair comp., dark hair and gray eyes. Occ. farmer, residing in Monongalia Co., W. Va. Post war rosters show service in Co. A. Post war resident of Monongalia Co., W. Va. Age 40, farmer, Clay Dist., Monongalia Co., W. Va. 1880 Census. NFR.

TENNANT, LEM - Pvt. Co. ?. Post war rosters only, which describe him as being a tall slim man. NFR.

THACKSTON, WILLIAM D. - Pvt. Co. C. b.c. 1836. Not on muster rolls. Cpd. Beverly, W. Va., 3/1/64. Confined at the Atheneum Prison, 3/24/64. Desc.: age 28, 5'10", fair comp., dark hair and blue eyes. Occ. carpenter, residing in Prince Edward Co. Took the oath of allegiance and was released, 3/25/64. NFR.

THOMPSON, GEORGE W. - Pvt. Co. I. b. Nicholas Co., W. Va., c. 1828. Resident of Clay Co., W. Va. Arrested and confined by 3/15/62. Charged with being a bushwhacker. Enl. Camp Northwest, W. Va., 4/20/63 (Lewisburg, W. Va., 2/1/63 or Warm Springs, 5/63). POW record shows enl. as Richmond, 3/63. Not stated if present or absent on muster-in roll dated 5/5/63. Ab. 11/1/63 - 8/31/64 (dated 1/6/65), missing in skirmish. Present 11/1/63 - 10/31/64 (dated 12/31/63). Clothing issued, 2/29/64. Cpd. Clay Co., W. Va., 12/20/64. Sent to Clarksburg, W. Va., 12/26/64, and was confined. Desc.: age 38, 5'9", sallow comp., brown hair and hazel eyes. Occ. farmer, residing in Clay Co., W. Va. Transf. to Wheeling, W. Va., 12/28/64. Confined at the Atheneum Prison, 12/28/64. Transf. to Camp Chase, 12/30/64. Confined at Camp Chase, 12/31/64, desires to take the oath of allegiance, being a deserter. Applied to take the oath of allegiance, 1/65. Took the oath and was released, 5/15/65. Desc.: age 38, 5'8", dark comp., dark hair and blue eyes, a resident of Clay Co., W. Va. Age 53, farmer, Henry Dist., Clay Co., W. Va. 1880 Census. NFR.

THOMPSON, PETER - Pvt. Co. B. Enl. Camp Northwest, W. Va., 6/10/63 (6/1/63). Not stated if present or absent on muster-in roll dated 7/25/63. Present 11/1/63 - 8/31/64 (dated 1/6/65), detailed as Blacksmith. Clothing issued 3/31/64. Present 9/1/64 - 10/31/64 (dated 12/30/64), detailed as Blacksmith; entitled to $100 bond. Wd. by 10/64 and in the Staunton Gen. Hosp., vulnus sclopeticum, left femur. DOW. Staunton, 10/21/64.

THORNHILL, WILLIAM A. - 1st Sgt. Co. ?. Post war rosters only, which show he was cpd./wd. at Jack's Shop, in the leg. Post war farmer and merchant. d. 1899.

THRASH, DAVID H. - Pvt. Co. D. Resident of Upshur Co., W. Va. Enl. Gnatty Creek, 5/1/63, in Co. D. Not stated if present or absent on muster-in roll dated 7/20/63. Enl. Bulltown, W. Va., 5/10/63, in Co. F. Not stated if present or absent on muster-in roll dated 7/20/63. Ab. 7/1/63 - 8/31/64 (dated 1/6/65), prisoner since 12/3/63; entitled to enl. bounty. Cpd. Alleghany Co., 12/20/63. Confined at the Atheneum Prison, 12/31/63. Desc.: age 21, 5'9", dark comp., dark hair and blue eyes. Occ. farmer, residing in Harrison Co., W. Va. Transf. to Camp Chase, 12/31/63. Confined at Camp Chase, 1/1/64. Transf. to Ft. Delaware, 3/14/64. Confined at Ft. Delaware, 3/17/64. Ab. 9/1/64 - 10/31/64 (dated 12/30/64), prisoner since 12/18/63; entitled to enl. bounty. Took the oath of allegiance and was released, 5/6/65. Desc.: age ?, 5'10", dark comp., dark hair and gray eyes, a resident of Harrison Co., W. Va. NFR.

TIMBERLAKE, WILLIAM E. - 2nd Sgt. Co. I. Enl. Camp Marlin's (Marlin's Bottom), W. Va., 8/15/63 (Greenbrier Bridge, 10/20/63). Ab., 3rd Sgt., 11/1/63 - 8/31/64 (dated 1/6/65), sick in a Richmond Hosp. Ab., 2nd Sgt., 11/1/63 - 10/31/64 (dated 12/31/64), sick in a Richmond Hosp. Clothing issued 2/29/64. Paroled at Richmond, 5/2/65. NFR.

TINGLER, H. S. - Pvt. Co. H. Enl. Camp Northwest, W. Va., 7/1/63. Not stated if present or absent on muster-in roll dated 8/63. Transf. to Lurty's Batty., 11/1/63. NFR.

TODD, ADAM P. - Pvt. Co. D. Enl. Weston, W. Va., 5/1/63. Not stated if present or absent on muster-in roll dated 8/63. NFR.

TODD, DAVID - Pvt. Co. I. Enl. Marlin's Bottom, W. Va., 9/1/63. Ab. 11/1/63 - 8/31/64 (dated 1/6/65), never reported. NFR.

TODD, JOHN - Pvt. Co. I. b.c. 1839. Enl. Camp Northwest, W. Va., 6/18/63, age 24. Not stated if present or absent on muster-in roll dated 5/5/63. NFR.

TOLBERT (TALBERT), SALATHIEL - Pvt. Co. D. Enl. Hightown, Highland Co., 3/1/64. Present 12/31/63 - 8/31/64 (dated 1/6/65). Present 9/1/64 - 10/31/64, entitled to $100 enl. bounty.

TOMS, JAMES S. - Pvt. Co. D. Enl. Camp Scott, 7/25/63. Not stated if present or absent on muster-in roll dated 8/63. Present 7/1/63 - 1/1/64 (dated 1/1/64), transf. to Co. E, 20th Va. Cav., 11/1/63; had his own horse; $50 enl. bounty due. Ab. 12/31/63 - 8/31/64 (dated 1/6/65), transf. to Co. E, 20th Va. Cav., 11/1/63. Ab. 9/1/64 - 10/31/64, transf. to Co. E, 20th Va. Cav., 11/1/63. Present in Co. E, 1/1/64 - 8/31/64 (dated 1/6/65), transf. to Co., 10/23/63; entitled to $100 bond. Present in Co. E, 9/1/64 - 10/31/64 (dated 12/29/64), entitled to $100 bond. NFR.

TOOTHMAN, BENJAMIN SMITH - 4th Sgt. Co. G. b. Coolville, O., 10/42. Enl. Wood Co., W. Va., 5/2/63 (5/12/63). Not stated if present or absent on muster-in roll dated 8/63, 4th Sgt. Present, Pvt., 11/1/63 - 2/29/64, had his own horse and equipment. Clothing issued 2/29/64. Not stated if present or absent 7/1/64 - 8/31/64, had his own horse; entitled to bond. Ab. 9/1/64 - 10/31/64 (dated 12/29/64), wd., date and place not stated; entitled to $100 bond. Post war sketch states he enl. 1861. Post war resident of Wood Co., W. Va. Age 37, railroad conductor, Parkersburg, Wood Co., W. Va. 1880 Census. Went to Tx., where he was killed by falling from a train. NFR.

TOOTHMAN, DAVIS - Pvt. Co. ?. b.c. 1820. David Poe, in his book, mentions that Davis Toothman accompanied him on his first recruiting trip into Northwestern Va. Toothman went to Marion Co., W. Va., and there surrendered. Age 60, farmer, Mannington Dist., Marion Co., W. Va. 1880 Census. NFR.

TRADER, JAMES H. - Pvt. Co. H. b.c. 1830. Enl. Camp Northwest, W. Va., 7/1/63 (6/27/63). Not stated if present or absent on muster-in roll dated 8/63. Ab. 10/31/63 - 8/31/64, in hands of enemy. Deserted. Confined at Parkersburg, W. Va., by 1/25/64. Ab. 9/1/64 - 10/31/64 (dated 12/30/64), prisoner, cpd. 1/63. Post war resident of Ritchie Co., W. Va. Age 48, farmer, Murphy Dist., Ritchie Co., W. Va. 1880 Census. NFR.

TRICKETT, EDWARD - Pvt. Co. A. Post war rosters only, which show he was a resident of Monongalia Co., W. Va. Could be Michael E. Trickett. NFR.

TRICKERT (TRICKER, TRICKATT), MICHAEL E. - Pvt. Co. A. b.c. 1828. Prior service, Co. D, 19th Va. Cav. Enl. Pocahontas Co., W. Va., 3/15/63 (3/6/63), age 35. Not stated if present or absent on muster-in roll dated 3/15/63. Present 7/1/63 - 9/1/63. Ab. 10/31/63 - 8/31/64, deserted 11/13/63, since d. in Camp Chase. Cpd. Fairmont, W. Va., 12/16/63 (Shenandoah Co., 12/16/63). Confined at the Atheneum Prison, 12/16/63. Desc.: age 37, 5'11+", fresh comp., dark hair and gray eyes. Occ. farmer, residing in Monongalia Co., W. Va. Transf. to Camp Chase, 12/17/63. Confined at Camp Chase, 12/18/63. DOD. Camp Chase, 9/10/64 (10/20/64), typhoid fever. Bur. Camp Chase Confederate Cem., grave no. 236.

TRIGETT (TRICKETT), WILLIAM S. - Pvt. Co. C. b. Preston Co., W. Va., c. 1843. Prior service, Co. C, 46th Battn. Va. Cav. Transf. to Co. C, 20th Va. Cav., 1/10/64. Not on muster rolls. POW record shows enl. as Highland Co., 7/62. Deserted. Cpd. Beverly, W. Va., 12/1/64, listed as a member of Co. C, 20th Va. Cav. Desc.: age 6', fair comp., dark hair and brown eyes. Occ. farmer, residing in Monongalia Co., W. Va. Took the oath of allegiance and was released, 12/22/64. NFR.

TRIMBLE, DRAPER - Pvt. Co. D. Enl. Elk, W. Va., 5/1/63. Not stated if present or absent on muster-in roll dated 8/63. NFR.

TYLER, JAMES - Pvt. Co. E. Enl. Camp Clover Lick, 7/11/63. Not stated if present or absent on muster-in roll dated 7/18/63. NFR.

UMPHREYS, WILLIAM C. - Pvt. Co. I. b.c. 1830. Enl. Lewisburg, W. Va., 3/20/64, age 34. Not stated if present or absent on muster-in roll dated 5/5/63. NFR.

UNDERWOOD, JOHN RILEY - Pvt. Co. H. b.c. 1829. Enl. Camp Northwest, W. Va., 7/1/63 (6/28/63). Not stated if present or absent on muster-in roll dated 8/63. Ab. 10/31/63 - 8/31/64, deserted 8/63. Cpd. Columbus, Ohio, 2/8/64. Confined at Camp Chase, 2/29/64. Adm. USA Gen. Hosp., Camp Chase, 3/15/64, smallpox. Returned to the prison, 4/4/64. Desires to take the oath of allegiance, 6/10/64, stating he was conscripted and deserted. Ab. 9/1/64 - 10/31/64 (dated 12/30/64), deserted 9/63. Took the oath of allegiance and was released, 12/1/64. Desc.: age 35, 5'11", dark comp., dark hair and gray eyes, a resident of Ritchie Co., W. Va. NFR.

UTTER, BRYANT - Pvt. Co. F. b.c. 1840. Age 10, 1850 Wirt Co., W. Va. Census. Enl. Camp Clover Lick (Camp Miller), 7/17/63. Not stated if present or absent on muster-in roll dated 7/20/63. Ab. 7/1/63 - 8/31/64 (dated 1/6/65), transf. to Co. C, 19th Va. Cav. Ab. 9/1/64 - 10/31/64 (dated 12/30/64), transf. to Co. C, 19th Va. Cav. Brother of Marion Utter. NFR.

UTTER, MARION - Pvt. Co. F. b.c. 1838. Age 12, 1850 Wirt Co., W. Va. Census. Enl. Camp Clover Lick (Camp Miller), 7/17/63. Not stated if present or absent on muster-in roll dated 7/20/63. Ab. 7/1/63 - 8/31/64 (dated 1/6/65), transf. to Co. C, 19th Va. Cav. Ab. 9/1/64 - 10/31/64 (dated 12/30/64), transf. to Co. C, 19th Va. Cav. Brother of Bryant Utter. NFR.

UTTERBACK, JOHN (JACOB) A. - Pvt. Co. D. b. Fauquier Co., 1847. Prewar resident of near Philippi, Barbour Co., W. Va. Prior service, Co. A, 25th Va. Inf. Enl. Weston, W. Va., 5/1/63. Not stated if present or absent on muster-in roll dated 8/63. Present 7/1/63 - 1/1/64 (dated 1/1/64), had his own horse. Present 12/31/63 - 8/31/64 (dated 1/6/65). Present 9/1/64 - 10/31/64, entitled to $100 enl. bounty. Cpd. and confined at Clarksburg, W. Va., by 4/14/65. Desc.: age 17, 5'6", fair comp., light hair and blue eyes. Occ. farmer, residing in Taylor Co., W. Va. Took the Amnesty oath and was released, 4/14/65. Post war rosters show he was wd./cpd. Winchester, 1864. Post war resident of Alexandria, 1902. d. 2/4/1929. Bur. Section 16, Arlington National Cem., Arlington.

VANCE, JAMES K. (R.) "Jim" - Pvt. Co. A. b. Highland Co., c. 1847. Enl. Highland Co., 4/5/63, age 16. POW record shows enl. as Bath Co., 4/62. Not stated if present or absent on muster-in roll dated 4/5/63. Present 7/1/63 - 9/1/63. Present 10/31/63 - 8/31/64. Clothing issued 2/29/64. Cpd. Beverly, W. Va., 10/29/64. Confined at Clarksburg, W. Va. Desc.: age 17, 5'3", fair comp., light hair and blue eyes. Occ. farmer, residing in Highland Co. Transf. to Wheeling, W. Va., 11/2/64. Confined at the Atheneum Prison, 11/2/64. Desc.: age 16, 5'3", fair comp., light hair and gray eyes. Transf. to Camp Chase, 11/3/64. Confined at Camp Chase, 11/4/64. Took the oath of allegiance and was released, 6/12/65. Desc.: age 16, 5'6", light comp., light hair and blue eyes. a resident of Highland Co. "Though a youth of seventeen, knew no fear." Post war resident of Highland Co. Moved to Ks. NFR.

VANDEVENDER, GEORGE A. (H.) - 3rd Sgt. Co. H. b.c. 1843. Enl. Camp Northwest, W. Va., 6/1/63 (4/9/63; Calhoun Co., W. Va., 5/9/63). Not stated if present or absent on muster-in roll dated 8/63, 3rd Sgt. Ab., Prov., 10/31/63 - 8/31/64, in hands of the enemy. Cpd. Calhoun Co., W. Va., 12/4/63. Confined at the Atheneum Prison, 1/12/64. Desc.: age 20, 5'8 3/4", fresh comp., dark hair and dark eyes. Occ. farmer, residing in Calhoun Co., W. Va. Took the oath of allegiance, gave his bond and was released, 1/28/64. Ab. 9/1/64 - 10/31/64 (dated 12/30/64), prisoner, cpd. 10/63. Age 37, farmer, Center Dist., Calhoun Co., W. Va. 1880 Census. NFR.

VANHORN, JOHN N. - Pvt. Co. D. Enl. Elk, W. Va., 5/1/63 (Hightown, Highland Co., 4/1/64). Not stated if present or absent on muster-in roll dated 8/63. Present 12/31/63 - 8/31/64 (dated 1/6/65), entitled to enl. bounty. Ab. 9/1/64 - 10/31/64, AWOL, not entitled to enl. bounty. NFR.

VANSENER, JOHN - Pvt. Co. E. Enl. Camp Clover Lick, 7/11/63. Not stated if present or absent on muster-in roll dated 7/18/63. NFR.

VESS, ANDREW JACKSON - Pvt. Co. K. b. Rockbridge Co., 4/30. Age 29, laborer, Kerr's Creek, Rockbridge Co. 1860 Census. Prior service, Co. G, 58th Va. Inf. Enl. Camp Cameron, Bath Co., 2/15/64. Present 11/1/63 - 2/29/64. Clothing issued 2/29/64. Ab. 2/29/64 - 8/31/64, AWOL. Post war resident of Millboro Springs, 1904. NFR.

VESS, JOHN T. - Pvt. Co. K. b. Va., c. 1847. Age 13, 4th Dist., Augusta Co. 1860 Census. Enl. Camp Northwest, W. Va., 6/16/63. Present 11/1/63 - 2/29/64. Clothing issued 2/29/64. Ab. 2/29/64 - 8/31/64, AWOL. Killed in logging accident on Little North Mtn., in upper Colliers Creek, 3/98.

VESS, Z. B. - Pvt. Co. K. b. 12/18/46. Enl. Camp Cameron, Bath Co., 2/15/64. Present 11/1/63 - 2/29/64. Ab. 2/29/64 - 8/31/64, deserted 6/16/64. Clothing issued 2/29/64 and 3/23/64. d. 9/16/1913. Bur. Mount Mary Cem., Bath Co.

VEST, DAVID J. - Pvt. Co. I. b. Rockbridge Co., 10/3/45. Age 17(?), Collierstown, Rockbridge Co. 1860 Census. Enl. Warm Springs, 4/20/63 (4/1/63, 4/1/64), age 18. Not stated if present or absent on muster-in roll dated 5/5/63. Ab. 11/1/63 - 8/31/64 (dated 1/6/65), AWOL. Ab. 11/1/63 - 10/31/64 (dated 12/31/64), wd., in the foot, date and place unknown. Farmhand, Buffalo Dist., Rockbridge Co. 1870 Census. Farmer, Goshen, Rockbridge Co., 1903. d. 9/19/1920. Bur. Lebanon Presbyterian Church Cem.

VEST, JAMES M. - Pvt. Co. I. b. Collierstown, Rockbridge Co., 9/16/41. Age 19, laborer, Collierstown, Rockbridge Co. 1860 Census. Enl. Warm Springs, 4/20/63 (4/1/63), age 21. Not stated if present or absent on muster-in roll dated 5/5/63. Ab. 11/1/63 - 8/31/64 (dated 1/6/65), transf. to the 60th Va. Inf. Ab. 11/1/63 10/31/64 (dated 12/31/64), transf. to the 60th Va. Inf. Wd. at Cloyd's Mtn., 5/13/64, lost the third finger of the left hand. Laborer, Buffalo Dist., Rockbridge Co. 1870 Census. d. Kerr's Creek, 9/7/1903. Bur. New Monmouth Presbyterian Church Cem.

VEST, JOHN M. - Pvt. Co. K. b.c. 1847. Enl. Camp Northwest, W. Va., 7/13/63, age 16. Not stated if present or absent on muster-in roll dated 7/21/63. Ab. 7/1/63 - 11/1/63 (dated 1/6/64), AWOL. Clothing issued 2/29/64. Order for his arrest issued by the Conscript Bureau, 2/17/64, stating he could be found in Rockbridge Co. The warrant was returned 2/29/64, with the note that Vest had returned to his command. NFR.

VEST, S. W. - Pvt. Co. ?. Not on muster rolls. In Chimborazo Hosp., 9/17/64. Note in his CSR shows residence as Albemarle Co. NFR.

VEST, SAMUEL G. Jr. - Pvt. Co. I. b. Rockbridge Co., c. 1845. Age 15, Collierstown, Rockbridge Co. 1860 Census. Enl. Warm Springs, 4/1/64 (1/65). Ab. 11/1/63 - 8/31/64 (dated 1/6/65), never reported. Ab. on furlough to get a horse, 4/?/65. Enl. Rockbridge Jr. Reserves, Collierstown, 4/1/65. Desc.: age 18, 5'6+", fair comp., dark hair and gray eyes, a farmer. Age 23, farmhand, Buffalo Dist., Rockbridge Co. 1870 Census. Age 65, farmer, Kerr's Creek Dist., Rockbridge Co. 1910 Census. d. Collierstown, 5/5/1933, age 84, while living in Clifton Forge. Bur. Union View Cem., Alleghany Co.

VEST, SAMUEL G. Sr. - Pvt. Co. I. Enl. Camp Marlin's Bottom, W. Va., 9/1/63 (Warm Springs, 5/1/63). Ab. 11/1/63 - 8/31/64 (dated 1/6/65), sick. Ab. 11/1/63 - 10/31/64 (dated 12/31/64), sick. NFR.

VINCENT, EDWARD FLETCHER - Pvt. Co. B / F&S QM Sgt. b. Marion Co., W. Va., 5/14/25. Prewar farmer. Prior service, Co. A, 31st Va. Inf. and Co. B, 19th Va. Cav. Transf. to Co. B, 20th Va. Cav., 8/1/63. Enl. Highland Co., 4/1/63. Present, QM Sgt., FS MR 1/1/64 8/31/64 (dated 1/6/65), has his own horse. Paroled at Staunton, 5/1/65, as a Pvt. in Co. B, 20th Va. Cav. Desc.: age 34, 5'9", fair comp., brown hair and blue eyes, a resident of Augusta Co. Post war member of Staunton Camp UCV, age 81 in 1906. d. Shutterlee Mill Road, Augusta Co., 7/11/1914 (7/10/1914).

VOGLE, CHARLES A. - Pvt. Co. K. b.c. 1846. Enl. Camp Northwest, W. Va., 6/10/63, age 17. Not stated if present or absent on muster-in roll dated 7/21/63. Present 7/1/63 - 11/1/63 (dated 1/6/64). Ab. 11/1/63 - 2/29/64, d. Camp Cameron, Bath Co., 3/3/64. Clothing issued 2/29/64. Ab. 2/29/64 - 8/31/64, d. Camp Cameron, Bath Co., 3/3/64.

WADE, HOWARD - Pvt. Co. C. b. 12/19/40. Age 18(?), farmhand, Meadow Dale, Highland Co. 1860 Census. Prior service, Co. F, 25th Va. Inf. Enl. Pocahontas Co., W. Va., 6/1/63 (Highland Co.) Not stated if present or absent on muster-in roll dated 8/63. Ab. 6/30/63 - 8/31/64 (dated 1/6/65), POW since 8/28/64. Clothing issued 3/10/64. Ab. 9/1/64 - 10/31/64 (dated 12/30/64), POW since 8/28/64. Cpd. Smithfield, 8/28/64. Sent to Harpers Ferry, W. Va., then to Camp Chase. Confined at Camp Chase, 9/2/64. Adm. Chase USA Gen. Hosp., 10/14/64, variola. Returned to the prison, 10/20/64, once vaccinated. Took the oath of allegiance and was released, 1/12/65. Desc.: age 23(?), 5'8", fair comp., light hair, gray eyes and sandy whiskers, a resident of Highland Co. Post war minister and resident of Highland Co. d. 10/15/1901. Bur. Wade Family Cem., Highland Co.

WAGNER (WAGGONER, WAGONER), JESSE - Pvt. Co. H. b.c. 1829. Farmer. Enl. Camp Northwest, W. Va., 7/1/63. Not stated if present or absent on muster-in roll dated 8/63. Ab. 10/31/63 - 8/31/64, sick in 1864; DOD. Highland Co., 8/64. Not stated if present or absent 9/1/64 - 10/31/64 (dated 12/30/64), deceased. d. Highland Co., 8/15/64, age 35.

WAGNER (WAGGONER, WAGONER), URIAH - Pvt. Co. D. b.c. 1845 (1847). Not on muster rolls. POW record shows he enl. in Highland Co., 4/64. Deserted. Reported at Beverly, W. Va., 10/26/64. Confined at Clarksburg, W. Va. Took the oath of allegiance and was released, 10/30/64. Desc.: age 20, 5'5", light comp., light hair and gray eyes. Occ. farmer, residing in Highland Co. Post war rosters show he enl. in 1864 and served 8 months. Post war resident of Highland Co. NFR.

WALTHALL, H. - Pvt. Co. C. Not on muster rolls. Cpd., date and place unknown. Was exchanged and landed at Dutch Gap, 3/3/65. Adm. Chimborazo Hosp. No. 1, 3/65. Furloughed 3/7/65, resident of Lexington, Rockbridge Co. NFR.

WALTON, WILLIAM R. - Pvt. Co. B. Enl. Williamsburg, Greenbrier Co., W. Va., 3/17/63. Not stated if present or absent on muster-in roll dated 7/25/63. Transf. to Lurty's Batty., 9/23/63. May have served in the 19th Va. Cav. NFR.

WAMSLEY, ENOCH - Pvt. Co. C. b. 1835. Age 25, farmer, Randolph Co., W. Va. 1860 Census. Prior service Co. F, 31st Va. Inf. Enl. Pocahontas Co., W. Va., 4/25/63 (Randolph Co., W. Va., 4/28/63). Not stated if present or absent on muster-in roll dated 8/63. Ab. 6/30/63 - 8/31/64 (dated 1/6/65), POW since 12/27/63; 6% bond due. Cpd. Pocahontas Co., W. Va., 12/26/63. Confined at the Atheneum Prison, 1/6/64. Desc.: age 24(?), 5'7", florid comp., light hair, blue eyes and sandy whiskers. Occ. farmer, residing in Preston Co., W. Va. Transf. to Camp Chase, 1/7/64. Confined at Camp Chase, 1/8/64. Transf. to Ft. Delaware, 3/14/64. Confined at Ft. Delaware, 3/17/64. Ab. 9/1/64 - 10/31/64 (dated 12/30/64), POW since 12/27/63. Took the oath of allegiance and was released, 6/21/65. Desc.: age ?, 5'7", ruddy comp., dark hair and blue eyes, a resident of Randolph Co., W. Va. Post war resident of Randolph Co., W. Va. Age 44, farmer, Mingo, Randolph Co., W. Va. 1880 Census. Resident of Monterville, W. Va., 1924. d. 12/22/1942. Bur. Heavener Cem., Monterville, W. Va.

WAMSLEY, WILLIAM H. - Pvt. Co. C. b. 3/29/44. Age 17, laborer, Randolph Co., W. Va. 1860 Census. Enl. Randolph Co., W. Va., 5/7/63 (5/1/63). Not stated if present or absent on muster-in roll dated 8/63. Ab. 6/30/63 - 8/31/64 (dated 1/6/65), inside enemy lines and never reported. Age 37, farmer, Mingo, Randolph Co., W. Va. 1880 Census. d. 3/1/1901. Bur. Wamsley Cem., Valley Bend, Randolph Co., W. Va.

WARD, WILLIAM J. - Pvt. Co. E. b.c. 1846. Enl. Bulltown, W. Va., 5/10/63. Not stated if present or absent on muster-in roll dated 7/18/63. Present 1/1/64 - 8/31/64 (dated 1/6/65), entitled to $100 bond. Ab. 9/1/64 - 10/31/64 (dated 12/29/64), entitled to $100 bond. Paroled at Staunton, 5/19/65, signs by x. Desc.: age 19, 6', dark comp., black hair and black eyes. NFR.

WARE, ALLEN B. - Pvt. Co. C. b. 6/20/30. Age 30, farmer, Randolph Co., W. Va. 1860 Census. Enl. Randolph Co., W. Va., 5/5/63. Not stated if present or absent on muster-in roll dated 8/63. Ab. 6/30/63 - 8/31/64 (dated 1/6/65), AWOL. Clothing issued 3/10/64. Ab. 9/1/64 - 10/31/64 (dated 12/30/64), AWOL. Age 49, farmer, Mingo, Randolph Co., W. Va. 1880 Census. d. 11/19/95. Bur. Ware Cem., Ware School, Randolph Co., W. Va.

WARE, ANDREW "Big Andy" - Pvt. Co. C. Enl. Randolph Co., W. Va., 3/1/64. Present 6/30/63 - 8/31/64 (dated 1/6/65), enl. bounty due. Ab. 9/1/64 - 10/31/64 (dated 12/30/64), AWOL. NFR.

WARE, BENONI (BENJAMIN) T. (F.) - Pvt. Co. C. b. 11/22/43. Age 16, farmer, Randolph Co., W. Va. 1860 Census. Enl. Pocahontas (Randolph) Co., W. Va., 3/19/63. Not stated if present or absent on muster-in roll dated 8/63. Ab. 6/30/63 - 8/31/64 (dated 1/6/65), AWOL. Clothing issued 3/10/64. Present 9/1/64 - 10/31/64 (dated 12/30/64). Surrendered at Buckhannon, W. Va., 5/11/65. Confined at Clarksburg, W. Va., 5/14/65. Paroled for exchange and was released, 5/15/65. Desc.: age 20, 6'+", florid comp., black hair and hazel eyes. Occ. farmer, residing in Randolph Co., W. Va. Age 37, farmer, Mingo, Randolph Co., W. Va. 1880 Census, listed as Benjamin T. Ware. Awarded Cross of Honor. Post war resident of Randolph Co., W. Va. Member of Gen. Pegram Camp, UCV, Valley Head, W. Va. d. 2/22/1914. Bur. Lower Mingo Cem., Randolph Co., W. Va.

WARE, GEORGE W. M. Jr. - Pvt. Co. C. b. Randolph Co., W. Va., 1838. Age 22, farmer, Randolph Co., W. Va. 1860 Census. Enl. Beverly, Randolph Co., W. Va., 5/5/63. Not stated if present or absent on muster-in roll dated 8/63. Ab. 6/30/63 - 8/31/64 (dated 1/6/65), AWOL. Clothing issued 3/10/64. Ab. 9/1/64 - 10/31/64 (dated 12/30/64), AWOL. Cpd. Beverly, W. Va., 11/10/64. Confined at Clarksburg, W. Va. Took the oath of allegiance and was sent North, 11/13/64. Desc.: age 26, 5'6", fair comp., light hair and brown eyes. Occ. farmer, residing in Randolph Co., W. Va. Age 42, farmer, Mingo, Randolph Co., W. Va. 1880 Census. Post war resident of Valley Head, Randolph Co., W. Va., 1924. d. 1925. Bur. Ware Cem., Ware Ridge School, Randolph Co., W. Va.

WARE, JAMES - Pvt. Co. C. Enl. Randolph Co., W. Va., 5/10/64. Ab. 6/30/63 - 8/31/64 (dated 1/6/65), sick; enl. bounty due; 6% bond due. Ab. 9/1/64 - 10/31/64 (dated 12/30/64), sick; 6% bond due. NFR.

WARE (WARD), JOHN R. - Pvt. Co. C. b.c. 1842. Age 18, farmer, Randolph Co., W. Va. 1860 Census. Enl. Randolph Co., W. Va., 5/5/63. Not stated if present or absent on muster-in roll dated 8/63. Ab. 6/30/63 - 8/31/64 (dated 1/6/65), AWOL. Clothing issued 3/10/64. Present 9/1/64 - 10/31/64 (dated 12/30/64). Age 41, farmer, Mingo, Randolph Co., W. Va. 1880 Census. NFR.

WARNER, JOHN - Pvt. Co. F. b. Lewis Co., W. Va., c. 1844. Enl. Camp Clover Lick (Camp Miller), 7/17/63. Not stated if present or absent on muster-in roll dated 7/20/63. Ab. 7/1/63 - 8/31/64 (dated 1/6/65), transf. to Co. C, 19th Va. Cav. Ab. 9/1/64 10/31/64 (dated 12/30/64), transf. to Co. C, 19th Va. Cav. NFR.

WAUGH, LEVI - Pvt. Co. C. b.c. 1839. Prior service, Co. I, 25th Va. Inf. Enl. Pocahontas Co., W. Va., 5/10/63. Not stated if present or absent on muster-in roll dated 8/63. Ab. 6/30/63 - 8/31/64 (dated 1/6/65), deserted 1/1/64. Cpd. Pocahontas Co., W. Va., 2/15/64. Confined at the Atheneum Prison, 2/21/64. Desc.: age 25, 6', fresh comp., light hair and dark eyes. Occ. farmer, residing in Pocahontas Co., W. Va. Transf. to Camp Chase, 3/4/64. Confined at Camp Chase, 3/5/64. Transf. to Ft. Delaware, 3/14/64. Confined at Ft. Delaware, 3/17/64. Took the oath of allegiance and was released, 6/21/65. Desc.: age ?, 6', sallow comp., light hair and brown eyes, a resident of Pocahontas Co., W. Va. Age 42, farmer, Edray, Pocahontas Co., W. Va. 1880 Census. NFR.

WAYBRIGHT, COLUMBUS P. - Pvt. Co. D. Enl. Hightown, Highland Co., 7/15/63. Not stated if present or absent on muster-in roll dated 8/63. NFR.

WEAVER, CHARLES B. - Pvt. Co. I. b.c. 1838. Enl. Camp Northwest, W. Va., 7/20/63, age 25. Not stated if present or absent on muster-in roll dated 5/5/63. NFR.

WEAVER, M. A. - Lt. Co. I. Not on muster rolls. Adm. CSA Gen. Hosp., Charlottesville, 11/24/64, gonorrhoea. RTD. 3/22/65. NFR.

WELLEN, D. C. - Pvt. Co. G. Post war rosters only, which show he was living in 1924. NFR.

WELSH (WELCH), MICHAEL - Pvt. Co. K. b.c. 1839. Enl. Warm Springs, 4/1/63, age 24. Not stated if present or absent on muster-in roll dated 7/21/63. Ab. 7/1/63 - 11/1/63 (dated 1/6/64), POW cpd. at Droop Mtn.; had his own horse since 7/1/63. Ab. 11/1/63 - 2/29/64, cpd. Droop Mtn., 11/6/63. Cpd. Lewisburg, W. Va., 11/7/63. Confined at the Atheneum Prison, 11/20/63. Desc.: age 25, 5'6+", ruddy comp., brown hair and gray eyes. Occ. laborer, residing in New Orleans, La. Transf. to Camp Chase, 11/20/63. Confined at Camp Chase, 11/21/63. Desires to take the oath of allegiance, 6/10/64, stating he was a conscript. Ab. 2/29/64 - 8/31/64, cpd. Droop Mtn., 11/6/63. Took the oath of allegiance and was released, 3/23/65. Desc.: age 27, 5'7", dark comp., dark hair and blue eyes. NFR.

WEST, CHARLES N. (W.) - Sgt. Co. B. b.c. 1834. Not on muster rolls. Cpd., date and place not stated, and confined at Camp Chase. Took the oath of allegiance and was released, 3/18/65. Desc.: age 31, 5'10", dark comp., dark hair and brown eyes. Reference jacket in CSR shows service in Co. C, 46th Battn. Va. Cav. NFR.

WEST, WILLIAM M. - Pvt. Co. E. b. Harrison Co., W. Va., c. 1835. Enl. Bulltown, Braxton Co., W. Va., 5/10/63. Not stated if present or absent on muster-in roll dated 7/18/63. Present 1/1/64 - 8/31/64 (dated 1/6/65), entitled to $100 bond. Present 9/1/64 - 10/31/64 (dated 12/29/64), entitled to $100 bond. Cpd. Beverly, W. Va., 10/29/64. Confined at Clarksburg, W. Va. Desc.: age 29, 5'10", fair comp., auburn hair and blue eyes. Occ. farmer, residing in Harrison Co., W. Va. Transf. to Wheeling and confined at the Atheneum Prison, 11/2/64. Desc.: age 29, 5'10", fair comp., red hair and hazel eyes. Transf. to Camp Chase, 11/3/64. Confined at Camp Chase, 11/4/64. Took the oath of allegiance and was released, 5/11/65, ordered to report to Gov. Bowman at Wheeling, W. Va. Desc.: age 29, 5'10", florid comp., light hair and blue eyes, a resident of Harrison Co., W. Va. Age 45, farmer, Grant Dist., Harrison Co., W. Va. 1880 Census. NFR.

WEST, WILLIAM O. (C.) - Pvt. Co. E. b. Harrison Co., W. Va., c. 1845. Enl. Bulltown, Braxton Co., W. Va., 5/10/63. Not stated if present or absent on muster-in roll dated 7/18/63. Present 1/1/64 - 8/31/64 (dated 1/6/65), entitled to $100 bond. Present 9/1/64 - 10/31/64 (dated 12/29/64), entitled to $100 bond. Cpd. Beverly, W. Va., 10/29/64. Confined at Clarksburg, W. Va. Desc.: age 19, 5'8", dark comp., dark hair and blue eyes. Occ. farmer, residing in Harrison Co., W. Va. Transf. to Wheeling, W. Va. and confined at the Atheneum Prison, 11/2/64. Desc.: age 19, 5'7+", fair comp., dark hair and gray eyes. Transf. to Camp Chase, 11/3/64. Confined at Camp Chase, 11/4/64. DOD. Camp Chase, 12/1/64, typhoid maline. Bur. Camp Chase Confederate Cem., grave no. 541.

WESTFALL, HARRISON - Pvt. Co. C. b. 1814. Enl. Randolph Co., W. Va., 4/27/63. Not stated if present or absent on muster-in roll dated 8/63. Ab. 6/30/63 - 8/31/64 (dated 1/6/65), POW since 12/27/63; 6% bond due. Cpd. Pocahontas Co., W. Va., 12/26/63. Confined at the Atheneum Prison, 1/6/64. Desc.: age 21, 5'5", fair comp., dark hair, hazel eyes and dark whiskers. Occ. farmer, residing in Randolph Co., W. Va. Transf. to Camp Chase, 1/7/64. Confined at Camp Chase, 1/8/64. Transf. to Ft. Delaware, 3/14/64, violated his oath of allegiance. Confined at Ft. Delaware, 3/17/64. Ab. 9/1/64 - 10/31/64 (dated 12/30/64), POW since 12/27/63. Paroled 2/27/65 and was sent to City Point, to be exchanged. Exchanged. Adm. Gen. Hosp. No. 9, 3/2/65. Transf. to Howard's Grove Hosp., 3/3/65, paroled prisoner. Adm. Gen. Hosp. No. 9, 3/5/65. Transf. to Chimborazo Hosp., 3/6/65. Adm. Chimborazo Hosp. No. 2, 3/5/65, loss of sight in right eye. Furloughed 3/12/65, 30 days. Post war resident of Randolph Co., W. Va. d. 1865. Bur. Brick Church Cem., Huttonsville, W. Va.

WHEELER, JOHN H. - Pvt. Co. K. b.c. 1846. Enl. Warm Springs, 4/1/63, age 17. POW record shows enl. as Hampton, 5/61. Not stated if present or absent on muster-in roll dated 7/21/63. Present 7/1/63 - 11/1/63 (dated 1/6/64). Ab. 11/1/63 - 2/29/64, deserted 3/24/64. Ab. 2/29/64 - 8/31/64, cpd. in Md., 7/29/64. Clothing issued 2/29/64 and 3/23/64. Deserter. Gave himself up at Weaverton, Md., 8/7/64. Sent to Harpers Ferry, W. Va., then to Washington, DC, 8/17/64; wishes to take the oath of allegiance. Confined at Washington, DC. Took the oath of allegiance and was released, 8/18/64, and was sent to Philadelphia, Pa. Desc.: age 16(?), 5'4", florid comp., brown hair and hazel eyes, a resident of Hampton. NFR.

WHITE, ALEXANDER - Pvt. Co. H. Enl. Camp Miller, 11/8/63 (Camp Northwest, W. Va., 6/18/63). Ab. 10/31/63 - 8/31/64, transf. to another command, 2/64. Ab. 9/1/64 - 10/31/64 (dated 12/30/64), transf. to another command, 2/64. NFR.

WHITE, ASARIAH - Pvt. Co. C. b.c. 1840. Enl. Pocahontas Co., W. Va., 3/1/64. Present 6/30/63 - 8/31/64 (dated 1/6/65), enl.- bounty due; 6% bond due. Clothing issued 2/29/64, signs by x. Ab. 9/1/64 - 10/31/64 (dated 12/30/64), on horse detail; 6% bond due. Paroled at Staunton, 5/16/65. Desc.: age 25, 5'8", dark comp., dark hair and gray eyes. NFR.

WHITE, FREDERICK (FREDERIC) P. "Fred" - Pvt. Co. C. b.c. 1845. Age 15, farmer, Randolph Co., W. Va. 1860 Census. Enl. Randolph Co., W. Va., 4/28/63. Not stated if present or absent on muster-in roll dated 8/63. Present 6/30/63 - 8/31/64 (dated 1/6/65), 6% bond due. Ab. 9/1/64 - 10/31/64 (dated 12/30/64), sick; 6% bond due. Post war resident of Randolph Co., W. Va. d. by 1916. NFR.

WHITE, WARREN - 4th Corp. Co. G. Enl. Wood Co., W. Va., 6/24/63. Not stated if present or absent on muster-in roll dated 8/63, Pvt. Present, Pvt., 11/1/63 - 2/29/64. Clothing issued 2/29/64. Not stated if present or absent, 4th Corp., 7/1/64 - 8/31/64. Ab., 4th Corp., 9/1/64 - 10/31/64 (dated 12/30/64), deserted 10/1/64. Clothing issued 3rd Qr. 1864. Post war resident of Wood Co., W. Va. Age 44, farmer, Steele Dist., Wood Co., W. Va. 1880 Census. NFR.

WHITE, WILLIAM BAXTER - Pvt. Co. C. b. 8/14/45. Prior service, Co. A, 62nd Va. Mtd. Inf. Enl. Pocahontas Co., W. Va., 3/1/64. Present 6/30/63 - 8/31/64 (dated 1/6/65), 6% bond due; transf. from Co. A, 62nd Va. Inf., 4/1/64. Ab. 9/1/64 - 10/31/64 (dated 12/30/64), on horse detail; 6% bond due. Paroled at Staunton, 5/27/65, signs by x. Desc.: age 20, 5'2", fair comp., light hair and blue eyes. Post war resident of Randolph Co., W. Va. Bur. Huttonsville Cem., Randolph Co., W. Va. NFR.

WHITE, WILLIAM S. - Pvt. Co. A. b.c. 1844. Resident of Marion Co., W. Va. Enl. Pocahontas Co., W. Va., 4/6/63, age 19. Not stated if present or absent on muster-in roll dated 4/6/63. Present 7/1/63 - 9/1/63. Ab. 10/31/63 - 8/31/64, cpd. in Md., 7/13/64. Clothing issued 2/29/64. Cpd. Rockville, Md., 2/13/63. Wd. Rockville, Md., 7/13/64, head. Adm. Campbell USA Hosp., Washington, DC, 7/16/64, gunshot wd. to head, by minnie ball, age 18. Released and sent to the Old Capitol Prison, 7/19/64. Confined at the Old Capitol Prison, 7/19/64. Transf. to Elmira, NY, 7/23/64. Confined at Elmira Prison, 7/25/64. DOD. Elmira Prison, 10/2/64, typhoid fever. Bur. Elmira, NY, grave no. 529.

WIGAL, HENRY CLAYTON - Pvt. Co. G. b.c. 1847. Enl. Wood Co., W. Va., 6/24/63. Not stated if present or absent on muster-in roll dated 8/63. Present 11/1/63 - 2/29/64. Clothing issued 2/29/64 and 8/25/64. Present 7/1/64 - 8/31/64, had his own horse; entitled to bond. Ab. 9/1/64 - 10/31/64 (dated 12/29/64), on detached service; entitled to $100 bond. Cpd. Parkersburg, W. Va., 4/21/65. Confined at Clarksburg, W. Va., 4/22/65. Desc.: age 18, 5'9", fair comp., yellow hair and blue eyes. Occ. farmer, residing in Wood Co., W. Va. Paroled 4/24/65, to be exchanged, and was released. Post war resident of Wood Co., W. Va. Age 33, teaches school, Clay Dist., Wood Co., W. Va. 1880 Census. NFR.

WIGAL, JOHN M. - Pvt. Co. G. b. Wood Co., W. Va., 2/19/29. Enl. Wood Co., W. Va., 6/24/63. Not stated if present or absent on muster-in roll dated 8/63. Present 11/1/63 - 2/29/64. Clothing issued 2/29/64. Present 7/1/64 - 8/31/64, had his own horse; entitled to bond. Ab. 9/1/64 - 10/31/64 (dated 12/29/64), in hosp.; entitled to $100 bond. Returned to his home in Wood Co., W. Va., 2/14/65. Post war sketch states he enl. at Camp Northwest, on the Greenbrier River. Post war resident of Wood Co., W. Va. Post war farmer, and resident of Harris Dist., Wood Co., W. Va. d. Wood Co., W. Va., 11/8/87. Bur. Bethany Cem., Wood Co., W. Va.

WILEY, JAMES CRAWFORD "Uncle Jim" - Pvt. Co. D. b. Jackson River, Highland Co., 3/15/45. Prior service, Co. C, 46th Battn. Va. Cav. Enl. in the Valley of Va., 6/1/64. POW record shows enl. as Highland Co., 6/63. Not stated if present or absent on 12/31/63 8/31/64 (dated 1/6/65). Ab. 9/1/64 - 10/31/64, AWOL. Deserted. Reported at Beverly, W. Va., 12/28/64. Confined at Clarksburg, W. Va. Desc.: age 16, 5'7", dark comp., black hair and gray eyes. Occ. farmer, residing in Highland Co. Took the oath of allegiance and was released, 12/31/64. Post war rosters show he was in a hospital at the time of the surrender. Post war roster shows he served as a courier for William L. Jackson, and rode a small brown mare. CSR listed as James D. Wiley. Post war account says he was wd. 5 times. Moved to Bartow, Pocahontas Co., W. Va., 1905. Then to Thornwood, remained there until 1925. Moved to Durbin, W. Va., then back to Bartow. Post war resident of Thornwood, W. Va., 1924. d. Traveler's Repose, W. Va., 9/15/1927, age 82 years, 6 months. Bur. Monterey Cem.

WILEY, OSCAR T. - Pvt. Co. C. b. Highland Co., 11/21/46. Enl. Pocahontas Co., W. Va., 1/1/64. POW record shows enl. as Highland Co., 4/64. Present 6/30/63 - 8/31/64 (dated 1/6/65), enl. bounty due. Ab. 9/1/64 - 10/31/64 (dated 1/6/65), sick. Deserted. Reported at Beverly, W. Va., 12/28/64. Confined at Clarksburg, W. Va. Desc.: age 15(?), 5'7", fair comp., dark hair and dark eyes. Occ. farmer, residing in Highland Co. Took the oath of allegiance and was released, 12/31/64. Post war resident of Highland Co. d. 8/17/1927. Bur. Old Terry Family Cem., Highland Co.

WILFONG, JOHN E. - Pvt. Co. E. Enl. Camp Clover Lick, 7/11/63. Not stated if present or absent on muster-in roll dated 7/18/63. NFR.

WILLIAMS, JOHN S. - Pvt. Co. D. Enl. Hightown, Highland Co., 7/15/63. Not stated if present or absent on muster-in roll dated 8/63. Post war roster shows he was wd. during the war. Post war resident of Fort Seybert, Pendleton Co., W. Va. W. Va. NFR.

WILLIAMS, JOHN W. - Pvt. Co. K. b.c. 1840. Enl. Warm Springs, 4/1/64, age 24. Not stated if present or absent on muster-in roll dated 7/21/63. Ab. 7/1/63 - 11/1/63 (dated 1/6/64), transf. to Walker's Battn. (Co. A, 47th Battn. Va. Cav.). NFR.

WILLIAMS, P. D. - Pvt. Co. K. b.c. 1834. Enl. Camp Northwest, W. Va., 6/1/63, age 29. Not stated if present or absent on muster-in roll dated 7/21/63. Ab. 7/1/63 - 11/1/63 (dated 1/6/64), detailed at Niter works. Ab. 11/1/63 - 2/29/64, AWOL. Ab. 2/29/64 - 8/31/64, detailed at Niter works and failed to report. NFR.

WILLIAMS, PASCHAL D. (B.) - Pvt. Co. D. b.c. 1822. Enl. Hightown, Highland Co., 7/15/63. Present 7/1/63 - 1/1/64 (dated 1/1/64). Not stated if present or absent 12/31/63 - 8/31/64 (dated 1/6/65). Ab. 9/1/64 - 10/31/64, AWOL. Paroled at Staunton, 5/22/65. Desc.: age 43, 5'10+", fair comp., black hair and blue eyes. NFR.

WILLIAMS, RICHARD - Pvt. Co. F. Enl. Camp Northwest (Camp Miller), W. Va., 7/19/63. Not stated if present or absent on muster-in roll dated 7/20/63. Ab. 7/1/63 - 8/31/64 (dated 1/6/65), transf. to Co. A, 19th Va. Cav. Ab. 9/1/64 - 10/31/64 (dated 12/30/64), transf. to Co. A, 19th Va. Cav. NFR.

WILLIAMS, THOMAS J. - Pvt. Co. D. b. Highland Co., c. 1839. Age 21, farmhand, Wilsonville, Highland Co. 1860 Census. Prior service, 2nd Co. B, 31st Va. Inf. Enl. Hightown, Highland Co., 7/15/63. Not stated if present or absent on muster-in roll dated 8/63. Post war rosters show service in Co. G. NFR.

WILMOTH, SAMUEL J. - Pvt. Co. C. 2/24/26. Post war rosters only, which show him as a resident of Randolph Co., W. Va. Age 54, farmer, New Interest, Randolph Co., W. Va. 1880 Census. d. 6/1/1900. Bur. Israel Cem., Kerens, W. Va.

WILSON, ELI J. - 1st Sgt. Co. D. b.c. 1845. Enl. Huntersville, W. Va., 6/1/63. Not stated if present or absent on muster-in roll dated 8/63, Pvt. Present, 1st Corp., 7/1/63 - 1/1/64 (dated 1/1/64), had his own horse. Present, 1st Corp., 12/31/63 - 8/31/64 (dated 1/6/65). Present 9/1/64 - 10/31/64, entitled to $100 enl. bounty. Paroled at Staunton, 5/25/65, listed as 1st Sgt. Desc.: age 20, 5'9", fair comp., light hair and gray eyes. NFR.

WILSON, GEORGE R. - Pvt. Co. B. b.c. 1843. Enl. Camp Northwest, W. Va., 5/24/63 (5/15/63). Not stated if present or absent on muster-in roll dated 7/25/63. Present 11/1/63 - 8/31/64 (dated 1/6/65), detailed as Blacksmith. Employed as a teamster at Warm Springs, 1/64. Employed as a blacksmith at Warm Springs, 2/64. Clothing issued 1/17/64, detailed as blacksmith and 2/29/64. Present 9/1/64 - 10/31/64 (dated 12/30/64), detailed as Blacksmith; entitled to $100 bond. Post war resident of Monongalia Co., W. Va. Age 37, farmer, Grant Dist., Monongalia Co., W. Va. 1880 Census. NFR.

WILSON, GEORGE W. - 4th Corp. Co. A. b. 1841. Enl. Highland Co., 11/4/62, age 19. Not stated if present or absent on muster-in roll dated 11/4/62, 4th Corp. Present, 4th Corp., 7/1/63 - 9/1/63. Present, 4th Corp., 10/31/63 - 8/31/64. Clothing issued 3/?/64. Paroled at Winchester, 5/10/65. Desc.: age 21, 5'9", light comp., dark hair and gray eyes, a resident of Monongalia Co., W. Va. Post war rosters show he carried a dispatch from Gen. Breckenridge to Gen. Rhodes, around Ft. Lincoln, near Washington, DC after 12 men had been killed trying to do so. Post war resident of Monongalia Co., W. Va. Post war rosters show him as Sgt. d. 1930. Bur. East Oak Grove Cem., Monongalia Co., W. Va.

WILSON, HENRY P. - Pvt. Co. B. b.c. 1845. Enl. Marion Co., W. Va., 2/17/63 (Monongalia Co., W. Va., 2/14/63). Not stated if present or absent on muster-in roll dated 7/25/63. Present 11/1/63 8/31/64 (dated 1/6/65). RTD from furlough to the Northwest 3/23/64, brought in 6 recruits. Present 9/1/64 - 10/31/64 (dated 12/30/64), entitled to $100 bond. Post war rosters show him as a Corp. Post war resident of Monongalia Co., W. Va. Age 35, farmer, Clay Dist., Monongalia Co., W. Va. 1880 Census. NFR.

WILSON (WILLISON), JAMES - 3rd Corp. Co. K. b.c. 1845. Enl. Camp Northwest, W. Va., 6/21/63 (6/19/63), age 18. Not stated if present or absent muster-in roll dated 7/21/63, Pvt. Present, Pvt., 7/1/63 - 11/1/63 (dated 1/6/64). Present, 4th Corp., 11/1/63 2/29/64, promoted 4th Corp., 1/1/64. Clothing issued 2/29/64. Ab., 3rd Corp., 2/29/64 - 8/31/64, AWOL. NFR.

WILSON, JOHN - 4th Sgt. Co. K. b.c. 1839. Enl. Camp Northwest, W. Va., 5/10/63 (5/1/63), age 24. Not stated if present or absent muster-in roll dated 7/21/63, 3rd Corp. Present, 2nd Corp., 7/1/63 - 11/1/63 (dated 1/6/64), promoted 2nd Corp., 8/1/63. Present, 1st Corp., 11/1/63 - 2/29/64, promoted 1st Corp., 1/1/64; had his own horse since 7/14/64. Clothing issued 2/29/64 and 3/23/64. Ab., 4th Sgt., 2/29/64 - 8/31/64, had his own horse since 7/1/64; missing since the Beverly, W. Va. fight; $100 enl. bounty due. NFR.

WILSON, JOHN R. - Pvt. Co. B. Enl. Marion (Monongalia) Co., W. Va., 2/17/63. Not stated if present or absent on muster-in roll dated 7/25/63. Present 11/1/63 - 8/31/64 (dated 1/6/65). Present 9/1/64 - 10/31/64 (dated 12/30/64), entitled to $100 bond. Post war resident of Monongalia Co., W. Va. NFR.

WILSON, JOSEPH - 2nd Sgt. Co. H. Prior service, 19th Va. Cav. Enl. Camp Northwest, W. Va., 6/1/63. Not stated if present or absent on muster-in roll dated 8/63, Pvt. Ab., 2nd Sgt., 10/31/63 8/31/64, in hands of the enemy. Ab., 2nd Sgt., 9/1/64 - 10/31/64 (dated 12/30/64), prisoner in hands of enemy; cpd. 10/63. No POW records. NFR.

WILSON, MARTIN M. - 2nd Lt. Co. D. b.c. 1843. Enl. Weston, W. Va., 5/1/63. Not stated if present or absent on muster-in roll dated 8/63, 4th Corp. Present, 3rd Corp., 7/1/63 - 1/1/64 (dated 1/1/64), had his own horse. Present, 3rd Corp., 12/31/63 - 8/31/64 (dated 1/6/65). Present, 3rd Corp., 9/1/64 - 10/31/64, entitled to $100 enl. bounty. Paroled at Staunton, 5/25/65, as 2nd Lt. Desc.: age 22, 6', fair comp., black hair and gray eyes. Post war rosters show him as N. M. Wilson, Sgt. Co. D. Post war resident of Buckhannon, W. Va. Bur. Heavener Cem., Buckhannon, W. Va.

WILSON, O. A. (A. O.) - Pvt. Co. A. b.c. 1843. Enl. Monongalia Co., W. Va., 4/1/64. Present 10/31/63 - 8/31/64, $50 enl. bounty due. Paroled at Winchester, 5/10/65. Desc.: age 22, 5'10", light comp., auburn hair and hazel eyes, a resident of Monongalia Co., W. Va. Post war resident of Monongalia Co., W. Va. Moved to Bates Co., Mo. Constable. Killed by a man named "Hardy" who was one of the Jesse James gang, while attempting to arrest him.

WILSON, ROBERT - Pvt. Co. H. b. Marion (Monongalia) Co., W. Va., 9/15/39. Age 21, Calhoun Co., W. Va. 1860 Census. Enl. Camp Northwest, W. Va., 6/1/63. Not stated if present or absent on muster-in roll dated 8/63. Served in Co. A, 19th Va. Cav. Age 40, farmer, Center Dist., Calhoun Co., W. Va. 1880 Census. Brother of William C. Wilson. d. 4/26/1916. Bur. Broomstick Cem., Calhoun Co., W. Va.

WILSON, WILLIAM C. - 2nd Lt. Co. H. b. Monongalia (Roane) Co., W. Va. 2/17/37. Age 24, Calhoun Co., W. Va. Enl. Camp Northwest, W. Va., 6/1/63. Elected 2nd Lt., 6/4/63. Not stated if present or absent on muster-in roll dated 8/63, 2nd Lt. Present, 2nd Lt., 10/31/63 - 8/31/64. Present, 2nd Lt., 9/1/64 - 10/31/64 (dated 12/30/64), entitled to $100 bond. Ab. 10/25/64, sick in hosp., 7 days. Served in Co. A, 19th Va. Cav. Age 43, farmer, Sheridan Dist., Calhoun Co., W. Va. 1880 Census. Brother of Robert Wilson. d. 9/19/1908. Bur Prosperity-Saunders Cem., Calhoun Co., W. Va.

WISE, RANDOLPH - Pvt. Co. C. b.c. 1843. Age 17, laborer, Randolph Co., W. Va. 1860 Census. Enl. Randolph Co., W. Va., 11/12/63. Ab. 6/30/63 - 8/31/64 (dated 1/6/65), POW since 7/11/64; enl. bounty due; 6% bond due. Clothing issued 3/20/64, signs by x. Cpd. Craigsville, Md., 7/11/64. Confined at the Old Capitol Prison, 7/12/64. Transf. to Elmira, NY, 7/23/64. Confined at Elmira Prison, 7/25/64. Ab. 9/1/64 - 10/31/64 (dated 12/30/64), POW since 7/10/64. Desires to take the oath of allegiance, 9/30/64. Paroled 3/14/65 and sent to the James River, to be exchanged, signs by x. Exchanged at Boulware's Wharf, James River, 3/?/65. Cpd. Beverly, W. Va., 5/18/65. Confined at Clarksburg, W. Va., 5/21/65. Paroled 5/22/65, to be exchanged, and was released, signs parole by x. Desc.: age 21, 6', florid comp., dark hair and blue eyes. Occ. farmer, residing in Randolph Co., W. Va. CSR shows service in Co. E. Age 36, Huttonsville, Randolph Co., W. Va. 1880 Census. NFR.

WISEMAN, JOSIAH - Pvt. Co. B. Post war rosters only, which show he was cpd., date and place not stated, and confined at Camp Chase. NFR.

WITHEROE (WITHROW), WILLIAM - Pvt. Co. K. b.c. 1838. Enl. Camp Northwest, W. Va., 6/18/63, age 25. Not stated if present or absent on muster-in roll dated 7/21/63. Ab. 7/1/63 - 11/1/63 (dated 1/6/64), AWOL. Ab. 11/1/63 - 2/29/64, AWOL. Ab. 2/29/64 - 8/31/64, AWOL. NFR.

WOLF, NEWTON J. - Pvt. Co. E. b.c. 1844. Enl. Bulltown, W. Va., 5/10/63. Not stated if present or absent on muster-in roll dated 7/18/63. Present 1/1/64 - 8/31/64 (dated 1/6/65), entitled to $100 bond. Present 9/1/64 - 10/31/64 (dated 12/29/64), entitled to $100 bond. Cpd. Harrisonburg, 9/25/64. Adm. Sheridan Depot Field Hosp., Winchester, 10/6/64, typhoid fever. Transf. to Gen. Hosp. at Martinsburg, W. Va., 10/12/64. Adm. USA Gen. Hosp., West's Building, Baltimore, Md., 10/13/64, convalescent from febris intermitten, age 20. Transf. to Gen. Hosp., 10/25/64 at Pt. Lookout. Confined at Pt. Lookout, 10/26/64. Paroled 10/30/64, to be exchanged. Exchanged at Venus Point, Savannah River, Ga., 11/15/64. Clothing issued 11/18/64, paroled prisoner. NFR.

WOOD, THOMAS K. - 2nd Sgt. Co. E. Enl. Bulltown, W. Va., 5/10/63. Not stated if present or absent on muster-in roll dated 7/18/63, 2nd Sgt. Ab., 2nd Sgt., 1/1/64 - 8/31/64 (dated 1/6/65), cpd. Harrison Co., W. Va., 8/1/63. Gave himself up at Clarksburg, 8/?/63. Confined at the Atheneum Prison, 8/9/63. Desc.: age 21, 5'11", florid comp., dark hair and dark eyes. Occ. farmer, residing in Harrison Co., W. Va. Transf. to Camp Chase, 8/11/63. Confined at Camp Chase, 8/12/63. Transf. to Ft. Delaware, 2/29/64. Confined at Ft. Delaware, 3/4/64 (3/2/64). Ab., 2nd Sgt., 9/1/64 - 10/31/64 (dated 12/29/64), cpd. 9/1/64. Took the oath of allegiance and was released, 5/15/65. Desc.: age ?, 5'11", fair comp., brown hair and hazel eyes, a resident of Clarksburg, W. Va. NFR.

WOODELL (WOODDELL), WILLIAM P. H. - Pvt. Co. E. Enl. Camp Clover Lick, 7/11/63. Not stated if present or absent on muster-in roll dated 7/18/63. Served in the 19th Va. Cav. NFR.

WOODLEY, WILLIS H. - Pvt. Co. D. b. 1843. Prior service, 25th Va. Inf. Enl. Camp Willy, 8/16/63. Present 7/1/63 - 1/1/64 (dated 1/1/64), member of the legislature. Ab. 12/31/63 - 8/31/64 (dated 1/6/65), member of the legislature. Clothing issued 1/13/

64 and 3/1/64. Ab. 9/1/64 - 10/31/64, member of the House of Delegates. Paroled at Ashland, 4/27/65, residence listed as Albemarle Co. d. 1929. Bur. Beverly Cem., Beverly, W. Va.

WOODS, JAMES M. - Pvt. Co. C. b. Highland Co., c. 1835. Age 25, farmer, Meadow Dale, Highland Co. 1860 Census. Enl. Highland Co., 7/1/64. Ab. 6/30/63 - 8/31/64 (dated 1/6/65), on detached service; enl. bounty due. Ab. 9/1/64 - 10/31/64 (dated 12/30/64), on detached service. NFR.

WOODS, PETER WESLEY - Pvt. Co. C. b. Mill Gap, Highland Co., 7/18/45. Enl. Highland Co., 6/27/63. POW record shows enl. as Pocahontas Co., W. Va., 8/62. Not stated if present or absent on muster-in roll dated 8/63. Present 6/30/63 - 8/31/64 (dated 1/6/65). Clothing issued 5/10/64. Deserted. Cpd. Beverly, W. Va., 8/7/64. Confined at Clarksburg, W. Va. Ab. 9/1/64 - 10/31/64 (dated 12/30/64), deserted 10/1/64; 6% bond due. Took the oath of allegiance and was released, 11/13/64. Desc.: age 20, 5'11+", gray comp., light hair and hazel eyes. Occ. farmer, residing in Highland Co. Post war farmer and resident of Mill Gap, Highland Co. d. Blue Grass, 4/15/1913 (4/24/1913). Bur. Green Hill Methodist Church Cem., Highland.

WOODS (WOOD), THOMAS J. - Pvt. Co. A. b. Highland Co., c. 1832. Age 28, farmhand, Meadow Dale, Highland Co. 1860 Census. Enl. Highland Co., 3/30/63. Not stated if present or absent on muster-in roll dated 3/30/63. Present 7/1/63 - 9/1/63. Ab. 10/31/63 - 8/31/64, cpd. 8/20/63. Cpd. Highland Co., 8/20/63. Confined at the Atheneum Prison, 8/30/63. Desc.: age 21 (?), 5'11", florid comp., dark hair and gray eyes. Occ. farmer, residing in Highland Co. Transf. to Camp Chase, 8/31/63. Confined at Camp Chase, 9/1/63. Transf. to Rock Island, Ill., 1/22/64. Confined at Rock Island Prison, 1/24/64. Transf. for exchange 2/15/64. Exchanged. Paroled at Staunton, 5/23/65. Desc.: age 32 (?), 5'11", dark comp., brown hair and blue eyes. Post war resident of Highland Co. NFR.

WOODYARD, JOHN PRESLEY (PRESLY) - 3rd Lt. Co. G. b. Ripley, Jackson Co., W. Va., 3/28/40. Farmer and miller, Wood Co., W. Va. Went south in company with Tom Stinchcomb to join the army. Enl. Belleville, Wood Co., W. Va., 6/24/63. Not stated if present or absent on muster-in roll dated 8/63, Pvt. Present, Pvt., 11/1/63 - 2/29/64. Clothing issued 2/29/64. Present, Pvt., 7/1/64 - 8/31/64, had his own horse; entitled to bond. Ab., Pvt., 9/1/64 - 10/31/64 (dated 12/29/64), in hosp.; entitled to $100 bond. Breveted Lieut. 5/4/65, for good conduct. Paroled at Staunton, 5/11/65, as 3rd Lt. Desc.: age 25, 5'10", fair comp., sandy hair and hazel eyes. Post war resident of Mo., Ks. and was a pensioner, residing at Garfield, Benton Co., Ark., 1908.

WREN, ALVERTON C. - 4th Sgt. Co. I. b.c. 1846. Enl. Camp Northwest, W. Va., 6/20/63, age 17. Not stated if present or absent on muster-in roll dated 5/5/63. NFR.

WRIGHT, DAVID - Pvt. Co. H. b. Barbour Co., W. Va., c. 1841. Enl. Camp Northwest, W. Va., 7/1/63 (6/28/63). Not stated if present or absent on muster-in roll dated 8/63. Ab. 10/31/63 - 8/31/64, in hands of enemy. Cpd. Ritchie Co., W. Va., 10/20/63. Confined at the Atheneum Prison, 10/24/63. Desc.: age 22, 5'9+", florid comp., brown hair and blue eyes. Occ. farmer, residing in Ritchie Co., W. Va. Transf. to Camp Chase, 10/26/63. Confined at Camp Chase, 10/27/63. Transf. to Rock Island, Ill., 1/22/64. Confined at Rock Island Prison, 1/24/64. Desires to take the oath of allegiance and go home, 3/18/64. Ab. 9/1/64 - 10/31/64 (dated 12/30/64), prisoner, cpd. 10/63. d. in the barracks, Rock Island Prison, 6/15/64. Bur. Rock Island, Ill., grave no. 1239. Brother of Lloyd and Zachariah Wright.

WRIGHT, LLOYD (LOYD, LOID) - Pvt. Co. H. b. Ritchie Co., W. Va., 5/22/44. Enl. Camp Northwest, W. Va., 7/1/63 (6/28/63). Not stated if present or absent on muster-in roll dated 8/63. Present 10/31/63 - 8/31/64. Ab. 9/1/64 - 10/31/64 (dated 12/30/64), in hosp.; entitled to $100 bond. Paroled at Charleston, W. Va., 5/10/65, signs by x. Desc.: age 20, 5'10", dark comp., black hair and blue eyes. Post war farmhand and resident of Ritchie Co., W. Va. Brother of David and Zachariah Wright. Age 35, farmer, East Union Dist., Ritchie Co., W. Va. 1880 Census. NFR.

WRIGHT, ZACHARIAH - Pvt. Co. H. b. Barbour Co., W. Va., 4/30/39. Enl. Camp Northwest, W. Va., 7/1/63 (6/28/63). POW record shows enl. as Pocahontas Co., W. Va., 6/63. Not stated if present or absent on muster-in roll dated 8/63. Ab. 10/31/63 - 8/31/64, AWOL since 5/31/64. Clothing issued 2/29/64. Ab. 9/1/64 10/31/64 (dated 12/30/64), AWOL. Cpd. Bone Creek, Ritchie Co., W. Va., 1/15/65, as a member of Co. E. Confined at Clarksburg, W. Va., 1/17/65. Took the oath of allegiance and was released, 1/17/65. Desc.: age 27, 5'5", dark comp., brown hair and blue eyes. Occ. farmer, residing in Ritchie Co., W. Va. Brother of David and Lloyd Wright. Post war farmer and resident of Ritchie Co., W. Va. Age 42, farmer, East Union Dist., Ritchie Co., W. Va. 1880 Census. d. 3/1/1915. Bur. Dunkard Cem., Racket, Ritchie Co., W. Va.

YEAGER, PETER DILLEY - Pvt. Co. E. b. Pocahontas Co., W. Va., 1831. Age 29, farmer, Traveler's Repose, Pocahontas Co., W. Va. 1860 Census. Enl. Camp Clover Lick, 7/11/63. Not stated if present or absent on muster-in roll dated 7/18/63. Served in Co. F, 19th Va. Cav. Post war farmer and hotel owner. Age 49, farmer, Green Banks, Pocahontas Co., W. Va. 1880 Census. Member of Pocahontas Co. Board of Education, 24 years. Postmaster, Traveler's Repose (Bartow), W. Va., 52 years. NFR.

YOKE, WILLIAM - Pvt. Co. D. Enl. Oakland Depot, Alleghany Co., 4/1/64. Ab. 12/31/63 - 8/31/64 (dated 1/6/65), drowned in Potts Creek, 5/14/64. Ab. 9/1/64 - 10/31/64, deceased.

YOKUM (YERKAM, YOLKAM, YOAKUM), JACOB Jr. - Pvt. Co. C. b.c. 1833. Age 27, farmer, Randolph Co., W. Va. 1860 Census. Enl. Randolph Co., W. Va., 5/6/63. Not stated if present or absent on muster-in roll dated 8/63. Ab. 6/30/63 - 8/31/64 (dated 1/6/65), inside enemy lines, never reported. CSR as Yerkham. Age 49, farmer, Valley Bend, Randolph Co., W. Va. 1880 Census. Bur. Warnsley Cem., Randolph Co., W. Va. NFR.

YOKUM, (YERKHAM, YOLKAM, YOAKUM), WASHINGTON - Pvt. Co. C. b.c. 1828. Age 23(?), Randolph Co., W. Va. 1860 Census. Enl. Beverly, W. Va., 5/6/63. Not stated if present or absent on muster-in roll dated 8/63. Ab. 6/30/63 - 8/31/64 (dated 1/6/65), inside enemy lines, never reported. CSR as Yerkham. Age 53, farmer, Valley Bend, Randolph Co., W. Va. 1880 Census. NFR.

YOST, JEHU - Pvt. Co. A. Post war rosters only. NFR.

YOST, TITUS - Pvt. Co. A. Post war rosters only, which show he was a resident of Marion Co., W. Va. NFR.

YOUNG, AARON BELL - 2nd Lt. Co. F. b. Gnatty Creek, Peel Tree, Harrison Co., W. Va., 4/22/32. Prior service, Co. C, 31st Va. Inf. Family lore states that he "stole" Little Sorrel for his friend, Maj. Gen. Thomas J. "Stonewall" Jackson. Enl. Bulltown, W. Va., 5/10/63. Elected 2nd Lt., Co. F, 20th Va. Cav., 5/10/63. Not stated if present or absent on muster-in roll dated 7/20/63, 2nd Lt. Present, 2nd Lt., 7/1/63 - 8/31/64 (dated 1/6/65). Present, 2nd Lt., 9/1/64 - 10/31/64 (dated 12/30/64). Pardoned by Pres. Andrew Johnson, 10/9/65. Post war farmer in Lewis, Gilmer and Wirt Co's., W. Va. Moved from Lewis Co., W. Va. to Troy Dist., Gilmer Co., W. Va., 1869. Had 6 children by his first wife, then married a widow with one child, and had 15 more by her, reared 22 children. Age 48, farmer, Troy Dist., Gilmer Co., W. Va. 1880 Census. Assessor in Gilmer Co., W. Va., 1896. Moved to Wirt Co., W. Va., 1902. Co. Commissioner, Wirt Co., W. Va. Referred to as "Capt." after the war. d. Wirt Co., W. Va., 3/15/1915. Bur. Pisgah Church Cem., near Palestine, W. Va. Brother of Granville and James N. Young.

YOUNG, GRANVILLE - Pvt. Co. F. b. 1/25/39. Enl. Camp Clover Lick, 7/11/63. Not stated if present or absent on muster-in roll dated 7/20/63. Ab. 7/1/63 - 8/31/64 (dated 1/6/65), prisoner since 7/13/63. Ab. 9/1/64 - 10/31/64 (dated 12/30/64), prisoner since 7/13/63. Moved to Gilmer Co., W. Va. Post war farmer, Big Cove Creek, Gilmer Co., W. Va. Brother of Aaron B. and James N. Young. Age 33, farmer, Troy, Gilmer Co., W. Va. 1880 Census. d. Gilmer Co., W. Va., 1926. Bur. Upper Big Run Cem., near Troy, Gilmer Co., W. Va.

YOUNG, JAMES NEAL - Pvt. Co. F. b. 3/1/41. Resident of Harrison Co., W. Va., 1850, age 10. Enl. Bulltown, W. Va., 5/10/63. Not stated if present or absent on muster-in roll dated 7/20/63 (7/27/63). Present 7/1/63 - 8/31/64 (dated 1/6/65), had his own horse; entitled to enl. bounty. Adm. Gen. Hosp., Winchester, 7/28/64, dysenteria. Transf. to Gen. Hosp., 8/7/64. Present 9/1/64 - 10/31/64 (dated 12/30/64), entitled to enl. bounty. Adm. CSA Gen. Hosp., Charlottesville, 9/1/64, chronic bronchitis. Transf. to Lynchburg, 9/26/64. d. 1/31/66.

YOUNG, JOHN W. - Capt. Co. E. b. Clarksburg, W. Va., 11/19/26. Resident of Harrison Co., W. Va. No enl. data. Appointed Capt., 5/10/63, confirmed by election. Present muster-in roll dated 7/18/63, commanding Co. Wd. Droop Mtn., W. Va., 11/6/63, while leading his co. in a charge. DOW. Lewisburg, W. Va., 11/7/63. Bur. Lewisburg, W. Va. Post war rosters show him as Capt. of Co. D. Called "brave and gallant" by Lt. Col. W. P. Thompson in his report of the battle of Droop Mtn., W. Va., 11/6/63. In Vol. 6, Bath Co. Will Book, there is a list and appraisal of his personal property, which included the following: 1 pair pistols with holsters - $50; Uniform coat and pants - $250; 1 halter and bridle rein - $8; 1 saddle - $40; and noted that one horse died prior to the inventory being taken on 1/16/64.

YOUST (YOST), AARON - Pvt. Co. A. b.c. 1825. Enl. Pocahontas (Monongalia) Co., W. Va., 4/1/63, age 38. Not stated if present or absent muster-in roll dated 4/1/63. Present 7/1/63 - 9/1/63. Ab. 10/31/63 - 8/31/64, deserted 11/4/63. NFR.

YOUST (YOST), FRANCIS MARION - Pvt. Co. A. b.c. 1836. Resident of Marion Co., W. Va. Arrested and confined at Wheeling, W. Va. Released on his oath by 3/13/62. Enl. Pocahontas Co., W. Va., 5/1/63, age 27 (Marion Co., W. Va., 5/4/63). Not stated if present or absent on muster-in roll dated 5/1/63. Present 7/1/63 - 9/1/63. Ab. 10/31/63 - 8/31/64, transf. to Co. B, 4/18/64. Ab., Co. B, 11/1/63 - 8/31/64 (dated 1/6/65), AWOL since 2/64. Ab., Co. B, 9/1/64 - 10/31/64 (dated 12/30/64), AWOL since 2/64. Cpd. Monongalia Co., W. Va., 4/16/64. Sent to Cumberland, Md., then to Wheeling, W. Va. Confined at the Atheneum Prison, 4/16/64. Desc.: age 27, 5'6+", florid comp., light hair and blue eyes. Occ. blacksmith, residing in Marion Co., W. Va. Transf. to Camp Chase, 2/7/65. Confined at Camp Chase, 2/8/65. DOD. Camp Chase, 3/16/65, dysenteria. Bur. Camp Chase Confederate Cem., grave no. 1678.

YOUST (YOST), JACOB - 1st Sgt. Co. A. b.c. 1829. Enl. Highland Co., 11/6/62, age 33. Not stated if present or absent on muster-in roll dated 11/6/62, 3rd Sgt. Cpd. near Grafton, W. Va., 5/17/63. Confined at Ft. McHenry. Paroled and sent to Ft. Monroe, 5/20/63, to be exchanged. Exchanged. Cpd. Preston Co., 7/11/63, listed as a member of Capt. Evans Co., 19th Va. Cav. Confined at the Atheneum Prison, 7/14/63. Desc.: age 44(?), 5'4", fresh comp., dark hair and blue eyes. Occ. farmer, residing in Marion Co., W. Va. Was sent to Fairmont, W. Va. for trial, 7/28/63. Present, 3rd Sgt., 7/1/63 - 9/1/63. Not stated if present or absent, 1st Sgt., 10/31/63 - 8/31/64, was ordered to appear before an examining board at Richmond, 9/1/64, not heard from since. RTD from a furlough to the Northwest, 4/23/64, bringing a "very beautiful flag" for the 20th Va. Cav. from the ladies of Marion Co., W. Va. "Did his duty." NFR.

YOUST (YOST, YOUNT), JAMES Jr. - Pvt. Co. A. b.c. 1838. Enl. Lewis Co., W. Va., 5/4/63. Not stated if present or absent muster-in roll dated 5/4/63. Present 7/1/63 - 9/1/63. Ab. 10/31/63 - 8/31/64, deserted 9/16/63. Cpd. Monongalia Co., W. Va., 5/26/64, charged with being a robber. Confined at the Atheneum Prison, 5/28/64. Desc.: age 26, 5'8", fair comp., light hair and gray eyes. Occ. farmer, residing in Marion Co., W. Va. Transf. to Camp Chase, 12/27/64. Confined at Camp Chase, 12/28/64, robber cpd. within our [Federal] lines. Took the oath of allegiance and was released, 6/11/65. Desc.: age 28, 5'8", fair comp., light hair and blue eyes, a resident of Marion Co., W. Va. NFR.

YOUST (YOST), JOHN - Pvt. Co. A. Enl. Marion Co., W. Va., 5/18/63. Present 10/31/63 - 8/31/64. Employed as a teamster at Warm Springs, 1/64. Clothing issued 3/64. Cpd. 4/2/65, place not stated. Confined at the Atheneum Prison, 4/3/65. Took the oath of allegiance at Clarksburg, W. Va. Resident of Marion Co., W. Va. NFR.

YOUST (YOST), LAMECH - Pvt. Co. A. Enl. Marion Co., W. Va., 2/13/64. Ab. 10/31/63 - 8/31/64, AWOL since 8/28/64. NFR.

YOUST (YOST), MATHIAS (MATHEW) D. - Pvt. Co. A. b.c. 1833. Enl. Pocahontas Co., W. Va., 6/10/63 (11/10/63). Not stated if present or absent on muster-in roll dated 6/10/63. Present 7/1/63 9/1/63. Ab. 10/31/63 - 8/31/64, deserted 6/20/64. Cpd. Marion Co., W. Va., 11/16/63. Confined at the Atheneum Prison, 11/22/63. Desc.: age 33, 5'8,", dark hair, brown hair and gray eyes, a resident of Marion Co., W. Va. Transf. to Camp Chase, 2/9/64. Confined at Camp Chase, 2/10/64. Desires to take the oath of allegiance, 6/10/64, stating he was a conscript and deserter. Took the oath of allegiance and was released, 6/12/65. Desc.: age 33, 5'8", dark comp., dark hair and gray eyes, a resident of Marion Co., W. Va. NFR.

YOUST, PERMENEUS W. (H.) - Pvt. Co. B. b.c. 1846. Enl. Marion Co., W. Va., 2/1/64. Present 11/1/63 - 8/31/64 (dated 1/6/65), entitled to enl. bounty. Present 9/1/64 - 10/31/64 (dated 12/30/64), entitled to enl. bounty; entitled to $100 bond. Clothing issued 9/2/64. Surrendered at Beverly, W. Va., 5/10/65. Confined at Clarksburg, W. Va., 5/13/65. Paroled 5/14/65, to be exchanged, and was released. Desc.: age 19, 5'9", fair comp., light hair and blue eyes. Post war resident of Marion Co. NFR.

YOUST (YOST), SAMUEL B. - Pvt. Co. A. Enl. Camp Northwest, W. Va., 6/10/63 (Monongalia Co., W. Va., 2/10/63). Not stated if present or absent on muster-in roll dated 7/25/63. Ab. 11/1/63 - 8/31/64 (dated 1/6/65), AWOL since 2/64. Clothing issued 3/31/64. Ab. 9/1/64 - 10/31/64 (dated 12/30/64), AWOL since 2/64. NFR.

YOUST, WESLEY - Pvt. Co. B. Not on muster rolls. Clothing issued 11/12/64, on the way to his command. NFR.

YOUST (YOST), WILLIAM Jr. - Pvt. Co. B. b.c. 1845. Enl. Camp Northwest, W. Va., 6/10/63. Not stated if present or absent on muster-in roll dated 7/25/63. Present 11/1/63 - 8/31/64 (dated 1/6/65). Clothing issued 3/1/64 and 3rd Qr. 1864. Present 9/1/64 10/31/64 (dated 12/30/64), entitled to $100 bond. Surrendered at Beverly, W. Va., 5/10/65. Confined at Clarksburg, W Va., 5/13/65. Paroled 5/14/65, to be exchanged, and was released. Desc.: age 20, 5'9", fair comp., light hair and blue eyes. Occ. farmer, residing in Marion Co., W. Va. Post war resident of Marion Co., W. Va. NFR.

YOUST (YOST), WILLIAM M. - Pvt. Co. A. b.c. 1833. Enl. Highland Co., 11/6/62, age 29. Not stated if present or absent muster-in roll dated 11/6/62. Present 7/1/63 - 9/1/63. Ab. 10/31/63 - 8/31/64, deserted 10/26/64. Clothing issued 3/?/64. NFR.

BIBLIOGRAPHY
19TH AND 20TH VIRGINIA CAVALRY

Manuscripts

Carrier Library, James Madison University, Harrisonburg, Va.
　George W. Manley Papers

Chicago Historical Society, Chicago, Ill.
　Ezra Warner Papers
　Letter of John W. Young, 20th Virginia Cavalry
　Last Days of the Confederacy, by E. R. Goggin

Cooper, Homer C., Athens, Ga.
　Letters of Jacob S. Hall

Corder, Lyle., Bridgeport, W. Va.
　Diary of Andrew J. Jones, 20th Virginia Cavalry

Eleanor S. Brockenbrough Library, The Museum of the Confederacy, Richmond, Va.
　Roll of Honor Books
　Dunlop Papers

Greenbrier Historical Society, Lewisburg, W. Va.
　Roster of Greenbrier Confederates

Harrisonburg - Rockingham County Historical Society, Dayton, Va.
　United Daughters of the Confederacy, Southern Cross of Honor Documents (Held at James Madison University Library, Harrisonburg, Va.)

Highland County Circuit Court, Monterey, Va.
　Roster of Highland County Confederates

Library of Congress, Washington, D. C.
　Jubal A. Early Papers

National Archives, Washington, D. C.
　Compiled Military Service Records, 19th Virginia Cavalry
　Compiled Military Service Records, 20th Virginia Cavalry

Compiled Military Service Records, 2nd Virginia State Line
Compiled Military Service Records, 3rd Virginia State Line
Letters Received by the Confederate Adjutant & Inspector General's Office
Letters Received by the Confederate Secretary of War
Compiled Military Service Records of Confederate General, Staff and Non-Commissioned Officers
Confederate Inspection Reports - Lomax's Division
Returns, Army of Western Virginia and East Tennessee
1860 Census, Pocahontas County, Va.
1860 Census, Randolph County, Va.
1860 Census, Braxton County, Va.
1860 Census, Webster County, Va.
1860 Census, Calhoun County, Va.
1860 Census, Gilmer County, Va.
1860 Census, Bath County, Va.
1860 Census, Highland County, Va.
Department of Western Virginia
    General and Special Orders

Pocahontas County Historical Society, Marlinton, W. Va.
    William T. Price Papers

Randolph County Historical Society, Beverly, W. Va.
    Special Orders, Army of Northern Virginia

United Daughters of the Confederacy, Stonewall Jackson Chapter No. 1333, Clarksburg, W. Va.
    Furlough of John S. Dennison

United States Army Military History Institute, Carlisle Barracks, Pa.
    Letter of James L. Sharp
    H. D. Ruffner Papers

University of Virginia Library, Special Collections Department, Charlottesville, Va.
    Gordonsville Hospital Prescription Book

Virginia Historical Society, Richmond, Va.
    Enrolling books of the Rockingham County, Va. Enrolling office
    CSA Army Department of Henrico Papers
        John Avis File
    Muster Roll, Company A, 20th Virginia Cavalry July -August 1863
    Holmes Conrad Papers (Mss1C7637a)

Virginia Military Institute, Lexington, Va.
   Cadet Files

Virginia State Library, Archives, Richmond, Va.
   Confederate Pension Records (1888, 1900, 1902)
   Letters of Seth Slocum
   Department of Military Affairs
      Records of the 19th Virginia Cavalry
      Records of the 20th Virginia Cavalry

West Virginia University, Morgantown, W. Va.
   Roy Bird Cook Papers
   Homer C. Cooper Papers
      Letter of Joseph William Cooper
   Jacob W. Marshall Papers
   D. Boston Stewart Papers

Published Sources

Armstrong, Richard L. *25th Virginia Infantry and 9th Battalion Virginia Infantry*. H. E. Howard, Inc., Lynchburg, Va. 1990.

_____. *11th Virginia Cavalry*. H. E. Howard, Inc., Lynchburg, Va. 1989.

Ashcraft, John M., Jr. *31st Virginia Infantry*. H. E. Howard, Inc., Lynchburg, Va. 1988.

Bishop, William H. *History of Roane County, West Virginia*. Spencer: W. H. Bishop, c. 1927.

Bohannon, Keith S. *The Giles, Alleghany and Jackson Artillery*. H. E. Howard, Inc., Lynchburg, Va. 1990.

Calhoun County Historical Society. *History of Calhoun County, W. Va. 1989*. Walsworth Publishing, Don Mills, Inc., Waynesville, N.C., 1990.

Cammack, John Henry. *Personal Recollections*. Paragon Printing & Publishing Co., Huntington, W. Va., 1923.

Chapla, John. *42nd Va. Infantry*. H. E. Howard, Inc., Lynchburg, Va. 1983.

Comstock, Jim, ed. *The West Virginia Heritage Encyclopedia*. Jim Comstock, Richwood, W. Va. 1974. 25 Vols.

_____. ed. *The West Virginia Heritage Encylopedia Supplement.* Jim Comstock, Richwood, W. Va. 1976. 25 Vols.

Cook, Roy Bird. *Lewis County in the Civil War, 1861 - 1865.* Jarrett Print. Co., Charleston, W. Va. 1924.

Delauter, Roger U., Jr. *62nd Virginia Infantry.* H. E. Howard, Inc., Lynchburg, Va. 1988.

Driver, Robert J., Jr. *1st Virginia Cavalry.* H. E. Howard, Inc., Lynchburg, Va. 1991.

_____. *14th Virginia Cavalry.* H. E. Howard, Inc., Lynchburg, Va. 1988.

_____. *58th Virginia Infantry.* H. E. Howard, Inc., Lynchburg, Va. 1990.

_____. *52nd Virginia Infantry.* H. E. Howard, Inc., Lynchburg, Va. 1986.

_____. *The Staunton Artillery - McClanahan's Battery.* H. E. Howard, Inc., Lynchburg, Va. 1988.

_____. *Lexington And Rockbridge County in the Civil War.* H. E. Howard, Inc., Lynchburg, Va. 1989.

Evans, Clement A., ed. *Confederate Military History.* 12 Volumes. Atlanta: Confederate Publishing Company, 1898.

Gilmor, Harry. *Four Years In The Saddle.* Harper & Brothers, Pub., New York, 1866.

Greenbrier County Historical Society. "The Diary of Colonel J. W. A. Ford," *The Journal of the Greenbrier Historical Society*, Volume II, Number 3, (1971), pp. 29-53.

Hawkins, Paul C. and Judith Hawkins. *Upshur County Death Records.* Heritage Books, Inc., Bowie, Md., 1993.

Hornbeck, Betty. *Upshur Brothers in the Blue and Gray.* The Republican Delta, Buckhannon, W. Va. 1962.

Johnston, A. S. *Capt. Beirne Chapman and Chapman's Battery.* The Monroe Watchman, Union, W. Va., 1991.

Knauss, William H. *The Story of Camp Chase.* Publishing House of the Methodist Episcopal Church, South, Nashville, Tenn. 1906.

Knotts, R. J., Jr. *Calhoun County in The Civil War.* Calhoun County Historical and Genealogical Society, Grantsville, W. Va., 1982.

Krick, Robert K. *Lee's Colonels: A Biographical Register of the Field Officers of the Army of Northern Virginia.* Morningside Bookshop, Dayton, O., 2nd Edition, 1984.

Lowry, Terry D. *22nd Virginia Infantry.* H. E. Howard, Inc., Lynchburg, Va. 1988.

Lowther, Minnie Kendall. *History of Ritchie County.* Wheeling News Lito. Co., Wheeling, W. Va., 1911.

Marsh, William A., Comp. *1880 Census of West Virginia.* 13 Volumes. McClain Print. Co., Parsons, W. Va., 1979.

Matheny, H. E. *Wood County, West Virginia, In Civil War Times.* Joseph M. Sakach, Jr., Trans-Allegheny Books, Inc., Parkersburg, W. Va., 1987.

Maxwell, Hu. *History cf Monongalia County.* N.p,n.d. Printed, but not published.

_____. *History of Barbour County, West Virginia, from Its Earliest Exploration and Settlement to the Present Time.* Acme Publishing Co., Morgantown, W. Va., 1899.

_____. *History of Randolph County, West Virginia.* Acme Publishing Co., Morgantown, W. Va., 1898.

Mickle, William E. *Well Known Confederate Veterans.* Wm. E. Mickle, New Orleans, La., 1915.

Miller, Thomas Condit and Hu Maxwell. *West Virginia and Its People.* 3 Volumes. Lewis Historical Pub. Co., New York, 1913.

Musick, Michael P. *6th Virginia Cavalry.* H. E. Howard, Inc., Lynchburg, Va. 1990.

Pocahontas County Historical Society, Inc. *History of Pocahontas West Virginia 1981.* Taylor Publishing Co., Dallas, Tx. 2nd Printing, May 1982.

Poe, David. *Personal Reminiscences of the Civil War.* Upshur Republican Print, Buckhannon, W. Va., 1911.

Potts, M. P. H. *A Boy Scout of the Confederacy.* Brown Printing Co., Montgomery, Ala., 1923.

Rice, Donald L. *Randolph 200: A Bicentennial History of Randolph County, West Virginia.* Walsworth Press, Inc., Waynesville, N. C. 1988.

Scott, J. L. 36th and 37th Battalions Virginia Cavalry. H. E. Howard, Inc., Lynchburg, Va. 1986.

_____. *23rd Battalion Virginia Infantry.* H. E. Howard, Inc., Lynchburg, Va. 1991.

Sutton, John Davidson. *History of Braxton and Central West Virginia.* N.p., 1919.

Thompson, R. L. *Webster County History - Folklore, From the Earliest Times to the Present.* Webster Springs: Star Printers, 1942.

U. S. War Department. *War of the Rebellion: Official Records of the Union and Confederate Armies.* 128 Volumes. U.S. Government Printing Office, Washington, D. C., 1880-1901.

Vandiver, Frank E., ed. *War Memoirs.* Indiana Univ. Press, Bloomington, Ind., 1960.

Wallace, Lee A., Jr. *Guide to Virginia Military Organizations, 1861-1865.* H. E. Howard, Inc., Lynchburg, Va., 1986.

_____. *1st Virginia Infantry.* H. E. Howard, Inc., Lynchburg, Va. 1985.

_____. *5th Virginia Infantry.* H. E. Howard, Inc., Lynchburg, Va. 1988.

Warner, Ezra. *Generals in Gray.* Louisiana State Univ. Press, Baton Rouge, La., 1959.

Wiley, Samuel T. *History of Monongalia Co., West Virginia.* Preston Publishing Co., Kingwood, W. Va., 1883.

Williams, C. R., comp. *Southern Sympathizers: Wood County Confederate Soldiers.* Inland River Books, Parkersburg, W. Va., 1983.

Writer's Program, West Virginia. *Of Stars and Bars.* Charleston, W. Va., 1940.

Newspapers

Braxton Democrat, Sutton, W. Va.
Pocahontas Times, Marlinton, W. Va.
Randolph Enterprise, Elkins, W. Va.
Staunton *Spectator,* Staunton, Va.
Staunton *Vindicator,* Staunton, Va.
The Recorder, Monterey, Va.
Wheeling *Daily Intelligencer,* Wheeling, W. Va.

Periodicals

Confederate Veteran. 40 Volumes, 1893 - 1932.
Magazine of History and Biography, Randolph County Historical Society. 13 Volumes.